...

Judge Diarmuid O'Scannlain Dissents

Edited by Robert Dittmer

"The addition of a separate right to "bear" arms, beyond keeping them, should therefore protect something more than mere carrying incidental to keeping arms. [. . .] Understanding "bear" to protect at least some level of carrying in anticipation of conflict outside of the home provides the necessary gap between "keep" and "bear" to avoid rendering the latter guarantee as mere surplusage. [. . .]

"The right to bear arms must include, at the least, the right to carry a firearm openly for self-defense."

-Young v. Hawaii (Ninth Circuit Court) (July 24, 2018)

Note on the text: most italics and bold has been removed.

Acknowledgements

Websites (in no particular order):

www.law.cornell.edu
supreme.justia.com
caselaw.findlaw.com
Public.Resource.Org
Openjurist.org
scholar.google.com
en.wikipedia.org

"In this highly charged area, we constitutionally inferior courts should be careful to apply established law. Failure to do so begets the very errors that plagued this case. That failure culminated in a ruling that invalidated a considered congressional policy and imposed a wholly novel view of constitutional liberty on the entire United States. The Supreme Court's cases tell us to exercise greater care, caution, and humility than that. Indeed, our constitutional system demands more respect than that. When judges sacrifice the rule of law to find rights they favor, I fear the people may one day find that their new rights, once proclaimed so boldly, have disappeared because there is no longer a rule of law to protect them."

-Judge O'Scannlain's concurrence in Log Cabin Republicans v. US (Sept 29, 2011)

Table of Contents
Contents

Note on the cases—All Ninth Circuit Court cases

Judge O'Scannlain is a judge for the ninth circuit court of appeals. Unless otherwise stated, all of the cases in this book are ninth circuit court of appeals cases.

Judge O'Scannlain's concurrence and dissent in Mullis v. US Bankruptcy Court, Dist. of Nevada (Sept 24, 1987)

O'SCANNLAIN, Circuit Judge, concurring in part and dissenting in part:

I concur in substantially all of the majority's opinion, but I must respectfully dissent from its analysis of judicial immunity from prospective injunctive relief set forth in part III C.

The majority believes that the Pulliam exception to judicial immunity should apply only to state judges, while federal judges should remain absolutely immune to challenges for prospective injunctive relief. In my view, the majority's approach misreads the Supreme Court's Pulliam opinion. Moreover, I believe the Court has already considered the majority's policy argument in Pulliam itself, concluding that there is no need to shield judges (state or federal) from injunctive relief challenges:

We never have had a rule of absolute judicial immunity from prospective relief, and there is no evidence that the absence of that immunity has had a chilling effect on judicial independence ... The limitations already imposed by the requirements for obtaining equitable relief against any defendant — a showing of an inadequate remedy at law and of a serious risk of irrevocable harm (citations omitted), — severely curtail the risk that judges will be harassed and their independence compromised by the threat of having to defend themselves against suits by disgruntled litigants.

Pulliam at 536-38, 104 S.Ct. at 1977-79.

The Supreme Court has previously held that it is inappropriate to create a distinction between state and federal officials for purposes of immunity:

There is no basis for according to federal officials a higher degree of immunity from liability when sued for a constitutional infringement as authorized by Bivens than is accorded state officials when sued for the identical violation under section 1983. The constitutional injuries made actionable by section 1983 are of no greater magnitude than those for which federal officials may be responsible.

Butz v. Economou, 438 U.S. 478, 500, 98 S.Ct. 2894, 2907, 57 L.Ed.2d 895 (1978). This circuit has also noted that "we make no distinction between a section 1983 action and a Bivens action for purposes of immunity." Lonneker Farms, Inc. v. Klobucher, 804 F.2d 1096, 1097 (9th Cir.1986). Until today, no court has sought to parse these otherwise plain statements of the law, and I can see no reason to do so in the present case. To extrapolate from Pulliam a rule which broadly discriminates between federal and state judges in the judicial immunity field is at best unwarranted and at worst potentially divisive to the goal of harmony in the administration of the American judicial system.

I would simply follow the reasoning of Affeldt which the majority cites with favor and then abandons. Both Affeldt and the majority here conclude that the litigant "cannot show an inadequate remedy `at law' and a serious risk of irreparable harm, prerequisites to injunctive relief under Pulliam" (Maj.Op. at 1392). In my view, this ends the matter; no injunction will lie against the federal judge in this case and his decision is properly affirmed on such grounds alone.

Judge O'Scannlain's dissent in Smith v. Endell (Nov 14, 1988) [Notes omitted]

O'SCANNLAIN, Circuit Judge, dissenting:

As I read the record in this case, defendant Smith never invoked his right to counsel after having been given unrestricted opportunity to do so. At most he was "thinking out loud" while making up his mind in a clearly non-coercive situation. In the Miranda-Edwards-Fouche I-Fouche-II context, I would summarize the record as comprising an initial Miranda waiver as the interrogation begins, a later ambiguous request for counsel[1] followed by clarifying questions, after which it becomes clear that defendant never did invoke his right to counsel. Therefore, I must dissent from the majority's decision to require suppression of the confession. I would concur in the four preceding court decisions (two Alaska state courts, a federal magistrate, and a federal district judge), which found no constitutional bar to the admissibility of Smith's confession.

The key issue is, of course, whether Smith's statements were sufficient, as a matter of constitutional law, to invoke his right to counsel. If Smith had stopped after "Can I talk to a lawyer?," he would have invoked unambiguously his fifth and fourteenth amendment rights and no doubt the Alaska troopers, following Miranda and Edwards, would have answered affirmatively and shown him the telephone as indeed they did in this case. In any event, "can I talk to a lawyer?" standing alone, would have been an unambiguous request for counsel.

The problem is that Smith did not stop there. He went on to say, without interruption, that he was only interested in talking to a lawyer if the police were looking at him as a suspect, whereupon he asked the question, "Are you looking at me as a suspect?" Although the majority feels otherwise, I find the trooper's answer to that question to be responsive and comprehensible: "Well, it ... it wouldn't be fair to you to say that we weren't Mike." Of course Smith was a murder suspect and Trooper Stearns told him so.

The troopers then began to clarify whether Smith, having received confirmation he was indeed a suspect, wanted to go on to invoke his right to counsel, as the following excerpt from the interrogation transcript makes clear.

STEARNS: And you signed [the rights sheet] and you're aware ... and you're aware that it says on there any time you feel that you want counsel, that's it, okay. So, don't misunderstand Chuck and I. You want counsel, well ... by God don't ... don't hesitate to get yourself counsel. You want to talk to us about Ron Cole's dealings, you want to talk to us about the murder and suspects, anybody, will [sic] talk to you. If you want a lawyer to do that, then feel free [gesturing to a nearby telephone].

These police statements were well within the clarification process because they were in response to Smith's own questions.[2] The majority attaches great significance to the troopers' explaining to Smith why he was a suspect, which it deems impermissible because it found a purpose to elicit incriminating statements in violation of the standard we established in Fouche I, 776 F.2d at 1405 ("Questions aimed at clarifying the desire for counsel must be strictly limited to that purpose; they may not be used to elicit incriminating information").[3] While the Fouche I standard is strict by its very terms, I do not believe it was intended to be used as a mechanism to pick apart every word that a police officer might utter during the course of an interrogation. Indeed, the actions of the troopers are at least as solicitous concerning the suspect's right to counsel, if not more so, as those of the FBI agent which we held to be proper in Fouche II. See also United States v. Nordling, 804 F.2d 1466, 1470-71 (9th Cir.1986). Even the majority concedes that the interrogation was conducted without the slightest trace of coercion.[4] Majority opinion at 1531.

In the clarification process, it became obvious that Smith did not intend to invoke his right to an attorney. Having been offered the telephone to call his lawyer, Smith chose instead to renew the dialogue. Indeed, Smith stated shortly before his confession, and long after having been told he was a suspect: "I don't know if I need [an attorney] or not. That's why I'm trying to make my mind up, if I need to go that route for myself, you know."

Certainly, if Smith's initial statements had been unequivocal, then I would not look beyond them in determining that he had properly invoked his right to counsel. Smith v. Illinois, 469 U.S. at 92, 105 S.Ct. at 491. But Smith's initial statements do not rise to the level of an unambiguous request, and therefore the Smith v. Illinois rule does not apply. See Grooms v. Keeney, 826 F.2d 883, 887 (9th Cir.1987) (court stating that "[t]he Smith rule does not apply here, because it concerned an unequivocal request for counsel, and there is no persuasive reason to extend or invert its rule to fit the facts of this case") (citation omitted).

Smith's latter statements merely show that he had no intention of unambiguously invoking his right to counsel before continuing to answer questions. In Fouche II, we did not require in the clarification process that the suspect affirmatively state that he would continue without a lawyer present. Rather, simply enough, we evaluated whether Fouche invoked his right to counsel. See Fouche II, 833 F.2d at 1287 ("Fouche voluntarily declined to invoke his right to counsel, choosing instead to answer [the agent's] questions").

Nothing in Edwards or its progeny mandates a reversal in this case. Smith made an ambiguous inquiry about right to counsel, to which the troopers responded properly by seeking to clarify Smith's true intentions. In so doing, the troopers did not stray from the limits we laid down in Fouche I. I am aware of no Supreme Court or Ninth Circuit precedent which freezes police in their tracks after the defendant says "I'm trying to make my mind up" in this context. I am concerned that the majority's analysis unnecessarily complicates this area of the law. I fear that the majority's holding does not accomplish what in large measure it sets out to do, i.e., provide a bright line for all concerned parties to follow. In fact, I think it may likely have the opposite effect. The analysis essentially injects a new concept into the fifth-fourteenth amendment lexicon: "conditional unequivocal request for counsel." In so doing, it confuses and diverts attention from whether right to counsel has been invoked. It also carries with it a potentially thorny new analytical requirement, i.e., whether a "condition" laid down by the suspect is satisfied.[5]

Even if my fears that the majority's "bright line" will become blurred are unjustified, I am concerned that it loses sight of the policy underlying that line. Until now, we have sought to maintain a delicate balance[6] between ensuring that suspects are properly insulated against police overreaching while allowing the law enforcement community to perform its duties effectively.[7]

Perhaps the majority's new "bright line" is only an accretion from the old. But one only has to look back less than a decade to the facts of Edwards (which extended Miranda) and compare them to the present case to see how accretion becomes avulsion. The Edwards Court was presented with detectives who went to the jail where defendant was being held to badger him into talking after he had unequivocally invoked both his right to counsel and his right to remain silent; the Court quite properly drew a line beyond which the police could not go and required suppression of the confession. Here, we delegate to a knowledgeable defendant during a Miranda -waived interrogation at trooper headquarters the right to lay down to police the conditions upon which his interrogation may or may not proceed. We have come a long way since Miranda and Edwards — too far, too fast, in my view.

Judge O'Scannlain's dissent in US v. Chatman (March 9, 1989)

O'SCANNLAIN, Circuit Judge, dissenting:

I dissent from the majority's holding, which follows the Fourth Circuit's recent holding that Congress intended to apply the common law definition of burglary for purposes of implementing the sentence enhancement statute. See United States v. Headspeth, 852 F.2d 753 (4th Cir.1988). Although, like the majority, I am loath to create an unnecessary circuit split, using the common law definition creates so many practical and interpretive difficulties that I am persuaded that Congress did not intend it. Instead, Congress clearly expected to take a state burglary conviction as it finds it on a defendant's rap sheet.

First, my survey of the laws of the fifty states and the District of Columbia indicates that only two states, Maryland and Virginia, retain all elements of the common law crime of burglary (and even these two states seem to use a definition of "nighttime" different from that used at common law). Thus, a burglary conviction in every jurisdiction except these two would require a federal court to conduct an inquiry into whether one or more of the elements has been satisfied. Not only is this procedure cumbersome, but it seems likely that if Congress had intended federal courts to follow the unusual procedure of investigating the factual circumstances of individual crimes for purposes of applying the sentence enhancement statute that it would have said so explicitly. In addition, I find it hard to believe that Congress would have included the term "burglary" in a federal statute merely to reach burglary convictions under the laws of Maryland and Virginia.

Second, the common law definition of burglary is so esoteric as to defy easy application, which suggests that Congress did not intend the federal courts to attempt to apply it. At common law, each element of the crime was elaborated in extreme detail, and most were defined so as to differentiate between types of action that seem practically indistinguishable, at least from the point of view of danger created. For example, an actual "breaking" was required — entry through an open door or window was insufficient, although coming down the chimney was considered breaking. Similarly, night was generally defined as the time during which there was enough daylight to discern a person's face. Common law decisions likewise interpreted "dwelling-house" in an extremely particularized sense, including buildings within the "curtilage," that is, nearby barns, stables, or dairy houses near, or within "bow-shot" of the main building. It seems unlikely that Congress contemplated that federal courts would attempt to reinstate these arcane distinctions between various types of offenses.

Theoretically, some of these difficulties might be avoided by using the catchall term "otherwise presents a serious potential risk of physical injury to another" to enhance the sentences of those convicted of a "burglary," that does not fit the common law definition. However, this approach has two problems. First, it essentially reads the term "burglary" out of the statute, because the term will now only apply to an extremely small number of cases which fit all the convolutions of the common law definition. Second, I think this approach will still not reach the vast majority of state burglary statutes, under the categorical analysis correctly adopted by the court. Most state statutes include offenses that do not necessarily involve any serious risk of physical injury to another, because, like the statute at issue in this case, they punish the burglary of unoccupied structures. Even the common law definition of burglary does not require that the dwelling house be occupied at the time of the burglary. Thus, contrary to congressional purposes, crimes generally defined as burglary would not qualify for sentence enhancement, unless we read the catchall provision in a much broader sense than in the proposed opinion.

In my view, it seems more probable to assume that Congress meant the federal courts to examine only the language of the relevant state statutes and generally accept the state statutory definitions of burglary. This does not mean that the courts would accept as burglary for purposes of section 924 whatever definition the state chooses to give it. As the Supreme Court has noted, when borrowing state law, "specific aberrant or hostile state rules do not provide appropriate standards for federal law." United States v. Little Lake Misere Land Co., 412 U.S. 580, 596, 93 S.Ct. 2389, 2398, 37 L.Ed.2d 187 (1973). Thus, for example, the fact that a state defined the offense of jaywalking as "burglary" would not satisfy the definition of burglary for purposes of section 924 if classifying such an offense as "burglary" was not Congress' intent. Where the state statute deviates sufficiently from what Congress intended the courts might be forced to state that no conviction under the statute would count for section 924(e)(1) enhancement purposes. As a practical matter, the likelihood of such event is remote, the majority's opinion to the contrary notwithstanding. In my view, none of the existing state statutory definitions of burglary fall into this category.

It is not at all surprising to me that California dignifies its citizen's car as highly as one's home. Indeed, in California one's car may indeed be more sacrosanct than one's dwelling. Congress could not possibly have meant to penalize the citizens of California for thinking that the contents of a locked car are entitled to as much protection from theft as the contents of an apartment.

For these reasons, I would affirm Judge Keller in his determination that the crime committed was a "burglary" and therefore a "violent felony" under the federal sentence enhancement statute.

Judge O'Scannlain's dissent in US v. Ant (July 27, 1989)

O'SCANNLAIN, Circuit Judge, dissenting:

Because I agree with Judge Battin that suppression in federal court of the guilty plea entered in tribal proceedings disparages the integrity of tribal courts, I must respectfully dissent. The majority concedes that Ant's plea in tribal court complied fully with tribal law and the Indian Civil Rights Act (ICRA). The majority points to no evidence of coercion, "shocking conduct," or inaccuracy in the transcript of the tribal proceedings. Because I find no constitutional prohibition against admission of the guilty plea in federal court, and because I find no bar to admissibility as an evidentiary matter, I would affirm Judge Battin's denial of the motion to suppress.

I agree with the majority that had the plea been entered in a state court it would have been constitutionally infirm. I agree with the majority that had the plea been made in a federal court, it would have been constitutionally infirm. I also agree that such a guilty plea, had it been made in a state trial or in another federal trial, would require suppression here for the reasons expressed in the majority opinion.

But none of these principles is relevant here. The plea occurred, not in a federal court, not in a state court, but in a tribal court whose proceedings are entitled to the dignity shown to foreign courts. See United States v. Wheeler, 435 U.S. 313, 328, 98 S.Ct. 1079, 1088, 55 L.Ed.2d 303 (1978). Generally, evidence of judicial proceedings in foreign courts is admissible in federal court. See Ennis v. Smith, 55 U.S. (14 How.) 400, 430, 14 L.Ed. 472 (1852); 30 Am.Jur.2d Evidence § 982 (1967). This includes evidence of guilty pleas received in a foreign jurisdiction. See United States v. Nolan, 551 F.2d 266 (10th Cir.), cert. denied, 434 U.S. 904, 98 S.Ct. 302, 54 L.Ed.2d 191 (1977) (evidence of defendant's British conviction, and his guilty plea leading up to it, even if they were obtained in manner inconsistent with U.S. Constitution, nonetheless held properly admitted in federal criminal trial under Fed.R.Evid. 404(b)); cf. United States v. Ogle, 587 F.2d 938 (8th Cir.1978) (even if Japanese system does not afford constitutional due process protections, Japanese conviction admissible to prove identity); cf. also La Victoire v. Kelly, 5 A.D.2d 548, 173 N.Y.S.2d 543, 547 (1958) (motorist's plea of guilty in Canada admissible in license revocation hearing to determine whether out-of-state driving violation occurred).

Granted, none of these cases directly addresses the admissibility of a guilty plea to a foreign criminal charge that has as its basis the very same activity as does the federal crime. Admissibility in the case before us is more compelling, however, because there is no danger of Ant's being convicted based on evidence of prior crimes designed to show bad character. See United States v. Lewis, 787 F.2d 1318, 1321 (9th Cir.1986); Fed.R.Evid. 404(b).

Furthermore, we have given great deference to search and seizure procedures satisfactory to foreign jurisdictions when they meet certain threshold tests. Generally, such evidence obtained by foreign officials is admissible in federal court. Cf. Stonehill v. United States, 405 F.2d 738, 743, 746 (9th Cir.1968), cert. denied, 395 U.S. 960, 89 S.Ct. 2102, 23 L.Ed.2d 747 (1969) (evidence seized by foreign officers in raids which would have violated fourth amendment held admissible in federal court). This is true even when the officials' conduct would violate the Constitution had they been state or federal agents, provided that the conduct (1) does not amount to coercion; (2) is not "shocking"; and (3) is valid in the jurisdiction where the evidence was secured. See United States v. Rose, 570 F.2d 1358, 1362 (9th Cir.1978). And, there is a fourth threshold consideration: the foreign jurisdiction must be "at least equally [as] civilized" as the United States. See United States v. Nagelberg, 434 F.2d 585, 587 n. 1 (2d Cir.1970), cert. denied, 401 U.S. 939, 91 S.Ct. 935, 28 L.Ed.2d 219 (1971). There is no reason not to apply this same four-part standard in cases involving uncounseled guilty pleas in foreign or tribal courts. Just as the fourth amendment is not binding on foreign officials in their evidence gathering activities, so too the sixth amendment is not binding upon foreign or tribal courts. See Flynn v. Shultz, 748 F.2d 1186, 1197 & n. 10 (7th Cir.1984), cert. denied, 474 U.S. 830, 106 S.Ct. 94, 88 L.Ed.2d 77 (1985) (court stating that "[o]bviously, the Mexican government is not bound by the requirements of our Constitution" and noting that there is "no indication from the debate leading to ratification of the Constitution and the Bill of Rights that application of the Sixth Amendment to foreign court prosecutions was contemplated").

What the majority opinion implies, regrettably, is that we simply are not willing to treat tribal courts with the same dignity as we do foreign courts. Whether the majority intends it or not, its opinion will be construed to mean that evidence from tribal court proceedings obtained in a way which clearly complies with ICRA and tribal law will be suppressed largely because we do not regard tribal courts to be as "civilized" as state and federal courts.[1]

Congress clearly intended that not all provisions of the Constitution be imposed upon the freedom of Indian tribes to conduct themselves in accordance with their own tribal laws — laws, incidentally, which have always been considered to be laws of a sovereign of equal dignity with the United States, not a subdivision of the federal government. Wheeler, 435 U.S. at 328, 98 S.Ct. at 1088.

The majority seems troubled by the fact that the sixth amendment is not binding upon tribal courts.[2] But that is exactly what the ICRA tells us. Compare U.S. Const. amend. VI ("In all criminal prosecutions, the accused shall ... have the Assistance of Counsel for his defense") with 25 U.S.C. § 1302(6) (1982) ("No Indian tribe in exercising powers of self-government shall ... deny to any person in a criminal proceeding the right ... at his own expense to have the assistance of counsel for his defense") (emphasis supplied).

Had Congress intended that the full panoply of sixth amendment protections be imposed upon tribal courts, it clearly could have said so in the ICRA. Because the nature of comity between tribal courts and federal courts — analogous to the relationship between sovereign states — is so sensitive and so delicately balanced, it is up to Congress, not this panel, to change the rules if they should be changed at all.

Notes

[1] There is potential for even greater disparagement. Under the ICRA, right to counsel is only guaranteed to the extent the defendant can afford an attorney. Under the majority's rationale, could it not be argued that evidence from a tribal proceeding in which an indigent defendant appears pro se would never be admissible in federal court? Indeed what policy, other than disparagement, is served by promulgation of the majority's new "policy" on suppression of evidence which by definition has not been obtained by unconstitutional means?

[2] Of course, I recognize that suppressing a tribal court guilty plea in a federal criminal trial is not equivalent to an imposition of the sixth amendment on tribal courts. Nonetheless, the majority's holding will have far-reaching consequences since virtually all tribal court guilty pleas will be inadmissible in federal court, given the less stringent requirements of the ICRA.

Judge O'Scannlain's dissent from the order rejecting the suggestion for rehearing en banc in US v. Cunningham (Nov 24, 1989)

O'SCANNLAIN, Circuit Judge, with whom Circuit Judges CYNTHIA HOLCOMB HALL, BRUNETTI, KOZINSKI, NOONAN, DAVID R. THOMPSON, and TROTT concur, dissenting from the order rejecting the suggestion for rehearing en banc.

By rejecting the government's suggestion to rehear this case en banc, the court lets stand an unfortunate and utterly needless hindrance to effective law enforcement. Congress has stated clearly, as a matter of national policy, that armed career criminals are a threat to the very health of our modern society. Sentence enhancement is the precise antidote identified by the legislative branch to deal with the problem nationwide. Nationwide except, it now becomes, for the states of Alaska, Arizona, California, Hawaii,

Idaho, Montana, Nevada, Oregon, and Washington, plus the territories of Guam and the Northern Mariana Islands. Nationwide, that is, except for about twenty percent of the population of this country and half its land mass. For this court now rules that burglary convictions in nine states and two territories can no longer be taken into account to enhance sentences under the Armed Career Criminal Act of 1984. Because this ruling offends common sense, is contrary to express congressional intent, and contravenes the overwhelming weight of authority from other circuits, I respectfully dissent.

I

Randall Cunningham was indicted on one count for possession of a firearm by a previously convicted felon, in violation of 18 U.S.C. § 922(g)(1) (Supp. V 1987). At the time of Cunningham's arraignment, the government filed an information alleging that he had three prior felony convictions for purposes of 18 U.S.C. § 924(e) (Supp. V 1987), which provides for enhanced sentences without parole where defendants, who are convicted under section 922(g)(1), have three or more previous convictions of a "violent felony." "Violent felony" is defined to include "burglary." 18 U.S.C. § 924(e)(2)(B)(ii).

One of Cunningham's three prior convictions was an Oregon conviction for second-degree burglary. Under Oregon law, a person commits burglary in the second degree if he "enters or remains unlawfully in a building with intent to commit a crime therein." Or.Rev.Stat. 164.215(1) (1985). Over Cunningham's objection that second-degree burglary under Oregon law is not a "violent felony," the district court imposed an enhanced sentence of twenty years imprisonment.

A panel of this court reversed the district court and held that the Oregon burglary could not be counted as one of the three predicate felonies. The panel was relying on this court's recent decision in United States v. Chatman, 869 F.2d 525 (9th Cir.1989), which held that the term "burglary" as used in 18 U.S.C. § 924(e)(2)(B)(ii) means common law burglary — "the breaking and entering of the dwelling house of another, in the nighttime, with the intent to commit a felony therein." Id. at 527. The Cunningham panel found that "[b]ecause [an] Oregon state conviction of second degree burglary does not fit the definition of burglary ... contained in section 924(2)(B)(ii) [sic], it cannot serve as a basis for sentence enhancement." U.S. v. Cunningham, 878 F.2d 311, 312 (9th Cir.1989). In other words, because a burglary might have occurred during the day in an office building, it cannot be counted.

Judges Skopil and McKibben specially concurred because they felt bound by Chatman. Both judges stated their belief that Chatman was wrongly decided, however, and they encouraged en banc review "to correct the error." Cunningham, at 312.

II

Contrary to the court's decision in Chatman, now compounded by its decision in Cunningham, Congress never intended to limit the definition of "burglary" in 18 U.S.C. § 924(e) to common law burglary.[1]

As originally conceived, the Armed Career Criminal Act of 1984 defined "burglary" in broad, generic terms as "any felony consisting of entering or remaining surreptitiously within a building that is property of another with intent to engage in conduct constituting a Federal or State offense." 18 U.S.C.App. § 1202(c)(9) (1982 & Supp. II 1984) (repealed). The legislative history reveals why the broad definition was chosen:

> Robberies and burglaries are the most damaging crimes to society. Robberies and burglaries occur with far greater frequency than other violent felonies, affect many more people, and cause the greatest losses. A person is forty times more likely to be a victim of robbery than of rape.
>
> * * * * * *
>
> Burglaries involve invasion of [innocent individuals'] homes or workplaces, violation of their privacy, and loss of their most personal and valued possessions.
>
> * * * * * *
>
> Most robberies and burglaries are committed by career criminals ... [who] commit robberies and burglaries interchangeably.

H.R.Rep. No. 1073, 98th Cong., 2d Sess. 3 (1984) (statement of Sen. Specter) (emphasis added).

The Career Criminal Amendments Act of 1986 eliminated the preexisting definition and provided no substitute. But the Amendment's legislative history shows that Congress intended to broaden rather than to restrict the number of offenses which would give rise to sentence enhancement. Senator Arlen Specter, who introduced the original career criminal bill, understood that the amendment would serve to "broaden the definition [of career criminal] so that we may have a greater sweep and more effective use of this important statute." Armed Career Criminal Act Amendments: Hearing on H.R. 4639 and H.R. 4768 Before the Subcomm. on Crime of the House Comm. on the Judiciary, 99th Cong., 2d Sess. 44 (1986). To achieve this goal, the Bill "broaden[ed] the so-called predicate crimes to include drug violations and certain other serious violent acts." 132 Cong.Rec. 7697 (1986) (statement of Sen. Specter). Representative Ron Wyden, the sponsor of H.R. 4639 (a House bill which was a precursor of the amendment), explained that while the Act had been a success, it "would be much more effective if the predicate offenses were extended beyond robbery and burglary to include crimes of violence and serious drug offenses." Armed Career Criminal Act Amendments: Hearing on S. 2312 Before the Subcomm. on Criminal Law of the Senate Comm. on the Judiciary, 99th Cong., 2d Sess. 6 (1986) (emphasis added).

Congress thus intended that burglary, as defined under the Armed Career Criminal Act of 1984, would continue to serve as a predicate offense. Moreover, Congress intended to expand the number and variety of offenses which would give rise to sentence enhancement under the Act. There is absolutely no indication that Congress sought to restrict the offenses giving rise to sentence enhancement. See United States v. Hill, 863 F.2d 1575, 1580 (11th Cir.1989). This court's decision to introduce such a restriction for the nine western states and two Pacific territories flies in the face of the will of Congress.

III

All circuit courts of appeals which have decided the issue since Chatman have held that the term "burglary" is not limited to its common law definition. These courts take two approaches to the issue. Three circuits simply carry forward the express definition of "burglary" contained in the original version of section 924(e). See Hill, 863 F.2d at 1581-82;[2] United States v. Dombrowski, 877 F.2d 520, 530 (7th Cir.1989); United States v. Palmer, 871 F.2d 1202, 1208 (3d Cir.1989).

The other approach is the one I recommended in my dissent in Chatman — to treat section 924(e) as applicable to any felony defined as "burglary" under state law. See Chatman, 869 F.2d at 530-31 (O'Scannlain, J., dissenting). Both the Fifth and Eighth Circuits take this tack. See United States v. Quintero, 872 F.2d 107, 115 (5th Cir.1989); United States v. Taylor, 864 F.2d 625, 626-27 (8th Cir.1989), cert. granted, 493 U.S. 889, 110 S.Ct. 231, 107 L.Ed.2d 183 (1989).

Defendant Cunningham's Oregon second-degree burglary conviction would qualify as a predicate crime under either of the rationales adopted by these five courts.

IV

By refusing to take Cunningham en banc, this circuit reaffirms its commitment to a medieval anachronism rejected by every state legislature in this circuit. Congress never intended ancient notions of common law pleading to control crime fighting in the twentieth century. Let us hope that the states of the Ninth Circuit do not become a haven for armed career criminals beyond the reach of the deliberate sentence enhancement policy set by Congress.

Notes

[1] The majority in Chatman erred because it misread the legislative history of section 924(e), and placed determinative weight on the fact that one of the House bills, H.R. 4768, limited the definition of "violent felony" to crimes involving "the use, attempted use, or threatened use of physical force against the person of another." 869 F.2d at 527-28. See also United States v. Headspeth, 852 F.2d 753, 756-58 (4th Cir.1988). Even under this definition of "violent felony," burglary surely must be included. Burglary is a crime that, by its nature, involves a substantial risk of physical force against the person of another.

The Fourth Circuit in Headspeth, in deciding that Maryland's "storehouse breaking" offense did not constitute "burglary" under section 924(e) as amended, limited "burglary" to its common law definition. At least Headspeth, unlike Chatman, has the merit of not rendering that part of the Armed Career Criminal Act a dead letter within its Circuit's boundaries. Two of the five states comprising the Fourth Circuit seem to retain in their "burglary" statutes all the elements of the common law crime. Indeed, they are the only two such states nationwide. See Chatman, 869 F.2d at 530 (O'Scannlain, J., dissenting).

[2] A subsequent decision of the Eleventh Circuit applying this principle is awaiting certiorari consideration by the Supreme Court in a petition filed by the convicted defendant urging reversal based on, inter alia, our Chatman decision. Carter v. United

States, 872 F.2d 434 (11th Cir.1989), petition for cert. filed, No. 88-7307 (May 22, 1989).

Judge O'Scannlain's concurrence and dissent in Mt. Adams Veneer Co. v. US (Feb 13, 1990)

O'SCANNLAIN, Circuit Judge, concurring in part and dissenting in part:

I respectfully dissent from Part II of the majority's disposition which affirms the district court's denial of injunctive relief to Puget Sound Plywood, Inc. ("Puget Sound") and Publishers Forest Products Company of Washington ("Publishers"). Puget Sound and Publishers sought injunctive relief to compel the Forest Service to permit them to amend their buy-out applications in order to include certain Mt. Adams Veneer Company's ("Mt. Adams") contracts in their respective applications.

The majority properly determines that Puget Sound and Mt. Adams are affiliates and that Publishers and Mt. Adams are affiliates. But somehow it fails to recognize the necessary implication of these conclusions: as affiliates of Mt. Adams, Puget Sound and Publishers are each entitled to include portions of Mt. Adams' contracts in their separate buy-out applications. Instead, the majority insists that Puget Sound and Publishers be relegated back to the Forest Service to start a new, and in my view needless, process seeking leave to amend their original filings. Even footnote 4 of the majority's disposition acknowledges that such process is likely to be a useless act, and counsel for the Forest Service said as much during oral argument. The majority simply prescribes an exercise in futility. The majority improperly and illogically divorces the findings on the merits from the determination of whether Puget Sound and Publishers may amend their applications in light of such findings. The Federal Timber Contract Payment Modification Act clearly provides that, for the purpose of determining a purchaser's buy-out limitation, affiliates "shall be treated as a single entity." 16 U.S.C. § 618(a)(7)(A). Obviously this means that an entity consisting of two affiliates is allowed only one buy-out entitlement rather than two and that such an entity may elect to buy out the most economically advantageous contracts held by either affiliate. Puget Sound/Mt. Adams and Publishers/Mt. Adams must therefore be treated as single entities; having been deemed affiliates of Mt. Adams, Puget Sound and Publishers are each necessarily entitled to include selected Mt. Adams' contracts in their buy-out applications.

The district court has the power to order equitable relief. See Sierra Pacific v. Lyng, 866 F.2d 1099, 1112 (9th Cir.1989) ("We find nothing in the statute to indicate that Congress intended to divest the [district] courts of their inherent equitable powers"). I believe the district court improperly failed to exercise its equitable powers by not requiring the Forest Service to permit Puget Sound and Publishers to amend their buy-out applications as a consequence of its ruling on the merits.

I would therefore remand to district court with instructions to grant such equitable relief.

Judge O'Scannlain's dissent in Bianchi v. Bellingham Police Dept. (July 26, 1990)

O'SCANNLAIN, Circuit Judge, dissenting:

I do not agree with the court that Bianchi's claims for unlawful arrest and detention are saved by the Washington Code's tolling provision. In my view, the statute of limitations has run on these claims and we must affirm the district court's order of dismissal. I therefore respectfully dissent.

The court notes that Bianchi has been continuously imprisoned since his arrest in 1979 and then "hold[s] that actual, uninterrupted incarceration is the touchstone for determining disability by incarceration." Ante at 1318. If Washington law provided for a general disability by incarceration, I would agree with this holding. The Washington legislature, however, has not so provided.

The Washington tolling statute teaches that if one entitled to bring an action is, "at the time the cause of action accrues either under the age of eighteen years, or incompetent or disabled [to a particular degree], or imprisoned on a criminal charge, or in execution under the sentence of a court for a term less than his natural life, the time of such disability" shall not be included for statute-of-limitations purposes. Wash.Rev.Code § 4.16.190 (West 1988). I agree with the court that Bianchi's causes of action accrued when he was allegedly unlawfully arrested and detained from January 12 to January 15, 1979. We also generally agree that Bianchi was "imprisoned on a criminal charge" during this time.

Yet the court goes on to give Bianchi the benefit of another disability: that of being "in execution under the sentence of a court for a term less than his natural life." Id. The court does so even though it concedes, in the words of the Washington statute, that Bianchi was not suffering from this second disability "at the time the cause of action accrue[d]." Id. Bianchi was not "in execution under the sentence of a court" until he was convicted and sentenced in Washington in October 1979. This conviction and sentencing took place several months after Bianchi's arrest — that is, several months after the incidents of which he complains had occurred and his causes of action had accrued.

In my view, the tolling provision ceased to be effective and the statute of limitations began to run on Bianchi's claims upon his conviction and sentencing. As the court concedes, Bianchi's disability of being "imprisoned on a criminal charge" was then removed. The Washington legislature has declared irrelevant the fact that another disability (viz., being "in execution under the sentence of a court") was put in its place. Section 4.16.250 of the Washington Code provides that "[n]o person shall avail himself of a disability unless it existed when his right of action accrued." Wash.Rev.Code § 4.16.250 (1988) (emphasis added). In light of the unambiguous language of sections 4.16.190 and 4.16.250, there is no basis for tacking together two separate disabilities.

The court would rely on "the purpose" of the Washington tolling statute, which is to "'protect those who are incapable of protecting themselves by reason of minority, insanity or actual imprisonment.'" Ante at 1318 (quoting Mitchell v. Greenough, 100 F.2d 184, 187 (9th Cir.1938), cert. denied, 306 U.S. 659, 59 S.Ct. 788, 83 L.Ed. 1056 (1939)) (emphasis court's). Yet, by giving Bianchi the benefit of a disability from which he was not suffering when his causes of action accrued, the court's holding runs against the plain language of sections 4.16.190 and 4.16.250. We should not rely on the "purpose" of statutes when to do so requires rendering meaningless unambiguous words. See Tennessee Valley Auth. v. Hill, 437 U.S. 153, 184 n. 29, 98 S.Ct. 2279, 2296 n. 29, 57 L.Ed.2d 117 (1978) ("When confronted with a statute which is plain and unambiguous on its face...., it is not necessary to look beyond the words of the statute.") (emphasis removed); Central Montana Elec. Power Coop. v. Administrator of the Bonneville Power Admin., 840 F.2d 1472, 1478 (9th Cir.1988) ("We avoid any statutory interpretation that renders any section superfluous and does not give effect to all of the words used by Congress.").

Judge O'Scannlain's concurrence and dissent in Bay Area Peace Navy v. US (Sept 14, 1990) [Notes omitted]

O'SCANNLAIN, Circuit Judge, concurring in part and dissenting in part:

I concur in the majority's opinion to the extent that it holds that the government's position was substantially justified and that the district court therefore abused its discretion in awarding plaintiffs attorneys' fees. In my view, however, the government's position was more than "substantially justified" — it was correct. I therefore dissent from that part of the majority's opinion which affirms the district court's grant of a permanent injunction against the United States. I would find that the 75-yard safety-and-security zone was a valid time, place, or manner restriction on speech in a public forum.

I

All three members of the panel agree as to the appropriate test for evaluating whether the three-hour safety-and-security zone violated the first amendment rights of the Peace Navy. It is the test for restrictions on the time, place, or manner of protected speech in a public forum.[1] As the majority notes, such restrictions may be imposed, provided that they "`are justified without reference to the content of the regulated speech, that they are narrowly tailored to serve a significant governmental interest, and that they leave open ample alternative channels for communication of the information.'" Ante at 1226 (quoting Ward v. Rock Against Racism, 109 S.Ct. 2746, 2753 (1989) (quotation omitted)).

This is a three-part test, requiring (1) content neutrality, (2) narrow tailoring to serve a significant governmental interest, and (3) the preservation of ample alternative channels for communication. Because both sides seem to agree that the zone regulation meets the first prong of content neutrality, see ante at 1227, our job becomes easier: we need to examine only the second and third prongs of the test. Unlike the majority, I conclude, for the reasons detailed below, that the challenged regulation satisfies both of these remaining prongs.

II

A

To withstand constitutional scrutiny, any restriction here must "serve a significant governmental interest." Rock Against Racism, 109 S.Ct. at 2753 (quotation omitted). The government here has two significant interests. First, it has a significant interest in ensuring the security of public officials. Second, the government has a significant interest in ensuring maritime safety.[2] I examine each of these interests in turn.[3]

Fleet Week is the largest annual Navy event in the United States.[4] One of its purposes is to demonstrate to certain invited visitors and to the public the view that the United States Navy is well-prepared and effective and represents a good investment of public funds. Fleet Week is not, however, merely a Navy event. It is an event that the Navy has conducted at the invitation of the Mayor of San Francisco. Some 500,000 people pack the shore to watch the Navy parade in the San Francisco Bay, while anywhere from 3,000 to 6,000 invitees, including high-ranking military officers, local government officials, and other dignitaries, watch from bleacher seats erected at the end of the Aquatic Park Pier. The Pier, which curves out into the San Francisco Bay, is about 500 yards long, but only 10 to 12 yards wide. At the very end of the Pier is constructed a reviewing platform, on which sit 60 of the guests who are considered the highest ranking.

The government's undeniable interest in protecting the people on the Pier must be considered, as it was by the district court and apparently by the majority here, to be significant. Since Fleet Week is an event partially intended to demonstrate the United States' military strength and preparedness, it attracts many people in this country to whom these characteristics are distasteful. The government has a significant interest in protecting its officials from the possibility of certain actions against them by such people.[5]

As half a million people jostle for position on the shore and thousands on the Pier also watch, hundreds, maybe thousands (according to uncontroverted testimony) of boats sail about the Bay. Many of these find themselves between the end of the Pier and the area through which the Navy's ships parade; this United States Navy parade consists of ships with quite limited maneuverability. Further, the countless boats of the Peace Navy, Greenpeace, and other protesters, as well as those of mere spectators, also sail about. Most of these vessels are operated by recreational boaters, who are subject to no licensing or supervision here. And as anyone familiar with the San Francisco Bay knows, the wind, tide, and currents are often treacherous; they are especially so toward the end of the Pier.

Given all this, the government's other asserted interest — maritime safety — must also be considered to be significant here. The Coast Guard testified that, based on its considerable experience and pursuant to its statutory mandate,[6] it determined that a safety zone was necessary in these circumstances to ensure maritime safety and to protect against accidents. It further testified that such a zone is necessary to allow easy access to the Pier and the shore to handle potential casualties from accidents.[7]

Ensuring maritime safety and protecting citizens in these circumstances clearly constitute significant governmental interests.

B

We must next ask whether the government's regulation is "narrowly tailored to serve" these significant interests. Rock Against Racism, 109 S.Ct. at 2753 (quotation omitted). For the reasons detailed below, I would find that the government has narrowly tailored its regulation.

It is important to describe what constitutes "narrow tailoring." As the majority points out, narrow tailoring does not require that the government adopt the least-restrictive means in promulgating its regulation. "Rather, `[s]o long as the means chosen are not substantially broader than necessary to achieve the government's interest, [ ] the regulation will not be invalid simply because a court concludes that the government's interest could be adequately served by some less-speech-restrictive alternative.'" Ante at 1227 (quoting Rock Against Racism, 109 S.Ct. at 2758) (emphasis and emendations added by majority); see also United States v. Albertini, 472 U.S. 675, 689, 105 S.Ct. 2897, 2906-07, 86 L.Ed.2d 536 (1985) (the validity of a regulation "does not turn on a judge's agreement with the responsible decisionmaker concerning the most appropriate method for promoting significant government interests").[8] Courts should be "loath to second-guess the Government's judgment" as to whether a regulation "`burden[s] substantially more speech than is necessary to further the government's legitimate interest.'" Board of Trustees of the State Univ. of New York v. Fox, ____ U.S. ___, 109 S.Ct. 3028, 3034, 106 L.Ed.2d 388 (1989) (quoting Rock Against Racism, 109 S.Ct. at 2758).

The regulation contested in this action is the Coast Guard's imposition of a 75-yard zone around the end of the Aquatic Park Pier within which no civilian maritime vessels were permitted; this safety-and-security zone was in effect for only a three-hour period. The district court struck this down and permanently enjoined the Coast Guard from imposing a zone any larger than 25 yards.

I would conclude that the government has narrowly tailored its regulation to serve its significant interest in protecting officials. Originally, the Navy pressed for a 100-yard safety-and-security zone, believing it the minimum necessary, but the Coast Guard disagreed. Balancing "the rights of free people to freely express themselves" against the need for "minimal" protection, Reporter's Transcript ("R.T.") at 109, 97 (Feb. 23, 1988) (testimony of David Zawadzki, Captain of the Port and Commanding Officer of the Coast Guard Marine Safety Office in Alameda), the Coast Guard arrived at the 75-yard zone.

As noted, the district court concluded that "there is no tangible evidence" that a 75-yard zone is necessary to promote the concededly significant governmental interests. Yet it is difficult to conceive of what "tangible evidence" the government could have introduced. It is desirable that precautions be taken to avert problems, and here a narrow precaution was taken. The majority's seeming assertion that the government has shown only "mere speculation about danger," ante at 1228, is unfair. The government has shown that a safety-and-security zone served significant interests and that the zone's size (75 yards) resulted from narrow tailoring. As the government points out, the Coast Guard should not be forced to wait until a catastrophe occurs before it can demonstrate that the security concerns are real.[9]

All around us are "tangible" reminders of constant threats to individual security. The House of Representatives recently noted that "[m]any special events that provide the potential for terrorist actions directed against American citizens occur on or near our nation's coasts." H.R.Rep. No. 494, 99th Cong., 2d Sess. 48 (1985) (emphasis added), reprinted in 1986 U.S.Code Cong. & Admin.News 1865, 1914. Because of this potential, Congress specifically charged the Coast Guard with ensuring safety and security in the nation's ports through the "establishment of security and safety zones, and the development of contingency plans and procedures, to prevent or respond to acts of terrorism." 33 U.S.C. § 1226(b)(1) (1988) (emphasis added). In response to that congressional directive, "each Captain of the Port around the country was tasked by Coast Guard Headquarters with doing vulnerability assessments.... to take a little broader look at safety and security issues." R.T. at 74 (Feb. 23, 1988) (testimony of Captain Zawadzki). As for the particular instance of Fleet Week and the crowd of dignitaries on the Aquatic Park Pier, the Coast Guard explained that "where you are out on a promontory, away from land, with a very narrow access or egress road, you're sitting out there and you have few options if something goes wrong or if someone poses a physical threat to those people out there.... The people out there would be vulnerable." Id. at 95 (testimony of Captain Zawadzki).

According to both the district court and the majority, "there was no showing that Fleet Week presents `any danger that is not present each time a public official appears in public.'" Ante at 1228 (quoting district court). Not so, I think — the dangers are magnified tremendously by the fact that all the public officials at this event are crowded onto a small pier, with no easy means of egress. They could be sitting ducks, as it were, for terrorists who could quickly sail in from only 75-feet away (the size of the maximum permissible safety-and-security zone under the permanent injunction). That the government also closes the Pier itself to the public for twenty-four hours before parade day for security purposes should be seen as a further indication of its genuine concern with security.[10]

The tailoring was also narrow to promote the government's interest in maritime safety. Both Coast Guard and Navy officers testified that this above-described goal of ensuring maritime safety was promoted by the establishment of a safety zone. They further gave uncontradicted testimony of the utility of a safety zone of at least 75 yards. The majority, however, again takes a begrudging view of the evidence, stating that "[t]here was no evidence presented that a 25-yard zone was insufficient" for the purpose of providing "a channel of access to the land by military vessels ... for handling law enforcement and medical emergencies." Ante at 1228. Yet there was much other evidence: for instance, testimony about the unpredictability of winds and currents, the lack of maneuverability of Navy (that is, United States Navy) ships, the number of vessels in the Bay, and many other factors relevant to the appropriate size of a safety zone. Given also the Coast Guard's expertise in maritime safety, I am satisfied that the 75-yard zone met the "narrow tailoring" test.

In short, the Coast Guard properly acted in an anticipatory fashion to ensure security and to promote maritime safety. In so doing, it was advancing significant governmental interests through a narrowly-tailored regulation. The majority's implication that a catastrophe must first occur before a sufficient safety-and-security zone may be established is not compelled by the first amendment.[11]

III

Because the government has satisfied the first contested prong of the test for time, place, or manner restrictions, the only remaining question is whether ample alternative channels for communication were left open. I think that such channels have been left open; in this, I disagree with the district court and the majority here.

First and most importantly, the Peace Navy is still free to sail. The fact that it would have to remain another 150 feet from the Pier — less than the distance from home plate to second base on a baseball diamond's basepaths — would not deprive it of its ability to mimic the United States Navy parade. The Peace Navy would still be in full view of the thousands of people on the Pier and the hundreds of thousands along the shore. Larger signs could still convey the Peace Navy's visual messages; indeed, permissible sound amplification — not proscribed by the safety-and-security zone because not affecting the above-described interests of the government — might make the Peace Navy heard, including a handful of children singing anti-war songs. The effective difference in communication between 25 yards and 75 yards would be minimal.[12]

Second, the use of handbills or pamphlets on land would enable protestors to reach the vast majority of those on shore. This traditional form of protest may be less inventive and clever than the use of boats only a few feet from shore, but that is not to say that it is therefore constitutionally inadequate.

Both the district court and the majority here base their findings of inadequacy on the idea that the alternatives would not allow the Peace Navy to deliver its message to the "3,000 or more Fleet Week official invitees on the pier." Ante at 1230. But as all its witnesses at trial testified, the Peace Navy is interested in reaching both the people on the Pier and the far-many more on the shore.

I do not gainsay that from 75 yards the Peace Navy would find it more difficult to present singing children and dramatic performances than would be the case from 25 yards. Nor do I argue that the Peace Navy's ability to present its message would not be affected in some ways by the requirement of a safety-and-security zone. Nevertheless, for the reasons set forth above, I am satisfied that the Peace Navy has ample alternative channels for communication of its message within the meaning of applicable constitutional principles.

IV

The Coast Guard here promulgated its regulation in part to enforce Congress's mandate that it ensure security on our nation's coasts; it also acted pursuant to its statutory authority to ensure maritime safety. The regulation was effective for a brief three-hour period when 500,000 people packed the shore, several thousand more crowded onto the Aquatic Park Pier, and the waters around the Pier teemed with hundreds, if not thousands, of boats. Because I would find in these circumstances that the government's creation of a safety-and-security zone of 75 yards was narrowly tailored to serve the government's significant interests of ensuring individual security and maritime safety, and because I would find that the regulation left the Peace Navy with ample alternative channels to communicate its message, I would conclude that the zone was a valid time, place, or manner restriction on speech in a public forum. I would therefore reverse the district court's order of a permanent injunction.

For these reasons, I must respectfully dissent from that part of the majority's opinion which upholds the action of the district court.

Judge O'Scannlain's dissent in Federal Sav. & Loan Ins. v. Molinaro (Jan 17, 1991) [Notes omitted]

O'SCANNLAIN, Circuit Judge, dissenting:

Respectfully, I dissent.

I

"It is now clear that the central purpose of Rule 11 is to deter baseless filings in the District Court and thus, consistent with the Rule Enabling Act's grant of authority, streamline the administration and procedure of the federal courts." Cooter & Gell v. Hartmarx Corp., ___ U.S. ___, 110 S.Ct. 2447, 2454 (1990); see also Pavelic & LeFlore v. Marvel Entertainment Group, ___ U.S. ___, 110 S.Ct. 456, 460, 107 L.Ed.2d 438 (1989) (Marshall, J., dissenting) ("One of the fundamental purposes of Rule 11 is to strengthen the hand of the trial judge in his [or her] efforts to police abusive litigation practices and to provide him [or her] sufficient flexibility to craft penalties to each case."). Management of complex litigation often depends on the power of the trial court to sanction attorney behavior in those rare instances where it is necessary to do so. In my view, Rule 11 sanctions played a crucial role in this blockbuster case ably managed by Judge Stotler, who used her authority with appropriate discretion.

The Supreme Court has recognized that the district court is in the best position to determine the propriety of Rule 11 sanctions. "A district court's ruling that a litigant's position is well grounded and legally tenable for Rule 11 purposes is ... fact-specific." Id. at 2460. Moreover, "[d]eference to the determination of courts on the front lines of litigation will enhance these courts' ability to control the litigants before them." Id.

This case well illustrates the propriety of these principles. As of April 1989, the sixty-seven-page docket sheet in this case reflected over 2,300 entries. The present litigation is anything but "streamlined." Moreover, one cannot help but note the irony underlying this entire litigation. The FSLIC essentially charges that John L. Molinaro (and, to some extent, Kimberleigh Ferm) has spent years creating trails of paper to hide his fraudulent dealings while director of Ramona Savings & Loan. The paper war seems to have continued in the district court and has apparently enlisted some of the attorneys in its frenzy.[1] Seldom has this court's need to reinforce the "front lines of litigation" — the district court — been more apparent than in the present case.

With the foregoing in mind, I turn to the merits of the appeal by Michael T. Morrissey, Ferm's attorney, and his law firm, against whom the sanctions were imposed.[2]

II

Our court has identified two separate and independent grounds for the imposition of Rule 11 sanctions. First, sanctions "must be imposed on the signer of a paper if either a) the paper is filed for an improper purpose, or b) the paper is `frivolous.'" Townsend v. Holman Consulting Corp., 914 F.2d 1136, 1140 (9th Cir.1990) (emphasis added). Although I suspect that Ferm's counsel may have violated both prongs of Rule 11, the district court considered primarily the frivolousness prong.[3] In any event, the district court was correct; the filing was frivolous and Morrissey, for having signed it, was properly sanctioned.[4]

A

Ferm's counterclaim and cross-claim was sanctionable as an unjustifiable (and therefore frivolous) collateral attack on the district court's earlier orders, including specifically the March 7 order. When FSLIC moved on February 1, 1988 for an order allowing it to take possession of the monies placed in the court clerk's custody, Ferm specifically opposed the motion on the ground that $489,000 of the funds were her separate property. The district court in its March 7 order considered, and rejected, Ferm's opposition. Ferm's counterclaim and cross-claim coming three weeks later is a blatant attempt to obtain indirectly what was clearly denied her directly.[5]

We have consistently upheld the imposition of sanctions based upon a party's attempts to relitigate the same issue before a district court. In Pipe Trades Council, Local 159 v. Underground Contractors Ass'n, 835 F.2d 1275 (9th Cir.1987), we upheld sanctions imposed upon a party who filed a repetitious motion, albeit styled as a "different" type of motion. See id. at 1280-81; see also Stewart v. American Int'l Oil & Gas Co., 845 F.2d 196, 201 (9th Cir.1988) (imposing sanctions upon a party for filing a third-party complaint which was not only frivolous but "nearly identical" to an earlier action).

B

The substantive counts in Morrissey's filing for Ferm are equally baseless.

1

The claim that the FSLIC conspired fraudulently to convey Ferm's money is "wacky, sanctionably so." See Szabo Food Serv., Inc. v. Canteen Corp., 823 F.2d 1073, 1080 (7th Cir.1987), cert. dismissed, 485 U.S. 901, 108 S.Ct. 1101, 99 L.Ed.2d 229 (1988). FSLIC's efforts to satisfy its own judgments cannot be "conspiracy" as a matter of law. A civil conspiracy is an agreement by two or more persons to perform a wrongful act, or to achieve a lawful result through unlawful means. See Pestin v. Squires, 156 Cal.App.2d 240, 319 P.2d 405, 409 (1958). The acts of which Ferm complained were performed pursuant to the express orders of the district court, with notice to Ferm and all other parties below. Its conduct could not possibly have been "wrongful" or "unlawful" as a matter of law in those circumstances. See Western State Bank v. Grumman Credit Corp., 564 F.Supp. 9, 19 (D.Mont.1982), aff'd, 701 F.2d 187 (9th Cir.1983) (distribution of proceeds to secured creditor not conspiracy because not illegal).

Moreover, Ferm's conspiracy claim is substantively groundless on its face. The purpose of the stipulation for the transfer between New Trend and FSLIC was, obviously, to satisfy partially FSLIC's judgment against Molinaro. The fact of Molinaro's ownership of these funds and FSLIC's entitlement thereto was already resolved by the district court against Ferm. Ferm's attempt to recharacterize the district court's rulings as a "conspiracy" by FSLIC is frivolous beyond doubt. See Agnew v. Parks, 172 Cal.App.2d 756, 343 P.2d 118, 123 (1959) ("in a civil conspiracy no cause can arise if one had a legal right to do the act complained of").

2

The irony in Ferm's abuse of process claim should be self-evident. To prevail in an abuse of process, one must show that the defendant had an ulterior motive, and performed a willful act to misuse the process to gain a collateral advantage over that person. See Slaughter v. Legal Process & Courier Serv., 162 Cal.App.3d 1236, 1247, 209 Cal.Rptr. 189, 195 (1984). For Ferm to have prevailed on this claim, Ferm would have had to set forth facts that FSLIC intentionally and with the purpose of taking advantage of Ferm used the process in a way that was improper in the regular course of proceedings.

FSLIC served its writ of execution to obtain assets held in the name of "John Cook," Molinaro's alias, to satisfy partially its outstanding judgments against Molinaro. A writ of execution is the proper method of enforcing judgments. Fed.R.Civ.P. 69(a); Cal.Code Civ.Proc. §§ 699.010-699.080. The district court properly found that Ferm could not, in good faith, plead an ulterior motive on FSLIC's part in the service of its writ of execution because its motive was to satisfy an outstanding judgment under relevant law. See Ion Equip. Corp. v. Nelson, 110 Cal.App.3d 868, 876-77, 168 Cal.Rptr. 361, 364-65 (no abuse of process by a party's use of a writ of execution, even if issuance of writ was improper, as no ulterior motive could be inferred).

3

The conversion and trespass claims which Morrissey made for Ferm are also frivolous. Conversion is an act of willful interference with personal property, without lawful justification, such that a person entitled thereto is deprived of the use and possession of the personal property. See De Vries v. Brumback, 53 Cal.2d 643, 647, 2 Cal.Rptr. 764, 767, 349 P.2d 532, 535 (1960). It is not sufficient that the party claiming possession is an owner of the property; she must also have a right to immediate possession. See Hartford Finan. Corp. v. Burns, 96 Cal.App.3d 591, 598, 158 Cal.Rptr. 169, 172 (1979). Moreover, an action for conversion will not lie if the person in possession has a right to the property superior to that of the person claiming conversion. See Stan Lee Trading, Inc. v. Holtz, 649 F.Supp. 577, 580 (C.D.Cal.1986); Silverstein v. Kohler & Chase, 181 Cal. 51, 54, 183 P. 451 (1919).

The claims of conversion were without foundation for all of these reasons. Ferm could not, in good faith, argue that FSLIC acted without "lawful justification" by serving the FBI with a writ of execution to obtain property held in the name of "John Cook," Molinaro's alias. It initiated this writ pursuant to final judgments against Molinaro granted by the district court. FSLIC had ample justification to execute on property concealed in safe deposit boxes under Molinaro's assumed name in these circumstances. Ferm could not, without distorting facts already in the district court's record and ignoring previous district court orders, claim that FSLIC willfully and voluntarily sought to deprive Ferm of property which it knew belonged to her.[6]

To state a claim for trespass to personal property, the person claiming trespass must establish an intentional interference by a person with physical possession of the property belonging to another, without justification or consent, proximately causing the damage. Itano v. Colonial Yacht Anchorage, 267 Cal.App.2d 84, 72 Cal.Rptr. 823, 827 (1968). Ferm's claim for trespass was irreparably deficient because Ferm could not plead and prove that FSLIC acted without legal justification in serving a writ of execution on the FBI as discussed above.

Ferm's claim was also baseless because a trespass contemplates the interference with possession, not ownership, of personal property. See Allen v. McMillion, 82 Cal.App.3d 211, 218, 147 Cal.Rptr. 77, 83 (1978). As noted above, the subject assets were in Molinaro's possession because they were held in a safe deposit box under his name alone. Accordingly, Molinaro was in possession of these assets at the time the FBI seized them. Even assuming some sort of trespass was committed, no party interfered with Ferm's possession of personal property, and accordingly Ferm had no standing to bring a trespass claim. Her assertions to the contrary were nothing short of frivolous.

III

The Supreme court identified several drawbacks inherent in a non-deferential appellate review of a district court's Rule 11 determinations, see Cooter & Gell, ____ U.S. at ____, 110 S.Ct. at 2460, and each of these difficulties is present in the majority's disposition today.

The majority disposition has the effect of "establishing circuit law in a most peculiar, second-handed fashion." Id. It detracts from the district court's "ability to control the litigants before them," id., a particularly troublesome result here. Finally, and most significantly, the majority's rationale seriously undercuts Rule 11's deterrence objectives. See id. at 2454 ("Although the rule must be read in light of concerns that it will spawn satellite litigation and chill vigorous advocacy, any interpretation must give effect to the rule's central goal of deterrence.") (citation omitted).

Judge Stotler admirably and judiciously applied Rule 11 in a measured manner in this thorny litigation. Our response should be approval and encouragement, not reversal, in this ongoing saga.

I would affirm the district court's imposition of sanctions in all respects.

**Judge O'Scannlain's concurrence and dissent in Confederated Tribes v. Lujan
(April 3, 1991) [Notes omitted]**

O'SCANNLAIN, Circuit Judge, concurring in part and dissenting in part:

The majority's analysis has two parts. First, the majority concludes that the
Quinault Indians are a necessary and indispensable party under Rule 19; the court then
concludes that because the Nation cannot be joined for reasons of sovereign immunity, the
suit must be dismissed. While I agree that some of plaintiffs' claims should have been
dismissed, I am not persuaded that dismissal of the complaint as a whole was proper. I
therefore can concur in only part of the court's judgment. Moreover, because I believe that
the majority has adopted a Draconian and overbroad interpretation of the compulsory
joinder rule — which unlike sovereign immunity is an equitable rule of discretion — I
respectfully dissent from the majority's reasoning.

I

As the majority explains, Rule 19 has two pertinent parts. Rule 19(a) prescribes
standards for determining whether a non-party is "necessary" to the litigation, and Rule
19(b) prescribes standards for determining whether a non-party is "indispensable," so that
litigation cannot proceed in that non-party's absence.[1]

A

Rule 19(a) states that a non-party:

who is subject to service of process and whose joinder will not deprive the court
of jurisdiction over the subject matter of the action shall be joined as a party in the action
if (1) in the person's absence complete relief cannot be accorded among those already
parties, or (2) the person claims an interest relating to the subject of the action and is so
situated that the disposition of the action in the person's absence may (i) as a practical
matter impair or impede the person's ability to protect that interest or (ii) leave any of the
persons already parties subject to a substantial risk of incurring double, multiple, or
otherwise inconsistent obligations by reason of the claimed interest.

Fed.R.Civ.P. 19(a). Applying these standards to the Quinaults, the majority
concludes that they are a necessary party. I disagree.

1

First, the majority reasons that the plaintiffs' success in this action would not
afford them "complete relief" without joinder of the Quinaults. The court's opinion offers a
one-sentence explanation: "Judgment against the federal officials would not be binding
upon the Quinault Nation, who could continue to assert sovereign powers and
management responsibilities over the reservation." Ante at 1498. It is, of course, true that
judgment against the named defendants would not bind the Quinaults — in the same
sense that judgment against a named defendant can never bind a non-party.[2] That
observation is definitional, but it says nothing about the unavailability of relief within the
meaning of Rule 19(a). The plaintiffs have alleged that federal officials have "denied their
rights in the Reservation," have failed to recognize their right "to be treated equally as

federally recognized Indian tribes," and have improperly recognized the Quinaults as "the exclusive governing body of the Reservation." Complaint at ¶¶ 31, 33, 43; see also id. at ¶¶ 21-51 (alleging six causes of action). It is not clear why declaratory or injunctive relief rendered against the named defendants on these claims would not be "complete" within the relevant level of generality.

The Confederated Tribes probably have no illusions that success in this action will afford them complete relief from all their troubles with the Quinaults, but defining "complete relief" in such expansive terms deprives it of meaning. The relevant question for Rule 19(a) must be whether success in the litigation can afford the plaintiffs the relief for which they have prayed. Again, the "completeness" of relief must be analyzed within the relevant level of generality: the four corners of the complaint.[3]

The majority places considerable weight on this circuit's recent decision in Makah Indian Tribe v. Verity, 910 F.2d 555 (9th Cir.1990), but Makah is clearly distinguishable. The plaintiff Indians in Makah sought to force the government to reallocate a limited number of fishing allotments. A panel of this circuit affirmed the district court's dismissal of the suit because the plaintiff tribe had failed to join the twenty-three other tribes which possessed allotted rights. As the court explained:

The [district] court, viewing the 1987 harvest as a trust fund, held that it could not grant complete relief to the Makah because it would violate the treaty rights of other tribes. It held the absent tribes had an interest in the suit because "any share that goes to the Makah must come from [the] other tribes."

Makah, 910 F.2d at 559 (quoting district court order) (emphasis added). It is appropriate to dispose of cases like Makah through Rule 19 because in such circumstances the court quite literally cannot give the plaintiff the interest that it seeks without simultaneously taking that interest away from the absent non-party. By contrast, the Confederated Tribes seek to vindicate rights to which they allege all Indians on the Quinault Reservation are entitled. There is no comparable "trust fund" or limited resource at issue in this case; here, there is "no pie to carve up."

The Makah court itself recognized this distinction. At the same time that the court affirmed dismissal of the plaintiffs' challenge to the fishing allotments, it reversed the district court's dismissal of their challenge to the administrative process that determines those allotments. The court held that an adjudication of these "procedural claims" could still be effective and would not prejudice the absent tribes "because all of the tribes have an equal interest in an administrative process that is lawful." Id.

The ruling that the Confederated Tribes seek would likewise be an adjudication of "procedural," rather than proprietary, claims. They seek — at least in part, if not entirely — a declaration and enforcement of their rights in the governmental processes that most immediately affect their lives. All the resident tribes of the Quinault Reservation have an equal interest in a fair and lawful administration of these processes; none would be legitimately prejudiced by a judgment regarding their respective rights under the laws and treaties that govern the reservation.[4]

2

The majority's determination that the Quinaults have an interest at risk under Rule 19(a)(2) is similarly overbroad. The court's opinion asserts that "the Quinault Nation undoubtedly has a legal interest in the litigation. Plaintiffs seek a complete rejection of the Quinault Nation's current status as the exclusive governing authority of the reservation." Ante at 1498. Certainly, on one level of analysis, an enhancement of the standing of the Confederated Tribes relative to that of the Quinaults must be viewed as an erosion of the Quinaults' current status, but to assert that the Quinaults have a legally protectable interest for that reason sufficient to make them a necessary party is to stretch the directive of Rule 19(a) very broadly indeed. It is indisputable that if the plaintiffs prevail, the Quinaults' "interests," broadly defined, will suffer. The relevant inquiry for Rule 19(a), however, must be whether cognizable legal rights of the absent non-party will be prejudiced by the suit's continuation.[5] "Prejudice to one's self-interest" and "prejudice to one's legally protected interests" are not synonymous.[6] An application of compulsory joinder principles as broad as the majority's would force dismissal of virtually every case in which the self-interest of a non-party is adversely affected and the non-party cannot be joined.

More importantly, the court's assertion that the plaintiffs seek "a complete rejection" of the Quinaults' "current status" both distorts and prejudges the plaintiffs' claim. What the plaintiffs seek is not a rejection of the Quinaults' current status but a declaration that the Quinaults are not and never have been entitled to that status. If the former were the case, then presumably the majority would be correct in concluding that the Quinaults have a vested legal interest and that Rule 19(a) applies, but to reach that same result when the plaintiffs seek a declaratory judgment is to give the Quinaults the benefit of an unfair bootstrap. The court is saying that whether or not the Quinaults actually have a right to their current status, they say that they do, and that is enough to qualify as a protectable interest under Rule 19(a)(2).[7]

The majority's final argument under Rule 19(a)(2) is that "[e]ven partial success by the plaintiffs could subject both the Quinault Nation and the federal government to substantial risk of multiple or inconsistent legal obligations." Ante at 1498. This sentence, which stands alone without reasoning or analysis, is cryptic. Again, unlike Makah, the controversy here does not involve a limited fund or resource. Vindicating any of the asserted rights of the Confederated Tribes would take nothing from the Quinaults (in any non-relative sense) and certainly nothing which they might later be asked to give to someone else. More importantly, the concern of the Rule is to protect "persons already parties" from the risk of inconsistent legal obligations. Fed.R.Civ.P. 19(a)(2)(ii) (emphasis added). The Quinaults are not already a party; therefore, any risk to them on this score is irrelevant. I respectfully suggest that the majority has simply misread the Rule.

B

Having determined that the Quinaults are a necessary party, the majority properly proceeds to determine whether they may be joined. The majority also correctly concludes that because they have sovereign immunity and have not consented to suit, they may not be. The court then proceeds to determine whether the Quinaults are an "indispensable" party within the meaning of Rule 19(b); but here too the analysis loses force.[8]

Rule 19(b) states that if a necessary party cannot be joined,

the court shall determine whether in equity and good conscience the action should proceed among the parties before it, or should be dismissed, the absent person being thus regarded as indispensable. The factors to be considered by the court include: [1] first, to what extent a judgment rendered in the person's absence might be prejudicial to the person or those already parties; [2] second, the extent to which, by protective provisions in the judgment, by the shaping of relief, or other measures, the prejudice can be lessened or avoided; [3] third, whether a judgment rendered in the person's absence will be adequate; [4] fourth, whether the plaintiff will have an adequate remedy if the action is dismissed for non-joinder.[9]

In applying these four factors, the district court concluded that the first three counsel dismissal of the suit. The majority endorses that determination, but in so doing, its reasoning, in my view, exhibits the same infirmities as its Rule 19(a) analysis.

1

First, the majority adopts the district court's reasoning that "a judgment in favor of the plaintiffs would clearly prejudice the Quinault Nation because it would presumably alter the Quinault[s'] existing authority to govern the reservation." Ante at 1499-1500. By equating "alteration" of the Quinaults' status with "prejudice" of their legal rights, the majority once again interprets the Quinaults' protectable interests too broadly, viewing "interests" in extra-legal terms. Moreover, by implicitly legitimizing the Quinaults' "existing authority to govern," the majority again prejudges the very substance of the plaintiffs' claim.[10]

2

Second, the majority adopts the district court's conclusion that "no relief could be fashioned to avoid that prejudice and that no compromise position would satisfy [the] plaintiffs without prejudice to the Quinault Nation." Ante at 1499. Without supporting reasoning or explanation, the majority insists that "[t]here is no partial or compromise remedy that will not prejudice the Quinault Nation." Id. at 1499. It is difficult to find these pronouncements persuasive without any discussion of the nature or substance of the plaintiffs' claims. When facing such a complicated complaint, how can a court be so sure — on the basis of the pleadings alone — that protective provisions cannot be worked into a final judgment to avoid unfair prejudice? Assuming that the plaintiffs prevail, why would the court be unable to fashion relief in a manner that would avoid prejudice to any legitimate rights of the Quinaults? The majority does not answer these questions.

3

With respect to the third factor, whether a judgment rendered in the Quinaults' absence would be adequate, the court's opinion is largely silent. The implicit argument is a non sequitur. My colleagues appear to suggest that because the Quinaults are immune from suit, there can be no effective relief. The plaintiffs, however, are not suing the Quinaults; they are suing the named federal officials, and the relief they seek would be summoned entirely from the hands of those officials. The Quinaults do not have to be a party in order for the requested relief to be adequate.[11]

4

The majority admits that the fourth factor weighs heavily in favor of the plaintiffs. Given the absence of an alternative forum, proceeding to the merits in this action is the plaintiffs' only hope of obtaining an adequate remedy. In my view, this single factor makes dismissal of the suit so harsh that it may outweigh the other three factors combined.[12]

5

Finally, Rule 19(b) states that the applicable standard by which to consider all four of its factors is whether "in equity and good conscience the action should proceed among the parties already before [the court]." I believe that under this standard the present action clearly should proceed and that a better question might be whether "in equity and good conscience" this action can be dismissed. Rule 19 does not grant absent non-parties a substantive legal right to joinder; it is an equitable rule of discretion, the purely pragmatic purpose of which is to effect justice in the immediate case. See Provident Tradesmens Bank & Trust Co., 390 U.S. at 116-25, 88 S.Ct. at 741-46 (Part II of the opinion). As we said in Makah, "[t]he inquiry is a practical one and fact specific, and is designed to avoid the harsh results of rigid application." Makah, 910 F.2d at 558 (citations omitted).

> The rule is that if the merits of the cause may be determined without prejudice to the rights of necessary parties, absent and beyond the jurisdiction of the court, it will be done; and a court of equity will strain hard to reach that result. [Citations omitted.]

> We refer to the rule established by these authorities because it illustrates the diligence with which courts of equity will seek a way to adjudicate the merits of a case in the absence of interested parties that cannot be brought in.... [T]he rule as stated is intended for the benefit of a plaintiff whose bill sets forth a cause of action which he should, if possible, be given an opportunity to prove....

Bourdieu v. Pacific W. Oil Co., 299 U.S. 65, 70-71, 57 S.Ct. 51, 53-54, 81 L.Ed. 42 (1936); see also Moore's Federal Practice ¶ 19.01-1[1], at 19-20 (quoting Bourdieu). Thus, even if a balancing of the Rule 19(b) factors were to favor dismissal, it is clear that when compulsory joinder presents a close question the court should err on the side of continuing the litigation. If necessary, the action can always be dismissed at a later date,[13] but dismissal now — with nowhere else for the plaintiffs to turn — terminates the asserted claims forever.[14]

C

In short, I cannot agree with the majority's conclusion that the action was properly dismissed for failure to join the Quinault Nation. I do not believe that the Quinaults are either necessary or indispensable under Rule 19. At the very least, it is too early to tell if the Quinaults are such a party. The complaint alleges six causes of action, and without analyzing the substantive law behind these claims and the various possibilities for relief, one cannot fairly determine that the suit cannot proceed.

II

To say that a Rule 19 dismissal is inappropriate begs the question of what is appropriate.

The answer to that question depends on how one reads the plaintiffs' complaint. Although the complaint alleges six causes of action, they can be reduced to essentially three sorts of claims.

A

Plaintiffs allege in their third cause of action that they are entitled to an injunction requiring defendant "to establish and recognize a governing body of the Reservation pursuant to the Indian Reorganization Act of June 18, 1934" and consistent with declaratory relief requested in other portions of their complaint. Complaint at ¶ 37. Plaintiffs allege in their sixth cause of action that they are entitled to an injunction prohibiting the defendant from "considering ... applications for construction within the Reservation ... proposed by or on behalf of the Quinault Tribe." Id. at ¶ 47.

I would affirm dismissal of these claims for reasons of non-justiciability. As defendants argued below, such claims present political questions that lie beyond the adjudicative powers of this court. To the extent that the plaintiffs seek a judgment declaring how the federal government should deal with them or the Quinaults as a forward-looking matter, they are asking this court for an impermissible encroachment upon the prerogatives of the other branches of government. The Constitution itself explicitly commits to Congress the task of "regulat[ing] Commerce ... with the Indian Tribes." U.S. Const. art. I, § 8, cl. 3. Congress, in turn, has explicitly assigned "the management of all Indian affairs and of all matters arising out of Indian relations" to the Executive Branch. 25 U.S.C. § 2 (1990). Indeed, in its seminal opinion in Baker v. Carr, 369 U.S. 186, 82 S.Ct. 691, 7 L.Ed.2d 663 (1962), in which it recast the political question doctrine, the Supreme Court pointed to cases that question the status of Indian tribes as "representative" of political controversies inappropriate for judicial resolution. See Baker, 369 U.S. at 211, 215-17, 82 S.Ct. at 706, 709-10.[15]

I therefore concur in the court's judgment to the extent that it affirms dismissal of the third and sixth causes of action. I would affirm, however, on the alternative ground of nonjusticiability. See Lee v. United States, 809 F.2d 1406, 1408 (9th Cir.1987) ("We may affirm on any ground fairly supported by the record."), cert. denied sub nom. Lee v. Eklutna, Inc., 484 U.S. 1041, 108 S.Ct. 772, 98 L.Ed.2d 859 (1988).

B

Plaintiffs allege in their first cause of action that "[t]he Quinault Tribe has never been lawfully and formally federally recognized as the exclusive governing body of the Reservation," and that plaintiffs "are entitled to judgment declaring that the Quinault Tribe is not the exclusive governing body of the Reservation." Complaint at ¶¶ 28, 32. They further allege that the defendants' favoring of the Quinaults denies "their rights in the Reservation" and that they "are entitled to judgment declaring that [the various tribes on the Reservation] have equal rights in the Reservation." Id. at ¶¶ 31, 33. Similarly, the plaintiffs allege in their fifth cause of action that the defendants "ha[ve] implemented and [are] enforcing the Indian Land Consolidation Act ... as though the Quinault Tribe is the exclusive governing body of the Reservation." Id. at ¶ 43.

To the extent that the plaintiffs simply seek a declaration of their rights and of the scope of the defendants' authority under the Treaty of Olympia and more recent federal legislation, I believe that the district court's dismissal of their claims should be reversed and that their claims should be reinstated. The Declaratory Judgment Act, upon which the plaintiffs have alleged jurisdiction, provides that "[i]n a case of actual controversy within its jurisdiction, ... any court of the United States, upon the filing of an appropriate pleading, may declare the rights and other legal relations of any interested party seeking such declaration, whether or not further relief is or could be sought." 28 U.S.C. § 2201(a) (emphasis added).[16] The Confederated Tribes have insisted repeatedly, both in their briefs and during oral argument, that what they seek above all else is a declaration of previously recognized and adjudicated rights. I believe that the district court has both the jurisdiction and the obligation to provide that declaration.

Indeed, federal courts have been favorable to similar claims in the past. Nine years ago, in Wahkiakum Band of Chinook Indians v. Bateman, 655 F.2d 176 (9th Cir.1981), this court acknowledged its obligation to interpret the rights of Indian litigants under the Treaty of Olympia and associated laws. In that case, the court affirmed the district court's summary judgment denying the plaintiff Indians' plea for declaratory and injunctive relief, but the court parsed the relevant laws and declared the parties' rights under those laws in the process. Sixty years ago, in Halbert v. United States, 283 U.S. 753, 51 S.Ct. 615, 75 L.Ed. 1389 (1930), the Supreme Court interpreted the Treaty of Olympia and associated laws and granted declaratory relief to a group of Indians seeking "to establish and enforce asserted rights to allotments ... in the Quinaielt [sic] Indian Reservation." 283 U.S. at 755, 51 S.Ct. at 615.[17]

In short, to the extent that the plaintiffs seek a declaration of what their rights are as opposed to what their rights should be, their claims appear to be justiciable, within the jurisdiction of the court, and not dependent upon the courtroom presence of the Quinaults. I therefore dissent from the majority's affirmance of the district court's dismissal of the first and fifth causes of action.

C

The third group of claims is the most troubling. In numerous statements sprinkled throughout their complaint, the plaintiffs have alleged violations of "rights" in the vaguest of terms. They have neglected to state with any specificity the substantive law upon which these claims are based. Presumably, this court could affirm dismissal of these allegations for failure to state a claim, but liberal pleading rules counsel against that approach. See Fed.R.Civ.P. 15(a) ("a party may amend the party's pleading only by leave of court or by written consent of the adverse party; and leave shall be freely given when justice so requires"); see, e.g., United States v. Hougham, 364 U.S. 310, 316, 81 S.Ct. 13, 18, 5

L.Ed.2d 8 (1960) (Rule 15 is a "liberal rule[] governing the amendment of pleadings" and "was designed to facilitate the amendment of pleadings except where prejudice to the opposing party would result"); Conley v. Gibson, 355 U.S. 41, 48, 78 S.Ct. 99, 103, 2 L.Ed.2d 80 (1957) ("The Federal Rules reject the approach that pleading is a game of skill in which one misstep by counsel may be decisive to the outcome.").

I believe that a fair reading of the complaint suggests that the plaintiffs may mean to raise civil rights claims, and if that is their intent, the district court surely should have allowed an opportunity to amend. The extraordinary judicial interest in vindicating civil rights, the absence of an alternative forum, and the embryonic stage of this litigation all add considerable weight to what should be an already strong bias in favor of a liberal treatment of the pleadings. Cases implicating the civil rights of Indians are especially sensitive and complex, and they should not be dismissed prematurely. I therefore believe that this court should reverse dismissal of and reinstate those claims which may appear to be civil rights claims with specific instructions that the district court direct the plaintiffs to amend their complaint.

D

Plaintiffs allege in their second cause of action that they "are entitled to a prohibitory injunction preliminarily and permanently enjoining defendant [Lujan] from recognizing and dealing with the Quinault Tribe as the exclusive governing body of the Reservation." Complaint at ¶ 35. They similarly allege in their fourth cause of action that they are entitled to an injunction prohibiting the defendants from recognizing the Quinaults as the exclusive Reservation authority for matters dealing with forest management, forest roads, law and order, Indian lands, and natural resources. Id. at ¶¶ 39, 41.

To the extent that these claims seek an interpretation of the relevant federal laws and a declaration of the plaintiffs' rights under those laws, I would apply the analysis suggested in part II-B above and reinstate their claims. To the extent, however, that these claims seek "prospective" relief that would encroach upon the discretion of Congress and the Secretary of the Interior, I would apply the analysis suggested under part II-A above and affirm dismissal for nonjusticiability.

III

In sum, I concur in the majority's judgment insofar as it affirms dismissal of some of the plaintiffs' claims, but I cannot endorse the majority's reasoning as to those claims. Specifically, I concur in affirming dismissal of all allegations the adjudication of which would require judicial encroachment upon the discretionary authority of the political branches of government.

I dissent from the majority's judgment insofar as it affirms dismissal of any other claims, and I dissent from the majority's interpretation and application of the compulsory joinder rule.

Judge O'Scannlain's dissent in Petrone v. HHS Secretary (June 14, 1991)

O'SCANNLAIN, Circuit Judge, dissenting:

I respectfully dissent.

I

As a general rule, disability benefits may be terminated when evidence shows that the disability has ceased. See 42 U.S.C. § 423(f). Prior to 1980, the Secretary of the Department of Health and Human Services employed the "medical improvement" standard to make this determination; under this standard, the Secretary would not find that a disability had ceased unless the claimant's condition had improved since the last determination of disability. Rhoten v. Bowen, 854 F.2d 667, 668 (4th Cir.1988). In 1980, the Secretary announced that he had abandoned the medical improvement standard and, in its place, established a "current disability" standard pursuant to which benefits were terminated if it was found, on the basis of new evidence, that the person was not presently disabled. Id.

Many Social Security disability benefit recipients filed suit in federal courts challenging the new regulations. See, e.g., Johnson v. Heckler, 606 F.Supp. 82 (S.D.N.Y.1984); Turner v. Heckler, 592 F.Supp. 599 (N.D.Ind.1984); Graham v. Heckler, 573 F.Supp. 1573 (N.D.W.Va.1983); Lopez v. Heckler, 572 F.Supp. 26 (C.D.Cal.1983). Thereafter, prompted at least partially by these numerous district court actions, Congress enacted the Social Security Disability Benefits Reform Act of 1984 ("Reform Act"). See Rhoten, 854 F.2d at 669 & n. 1. The Reform Act did not establish a presumption of continuing disability. However, it did provide that terminations must be based on substantial evidence of medical improvement. In addition, the Reform Act specifically provided for automatic remand of all requests for judicial review pending on September 19, 1984. See id.

Unfortunately, Congress apparently did not consider the relationship between this automatic remand provision and the Equal Access to Justice Act ("EAJA"), 28 U.S.C. § 2412. Needless to say, claimants whose benefits were restored upon remand sought attorney's fees under the EAJA. Courts have since grappled with the question of whether such claimants are "prevailing parties" within the meaning of the EAJA.[1] Three theories have been proposed. Under the first theory, claimants who received benefits as a result of the Reform Act's automatic remand provision can never be prevailing parties, as the "clear causal relationship" between the lawsuit and the relief is lacking. In addition to the majority here, this reasoning has been endorsed by the First Circuit, see Guglietti v. Secretary of HHS, 900 F.2d 397 (1st Cir.1990), the Seventh Circuit, see Hendricks v. Bowen, 847 F.2d 1255 (7th Cir.1988), and the Eighth Circuit, see Truax v. Bowen, 842 F.2d 995 (8th Cir.1988).

The second theory is the obverse of the first; under this view, a claimant may be a prevailing party for purposes of the EAJA simply by bringing the lawsuit that enabled retroactive application of the Reform Act. See Perket v. Secretary of HHS, 905 F.2d 129 (6th Cir.1990); Guglietti, 900 F.2d at 405-08 (Breyer, J., dissenting). The rationale for this viewpoint was encapsulated by Judge Breyer:

> In my view, the following circumstances make it proper, as a matter of ordinary English usage, as well as a matter of law, to say that the claimant "prevailed" in her legal action. First, she did get the relief she wanted. Second, her legal action was a necessary condition for her obtaining it.... Third, the outside event — the Congressional action — was not an unrelated, extra-judicial event. Rather, Congress acted, in part, because this claimant, and other claimants similarly situated, had filed lawsuits.

Guglietti, 900 F.2d at 405 (Breyer, J., dissenting) (citations omitted).

The third theory is an intermediate approach, aptly entitled as the "inevitable victory" theory. See Perket, 905 F.2d at 133. Under this theory, a claimant is a prevailing party under the EAJA if she would have otherwise prevailed in the absence of the Reform Act. Id.; see also Lopez v. Sullivan, 882 F.2d 1533, 1537 (10th Cir.1989); Rhoten, 854 F.2d at 670; Hendricks, 847 F.2d at 1259 (Easterbrook, J., concurring) ("An award is both appropriate and necessary when the claimant would have prevailed in his quest for benefits, and would have recovered fees, had the Reform Act never existed.").

It is this latter approach which I believe we should adopt today. This approach avoids the problem of rewarding lawyers for mere "serendipity." See Hendricks, 847 F.2d at 1259 (Easterbrook, J., concurring). However, it also avoids the equally unfortunate result of failing to compensate claimants who have brought meritorious lawsuits. See id. at 1261 ("When the EAJA otherwise would have required the government to pay, ... the creation of a new entitlement in the Reform Act should not make the claimants worse off."). Indeed, this approach best harmonizes Congress's objectives in both the Equal Access to Justice Act and the Disability Benefits Reform Act.

II

In the present case, the district court concluded that a disability claimant who received benefits as a result of passage of the Reform Act could not be a prevailing party under the EAJA. Applying the "inevitable victory" theory, I would remand this case to the district court to determine whether Petrone would have prevailed in the absence of the Reform Act. If so, the district court should next determine whether the government's position was not substantially justified. If both of these inquiries are resolved in Petrone's favor, I believe she should be entitled to attorney's fees under the Equal Access to Justice Act.

Notes

[1] In order to receive attorney's fees under the EAJA, the requester must be a prevailing party, the government's position cannot be substantially justified, and no special circumstances may exist that would make such an award unjust. See Bay Area Peace Navy v. United States, 914 F.2d 1224, 1230 (9th Cir.1990).

Judge O'Scannlain's dissent in US v. Perkins (July 1, 1991)

O'SCANNLAIN, Circuit Judge, dissenting:

Ernest Perkins has raised eight independent challenges to his bank robbery conviction. The court rejects all eight and affirms the conviction. I concur in the court's analysis in all respects but one; I am not persuaded that the district court's change-of-appearance instruction, which everyone but the government concedes was improper,[1] constituted harmless error beyond a reasonable doubt. I therefore must dissent.

I

The court has properly identified the problem: "A change of appearance instruction contemplates some independent evidence indicating that the defendant himself actually changed his appearance." Ante at 1403 (emphasis in original). Here, there is no such independent evidence. The bank surveillance photographs demonstrate that the robber, during the commission of the crime, had a long, thick moustache. A distinct photograph of the defendant demonstrates that he, at the time of his booking, had only a slight amount of growth over his lip. By themselves, these two sets of images offer no meaningful inference; there is nothing to tie them together. The missing link that would have justified a change-of-appearance instruction would be a photograph of Perkins before the robbery (or at least, before the trial) demonstrating that formerly he too, like the robber, had a long, thick moustache. Only then would there be a demonstrable change in the defendant's appearance from which one might fairly infer a consciousness of guilt and thus ultimately conclude that Perkins and the robber are the same man. As it was, the government had only two of the three snapshots it needed to warrant the challenged instruction: the all-important "before" picture either does not exist or is inexplicably absent from the record.

II

Under the rule articulated by the Supreme Court in Chapman v. California, 386 U.S. 18, 87 S.Ct. 824, 17 L.Ed.2d 705 (1967), an error striking at the fundamental fairness of a criminal trial may be deemed harmless only if "the court [is] able to declare a belief that it was harmless beyond a reasonable doubt." Chapman, 386 U.S. at 24, 87 S.Ct. at 828.[2] The beneficiary of the constitutional error bears the burden of proving that "the error complained of did not contribute to the verdict obtained." Id. Unlike the court, I am not convinced that the trial court's erroneous instruction was harmless beyond a reasonable doubt, and I am not persuaded that the government has met its burden of proving otherwise.

The court bases its conclusion on two observations. First, the court contends that "[i]n order for the jury to have attached significance to any change of appearance, the jury already would have [to have] concluded that the defendant was the robber." Ante at 1403. According to this reasoning, the instruction was harmless because a logical jury would have had no rational basis for connecting the bank photographs with the booking photograph in order to infer a change of appearance. Either the jury already had concluded that both images depicted the same man, or absent the "missing link," they simply disregarded the instruction as nonsensical.

This reasoning, however, merely assumes away the problem. Presumably, a change-of-appearance instruction was only necessary because it was not abundantly clear that both sets of pictures depicted the same man. The purpose of a change-of-appearance instruction is, after all, to guide the jury's consideration of circumstantial evidence that may help to identify the defendant as the criminal; if direct evidence already sufficiently identifies the criminal, then the prosecution has no need for such an instruction. Indeed, in this case the government did not attempt (and apparently was unable) to make an in-court identification.[3]

Moreover, the fact that the instruction makes no sense without a picture of what Perkins looked like before the robbery does not suggest that the jury ignored it or placed no value upon it. It is precisely when reason does not support the giving of a jury instruction that consideration of that instruction may prove prejudicial. A logical jury might well have assumed that the trial court would not have given it illogical directions, thus concluding that the court at least was satisfied that the missing link had been supplied. In this way, Perkins may have been prejudiced — literally "pre-judged" — by the trial court.

Second, the court concludes that the evidence of Perkins's guilt was overwhelming. Ordinarily, when there is overwhelming evidence of guilt, there can be no reasonable doubt that the error was harmless. See, e.g., Harrington v. California, 395 U.S. 250, 254, 89 S.Ct. 1726, 1728, 23 L.Ed.2d 284 (1969); Rose, 478 U.S. at 584, 106 S.Ct. at 3109 (Burger, C.J., concurring); Echavarria-Olarte, 904 F.2d at 1398-99. "[T]he Constitution entitles a criminal defendant to a fair trial, not a perfect one." Van Arsdall, 475 U.S. at 681, 106 S.Ct. at 1436 (citations omitted).

I cannot agree, however, that the government's evidence in this case is overwhelming. In support of its conclusion to the contrary, the court recites the following:

Alamond [an eye-witness] identified Perkins as the man he saw running from the bank and getting in a blue Datsun; the police found in the bank a parking citation issued to the blue Datsun which was registered to Perkins, and found a delinquent notice for the ticket in Perkins's apartment; Perkins lied about his ownership of the car when he actually drove the blue Datsun to the place where he was arrested and had the keys to that car in his pocket, showing his consciousness of guilt; and the police found in Perkins's apartment a rust-colored 1970's style suit and maroon briefcase matching those used in the robbery.

Ante at 1404. The defense has raised powerful challenges to all of this evidence.

First of all, in his initial police interview, Chris Alamond described the Datsun he saw as brown, not blue — a discrepancy that casts considerable doubt upon the accuracy of his observation. He also described the fugitive whom he saw as having no facial hair — a fact that casts further doubt upon his identification or, perhaps, suggests that the man whom he saw was not the robber. Alamond, moreover, did not identify Perkins as the robber in open court. In fact, he admitted at trial that his observation was insufficient to permit such an identification. Alamond did positively identify Perkins sometime before trial in a live police lineup, but even that identification is questionable. At the time, Alamond conceded that he was "not sure" about his identification because the man he observed had been both on the run and across the street. Furthermore, two days prior to the lineup, Alamond had examined a police photospread and had described a picture of Perkins as being "similar" to the man he had seen; Perkins, however, was the only person common to both the photospread and the subsequent lineup.

Nearly all the remaining evidence cited by the court relates to the getaway car and its connection to Perkins.[4] The defense, however, has offered an explanation for this connection that, if not convincing, is at least sufficient to render this evidence less than "overwhelming" in its implication of guilt. See Dudley v. Duckworth, 854 F.2d 967, 972 (7th Cir.1988) (error not harmless where evidence of guilt was "impressive but not overwhelming"), cert. denied, 490 U.S. 1011, 109 S.Ct. 1655, 104 L.Ed.2d 169 (1989). Perkins contends that he sold the car to a fellow boarder at his rooming house, Harold McGee. He admits that he continued to have "periodic access" to the car because McGee had not finished paying for it, but he insists that McGee also used the vehicle and that McGee was the driver on the day of the robbery. Perkins further insists that McGee, whom Perkins had known from his days at a halfway house, looks deceptively similar to Perkins and more closely fits the witnesses' descriptions of the robber. Like Perkins, McGee allegedly has a medium complexion, slim build, and short-cropped hair. Moreover, McGee is 5' 10", the same height as the robber in the estimation of Linda Purmont, the bank teller who had the closest view. Perkins, on the other hand, is 5' 5 1/2", an inch shorter than Purmont herself.

If McGee did commit the crime, he may well have dropped the parking citation on the bank floor in an effort to implicate Perkins and divert attention from himself. Indeed, if he were a calculating felon, he could have purchased Perkins's car with this whole scheme in mind, never intending to change the vehicle's registration or to assert exclusive ownership. He may also have planted the clothes worn during the robbery in Perkins's closet. As the defense points out, McGee was a resident of the same rooming house and had access to Perkins's room. One might also reasonably wonder whether Perkins, if he was the actual robber, would have been careless enough to have dropped the parking citation on the bank floor and to have kept the incriminating clothes in his closet.

The purpose of these speculations is, of course, not to cast any suspicion upon Mr. McGee, whom we may presume to be a model citizen. Nor do I mean to usurp the function of the jury, who alone must weigh competing views of the evidence. Rather, I mean only to suggest that no single view of the evidence here is overwhelming. A reasonable doubt persists over whether the prejudicial inference in an admittedly improper jury instruction may have tipped the delicate balance of considerations. I simply cannot conclude without a doubt that the erroneous change-of-appearance instruction did not contribute to the verdict.

I would therefore vacate the conviction and remand this case for a new trial.

Notes

[1] "We review a district court's decision to submit [a change-of-appearance] instruction[] for abuse of discretion." United States v. Feldman, 788 F.2d 544, 555 (9th Cir.1986), cert. denied, 479 U.S. 1067, 107 S.Ct. 955, 93 L.Ed.2d 1003 (1987).

[2] We recognize at least three levels of harmless-error scrutiny in the criminal context. See generally United States v. Valle-Valdez, 554 F.2d 911, 914-17 (9th Cir.1977). First, when the error is not of a constitutional dimension, we will deem it harmless if it is "more probable than not" that the verdict would have been the same without the error. See United States v. Echavarria-Olarte, 904 F.2d 1391, 1398 (9th Cir.1990).

Second, when the error is constitutional in nature, we will apply the Chapman rule and deem it harmless if, but only if, it is clear that the error was harmless beyond a reasonable doubt. See, e.g., Delaware v. Van Arsdall, 475 U.S. 673, 106 S.Ct. 1431, 89 L.Ed.2d 674 (1986); Rose v. Clark, 478 U.S. 570, 106 S.Ct. 3101, 92 L.Ed.2d 460 (1986); see also id. at 576-77, 106 S.Ct. at 3105 (describing numerous Supreme Court cases that have applied the Chapman rule).

Finally, when the error is constitutional in nature and it implicates a "structural" right so basic to a fair trial that, by definition, it can never be harmless, we will deem the error harmful per se. See Chapman, 386 U.S. at 23 & n. 8, 87 S.Ct. at 823 & n. 8; Rose, 478 U.S. at 577-80, 106 S.Ct. at 3105-07 (describing numerous Supreme Court cases that have applied this rule); id. at 586-89, 106 S.Ct. at 3110-12 (Stevens, J., concurring) (suggesting that some errors are harmful per se because they implicate principles beyond the immediate case and affect values other than the accuracy and reliability of the verdict).

As Chief Judge Wallace pointed out for this court in Valle-Valdez, it is not always clear what level of scrutiny should apply to an erroneous jury instruction. See Valle-Valdez, 554 F.2d at 916-17 (citing Ninth Circuit cases that have applied both the first and the second tests). The majority has elected to apply the Chapman rule, the intermediate level of scrutiny, to the change-of-appearance instruction at issue here. I agree that Chapman represents the appropriate standard because the error in the present instruction has a prejudicial quality that implicates due process concerns. See infra; see also Rose, 478 U.S. at 572, 576-84, 106 S.Ct. at 3103, 3105-09 (applying Chapman rule to an improper jury instruction); Feldman, 788 F.2d at 555-56 (applying Chapman rule to an improper change-of-appearance instruction). I therefore agree with the majority's choice of standard; I disagree with its conclusions under that standard.

[3] Linda Purmont, the bank teller whom the robber directly confronted, initially told the police that she was confident in her ability to identify the robber if presented the opportunity. At a live police lineup seven days after the crime, however, she positively identified a random participant who was standing immediately beside the defendant as the robber. At the time, she said that she recognized this man as the robber "the moment that he came in" and that she "knew it was him."

[4] The court also mentions Perkins's false exculpatory statement as part of the overwhelming evidence of his guilt. As the court concedes and as its earlier discussion of

this issue explains, however, such statements may not properly be regarded as direct evidence of guilt. They are at best circumstantial evidence of a consciousness of guilt. See ante at 1402.

Judge O'Scannlain's dissent in Schneider v. TRW (July 10, 1991) [Notes omitted]

O'SCANNLAIN, Circuit Judge, dissenting:

I respectfully dissent.

First, I believe that the district court abused its discretion in reaching the merits of Schneider's pendent state law claims. Having determined preliminarily that the federal claims lacked merit, the court should have dismissed the state claims without prejudice pursuant to the Gibbs doctrine. See United Mine Workers v. Gibbs, 383 U.S. 715, 86 S.Ct. 1130, 16 L.Ed.2d 218 (1966).

Second, given that the district court did address the state law claims, I believe that the court erred in concluding that Schneider has failed to raise a genuine issue of material fact with respect to those claims. Under a proper understanding of the complaint, the record, and the relevant state law, Schneider has indeed presented a litigable controversy — both in contract and in tort. The majority reaches the opposite conclusion, in my view, only through a questionable application of evidentiary rules and local rules of practice that effectively excludes from consideration the "smoking-gun" deposition of a TRW employee.

I

According to United Mine Workers v. Gibbs, federal courts may assert federal-question jurisdiction over pendent state-law claims only if those claims satisfy a three-pronged test.[1] First, "[t]he state and federal claims must derive from a common nucleus of operative fact ... such that [the plaintiff] would ordinarily be expected to try them all in one judicial proceeding." Gibbs, 383 U.S. at 725, 86 S.Ct. at 1138. This first requirement is constitutional. If the various claims do not form one integrated "case or controversy," then a federal court lacks article III authority to adjudicate the state claims. See id.; U.S. Const. art. III, § 2, cl. 1. Schneider's claims, however, are all closely related. They all arise out of and concern the circumstances of her hiring and firing by TRW. Her complaint therefore satisfies this first prong.

Second, Gibbs states that "[t]he federal claim [upon which pendent jurisdiction is premised] must have substance sufficient to confer subject matter jurisdiction on the court." Gibbs, 383 U.S. at 725, 86 S.Ct. at 1138 (citing Levering & Garrigues Co. v. Morrin, 289 U.S. 103, 53 S.Ct. 549, 77 L.Ed. 1062 (1933)). This requirement is also constitutional.

If the claims all arise from a common transaction or occurrence, then, "assuming substantiality of the federal issues, there is power in federal courts to hear the whole." Id. (emphasis in original; footnote omitted). In the present case, the federal claims are arguably insubstantial, although not to the point of depriving the court of jurisdiction. See Levering & Garrigues Co., 289 U.S. at 105, 53 S.Ct. at 550 ("the federal question averred may be plainly insubstantial [if it is] obviously without merit"); see also Hagans v. Lavine, 415 U.S. 528, 539-41, 543, 94 S.Ct. 1372, 1380-81, 1382, 39 L.Ed.2d 577 (1974).

The problem in this case arises when one focuses upon the third prong of the Gibbs test. Even when a federal court has the constitutional power to hear pendent claims under the first two prongs, Gibbs holds that the court may (and should) refrain from ruling on those claims in certain circumstances. The court must weigh "considerations of judicial economy, convenience and fairness to litigants; if these are not present a federal court should hesitate to exercise jurisdiction over state claims." Gibbs, 383 U.S. at 726, 86 S.Ct. at 1139. As the Gibbs Court explained:

Needless decisions of state law should be avoided both as a matter of comity and to promote justice between the parties, by procuring for them a surer-footed reading of applicable law. Certainly, if the federal claims are dismissed before trial, even though not insubstantial in a jurisdictional sense, the state claims should be dismissed as well. Similarly, if it appears that the state issues substantially predominate, ... the state claims may be dismissed without prejudice and left for resolution to state tribunals.

Id. at 726-27, 86 S.Ct. at 1139 (footnotes omitted).[2] Pendent jurisdiction is ultimately a doctrine of discretion, and in the present case, I am persuaded that the district court abused that discretion. See id. at 728, 86 S.Ct. at 1140.

There is no indication that the district court ever considered any of the Gibbs factors before ruling on the merits of Schneider's state law claims. A weighing of the Gibbs factors, however, indisputably favors dismissal of those claims. First of all, fairness to the litigants clearly counsels dismissal because a surer-footed reading of state law would be available in state court. The apparent split within this panel over how to read California law attests to that. Secondly, concerns about comity and respect for the state judicial system also favor dismissal. Recent landmark developments in the state's contract and tort law strongly urge federal judicial restraint. See, e.g., Foley v. Interactive Data Corp., 47 Cal.3d 654, 765 P.2d 373, 254 Cal.Rptr. 211 (1988).

Thirdly, interests of economy and convenience are not significantly advanced by federal adjudication. The federal claims were all dismissed before trial, and accumulated evidence bearing on the state claims may easily be carried "across the street" to the courtroom of a state superior court judge presumably better versed in the relevant law.

Finally, there can be no doubt that "state issues substantially predominate." Schneider voluntarily withdrew her section 1983 claim when it became clear that there was no evidence of state action to support it, and the district court properly and swiftly rejected her two remaining federal claims — alleging discrimination on the basis of age and national origin — because Schneider "failed to specify any acts which can be regarded as discriminatory in nature." Schneider v. TRW, Inc., No. 86-2369 at 3-4 (S.D.Cal. Aug. 3, 1989). Indeed, Schneider has abandoned all three of her federal claims on appeal, apparently conceding their insubstantiality. "When the state issues apparently predominate and all federal claims are dismissed before trial, the proper exercise of jurisdiction requires dismissal of the state claim[s]." Wren v. Sletten Constr. Co., 654 F.2d

529, 536 (9th Cir.1981) (per curiam) (citations omitted); see also Kitchens v. Bowen, 825 F.2d 1337, 1342 (9th Cir.1987), cert. denied, 485 U.S. 934, 108 S.Ct. 1109, 99 L.Ed.2d 270 (1988); Otto v. Heckler, 802 F.2d 337, 338, amending 781 F.2d 754 (9th Cir.1986); Schultz v. Sundberg, 759 F.2d 714, 718 (9th Cir.1985) (per curiam).

In response to these arguments, my colleagues appear to advance the dubious proposition that a district court's decision to retain jurisdiction over pendent claims is essentially unreviewable so long as it does not violate article III — i.e., the first two prongs of the Gibbs test. See ante at 995 ("The district court had the power to decide the pendent claims in this case, and presumably thought it best to decide them.") (emphasis added), 995 ("Unless the district court was without power to hear the case, which is not the situation here, we ought not surprise the district court [by reversing its decision to retain jurisdiction]") (emphasis added). They therefore do not necessarily disagree with the results of my Gibbs analysis; they simply contend that it is not our role to engage in that analysis in the first place. I disagree. While it is clear that Gibbs commits the determination of whether to exercise pendent jurisdiction to the sound discretion of the district court, it is equally clear that we must review the district court's determination for an abuse of that discretion. See Gibbs, 383 U.S. at 728, 86 S.Ct. at 1140; Mackey v. Pioneer Nat'l Bank, 867 F.2d 520, 523 (9th Cir.1989); Aydin Corp. v. Loral Corp., 718 F.2d 897, 903-04 (9th Cir.1983); Arizona v. Cook Paint & Varnish Co., 541 F.2d 226, 227 (9th Cir.1976) (per curiam), cert. denied, 430 U.S. 915, 97 S.Ct. 1327, 51 L.Ed.2d 593 (1977). I find such an abuse here. The district court completely failed to consider the question, and on the record before us, its tacit determination to proceed with the state claims was, in my view, clearly in error.

My colleagues also insist that, even if it would have been a preferable course of action originally, dismissal of the pendent claims at this late stage is unwarranted given the passage of time and the current consumption of judicial resources. Ante at 995. They further point out that neither party has challenged the district court's retention of jurisdiction here, and they argue that it is inappropriate for us to raise the issue on our own initiative. Id.

These arguments are equally unpersuasive. As we recognized in Wren, "'the issue whether pendent jurisdiction has been properly assumed is one which remains open throughout the litigation.'" 654 F.2d at 536 (quoting Gibbs, 383 U.S. at 727, 86 S.Ct. at 1139). Despite the majority's exclusive focus upon the interests of judicial economy, those interests are not the only or even the most important factor for us to consider. Sunk costs can rarely justify injustice, and they do not outweigh the wrong wrought by a potentially incorrect and unfair application of state law. Moreover, jurisdictional matters and questions of comity require a court's own constant vigilance, and where dismissal is clearly appropriate, a court need not wait for action by the parties.[3]

In short, this litigation essentially concerns contract and tort law and the inchoate principles of California employment law. It probably should not have been in federal court in the first place, and it certainly should not have stayed here so long. I would therefore vacate the district court's entry of summary judgment on the pendent claims and remand for entry of an order dismissing those claims without prejudice.

II

Notwithstanding the Gibbs problem, and turning nonetheless to the merits of the pendent claims, I believe that Schneider has successfully presented triable issues, both in contract and in tort, when one views the evidence in the light most favorable to her case. I address the contract claim first and the tort claim thereafter.

A

1

Schneider disputes TRW's contention and the district court's conclusion that she was an at-will employee. Under California law, an at-will employee is terminable with or without good cause upon notice by either party. See Cal.Lab.Code § 2922 (West 1989); Foley, 47 Cal.3d 654, 665, 765 P.2d 373, 376, 254 Cal.Rptr. 211, 214. California law presumes that employment is terminable at will, but the presumption is rebuttable by evidence of an oral or written agreement to the contrary. The California Supreme Court's seminal decision in Foley recognized two sorts of contractual promises that can trump the presumption: (1) express promises and (2) promises that are "implied in fact" by the employer's representations or conduct.[4] In short, to survive summary judgment on her breach of contract claim (and on any other claim whose success depends upon the refutation of at-will status), Schneider must establish a prima facie case sufficient to allow a jury to infer the existence of a promise qualifying TRW's right to terminate her without good cause — a promise that may be oral or written, express or implied.[5] This much she has done.

In her complaint, briefs, and supporting affidavits, Schneider has maintained consistently that she was not entirely confident in her ability to perform the job that TRW originally had in mind for her and that she accepted the offer upon the receipt of three assurances: (1) that the company would provide necessary training and supervision, (2) that the company would place her in an entry-level position for which someone with her background would normally be regarded as overqualified, and (3) that her poor command of the English language would not be a hindrance to her progress. At no point have the defendants purported to contradict or rebut Schneider's claim that she received these specific assurances — assurances which, if proven to exist to the finder of fact, presumably would proscribe any decision to terminate her on the basis of inadequate training or poor language skills.[6]

On the other hand, the sworn statements of several TRW employees who worked with Schneider lend prima facie support to her claim that she did receive such assurances. Most notable among these statements is the deposition of Robert Mangum, who served as Schneider's immediate supervisor during much of the period in question. Mangum, who is a codefendant in this action, has provided strong evidence in the case against the company and his superior, Don Rohner, the man whom Schneider mostly credits with having hired and fired her. In his deposition, Mangum explains:

Don Rohner wanted to talk to me concerning what to do with Maria Schneider. One of the requests that he made of me was, "Whatever," quote, unquote, he said, "Whatever it takes, Bob, get rid of her." And I didn't really question him about it. I didn't — in fact, I sort of ignored him. Within that week after that Don made it very clear to me that he wanted to get rid of Maria Schneider even though she was on a probationary status. He said, "Whatever it takes, Bob, get rid of her." He says, "I don't want her working here any more.["] And I questioned him; and specifically he wanted me to not give her a chance to perform, not to fulfill our agreement in the verbal warning that we gave Maria. We contracted with her to give her 30 days to improve, to meet certain standards; and he said that, "That's unnecessary, Bob. I want you to get rid of her."

Deposition of Robert Mangum at 22 (Sept. 26, 1988) (emphasis added). Later in his deposition, Mangum states:

I was upset by the fact that [Rohner] was going to invalidate or void a contract we made with Maria in her verbal review to give her a chance to perform. That's what I was upset about.... I was ... upset with the fact that we were going to get rid of someone in a somewhat unethical manner. In other words, I was told to fire her, not give her a chance to actually learn something.

[T]he personnel department ... agreed that there would be no disciplinary action taken on Maria, or in other words, Maria would not have to perform to her 30 day verbal warning, that was wiped clean.

Id. at 25, 27 (emphasis added). On the basis of this deposition alone, Schneider has presented a genuine issue of material fact regarding the company's conduct and its promissory obligations.[7]

2

The court, however, excuses the district court's failure to acknowledge this and several other inculpatory depositions by declaring that this critical evidence (a) is not part of the district court's record, (b) is inadmissible hearsay, and (c) was not lodged with the district court in compliance with its local rules of practice. See ante at 990 n. 2. All three of these arguments are unpersuasive.

First, the district court itself has made none of these determinations, and yet all three involve matters that lie wholly within that court's exclusive domain. An appellate court has neither the authority nor the occasion to make evidentiary rulings or to apply a district court's local rules of practice. Nor has TRW advanced any of these arguments in this appeal. My colleagues have simply substituted their own judgment for that of the district court on matters that only relate to the district court and that, as far as the immediate record reveals, clearly did not concern the district court here. In so doing, they have subverted the time-honored principle that courts reviewing summary judgments must view the evidence and resolve any conflicts in the light most favorable to the nonmoving party.

3

Even assuming that it is appropriate for an appellate court to decide to exclude evidence on its own motion, my colleagues' arguments are still unpersuasive. First, the depositions at issue are indeed part of the district court's record: they are all file-stamped as having been lodged with the district court in a timely fashion; they appear as an entry on the district court's docket sheet; and they comprise exactly fifty percent of Schneider's excerpts of record, the contents of which TRW has never challenged. It is simply indisputable that the depositions relied upon were "on file" with the district court when it heard and ruled upon TRW's motion. See Fed.R.Civ.P. 56(c).

4

Second, there is absolutely no indication that the district court ever regarded the depositions in question to be inadmissible hearsay, and TRW has not challenged them as hearsay. The reason for this is understandable: to exclude these depositions on hearsay grounds would be (and is) simply wrong as a matter of law. Admittedly, they are out-of-court statements, and they therefore satisfy the technical definition of hearsay contained in Rule 801 of the Federal Rules of Evidence. See Fed.R.Evid. 801(c) (defining hearsay as "a statement, other than one made by the declarant while testifying at the trial or hearing, offered in evidence to prove the truth of the matter asserted.") (emphasis added). Yet virtually all depositions are out-of-court statements; if Rule 801 governed their admissibility in civil actions, their value as a discovery tool would be largely ephemeral. Rule 801 therefore does not control the admissibility of depositions; rather, Rule 32 of the Federal Rules of Civil Procedure controls.[8] That rule states in pertinent part that:

[a]t the trial or upon the hearing of a motion ..., any part or all of a deposition, so far as admissible under the rules of evidence applied as though the witness were then present and testifying, may be used against any party who was present or represented at the taking of the deposition or who had reasonable notice thereof....

Fed.R.Civ.P. 32(a); see also id. 32(b) (the absence or unavailability of the deponent is not a ground upon which to object to the admission of a deposition). The fact that the depositions were taken out of court is, therefore, not a bar to their admissibility. See id. advisory committee's note on 1970 amendment (explaining that the italicized language quoted above "eliminates the possibility of certain technical hearsay objections which are based, not on the contents of [the] deponent's testimony, but on his absence from court.").

To the extent that my colleagues actually mean to suggest that certain statements within the depositions — rather than the depositions themselves — are inadmissible hearsay, their argument is equally uncompelling. Most of the inculpatory testimony within the depositions is not hearsay at all but represents the first-hand, personal observations of the deponents themselves. Most of that which does not (for example, Mangum's accounts of what Rohner said) is not hearsay either but constitutes the admissions of a party-opponent. See Fed.R.Evid. 801(d)(2), 805.

Nor are any non -hearsay challenges to the content of the depositions well taken. The depositions contain indisputably relevant and material testimony by apparently competent witnesses, and on that basis, the testimony they embody is admissible. See 6 J.

Moore, W. Taggart & J. Wicker, Moore's Federal Practice ¶ 56.11[1.-3] (2d ed. 1991).
Moreover, TRW has made no objection to Schneider's reliance on this testimony, and any
objections at this stage would be untimely. See Fed.R.Civ.P. 32(d)(3); Fed.R.Evid.
103(a)(1). As an appellate court obligated to view the evidence in the light most favorable
to Schneider, we are certainly in no position to raise objections of our own.

5

The court's invocation of the district court's local rules of practice is similarly
inappropriate. The local rule in question requires that a party opposing another party's
motion file a written opposition that "contain[s] ... copies of all documentary evidence
upon which the party in opposition relies." S.D.Cal.R. 220-8(b)(3), quoted ante at 990 n.
2. The court implies that because Schneider did not physically attach the relevant portions
of the most damning depositions to her memorandum, the testimony in those depositions
was not properly before the district court. I disagree.

The Mangum deposition and the others upon which Schneider relies were lodged
with the district court on April 17, 1989, only seven days after Schneider filed her original
memorandum in opposition to summary judgment and seven days before the district
court's first hearing on the motion.[9] Schneider clearly intended this later filing to amend
her earlier memorandum, which is replete with specific references to the depositions. To
deny her reliance on this critical evidence upon the mere technicality that the two
documents were filed one week apart and were not physically attached — or alternatively,
on the technicality that she did not refile or re-cite the depositions when she opposed
TRW's renewal of its motion less than three months later — is harsh justice indeed. See
supra note 9; see also 10A C. Wright, A. Miller & M. Kane, Federal Practice and Procedure
§ 2721, at 44 (1983) (court "will consider all papers of record" before granting summary
judgment); Higgenbotham v. Ochsner Found. Hosp., 607 F.2d 653, 656-57 (5th Cir.1979)
("The rule [Fed.R.Civ.P. 56(c)] does not distinguish between depositions merely filed and
those singled out by counsel for special attention. Nor is this a case where the deposition
that created the dispute was a needle in a paper haystack; the docket sheet shows that only
five depositions were filed.") (footnote omitted).

To bolster its invocation of the district court's local rules, the court cites Nilsson,
Robbins, Dalgarn, Berliner, Carson & Wurst v. Louisiana Hydrolec, 854 F.2d 1538 (9th
Cir.1988), for its holding that the district court was "under no obligation to mine the full
record" for triable issues of fact. Ante at 991 n. 2. In light of the original opposing
memorandum's very specific citations to the relevant depositions, however, no such
mining operation is called for in this case. Nilsson, moreover, is distinguishable. There,
the non-moving party had twice failed to answer the movant's pleadings and had
"repeatedly refused to conform to the Local Rules and the Federal Rules of Civil
Procedure." Nilsson, 854 F.2d at 1541. The district court had entered four orders for
monetary sanctions and had imposed and lifted three default judgments, and these
measures still "did not alleviate this behavior." Id.; see id. at 1541-42. In addition, the non-
moving party

w[as] put on notice by [the movant] eleven months before the summary
judgment motion was ruled upon, that its memorandum in opposition to the motion for
summary judgment was legally insufficient because of the lack of evidentiary support[,
and t]he trial judge, in her tentative ruling, [had] highlighted for [the non-moving party]
the flaws in their opposition .... [The non-moving party], in the face of all these warnings
that summary judgment would be granted unless they adequately supported their
opposition to the ... motion, neglected to cite the court to a single evidentiary fact.

Id. at 1545 (emphasis added).[10]

To equate Schneider's slight oversight, which was swiftly remedied, with this
pattern of persistent misconduct is patently strained. Moreover, there is no evidence in
this case that the district court ever gave Schneider any comparable warnings. In any
event, the Nilsson court clearly based its holding first and foremost on the non-moving
party's failure to cooperate and only secondarily on the relevant local rule of practice. See
id. at 1545. There can be no doubt that an obstructive failure to cooperate is costly and
prejudicial to the movant; there is, however, no similar sign of prejudice in the current
case.

In no way do I mean to imply that the observance of local rules of practice need
not be strict, and I would not suggest that one can disregard such rules with impunity.
Local rules serve a necessary and important function. My complaint is not with the rules
themselves but with the present application of one of those rules. The court has applied
this rule unfairly and in a manner wholly inconsistent with the Federal Rules of Civil
Procedure. See Fed.R.Civ.P. 83 (a district court may "make and amend rules governing its
practice not inconsistent with these rules."); see also id. 1 (purpose of federal rules is to
secure outcomes that are both efficient and just); 56(c) (summary judgment not proper
where "pleadings, depositions, answers to interrogatories, and admissions on file, together
with the affidavits, if any," reveal a genuine issue of material fact). Perhaps most
importantly, the court has undertaken to apply this rule retroactively from the appellate
stage — even though the district court's record is devoid of any reference to its local rules
and even though there is no indication that the district court would have applied this
particular rule to the same end.

6

Finally, in addition to denying Schneider's reliance on critical depositions, the
court affirms the district court's conclusion that her evidence has failed to rebut
California's at-will presumption. For this holding, the court cites Pugh v. See's Candies,
Inc., 116 Cal.App.3d 311, 171 Cal.Rptr. 917 (1981). See ante at 990. In Pugh, a case
favorably cited by the Foley court, the California Court of Appeal reinstated a former
employee's suit against his former employer on grounds that the trial judge had
prematurely terminated the action. The court held that the plaintiff had successfully
demonstrated a prima facie case of wrongful termination by introducing evidence from
which a reasonable jury could infer (a) the existence of an implied promise not to fire him
without cause and (b) an unlawful breach of that promise. See Pugh, 116 Cal.App.3d at

329, 171 Cal.Rptr. at 927.

I agree that Pugh is on point. I further believe that, like Wayne Pugh, Maria Schneider has demonstrated a prima facie case from which a jury might infer both the existence and the breach of a promise not to terminate her for certain reasons. The court reaches the opposite conclusion by focusing upon four "factors" mentioned by the Pugh court as indicative of whether the parties have an implied agreement modifying their ability to terminate their relationship at will.[11] As the Pugh court itself explained, however, these four factors are neither dispositive nor all-inclusive. "[I]t is appropriate to consider the totality of the parties' relationship: Agreement may be `shown by the acts and conduct of the parties, interpreted in the light of the subject matter and the surrounding circumstances.'" Id., 116 Cal.App.3d at 329, 171 Cal.Rptr. at 927 (quoting Marvin v. Marvin, 18 Cal.3d 660, 678 n. 16, 557 P.2d 106, 118 n. 16, 134 Cal.Rptr. 815, 827 n. 16 (1976)); see also Foley, 47 Cal.3d at 681, 765 P.2d at 388, 254 Cal.Rptr. at 226 ("the totality of the circumstances determines the nature of the contract") (citing Pugh).

Thus, although the majority correctly points out that Schneider has admitted an awareness of "no TRW policies suggesting assurances of continued employment," that observation does nothing to deny her contention that TRW made particular contractual assurances in her case. Similarly, the absence of an industry-wide custom of terminating employees only for good cause is relevant but not dispositive, and the fact that Schneider was only with the company for nine months does not necessarily mean that she had no reasonable expectations of job security. In fact, in light of Schneider's claim that TRW promised to train her, the shortness of her tenure would, if anything, seem to support an inference that the company reneged on that promise. See supra note 7. Finally, despite the majority's contention to the contrary, Schneider clearly does argue that TRW's actions and communications conveyed contractual obligations. See Brief for Appellant at 14-17.

In short, to have granted summary judgment on Schneider's breach of contract claim, the district court must have concluded that Schneider failed to present even a prima facie case sufficient to support the finding of a promise modifying the company's right to fire her. I do not believe that the record supports such a conclusion. I would therefore reverse the district court's entry of summary judgment on the breach of contract claim.

B

With respect to Schneider's tort claims, the district court essentially held that Schneider's status as an at-will employee precluded these theories of recovery. See Schneider, No. 86-2369 at 3. If the court is correct in concluding that Schneider was an at-will employee, then its tort analysis is also largely correct. The at-will concept would be ephemeral if employees who, as a matter of contract, are legally terminated without good cause could turn around and sue their employers in tort. The California Supreme Court recognized this fact in Foley. See Foley, 47 Cal.3d at 698 n. 39, 765 P.2d at 400 n. 39, 254 Cal.Rptr. at 238 n. 39. It therefore held that, absent a specific public policy or legislation to the contrary, an at-will employee who seeks to challenge a termination decision cannot sue his former employer for tort damages or for breach of implied covenants of good faith and fair dealing.[12]

Two aspects of the district court's analysis, however, call its reliance on Foley into question. First, as I have already mentioned, the evidence does not indisputably establish that Schneider was an at-will employee. In my view, she has presented a prima facie case sufficient to put the question before a jury. Second, the district court has fundamentally misconstrued the nature of her tort claims. The company, she contends, was not fraudulent and deceitful when it fired her; it was fraudulent and deceitful when it hired her. In her view, TRW held out assurances to induce her to accept its offer and to move from San Francisco to San Diego without ever intending to honor those assurances. See Complaint at ¶¶ 18-19; Memorandum of Points and Authorities in Opposition to Defendants' Motion for Summary Judgment at 8. A tort claim based upon such allegations remains unaffected by the logic of Foley because it concerns what is in essence pre-contractual conduct. Even if Schneider was an at-will employee, she presumably can still sue the defendants in tort with respect to actions that preceded their employment relationship. Allowing such claims to proceed does not erode an employer's ability to fire at will.[13]

Recognizing that Foley does not foreclose these claims, however, only answers half the question. One must still determine whether Schneider has introduced evidence of tortious conduct sufficient to survive summary judgment. I believe that she has, and the Mangum deposition, alone, is sufficient to present a prima facie case. First, Mangum's statement makes it clear that TRW knew about Schneider's inexperience and her poor command of the English language when it hired her and that the company assured her, both at the time of hiring and subsequently, that it would provide adequate training. Then, in a critical portion of the deposition, Mangum states:

Mr. Rohner believed that once he was given an approved requisition, in other words, a promise by ... upper management to alot [sic] certain dollars for a hire, he thought if he didn't fill it within seven days he would lose his requisition. I'm serious. This is why he hired Maria. She was the first warm body that he saw that would fit the bill and he was scared to death he would lose that money, and so he was trying to build a kingdom or, I don't know, he's not the best manager in the world; but he definitely — I swear to God I couldn't believe it.

Q. Did he tell you that?

A. Yes, he was scared to death he was going to lose that requisition, so he wanted to fill it. See, Don Rohner's position was, you can always fire someone who doesn't work out, and guess what, you still have an opening to fill. I am not making that up, that's Don Rohner's philosophy[.]

Deposition of Robert Mangum at 36 (Sept. 26, 1988). Again, on the basis of this deposition alone, Schneider has presented triable issues in tort sufficient to survive summary judgment.

III

In sum, I would affirm the district court's judgment for the defendants on the federal claims. I would reverse its judgment for the defendants on the pendent state-law claims and would remand for entry of an order dismissing those claims without prejudice. Alternatively, I would remand for further proceedings in the district court on the merits of the pendent claims.[14] Summary judgment is summary justice, and the record in this case does not warrant summary justice.

Judge O'Scannlain's dissent in Collazo v. Estelle (July 18, 1991) [Notes omitted]

O'SCANNLAIN, Circuit Judge, with whom BEEZER and NOONAN, Circuit Judges join, dissenting:

To paraphrase the great Bard of Avon, "[t]he [majority] doth protest too much, methinks." W. Shakespeare, Hamlet, III, ii. In a noble attempt to vindicate important legal principles, my colleagues have misinterpreted and exaggerated the essential and dispositive facts of this case. More importantly, they have unjustifiably expanded the prophylactic rules that govern the waiver of an accused's constitutional rights to legal assistance and against self-incrimination. I therefore respectfully dissent.

I

A

In Edwards v. Arizona, 451 U.S. 477, 101 S.Ct. 1880, 68 L.Ed.2d 378 (1981), the Supreme Court held that "an accused ..., having expressed his desire to deal with the police only through counsel, is not subject to further interrogation by the authorities until counsel has been made available to him, unless the accused himself initiates further communication, exchanges, or conversations with the police." Id. at 484-85, 101 S.Ct. at 1884-85 (emphasis added). Elaborating upon the importance of this italicized language, which my colleagues now excise from the Court's holding, the Court wrote:

In concluding that the fruits of [a second] interrogation initiated by the police on January 20 could not be used against Edwards, we do not hold or imply that Edwards was powerless to countermand his election [to remain silent and to consult an attorney] or that the authorities could in no event use any incriminating statements made by Edwards prior to his having access to counsel. Had Edwards initiated the meeting on January 20, nothing in the Fifth and Fourteenth Amendments would prohibit the police from merely listening to his voluntary, volunteered statements and using them against him at the trial. The Fifth Amendment right identified in Miranda is the right to have counsel present at any custodial interrogation. Absent such interrogation, there would have been no infringement of the right that Edwards invoked and there would be no occasion to determine whether there had been a valid waiver. Rhode Island v. Innis, [446 U.S. 291, 298 n. 2, 100 S.Ct. 1682, 1688 n. 2, 64 L.Ed.2d 297 (1980)], makes this sufficiently clear.

Id. at 485-86, 101 S.Ct. at 1885 (emphasis added).

Two years after Edwards, in Oregon v. Bradshaw, 462 U.S. 1039, 103 S.Ct. 2830, 77 L.Ed.2d 405 (1983), a plurality of the Court announced a two-part test by which to gauge the admissibility of a confession offered by a suspect after his invocation of the right to counsel. The confession is admissible, the Court held, if (a) the suspect initiates the discussion that leads to it and (b) the totality of the circumstances reveals that the purported waiver is both voluntary and intelligent. Id. at 1044-46, 103 S.Ct. at 2834-35 (plurality opinion); see also id. at 1048-50, 103 S.Ct. at 2836-37 (Powell, J., concurring in the judgment).

More recently, in Arizona v. Roberson, 486 U.S. 675, 108 S.Ct. 2093, 100 L.Ed.2d 704 (1988), in language that the majority surprisingly quotes and emphasizes, the Supreme Court held that in the wake of a request for counsel "it is presumed that any subsequent waiver that has come at the authorities' behest, and not at the suspect's own instigation, is itself the product of the `inherently compelling pressures' and not the purely voluntary choice of the suspect." Id. at 681, 108 S.Ct. at 2097-98, quoted ante at 421 (with same emphasis added). Mirroring the more explicit language of Edwards and Bradshaw, Roberson's tacit suggestion is that a subsequent waiver "at the suspect's own instigation" is not subject to such presumption.

Similarly, in Minnick v. Mississippi, ___ U.S. ___, 111 S.Ct. 486, 112 L.Ed.2d 489 (1990), a recent decision wholly neglected by my colleagues, the Supreme Court held that when an accused requests counsel, "interrogation must cease, and officials may not reinitiate interrogation without counsel present, whether or not the accused has consulted with his attorney." Id. 111 S.Ct. at 491 (emphasis added). Like Bradshaw and Roberson, Minnick is a conscious and careful echo of Edwards. Writing for the Court in Minnick, Justice Kennedy repeatedly stressed that the prophylactic protection of these several rulings only extends to situations involving "police-initiated questioning." Id.; see also id. ("a fair reading of Edwards and subsequent cases demonstrates that we have interpreted the rule to bar police-initiated interrogation unless the accused has counsel with him at the time of questioning") (emphasis added); id. at 489 ("`a valid waiver of th[e] right [to have counsel present during questioning] cannot be established by showing only that [the accused] responded to further police-initiated custodial interrogation ...'") (quoting Edwards, 451 U.S. at 484, 101 S.Ct. at 1884) (emphasis added).

Indeed, the Minnick Court went out of its way to explain that "Edwards does not foreclose finding a waiver of Fifth Amendment protections after counsel has been requested, provided that the accused has initiated the conversation or discussions with the authorities; but that is not the case before us." Id. at 492 (emphasis added). I respectfully submit that what was not before the Supreme Court in Minnick is before this court today.

B

Given that the Supreme Court itself has denied that Edwards compels the majority's holding, it is curious indeed for the majority to suggest that the officers' conduct represented a "textbook violation of Edwards v. Arizona." Ante at 417.[1] Even the majority admits that Collazo initiated the conversation that immediately led to his confession of guilt:

Collazo requested to talk to a lawyer. Instead of respecting his request, however,

Officer Destro (Officer Rolen's partner) attempted to pressure him into dispensing with counsel and talking to them about the homicide....

The police then departed....

Collazo was then permitted to call and to see his wife, a legal secretary. She came to the police station and had a lengthy discussion with him, the substance of which is unknown. Some three hours after the officers' departure, Collazo contacted a sergeant and asked, "Where are the investigators?" The sergeant correctly construed this as a request to talk to them, and they were so notified and returned to the station. Collazo was again advised of his Miranda rights, and indicated he had changed his mind and was now willing to talk. He then essentially confessed to his non[-]shooting role in the crimes for which he had been charged and arrested.

Ante at 413-14 (footnote omitted).

Under a plain reading of these facts and the Bradshaw and Edwards rules, Collazo's confession was both voluntary and legally admissible in the case against him. After a three hour hiatus, during which time he had the opportunity to (and did) have "a lengthy discussion" with a trusted confidante, Collazo actively sought out the police officers who were investigating the Metzger homicide.[2] The officers, who had long since left the police station, were then summoned back upon his request. Once again, and notably without making any impermissible suggestions this time, the officers advised Collazo of his Miranda rights. Only after affirmatively acknowledging that he understood those rights four times and that he voluntarily had changed his mind, did Collazo confess.[3]

No one disputes that the officers' conduct during the initial conversation was improper and reprehensible. The issue, however, is whether that improper conduct produced Collazo's later confession. As the Supreme Court opined in Rhode Island v. Innis, 446 U.S. 291, 100 S.Ct. 1682, 64 L.Ed.2d 297 (1980):

[I]t may be said ... that the [petitioner] was subjected to "subtle compulsion." But that is not the end of the inquiry. It must also be established that a suspect's incriminating response was the product of words or actions on the part of the police that they should have known were reasonably likely to elicit an incriminating response. This was not established in the present case.

Id. at 303, 100 S.Ct. at 1691 (footnote omitted and emphasis added). On the contrary, California carried its burden at the trial level of proving by a preponderance of the evidence that Collazo's waiver and confession were voluntary. See Colorado v. Connelly, 479 U.S. 157, 168, 107 S.Ct. 515, 522, 93 L.Ed.2d 473 (1986) ("Whenever the State bears the burden of proof in a motion to suppress a statement that the defendant claims was obtained in violation of our Miranda doctrine, the State need prove waiver only by a preponderance of the evidence."); see generally Lego v. Twomey, 404 U.S. 477, 92 S.Ct. 619, 30 L.Ed.2d 618 (1972). In fact, as the majority points out, "the trial court found Collazo's confession `voluntary beyond a reasonable doubt,' and that there was `no taint whatsoever to his ultimate statement.'" Ante at 415 n. 3 (quoting trial transcript).

Even if the state had not met its burden, however, the "totality of the circumstances" plainly reveals that Collazo voluntarily initiated the discussion during which he confessed and, further, that he initiated that discussion precisely in order to confess. See Colorado v. Spring, 479 U.S. 564, 573, 107 S.Ct. 851, 857, 93 L.Ed.2d 954 (1987) ("`Only if the "totality of the circumstances surrounding the interrogation" reveal[s] both an uncoerced choice and the requisite level of comprehension may a court properly conclude that the Miranda rights have been waived.'") (quoting Moran v. Burbine, 475 U.S. 412, 421, 106 S.Ct. 1135, 1140, 89 L.Ed.2d 410 (1986) (quoting Fare v. Michael C., 442 U.S. 707, 725, 99 S.Ct. 2560, 2572, 61 L.Ed.2d 197 (1979))). As a prior panel of this court observed:

Collazo had a prior criminal history, and was experienced in the routine of police interrogation. He was a paid informant of the DEA. There was a lapse of approximately three hours between the first interrogation session and Collazo's subsequent confession. Collazo conferred with his wife in the interim. Finally, at the time of his confession, Collazo stated that he was not acting under pressure of any promise or threat.

Collazo v. Estelle, 898 F.2d 87, 89 (9th Cir.1989), reh'g en banc granted, id. at 91. Collazo's familiarity with the legal process, his ability to consult his wife, his affirmation that he understood and yet still wished to waive his rights, the passage of a considerable period of time, and the complete absence of any evidence to suggest that he was acting under duress — when weighed together — demonstrate "a break in the chain of events sufficient to insulate the statement from all that went on before." United States v. Patterson, 812 F.2d 1188, 1192 (9th Cir.1987) (citing Clewis v. Texas, 386 U.S. 707, 710, 87 S.Ct. 1338, 1340, 18 L.Ed.2d 423 (1967)), cert. denied, 485 U.S. 922, 108 S.Ct. 1093, 99 L.Ed.2d 255 (1988).[4]

To borrow from the language of torts, a preponderance of the evidence indicates that Collazo's own free will was the "supervening cause" of his confession. Under such circumstances and where the accused, rather than the police, initiates the relevant discussion, Edwards and its progeny clearly indicate that a confession is properly admissible. Virtually all other circuits that have addressed this question have so concluded, and a district court within this circuit has agreed. See United States v. Velasquez, 885 F.2d 1076, 1083-89 (3d Cir.1989) (suspect who initiated further discussion and confessed after first invoking Miranda rights effectively waived those rights), cert. denied, ____ U.S. ____, 110 S.Ct. 1321, 108 L.Ed.2d 497 (1990); Plazinich v. Lynaugh, 843 F.2d 836 (5th Cir.1988) (same), cert. denied, 488 U.S. 1031, 109 S.Ct. 841, 102 L.Ed.2d 973 (1989); United States v. Comosona, 848 F.2d 1110, 1112-13 (10th Cir.1988) (same); Fike v. James, 833 F.2d 1503 (11th Cir.1987) (same); Robinson v. Percy, 738 F.2d 214, 221 (7th Cir.1984) (same); Fetterly v. Paskett, 744 F.Supp. 966, 970-71 (D.Idaho 1990) (same); cf. United States v. Gomez, 927 F.2d 1530, 1539 (11th Cir.1991).

C

The majority is only able to avoid this conclusion through a combination of dubious factfinding and wordplay that purportedly permits the court to say that Collazo did not really "initiate" the discussion that led to his confession.

First, the majority claims that there is an "evident linkage between the [initial] coercion and the [subsequent] confession." Ante at 420. In the majority's words, "we find ... that Collazo's initiation of the communication leading to the second interrogation was the product of the coercive statements made by the police during the first, illegal interrogation." Ante at 420. Appearing as it does for the first time in the long history of this case in the latter pages of the majority's opinion, this purely factual finding is hardly believable. Indeed, in four previous decisions in this very case, the state trial and appellate courts, the district court, and a prior panel of this court all expressly found that there was no linkage — evident or otherwise — between the officers' initial comments and Collazo's later confession.[5] Again, as the majority concedes, the trial court found that Collazo's confession was "voluntary beyond a reasonable doubt." See ante at 415 n. 3; see also Sumner v. Mata, 449 U.S. 539, 546-47, 101 S.Ct. 764, 768-69, 66 L.Ed.2d 722 (1981) (in habeas proceedings, the factual findings of state trial and appellate courts are presumed correct if fairly supported by the record). Indeed, as the state points out, Collazo himself repeatedly affirmed at the time of his confession that his waiver was the product of his own free will, and the trial court agreed. My colleagues, however, dispense with that finding and substitute their own judgment, determining on the basis of a cold record that those affirmations are not credible but that Collazo's subsequent, counsel-guided testimony at the suppression hearing is. See ante at 429. Credibility determinations, though, are not the province of this court. We must accept those determinations as they appear in the record, and the majority is unable to demonstrate where in the record there is any affirmative evidence of their alleged "evident linkage." The facts simply do not support the finding.[6]

Moreover, the majority's characterization of the second discussion as a "second interrogation" is itself inappropriate: "`Interrogation,' as conceptualized in the Miranda opinion, must reflect a measure of compulsion above and beyond that inherent in custody itself." Innis, 446 U.S. at 300, 100 S.Ct. at 1689 (footnote omitted). "By custodial interrogation, we mean questioning initiated by law enforcement officers after a person has been taken into custody or otherwise deprived of his freedom of action in any significant way." Miranda v. Arizona, 384 U.S. 436, 444, 86 S.Ct. 1602, 1612, 16 L.Ed.2d 694 (1966) (emphasis added). Collazo initiated the second discussion and was not subjected to substantial pressures during that discussion before he actually confessed. Under similar circumstances, this court has held that a discussion may not be characterized as an "interrogation" for purposes of Miranda. See Shedelbower v. Estelle, 885 F.2d 570, 573 (9th Cir.1989), cert. denied, ___ U.S. ___, 111 S.Ct. 975, 112 L.Ed.2d 1060 (1991); United States v. Thierman, 678 F.2d 1331, 1334-35 (9th Cir.1982); see also United States ex rel. Church v. DeRobertis, 771 F.2d 1015, 1017-20 (7th Cir.1985); Robinson v. Percy, 738 F.2d at 218-19. Under similar circumstances, the Supreme Court has also suggested that Miranda rights may not even be implicated. See Innis, 446 U.S. at

298 n. 2, 100 S.Ct. at 1688 n. 2; Edwards, 451 U.S. at 485-86, 101 S.Ct. at 1885; see also Arizona v. Mauro, 481 U.S. 520, 107 S.Ct. 1931, 95 L.Ed.2d 458 (1987).

By declaring the existence of an "evident linkage" between the two discussions, the majority seeks to do with the facts what it clearly cannot do with the law: escape the unmistakable implication of Edwards, Bradshaw, Roberson, Innis, and Minnick that when the accused initiates the conversation, he may thereby render harmless prior police improprieties and render admissible subsequent incriminating statements. By holding, as a factual matter, that Collazo was acting under the undue influence of the officers' earlier comments when he later requested to speak with them, the majority concludes that Collazo did not actually "initiate" the second conversation at all but that, in fact, the police did. Ante at 422. This cannot be believed, and as a result, neither can the court's holding that Collazo's confession was coerced.

This, then, is the critical flaw in the majority's analysis: Part III of the court's opinion presents a compelling but largely irrelevant survey of our Miranda jurisprudence and its underlying policy rationales only to conclude, in dicta, that the conduct of the police during the first conversation was not "compatible with a system of justice that does not permit police coercion" and typifies behavior that "offends due process as guaranteed by the Fourteenth Amendment." Ante at 416, 419-20. Part IV then attempts to resuscitate Part III, which is otherwise entirely dicta, by finding the all-important "evident linkage": the ethereal thread of coercion that ties the two conversations — and the two parts of the majority's analysis — together. The structure of the argument is inherently seductive. Surely no one disagrees with Part III and its broad affirmations of an accused's rights, but properly understood, Part III has no bearing on the specific facts or question before us.

In short, because there was no appreciable foul play associated with the incriminating second conversation and because Collazo himself initiated that conversation in order to confess, the majority's holding cannot stand unless one is able to impute the impropriety that occurred during the first conversation into the second one as well. This requires a finding of not one, but two involuntary acts on Collazo's part. First, one must find that Collazo's request to speak with the officers — after the three-hour hiatus and after the lengthy discussion with his wife — was itself coerced, and then one must find that his subsequent confession was also coerced. The facts support neither finding. Collazo affirmatively initiated the second conversation and voluntarily admitted his guilt.[7]

D

If the majority's misreading of the facts were my only complaint, this would be a briefer dissent. A view of police coercion as expansive as the majority's, however, has greater ramifications. If allowed to stand, the majority's holding will unjustifiably extend the current reach of Miranda's prophylactic protections. See Connelly, 479 U.S. at 166, 107 S.Ct. at 521 (cautioning against "expanding `currently applicable exclusionary rules by erecting additional barriers to placing truthful and probative evidence before state juries'") (quoting Lego, 404 U.S. at 488-89, 92 S.Ct. at 626).

The "unless" clause in the Edwards holding, the qualification in the Roberson holding, the very essence of the Bradshaw and Innis holdings, and the careful caveat in Minnick — which all suggest that suspect-initiated discussions may produce admissible confessions in the wake of police improprieties — are at risk of becoming dead letters within this circuit. If a court can find upon these facts that the accused did not "initiate" the relevant discussion and did not voluntarily confess thereafter, then one wonders under what conditions a confession in the wake of prior police misconduct will ever be admissible in court. In short, the majority's holding goes a long way toward establishing the proposition that police misconduct creates a per se violation of Miranda that subsequent voluntary acts of the accused can never render harmless. See United States v. Anderson, 929 F.2d 96, 99 (2d Cir.1991) ("the application of a per se rule is inappropriate"). Because Miranda is a prophylactic rule — and not a constitutional right — such a proposition of law has no rationale to recommend it. See ante at 418 (acknowledging that "Miranda `rights' are `not themselves rights protected by the Constitution'") (quoting Michigan v. Tucker, 417 U.S. 433, 444, 94 S.Ct. 2357, 2363, 41 L.Ed.2d 182 (1974)); see also Roberson, 486 U.S. at 688-93, 108 S.Ct. at 2101-04 (Kennedy, J., dissenting).

II

Courts must be wary of exaggerating what are properly recognized as contemptible improprieties into grandiose visions of injustice. The temptation to entertain such visions is especially great in cases that pit lonely criminal defendants against the police and prosecutorial powers of their state governments. The danger in succumbing to such temptation is that rules designed to secure the integrity of the legal process can gradually take the form of escape valves whose only notable effect is to provide safe haven for indisputably guilty persons. Cf. Fulminante, 111 S.Ct. at 1264 (holding that even the admission of a coerced confession may be harmless error and noting that "`the central purpose of a criminal trial is to decide the factual question of the defendant's guilt or innocence'") (quoting Delaware v. Van Arsdall, 475 U.S. 673, 681, 106 S.Ct. 1431, 1436, 89 L.Ed.2d 674 (1986)); see also Robinson v. Borg, 918 F.2d 1387, 1394 (9th Cir.1990) (Trott, J., dissenting) (warning against the dangers of expansive judicial applications of the Miranda rules and urging the judiciary "to monitor carefully the costs of these rules as they are applied to the cases that come before us").

In my view, that is precisely what has happened in this case and what could happen to this court's Miranda jurisprudence generally. Through a dramatic envoy, our thoughtful bard once warned:

> We must not make a scarecrow of the law,
> Setting it up to fear the birds of prey,
> And let it keep one shape till custom make it,
> Their perch, and not their terror.

W. Shakespeare, Measure for Measure, II, i. The majority has rallied behind such a straw man here, and I therefore earnestly hope that the tenure of today's ruling as the law of this circuit will be short-lived.

Judge O'Scannlain's concurrence and dissent in US v. Smith (Sept 17, 1991)

O'SCANNLAIN, Circuit Judge, concurring in part and dissenting in part:

I concur wholeheartedly in the judgment and in all but two Parts of the majority's opinion. I dissent, however, from Parts IV and V-A.

In Part IV, the majority holds that the district court adequately considered Smith's ability to pay before it found, as a factual matter, that he will be able to produce one of the largest restitution awards ever imposed in this circuit — nearly $12.8 million — within five years of his release from prison. Because I do not believe that the record supports either the majority's holding or the district court's finding, I would reverse the district court on this ground.[1]

In Part V-A, the majority holds that the district court under-valued the collateral held by Smith's institutional victims when it calculated the total loss attributable to his criminal conduct. The majority thus concludes that the court overstated the amount properly compensable by restitution to this extent. Because I believe that the majority mischaracterizes the nature of the victims' loss and because I believe that the district court's valuation of the collateral was proper, I would affirm the district court on this ground.

I

A

The Victim and Witness Protection Act of 1982 ("VWPA") provides that:

The court, in determining whether to order restitution under section [3663] of this title and the amount of such restitution, shall consider the amount of the loss sustained by any victim as a result of the offense, the financial resources of the defendant, the financial needs and earning ability of the defendant and the defendant's dependents, and such other factors as the court deems appropriate.

18 U.S.C. § 3664(a) (1988) (emphasis added). In determining whether district courts have satisfied this obligation, at least three of our sister circuits "have invoked their supervisory power to require district courts to make specific factfindings" on the considerations identified in this provision. United States v. Bruchey, 810 F.2d 456, 458-59 (4th Cir.1987) (citing United States v. Hill, 798 F.2d 402, 406-07 (10th Cir.1986), and United States v. Palma, 760 F.2d 475, 480 (3d Cir.1985)). We, however, have rejected their lead.

In United States v. Cannizzaro, 871 F.2d 809 (9th Cir.), cert. denied, 493 U.S. 895, 110 S.Ct. 245, 107 L.Ed.2d 195 (1989), we noted that "[t]here is no textual support for [the] contention that the district court must make findings of fact concerning [the defendant's] financial condition before imposing restitution [under the VWPA]." Id. at 810. We explained:

There is a material difference between requiring a district court to make findings of fact and requiring it to consider certain factors. Findings of fact can only be made on the basis of a formal adversarial record; the parties must be permitted to present testimonial and documentary evidence; one party or the other must carry the burden of proof as to each contested issue. For example, where the amount or type of restitution is disputed, the government must demonstrate, by a preponderance of the evidence, the loss sustained by the victim; the defendant carries the burden, again by a preponderance of the evidence, of demonstrating his financial resources (or lack thereof), as well as the financial needs of his dependents. 18 U.S.C. § 3664(d).

On the other hand, requiring the district court to consider certain factors grants the court broad discretion to determine the type and amount of evidence it deems relevant. We have no authority to modify the statutory scheme by narrowing that discretion. "The test is whether the district court complied with the applicable [statute]. If the [statute] do[es] not require a detailed explanation of the court's decision, the district court need not volunteer one...." United States v. Gomez, 846 F.2d 557, 560 (9th Cir.1988).

Id.

The majority is therefore correct to hold that the district court had no obligation to state on the record the reasons that led it to conclude why $12.8 million was an appropriate sum. See ante at 623. The court had an obligation only to consider the factors enumerated in the statute, and the court expressly stated that it undertook the proper considerations when it announced its decision.

B

The majority's holding on this point, however, only answers half of Smith's argument. Smith has not simply tried to persuade us to adopt the procedural prophylactic — the explicit factfinding requirement — that some of our sister circuits have endorsed; he has also argued that there is inadequate support in the record for the district court's order. On this score, his argument is persuasive.

Cannizzaro did not and could not hold — as the majority implicitly does here — that a restitution order is essentially unreviewable so long as the district court simply states on the record that it has weighed the appropriate statutory considerations. If the court's order utterly lacks factual support in the record, then a mere conclusory assertion that the court has engaged in the required analysis cannot suffice to uphold the order. Even though the manner by which the court reached its result may not be an abuse of discretion, the substantive result itself still can be. See United States v. Angelica, 859 F.2d 1390, 1392 (9th Cir.1988) (court still reviews restitution orders that comply with the statutory limits and procedural requirements of the VWPA for an abuse of discretion); Schmidt v. Herrmann, 614 F.2d 1221, 1224 (9th Cir.1980) (abuse of discretion standard means that court will reverse where it has "`a definite and firm conviction that the court below committed a clear error of judgment in the conclusion it reached upon a weighing of the relevant factors'" (citations omitted). Such is the case here.

Indeed, the apparent divergence between the defendant's ability to pay and the amount of the restitution order is more extreme in this case than in any decision cited by either party and than any reported decision of which I am aware — including all the decisions that have vacated restitution orders. For example, in United States v. Mahoney, 859 F.2d 47 (7th Cir.1988), the Seventh Circuit invalidated an order that had been entered against a defendant who, like Smith, had been convicted of defrauding financial institutions. The district court had ordered the defendant, who was free on probation, to pay $288,655 over the course of a five-year period despite an annual salary of only $30,000. In reversing, a unanimous court of appeals explained:

the restitution order itself — which requires the defendant to make full restitution (totalling over $288,000) over the requisite five-year period of payment — leaves little doubt that the judge simply forgot or disregarded the defendant's ability to pay and the needs of his dependent wife as well. We fail to perceive how this defendant, a man without any tangible assets and a $30,000 annual salary — will somehow be able to repay a debt totalling more than nine times his annual salary in five years.

859 F.2d at 51 (emphasis in original); see also United States v. Clark, 901 F.2d 855 (10th Cir.1990) (district court abused its discretion in requiring defendant with negative cash flow to pay over $153,000 in restitution). By comparison, the district court in this case has ordered an incarcerated defendant with current liabilities of $10.8 million and an annual cash flow of negative $183,000 to produce $12.8 million within five years of his release from prison at the age of fifty-eight. To comply with this order, Smith will have to produce a monthly income of over $213,000 — after taxes and necessary living expenses — in each of the first sixty months after his release from prison. The contrast to the order in Mahoney hardly counsels affirmance.

Nor is the Mahoney decision only illustrative on a factual level. Like this court in Cannizzaro, the Mahoney court explicitly rejected the idea that district courts must make specific factfindings on the considerations enumerated in the VWPA. See Mahoney, 859 F.2d at 49-50; see also United States v. Gomer, 764 F.2d 1221, 1222 (7th Cir.1985). Nonetheless, the court refused to accept at face value the district court's bare assertion that it had properly discharged its statutory obligation; the court recognized its own obligation to look behind the district court's order to evaluate the sufficiency of the evidence in the record. Because that evidence could in no way support the restitution order, the court reversed.

Here, too, one can only conclude that the district court "simply forgot or disregarded" the evidence that was put before it regarding Smith's ability to pay. Mahoney, 859 F.2d at 51. Like the order at issue in Mahoney, the order at issue here also requires the defendant to make full restitution, which is at least prima facie evidence of a failure to balance the statute's competing considerations.[2] Even a summary glance at the presentence report, which the government has not challenged, indicates that the order is wholly unrealistic. At the time of sentencing, Smith claimed total assets of only $7,750; liabilities of $10.8 million; a monthly income of $5,000; and monthly expenses of $20,250. He claimed to have thirty-seven personal debts and no remaining corporate ownership interests. His federal tax returns for the three years immediately preceding the court's order, which are also part of the record, demonstrate negative personal income for each of those years as well. In addition, as Smith's counsel has argued, it is clear that Smith will have even less of the youth, credit, and assets necessary to support the court's order when he finally is released from custody at the end of his ten-year term, and at that point, his felony conviction will likely handicap his employment efforts and earning potential even further.

The government has challenged none of this evidence. Nor has it presented any contrary evidence of its own to suggest that Smith may have access to additional assets or funds currently hidden from the court's view. Rather, in its effort to justify the district court's order, the government has simply pointed to two prior decisions by this court that have upheld restitution awards — United States v. Ruffen, 780 F.2d 1493 (9th Cir.), cert. denied, 479 U.S. 963, 107 S.Ct. 462, 93 L.Ed.2d 407 (1986), and United States v. Keith, 754 F.2d 1388 (9th Cir.), cert. denied, 474 U.S. 829, 106 S.Ct. 93, 88 L.Ed.2d 76 (1985) — and to Smith's past fortunes, which it claims are strong evidence of his ability to accumulate wealth.

Neither of these arguments, however, is persuasive. First, our decisions in Ruffen and Keith simply stand for the proposition that the VWPA does not bar sentencing courts from imposing restitution upon defendants who are indigent at the time of sentencing. Neither case denies the fact that the VWPA requires courts to balance competing considerations and to weigh factors relating to the defendant's ability to pay. Indeed, both cases explicitly recognize the Act's affirmative balancing requirement. See Ruffen, 780 F.2d at 1495; Keith, 754 F.2d at 1393. Second, courts have made clear that evidence of past earnings alone will not suffice to satisfy the Act; the relevant question is whether the defendant's present condition and future prospects, when viewed at the time of sentencing, support the inference of an ability to fulfill the court's order. See, e.g., United States v. Atkinson, 788 F.2d 900, 903 (2d Cir.1986). It is simply beyond dispute that the conditions which produced Smith's high-flying days in the seventies have irretrievably passed.

C

Nonetheless, the majority refuses to grant — or even to deny — that the overwhelming weight of the evidence leads to the "`definite and firm conviction that the court below committed a clear error of judgment in the conclusion it reached upon a weighing of the relevant factors.'" Schmidt, 614 F.2d at 1224 (defining abuse of discretion standard) (citations omitted). Rather, the majority effectively holds that by reciting the magic words — by simply stating that it "`consider[ed] the financial resources of [Smith], and the financial needs and earning ability of [Smith] and his dependents'" — the district court "satisfied the requirements of the Act." Ante at 623 (quoting district court's order). Although acknowledging, as it must, that the prospects for Smith's compliance with the order are not great, the majority discounts this concern by noting that Smith can always petition for an extension of time or seek a "remittitur" when the deadline for final payment approaches. See ante at 624.

Under the majority's holding, therefore, a district court in the Ninth Circuit may now order full restitution under the VWPA — even where the evidence before it overwhelmingly indicates that the defendant will not be able to pay — so long as it performs the procedural formality of stating that it has considered the defendant's ability to pay. I cannot agree. Courts that elect to impose the criminal penalty that the VWPA authorizes must have an adequate basis in the record for doing so. Where they do not, it is no answer to the claim that they have abused their discretion to suggest that they might later retreat from their orders in subsequent proceedings. Indeed, the prospect of a future retreat from the order we uphold today in no way rebuts the contention that that order lacks support in the record and constitutes an abuse of discretion; if anything, the majority's invocation of that prospect supports Smith's contentions.

In my view, the majority has elected to emphasize one purpose of the VWPA to the detriment of its other, competing purposes. An award under the VWPA, it must be remembered, is a criminal, not a civil penalty. Its primary function is to serve "the traditional purposes of punishment — it can deter potential offenders, serves society's legitimate interest in peaceful retribution, and can be a useful step toward rehabilitation." United States v. Ciambrone, 602 F.Supp. 563, 568 (S.D.N.Y.1984). Congress did not intend for the VWPA to serve as a substitute for a civil damages award. See id.; United States v. Satterfield, 743 F.2d 827, 836-37 (11th Cir.1984) (referring to the VWPA's legislative history); United States v. Brown, 744 F.2d 905, 908-11 (2d Cir.) (same), cert. denied, 469 U.S. 1089, 105 S.Ct. 599, 83 L.Ed.2d 708 (1984). As the Seventh Circuit explained in Mahoney:

it is most paramount that the defendant, in the all-important rehabilitative process, have at least a hope of fulfilling and complying with each and every order of the court. Thus, an impossible order of restitution, as made in this case, is nothing but a sham, for the defendant has no chance of complying with the [order], thus defeating any hope of restitution and impeding the rehabilitation process.

Mahoney, 859 F.2d at 52.

I therefore dissent from Part IV of the majority's opinion.

II

As the foregoing indicates, I believe that the district court's $12.8 million figure is impermissibly high in light of the available evidence regarding Smith's ability to pay. Unlike my colleagues, however, I would affirm the district court's order if the evidence did suggest an ability to pay.

The majority reverses because it concludes, in Part V-A, that the district court undervalued the collateral property held by Smith's victims when it attempted to calculate the total loss that they incurred from his fraud. In the majority's view:

Smith should receive credit against the restitution amount for the value of the collateral property as of the date title to the property was transferred to either [Queen City] Savings & Loan or Gibraltar. As of that date, the new owner had the power to dispose of the property and receive compensation.

Ante at 625 (emphasis added). I disagree and therefore dissent from Part V-A of the majority's opinion as well.

A

A restitution order under the VWPA may require that the defendant:

(1) in the case of an offense resulting in damage to or loss or destruction of property of a victim of the offense —

(A) return the property to the owner of the property or someone designated by the owner; or

(B) if return of the property under subparagraph (A) is impossible, impractical, or inadequate, pay an amount equal to the greater of —

(i) the value of the property on the date of the damage, loss, or destruction, or

(ii) the value of the property on the date of sentencing, less the value (as of the date the property is returned) of any part of the property that is returned....

18 U.S.C. § 3663(b)(1) (1988).[3]

Smith's argument, which the majority accepts, is that the district court failed to give adequate credit under this provision for the value of the real estate that secured his five fraudulent loans. See ante at 625. It is no secret that the value of West Texas real estate steadily declined during the 1980's, and Smith essentially contends that the court calculated the restitutionary value of the collateral properties at an unfairly late date during the course of that decline. The result, Smith implies, is that the restitution order improperly ascribes to his illegal conduct losses that are actually attributable to market forces. In Smith's view, the appropriate setoff date for each of the five respective properties is the date on which Queen City "took control" of that particular property upon foreclosure.

To assess the validity of Smith's argument, however, one must first understand precisely what loss the court's restitution order is meant to restore. In this case, the "stolen property" was capital — loan proceeds that were fraudulently procured and interest payments that were fraudulently denied. Because Smith cannot return the actual loan proceeds that he fraudulently took and because the value of capital increases with time, it follows that Smith's victims are entitled to an award of restitution under subsection 3663(b)(1)(B)(ii). In other words, they are entitled to the present value of the stolen capital: whatever amount of money Queen City would have had on the date of Smith's sentencing if it had not been defrauded into loaning its money to Smith. See 18 U.S.C. § 3663(b)(1)(B)(ii) (1988).[4]

Understanding that what Smith stole was capital, the district court did not abuse its discretion. It declined to grant Smith credit for some of the collateral property until after his victims had recovered proceeds from the disposition of that property, and it valued any property that remained unsold at sentencing as of that date. As a matter of dollars and cents, the court's valuation was correct.

B

The majority reaches the opposite conclusion only because it erroneously treats the five collateral properties as if they are somehow equivalent to the stolen capital. In the majority's view, when Queen City and Gibraltar assumed title to those properties, they effectively received some of their money back. See ante at 624-25. That suggestion cannot withstand scrutiny. After all, Queen City would not have invested in Smith's Texas properties if it had not been defrauded into believing that they were reasonable investments. As it turned out, the cash-flow projections for the five borrowing corporations were largely fictional, and the mortgage proceeds, which were in every case designated for development of the underlying property, were substantially diverted to Smith's previous creditors and to other illegitimate uses. To allow Smith to claim credit for the collateral properties as of the date Queen City took title is to allow him some of the benefit of his fraudulent bargain. What Smith stole was capital, and to restore his victims to the status quo ante, he must return the present value of that capital. See United States v. Angelica, 859 F.2d 1390, 1394 (9th Cir.1988) (no abuse of discretion in denying credit for defendant's offer of unwanted substitute property).

Moreover, Smith has not argued that he deserves credit for the value of the collateral as of the date his victims assumed title to the property. If that were the applicable rule of law, then a mortgagee who possessed title before he became aware of a fraudulent borrower's scam would ultimately be forced to set off the value of the collateral he received in that scam at a point before he even knew that he should be trying to get rid of it. What Smith has argued is that he deserves credit for the collateral as of the date his victimized mortgagees "took control" of the properties. But such argument misses the mark as well. A setoff valuation at that time would also be inappropriate because, as the majority's holding implies, "control" cannot be remunerative without title.

Nor does our decision in United States v. Tyler, 767 F.2d 1350 (9th Cir.1985), upon which both the majority and Smith rely, support the court's holding. See ante at 624-25. A defrauded lender's assumption of title over collateral property that is itself part of the fraud is in no way analogous to a timber owner's recovery of stolen timber.

In my view, the district court acted well within its authority when it determined that Queen City "received" compensation when it received actual, capital proceeds and not on the earlier dates when it "took control" of or title to the five Texas properties. See 18 U.S.C. § 3663(e)(1) (1988). I would therefore affirm the district court's valuation of the victims' losses, and I dissent from my colleagues' contrary conclusion.

III

In light of the foregoing, I concur in the judgment and in Parts I, II, III, and V-B of the court's opinion. I dissent from Parts IV and V-A.

Notes

[1] As appellant's counsel noted during oral argument, we review the district court's findings of fact for clear error and its decision to order restitution on the basis of those findings for an abuse of discretion.

[2] See Bruchey, 810 F.2d at 458 ("the VWPA implicitly requires the district judge

to balance the victim's interest in compensation against the financial resources and circumstances of the defendant — all while remaining faithful to the usual rehabilitative, deterrent, retributive, and restrictive goals of criminal sentencing"); Mahoney, 859 F.2d at 49 (quoting Bruchey); United States v. Peden, 872 F.2d 1303, 1310 (7th Cir.1989) (same); United States v. Atkinson, 788 F.2d 900, 903 (2d Cir.1986) (VWPA requires "balancing of the victim's loss against the defendant's resources and circumstances"); cf. United States v. Mitchell, 893 F.2d 935, 936 (8th Cir.1990) (order of restitution under Federal Sentencing Guidelines must be based upon "an informed decision" regarding the defendant's ability to pay).

[3] The parties apparently agree — and logic suggests — that this is the applicable provision. Compare 18 U.S.C. § 3663(b)(1) with 18 U.S.C. §§ 3663(b)(2)-(4).

[4] As an economic and arithmetical matter, one should be able to determine this number by multiplying the total proceeds loaned to Smith by the real rate of return on all of Queen City's "non-Smith" capital from the respective dates on which the loans closed until the date of sentencing.

Judge O'Scannlain's concurrence and dissent in Montana v. US Dept. of Commerce (District Court, D. Montana, Helena Division) (Oct 18, 1991)

O'SCANNLAIN, Circuit Judge, concurring in part and dissenting in part:

I join in the majority opinion to the extent it holds that the three-judge district court was properly convened, that plaintiffs have standing, and that plaintiffs' claims are justiciable.[1] On the merits, however, I am of the view that plaintiffs have failed to show that Congress' present method for allocating House of Representative seats to the states violates the Constitution, and hence I respectfully dissent from the order granting plaintiffs' motion for summary judgment.

I

The State of Montana, and its governor, attorney general, secretary of state and congressional delegation (the "State"), allege that the equal proportions formula used to allocate House seats among the states violates Article I, Section 2, of the Constitution. In the history of the Republic, Congress has used four different mathematical formulae[2] to apportion House of Representatives seats among the states. Bureau of the Census, U.S. Dep't of Commerce, Counting for Representation: The Census and the Constitution 3-5 (1990). Following the 1920 census, Congress failed to reapportion House seats among the states. This failure was due in part to a lack of confidence in the population figures presented to Congress by the Census Bureau, but was also due in part to increasing doubts that the then-used "major fractions" formula accurately assigned House seats to states based on population. H.Rep. No. 1314, 91st Cong., 2d Sess. 16-17 (1970).

Hence in 1929, Congress commissioned the National Academy of Sciences (the "NAS") to determine which mathematical formula for allocating House seats among the states would best accomplish such allocation consistent with the constraint that states cannot be assigned fractions of a representative. See Report of the Nat'l Academy of Sciences Comm. on Apportionment (1929), reprinted in H.Rep. No. 1314, 91st Cong., 2d Sess. 19-21 (1970). The NAS recommended to Congress that it abandon the major fractions formula and adopt the Hill "equal proportions" formula. Id. The committee of four prominent mathematicians convened by the NAS to respond to Congress' inquiry studied five allocation formulae, including all of the formulae before the court in this matter. Id. The NAS study determined that the Hill formula was not only the least biased as between large states and small, but also led to the least percentage discrepancy in "sizes of congressional districts or ... numbers of Representatives per person." Id.

In 1941, Congress passed into law a requirement that the method of equal proportions, the Hill formula, was to be used to apportion representatives among the states. See 2 U.S.C. § 2a(a). Congress has revisited the issue of allocation methodology several times since 1941. In 1948, Congress commissioned another NAS study, which concurred in the 1929 study, again finding the Hill formula superior. In 1971, a House subcommittee stated that the Hill formula served the objective of keeping "the average number of persons per congressional district ... as nearly equal as possible among the States," and hence declined to change it. H.Rep. No. 1314, 91st Cong., 2d Sess. 5-6 (1970). In 1981, the House considered a bill that would have replaced the Hill "equal proportions" formula with the Hamilton-Vinton formula, but the bill was never passed. In the latest allocation of House seats, conducted earlier this year and based on the 1990 census figures, the Hill formula was used, as it has been since 1941.

II

The Supreme Court has never set forth the standard for evaluating claims that Congress has misapportioned House seats among the several states. However, as early as Yick Wo v. Hopkins, 118 U.S. 356, 6 S.Ct. 1064, 30 L.Ed. 220 (1886), voting had been held to be a "fundamental right." Id. at 370, 6 S.Ct. at 1071. More recently, the Court has stated: "Our Constitution leaves no room for classification of people in a way that unnecessarily abridges" the right to vote. Wesberry v. Sanders, 376 U.S. 1, 17, 84 S.Ct. 526, 535, 11 L.Ed.2d 481 (1964). A court, therefore, should center its inquiry on the question of whether disparities in voting power are "unnecessary." Heightened scrutiny attends allegations of deprivation of voting rights. Reynolds v. Sims, 377 U.S. 533, 562, 84 S.Ct. 1362, 1381, 12 L.Ed.2d 506 (1964).

Karcher v. Daggett, 462 U.S. 725, 103 S.Ct. 2653, 77 L.Ed.2d 133 (1983), concerned the mapping of congressional districts within one state and hence is not directly applicable here. Nonetheless, the Court there set forth a burden shifting scheme that provides a helpful analytic framework for evaluating the claims brought before us. Under this scheme, the plaintiff has the initial burden of showing that population differences exist among districts, and, more important, that such "differences were not the result of a good faith effort to achieve equality" and could have been avoided by use of a different districting plan. Karcher, 462 U.S. at 731, 103 S.Ct. at 2658. If the plaintiff meets this burden, the burden shifts to the defenders of the districting plan: "[T]he State must bear the burden of proving that each significant variance between districts was necessary to achieve some legitimate goal." Id.

III

Article I, Section 2, of the Constitution, as amended by Section 2 of the Fourteenth Amendment, requires that "Representatives shall be apportioned among the several States according to their respective numbers." The manifest command of this text is that House seats are to be allocated to the states based on population. It is also the clear implication of this text, however, that House seats may not straddle state lines; seats must be apportioned to a particular state. Moreover, Article I, Section 2, also provides that "each State shall have at Least one Representative." Hence, while population is an important factor in allocating House seats, other constraints affect the allocation. Because the Constitution provides for these additional constraints, Justice Harlan observed that it "is not strictly true" that "in allocating Congressmen the number assigned to each State should be determined solely by the number of the State's inhabitants." Wesberry, 376 U.S. at 26-27 n. 8, 84 S.Ct. at 540 n. 8 (Harlan, J., dissenting) (emphasis added).

Contemporaneous accounts of the drafting of the Constitution similarly evince the Framers' intent that the House be apportioned according to population, subject to the constraints inherent in the Constitution's federal structure. One of the great debates at the Constitutional Convention centered on how to allocate seats in the National Legislature. Although each state, regardless of population, had been equally represented in the Continental Congress, many now argued that "equal numbers of people ought to have an equal no. of representatives." 1 The Records of the Federal Convention of 1787 at 179 (Farrand ed. 1937) (statement of James Wilson of Pennsylvania). This debate culminated in the Great Compromise, which allocated seats to the states on the basis of population in one chamber, and irrespective of population in the other.

James Madison confirmed the Framers' intent that House seats should be allocated by population. He expressed the view that "[i]t is a fundamental principle of the proposed Constitution, that ... the aggregate number of representatives allotted to the several States[] is to be determined by a federal rule, founded on the aggregate number of inhabitants." The Federalist, No. 54 at 368 (Van Doren ed. 1945).

Hence it is clear that the general principle for allocation is that House seats are to be assigned to states based on population. Unlike in the intrastate context, however, this is not the end of the analysis in the interstate context. For the Constitution requires that the general principle of allocation by population be subject to the following constraints: there must be at least one representative per state, and congressional districts cannot cross state lines. These constraints create the so-called fractional interest problem. For instance, when Montana's percentage of the total U.S. population is multiplied by 435, it should receive 1.404 representatives.[3] Since the Constitution does not permit a representative to be shared between two states, Montana cannot have four-tenths of a representative in Congress. It is impossible, therefore, to follow precisely the general principle of apportionment by population.

James Madison's notes of the Constitutional Convention debate show that the Framers were aware that the scheme they were creating would lead to the fractional interest problem: "A State might have one Representative only, that had inhabitants enough for 1½ or more, if fractions could be applied...." 2 The Records of the Federal Convention of 1787 at 358 (Farrand ed. 1937) (statement of Oliver Elsworth of Connecticut). The Framers, however, did not include in the Constitution a specific mathematical formula to address the fractional interest problem, and the allocation formula to be used became a point of contention between the First Congress and President Washington. See Joseph Story, 2 Commentaries on the Constitution § 678-79 (1833).

Justice Story addressed the fractional interest problem in his Commentaries on the Constitution. He first noted that "there can be no subdivision of [a representative]; each state must be entitled to an entire representative, and a fraction of a representative is incapable of apportionment." Id. at § 676. Yet Justice Story rejected the notion that if the allocation of House seats could not be accomplished strictly proportionate to population, population should be entirely disregarded. Instead, he reasoned:

the truest rule seems to be, that the apportionment ought to be the nearest practical approximation to the terms of the constitution; and the rule ought to be such, that it shall always work the same way in regard to all the states, and be as little open to cavil, or controversy, or abuse, as possible.

Id. Thus, in evaluating the State's claims, this court must be mindful that representation in the House precisely proportionate to population is impossible under the constitutional plan. Because the goal of any apportionment formula is to be a "practical approximation" to a population-based allocation, merely pointing out that the equal proportions formula leads to population disparities is insufficient to condemn it. Rather, it must be shown that lesser population disparities are possible using another formula.

IV

The State alleges that the equal proportions formula used to allocate House seats among the states is unconstitutional under Article I, Section 2, of the Constitution. The initial burden is on the State to show that the population differences under the equal proportions formula are avoidable, and that they result from the lack of a good faith effort by Congress to achieve population equity among districts, subject to the constitutional provisions requiring at least one representative per state and barring congressional districts from straddling state boundaries. In my view, the State has failed to meet that burden.

Although the Supreme Court has indeed had occasion to evaluate intra state apportionment plans in cases such as Wesberry and Karcher, the standard of precise numerical equality announced in those cases is impossible to apply here. We engage in a fundamentally different inquiry. Although population equity among districts is a guiding principle, because of the constraints imposed by the Constitution it is impossible to have districts that are even approximately equal in size. Indeed, application of any of the apportionment formulae before this court results in congressional district populations varying by hundreds of thousands of people between states. In intrastate apportionment cases, we must ask the relatively straightforward question: do the districts have the same population? This court has the more complex task of evaluating the relative merits of plans which, by necessity, all fall far short of population equality.[4]

Three different formulae for addressing the fractional interest problem are before this court. The currently used Hill "equal proportions" formula rounds upward all fractions that are greater than the geometric mean of the two whole numbers the fraction falls between. The State offers two alternative allocation formulae it contends would reduce population differences among districts. The Adams "smallest divisors" formula rounds all fractions up no matter how small. The Dean "harmonic means" formula rounds fractions upward if the fraction exceeds the harmonic mean of the two whole numbers the fraction falls between. The Adams and Dean formulae, which have in common the fact that their use would result in two House seats being allocated to Montana, are alleged by the State better to serve the constitutional requirement that House seats be allocated by population.

The Adams "smallest divisors" formula, in my view, is clearly inconsistent with the principle that House seats should be allocated to the states by population. Its most obvious defect is that it violates "quota" for four states. That is, it assigns a number of representatives to a state that is neither of the two closest whole numbers to that state's exact, unrounded share of representation. For instance, California's unrounded quota is 52.124; that is, if representatives could be apportioned in fractions, California would be entitled to exactly 52.124 representatives in the next Congress, based on its 1990 census population. Defs.' Ex. 1 at 12 (declaration of Ernst). While there may be room for argument whether California's quota should be rounded down to 52 or up to 53 representatives, surely it could not be plausibly argued that the House was apportioned according to population if California were allocated only 50 House seats. Yet that is exactly the result compelled by adoption of the Adams plan. Id. And California is not an isolated case. Using the Adams formula, Illinois, New York, and Ohio would also receive an apportionment of House seats in violation of their quotas, under the 1990 census. Id. at 13.

The Hill "equal proportions" formula, by contrast, has never violated quota in the fifty years it has been in use. Id. Every state has always been assigned a number of House seats that is one of the two closest whole numbers to its exact quota. I fail to see how the Adams formula could be said to be more consistent than the Hill formula with the command of Article I, Section 2, that House seats be apportioned to the states based on population.

Nor does application of the Dean "harmonic means" formula show that the Hill "equal proportions" formula leads to unnecessary population differences. The result under the Dean formula is relatively easy to compare to that under the Hill formula because the only difference in seat allocation would be that Washington state's ninth House seat would be reassigned and added to Montana. Pls.' Hill Aff.Ex. G at 1. All other House seat assignments would remain the same under both formulae. This switch of one House seat would increase the population variance between the only two states affected. Under the current apportionment using the Hill formula, Montana's congressional district is 48.0% larger than Washington's average district. Using the Dean formula, Washington's districts would become 52.1% larger than Montana's.

The majority states that the "absolute difference from the ideal district is the proper criterion to use in determining whether Congress has met the goal of equal representation for equal numbers of people." Ante at 1364. Yet under this criterion, the Hill "equal proportions" formula also performs better than the Dean "harmonic means" formula. Under the Hill formula, Montana has one district that is 231,189 persons larger than the ideal district size. If the Dean formula were used, Montana would have two districts, each 170,638 persons smaller than the ideal, for a total absolute variance of 341,276 from the ideal district size. Likewise, Washington's absolute population variance would increase by shifting from the Hill formula to the Dean formula. Under the Hill formula, Washington has nine districts, each 29,361 persons too small, for a total absolute variance of 264,249, while adopting the Dean formula would create eight districts, each 38,527 persons too large, increasing the total absolute variance to 308,216. Interestingly, Montana apparently argues that it can live with a variance of 341,276 persons under the Dean formula, while it insists that its 231,189 person variance under the Hill formula is clearly unconstitutional.

The State puts great stock in the fact that under one measure, the Dean and Adams formulae do perform better than the Hill formula: both the Dean and Adams formulae produce a narrower range between the smallest district and the largest. That is, if one selects the single biggest district and the single smallest district in the country, and compare just those two, the disparity is smaller when using the Dean or Adams formulae than when using the Hill formula.

The analysis cannot be limited, however, to only two of the nation's congressional districts to the exclusion of the other 433. Instead of examining the degree to which just two districts vary from the ideal, a rigorous analysis looks at the variance of every district in the nation. When all 435 districts are considered, the Hill method has the least absolute population variance from the ideal district size, compared to either the Dean or Adams methods. Defs.' Ex. 1 at 13 (declaration of Ernst). Moreover, "it can be shown mathematically that the [Hill] equal proportions method minimizes this variance among all apportionment methods and all sets of populations." Id. at 14.

In my view, the majority is mistaken in stating that "[t]he Dean method ... best accomplishes the goal of creating districts closest to the ideal district size." Ante at 1364. The State's expert did originally claim that "the Dean method produces the smallest variance or standard deviation." Pls.' Tiahrt Aff. at 5. The Census Bureau's expert, however, has pointed out that the State erred by "fail[ing] to take into account the number of districts in each state" when computing their variance analysis.[5] Defs.' Ex. 1 at 13 (declaration of Ernst). The State has conceded this error. See Pls.' Br. in Opp'n to Defs.' Mot. for Summ.J. 2 n. 1 ("Plaintiffs do not dispute the factual allegations contained in the

Declaration of Lawrence Ernst."). The Census Bureau has persuasively shown that the Hill formula is superior, notwithstanding the State's mistaken belief that the Dean formula produced the least absolute variance. See Defs.' Ex. 1 at 13 (declaration of Ernst).

In sum, neither of the formulae proposed by the State lead to less population variance than the Hill "equal proportions" formula in use for the past fifty years. The State, in my view, has failed to demonstrate that a better formula exists than the one chosen by Congress. Surely when the Hill formula leads to the least population variance from the ideal, among the formulae put before this court, it cannot be said that Congress has failed to make a good faith effort to achieve population equality among congressional districts. Karcher requires just such a showing by the State, and therefore I conclude that the State has failed to meet its burden of proof.

V

The State also claims that section 2a of Title 2 of the United States Code is unconstitutional under Article I, Sections 2 and 7, by not allowing legislative consideration of reapportionment. The majority did not reach this claim, but in my view it should be dismissed for failing to state a claim upon which relief can be granted.

First, there is no textual support in Article I, Sections 2 or 7, for the proposition that at each census, Congress must reexamine the mathematical formula it uses to allocate House seats.[6] Article I, Section 2, mandates an "actual Enumeration" every ten years, but gives no hint that Congress must reexamine every ten years the formula it uses to address the fractional interest problem. Section 7 merely recites the process which must be followed for a bill to be enacted into law. It is not alleged that section 2a of Title 2 was enacted in violation of Article I, Section 7, and nothing in section 2a interferes with the process set forth in Section 7 for enacting law. Hence, the constitutional basis for the State's second claim is most unclear.

Second, even if the Constitution does require Congress to reexamine the allocation methodology every ten years, nothing about section 2a of Title 2 prevents such a reexamination. As with any federal statute, Congress is always free to pass superseding legislation that expressly or impliedly repeals section 2a. Indeed, on at least three occasions since section 2a was passed in 1941, Congress has reconsidered use of the Hill "equal proportions" formula specified in section 2a. In 1948, Congress commissioned a NAS study on allocational formulae, and in 1971 and 1981, subcommittee hearings were held on whether section 2a should be amended. Moreover, to the extent the Montana congressional delegation is alleging that the action of their House and Senate colleagues has prevented consideration and passage of a replacement to the Hill formula, we lack jurisdiction because such claim presents a non-justiciable political question.

Despite the State's characterization of section 2a as an "automatic" allocation scheme that is somehow beyond congressional control, nothing but a lack of political will prevents Congress from repealing or amending section 2a now or in the future to change the allocation formula. That Congress has chosen for the time being not to amend section 2a of the statute does not violate either Sections 2 or 7 of Article I. I would dismiss the

State's second claim.

VI

The Framers could have created a system where congressional districts disregarded state boundaries, in the same way intrastate districts are now drawn across county lines or city limits. This would have largely eliminated the fractional interest problem, since without the constraint of staying within state boundaries, the nation could be divided up into 435 districts each of equal population. But although they recognized the fractional interest problem, the Framers persisted in creating a scheme whereby House seats are assigned to states, not directly to groups of 572,466 people (the current ideal district size), because of the sovereign role the states play in our federal system. Under our scheme of federalism the population within congressional districts must inevitably vary from state to state, and as Justice Story instructs us, the best we can seek is "the nearest practical approximation" to the ideal of apportionment exactly proportionate to population. Either of the alternative formulae put forward by the State creates a greater absolute population variance from the ideal district size than the Hill "equal proportions" formula. The State, in my view, has failed to show that the formula mandated by Congress is not "the nearest practical approximation," and hence I would grant defendants' motion for summary judgment.

Notes

[1] To the extent, however, that plaintiffs' second claim alleges that the internal organization or processes of Congress have denied the Montana congressional delegation the opportunity to vote on apportionment issues, it is a non-justiciable political question. See United States v. Munoz-Flores, 495 U.S. 385, 110 S.Ct. 1964, 1970, 109 L.Ed.2d 384 (1990) (political question "doctrine is designed to restrain the judiciary from inappropriate interference in the business of the other branches of government"); see also Armstrong v. United States, 759 F.2d 1378, 1380 (9th Cir.1985) (matter is justiciable because it "does not require delving into the internal records or workings of Congress").

[2] These are: Jefferson "greatest divisors" (1792-1830); Webster "major fractions" (1840, 1910, and 1930); Hamilton-Vinton "simple rounding" (1850-1900); and Hill "equal proportions" (1941-present).

[3] This number, the exact, unrounded proportion of representation a state would be entitled to if fractions of representatives could be apportioned, is referred to by statisticians as the state's "quota."

[4] Variance analysis is a less than straightforward inquiry. In testimony before the House Subcommittee on Census and Population in 1980, a former Census Bureau statistician observed that there are at least three ways in which the constitutional command of representation based on population could be translated into a statistical test for allocation formulae: (1) variability from the ideal number of persons per district, (2) variability from the ideal share each person should have of his representative's vote, or (3) variability of nearness to quota. H.Rep. No. 18, 97th Cong., 1st Sess. 58 (1981). Moreover,

variability could be measured both as the absolute variance, or as the variance of the mean squared, which is more typically used by statisticians. Id. When the statistician evaluated several allocation formulae, no one formula proved best under all of these measures. Id.

[5] The reason a variance analysis must account for the number of districts per state is not that there could be variance among the districts within a given state. Indeed, Dr. Ernst's calculations assume that districts within a given state will be evenly sized, as required under Karcher. Rather, the necessity of accounting for the number of districts per state is illustrated by the following hypothetical: State A has one district which is 100,000 persons larger than the ideal district. State B has fifty districts, each 10,000 persons larger than the ideal. Under the State's incorrect variance analysis using the average variance for each state, State A's average variance of 100,000 persons is greater than State B's average variance of 10,000 persons. When the number of districts in each state is accounted for, however, State B's variance of 500,000 persons (50 × 10,000) is much larger than State A's variance of 100,000 persons (1 × 100,000).

[6] Seldom in constitutional jurisprudence does a court encounter a claim, as here, where there is an utter void of case law. We must perforce make direct recourse to the naked text of the Constitution, a daunting prospect indeed.

Judge O'Scannlain's dissent in Clow v. US Dept. of Housing & Urban Dev. (Nov 5, 1991)

O'SCANNLAIN, Circuit Judge, dissenting:

Because it is clear that this court lacks jurisdiction to address the merits of this action, I respectfully dissent. The Clows' claims for declaratory and injunctive relief to compel HUD to provide mortgage assistance and to prevent the loss of their home are regrettably but undeniably moot (see infra Part II), and the court lacks the statutory authority to entertain their alternative prayer for a replacement home (see infra Part III).

Surprisingly, my colleagues dispute neither of these assertions but nonetheless conclude that we may reach the merits of the Clows' appeal. They reach this conclusion by invoking a vaguely defined and highly questionable theory that some have referred to as "hypothetical jurisdiction." See, e.g., Comment, Assuming Jurisdiction Arguendo: The Rationale and Limits of Hypothetical Jurisdiction, 127 U.Pa. L.Rev. 712 (1979). According to this theory, a court may assume — without deciding — that it has proper jurisdiction to entertain an appeal "where the jurisdictional question is complex and the appeal is clearly without merit." Wolder v. United States, 807 F.2d 1506, 1507 (9th Cir.1987) (per curiam), cited ante at 616.

In short, the court today perpetuates a dubious notion, premised largely upon a misreading of the Supreme Court's decision in Norton v. Mathews, 427 U.S. 524, 96 S.Ct. 2771, 49 L.Ed.2d 672 (1976), which posits that if a case is especially easy to decide on the merits, it need not satisfy a statutory grant of jurisdiction or meet the case-or-controversy requirement of article III. Because I perceive no such exception to the important constitutional and statutory limitations on judicial power and because the theoretical and practical dangers of recognizing such an exception are immense (see infra Part IV), I must dissent.

I

A

The Department contends that because the home now belongs to an innocent third party the case is moot. Although not for the reasons advanced by HUD,[1] I find this argument both persuasive and dispositive. A case becomes moot when a judicial determination of the legal issues tendered by the parties would no longer affect the practical result. See DeFunis v. Odegaard, 416 U.S. 312, 317, 94 S.Ct. 1704, 1706, 40 L.Ed.2d 164 (1974) (per curiam) ("`Where the activities sought to be enjoined have already occurred, and the appellate courts cannot undo what has already been done, the action is moot.'"); Headwaters, Inc. v. Bureau of Land Management, 893 F.2d 1012, 1015 (9th Cir.1989) (quoting Friends of the Earth, Inc. v. Bergland, 576 F.2d 1377, 1379 (9th Cir.1978)); see also United States v. Alder Creek Water Co., 823 F.2d 343, 345 (9th Cir.1987) ("A case becomes moot when interim relief or events have deprived the court of the ability to redress the party's injuries.").

Even if the court were to conclude that HUD acted arbitrarily and capriciously in denying the Clows' application, such a ruling would offer the Clows no meaningful relief. The Department can no longer provide the mortgage assistance for which the Clows applied. The mortgage in question no longer exists. The home in question is apparently in the hands of a bona fide purchaser who is not a party to the action and who presumably offered good value for the property without notice of the Clows' claim. To dispossess that owner in order to reinstall the Clows would exceed the equitable powers of the court. In short, the Clows cannot possibly profit from a declaratory or injunctive ruling in their favor.

B

Diverting attention from the apparent absence of meaningful relief, the Clows frame their argument in the language of fairness. To adjudge the case moot, they insist, would be unjust. It would allow HUD to benefit unfairly from its ability to dispose of property before the courts have had an opportunity to act. The Clows point to two decisions of this circuit in support of their contention: People of Saipan v. Department of Interior, 502 F.2d 90 (9th Cir.1974), cert. denied, 420 U.S. 1003, 95 S.Ct. 1445, 43 L.Ed.2d 761 (1975), and National Forest Preservation Group v. Butz, 485 F.2d 408 (9th Cir.1973). Both cases are distinguishable.

In People of Saipan, citizens of the Trust Territory of the Pacific Islands sued to prevent the execution of a lease that was designed to allow an American airline to build a hotel on public land that had special cultural importance to the Islanders. In the words of the court, the airline contended that it "ha[d] acquired some equities by proceeding with the construction of its hotel while its right to do so [was] being litigated." 502 F.2d at 100. Noting that the airline had apparently commenced building in anticipation of the litigation, the court rejected this contention.

Similarly, in National Forest Preservation Group, the plaintiff organization challenged the government's conveyance of certain public lands to a major corporation. The district court granted summary judgment for the defendant and denied the plaintiff's request for an injunction pending appeal. Two days later, the government conveyed the land to the corporation, and the corporation immediately transferred a large portion of it to an independent third party. On appeal, this court ruled that such speedy transfers during the pendency of the appeal could not put the legality of the conveyances beyond the jurisdiction of the court.

For its holdings in both People of Saipan and National Forest Preservation Group, the court relied on a passage from the Supreme Court's decision in Jones v. Securities and Exchange Comm'n:

[A]fter a defendant has been notified of the pendency of a suit seeking an injunction against him, even though a temporary injunction be not granted, he acts at his peril and subject to the power of the court to restore the status, wholly irrespective of the merits as they may be ultimately decided.

Jones, 298 U.S. 1, 17-18, 56 S.Ct. 654, 658, 80 L.Ed. 1015 (1936); see People of Saipan, 502 F.2d at 100 (quoting this passage); National Forest Preservation Group, 485 F.2d at 411 (same).

The Clows thus contend that HUD "acted at its peril" when it sold their former home and that HUD cannot fairly claim that the case is now moot because of that transfer. As a matter of fundamental fairness, the Clows' argument has great appeal. As a rebuttal to the doctrine of mootness, however, it does not. Both Ninth Circuit cases, as well as the Supreme Court case, are distinguishable.

Jones, for example, did not involve a question of mootness at all. In fact, neither the majority nor the dissenting opinion ever mentions that word. The relevant issue in Jones was what effect the pendency of a stop-order proceeding should have on the target of the prospective stop order — in that case, a securities registration statement that had been filed but had not yet become effective. The Supreme Court held that a stop-order proceeding is analogous to a suit for an injunction in equity and that once on notice, the defendant acts at his peril when he relies on his assumed rights in the target of the prospective order. In short, the Court's holding simply stands for the proposition that claims of detrimental reliance will fall on deaf ears when the party seeking sympathy had notice of the pending litigation before the asserted acts of reliance occurred. The Jones holding thus defangs a particular argument that defendants have commonly used in equity actions, but it does not at all affect the law of mootness. The Court did not say that future acts of the defendant have no capacity to render proceedings on the subject moot or that an irrevocable disposal of the target of the court's order has no effect on the viability of pending litigation. Indeed, the Court explicitly recognized the inherent limitation in its holding: "[A]fter a defendant has been notified of the pendency of a suit seeking an injunction against him, ... he acts at his peril and subject to the power of the court to restore the status." Jones, 298 U.S. at 17-18, 56 S.Ct. at 658 (emphasis added). Where the court is without power to restore the status, it follows that the defendant does not act at his peril.

National Forest Preservation Group was a straightforward application of the Jones rule. There, the defendant corporation claimed that because it had transferred much of the land in question to an independent third party, the court had lost jurisdiction to adjudicate the dispute. The court rejected this contention as "[n]onsense" because it still possessed the capacity to render effective relief. National Forest Preservation Group, 485 F.2d at 411. Indeed, the court still had jurisdiction over the land and all the relevant parties, including the independent third party: the transfers had only been "from one party to the litigation to another." Id. These facts distinguish National Forest Preservation Group from the present case and demonstrate that, like Jones, it did not involve mootness at all.[2]

Similarly, in People of Saipan, the question was whether the defendant airline could escape operation of a future court order by commencing construction of the challenged project. So long as both the airline and the site remained within the jurisdiction of the court, the answer was dictated by Jones: having been on notice of the litigation, the defendant could not fairly escape the force of the order. Such a holding, however, suggests nothing about mootness.

C

By relying on cases that have applied the Jones rule, which is essentially an equitable rule of fairness, the Clows have side-stepped the jurisdictional issue to focus upon fairness concerns. Their desire to do so is understandable: considerations of fairness do seem to weigh in the Clows' favor. If there is any merit to the Clows' claims, dismissal could reward government misconduct. Dismissal also suggests that HUD may escape judicial review through its own quick actions. In light of the underlying claims and policies here, that prospect seems especially disturbing. The mortgage assistance program was established to assist homeowners in dire straits, who have an especially earnest need for effective review of their claims. Moreover, because HUD is a government agency whose guiding aim is to serve the public interest, there is no justifiable profit motive driving its actions; to an even greater degree than the average litigant, HUD should have the capacity and the obligation to defer action on a matter that it knows to be the subject of a pending dispute.

As a matter of policy, these arguments may seem persuasive, but mootness is not a matter of policy; it is a matter of power. "[F]ederal courts are without power to decide questions that cannot affect the rights of litigants in the case before them." North Carolina v. Rice, 404 U.S. 244, 246, 92 S.Ct. 402, 404, 30 L.Ed.2d 413 (1971) (per curiam). Mootness is a doctrine of jurisdiction; it is not a doctrine of discretion. See id. ("Mootness is a jurisdictional question because the Court `is not empowered to decide moot questions or abstract propositions.'") (quoting California v. San Pablo & Tulare Ry. Co., 149 U.S. 308, 314, 13 S.Ct. 876, 878, 37 L.Ed. 747 (1893), quoted in United States v. Alaska S.S. Co.,

253 U.S. 113, 116, 40 S.Ct. 448, 449, 64 L.Ed. 808 (1920)); see also id. ("the question of mootness is a federal one which a federal court must resolve before it assumes jurisdiction").

The federal courts' "impotence `to review moot cases derives from the requirement of Article III of the Constitution under which the exercise of judicial power depends upon the existence of a [live] case or controversy.'" Id. (quoting Liner v. Jafco, Inc., 375 U.S. 301, 306 n. 3, 84 S.Ct. 391, 394 n. 3, 11 L.Ed.2d 347 (1964)). When the court ceases to be able to affect the legal relationship between the parties upon the complaint before it, that is the end of the inquiry. The court stands like an unplugged appliance. The judicial power is lost, and there is no jurisdiction for a consideration of the equities.

D

1

The Supreme Court has yielded its adherence to this firm position in only two sorts of cases. The first category includes disputes "capable of repetition, yet evading review." Southern Pac. Terminal Co. v. ICC, 219 U.S. 498, 515, 31 S.Ct. 279, 283, 55 L.Ed. 310 (1911). In these cases the duration of litigation invariably exceeds the life of the underlying dispute, and the Court has held that an exception to traditional mootness analysis is necessary to afford the complaining party an opportunity to litigate its rights. See, e.g., Roe v. Wade, 410 U.S. 113, 125, 93 S.Ct. 705, 713, 35 L.Ed.2d 147 (1973) (because usual appellate process exceeds nine months, litigation of right to abortion does not become moot when claimant's pregnancy comes to term).

This narrow exception does not apply to the current case for two reasons. First, the type of dispute involved must be one that would invariably evade review if adjudged moot. See id.; see also Southern Pac. Terminal Co., 219 U.S. at 516, 31 S.Ct. at 284. The Clows have not alleged that HUD's policies, by their nature, will always preempt appellate review of a denial of mortgage assistance. Second, the dispute must have a capacity for repetition between the current parties; it is not enough that the same issue might provoke a similar dispute between the defendant and a third party. See DeFunis, 416 U.S. at 319, 94 S.Ct. at 1707 (dismissing case as moot) ("the question is certainly not `capable of repetition' so far as [the plaintiff] is concerned"); Roe, 410 U.S. at 125, 93 S.Ct. at 713 (adjudging case not moot) ("[p]regnancy often comes more than once to the same woman"); H. Hart & H. Wechsler, The Federal Courts & the Federal System 208 (3d ed. 1988) ("Recent decisions emphasize that, in the absence of a class action, the question in such cases is the possibility of recurrence with respect to the complaining party.") (citing Murphy v. Hunt, 455 U.S. 478, 482, 102 S.Ct. 1181, 1183, 71 L.Ed.2d 353 (1982) and Weinstein v. Bradford, 423 U.S. 147, 149, 96 S.Ct. 347, 348, 46 L.Ed.2d 350 (1975)). The Clows have not suggested that this problem is likely to plague them again.

2

The second category of exceptional cases includes the so-called "voluntary cessation" cases. These cases stand for the proposition that "voluntary cessation of allegedly illegal conduct does not deprive the tribunal of power to hear and determine the case, i.e., does not make the case moot." United States v. W.T. Grant Co., 345 U.S. 629, 632, 73 S.Ct. 894, 897, 97 L.Ed. 1303 (1953). The logic that supports this rule is plain: a controversy does not cease to be "live" when the defendant voluntarily and temporarily suspends the challenged practice in an effort to evade judicial review. If there is "a sufficient possibility of a recurrence" once the litigation subsides, the controversy is not moot. H. Hart & H. Wechsler, supra, at 206 (citations omitted). In this case, "`there is no reasonable expectation that the wrong will be repeated'" once the action is dismissed, and HUD has not voluntarily suspended any challenged conduct in an effort to render the action moot. DeFunis, 416 U.S. at 318, 94 S.Ct. at 1706 (quoting W.T. Grant Co., 345 U.S. at 633, 73 S.Ct. at 897). Accordingly, neither of the recognized exceptions to the mootness doctrine applies here.

II

The majority nonetheless concludes that the Clows' action is not moot because "even after their home had been sold to an innocent third party, the Clows' complaint assert[ed] an avenue of relief which they claimed was available to them; HUD's providing them with a [substitute] home of similar value to their own under the same terms and conditions [as] their previous mortgage." Ante at 616. This argument misses the mark. The Clows' prayer for a replacement home cannot confer power upon the court to decide an otherwise moot action because the court lacks the statutory power to entertain such a prayer. A request for a replacement home is in effect a request for damages, and the Administrative Procedure Act ("APA"), upon which the Clows' right to judicial review is predicated, expressly retains the government's sovereign immunity and precludes judicial review with respect to damages claims.

Section 10 of the APA provides in pertinent part:

A person suffering legal wrong because of agency action, or adversely affected or aggrieved by agency action within the meaning of a relevant statute, is entitled to judicial review thereof. An action in a court of the United States seeking relief other than money damages and stating a claim that an agency or an officer or employee thereof acted or failed to act in an official capacity or under color of legal authority shall not be dismissed nor relief therein be denied on the ground that it is against the United States or that the United States is an indispensable party.

5 U.S.C. § 702 (1988) (emphasis added); see also id. § 701(a)(1) ("This chapter applies ... except to the extent that statutes preclude judicial review."). Courts have repeatedly construed this provision to mean that the APA does not confer power on the federal courts to entertain actions against the United States for money damages. See, e.g., Rowe v. United States, 633 F.2d 799, 801 (9th Cir.1980), cert. denied, 451 U.S. 970, 101 S.Ct. 2047, 68 L.Ed.2d 349 (1981); Hill v. United States, 571 F.2d 1098, 1102 & n. 7 (9th Cir.1978); see also Bowen v. Massachusetts, 487 U.S. 879, 108 S.Ct. 2722, 101 L.Ed.2d 749 (1988).

Courts have also repeatedly held that "a plaintiff may not transform a claim for monetary relief into an equitable action simply by asking for an injunction that orders the payment of money." New Mexico v. Regan, 745 F.2d 1318, 1322 (10th Cir.1984) (citing Jaffee v. United States, 592 F.2d 712, 715 (3d Cir.1979)), cert. denied, 471 U.S. 1065, 105 S.Ct. 2138, 85 L.Ed.2d 496 (1985). Indeed, courts "have emphasized that if the `prime objective' or `essential purpose' of the claim is to recover money from the federal government, the action [is not cognizable under the APA]." Hamilton Stores, Inc. v. Hodel, 925 F.2d 1272, 1278 (10th Cir.1991); see also id. at 1276-79; New Mexico, 745 F.2d at 1322 (citing, inter alia, Bakersfield City School Dist. v. Boyer, 610 F.2d 621, 628 (9th Cir. 1979)). As the Tenth Circuit explained in Hamilton Stores, even when "[the plaintiff's] prayer for relief does not request money damages, we scrutinize claims against the United States to be certain that the plaintiff has not endeavored to `transform a claim for monetary relief into an equitable action simply by asking for an injunction that orders the payment of money.'" Hamilton Stores, 925 F.2d at 1278 (quoting New Mexico, 745 F.2d at 1322)).

Our scrutiny in this regard must be strict not only because the issue is jurisdictional in nature but also because it implicates concerns of sovereign immunity; the federal government has elected not to waive its immunity to damage awards under the APA, and the courts must honor that decision. See General Atomic Co. v. United Nuclear Corp., 655 F.2d 968, 968-69 (9th Cir.1981) (jurisdictional statutes are to be interpreted strictly; federal courts are courts of limited jurisdiction, and doubts are to be resolved against the assumption of such jurisdiction), cert. denied, 455 U.S. 948, 102 S.Ct. 1449, 71 L.Ed.2d 662 (1982); Woodbridge Plaza v. Bank of Irvine, 815 F.2d 538, 544 (9th Cir.1987) (Fletcher, J., dissenting) (same); see also Irwin v. Veterans Admin., ____ U.S. ____, 111 S.Ct. 453, 456, 112 L.Ed.2d 435 (1990) (a waiver of sovereign immunity "must be strictly construed").

Here, there can be no doubt that the Clows' request for a replacement home constitutes a request for money damages within the meaning of the APA. The Supreme Court itself has made this clear. The Court recently defined the term "money damages" within the context of section 702 in Bowen v. Massachusetts, 487 U.S. 879, 108 S.Ct. 2722, 101 L.Ed.2d 749 (1988). Writing for the Court, Justice Stevens adopted the reasoning and analysis of a District of Columbia Circuit decision:

Judge Bork's explanation of the plain meaning of the critical language in this statute merits quotation in full. In his opinion for the Court of Appeals for the District of Columbia Circuit in Maryland Dept. of Human Resources v. Department of Health & Human Services, 246 U.S.App.D.C. 180, 763 F.2d 1441 (1985), he wrote:

We turn first to the question whether the relief Maryland seeks is equivalent to money damages....

We begin with the ordinary meaning of the words Congress employed. The term "money damages," 5 U.S.C. § 702, we think, normally refers to a sum of money used as compensatory relief. Damages are given to the plaintiff to substitute for a suffered loss, whereas specific remedies "are not substitute remedies at all, but attempt to give the plaintiff the very thing to which he was entitled." D. Dobbs, Handbook on the Law of Remedies 135 (1973).

Bowen, 487 U.S. at 894-95, 108 S.Ct. at 2732 (quoting Maryland Department of Human Resources, 763 F.2d at 1446 (emphasis in original)) (footnote omitted); see also Bowen, 487 U.S. at 914, 108 S.Ct. at 2742 (Scalia, J., dissenting) ("Whereas damages compensate the plaintiff for a loss, specific relief prevents or undoes the loss — for example, by ordering return to the plaintiff of the precise property that has been wrongfully taken, or by enjoining acts that would damage the plaintiff's person or property.") (citing 5A A. Corbin, Contracts § 1141, at 113 (1964), and Dobbs, supra, at 135).[3]

The Clows' request for a replacement home is a request for compensatory relief intended to substitute for a suffered loss; it is not a request for specific relief intended to return to the Clows the actual "specie" to which they claim they are entitled and of which they claim they were wrongfully deprived. See Dobbs, supra, at 135. Indeed, it is literally definitional that a request for a substitute home is, in Professor Dobbs's words, a request for a "substitutionary" remedy. Id. It follows, therefore, that we must regard the Clows' request as a prayer for money damages which the federal courts have no authority to entertain under the APA.

III

My colleagues do not directly dispute this reasoning. Rather, they conclude that the court may assume jurisdiction over the Clows' claim for a replacement home without deciding whether such jurisdiction is proper. The court, they hold, may exercise what some have dubbed "hypothetical jurisdiction." See Comment, supra, 127 U.Pa. L.Rev. at 713.

A

For reasons eloquently expressed by Judge Clarence Thomas in a recent case before the District of Columbia Circuit, I cannot agree:

Federal courts are courts of limited jurisdiction. When federal jurisdiction does not exist, federal judges have no authority to exercise it, even if everyone — judges, parties, members of the public — wants the dispute resolved. [Citations omitted.] It follows that federal courts have a "`special obligation'" to appraise at the outset their own jurisdiction, even when the parties, or the lower courts, have not raised any jurisdictional questions themselves. FW/PBS, Inc. v. City of Dallas, [493 U.S. 215] 110 S.Ct. 596, 607 [107 L.Ed.2d 603] (1990) (citation omitted). This tenet is as solid as bedrock and almost as old. [Citations omitted].

Cross-Sound Ferry Servs., Inc. v. ICC, 934 F.2d 327, 339 (D.C.Cir.1991) (Thomas, J., dissenting in relevant part); see also Mansfield, Coldwater & Lake Mich. Ry. v. Swan, 111 U.S. 379, 382, 4 S.Ct. 510, 511, 28 L.Ed. 462 (1884) (rule requiring courts to examine their own jurisdiction "is inflexible and without exception"); Fed.R.Civ.P. 12(h)(3) ("Whenever it appears by suggestion of the parties or otherwise that the court lacks jurisdiction of the subject matter, the court shall dismiss the action.").

Without assuring itself that it has actual jurisdiction, a court has no power to proceed further. It has no power even to suggest that the action may be insubstantial on the merits. The concept of hypothetical jurisdiction is therefore nonsensical: without actual jurisdiction, the court cannot act, and it is illogical to suggest that "hypothetical" jurisdiction may exist where actual jurisdiction may not.

The truistic constraint on the federal judicial power, then, is this: A federal court may not decide cases when it cannot decide cases, and must determine whether it can, before it may. The majority here changes this fundamental precept to read, in effect, that under certain circumstances a federal court should decide cases regardless of whether it can, and need not determine whether it can, before it does. This revision seems to me difficult to square with the Supreme Court's regular warnings to the federal courts to fulfill their "special obligation" to inquire into their own jurisdiction at the outset....

The Supreme Court reiterated this principle twice last Term. [See Carden v. Arkoma Associates, [494 U.S. 185] 110 S.Ct. 1015 [108 L.Ed.2d 157] (1990), and FW/PBS, 110 S.Ct. 596].

* * * * * *

Read in light of one hundred and eighty-seven years of other precedents, the Supreme Court's opinions in FW/ PBS and Carden confirm that federal courts must first assure themselves that they have the authority to hear a dispute before they may decide the dispute on the merits. See FW/PBS, 110 S.Ct. at 607-08; Carden, 110 S.Ct. at 1021. Federal courts simply may not assume jurisdiction hypothetically. Some cases might cry out for decision on the merits; some might pose difficult jurisdictional problems. Our threshold duty to examine our own jurisdiction is no less obligatory in either instance.

Cross-Sound Ferry, 934 F.2d at 340, 345-46 (Thomas, J., dissenting in relevant part).

B

Norton v. Mathews, 427 U.S. 524, 96 S.Ct. 2771, 49 L.Ed.2d 672 (1976), upon which the majority relies, does not suggest otherwise. Norton involved a direct appeal from a three-judge district court, and it presented a difficult jurisdictional question conjoined with an extremely simple merits question. The answer to the merits question was clear because the Court had just decided the identical issue in a companion case. Mathews v. Lucas, 427 U.S. 495, 96 S.Ct. 2755, 49 L.Ed.2d 651 (1976). The jurisdictional question, on the other hand, was quite subtle and concerned whether the three-judge district court had been properly convened.

Writing for the Court, Justice Blackmun concluded that it was unnecessary to decide the jurisdictional question because it was obvious after Lucas that there was no merit to the underlying appeal. Justice Blackmun, however, did not conclude (and the Court did not hold) that a decision on the merits of an appeal can be entered without the usual inquiry into the propriety of jurisdiction — or, for that matter, without proper jurisdiction itself. Rather, the Court held that it did not need to decide the particular jurisdictional question at issue in Norton in order to affirm on the merits there because under either possible answer to that question, the outcome would be the same. As Justice Blackmun explained:

Assuming that the three-judge district court was correctly convened, and that we have jurisdiction over the appeal, the appropriate disposition, in the light of Mathews v. Lucas, plainly would be to affirm.... Assuming, on the other hand, that we lack jurisdiction because the three-judge district court was needlessly convened, the appropriate disposition would be to dismiss the appeal. When an appeal to this Court is sought from an erroneously convened three-judge district court, [however,] we retain the power "'to make such corrective order as may be appropriate to the enforcement of the limitations'" which 28 U.S.C. § 1253 imposes. What we have done recently, and in most such cases where the jurisdictional issue was previously unsettled ... has been to vacate the district court judgment and remand the case for the entry of a fresh decree from which an appeal may be taken to the appropriate court of appeals.... In the present case, however, the decision in Lucas has rendered the [underlying] issues insubstantial and so much so as not even to support the jurisdiction of a three-judge district court to consider their merits on remand. Thus, there is no point in remanding to enable the merits to be considered by a court of appeals.

Norton, 427 U.S. at 531-32, 96 S.Ct. at 2775 (citations omitted and emphasis added).

In other words, a determination that the three-judge district court was improperly convened in Norton would not have meant the absence of district court jurisdiction altogether; it would only have meant that there was no jurisdiction for a three-judge district court. Jurisdiction in an ordinary, one-judge district court would presumably still lie. Given that fact, rather than dismiss the appeal outright, the Supreme Court ordinarily would be inclined to remand "for the entry of a fresh decree [by a one-judge district court] from which an appeal [could then] be taken to the appropriate court of appeals." Id. In Norton, however, remanding for the entry of an appropriately appealable decree made little sense because the outcome of any such appeal was already foreordained by Lucas.

In short, the knotty jurisdictional question that the Norton Court abstained from deciding was not a question of jurisdiction vel non, but a question of which of two jurisdictional schemes, both of which were equally capable of conferring power on the district court, properly applied. Indeed, it was clear that the district court did have proper jurisdiction in one form or another. The only question was whether a one-judge court or a three-judge court was the appropriate form. Given the nature of that question, the Supreme Court could either (a) resolve its doubts in favor of jurisdiction and affirm on the merits or (b) vacate and remand for further proceedings that would cure the jurisdictional problem but that would ultimately have to favor the same party on the merits. Either way, the same party would prevail and would do so on the merits. In choosing the first and more efficient option, therefore, the Supreme Court did not ignore or pass over the threshold question of jurisdiction vel non, as the majority has here. On the contrary, it implicitly acknowledged that the district court's jurisdiction — in one form or another — was certain and that nothing depended upon a resolution of the precise nature of that jurisdiction because the same party would prevail on the merits in either event.

C

Unfortunately, several very recent decisions by this court have suggested — as the majority again does here — that Norton stands for some broader notion of hypothetical jurisdiction. See Federal Ins. Co. v. Scarsella Bros., 931 F.2d 599, 602 (9th Cir.1991) ("Where an appeal presents difficult questions concerning jurisdiction, we may forego the resolution of such issues if the merits of the appeal are insubstantial.") (citing Norton); Forster v. County of Santa Barbara, 896 F.2d 1146, 1147 n. 2 (9th Cir.1990) (per curiam); Sundance Land Corp. v. Community First Fed. Sav. & Loan Ass'n, 840 F.2d 653, 666 n. 15 (9th Cir.1988); Wolder, 807 F.2d 1507; Lehner v. United States, 685 F.2d 1187, 1190 (9th Cir.1982), cert. denied, 460 U.S. 1039, 103 S.Ct. 1431, 75 L.Ed.2d 790 (1983). Standing alone, these decisions would perhaps command our allegiance as circuit law. Not one of these decisions, however, provides any analysis to support such a reading of Norton — especially in light of both pre- and post-Norton decisions by the Supreme Court which have implicitly rejected the concept of hypothetical jurisdiction. Indeed, not one endeavors to explain the nature or limits of this novel theory. The decisions simply cite Norton (and each other) as authority. Cf. Comment, supra, 127 U.Pa.L.Rev. at 713 ("This practice of assuming jurisdiction arguendo, here dubbed `hypothetical jurisdiction,' has developed for the most part without examination.").[4]

Norton, however, does not support such a principle. To read Norton so broadly is to misconstrue the nature of the jurisdictional question presented in that case: Norton involved concerns that are unique to the convening of a three-judge district court and did not implicate the question of jurisdiction vel non. More importantly, such an understanding of Norton contradicts time-worn principles and innumerable precedents that exhort federal courts to examine the sources of their presumed authority before acting upon them. See Cross-Sound Ferry, 934 F.2d at 339-45 (Thomas, J., dissenting in relevant part) (citing and discussing many of these innumerable precedents and criticizing similar readings of Norton by the District of Columbia Circuit). Indeed, one advocate of hypothetical jurisdiction has conceded as much. After analyzing all the Supreme Court decisions from which one could infer even a hint of approval for the notion, this student candidly concluded that "there is thus no Supreme Court opinion unequivocally holding that it is permissible to assume justiciability and rule on the substantive merits." Comment, supra, 127 U.Pa. L.Rev. at 745.[5]

Within the context of our constitutional system, the concept of hypothetical jurisdiction simply has no place. A court has no discretion where it has no power, and to suggest otherwise is to erode a fundamental limitation on the exercise of judicial authority. Without a coherent rationale to justify its application or to limit its reach, the concept of hypothetical jurisdiction threatens to swallow numerous statutory restraints on the federal courts. In fact, the continued proliferation of this notion could lead to a regime in which the only check on judicial power is a court's own disinclination to reach the merits. That, I would suggest, invites judicial arrogance.

In a wholly different context, a wiser lawyer than most once warned: "It is as much the duty of Government to render prompt justice against itself, in favor of citizens, as it is to administer the same between private individuals." Cong.Globe, 37th Cong., 2d Sess. (1861 App.2d) (quoting President Lincoln). As an instrument of government, the federal courts have a "`special obligation'" to restrain themselves when the law indicates that they have no power. FW/PBS, 110 S.Ct. at 607 (quoting Mitchell v. Maurer, 293 U.S. 237, 244, 55 S.Ct. 162, 165, 79 L.Ed. 338 (1934)). We have no power here.

IV

The Clows' primary requests for declaratory and injunctive relief are moot: the mortgage in question no longer exists, and the home in question is no longer before the court. The Clows' alternative prayer for a replacement home does nothing to cure this problem because the court lacks the statutory authority to entertain that claim under the APA. Finally, despite the majority's contrary conclusion, hypothetical jurisdiction cannot lie where actual jurisdiction is clearly absent. Indeed, the very concept of hypothetical jurisdiction is indefensible.

I would therefore vacate the district court's judgment and remand with instructions to dismiss the Clows' complaint pursuant to Rule 12(b)(1) of the Federal Rules of Civil Procedure.

Notes

[1] The Department relied on one case for its mootness argument: Fair v. EPA, 795 F.2d 851 (9th Cir.1986). That case is clearly distinguishable. In Fair, the plaintiff sought a judgment declaring that the defendant had a duty to conduct further study before approving construction of a sewer line. The district court dismissed the complaint, and the plaintiff appealed. On appeal, this court dismissed the action as moot because the sewer line had been fully constructed in the meantime. It is, of course, virtually impossible to conduct a pre-approval study after completion of the project in question. The Clows, on the other hand, do not ask for a virtual impossibility. They appear, however, to ask for a legal impossibility — as I explain herein.

[2] The court's discussion of Jones appears under the heading "MOOTNESS," but there is no discussion of the mootness doctrine per se in the court's opinion and no other mention of the word. See National Forest Preservation Group, 485 F.2d at 410-11. Moreover, in addition to citing Jones, National Forest Preservation Group cited the Supreme Court's decision in Porter v. Lee, 328 U.S. 246, 66 S.Ct. 1096, 90 L.Ed. 1199 (1946). See 485 F.2d at 411. Porter was also an application of the Jones rule and not a mootness case. There, the Court held that "where a defendant with notice in an injunction proceeding completes the acts sought to be enjoined the court may by mandatory injunction restore the status quo." 328 U.S. at 251, 66 S.Ct. at 1099 (citation omitted).

[3] Thus, under Bowen, the fact that a claimant has not requested money per se does not necessarily mean that he has not requested "money damages." Nor, for that matter, is the converse necessarily true: a claim that does specify money is not by virtue of that fact alone always a claim for money damages. See Bowen, 487 U.S. at 893, 108 S.Ct. at

2731 ("The fact that a judicial remedy may require one party to pay money to another is not a sufficient reason to characterize the relief as `money damages.'"); id. at 895, 108 S.Ct. at 2732 ("`while in many instances an award of money is an award of damages, "[o]ccasionally a money award is also a specie remedy."'") (quoting Maryland Department of Human Resources, 763 F.2d at 1446 (quoting D. Dobbs, supra, at 135)). For example, a claim for back wages or for the provision of Medicaid benefits that were improperly disallowed is a request for specific relief that just happens to be monetary. See id. 487 U.S. at 900, 108 S.Ct. at 2735; D. Dobbs, supra, at 135.

Bowen therefore places critical emphasis on the substantive nature of the remedy, rather than its specific form. In order to give the waiver of sovereign immunity contained in section 702 its proper effect, courts must regard claims for money as claims for specific relief when the money is, in fact, the specie — "the very thing" — to which the plaintiff claims he is entitled. Id. On the other hand, in order to prevent artful pleaders from eroding the sovereign immunity that section 702 expressly retains, courts must treat nonmonetary relief as money damages when, as here, the relief is purely compensatory in nature.

[4] Some have suggested that where the party seeking jurisdiction would not prevail in either event, it is irrelevant whether the court decides the case on jurisdictional grounds or on the merits. See, e.g., Browning-Ferris Indus. v. Muszynski, 899 F.2d 151, 159, 160 (2d Cir.1990); Comment, supra, 127 U.Pa.L.Rev. at 736-37, 748. That suggestion is demonstrably untrue. The collateral ramifications of a decision on the merits are clearly different from those that attend a dismissal on jurisdictional grounds. Res judicata, for example, will only attach to a decision on the merits. Private agreements among the parties or between the parties and their attorneys or indemnitors may also be affected by the form of the court's decision.

[5] Courts in this circuit that have invoked the notion of hypothetical jurisdiction have generally relied upon Norton as their primary authority for doing so. In other circuits, courts that have invoked the theory have generally relied upon three other Supreme Court decisions, in addition to Norton: (1) Secretary of the Navy v. Avrech, 418 U.S. 676, 94 S.Ct. 3039, 41 L.Ed.2d 1033 (1974) (per curiam); (2) Chandler v. Judicial Council, 398 U.S. 74, 90 S.Ct. 1648, 26 L.Ed.2d 100 (1970); and (3) United States v. Augenblick, 393 U.S. 348, 89 S.Ct. 528, 21 L.Ed.2d 537 (1969). These cases are among those discussed in the Pennsylvania Comment. See Comment, supra, 127 U.Pa.L.Rev. at 733-53. Judge Thomas has persuasively explained why a similar reliance on these decisions is also unjustified. See Cross-Sound Ferry, 934 F.2d at 342-45 (Thomas, J., dissenting in relevant part).

Judge O'Scannlain's dissent in Silver v. US PS (Dec 11, 1991)

O'SCANNLAIN, Circuit Judge, dissenting:
In my view, the Postmaster General and Deputy Postmaster General are not

appointed in a manner consistent with the Appointments Clause, art. 2, § 2, cl. 2. Thus, I respectfully dissent from part IIB of the opinion of the court.

I

The Appointments Clause describes two processes for appointments of officers of the United States, and those appointed by the respective processes have come to be known as "principal" or "inferior" officers. Principal,[1] i.e., non-"inferior," officers must be appointed by the President with the advice and consent of the Senate. For inferior officers, "the Congress may by Law vest the Appointment of such inferior Officers, as they think proper, in the President alone, in the Courts of Law, or in the Heads of Departments." Id.

In our scheme of separation of powers the duty to enforce the laws of the United States falls upon the President. The President may delegate his enforcement duties to members of the executive branch, but the Appointments Clause serves as a check on such delegation. See Myers v. United States, 272 U.S. 52, 117-18, 47 S.Ct. 21, 25-26, 71 L.Ed. 160 (1926). Executive branch enforcement powers may only be exercised by officers of the United States appointed in accordance with the Appointments Clause. Buckley v. Valeo, 424 U.S. 1, 140, 96 S.Ct. 612, 691, 46 L.Ed.2d 659 (1976) (per curiam).

Silver argues that the Postal Service Board of Governors (the "Board") was not appointed in accordance with the Appointments Clause, and hence may not lawfully exercise executive branch enforcement powers. The eleven-person Board consists of nine Governors, the Postmaster General, and the Deputy Postmaster General. 39 U.S.C. § 202. The constitutionality of the appointment process set forth in section 202 for each of these Board members shall be examined in turn.

A

Each Governor is appointed to a nine year term by the President, with the advice and consent of the Senate. 39 U.S.C. § 202(a), (b). This clearly comports with the constitutional requirements for the appointment of principal officers. Buckley, 424 U.S. at 126, 96 S.Ct. at 685.

B

The Postmaster General (the "PG") is appointed by the nine Governors. 39 U.S.C. § 202(c). Since the PG is not appointed by the President with the advice and consent of the Senate, his appointment manifestly violates the Appointments Clause if he is a principal officer. For purposes of this analysis, however, it can be assumed that the PG is merely an inferior officer.[2] The Appointments Clause permits inferior officers to be appointed by "Heads of Departments." Hence the constitutionality of the PG's appointment turns on whether the Governors alone, as opposed to the full Board, can be considered a Head of Department.

Silver contends that the term Heads of Departments as used in the Appointments Clause can only apply to those who head executive departments, that is, to members of the Cabinet. The Supreme Court recently declined to address the question of whether "the head of one of the principal agencies" was a "Head of Department" for purposes of the Appointments Clause. See Freytag v. Commissioner, ____ U.S. ____, 111 S.Ct. 2631, 2643 n.

4, 115 L.Ed.2d 764 (1991). Justice Scalia, concurring in part and joined by three other Justices, forcefully argued, however, that "there is no reason, in text, judicial decision, history or policy, to limit the phrase `the Heads of Departments' in the Appointments Clause to those officials who are members of the President's Cabinet." Id. 111 S.Ct. at 2660 (Scalia, J., concurring in part and concurring in the judgment). Justice Scalia pointed out that the Cabinet did not even exist in the original Constitution, id. at 2658-59, and that the definition of "department" in an American dictionary roughly contemporaneous with the drafting of the Constitution was stated in terms of having a separate function, and was not dependent on size or status, id. at 2660.

Thus the mere fact that the Governors do not sit in the President's Cabinet would not prevent them from collectively[3] constituting a Head of Department. But a closer examination shows that the Governors by themselves, as distinct from the full Board, simply do not function as a Head of Department within the management scheme of the Postal Service.

The government contends in its brief that "[t]he nine Governors of the Postal Service are the "head of department in the sense that they are the highest authority within the Postal Service." In my view, this cannot be correct. The nine-member Governors alone do not manage and govern the Postal Service; only the full eleven-member Board, of which the Governors comprise a part, is granted the authority under statute to "exercise the power of the Postal Service." 39 U.S.C. § 202(a). The Board, not the Governors alone, "shall direct and control the expenditures and review the practices and policies of the Postal Service." 39 U.S.C. § 205(a). It is the Board that is given plenary power to delegate the authority vested in it to the PG. 39 U.S.C. § 402. Although the Governors alone vote on rate increases and new classes of mail, 39 U.S.C. § 3621, all other functions and powers of the Postal Service are directed by the full Board.

Under this statutory scheme, clearly the full Board governs and controls the Postal Service, and I am not persuaded that the Governors, a mere subset of the Board, can be regarded as the Head of Department. Hence the Governors alone cannot be empowered to appoint officers of the United States consistent with the Appointments Clause. The statutory scheme for appointment of the PG is unconstitutional because, in my view, it does not have as its source one of the only three options the Constitution permits: the President alone, the Courts of Law, or the Heads of Departments. Congress could not have intended nine members of the Board to be the head of department for Appointments Clause purposes while intending all eleven members to be head of department for purposes of running the Postal Service.

C

The provision for appointment of the Deputy Postmaster General (the "DPG") is likewise flawed. The DPG is appointed by the Governors and the PG. By the reasoning applicable to the PG's selection, appointment of the DPG by the Governors alone would be inconsistent with the Appointments Clause. The additional participation of the PG, arguably an inferior officer, merely compounds the irregularity of the DPG's appointment process.

The DPG might not be subject to the Appointments Clause if, instead of being an inferior officer, he were a mere employee of the United States. See Buckley, 424 U.S. at 126, 96 S.Ct. at 685. All indications point, however, toward the DPG not being a mere employee. In Buckley, the Court defined employees in the Appointments Clause context as being "lesser functionaries subordinate to officers of the United States." Buckley, 424 U.S. at 126 n. 162, 96 S.Ct. at 685 n. 162. On the other hand, "any appointee exercising significant authority pursuant to the laws of the United States" must be appointed in the manner prescribed by the Appointments Clause. Id. at 126, 96 S.Ct. at 685.

The DPG is clearly not a "lesser functionary." The DPG by statute and regulation exercises significant authority.[4] He serves as an alternate to the PG when the PG cannot perform his duties. 39 U.S.C. § 203. He is chief operating officer of the Postal Service, 39 C.F.R. § 225.1, and the three Postal Service operations departments report to him, 39 C.F.R. § 225.2. Significantly, the DPG reports to the Board, not to the PG. See 39 C.F.R. § 224 (DPG is not on list of parties reporting to PG). Most important, the DPG serves as a voting member of the Board of the Postal Service. 39 U.S.C. § 202(d).

Justice Scalia has speculated that the DPG was likely an officer of the United States even as early as the administration of George Washington. Freytag, 111 S.Ct. at 2659 (Scalia, J., concurring in part and concurring in the judgment). And while the Supreme Court has never addressed whether the DPG is an officer of the United States, it has found the postmaster of Portland, Oregon, to be an officer of the United States. Myers v. United States, 272 U.S. 52, 47 S.Ct. 21, 71 L.Ed. 160 (1926). See also United States v. McCrory, 91 F. 295 (5th Cir.1899) (letter carrier is officer of United States). Given the important role of the DPG in the statutory scheme of the Postal Service, the DPG cannot be a mere employee immune from the Appointments Clause.

II

Although in my view the statute setting forth the appointment process for the PG and the DPG violates the Appointments Clause, the effect of this unconstitutionality on the enforcement action against Silver is initially unclear.[5] The PG and DPG were not personally involved in Silver's enforcement action. The PG and the DPG are, however, voting members of the Postal Service Board of Governors (39 U.S.C. § 202(d)) and thus the question remains what effect the existence of unconstitutionally appointed members has on that Board and therefore the Postal Service. As previously discussed, the power to execute the laws of the United States is lodged in the President. U.S. Const. art. II, § 3. In postal matters, that power is delegated to the Board. 39 U.S.C. § 202(a). They in turn are authorized to delegate their authority to the PG "as [the Board] deems desirable." 39 U.S.C. § 402. In the final link in the chain of delegation, the PG is permitted under Postal Service regulations to delegate "any function vested in the Postal Service, [or] in the [PG]" to "any employee or agent" of the Postal Service. 39 C.F.R. § 222.1.

Hence the constitutional power to execute the laws of the United States, if it is to be effective, must flow from the President through the Board and PG to the Judicial

Officer and the ALJ involved in the Silver enforcement action. The Appointments Clause serves as a "limiting principle" on this flow of power, however. See Freytag, 111 S.Ct. at 2639. Executive authority cannot be handed down to those who hold office in violation of the Appointments Clause. Buckley, 424 U.S. at 140, 96 S.Ct. at 691.

Because the Board has members whose appointment violates the Appointments Clause, in my view, the Board cannot exercise executive authority. The fact that the PG and the DPG are just two of the eleven members of the Board does not eliminate the constitutional infirmity. As a practical matter, the actions of the Board may be dependent on the PG and the DPG, as when they are needed to form a quorum, or where they cast the deciding votes. More fundamentally, the command of the Appointments Clause is not mere "etiquette or protocol," Buckley, 424 U.S. at 125, 96 S.Ct. at 685, and to allow powerful boards or commissions to be composed, even in part, by members appointed in an unconstitutional manner would vitiate the Appointments Clause.

This constitutional infirmity of the Board interrupts the chain of enforcement authority from the President to the Judicial Officer and ALJ. Because of its unconstitutional composition, the Board is bereft of any executive enforcement authority to delegate to the PG, let alone to the Judicial Officer and ALJ. Moreover, even if the Board were thought not to be undermined by the unconstitutionality of two of its members, the constitutional infirmity of the PG himself would still break the chain of authority from the President to the Postal Service Judicial Officer and ALJ.

The Appointments Clause speaks to "the fundamental principles of the Government established by the Framers of the Constitution, ... [to] the intent of the Framers that the powers of the three great branches of the National Government be largely separate from one another." Buckley, 424 U.S. at 120, 96 S.Ct. at 682. "The Appointments Clause prevents Congress from dispensing power too freely; it limits the universe of eligible recipients of the power to appoint. * * * The structural interests protected by the Appointments Clause are not those of any one Branch of government but of the entire Republic." Freytag, 111 S.Ct. at 2639. Given the profound interests at stake, even seemingly minor violations of the Appointments Clause cannot be ignored. I would reverse.

Notes

[1] The term "principal officer" is found nowhere in the text of the Constitution, but has been adopted by the Supreme Court in its Appointments Clause jurisprudence. See, e.g., Freytag v. Commissioner, ____ U.S. ____, 111 S.Ct. 2631, 115 L.Ed.2d 764 (1991).

[2] As the chief executive officer of the Postal Service (39 C.F.R. § 225.1), it can hardly be doubted that the PG is at least an "inferior" officer of the United States.

[3] Although the Supreme Court has never addressed the question of whether a group, as opposed to an individual, could be a department head, many independent regulatory agencies are headed by groups with no apparent constitutional infirmity, and the Attorney General determined as early as 1933 that groups could be "Heads of

Departments." See 37 Op. Att'y Gen. 227, 229-30 (1933).

[4] In its determination that the appointee in question in Freytag was an inferior officer, the Court found it significant that the appointee's "duties, salary, and means of appointment ... are specified by statute." Freytag, 111 S.Ct. at 2640.

[5] I adhere to the principle of finding unconstitutional as narrow and discrete a part of a statute as possible. In my view, only those parts of section 202 concerning the appointment of the PG and the DPG, and not those parts concerning the appointment of the Governors, are unconstitutional. Even with this narrow conclusion, however, the implications of the flawed appointment of the PG and DPG on the Board as a whole must be explored.

Judge O'Scannlain's concurrence and dissent in Jordon v. Gardner (Jan 10, 1992, amended April 2, 1992)

O'SCANNLAIN, Circuit Judge, concurring in part and dissenting in part:

While I concur in the court's analysis of plaintiffs' First and Fourth Amendment claims, I must respectfully dissent from its analysis and conclusions on the Eighth Amendment issue. I conclude that Judge Bryan's findings of fact were correct and were not "clearly erroneous" and with one exception, see ante at 1142, apparently the court does as well;[1] we differ in the legal conclusions flowing from such findings so far as current "cruel and unusual punishment" doctrine is concerned.

I

When Superintendent Eldon Vail took over the stewardship of the Washington Corrections Center for Women ("WCCW"), he was confronted with a problem. The guards' union, the Washington State Corrections Employees Association, had filed a grievance against the institution's policy of forbidding cross-gender so-called "pat" searches of the inmates. The female guards were unhappy that their food breaks, taken while they were still officially on duty, were occasionally interrupted in order to conduct a one-minute search. Shortly after his assumption to the role of superintendent, Vail decided to deny the grievance but moot the issue by implementing random, cross-gender searches.

During the so-called "pat" search, a guard is to "[u]se a flat hand and pushing motion across the [inmate's] crotch area." Plaintiff's Exhibit No. 16, Jordan v. Gardner, No. C89-399TB (W.D.Wash.) (guard training material). The guard must "[p]ush inward and upward when searching the crotch and upper thighs of the inmate." Id. All seams in the leg and the crotch area are to be "squeez[ed] and knead[ed]." Id. Using the back of the hand, the guard also is to search the breast area in a sweeping motion, so that the breasts will be "flattened." Id. Superintendent Vail estimated that the searches take forty-five seconds to one minute.

Judge Bryan understandably refused to use the term "pat" search to describe the new policy which was instituted on July 5, 1989. Transcript of Court's Oral Decision, Dec. 22, 1989 at 18. Several inmates were searched by male guards on that first (and only) day of its implementation. One, who had a long history of sexual abuse by men, unwillingly submitted to a cross-gender search and suffered severe distress: she had to have her fingers pried loose from bars she had grabbed during the search, and she vomited after returning to her cell block.[2] Later that day, the inmates obtained a preliminary injunction, which was transformed into a permanent injunction after an expedited trial. Random cross-gender searches have not occurred at WCCW since that day, over two years ago.

The district court issued its order permanently enjoining the searches following a seven-day trial. The district court record includes over 1000 pages of trial testimony transcripts and about 300 court documents. In reaching its decision, the district court heard six days of live testimony, reviewed eight written or videotaped depositions, and received fifty-six exhibits.

II

"After incarceration, only the `unnecessary and wanton infliction of pain' ... constitutes cruel and unusual punishment forbidden by the Eighth Amendment." Ingraham v. Wright, 430 U.S. 651, 670, 97 S.Ct. 1401, 1412, 51 L.Ed.2d 711 (1977) (quoting standard originally described in Gregg v. Georgia, 428 U.S. 153, 183, 96 S.Ct. 2909, 2929, 49 L.Ed.2d 859 (1976) (joint opinion of Stewart, Powell, and Stevens, JJ.)) (internal citation omitted), quoted in Whitley v. Albers, 475 U.S. 312, 319, 106 S.Ct. 1078, 1084, 89 L.Ed.2d 251 (1986). While none dispute that our inquiry should focus upon whether the search policy at issue constitutes the "unnecessary and wanton infliction of pain," there appears no consensus as to the means to determine whether the policy meets that description.

A

Under traditional Eighth Amendment analysis, we consider whether there is an "infliction of pain," and, if so, whether that infliction is "unnecessary and wanton."

1

The district court made a number of findings of fact on the issue of pain. Noting that many of the inmates at WCCW have suffered sexual or physical abuse by men, the district court found that physical, emotional, and psychological differences between men and women "may well cause women, and especially physically and sexually abused women, to react differently to searches of this type than would male inmates subjected to similar searches by women." Findings of Fact & Conclusions of Law at 3, Jordan v. Gardner, No. C89-339TB (W.D.Wash. Feb. 28, 1990) [hereinafter Findings & Conclusions] (¶ 6). The district court found that "[t]here is a high probability of great harm, including severe psychological injury and emotional pain and suffering, to some inmates from these searches, even if properly conducted." Id. (¶ 8). This finding was buttressed by testimony regarding the inmate witnesses' personal history, which the court found to be credible. Id. (¶ 7).

The record in this case, including the depositions of several inmates and the live testimony of one, describes the shocking background of verbal, physical, and, in particular, sexual abuse endured by many of the inmates at WCCW. For example, one inmate, who gave live trial testimony, described rapes by strangers (twice) and by husbands or boyfriends. She was also beaten by various men in her life; two deprived her of adequate food; one pushed her out of a moving car. Her story is not particularly unique. Eighty-five percent of the inmates report a history of such abuse to WCCW counselors, including rapes, molestations, beatings, and slavery.

Another inmate testified by deposition that her second husband beat her, strangled her, and ran over her with a truck. As she grew up, another inmate was frequently strapped or handcuffed to a bed by her half-brother, who beat or raped her; inmate's mother told her that there was nothing wrong with her half-brother's conduct. The inmate's mother once directed her to masturbate her stepfather, and in her later teens she was pushed into sexual liaisons by her mother, who would then blackmail the men. Another inmate's hand was broken by one of her two wife-beating husbands. Another inmate was sixteen when her uncle impregnated her; after the failure of the uncle's attempts to induce an abortion using a broom handle, screwdriver, bleach, and Lysol, the uncle paid a man to marry her. During that marriage, she was frequently raped by her husband and his friends, one time ending up in the hospital after they beat her and "ripped [her] behind."

The inmates presented testimony from ten expert witnesses on the psychological impact of forced submission to these searches by male guards, and related issues. The experts included WCCW staff members, social workers, psychologists, an anthropologist, and the former Director of Corrections for four different states (Raymond Procunier). The testimony described the psychological fragility and disorders found in abused women. A psychologist specializing in psychotherapy for women testified that the unwilling submission to bodily contact with the breasts and genitals by men would likely leave the inmate "revictimiz[ed]," resulting in a number of symptoms of post-traumatic stress disorder.

Although the majority points to some expert testimony that expresses uncertainty as to the magnitude of the harm suffered by the inmates, this court is not in the position of weighing evidence in the first instance. On appeal we look for clear error. Only if we are left "with the definite and firm conviction that a mistake has been committed," McConney, 728 F.2d at 1201, may we overturn Judge Bryan's factfinding. Based on the record just summarized, Judge Bryan's findings are fully justified. And despite its discussion casting doubt on Judge Bryan's factfinding, in the final analysis the majority too is apparently unwilling to disturb the trial court's findings of fact regarding the impact of the searches on the inmates. See ante at 1142.

Although the majority states that the inmates' experts "admitted uncertainty about the effect of the searches," id. at 1142, apparently because they were unable to identify the extent of harm which would be suffered by any particular inmate or how many would suffer great harm, the inmates' experts unanimously were of the view that some would suffer substantially. Given the inmates' own testimony and the fact that many of the inmates' experts were actually employed at WCCW and familiar with the inmates, the majority's skepticism of the district court's findings is not well placed.[3]

Once the district court's findings are accepted, there is no doubt that the constitutional standard for a finding of "pain" has been established. In most other search cases, the court has not been presented with evidence pointing to more than momentary discomfort caused by the search procedures. Compare Tribble v. Gardner, 860 F.2d 321, 325 n. 6 (9th Cir.1988) (digital rectal searches may inflict pain for Eighth Amendment purposes), cert. denied, 490 U.S. 1075, 109 S.Ct. 2087, 104 L.Ed.2d 650 (1989) with Grummett v. Rushen, 779 F.2d 491, 493 n. 1 (9th Cir.1985) ("pat-down" searches (including groin area) of male inmates by female guards does not describe sufficient harm for Eighth Amendment protection) and Smith v. Fairman, 678 F.2d 52, 53 (7th Cir.1982) (per curiam) ("pat" searches of male inmates by female guards, during which the guards simply pat the clothing and avoid genital areas, are not sufficiently barbarous to violate the Eighth Amendment), cert. denied, 461 U.S. 907, 103 S.Ct. 1879, 76 L.Ed.2d 810 (1983). However, none of these cases presented a record of potential serious psychological harm anything like that presented by the WCCW inmates.

We have previously recognized that conditions of confinement that seriously threaten the health and safety of the inmates are unconstitutional, even if these conditions have not caused actual illness but merely pose an unreasonable risk of harm. See Hoptowit v. Spellman, 753 F.2d 779, 783-84 (9th Cir.1985). If stagnant air or poor lighting are a sufficient harm for Eighth Amendment purposes, see id., then the inmates doubtless have established sufficient harm here.

2

Whether the infliction of pain is "unnecessary and wanton" involves an inquiry into the justification for the measure complained of and the intent behind the measure. Where "[t]here is no purpose to inflict unnecessary pain nor any unnecessary pain involved," Louisiana ex rel. Francis v. Resweber, 329 U.S. 459, 464, 67 S.Ct. 374, 376, 91 L.Ed. 422 (1947) (plurality), there is no cruelty.

In the majority's view, the inmates' Eighth Amendment claim fails on the "unnecessary and wanton" portion of the test. The majority offers the following reasoning in support of its conclusion that the prison officials have advanced a sufficient justification for the search policy:

In this case, the district judge stated that he had "no doubt" that prison officials implemented the policy to address "the legitimate governmental interest of security." In light of this finding, we cannot conclude that the searches are "so totally without penological justification that [they amount to] the gratuitous infliction of suffering." Hoptowit, 682 F.2d at 1246 (quotations omitted); see also Vigliotto v. Terry, 873 F.2d 1201, 1203 (9th Cir.1989) (eighth amendment protects prisoners from searches performed solely for "calculated harassment").

Ante at 1142-43. I am not persuaded.

a

First, it is far from clear that any policy will withstand an Eighth Amendment challenge so long as it is not "totally without penological justification." The quotation from Hoptowit in the passage set forth above, like the discussion in Vigliotto, does not purport to describe the constitutional minima. Rather, the class of activities prohibited by the Eighth Amendment "includes those sanctions that are `so totally without penological justification that [they] result[] in the gratuitous infliction of suffering.'" Hoptowit, 682 F.2d at 1246 (quoting Gregg, 428 U.S. at 183, 96 S.Ct. at 2929 (joint opinion)) (emphasis added); see also Rhodes v. Chapman, 452 U.S. 337, 346, 101 S.Ct. 2392, 2399, 69 L.Ed.2d 59 (1981) ("Among `unnecessary and wanton' inflictions of pain are those that are `totally without penological justification.'") (quoting Gregg) (emphasis added); Michenfelder v. Sumner, 860 F.2d 328, 335 (9th Cir. 1988) (same). Nothing in these cases requires that a policy be completely worthless to penological purposes in order for an Eighth Amendment claim to be sustained, no matter how serious the harm generated by the policy.

Nonetheless, the record here supports the district court's conclusion that the cross-gender searches were "without penological justification," Findings & Conclusions at 12 (¶ 28). The record reflects, and the district court found, that WCCW's security is not dependent upon cross-gender searches. The prison officials do not argue that WCCW's security has been impaired in the slightest during the pendency of the district court's injunctions, preliminary and permanent, which have now been in effect for two years. Although Superintendent Vail's predecessor voiced concerns about internal security and the need for random searches, these concerns have been met by the establishment of random and routine searches by female guards. Superintendent Vail himself confirmed as much at trial.

Nor do cross-gender searches ensure equal employment opportunities for male guards. The conflict between the right of one sex not to be discriminated against in job opportunities and the other to maintain some level of privacy "has normally been resolved by attempting to accommodate both interests through adjustments in scheduling and job responsibilities for the guards." Smith, 678 F.2d at 55; see also Gunther v. Iowa State Men's Reformatory, 612 F.2d 1079, 1087 (8th Cir.), cert. denied, 446 U.S. 966, 100 S.Ct. 2942, 64 L.Ed.2d 825 (1980), overruled on other grounds, Kremer v. Chemical Constr. Corp., 456 U.S. 461, 102 S.Ct. 1883, 72 L.Ed.2d 262 (1982). At trial, the prison officials' own witnesses testified that not a single bid had been refused, promotion denied, nor guard replaced as a result of the ban on routine cross-gender searches.

Thus, no penological purpose for the cross-gender searches remains. Although the district court found that the random search policy was "addressed" to security, it also noted that the evidence demonstrated "that the security interests of the [WCCW] have been adequately fulfilled by the actions of its administrative officials, prior to the proposed policy change and during the period in which a preliminary injunction has been in effect in this case." Findings & Conclusions at 6 (¶ 19). And, of course, the district court concluded that "[t]he proposed random or routine cross-gender clothed body searches constitute the infliction of pain without penological justification, and cruel and unusual punishment in violation of the Eighth Amendment." Id. at 12 (¶ 28) (emphasis added).

These latter findings were entirely consistent with the evidence.[4]

It appears that none of the Eighth Amendment cases decided by the Supreme Court, this circuit, or any other court of appeals has upheld a pain-inflicting measure simply because prison officials implemented the policy to "address" a legitimate governmental interest. Rather, other courts (and other panels within this court) have placed far more teeth in the "unnecessary and wanton" infliction test than the majority does today.

b

Although I agree with Judge Bryan that the cross-gender aspect of the search policy is "without penological justification," I do not believe that the Eighth Amendment demands so little of prison officials. In formulating its test, the majority has simply disregarded the "unnecessary and wanton" terminology which all courts have agreed is the appropriate test in this area.

From the discussion above, it should be evident that the cross-gender searches are "unnecessary," as I am sure the majority would agree. The tougher inquiry is whether the infliction of pain here could be considered "wanton." "Eighth Amendment claims based on official conduct that does not purport to be the penalty formally imposed for a crime require inquiry into [the prison officials'] state of mind . . . ." Wilson v. Seiter, ____ U.S. ____, 111 S.Ct. 2321, 2326, 115 L.Ed.2d 271 (1991). "It is obduracy and wantonness ... that characterize the conduct prohibited by the Cruel and Unusual Punishments Clause." Whitley, 475 U.S. at 319, 106 S.Ct. at 1084.

"[W]antonness does not have a fixed meaning but must be determined with `due regard for differences in the kind of conduct against which an Eighth Amendment objection is lodged.'" Wilson, 111 S.Ct. at 2326 (quoting Whitley, 475 U.S. at 320, 106 S.Ct. at 1084). In Whitley, a prisoner was shot in the kneecap during or immediately following a prison riot. In an emergency, the prison guard's actions "are necessarily taken `in haste, under pressure,' and balanced against `competing institutional concerns for the safety of prison staff or other inmates.'" Id. (quoting Whitley, 475 U.S. at 320, 106 S.Ct. at 1084). In such extreme circumstances, the Court defined wantonness as "acting `"maliciously and sadistically for the very purpose of causing harm."'" Id. (quoting Whitley, 475 U.S. at 320-21, 106 S.Ct. at 1085 (quoting Johnson v. Glick, 481 F.2d 1028, 1033 (2d Cir.) (Friendly, J.), cert. denied, 414 U.S. 1033, 94 S.Ct. 462, 38 L.Ed.2d 324 (1973))).

In non-emergency situations, there is ordinarily not a clash with other important governmental responsibilities but rather plenty of time for reflection; then, "`deliberate indifference' would constitute wantonness." Id. (quoting Estelle v. Gamble, 429 U.S. 97, 97 S.Ct. 285, 50 L.Ed.2d 251 (1976)). In Wilson, the Court extended use of the "deliberate indifference" standard from cases of deprivation of medical care to all "prison conditions" cases. See id.

As in a prison conditions case, where prison officials formulate a policy in a nonemergency, there are no particular constraints on the officials' decisionmaking process which justify a requirement of "malice" for culpability. See Redman v. County of San Diego, 942 F.2d 1435, 1442 (9th Cir.1991) (en banc). Thus, the Supreme Court would apply the "deliberate indifference" standard to this circumstance to determine "wantonness."[5]

The record supports the conclusion that the inmates met their burden of establishing "deliberate indifference." Superintendent Vail indicated that he adopted the policy without a great deal of knowledge about the impact of the searches upon the inmates, see supra note 4, and that the policy was not required for security purposes. Yet long before the policy was actually implemented, Superintendent Vail was urged by members of his own staff not to institute cross-gender searches due to the psychological trauma which many inmates likely would suffer. Further, once the policy took effect, a court order was necessary to prevent the searches although one of the first inmates to be searched suffered a severe reaction. See supra note 2 and accompanying text. Even now, despite ample testimony of the harmful effects of this policy, the prison officials are intent upon reversing the district court injunction. See Redman, 942 F.2d at 1443 (prison officials may not act with reckless indifference to a particular vulnerability of which the officials know or should know).[6]

Under these circumstances, one must conclude that the prison officials' conduct in this matter has been "wanton." Judge Bryan properly found that the policy is "unnecessary and wanton," and that it lacks a penological justification.

B

The prison officials propose use of another test altogether. They argue that the Eighth Amendment challenge, like all of the inmates' other assertions, should be measured under the "reasonableness" standard of Turner v. Safley, 482 U.S. 78, 107 S.Ct. 2254, 96 L.Ed.2d 64 (1987), rather than by the traditional Eighth Amendment approach. I agree with the majority's tacit rejection of this approach.

Although the Supreme Court has stated broadly that "the standard of review we adopted in Turner applies to all circumstances in which the needs of prison administration implicate constitutional rights," Washington v. Harper, 494 U.S. 210, 110 S.Ct. 1028, 1038, 108 L.Ed.2d 178 (1990), Turner has been applied only where the constitutional right is one which is enjoyed by all persons, but the exercise of which may necessarily be limited due to the unique circumstances of imprisonment. See, e.g., id. (due process under Fourteenth Amendment); Turner, 482 U.S. at 91-99, 107 S.Ct. at 2262-67 (free association under First Amendment); Michenfelder, 860 F.2d at 332-36 (applying Turner to privacy and Fourth Amendment claims, but not to Eighth Amendment claim); Griffin v. Coughlin, 743 F.Supp. 1006, 1010-19 (N.D.N.Y.1990) (applying Turner to equal protection claim but not to Eighth Amendment claims); see also Vigliotto, 873 F.2d at 1203 (examining Eighth Amendment claim without reference to Turner).[7] Eighth Amendment rights do not conflict with incarceration; rather, they limit the hardships which may be inflicted upon the incarcerated as "punishment." See Spain v. Procunier, 600 F.2d 189, 193-94 (9th Cir.1979) (Kennedy, J.) ("Whatever rights one may lose at the prison gates, ... the full protections of the eighth amendment most certainly remain in force.") (citations omitted).

Perhaps for this reason, the Supreme Court has not applied Turner to an Eighth Amendment case.

Nonetheless, if one were to apply a Turner analysis to the inmates' Eighth Amendment claim, one should reach the same result. Nothing is "reasonable" about a policy which is "cruel and unusual," "unnecessary and wanton." Cf. Tribble, 860 F.2d at 325 n. 6 (noting that if searches violate Fourth Amendment under Turner, they may also violate Eighth Amendment to the extent they are shown to inflict pain). Although there is a rational connection between a random-search policy and security, there is no security or other reason for permitting cross-gender searches absent suspicion or emergency. The present policy of random searches by female guards suffices as a fully adequate alternative. Cf. Turner, 482 U.S. at 97-98, 107 S.Ct. at 2265-66 ("No doubt legitimate security concerns may require placing reasonable restrictions upon an inmate's right to marry.... The [challenged] regulation, however, represents an exaggerated response to such security objectives."). Nor does the record reflect that the injunction has resulted or would result in "a tremendous rearrangement of work schedules," Grummett, 779 F.2d at 494, or otherwise resulted in a negative "ripple effect," Michenfelder, 860 F.2d at 336, on the institution.

C

Under any possible test, the inmates have established a violation of their Eighth Amendment right to be free from "cruel and unusual punishments." The record more than adequately supports the district court's finding of psychological harm, and the harm is sufficient to meet the constitutional minima. Furthermore, the infliction of this pain is "unnecessary and wanton" under the applicable legal standards. The district court's conclusion of law with regard to this claim should be upheld.

III

Having identified an Eighth Amendment violation, one must then consider the propriety of the district court's remedy. "The district judge ha[s] the power only to correct the constitutional defects that he [or she] [finds]." Hoptowit, 682 F.2d at 1253; see also Toussaint v. McCarthy, 801 F.2d 1080, 1107-08 (9th Cir.1986) ("An injunction must be narrowly tailored to cure the constitutional violation and must not intrude on the functions of state officials unnecessarily."), cert. denied, 481 U.S. 1069, 107 S.Ct. 2462, 95 L.Ed.2d 871 (1987).

The district court designed its injunction narrowly. The prison officials are enjoined only from conducting "routine or random clothed body searches of female inmates which include touching of and around breasts and genital areas[] by male corrections officers" at WCCW. Findings & Conclusions at 14 (¶ 1) (issuing order of injunction). The court specifically noted that its decision "does not extend to cross gender searches under emergency conditions, cross gender searches of men by women, or cross gender searches at female institutions other than [WCCW]." Id. at 13 (¶ 33).

The prison officials have not challenged the scope of the injunction, instead focusing upon its raison d'etre. The injunction was appropriately tailored to prohibit the identified constitutional violation. The district court has not barred the implementation of random or routine suspicionless searches; in fact, these have continued during the two years since the cross-gender search policy was enjoined. Only non-emergency, suspicionless searches by male guards are forbidden.

IV

It cannot be gainsaid that incarceration "`brings about the necessary withdrawal or limitation of many privileges and rights,'" Pell v. Procunier, 417 U.S. 817, 822, 94 S.Ct. 2800, 2804, 41 L.Ed.2d 495 (1974) (quoting Price v. Johnston, 334 U.S. 266, 285, 68 S.Ct. 1049, 1060, 92 L.Ed. 1356 (1948)), or that some conditions that are "restrictive and even harsh" can be "part of the penalty that criminal offenders pay for their offenses against society," Rhodes, 452 U.S. at 347, 101 S.Ct. at 2399. In this case we are presented with the prospect of serious psychological suffering, the infliction of which is demonstrably "unnecessary" and, in the constitutional sense of the word, "wanton." I seriously doubt that "standards of decency in modern society," Baumann v. Arizona Dep't of Corrections, 754 F.2d 841, 846 (9th Cir.1985), are met by the indifferent imposition of needless harm such as here.

The inmates have established a violation of their Eighth Amendment rights, justifying the district court's issuance of an injunction.

I respectfully dissent.

Notes

[1] The majority and both parties agree that the district court's findings of fact are subject to the "clearly erroneous" standard of review. See United States v. McConney, 728 F.2d 1195, 1200 & n. 5 (9th Cir.) (en banc), cert. denied, 469 U.S. 824, 105 S.Ct. 101, 83 L.Ed.2d 46 (1984). We must accept the district court's findings unless our review of the record leaves us "`with the definite and firm conviction that a mistake has been committed.'" Id. at 1201 (quoting Pullman-Standard v. Swint, 456 U.S. 273, 285 n. 14, 102 S.Ct. 1781, 1788 n. 14, 72 L.Ed.2d 66 (1982) (quotation omitted)). The remarkable frequency with which the majority's view of the record is supported with citations to isolated expert and witness testimony, rather than to findings of fact, is troubling in light of our circuit's longstanding tradition of deference to district court credibility and fact determinations.

[2] This inmate, Sharon Hanson, later settled a suit for damages against the guard and prison officials for $1,000 plus $10,000 in attorney fees.

[3] The majority's observation that "expert opinions do `not ordinarily establish constitutional minima'" is somewhat baffling. Ante at 1142 (parenthetical to, and quotation from, Hoptowit v. Ray, 682 F.2d 1237, 1246 (9th Cir.1982)). The inmates offered more than just expert testimony; some of them gave testimony themselves, see Findings & Conclusions at 3 (¶ 7), and the district court also considered the disastrous results of the cross-gender search of Sharon Hanson, see supra note 2 and accompanying text. In any event, that portion of Hoptowit to which the majority refers discusses the inadequacies of

expert testimony on the issue of "evolving standards of decency," which is determined not by what experts would prefer but by "what the general public would consider decent." See Hoptowit, 682 F.2d at 1246. The reference has no relevance to an attempt to establish "probability of harm."

[4] The Supreme Court has instructed us that "neither judge nor jury freely [may] substitute their judgment for that of officials who have made a considered choice." Whitley, 475 U.S. at 322, 106 S.Ct. at 1085, quoted in ante at 1142. By concluding that cross-gender searches are unjustifiable on this record, Judge Bryan has not violated this stricture. It is difficult to describe the new policy as a "considered choice"; Superintendent Vail noted at trial that he had formulated his policy "[n]ot with anywhere near the amount of knowledge I have at this point" concerning the likely impact on the inmates. Cf. Tribble, 860 F.2d at 327 n. 9 ("In view of the substantial evidence that ... defendants have exaggerated their response to purported security considerations, we do not defer to their expert judgment in these matters.") (citations omitted).

[5] The majority concludes that the deliberate indifference standard may not apply here because of the existence of "equally important governmental responsibilities." Ante at 1144 n. 3. Judge Bryan, however, found that no penological purpose was served by cross-gender searches. Findings & Conclusions at 12 (¶ 28). The record simply does not support the notion that equally important governmental interests are presented in this case.

[6] Although Redman involves the Fourteenth Amendment's protections, the Eighth Amendment imposes a duty on prison officials at least as rigorous. Redman, 942 F.2d at 1442-43.

[7] But see Walker v. Sumner, 917 F.2d 382, 385-88 (9th Cir.1990) (applying one Turner factor to assertion that forced blood test violated Fourth, Eighth, and Fourteenth Amendments, without analyzing constitutional arguments separately); Michenfelder, 860 F.2d at 331 n. 1 (suggesting Turner's applicability to Eighth Amendment analysis, although later using traditional Eighth Amendment approach).

Judge O'Scannlain's partial dissent in Romberg v. Nichols (Jan 13, 1992)

O'SCANNLAIN, Circuit Judge, dissenting in part:

I dissent only from Part IIIA of the court's opinion which affirms the forty percent reduction of the fee award. In my view, the reasons cited by the district court were insufficient to justify departure from the presumptively reasonable lodestar figure.

I

In calculating the fee award, the district court first set a lodestar figure of $48,562.50, representing all of the hours claimed by the Rombergs' attorney (277.5) compensated at the rate of $175 per hour. In so doing, the court expressly "accepted at face value" the hours submitted by the Rombergs' attorney and expressly selected the $175 rate. Romberg v. Nichols, No. 83-8448 at 2, 3 (C.D.Cal. Jan. 20, 1989). The court then specifically addressed all twelve of the factors identified by the Kerr court as relevant to any departure from the lodestar.[1] See Kerr v. Screen Extras Guild, Inc., 526 F.2d 67, 69-70 (9th Cir. 1975) (adopting twelve factors identified by the Fifth Circuit as appropriate for this purpose in Johnson v. Georgia Highway Express, 488 F.2d 714 (5th Cir.1974)), cert. denied, 425 U.S. 951, 96 S.Ct. 1726, 48 L.Ed.2d 195 (1976); see also Hensley v. Eckerhart, 461 U.S. 424, 429-30, 103 S.Ct. 1933, 1937-38, 76 L.Ed.2d 40 (1983) (noting that the Senate and House Reports on section 1988 both favorably cited the twelve Johnson factors).

The court determined that three of the factors justified a reduction of the fee: (a) the novelty and difficulty of the questions involved, (b) the skill requisite to perform the legal services properly, and (c) the amount involved and the results obtained. See Kerr, 526 F.2d at 70 (the second, third, and eighth factors). The Rombergs now contend that the district court abused its discretion in using these three factors to reduce the lodestar by forty percent. I agree.

In Jordan v. Multnomah County, 815 F.2d 1258 (9th Cir.1987), we acknowledged that "[a] `strong presumption' exists that the lodestar figure represents a `reasonable' fee." Id. at 1262 (quoting Pennsylvania v. Delaware Valley Citizens' Council for Clean Air, 478 U.S. 546, 565, 106 S.Ct. 3088, 3098, 92 L.Ed.2d 439 (1986)). Although the district court has broad discretion to determine the amount of a fee award, it must justify any departure from the lodestar figure if the hours and rate that determine the lodestar are themselves reasonable. See Delaware Valley Citizens' Council, 478 U.S. at 564-65, 106 S.Ct. at 3098; Blum v. Stenson, 465 U.S. 886, 897, 104 S.Ct. 1541, 1548, 79 L.Ed.2d 891 (1984); see also Long v. IRS, 932 F.2d 1309, 1313-14 & n. 4 (9th Cir.1991) (per curiam). This justification must include more than a bare statement of the Kerr factors relied on; the district court must also supply an explanation of the application of those factors to the case. See Cunningham v. County of Los Angeles, 879 F.2d 473, 488 (9th Cir.1988). Here, in light of the district court's own admission of the reasonableness of both the hours claimed and the rate to be applied, I conclude that the court's purported justifications are inadequate to support its forty-percent downward departure.

A

In discussing the second Kerr factor, the district court explained:

2. The case was not novel. It did take skill under the circumstances, but the above observation about the jury's option [to produce a Solomonic solution by awarding nominal damages] is a reducing factor.

Romberg v. Nichols, No. 83-8448 at 2 (C.D.Cal. Jan. 20, 1989). The court's analysis here is a non sequitur that appears to penalize the Rombergs for having prevailed in the first place. The court first states that "[t]he case was not novel" and then concludes that because the Rombergs' attorney invited nominal damages, that invitation constitutes a reducing factor. An attorney's request for nominal damages at the end of a trial, however, says nothing about the "novelty and difficulty of the questions involved"; there is no logical connection here. More importantly, reducing the fee award on the basis of a belief that the jury would have found for the defendants if not presented with the option of awarding nominal damages is clearly impermissible. As we explained ante, at Part II-D of the court's opinion, if a district court concludes that the evidence does not support the jury's verdict, the appropriate course of action is to set aside the verdict — not to penalize the prevailing attorney.

B

With respect to the third Kerr factor — "the skill requisite to perform the legal services properly" — the district court explained:

3. Mr. Yagman is a skilled and effective civil rights lawyer. As such, however, he should have realized that there was little or nothing to support the claims that never got to the jury — again, a significant reducing factor.

Romberg v. Nichols, No. 83-8448 at 3 (C.D.Cal. Jan. 20, 1989). The Rombergs maintain that this reduction is also impermissible because none of the 277.5 hours billed was spent on claims that did not proceed to trial. This argument is equally meritorious. If the lodestar does not include the hours spent on dismissed claims, then any subsequent reduction for those hours constitutes double discounting. In any event, the proper stage at which to reduce a fee award for time that is not compensable is during the calculation of the lodestar. Here, the court expressly found that the elements comprising the lodestar were reasonable. A subsequent discount by an undefined percentage on the basis of alleged overbilling is inconsistent with that determination and cannot suffice to rebut the presumption of correctness acknowledged by this court in Jordan.

C

Finally, in applying the eighth Kerr factor — "the amount involved and the results obtained" — the district court concluded:

8. The results obtained were (i) $2.00 in cash and (ii) "vindication." If all plaintiffs wanted was vindication they could have made the case a straight-forward Fourth Amendment claim from the outset. This is clearly a reducing factor.

Romberg v. Nichols, No. 83-8448 at 3 (C.D.Cal. Jan. 20, 1989). The Supreme Court, however, has expressly "reject[ed] the proposition that fee awards under 1988 should necessarily be proportionate to the amount of damages a civil rights plaintiff actually recovers." City of Riverside v. Rivera, 477 U.S. 561, 574, 106 S.Ct. 2686, 2694, 91 L.Ed.2d 466 (1986) (plurality opinion); see also id. at 585, 106 S.Ct. at 2699-2700 (Powell, J., concurring in judgment and similarly rejecting a proportionality rule). This court has gone even one step further, recognizing that although the size of an award can be a permissible consideration, the smallness of an award alone cannot justify reduction of the attorney's fee. See Jordan, 815 F.2d at 1262 & n. 6 (citing Hensley and noting that the second, third, eighth, and ninth factors identified in Johnson and Kerr "cannot serve as independent bases for adjusting fee awards"); see also Long, 932 F.2d at 1314 & n. 4 (explaining same). The substance of the prevailing claim, rather than the amount of relief received, is the central concern for section 1988 purposes. See Greater Los Angeles Council on Deafness v. Community Television, 813 F.2d 217, 222 (9th Cir.1987). Indeed, as the Supreme Court recently explained, "[t]he intention of Congress [in enacting section 1988] was to encourage successful civil rights litigation, not to create a special incentive to prove damages ..." Blanchard v. Bergeron, 489 U.S. 87, 95, 109 S.Ct. 939, 945, 103 L.Ed.2d 67 (1989). What the attorney has earned is a wholly independent consideration from what the jury believes his clients have suffered.

II

In light of these considerations, I would reverse the district court's fee determination, and remand for recalculation in a manner consistent with the foregoing analysis of the law of this circuit.

Notes

[1] The majority interprets the district court's order as considering the Kerr factors simultaneously with setting the lodestar. Although I disagree with this interpretation, it is immaterial to the result. Whatever the order in which the award amount was calculated, the reducing factors relied on were impermissible in light of the district court's concession that the hours claimed and fee set were reasonable.

Judge O'Scannlain's dissent in Stock West Corp. v. Taylor (May 18, 1992)

O'SCANNLAIN, Circuit Judge, dissenting:

Because the majority improvidently extends the National Farmers Union-LaPlante abstention doctrine far beyond the scope intended by the Supreme Court, and because the record is inadequate to determine whether defendant Taylor's actions fall within the scope of tribal immunity, I respectfully dissent.

I

A

Talismanic invocation of tribal court jurisdiction is surely insufficient to mandate federal court abstention. Yet that is all that is present here. This is a tort action for alleged malpractice committed in Portland, Oregon. Neither party to this litigation is a member of the Colville Tribes, nor is even Native American. Indeed, the only connection to an Indian tribe is that the alleged tortfeasor, Taylor, was employed by a tribal corporation and was in Portland on his client's business when he allegedly committed the tort. The majority would close the door to the federal court whenever a suit had any connection to a tribe, no matter how removed or remote. I simply cannot read National Farmers Union and LaPlante so expansively as to require federal court abstention in this situation.

There are two fundamentals of this case that the majority seems unwilling to accept. First, Stock West is alleging a tort, a negligent misrepresentation in the opinion letter. Stock West's claim is not based on the contracts to build and operate the sawmill on the reservation. The sawmill contracts are a legal nullity and could not possibly form the basis of a cause of action; indeed, a tribal court has so held. See Confederated Tribes of the Colville Reservation v. Stock West Inc., 15 Indian L.Rptr. 6019 (Colville Tribal Ct. May 2,

1988).

Nor was the transaction underlying the opinion letter the sawmill contracts. In fact, the sawmill contracts had been executed one year earlier. Rather, the opinion letter was prepared in connection with the loan agreement, which was entered into in Portland. Stock West's tort claim against Taylor stands independent of the sawmill contracts with the tribes.[1]

Second, the tort alleged by Stock West occurred hundreds of miles from the Colville Tribes' reservation, in Portland, Oregon. The majority apparently believes that Stock West's malpractice and misrepresentation claim may have arisen on the Colville reservation because the allegedly fraudulent opinion letter was researched and drafted on the reservation. I cannot agree. It is not malpractice to write a fraudulent letter and then discard it. Nor was there any misrepresentation until Taylor travelled to Portland, Oregon and delivered the opinion letter to Stock West at the loan closing. Under Oregon law, the delivery of the opinion letter is the tort. Rice v. McAlister, 268 Or. 125, 519 P.2d 1263, 1265 (1974). See also Heil v. Morrison Knudsen Corp., 863 F.2d 546, 550 (7th Cir.1988) ("[A] tort is not wrongful conduct in the air; the arrow must hit its mark."). It is beyond peradventure, in my view, that the tort upon which Stock West's action is based occurred in Portland, when the allegedly fraudulent legal opinion was presented to Stock West. See Cavalier Label Co. v. Polytam, Ltd., 687 F.Supp. 872, 879 (S.D.N.Y.1988) ("The tort of fraud is considered to be committed where the misrepresentation is uttered.").

Because the cause of action alleged by Stock West did not arise on the Colville Tribes' reservation, the Supreme Court cases announcing a doctrine of abstention for exhaustion of tribal remedies, National Farmers Union Ins. Cos. v. Crow Tribe, 471 U.S. 845, 105 S.Ct. 2447, 85 L.Ed.2d 818 (1985) and Iowa Mut. Ins. Co. v. LaPlante, 480 U.S. 9, 107 S.Ct. 971, 94 L.Ed.2d 10 (1987), and the cases in this circuit following them, simply do not apply here. In both National Farmers Union and LaPlante it was undisputed that the transaction or occurrence underlying the plaintiff's claim occurred within the boundaries of a reservation. To extend the extraordinary doctrine of abstention to a claim based on an occurrence that happened off the reservation is, in my view, unwarranted.

In National Farmers Union, the suit arose out of a motorcycle-pedestrian accident that occurred in a school parking lot "located on land owned by the State within the boundaries of the Crow Indian Reservation." National Farmers Union, 471 U.S. at 847, 105 S.Ct. at 2449. The pedestrian sued the school and obtained a default judgment in tribal court. Id. at 847-48, 105 S.Ct. at 2449. The school (and its insurer) then sought a temporary restraining order in federal court to prevent the issuance of a writ of execution against school property. Id. Because the underlying incident occurred on the reservation, the existence of civil tribal court jurisdiction over the school and its insurer — non-Indian parties — seemed likely, and the Court held that the determination of whether jurisdiction existed "should be conducted in the first instance in the Tribal Court itself." Id. at 856, 105 S.Ct. at 2454. Nowhere did the Court suggest that the bare assertion of tribal jurisdiction by one of the parties, even where the claim did not arise on the reservation, would be sufficient to require abstention by the district court.

Two years later, the Supreme Court revisited the tribal court abstention doctrine in LaPlante. There too, the Court pointed out that the cause of action was based on an accident that occurred "within the boundaries of the Reservation." LaPlante, 480 U.S. at 11, 107 S.Ct. at 974. The Court extended the abstention doctrine of National Farmers Union, a federal question case, to matters arising under a district court's diversity jurisdiction, id. at 16, 107 S.Ct. at 976, but again gave no indication that such doctrine would apply to actions that did not arise on the reservation.

This circuit too has always limited its application of the National Farmers Union-LaPlante abstention doctrine to causes of action that arose on an Indian reservation. See United States v. Plainbull, 957 F.2d 724, 725 (9th Cir.1992) (action for "trespass by [defendants'] livestock on tribal lands"); Crawford v. Genuine Parts Co., 947 F.2d 1405, 1406 (9th Cir.1991) ("action arose when an automobile accident occurred on ... the Blackfeet Indian Reservation"), cert. denied, ____ U.S. ____, 112 S.Ct. 1174, 117 L.Ed.2d 419; Burlington Northern R.R. Co. v. Crow Tribal Council, 940 F.2d 1239, 1241 (9th Cir.1991) (action to challenge tribal ordinance that "establishe[d] `general duties' for common carriers operating on the Crow Reservation"); Stock West, Inc. v. Confederated Tribes of the Colville Reservation, 873 F.2d 1221, 1222 (9th Cir.1989) (action to compel arbitration of contract "to construct and later manage a sawmill on the Colville reservation"); White Mountain Apache Tribe v. Smith Plumbing Co., 856 F.2d 1301, 1303 (9th Cir.1988) ("The parties agree that all relevant subcontracts were entered into, and all relevant deliveries were made on the Fort Apache Indian Reservation."); Wellman v. Chevron U.S.A, Inc., 815 F.2d 577, 578 (9th Cir.1987) ("suit ... concerning a contract with a non-Indian corporation for work on tribal lands"); A & A Concrete, Inc. v. White Mountain Apache Tribe, 781 F.2d 1411, 1416 (9th Cir.) ("undisputed that the transactions which form the bases for appellants' claims occurred or were commenced on tribal territory"), cert. denied, 476 U.S. 1117, 106 S.Ct. 2008, 90 L.Ed.2d 659 (1986).

National Farmers Union-LaPlante abstention applies only to civil actions that arise on the reservation because a presumption arises that tribal courts have jurisdiction. "Tribal authority over the activities of non-Indians on reservation lands is an important part of tribal sovereignty. Civil jurisdiction over such activities presumptively lies in the tribal courts unless affirmatively limited by a specific treaty provision or federal statute." LaPlante, 480 U.S. at 18, 107 S.Ct. at 977 (emphasis added) (internal citations omitted). Where the presumption of tribal jurisdiction is absent, abstention cannot be justified.

In my view, there can be no question that this suit arose off the reservation. Further, I disagree with the majority that a merely "colorable question" as to whether the suit is somehow connected to another transaction that did arise on the reservation can be sufficient to prevent a federal court from exercising its jurisdiction. Abstention comes at a high cost. It deprives the plaintiff of his statutory entitlement to choose a federal court as his forum. Moreover, it ordinarily delays the final resolution of the case, and increases the costs of litigation. See England v. Louisiana State Bd. of Medical Examiners, 375 U.S. 411,

418, 84 S.Ct. 461, 466, 11 L.Ed.2d 440 (1964) (acknowledging the "delay and expense to which application of the abstention doctrine inevitably gives rise"). "The Supreme Court has stated that the doctrine of abstention `is an extraordinary and narrow exception to the duty of a District Court to adjudicate a controversy properly before it.'" Plainbull, 957 F.2d at 727 (quoting County of Allegheny v. Frank Mashuda Co., 360 U.S. 185, 188, 79 S.Ct. 1060, 1063, 3 L.Ed.2d 1163 (1959)). The fact that there may be some question that Stock West's suit may be remotely related to a previous transaction that did occur on the reservation cannot be sufficient to abrogate this duty.

B

That Taylor was employed by tribal corporations as attorney when he committed the alleged tort does not change the result. Taylor was not executing tribal policy when he rendered the opinion letter, but rather simply complying with subsection 4.2.18 of the loan agreement, which required the tribal corporations, as borrowers, to "deliver[] to [the] Bank the opinion of Borrower's counsel." Although Taylor was the senior attorney in the Reservation Attorney's office, there is no evidence in the record that he participated in tribal governance or held a policy-making position in tribal government akin to the role an attorney general plays in state or federal government. Nor is Taylor even a member of the Colville Tribes.

In any event, Taylor is not being sued in his role as senior attorney in the Reservation Attorney's office, or even as counsel to the tribal corporations. Taylor is being sued for violating his duties to third parties as a member of the Washington bar, and his attorney-client relationship with the tribal corporations is not at issue. The Colville Tribes are not a party to this suit. Stock West does not challenge tribal actions or policies, or seek damages from the Tribes. However this suit comes out, the Tribes cannot be liable to judgment.

Thus, the only connection between this suit and Taylor's employer, the tribal corporations, is that Taylor was travelling on tribal corporation business when the tort allegedly was committed in downtown Portland, Oregon. Surely if Taylor had negligently hit someone with a Tribe-owned car in Portland while driving to his meeting, abstention would not be mandated (even if the Colville Tribal court asserted jurisdiction) if the injured party brought suit in federal court in Portland. The negligent tort alleged here is in substance no different.

Regardless of who his client is, Taylor has certain independent duties as a member of the state bar, and it is these duties he is alleged to have violated. The identity of Taylor's employer or client is immaterial in an action of this kind since the alleged tort occurred off the reservation. Under these circumstances, National Farmers Union-LaPlante abstention simply does not apply.

II

The district court denied discovery on the question of Taylor's alleged immunity. The issue is far from clear. "[W]hen tribal officials act in their official capacity and within the scope of their authority, they are immune." Imperial Granite Co. v. Pala Band of

Mission Indians, 940 F.2d 1269, 1271 (9th Cir.1991). Whether Taylor is a "tribal official," and if so whether the rendering of a negligent legal opinion as part of a commercial transaction is within his official capacity and the scope of his authority, cannot be determined on this record. I would remand for further discovery.

I cannot agree with the majority that the district court erred in even considering the question of sovereign immunity. While it cannot be gainsaid that tribal courts are best qualified to interpret tribal law, tribal official immunity is governed by federal law. Both before and after development of the National Farmers Union-LaPlante abstention doctrine, this court has had many occasions to consider whether tribal immunity extends to individual tribal officials. See Imperial Granite, 940 F.2d at 1271-72; Burlington Northern R.R. Co. v. Blackfeet Tribe, 924 F.2d 899, 901-02 (9th Cir.), petition for cert. filed, 60 U.S.L.W. 3294 (Oct. 2, 1991); Evans v. McKay, 869 F.2d 1341, 1348 n. 9 (9th Cir.1989); Hardin v. White Mountain Apache Tribe, 779 F.2d 476, 479-80 (9th Cir.1985); Snow v. Quinault Indian Nation, 709 F.2d 1319, 1322 (9th Cir.1983), cert. denied, 467 U.S. 1214, 104 S.Ct. 2655, 81 L.Ed.2d 362 (1984); Davis v. Littell, 398 F.2d 83, 84-85 (9th Cir.1968), cert. denied, 393 U.S. 1018, 89 S.Ct. 621, 21 L.Ed.2d 562 (1969). In none of these cases did we hold that the district court was barred from addressing the question of tribal official immunity. Hence, I would permit the district court to consider whether tribal immunity extends to Taylor's actions here.

Accordingly, I respectfully dissent.

Notes

[1] Interestingly, the tribal corporations expressly waived sovereign immunity from suit in any court of competent jurisdiction under both the sawmill contracts, see Stock West, Inc. v. Confederated Tribes of the Colville Reservation, 873 F.2d 1221, 1224 n. 6 (9th Cir.1989), and the loan agreement. Presumably, such waiver extends to Mr. Taylor as attorney for the tribal corporations which the Colville Tribal court will honor if it now assumes jurisdiction in this case.

Judge O'Scannlain's concurrence and dissent in NRDC v. EPA (June 4, 1992)

O'SCANNLAIN, Circuit Judge, concurring in part and dissenting in part:

I concur in Parts I, II.A, II.C.1, II.C.4, II.E, and much of Part II.B of the majority opinion. I dissent from Part II.B.2.c, directing EPA to issue supplemental regulations. I dissent also from Parts II.C.2 and II.C.3, in which the court invalidates EPA's exclusion of storm water discharges from certain light industrial and small construction sites from the definition of "discharges associated with industrial activity." Finally, I concur in the result, but not the reasoning, of Part II.D, holding that EPA has not acted unlawfully by failing to include specific control requirements in the permit application regulations.

I

The majority holds that EPA has violated statutory requirements by failing to set dates for approval of, and compliance with, permits as part of its permit application program. Ante at 1300. Despite the holding in Part II.B.2.b that injunctive relief is inappropriate (with which I agree), the majority in Part II.B.2.c orders EPA to issue supplemental regulations setting such deadlines immediately.

I am not convinced that the statute requires EPA to set these deadlines as part of the permit application process. The provision at issue reads, in relevant part:

(4) Permit application requirements

(A) Industrial and large municipal discharges

Not later than 2 years after February 4, 1987, the Administrator shall establish regulations setting forth the permit application requirements for stormwater discharges described in paragraphs (2)(B) and (2)(C). Applications for permits for such discharges shall be filed no later than 3 years after February 4, 1987. Not later than 4 years after February 4, 1987, the Administrator or the State, as the case may be, shall issue or deny each such permit. Any such permit shall provide for compliance as expeditiously as practicable, but in no event later than 3 years after the date of issuance of such permit.

(B) Other municipal discharges

Not later than 4 years after February 4, 1987, the Administrator shall establish regulations setting forth the permit application requirements for stormwater discharges described in paragraph (2)(D). Applications for permits for such discharges shall be filed no later than 5 years after February 4, 1987. Not later than 6 years after February 4, 1987, the Administrator or the State, as the case may be, shall issue or deny each such permit. Any such permit shall provide for compliance as expeditiously as practicable, but in no event later than 3 years after the date of issuance of such permit.

CWA § 402(p)(4); 33 U.S.C. § 1342(p)(4) (1988).

While the statute establishes a time line EPA must follow, it does not, in my view, require that EPA include the deadline for permit approval in the permit application regulations. I agree that, given EPA's past delays and the fact that the statutory dates for issuance or denial of permits are now long past, it is appropriate for this court to declare that the statute requires EPA to issue or deny permits within one year of the application deadline. I do not, however, see that any purpose is served by requiring EPA to issue supplemental regulations setting out these deadlines, and I doubt our authority to do so.

With respect to compliance deadlines, the statute contemplates that such deadlines will be set in individual permits as they are issued. See CWA § 402(p)(4)(A), (B) ("Any such permit shall provide for compliance. ..."). Each permit must contain a compliance deadline, which may not exceed three years from the date of issuance. Nothing in the statute requires EPA to establish compliance deadlines now, before any permits have been issued. Accordingly, in my view, NRDC's challenge to the lack of compliance deadlines in EPA's current regulations is premature. I therefore dissent from Part II.B.2.c of the majority opinion.

II

I dissent also from Parts II.C.2 and II. C.3. In my view, EPA's definition of "discharge associated with industrial activity" is a reasonable construction of an ambiguous statute, entitled to deference. While my colleagues acknowledge that we may not overturn an agency rule that represents a "permissible construction" of a statute, ante at 1297 (quoting Chevron, U.S.A., Inc. v. NRDC, 467 U.S. 837, 843, 104 S.Ct. 2778, 2781, 81 L.Ed.2d 694 (1984)), they fail to apply that axiom.

A

EPA's rule excludes from the permitting requirement certain light industry facilities at which "areas where material handling equipment or activities, raw materials, intermediate products, final products, waste materials, byproducts, or industrial machinery" are not exposed to storm water. See 40 C.F.R. § 122.26(b)(14). EPA determined that discharges from such facilities do not fall within the definition of "discharges associated with industrial activity." In my view, this determination was reasonable.

The majority concedes that the statute does not define "discharge associated with industrial activity." Ante at 1304. The operative phrase, as my colleagues note, is "associated with." See id. For purposes of evaluating the light industry exemption, I concede that manufacturing falls within the generally accepted meaning of "industrial activity," and that many of the facilities exempted by the EPA rule are manufacturers. Nonetheless, that concession does not compel the conclusion that discharges from such facilities are "associated with industrial activity."

The majority concludes, without explanation, that the phrase "discharges associated with industrial activity" is "very broad." Ante at 1304. Neither the plain meaning of the term "associated" nor the legislative history of the statute support this conclusion. "Associated with" means closely related to or connected with. See Webster's Ninth New Collegiate Dictionary 110 (1986). To the extent it casts any light on the subject, the legislative history supports a narrow reading of the phrase "associated with." Four members of the House, in the course of floor debates on the measure both before and after President Reagan's veto, explained that:

[a] discharge is associated with industrial activity if it is directly related to manufacturing, processing or raw materials storage areas at an industrial plant. Discharges which do not meet this definition include those discharges associated with parking lots and administrative and employee buildings.

133 Cong.Rec. 985 (1987) (statement of Rep. Hammerschmidt) (emphasis added).[1] The underscored language suggests that Congress intended to regulate only discharges directly related to certain activities at industrial facilities. EPA's interpretation, that discharges are "directly related" to these activities only if storm water may reasonably be expected to come into contact with them before its discharge, is eminently logical.

The majority opinion interprets the exclusion of parking lots as an expression of congressional intent "to exclude only those facilities or parts of a facility that are completely nonindustrial." Ante at 1304. My colleagues' reliance on the second sentence of the statement quoted above to establish this intent, however, is misplaced. The sentence relied on cannot assist us in our search for the meaning of "associated with" because it employs that very term. Moreover, it does not pretend to establish an exhaustive list of areas excluded from regulation. Legislators listed discharges from parking lots and administrative and employee buildings as among those not directly related to industrial activity; no one suggested that only discharges associated with those structures were to be excluded.

EPA's definition is consistent with the plain words of the statute and, to the extent any intent is discernible, the congressional intent. EPA has defined the term "storm water discharge associated with industrial activity" to cover only those discharges reasonably expected to come into contact with industrial activities. A large number of facilities automatically fall within EPA's definition and are required to apply for permits. Because facilities falling within certain specified classifications under the Standard Industrial Classification manual generally conduct their operations entirely indoors, minimizing the likelihood of contact with storm water, EPA has not automatically included them within the regulations. However, these facilities are required to apply for permits if "areas where material handling equipment or activities, raw materials, intermediate products, final products, waste materials, byproducts, or industrial machinery at these facilities are exposed to storm water." 40 C.F.R. § 122.26(b)(14). If a storm water discharge is in fact directly related to or associated with the industrial activity carried on at a facility falling within the light industry category, the facility must obtain a permit.[2]

In my view, the statute's treatment of oil and gas facilities supports EPA's reading of the term "associated with industrial activity." Congress specifically exempted from the permit requirement discharges from oil and gas facilities and mining operations which have not come in contact with raw materials, finished products, or waste products. CWA § 402(l)(2). This section indicates a congressional intent to exempt uncontaminated discharges which have not come into contact with "industrial activities" from regulation. For oil, gas, and mining operations, Congress in this section supplied a specific, and quite limited, definition of "industrial activities." For other facilities, that definition was left to the discretion of EPA, which has adopted a much broader definition, encompassing contact with such things as industrial machinery and materials handling equipment. See 40 C.F.R. § 122.26(b)(14).

I do not mean to suggest that the majority's construction of the statute is untenable. It may even be preferable to the reading chosen by the agency. Nonetheless, in my view the statute is ambiguous and the legislative history does not demonstrate any clear congressional intent. The question before this court, therefore, is not whether "the agency construction was the only one it permissibly could have adopted" or even whether it is the "reading the court would have reached if the question initially had arisen in a judicial proceeding." Chevron, U.S.A. v. NRDC, 467 U.S. 837, 843 n. 11, 104 S.Ct. 2778, 2782 n. 11, 81 L.Ed.2d 694 (1984). We need only inquire if the agency's construction is a permissible one. Id. at 843, 104 S.Ct. at 2781. EPA's definition falls well within permissible bounds, and should be upheld.

B

Although the issue is closer, I also am not persuaded that EPA's exemption for construction sites under five acres should be struck down. EPA has not conceded that "construction activity is industrial in nature." Ante at 1306. In the preamble to its final rule, EPA noted that "Construction activity at a high level of intensity is comparable to other activity that is traditionally viewed as industrial, such as natural resource extraction."[3] 55 Fed.Reg. 48,033 (1990) (emphasis added). EPA explained that it was "attempting to focus [regulation] only on those construction activities that resemble industrial activity." 55 Fed.Reg. at 48,035 (emphasis added).

Neither NRDC nor the majority point to anything in the statute or the legislative history that would require the agency to define "industrial activity" as including all construction operations. Accordingly, I believe deference is due EPA's definition, provided it is not arbitrary, capricious, or manifestly contrary to the statute. Chevron, U.S.A., 467 U.S. at 844, 104 S.Ct. at 2782.

In trying to determine when construction should be treated as industrial activity, EPA considered a number of possible approaches. See 55 Fed.Reg. at 48,035. Exempting construction that would be completed within a certain designated time frame was deemed inappropriate, because the work could be both intensive and expansive but nonetheless take place over a short period of time. Basing the limit on quantity of soil removed was also rejected as not relating to the amount of land surface disturbed. EPA finally settled on the surface area disturbed by the construction project as a feasible and appropriate mechanism for "identifying sites that are [sic] amount to industrial activity." 55 Fed. Reg. at 48,036.

Having determined that not all construction amounts to industrial activity, and that the appropriate basis for differentiation is land area disturbed, EPA then had to determine where to draw the line. Initially, EPA proposed to exempt all construction operations disturbing less than one acre of land, as well as single family residential projects disturbing less than five acres. 53 Fed.Reg. 49,431 (1988). In the final rule, however, EPA adopted a five-acre minimum for all construction projects. 55 Fed. Reg. 48,066 (1990); 40 C.F.R. § 122.26(b)(14)(x).

Admittedly, the final rule contains little in the way of justification for treating two-acre sites differently than five-acre ones, but that does not necessarily make it arbitrary and capricious. Line-drawing is often difficult. NRDC was apparently willing to accept EPA's proposed one-acre/five-acre rule. Although NRDC now challenges the blanket five-acre rule, it offers no evidence that sites excluded from the permitting requirement constitute "industrial activity." In such absence of any evidence in the record undermining EPA's conclusion on an issue squarely within its expertise, I believe the rule must be upheld.[4]

III

Finally, while I concur in the result reached by the majority in Part II.D, rejecting NRDC's claim that EPA has unlawfully failed to require substantive controls on municipal discharges, I disagree with the majority's reasoning. In my view, NRDC's claim is premature, and we should decline to address its merits.

NRDC contends that the 1987 amendments require EPA to establish substantive controls for municipal storm water discharges. In support of this argument, NRDC relies on CWA § 402(p)(3)(B), 33 U.S.C. § 1342(p)(3)(B), which provides:

> Permits for discharges from municipal storm sewers —
> * * * * * *
>
> (ii) shall include a requirement to effectively prohibit non-stormwater discharges into the storm sewers; and
>
> (iii) shall require controls to reduce the discharge of pollutants to the maximum extent practicable....

This section refers only to permits, and says nothing about permit applications. Because EPA has yet to issue any permits, NRDC's claim on this point is premature. In the absence of any indication to the contrary, we must assume that any permit issued will comply with all applicable statutory requirements. The statute does not require that EPA detail the substantive controls to be imposed when establishing permit application requirements. Accordingly, I would reject NRDC's claim without reaching the issue of the Administrator's discretion in selecting those controls.

IV

In sum, I join much of my colleagues' opinion. However, I would not require EPA to issue supplemental regulations detailing the time line for issuance of and compliance with permits, and I would uphold EPA's definition of "discharge associated with industrial activity." Finally, I would reject NRDC's claim that EPA is required to detail control measures in the permit application regulations on the grounds that the statute requires control measures only in the permits themselves.

Notes

[1] This statement was repeated verbatim by Reps. Stangeland and Snyder. 133 Cong. Rec. at 991-92; 132 Cong. Rec. at 31,959, 31,964 (1986). Rep. Rowland offered a slight variation on the theme:

> One of the discharge categories is "a discharge associated with an industrial activity." A discharge is not considered to be associated with industrial activity unless it is directly related to manufacturing, processing, or raw materials storage areas at an industrial plant. Such discharges include [sic] those from parking lots and administrative areas and employee buildings.

132 Cong. Rec. at 31,968. Rep. Rowland apparently misspoke; he probably meant, like the other legislators who addressed the topic, to say "[s]uch discharges do not include" those from parking lots.

[2] Thus, nothing turns on the assumption, attacked by my colleagues as unsupported by the record, ante at 1304, that industrial activities at this category of facilities will take place largely indoors. Where the assumption does not hold true, the

permit requirement applies with full force. I also note that NRDC has pointed us to no evidence undermining EPA's assumption.

Unlike my colleagues, I decline to assume that EPA will not carry out its responsibility to identify and to require permits of facilities where industrial activities are in fact exposed to storm water, or that such facilities will ignore their statutory duty to apply for permits. Should that occur, a lawsuit challenging EPA's failure to enforce its regulations might well be in order. An unsubstantiated suspicion that EPA may not vigorously enforce its regulations, however, does not make those regulations arbitrary or capricious.

[3] EPA did admit that "[e]ven small construction sites may have a significant negative impact on water quality in localized areas," 55 Fed.Reg. at 48,033. In the absence of any indication of what EPA meant by "small," however, that statement does not undermine EPA's exemption of sites under five acres.

[4] Because I conclude that the rule falls within the permissible bounds of the statutory definition of "discharges associated with industrial activity," I need not consider the applicability of the de minimis exception.

Judge O'Scannlain's dissent in Sepulveda v. Ramirez (June 26, 1992)

O'SCANNLAIN, Circuit Judge, dissenting:

Any constitutional right that Sepulveda may have had not to be observed by a parole officer of the opposite sex while producing a urine sample was not, in my view, "clearly established" at the time of the incident, as required by Harlow v. Fitzgerald, 457 U.S. 800, 102 S.Ct. 2727, 73 L.Ed.2d 396 (1982). Hence, I respectfully dissent from the denial of qualified immunity for appellants.

The only question we face on this appeal is whether the district court erred in denying appellants' summary judgment motion on the issue of qualified immunity. This case is not about whether appellants exercised "common sense." Nor is it about whether they violated state regulations. See Davis v. Scherer, 468 U.S. 183, 194, 104 S.Ct. 3012, 3019, 82 L.Ed.2d 139 (1984) ("Officials sued for constitutional violations do not lose their qualified immunity merely because their conduct violates some [state] statutory or administrative provision."). Most important, the merits of Sepulveda's constitutional claim are not before us; our review is narrow. We must merely determine whether appellants' conduct "violate[d] clearly established statutory or constitutional rights of which a reasonable person would have known." Harlow, 457 U.S. at 818, 102 S.Ct. at 2738.

Critical to determining whether a constitutional right was "clearly established" is properly framing such right. As Justice Scalia has observed, "[t]he operation of [the Harlow] standard ... depends substantially upon the level of generality at which the relevant `legal rule' is to be identified." Anderson v. Creighton, 483 U.S. 635, 639, 107 S.Ct. 3034, 3038, 97 L.Ed.2d 523 (1987); see also Michael H. v. Gerald D., 491 U.S. 110, 109 S.Ct. 2333, 2344 n. 6, 105 L.Ed.2d 91 (1989) (Scalia, J., joined by Rehnquist, C.J.)

(discussing the significance of the level of generality with which a right is defined in concluding whether an asserted right is so rooted in history and tradition as to be protected under the "liberty" term of the Due Process Clause). For instance, at a highly generalized level, one might characterize the right allegedly violated here as the "right to bodily privacy." At this level of generality, a case could be made that the right is "clearly established." See York v. Story, 324 F.2d 450, 455-56 (9th Cir.1963), cert. denied, 376 U.S. 939, 84 S.Ct. 794, 11 L.Ed.2d 659 (1964) (complaining witness who is forced by the police to be photographed unclothed has stated a constitutional claim).

But virtually any alleged right could be recast as a part of a very broad right that is more generally recognized. If courts were simply to accept these characterizations, however, "Harlow would be transformed from a guarantee of immunity into a rule of pleading." Anderson, 483 U.S. at 639, 107 S.Ct. at 3039. Thus, "the right the official is alleged to have violated must have been `clearly established' in a more particularized, and hence more relevant, sense: The contours of the right must be sufficiently clear that a reasonable official would understand that what he is doing violates that right.... [I]n the light of pre-existing law the unlawfulness must be apparent." Id. at 640, 107 S.Ct. at 3039. Thus, in Anderson, while it was manifest that the right to be free from warrantless searches of one's home absent exigent circumstances was "clearly established," the lower court erred in not looking at the particular circumstances of the challenged search to determine whether it was clearly established under those circumstances that exigency did not exist, and that accordingly the search was unconstitutional. Id. at 640-41, 107 S.Ct. at 3039.

Assuming that a generalized right to bodily privacy is "clearly established" under decisional law, whether such right existed under the particular circumstances presented here is most uncertain under our case law. Prior to this case, there appear to be no decisions in our circuit recognizing parolees' privacy rights in these circumstances, let alone any cases attempting to strike a balance between the privacy interests of parolees and the interests of the state in accurate drug testing of its parolees.

We are left to attempt to draw analogies from prisoner cases, and these decisions hardly make a compelling case that a fundamental right of prisoners to bodily privacy has been "clearly established." Indeed, both times this circuit has addressed the question, it has permitted prison officials to view unclothed inmates of the opposite sex. We have engaged in balancing of inmates' interest in not being viewed unclothed with the administrative needs of the prison. Thus, we have permitted female guards to view unclothed male prisoners, where "the positions to which they are assigned require infrequent and casual observation, or observation at a distance." Grummett v. Rushen, 779 F.2d 491, 494 (9th Cir.1985). We also have held that the Constitution does not bar female guards from occasionally being present at strip searches of men or from routinely serving on shower duty in a men's prison. Michenfelder v. Sumner, 860 F.2d 328, 330, 334 (9th Cir.1988). In sum, this circuit has never held that the Constitution is violated by the mere fact of a prison official viewing the unclothed body of an inmate of the opposite sex, and has not even addressed the question of bodily privacy rights parolees may have in connection with drug testing.

Looking at the particularized circumstances of this case, in my view appellants did not violate a "clearly established" constitutional right. Whatever due process right a prisoner or parolee may have against his or her unclothed body being viewed by an official of the opposite sex, the contours of such right are not sufficiently clear that a reasonable officer here would understand that what he was doing violated that right.

The merits of Sepulveda's case are not before us and I express no views on whether she has stated a constitutional claim. Any right she may have in not having a parole officer observe her while she produced a urine sample, however, in my view is not so "clearly established" as to abrogate appellants' qualified immunity.

Hence, I respectfully dissent.

Judge O'Scannlain's concurrence and dissent in US v. Sneezer (Dec 30, 1992)

O'SCANNLAIN, Circuit Judge, concurring in part and dissenting in part:

I concur in the remand for resentencing, but dissent from the affirmance of admissibility of the prior attempted rape incident.

I

While I agree we must remand for resentencing because the district court erroneously concluded that the two counts of aggravated sexual abuse should not be grouped together, I write separately because I cannot subscribe to my colleagues' reasoning.

Whether the two counts of aggravated sexual abuse should be grouped together under section 3D1.2(b) of the Sentencing Guidelines is a difficult question to resolve. The Guidelines recognize that "even if counts involve a single victim, the decision as to whether to group them together may not always be clear cut." U.S.S.G. § 3D1.2 at commentary (background). We are advised that "[i]n interpreting this Part and resolving ambiguities, the court should look to the underlying policy of this Part." Id. That policy is that "[a]ll counts involving substantially the same harm shall be grouped together into a single Group." U.S.S.G. § 3D1.2.

I recognize that there is a certain artificiality inherent in a judicial inquiry into whether two counts of aggravated sexual abuse form the same harm to the victim, but just such an inquiry is demanded by the Guidelines. The inquiry must begin, as always, with the explicit language of the Guidelines. Section 3D1.2(b) states that "[c]ounts involve substantially the same harm within the meaning of this rule ... when [they] involve the same victim and two or more acts or transactions connected by a common criminal objective...." Id. Accordingly, the proper inquiry is whether the two counts of aggravated sexual abuse were connected by a common criminal objective.

Remarkably, the Guidelines clearly envision circumstances under which two or more rapes will be grouped together for sentencing purposes. To illustrate, the examples provided in the commentary to section 3D1.2 state that two counts of assault on a federal officer for shooting at the same officer twice while attempting to prevent apprehension as part of a single criminal episode are to be grouped. Id. at commentary (note 3, example 4). In contrast, two counts of rape for raping the same person on different days are not to be grouped together. Id. (note 4, example 5). There must be circumstances, therefore, in which two counts of rape for raping the same person are to be grouped together.

The commentary to section 3D1.2 suggests that it is useful to ask how contemporaneous were two assaults in order to determine whether there was one composite harm. Placing too great an emphasis on elapsed time, however, obscures the proper inquiry under section 3D1.2(b). That inquiry is whether the counts are "part of a single course of criminal conduct with a single criminal objective and represent essentially one composite harm." Id. (note 4). If so, the counts must be grouped.

In this case, Sneezer abducted the victim, drove to an isolated area, and parked. After unsuccessfully attempting rape inside the car he forced the victim outside, ordered her to lie on the ground, and began having sexual intercourse. After she complained about being cold and about the rocky surface, he gave her his shirt. He then had the victim lie on the hood of the car where he continued to have sexual intercourse with her. The victim again complained about being cold and the defendant told her to get into the car. As they were getting into the car, she escaped. Under these facts, I conclude that the two counts of aggravated sexual abuse form part of a single course of conduct with a common criminal objective — rape — and represent essentially the same harm.[1]

II

The majority holds that evidence of a rape three years prior to this incident was admissible under Rule 404(b). I fail to see any other purpose for the introduction of the five-year-old attempted rape charge than to demonstrate that the defendant acted in conformity with that prior bad act on this occasion. Therefore, I respectfully dissent.

I agree that Rule 404(b) is inclusionary. That is, evidence of prior crimes is not excluded unless its sole purpose is to "prove the character of a person to show action in conformity therewith." Fed. R.Evid. 404(b); accord United States v. Diggs, 649 F.2d 731, 737 (9th Cir.), cert. denied, 454 U.S. 970, 102 S.Ct. 516, 70 L.Ed.2d 387 (1981). Under the law of this circuit, however, evidence of a prior bad act can only be introduced to prove a material issue, or essential element, of the crime. United States v. Ross, 886 F.2d 264, 267 (9th Cir.1989); United States v. Houser, 929 F.2d 1369, 1373 (9th Cir.1990).

The majority has failed to identify convincingly what material elements of the crime this evidence goes to prove. The trial court expressly held that knowledge and identity were not issues in dispute. The majority contends that the fact that Sneezer had previously been arrested and charged with attempted rape shows "motive, intent and the fact of a plan." Opinion at 924. Those words, however, are not talismanic, the mere utterance of which enables the prosecution to introduce evidence of a prior crime. I am forced to conclude that the sole purpose for the introduction of this evidence was to show conformity with a prior bad act.

Intent was not a disputed issue in this case. Neither crime charged is a specific intent crime. In fact, the trial court refused to instruct the jury on voluntary intoxication because it held that kidnapping under 18 U.S.C. § 1201(a)(2) is a general intent crime, a conclusion this court affirms. In light of that, the majority cannot now validly hold that the defense made intent a material issue in this case. The evidence cannot be admissible to show intent. Cf. United States v. Hadley, 918 F.2d 848, 851 (9th Cir.1990) (evidence of prior sexual abuse relevant to material element because government had to demonstrate specific intent); United States v. Bradshaw, 690 F.2d 704, 709 (9th Cir.1982), cert. denied, 463 U.S. 1210, 103 S.Ct. 3543, 77 L.Ed.2d 1392 (1983) (in kidnapping case, evidence of prior sexual relations and drug use relevant to issue of consent, "the defendant's chief defense at trial").

Moreover, if admissible to prove intent, the prior crime must necessarily be similar to the charged offense. Ross, 886 F.2d at 267. The majority asserts that the prior incident was "nearly identical" to this incident. Opinion at 924. I am troubled by the vagueness of the characteristics listed in support of that assertion. For example, that Sneezer, "took off his clothes and hers, [and] laid on [each woman]" is hardly persuasive of such similarity as to be admissible here.

The lack of distinct similarities between the two incidents also undercuts the notion that they show a plan. True, the earlier incident also took place on the Navajo Reservation and involved abduction and transport by car to a remote area. But, no common scheme united these two crimes nor was there evidence they were part of an ongoing conspiracy. See United States v. Powell, 587 F.2d 443, 448 (9th Cir.1978). The earlier attempted rape charge was not connected in any way with the crimes charged here and, therefore, cannot be admitted under the "plan" exception to Rule 404(b).

"Motive" provides no better basis for introducing this evidence. Specific motive is not an element of either of the offenses charged. I do not see, and the majority has not explained, how motive is relevant to a disputed material issue in this particular case. See United States v. Brown, 880 F.2d 1012, 1014 (9th Cir.1989). Evidence of motive is therefore inadmissible. Moreover, at least in relation to the aggravated sexual abuse charges, I do not see how evidence of an attempted rape five years before the trial would tell us anything about Sneezer's motive in this case.

Because I am persuaded that it was an abuse of discretion to admit the evidence, I conclude that Sneezer's convictions must be reversed unless its introduction was harmless error. Id. at 1016. The very purpose of Rule 404 is to exclude the inference that because the defendant had attempted rape before he is guilty of rape now. This particular type of bad character evidence is so prejudicial, and so likely to infect the jury, that I cannot conclude that its admission was harmless.

Notes

[1] The majority offers a reductio ad absurdum by urging that multiple rapes over several days might be grouped if the defendant had a uniform objective and plan to

"abuse" his victim. The commentary itself lays such concern to rest. The problem is that "elapsed time" between events is not dispositive and such a test is useless to apply. Moreover, in a case like this, not only is the timing inquiry "repulsive and dispiriting," but it asks the court to draw lines where there is no principled basis upon which to do so. My colleagues group these rapes because they were separated by only "a few minutes." Where in the Guidelines or commentary can we find whether a few more minutes should matter? Is a fifteen minute separation between counts sufficient not to group them? An hour? Two hours separated by lunch? I suggest that the better view is that timing is merely one factor which helps us determine whether the counts involved substantially the same harm.

Judge O'Scannlain's dissent from the order of denial of rehearing en banc in US v. Lopez-Vasquez (Feb 8, 1993)

O'SCANNLAIN, Circuit Judge, with whom HALL, WIGGINS, KOZINSKI, TROTT, T.G. NELSON, and KLEINFELD, Circuit Judges join, dissenting from the order of denial of rehearing en banc:

When a panel of this court announces a new per se rule — indeed, one that misreads an en banc decision we rendered less than a year ago, that rests on an empirical foundation consisting entirely of unsubstantiated speculation, and that in any event adds nothing in the way of real protection for the right it is intended to safeguard — reasonably good cause exists to assemble the en banc court. When that new per se rule stands controlling Supreme Court precedent on its head, and introduces the altogether remarkable notion of a fundamental constitutional right to appeal, the case for en banc rehearing becomes overwhelming. Our court has decided otherwise, and from that decision I must respectfully dissent.

I

Let us begin where the panel should have, with an examination of the Supreme Court's decision in United States v. Mendoza-Lopez, 481 U.S. 828, 107 S.Ct. 2148, 95 L.Ed.2d 772 (1987), and that of our en banc court in United States v. Proa-Tovar, 975 F.2d 592 (9th Cir.1992) (en banc). For while the panel's opinion indeed quotes the language of Mendoza-Lopez, it fails to follow its reasoning. In particular, the panel ignores the implications of the interpretation of Mendoza-Lopez upon which we settled in Proa-Tovar.

Mendoza-Lopez holds that "where the defects in an administrative proceeding foreclose judicial review of that proceeding, an alternative means of obtaining judicial review must be made available before the administrative order may be used to establish conclusively an element of a criminal offense." 481 U.S. at 838, 107 S.Ct. at 2155. For this reason, a defendant charged with the crime of re-entering this country after deportation under 8 U.S.C. § 1326 who "was effectively denied his right to direct review" must be permitted "to mount a collateral attack on the deportation proceeding when he [is] prosecuted under section 1326." Proa-Tovar, 975 F.2d at 594. So much is clear from Mendoza-Lopez itself.

To succeed in his collateral attack, the section 1326 defendant must show that his prior deportation proceeding violated due process — that is, (1) that the proceeding was marked by "fundamental procedural defects," Mendoza-Lopez, 481 U.S. at 841, 107 S.Ct. at 2157, and (2) that these defects resulted in prejudice to the alien. The prejudice requirement, obscure in Mendoza-Lopez, was made clear in Proa-Tovar. See Proa-Tovar, 975 F.2d at 595 ("the Court has not eliminated prejudice from the equation").

But the panel here misses the point that underlies both Mendoza-Lopez and Proa-Tovar: the section 1326 defendant's entitlement to mount a collateral attack on his prior deportation is one thing, the merits of that collateral attack something entirely different. Perhaps the panel errs because, in this case, whether Lopez-Vasquez validly waived his right to appeal plays a role in both these determinations. Nevertheless, two distinct questions are involved here. First is the question whether Lopez-Vasquez was deprived of his right to direct review, thus entitling him to mount his collateral attack in this proceeding. Second is the (wholly separate) question whether his deportation was in fact fundamentally unfair.

The panel would have done well to seek guidance from the other circuits that have been forced to "unravel the riddle" of Mendoza-Lopez. Proa-Tovar, 975 F.2d at 594. All of these courts have interpreted the Court's decision precisely as outlined above. All agree, that is, that "Mendoza-Lopez presupposes a two-step process for determining when an alien can prevent his deportation from being used as a basis for conviction under 8 U.S.C. § 1326." United States v. Encarnacion-Galvez, 964 F.2d 402, 406 (5th Cir.1992). "[T]he alien must show not only that he was [1] effectively deprived of his right to direct appeal, but also that [2] the administrative proceedings were fundamentally unfair in some respect that would have entitled him to relief on appeal." United States v. Fares, 978 F.2d 52, 57 (2d Cir.1992). Accord United States v. Santos-Vanegas, 878 F.2d 247, 251-52 (8th Cir.1989); United States v. Holland, 876 F.2d 1533, 1536 (11th Cir.1989) ("The defendant must show that he was deprived of judicial review of the proceeding and that the proceeding was fundamentally unfair.") (emphasis supplied).

II

Against this backdrop, the shortcomings of the panel's opinion emerge starkly.

Although a deportee may waive his right to judicial review of his deportation order, that waiver must be "considered and intelligent." [Mendoza-Lopez, 481 U.S. at 837-38, 107 S.Ct. at 2154-55] ... The government bears the burden of proving the waiver. See Brewer v. Williams, 430 U.S. 387, 404 [97 S.Ct. 1232, 1242, 51 L.Ed.2d 424] (1977) ("it is incumbent upon the State to prove `an intentional relinquishment or abandonment of a known right or privilege.'") (emphasis supplied, citation omitted).

United States v. Lopez-Vasquez, 1 F.3d 751. With all due respect, this is not merely nonsense. It is nonsense on stilts.

A

First, the nonsense. The panel assigns the government the burden of proving that Lopez-Vasquez validly waived his right to appeal his deportation. As explained above, however, the validity of such a waiver goes to two different legal questions. Consequently, when the panel says that the government bears the burden of proving a valid waiver, it is really saying two different things. Neither can withstand scrutiny.

On the one hand, the panel is saying that the government bears the burden of proving that Lopez-Vasquez was not deprived of judicial review of his deportation proceeding, and is therefore not entitled to mount a collateral attack upon that proceeding. In effect, the panel creates a presumption that the defendant was improperly denied review and therefore is entitled to mount a collateral attack, in every section 1326 prosecution. This is simply irrational, and Mendoza-Lopez clearly does not envision any such thing. The Court did not mandate that collateral attacks be entertained as a matter of course, but said rather that they must be permitted in exceptional circumstances, that is, where judicial review is actually foreclosed because of defects in the deportation proceeding. See Mendoza-Lopez, 481 U.S. at 838-40, 107 S.Ct. at 2155-56.

On the other hand, by insisting that the government prove a valid waiver of appeal, the panel is effectively bifurcating the burden of proof as to the fundamental fairness of the underlying deportation proceeding. For Lopez-Vasquez holds that it is up to the government to prove that the defendant's deportation proceeding was not marred by any fundamental procedural defect — here, a defect implicating the defendant's right to appeal. Yet we held in Proa-Tovar that "[t]he defendant ... bears the burden of proving prejudice" from any such defect. 975 F.2d at 595. The result is simply irrational. Nothing can justify carving up the burden of proof on the single issue of fundamental fairness in this ad hoc manner. Because the panel has failed to consider the implications of its decision within the framework provided by Mendoza-Lopez and Proa-Tovar, it makes a hodge-podge of the assignment of burdens of proof.

B

Now the stilts. As authority for the proposition that the government bears the burden of proving waiver here, the panel cites Brewer v. Williams. The citation is obviously intended as more than merely illustrative; the panel clearly regards Brewer as controlling precedent. Thus we are told in a footnote that "[o]ther circuits that may appear to have placed the burden of proof on the defendant did not consider the allocation of burden of proof in Brewer." Lopez-Vasquez, op. at 754 n. 3. (citing cases).

But Brewer controls nothing in this context. At issue in that famous case was a purported waiver of the Sixth Amendment right to counsel. The criminal defendant's right to counsel, of course, is a fundamental constitutional right, "indispensable to the fair administration of our adversary system of criminal justice." Brewer, 430 U.S. at 398, 97 S.Ct. at 1239 (emphasis supplied). Accordingly, the Brewer Court employed the "strict standard" of waiver set forth in Johnson v. Zerbst, 304 U.S. 458, 464, 58 S.Ct. 1019, 1023, 82 L.Ed. 1461 (1938), Brewer, 430 U.S. at 404, 97 S.Ct. at 1242, which is, indeed, "[t]he strictest test of waiver which might be applied." Id. at 433, 97 S.Ct. at 1257 (White, J., dissenting). In this context, it is no surprise that the government "bears a heavy burden" of proof. Id. at 402, 97 S.Ct. at 1241 (citation omitted).

At issue in this case, however, is a waiver of the statutory right to judicial review of the result of a civil deportation proceeding. Such a right is in no sense indispensable to the fair administration of justice — it is not guaranteed as a matter of due process. Indeed, the right to an appeal is simply not protected by the Constitution, in this or any conte. So well established is this principle that fully a century ago the Supreme Court could say that "[a] citation of authorities on the point is unnecessary." McKane v. Durston, 153 U.S. 684, 687, 14 S.Ct. 913, 915, 38 L.Ed. 867 (1894).

What, then, justifies the panel's reliance on Brewer? Why must an alien's alleged waiver of the statutory right to appeal a deportation order be tested according to "the strictest possible" standard of waiver, the standard applied by the Court to waivers of fundamental constitutional rights in a criminal context, a standard under which "it is incumbent upon the State" to prove waiver? The panel does not explain.[1]

C

Under the stilts, we may add a pair of skates:

"Courts should `indulge every reasonable presumption against waiver,' and they should `not presume acquiescence in the loss of fundamental rights.'" Barker v. Wingo, 407 U.S. 514, 525 [92 S.Ct. 2182, 2189, 33 L.Ed.2d 101] (1972) (citations omitted).

Lopez-Vasquez, op. at 754. The problem with this passage is that Barker v. Wingo has no application in this context. Like Brewer, Barker was a case involving a purported waiver of fundamental constitutional rights — here, the right to a speedy trial under the Sixth Amendment. The Supreme Court's injunction to "indulge every reasonable presumption against waiver" was thus premised on fear of "acquiescence in the loss of fundamental rights." Indeed, if we look again to Johnson v. Zerbst, which is the source of the language quoted in Barker and relied upon by the panel here, this very point comes through loud and clear:

It has been pointed out that "courts indulge every reasonable presumption against waiver" of fundamental constitutional rights and that we "do not presume acquiescence in the loss of fundamental rights."

304 U.S. at 464, 58 S.Ct. at 1023 (citations omitted, emphasis supplied).

Let us repeat: the right to an appeal is not protected by the Constitution, even for criminal defendants. The right to an appeal is a statutory right ... period. What is it, then, that justifies "indulging every reasonable presumption against waiver" of the right to appeal, as we would waiver of the right to counsel, or the right to jury trial, or the right to confront one's accusers? Again, the panel does not provide an answer.

D

The panel has imported the strict standard applicable to the waiver of fundamental constitutional rights, and the presumption against waiver of such rights, into a context where the waiver of constitutional rights is not even remotely at issue. Under Mendoza-Lopez, Lopez-Vasquez enjoys three different due process rights: (1) his right as a section 1326 defendant to collateral review of a prior deportation where direct appeal was improperly denied him; (2) his right as a deportation proceeding respondent to a fundamentally fair deportation proceeding; (3) his right as a section 1326 defendant not to be subject to criminal penalties on the basis of a prior deportation that was not fundamentally fair. No one claims that Lopez-Vasquez waived any of these rights, whether validly or invalidly. All of these rights are alive and well in this proceeding, the very point of which is to vindicate those rights if they are indeed at risk. The only right Lopez-Vasquez is alleged to have waived is his unenumerated statutory right to an appeal.

Yet the panel proceeds as if Mendoza-Lopez made the right to appeal a deportation order a necessary aspect of due process, such that a waiver of the right to appeal such an order is a waiver of a due process right. If this were true, it would indeed follow, as the panel seems to think, that the burden of proving waiver should be placed on the government, and that the presumption against such waiver should apply. But it is not true. Mendoza-Lopez does not say that due process guarantees the right to appeal a deportation order; it says that due process guarantees the right to some kind of judicial review of the deportation proceeding before the order may be relied upon to establish an element of a criminal offense. Mendoza-Lopez does not say that an alien who is denied the right to appeal his deportation order is thereby denied due process; it says that an alien who is prejudiced by the denial of his right to appeal in such a way as to render his deportation proceeding fundamentally unfair is denied due process.

Mendoza-Lopez does not, in short, say that the right to an appeal is guaranteed as a matter of due process of law. The waiver of the right to an appeal is not the waiver of a constitutional right. Cases setting forth standards for reviewing waivers of fundamental constitutional rights are not controlling here — indeed, they are not even relevant. The reasoning of Lopez-Vasquez, then, is just plain wrong.

E

This lengthy analysis is necessary because the panel's holding is entirely dependent upon the presumption against waiver: "We conclude mass silent waiver impermissibly `presume[s] acquiescence' in the loss of the right to appeal and fails to overcome the `presumption against waiver.' See Barker, 407 U.S. at 525 [92 S.Ct. at 2189]." The presumption indulged in by the panel is the only basis for thinking that a per se rule can or should govern here. That rule is utterly compromised by its reliance on this nonexistent presumption, and it should not have been allowed to stand.

III

There's more. The panel has entirely overlooked the significance of the fact that what is involved here is a collateral attack on the constitutionality of a prior adjudication. The government here introduced a facially valid deportation order in an effort to establish one element of the offense defined by section 1326. Lopez-Vasquez "sought to deprive [the order] of [its] normal force and effect in a proceeding that had an independent purpose other than to overturn the prior judgment[]." Parke v. Raley, ____ U.S. ____, ____, 113 S.Ct. 517, 523, 121 L.Ed.2d 391 (1992). "[B]y definition," that is a collateral attack. Id.

This makes a world of difference, as Justice O'Connor recently explained in Parke v. Raley. At issue was a Kentucky sentence enhancement scheme which placed upon the defendant the burden of proving the invalidity of any prior convictions once the state produced a facially valid prior judgment. The Sixth Circuit had held that this scheme was unconstitutional when applied to a defendant who claimed his prior convictions were based on guilty pleas entered in violation of the rule in Boykin v. Alabama, 395 U.S. 238, 89 S.Ct. 1709, 23 L.Ed.2d 274 (1969).

The Sixth Circuit thought rejection of Kentucky's burden-shifting scheme compelled by Boykin's statement that the waiver of rights resulting from a guilty plea cannot be "presume[d] ... from a silent record." [395 U.S.] at 243 [89 S.Ct. at 1712].

We see no tension between the Kentucky scheme and Boykin. Boykin involved direct review of a conviction allegedly based upon an uninformed guilty plea. Respondent, however, never appealed his earlier convictions. They became final years ago, and now he seeks to revisit the question of their validity in a separate recidivism proceeding. To import Boykin's presumption of invalidity into this very different context would, in our view, improperly ignore another presumption deeply rooted in our jurisprudence: the "presumption of regularity" that attaches to final judgments, even when the question is waiver of constitutional rights. Although we are perhaps most familiar with this principle in habeas corpus actions, it has long been applied equally to other forms of collateral attack.

Raley, ____ U.S. at ____, 113 S.Ct. at 523 (emphasis supplied, citations omitted).

These principles have been unvaryingly followed in our own cases. See, e.g., United States v. Pricepaul, 540 F.2d 417, 423 (9th Cir.1976) (defendant bears the burden of proving invalidity of guilty plea for purposes of defending against charge of being felon in possession of firearm); United States v. Carroll, 932 F.2d 823, 825 (9th Cir.1991) (defendant bears burden of proving constitutional invalidity of prior convictions used in sentencing under the Guidelines). The decisions of the other courts of appeals are to the same effect. See Raley, ____ U.S. at ____, 113 S.Ct. at 525 (citing examples in different contexts).

The panel has simply ridden roughshod over the "presumption of regularity" that ought to attach to a final, facially valid deportation order. Once the government produced such an order, it was up to Lopez-Vasquez to rebut that presumption, and to prove the existence of fundamental unfairness in the underlying deportation proceeding. The panel, however, has gone in precisely the opposite direction: it has conjured up a presumption of irregularity. This presumption stands in turn upon the "presumption against waiver" of the "fundamental constitutional" right to appeal, which does not exist, and which, even if it did exist, would not justify shifting the entire burden of proof to the government: "even when a collateral attack on a final [adjudication] rests on constitutional grounds, the presumption of regularity that attaches to final judgments makes it appropriate to assign a proof burden to the defendant." Id. at ____, 113 S.Ct. at 524 (citation omitted).

Nonsense on stilts on skates ... and on thin ice to boot.

IV

And there's still more. The panel has crafted a per se rule to govern the question of waiver. Yet the Supreme Court has repeatedly stressed that "inflexible per se rule[s]" are all but entirely out of place in this context, because the question of waiver is inherently fact-specific:

> A waiver is ordinarily an intentional relinquishment or abandonment of a known right or privilege. The determination of whether there has been an intelligent waiver ... must depend, in each case, upon the particular facts and circumstances surrounding that case, including the background experience and conduct of the accused.

Johnson v. Zerbst, 304 U.S. 458, 464, 58 S.Ct. 1019, 1023, 82 L.Ed. 1461 (1938). Over and over again, the Court has approved this approach, under which the validity of a purported waiver is to be determined "under the totality of the circumstances" bearing on that waiver. See, e.g., Solem v. Stumes, 465 U.S. 638, 647, 104 S.Ct. 1338, 1343, 79 L.Ed.2d 579 (1984); Oregon v. Bradshaw, 462 U.S. 1039, 1046, 103 S.Ct. 2830, 2835, 77 L.Ed.2d 405 (1983) (plurality opinion); Fare v. Michael C., 442 U.S. 707, 724-25, 99 S.Ct. 2560, 2571-72, 61 L.Ed.2d 197 (1979); North Carolina v. Butler, 441 U.S. 369, 374-75, 99 S.Ct. 1755, 1757-58, 60 L.Ed.2d 286 (1979). This fact specific approach to waiver is the rule "[e]ven when a right so fundamental as that to counsel at trial is involved." Butler, 441 U.S. at 374, 99 S.Ct. at 1758. Indeed, it has been observed that there is but "a solitary exception to [the Court's] waiver jurisprudence," in which the case-by-case approach has been abandoned in favor of a per se rule. Minnick v. Mississippi, 498 U.S. 146, 160-62, 111 S.Ct. 486, 495, 112 L.Ed.2d 489 (1990) (Scalia, J., dissenting).[2]

If the validity of an individual's waiver even of fundamental constitutional rights is all but invariably to be determined according to "the totality of the circumstances," what justifies a per se rule of invalidity here, where the statutory right to appeal is in question? The panel doesn't say.

Indeed, while the panel has gone out of its way to import Zerbst's strict standard of waiver (by way of Brewer) and its indulgence of every presumption against waiver (by way of Barker), it has gone equally out of its way to ignore Zerbst's injunction that the validity of a waiver "must depend, in each case, on the particular facts and circumstances surrounding that case." Nonsense on stilts, skating on thin ice ... blindfolded.

V

Teetering awkwardly on such a precarious legal foundation, the panel's per se rule is a bad rule, untenable as a matter of logic and undesirable as a matter of policy.

The panel holds that the procedure employed by the immigration judge, whereby the respondents were invited to stand up if they wished to appeal, always "makes it impossible to determine whether aliens who do not stand have made a voluntary and intelligent decision to waive their right to appeal." Lopez-Vasquez, op. at 754 n. 5. But this is plainly false, as anyone with experience in these kinds of cases must understand. To be sure, the use of this procedure will sometimes prevent a reviewing court from determining that an individual made a considered and intelligent decision not to appeal. But this is by no means invariably the case. In some cases, the record will demonstrate that a particular individual's waiver of appeal is fully informed and eminently rational, even though the transcript does not record him as saying, "I understand that I may appeal, but I do not wish to do so." By the same token, one can easily imagine instances in which the record will contain just such a statement, yet a reviewing court will be firmly convinced that the words did not reflect a voluntary decision intelligently made. The point is simply that it is not always (or even usually) impossible for us to judge the character of a decision not to appeal just because that decision is expressed non-verbally. See United States v. Ortiz-Rivera, 1 F.3d 763 (9th Cir. 1993) (per curiam).[3]

This is a fact we have unambiguously acknowledged in cases treating a criminal defendant's waiver of the right to appeal. Thus we have held that "a Rule 11 colloquy on the waiver of the right to appeal is not a prerequisite to a finding that the waiver is valid; a finding that the waiver is knowing and voluntary is sufficient." United States v. DeSantiago-Martinez, 980 F.2d 582, 583 (9th Cir. 1992). The panel's decision therefore gives rise to a staggering anomaly whereby, in this circuit, the appeal rights of the respondents in a deportation proceeding, being waivable only by express declaration in open court, are thus subject to greater procedural protections than are the analogous rights of the defendant in a criminal case. Cf. United States v. Nicholas-Armenta, 763 F.2d 1089, 1090 (9th Cir.1985) ("Respondents in a civil deportation hearing ... are not entitled to the same ... rights afforded a criminal defendant.").

Moreover, the empirical basis on which the panel erects its rule is dubious at best. The panel assumes that eliciting waiver by inviting an alien to stand if he wishes to appeal "creates a risk that individual detainees will feel coerced by the silence of their fellows," and "tend[s] to stigmatize detainees who wish[] to appeal and to convey a message that appeal was disfavored." Lopez-Vasquez, slip op. at 6638. Where do these assumptions come from?

Given the facts of this case, and of the many similar cases we review, it is entirely plausible to indulge a quite different set of assumptions. Lopez-Vasquez surely knew at the time of his deportation hearing that he had "been convicted six times for theft of property, driving under the influence, burglary, and possession of a controlled substance." Id. at 755 n. 8. In addition, "the immigration judge explained the right to appeal, and Lopez-Vasquez was provided with a form explaining his right to appeal in Spanish." Id. at 754. Thus even the panel must admit that "Lopez-Vasquez apparently knew what an appeal was, and was aware he had some right to appeal." Id. at 754 n. 6. It is not at all unreasonable to think that Lopez-Vasquez remained seated when asked if he wished to appeal his deportation because he knew full well that an appeal could not possibly help him, and did not wish to be confined in a detention center for as long as it might take to process such a fruitless effort. If we are to traffic in assumptions, then we might very well assume that an alien's decision not to appeal generally rests on rational self-interest that counsels the hopelessness of an appeal rather than the "coercion" or "stigma" identified by the panel. See Ortiz-Rivera, supra.[4]

Even if the panel is right to be concerned about "coercion" and "stigma" in these circumstances, the per se rule it has crafted does precious little to address these concerns.

Lopez-Vasquez was one of twelve respondents in the underlying deportation proceeding. The procedure mandated by the panel here would require an immigration judge to ask each respondent individually whether he wished to appeal. Suppose Lopez-Vasquez had been the twelfth respondent so questioned, and suppose (as is not unlikely) that each of his fellows had declined to appeal before him. Now suppose that the immigration judge turns his attention to Lopez-Vasquez: "And you, sir, do you wish to appeal my ruling?" Might this not be even more coercive than the procedure actually employed here, making it even harder for the respondent to assert his desire for review? The coercion and stigma the panel fears is inherent in any group deportation proceeding. Such proceedings, however, unquestionably do not offend due process. See, e.g., Nicholas-Armenta, 763 F.2d at 1091. By its oversolicitous concern for one aspect of these proceedings, the panel may have actually done more harm than good to the rights it means to protect.

In any event, if the panel believed that it could not find a valid waiver on these facts, as it evidently did, then it should have predicated its order of remand on these facts. The general assumptions advanced by the panel in no way support a per se rule that forces us to disregard the specific facts of particular cases. The rule itself, meanwhile, will inevitably foster results that are both silly and unjust. Indeed, it has already happened. See Ortiz-Rivera, supra.

VI

Kersplat! Nonsense on stilts, skating blindfolded on thin ice must topple in the end.

The law of this circuit now states that, in every section 1326 prosecution, the government must rebut the presumption that the defendant was deprived of his right to review of the underlying deportation order. The government must further rebut the presumption that the deportation proceeding was not marred by any fundamental procedural defect. The government's failure to carry its burden as to either of these two presumptions has the absurd consequence of shifting the burden to the defendant, who then, mysteriously, must prove prejudice. The law of this circuit also now holds that a non-verbal waiver of the right to appeal is per se unknowing, unconsidered, and unintelligent, and that reviewing courts lack the means to discern a valid waiver from a record that does not contain some approximation of the verbal ritual, "I do not wish to appeal." To arrive at this weird state of affairs, we have had to suffer one of our three-judge panels to cast aside, wittingly or not, the authority of the Supreme Court and of our own en banc court.

Our law should be otherwise. Our sufferance should not extend so far. We have passed up the opportunity to set things right. I respectfully dissent.

Notes

[1] In Proa-Tovar, the en banc court concluded that "[a] defendant who seeks to exclude evidence of a deportation order in a prosecution under 8 U.S.C. § 1326 must do more than demonstrate deprivation of the right to a direct appeal from that order. The defendant also bears the burden of proving prejudice." Proa-Tovar, 975 F.2d at 595. In the

face of this unambiguous statement to the contrary, the panel maintains that the government bears the burden of proving the validity of Lopez-Vasquez's waiver of appeal. How can the panel take a position that is flatly inconsistent with an en banc decision on which the ink is scarcely dry without even attempting to explain itself?

[2] Justice Scalia was referring to Edwards v. Arizona, 451 U.S. 477, 101 S.Ct. 1880, 68 L.Ed.2d 378 (1981), which held that a criminal suspect's invocation of his Miranda right to have counsel present gives rise to an "irrebuttable presumption" against voluntary waiver of that right in response to police-initiated interrogation. Minnick itself, of course, is to the same effect.

[3] Ortiz-Rivera provides as good an example as could be wished of just how misguided is the per se rule of Lopez-Vasquez, and just how foolish and wasteful are the results it forces upon us.

That case, like this one, was a section 1326 prosecution in which the defendant sought to mount a collateral attack upon his underlying deportation proceeding. The facts were not disputed: Ortiz-Rivera entered a conditional guilty plea in which he stipulated that he had suffered previous state convictions for armed robbery, the sale or transportation of cocaine, and the unlawful driving or taking of a vehicle, that he had been twice deported in the past, and that he had illegally entered the United States on three separate occasions. 1 F.3d at 752.

In the deportation hearing he challenged as fundamentally unfair, meanwhile, Ortiz-Rivera was one of seven respondents. All were twice advised by the immigration judge ("IJ") that they had a right to appeal his decision as to their deportability. Ortiz-Rivera, along with all other respondents, individually stated that he understood that he had such a right. Id. at 766.

He then engaged in an individual colloquy with the IJ, in English, which the IJ observed he spoke well. During that colloquy, Ortiz-Rivera declined the offer of a free lawyer, admitted that he had been convicted of the cocaine offense, and further admitted that he was deportable as charged. He was then informed that, having lived in this country for some time, he might be eligible for a waiver of deportation, and asked whether he had ever had any legal immigration papers. He answered in the negative, explaining that he "was in trouble" — apparently a reference to his criminal record. Finally, he was asked whether there was "any argument at all" that he had a legal right to be in this country. He said no. Id. at 766-68.

After the IJ had questioned the other six respondents, all of whom conceded deportability, he informed them that he was going to sign an order for their deportations. He then re-advised the respondents that they had a right to appeal his decision, and invited anyone who wished to appeal to stand so that he could "explain the appeal process in more detail and have someone help you fill out the appeal application." None of the respondents stood up. Id. at 768.

Despite such a record, Lopez-Vasquez compelled us to hold that Ortiz-Rivera's decision to remain seated when invited to exercise his right to appeal did not manifest a considered and intelligent decision to waive that right. That conclusion defies reality in a fashion too obvious to require further comment.

[4] Again, Ortiz-Rivera exposes the flaws in the panel's opinion here. There exists not even the remotest chance that, when invited to stand if he wished to appeal, Ortiz-Rivera failed to do so because he felt "coerced by the silence of [his] fellows," or feared being "stigmatized" by his desire for justice. Ortiz-Rivera didn't stand because he knew he had no legal right to be in this country in the first place, and knew as well that, given his criminal record, he had no hope of remaining. He made a "considered" and "intelligent" decision — indeed, a downright sensible decision — to accept immediate deportation, and freedom in his native Mexico, rather than to remain in a detention center for who-knows-how-long while an obviously futile appeal wound its way through the system. And yet we were compelled by Lopez-Vasquez to hold that Ortiz-Rivera was improperly deprived of his right to judicial review, and to remand the case to the district court for further proceedings. District courts have many more important things to do.

Judge O'Scannlain's partial concurrence in US v. Aguilar (May 12, 1993, amended August 9, 1993)

O'SCANNLAIN, Circuit Judge, concurring in part:

I would affirm Judge Aguilar's conviction for disclosure of a wiretap under 18 U.S.C. § 2232(c) but would reverse his conviction for obstruction of justice under 18 U.S.C. § 1503. Thus, I concur in the result reached by Judge Hall as to Count Six and in the result reached by Judge Hug as to Count Eight.

As to the appeal of the sentence, we reject the government's challenge to the district court's decision to depart downward from the Sentencing Guidelines. However, the court failed to follow the procedure set forth in United States v. Lira-Barraza, 941 F.2d 745 (9th Cir.1991) (en banc). Consequently, we must vacate the sentence on Count Six and remand for resentencing.

I

I agree with Judge Hall that a rational trier of fact could find beyond a reasonable doubt that Judge Aguilar had knowledge of the wiretap application; there clearly was sufficient evidence in the record. Accordingly, I concur in part II.A of her opinion. I also agree that section 2232(c) does not violate the First Amendment as applied to Judge Aguilar. Accordingly, I concur in part II.B of her opinion. I cannot agree, however, with Judge Hall's analysis of the knowledge instruction in parts II.C and II.D of her opinion. I believe that the district court's knowledge instruction was erroneous for the reasons set forth by Judge Hug in section C of his opinion; nevertheless, I conclude that the error, fatal as to Count Eight, was harmless as to Count Six.

I believe that Judge Hug's analysis of the knowledge instruction is correct. Therefore, reversal on both counts is required unless the error was logically harmless beyond any reasonable doubt because the record compels a guilty verdict. United States v.

Sanchez-Robles, 927 F.2d 1070, 1075 (9th Cir.1991); see also United States v. Alvarado, 838 F.2d 311, 317 (9th Cir.) ("Application of the harmless error doctrine is appropriate where the evidence of guilt is so overwhelming that a conviction is compelled."), cert. denied, 487 U.S. 1222, 108 S.Ct. 2880, 101 L.Ed.2d 915 and 488 U.S. 838, 109 S.Ct. 103, 102 L.Ed.2d 78 (1988). Applying any other standard of review to this erroneous instruction would allow for conviction without establishment of knowledge, an essential element of the offense, beyond a reasonable doubt. See In re Winship, 397 U.S. 358, 364, 90 S.Ct. 1068, 1072, 25 L.Ed.2d 368 (1970) (due process requires that each element of an offense be proved beyond reasonable doubt). But see United States v. Valle-Valdez, 554 F.2d 911, 915-16 (9th Cir.1977) (noting some confusion in the cases, but observing that errors in jury instructions are generally considered nonconstitutional and therefore the standard from Chapman v. California, 386 U.S. 18, 87 S.Ct. 824, 17 L.Ed.2d 705 (1967), need not apply).

A

After examination of the record, I conclude that the error was harmless beyond a reasonable doubt with respect to Count Six, the wiretap count. The evidence of Judge Aguilar's knowledge consisted of the following:

(1) Both Judge Peckham and Judge Aguilar testified that Judge Peckham had told Judge Aguilar that Chapman's name had come up "in connection with" a wiretap;

(2) Judge Aguilar saw an FBI agent photographing Chapman outside Aguilar's house;

(3) Steve Aguilar testified that Judge Aguilar told him that he had overheard at work that Chapman was being wiretapped;

(4) Three months after Judge Aguilar revealed the wiretap to Chapman, he repeatedly told Solomon in recorded conversations that he knew Chapman's phone was tapped.

The strongest evidence against Judge Aguilar is the transcript of his May 17 conversation with Solomon. Because it postdates Judge Aguilar's alleged violation of section 2232(c) by more than three months, I am reluctant to assign "overwhelming" weight to this evidence. See Judge Hall's Opinion, at 622. Nonetheless, the combination of what Judge Peckham told Judge Aguilar and what Judge Aguilar told Steve Aguilar shows conclusively that Judge Aguilar was substantially certain that Chapman had been or was being tapped. It does not appear that Judge Aguilar received any additional information between the disclosure and his self-incriminating statements. I therefore conclude that the erroneous instruction was harmless beyond a reasonable doubt with regard to Count Six.

B

On the other hand, I cannot conclude that the error was harmless beyond a reasonable doubt as to Count Eight, the obstruction of justice count. The obstruction count requires a showing that the defendant knew: (1) that a grand jury was meeting, and (2) that the person tampered with was expected to be called as a witness before the grand jury. United States v. Washington Water Power Co., 793 F.2d 1079, 1084 (9th Cir.1986).

There appears to be no room to doubt that Judge Aguilar knew a grand jury was meeting. Solomon told Judge Aguilar, in a recorded conversation on May 26, 1988, one month before the alleged violation, that the FBI had told him a grand jury was in session. Judge Aguilar indicated his understanding of this information by observing, later in the same conversation, "if they subpoena me I may have a problem."

However, the evidence is considerably thinner that Judge Aguilar knew that the FBI agents to whom he lied were expected to be witnesses before the grand jury. There is no direct evidence at all. Nor do Judge Aguilar's prevarications support an unequivocal inference of knowledge. It is equally plausible that he hoped his lies would dissuade the government from seeking an indictment against him.

Certainly, as the government points out, the jury could infer that Judge Aguilar, an experienced federal judge, deduced that the investigating FBI agents were likely to be witnesses before the grand jury. The availability of this inference, however, points up the danger of the "high probability" jury instruction. The jury could have concluded that Judge Aguilar did not know the agents were likely witnesses, but should have. In the absence of an instruction precluding conviction for negligence, I cannot be confident the jury did not convict for negligence.

Jury instructions are not to be examined in isolation. Maddox v. City of Los Angeles, 792 F.2d 1408, 1412 (9th Cir.1986). The erroneous knowledge instruction could theoretically have been cured by the trial judge's instruction on intent to "impede, interfere with or obstruct the functioning of that grand jury." In my view, however, the intent instruction does not ameliorate the flaw in the knowledge instruction. The jurors may have concluded that Judge Aguilar intended to "obstruct the functioning of the grand jury" by inducing the government not to seek an indictment against him. Yet the government does not argue, and I do not believe, that such a showing is sufficient to violate section 1503. I therefore conclude that the erroneous knowledge instruction requires reversal of the conviction on Count Eight.

II

In imposing sentence, the district court assigned Judge Aguilar an offense level of 16,[1] which carries a sentence of twenty-one to twenty-seven months and a fine of $5000 to $50,000 for persons in criminal history category I. The court then departed downward and assigned Judge Aguilar an offense level of 10 and sentenced him to two six month terms of imprisonment, to be served concurrently, and fined him $1000 on each count. The government appeals the district court's downward departure from the Sentencing Guidelines.

Under 18 U.S.C. § 3553(b), the district court must sentence a defendant within the applicable Guidelines range unless "the court finds there exists an aggravating or mitigating circumstance of a kind, or to a degree, not adequately taken into consideration by the Sentencing Commission in formulating the guidelines that should result in a sentence different from that described." Here, the court offered the following reasons for its departure:

I do think Judge Aguilar now commences a long course of adversarial proceedings, ... beginning with the Ninth Circuit Judicial Council, with the state and local bar associations, with the House of Representatives, with the United States Senate. Those proceedings will be long, humiliating, and burdensome and may even bring into play a number of events that are not part of the convictions for which he stands convicted before the court at this time. I think that burden is a major and substantial punishment that warrants some degree of departure downward.

The district court emphasized that its willingness to depart was limited only to those features that it believed "are so different and unique with this defendant, ... and are so extensive and will be so enduring that it would be the sort of ground upon which a sentencing commission would favor a court sitting here today using it as a basis for departure."

Our review of the departure imposed by the district court involves three steps. United States v. Lira-Barraza, 941 F.2d 745, 746-47 (9th Cir.1991) (en banc). First, we must determine whether the district court had the legal authority to depart from the Sentencing Guidelines. Id. at 746. Second, we review for clear error factual findings supporting the existence of the identified circumstance. Id. at 746-47. Third, we must determine whether a six level departure downward was unreasonable. Id. at 747. Here, because the district court's statement did not include "a reasoned explanation of the extent of the departure founded on the structure, standards and policies of the Act and Guidelines," id., the district court failed to comply with the underlying requirements of the third step of Lira-Barraza and we must remand.

On remand, the district court may again choose to depart downward based on the additional punishment awaiting Judge Aguilar. The government vigorously contends that the district court does not have the legal authority to do so. We therefore believe that some comment on the appropriateness of departure is warranted.

The district court may depart if it identifies a mitigating circumstance of a kind or to a degree the Commission did not adequately take into account when formulating the Guidelines. Id. at 746. Even if the circumstance is one not adequately considered, the court cannot depart if the circumstance is inconsistent "with the sentencing factors prescribed by Congress in 18 U.S.C. § 3553(a), [and] with the Guidelines..." Id.

The mitigating circumstance upon which the district court based its downward departure was the additional punishment it anticipated Judge Aguilar would suffer during the course of potential disbarment and impeachment hearings. The government argues that the Guidelines account for that circumstance in sections 3B1.3 and 3E1.1, which respectively establish an upward adjustment if the defendant has abused a position of trust and a downward adjustment if the defendant accepts responsibility for his actions by resigning his office. See U.S.S.G. §§ 3B1.3, 3E1.1 and comment. (n.1(f)). The court's ruling, however, was not based solely on the likelihood of impeachment, but on the likelihood that Judge Aguilar will suffer additional punishment throughout the course of several disciplinary hearings. The provisions cited by the government cannot be said to account for this circumstance.

Nor was this departure "inconsistent with the Guidelines' policy that disparity in sentencing should never be occasioned by socioeconomic factors." The district court did not rely on socioeconomic status to support its departure. Rather, the district court relied upon a determination that Judge Aguilar, because he is a federal judge, would be subject to punishment in addition to the court-imposed sentence. Judge Aguilar's job accounts for this extra punishment; the departure was not based on his level of wealth, privilege, or "status in society."[2] Cf. United States v. Lopez, 938 F.2d 1293, 1297 (D.C.Cir. 1991). Additional punishment appears to be a valid mitigating factor. Cf. United States v. Lara, 905 F.2d 599, 601-03 (2d Cir.1990) (departure upheld where defendant's vulnerability required prison officials to place him in solitary confinement, increasing the severity of his punishment).[3] Moreover, unlike Judge Hall, we do not consider each particular aspect of the additional punishment facing Judge Aguilar "abstractly and alone," United States v. Cook, 938 F.2d 149, 153 (9th Cir. 1991), but instead recognize the "unique combination of factors" that comprises the mitigating circumstance in this case. Id.

Judge Aguilar, if he is subjected to impeachment proceedings, will suffer additional punishment by the government, imposed in a public, quasi-judicial proceeding. If convicted upon impeachment, not only will he be removed from his otherwise life-tenured position, he will be disqualified from holding any future government appointive position. See United States v. Brown, 381 U.S. 437, 448, 85 S.Ct. 1707, 1714, 14 L.Ed.2d 484 (1965) ("Disqualification from office may be punishment, as in cases of conviction upon impeachment.") (quoting Cummings v. Missouri, 71 U.S. (4 Wall) 277, 320, 18 L.Ed. 356 (1866)). If convicted upon impeachment, Judge Aguilar will also suffer full forfeiture of his pension rights, a loss of considerable economic significance.[4] Unlike most federal officers and employees, an Article III judge's pension does not vest until he attains at least age sixty-five and meets certain service requirements, typically fifteen years. See 28 U.S.C. § 371. In contrast, had he been an Article I judge such as a bankruptcy judge, or a magistrate judge, Judge Aguilar would have begun vesting upon completion of eight years of service and by now would be nearly fully vested in his right to receive the salary of the office for life beginning at age sixty-five. See 28 U.S.C. § 377. Therefore, unlike an Article I judge, or any other federal official or employee for that matter, an Article III judge who leaves office for any reason prior to the age of sixty-five forfeits all pension rights no matter how many years he may have served. From publicly available material, it appears that Judge Aguilar has served on the bench since 1980; should he leave office before April 15, 1996, the date of his sixty-fifth birthday, he will receive no retirement benefits whatsoever. This will be true whether he resigns voluntarily or suffers impeachment.

Thus, the additional formal punishment to be imposed upon Judge Aguilar as a result of his conviction can be distinguished, both qualitatively and quantitatively, from the "substantial pain and humiliation" suffered by criminal defendants who are "well-known figures in the worlds of government and finance." For that reason we reject the suggestion that the additional punishment Judge Aguilar will suffer is not "atypical."[5]

See U.S.S.G. Ch. 1, Pt. A4(b). While Judge Hall may be right that "well-known figures" of high social standing appear as criminal defendants all too frequently, the criminal conviction of an Article III judge is, thankfully, still a rare occurrence. Notwithstanding the recent impeachments of several federal judges,[6] Judge Aguilar is the first convicted federal judge to be sentenced under the Guidelines. As such, his case does not appear to fall within the heartland of cases for which the Guidelines were designed. Moreover, we reiterate that the additional punishment identified by the district court is not based upon Judge Aguilar's "personal financial hardship," "foreclosure of career opportunities," or, especially, "loss of position." Judge Hall's Opinion, at 624-25. Thus, we are satisfied that Judge Bechtle had the legal authority to depart; the first element of Lira-Barraza was met.

Lira-Barraza also requires us to review for clear error the district court's factual findings supporting the existence of the identified circumstance. Lira-Barraza, 941 F.2d at 746-47. The government argues, in effect, that no factual findings were made as to the possibility that Judge Aguilar might avoid the humiliation of impeachment by resigning. The government's argument, as to step two, is well taken but may be ultimately moot. On remand, the district court should specifically consider whether other additional punishment, such as forfeiture of pension and disbarment, will result in the event of Judge Aguilar's potential resignation to avoid impeachment.

"The Guidelines are not a straightjacket for district judges. They do provide discretion to depart." Cook, 938 F.2d at 152. Congress has instructed sentencing courts "to provide just punishment for the offense." 18 U.S.C. § 3553(a)(2)(A). In this case, Judge Hall would have us remand for the imposition of a more severe sentence even though we reverse one count of conviction. To do so without allowing the district court to consider in its discretion the additional formal punishment and the unusual financial ramifications that arise because of the appellant's job as an Article III judge would violate Congress's mandate to provide just punishment.

In sum, we agree that additional punishment is a permissible basis for downward departure. We remand, however, for the district court to follow the procedures established in Lira-Barraza. In particular, the court must consciously measure the extent of its departure against the sentencing structure established by the Act and the Guidelines. Lira-Barraza, 941 F.2d at 748.

III

In conclusion, I would affirm Judge Aguilar's conviction as to Count Six, reverse his conviction as to Count Eight, and remand for resentencing in accordance with the foregoing opinion.

Notes

[1] The district court increased the offense level for Count Six from 12 to 14 for abuse of public trust under U.S.S.G. § 3B1.3. Judge Aguilar was convicted of multiple counts. Therefore, in calculating the combined offense level under U.S.S.G. § 3D1.4, the district court added two levels, resulting in a combined offense level of 16. Because we

vacate one count of conviction, § 3D1.4 no longer applies. The maximum offense level applicable is 14, rather than 16.

[2] Although Judge Aguilar's job may constitute one component of his socioeconomic status, see Lopez, 938 F.2d at 1297, unlike Judge Hall, we are not convinced that one component of his socioeconomic status, his job, defines his socioeconomic status. See Judge Hall's Opinion, at 624.

We note in passing that, although the Guidelines specifically state that "socioeconomic status" is not a relevant factor in sentence determination, U.S.S.G. § 5H1.10, this court has recently suggested that consideration of socioeconomic "factors" may not always be precluded. United States v. Valdez-Gonzalez, 957 F.2d 643, 649 n. 3 (9th Cir.1992).

[3] The extra punishment identified by the district court can be distinguished from other collateral effects arising from conviction. For example, our court has held that the likelihood of deportation is not a valid basis for departure. United States v. Alvarez-Cardenas, 902 F.2d 734, 737 (9th Cir.1990); United States v. Ceja-Hernandez, 895 F.2d 544 (9th Cir.1990). These deportation cases, however, are distinguishable in two respects. First, despite its undeniable impact, deportation is not considered punitive. See Galvan v. Press, 347 U.S. 522, 531, 74 S.Ct. 737, 742, 98 L.Ed. 911 (1954). Second, Alvarez-Cardenas involved a drug conviction, and Ceja-Hernandez a conviction for illegal presence in the United States. Deportation as a consequence of the former is not rare, and as a consequence of the latter is the rule. We must therefore assume that the Sentencing Commission took the possibility of deportation into account when determining the appropriate offense level for these crimes. See Ceja-Hernandez, 895 F.2d at 545.

[4] The right to receive, beginning at age sixty-five, the salary of the office (presently $133,600 per annum) for life, can be calculated from actuarial tables; the value of such annuity is likely to exceed $1.3 million dollars. See 28 U.S.C. § 371(a); cf. 5 U.S.C. § 8339.

[5] Similarly, a forfeiture proceeding following a drug or racketeering conviction, or a civil damage award after a conviction for a white collar crime, simply is not "atypical." We cannot presume the Sentencing Commission did not anticipate these common collateral effects of conviction for such crimes when designing the Guidelines.

[6] See Nixon v. United States, 938 F.2d 239, 248, 250 (D.C.Cir.1991) (Edwards, J., dissenting in part and concurring in judgment) (noting the recent impeachments of Harry E. Claiborne and Alcee Hastings, as well as Walter Nixon), aff'd, ____ U.S. ____, 113 S.Ct. 732, 122 L.Ed.2d 1 (1993); see also United States v. Claiborne, 765 F.2d 784 (9th Cir.1985), cert. denied, 475 U.S. 1120, 106 S.Ct. 1636, 90 L.Ed.2d 182 (1986); United States v. Nixon, 816 F.2d 1022 (5th Cir.), reh'g denied, 827 F.2d 1019 (5th Cir.1987), cert. denied, 484 U.S. 1026, 108 S.Ct. 749, 98 L.Ed.2d 762 (1988); and United States v. Collins, 972 F.2d 1385 (5th Cir.1992), cert. denied, ____ U.S. ____, 113 S.Ct. 1812, 123 L.Ed.2d 444 (1993).

Judge O'Scannlain's concurrence in Koff v. US (Sept 1, 1993)

O'SCANNLAIN, Circuit Judge, concurring in the judgment:

I agree that Part II of the per curiam opinion represents the proper resolution of the merits of the taxpayers' arguments in this case. I believe, however, that this panel ought never to have reached the merits. In my view, there is a conflict in this court's precedents that prevents us from asserting jurisdiction here, and requires that we recommend that this case be decided by our en banc court.

I

It is settled that 28 U.S.C. § 2410 serves to abrogate the United States' sovereign immunity from suit only with respect to challenges to "the procedural validity of a tax lien" — "[a] taxpayer may not use a section 2410 action to collaterally attack the merits of an assessment." Elias v. Connett, 908 F.2d 521, 527 (9th Cir.1990). See Powelson v. United States, 979 F.2d 141, 145 (9th Cir.1992); Hughes v. United States, 953 F.2d 531, 538 (9th Cir.1992); Arford v. United States, 934 F.2d 229, 232 (9th Cir.1991). Our cases agree on this much. They differ, however, with respect to how the line is to be drawn between a challenge to "the procedural validity of a tax lien" and a challenge to "the merits of an assessment."

A

In Elias, we held that a taxpayer's allegation that "a lawful assessment against him does not exist" goes to "the merits of [his] assessment rather than the procedural validity of the IRS's lien," and thus does not state a claim cognizable under section 2410. Elias, 908 F.2d at 527. The Koffs allege that the tax lien placed on their property is invalid because the IRS did not properly follow its internal procedures in effecting the assessment upon which the lien is based. Although the legal result for which the Koffs contend is that the lien is invalid, the basis of this contention is that "a lawful assessment against [them] does not exist." Under Elias, then, the Koffs' suit constitutes an attack on the merits of their assessment, to which the waiver of sovereign immunity in section 2410 does not extend.

B

In Arford, the taxpayers "alleged that the government [] did not assess their taxes as required by [section] 6203." 934 F.2d at 231. Without discussing Elias, we held that this allegation stated a claim cognizable under section 2410: "to the extent [the Arfords] are challenging the procedural lapses of the assessment under § 6203, 28 U.S.C. § 2410 does serve as a waiver of sovereign immunity." Id. at 232. The Koffs' allegation that the IRS did not properly follow its internal assessment procedures is indistinguishable from the Arfords' claim "that the government [] did not assess their taxes as required by" law. Under Arford, then, the Koffs' suit presents a claim of "procedural lapse[]" which falls within the waiver of sovereign immunity in section 2410.

II

To my mind, Elias and Arford are plainly in conflict. Moreover, I believe that en banc resolution of this conflict is unavoidable, for I am unable to agree with either of the approaches my colleagues have taken in this matter.

Judge Ferguson would avert the need to recognize the conflict between Elias and Arford by assuming for purposes of decision that we have jurisdiction, and deciding this case on the merits. This sort of solution is undeniably an attractive and, in general, a useful one. Under the circumstances, however, I believe it is unavailable to us. As I have explained at length elsewhere, I believe we are forbidden to assume we have jurisdiction to exercise the judicial power created by Article III and vested in us by statute. See Clow v. United States Dep't of Housing & Urban Dev., 948 F.2d 614, 619 (9th Cir.1991) (O'Scannlain, J., dissenting).

Judge Rymer, meanwhile, would attempt to reconcile Elias and Arford. With respect, I think her attempt does not succeed. Section 6203 provides (1) that assessments must "be made ... in accordance with rules and regulations prescribed by the Secretary," and (2) that "a copy of the record of the assessment" must be given the taxpayer "upon request." Arford held that a claim of "procedural lapses of the assessment under § 6203" is cognizable under section 2410. Judge Rymer would "read th[is] language ... to mean that § 2410 allows a taxpayer to make the procedural argument that she did not receive notice of her assessment which is required by § 6203 and that a tax lien is therefore invalid." That is, Judge Rymer would read Arford as extending only to the second requirement of section 6203, not to the first.

I cannot accept this approach for, unfortunately, this is assuredly not what Arford actually held. Neither the language of the opinion nor the facts in Arford provide any basis for reading the phrase "procedural lapses in the assessment" to mean only "failure to provide a copy of the record of the assessment upon request." The Arfords did not allege only the latter sort of failure. They allege that the government "did not assess their taxes as required" by law. In holding that this allegation stated a claim under section 2410, Arford in no way implied that the only "procedural lapses" that counted were those that involved failure to provide the taxpayer with required documentation.

III

Sitting as a three-judge panel, we have no authority to overrule the decision of any other three-judge panel of this court. See, e.g., United States v. Washington, 872 F.2d 874, 880 (9th Cir.1989). Neither do we have the power to "make [a] choice between two opposing lines of authority." Greenhow v. Secretary of Health & Human Servs., 863 F.2d 633, 636 (9th Cir.1988), overruled en banc, United States v. Hardesty, 977 F.2d 1347, 1348 (9th Cir.1992) (en banc). Further, in this instance, we are not permitted to assume the irrelevance of the conflict for purposes of decision, because the conflict goes to our very jurisdiction to hear this appeal. Finally, I see no way to bring about a persuasive and final reconciliation between the cases that are the source of the conflict.

I believe we do ourselves little credit, and the lawyers and litigants who practice before us little good, when we ignore an irreconcilable conflict in our decisions. We must inevitably produce such conflicts. To be sure, we can paper them over easily enough. But in doing so we tolerate and, indeed, encourage, abiding uncertainties in our circuit law, undermining the predictability and uniformity of treatment for which we are bound to strive. The law of this circuit, in short, is far more likely to develop in a rational fashion when we acknowledge our mistakes and move quickly to correct them than when we contrive to disavow them.

In any event, we have declared that "the appropriate mechanism for resolving an irreconcilable conflict is an en banc decision," and that "[a] panel faced with such a conflict must call for an en banc review." Hardesty, 977 F.2d at 1348 (quoting Atonio v. Wards Cove Packing Co., 810 F.2d 1477, 1478-79 (9th Cir.1987) (en banc), cert. denied, 485 U.S. 989, 108 S.Ct. 1293, 99 L.Ed.2d 503 (1988)) (emphasis in Hardesty). Although the legal issue presented here is not as significant as many we face, en banc reconsideration is nonetheless "necessary to secure ... uniformity of [our] decisions." Fed.R.App.P. 35. We are thus bound to recommend that this case be heard by the en banc court. Rather than render a decision in this matter, I would make such a recommendation.

Judge O'Scannlain's dissent in Hartooni v. INS (April 7, 1994)

O'SCANNLAIN, Circuit Judge, dissenting:

While I believe that this is a close case, especially given the majority's admission that doubts have been raised about the petitioner's credibility, Majority Opinion at 343, I am persuaded that the immigration judge ("IJ") made implicit findings concerning the petitioner's credibility. Because these findings are entitled to "considerable deference," De Valle v. INS, 901 F.2d 787, 792 (9th Cir. 1990), I would affirm the BIA's decision that Ms. Hartooni does not qualify for asylum.

The majority maintains that the IJ did not make findings on the credibility of Ms. Hartooni's claims because he did not "make findings of fact regarding which, if any, of her specific claims were questionable." Majority Opinion at 342. However, the IJ did state, after a detailed exposition of Ms. Hartooni's allegations of persecution, that "[t]he cumulative effect of the respondent's testimony and application therefore leads me to conclude that the respondent has not established a credible claim to persecution." IJ Opinion at 8-9. This conclusion establishes that the IJ did not find credible the petitioner's claim of fear of persecution based on the facts of her story. It is evident from the IJ's recitation of Ms. Hartooni's allegations of fear and her contradictory statements, that the IJ considered her story fully and found that conflicting facts destroyed the credibility of each of her claims of fear. Since the petitioner has not provided any explanation for the inconsistency of her statements, the only conclusion the IJ could draw was that her testimony was not credible. The IJ's conclusory statement should be enough. This court should not require that an IJ recite some talismanic rote on credibility to meet the burden.

The BIA did not err in according considerable deference to the IJ's conclusion on Ms. Hartooni's credibility since it was supported by substantial evidence. The facts that Ms. Hartooni's parents are practicing Christians living in Iran, that they run a successful business without any apparent government interference, and that they are allowed to send a considerable amount of money to their children living in the United States suggest that Ms. Hartooni could live safely with her parents in Iran. This is more than enough to support the BIA's determination that Ms. Hartooni did not qualify for asylum. INS v. Elias-Zacarias, ____ U.S. ____, ____, 112 S.Ct. 812, 815, 117 L.Ed.2d 38 (1992) (BIA's decision cannot be reversed unless petitioner presented such evidence that reasonable factfinder would have to conclude that requisite fear of persecution existed).

I respectfully dissent.

Judge O'Scannlain's dissent in Padilla-Agustin v. INS (April 21, 1994)

O'SCANNLAIN, Circuit Judge, concurring in part and dissenting in part:

Relying upon what it calls the "normal way to approach forms," the majority finds that the absence of a large blank space on the printed notice of appeal form deprived Padilla of procedural due process guaranteed by the United States Constitution. Unfortunately, it is the presence of a large blank space in the reasoning of its opinion which leads the majority to such a bizarre conclusion. Because I believe that form EOIR-26 provided reasonable notice to Padilla, I must dissent from that part of the majority's opinion denominated "A. Adequacy of the Summary Dismissal Procedures"; I concur in the remainder.

I

The Board of Immigration Appeals ("BIA") requires a petitioner appealing an adverse immigration judge ("IJ") decision to state the specific grounds for the appeal. A petitioner may not merely assert that an IJ erred in denying an application for relief from deportation. Instead, as the majority observes, he or she must identify the IJ's alleged error and discuss either the legal standards that the IJ contravened or the particular details of any factual error. Matter of Valencia, 19 I. & N.Dec. 354 (BIA 1986).

Form EOIR-26 adequately alerts petitioners to this "specificity" requirement. On its front, the form instructs a petitioner to "[s]pecify [the] reasons for this appeal and continue on separate sheets if necessary. If the factual or legal basis for the appeal is not sufficiently described the appeal may be summarily dismissed." This statement is followed by a blank area approximately 1.75 inches in length. On the reverse side, the form again cautions: "Summary dismissal of appeals. The BIA may ... summarily dismiss any appeal in which ... the party concerned fails to specify the reasons for his/her appeal on the [other] side of this form...." [Bold in original].

These statements reasonably satisfy the government's due process obligation to notify a petitioner of the BIA's specificity requirement. Due process requires that "[t]he BIA's procedures in summarily dismissing appeals must not be so arbitrary as to undermine the principles of due process." Toquero v. INS, 956 F.2d 193, 196 (9th Cir.1992). The BIA thus must provide petitioners with adequate notice of the steps that they must take to avoid summary dismissal. See id. at 197; Nazakat v. INS, 981 F.2d 1146,

1148-49 (10th Cir.1992). This "right to adequate notice simply requires that [a] proposed form of notification be reasonably certain to inform those affected" of their obligations. Vancouver Women's Health Collective Soc. v. A.H. Robins Co. Inc., 820 F.2d 1359, 1364 (4th Cir.1987). Form EOIR-26 meets this standard. It tells a petitioner to specify the reasons for his or her appeal, including all legal and factual bases. It then twice warns a petitioner of the consequences of a failure to comply with this directive.

The only case to address the sufficiency of notice in immigration appeal procedures, Nazakat, 981 F.2d 1146, confirms this conclusion. In Nazakat, the BIA summarily dismissed an appeal because the petitioner's I-290A form was insufficiently specific. The petitioner asserted that the dismissal violated procedural due process. The Tenth Circuit disagreed, observing that an immigration judge had:

warned the petitioner to prepare an adequate Notice of Appeal: "Don't just say, `I disagree.' As I explained to you ... you've got to put the reasons.... grounds that an error was made, in this area, or that area, whatever grounds that you're appealing on. You have to be specific."

Id. at 1148 (ellipses in original).

Form EOIR-26 gives the same instructions to a petitioner. Its directives and warnings of summary dismissal are equivalent to, if not greater than, the Nazakat IJ's warning that Nazakat's appeal had to be "specific" and had to state his reasons for appealing.[1] Form EOIR-26 does not violate the Constitution.

II

Curiously, the majority finds greatest fault with form EOIR-26 not because of what it says or does not say, but because of an absence of empty space.

Form EOIR-26 provides a blank area 1.75 inches in length beneath its instructions regarding a petitioner's statement of reasons for his or her appeal. The majority finds this space so misleading to immigrants that it denies them due process. The majority explains that, "[b]ecause minimal space is provided for petitioners to state their reasons for appeal, this creates the misimpression that most petitioners are expected to state those reasons within the space of 1.75 inches and can do so with sufficient clarity. That simply is a normal way to complete forms...." [Opinion at 3433.]

This view is faulty because petitioners are not, in fact, limited to the 1.75-inch area. Form EOIR-26 plainly informs petitioners that they may continue onto additional sheets of paper if necessary. Petitioners thus are not restricted to a "minimal space" to complete the form.

The majority nevertheless suggests that, because form EOIR-26 merely gives petitioners the option to continue on to additional pages (as well as the related option to file, or not file, a brief), it lulls petitioners into believing that they need not do so, regardless of the specific issues involved in their appeals. [Opinion at 3433.] This view presumes that petitioners will ignore the form's explicit directive to specify the reasons, including all legal and factual bases, for an appeal.

I see no reason to make this presumption. It seems much more likely that petitioners, who are one step closer to deportation after losing before an IJ, will take the form's directive seriously and will write to whatever length they deem necessary to comply with it. Consequently, if the option to attach additional pages to form EOIR-26 has any effect on petitioners' behavior, it is to encourage, rather than to deter, the inclusion of details explaining the basis for an appeal.

Further, to the extent that the majority relies on Toquero, 956 F.2d at 197, and Escobar-Ramos v. INS, 927 F.2d 482, 484 (9th Cir.1991), to find form EOIR-26 defective, such reliance is misplaced. In both cases, this court signaled concern that form I-290A provided insufficient notice of specificity requirements while nevertheless affirming BIA action.

These cases are distinguishable from the present one because form EOIR-26 provides better notice than form I-290A. For example, instructions and an accompanying warning of summary dismissal are more prominent on form EOIR-26. Form EOIR-26 states, on its front, that failure to describe the basis of the appeal sufficiently may lead to summary dismissal. Form I-290A, in contrast, buries the same warning on its reverse side.

Form EOIR-26 also prompts a petitioner to write his or her reasons for appeal "on separate sheets if necessary." As explained above, the form thus encourages a petitioner to elaborate on the reasons for an appeal. Form I-290A does the opposite. Not only does it fail to suggest the attachment of additional pages, but it also instructs a petitioner "[b]riefly" to state the reasons for his or her appeal.

Rather than acknowledge the improvements made to form EOIR-26 in these important respects, the majority focuses on the fact that form EOIR-26 contains a smaller blank space than form I-290A, which provides a 3-inch area for identifying the reasons for an appeal. [Opinion at 3433.] As explained above, however, the "concatenation" of form EOIR-26 in this manner does not mislead a petitioner into limiting his or her reasons for appeal to a 1.75-inch space where such a limitation would be inappropriate.

Consequently, I must conclude that form EOIR-26 does not mislead petitioners nor deprive them of due process.[2]

III

Padilla did not comply with the instructions on form EOIR-26. In his two-sentence explanation of his appeal, Padilla stated only that he has fled his home country because he had been persecuted and that he would be mistreated or killed if he returned. He nowhere identified what errors, factual or legal, the IJ purportedly made and never described the facts underlying his objections to the IJ's decision.

I thus would hold that the BIA's summary dismissal of Padilla's appeal did not violate Padilla's procedural due process rights. While I might agree with the majority's assessment that the BIA should continue to improve its forms, the Constitution does not require the BIA to make improvements on a form that already provides at least minimal satisfactory notice. See Vancouver, 820 F.2d at 1364.

I thus respectfully dissent.

Notes

[1] The majority misreads Nazakat to reach the opposite conclusion, asserting that Nazakat "exuded discomfort with the idea that, taken alone, the Notice of Appeal Form adequately apprises immigrants of the relevant specificity requirements." [Opinion at 3431.] This analysis of the gestalt of the Tenth Circuit's opinion is simply wrong. Nowhere in Nazakat does the Tenth Circuit criticize or express dissatisfaction with form I-290A. Instead, without mentioning the instructions on form I-290A, the court simply held that an IJ's warning to Nazakat was sufficient notice.

[2] The majority also observes that Immigration and Naturalization Service ("INS") regulations regarding the appeal requirements for forms EOIR-26 and I-290A are confusing. Padilla, however, does not claim that he was misled by, or has ever read, these regulations. In fact, at oral argument he made the opposite contention that pro se immigrants cannot be expected to be familiar with the regulations and decisions of the INS and BIA. Further, the cases cited by the majority, Vlaicu v. INS, 998 F.2d 758 (9th Cir. 1993), and Shamsi v. INS, 998 F.2d 761 (9th Cir.1993), are inapposite. In those cases the court remanded to the BIA because both INS forms and INS regulations misled petitioners into believing that they had timely appealed. Here, however, form EOIR-26 simply is not misleading.

Judge O'Scannlain's special concurrence in Chlorine Institute, Inc. v. California Highway Patrol (July 11, 1994)

O'SCANNLAIN, Circuit Judge, specially concurring:

The result of this case is an unfortunate defeat of the legitimate interests of the people of California who wish to protect themselves from the risks of hazardous materials. Nevertheless, with reluctance and based solely on the binding precedent of our court's decision in Southern Pacific Transportation Co. v. Public Service Commission of Nevada, 909 F.2d 352 (9th Cir.1990), I must concur in the court's opinion.

Although I believe that Southern Pacific dictates that the court affirm the district court's ruling that California's regulation is preempted by the Hazardous Materials Transportation Uniform Safety Amendments, I regret the result and the implications it carries for federalism. Our Constitution is based on a healthy respect for the sovereignty of the state. As Chief Justice John Marshall observed: "The genius and character of the [federal] government seem to be, that its action is to be applied to all the external concerns of the nation, and to those internal concerns which affect the states generally; but not to those which are completely within a particular state, which do not affect other states, and with which it is not necessary to interfere, for the purpose of executing some of the general powers of the government." Gibbons v. Ogden, 22 U.S. 1, 86, 9 Wheat. 1, 195, 6 L.Ed. 23 (1824). State sovereignty is only to be infringed when necessary. Goldstein v. California, 412 U.S. 546, 554, 93 S.Ct. 2303, 2308-09, 37 L.Ed.2d 163 (1973). "Necessary" should entail a higher hurdle than a mere stated desire for uniformity because the diminution of state rights does not come without a cost.

Justice O'Connor has repeatedly articulated the history and purposes behind our federalist structure. Federalism "assures a decentralized government that will be more sensitive to the diverse needs of a heterogenous society; it increases opportunity for citizen involvement in democratic processes; it allows for more innovation and experimentation in government; and it makes government more responsive by putting the States in competition for a mobile citizenry." Gregory v. Ashcroft, 501 U.S. 452, 458, 111 S.Ct. 2395, 2399, 115 L.Ed.2d 410 (1991).

The effect of the erosion of state authority is particularly ironic in the area of environmental regulation. Within our federal system, states are intended to be laboratories of experimentation in which various policies are debated, implemented, and refined. The modern environmental movement started in the states. The federal government has followed the lead of the states, evaluating different state programs and borrowing the best ideas in order to form a comprehensive federal law. It is incongruous that in adopting the ideas that states have already developed, federal law should prevent further innovation by prohibiting states from expanding their environmental programs, be they regulation of hazardous materials transportation or other initiatives. By preempting state authority in this case, we effectively eliminate the ability of states to develop new and better ways of protecting the public health, safety, and environment. And we prevent innovative state programs from percolating up to the federal level.

At oral argument counsel for the Chlorine Institute made the curious assertion that the Hazardous Materials Transportation Uniform Safety Act did not constitute 100% preemption of the regulation of hazardous materials by the receiving state. Yet he argued, persuasively, that the issue was whether the state regulation would violate the principle of "uniformity." But for Southern Pacific, I would remand this case for a factfinding determination by the trial court in California as to whether the state regulations were indeed an obstacle to national uniformity. On a clean slate, they may be or they may be not. In any event, it is bleak consolation to be offered recourse to a federally-constituted board sitting in Washington, D.C. for responsive resolution of California's legitimate safety concerns in this case.

Judge O'Scannlain's dissent in Beno v. Shalala (July 13, 1994)

O'SCANNLAIN, Circuit Judge, dissenting:

I respectfully dissent. For the reasons expressed in Judge Levi's well-crafted memorandum of decision and order (unpublished), I would affirm. Given the extremely deferential standard under which we review the Secretary's decisions under 42 U.S.C. § 1315, I believe that the agency record provides more than sufficient support for the Secretary's waiver.

As the court's opinion rightly states, an agency's decision is arbitrary and capricious, and may be reversed, only if:

the agency has relied on factors which Congress has not intended it to consider, entirely failed to consider an important aspect of the problem, offered an explanation for its decision that runs counter to the evidence before the agency, or is so implausible that it could not be ascribed to a difference in view or the product of agency expertise.

Motor Vehicle Mfr. Ass'n v. State Farm Ins., 463 U.S. 29, 44, 103 S.Ct. 2856, 2867, 77 L.Ed.2d 443 (1983). The court misconstrues this rule. It fails to recognize that the rule severely narrows the scope of this court's review. Recall the Supreme Court's language: "entirely failed" and "so implausible." These are words of extremes; they indicate that an agency decision should be reversed only in the rare case when it is utterly unsupported by the record.

This is not such a case. Rather, the instant proceeding is very similar to Aguayo v. Richardson, 473 F.2d 1090 (2d Cir.1973), the only other appellate case to review the Secretary's waiver of federal requirements under Section 1315 and approval of an experimental welfare project. In Aguayo, as here, the Secretary approved New York's proposed welfare program without a statement of the grounds for its decision. Id. at 1103. Nevertheless, Judge Henry J. Friendly, writing for the court, concluded that "[w]e are satisfied that the materials before the Secretary sufficed for `a consideration of the relevant factors' by him and that there was no `clear error of judgment' on his part." Id. at 1106 (quoting Citizens to Preserve Overton Park, Inc. v. Volpe, 401 U.S. 402, 426, 91 S.Ct. 814, 851, 28 L.Ed.2d 136 (1971)).

The majority attempts to distinguish Aguayo because the Aguayo agency record included not only the plaintiffs' objections to the welfare plan, but also a memorandum prepared by the state responding to these objections. This is both true and irrelevant. Although California did not similarly respond to the appellants' objections, the agency record does include extensive information on the proposed program. Besides California's application for the waiver, the Secretary had before her the appellants' "voluminous materials" about the claimed harms the program would cause. Here, as in Aguayo, the Secretary had sufficient data — including information and arguments supporting both sides of the dispute — for a consideration of the relevant factors in making her decision. I would not presume, as the majority does, that the Secretary simply ignored these materials. The lack of a memorandum from the state responding to the appellants' materials means nothing. Nor would I presume, as the majority infers, that the record is underdeveloped. Quoting Judge Friendly once again, "the statute ... does not require that, before the Secretary approves an experiment, every i must be dotted and every t crossed." Id. at 1107.

Further, the Supreme Court has held that a reviewing court may "uphold a decision of less than ideal clarity if the agency's path may reasonably be discerned." Motor Vehicle, 463 U.S. at 43, 103 S.Ct. at 2867. The Secretary's path is discernible here. She was presented with information and arguments for and against the waiver. She accepted California's position and granted the waiver. This court is not empowered to review the merits of that decision. It certainly has no power to nit-pick nor second guess the policy judgment inherent in the scheme.

Because the extremely deferential standard for reviewing the agency's process controls the decision in this case, I need not comment on other issues discussed in the court's opinion.

Judge O'Scannlain's dissent in Chitkin v. Lincoln Nat. Ins. Co. (Dist. Court, SD California) (March 2, 1995)

O'SCANNLAIN, Circuit Judge, dissenting:

We are faced with a reimbursement provision of an insurance policy, issued as part of an ERISA plan, that we all agree is rather poorly drafted. The majority believes, however, that there is only one reasonable interpretation of the provision and therefore reverses and orders that judgment be entered in favor of the insurance company that drafted the provision. I cannot agree with the majority that the insurer's interpretation of the provision is reasonable. For that reason, I respectfully dissent.

To recapitulate, the provision at issue here provides, in pertinent part, that:

Payment made for charges must be returned to Lincoln National if:

. . . . .

2. a third party is determined to be liable for such charges.

If an individual insured under the policy has

a. medical or dental charges ...

as a result of the negligence or intentional act of a third party, and makes a claim to Lincoln National for benefits under the policy for such charges ..., the insured individual (or legal representative of minor ...) must agree in writing to repay Lincoln National from any amount of money received by the insured individual from the third party, or its insurer....

The repayment agreement will be binding upon the insured individual (or legal representative of a minor ...) whether:

a. the payment received from the third party, or its insurer, is the result of:

...

3) a compromise settlement

(Emphasis added). While this provision is far from pellucid, it is clear that the insured "must agree in writing to repay Lincoln National from any amount of money received by the insured individual from the third party, or its insurer." Once signed, this repayment agreement is binding on the insured.

I must confess to grave doubts when an insurance company tells me that express language in an ERISA plan drafted by that company serves no true purpose and is to be ignored. At oral argument before this court, Lincoln National was unable to identify for us the purpose underlying the requirement that a repayment agreement be executed by the insured. In fact, Lincoln National insisted that the requirement that a written repayment agreement be executed was merely an "historical relic" which we should disregard. I find Lincoln National's argument rather unpersuasive.

The district court read the reimbursement provision to require execution of a repayment agreement as a prerequisite to recovery. Accordingly, the district court held that Lincoln National's failure to request that the Chitkins sign a repayment agreement prevented the insurer from recovering under this provision of the ERISA plan.[1] The majority concludes that the district court's interpretation of the provision is unreasonable. To reach such a conclusion, the majority must agree with Lincoln National that the express requirement that the insured sign a repayment agreement, quoted above, is of no import. We are told, instead, that the only language that matters is that which suggests a general obligation to reimburse Lincoln National arises whenever payment is received from a third party. However, the language of the provision expressly indicates that the insured is obligated to sign a repayment agreement. Thus, I cannot agree with Lincoln National's characterization of the reimbursement provision.

We often apply the axiom that when the terms of an insurance policy are ambiguous they are construed against the insurer and in favor of the insured. See Commercial Union Ins. Co. v. Sponholz, 866 F.2d 1162, 1163 (9th Cir.1989). Lincoln National suggests that such a presumption carries no force when we interpret a provision in an ERISA plan. Regardless of the validity of that presumption in this context, Lincoln National agrees that we are to "interpret terms in ERISA insurance policies in an ordinary and popular sense as would a person of average intelligence and experience." Evans v. Safeco Life Ins. Co., 916 F.2d 1437, 1441 (9th Cir.1990) (quotation omitted). Here, the reimbursement provision clearly suggests that execution of a written repayment obligation is a prerequisite to reimbursement. I believe that a person of average intelligence and experience would not suspect that the written repayment agreement is merely a meaningless relic. In short, I believe the district court's interpretation of the reimbursement provision was reasonable.

Furthermore, the majority argues that the ambiguous language does serve a purpose, indeed that it is a condition precedent. Ironically, it took the majority to do what Lincoln National itself could not: come up with a justification for its own sloppy contractual language. The majority asserts that the language is a condition precedent but it has created this post hoc rationalization out of whole cloth. Lincoln National never even argued that the language was a condition precedent. Therefore, it is straining credulity to divine that the parties had this justification in mind when they signed this contract. It is incorrect to grant summary judgment to Lincoln National based on a contract interpretation which even it never envisioned.

Not only do I disagree with the majority that Lincoln National's interpretation is reasonable, I also believe that the majority should have remanded this case for trial rather than ordering summary judgment entered in favor of Lincoln National. See Evanston Ins. Co. v. Fred A. Tucker & Co., Inc., 872 F.2d 278, 279 (9th Cir.1989) ("if, on the face of the contract, two reasonable and fair interpretations are possible, an ambiguity exists"); International Brotherhood of Elec. Workers v. Southern Cal. Edison Co., 880 F.2d 104,

107 (9th Cir.1989) ("When the meaning of an agreement is ambiguous on its face and contrary references as to the intent are possible an issue of material fact exists for which summary judgment ordinarily is inappropriate.") The best that can be said for the policy provision before us is that it is ambiguous. Thus, summary judgment in favor of Lincoln National is inappropriate.

I would go further. I would affirm. It is, it seems to me, more than reasonable to assume that the written repayment agreement requirement exists for a purpose. Thus, I believe that Lincoln National's interpretation, requiring us to read that obligation out of the provision, is simply unreasonable. I refuse to treat the express language of a provision drafted by a sophisticated insurance company as mere surplusage, especially where that language can only confuse plan participants. If the repayment agreement is truly a relic, entirely irrelevant to the insured's reimbursement obligation as Lincoln National contends, then Lincoln National should remove it from the reimbursement provision. See Slottow v. American Casualty Co., 10 F.3d 1355, 1358 (9th Cir.1993). Under these circumstances, I am particularly unsympathetic to Lincoln National's characterization.

Thus, while I join my colleagues in condemning the sloppy drafting of this reimbursement provision, I would do more than express disapproval. I see no reason to rescue Lincoln National from its own careless drafting.

I respectfully dissent.

Notes

[1] Presumably, if the company had requested that the Chitkins sign a repayment agreement prior to its payment of benefits or termination of their coverage and the Chitkins had refused, the Chitkins would have breached the provision and would be liable. The Chitkins concede as much in their brief. Thus, Lincoln National is not left without a remedy if it pays benefits before the execution of a repayment agreement. To receive reimbursement, it must simply request compliance with the provision's requirement before terminating coverage.

Judge O'Scannlain's partial dissent in Leslie Salt Co. v. US (May 22, 1995)

O'SCANNLAIN, Circuit Judge, dissenting in part:

I respectfully dissent from Part IV of the majority opinion.

Section 309(d) of the Clean Water Act ("the Act") provides:

Any person who violates [one of the enumerated sections of the Act] shall be subject to a civil penalty not to exceed $25,000 per day for each violation.

33 U.S.C. § 1319(d) (emphasis added). The majority reads this language to mean that civil penalties are mandatory for proven violations of the Act. If section 309(d) had provided "Any person who violates ... shall pay a civil penalty," I would readily agree with the majority's interpretation. However, it does not so provide, and we cannot ignore the three words following the word "shall." To do otherwise "violates the settled rule that a

statute must, if possible, be construed in such a fashion that every word has some operative effect." United States v. Nordic Village, Inc., 503 U.S. 30, 35, 112 S.Ct. 1011, 1015, 117 L.Ed.2d 181 (1991).

Section 309(d) did not use the words "shall pay"; it used the words "shall be subject to." The latter phrase is synonymous with "shall be liable to" or "shall be answerable to." Black's Law Dictionary 1278 (5th ed. 1979). Read literally, the section merely states that a violator is liable to be assessed a civil penalty, not that he or she must be. In other words, civil penalties are discretionary. Several district courts facing this question have come to this conclusion as well. See, e.g., Hawaii's Thousand Friends v. Honolulu, 149 F.R.D. 614, 617 (D.Haw.1993); United States v. Bradshaw, 541 F.Supp. 880, 883 (D.Mass.1981). See also United States v. Winchester Mun. Util., 944 F.2d 301, 306 (6th Cir.1991) (suggesting that district courts that found civil penalties discretionary are correct).

If Congress had meant civil penalties to be mandatory, it could have written section 309(d) to state that a violator "shall pay" a civil penalty. Indeed, these are precisely the words it has chosen in numerous civil penalty provisions. See, e.g., 7 U.S.C. § 1596(a) ("Any person who ... violates any provision of this chapter ... shall pay a fine of not more than $1,000 ...") (emphasis added); 26 U.S.C. § 6038(b)(1) ("If any person fails to furnish ... any information ... required under [this section], such person shall pay a penalty of $1,000 ...") (emphasis added).

In addition, to the extent it might be relevant, the Act's legislative history reveals no congressional intent whatsoever to make civil penalties mandatory. The House Report to the 1972 Amendments simply states that "the courts are authorized to apply appropriate civil penalties under Section 309(d)." H.R.Rep. No. 911, 92nd Cong., 2d Sess. 133 (1972) (emphasis added). It does not suggest that Congress believed the courts are required to do so.

Even if section 309(d) were found to be ambiguous, the rule of lenity should counsel us to choose the interpretation least likely to impose penalties unintended by Congress. See National Org. for Women, Inc. v. Scheidler, ____ U.S. ____, ____, 114 S.Ct. 798, 806, 127 L.Ed.2d 99 (1994). The rule of lenity has not been limited to criminal statutes, particularly when the civil sanctions in question are punitive in character. See United States v. Thompson/Center Arms Co., 504 U.S. 505, 518 n. 10, 112 S.Ct. 2102, 2110 n. 10, 119 L.Ed.2d 308 (1992). The penalties contemplated by section 309(d) clearly have punitive purposes. Tull v. United States, 481 U.S. 412, 422-23, 107 S.Ct. 1831, 1838, 95 L.Ed.2d 365 (1987). Thus, section 309(d) should not be read to require civil penalties in all cases but only where the district court, in its discretion, finds them appropriate.

Undoubtedly, civil penalties will be imposed in most cases of proven violations of the Act; however, by leaving them to the district court's discretion, more appropriate remedies may be fashioned in exceptional cases. For example, the district court may encounter situations in which the purposes of the Act are better served by seeing to it that the violator undertakes comprehensive corrective actions. See, e.g., Gwaltney v.

Chesapeake Bay Found., 484 U.S. 49, 60-61, 108 S.Ct. 376, 382-83, 98 L.Ed.2d 306 (1987) (suggesting that civil penalties might be inappropriate where violator agrees to take some extreme corrective action).

I would therefore reverse the district court's "order regarding remedies" to the extent that it held that section 309(d) of the Act mandated that a civil monetary penalty be imposed for every violation of the Act.

Judge O'Scannlain's dissent in Moore v. Calderon (May 26, 1995)

O'SCANNLAIN, Circuit Judge, dissenting:

I respectfully disagree that we should order the release pending appeal of a double murderer who was sentenced to death by a jury of his peers and whose conviction was affirmed in a lengthy decision by the California Supreme Court.

I have no doubt that Moore's habeas corpus petition raises substantial constitutional questions, as identified in the district court's opinion. Nor can I condone the state's failure to file this motion for stay until almost the last minute before Moore's scheduled release date. Nonetheless, I believe that principles of comity and federalism require us to afford the state the opportunity for full appellate consideration of the district court's decision. Thus, instead of rushing to judgment, the appropriate course would be to permit full briefing and oral argument on the merits before taking further action. I am convinced that we can expedite the process sufficiently to minimize any prejudice to Moore while still providing the state the careful appellate review properly due it.

However, the majority has determined that a stay is inappropriate because the state has not made a sufficiently strong showing that it is likely to succeed on the merits pursuant to Hilton v. Braunskill, 481 U.S. 770, 776, 107 S.Ct. 2113, 2119, 95 L.Ed.2d 724 (1987). Although it is very possible that Moore's reliance on Fritz v. Spalding, 682 F.2d 782 (9th Cir.1982), is well-placed, I am not willing effectively to decide that California violated Moore's constitutional rights based on only the most cursory review in this court, without the benefit of appropriate briefing, let alone oral argument. The California courts which examined and upheld Moore's conviction are entitled to a more considered treatment. Indeed, the fact that the district court proceedings consumed almost three-and-one-half years indicates that the issues are deserving of careful analysis by this court.

In addition, by focusing solely on the state's likelihood of success on the merits, the majority ignores the other factors that the Hilton Court deemed worthy of consideration in deciding a motion for a stay. For instance, the Court explicitly stated that a court may take into account the "possibility of flight" and "the risk that the prisoner will pose a danger to the public if released." Id. at 777, 107 S.Ct. at 2119. Further, we may consider the state's interest in continuing custody over the defendant. That interest "will be strongest where the remaining portion of the sentence to be served is long." Id. Here, these factors weigh strongly in favor of granting the stay.

Moore has been convicted of two coldblooded murders. A jury determined that

Moore and two cohorts bound and gagged Mr. and Mrs. Robert Crumb of Long Beach, California, robbed them, and then brutally beat and stabbed them to death. Moore has also been identified as the murderer of a Woolworth's store manager during another robbery in Kansas. Moore was accused of abducting the manager at gunpoint, and, after ignoring the manager's pleas for his life, shooting him to death. That Moore poses a danger to the public is without question.

Further, Moore is under a death sentence. Consequently, he poses a substantial risk of flight as he has nothing to lose and everything to gain by fleeing. Releasing Moore under such circumstances is likely to have disastrous consequences. Finally, because Moore's sentence is so severe, the state has a substantial interest in continuing to confine him.

I recognize that a district court's finding of a constitutional violation is not a matter to be taken lightly. However, the Supreme Court has set forth common-sense considerations to guide a federal court in determining whether or not to order release of a state prisoner before it can give full consideration to the merits. Such considerations are compelling here and require grant of the state's motion for stay pending appeal.

Judge O'Scannlain's dissent in Gotro v. R & B Realty Group (Nov 14, 1995)

O'SCANNLAIN, Circuit Judge, dissenting:

The statute at issue, 28 U.S.C. § 1447(c), sets forth procedures for plaintiffs to remand a case to state court when the defendant improperly removed the case to federal court. Of relevance here, that section provides that "[a]n order remanding the case may require payment of just costs and any actual expenses, including attorney fees, incurred as a result of the removal." The majority maintains that under such language a district court must award attorneys' fees to a litigant who had not actually incurred an obligation to pay those fees. I respectfully dissent from that portion of the opinion.

This issue appears to be one of first impression. The majority points to Moore v. Permanente Medical Group, Inc., 981 F.2d 443 (9th Cir.1992), where we awarded attorneys' fees under section 1447(c) to an attorney who was hired on a contingency fee basis; however, that case did not present the question of statutory interpretation at issue here. Here, the question is whether a statute which provides for the award of "any actual expenses" (expressly including attorneys' fees) that are "incurred" as a result of an improper removal, contemplates an award of fees to a plaintiff who had no obligation to pay for legal services performed in connection with the removal. I believe that if any weight is to be given to the words chosen by Congress, then to ask the question is to answer it.

It must be assumed that when Congress chose the words "just costs and any actual expenses, including attorney fees, incurred as a result of the removal," it meant what it said. Consequently, the statute means that a defendant who improperly removes a case to federal court may be liable for costs but only for such attorneys' fees that the plaintiff is actually obligated to pay as a result of the removal episode. I find support for this construction of section 1447(c) in a comparison with other federal statutes awarding attorneys' fees.

The language of section 1447(c) is quite different from that of numerous other federal fee-shifting statutes, which provide for an award of "a reasonable attorney's fee" to the prevailing party without any further qualification.[1] Under most such statutes, reasonable attorneys' fees are expressly included as "costs" or separately listed. My research has revealed no other federal fee-shifting statute which limits attorney fee awards, "reasonable" or otherwise, to "actual expenses ... incurred." Obviously, when the statute permits an award of "reasonable" attorneys' fees, it makes no difference whether a plaintiff has a contingency fee agreement with his or her attorney, and courts have devised various formulas for determining what is a "reasonable fee." See Hensley v. Eckerhart, 461 U.S. 424, 433-37, 103 S.Ct. 1933, 1939-41, 76 L.Ed.2d 40 (1983); Kerr v. Screen Extras Guild, Inc., 526 F.2d 67, 69-70 (9th Cir.1975), cert. denied, 425 U.S. 951, 96 S.Ct. 1726, 48 L.Ed.2d 195 (1976). In drafting section 1447(c), however, Congress elected to diverge both from the "reasonable attorneys' fee" language almost universally used and the inclusion of such fees as costs. Given this divergence, I cannot help but conclude that Congress' choice of language in section 1447(c) was significant.

Gotro first argues that the contingency fee agreement that she entered into did impose on her an obligation to pay attorneys' fees under circumstances such as this one. Gotro points to the "Statutory Fees" provision of her contingency fee agreement, particularly the provision that "all attorney fees that may be recovered from defendants, by settlement or litigation, pursuant to any law ... shall belong to the attorney." Gotro maintains that the quoted provision is an assignment of a contingent benefit under contract law. According to Gotro, the provision means that as soon as the contingency occurs — that is, when attorneys' fees are awarded — then she incurred the obligation of paying her attorneys the fees that were awarded. The fact that she arranged to discharge that obligation by an advance assignment, she argues, does not change the fact that upon the occurrence of the contingency, the obligation for payment was incurred.

Such an interpretation of Gotro's contingency fee agreement is implausible. The fact is, if Gotro were eventually to recover damages, she would owe her attorneys the same percentage of the damages regardless of whether the case had previously been improperly removed. Similarly, if Gotro were later to recover nothing, then she would owe her attorneys nothing, despite their having contested the improper removal. Thus, it is clear that Gotro incurred no expenses (including attorney fees) as a result of the removal and consequently was entitled to no award under section 1447(c).

Gotro next contends that section 1447(c) was intended to deter improper removals and that this purpose would be poorly served if the statute were read to eliminate a defendant's obligation to pay attorneys' fees for improperly removed cases whenever the defendant's opponent was represented by an attorney on a contingency fee. There are two obvious replies to such contention. First, given the clear language of the statute, it must have been designed primarily to reimburse plaintiffs for unnecessary litigation costs. Thus, plaintiffs who actually incur litigation costs should be reimbursed while those who have not incurred any costs should have no such claim. Second, an attorney who is entering into a contingency fee arrangement with a client can easily draft the contingency fee agreement to provide that in the event of a section 1447(c) prevailing result, the client shall be obligated to pay actual fees. Such a provision will, in turn, trigger the defendant's obligation for attorneys' fees under section 1447(c) and thus will make the attorney whole and will not unfairly prejudice the client.

In this case, however, Gotro had not incurred an obligation to pay her attorneys any fees as a result of the removal;[2] thus, I would hold that the district court erred in making an attorney fee award to her.

Notes

[1] See, e.g., 5 U.S.C. § 5596(b)(1)(A)(ii) ("[Plaintiff] ... is entitled ... to receive ... reasonable attorney fees related to the personnel action."); 11 U.S.C. § 523(d) ("The court shall grant judgment ... for the costs of, and a reasonable attorney's fee for the proceeding."); 12 U.S.C. § 3417(a)(4) ("[Defendant] is liable to the customer ... in an amount equal to ... the costs of the action together with reasonable attorney's fees as determined by the court."); 15 U.S.C. § 78u(h)(7)(A)(iii) ("[Plaintiff is entitled to] ... the costs of the action and reasonable attorney's fees as determined by the court."); 15 U.S.C. § 1640(a) ("[Defendant is liable for] ... the costs of the action, together with a reasonable attorney's fee as determined by the court."); 15 U.S.C. § 1692K(a)(3) ("[Defendant is liable for] ... the costs of the action, together with a reasonable attorney's fee as determined by the court."); 16 U.S.C. § 1540(g)(4) ("The court ... may award costs of litigation (including reasonable attorney and expert witness fees) to any party."); 18 U.S.C. § 1964(c) ("[Plaintiff] shall recover threefold the damages he sustains and the cost of the suit, including a reasonable attorney's fee."); 18 U.S.C. § 2520(c) ("Plaintiff shall ... be entitled to recover ... a reasonable attorney's fee and other litigation costs reasonably incurred."); 29 U.S.C. § 216(b) ("The court shall ... allow a reasonable attorney's fee to be paid by the defendant, and costs of the action."); 42 U.S.C. § 1988(b) ("The court ... may allow ... a reasonable attorney's fee as part of the costs."); 42 U.S.C. § 2000e-5(k) ("The court may allow ... a reasonable attorney's fee (including expert fees) as part of the costs...."); 42 U.S.C. § 6305(d) ("The court ... may award costs of litigation (including reasonable attorney and expert witness fees) to any party....").

[2] Gotro's contingency fee agreement obligates her to pay "Litigation Costs and Expenses." Thus, of course, Gotro should be entitled to be reimbursed for the costs of photocopying, amounting to $47.55, that are detailed in the affidavit, under either the "just costs" or "actual expenses ... incurred" portions of section 1447(c).

Judge O'Scannlain's dissent from rejecting rehearing en banc in Northwest Environmental Advocates v. City of Portland (Jan 24, 1996)

O'SCANNLAIN, Circuit Judge, joined by HALL, T.G. NELSON, and KLEINFELD, Circuit Judges, dissenting from order rejecting suggestion for rehearing en banc:

By failing to rehear this case en banc, we have significantly reshaped federal environmental law, without consent of Congress, to the curious end that any citizen will now be permitted to bring a lawsuit at government expense for the enforcement of state water quality standards that have not been translated into effluent limitations in federal permits. Such unwarranted expansion of citizen standing conflicts with the plain language of the Clean Water Act and with prior decisions of this circuit and others.

It should go without saying that the environment faces real and growing dangers that warrant protective measures and challenge us to develop innovative solutions. Nevertheless, by allowing citizens to enforce standards that Congress specifically allocated to government agencies to monitor, the court has upset the delicate balance envisioned by Congress in its promulgation of the current enforcement regime for environmental law. The result promises to invite excessive, costly, and counterproductive citizen suits, funded by the taxpayers, for the enforcement of standards that are imprecise and astronomically costly to the municipalities affected.

The Clean Water Act allows citizens to enforce effluent limitations contained in federal permits, but the Act does not permit citizens to enforce general water quality provisions. 33 U.S.C. § 1365. There is more than a technical distinction involved; there are significant consequences at stake. Water quality standards address the level of pollutants found in a body of water, while effluent limitations focus on the level of pollutants in the effluent discharged into a body of water by a particular discharger. As Judge Kleinfeld notes in his well-articulated dissent, "[w]ater quality standards are a useful device for government enforcement authorities ... because they provide standards for effluent limitations [but water quality standards] are too uncertain and amorphous ... for use against specific polluters." Northwest Environmental Advocates v. Portland, 56 F.3d 979, 992 (9th Cir.1995) (Kleinfeld, J., dissenting) ("NWEA II"). While state water quality standards may serve as an important source of authority for a state to impose additional pollution control requirements, they should not be used as a vehicle for flooding the federal courts with citizen suits against permittees who are meeting the specific requirements (i.e. effluent limitations) outlined in their permits.

In its original opinion released more than two years ago, the same panel, writing for the court, held the exact opposite of what it now holds. There, the then-majority opined that citizens do not have a private right of action to enforce water quality standards contained in Portland's permit because such standards do not constitute an "effluent standard or limitation" under 33 U.S.C. § 1365(a) and (f) and ruled for the City of Portland. Northwest Environmental Advocates v. Portland, 11 F.3d 900 (9th Cir.1993) ("NWEA I"). Judge Pregerson dissented.

The citizen plaintiffs then filed a suggestion for rehearing en banc which failed to receive a majority of votes of the active judges of the full court. On April 25, 1994, the panel resumed control of the case. Instead, however, of entering the order denying the petition for rehearing and rejecting the suggestion for rehearing en banc, and thereby allowing the mandate to issue seven days later under FRAP 41(a), the panel held on to the case and reconsidered its holding in light of PUD No. 1 of Jefferson County v. Washington Department of Ecology, ____ U.S. ___, 114 S.Ct. 1900, 128 L.Ed.2d 716 (1994) ("Jefferson County"), which the Supreme Court decided one month after rejection of the en banc call in NWEA I. Relying on Jefferson County, the panel developed a new majority and thereupon vacated its original opinion and substituted a new one holding that citizens indeed do have standing under the Clean Water Act to enforce water quality standards. NWEA II, 56 F.3d 979, filed June 7, 1995.

In my view, the panel erred by reversing its original position, because Jefferson County simply does not support such reversal and the panel's new holding conflicts not only with a prior decision of our own court, but also with the law of other circuits. The court now cites Jefferson County in support of the view that Congress intended to confer standing on citizens to enforce water quality standards. NWEA II, 56 F.3d at 987. However, as the majority eventually acknowledges, id. at 988, and as the dissent emphasizes, Jefferson County has nothing to do with citizens' standing. Id. at 990 (Kleinfeld, J., dissenting) ("Jefferson County does not involve a citizens' suit, says nothing about citizens' suits, and implies nothing about citizens' suits.").

Instead of addressing citizen standing to enforce a permit condition, Jefferson County concerns a local utility district's appeal of a stream flow condition imposed by the state as part of the state's certification of the district's application for a federal permit to build a hydroelectric power plant. ____ U.S. at ____-____, 114 S.Ct. at 1907-08. The Supreme Court held that "States may condition certification [of projects] upon any limitations necessary to ensure compliance with state water quality standards or any other `appropriate requirement of State law,'" and that the minimum flow condition imposed by Washington was an appropriate requirement of state law. Id. at ____, 114 S.Ct. at 1910. This holding merely indicates that states may impose certain water quality requirements as conditions for granting the state certification that must be obtained by an applicant seeking a federal permit. In no way does this holding support the notion that citizens have a private right of action to challenge permit conditions that have not been translated into effluent limitations.

Section 505 of the Clean Water Act authorizes federal jurisdiction over citizen suits "(1) against any person ... who is alleged to be in violation of (A) an effluent standard or limitation under this chapter...." 33 U.S.C. § 1365(a)(1). In defining "effluent standard or limitation," the section refers to various discharge-related limitations that may be imposed by other sections of the Act or by a federal permit. 33 U.S.C. § 1365(f); see 33 U.S.C. § 1365(f)(6) ("effluent standard or limitation" means "a permit or condition thereof"); Jefferson County, ____ U.S. at ____, ____-____, 114 S.Ct. at 1915, 1916-17 (Thomas, J., dissenting) (describing discharge-related limitations in the Act).

Since the citizen-plaintiffs in this litigation allege violations, not of effluent limitations, but rather of a state water quality provision contained in Portland's permit, the citizens fail to meet the Clean Water Act's requirements for citizen standing. By holding otherwise, NWEA II conflicts with our decision in Oregon Natural Resources Council v. U.S. Forest Service, 834 F.2d 842 (9th Cir.1987) ("ONRC"), in which we stated that citizens may file suit to enforce permit limitations derived from water quality standards, but not water quality standards themselves. Id. at 850 ("[E]ffluent limitations may be derived from state water quality standards and may be enforced when included in a discharger's permit. We agree with defendants that it is not the water quality standards themselves that are enforceable....").

Granted, ONRC involved citizens attempting to enforce state water quality standards under 33 U.S.C. § 1311(b)(1)(C), as opposed to state water quality standards contained in a permit. However, the court's conclusion that the Clean Water Act forbids citizens from suing to enforce water quality standards under section 1311(b)(1)(C) may logically be extended to suits by citizens to enforce water quality standards in permits. See NWEA I, 11 F.3d at 907 (citing authorities indicating that "whenever courts have been faced with the question, the answer has been that citizen suits cannot be used to enforce water quality standards").

As the same panel declared in NWEA I, "[The plaintiffs] have not been able to find a single case in which a court held that citizen suits could be used to enforce water quality standards, whether the water quality standards were incorporated in a NPDES [National Pollution Discharge Elimination System] permit or not." Id. at 907-08; see also id. at 909-11 (outlining legislative history supporting conclusion that citizens lack standing to enforce water quality standards that have not been translated into effluent limitations).

No other circuit has recognized a right of citizens to sue for the enforcement of state water quality standards contained in permits. In fact, other circuits have explicitly and implicitly ruled out such suits. See Save Our Community v. United States Environmental Protection Agency, 971 F.2d 1155, 1162 (5th Cir.1992) ("Without the violation of either (1) an effluent standard or limitation under the CWA, or (2) an order issued with respect to these standards and limitations, the district court lacks jurisdiction to act [in a citizen suit]."); United States v. Hooker Chemicals & Plastics Corp., 749 F.2d 968, 979 (2d Cir. 1984) ("`[a]uthority granted to citizens to bring enforcement actions under this section is limited to effluent standards or limitations established administratively under the Act'" (quoting S.Rep. No. 414, 92d Cong., 2d Sess. 80 (1972), reprinted in 1972 U.S.C.C.A.N. 3668, 3747)).

Furthermore, the holding in NWEA II directly conflicts with the Second Circuit's decision in Atlantic States Legal Foundation v. Eastman Kodak, 12 F.3d 353 (2d Cir. 1993), cert. denied, ____ U.S. ____, 115 S.Ct. 62, 130 L.Ed.2d 19 (1994). In Atlantic States, the Second Circuit held that "state regulations, including the provisions of SPDES [State Pollutant Discharge Elimination System] permits, which mandate `a greater scope of coverage than that required' by the federal CWA and its implementing regulations are not enforceable through a citizen suit under 33 U.S.C. § 1365." Id. at 359 (citation omitted). In addition, the court noted:

States may enact stricter standards for wastewater effluents than mandated by the CWA and federal EPA regulations. 33 U.S.C. § 1342(b). These states' standards may be enforced under the CWA by the states or the EPA, 33 U.S.C. § 1342(h), but private citizens have no standing to do so.

Id. at 358.

In short, NWEA II contradicts the plain language of the Clean Water Act, conflicts with a prior decision of this circuit, and creates a needless intercircuit conflict with all courts of appeals that have addressed the issue. The decision establishes a citizens' cause of action that Congress never intended and that no other circuit has felt compelled to recognize.

Failure to rehear this case en banc is a most unfortunate and unsettling misstep in the orderly development of federal environmental law. I respectfully dissent.

Judge O'Scannlain's dissent in Crowder v. Kitagawa (April 30, 1996) [Notes omitted]

O'SCANNLAIN, Circuit Judge, dissenting:

I cannot agree that the State of Hawaii has violated its obligation to blind people under federal law. Because the plaintiffs have failed to offer any evidence to satisfy two of the three elements required to be proven by the plain language of the statute at issue in this case, I respectfully dissent.

I

To state a claim under section 202 of Title II of the Americans with Disabilities Act ("ADA"), 42 U.S.C. § 12132, a plaintiff bears the burden of proving: (1) that he is a "qualified individual with a disability" as defined in section 12131(2); (2) that he was either excluded from participation in or denied the benefits of some public entity's services, programs or activities, or was otherwise discriminated against by the public entity; and (3) that such exclusion, denial of benefits, or discrimination was by reason of the plaintiff's disability. Tyler v. City of Manhattan, 857 F.Supp. 800, 817 (D.Kan.1994) (citation omitted); Concerned Parents to Save Dreher Park Center v. City of West Palm Beach, 846 F.Supp. 986, 990 (S.D.Fla.1994).

As to the first requirement, the blind plaintiffs in this case are clearly disabled. However, it is not clear whether they meet the "qualified" prong because, as noted infra, they have failed to identify a specific program, activity, or benefit for which they are "qualified," i.e. for which they "meet[] the essential eligibility requirements." 42 U.S.C. § 12131(2). Unless the plaintiffs identify such a program, activity, or benefit, this court cannot even determine what the "essential eligibility requirements" are, much less whether the plaintiffs have met them.[1] I need not address this first requirement, however, because in my view the plaintiffs have clearly failed to raise an issue of material fact with regard to either of the last two elements. These two requirements will be discussed in turn.[2]

II

A

The record discloses that the plaintiffs have failed to offer any evidence whatsoever that Hawaii's quarantine has excluded them from participation in, or denied them the benefits of, any specific public entity's services, programs, or activities. As the district court noted, Hawaii's quarantine is a public health measure, and it does not provide any "benefits" to which the plaintiffs could be denied. In addition, to the extent that the quarantine is a "service, program or activity," it is clear that they have been allowed to "participate." The plaintiffs therefore must prove that they have been excluded from, or denied the benefits of, some particular state service, program or activity other than the quarantine.

In opposition to the defendants' summary judgment motion, the plaintiffs filed at least 15 declarations in the district court. One searches these declarations in vain for even a solitary reference to a specific program, activity, or service to which the plaintiffs have been denied access or benefits. The plaintiffs have thus failed to meet their burden of proof. See Lincoln Cercpac v. Health and Hosps. Corp., 920 F.Supp. 488, 498 (S.D.N.Y. Mar. 21, 1996) ("[P]laintiffs here have not defined a service available to the non-disabled that they are being denied by reason of their disability. Accordingly, we find plaintiffs have no substantial likelihood of success on their ADA claims."); Casey v. Lewis, 834 F.Supp. 1569, 1585 (D.Ariz.1993) (plaintiffs failed to establish Rehabilitation Act claim in part because they "did not identify particular programs from which any of the handicapped inmates were excluded because of their handicaps").

In spite of plaintiffs' failure of proof, the majority concludes that "[t]he evidence produced in support of the parties' motions for summary judgment established that the state's quarantine requirement denies visually-impaired persons the ability to make meaningful use of services the state provides." Op. at 1482. There are at least two immediate problems with this conclusion.

First, undoubtedly because the plaintiffs have failed to do so, the majority does not identify a particular state service, program, or activity to which the plaintiffs have been denied benefits or access. Instead, the opinion makes only a broad reference to "a variety of public services, such as public transportation, public parks, government buildings and facilities, and tourist attractions...." Op. at 1485. The court's conclusion that the blind have been denied access to such services is simply unsupported by the record.[3]

Second, the plaintiffs' claims are defeated by their own evidence. In the extremely limited section of their appellate brief addressing this issue, the plaintiffs list a broad range of public programs geared specifically to the blind. After listing these services, they offer only the following argument:

Only blind users of guide dogs allowed to enter Hawaii can benefit from the foregoing. Those unable to travel because of quarantine are foreclosed from them. The blind in Hawaii cannot leave with their guide dogs, thereby preventing them from public services, programs and activities on the mainland U.S.

(Emphasis added.)

Plaintiffs' entire argument on appeal, therefore, boils down to the assertion that the quarantine, by depriving them of access to their guide dogs, deprives them of the ability to travel, and because they cannot travel they are excluded from virtually all public programs provided to the blind.[4] Even assuming that the plaintiffs may use such an argument to overcome their otherwise clear obligation to identify a particular program from which they have been excluded or denied benefits, it is entirely undermined by their admissions that they have traveled, albeit at times with difficulty, without guide dogs.[5] Accordingly, their only argument on this point, i.e. that the quarantine excludes them from participation in or denies them the benefits of all state services, programs, or activities provided to the blind because it makes them unable to travel, simply fails.

I am not unmindful of the difficulties which the plaintiffs may encounter when traveling without their guide dogs. However, the plaintiffs have (1) failed to offer any evidence establishing that they have been denied the benefits of, or participation in, any particular state program, service, or activity, and (2) failed to offer evidence supporting their novel alternative argument that they have been excluded from all such programs because the quarantine prohibits them from traveling. As such, I have no choice but to conclude that they have failed to raise an issue of material fact regarding whether the quarantine violates Title II of the ADA.

B

Plaintiffs have also failed to offer evidence establishing that they have suffered "discrimination" within the meaning of the statute. The Hawaii quarantine is a facially-neutral public health measure of general applicability. Nothing in the legislation or regulations enacting the quarantine creates any classification whatsoever; there is thus no facial discrimination.

The majority, relying in large part on Alexander v. Choate, 469 U.S. 287, 105 S.Ct. 712, 83 L.Ed.2d 661 (1985), states that "[i]t is ... clear that Congress intended the ADA to cover at least some so-called disparate impact cases of discrimination...." Op. at 1483. Applying disparate impact analysis, the majority concludes that "Hawaii's quarantine requirement is a policy, practice or procedure which discriminates against visually-impaired individuals by denying them meaningful access to state services, programs or activities in violation of the ADA." Op. at 1485.[6]

I respectfully disagree both with the majority's application of Choate and also with its finding of discrimination in this case. In Choate, the State of Tennessee proposed to cut back the number of annual inpatient hospital days that the state Medicaid program would pay on behalf of Medicaid recipients. Disabled recipients alleged that the proposal would have a disproportionate effect on the disabled, and that it therefore discriminated against them in violation of section 504 of the Rehabilitation Act. The Supreme Court stated that "[w]hile we reject the boundless notion that all disparate-impact showings constitute prima facie cases under section 504, we assume without deciding that section 504 reaches at least some conduct that has an unjustifiable disparate impact upon the handicapped." Id. at 299, 105 S.Ct. at 719 (emphasis added). Proceeding from that assumption, the Court then stated that "[t]o determine which disparate impacts § 504 might make actionable, the proper starting point is Southeastern Community College v. Davis, 442 U.S. 397, 99 S.Ct. 2361, 60 L.Ed.2d 980 (1979)." Id. at 299-300, 105 S.Ct. at 719-20. "The balance struck in Davis requires that an otherwise qualified handicapped individual must be provided with meaningful access to the benefit that the grantee offers." Id. at 301, 105 S.Ct. at 720.

The Court then examined whether the proposed program would deny the disabled "meaningful access" to Medicaid services in Tennessee, and concluded that it would not:

The 14-day rule challenged in this case is neutral on its face, is not alleged to rest on a discriminatory motive, and does not deny the handicapped access to or exclude them from the particular package of Medicaid services Tennessee has chosen to provide. The State has made the same benefit-14 days of coverage-equally accessible to both handicapped and nonhandicapped persons, and the State is not required to assure the handicapped "adequate health care" by providing them with more coverage than the nonhandicapped.

Id. at 309, 105 S.Ct. at 724.

Rather than supporting the majority's position, the Court's analysis suggests that the ADA does not reach the claim asserted in this case. The quarantine is neutral on its face, and is not alleged to rest on a discriminatory motive. Moreover, as explained infra, the plaintiffs have failed to provide any evidence showing that the quarantine excludes the blind from any public benefit. I therefore disagree with the majority's conclusion that Choate supports the proposition that the ADA reaches the plaintiffs' claim.

It is worth noting that Patton v. TIC United Corp., 77 F.3d 1235 (10th Cir.1996) also suggests that the ADA does not apply here. In Patton, the plaintiff claimed that a Kansas law placing a cap on punitive damage awards was void as superseded by section 202. Applying Choate, the Tenth Circuit concluded that the ADA did not apply to the claim:

Interpreting the Rehabilitation Act, the Supreme Court has held that a facially neutral governmental restriction does not deny "meaningful access" to the disabled simply because disabled persons are more likely to be affected by it. Even if the burden of the .... damage cap falls disproportionately on the disabled, [Choate] requires only that Patton have the same access to a jury determination of damages as everyone else. He did. Because the damages limitation applies to all victorious plaintiffs, Patton was not denied access to a jury determination of damages by reason of disability.

Id. at 1245 (emphasis added) (citations omitted). This reasoning suggests that even if the burden of Hawaii's quarantine is found to fall disproportionately on the blind (a proposition which I discuss in Part III), the ADA is not violated so long as the blind have equal access to their animals as everyone else.[7] This condition is clearly met here. Accordingly, I am persuaded that the ADA does not reach the plaintiffs' discrimination claim.

III

Even assuming that the plaintiffs have raised an issue of material fact regarding whether they were discriminated against, they have failed to offer evidence showing that any such discrimination occurred "by reason of their disability," the remaining hurdle to be overcome.

The ADA defines "disability" in relevant part as "a physical or mental impairment that substantially limits one or more of the major life activities of" an individual. 42 U.S.C. § 12102(2)(A). Properly characterized, therefore, the plaintiffs' disability is their blindness. In order to prevail under Title II, they must therefore show that the quarantine discriminates against them, or denies them access to state benefits, by reason of their blindness. This they have not done.

The primary flaw in the plaintiffs' argument is the erroneous, implicit assumption that dependence upon a guide dog constitutes a "disability" under Title II. For example, the plaintiff classes in this case were defined as follows:

The Plaintiff Vernon Crowder class shall be defined as non-residents of Hawaii who are blind and who desire to freely travel to Hawaii for business and/or pleasure with their certified guide dogs .... The Plaintiff Stephanie Good class shall be defined as residents of Hawaii who are blind and who desire to freely travel for business and/or pleasure from Hawaii to the mainland United States and/or foreign countries and return to Hawaii with their certified guide dogs ....

(Emphasis added). The members of the plaintiff classes thus have two distinguishing characteristics: (1) they are blind, and (2) they desire to travel with their guide dogs. Even assuming arguendo that the quarantine has a disparate impact on the plaintiffs, it does so only because of the latter characteristic.[8] However, in order to state a claim under Title II, the plaintiffs must show that the disparate impact occurred because of the former characteristic; only the former is a "disability" under Title II.

This conclusion is supported by Flight v. Gloeckler, 68 F.3d 61 (2d Cir.1995). The plaintiff in Flight, who suffered from multiple sclerosis and was restricted to a wheelchair, was a client of the New York State Office of Vocational and Educational Services for Individuals with Disabilities ("VESID"). The plaintiff decided to purchase a van, and he petitioned VESID for financial assistance to make necessary modifications to the van. VESID's policies allowed it to spend $10,500 to modify a van for a client who was to able to drive, but only $4,000 if the client planned to be a passenger. VESID found that the plaintiff was too severely disabled to drive, and thus authorized allocation of only $4,000. The plaintiff sued, alleging a violation of both section 504 of the Rehabilitation Act and section 202 of the ADA.

The Second Circuit rejected the plaintiff's claim. After noting that the Rehabilitation Act "does not require all handicapped persons to be provided with identical benefits" but "mandates only that services provided nonhandicapped individuals not be denied [to a disabled person] because he is handicapped," id. at 63-64 (quoting P.C. v. McLaughlin, 913 F.2d 1033, 1041 (2d Cir. 1990)) (emphasis added), the court stated that

"Flight was not denied the additional subsidy `solely by reason of ... his disability' within the meaning of § 504." Id. at 64. The court noted that "[t]he denial of the increased allowance was not based upon Flight's classification as a victim of multiple sclerosis, but rather upon the type of modification that he requested." Id.

In reaching this conclusion, the court rejected a claim similar to the claim implicitly made by the plaintiffs here:

Flight contends that his disability is not multiple sclerosis, but rather an inability to drive, but this argument is unpersuasive. A disability is a "physical or mental impairment," ... i.e., "any physiological disorder or condition ... affecting" the neurological system. Clearly, an inability to drive is not a physiological condition, but rather a result of a physiological condition, viz., Flight's neurological disorder.

Id. (emphasis in original) (citations omitted). The court thus rejected the plaintiff's Rehabilitation Act claim. Importantly, the court rejected his ADA claim on similar grounds:

[The ADA] is inapplicable because the distinction in the present case is not based upon Flight's disability, multiple sclerosis, but rather upon his inability to drive. Thus, VESID does not provide varying services or benefits "on the basis of disability" within the meaning of § 35.130(b)(1)....

Id.

This reasoning is equally applicable here. The plaintiffs' dependence on their guide dogs is, properly considered, a result of their physical impairment, rather than a physical impairment in its own right. Accordingly, even if the quarantine is found to have a disparate impact on the plaintiffs, it does not do so by reason of their disability.

The fact that the quarantine does not discriminate on the basis of blindness is also borne out by the fact that the record is devoid of any allegation or evidence that the quarantine discriminates against blind people generally.[9] Indeed, the plaintiff class members represent only a tiny portion of the blind; reports in various newspapers[10] indicate that only somewhere between 1-5% of the blind use guide dogs.[11] If the quarantine does, as the plaintiffs allege, discriminate or deny state services by reason of blindness, then all people who are blind could constitute members of the plaintiff class and could assert ADA claims. The fact that the plaintiffs have chosen to file suit while other blind individuals have not simply points out that the quarantine does nothing by reason of blindness; it affects the plaintiffs only because of their use of guide dogs.

Because the plaintiffs are unable to show that the quarantine discriminates against them by reason of their blindness, they have failed to establish an issue of material fact on an essential element of their claim.

IV

For the foregoing reasons, I would affirm the district court's grant of summary judgment to the defendants on the plaintiffs' ADA claim.[12]

Judge O'Scannlain's dissent from rejecting rehearing en banc in Compassion

in Dying v. WA (June 12, 1996) [Excerpt]

O'SCANNLAIN, Circuit Judge, joined by TROTT and KLEINFELD, Circuit Judges, dissenting from order rejecting request for rehearing en banc by the full court:

[. . .] As the Second Circuit recently concluded: "The right to assisted suicide finds no cognizable basis in the Constitution's language or design, even in the very limited cases of those competent persons who, in the final stages of terminal illness, seek the right to hasten death." Quill v. Vacco, 80 F.3d 716, 724-25 (2d Cir. 1996); [. . .]. [. . .]

B

The majority goes on to err by concluding that there is no constitutionally permissible distinction between suicide and refusing medical treatment; such a conclusion ignores a long line of judicial decisions that recognize the distinction.[12] The right to refuse medical treatment is grounded in the common law right to be free of unwanted bodily contact; in contrast, the common law has never recognized a right to assistance in deliberately taking one's life. The removal of life-support is not the actual cause of death; there, death results from natural causes. See Stephen Carter, The Culture of Disbelief 236 (1993) ("[assisted suicide] involves not letting the patient die, but making the patient die"). [. . .]

C

Contrary to the conclusions contained in the majority's lengthy exegesis, neither the Constitution nor history supports the notion that this court may compel the State of Washington (and eight other western states) to recognize an individual's right to physician-assisted suicide.

Considering the pains to which the majority has gone to assert the redemptive nature of Judas Iscariot's suicide and to attribute utilitarian motivations to St. Augustine's writings on suicide,[13] I feel obliged to observe that no amount of historical revisionism can cure the constitutional infirmities that plague the majority's holding. Moreover, the majority's extensive discussion of historical attitudes toward suicide is beside the point; the proper focus should be on whether a right to assisted suicide is rooted in American history and tradition. Clearly it is not. See, e.g., Cruzan, 497 U.S. at 292-94, 294-96, 110 S.Ct. at 2859, 2860 (Scalia, J., concurring) ("Case law at the time of the adoption of the Fourteenth Amendment generally held that assisting suicide was a criminal offense."); Quill, 80 F.3d at 724 ("Nor can it be said that the right to assisted suicide claimed by plaintiffs is deeply rooted in the nation's traditions and history. Indeed, the very opposite is true.").

The most comprehensive study available on the history of suicide unequivocally concludes that "the weight of authority in the United States, from colonial days through at least the 1970s has demonstrated that the predominant attitude of society and the law has been one of opposition to suicide. It follows that courts should not hold suicide or its assistance to be a protected right under the United States Constitution." Thomas J. Marzen et al., Suicide: A Constitutional Right?, 24 Duq.L.Rev. 1, 100 (1985).[14]

The Supreme Court has never recognized a substantive due process right without first finding that there is a tradition of protecting that particular interest. Here, there is absolutely no tradition of protecting assisted suicide. Almost all states forbid assisted suicide and some states even permit the use of nondeadly force to thwart suicide attempts. No state has ever accepted consent of the victim as a defense to a charge of homicide. These are the political judgments made by the democratic process; if they are no longer "politically correct," let the legislatures act to change them, not life-tenured judges immune from the voters' reach.

IV

Finally, let no one be beguiled into misconceptions concerning Compassion's actual holding; this case is not about aggressive pain management.

Long before the eight-judge opinion was issued, pain treatments — such as the injection of morphine — have been legal and well-established in the medical community. See American Medical Ass'n, Current Opinions of the Council on Ethical & Judicial Affairs, Code of Medical Ethics § 2.20, at 14 (1992) ("For humane reasons, with informed consent, a physician may do what is medically necessary to alleviate severe pain, or cease or omit treatment to permit a terminally ill patient to die when death is imminent. However, the physician should not intentionally cause death.").

Furthermore, no physician has ever been imprisoned for properly prescribing pain killers. It is common knowledge that physicians, with the tacit consent of the family, may over-medicate for pain with the risk of accelerating death. So long as the primary intention is to lessen pain, there is no danger of imprisonment. As Judge Kleinfeld emphasizes, under these circumstances, there is a fundamental distinction between putting one in harm's way and intending death:

Knowledge of an undesired consequence does not imply that the actor intends that consequence. A physician who administers pain medication with the purpose of relieving pain, doing his best to avert death, is no murderer, despite his knowledge that as the necessary dosage rises, it will produce the undesired consequence of death.

Compassion, 79 F.3d at 858 (Kleinfeld, J., dissenting). Clearly, Compassion's constitutionalization of the right of physicians to prescribe lethal doses for the express purpose of ending the lives of their consenting patients goes far beyond the most aggressive, medically approved pain treatments.

V

The eight-judge majority has not sustained its burden of proving that the Constitution compels a state to recognize, against the will of its people, a right to assisted suicide. However much judges, as individuals, may desire such a right for the terminally ill, we, as judges, are limited by the text of the Constitution and by the Framers' clear intent that the judiciary be "disassociated from direct participation in the legislative process." See Dennis v. United States, 341 U.S. 494, 517, 552, 71 S.Ct. 857, 871, 889, 95 L.Ed. 1137 (1951) (Frankfurter, J., concurring). In the words of Justice Frankfurter: "Our duty to abstain from confounding policy with constitutionality demands perceptive humility as well as self-restraint in not declaring unconstitutional what in a judge's private judgment is deemed unwise and even dangerous." Id. at 552, 71 S.Ct. at 889.

The constitutionalization of a right to physician-assisted suicide is nothing short of pure invention — constitutionally untenable and historically unprecedented. It is especially egregious when only eight of the twenty-four active judges on our court can nullify the will of the voters of Washington who rejected a physician-assisted suicide law just five years ago. [. . .]

Judge O'Scannlain's dissent in Air One Helicopters v. FAA (June 12, 1996)

O'SCANNLAIN, Circuit Judge, dissenting:

I respectfully dissent. While I empathize with Air One's plight, I conclude that (1) this court lacks jurisdiction to entertain Air One's petition for review, (2) the court lacks authority to rule that the Spanish registration is invalid (and has erred by doing so without applying Spanish law), and (3) the majority's opinion ordering the FAA to register Air One's helicopter in the United States directly conflicts with both a statute and a treaty.

I

The appropriate jurisdictional test is that outlined in Air California v. U.S. Dept. of Transportation, 654 F.2d 616 (9th Cir.1981). In that case, this court stated that under 49 U.S.C.App. § 1486(a),[1] FAA "[a]dministrative orders are not final and reviewable `unless and until they impose an obligation, deny a right, or fix some legal relationship as a consummation of the administrative process.'" Id. at 621 (citations omitted).

Air One argues that the FAA letters in this case are final orders because they effectively deny Air One its right to register its helicopter. I disagree. None of the letters denied Air One's registration application; to the contrary, the letters merely told Air One what it needed to provide in order to get the application approved, namely a certificate from a Spanish authority (either the Spanish National Aircraft Registry or a Spanish court) that the Spanish registration was invalid. Accordingly, the letters do not impose any obligation, deny any right or fix any legal relationship as the consummation of the administrative process.

The majority states that "[w]hether or not the [FAA] letters amount to final agency action," this court has jurisdiction to review the FAA's alleged "failure to register the helicopter" because exhaustion of administrative remedies would be futile. In support of its conclusion on this point, it states that "[t]he FAA has admitted that any further attempts by Air One to obtain a different decision will be futile."

I cannot agree with this latter statement. The FAA has not conceded that exhaustion of administrative remedies would be futile; to the contrary, the FAA has said that it would accept a final judgment or decree from a court of competent jurisdiction in Spain that the registration is invalid. See Appellee's Brief at 26-27; Jan. 3, 1996 memorandum from Kenneth G. Caplan, Special Attorney to the U.S. Attorney General. The relevant federal regulations state that such a judgment would constitute "satisfactory evidence of termination of the foreign registration." 14 C.F.R. § 47.37(b)(2). Air One cannot argue that any efforts to obtain a different decision from the FAA would be "futile" when it refuses to pursue the very remedy which the FAA has suggested and which is mandated by the relevant federal regulations.[2]

Accordingly, Air One has a remedy available to it, and the FAA's letters do not "impose an obligation, deny a right, or fix some legal relationship as a consummation of the administrative process." Air California, 654 F.2d at 621. For that reason, they "are not final and reviewable," id., and this court lacks jurisdiction to hear Air One's appeal.

II

Even if this court has jurisdiction to consider Air One's appeal, I do not believe that we have authority to hold that the Spanish registration is invalid.

The majority states that "we can determine when and if a registration in a foreign country remains valid." Op. at 883 (emphasis added). In doing so, the majority apparently relies on 14 C.F.R. § 47.37(b)(2). However, it has misapplied the provision. That regulation states that

> satisfactory evidence of termination of the foreign registration may be —
>
> ....
>
> (2) A final judgment or decree of a court of competent jurisdiction that determines, under the law of the country concerned, that the registration has become invalid.

14 C.F.R. § 47.37(b)(2) (emphasis added). I strongly doubt that this court is one of "competent jurisdiction" to determine that the Spanish registration is invalid; I suspect that only a Spanish court so qualifies.

More important, however, is the fact that the majority does not even purport to apply Spanish law in holding the Spanish registration invalid, as is clearly required by the regulation. Even assuming that we are a "court of competent jurisdiction" to decide the issue, the parties have not provided any briefing on Spanish law, and we should not decide such an issue in a vacuum.

III

Finally, the majority's opinion also forces the FAA to register Air One's helicopter even though the FAA can do so only by violating both a statute and a treaty. First, under federal law, "[a]n aircraft [owned by a citizen of the United States] may be registered [in the United States] only when the aircraft is — (1) not registered under the laws of a foreign country...." 49 U.S.C. § 44102(a) (emphasis added). As Air One concedes, its helicopter is in fact "registered under the laws of a foreign country."[3] The majority's opinion ordering the FAA to register Air One's helicopter in the United States clearly contravenes this statute.

Second, as the majority notes, Chapter III, Article 18 of the Chicago Convention states that "[a]n aircraft cannot be validly registered in more than one State...." The only Spanish authority yet to rule on the subject has stated that the aircraft is in fact "validly registered" in Spain. Accordingly, the majority's opinion clearly places the United States in violation of this treaty. In addition, the majority's decision to invalidate the Spanish registration, before the Spanish courts have even been given an opportunity to rule on the subject, contravenes basic principles of international comity. Finally, the majority's opinion provides a dangerous precedent which may encourage foreign courts to rule, in subsequent cases, that aircraft registered by the FAA in the United States are not in fact "validly" registered here. The practical effect of the majority's ruling is thus to render the treaty a virtual nullity.

IV

There is no question that Air One has been the victim of a protracted, intercontinental bureaucratic nightmare, and I empathize completely with Air One's plight and with the majority's strong desire to remedy it. However, federal courts are courts of limited jurisdiction. Because of that fact, we sometimes confront cases, such as the one at bar, where we simply lack authority to act. And even if we do act, we must always do so in a manner consistent with federal laws and regulations. Because I fear that the majority's opinion may be inconsistent with these principles, I respectfully dissent.

Notes

[1] This provision has since been repealed and recodified, without significant change, at 49 U.S.C. § 46110.

[2] In addition, in light of Air One's decision not to pursue such a judgment in the Spanish courts, I respectfully submit that the majority's statement that "bringing a court challenge will be unsuccessful" is nothing more than pure speculation.

[3] In spite of the majority's holding that the Spanish registration is invalid, this conclusion cannot and does not alter the basic fact that the helicopter remains "registered under the laws of a foreign country."

Judge O'Scannlain's concurrence in Separation of Church and State Committee v. City of Eugene (Aug 20, 1996) [Excerpt]

O'SCANNLAIN, Circuit Judge, concurring in the result:

[. . .] Ironically, the will of the majority of voters of Eugene, Oregon who approved use of the cross for a benign purpose must be overruled, while the Ku Klux Klan receives constitutional protection when it uses the cross as a message of hate. As judges of the inferior courts of the federal system, we do our best to resolve cases in the light of Supreme Court guidance. Alas, its instructions on implementation of the Establishment Clause are not always clear, consistent or coherent.

Judge O'Scannlain's concurrence and dissent in US v. Baramdyka (Sept 10, 1996)

O'SCANNLAIN, Circuit Judge, concurring in part and dissenting in part:

I agree that Baramdyka's ineffective assistance of counsel claims, his double jeopardy claim, and his claim on direct appeal that the district court erred by failing to reduce his sentence for time served in Chile have all either been waived or lack merit. My disagreement with the majority is limited only to the disposition of Count 8 in his habeas appeal.

I would vacate Baramdyka's conviction and five-year probationary sentence because in my view, Chile has not waived its rights under the United States-Chilean extradition treaty, nor under the doctrines of specialty and dual criminality incorporated in that treaty, to preclude the United States from prosecuting Baramdyka on that count. Because, as a matter of treaty, the United States was barred from prosecuting Count 8, I respectfully dissent from part of the court's opinion.

"As a matter of international comity, the doctrine of specialty prohibits the requesting nation from prosecuting the extradited individual for any offense other than that for which the surrendering state agreed to extradite." United States v. Khan, 993 F.2d 1368, 1373 (9th Cir.1993) (citations, internal quotations omitted). In Securities Exchange and Commission v. Eurobond Exchange, Ltd., 13 F.3d 1334 (9th Cir.1994), this court held that the specialty defense is one of personal, rather than subject matter jurisdiction, and further held that a defendant who had failed to raise the defense in his answer had waived it. Id. at 1337. Even though the defendant had waived his own rights, this court nonetheless went on to consider whether the Swiss government, which had extradited the appellant in that case, would object to the institution of civil proceedings against him. Noting that "the protection [of the rule of specialty] exists only to the extent that the surrendering country wishes," id. (quoting United States v. Najohn, 785 F.2d 1420, 1422 (9th Cir.) (per curiam), cert. denied, 479 U.S. 1009, 107 S.Ct. 652, 93 L.Ed.2d 707 (1986)), we took pains to observe that the Swiss had explicitly represented to the United States that they would not object if the United States instituted civil proceedings against the appellant. As a result, we were able safely to conclude that "as a matter of international comity a trial in this civil matter will not offend the Swiss." Id. We further noted that in Van Cauwenberghe v. Biard, 486 U.S. 517, 108 S.Ct. 1945, 100 L.Ed.2d 517 (1988) the Supreme Court had observed that "[i]n the absence of an explicit agreement obligating the United States to protect the extradited person from the burdens of a civil suit, we believe that there is little potential that the extraditing state ... will view the mere conduct of a private civil trial as a breach of an obligation by the United States not to abuse the extradition process." Id. at 525, 108 S.Ct. at 1951. Relying on Biard, we thus concluded that "[h]ere, there is no question of an abuse of the extradition process on the part of the United States where the Swiss have made known their belief that the Treaty does not apply to this action." Eurobond, 13 F.3d at 1337.

This case is clearly distinguishable from Eurobond. Here, there is nothing in the record which suggests that Chile has surrendered its right to prevent the United States from prosecuting Baramdyka on Count 8. To the contrary, there is evidence in the record suggesting that Chile would in fact object: Chile specifically declined this country's request to prosecute Baramdyka on Count 8. Accordingly, it is difficult to see how Chile will interpret the United States government's decision to prosecute Baramdyka on Count 8, and this court's decision to affirm that conviction, as anything other than "an abuse of the extradition process on the part of the United States," Eurobond, 13 F.3d at 1337, and as a breach of the treaty.

This court has repeatedly emphasized the importance of ensuring the continued vitality of the specialty doctrine. In United States v. Andonian, 29 F.3d 1432 (9th Cir.1994), cert. denied, ____ U.S. ____, 115 S.Ct. 938, 130 L.Ed.2d 883 (1995), we noted that "[t]he doctrine is based on principles of international comity: to protect its own citizens in prosecutions abroad, the United States guarantees that it will honor limitations placed on prosecutions in the United States. Our concern is with ensuring that the obligations of the requesting nation are satisfied." Id. at 1435 (citations omitted) (emphasis added).[1] Similarly, in Najohn, supra, we noted that "preservation of the institution of extradition requires that the petitioning state live up to whatever promises it made in order to obtain extradition." Najohn, 785 F.2d at 1422.

In my view, by failing to set aside Baramdyka's conviction on Count 8 we unnecessarily undermine these principles. Not only will we potentially inhibit the United States' ability to "protect its own citizens in prosecutions abroad" in future cases, but we will also unnecessarily provide Chile and other countries with reason to demur in future cases in which the United States requests the extradition of other major drug dealers. Accordingly, I would grant Baramdyka's section 2255 petition to set aside his conviction on Count 8.

Notes

[1] We emphasized in Andonian that "[a]n extradited person ... may be tried for a crime other than that for which he was surrendered, if the asylum country consents." Id. (citations, internal quotations omitted) (emphasis added by Andonian).

Judge O'Scannlain's dissent in In re Bernard (Sept 25, 1996)

O'SCANNLAIN, Circuit Judge, dissenting:

Because I am not persuaded that the Bernards "disposed of" or "parted with" property, I respectfully dissent.

Section 727 is at the heart of the Bankruptcy Code's provisions designed "to relieve the honest debtor from the weight of oppressive indebtedness and permit him to start afresh free from the obligations and responsibilities consequent upon business misfortunes." Williams v. U.S. Fidelity Co., 236 U.S. 549, 554-55, 35 S.Ct. 289, 290, 59 L.Ed. 713 (1915), quoted in In re Devers, 759 F.2d 751 (9th Cir.1985). As such, it is "construed liberally in favor of the debtor and strictly against those objecting to discharge." In re Adeeb, 787 F.2d 1339, 1342 (9th Cir.1986).

The majority is correct to observe that the definition of "transfer" in the

Bankruptcy Code is very broad; it would be a mistake, however, to read it even more broadly than it is written. "`[T]ransfer' means every mode ... of disposing of or parting with property or with an interest in property...." 11 U.S.C. § 101(54). If there is no "disposing of" or "parting with" property, then there is no transfer. The question in this case is whether the simple act, without more, of withdrawing money from bank accounts and money market accounts is "disposing of" or "parting with" property.

When the Bernards withdrew money from their own accounts in early 1991, they did not relinquish an interest in property; they merely changed the location of identifiable cash funds. No third party gained an interest in the cash, and the total value of the Bernards's assets did not change. Just as a transfer would occur neither when a debtor breaks a twenty-dollar bill into two ten-dollar bills nor when he cashes his paycheck at his employer's bank, no transfer occurred here. The cash received by the Bernards was exactly equivalent to and easily identifiable as the sums previously deposited in their accounts.

The majority breaks with the Seventh Circuit in interpreting section 727(a)(2), claiming that this court's decision in In re Adeeb, 787 F.2d 1339 (9th Cir.1986), controls. With respect, I read Adeeb as holding only that "lack of injury to creditors is irrelevant for purposes of denying a discharge in bankruptcy." Id. at 1343. In contrast to the case before us, however, Adeeb dealt with an unambiguous transfer of property to third parties, followed by a re-transfer back to the debtor. Id. at 1341-42. Adeeb says nothing about whether there must be injury to creditors for a transfer to occur; the first transfer did indeed harm Adeeb's creditors. Adeeb merely held that later retransfers were not a defense to a denial of discharge.

The Seventh Circuit has addressed directly whether a transfer can occur if a transaction did not harm creditors. In Matter of Agnew, it held that "to justify the refusal of discharge under a section 727(a)(2) transfer, `it must be shown that there was an actual transfer of valuable property belonging to the debtor which reduced the assets available to creditor and which was made with fraudulent intent.'" Matter of Agnew, 818 F.2d 1284, 1289 (7th Cir.1987) (quoting 4 Collier on Bankruptcy, ¶ 727.02[5] (15th ed. 1986)).

The Agnew approach is consistent with decisions of bankruptcy courts in this circuit. For example, in In re Harris, 101 B.R. 210 (Bankr.S.D.Cal.1989), a bankruptcy court concluded that a debtor did not "transfer" property when he conveyed assets to a trust naming the debtor as sole beneficiary because "the assets were no less susceptible under the Trust to the claims of the Debtors' creditors than they would have been had no trust ever been created." Id. at 216. See In re Garcia, 168 B.R. 403, 407 (D.Ariz.1994) (recording declaration of homestead is not a transfer because there was no reduction of assets available to creditor).

It seems to me that debtors should not be punished for transferring assets available to creditors unless the record establishes that they are actually disposing of or parting with those assets. The bankruptcy court found only that the Bernards withdrew $44,010.61 from a money market account and $20,000 from a checking account in early 1991; it made no findings as to what happened to the money after that and the testimony was controverted.

Based on the record in this case, the only question before us is whether the withdrawals, as such, were "transfers" as a matter of law. On this issue, I respectfully dissent from the majority's opinion.

Judge O'Scannlain's dissent in Howard v. Shay (Nov 22, 1996)

O'SCANNLAIN, Circuit Judge, dissenting:

I agree with the majority that ERISA fiduciaries are held to the standard not of a "prudent lay person" but rather of a "prudent fiduciary with experience dealing with a similar enterprise." Whitfield v. Cohen, 682 F.Supp. 188, 194 (S.D.N.Y.1988). If they do not have all of the knowledge and expertise necessary to make a prudent decision, they have a duty to obtain independent advice. Of course, the mere seeking of an independent appraisal does not, by itself, satisfy the prudence requirement. As the Fifth Circuit noted in an oft-quoted passage, "[a]n independent appraisal is not a magic wand that fiduciaries may simply waive over a transaction to ensure that their responsibilities are fulfilled. It is a tool, and, like all tools, is useful only if used properly." Donovan v. Cunningham, 716 F.2d 1455, 1474 (5th Cir. 1983).

Nevertheless, I know of no case in which ERISA fiduciaries were adjudged to have breached their duty when they carefully selected and accurately informed the independent appraiser of the relevant data. In fact, the Fifth Circuit has held that

> [t]o use an independent appraisal properly, ERISA fiduciaries need not become experts in the valuation of closely-held stock-they are entitled to rely on the expertise of others. However, as the source of the information upon which the experts' opinions are based, the fiduciaries are responsible for ensuring that that information is complete and up-to-date.

Cunningham, 716 F.2d at 1474 (citation omitted).

The majority cites this Fifth Circuit case to support the creation of a new and unwarranted requirement for ERISA fiduciaries who would obtain expert opinions-that fiduciaries must make certain that reliance on an expert's advice is reasonably justified under the circumstances. Cunningham simply does not stand for this proposition. The fiduciaries in that case had relied on an expert's valuation of the stock made 13 and 20 months before the ESOP transactions. By the time of the ESOP transactions, the fiduciaries knew that the growth projections used by the expert were incorrect-the company had not actually done as well as projected. The fiduciaries nonetheless used the expert's valuation opinion to set the price of the stock for the ESOP transaction. The Fifth Circuit held that the fiduciaries had breached their duties-that they must provide complete and up-to-date information to experts before relying on the experts' opinion.

The crucial distinction between Cunningham and the case before us is that the Cunningham fiduciaries-the company's board of directors-knew that the company had not performed as well as the growth projections. In effect, they knew that the expert's appraisal was out of date. In this case, however, the majority faults the fiduciaries not for providing inaccurate data to the expert, but for failing to question the expert's methodology and valuation assumptions.

The district court specifically found that the fiduciaries in this case used an appropriate selection process in choosing Arthur Young, and that they provided Arthur Young with all relevant, material information. Unless that finding is clearly erroneous, this court should hold that the fiduciaries acted prudently. The majority's unprecedented rule essentially requires the fiduciaries to be experts in subjects in which they admittedly have insufficient knowledge or experience. Fiduciaries use experts precisely because they are not qualified to do the appraisal themselves; once they have carefully selected and adequately informed the expert, they should be able to rely on the expert's conclusions.

The district court also found that Arthur Young's valuation was appropriate, and that the price Arthur Young recommended was adequate and fair. Unless that finding is also clearly erroneous, there is little basis for claiming that the fiduciaries' reliance on Arthur Young's valuation was unreasonable or imprudent.

I respectfully dissent.

Judge O'Scannlain's concurrence and dissent in New Breed Leasing Corp. v. NLRB (April 30, 1997)

O'SCANNLAIN, Circuit Judge, concurring and dissenting in part:

I respectfully dissent from Part V of the court's opinion, which concludes that the law of the case doctrine is inapplicable to our review of the National Labor Relations Board's final remedies and requires New Breed Leasing Corporation to restore the status quo ante with respect to wages and terms and conditions of employment. I concur in the remainder of the opinion without reservation.

I

The majority concludes that the law of the case doctrine is inapplicable to our review of the National Labor Relations Board's ("NLRB" or "Board") final remedies, because "we have not previously considered or decided the legal issues now before us." Supra, at 1467. In Aguayo v. New Breed Leasing Corp., 46 F.3d 1138, 1995 WL 7506, *1 (9th Cir.1995) (unpublished disposition), which arises out of the same facts as the instant appeal, indeed it is an earlier stage in this very case, this court reviewed the district court's grant of an interim injunction in favor of the Regional Director of Region 21 of the NLRB, pursuant to 29 U.S.C. § 160(j). The district court's injunction required New Breed Leasing Corporation ("New Breed"), inter alia, (1) to recognize and bargain with the unions, (2) to hire all (eleven) of the Maersk employees, and (3) to restore the Maersk employees' initial wages and conditions of employment, pending resolution of the unfair labor practice charges subject to this appeal. This court upheld the injunction, but remanded to the district court to "provide New Breed an opportunity to establish that fewer than eleven jobs would have been available for former Maersk employees regardless of New Breed's alleged unfair labor practice and modify the injunction to permit New Breed to set initial wages and conditions of employment." Aguayo, 1995 WL 7506 at *1 (emphasis added). We held in no uncertain terms that the district court erred with respect to its status quo ante remedies:

> The district court did err, however, in requiring New Breed to restore the former wages and conditions of employment at the Compton site. Requiring New Breed to set initial wages at the union rate is not necessary to "protect the integrity of the collective bargaining process [or] to preserve the Board's remedial power."

Id. (internal citation omitted). I am at a loss to understand how the majority can so easily wipe the procedural slate clean and ignore this court's earlier holding on the same issue and facts.

The law of the case doctrine indeed precludes our review of the Board's remedies. See, e.g., Lindy Pen Co. v. Bic Pen Corp., 982 F.2d 1400, 1404 (9th Cir.), cert. denied, 510 U.S. 815, 114 S.Ct. 64, 126 L.Ed.2d 34 (1993) ("Undeniably, the decision of the circuit court in a prior appeal must be followed in all subsequent proceedings in the same case under the law of the case doctrine."); Eichman v. Fotomat Corp., 880 F.2d 149, 157 (9th Cir.1989) ("Under the law of the case doctrine a decision of the court in a prior appeal must be followed in all subsequent proceedings in the same case."). The majority's decision on the Board's remedies simply does not square with this court's earlier disposition of the case.

II

Assuming arguendo that we are not precluded from reviewing the Board's remedies under the law of the case doctrine, the majority nonetheless errs in upholding the Board's status quo ante remedies. A successor employer violates section 8(a) of the National Labor Relations Act ("NLRA" or "Act") if it makes discriminatory hiring decisions and refuses to employ a predecessor's employees in order to avoid this obligation. 28 U.S.C. § 158(a). Substantial evidence supports the Board's conclusion that New Breed was (i) a successor employer who (ii) refused to hire its predecessor's employees because of their union affiliation and (iii) refused to recognize and bargain with the unions representing the employees. Because New Breed violated section 8(a)(3) and (1) of the Act, the Board may impose a remedial remedy to restore the situation to what it would have been absent the violation. The Board, however, may not impose a remedy that is punitive in nature. New Breed properly maintains that the Board's order requiring it to restore the wages, hours, and working conditions of the Maersk employees is punitive.

The Board's order reads, in relevant part:

> I shall order Respondent to offer the former Maersk unit employees in writing immediate, full, and unconditional employment in the unit positions they occupied when employed by Maersk, terminating unit employees not formerly employed by Maersk as necessary, if such positions no longer exist, they shall be offered substantially equivalent positions, without prejudice to their seniority and other rights and privileges they would have enjoyed if initially hired at the commencement of Respondents operations, and to

make them whole for any loss of earnings and benefits....

I shall also order Respondent, on the Unions' request, to restore the status quo ante with respect to each unit, to rescind the unilateral changes, including all initial terms and conditions of employment different from those in place under Maersk's agreement with the Unions, in unit employees' wages, hours, and terms and conditions of employment implemented on and before April 1, 1994, and subsequently; and to make all affected unit employees whole for losses they incurred by virtue of its unilateral changes in their wages, fringe benefits, and other terms and conditions of employment....

The majority's decision is contrary to the weight of authority construing the Board's remedial power.

A

First, the majority's holding is not supported by the United States Supreme Court's decision in NLRB v. Burns Int'l Security Services, Inc., 406 U.S. 272, 92 S.Ct. 1571, 32 L.Ed.2d 61 (1972), where the Court first examined whether a successor employer is bound by its predecessor's collective bargaining agreement. The Supreme Court held that requiring a successor to accept its predecessor's agreement goes beyond remediation, because the successor's only obligation is to bargain with the predecessor's employees. The "parties need not make any concessions as a result of Government compulsion and ... they are free from having contract provisions imposed upon them against their will.... [H]olding ... [the] employer bound to the substantive terms of an old collective-bargaining contract may result in serious inequities." Burns, 406 U.S. at 287, 92 S.Ct. at 1582. The Supreme Court carved out the "perfectly clear" exception to its rule when it is perfectly clear that all or substantially all of the predecessor's employees will be rehired. The exception only imposes a duty on the successor to "consult" with the union before it sets the initial terms and conditions of employment. The duty to consult however does not imply an obligation to accept the old terms of employment. See also Fall River Dyeing & Finishing Corp. v. NLRB, 482 U.S. 27, 36-42, 107 S.Ct. 2225, 2232-35, 96 L.Ed.2d 22 (1987) (discussing and reaffirming Burns).

B

Second, this court has consistently held that a successor employer is free to set the initial terms and conditions of employment. New England Mechanical, Inc. v. Laborers Local Union 294, 909 F.2d 1339, 1342 (9th Cir.1990); Sheet Metal Workers Int'l Ass'n Local No. 359 v. Arizona Mechanical & Stainless, Inc., 863 F.2d 647, 651 (9th Cir. 1988); NLRB v. World Evangelism, Inc., 656 F.2d 1349, 1355 (9th Cir.1981); Kallmann v. NLRB, 640 F.2d 1094, 1103 (9th Cir.1981); NLRB v. Edjo, Inc., 631 F.2d 604, 606 (9th Cir.1980); NLRB v. Dent, 534 F.2d 844, 847 (9th Cir.1976). The majority seeks to avoid the application of these precedents by reframing the issue into an issue of first impression. However, its reasoning is not persuasive because our circuit has already determined that a successor employer has a duty to consult with the union before unilaterally changing the terms of employment but has no obligation to accept its predecessor's labor agreement.

Under Kallmann, in particular, New Breed should not be required to restore the wages, hours, and working conditions of the Maersk employees. This court held in no uncertain terms that a successor has no obligation to accept its predecessor's labor agreement and reinstate the predecessor's terms and conditions of employment. Contrary to the majority's pronouncement, Kallmann states that such an order indeed constitutes a penalty.

> Nevertheless, we disagree with the extent of the remedial order. Even though under the facts of this case Kallmann had a duty to consult with the union before unilaterally charging the terms of employment, as a successor employer he had no obligation to accept his predecessor's labor agreement. The effect of the Board's order is to force Kallmann to abide by the terms of his predecessor's contract with the employees for the entire period of time Kallmann has owned the enterprise.

Id. (citations omitted) (emphasis added). The majority's attempt at distinguishing Kallmann on these facts is unavailing.

C

And finally, the Second, Fourth and District of Columbia Circuits have held that successors may set their own terms and conditions. Saks & Co. v. NLRB, 634 F.2d 681, 687-88 (2d Cir.1980); Nazareth Reg'l High Sch. v. NLRB, 549 F.2d 873, 881-82 (2d Cir.1977);[1] NLRB v. Spruce Up Corp., 529 F.2d 516 (4th Cir.1975); International Ass'n of Machinists & Aerospace Workers v. NLRB, 595 F.2d 664, 672-76 (D.C.Cir.1978). The majority, however, concludes that the Seventh Circuit's reasoning in U.S. Marine Corp. v. NLRB, 944 F.2d 1305 (7th Cir.1991) (enbanc) is persuasive and should be adopted in the instant case. The Seventh Circuit held that where a successor employer illegally refused to bargain with a predecessor's union, the Board's order to reinstate the contract in effect under the predecessor was a proper status quo ante remedy. It concluded that this was appropriate because, under the "perfectly clear" exception delineated in Burns, a successor that would have retained all or substantially all of its predecessor's employees, absent its discriminatory hiring practice, "loses the right to set the initial terms and conditions of employment and violates the Act if it unilaterally alters the predecessor's terms without first consulting the union." Id. at 1320.

In reaching its decision, the court split six to five. I cast my lot with the Seventh Circuit dissenters because (i) the majority's interpretation of the "perfectly clear" exception is inconsistent with the rationale in Burns; and (ii) the status quo ante remedy contravenes certain policies embedded within the NLRA regarding successor ownership. In his dissent, Judge Easterbrook properly argued that a bona fide sale of a business enables the successor to impose its own terms. He emphasized that the forfeiture of a successor's privilege to set the initial terms and conditions of employment is contrary to such policies as freedom of contract and the need to resuscitate ailing business.

They have received wages from U.S. Marine to compensate them for the elimination of the antique manning tables and work rules. Now they receive a third salve, in back pay, for the loss of the work rules they enjoyed when Chrysler ran the plant, and U.S. Marine must use those rules from now on. None of this is remedial, and as a penalty it is not only too high but also interferes with the future operation of the plant. How much cleaner if the Board could levy a hefty fine, distribute the money to the workers, and be done. Instead, the Board's pretense of "remedy" has produced an order that may make profitable production impossible. By approving this masquerade we preserve featherbedding, increase the risks of taking over foundering firms, and frustrate the revival of aging plants. Neither American workers nor American consumers will welcome this consequence.

Id. at 1331.

Here, the remedy for discriminating against the eleven Maersk employees would be an order to hire them. It goes beyond mere remediation to impose the prior contract because New Breed would have had the right to set its own terms and conditions had it hired those employees initially. Because New Breed violated its obligation as a successor to bargain, the proper remedy is a bargaining order, not reinstatement of the contract that existed under Maersk.

III

Because the majority's decision is contrary to the weight of authority construing both the law of the case doctrine and the Board's remedial power, I dissent from that part of the court's opinion which orders the status quo ante remedy.

Notes

[1] The majority relies on NLRB v. Staten Island Hotel Ltd. Partnership, 101 F.3d 858 (2d Cir. 1996), for the proposition that imposing a predecessor's employment agreement is remedial rather than punitive. However, Staten Island is distinguishable: "[T]he requirement that the Company pay former employees at the prior rates was plainly intended to be remedial, for it is temporally limited: (the Board's order requires payment at the prior rates only until the Company negotiates in good faith with the Union, either to agreement or to impasse.") Id. at 862 (emphasis added).

Judge O'Scannlain's dissent from the order rejecting the suggestion for rehearing en banc in Finley v. National Endowment for the Arts (May 1, 1997)

O'SCANNLAIN, Circuit Judge, joined by KOZINSKI and KLEINFELD, Circuit Judges, dissenting from order rejecting suggestion for rehearing en banc:

This case should be reheard en banc because our three judge panel split decision conflicts with two other circuits, is wrong on the merits, and turns the First Amendment on its head.

The plaintiffs are artists, who, along with 5,164 others, applied for a Visual Arts Fellowship from the National Endowment for the Arts ("NEA") in 1994. The plaintiffs weren't awarded fellowships (although 88 others were) so they sued, claiming that their First Amendment rights had been violated because Congress required the NEA, in addition to judging applications by "artistic excellence" and "artistic merit," to "tak[e] into consideration general standards of decency and respect for the diverse beliefs and values of the American public." 20 U.S.C. § 954(d). In ruling that the "decency and respect" provision offends the First Amendment, our divided court commits three grave errors.

First, the panel majority gave the NEA statute an implausible construction. According to the panel, rather than merely take "decency and respect" into consideration, as the statute says, the NEA must use "decency and respect" as the decisive criterion for awarding grants. Finley v. NEA, 100 F.3d 671, 680 (9th Cir.1996). There simply is no warrant for manufacturing such an imagined conflict with the First Amendment.[1]

The panel's second error aggravates the first by applying the "void for vagueness" doctrine where it does not belong, and without regard for the purposes underlying it. A vague law is not as dangerous when the government is handing out a prize instead of meting out a punishment. The "decency and respect" provision neither "trap[s] the innocent," nor "impermissibly delegates basic policy matters to policemen, judges, and juries for resolution on an ad hoc and subjective basis." Grayned v. City of Rockford, 408 U.S. 104, 108-109, 92 S.Ct. 2294, 2299, 33 L.Ed.2d 222 (1972).

As the panel majority would have it, however, simply because the statute is vague and has something to do with speech, it must offend the First Amendment. See Finley, 100 F.3d at 679. In my view, this is wrong: a law must actually threaten or chill protected speech before we strike it down.

How does the "decency and respect" provision inhibit First Amendment rights? Tellingly, the majority doesn't say. It merely points to the heightened need for specific standards when a statute's provisions "touch upon speech." Finley, 100 F.3d at 679. The need "may be even greater when a statute subsidizes speech and the risk that the provision on its face will inhibit speech remains." Id. This confusing (and doubtful) statement utterly fails to explain how First Amendment liberties are threatened when the government awards a prize.

The majority might well have thought that a government award for certain types of art will subtly coerce artists to produce art of that type, thereby chilling creation of "other" art. Or it could have thought that artists cannot be denied a government benefit because they express themselves in a particular way, i.e., indecently. Neither theory fits here, however.

If the first argument were true, the government could never hand out awards for any specific type of art without chilling other artistic expression. Under such reasoning, it would be unconstitutional for the government to award a prize for the best performance of Mozart's "Magic Flute" because it might coerce opera companies across the nation to perform that opera in preference to another.

The second argument is equally problematic. The Supreme Court has repeatedly instructed that the First Amendment is not violated when Congress subsidizes some speech, but not all speech. Rust v. Sullivan, 500 U.S. 173, 193, 111 S.Ct. 1759, 1772, 114 L.Ed.2d 233 (1991); Regan v. Taxation with Representation of Wash., 461 U.S. 540, 549, 103 S.Ct. 1997, 2002-03, 76 L.Ed.2d 129 (1983); Harris v. McRae, 448 U.S. 297, 317 n. 19,

100 S.Ct. 2671, 2688 n. 19, 65 L.Ed.2d 784 (1980); Maher v. Roe, 432 U.S. 464, 475, 97 S.Ct. 2376, 2383, 53 L.Ed.2d 484 (1977); Buckley v. Valeo, 424 U.S. 1, 96 S.Ct. 612, 46 L.Ed.2d 659 (1976). Moreover, Rosenberger v. Rector & Visitors of the Univ. of Virginia, ___ U.S. ___, 115 S.Ct. 2510, 132 L.Ed.2d 700 (1995), cannot be stretched to cover this case: the government benefit here is given out to a select few artists on the basis of the content of their expression. Rosenberger should not be read to apply to prizes.

The panel's third error comes in its alternate holding: that the statute is impermissible because it contains content-based and viewpoint-based restrictions. The panel applies standard First Amendment principles to a situation that the First Amendment doesn't cover. When the government awards a special prize to a select few artists, it necessarily will distinguish between the artists on the basis of the content of their speech. Indeed, content-based distinctions are the whole reason for NEA grants. Considerations of viewpoint are also a necessary element of the decision of whether art is "excellent" or meritorious. What art critic would contend that the subject matter of a work of art is irrelevant to deciding whether it is "excellent"? In any event, the terms "artistic excellence" and "artistic merit" are vague enough to allow an NEA official to consider an artist's viewpoint, but that doesn't bother the majority. It shouldn't, because the First Amendment does not prohibit that. Neither does the Amendment prohibit "taking into consideration general standards of decency and respect" when awarding a prize.

The majority's opinion does far more than give a hostile construction to a Congressional enactment in order to create a conflict with other circuits and Supreme Court precedent, and overturn a law. It sows the seeds of an imprudent First Amendment jurisprudence which will entangle and choke Congress' ability to control public funds used to sponsor any sort of free expression.

Because this case should have been reheard en banc, I respectfully dissent from the court's order not to do so.

Notes

[1] The panel creates more than an imagined conflict with two of our sister circuits. See Piarowski v. Illinois Community College, 759 F.2d 625 (7th Cir.1985); Advocates for the Arts v. Thomson, 532 F.2d 792 (1st Cir.). cert. denied, 429 U.S. 894, 97 S.Ct. 254, 50 L.Ed.2d 177 (1976).

Judge O'Scannlain's concurrence and dissent in Richardson v. City and County of Honolulu (Sept 8, 1997)

O'SCANNLAIN, Circuit Judge, concurring in part and dissenting in part.

I join the court's opinion regarding the constitutionality of Ordinance 91-96. With respect to Ordinance 91-95, I concur in the court's conclusion in Part II-B that there is no violation of the Public Use Clause, but write separately to express concern about Hawaii Housing Authority v. Midkiff, 467 U.S. 229, 104 S.Ct. 2321, 81 L.Ed.2d 186 (1984). I respectfully dissent from Part II-C, however, because I believe that the challenge to Ordinance 91-95's compensation provision is ripe, and that the provision does not provide just compensation.

I

In Part II-B the court concludes that Ordinance 91-95 does not violate the Public Use Clause and relies heavily on Hawaii Housing Authority v. Midkiff.

A

The Fifth Amendment to the Constitution states: "... nor shall private property be taken for public use without just compensation." U.S. Const., amend V. The Public Use Clause is an explicit limit on the power of the government to take private property for, as the Supreme Court has long recognized, a taking must be for public use; a taking for a purely private use is unconstitutional. See Thompson v. Consolidated Gas Corp., 300 U.S. 55, 80, 57 S.Ct. 364, 376, 81 L.Ed. 510 (1937).

Notwithstanding this principle, however, the Supreme Court in Midkiff gave the Public Use Clause an exceedingly broad reading: to satisfy the Clause, a taking need only be "rationally related to a conceivable public purpose." Midkiff, 467 U.S. at 241, 104 S.Ct. at 2329. "The `public use' requirement is thus coterminous with the scope of a sovereign's police powers." Id. at 240, 104 S.Ct. at 2329; Nat'l R.R. Passenger Corp. v. Boston & Maine Corp., 503 U.S. 407, 422-24, 112 S.Ct. 1394, 1404-05, 118 L.Ed.2d 52 (1992).

Since Midkiff was decided, however, the Supreme Court's regulatory takings jurisprudence has undergone considerable change.

See Dolan v. City of Tigard, 512 U.S. 374, 114 S.Ct. 2309, 129 L.Ed.2d 304 (1994); Lucas v. South Carolina Coastal Council, 505 U.S. 1003, 112 S.Ct. 2886, 120 L.Ed.2d 798 (1992); Nollan v. California Coastal Comm'n, 483 U.S. 825, 107 S.Ct. 3141, 97 L.Ed.2d 677 (1987). Nollan, Lucas, and Dolan, of course, dealt with a different area of takings jurisprudence, subject to a different set of rules than the one before us: here we have a challenge under the Public Use Clause whereas that trio dealt with regulatory takings.

Notwithstanding that the Nollan-Lucas-Dolan trio dealt with a different part of the Takings Clause, the landowners argue that these cases have modified Midkiff's deferential review of a legislature's public use determination. The court rejects this argument, and I agree: the Nollan-Lucas-Dolan trio does not expressly modify or overrule Midkiff, and therefore we must apply Midkiff in this case. Indeed, recent Ninth Circuit authority confirms that Midkiff is still viable. See Bay View, Inc. v. AHTNA, Inc., 105 F.3d 1281, 1286 (9th Cir.1997) ("After [Midkiff], a legislative determination of what constitutes `public use' is subject to `an extremely narrow' review, and will be upheld so long as it's rational."). Midkiff's deferential standard compels me to conclude that Ordinance 91-95's taking serves a "conceivable public purpose."

B

Although Midkiff has not been overruled, and although Nollan, Lucas, and Dolan deal with a different part of the Takings Clause, I nevertheless believe that there is tension between these two lines of authority. The underlying thrust of the Nollan-Lucas-Dolan decisions — increasing the scrutiny of regulations to determine if they go "too far" (enough to require compensation) — is inconsistent with Midkiff's sweeping deference. It may be time for the Supreme Court to reconsider Midkiff.

To provide the context for this observation, I must take a brief detour. It seems to me that, speaking in broad terms, there are three ways the government can exercise control over property, especially real property. First, it can regulate pursuant to its broad police powers. Second, it can use its power of eminent domain to take the property without the consent of the owner as long as it pays just compensation. Third, it can buy land from a voluntary seller after negotiating a price — that is, it can use its revenues to behave like any other arm's length purchaser of private property. See Thomas W. Merrill, The Economics of Public Use, 72 Cornell L.Rev. 61, 72 (1986).

Nollan, Lucas, and Dolan dealt with the relationship between the first two categories. Lucas established when a government regulation goes too far. See Lucas, , 505 U.S. at 1030, 112 S.Ct. at 2901 ("When ... a regulation that declares "off-limits" all economically productive or beneficial uses of land goes beyond what the relevant background principles would dictate, compensation must be paid to sustain it."). Nollan and Dolan tightened the required fit between the legitimate purpose sought to be accomplished by a government regulation and the means chosen — thereby identifying some exercises of the police power as takings. A police power regulation will be treated as a taking — an exercise of eminent domain — requiring compensation unless it adequately fits its purposes; that is, unless there is an "essential nexus" between a legitimate state interest and the regulation. See Dolan, 512 U.S. at 385-87, 114 S.Ct. at 2317; Nollan, 483 U.S. at 837, 107 S.Ct. at 3148-49.

The Nollan-Lucas-Dolan trio therefore established that the Takings Clause is a limitation upon the state's police powers; if a regulation goes too far, or does not have the right fit, then it must be treated as an exercise of eminent domain — a taking — which requires compensation. The Public Use Clause appears to serve the same sort of function, but with respect to the second and third categories — it limits the state's power of eminent domain. If an exercise of eminent domain goes too far — if it is for a private purpose, not a public one — then it cannot stand. If the state wants to acquire property in such circumstances (and has the statutory authority to do so), it may negotiate with the landowner to purchase the property at an agreed price, but it may not use its condemnation power.[1]

Because the Nollan-Lucas-Dolan trio increased the level of scrutiny given to police power regulations, identifying some of them as takings, it stands to reason that the same increased scrutiny should be given to outright condemnation. If a taking does not have the required fit — perhaps something like Nollan's "essential nexus" — between its proclaimed public use and its actual effect, then it should be invalid under the Public Use Clause.

The court's opinion seeks to distinguish these cases, but I am unpersuaded. To the majority, the distinction is the provision of compensation: "[W]e see nothing inconsistent in applying heightened scrutiny when the taking is uncompensated, and a more deferential standard when the taking is fully compensated." Whereas the majority is correct that there is less reason to be suspicious of a fully compensated taking than an uncompensated one, more deference does not imply absolute deference. We ought not vitiate the public use requirement because, even if a landlord does receive the "fair market value" of the property, the landlord loses his right to exclude. Whether because of a sentimental attachment to his property or a conviction that the property is actually worth more than what the market will currently bear, a landlord might choose not to sell, even at the "fair market value." The landlord who refuses to sell is asserting his right to exclude. As the Dolan Court recognized, "th[e] right to exclude others is `one of the most essential sticks in the bundle of rights that are commonly characterized as property.'" Dolan, 512 U.S. at 393, 114 S.Ct. at 2320 (quoting Kaiser Aetna v. United States, 444 U.S. 164, 176, 100 S.Ct. 383, 391, 62 L.Ed.2d 332 (1979)). The public use requirement protects this right by limiting government encroachment on private property — by forcing the government to prove that it is upholding the public welfare and not merely transferring wealth to a class of persons with a stronger political voice.

Therein lies the mischief of Midkiff. Hopefully the Supreme Court will have the opportunity to extend its emerging takings jurisprudence to protect the right to exclude and to add vitality to the public use requirement. If the Clause is to have any effect at all, it must mean that a court will not feign blindness when it sees through a patently transparent legislative recital that a taking is for a public use. When the government uses eminent domain to take real property from A and give it to B, with no meaningful impact on anyone else or on the community at large, the taking is purely private and should violate the Public Use Clause.

In my view, Ordinance 91-95, unlike the statute in Midkiff, is a purely private taking. In Midkiff, the legislature was attempting to break up an oligopoly in land ownership — a remnant of Hawaii's feudal past — to allow single family home ownership. Breaking apart large blocks of land held by a small group of landowners — blocks which encompassed almost half the entire State of Hawaii — could be reasonably expected to spark more land transactions and lead to a more fluid real estate market. See Midkiff, 467 U.S. at 232-33, 104 S.Ct. at 2324-25. That some economists might disagree with the legislature's remedy does not mean that the statute would be invalid — it retained an "essential nexus" to its purpose and would be constitutional.

In this case, however, the Honolulu City Council found no land oligopoly, but a mere concentration of land ownership in the hands of landowners (a tautology), many of whom refused to sell their land to their leasehold tenants (typically groups of highrise condominium owners), which in turn led to increased real property prices. As a remedy, when properly triggered, Ordinance 91-95 would condemn the property of the landowners and transfer it in pro rata shares to the condominium owners. It seems to me that the ordinance is nothing more than a naked transfer from one property owner to another — from landlords to tenants. To be sure, because tenants will be able to own land that they could not purchase in the open market, the ordinance might well make today's tenants better off, and will certainly eliminate their need to pay rent altogether. But transferring title to the tenants will not change the value of the property — which will still equal the combined value of the leasehold interest and the reversionary interest — and hence should not lower the price a seller will demand. If the landlords constituted an oligopoly, then the division of the ownership of the land could have the effect of lowering land prices from an oligopolistic level to something approaching the free-market level. In the absence of a showing of an oligopoly, however, Ordinance 91-95 has nothing to do with changing the structure of Hawaii's real estate market.

Nevertheless, Midkiff's language limits the public use inquiry to whether there is a conceivable public purpose behind the law. Applying that deferential standard, I conclude that Ordinance 91-95 barely passes muster, and therefore I reluctantly concur in the court's conclusion that it does not violate the Public Use Clause.

II

In Part II-C of its opinion, the court concludes that the landowners' compensation claims are not ripe. It does so while theoretically recognizing the well-established rule that a party need not seek compensation when doing so would be futile under existing state law. See Levald, Inc. v. City of Palm Desert, 998 F.2d 680, 686 (9th Cir.1993); see also Williamson County Regional Planning Comm'n v. Hamilton Bank, 473 U.S. 172, 196-97, 105 S.Ct. 3108, 3121-22, 87 L.Ed.2d 126 (1985).

Ordinance 91-95 sets the compensation for the taking as "the current fair market value of the leased fee interest." Ordinance 91-95, § 5.3. It defines the "leased fee interest" as the "reversionary interests of the fee owner." Id. at § 1.2.

By its plain meaning, the ordinance pays only the current fair market value of the landowner's reversionary interest. In other words, the landowner gets paid only for his interest in the property which excludes the leasehold. Conspicuously absent from this formula is any payment for the current stream of rental payments from the tenants to the landlord. Undoubtedly, the landlord has a protected property interest in the rental payments — a lessor's interest distinct from the reversionary interest in the land. Currently, the tenants pay rent to the landlord for the lease term. Under the ordinance, the tenants stop paying rent immediately upon condemnation. The landlord loses the stream of payments for the leasehold period but is not compensated for the loss.

In the court's view, Honolulu's Department of Housing and Community Development could interpret the compensation provision broadly and include the lost rental payments in the compensation formula. I do not think a fair (or even generous) reading of the ordinance will sustain that conclusion. The ordinance is clear: the landowners will get paid only for their "reversionary interests," which, as a matter of basic property law, do not include the current income from the property. See Black's Law Dictionary 1186 (5th ed. 1979) (defining "reversionary interest" as "[t]he property that reverts to the grantor after the expiration of an intervening income interest"). The Supreme Court has recognized that merely compensating a lessor for the reversionary interest is insufficient:

"[W]hen a lease of trust land is made, ... upon a subsequent condemnation by the United States, the trust must receive the then full value of the reversionary interest that is subject to the outstanding lease, plus, of course, the value of the rental rights under the lease."

Alamo Land & Cattle Co., Inc. v. Arizona, 424 U.S. 295, 303, 96 S.Ct. 910, 916, 47 L.Ed.2d 1 (1976) (emphasis added). The landlord must receive the value of the leased payments because that is the difference between what is taken by the government (a present fee simple) and the fair market of the "reversionary interests."

The court reaches the incorrect result because its analysis is incomplete. After noting that what reverts back to the landlord is a fee interest, the court states that "[t]he projected earning of that property would be a normal factor in determining the value of the property that reverts to the lessor." The court is correct in that what reverts back is a fee interest, and that the value of a fee interest takes into account all projected earnings. The court does not recognize, however, that a reversionary interest in fee simple is a lesser estate than a present fee simple, and that the difference is the interim lease payments. One can view the value of property as the sum of the discounted future cash flows. A reversionary interest is less valuable than a present fee simple because the value of a reversionary interest does not include the rent payments made prior to reversion, as those would be past cash flows.

Thus, to provide just compensation, Hawaii must pay the landlords the value of the reversionary interest plus the present value of the lease payments. There is no need to wait and see how the Department administers Ordinance 91-95, for unless the ordinance means something other than what it very clearly says, it does not authorize the Department to give landowners just compensation. In light of the plain meaning of the ordinance, any compensation paid by Honolulu to the landowners would be constitutionally inadequate. The formality of pursuing such compensation would therefore be futile. For that reason, I would conclude that the landowners' compensation claims are ripe for review, and that the district court's order should be reversed to that extent.

Notes

[1] This is not to say that the Public Use Clause prohibits the government from possessing property for a non-public use; if the government with the statutory power to do so purchases the property from a voluntary seller, there is no taking at all because there is no use of eminent domain. The government becomes the owner with the consent of the seller.

Judge O'Scannlain's dissent in Epstein v. MCA, Inc. (Oct 22, 1997)

O'SCANNLAIN, Circuit Judge, dissenting:

Because I wholeheartedly agree with the Supreme Court's determination that the adequacy of representation issue was fully and fairly litigated and necessarily decided in the Delaware courts, I must respectfully dissent from the opinion this court announces today. In fashioning its own version of the events as they unfolded before the Delaware courts, the majority posits that the plaintiffs' adequacy claims were neither "actually litigated" before the Chancery Court nor "finally decided" by that court. With all deference, I believe that the undisputed facts tell a different story.

I

The argument urged upon us by the Epstein plaintiffs certainly engenders sympathy and has some force. Irrespective of whether the Delaware attorneys' conduct in the state court rose to the level of constitutional deprivation, their act of referring, in a single breath, to their own clients' claims as "fraught with uncertainty," "weak," and "horrendous" suggests less than dynamic advocacy. Regrettably, however, and unlike my colleagues, I do not believe that we are in a position to pass judgment on the merits of this appeal. The very issue presented to our court for decision today — whether or not the Epstein plaintiffs received constitutionally adequate representation in the Delaware courts — has been fully and fairly litigated before a state court of competent jurisdiction and finally decided by that court. Consequently, under the Full Faith and Credit Act, 28 U.S.C. § 1738, and the policies of federalism, comity, and finality that give it life, our court is not, in my mind, free simply to revisit the issue.

I do agree with my colleagues that the Supreme Court did not conclusively resolve the due process issue before it remanded the case to us. Indeed, as our court's opinion points out, the Supreme Court specifically disclaimed any interest in resolving the merits of the inadequacy claim. See Matsushita Elec. Indus. Co. v. Epstein, ____ U.S. ____, ____ n. 5, 116 S.Ct. 873, 880 n. 5, 134 L.Ed.2d 6 (1996). However, the fact that the Supreme Court chose not to reach the due process challenge does not inexorably lead to the conclusion that this court may decide the issue. Quite the contrary, after reviewing the record, the Supreme Court concluded — in three separate passages and in no uncertain terms — that the Delaware courts had already conclusively resolved the due process issue. First, in Part I, in which it described the procedural posture of the case, the Court stated, rather matter-of-factly, that "[a]fter argument from several objectors, the [Chancery] Court found the class representation adequate...." Id. at ____, 116 S.Ct. at 876 (emphasis added). Several pages later, the Court reiterated its conclusion: citing the decisions of the Delaware courts approving the second MCA settlement, the Supreme Court specifically found that the Chancery Court, in accordance with Delaware Court of Chancery Rule 23, had "determined that the plaintiffs[,] ... as representatives of the Settlement Class, have fairly and adequately protected the interests of the Settlement Class." Id. at ____, 116 S.Ct. at 880 (quoting Order and Final Judgment at 2, In re MCA, Inc. Shareholders Litig., C.A. No. 11740, 1993 WL 43024 (Del.Ch. Feb. 22, 1993)) (internal quotation marks omitted) (emphasis added). Finally, in its now famous footnote five, the Court expressed its skepticism at plaintiffs' decision even to press the due process issue "in spite of the Chancery Court's express ruling, following argument on the issue, that the class representatives fairly and adequately protected the interests of the class." Id. at ____ n. 5,

116 S.Ct. at 880 n. 5 (emphasis added).

Consequently, it is scarcely debatable that in the eyes of the Supreme Court, the Epstein plaintiffs' due process challenge was presented to and rejected by the Delaware state courts. The trouble, I suppose, is that the majority and the Supreme Court do not share the same vision.

A

In support of its "no-actual-litigation" argument, the majority first complains that, despite the fact that the form of notice sent to class members explicitly provided the rights to opt out and to object,[1] that notice "said nothing about adequacy of representation." Maj. Op. at 1240. Of course, the first, most obvious, and most decisive response to the majority's complaint is that the doctrine of collateral estoppel simply does not demand that an issue be actually noticed for argument, only that it be actually litigated at argument. See, e.g., Messick v. Star Enter., 655 A.2d 1209, 1211 (Del.1995) ("The test for applying collateral estoppel requires that (1) a question of fact essential to the judgment, (2) be litigated and (3) determined (4) by a valid and final judgment." (quoting Taylor v. State, 402 A.2d 373, 375 (Del.1979))). Secondly, even if lack of notice were somehow independently relevant to a proper collateral estoppel analysis, the court's no-notice argument fails to account for the fact that the form of notice mailed to each of the class members detailed the precise terms of the settlement. The very terms of that settlement — so pungently characterized by the majority as "a bare 2 a share, inclusive of attorney fees" and a release of all claims, state and federal — are prima facie evidence that something was amiss. See Maj. Op. at 1252-53. That fact — that the settlement on its face raises eyebrows — was no less true on October 27, 1992, when the notice was mailed, than our court finds it today. Consequently, the Epstein plaintiffs "were not forced into a position of having to predict whether their interests would be adequately represented. They could determine whether there had been adequate representation of their interests by reviewing the terms of the settlement." Marshall v. Holiday Magic, Inc., 550 F.2d 1173, 1177 (9th Cir.1977); accord In re Four Seasons Sec. Laws Litig., 502 F.2d 834, 843 (10th Cir.1974). They knew that they could object in the Delaware courts to the settlement, and, by implication, to the representation that had produced the settlement; they simply declined to do so.[2]

Closer to the heart of the appropriate collateral estoppel standard, the court claims — inexplicably, in my view — that the objectors who did elect to appear at the settlement hearing did not "actually litigate" the adequacy of their representation. To the contrary, one of the objectors, William Krupman, explicitly stated (as the majority itself acknowledges) that he opposed the settlement because "the purported class representatives ... had proposed a settlement that benefitted no one but their own attorneys. They did not provide adequate representation to the class." Affidavit of William A. Krupman at 2–3, In re MCA, Inc. Shareholders Litig., Civ. A. No. 11740, 1993 WL 43024 (Del.Ch. Feb. 16, 1993) (emphasis added). The majority attempts to cushion the blow of Mr. Krupman's explicit statement by accusing it of "conflating the non-constitutional question of the fairness of the settlement with the constitutional question of the adequacy of representation." Maj. Op. at 1241. Its criticism, however, rings particularly hollow for one salient reason, alluded to briefly above: the court's own conclusion of inadequacy rests substantially on precisely the same logic, namely, that, under the terms of the settlement, the Delaware plaintiffs' attorneys who profited so well did so at the expense of their class-member clients. See generally Maj. Op. at 1250-55.

The majority dismisses the arguments of another of the objectors, Pamela Minton de Ruiz, out of hand because she failed to use the magic word "inadequacy." Rather, the court notes, Minton de Ruiz "framed her objection in terms of collusion." Maj. Op. at 1240 (emphasis added). The court simply brushes Minton de Ruiz's objection aside because, it complains, she did not "focus[] on the much broader issue of whether representation was constitutionally adequate." Maj. Op. at 1240. Formalistic labels and logic games[3] aside, however, it appears that the court has either failed to recognize for itself or failed to admit to itself that the Epstein plaintiffs bottom their inadequacy of representation argument on virtually the identical factual predicate upon which Minton de Ruiz based her "collusion" objection. For instance, the Delaware Chancery Court characterized Minton de Ruiz's argument in the following terms:

She argues ... that the Delaware plaintiffs have colluded with the defendants to settle this action and dispose of the supposedly meritorious federal claims in exchange for an award of attorneys' fees and a de minimis benefit to the class.

In re MCA, Inc. Shareholders Litig., Civ. A. No. 11740, 1993 WL 43024, at *3 (Del.Ch. Feb.16, 1993). When one compares Minton de Ruiz's contention with one of the plaintiffs' central arguments from their opening brief in this appeal, the perceived distinction between "inadequacy of representation" and "collusion" quickly begins to fade:

Delaware counsel — paid only on a contingency basis — had no incentive other than to "compromise" other litigants' substantial federal claims. Counsel knew that, if they settled the federal claim they would get paid; if they attempted to litigate, they would get nothing. Such a one-sided incentive structure is surely a constitutionally disabling conflict of interest....

Appellants' Opening Brief at 27 (emphasis in original). And once one recognizes that even this court's own inadequacy holding invokes the very same attorney-client antagonism, the majority's effort to obscure substantive identity in semantic minutiae is laid bare:

Matsushita ... knew that class counsel had an extraordinary incentive to settle and settle quickly because that was the only way they could extract a fee out of the federal claims.

....

... Indeed, the misalignment of interests and incentives between class counsel and their clients in these circumstances was so great that it is fair to say that counsel's interests were more in line with the interests of Matsushita than those of their clients.

Maj. Op. at 1250 (emphasis in original). In sum, try as it may to "label away" objector Minton de Ruiz's argument, the fact remains that a rose by any other name is still a rose: in this case, as the court's opinion amply demonstrates, the primary reason that the class representatives were alleged to have been inadequate was the self-interested and, dare I say, collusive, conduct of the Delaware class attorneys.

B

In addition to holding that the inadequacy issue was not "actually litigated" in the Delaware system, this court cites Prezant v. De Angelis, 636 A.2d 915 (Del.1994), and suggests that the Delaware courts did not "finally determine" the question of inadequacy in a manner consistent with Delaware law. Maj. Op. at 1241 n. 6. Again, I must agree with the United States Supreme Court's assessment that the available evidence counsels otherwise. In Prezant, the Delaware Supreme Court announced the following holding: "[I]n every class action settlement, the Court of Chancery is required to make an explicit determination on the record of the propriety of the class action according to the requisites of Rule 23(a) and (b)," including the mandate that class representation was adequate. Prezant, 636 A.2d at 925. Contrary to the majority's suggestion, the Vice Chancellor in this case specifically made the "explicit determination" contemplated by Prezant, when he declared that "it is ... hereby determined that the plaintiffs in the Actions, as representatives of the Settlement Class, have fairly and adequately protected the interests of the Class...." Order and Final Judgment at 2, In re MCA, Inc. Shareholders Litig., Civ. A. No. 11740, 1993 WL 43024 (Del.Ch. Feb. 16, 1993). His "determination," I submit, could not have been more "explicit." What is more, the Delaware Supreme Court — the very court that issued the Prezant guidelines — entertained additional argument on the inadequacy matter, and expressly and unanimously affirmed the Chancery Court's determination that the class had been adequately represented. See In re MCA, Inc. Shareholders Litig., No. 126,1993, 1993 WL 385041, at *1 (Del. Sept. 21, 1993).[4]

In sum, I conclude, as did the United States Supreme Court, that the question of adequate representation (1) was actually litigated before the Delaware Chancery Court and (2) was decided by that court in a valid and final judgment. Although the plaintiffs in this action were not themselves present before the Vice Chancellor, their grievances were ably litigated through their surrogates, objectors Krupman and Minton de Ruiz. Moreover, as the settlement notice made explicit, the plaintiffs themselves were presented with a "full and fair opportunity" to participate personally in the settlement hearing if they so desired. Consequently, under long-established principles of Delaware preclusion law, I believe that the Delaware courts would give collateral estoppel effect to the Chancery Court's judgment and would forbid plaintiffs from relitigating the merits of the inadequacy issue. See Messick v. Star Enter., 655 A.2d 1209, 1211 (Del.1995); Evans v. Frank E. Basil, Inc., 1986 WL 3973, at *2 (Del.Super.Ct. Mar. 20, 1986). Pursuant to the plain — and now universally acknowledged — meaning of the Full Faith and Credit Act, 28 U.S.C. § 1738, we must do the same. See Matsushita, ____ U.S. at _____, 116 S.Ct. at 877 ("The Act ... directs all courts to treat a state court judgment with the same respect it would receive in the courts of the rendering state."); accord Marrese v. American Academy of Orthopaedic Surgeons, 470 U.S. 373, 380, 105 S.Ct. 1327, 1331-32, 84 L.Ed.2d 274 (1985); Migra v.

Warren City Sch. Dist., 465 U.S. 75, 81, 104 S.Ct. 892, 896, 79 L.Ed.2d 56 (1984); Kremer
v. Chemical Constr. Corp., 456 U.S. 461, 481–82, 102 S.Ct. 1883, 1897-98, 72 L.Ed.2d 262
(1982); Allen v. McCurry, 449 U.S. 90, 96, 101 S.Ct. 411, 415-16, 66 L.Ed.2d 308 (1980).

II

As to the majority's last-gasp invocation of Phillips Petroleum Co. v. Shutts, 472
U.S. 797, 105 S.Ct. 2965, 86 L.Ed.2d 628 (1985), to deny the Delaware judgment issue
preclusive effect, I most emphatically protest. The court cites Shutts in support of its per se
rule that class settlement objectors — such as Krupman and Minton de Ruiz — may never,
consistent with the Due Process Clause, finally litigate absent class plaintiffs' rights to
adequate representation. Shutts simply cannot, in my view, bear the weight of such an
extreme interpretation.[5] The concerns that impelled the Shutts Court's recognition of
the prerogative of absent plaintiffs generally to "sit back and allow the litigation to run its
course," Shutts, 472 U.S. at 810, 105 S.Ct. at 2974, plainly are not in play in this case.

The Shutts Court was motivated by a concern for fairness to parties who, without
the right to "sit back," might be forced to forfeit their claims altogether. The Shutts Court
found that in light of financial constraints, some plaintiffs, if forced to litigate their own
claims, might "have no realistic day in court." Id. at 809, 105 S.Ct. at 2973. However, as
the following colloquy, which occurred during oral argument before the Supreme Court,
makes clear, the Epstein plaintiffs (quite unlike the "absent" class plaintiffs in Shutts)
absented themselves from the Delaware fairness hearing not for financial reasons, but for
tactical reasons:

[COURT]: What about the argument that you should have come into Delaware
to make [the inadequacy of representation] objection and not stayed out of it?

[COUNSEL]: ... If we stayed out ... we knew that we could make collaterally the
attack on lack of adequate representation [and] due process....

Transcript of Oral Argument at 47, Matsushita Elec. Indus. Co. v. Epstein, ____
U.S. ____, 116 S.Ct. 873, 134 L.Ed.2d 6 (1996). What is more, the Epstein plaintiffs lost
absolutely nothing by not attending the settlement hearing. As they sat idly by, content in
the notion that they had preserved their right collaterally to attack the Delaware judgment,
their substantive arguments were, as detailed above, simultaneously being presented by
objectors Krupman and Minton de Ruiz. (Indeed, this fact very likely was known to the
Epstein lawyers, in light of objector Krupman's lawyer's admission that his client's
objection had originally been drafted by the attorneys representing the Epstein plaintiffs.)

The Epstein plaintiffs have managed, quite literally, to have their cake and eat it
too. They now get two bites at the proverbial apple. Today, this court not only condones
such gluttony, it constitutionalizes it. We are constantly reminded that "no single model of
procedural fairness, let alone a particular form of procedure, is dictated by the Due
Process Clause." Kremer v. Chemical Constr. Corp., 456 U.S. 461, 483, 102 S.Ct. 1883,
1898, 72 L.Ed.2d 262 (1982). Rather, "due process is flexible and calls for such procedural
protections as the particular situation demands." Morrissey v. Brewer, 408 U.S. 471, 481,
92 S.Ct. 2593, 2600, 33 L.Ed.2d 484 (1972). For the court to have co-opted the salutary

principle announced in Shutts and applied it in rote fashion to the facts of this case undermines, in my view, the very concept of due process of law.

III

The majority seeks to hush Matsushita's "alarmist cry" that the opinion announced today "will sound the death knell to finality in class actions if individual objectors cannot bind absentees on the issue of adequate representation." Maj. Op. at 1242. The court rejects Matsushita's argument as "hyperbole." Maj. Op. at 1242. To allay Matsushita's fears, the court directs its attention to the following passage in the Delaware Supreme Court's opinion in Prezant:

[The approach we announce today] will serve to benefit both class members and defendants. Class members ... will ... have their interests protected by the requirement that their claims cannot be compromised without ... a judicial determination that the Rule 23 criteria have been satisfied.... Such a determination will include a finding that their due process right to adequate representation has in fact been satisfied. Defendants will be protected from a possible collateral attack on the validity of the settlement by a class member claiming the settlement did not meet the requirements of Rule 23. This protection will help insure that the final release sought by defendants in settlements is indeed final.

Prezant, 636 A.2d at 925—26. I sincerely doubt that the court's reassurance is of any consolation whatsoever to Matsushita or to other potential class action defendants. If anything, it is a source of consternation. Matsushita, after all, did precisely what the Prezant court (and now this court) instructed it to do: It asked for and got a judicial finding — an "express ruling," in the words of the United States Supreme Court — that the representation of the plaintiff class had been constitutionally adequate. Curiously, today this court tells both Matsushita and the Delaware judiciary that, alas, they did not do enough.

Because I believe that today's decision not only threatens finality, but also contravenes "the elementary principles of federalism and comity," Growe v. Emison, 507 U.S. 25, 35, 113 S.Ct. 1075, 1082, 122 L.Ed.2d 388 (1993), that animate the Full Faith and Credit Act, I respectfully dissent.

Notes

[1] A number of the class plaintiffs exercised their procedural rights pursuant to the notice: eighteen shareholders opted out of the class, and three class members appeared in the Delaware Chancery Court to object to the settlement. See In re MCA, Inc. Shareholders Litig., Civ. A. No. 11740, 1993 WL 43204, at *3 (Del. Ch. Feb. 16, 1993).

[2] I might add that the Epstein plaintiffs' counsel's candid admission to the Supreme Court that his clients stayed out of the Delaware proceedings for purely strategic reasons, see infra page 1259-60, is conclusive proof that any perceived notice failure was illusory.

[3] The majority would have us read Minton de Ruiz's objection as if it belonged in

a Venn diagram: "All collusion is inadequacy; some inadequacy is collusion...."

[4] The majority accuses the Delaware Chancery Court of failing properly to support its conclusion of adequacy, citing language from the Prezant opinion suggesting that a court should "articulate on the record its findings regarding the satisfaction of the Rule 23 criteria and supporting reasoning in order to facilitate appellate review." Prezant, 636 A.2d at 925. Even if I believed that the quoted language represented the holding of the Delaware Supreme Court — which I do not, see Goodrich v. E.F. Hutton Group, Inc., 681 A.2d 1039, 1045 (Del.1996) (reaffirming that the "essential" requirement recognized in Prezant is "a judicial determination that the adequate representation requirement of Rule 23(a)(4) has been satisfied") — I believe that the Chancery Court discharged its responsibility of articulating the reasons for its holding; it found that although the objectors had alleged that the settlement was collusive, "[s]uspicion ... is not enough." In re MCA, Inc. Shareholders Litig., Civ. A. No. 11740, 1993 WL 43024, at *5 (Del.Ch. Feb. 16, 1993); see also Youngman v. Tahmoush, 457 A.2d 376, 381 (Del.Ch.1983) (suggesting that, under Delaware law, the party challenging the adequacy of the class members' representation bears the burden of demonstrating inadequacy). That finding was specifically affirmed by the Delaware Supreme Court.

[5] It is certainly worthy of note, in this respect, that the majority itself recognizes that the Third Circuit's recent, post-Shutts, decision in Grimes v. Vitalink Communications Corp., 17 F.3d 1553 (3d Cir.1994), patently rejects such view. Maj. Op. at 1242.

Judge O'Scannlain's concurrence in Bates v. Jones (Dec 19, 1997) [Excerpt]

O'SCANNLAIN, Circuit Judge, concurring in the result:

[. . .] Judge Fletcher argues in her dissent that Proposition 140 is defective because the voters were not provided with "notice that they were voting on a severe limitation to their fundamental right to vote for candidates of their choice." See infra, Judge Fletcher dissenting opinion at 867; see also infra, Judge Fletcher dissenting opinion at 866 (incorporating Bates, 127 F.3d at 856-63). Although the court's opinion avoids this issue by assuming, without deciding, that a federal court may determine whether a state has given adequate "notice" to its voters in connection with a statewide initiative ballot measure, I feel that Judge Fletcher's analysis should not go unchallenged. First, I will examine whether the people have a "fundamental right to vote for candidates of their choice," and then I will consider whether some special "notice" is necessary when the voters of a state enact legislation via the initiative process.

[. . .] The necessary corollary to the notion that the people have a fundamental right to vote for candidates of their choice is that there exists a constitutional right to vote for a particular candidate. It seems beyond cavil that the former cannot survive without the latter. The right to vote for a particular candidate, in turn, perforce implicates the right to stand for elective office. The district court in Bates v. Jones, 958 F.Supp. 1446, 1460

(N.D.Ca.1997), in identifying the constitutional rights implicated by Proposition 140's lifetime legislative term limits, gleaned from the Supreme Court's decision in Burdick, 504 U.S. at 441, 112 S.Ct. at 2067 a "right to vote for [a] particular candidate." The district court proclaimed that voters can be denied the opportunity to vote for a particular candidate only if "constitutionally adequate" means existed for that candidate to appear on the ballot. See Bates, 958 F.Supp. at 1460. I must respectfully disagree. The district court reads far too much into Burdick's discussion of the means of gaining access to the Hawaii ballot. Indeed, it is well-established that "[a]lthough [a voter] is guaranteed an equal voice in the election of those who govern, [he or she] does not have an unlimited right to vote for any particular candidate." Burdick v. Takushi, 937 F.2d 415, 418 (9th Cir.1991), aff'd, 504 U.S. 428, 112 S.Ct. 2059, 119 L.Ed.2d 245 (1992). As we noted in Burdick, the Supreme Court has upheld numerous restrictions imposed by the states on who may run for certain state offices. Id.; see e.g., Munro v. Socialist Workers Party, 479 U.S. 189, 196-97, 107 S.Ct. 533, 537-38, 93 L.Ed.2d 499 (1986) (upholding state requirement that minor-party candidates receive at least 1% of votes in state's multi-party primary election for candidate to appear on ballot); Clements, 457 U.S. at 972, 102 S.Ct. at 2848 (upholding provisions of state constitution which provided for automatic resignation of certain state and local officeholders who became candidates for any other state office and which prevented most government officials from becoming eligible to serve in state legislature before completing current term of office); Storer, 415 U.S. at 728-29, 94 S.Ct. at 1278-79 (upholding state disaffiliation provision which prevented person from running as independent candidate if he registered with political party during year prior to immediately preceding primary); American Party of Texas, 415 U.S. at 782, 94 S.Ct. at 1306 (state can deny place on ballot to frivolous candidate by requiring all candidates to "demonstrate a significant, measurable quantum of community support.") Consequently, while there is a right to equal participation in voting, a constitutional right to vote for a particular candidate simply does not exist.[3]

   Further, if there is a right to vote for a particular candidate, such right necessarily implicates a corresponding constitutional right to be a candidate. Judge Fletcher suggests in her dissent that "every attempt by a state to set restrictive qualifications concerning who can and who cannot serve as a candidate for elective office implicates rights that are `fundamental' and requires careful scrutiny." See infra, Judge Fletcher dissenting opinion at 868. The district court also suggested that there is a "right to run for a particular office" that requires protection akin to that afforded the right to vote. See Bates, 958 F.Supp. at 1461 (citing Lubin, 415 U.S. at 716, 94 S.Ct. at 1320). Once again, I respectfully disagree both with Judge Fletcher and the district court. The interest of an individual in being a candidate is of no exceptional constitutional significance; it does not merit a departure from traditional equal protection principles. "Far from recognizing candidacy as a `fundamental right,' we have held that the existence of barriers to a candidate's access `does not of itself compel close scrutiny.'" Clements, 457 U.S. at 962, 102 S.Ct. at 2843 (quoting Bullock, 405 U.S. at 143, 92 S.Ct. at 855).

For the foregoing reasons, the asserted constitutional right of the people "to vote for the candidates of their choice" simply does not exist. Consequently, it is evident that no "fundamental right" was "severely limited" by Proposition 140 and thus, the dissent's analysis is fatally flawed.

B

As to the contention that Proposition 140's lifetime legislative term limits must fail because the voters of California were not provided with adequate "notice" of the "severe limitation" the provision would impose on their fundamental rights, there is even less foundation in law or tradition. While I agree with the court's opinion that sufficient "notice" of the extent of the term limits provision was provided to the voters of the State of California, I hesitate to assume for even a moment that such "notice" was required or even within the province of a federal court to determine.[4] See, supra majority opinion at 845-846.

Judge Reinhardt, writing for the original panel, held that, although the proper interpretation of Proposition 140 is purely a matter of state law, "the issue whether the people's fundamental political rights may be severely burdened by means of an `ambiguous' initiative that `the average voter' would only `likely' understand is ... a question of federal law." Bates, 127 F.3d at 857. Judge Fletcher argues in her dissent that, while the California Supreme Court in Eu was only concerned with what the "average" voter "likely" believed about Proposition 140, "surely the adequacy of notice cannot turn on what a person of average intelligence `likely' understood." See infra, Judge Fletcher dissenting opinion at 866. According to Judge Fletcher, evidently, the federal standard for adequate "notice" when fundamental rights are at stake requires a different and more stringent inquiry than the state standard. Searching the Constitution, however, I am unable to locate an "ignorant voter clause" that vests federal courts with the power to review voter-enacted legislation to ensure that enough people were capable of understanding what they voted for at the ballot. In all fairness, Judge Fletcher does not attempt to ground this newly-discovered right in the Constitution. Instead, it appears to be simply yet another novel right that "implicates due process concerns," see Bates, 127 F.3d at 857, created by weaving together snippets from various cases,[5] none of which would seem to betray that it would one day have the dubious distinction of being called upon for this purpose.

Such "notice" requirement is most likely grounded in an antipathy for and distrust of the initiative process which finds support in neither the Constitution nor Supreme Court precedent. Although it has been argued that the Supreme Court reviews popular legislation more closely than legislation enacted by representatives, see Julian N. Eule, Judicial Review of Direct Democracy, 99 Yale L.J. 1503, 1562-65 (1990); Mark Slonim & James H. Lowe, Comment, Judicial Review of Laws Enacted by Popular Vote, 55 Wash. L.Rev. 175, 194-96 (1979), an examination of the case law does not bear out such assertion. As noted in City of Eastlake v. Forest City Enterprises, Inc., 426 U.S. 668, 672-73, 96 S.Ct. 2358, 2361-62, 49 L.Ed.2d 132 (1976), "[i]n establishing legislative bodies, the people can reserve to themselves power to deal directly with matters which might otherwise be assigned to the legislature." The Supreme Court applies the very same standard of review both to popular and to representative legislation and has held that the fact that legislation was enacted by initiative "is without constitutional significance."[6] Lucas v. Forty-Fourth General Assembly, 377 U.S. 713, 737, 84 S.Ct. 1459, 1474, 12 L.Ed.2d 632 (1964) (striking down, on equal protection grounds, apportionment scheme that violated "one person-one vote" principle notwithstanding approval by voters of state).

To engraft a due process "notice" requirement on popular legislation is to invite the federal courts to look behind initiatives to ensure that voters were capable of understanding the potential consequences of their actions and acted accordingly. This is simply beyond our province. The Supreme Court has historically presumed that legislators are aware of the consequences of the laws which they enact and has declined to invalidate legislation on the ground that "Congress was unaware of what it accomplished or ... was misled by the groups that appeared before it." See United States Railroad Retirement Bd. v. Fritz, 449 U.S. 166, 179, 101 S.Ct. 453, 461, 66 L.Ed.2d 368 (1980) ("The language of the statute was clear and we have historically assumed that Congress intended what it enacted."); see also Taxpayers to Limit Campaign Spending v. Fair Political Practices Comm'n, 51 Cal.3d 744, 274 Cal.Rptr. 787, 801, 799 P.2d 1220, 1235 (1990) ("In order to further the fundamental right of the electorate to enact legislation through the initiative process, this court must on occasion indulge in a presumption that the voters thoroughly study and understand the content of complex initiative measures.") Further, it has long been established that there is no due process right to "notice" in the enactment of legislation. See Bi-Metallic Investment Co. v. State Board of Equalization, 239 U.S. 441, 445, 36 S.Ct. 141, 142, 60 L.Ed. 372 (1915) (no due process right to notice before government acts in legislative capacity). In light of the fact that there is no constitutionally significant difference between popular legislation and representative legislation, see Lucas, 377 U.S. at 737, 84 S.Ct. at 1474, we must reject the temptation to create a due process right to "notice" in the initiative process. We simply have no franchise to presume that the citizens of California could not understand what they were doing at the ballot box on November 6, 1990.

III

Like Judge Thompson, I would not interfere with the will of the people of California in adopting Proposition 140; I would reach such result, however, by the route charted by Judge Rymer or Part I of the foregoing analysis. With respect, for the reasons expressed in Part II, I must fundamentally reject the view expressed by Judge Fletcher that federal courts have a writ to impose a newly-minted "notice" requirement on the voters of California.

Judge O'Scannlain's dissent from denial of rehearing en banc in American-Arab Anti-Discrimination Committee v. Reno (Dec 23, 1997)

O'SCANNLAIN, Circuit Judge, with whom KOZINSKI and KLEINFELD, Circuit Judges, join, dissenting from denial of rehearing en banc:

Congress unambiguously revoked judicial review of deportation proceedings — with but one exception — when it passed, and the President signed into law, the Illegal Immigration Reform and Immigrant Responsibility Act of 1996 ("IIRIRA"), Pub.L. No. 104-208, div. C, 110 Stat. 3009 (1996). Today, the Ninth Circuit nullifies the express intent of the elected branches of our government by carving out yet another exception, one which is neither contemplated nor permitted by the plain language of the statute. In so doing, we are in tension with the two other circuits which have addressed IIRIRA's jurisdiction-stripping provisions, see Auguste v. Attorney General, 118 F.3d 723 (11th Cir.1997); Ramallo v. Reno, 114 F.3d 1210 (D.C.Cir.1997), as well as a prior decision of this court itself, Duldulao v. INS, 90 F.3d 396 (9th Cir.1996). Because I fear today's action inflicts mischief on the sound administration of our nation's immigration laws in the nine western states, I respectfully dissent from the court's decision not to review this case en banc.

I

In IIRIRA, Congress stated:

Except as provided in this section and notwithstanding any other provision of law, no court shall have jurisdiction to hear any cause or claim by or on behalf of any alien arising from the decision or action by the Attorney General to commence proceedings, adjudicate cases, or execute removal orders against any alien under this chapter.

8 U.S.C. § 1252(g) (emphasis added). As the opening clause suggests, Congress's elimination of jurisdiction over removal cases is not absolute. Another portion of section 1252, with unmistakable clarity, limits the number of exceptions to but one:

Judicial review of all questions of law and fact, including interpretation and application of constitutional and statutory provisions, arising from any action taken or proceeding brought to remove an alien from the United States under this chapter shall be available only in judicial review of a final order under this section.

8 U.S.C. § 1252(b)(9) (emphasis added).

At the risk of belaboring the obvious, when Congress says "only," it usually means "only." The only permitted judicial review of removal proceedings is the review of final orders. Under the plain language of IIRIRA, decisions by the Attorney General to commence proceedings and to adjudicate cases are simply not reviewable until the final order stage.

Nevertheless, this court now "finds" a second exception,[1] because "[a]ny other reading would present serious constitutional problems." American-Arab Anti-Discrimination Committee v. Reno, 119 F.3d 1367, 1373 (9th Cir.1997). Our circuit apparently believes that the narrowing of judicial review of deportation proceedings may violate the Constitution. To avoid these perceived problems, the court called upon "the well-established principle that where possible, jurisdiction-limiting statutes should be interpreted to preserve the authority of the courts to consider constitutional claims." Id. at 1372 (emphasis added).

With respect, the opinion's reliance on this principle of constitutional avoidance — interpreting statutes to avoid perceived constitutional infirmities — is without foundation in the facts of this case. As the opinion itself admits, the principle is to be invoked only "where possible." Whatever the merits of constitutional avoidance might be, no court may "avoid" a perceived conflict when the text is unambiguous, as it is here. The avoidance canon, invoked with such abandon, amounts to nothing less than rewriting the statute.[2]

Moreover, judicial decisions based on constitutional avoidance are all the more suspect, quite frankly, when there is no constitutional infirmity to avoid. That is precisely the scenario in this case. As the Supreme Court has stated:

Deportation is not a criminal proceeding and has never been held to be punishment. No jury sits. No judicial review is guaranteed by the Constitution.

Carlson v. Landon, 342 U.S. 524, 537, 72 S.Ct. 525, 533, 96 L.Ed. 547 (1951) (emphasis added). Just four years ago, the Supreme Court reminded us that, "[f]or reasons long recognized as valid, the responsibility for regulating the relationship between the United States and our alien visitors has been committed to the political branches of the Federal Government. [O]ver no conceivable subject is the legislative power of Congress more complete." Reno v. Flores, 507 U.S. 292, 305, 113 S.Ct. 1439, 1449, 123 L.Ed.2d 1 (1993) (quoting Mathews v. Diaz, 426 U.S. 67, 81, 96 S.Ct. 1883, 1892, 48 L.Ed.2d 478 (1976); Fiallo v. Bell, 430 U.S. 787, 792, 97 S.Ct. 1473, 1478, 52 L.Ed.2d 50 (1977)) (internal quotation marks omitted) (citations omitted) (alteration in original). Heeding these very words, this court has previously declared that "aliens have no constitutional right to judicial review of deportation orders." Duldulao v. INS, 90 F.3d 396, 400 (9th Cir.1996).

But alas, today's decision now creates an exception to this long-established rule. According to the opinion, the distinguishing factor in this case is that the plaintiffs have raised a First Amendment claim of selective enforcement. What the opinion overlooks, however, is that such exception swallows the constitutional principle. To fit within the exception, a potential deportee need only assert a First Amendment violation. Even if the claim were frivolous, no court can so rule until after obtaining jurisdiction. Because the question of jurisdiction logically precedes the question of merit, today's decision, which purports to expand jurisdiction only to meritorious First Amendment claims, actually broadens jurisdiction to all such claims, frivolous and meritorious alike. By artful pleading, a potential deportee now is entitled to judicial review notwithstanding the statute and the cases holding that there exists no constitutional right to judicial review in deportation matters. Nothing could be more contrary to both Supreme Court precedent and this court's decision in Duldulao.[3]

II

By finding a constitutional infirmity where none exists and then engrafting onto the statute an exception of our own creation, we undermine the unambiguous intent of Congress.

I respectfully dissent.

Notes

[1] The opinion locates this exception in § 1252(f)(1), which reads:

Regardless of the nature of the action or claim or of the identity of the party or parties bringing the action, no court (other than the Supreme Court) shall have jurisdiction or authority to enjoin or restrain the operation of the provisions of part IV of this subchapter, as amended by the Illegal Immigration Reform and Immigrant Responsibility Act of 1996, other than with respect to the application of such provisions to an individual alien against whom proceedings under such part have been initiated.

8 U.S.C. § 1252(f)(1). Contrary to the panel's interpretation, subsection (f) is not a grant of jurisdiction of any kind, but rather an additional restriction on jurisdiction that applies unless proceedings have been brought against an individual alien under part IV of this subchapter. Appropriately, subsection (f) is entitled "Limit on injunctive relief." The exception within this subsection is clearly only an exception to this subsection.

[2] To be sure, it is the duty of the courts, when they have jurisdiction, to declare unconstitutional any law that violates a protected right. Even then, the power to strike down a statute as unconstitutional does not include the power to amend it. See Frederick Schauer, Ashwander Revisited, 1995 Sup.Ct. Rev. 71, 74, 97-98.

[3] Not surprisingly, the only other circuits to have dealt with the issue have upheld IIRIRA's limitations on federal court jurisdiction. See Auguste, 118 F.3d at 726-27; Ramallo, 114 F.3d at 1214.

Judge O'Scannlain's concurrence and dissent in Gulliford v. Pierce County (Feb 27, 1998)

O'SCANNLAIN, Circuit Judge, concurring in part and dissenting in part.

I would affirm the judgment of the district court. Regrettably, I cannot join Section II.A's discussion of the jury instruction on verbal opposition to police action, which, in my view, threatens "[t]his court['s] ... reputation as the strictest enforcer of Rule 51," Hammer v. Gross, 932 F.2d 842, 847 (9th Cir.1991), and creates a direct intra-circuit conflict with Grosvenor Properties Ltd. v. Southmark Corp., 896 F.2d 1149 (9th Cir. 1990). Therefore, I respectfully dissent and would not reach the question of qualified immunity, which the majority discusses in Part III.

I

Federal Rule of Civil Procedure 51 states:

No party may assign as error the giving or the failure to give an instruction unless that party objects thereto before the jury retires to consider its verdict, stating distinctly the matter objected to and the grounds of the objection.

Fed.R.Civ.P. 51 (emphasis added). Our court has "interpreted this rule strictly and ha[s] stated that, `[i]n a civil case, we may not review a jury instruction in the absence of a proper objection.'" McGonigle v. Combs, 968 F.2d 810, 823 (9th Cir.1992) (quoting Larez

v. City of Los Angeles, 946 F.2d 630, 638 (9th Cir.1991)); see also 9 C. Wright & A. Miller, Federal Practice and Procedure § 2558, at 674 (1971) ("[T]he Ninth Circuit stands alone in reading Civil Rule 51 literally and denying that there is any power to reverse for plain error in an unobjected-to instruction in a civil case.") The party objecting to the instruction must bring "into focus the precise nature of the alleged error in the district court's instruction." McGonigle, 968 F.2d at 824 (emphasis added).

Gulliford now argues that he was arrested for obstructing a police officer without probable cause in violation of the Fourth Amendment. He does not claim on appeal that his First Amendment right verbally to hinder, delay, or obstruct the police was also violated.

Gulliford correctly argues before this court that jury instruction 15[1] was flawed because it failed to inform the jury that the police lacked probable cause to arrest him for speech that "knowingly hinder[ed], delay[ed], or obstruct[ed]" the police but did not include "fighting words []or ... obscene or opprobrious language." Houston v. Hill, 482 U.S. 451, 461, 107 S.Ct. 2502, 2509, 96 L.Ed.2d 398 (1987). Gulliford's objection to jury instruction 15 at trial rested on an entirely different ground. Gulliford's argument was as follows:

[The instruction] does not include a claim for a specific First Amendment violation, and as we indicated in our trial brief and in discussions previously with the court, we believe that both the First Amendment and the Fourth Amendment are implicated and that a violation of either would give rise to a cause of action.

In other words, Gulliford argued at trial that instruction 15 did not separately address his (now abandoned) claim that his First Amendment rights had been violated as well. Gulliford's (perhaps incorrect) argument was that the instruction was exclusively concerned with his Fourth Amendment claim — not that the instruction misstated the elements of that claim.

Of course, the contours of Gulliford's Fourth Amendment claim are shaped both by Wash. Rev.Code § 9A.76.020 — the Washington statute that prohibits obstruction of law enforcement officers — and by the First Amendment. Section 9A.76.020 provides: "Every person who ... (3) shall knowingly hinder, delay, or obstruct any public servant in the discharge of his official powers or duties; shall be guilty of a misdemeanor." Meanwhile, the First Amendment gives individuals the right to verbally obstruct public servants as long as they do not use "fighting words []or ... obscene or opprobrious language." Houston v. Hill, 482 U.S. 451, 462, 107 S.Ct. 2502, 2509, 96 L.Ed.2d 398 (1987). Viewed in conjunction with Wash. Rev.Code § 9A.76.020, the First Amendment helps to define Gulliford's right under the Fourth Amendment not to be arrested for obstructing the police without probable cause.

However, Gulliford's objection at trial to jury instruction 15 had nothing to do with his rights under the Fourth Amendment. Rather, Gulliford wanted the district court to instruct the jury separately regarding an alleged violation of his First Amendment right to verbally obstruct police officers. Because Gulliford failed to "stat[e] distinctly the matter objected to and the grounds of [his] objection [at trial]," Fed.R.Civ.P. 51 (emphasis added), he is precluded from raising his Fourth Amendment argument on appeal.

II

The majority invokes the "pointless formality" exception to Rule 51. As we explained in United States v. Payne, 944 F.2d 1458 (9th Cir.1991), "an objection may be a `pointless formality' when (1) throughout the trial the party argued the disputed matter with the court, (2) it is clear from the record that the court knew the party's grounds for disagreement with the instruction, and (3) the party offered an alternative instruction." Id. at 1464.

It is undisputed by the parties that Gulliford offered an alternative instruction. Gulliford has failed to demonstrate, however, either that "throughout the trial [he] argued the disputed matter with the court," or that "it is clear from the record that the court knew [Gulliford's] grounds for disagreement with the instruction." Id. (emphasis added). Apart from noting that Gulliford submitted an alternative instruction (thereby satisfying only the third element of the pointless formality test), the majority does not point to anything in the trial record to support its conclusion that the pointless formality exception to Rule 51 applies here.

In Grosvenor Properties Ltd. v. Southmark Corp., 896 F.2d 1149 (9th Cir.1990), the defendants submitted an alternative jury instruction that was rejected by the district court. See id. at 1152. At a sidebar conference called to consider the instructions, the defendants stated that their proposed instruction had not been given. See id. The district court responded that it had rejected the instruction and that it was unnecessary for counsel to repeat previously submitted instructions or objections. See id. We held that such a "sequence of events is not sufficient to constitute a sufficient objection to the instructions that were given, as Rule 51 is applied in this circuit." Id. If the defendants in Grosvenor did not succeed in preserving their objection despite complaining that their proposed instruction had not been given, then certainly Gulliford, who did nothing to call attention to the district court's rejection of his instruction, failed to preserve his objection.

In an attempt to distinguish Grosvenor, the majority relies upon a sentence from that opinion. See Majority Opinion at 1621 n. 6 ("However, in contrast to the instant case, the alternative jury instruction in Grosvenor failed `to state distinctly the matter objected to and the ground of the objection as required by Rule 51.'") (quoting Grosvenor, 896 F.2d at 1153). The relevant passage in Grosvenor, however, states, in full:

Southmark argues that it made the required specific objection to the instruction that failed to state that termination of the joint venture would end fiduciary duty, and that it submitted alternative theories of liability to the jury by way of special verdict questions. It contends that it did so by its submission of proposed jury instruction 22. In addition, at a sidebar conference called to consider corrections and additions to the instructions, Southmark's counsel stated that instruction 22 had not been given and the court responded that it had rejected that instruction. At that same conference the court noted that it was not necessary for counsel to repeat previously submitted instructions or objections.

However, this sequence of events is not sufficient to constitute a sufficient objection to the instructions that were given, as Rule 51 is applied in this circuit. This court has held that remarks made by counsel in chambers, discussion of law in pretrial memoranda and mere submission of proposed instructions did not clearly show that the issue was focused before the court.

In addition, an examination of proposed instruction 22 suggests that it was not sufficient to state distinctly the matter objected to and the ground of the objection as required by Rule 51.

Id. at 1152-53 (internal citations omitted). As the above passage demonstrates, our holding in Grosvenor, that a "sequence of events" which includes the submission of an alternative jury instruction does not "constitute a sufficient objection to the instructions that were given," did not turn on whether that alternative instruction "state[d] distinctly the matter objected to and the ground of the objection." Id. Although we observed ("addition[ally]") in Grosvenor that the alternative instruction was unclear, id. at 1153 (citing Brown v. AVEMCO Inv. Corp., 603 F.2d 1367, 1371 (9th Cir.1979)), the clarity of the alternative instruction was irrelevant to Grosvenor's analysis of the "sufficien[cy]" of the relevant "sequence of events." Id. at 1152. Far from distinguishing Grosvenor, the majority's discussion of that case demonstrates why the majority opinion is in direct conflict with it.

I respectfully dissent.

Notes

[1] Jury instruction 15 stated:

The First Amendment protects the right of citizens to verbally oppose and/or challenge police action without risking arrest so long as that challenge does not knowingly hinder, delay, or obstruct any public servant in the discharge of the public servant's official powers or duties.

Judge O'Scannlain's partial dissent in General Dynamics v. US (March 27, 1998)

O'SCANNLAIN, Circuit Judge, dissenting in part.

Prosecutors are understandably enticed by the lure of the big fish. But when an unsubstantiated indictment can lead to the imposition of over $25,000,000 in attorney's fees on an innocent party without recompense, we should hope for — nay, we expect — more responsible conduct by the government, regardless how attractive the quarry.

Unfortunately for General Dynamics, the government failed to observe basic precautions. It conducted an investigation of the alleged defense-contract fraud which was either unconscionably inadequate at best or recklessly arrogant at worst. As former Assistant Attorney General William Weld frankly conceded, the Department of Justice

("DOJ") blindly relied upon the faulty interpretation of the contract that the Defense Contract Audit Agency ("DCAA") had provided:

The audit of General Dynamics was predicated upon the DCAA's belief that the DIVAD contract was a firm fixed price contract which had specific, mandatory requirements. The audit report and the advice of DCAA personnel in connection therewith were critical to the prosecution's early understanding of the contract as a firm fixed price type.... This understanding formed the premise upon which the entire investigation was conducted and the indictment presented to the grand jury.

Securities Laws Enforcement and Defense Contractors: Joint Hearings Before the Sub-comm. on Oversight and Investigations of the House Comm. on Energy and Commerce, and the Subcomm. on Criminal Justice of the House Comm. on the Judiciary, 100th Cong. 39 (1987) (statement of William Weld, Assistant Attorney General, Criminal Division, U.S. Dept. of Justice) (emphasis added).

The government did not engage in a dispassionate, independent analysis of the DIVAD contract.[1] Had it done so — or had it simply given more careful analysis to General Dynamics's position ab initio — the DOJ would have realized quite clearly that the document at issue was not a "fixed-price" contract at all, but rather one of "best-efforts," the terms of which General Dynamics had completely satisfied. Too willing to discount the company's explanation as a mere post-hoc rationalization, the DOJ wrongfully pursued its ill-based prosecution for three-and-a-half years. That the Department is immune from suit in this case does not mean that it is also immune from criticism.

I

Yet this case is not about finger-pointing. It is about the jurisdiction of the federal courts. We lack jurisdiction when a claim is "based upon the exercise or performance or the failure to exercise of perform a discretionary function." 28 U.S.C. § 2680(a) (emphasis added). As this court has previously recognized, "[t]he decision whether or not to prosecute a given individual is a discretionary function for which the United States is immune from liability." Wright v. United States, 719 F.2d 1032, 1035 (9th Cir.1983). The DOJ's misconduct, therefore, cannot be the basis for General Dynamics's cause of action. To that extent I agree with the court.

The misconduct of the DCAA, however, is a different story. Although the court holds that the DOJ's immunity shields the DCAA, I am unfortunately unable to join in such conclusion and therefore respectfully dissent as to that portion of the court's opinion. Were we deciding this case on a blank slate, I might see things differently. Indeed, I share my colleagues concern that, because "[p]rosecutors do not usually do all of their own investigation," a litigant could almost always resort to the argument "that this or that report was negligently prepared," thereby "swallow[ing] up a large part of the discretionary function exemption." (Opinion at 2748, 2751). However, this is not an issue of first impression for our court, and we must decide General Dynamics's claim against the backdrop of precedent.

In United Cook Inlet Drift Assoc. v. Trinidad Corp. (In re The Glacier Bay), 71 F.3d

1447 (1995), we held that a discretionary review of a negligent hydrographic report did not shield the drafters of that report from liability. See id. at 1451. The court held, in no uncertain terms:

> Each separate action must be examined to determine whether the specific actor had discretion of a type Congress intended to shield.

Id. at 1451. My colleagues conclude that the discretionary reviewers in Glacier Bay did not have the "broad based discretion" that the DOJ had in this case. To them, it would seem, the distinction is a matter of degree. The DOJ was more independent than Glacier Bay's hydrographic reviewers; it had more information on which to base its decision.

Although my colleagues are correct that this is a distinction, it is a distinction without a difference. The Glacier Bay court was unequivocal: "[T]he proper level of inquiry must be act by act.... [W]e must determine whether each person taking an allegedly negligent act had discretion." Id. There was no suggestion that the result depended at all on the amount of discretion possessed by reviewers. To the contrary, "[e]ven if [the hydrographic] reviewers had discretion to approve the final charts, such discretion would not shield allegedly negligent non-discretionary acts by [those who prepared the charts]." Id.

To be sure, there is reason to be skeptical of Glacier Bay's reasoning, which could have the tendency to "bog down the government" and "elide what Congress has written." (Opinion at 1283, 1284-85). However, Glacier Bay's net, as described by the panel that decided that case, is wide enough to encompass the DCAA's negligence. I am thus unable to join the court's application of discretionary-function immunity. The DCAA clearly was not immune.

II

I nevertheless concur in the result because, in my view, General Dynamics's otherwise valid claim is time-barred. The Federal Tort Claims Act provides that a claim against the United States is barred unless the plaintiff presents it in writing to the appropriate federal agency within two years of accrual. See 28 U.S.C. § 2401(b). The claim accrues once the plaintiff knows of his injury and its cause, see United States v. Kubrick, 444 U.S. 111, 122, 100 S.Ct. 352, 359-60, 62 L.Ed.2d 259 (1979); Gibson v. United States, 781 F.2d 1334, 1344 (9th Cir.1986), irrespective of whether the plaintiff is also aware of the government's negligence or the full extent of the damages, see Kubrick, 444 U.S. at 123, 100 S.Ct. at 360.

In this case, identifying the injury for which General Dynamics seeks relief is simple: the injury is the indictment. In defending itself against the erroneously premised indictment, General Dynamics spent over $25,000,000 in attorney's fees. Identifying the "cause" of this injury is a more complicated issue because, in fact, there were two causes attributable to the government: the DCAA's release of its audit report and the DOJ's conduct during the course of its inadequate investigation. However, of these two causes, only the former is actionable. We all agree that the other, the DOJ's misjudgment, is shielded by discretionary immunity. Therefore, the operative question for determining the accrual of General Dynamics's cause of action is just the following: When did the company know that the audit report was a cause of the indictment? The answer, it seems to me, is December 1985, the time of the indictment. Because the company did not file its administrative claim until over three years later, in March 1989, and because equitable tolling was unavailable, the claim was untimely.

A

At the time of the indictment, General Dynamics knew that the DCAA's report was a cause of its injury. By then, it had already received the audit report, which notified the company that "[c]ertain of the matters addressed [therein were] currently under investigation by the Naval and Investigative Service and the Department of Justice." Also by that time, General Dynamics had made numerous written and oral appeals to the DOJ urging the Department to disregard the audit report and to acknowledge that the contract was one of "best efforts." Although the company might not have understood why the DOJ was confused despite the clear "best efforts" language in the contract, there can be no doubt that General Dynamics knew that the audit report was at the root of the problem, as is evidenced by its flurry of communications with the government. General Dynamics did not have to know the existence and extent of the DOJ's negligence, or even the DCAA's negligence, in order to file a claim based on the DCAA's report, see Kubrick, 444 U.S. at 123, 100 S.Ct. at 360; all it had to know was that the DCAA's report was a cause of its injury. It therefore seems clear that General Dynamics had sufficient knowledge at the time of the indictment in December 1985, and its claim accrued thereupon.

B

The limitations period began to run immediately upon indictment. The district court abused its discretion by tolling the statute of limitations before the dismissal of the indictment. Equitable tolling is generally available only "where the claimant has actively pursued his judicial remedies by filing a defective pleading during the statutory period, or where the complainant has been induced or tricked by his adversary's misconduct into allowing the filing deadline to pass." Irwin v. Department of Veterans Affairs, 498 U.S. 89, 96, 111 S.Ct. 453, 458, 112 L.Ed.2d 435 (1990). General Dynamics does not fall within either category. The company contends that filing its claim sooner than it did might have impeded its efforts to convince the government to dismiss the indictment, and also might have resulted in the suspension of its business with the government. Perhaps so, but the mere difficulty of such strategic choices does not authorize tolling; the government engaged in no "misconduct" during this period.

The district court also abused its discretion by tolling the statute of limitations after the dismissal of the indictment, during the period of negotiations between the company and the government for reimbursement of attorney's fees. Because these negotiations in no way precluded General Dynamics from filing a tort challenge, they should not have been the basis for tolling the statute of limitations. Thus, the limitations period continued to run, and it expired prior to General Dynamics's filing of its administrative claim.

III

Glacier Bay supports the district court's conclusion that the government was not immune in this case and should have reimbursed the $25,880,752 in resulting attorney's fees. Because General Dynamics's claim was time-barred, however, I must concur in the result of reversal.

Notes

[1] In fairness, Mr. Weld did eventually own up to the government's shortcomings. In testifying before Congress, he stated: "[B]ecause of the relatively limited function performed by DCAA, it is all the more important for the Justice Department to conduct, in essence, a de novo investigation and evaluation of the evidence." Id. at 50. Alas, too little, too late.

Judge O'Scannlain's partial dissent in Lucas Automotive Engineering v. Bridgestone/Firestone (March 31, 1998)

O'SCANNLAIN, Circuit Judge, dissenting only as to Part II.B.2.

I respectfully dissent from Part II.B.2 of the opinion, written by Judge Tashima.

The majority holds that Lucas Automotive has consumer standing to assert a section 7 claim for equitable relief, including divestiture, under section 16 of the Clayton Act. However, our decision in Rebel Oil Co., Inc. v. Atlantic Richfield Co., 51 F.3d 1421 (9th Cir.1995), viewed in conjunction with the Supreme Court's decision in Cargill, Inc. v. Monfort of Colorado, Inc., 479 U.S. 104, 107 S.Ct. 484, 93 L.Ed.2d 427 (1986), compels the opposite conclusion.

As the Supreme Court held in Cargill, in order to establish antitrust standing to sue for divestiture under section 16 of the Clayton Act, a plaintiff is required to "allege threatened loss or damage `of the type the antitrust laws were designed to prevent and that flows from that which makes defendants' acts unlawful.'" Cargill, 479 U.S. at 113, 107 S.Ct. at 491 (quoting Brunswick Corp. v. Pueblo Bowl-O-Mat, Inc., 429 U.S. 477, 489, 97 S.Ct. 690, 697-98, 50 L.Ed.2d 701 (1977)). The majority concludes that, as a purchaser of tires at the subdistributor level, Lucas Automotive is threatened with antitrust injury resulting from Coker Tire's acquisition of market power at the distributor level. I respectfully disagree with the majority's conclusion, as it conflicts with our decision in Rebel Oil.

In Rebel Oil, we held that market power may be demonstrated in one of two ways. First, the plaintiff may offer "direct evidence of the injurious exercise of market power." Id. at 1434. Lucas Automotive offers no direct evidence of a threat of the injurious exercise of market power by Coker Tire.

Second, the plaintiff may offer "circumstantial evidence pertaining to the structure of the market." Id. To demonstrate market power circumstantially, a plaintiff must: "(1) define the relevant market, (2) show that the defendant owns a dominant share of that market, and (3) show that there are significant barriers to entry and show that existing competitors lack the capacity to increase their output in the short run." Id. at 1434 (emphasis added).

The majority concludes that, after its acquisition of the right to distribute Firestone tires, Coker Tire possessed market power at the distributor level. However, although the majority does offer support for its conclusions that Coker Tire owns a dominant share of the relevant market and that there are significant barriers to entry, it fails to point to evidence in the record sufficient to demonstrate that Coker Tire's competitors, including Kelsey Tire, lack the capacity to expand their output in response to a price increase by Coker Tire.

Lucas Automotive argues in its brief that "Coker ... has the power to restrict output and raise prices without a competitive response, and to exclude competition." In support of this assertion, Lucas Automotive cites only a conclusory statement by Stanley Lucas. However, conclusory allegations unsupported by factual data are insufficient to defeat a motion for summary judgment. See Angel v. Seattle-First Nat'l Bank, 653 F.2d 1293, 1299 (9th Cir. 1981).

The only support that the majority offers for its tenuous (but essential to its holding) conclusion that Kelsey Tire "lack[s] the capacity to increase [its] output in the short run," Rebel Oil, 51 F.3d at 1434, is that "the Goodyear brand of vintage tires controlled by Kelsey is limited in terms of size." See Majority Opinion at 2898. Lucas Automotive has offered not a shred of evidence as to the cross elasticity of demand[1] between original equipment vintage tires of different sizes. Consequently, it is difficult to understand (based on the record before us) how the fact that Coker Tire distributes a greater range of tire sizes than Kelsey Tire suggests that Kelsey Tire cannot "increase [its] output in the short run" following a price increase by Coker Tire.[2] See Rebel Oil, 51 F.3d at 1434. Indeed, the majority's analysis only seems to underscore why Lucas Automotive failed to produce sufficient evidence to survive summary judgment.

I would affirm the district court's holding that Lucas Automotive lacks standing under section 16 of the Clayton Act.

Notes

[1] The cross elasticity of demand measures the percentage change in the quantity of a good demanded for each one-percent change in the price of a substitute good. See H. Hovenkamp, Economics and Federal Antitrust Law ¶ 1.1, at 62 (1985).

[2] I do not take the majority's analysis as challenging the district court's conclusion that the relevant market is that of original equipment vintage tires, as distinguished from original equipment vintage tires of a particular size.

Judge O'Scannlain's concurrence in US v. McKittrick (April 28, 1998)

O'SCANNLAIN, Circuit Judge, concurring:

I concur. I write separately only to emphasize that I find recourse to legislative history and arguments from statutory "purpose," see Maj. Op. 3956-61, unnecessary to the resolution of this appeal.

McKittrick's contention that the Fish and Wildlife Service was not authorized to create an experimental population from an "unlisted" population (i.e., Canadian gray wolves) is, in my view, answered by the plain language of the Endangered Species Act:

The Secretary may authorize the release ... of any population ... of an endangered species or a threatened species outside the current range of such species if the Secretary determines that such release will further the conservation of such species.

16 U.S.C. § 1539(j)(2)(A) (emphasis added). Boiled down to its essence, the statute provides that the Secretary may, upon making certain findings, authorize the release of "any population" of an "endangered species" or a "threatened species." The gray wolf is endangered and threatened as a species, even if the sub species that roams Canada is not. The statutory language refers to species, not subspecies. Consequently, in the end, the interpretive calculus is straightforward. Is the gray wolf an endangered or threatened species? Yes. Did the Secretary release "any population" of that species? Yes. Was the Secretary's action authorized by the plain language of § 1539(j)(2)(A)? It would certainly appear so.

Text alone also suffices, in my mind, to resolve McKittrick's claim that the Yellowstone designation violated § 1539(j)(1). That statute authorizes the release of experimental populations "only when, and at such times as, the population is wholly separate geographically from nonexperimental populations of the same species." Pointing to isolated past sightings of a few stray wolves in the Yellowstone area, McKittrick claims that the released experimental population at issue here was not sufficiently "separate geographically" from existing wolves under § 1539(j)(1). The statute, however, requires only that newly introduced experimental populations be separate geographically "from nonexperimental populations of the same species." 16 U.S.C. § 1539(j)(1) (emphasis added). And although the term "populations" is not specifically defined in the statute, its ordinary meaning undoubtedly denotes a group of more than one animal. See, e.g., Webster's Third New International Dictionary 1766 (1986) (defining "population" as "the organisms inhabiting a particular area or biotype"). A single straggler does not a population make.

Judge O'Scannlain's dissent in Stillwater Mining Co. v. Federal Mine Safety and Health Review Commission (April 28, 1998)

O'SCANNLAIN, Circuit Judge, dissenting.

Following an accident that killed one of Stillwater Mining Company's employees, an Administrative Law Judge ("ALJ") assessed a fine against Stillwater for violating a federal regulation that prohibits the use of equipment beyond its design capacity. See Stillwater Mining Co. v. Secretary of Labor, 18 F.M.S.H.R.C. 1291, 1298 (1996). The majority holds that the ALJ's conclusion is supported by substantial evidence; I respectfully disagree.

After Stillwater's employees bring ore up to the surface, they load it into long chutes. Located at the bottom of each chute is a gate assembly through which the ore is funneled into railcars. On August 21, 1995, the gate assembly on one of Stillwater's chutes collapsed, allowing ore to rush through the chute and to kill one of Stillwater's workers. At the time of the accident, the chute had been in operation for five years, during which time over 200,000 tons of ore had been pulled through without incident.

Following the accident, Stillwater was charged with violating 30 C.F.R. § 57.14205, which provides that "[m]achinery, equipment, and tools shall not be used beyond the design capacity intended by the manufacturer, where such use may create a hazard to persons." 30 C.F.R. § 57.14205. In determining that Stillwater had violated this regulation, the ALJ focused on eight one-inch diameter bolts that had been used to hold the collapsed gate assembly. See Stillwater Mining, 18 F.M.S.H.R.C. at 1296. Notably, the ALJ's focus on the bolts, as opposed to other components of the chute or gate assembly, was prompted at least in part by the fact that the bolts are "the only component of the chute and gate assembly for which there is any evidence regarding the design capacity intended by the manufacturer."[1] Id. Finding that Stillwater had used the bolts beyond their design capacity, the ALJ concluded that Stillwater had violated 30 C.F.R. § 57.14205 and assessed a $1500 fine. Id. at 1298.

Contrary to what the majority opinion concludes, the record does not contain substantial evidence to support the ALJ's finding that the bolts holding the gate assembly were used beyond their design capacity. Expert testimony established that the bolts were designed to withstand 408,408 pounds. Id. at 1296-97. The Mine Safety and Health Administration ("MSHA") failed to establish, however, what weight the bolts were actually subject to prior to the accident. Id. at 1297. Indeed, the ALJ found it "impossible to calculate the force applied to the bolts." Id.

Despite being unable to determine the force to which the bolts were subjected, the ALJ held that Stillwater had used the bolts in violation of 30 C.F.R. § 57.14205. The bolts must have been used beyond their design capacity, the ALJ concluded, because the chute gate assembly failed. Id. at 1297-98. The ALJ explained: "Whatever load was applied to the bolts on August 21, 1995, had to have exceeded the design capacity of the bolts; otherwise the chute would not have failed and Mr. Goode might not be dead."[2] Id. (emphasis added).

In defending the ALJ's decision, the majority incorrectly focuses upon the level of culpability required to prove violations of the Federal Mine Safety and Health Act ("FMSHA"). The majority contends that "the FMSHA imposes `a kind of strict liability on employers to ensure worker safety.'"[3] Maj. Op. at 1184 (quoting Miller Mining Co. v. Federal Mine Safety & Health Review Comm'n, 713 F.2d 487, 491 (9th Cir.1983)). Applying this standard, the majority holds that the ALJ's conclusion that Stillwater violated 30 C.F.R. § 57.14205 is supported by substantial evidence. See Maj. Op. at 1183-

1184.

However, even assuming arguendo that it were appropriate to impose strict liability for violations of the FMSHA, doing so would not help us to reach the majority's conclusion. The federal regulation at issue does not prohibit fatal accidents; rather, it prohibits the use of equipment beyond its design capacity. See 30 C.F.R. § 57.14205. The majority bases its reasoning upon a flawed conception of strict liability. Strict liability means that the plaintiff need not show recklessness, negligence, or any other mental state, see Winter v. G.P. Putnam's Sons, 938 F.2d 1033, 1035 (9th Cir.1991); it does mean that the plaintiff need not prove the elements of the underlying violation. Before we can hold Stillwater strictly liable for a violation of the regulation, we must decide whether a violation of that regulation occurred; that is, we must determine whether the bolts were used in excess of their design capacity. Apart from documenting the occurrence of the accident, the majority fails to point to any evidence of Stillwater's illegal use of the bolts.

The majority contends that Stillwater's argument — that the ALJ's ruling is not supported by substantial evidence — "disintegrates with the allocation of the burdens of proof."[4] Maj. Op. at 1184 (quoting Miller Mining, 713 F.2d at 490). The majority maintains that, by demonstrating that an accident occurred, MSHA "carried its initial burden of establishing a prima facie case of violation," thereby shifting the burden of proof to Stillwater. Id. Because Stillwater "offered no alternative explanation for the failure of the bolts or the gate assembly," it "failed to carry its burden of demonstrating compliance with the safety regulation." Id.

In support of its contention that the mere occurrence of an accident shifts the burden of proof with respect to whether a violation of 30 C.F.R. § 57.14205 has occurred, the majority inappropriately relies on our decision in Miller Mining. See Majority Opinion at 1184 (citing Miller Mining, 713 F.2d at 490). In Miller Mining, a mine was evacuated after a fire broke out in the main mine tunnel. See Miller Mining, 713 F.2d at 488. Acting pursuant to 30 U.S.C. § 813(k), the MSHA issued an order requiring all personnel to be withdrawn from the mine and giving the MSHA control over recovery efforts. See id. After the MSHA faltered in its efforts to fix the mine's ventilation fan (much to the dismay of local citizens), the mine was surreptitiously entered and the problem fixed. See id. at 489. We held that the MSHA's "uncontradicted evidence that the mine had been entered, and the ventilation system altered," was sufficient to establish "[a] prima facie case of violation." See id. at 491.

Our decision in Miller Mining is not controlling here. In Miller Mining, evidence that a mine had been entered was used to shift the burden of proof with respect to the alleged violation of an order which made such entry illegal. See id. Applying Miller Mining, we might reasonably hold that evidence that an accident occurred shifts the burden of proof with respect to a hypothetical regulation that simply prohibited accidents. However, it is quite another thing to hold, as my colleagues do, that mere evidence of an accident shifts the burden of proof with respect to a regulation that prohibits equipment from being used beyond its design capacity.

Apart from documenting the accident, the MSHA has failed to offer sufficient evidence that the bolts supporting the gate assembly were used beyond their design capacity in violation of 30 C.F.R. § 57.14205. Therefore, I would reverse the imposition of a civil penalty against Stillwater.

I respectfully dissent.

Notes

[1] The ALJ also noted that the parties agreed that the "immediate cause" of the accident was "the failure of the bolts that held the chute gate assembly...." Stillwater Mining, 18 F.M.S.H.R.C. at 1294. Saying that "the failure of the bolts" holding the gate assembly was the "immediate cause" of the accident is analogous to saying that heart failure is the "immediate cause" of every human death.

[2] Besides Stillwater's alleged use of the bolts beyond their design capacity, there are other possible explanations for the incident. For example, any component of the chute or gate assembly other than the bolts could have been defectively designed or defectively manufactured. Absent more compelling evidence of a violation of 30 C.F.R. § 57.14205, Stillwater should not be required to establish the validity of any such alternative explanation. See infra at 4063-65.

[3] In support of its position, the majority cites Miller Mining Co. v. Federal Mine Safety & Health Review Comm'n, 713 F.2d 487, 491 (9th Cir.1983). However, the passage from Miller Mining that the majority quotes for the proposition that the FMSHA imposes strict liability merely describes the Fifth Circuit's decision in Allied Products Co. v. Federal Mine Safety & Health Review Comm'n, 666 F.2d 890 (5th Cir. 1982). The relevant passage from Miller Mining states: "Imposing a kind of strict liability on employers to ensure worker safety, the [Fifth Circuit] pointed out there are no exceptions for fault, only harsher penalties for willful violations." Id. at 491.

[4] This allocation of burdens, according to the majority, "reflect[s]" the FMSHA's imposition of strict liability. Maj. Op. at 1184.

Judge O'Scannlain's concurrence and dissent in Garneau v. City of Seattle (May 4, 1998) [Notes omitted]

O'SCANNLAIN, Circuit Judge, concurring in part and dissenting in part.

I join Part IV of the court's opinion regarding the district court's discovery rulings. As to Parts II and III, however, which discuss the constitutionality of the Tenant Relocation Assistance Ordinance ("TRAO"), I respectfully dissent.

I

Nollan v. California Coastal Commission, 483 U.S. 825, 831-37, 107 S.Ct. 3141, 97 L.Ed.2d 677 (1987), and Dolan v. City of Tigard, 512 U.S. 374, 386-91, 114 S.Ct. 2309, 129 L.Ed.2d 304 (1994), outline the steps a court should take in determining the constitutionality of a government's exaction of private property made in exchange for a development permit. In essence, the exaction is unconstitutional when it (a) would be an outright taking in the absence of any exchange for the development permit, and (b) is not "roughly proportional" to the harms caused by the proposed development. Regrettably, the court finds Nollan and Dolan to be inapplicable for two reasons, which I shall address in turn.

A

The court first concludes that Nollan and Dolan pertain only to as-applied takings challenges, not to facial takings challenges. The analysis goes as follows: (1) the Nollan "nexus" test and the Dolan "rough proportionality" test require a court to compare the government's demanded exaction with the expected harm of the landlord's proposed development; (2) before making this comparison, a court must calculate the total amount of the exaction to be levied against the landlord bringing the suit; (3) in facial challenges, courts do not look at the total actual amount of the exaction, but rather only at the ordinance which permits the exaction; (4) consequently, Nollan and Dolan are not applicable to facial challenges. The weak link in this logical chain is the second step. The court incorrectly assumes that no comparison between exaction and harm can ever be made without first determining the total actual amount of the exaction. What the court disregards is this: When the harm is zero, an exaction can never be roughly proportional to, or even have a nexus with, the harm. Irrespective of the total actual amount of the exaction — whether it be $1,000 or $50,000 — it is not roughly proportional to zero. For this reason, I must part company with my colleagues.

The proposed development in this case causes no discernible harm whatsoever. When the city claims that the development would cause the tenants' moving expenses, the city is patently incorrect. Whether or not a landlord develops his land, the tenants must bear moving expenses when they vacate the premises. This burden should come as no surprise to tenants, who, by definition, are legally obliged to move out eventually, perhaps involuntarily. In its conventional sense, a "tenant" is "one who has the temporary use and occupation of real property" owned by someone else. Black's Law Dictionary 1314 (1979) (emphasis added). A landlord retains a right to evict the tenant at the expiration of the lease.[1] In constitutional parlance, this right is known as the "right to exclude," which, the Supreme Court has explained, is "one of the most essential sticks in the bundle of rights that are commonly characterized as property." Kaiser Aetna v. United States, 444 U.S. 164, 176, 100 S.Ct. 383, 62 L.Ed.2d 332 (1979). It is the landlord's exercise of his constitutionally protected right—and not the subsequent development — that causes the tenant's moving expenses. If the landlord chooses not to renew a lease, the tenants must pay moving expenses, regardless of what the landlord does to his land after eviction.

Moreover, even were I to accept the city's argument that the proposed development could constitute the cause of the tenant's moving expenses, I would still have to conclude that this "harm" is facially not roughly proportional to the requested exaction. Put simply, the magnitude of the relocation payments under the TRAO bears no relation whatsoever to the tenants' actual or even expected moving costs. Estimated moving costs should not include first or last month's rent, future rent increases, security deposits, or utility deposits because these amounts are not marginal costs. There is little reason to expect these amounts to be greater, on average, as a result of the proposed development.[2] Because only $391 of the relocation expenses is attributable to marginal costs,[3] the landlords' $1,000 share of each payment is assuredly not "related both in nature and extent to the impact of the proposed development." Dolan, 512 U.S. at 391, 114 S.Ct. 2309. Whether the landlord has to pay relocation expenses for one tenant or fifty, the monetary exaction is not roughly proportional to the costs of moving.

Thus, I cannot agree with the court's first conclusion that Nollan and Dolan pertain only to as-applied takings challenges. Although the court is correct that the government may seek land, money, or other concessions in return for a building permit, the exactions in this case are impermissible because they are not roughly proportional to the harm caused by the landlords, regardless of the total amount of the exactions. There is no need to determine how many relocation payments the landlords would have to make.

B

The court's second reason for holding Nollan and Dolan inapplicable is that these cases "do[] not address when a taking has occurred, [but] only how close a fit the exaction ... must have to the harms caused by development." Maj. Op. at 811. The first step in the Nollan-Dolan analysis, as the court notes, is to determine whether a government exaction would be a taking if made outright, in the absence of any exchange for a development permit. The court apparently believes that, because Nollan and Dolan do not articulate when an outright exaction can constitute a "taking," there could not be a taking under the facts of the present case.[4]

1

The problem with the court's analysis, quite simply, is that the court's conclusion does not follow from its premise. The question before us is whether a monetary exaction can constitute a taking. Nollan and Dolan's silence on this question does not imply that the question should be answered in the negative; it merely indicates that the question was not before the Court in either case. Moreover, the Supreme Court has, on other occasions, given us sufficient indication that the monetary exactions authorized by the TRAO are indeed takings. See Ehrlich v. City of Culver City, 512 U.S. 1231, 1231, 114 S.Ct. 2731, 129 L.Ed.2d 854 (1994); Webb's Fabulous Pharmacies, Inc. v. Beckwith, 449 U.S. 155, 163, 101 S.Ct. 446, 66 L.Ed.2d 358 (1980).

a

First, after deciding Dolan, the Supreme Court granted certiorari and summarily vacated a takings decision of the California Court of Appeal, remanding for consideration in light of Dolan. See Ehrlich v. City of Culver City, 512 U.S. 1231, 114 S.Ct. 2731, 129 L.Ed.2d 854 (1994). Ehrlich involved a fee charged by the city (to pay for more city parks) in exchange for a building permit. If Dolan were not applicable to monetary exactions, as my colleagues suggest, then it would have been an unnecessary waste of judicial resources to vacate and to remand Ehrlich. The Supreme Court's action suggests that the Court would apply Dolan to the monetary exactions at issue today.[5]

b

Second, in Webb's Fabulous Pharmacies, Inc. v. Beckwith, 449 U.S. 155, 101 S.Ct. 446, 66 L.Ed.2d 358 (1980), the Supreme Court found a Takings Clause violation in a monetary exaction that was "a forced contribution to general governmental revenues, ... not reasonably related to the costs of [any government service]." Id. at 163, 101 S.Ct. 446. If the exaction had been a "user fee" — a price for particular government services — then it quite likely would have been constitutional. See United States v. Sperry Corp., 493 U.S. 52, 60, 110 S.Ct. 387, 107 L.Ed.2d 290 (1989). Indeed, to pass Takings Clause scrutiny, a user fee need only be a "fair approximation of the cost of [government] benefits supplied." Id. (quoting Massachusetts v. United States, 435 U.S. 444, 463, 98 S.Ct. 1153, 55 L.Ed.2d 403 (1978)) (internal quotation marks omitted). The exaction in Webb's, however, was not a user fee; rather, it was nothing more than an uncompensated transformation of private property to public property in an attempt to "forc[e] some people alone to bear public burdens which, in all fairness and justice, should be borne by the public as a whole." Webb's, 449 U.S. at 163, 101 S.Ct. 446 (quoting Armstrong v. United States, 364 U.S. 40, 49, 80 S.Ct. 1563, 4 L.Ed.2d 1554 (1960)) (internal quotation marks omitted). Consequently, the exaction at issue in Webb's was unconstitutional.

For the same reason, the forced relocation payments at issue today also violate the Takings Clause. The landlords do not receive any government service in exchange for the exaction. The city of Seattle does not even contend that they do. Because the TRAO is not a "user fee," but rather a device for compelling landlords to bear a public burden, the TRAO cannot pass constitutional muster.

2

Moreover, even were I to accept the court's unsubstantiated assumption that ordinary monetary exactions cannot constitute takings, I would still have to disagree with its conclusion that the unique exactions authorized by the TRAO are not takings. The TRAO does not merely exact money.[6] Quite the contrary, a TRAO exaction is tantamount to a physical occupation of land because it has the effect of depriving landowners — without just compensation — of their constitutional right to exclude.

a

The TRAO is the economic equivalent of a hypothetical statute that

(a)"takes" the landowner's right to exclude; and

(b) inadequately "compensates" the landowner by granting him the option to buy back the right to exclude, an option whose value is necessarily less than the value of the right to exclude.

This hypothetical law has precisely the same effect as the TRAO: the landowner has to pay money to retain his right to exclude.[7] Because the two laws are functional equivalents, the constitutionality of the TRAO should follow the constitutionality of the hypothetical statute. Otherwise, we would be valuing form over function. Hence, if an out-and-out deprivation (without just compensation) of a landowner's right to exclude tenants violates the Takings Clause, then so should the Seattle ordinance.

b

A deprivation of the right to exclude most certainly violates the Takings Clause, as it constitutes a physical occupation of land. In Yee v. City of Escondido, 503 U.S. 519, 112 S.Ct. 1522, 118 L.Ed.2d 153 (1992), the Supreme Court made clear, albeit in dictum, that a deprivation of a landowner's right to exclude tenants, in the absence of just compensation, is unconstitutional: "Had the city required [landlords to permit] such an occupation, of course, the petitioners would have a right to compensation...."[8] Id. at 532, 112 S.Ct. 1522. Because a taking of the right to exclude without payment of just compensation is a violation of the Takings Clause, and because the TRAO accomplishes as much, I would hold that the ordinance constitutes an unconstitutional taking.[9]

II

To paraphrase the Supreme Court, the government may not obtain by extortion that which it cannot legitimately take outright. See Nollan, 483 U.S. at 837, 107 S.Ct. 3141. Because I view the Tenant Relocation Assistance Ordinance as akin to extortion, violative of the Takings Clause, I respectfully dissent.

Judge O'Scannlain's dissent in Dyer v. Calderon (Aug 6, 1998) [Notes omitted]

O'SCANNLAIN, Circuit Judge, with whom BRUNETTI, DAVID R.THOMPSON, and KLEINFELD, Circuit Judges, join, dissenting.

I respectfully dissent from the majority's holding that we are not foreclosed by Teague v. Lane, 489 U.S. 288, 109 S.Ct. 1060, 103 L.Ed.2d 334 (1989), from declaring that the entire hierarchy of California courts committed constitutional error by not implying juror bias.[1]

State court judges are our co-equal partners in the protection of federal constitutional rights.[2] Although Congress has granted us the authority to grant habeas corpus relief to state prisoners, due consideration of our circumscribed role in the federal system counsels prudent restraint in exercising that extraordinary power to second-guess state courts. Lest we forget, in Teague, the Supreme Court instructed us not to impose constitutional rules on our state court brethren that were not compelled by existing precedent when a habeas petitioner finished raising his claims on direct review. As the Court explained in Gilmore v. Taylor, 508 U.S. 333, 113 S.Ct. 2112, 124 L.Ed.2d 306 (1993), Teague "`validates reasonable, goodfaith interpretations of existing precedents made by state courts,' and thus effectuates the States' interest in the finality of criminal convictions and fosters comity between federal and state courts." Id. at 340, 109 S.Ct. 1060 (quoting Butler v. McKellar, 494 U.S. 407, 414, 110 S.Ct. 1212, 108 L.Ed.2d 347 (1990)) (internal citation omitted).

Under Teague, the reviewing federal court must inquire whether "`a state court considering [the petitioner's] claim at the time his conviction became final would have felt compelled by existing precedent to conclude that the rule [he] seeks was required by the Constitution.'" Lambrix v. Singletary, 520 U.S. 518, 117 S.Ct. 1517, 1524, 137 L.Ed.2d 771 (1997) (quoting Saffle v. Parks, 494 U.S. 484, 488, 110 S.Ct. 1257, 108 L.Ed.2d 415 (1990)) (emphasis added). That is to say, in order to conclude that application of a rule is not barred by Teague, the federal court must determine not only that the rule was "a reasonable interpretation of prior law," or even the "most reasonable" interpretation, but also that "no other interpretation was reasonable." Id. 117 S.Ct. at 1530. Because state courts would not have felt compelled by precedent (existing on the date Dyer's conviction became final) to conclude that the "implied-bias rule" developed by the majority was required by the Constitution, application of that rule is barred by Teague.

I

In Teague, the Supreme Court held, "[s]ubject to two narrow exceptions," Gilmore v. Taylor, 508 U.S. 333, 339, 113 S.Ct. 2112, 124 L.Ed.2d 306 (1993), that "new constitutional rules of criminal procedure will not be applicable to those cases which have become final before the new rules are announced." Teague, 489 U.S. at 310, 109 S.Ct. 1060. The federal court's inquiry under Teague must be conducted in three steps. First, the federal court must determine the date on which the petitioner's conviction became final. See Caspari v. Bohlen, 510 U.S. 383, 390, 114 S.Ct. 948, 127 L.Ed.2d 236 (1994). Second, it must "[s]urvey the legal landscape as it then existed," Graham v. Collins, 506 U.S. 461, 468, 113 S.Ct. 892, 122 L.Ed.2d 260 (1993), to "determine whether a state court considering [the petitioner's] claim at the time his conviction became final would have felt compelled by existing precedent to conclude that the rule [he] seeks was required by the Constitution." Saffle, 494 U.S. at 488, 110 S.Ct. 1257. Finally, "if the court determines that the habeas petitioner seeks the benefit of a new rule, the court must consider whether the relief sought falls within one of the two narrow exceptions to nonretroactivity."[3] Lambrix, 117 S.Ct. at 1524-25.

Dyer's conviction became final on October 31, 1988, the date on which the United States Supreme Court declined to review the California Supreme Court's decision affirming Dyer's conviction on direct review. See People v. Dyer, 45 Cal.3d 26, 246 Cal.Rptr. 209, 753 P.2d 1, cert. denied, 488 U.S. 934, 109 S.Ct. 330, 102 L.Ed.2d 347 (Oct. 31, 1988).

In surveying the legal landscape as it existed on that date, it is necessary to determine whether "precedent" would have "compelled" a state court to conclude that the Constitution "required" the implied-bias rule applied by the majority. Saffle, 494 U.S. at 488, 110 S.Ct. 1257. The majority purports to rely on three sources of precedent in support of its conclusion that juror bias may be implied: (1) decisions of the United States Supreme Court; (2) decisions of the lower federal courts; and (3) the common law.

II

Our survey of the decisions of the Supreme Court begins with Smith v. Phillips, 455 U.S. 209, 102 S.Ct. 940, 71 L.Ed.2d 78 (1982). In Smith, the Court examined whether a habeas petitioner's right to an impartial jury had been violated because a juror submitted an application for employment as an investigator in the District Attorney's Office during the petitioner's trial. See id. at 212, 102 S.Ct. 940. The petitioner argued that "[g]iven the human propensity for self-justification ... the law must impute bias to jurors in [such a] position." Id. at 215, 102 S.Ct. 940. The Supreme Court "disagree[d]," explaining that it had "long held that the remedy for allegations of juror partiality is a hearing in which the defendant has an opportunity to prove actual bias." Id.; see also id. at 215-17, 102 S.Ct. 940 (discussing Chandler v. Florida, 449 U.S. 560, 101 S.Ct. 802, 66 L.Ed.2d 740 (1981), Remmer v. United States, 347 U.S. 227, 74 S.Ct. 450, 98 L.Ed. 654 (1954), and Dennis v. United States, 339 U.S. 162, 70 S.Ct. 519, 94 L.Ed. 734 (1950)).

Justice O'Connor concurred in the Court's opinion in Smith. Justices Marshall, Brennan, and Stevens dissented. The concurring and dissenting Justices disagreed as to whether the Smith majority had in fact precluded the possibility that an implied-bias rule is required by the Constitution. In her concurring opinion, Justice O'Connor wrote "to express [her] view that the [majority] opinion does not foreclose the use of `implied bias' in appropriate circumstances." Id. at 221, 102 S.Ct. 940 (O'Connor, J., concurring). However, Justice Marshall, joined by Justices Brennan and Stevens, expressed a different view of the majority opinion: "According to the majority, the Constitution requires only that the defendant be given an opportunity to prove actual bias." Id. at 228, 102 S.Ct. 940 (Marshall, J., joined by Brennan and Stevens, JJ., dissenting) (emphasis added).

For Teague purposes, it matters little whether Justice O'Connor or the dissenting Justices in Smith arrived at the correct interpretation of the majority opinion; what does matter, quite simply, is that reasonable jurists could disagree. I posit what should be considered a most unremarkable point: Justices Marshall, Brennan, and Stevens are reasonable jurists. Because they could read a majority opinion of the United States Supreme Court as precluding the possibility of a constitutional implied-bias rule, I cannot conclude, unlike my majority colleagues, that all reasonable jurists would be compelled to locate such a rule in the Constitution.[4]

Would reasonable jurists have been compelled to change their minds between 1982, when Smith was decided, and October 31, 1988, when Dyer's conviction became final? To answer this question, we first look to the Supreme Court's decision in McDonough Power Equip., Inc. v. Greenwood, 464 U.S. 548, 104 S.Ct. 845, 78 L.Ed.2d 663 (1984). In McDonough, a four-Justice plurality stated that, in order to obtain a new trial on account of juror bias, "a party must first demonstrate that a juror failed to answer honestly a material question on voir dire, and then further show that a correct response would have provided a valid basis for a challenge for cause." Id. at 556, 104 S.Ct. 845. In a concurring opinion, Justice Blackmun, joined by Justices Stevens and O'Connor, observed that the plurality opinion did not "foreclose" the possibility that bias may be implied. Id. at 556, 104 S.Ct. 845 (Blackmun, J., joined by Stevens and O'Connor, JJ., concurring). In yet another concurring opinion, Justice Brennan, joined by Justice Marshall, expressed disagreement with the plurality's analysis, arguing that courts may consider whether there are "any facts in the case suggesting that bias should be conclusively presumed." Id. at

558, 104 S.Ct. 845 (Brennan, J., joined by Marshall, J., concurring).

State courts would not have felt compelled by these concurring opinions to conclude that bias may be implied as a matter of federal law. The McDonough Court reversed the Tenth Circuit's holding that a new trial was required on account of juror bias, see McDonough, 464 U.S. at 549, 104 S.Ct. 845; therefore, the statements in both concurring opinions regarding implied bias were dicta not necessary to the holding. See United States v. Boatwright, 822 F.2d 862, 864 (9th Cir.1987) (Kennedy, J.) ("The requirement [in United States v. Echegoyen, 799 F.2d 1271 (9th Cir.1986)], that two independent searches be in progress [for the challenged evidence to be admitted] is dictum, as the case admits the challenged evidence."); Hutchison v. Amateur Elec. Supply, 42 F.3d 1037, 1047 (7th Cir.1994) ("Any authority for denying prejudgment interest in [Donnelly v. Yellow Freight Sys., Inc., 874 F.2d 402 (7th Cir.1989)] thus is dicta, since the Donnelly court reversed the district court's denial of interest."); United States v. Helmsley, 985 F.2d 1202, 1207 (2d Cir.1993) ("The statement in [Mills v. Scully, 826 F.2d 1192 (2d Cir.1987), regarding potential deprivations of due process] was dictum since Mills reversed the grant of a writ of a habeas corpus."). Dicta in Supreme Court opinions are not binding, see McDaniel v. Sanchez, 452 U.S. 130, 141, 101 S.Ct. 2224, 68 L.Ed.2d 724 (1981); Ayala v. United States, 550 F.2d 1196, 1200 (9th Cir.1977), and are certainly insufficient to compel state courts to conclude that a rule is required by the Constitution under Teague. See Lambrix, 117 S.Ct. at 1525 (authority that supports point "in dictum" does not "`control[ ]' or `dictate[ ]' the result" for Teague purposes).

Between its decision in McDonough and 1988, the Supreme Court did not directly address the issue of implied bias. Thus, the decisions of the Supreme Court could not have "compelled" state courts to conclude that the Constitution requires the majority's implied-bias rule.[5]

III

The majority would apparently hold that, irrespective of whether there is a "Supreme Court case announcing" a constitutional rule of criminal procedure, the rule is not barred by Teague if it is "so deeply embedded in the fabric of due process that everyone takes it for granted." Maj. Op. at 984. I am unable to agree. A rule is "new" under Teague unless "a state court considering [the petitioner's] claim at the time his conviction became final would have felt compelled by existing precedent to conclude that the rule [the petitioner] seeks was required by the Constitution." O'Dell, 521 U.S. at ___, 117 S.Ct. at 1973 (holding that rule is not "new" only if this standard is met); Lambrix, 117 S.Ct. at 1524 (using same language to describe standard); Caspari, 510 U.S. at 390, 114 S.Ct. 948 (same); Saffle, 494 U.S. at 488, 110 S.Ct. 1257 (same). As the Supreme Court's repeated formulation of the Teague inquiry has made clear, Teague asks not only (1) whether a rule is required by (or deeply embedded in)[6] the Constitution, but also (2) whether existing precedent compelled that conclusion at the time the petitioner's conviction became final.

By "existing precedent," the Court could not have meant the Constitution itself. Otherwise, the Teague inquiry would not only be rendered circular (that is, Teague would ask whether "the Constitution compelled the conclusion that the rule the petitioner seeks is required by the Constitution"), but also toothless. Even if a rule was not compelled by Supreme Court decisions, a federal court would always be able to circumvent Teague simply by concluding that the rule had always been "deeply embedded in the fabric" of the Constitution. (Indeed, it is the rare case in which a federal court applies a constitutional rule of criminal procedure that the court does not believe to be "deeply embedded in the fabric" of some constitutional provision, or combination thereof.) If the Supreme Court had intended the result reached by the majority, it would simply have omitted the words "by existing precedent" from the Teague inquiry, and would have stated that a rule is not barred by Teague if state courts would "have felt compelled [ ] to conclude that the rule the petitioner seeks was required by the Constitution."[7] But see Saffle, 494 U.S. at 488, 110 S.Ct. 1257 (Teague asks whether state courts would "have felt compelled by existing precedent to conclude that the rule [the petitioner] seeks was required by the Constitution.") (emphasis added).

Even if there were a "deeply-embedded-in-the-fabric" exception to Teague, the Supreme Court's summary of its juror-bias decisions in Smith v. Phillips makes it clear that it would not apply here. The Smith Court stated, in pertinent part:

In argument before this Court, respondent ... contends that a court cannot possibly ascertain the impartiality of a juror by relying solely upon the testimony of the juror in question. Given the human propensity for self-justification, respondent argues, the law must impute bias to jurors in Smith's position. We disagree.

This court has long held that the remedy for allegations of juror partiality is a hearing in which the defendant has the opportunity to prove actual bias. For example.... Smith, 455 U.S. at 215, 102 S.Ct. 940 (emphasis added). Significantly, the Smith Court then proceeded to support this view by summarizing the Court's juror-bias jurisprudence, including its decisions in Dennis v. United States, 339 U.S. 162, 70 S.Ct. 519, 94 L.Ed. 734 (1950), Remmer v. United States, 347 U.S. 227, 74 S.Ct. 450, 98 L.Ed. 654 (1954), and Chandler v. Florida, 449 U.S. 560, 101 S.Ct. 802, 66 L.Ed.2d 740 (1981).[8] Even if the majority's historical sketch of juror-bias cases were somehow more accurate than that provided by the Smith Court (I respectfully submit that it is not), reasonable state judges sitting in 1988 were entitled to rely on the Smith majority's interpretation of precedent for the proposition that implied bias is not constitutionally required. Such state judges certainly could not have been expected to foresee our own interpretation of that precedent, decreed a decade later in 1998!

The majority's contention that "[n]o opinion in the two centuries of the Republic- except the dissent in our case-has suggested that a criminal defendant might lawfully be convicted by a jury tainted by implied bias," Maj. Op. at 985, is beside the point for three reasons. First, even assuming that the Supreme Court had not said that "the Constitution does not require an implied-bias rule," it certainly does not follow that the Court has said that "the Constitution does require an implied-bias rule"; only the second proposition is important under Teague. Second, while no court has uttered the precise words used by the majority, many reasonable jurists have concluded, in light of existing precedent, that defendants must demonstrate actual bias to obtain a new trial. See, e.g., Irons v. Lockhart, 741 F.2d 207, 208 (8th Cir.1984) ("In Smith v. Phillips ... the Supreme Court held that a petitioner who seeks habeas corpus relief based on an allegation of juror bias must prove actual bias, either in a state court or federal court hearing, and that a court cannot impute bias based on the petitioner's bare allegations."); Rogers v. McMullen, 673 F.2d 1185, 1189 (11th Cir. 1982) ("The Supreme Court [in Smith v. Phillips] rejected the implied bias argument and held that due process requires only that a defendant have the opportunity at a posttrial hearing to prove actual bias."); United States v. Whiting, 538 F.2d 220, 223 (8th Cir.1976) ("Where an attack is made upon the integrity of the trial by reason of alleged misconduct on the part of a juror in failing to disclose information pertinent to the issue of prejudice, the defendant's burden of proof must be sustained not as a matter of speculation, but as a demonstrable reality. No demonstration of intentional or knowing withholding of information by [the juror] is made here."). Finally, contrary to what the majority suggests, nowhere does this dissent take a position on whether the Constitution actually requires an implied-bias rule; rather, it simply observes that reasonable jurists could conclude that such a rule was not required at the time Dyer's conviction became final.

Buried beneath the majority's "fabric of due process" lies one relevant enduring fact. That is, Supreme Court precedent did not compel the conclusion that an implied-bias rule was required by the Constitution at the time Dyer's conviction became final. Cf. Tinsley v. Borg, 895 F.2d 520, 527 (9th Cir. 1990) ("The Supreme Court has never explicitly adopted or rejected the doctrine of implied bias.").

IV

We next examine whether, as of the date Dyer's conviction became final, the decisions of the lower federal courts would have compelled state courts to conclude that an implied-bias rule was constitutionally required. Because a state court could reasonably have concluded — and perhaps should have concluded—that it was not bound by any lower federal court's interpretation of the United States Constitution on any matter, it follows a fortiori that lower federal court decisions would not have bound that state court with respect to the specific question of implied bias.

As of 1988,[9] at least three federal courts of appeals had concluded that, with respect to the interpretation of federal law, state courts are bound only by the decisions of the United States Supreme Court, and not by the decisions of the lower federal courts.[10] See Bromley v. Crisp, 561 F.2d 1351, 1354 (10th Cir.1977) ("[T]he Oklahoma Courts may express their differing views on the retroactivity problem or similar federal questions until we are all guided by a binding decision of the Supreme Court."); United States ex rel. Lawrence v. Woods, 432 F.2d 1072, 1074 (1970) ("The federal Circuit Courts of Appeals and, in respect to federal law, the state courts of last resort, are subject to the supervisory jurisdiction of the Supreme Court of the United States. They are, however, as to the laws of the United States, co-ordinate courts.") (quoting Iowa Nat'l Bank v. Stewart, 214 Iowa

1229, 232 N.W. 445, 454 (1930)); Owsley v. Peyton, 352 F.2d 804, 805 (4th Cir.1965) ("Though state courts may for policy reasons follow the decisions of the Court of Appeals whose circuit includes their state, they are not obliged to do so.") (internal citation omitted). Although the Supreme Court had, as of 1988, neither adopted nor rejected this position, several individual Justices had expressed a similar view. See Steffel v. Thompson, 415 U.S. 452, 482 n. 3, 94 S.Ct. 1209, 39 L.Ed.2d 505 (1974) (Rehnquist, J., joined by Burger, C.J., concurring); Perez v. Ledesma, 401 U.S. 82, 125, 91 S.Ct. 674, 27 L.Ed.2d 701 (1971) (Brennan, J., joined by White and Marshall, JJ., dissenting).

Further, a substantial majority of the state courts that had addressed this issue, including California's, had concluded that they were not bound by the decisions of the lower federal courts on federal questions. Compare, e.g., Cowan v. Myers, 187 Cal.App.3d 968, 985, 232 Cal.Rptr. 299 (1986) ("[T]he decisions of the lower federal courts, even on federal questions, are not binding on this court."); State v. Webster, 114 Wis.2d 418, 426 n. 4, 338 N.W.2d 474 (1983); State v. Glover, 60 Ohio App.2d 283, 287, 396 N.E.2d 1064 (1978); Greene v. State, 11 Md.App. 106, 110, 273 A.2d 830 (1971), with Handy v. Goodyear Tire & Rubber Co., 230 Ala. 211, 160 So. 530 (1935); Kuchenmeister v. Los Angeles & S.L.R., 52 Utah 116, 172 P. 725 (1918). In light of this line of authority, a state court could reasonably have concluded that it was not bound by the decisions of any lower federal court on any federal constitutional issue. Accordingly, such lower federal court decisions could not "compel" state courts within the meaning of Teague. Compare Clemmons v. Delo, 124 F.3d 944, 955 n. 11 (8th Cir.1997) (assuming without deciding that "when the [Supreme] Court says `firmly dictated by precedent,' it means Supreme Court precedent"); Glock v. Singletary, 65 F.3d 878, 885 (11th Cir.1995) (en banc) (courts of appeals do not "dictate" particular rule to state courts for Teague purposes), with Jiminez v. Myers, 40 F.3d 976, 979-81 (9th Cir.1994) (using Ninth Circuit decisions to support conclusion that "totality of the circumstances" rule was not "new" under Teague). For this reason, the majority errs in relying upon United States v. Burr, 25 F. Cas. 49, 50 (D.Va.1807), a federal district court opinion, for the proposition that Teague is inapplicable.

Indeed, even assuming that all reasonable state court judges would have concluded, contrary to the weight of the authority, that they were bound to follow lower federal court precedent, Teague would still dictate that such judges were not compelled to recognize an implied-bias rule. At the time Dyer's conviction became final, the federal courts of appeals were split on the issue of implied bias. Compare United States v. Eubanks, 591 F.2d 513, 517 (9th Cir.1979) (holding that bias could be implied as a matter of law), with United States v. Malloy, 758 F.2d 979, 982 n. 6 (4th Cir.1985) (rejecting implied-bias theory and collecting cases in which other lower federal courts had done so); see also Debtor Reorganizers, Inc. v. State Bd. of Equalization, 58 Cal.App.3d 691, 696, 130 Cal.Rptr. 64 (1976) ("As between the decisions of the Ninth Circuit and [those] of the Fifth Circuit [on federal law], no primacy inheres in the former, so the persuasiveness of the conflicting views must depend upon the validity of the arguments made therein."). A state court judge sitting in 1988 could reasonably have followed those lower federal courts that had held that a defendant must establish actual bias to obtain a new trial; perforce, state court judges were not compelled to adopt the implied-bias rule. See Lambrix, 117 S.Ct. at 1530 ("[Teague asks] whether no other interpretation [of existing precedent] was reasonable.").

V

As of the time Dyer's conviction became final, the conclusion that an implied-bias rule was required by the Constitution was not compelled by either: (1) the decisions of the Supreme Court; or (2) the decisions of the lower federal courts.

Today the court holds that there is a third source of compelling authority: Sir Edward Coke's dictum in Dr. Bonham's Case, 77 Eng. Rep. 646, 652 (C.P.1610).[11] See Maj. Op. at 8601. Not likely! Our own Supreme Court has stated that "authority that supports the point in dictum" does not "`control[]' or `dictate[]' the result" under Teague. See Lambrix, 117 S.Ct. at 1525. The Court could hardly have intended an exception to this Teague-based rule, which applies even to the Court's own opinions, for the dictum of a seventeenth-century English common-law judge.

I respectfully dissent.

Judge O'Scannlain's concurrence and dissent in Bean v. Calderon (Dec 15, 1998)

O'SCANNLAIN, Circuit Judge, concurring in part and dissenting in part:

I join in most of the Court's opinion but respectfully dissent from Parts III and V. I agree that Bean did not procedurally default his claim of ineffective assistance of counsel, that Bean received effective assistance of counsel at the guilt phase of the trial and that there was sufficient evidence to convict Bean of the Fox murder. I disagree, however, on the two remaining issues: I conclude that Bean received effective assistance of counsel at the penalty phase and that joinder of the Schatz and Fox indictments did not deprive Bean of a fundamentally fair trial.

I

While I recognize that Bean's representation at the penalty phase was by no means flawless, it did not "so undermine[ ] the proper functioning of the adversarial process that the trial cannot be relied on as having produced a just result." Strickland v. Washington, 466 U.S. 668, 686, 104 S.Ct. 2052, 80 L.Ed.2d 674 (1984).

The Supreme Court has read the Sixth Amendment right to trial to include a right to counsel. See id. at 685, 104 S.Ct. 2052. To satisfy this right to counsel, it is not enough "that a person who happens to be a lawyer is present at trial alongside the accused." Id. Rather, the "accused is entitled to be assisted by an attorney . . . who plays the role necessary to ensure that the trial is fair." Id. The Supreme Court has set a low standard for counsel to qualify as effective because "the purpose of the effective assistance guarantee of the Sixth Amendment is not to improve the quality of legal representation . . . [but] is simply to ensure that criminal defendants receive a fair trial." Id. at 689, 104 S.Ct. 2052.

The Court, therefore, has stated:

> Judicial scrutiny of counsel's performance must be highly deferential. It is all too tempting for a defendant to second-guess counsel's assistance after conviction or adverse sentence, and it is all too easy for a court examining counsel's defense after it has proved unsuccessful, to conclude that a particular act or omission of counsel was unreasonable.

Id. The Court cautioned that

> The availability of intrusive post-trial inquiry into attorney performance . . . would encourage the proliferation of ineffectiveness challenges. Criminal trials resolved unfavorably to the defendant would increasingly come to be followed by a second trial, this one of the counsel's unsuccessful defense. Counsel's performance and even willingness to serve could be adversely affected.

Id. at 690, 104 S.Ct. 2052. Thus, while we must ensure that an accused has effective counsel at trial and, in Bean's case, at his sentencing hearing, we can do no more than require that the counsel provided was adequate.

The Supreme Court's two part Strickland test governs our review of an accused's counsel. It provides that a defendant claiming ineffective assistance must demonstrate that (1) counsel's actions were outside the wide range of professionally competent assistance, and (2) there is a reasonable probability that, but for counsel's unprofessional errors, the result of the proceeding would have been different. See id. at 687-694, 104 S.Ct. 2052.

Bean's counsel was not constitutionally ineffective during the penalty phase. Bean's counsel presented nine witnesses with more than 200 pages of witness testimony (page number includes cross-examination of witnesses), including two psychiatric experts, Dr. Weissman and Dr. Blunt. Dr. Blunt testified that, after performing five neurological tests, she was convinced that Bean was organically brain damaged from three lesions on the brain. This brain damage, she testified, involved an inability to think, to form judgments, to plan or to appreciate the criminality of conduct. Dr. Weissman testified that he had used six different tests on Bean and discovered that Bean was suffering from organic personality disorder and mental retardation (Bean had the mental age of an eight to eleven-year old in terms of "thinking" and "capacity to understand his environment"). Dr. Weissman testified further that, although he had reached no firm conclusion, he found that Bean had "soft signs" of "potentially mild to moderate degree of organic . . . brain damage." Counsel's presentation of the two psychiatrists was not, as the majority claims, a "failure to elicit mitigating testimony from mental health experts."

Bean's counsel also presented testimony from Bean's family and friends which showed a very poor upbringing. The jury knew that Bean was whipped by his mother, was placed in classes for "slow learners," was suspended from school several times, was made a ward of juvenile court at an early age, left home at age fifteen, and was interned at "Boys Ranch," some sort of juvenile detention center. The jury could also have gleaned from the testimony that Bean's father hit or whipped Bean, even though Bean's father denied beating Bean when asked directly.[1]

Bean alleged that his counsel inadequately investigated his background, inexcusably delayed his neuropsychological testing, inadequately prepared the witnesses, asked the expert witnesses the wrong questions and, overall, failed to present a compelling or reliable mitigation argument. Bean is correct that his counsel did a less than perfect job during the penalty phase. They could have presented Bean's mitigating evidence in greater and more compelling detail. Their inadequacies, however, do not "`amount[] in every respect to no representation at all.'" Clabourne v. Lewis, 64 F.3d 1373, 1387 (9th Cir.1995) (quoting Blake v. Kemp, 758 F.2d 523, 533 (11th Cir.1985)). Bean's arguments would have greater merit if the issue before this court were whether Bean's counsel did a good job during the penalty phase of his trial. The issue here is, however, whether Bean's counsel was constitutionally competent, a much lower standard.

This case differs markedly from other recent cases in which this court has held that counsel was constitutionally deficient during the penalty phase. In Smith v. Stewart, 140 F.3d 1263 (9th Cir.), cert. denied, ____ U.S. ____, 119 S.Ct. 336, 142 L.Ed.2d 277 (1998), this court held that trial counsel provided ineffective assistance because counsel "provided no evidence at the penalty phase and virtually no argument," despite the fact that evidence of mitigating circumstances "was rather near the surface." Id. at 1269 (emphasis added). Counsel's only argument involved "a few asthenic comments to the effect that Smith still denied his guilt and that he was just 30 years of age. Nothing else!" Id. at 1268.

In Correll v. Stewart, 137 F.3d 1404 (9th Cir.), cert. denied, ____ U.S. ____, 119 S.Ct. 450, ____ L.Ed.2d ____ (1998), counsel failed to present any evidence of the petitioner's purported mental illness as a mitigating factor. Defense counsel's argument at the sentencing hearing took a total of eight transcript pages. We held that "[t]his almost complete absence of effort on the part of Correll's counsel to investigate, develop, and present mitigating evidence, including evidence of Correll's psychiatric history and his condition at the time of the murders, constitutes deficient performance `outside the wide range of professionally competent assistance.'" Id. at 1412 (quoting Strickland, 466 U.S. at 690, 104 S.Ct. 2052). In addition, defense counsel met with his client for just five minutes in the month between the jury verdict and the pre-sentencing hearing.

Other cases are to the same effect. In Hendricks v. Calderon, 70 F.3d 1032 (9th Cir.1995), counsel failed to conduct any investigation into mitigating evidence without a strategic rationale to justify the lack of preparation. See id. at 1043. In Clabourne, counsel "did not call any witnesses, introduce any evidence of Clabourne's history of mental illness, or argue any mitigating circumstances beside Clabourne's mental condition at the time of the offense." Clabourne, 64 F.3d at 1384. Clabourne's entire mitigation argument took up six pages of the sentencing hearing transcript. We held that "the total absence of advocacy [fell] outside Strickland's `wide range of professionally competent assistance,'" and that counsel's representation at the sentencing hearing "amounted in every respect to no representation at all." Id. at 1387 (citations and internal quotation marks omitted).

These cases are instructive; Bean's counsel was not derelict in their duties compared to any of them. In these cases, counsel generally conducted no investigations, presented no mitigating evidence, made no arguments on behalf of their clients, and brought few (or no) witnesses to the stand. Of course, these cases do not stand for the proposition that only a complete failure to present mitigating evidence during the penalty phase will be sufficient to warrant a writ of habeas corpus for ineffective assistance of counsel, but they do serve as a valuable comparison. Bean's counsel did offer mitigating evidence to show Bean's background information and mental deficiencies and did make reasonable arguments on Bean's behalf. Although it would have been preferable for counsel to have asked different questions, presented more detailed mental health evidence, and investigated Bean's family background more carefully, the Constitution does not demand as much. Bean's counsel was not guilty of a "total absence of advocacy" amounting to no representation at all. Clabourne, 64 F.3d at 1387. In my opinion, therefore, Bean does not satisfy the first prong of the Strickland test.

Furthermore, under the second prong of the Strickland test, it is unlikely that, had the more detailed evidence now available regarding Bean's background and mental health been presented to the jury, the outcome of the trial would have changed. The jury was exposed to the majority of the evidence this court now points to as mitigating factors. Certainly, some of the more graphic details of Bean's childhood were not shared with the jury. The jury knew, however, that Bean spent time in juvenile detention, was whipped by his parents and left home at fifteen. Similarly, while the jury did not hear all the possible evidence of Bean's mental difficulties, the jury did hear two experts testify to Bean's brain damage. The added details discussed by the majority do not sufficiently change the overall picture of Bean's condition and history such that there is a reasonable probability that the outcome of the sentencing hearing would be different. In my opinion, therefore, Bean does not satisfy the second prong of the Strickland test.

I believe that the district court's decision to grant Bean a writ of habeas corpus for ineffective assistance of counsel during the penalty phase was error and should be reversed. I, therefore, respectfully dissent from Part III.

II

Nor do I believe Bean has demonstrated that he suffered actual prejudice from the district court's discretionary refusal to sever Bean's two murder counts. We address this issue on collateral review after the California Supreme Court has thoroughly considered the facts and arguments. People v. Bean, 46 Cal.3d 919, 251 Cal.Rptr. 467, 760 P.2d 996 (1988). Out of respect for important notions of federalism, comity and finality, our review should be deferential to the state court findings.

As a general matter, "[t]he propriety of a consolidation rests within the sound discretion of the state trial judge." Featherstone v. Estelle, 948 F.2d 1497, 1503 (9th Cir.1989) (quoting Tribbitt v. Wainwright, 540 F.2d 840, 841 (5th Cir.1976)). In order for this court to issue a writ of habeas corpus, Bean must have shown that the trial court's failure to sever the counts against him "actually render[ed][his] state trial fundamentally unfair and hence, violative of due process." Id. at 1502 (emphasis added); see also Herring v. Meachum, 11 F.3d 374, 377 (2nd Cir.1993) ("In considering whether a violation of due process occurred, the emphasis must be on the word `actually.'") Neither the potential for prejudice nor even a high probability of prejudice will suffice; Bean must establish that prejudice actually resulted "from the events as they unfolded during the joint trial." Herring, 11 F.3d at 377-378. The Second Circuit has clearly articulated the procedural posture for this habeas corpus review:

[H]abeas petitioners challenging their state convictions under the general fairness mandate of the due process clause bear an onerous burden. Because of the significant procedural protection provided by direct review through the state system, we will not lightly conclude that state court proceedings were so arbitrary as to violate due process.

Herring, 11 F.3d at 378 (citing Brecht v. Abrahamson, 507 U.S. 619, 113 S.Ct. 1710, 123 L.Ed.2d 353 (1993) (presumption of fidelity and legality attaches to state criminal proceedings)).

Bean alleges, and the majority agrees, that Bean was prejudiced because joinder allowed evidence of the Schatz crime, evidence that otherwise would not have been admitted, to be used by the prosecution to bolster its weak Fox case. The California Supreme Court found that the evidence for the two murder counts was not cross-admissible. Certainly, this finding heightens the likelihood of prejudice because joinder risks tainting the jury's view of the accused with evidence that would not otherwise have been admissible. It does not lead, however, to an automatic finding of actual prejudice. Also, as Bean and the majority point out, joinder in these cases can be especially dangerous when strong evidence of one crime is used to bolster weak evidence of a second crime. The California Supreme Court considered all these arguments and still concluded, I think correctly, that Bean did not show that there was a substantial danger of prejudice from the joinder of the two offenses.

We have not directly addressed this issue in a habeas case. In United States v. Johnson, 820 F.2d 1065 (9th Cir.1987), a direct review case, however, we noted in dictum that:

Even if the evidence would not have been admissible, the district court did not abuse its discretion because the jury was not likely in this case to confuse which count particular evidence was introduced to establish. When evidence concerning the other crime is limited or not admissible, our primary concern is whether the jury can reasonably be expected to "compartmentalize the evidence" so that evidence of one crime does not taint the jury's consideration of the other crime.

Johnson, 820 F.2d at 1071 (emphasis added). The court elaborated further, "[e]ven where evidence of one of the crimes is particularly weak, ... we consider[ ] principally whether the jury was likely to have been confused." Id. at 1071 n. 6 (citations omitted). The main issue we must decide is, therefore, whether the jury was reasonably able to distinguish evidence introduced in one case from evidence introduced in the other.

The California Supreme Court found that the evidence against Bean was sufficient on both counts and that "no spillover effect" of the evidence occurred. Bean, 46 Cal.3d at 940, 251 Cal.Rptr. 467, 760 P.2d 996. I agree. The evidence introduced for both the Fox offense and Schatz offense was simple and distinct, making it likely that the jury was able to keep the evidence separate when considering the various counts against Bean. See Herring, 11 F.3d at 378 ("Moreover, because the evidence with respect to each murder was distinct and easily compartmentalized, the risk of jury confusion at petitioner's trial was significantly limited."). The evidence of the Fox offenses consisted of Bean's fingerprint on a pair of sunglasses, witness testimony that Bean had been seen multiple times "casing" the Fox residence, and Bean's inconsistent testimony regarding ownership of the sunglasses. The evidence in the Schatz charge consisted of witnesses testifying to Bean's incriminating statements, a partial palm print, fingerprint, and footprints at the Schatz residence, and witness testimony. Neither the Fox nor the Schatz crimes involved complicated scenarios or crimes that involved confusing scientific evidence or complex transactions.

In addition, the two crimes were distinctly different. The Schatz crime involved two assailants breaking into a mobile home at night and attacking two victims with a hammer. The Fox crime involved a single assailant attacking a single woman with his fist or foot as she entered her house during the day. The evidence used to prove such distinctly distinguishable crimes is unlikely to have confused the jury. The majority, for example, is concerned that the jury would have been confused as to which crime the instructions regarding aiding and abetting, and conspiracy applied. This, I think, underestimates jury intelligence. Surely a jury would be able to realize that instructions regarding aiding and abetting, or conspiracy apply to the crime involving multiple assailants and not to the crime involving a single assailant. The majority also suggests that acquittal as to one of the counts would have established that the jury had compartmentalized the evidence. This is not an appropriate guide where, as here, there is sufficient evidence to convict the accused on both counts. In any event, the jury did bring in separate verdicts for the two murders and decided Bean should be sentenced to death for the Schatz murder and should get life imprisonment for the Fox murder.

The majority also worries that the trial court did not properly instruct the jury. It cites Johnson for the proposition that a jury can only compartmentalize the evidence if properly instructed to do so by the court. The jury instruction we found to be sufficient in Johnson was "[e]ach count charges a separate crime. You must decide separately what the evidence in the case shows about the crime." Id. at 1071. This instruction is not significantly more explicit than the instruction in Bean's trial. Although the trial court's instructions to the jury were certainly limited regarding the separateness of the crimes and their evidence, the jury was told it must "decide each count separately" and that "[e]ach count charges a distinct offense."

While I realize that the joinder of two counts always includes the risk that the jury will be prejudiced against a defendant charged with multiple crimes or that the jury will consider the evidence cumulatively, "joinder of offenses has long been recognized as a constitutionally acceptable accommodation of the defendant's right to a fair trial." Herring, 11 F.3d at 377. In this case, I am not convinced that Bean has presented evidence to show that he suffered actual prejudice as a result of the joinder of his two murder counts. I, therefore, must dissent from Part V. I would not second-guess the California Supreme Court's holding that joinder was not an abuse of discretion, and would affirm Bean's conviction for the Fox murder.

Notes

[1] When asked at the Sentencing Hearing what he would have done to Bean if he had not come home, Bean's father answered "I was going to whip him." In addition, when asked if he had anything to do with Bean leaving home, Bean's father answered "Well, I tell you, when you got kids you got to have a firm hand with them, you know, when you are raising them up. See, when the boys get a certain age they don't want to mind, see. But at my house, when they come up, I was the boss of the house. I don't let my kids rule my house. I'm the one that rules the house."

Judge O'Scannlain's dissent in Briones v. INS (April 30, 1999)

O'SCANNLAIN, Circuit Judge, dissenting:

Of course the majority is correct in concluding that the discrepancies in Briones's testimony suggest that his story is incredible; the immigration judge so found. The problem is that the purported facts in the record, if taken to be true, do not compel the conclusion that Briones was persecuted on account of political opinion. Therefore, we need not reach the issue of credibility, remand is unnecessary and, for these reasons, I must respectfully dissent.

Let us recall the standards established by the Supreme Court in INS v. Elias-Zacarias, 502 U.S. 478, 112 S.Ct. 812, 117 L.Ed.2d 38 (1992). First, our review of BIA decisions is highly deferential; we may reverse only if the evidence "was so compelling that no reasonable factfinder could fail to find the requisite fear of persecution." Id. at 483-484, 112 S.Ct. 812 (emphasis added). Second, to be statutorily eligible for asylum, Briones must demonstrate a well-founded fear of future persecution "on account of race, religion, nationality, membership in a particular social group, or political opinion." 8 U.S.C. § 1101(a)(42). The words "on account of" require an inquiry into the persecutor's motives, and the political opinion we investigate is that of the victim, and not that of the persecutor. Id. at 482, 483, 112 S.Ct. 812. Recall further that "political opinion is ... a narrow term, encompassing beliefs but not activities." Canas-Segovia v. INS, 970 F.2d 599, 601 (9th Cir.1992) (emphasis in original).

Briones sought asylum because of threats made against him by the NPA due to his service as a confidential informant for the Philippine government. As Briones stated in his opening brief, the NPA "is out to kill him because of his works as confidential agent of the military." Even the majority states that Briones's story indicates "he faces future persecution on account of his past activities as a government informer." Briones and the majority are correct to that extent; substantial evidence certainly supports the BIA's determination that the persecutors' interest was retaliation against a perceived informer. But it fails to establish that the NPA was motivated to persecute Briones on account of Briones's political opinion. Rather it demonstrates retaliation and self-protection by the NPA and, in my view, "it is reasonable to assume that the retaliation would occur regardless of what political opinion, if any, the respondent held." Adhiyappa v. INS, 58 F.3d 261, 265 (6th Cir.1995) (quoting the BIA decision).

Indeed, in a similar case, the Sixth Circuit held that the BIA's "determination that Petitioner's persecution was not on account of his political opinion" was supported by substantial evidence. Id. at 268. Adhiyappa, an Indian Tamil working at a Sri Lankan university, acted as a government informant by passing on information about student activists who supported the Tamil separatist cause. When the Tamil separatists threatened Adhiyappa, Adhiyappa fled to the United States and claimed asylum based on political opinion. In affirming the denial of Adhiyappa's asylum petition, the court explained that "the evidence would support a conclusion ... that it was his status as an informant, not his political opinion, that spurred their hatred." Id. The court noted that 8 U.S.C. § 1101(a)(42)(A) "provides protection for individuals who are persecuted on account of their political opinion, but it does not include all individuals who are persecuted because their actions tend to obstruct the activities of politically-motivated organizations, even where those activities may be in part motivated by political opinion." Id.

The attack on Briones can easily be analogized to the attack on Elias-Zacarias. In Elias-Zacarias, the Court held that a guerilla organization's attempt to conscript a Guatemalan native into its military forces did not necessarily constitute "persecution on account of political opinion." Elias-Zacarias, 502 U.S. at 481-482, 112 S.Ct. 812. Rejecting the argument that a political opinion should be imputed per se in such situations, the Court noted: "Even a person who supports a guerilla movement might resist recruitment for a variety of reasons — fear of combat, a desire to remain with one's family and friends, a desire to earn a better living in civilian life, to mention only a few." Id. at 482, 112 S.Ct. 812. Confronting Elias-Zacarias's argument that the persecutor's motives in forcibly recruiting members were necessarily political, the Court stated first, that the emphasis must be on the "victim's political opinion, not the persecutor's," and second, that "the mere existence of a generalized `political' motive underlying the guerillas' forced recruitment is inadequate to establish ... the proposition that Elias-Zacarias fears persecution on account of political opinion, as § 101(a)(42) requires." Id. (emphasis in original).

Likewise in Adhiyappa, as in Briones's case, it is doubtful that the petitioners' political opinions played any role at all. "One might undertake to inform government officials of the names of members of a militant separatist group for reasons other than political opinion." Adhiyappa, 58 F.3d at 267. In fact, as in Elias-Zacarias, Briones's testimony actually demonstrates that he was not motivated by political opinion. Briones testified that he agreed to serve as an informant because of concerns about the damage the NPA had caused to his hometown. Briones was motivated to protect his home town from the destruction caused by the NPA; there is no evidence he was motivated by a disagreement with the NPA's communist mission. Cf. Elias-Zacarias, 502 U.S. at 482, 112 S.Ct. 812 (Elias-Zacarias "testified that he refused to join the guerillas because he was afraid that the government would retaliate against him and his family if he did so.").

Even if we were to consider Briones's actions as politically motivated, he "still has to establish that the record ... compels the conclusion that he has a `well-founded fear' that the guerillas will persecute him because of that political opinion, rather than because of his" acts as a government informer. Id. at 483, 112 S.Ct. 812 (emphasis in original). Briones did not present any evidence suggesting that the guerillas erroneously believed that his informant service was politically based. See id. at 482, 112 S.Ct. 812. Moreover, even though the NPA was certainly forwarding its own political agenda by attempting to rid itself of a spy, this appears to be "the mere existence of a generalized `political' motive" and "is inadequate to establish ... the proposition that [Briones] fears persecution on account of political opinion, as § 101(a)(42) requires." Id. (emphasis in original).

The majority interestingly ignores the BIA's finding that Briones failed to present evidence that the Philippine government would be either unable or unwilling to protect him or that he ever sought such protection. This court has held that persecution may be "inflicted either by the government or by persons or organizations which the government is unable or unwilling to control." Sangha v. INS, 103 F.3d 1482, 1487 (9th Cir.1997). See also Korablina v. INS, 158 F.3d 1038, 1044 (9th Cir.1998) ("Persecution may be found by cumulative, specific instances of violence and harassment toward an individual ... not only by the government, but also by a group the government declines to control."); Singh v. INS, 134 F.3d 962, 967 n. 9 (9th Cir.1998) ("[P]rivate individuals that the government is unable or unwilling to control can persecute someone."). Because the NPA is not the government, Briones had the burden of showing that the Philippine government was "unable or unwilling" to control the NPA. As the BIA correctly found, Briones failed to present evidence to this effect.

The record in this case does not compel a conclusion that the findings of the BIA were wrong. The record presents no evidence to suggest that the NPA threatened Briones's life because he held political opinions antithetical to its own. Rather, the evidence shows that the NPA was attempting to shut off an information source that was exceedingly damaging to its operations and to retaliate against a man who had wreaked so much havoc to its plans. Indeed, even the majority acknowledges that "[i]t is a case of threatened retaliatory death for causing death." On these facts, I simply cannot say that "no reasonable factfinder could fail to find" that the persecution was on account of Briones's political opinions.

I would deny the petition for review and affirm the decision of the BIA in this case.

Judge O'Scannlain's dissent in Borja v. INS (April 30, 1999)

O'SCANNLAIN, Circuit Judge, with whom KLEINFELD, Circuit Judge, joins, dissenting:

I agree with the majority that the central question in this case is: "Does the evidence Ms. Borja presented compel the conclusion that the NPA subjected her to persecution on account of her political opinion under the Immigration and Nationality Act[?]" (emphasis added). Notwithstanding its disclaimers, however, the majority's analysis wholly distorts the "compelled" test and, instead, effectively applies "de novo" review of the BIA's decision, contrary to Supreme Court guidance. For this reason, I must respectfully dissent.

Two preliminary observations control. First, an appellate court reviews decisions of the BIA under a highly deferential standard; we may reverse the BIA only if the evidence in the record compels a contrary result. See INS v. Elias-Zacarias, 502 U.S. 478, 482, 112 S.Ct. 812, 117 L.Ed.2d 38 (1992). Second, the Supreme Court's decision in Elias-Zacarias makes clear that a petitioner must provide evidence, either direct or circumstantial, of her persecutors' motives. As the Court noted:

[The petitioner] objects that he cannot be expected to provide direct proof of his persecutors' motives. We do not require that. But since the statute makes motive critical, he must provide some evidence, direct or circumstantial.

Id. at 483, 112 S.Ct. 812 (emphasis added).

This case turns on the NPA's motives in persecuting Borja. Was the NPA motivated by Borja's politics or her money? Under Elias-Zacarias, Borja must present evidence that the NPA was motivated to persecute her, at least in part, because of her political opinion. See id. at 483-84, 112 S.Ct. 812. The BIA denied asylum to Borja because it concluded that the NPA's "imposition of `revolutionary taxes' (enforced by threats of harm and enforced by actual harm) was extortion ..., not [related] to the respondent's political opinion, but rather to her ability to pay." In other words, the NPA would have approached her, extorted money from her, and assaulted her regardless of her political opinions.

The BIA based its conclusion that the NPA persecuted Borja to get her money, not on account of political opinion, on several well-founded observations. First, Borja is from a family of means and was thus in a position to supply the NPA with needed resources. Second, the NPA approached Borja only at her parents' place of business; Borja provided no evidence that the NPA sought her at home or at the hospital at which she worked for fifteen years before leaving the Philippines. Third, Borja failed to demonstrate that she was treated any differently from others who were similarly situated economically. And fourth, as the country profile submitted by the Department of State's Bureau of Democracy reveals:

A large portion of Philippine asylum applicants allege that the NPA threatens them with death or other harm for refusing to support that organization financially. In most instances, the NPA is not interested in the political opinion of its intended victim but in the victim's wealth.

U.S. Dep't of State, The Philippines: Profile of Asylum Claims and Country Conditions 4 (1995) (emphasis added).

In contrast, the only evidence that the majority finds in support of its conclusion that the NPA was motivated to persecute Borja because of her political opinion is one threatening gesture against Borja that followed on the heels of Borja's statement of opposition to the NPA.[1] While Borja's statement obviously angered the two NPA members, they left the store as soon as she agreed to pay the requested so-called "revolutionary tax." Furthermore, over the following months, as long as Borja paid the NPA the money it demanded, the NPA did not harm her. When the NPA finally did harm Borja, the evidence is undisputed that it was on account of her refusal to pay the "double tax."[2] There is absolutely no evidence that the NPA cut Borja's arm because of her political hostility toward them. Thus, it appears that the NPA was concerned only with "tax" collection. Certainly, a reasonable fact finder would not be compelled to decide otherwise.[3]

I simply am not persuaded that Borja's evidence is so convincing that we are "compelled" to conclude that her persecution was on account of political opinion. See Elias-Zacarias, 502 U.S. at 483-84, 112 S.Ct. 812. There is no evidence that the NPA singled Borja out for extortion because of her political opposition to its cause.[4] Indeed, in all likelihood, the NPA knew nothing of Borja's political opinions, but approached Borja because it knew she was wealthy.[5] Moreover, Borja mentioned her political opinion only once, several months prior to the assault; the NPA actually harmed Borja only once, when Borja refused to make payment. Based on this record, the BIA's conclusion that the NPA was not motivated by Borja's political opinion is supported by substantial evidence.[6]

Sweeping aside the substantial evidence that supports the BIA's conclusion, the majority places emphasis on Borja's professed opposition to the NPA. As the Sixth Circuit has recognized, under Elias-Zacarias, it is of little concern whether the victim acts on the basis of political opinion: "[T]he motives of the asylum seeker are relevant only to the extent that they illuminate the motives of the alleged persecutors." Adhiyappa v. INS, 58 F.3d 261, 267 (6th Cir.1995). While I do not dispute that Borja professed her opposition to the NPA, the issue is whether her statements illuminate the NPA's motives. Given the substantial evidence that supports the BIA's conclusion that those motives were non-political, the illumination her statements provide is negligible.

Moreover, the majority ignores the State Department's finding that "[i]n most instances, the NPA is not interested in the political opinion of its intended victim but in the victim's wealth." This court has held that State Department reports are "`the most appropriate and perhaps the best resource' for `information on political situations in foreign nations.'" Kazlauskas v. INS, 46 F.3d 902, 906 (9th Cir.1995) (quoting Rojas v. INS, 937 F.2d 186, 190 n. 1 (5th Cir.1991)). While not dispositive, the report provides additional support for the BIA's conclusion that Borja's persecution was non-political.[7]

While the majority claims that it has "taken care . . . not to second-guess the BIA," I regret that is exactly what it has done. The BIA's decision is correct. The NPA, in need of financial support, by threats and force, made one wealthy Filipino after another give money to its cause. Borja, as a wealthy woman, was one of the NPA's targets. When Borja refused to pay, the NPA slashed her arm. Borja's story is disturbing and sad, as the majority eloquently and dramatically describes, but it does not establish persecution on account of political opinion. Borja was a victim of extortion and thievery, not political persecution. Borja's evidence that the NPA was motivated by her political opinion is weak at best; it is certainly not "so compelling that no reasonable fact finder could fail to find" in her favor. Elias-Zacarias, 502 U.S. at 483-84, 112 S.Ct. 812.

I would deny the petition for review and affirm the decision of the BIA in this case.

Notes

[1] The majority claims that this action by the NPA members proves that they were motivated to persecute Borja based on her political opinion. However, it is just as reasonable to infer that this action was motivated by a desire to scare Borja into paying over money.

[2] This case is distinguishable from Vera-Valera v. INS, 147 F.3d 1036 (9th Cir.1998), because, in that case, the guerillas told the asylum seeker that they wished to "cut off [his] ideas" which they accurately characterized as those of a "capitalist bureaucrat." It is also distinguishable from Gonzales-Neyra v. INS, 122 F.3d 1293, 1294 (9th Cir.1997), because in that case, the persecution changed in character after the guerillas learned of the asylum seeker's political opinion, from ordinary criminal extortion, to a threat to destroy his video arcade with him inside it because the games "distracted the youth, made them stupid, and `diverted their attention from national problems.'"

[3] We must keep in mind that we cannot "reverse the BIA `simply because we disagree with its evaluation of the facts, but only if we conclude that the BIA's evaluation of the facts is not supported by substantial evidence.'" Aruta v. INS, 80 F.3d 1389, 1393 (9th Cir. 1996) (quoting DeValle v. INS, 901 F.2d 787, 790 (9th Cir.1990) (quoting Diaz-Escobar v. INS, 782 F.2d 1488, 1493 (9th Cir.1986))); see also Mikhailevitch v. INS, 146 F.3d 384, 388 (6th Cir.1998) ("[W]e may not reverse the Board's determination simply because we would have decided the matter differently.").

[4] Borja testified that she was never involved in any political activities.

[5] This conclusion is supported by Borja's testimony. She testified that the NPA sought financial assistance from other businesses located in the same area as her parents' business. And she suspected that the NPA sought her out because of her parents' successful business, as well as her family's high standard of living.

[6] Frankly, I am greatly concerned about the consequences of the majority opinion. From now on every victim of extortion in the Philippines (and according to the State Department country profile, there may be many) need only allege that when the NPA approached them for money, they expressed support for the government. Any negative

reaction by the NPA necessarily would mean that all subsequent conduct of the NPA was motivated by the petitioner's political opinion. Whether the NPA cared one iota about that opinion would be irrelevant, and whether they were motivated by that opinion would be inconsequential, despite the Supreme Court's holding otherwise.

[7] The majority states that persecution can emanate from sections of the population that the government of that country is either unable or unwilling to control. See Korablina v. INS, 158 F.3d 1038, 1044 (9th Cir.1998). While I agree with this statement, Borja presented no evidence that the Philippine government is unable or unwilling to control the NPA. Borja testified that she never reported any of the incidents with the NPA to the Philippine authorities.

Judge O'Scannlain's concurrence in US v. Dutkel (Sept 17, 1999)

O'SCANNLAIN, Circuit Judge, concurring in the result:

I concur in the result ordered by the court's opinion but not entirely in its legal analysis. I write separately to express my view that in criminal cases involving jury tampering by a co-defendant, the defendant must establish that prejudice was likely to have resulted before the government should be required to prove the harmlessness of the intrusion. In this case, I agree we should reverse and remand for a harmlessness hearing because Dutkel has presented evidence sufficient to establish that some prejudice to himself was a likely result of Washington's jury tampering. Nevertheless, I would leave the burden of proof with the defendant rather than shift it to the government.

The opinion places the burden of proof in jury tampering cases upon the government, requiring the government to "show that there is no reasonable possibility that [any juror] `was ... affected in his freedom of action as a juror' as to [the defendant]." Op. at 899 (quoting Remmer v. United States, 350 U.S. 377, 379, 76 S.Ct. 425, 100 L.Ed. 435 (1956)) (Remmer II) (emphasis added). In allocating this burden to the government, the opinion relies heavily upon Remmer v. United States, 347 U.S. 227, 74 S.Ct. 450, 98 L.Ed. 654 (1954). In Remmer, the Supreme Court stated that "[i]n a criminal case, any private communication, contact, or tampering, directly or indirectly, with a juror during a trial about the matter pending before the jury is, for obvious reasons, deemed presumptively prejudicial." Id. at 229, 74 S.Ct. 450.

In more recent cases, however, the Supreme Court has retreated from Remmer's presumption of prejudice and the sweeping language of that opinion. In Smith v. Phillips, 455 U.S. 209, 102 S.Ct. 940, 71 L.Ed.2d 78 (1982), the defendant argued that he was entitled to a new trial because of the possible partiality of a juror who had applied for a job in the prosecutor's office during the defendant's trial. The Court rejected his argument, explaining that "[t]his Court has long held that the remedy for allegations of juror partiality is a hearing in which the defendant has the opportunity to prove actual bias." Id. at 215, 102 S.Ct. 940 (emphases added).[1] It is difficult to reconcile this language in Phillips with Remmer's presumption of prejudice: "[A]ssuring the defendant `an opportunity to prove actual bias' is out of synch with the Remmer presumption; why would a defendant enjoying a presumption in his favor need such an opportunity?" United States v. Williams-Davis, 90 F.3d 490, 496 (D.C.Cir.1996). Under Phillips, then, it would appear that the burden rests upon the defendant to prove prejudice in cases involving improper interference with the jury.

In United States v. Olano, 507 U.S. 725, 113 S.Ct. 1770, 123 L.Ed.2d 508 (1993), the Supreme Court reversed the Ninth Circuit's holding that the defendant was entitled to a new trial because two alternate jurors were present in the jury room during deliberations. The Olano Court stated that "[t]here may be cases where an intrusion should be presumed prejudicial, but a presumption of prejudice as opposed to a specific analysis does not change the ultimate inquiry: Did the intrusion affect the jury's deliberations and thereby its verdict?" Id. at 739, 113 S.Ct. 1770 (emphasis added and citations omitted). This language from Olano, deemphasizing the importance of presumptions of prejudice, seems inconsistent with Remmer's categorical directive. See Williams-Davis, 90 F.3d at 496 ("[T]he Olano Court appeared to see Remmer largely as a case illustrating the importance of weighing the likelihood of prejudice rather than as a source of rigid rules.").

In sum, the Supreme Court's post-Remmer cases suggest that allegations of improper interference with jury deliberations should be addressed through case-specific investigation into the existence of actual prejudice, rather than automatic application of Remmer's inflexible presumption. Our sister circuits have recognized the Court's retreat from, or narrowing of, the Remmer presumption. See United States v. Sylvester, 143 F.3d 923, 934 (5th Cir. 1998) ("[T]he Remmer presumption of prejudice cannot survive Phillips and Olano."); Williams-Davis, 90 F.3d at 496-97 (noting language in Phillips that is "out of synch with the Remmer presumption," and pointing to Olano's apparent "reconfigur[ation]" of Remmer).[2] While it is not our place to "second-guess" the Supreme Court, op. at 895, we certainly can—and must—follow the Court's modification of its own opinions. In light of Phillips and Olano, I would follow the Fifth and D.C. Circuits in holding that "only when the court determines that prejudice [from a suspected intrusion] is likely should the government be required to prove its absence." Sylvester, 143 F.3d at 934; see also Williams-Davis, 90 F.3d at 497 ("[T]he district court was correct under the Supreme Court's and our cases to inquire whether any particular intrusion showed enough of a `likelihood of prejudice' to justify assigning the government a burden of proving harmlessness.").

Our own decision in United States v. Angulo, 4 F.3d 843 (9th Cir.1993), similarly recognizes that Remmer has been modified since being handed down over four decades ago. The court characterizes Angulo as "reaffirming" the Remmer presumption in a case of jury tampering, op. at 895; careful examination of Angulo, however, cannot support such analysis. Rather than reaffirming Remmer, Angulo subtly reconfigures the Remmer presumption, applying a flexible multifactor test in place of a pure Remmer analysis.

If the court's reading of Angulo were correct, one would expect Angulo to conduct a straightforward Remmer analysis like the one undertaken here. Such an analysis would contain the following three steps: (1) classification of the case as a jury tampering case, (2) application of the Remmer presumption, and (3) remand for an evidentiary hearing pursuant to Remmer. But the Angulo court proceeded down a different path. After briefly summarizing Remmer, see Angulo, 4 F.3d at 846, it noted that "not every improper ex parte contact with a juror requires a mistrial." Id. at 847. It further observed that "[a]n evidentiary hearing is not mandated every time there is an allegation of jury misconduct or bias." Id. The Angulo court then stated:

> [I]n determining whether a hearing must be held, the court must consider the content of the allegations, the seriousness of the alleged misconduct or bias, and the credibility of the source. Considering these factors, we deem it clear that the district court abused its discretion in failing to hold a hearing under the facts presented in this case.

Id. (emphases added and citation omitted). Thus, instead of undertaking a conventional Remmer analysis, the Angulo court applied a more flexible, multi-faceted test that led it to conclude that a hearing should have been held in light of the specific circumstances present in that case.

Although the Angulo test may produce results similar to a pure Remmer analysis in many (but not all) jury tampering cases, as an analytical matter the Angulo approach is clearly distinct from the court's application of the Remmer presumption here. A Remmer analysis calls upon courts to classify the type of interference presented and apply a presumption if jury tampering is involved. In contrast, the Angulo test focuses not on interference classification but on evaluation of "the seriousness of the alleged misconduct or bias," Angulo, 4 F.3d at 847. Thus the Angulo test is much closer to the views of the Fifth Circuit in Sylvester and the D.C. Circuit in Williams-Davis than it is to the approach taken by the court in this case. See Sylvester, 143 F.3d at 934 (calling for trial courts to "assess the severity of the suspected intrusion"); Williams-Davis, 90 F.3d at 497 (calling for trial courts to assess the "likelihood of prejudice" from an intrusion). While the outcome of Angulo might simulate the court's result, Angulo's reasoning cannot bear the interpretation the court's analysis seeks to place upon it.

Like my colleagues, I reject Dutkel's argument that Washington's jury tampering constituted a structural error entitling Dutkel to a new trial. In light of the considerable evidence suggesting the likelihood of some prejudice to Dutkel, I agree that the district court erred by failing to hold a hearing to determine the harmlessness of Washington's jury tampering vis-a-vis Dutkel.[3] I part with the majority only to the extent that I would leave the burden of proof at such harmlessness hearing with Dutkel, giving him "the opportunity to prove actual bias" called for by Phillips.

Notes

[1] Phillips was not a jury tampering case, as the opinion points out. See op. at 894-95. The Phillips Court explicitly referred to Remmer, however, as an example of a case "in which the defendant [was properly given] the opportunity to prove actual bias," 455

U.S. at 215, 102 S.Ct. 940. The Phillips Court's citation of Remmer suggests that its modification of the Remmer presumption extends to jury tampering cases. The majority's attempt to distinguish Phillips as applicable only to cases not involving jury tampering, see op. at 894-95, is difficult to sustain in light of Phillips's express citation of Remmer.

[2] I am not persuaded by the Fourth Circuit's unqualified retention of the Remmer presumption in United States v. Cheek, 94 F.3d 136, 142 (4th Cir.1996). The Cheek opinion discusses neither Phillips nor Olano, suggesting that the Cheek court may have overlooked the possibility that these cases reconfigured Remmer.

[3] The evidence suggesting the possible ways in which Dutkel may have been prejudiced by his co-defendant's jury tampering is amply discussed in the opinion, op. at 897-99, and therefore I do not repeat it here.

Judge O'Scannlain's dissent in Planned Parenthood of Southern Arizona v. Lawall (Oct 22, 1999)

O'SCANNLAIN, Circuit Judge, with whom T.G. NELSON and KLEINFELD, Circuit Judges, join, dissenting:

The court's refusal to reconsider this case en banc allows a federal court to invalidate, for the second time, a duly enacted Arizona statute regulating abortion.[1] This time around, the court flouts Supreme Court precedent. I respectfully dissent.

It is difficult to imagine a decision more appropriate for en banc reconsideration than this one. First, the case is one of the utmost gravity. Federal courts must act with the greatest circumspection when we override a state's democratic processes to strike down its enactments as unconstitutional. We are legitimately charged with interpreting and enforcing the supreme law of the land-even at the cost of frustrating the will of electoral majorities-but it has never been doubted that on such occasions we must do so with heightened deliberation. Second, the panel's opinion all but ignores a Supreme Court precedent that compels the conclusion that Arizona's statute is, in fact, perfectly constitutional. Third, the panel's opinion introduces, without much deliberation at all, a novel and untenable standard in this circuit for facial attacks upon statutes regulating abortion. This new standard defies Supreme Court precedent and turns the law of facial challenges to statutes on its head. If consistently applied, this standard will render almost any statute regulating abortion impossible to defend against facial attack.

I

Under Arizona's judicial bypass procedure, a minor seeking an abortion who does not want to tell her parents or cannot obtain their consent may obtain permission from a judge. The judicial bypass procedure provides that a hearing to determine whether a minor may obtain an abortion "shall have precedence over other pending matters," A.R.S. § 36-2152(D), and that "[t]he court shall reach the decision promptly and without delay to serve the best interest of a pregnant minor," id. (emphases added). A minor may make an "expedited" appeal from a judge's denial of permission and has access to the courts for the purpose of making this appeal "twenty-four hours a day, seven days a week." Id. § 36-2152(E).

In Bellotti v. Baird, 443 U.S. 622, 99 S.Ct. 3035, 61 L.Ed.2d 797 (1979) (plurality opinion) ("Bellotti II"), the Supreme Court indicated that a state must provide a judicial bypass procedure in parental-consent statutes that "assure[s] that a resolution of the issue, and any appeals that may follow, will be completed with anonymity and sufficient expedition to provide an effective opportunity for an abortion to be obtained." Id. at 644, 99 S.Ct. 3035 (emphases added). In applying the requirements of Bellotti II in this case, the panel held that the Arizona statute's lack of specific time-limits at the trial court level "hinders any effective opportunity for obtaining an abortion, because the trial court could delay the bypass procedure for a sufficient period to render it practically unavailable." 180 F.3d at 1028.

This holding flies in the face of the Supreme Court's decision in Hodgson v. Minnesota, 497 U.S. 417, 110 S.Ct. 2926, 111 L.Ed.2d 344 (1990) (plurality opinion). In Hodgson, five Justices (with Justice O'Connor writing separately) upheld the judicial bypass provision of a Minnesota parental-notice statute that imposed no specific time-limits on the courts' disposition of bypass petitions. Hodgson must control the case before us, for the relevant language of Minnesota's bypass provision was essentially identical to that of the Arizona statute invalidated by the panel in this case. Compare Ariz.Rev.Stat. § 36-2152(D) (1996) ("The court shall reach the decision promptly and without delay . . . ." (emphases added)) with Minn.Stat. § 144.343(6)(iii) (1980 & Supp.1981) ("Proceedings in the court ... shall be given such precedence over other pending matters so that the court may reach a decision promptly and without delay . . . ." (emphases added)).

The panel held that Hodgson was distinguishable because there was evidence that Minnesota's courts processed bypass applications in a timely fashion, whereas in the instant case there is no evidence that Arizona processes judicial bypass applications in a manner that is timely or otherwise.[2]

180 F.3d at 1028. The panel's attempt to distinguish Hodgson is profoundly unpersuasive and represents a novel and utterly untenable deviation from the settled law of facial challenges.

First, none of the Justices who voted in Hodgson to uphold the judicial bypass provision without time-limits relied on-or even noted-any evidence that Minnesota processed judicial bypass petitions in a timely fashion. The Justices simply concluded as a matter of course that the statute passed constitutional muster both on its face and as applied. The citation to the evidence of timely processing of petitions in Hodgson was made by Justice Stevens, see Hodgson 497 U.S. at 440-42, 110 S.Ct. 2926 who voted (unlike the Hodgson majority) to invalidate Minnesota's judicial bypass provision. It is simply disingenuous for the panel to have declared as central to the Hodgson Court's judgment facts that were adduced solely by a Justice who dissented from that judgment. The plain meaning of the majority's opinions in Hodgson compels the conclusion that the Supreme Court's decision squarely controls the case before us.

Even more troubling is the panel's suggestion that, in order to defend against a facial attack upon a statute regulating abortion, the State now bears the burden of showing that there is no significant risk of the statute's unconstitutional application.[3] This cannot be correct. The panel's apparent reallocation of the evidentiary burden on a facial challenge is a fundamental deviation from established constitutional jurisprudence. If the State bore the burden, as the panel mistakenly believed was implied in Hodgson, a facial challenge to a state statute would not be "the most difficult challenge to mount successfully," Rust v. Sullivan, 500 U.S. 173, 183, 111 S.Ct. 1759, 114 L.Ed.2d 233 (1991), but the easiest. Indeed, a facial challenge to any newly effective statute regulating abortion would be, under the panel's ruling, absolutely indefeasible. Before it has enforced its new statute, the State would have no opportunity to show that its efforts to do so would be consistently constitutional. The result is tantamount to holding that every facial challenge to a reasonably drafted statute regulating abortion is a surefire winner-an obviously extravagent contention, but perhaps one intended by the panel.

Put another way, the panel's attempt to distinguish Hodgson by relying on the fact that Minnesota's statute was constitutionally applied suggests that a statute's constitutionality as applied is unrelated to the statute's facial validity. Au contraire! A statute that is constitutional as applied is perforce constitutional on its face. To hold otherwise is to imply that the State of Arizona might well have been able to legitimate a facially unconstitutional statute—simply by enforcing it for a while.[4] Merely to state so ludicrous a proposition suffices to refute it.

II

The panel also deviated from the law of facial challenges when it declared that the Supreme Court's decision in United States v. Salerno, 481 U.S. 739, 107 S.Ct. 2095, 95 L.Ed.2d 697 (1987), no longer sets the standard for facial challenges to statutes regulating abortion and held instead that the appropriate standard was adumbrated in Planned Parenthood v. Casey, 505 U.S. 833, 112 S.Ct. 2791, 120 L.Ed.2d 674 (1992). Salerno and pre-Casey cases like Ohio v. Akron Center for Reproductive Health, 497 U.S. 502, 514, 110 S.Ct. 2972, 111 L.Ed.2d 405 (1990), explicitly held that a facial challenge to a statute will fail if the statute has any constitutional application or, at the very least, if the challenge relies on supposition of "a worst-case [scenario] that may never occur," id. Casey, on the other hand, implied that a factual showing of unconstitutional application in "a large fraction of cases" in which the law applies is sufficient to render the law facially unconstitutional, even if the law has constitutional applications. Casey, 505 U.S. at 895, 112 S.Ct. 2791. The mysterious and unexplained deviation from the Court's rule on facial challenges in the plurality decision in Casey, however, never purported to overrule Salerno or Akron. Moreover, no decision of the Supreme Court has ever abrogated the explicit Salerno standard. Because the general standard for facial challenges to abortion regulations applicable under Salerno and Akron has not been authoritatively abandoned, we are simply bound to follow it.

In anticipatorily rejecting the standard laid out in Salerno and Akron, the panel forgot this court's role in the scheme of things. We apply, where applicable, the precedents of the Supreme Court unless it has overturned them. Clearly, we are not authorized to disregard the high court's decisions just because we conclude, on the basis of an unofficial tally of probable votes, that a majority of the Justices will decline to overrule us. This is, nevertheless, exactly what the panel did when it justified its application of Casey's standard with a survey of the views on the relationship between Casey and Salerno that individual Justices have expressed in non-authoritative writings. See 180 F.3d at 1025 ("Although the Court has yet to address the conflict between Casey and Salerno in a majority decision, members of the Court have offered their opinions in memoranda denying petitions for certiorari and applications for stays and injunctions pending appeals.").[5] Even when decisions of the Supreme Court suggest, but do not state, that one of its prior decisions has been vitiated, it is not our place to pronounce that decision's demise. The Court has repeatedly admonished "other courts" against "conclud[ing]" that its recent cases have, by implication, overruled an earlier precedent." Agostini v. Felton, 521 U.S. 203, 237, 117 S.Ct. 1997, 138 L.Ed.2d 391 (1997); see also State Oil Co. v. Khan, 522 U.S. 3, 118 S.Ct. 275, 284, 139 L.Ed.2d 199 (1997) ("The Court of Appeals was correct in applying th[e] principle [of stare decisis] despite disagreement with Albrecht, for it is this Court's prerogative alone to overrule one of its precedents."); Quijas v. Shearson/American Express, 490 U.S. 477, 484, 109 S.Ct. 1917, 104 L.Ed.2d 526 (1989) ("If a precedent of [the Supreme] Court has direct application in a case, yet appears to rest on reasons rejected in some other line of decisions, the Court of Appeals should follow the case which directly controls, leaving to [the Supreme] Court the prerogative of overruling its own decisions."). The panel erred egregiously in declaring—when the Supreme Court has not—that Salerno and Akron are overruled and that Casey supplies the standard for facial challenges to statutes regulating abortion. The panel should have followed the Salerno standard, which directly controls.

It is undisputed that, under Salerno and Akron, this court is required by Supreme Court precedent to reject a facial attack on a statute regulating abortion unless the party challenging the statute can "show that `no set of circumstances exists under which the Act would be valid.'" Akron, 497 U.S. at 514, 110 S.Ct. 2972 (quoting Webster v. Reproductive Health Servs., 492 U.S. 490, 524, 109 S.Ct. 3040, 106 L.Ed.2d 410 (1989) (O'Connor, J., concurring)). Because the plaintiff in this case could make no such showing, the plaintiff's attack must be rejected.

Furthermore, even if Casey logically, albeit sub silentio, overruled the Salerno standard applied in Akron, it obviously did so only to the extent of the burden actually borne by the plaintiffs in Casey. Hence, under Casey, the plaintiffs in this case would still have to establish that the Arizona statute is so overbroad that, "in a large fraction of the cases in which [the challenged regulation] is relevant, it will operate as a substantial [and otherwise impermissible] obstacle to a woman's choice to undergo an abortion." Casey, 505 U.S. at 895, 112 S.Ct. 2791 (emphasis added). The plaintiffs in this case have not shown that Arizona's trial courts will impermissibly drag out their consideration of a "large fraction" of minors' petitions for judicial bypasses. There is simply no basis in the record for such a presumption, and it is highly inappropriate for a federal court to be indulging in such an arrogant surmise. Even under Casey's lower standard for facial challenges, the plaintiffs in this case did not meet their burden, and the panel grievously erred in invalidating Arizona's statute.

III

The panel's opinion in this case was a lawless assault on a legitimate exercise in democratic government by the people of Arizona. It should have been reheard en banc and corrected; because the court declines to do so, I must respectfully dissent.

Notes

[1] A federal district court permanently enjoined the enforcement of a prior version of this statute in 1992. See Planned Parenthood v. Neely, 804 F.Supp. 1210 (D.Ariz.1992). Four years later, the Arizona legislature enacted the amended version that the panel invalidated in this case. See Ariz.Rev.Stat. § 36-2152 (1996); Planned Parenthood v. Neely, 130 F.3d 400, 402 (9th Cir.1997).

[2] Although Minnesota's statute required parental notification rather than parental consent (which Arizona's statute requires), the panel correctly declined to rely on that distinction. The Supreme Court has in the past acknowledged a possible difference between constitutional requirements for the judicial bypass provisions of parental-consent statutes and of parental-notification statutes, but that distinction was explicitly not dispositive in the Court's approval of the Minnesota statute's judicial bypass provision. Instead, the Court approved the Minnesota provision because it satisfied the arguably stricter standards articulated in Bellotti II for judicial bypass provisions in parental-consent statutes and therefore a fortiori satisfied constitutional requirements for judicial bypass provisions in parental-notice statutes. See Hodgson, 497 U.S. at 497-98, 110 S.Ct. 2926 (Kennedy, J., dissenting and concurring) ("The simple fact is that our decision in Bellotti II stands for the proposition that a two-parent consent law is constitutional if it provides for a sufficient judicial bypass alternative, and it requires us to sustain the statute before us here."); id. at 499-500, 110 S.Ct. 2926 (Kennedy, J., concurring and dissenting) ("As Bellotti II dealt with the far more demanding requirements of two-parent consent, and approved of such a requirement when coupled with a judicial bypass alternative, I must conclude that these same principles validate a two-parent notice requirement when coupled with a judicial bypass alternative.") (emphasis added); see also id. at 461, 110 S.Ct. 2926 (O'Connor, J., concurring) (citing only cases deciding the constitutionality of judicial bypass provisions of parental-consent statutes before concluding that Minnesota's judicial bypass provision "passes constitutional muster").

[3] The panel plainly implied that the burden was the State's when the panel determined that Arizona's statute had to fall in light of a dearth of evidence supporting consistently constitutional applications—for the plaintiffs in this case certainly offered no evidence whatsoever that Arizona's new statute had been un constitutionally applied

(much less that it had been or would be unconstitutionally applied in a significant number of cases).

[4] In the panel's view, this is exactly what must have happened (with the Supreme Court's approval) in Minnesota. The federal district court declined to grant a preliminary injunction barring the enforcement of the challenged Minnesota statute. See Hodgson, 648 F.Supp. at 760. The district court's decision against granting an injunction was presumably wrong, from the panel's perspective, for Minnesota's statute was practically identical to Arizona's, the preliminary injunction against which the panel unanimously affirmed. The panel thus seems to have believed that, in light of the Minnesota statute's consistently constitutional enforcement during the state's reprieve (enjoyed purely as a result of the federal district court's serendipitous bungling of constitutional law) the statute was—what luck!-no longer facially invalid by the time the case was tried.

[5] The panel admitted that its survey was non-authoritative, see 180 F.3d at 1025 n. 3, but the only other authorities for abandoning Salerno's explicit standard that the panel adduced were the decisions of lower courts, which, it hardly need be said, are not sufficient authority.

Judge O'Scannlain's concurrence and dissent in US v. Messer (Dec 14, 1999)

O'SCANNLAIN, Circuit Judge, concurring in part and dissenting in part:

Because I can find no instance of reversible error in the trial record to suggest that the Speedy Trial Act was violated, I must respectfully dissent from Part II of the majority's opinion. I concur in the sufficiency of the evidence analysis in Part III which moots my Speedy Trial Act analysis as to Khachatrian.

The majority does not point to a single instance of error in any of the five district court orders continuing the trial. Instead, it simply declares that the "sheer length of the delay" itself is grounds enough for finding a violation of the Speedy Trial Act, as though this excuse for reversal rises like an emergent property from the trial record. Maj. op. at 339. Examining each of these orders in detail, I conclude that district court ruled properly on each occasion. I respectfully decline to join the majority in aggregating five correct rulings into one transcendent incorrect one.

I

Let us first review the reasonableness of the individual continuances that were premised on Saccoccia's unavailability for trial. In its March 30, 1992 order, the district court granted a continuance, under 18 U.S.C. § 3161(h)(7), on the ground that Saccoccia was a fugitive in Switzerland. The majority itself cites to United States v. Tobin, 840 F.2d 867 (11th Cir.1988), a case in which the Eleventh Circuit held that an eight-month delay to apprehend a co-defendant was reasonable to apply to the appellant in that case. See id. at 869-70. Likewise, a delay of over three months to apprehend a co-defendant was held reasonable by the Eighth Circuit. See United States v. Cordova, 157 F.3d 587, 598-99 (8th

Cir.1998). Thus, the five-month delay granted to the government, continuing trial to September 15, 1992, to apprehend and to extradite Saccoccia was not unreasonable. In any event, the sheer complexity of the case and the need for foreign evidence were adequate factors upon which to validate the first continuance.

In its July 31, 1992 order, the district court found that a continuance to February 9, 1993 was necessary because Saccoccia was to be tried first in Rhode Island rather than California. The district court thoroughly investigated the government's decision and the district court's findings are compelling. First, the Rhode Island indictment was filed prior to the California indictment. It would seem strange, therefore, that the California trial should take precedence over this earlier indictment. Second, the Rhode Island indictment joined Saccoccia with other co-defendants. Thus, the Rhode Island district court would be faced with the same speedy trial issues that the Central District of California faced. In addition, three of the Rhode Island co-defendants were incarcerated pending trial. The government understandably preferred to compel to await trial the co-defendants out on bail rather than the co-defendants who were incarcerated. Thus, because the delay issues were similar in Rhode Island and in California, the government's decision to try the Rhode Island indictment first was eminently justifiable.

In United States v. Dennis, 737 F.2d 617, 621 (7th Cir.1984), the Seventh Circuit held that a 144-day delay was reasonable under § 3161(h)(7) to allow for Dennis' co-defendant to be "transported out of district on a preceding writ of habeas corpus . . . for prosecution on a different charge" in a different district. Id. at 620. The court reasoned that Dennis's co-defendant "was in custody and his whereabouts known at all times; while the government did not know precisely when [the co-defendant] could be produced, there was never any doubt that he would be produced; the delay was necessary to insure a joint trial." Id. at 621. Similarly, in this case, once Saccoccia was extradited to Rhode Island, Saccoccia was in custody and his whereabouts were known. Furthermore, the government also knew that he would be produced eventually. Finally, the delay was necessary for Saccoccia to finish his trial in Rhode Island so that he could then be transported to California to face trial with Appellants. See also United States v. Piasecki, 969 F.2d 494, 501 (7th Cir.1992) (holding that the time taken for a co-defendant to face trial before another judge was excludable as to that co-defendant and, because the co-defendant "was an unsevered co-defendant whose time for trial had not run, this time, likewise, constituted excludable delay as to Piasecki").

The district court's December 11, 1992 order continuing trial to May 18, 1993 was justified by the delay in Saccoccia's Rhode Island trial. The sudden illness of Saccoccia's counsel caused a mistrial and a continuance of the Rhode Island trial to February 1993. Appellants argue that Saccoccia could have been transported to California to stand trial before returning to Rhode Island for retrial. The Rhode Island district judge, however, specifically requested that Saccoccia remain in his district pending retrial, a request the government "felt obliged to respect." Compliance with the Rhode Island judge's request was completely reasonable. First, the Rhode Island trial had started. Thus, the judge and government were fully prepared to go forward with the trial. Second, Appellants did not oppose the government's motion for this continuance with any vigor. In fact, defense counsel "indicated that, while [they] continue[d] to oppose any continuance based upon the arguments [they] originally put forth in March, 1992, . . . [they] recognize[d] that the reasons stated in the court's March 30, 1992 order still appl[ied] in this case as a basis to continue the trial." In light of this evidence, the additional three-month delay occasioned by the court's order was perfectly understandable.

The final continuance granted by the district court in its April 5, 1993 order, which moved the trial date to September 1993, was justified by Saccoccia's need to retain counsel in Los Angeles and for the new counsel to prepare for trial. This circuit has held that four months of excludable delay while a co-defendant prepares for trial can be reasonably applied to another defendant. See United States v. Butz, 982 F.2d 1378, 1381-82 (9th Cir. 1993). Thus, the four-month delay to allow Saccoccia to prepare for trial was clearly reasonable especially given the complexity of the case and volume of the evidence.

Not one of these five orders involved reversible error, and the majority opinion makes no attempt to argue the contrary. How the majority can then prestidigitate a reversal is baffling. Certainly, the seventeen-month delay in this case is significant, but as the majority concedes, this is not the longest delay the courts have found reasonable under § 3161(h)(7) of the Speedy Trial Act. In United States v. Salerno, 108 F.3d 730 (7th Cir.1997), for example, the Seventh Circuit found a seventeen-month delay between Salerno's first trial, in which the jury could not reach a verdict, and his second trial to be reasonable. In Salerno, the delay was caused by a flurry of post-conviction motions filed by Salerno's co-defendants. Salerno, who had not been convicted in the first trial, was not a party to any of those motions. In the end, only Salerno was tried on the additional counts not decided in the first trial. Like Appellants, Salerno's long delay was for nought because he was ultimately not tried with the co-defendants for whom he had waited so long. The Seventh Circuit decided, nevertheless, that the delay excludable as to Salerno's co-defendants was attributable to Salerno because the co-defendants were subject to retrial on the remaining counts along with Salerno. See id. at 736. Likewise, in this case, the almost seventeen-month delay is long but, because it was excludable to Saccoccia, it was also excludable to Masino and Messer.[1]

II

Let us turn next to the majority's prejudice analysis. Regarding this element of the Speedy Trial Act, the Fifth Circuit has recently provided illumination: "With respect to the prejudice analysis, relevant considerations include whether the delay impaired the appellant's ability to defend himself or resulted in excessive pretrial incarceration." United States v. Franklin, 148 F.3d 451, 457 (5th Cir.1998).

Appellants proffer three arguments to support their claims of prejudice: (1) the delay gave the government substantially more evidence to prove its case than was available at the original trial date; (2) the delay removed any pressure from the United States attorney in Rhode Island to plea bargain with the Los Angeles defendants; and the only argument revealed by the majority, (3) that an important witness had died before trial.

The first two arguments are devoid of merit, as the majority's failure even to mention them suggests. Their first concern — that the government's additional time to prepare made its case stronger against Appellants — is simply not a valid showing of prejudice. See Salerno, 108 F.3d at 738 (stating that "`prejudice is not caused by allowing the Government properly to strengthen its case, but rather by delays intended to hamper defendant's ability to present his defense'" (quoting United States v. Tedesco, 726 F.2d 1216, 1221 (7th Cir.1984))). The second claim — regarding plea bargaining ability — is impossible to comprehend because of Appellants' inadequate development of the argument. Appellants provide no explanation of why passage of time would affect their plea bargaining ability. Nor do Appellants indicate whether they ever approached the government to initiate plea bargaining or if they would have been willing to accept a plea had the opportunity presented itself.

Like the majority, I conclude that the third allegation of prejudice is the only one worth exploring. Certainly the loss of a potential witness goes to Appellants' ability to defend themselves at trial. Mr. Aghabegian, however, was an outsider who would not have known the details of IMM, Clinton, and RGE. In addition, it is somewhat suspicious that the only witness Appellants would have called at trial died. Messer and Masino provided the defense's only testimony at trial.

Furthermore, generalized complaints about the overall length of the delay are similarly weak. We must remember that Appellants were not subjected to lengthy pretrial incarceration. See Salerno, 108 F.3d at 738 ("[D]efendant cannot convincingly claim that he was prejudiced by the unresolved criminal charges looming over his head. He was neither incarcerated during the seventeen-month period, nor did he seek to modify his bond conditions during that time." (internal citation and quotation omitted)); United States v. Mobile Materials, Inc. 871 F.2d 902, 917 (10th Cir.1989) ("[W]e cannot ignore that prior to trial . . . Mr. Philpot was free on bond."). These Appellants suffered far less inconvenience than defendants incarcerated while awaiting trial.

III

Finally, the majority's newly announced rule regarding severance is an unjustifiable pronouncement on this issue. See maj. op. at 340. With very good reason, courts frequently consider a defendant's efforts to sever trial a vital factor in evaluating prejudice. See Franklin, 148 F.3d at 457 ("A defendant's failure to move for severance, or otherwise to pursue a speedy trial in the district court, can undermine prejudice allegations made on appeal."); Mobile Materials, 871 F.2d at 917 ("Nor can we overlook the fact that throughout the protracted history of this prosecution Mr. Philpot has never filed a motion for severance."). Indeed some circuits have held that a defendant must make a motion to sever in order to rely on the reasonableness requirement of subsection (h)(7). See, e.g., United States v. Vasquez, 918 F.2d 329, 337 (2d Cir.1990). In this case, Appellants did not move to sever their case from Saccoccia's and now argue that a motion to sever would have been pointless. Their decision not to do so, however, could easily be interpreted as a tactical decision — an attempt to take advantage of the Speedy Trial Act. As the district court noted, "because the defendants were represented by able and experienced counsel, the Court can only assume that counsels' decision not to move for severance was a strategic one." I cannot agree with the majority's assertion that a defendant's failure to file a motion for severance is not a critical issue in evaluating his appeal based on the Speedy Trial Act. If the defendant himself is in no hurry to proceed to trial, why should we entertain his assertions later that he was prejudiced by the wait? I respectfully maintain that we should not.

IV

While the overall delay in this case may have been lengthy, each individual postponement was amply supported by the circumstances at the time. In each case, the district court filed well-considered orders establishing the necessity and reasonableness of the continuances. The government's and district court's emphasis on bringing a single trial against all four defendants was entirely rational. In light of the resources involved in Appellants' three-month trial, an unnecessary repeat performance would indeed have been a waste of judicial and prosecutorial resources. Yet, pointing to no mistakes by the district court, the majority now nevertheless orders just that.

I respectfully dissent.

Notes

[1] In addition, only the final twelve months of delay were attributable solely to Saccoccia's delays. The first continuances were justified by other factors.

Judge O'Scannlain's special concurrence in Ip v. US (March 7, 2000)

O'SCANNLAIN, Circuit Judge, specially concurring:

I concur in the eloquent and persuasive opinion of the court, which correctly interprets a difficult and opaque statute. I write separately only to note that this is a highly unusual case involving a highly unusual statute, and as such may be of only limited instructional value with respect to the enterprise of statutory interpretation as a whole.

The Supreme Court has instructed us that "[t]he plain meaning of legislation should be conclusive, except in the rare cases in which the literal application of a statute will produce a result demonstrably at odds with the intention of its drafters." United States v. Ron Pair Enters., 489 U.S. 235, 242, 109 S.Ct. 1026, 103 L.Ed.2d 290 (1989) (internal quotation marks omitted). For the reasons set forth in the court's thorough and careful analysis, I believe that the case before us is just such a rare case.

In joining the opinion (including Part III) of the court, then, I am in no way departing from my previously expressed views regarding the proper approach to statutory interpretation in the typical case. See, e.g., Rucker v. Davis, 203 F.3d 627 (9th Cir.2000) ("We begin, as we must, with the express language of the statute. . . . Where, as here, the language of the statute is plain and unambiguous, resort to legislative history is unnecessary."); Rumsey Indian Rancheria of Wintun Indians v. Wilson. 64 F.3d 1250, 1257 (9th Cir.1994); Citizens Action League v. Kizer, 887 F.2d 1003, 1006 (9th Cir.1989) ("In construing a statute, we look first to its plain meaning.").

Judge O'Scannlain's concurrence and dissent in NLRB v. Advanced Stretchforming Intern. (April 4, 2000)

O'SCANNLAIN, Circuit Judge, concurring in part and dissenting in part:

I concur in Part I of the court's opinion, granting summary enforcement to the National Labor Relations Board's ("Board") order of prospective relief to redress Advanced Stretchforming International, Inc.'s ("ASI") violations of the National Labor Relations Act ("NLRA").

I must respectfully dissent, however, from Parts II and III. In my view, the Board's award of back pay under the terms of the collective bargaining agreement of ASI's predecessor violates the holding of NLRB v. Burns Int'l Security Services, Inc., 406 U.S. 272, 92 S.Ct. 1571, 32 L.Ed.2d 61 (1972). This award does nothing to redress ASI's actual violations and does not restore the status quo ante. It constitutes a penalty well in excess of the Board's legal authority. In holding that this award is presumptively appropriate, the majority opinion misconstrues and misapplies the so-called "forfeiture doctrine," transforming it into a broad new exception capable of swallowing the rule set forth in Burns that a successor employer is not bound by its predecessor's collective bargaining agreement and is ordinarily free to set the initial terms of employment unilaterally. By arming the Board with an unauthorized power to punish, the majority has impermissibly upset the balance of power between management and labor that Congress established in the Act. I respectfully dissent.

I

The majority's analysis begins innocently enough by restating the general rule from Burns that a successor employer is not bound by its predecessor's collective bargaining agreement ("CBA") and is free to set the initial terms of employment for its workers without first consulting with their union. See Burns, 406 U.S. at 287-88, 92 S.Ct. 1571. According to the majority, however, an employer's "rights under Burns" to take such unilateral action can be forfeited if the successor "has failed to fulfill its corresponding Burns obligations." Supra at 1180. The majority reasons that, in the present case, ASI "`blocked the process by which the obligations of a successor are incurred'" by telling prospective workers that there would be "no union" at ASI and thus it forfeited its "Burns rights." Supra at 1181 (quoting the Board's decision, Advanced Stretchforming Int'l, 323 N.L.R.B. 529, 531 (1997)).

Somewhat surprisingly, the majority does not bother to tell us what exactly ASI's "Burns obligations" were and why its failure to fulfill such obligations might possibly be remedied by the forfeiture of ASI's "Burns rights" ordered by the NLRB-namely, an award of back pay under the terms of its predecessor's CBA. In fact, the reason for the majority's evasion is clear enough; the forfeiture doctrine is simply inapplicable here. The forfeiture doctrine is premised on the theory that an employer should forfeit its right to set the initial terms of employment only where it evades an actual legal obligation to consult with a union before imposing initial terms. In contrast, ASI was under no such obligation to consult with the UAW prior to imposing its initial terms of employment. In the majority's hands, the forfeiture doctrine becomes a punishment rather than a remedy.

A

In Burns, the Supreme Court addressed the obligations under the NLRA of successor employers such as ASI. The Court held that when a new employer acquires a business, it is free, generally, to set the initial terms and conditions of employment, and is not bound by its predecessor's CBA. See id. at 281-82, 287-88, 294-95, 92 S.Ct. 1571. The successor employer is, however, obligated to bargain with the union after setting initial terms. See id. at 281, 92 S.Ct. 1571.

There are three established exceptions to the Burns rule. A successor employer's right to set initial terms is limited if (1) the successor employer is the "alter ego" of the predecessor, see Sheet Metal Workers Int'l Assoc. v. Arizona Mechanical & Stainless, Inc., 863 F.2d 647, 651 (9th Cir. 1988); (2) the successor employer assumes or adopts the obligations of the predecessor's CBA, see id.; or (3) if "it is perfectly clear that the new employer plans to retain all of the employees in the [bargaining] unit," Burns, 406 U.S. at 294-95, 92 S.Ct. 1571 (emphasis added).

The third exception to the Burns rule, the "perfectly clear" exception, requires a successor to consult with an incumbent union before altering the predecessor's terms and conditions of employment when it is "perfectly clear that the new employer plans to retain all of the employees in the [bargaining] unit." Burns, 406 U.S. at 294-95, 92 S.Ct. 1571. The Court established this exception in Burns, stating:

Although a successor employer is ordinarily free to set the initial terms on which it will hire the employees of a predecessor, there will be instances in which it is perfectly clear that the new employer plans to retain all of the employees in the unit and in which it will be appropriate to have him initially consult with the employees' bargaining representative before he fixes terms.

Id. (emphasis added). An employer subject to this exception is not bound by its predecessor's CBA, nor is it required to agree to the terms the union proposes. See Burns, 406 U.S. at 282, 92 S.Ct. 1571. Rather, the successor employer must simply "consult" with the union before setting the initial terms and conditions of employment. See id. at 295, 92 S.Ct. 1571; Kallmann v. NLRB, 640 F.2d 1094, 1102 (9th Cir.1981).

The majority has sensibly abandoned its previous attempt to justify the Board's award under the Burns perfectly clear exception.[1] This is prudent, given that the ALJ correctly concluded that the exception is simply not implicated on these facts and the Board itself specifically disavowed any reliance on it, stating that the exception "was not determinative of the legality of [ASI's] conduct." Advanced Stretchforming, 323 NLRB at

529. Unfortunately, the Burns perfectly clear exception remains lurking in the background. The Board's award can only be justified if ASI breached a duty to negotiate with the UAW prior to setting the initial terms of employment. Despite its new reliance on the forfeiture doctrine without reference to the perfectly clear exception, the majority (to borrow from its quotation of the Rubaiyat of Omar Khayyam) has failed to "cancel half a Line" or "wash out a Word" of its previous ill-starred attempt to apply the Burns perfectly clear exception to this case.

In actuality, given that the perfectly clear exception does not apply here, ASI's only obligation under Burns was to negotiate with the UAW after it had unilaterally set initial terms of employment. It is not contested that ASI breached this obligation. Nevertheless, as the majority concedes, the Board's award of back pay was premised on the notion that "ASI unlawfully and unilaterally changed the employment terms without first bargaining with the union." See supra at 1179 (citing Advanced Stretchforming Int'l, 323 N.L.R.B. 529, 531 (1997)) (emphasis added). Because ASI was punished for violating an obligation it did not, in fact, have, the Board's award of back pay should be rejected.

B

In its attempt to justify the Board's award, the majority invokes the so-called "forfeiture doctrine," which courts have properly characterized as a "corollary" to the perfectly clear exception. See Capital Cleaning Contractors, Inc. v. NLRB, 147 F.3d 999 (D.C.Cir.1998).

The majority views the doctrine differently. Quoting the Board, the majority describes the forfeiture doctrine as follows:

The fundamental premise for the forfeiture doctrine is that it would be contrary to statutory policy to "confer Burns rights on an employer that has not conducted itself like a lawful Burns successor because it has unlawfully blocked the process by which the obligations and rights of such a successor are incurred." ... In other words, the Burns right to set initial terms and conditions of employment must be understood in the context of a successor employer that will recognize the affected unit employees' collective-bargaining representative and enter into good-faith negotiations with that union about those terms and conditions.

See supra at 1180 (quoting Advanced Stretchforming, 323 NLRB 529, 530) (emphasis added). Thus, in the Board's view, a view which the court today adopts, another exception to the Burns rule exists when a new employer attempts to avoid becoming a successor employer or fails to fulfill its duty to recognize and to bargain with the incumbent union. Apparently, only a successor who complies with all of its obligations under the NLRA can set the initial terms of employment; any unfair labor practice that "block[s] the process by which the obligations and rights of [] a successor are incurred," id., causes the employer to forfeit its rights. Hence, the majority opinion concludes that ASI's "no union" statement caused ASI to forfeit its right to set initial terms without first bargaining with UAW. The majority has it wrong.

As the majority implicitly acknowledges, see supra at 1181, courts have previously applied the forfeiture doctrine only in cases in which a successor employer discriminatorily refused to hire its predecessor's employees because of their union membership. See Kallmann, 640 F.2d at 1102-03; U.S. Marine Corp., 293 NLRB 669 (1989), enforced, 944 F.2d 1305 (7th Cir.1991). Indeed, courts have held that a successor employer who discriminatorily refuses to hire its predecessor's employees based on their union membership forfeits its right to set the initial terms of employment. See, e.g., Kallmann, 640 F.2d at 1102-03; U.S. Marine Corp. v. NLRB, 944 F.2d 1305, 1320 (7th Cir.1991); NLRB v. Horizons Hotel Corp., 49 F.3d 795, 806 (1st. Cir.1995); Capital Cleaning Contractors, Inc. v. NLRB, 147 F.3d 999, 1008 (D.C.Cir.1998). The majority now seeks to expand, for the first time, the scope of the forfeiture doctrine outside the discriminatory hiring context.

The majority justifies its application of the forfeiture doctrine here because ASI's violation of the NLRA by making "no union" statements is "similar" to the discriminatory hiring practices of employers such as Kallmann. This is simply not the case. The discriminatory hiring cases are distinguishable because the "fundamental premise" behind the forfeiture doctrine in the discriminatory hiring cases is that but for the successor employer's discriminatory refusal to hire its predecessor's employees, the employer would have come within the perfectly clear exception to the Burns rule, and thus would have been obligated to consult the union before setting the initial terms of employment. See U.S. Marine, 944 F.2d at 1320 ("Where all or substantially all of the predecessor's employees would have been retained but for the successor's unlawful discrimination, the successor loses the right to set initial terms and conditions of employment and violates the [NLRA] if it unilaterally alters the predecessor's terms without first consulting with the union.... But for its unlawful conduct, U.S. Marine would have hired substantially all of [its predecessor's] employees and therefore would have been obligated to consult with the Union before setting the terms and conditions of employment."); Capital Cleaning, 147 F.3d at 1008 ("[B]ecause Capital refused to hire the Ogden employees based upon their union membership, the Board properly presumed that but for such discrimination Capital would have hired a majority of the Ogden employees from the outset. Accordingly, Capital had a duty to bargain with Local 32 and therefore did not have the right unilaterally to set the terms and conditions upon which it offered employment.").

Applying the forfeiture doctrine in these types of cases prevents the successor employer from avoiding the perfectly clear exception through his "unlawful conduct." See Kallmann, 640 F.2d at 1102-03 (holding that the Board correctly found that the perfectly clear exception applied because "any uncertainty regarding whether substantially all the former employees would have been retained had to be resolved against [the successor employer] because he could not benefit from his ... [discriminatory] conduct" (footnote omitted)). More precisely, because the employers in such cases never would have had the right unilaterally to set the initial employment terms absent their discriminatory hiring, holding that they forfeit their right to set the initial terms of employment simply restores the status quo ante. Cf. Sure-Tan, Inc. v. NLRB, 467 U.S. 883, 900, 104 S.Ct. 2803, 81

L.Ed.2d 732 (1984) (noting that the Board's remedial authority includes the ability "to restore the situation `as nearly as possible, to that which would have obtained' but for" any unfair labor practice (quoting Phelps Dodge Corp. v. NLRB, 313 U.S. 177, 194, 61 S.Ct. 845, 85 L.Ed. 1271 (1941))).

Such rationale, however, does not justify holding that ASI forfeited its right to set initial terms. The majority falls far short in explaining how the application of the forfeiture doctrine here restores the situation to the status quo ante. But for ASI's unlawful conduct, i.e., its "no union" statement, it still would not have been subject to the "perfectly clear" exception and hence did not have any duty to consult with UAW before setting the initial terms of employment. Thus, the majority's "hypothesis," see supra at 1182, that ASI might have bargained to impasse before setting initial terms had it not made the "no union" statement is patently unreasonable.

Clearly, then, because the rationale underlying the forfeiture doctrine is inapplicable to this case, the discriminatory hiring cases provide absolutely no authority for the court's argument that ASI should be held to have forfeited its right to set initial hiring terms. The remedy that the Board misapplied in this case is one specifically designed to redress an employer's violation of the obligation created by the "perfectly clear" exception, nothing more. The majority utterly fails to justify extending its application here.

C

Given this close link between the forfeiture doctrine and the perfectly clear exception of Burns, could it be that, despite its disclaimer in footnote 3, the majority has persisted in its attempt to apply the perfectly clear exception to the instant case, this time sub silentio? The majority justifies its application of the forfeiture doctrine thus:

Here, no discriminatory hiring practices prevented ASI's "perfectly clear" obligation from arising. Instead, the "no union" statement chilled the invocation of that obligation once it had arisen. Having been informed when invited to apply for work with ASI that there would be no union at the new company, Aero's workers may well have believed that employment with ASI was contingent on abstaining from union representation, including insistence on the right to bargain before ASI imposed initial terms.

Supra at 1181-82 (emphasis added). The majority misses the point. Because none of the exceptions to the Burns rule applies here, Aero's workers had, in fact, no right to union bargaining before ASI imposed initial terms. While the majority now explicitly disclaims any reliance on the Burns "perfectly clear" exception, it nonetheless denies that ASI had the right unilaterally to set its initial terms of employment. The latter simply cannot be true.

II

The majority's application of the forfeiture doctrine is not only fundamentally inconsistent with the doctrine's underlying rationale, it is irreconcilable with Burns itself. In that case, Burns, as a successor employer, had violated the NLRA by unlawfully assisting a union which was a rival of its predecessor's employees' union and failing to recognize and to bargain with the incumbent union. See 406 U.S. at 276, 92 S.Ct. 1571. However, the Court rejected the Board's finding that Burns was bound by its predecessor's CBA or that it had violated the NLRA by setting initial employment terms. See id.

The Court viewed a successor's duty to bargain and the right to set initial terms as separate issues:

> Although Burns had an obligation to bargain with the union concerning wages and other conditions of employment when the union requested it to do so, ... [i]t is difficult to understand how Burns could be said to have changed unilaterally any pre-existing terms or condition of employment without bargaining when it had no previous relationship whatsoever to the bargaining unit and, prior to [the date Burns began operations], no outstanding terms and conditions of employment from which a change could be inferred.

Id. at 294, 92 S.Ct. 1571 (italics in original) (emphasis added). Thus, the Court rejected the Board's position that Burns violated the NLRA by setting the initial terms of employment, even though Burns can be said to have attempted to "block[] the process by which the obligations and rights of [] a successor are incurred," see supra at 1180, by refusing to bargain with the incumbent union and by unlawfully assisting a rival union. See Burns, 406 U.S. at 295-96, 92 S.Ct. 1571.

Burns directly controls this case. In Burns, the employer violated the NLRA by failing to bargain with the incumbent union and interfering with its employees' organizational rights by assisting a rival union, and yet the Court held that Burns retained the right to set initial hiring terms. See 406 U.S. at 294, 92 S.Ct. 1571. Here, ASI similarly violated the NLRA by failing to bargain with the incumbent union and by interfering with its employees' organizational rights through its "no union" statement. Yet, contrary to Burns, the court today holds that ASI forfeited the right to set initial hiring terms. The court appears to confuse a successor employer's obligations under the NLRA, and its right to set the initial terms of employment. Burns made clear that these issues are not inter-linked.

III

The Board has only remedial power and does not have the power to impose punishment for violations of the NLRA. See Phelps Dodge, 313 U.S. at 194, 61 S.Ct. 845. This limitation on the Board's authority "at a minimum ... encompasses the requirement that a proposed remedy be tailored to the unfair labor practice it is intended to redress." Sure-Tan, Inc., 467 U.S. at 900, 104 S.Ct. 2803. The majority has not even come close to explaining how forfeiture of ASI's right unilaterally to establish employment terms redresses ASI's unlawful "no union" statements. ASI never had, and never would have had, an obligation to consult with the UAW prior to imposing initial terms. The appropriate remedy for ASI's "no union" statement is an order directing ASI to cease and to desist telling potential applicants that ASI intends to operate with no union. The Board's order does so in this case. To add that ASI forfeited its right to set the initial terms of employment because of this unfair labor practice is "a penalty by another name — and not a much different name at that." U.S. Marine, 944 F.2d at 1328 (Easterbrook, J., dissenting). Indeed, a synonym of forfeit is "penalty." See Webster's Ninth New Collegiate Dictionary 484 (1987) (defining forfeit as "something forfeited or subject to being forfeited... PENALTY").

This court cannot authorize the Board to impose penalties. I respectfully dissent.

Notes
[1] The majority affirmed the Board's award on the basis of the perfectly clear exception in a now-withdrawn opinion. See NLRB v. Advanced Stretchforming Int'l, Inc., 208 F.3d 801 (9th Cir.2000).

Judge O'Scannlain's concurrence and dissent in Young v. City of Simi Valley (June 20, 2000)

O'SCANNLAIN, Circuit Judge, concurring in part and dissenting in part:
The City of Simi Valley enacted a reasonable zoning ordinance regulating the location of adult businesses. Philip Young, who was denied a permit to open a nude dancing club in a shopping center, challenged the ordinance on First Amendment grounds. A jury that heard Young's claims unanimously concluded that the ordinance, as applied by Simi Valley officials in this case, did not violate Young's First Amendment rights.

The jury was, however, unable to reach a decision as to whether the ordinance as a general matter effectively denies persons a reasonable opportunity to own and to operate adult businesses in Simi Valley. Accordingly, no verdict was rendered and the district court declared a mistrial. The district court then granted Young judgment as a matter of law, finding the City's ordinance unconstitutional both on its face and as applied. See Young v. City of Simi Valley, 977 F.Supp. 1017, 1022 (C.D.Cal. 1997).

The court now sustains Young's constitutional challenge to the "sensitive use" provision of Simi Valley's ordinance, which prohibits the opening of adult businesses near certain sensitive uses such as youth-oriented businesses, schools, and churches. Based on the theoretical possibility that a sensitive use might apply for a zoning permit and disqualify a pending application for an adult use located nearby, the court concludes that the ordinance gives private parties a so-called "sensitive use veto" over the opening of adult businesses in Simi Valley. Taking this hypothetical and running with it, the court declares the sensitive use provision unconstitutional on its face. The majority reaches this conclusion even though there is no dispute that the provision was not applied unconstitutionally against Young, whose own attempt to secure an adult use permit was in any event precluded by a preexisting sensitive use—a youth-oriented karate studio located in close proximity to Young's proposed site for a nude dance establishment.

As a plaintiff raising a facial challenge, Young bears "a heavy burden" in advancing his claim. National Endowment for the Arts v. Finley, 524 U.S. 569, 580, 118 S.Ct. 2168, 141 L.Ed.2d 500 (1998) (internal quotation marks omitted). As the Supreme Court has recently reminded us, "[f]acial invalidation `is, manifestly, strong medicine' that `has been employed by the Court sparingly and only as a last resort.'" Id. (quoting Broadrick v. Oklahoma, 413 U.S. 601, 613, 93 S.Ct. 2908, 37 L.Ed.2d 830 (1973)); see also Los Angeles Police Department v. United Reporting Publishing Corp., ____ U.S. ____, ____ _ ____, 120 S.Ct. 483, 489-90, 145 L.Ed.2d 451 (1999). Because I cannot agree with the court's facial invalidation of Simi Valley's ordinance, I must respectfully dissent.

I

The district court struck down Simi Valley's zoning ordinance on two grounds. Neither constitutes an adequate basis for holding the ordinance unconstitutional.

A

The district court held that the ordinance's sensitive use provision unconstitutionally gives such uses a de facto veto power over adult business permit applications. The majority agrees, finding the provision facially invalid for failing to provide would-be adult business owners with "reasonable alternative avenues of communication" as required under City of Renton v. Playtime Theatres, Inc., 475 U.S. 41, 50, 106 S.Ct. 925, 89 L.Ed.2d 29 (1986).

Under the Renton test, Simi Valley's ordinance is constitutional, as long as it "is designed to serve a substantial government interest and allows for reasonable alternative avenues of communication." Id. at 50, 106 S.Ct. 925. Young concedes that the ordinance is designed to serve a substantial government interest, namely, Simi Valley's strong interest in "combat[ing] the undesirable secondary effects" of adult businesses. Id. at 49, 106 S.Ct. 925. The only issue in this appeal, then, is whether the ordinance "effectively deni[es] [Young] a reasonable opportunity to open and operate an adult [business] within the city." Id. at 54, 106 S.Ct. 925.

The district court concluded that the theoretical possibility that a sensitive use might act to disqualify Young's application in itself renders the ordinance unconstitutional by "mak[ing] it unreasonably difficult, if not impossible, for an adult usage applicant to complete the permit process." 977 F.Supp. 1017, 1020 (C.D.Cal.1997). The majority apparently agrees. See maj. op. at 818.

The possibility that a sensitive use might attempt to exercise a de facto veto power over adult business applications does exist; how this deprives Young of a reasonable opportunity to open an adult business, however, is not apparent. Under the majority's reasoning, the mere potential for an ordinance to be applied in an unconstitutional manner renders the ordinance altogether unconstitutional. Under such a theory, almost any adult business zoning ordinance—including the one upheld in Renton—would be unconstitutional. For example, an ordinance that left half of a city's space available to adult businesses and did not contain any buffer zone requirements could still be attacked based on the possibility that a sensitive use (or the city itself) could purchase all property zoned for adult businesses, leaving such businesses without any available properties at which to locate and thus depriving them of a reasonable opportunity to operate an adult business. Such a theory is untenable in light of Renton, where the Supreme Court reversed this court to uphold the City of Renton's ordinance as constitutional—without pausing to speculate about possible scenarios in which the ordinance might be applied unconstitutionally.

Upholding the facial constitutionality of the sensitive use provision would not place the ordinance beyond constitutional scrutiny. The provision would still be fully subject to constitutional challenge on an "as applied" basis. In this case, for example, a reasonable jury could have found a high likelihood that a sensitive use would act to disqualify a future permit application by Young—even though the jury that did hear the case apparently did not do so. At trial Young introduced evidence from which it might be inferred that the Joshua Institute was a sham opened by Norman Walker to disqualify Young's application. Based on this circumstantial evidence, a jury could have believed that Walker would act similarly with respect to Young's future adult business permit applications.

This is not, however, the only reasonable conclusion to be drawn on the evidence. Significant evidence in the record—of a direct rather than circumstantial nature— points in the opposite direction. For instance, Walker testified that the opening of the Bible study class had nothing to do with Young's permit application; that any interaction between the Joshua Institute's application for a zoning permit and Young's application was "coincidental" and "unintentional"; and that Walker "had no idea," at the time that the Joshua Institute applied for a zoning permit, "that the effect of what [the Institute] did could stop Mr. Young" from obtaining a zoning permit for his proposed adult theater. Furthermore, the proposed location of Young's adult business was in any case already disqualified by the presence of a nearby youth-oriented business. In light of this evidence, it is not surprising that the jury found that the ordinance had not been applied unconstitutionally against Young.

In sum, the likelihood of a sensitive use acting to manipulate Simi Valley's zoning ordinances is a factual question for a jury to decide. This determination should be made on a case-by-case basis, in light of the facts and circumstances surrounding a particular adult use permit application. The district court erred in finding the ordinance facially unconstitutional and enjoining its enforcement.

B

The district court struck down the ordinance on another ground. Under the buffer zone requirements of the ordinance, approximately four potential adult use sites exist simultaneously in Simi Valley— a city in which only one application for an adult use is pending. The district court held, as a matter of law, that four possible sites "simply does not amount to a reasonable number of alternative means of communication." 977 F.Supp. at 1022. As the majority points out, see maj. op. at 821-22, the district court reached this conclusion without conducting the fact-specific inquiry into reasonableness required under Renton.

I agree with the majority that the district court's holding on this issue was erroneous. I would, however, proceed one step further. In Topanga Press, Inc. v. City of Los Angeles, 989 F.2d 1524, 1532-33 (9th Cir.1993), we strongly suggested (but did not explicitly hold) that the constitutionality of an ordinance like Simi Valley's can be determined by comparing the supply of locations available for adult businesses to the demand for such sites. Based on the Topanga Press analysis, I would expressly hold that, as a matter of law, an adult business zoning ordinance violates the First Amendment if, and only if, the ordinance restricts the number of sites available to adult businesses below the demand for such properties. Such a rule has already been explicitly adopted by the Fifth Circuit, see Woodall v. City of El Paso, 49 F.3d 1120, 1126-27 (5th Cir.1995), and it finds support in the case law of other circuits as well, see, e.g., Buzzetti v. City of New York, 140 F.3d 134, 140-41 (2d Cir.1998); Alexander v. City of Minneapolis, 928 F.2d 278, 283-84 (8th Cir.1991). This rule provides a sensible, workable test for conducting what might otherwise be an unwieldy (and arguably standardless) inquiry into First Amendment reasonableness under Renton.

The majority expressly declines to adopt such a rule, reasoning that "`supply and demand' analysis is insufficient to account for the chilling effect that an adult use zoning ordinance may have on prospective business owners." Maj. op. at 823. While the majority's concerns are legitimate, I simply fail to see how an individual can claim that he has been denied a reasonable opportunity to open an adult business as long as there exists a site within the municipality available for his business. Under Renton, of course, the aspiring operator of an adult establishment has no right to his preferred business location within the city. Regulating the location of certain types of businesses is, after all, "the essence of zoning." Renton, 475 U.S. at 54, 106 S.Ct. 925.

Young is the only individual who has ever sought to establish an adult business in Simi Valley. The number of sites available in the City for such businesses exceeds the demand for such sites (by a multiple of three to four). The Supreme Court's decision in Renton, the decisions of our sister circuits, and common sense all suggest that the number of available locations is reasonable as a matter of law.

II

Subsequent to oral argument in this case, the Supreme Court decided City of Erie v. Pap's A.M., ____ U.S. ____, 120 S.Ct. 1382, 146 L.Ed.2d 265 (2000). The city of Erie, Pennsylvania, enacted an ordinance prohibiting nudity in public places. Because the ordinance's definition of "public place" included "all buildings and enclosed places owned by or open to the general public, including . . . places of entertainment," the ordinance had the effect of banning nude erotic dancing. Id. at 1387-88 (quoting Erie, Pa., Code art. 711 (1994)).[1]

Although the members of the Court divided as to their reasoning, a majority voted to uphold the ordinance as "a content-neutral regulation that satisfies the four-part test of United States v. O'Brien, 391 U.S. 367, 88 S.Ct. 1673, 20 L.Ed.2d 672 (1968)." ____ U.S. at ____, 120 S.Ct. at 1388. Under Erie, then, municipalities have the right to ban nude dancing entirely if they were to choose to do so in an effort to combat the negative secondary effects of adult entertainment establishments. If municipalities can prohibit nude dancing outright through content-neutral restrictions on conduct aimed at fighting "crime and the other deleterious effects caused by the presence of [an adult] establishment in the neighborhood," they presumably can certainly use their zoning power to achieve the same ultimate effect as a total ban. Id. at 1393 (O'Connor, J.) (plurality opinion).

In light of evidence in the record suggesting that Young would still seek to present erotic strip tease dancing at his proposed adult entertainment establishment, Erie does not control this case. It does, however, have important implications for the constitutionality of adult use zoning ordinances.

Because Erie did not overrule Renton— Justice O'Connor's plurality opinion in Erie relied upon Renton for its analysis— the two decisions must be read as consistent with each other (despite the dissent's claim of irreconcilability, see id. at 1407-09 (Stevens, J., dissenting)). When read together, Erie and Renton establish somewhat different frameworks for evaluating the constitutionality of content-neutral regulations of nude dancing as opposed to other forms of adult entertainment. Under Erie, a municipality can enact a content-neutral ordinance banning nude dancing entirely. See id. at 1388. Under Renton, however, a municipality can enact a content-neutral ordinance regulating adult entertainment only to the extent that the ordinance does not deny an individual "a reasonable opportunity to own and operate an adult theater within the city." 475 U.S. at 54, 106 S.Ct. 925. Thus, after Erie, the extent to which cities like Simi Valley may ban or otherwise regulate adult entertainment would appear to depend upon the specific type of entertainment being regulated. Although I believe, for the reasons set forth above, that Young's challenge to the City's ordinance fails under Renton, I am persuaded that his challenge would indisputably fail if governed by the Erie standard.

In sum, the Supreme Court's recent decision in Erie reaffirms the important principle that "the government should have sufficient leeway to justify [content-neutral restrictions regulating conduct] based on secondary effects" of such conduct. Id. at 1396. The City would do well to consider both the holding and reasoning of Erie carefully in any attempt to refashion its ordinance in the wake of today's decision.

III

Simi Valley's adult business zoning ordinance allows for "reasonable alternative avenues of communication" and does not offend First Amendment standards. Although its sensitive use provision raises constitutional concerns and may be subject to challenge on an "as applied" basis, it is not unconstitutional on its face. Furthermore, as the majority recognizes, the ordinance's distance and buffer requirements undoubtedly pass constitutional muster. I would reverse and remand for vacation of the injunction in its entirety.

Notes

[1] "To comply with the ordinance, . . . dancers must wear, at a minimum, `pasties'

and a `G-string.'" _____ U.S. at _____, 120 S.Ct. at 1388.

Judge O'Scannlain's dissent in Robinson v. Solano County (July 12, 2000)

O'SCANNLAIN, Circuit Judge, dissenting:

The district court granted the sheriff's deputies in this case qualified immunity after concluding that "[p]olice have no dependable guidance [regarding] the constitutional limitations, if any, upon a mere threat or display of force to effect a seizure." This court now reverses, finding that clearly established law put the officers on notice as to the potential illegality of their conduct. Because the majority finds "clearly established law" where none exists, I must respectfully dissent.

I

Before proceeding to the specific facts of this case, a few brief observations regarding qualified immunity are in order. For purposes of qualified immunity analysis, a right is clearly established if "the contours of the right [are] sufficiently clear that a reasonable official would understand that what he is doing violates that right." Anderson v. Creighton, 483 U.S. 635, 640, 107 S.Ct. 3034, 97 L.Ed.2d 523 (1987). We have previously described the scope of the doctrine in the following terms:

[T]he qualified immunity "defense" has been defined quite broadly: "[I]t provides ample protection to all but the plainly incompetent or those who knowingly violate the law.... [I]f officers of reasonable competence would disagree on th[e] issue [whether or not a specific action was constitutional], immunity should be recognized."

Moran v. Washington, 147 F.3d 839, 844 (quoting Malley v. Briggs, 475 U.S. 335, 341, 106 S.Ct. 1092, 89 L.Ed.2d 271 (1986)). Although the qualified immunity inquiry would appear to be fairly straightforward, our cases defining the scope of the defense are less than pellucid. This is in large part due to the difficulty of selecting the appropriate level of generality for purposes of qualified immunity analysis. Fortunately, the Supreme Court has recognized this difficulty and provided the following guidance:

The operation of this standard, however, depends substantially upon the level of generality at which the relevant "legal rule" is to be identified. For example, the right to due process is quite clearly established by the Due Process Clause, and thus there is a sense in which any action that violates that Clause (no matter how unclear it may be that the particular action is a violation) violates a clearly established right. Much the same could be said of any other constitutional or statutory violation. But if the test of "clearly established law" were to be applied at this level of generality, it would bear no relationship to the "objective legal reasonableness" that is the touchstone of Harlow. Plaintiffs would be able to convert the rule of qualified immunity ... into a rule of virtually unqualified liability simply by alleging violation of extremely abstract rights. Harlow would be transformed from a guarantee of immunity into a rule of pleading. Such an approach, in sum, would destroy [the balance struck by the doctrine of qualified immunity].

Anderson, 483 U.S. at 639, 107 S.Ct. 3034. Thus, in qualified immunity cases, the crucial inquiry should not be the somewhat academic question of "how do we define the right allegedly violated" (such as the rather general "right to be free from excessive force"). Rather, the key question is "did the challenged actions fall short of objective legal reasonableness," such that "in light of pre-existing law the unlawfulness [of the official's actions was] apparent." Id. at 640, 107 S.Ct. 3034.

II

Here, the majority defines the right at issue—"the right to be free from excessive force"—at such a high level of generality that the resulting qualified immunity analysis "bear[s] no relationship to the `objective legal reasonableness' that is the touchstone of Harlow." Id. at 639, 107 S.Ct. 3034. The question here is not whether Robinson enjoys a "right to be free from excessive force," which, of course, he does (doesn't everyone?); rather, the issue is whether, "in light of pre-existing law, the unlawfulness [of the deputies' specific actions was] apparent." Id. at 640, 107 S.Ct. 3034 (emphasis added). Based on our cases, as well as those of our sister circuits, I must conclude that such unlawfulness—if any—was far from apparent.

Although the majority is correct in noting that it is not necessary for the very actions in question to have been held unlawful, the state of the law must be "sufficiently clear that a reasonable official would understand that what he is doing violates [the law]." Id. I find the requisite clarity sorely lacking in this case. We have never squarely addressed the extent to which merely pointing a weapon at a suspect, unaccompanied by the use of physical force, can give rise to § 1983 liability for violating the Fourth Amendment's prohibition against unreasonable seizures. The majority relies upon McKenzie v. Lamb, 738 F.2d 1005, 1010 (9th Cir.1984), for the proposition that pointing a service revolver at a suspect may constitute excessive force. The facts of McKenzie, however, are very different from those in the case at bar. The McKenzie panel reversed a grant of summary judgment in favor of police officers in a § 1983 action alleging the use of excessive force. In contrast to this case, where a weapon was pointed at Robinson but no physical force was used against him, the pointing of weapons in McKenzie was accompanied by significant force: Police officers "burst into the hotel room with weapons drawn, forced appellants against the wall, handcuffed them, and threw them to the floor." Id. at 1010 (emphases added). In light of the additional conduct of the officers in McKenzie that accompanied the pointing of weapons at the suspect, McKenzie does not establish—clearly or otherwise—that the actions of the officers in this case might be illegal.

Furthermore, persuasive authority from other circuits supports the proposition that merely pointing a weapon at a person does not give rise to § 1983 liability for violating the Fourth Amendment's prohibition against excessive force. See, e.g., Sharrar v. Felsing, 128 F.3d 810 (3d Cir.1997) (finding no Fourth Amendment violation when officers required plaintiffs to lie face down in dirt, with guns at their heads); Wilkins v. May, 872 F.2d 190, 194 (7th Cir.1989) ("[T]he action of a police officer in pointing a gun at a person is not, in and of itself, actionable [under the Fourth Amendment].")); Hinojosa v. City of Terrell, 834 F.2d 1223, 1229-31 (5th Cir.1988) (overturning a jury verdict against an officer for constitutionally excessive use of force, stating that "we are unwilling to say that merely pointing the gun was grossly disproportionate to the need for action"). In light of these precedents, the district court was correct in reaching the following conclusion: "Police have no dependable guidance [regarding] the constitutional limitations, if any, upon a mere threat or display of force to effect a seizure, and accordingly defendants are entitled to qualified immunity from suit." This conclusion makes particular sense in a case like this one, where the suspect to be seized was known to be in possession of a deadly weapon that he had recently used (even if only against dogs).[1]

III

While the treatment of Robinson by the defendant officers is certainly regrettable, sympathy for an attractive plaintiff does not justify distorting the law of qualified immunity. It is difficult to imagine how police officers can be held liable for alleged failure to adhere to law that was so "clearly established" that not even our district courts can divine its contours.[2] I respectfully dissent.

Notes

[1] This case is therefore quite distinguishable from McDonald v. Haskins, 966 F.2d 292 (7th Cir.1992), where an officer pointed his gun at the head of a nine-year-old child who was not suspected of any crime or of being armed. It is also very different from Black v. Stephens, 662 F.2d 181, 189 (3d Cir.1981), where an unidentified police officer "brandish[ed] his revolver" only eighteen inches away from the head of a man the officer had no cause to believe armed—with the man's wife "in the precise line of fire"—and threatened to shoot.

[2] "If judges thus disagree on a constitutional question, it is unfair to subject police to money damages for picking the losing side of the controversy." Wilson v. Layne, 526 U.S. 603, 618, 119 S.Ct. 1692, 143 L.Ed.2d 818 (1999).

Judge O'Scannlain's concurrence and dissent in US v. Matthews (Sept 14, 2000, amended Feb 21, 2001)

O'SCANNLAIN, Circuit Judge, concurring in part and dissenting in part:

I concur in the court's affirmance of Matthews's conviction, but I must respectfully dissent from its disposition of the sentencing issue in this case. Even assuming that the district court erred in applying the Armed Career Criminal ("ACC") enhancement of 18 U.S.C. § 924(e),[1] I cannot concur in the drastic step of remanding for resentencing on the record as it now stands, i.e., barring the trial court from further developing the record as appropriate. There is simply no reason in this case for deviating from our "general practice" of allowing the district court to conduct further appropriate proceedings on remand for purposes of resentencing. United States v. Washington, 172 F.3d 1116, 1118 (9th Cir.1999); see also United States v. Parrilla, 114 F.3d 124, 128 (9th Cir.1997) ("On remand, the district court should conduct further proceedings as may be necessary to enable it to make appropriate findings to resolve the factual dispute....."); United States v. Hedberg, 902 F.2d 1427, 1429 (9th Cir.1990) (remanding for de novo sentencing proceedings).

The Eighth Circuit opinion cited by the majority, United States v. Hudson, 129 F.3d 994 (8th Cir.1997), is rather cryptic and not very helpful in justifying this highly unusual step. The Hudson court supported its closing of the record by claiming that "we have clearly stated the governing principles as to when and how disputed sentencing facts must be proved." Id. at 995. The D.C. and Fourth Circuit cases cited by the majority did not involve statutes as complex as the ACC provision. Instead, those cases involved failures by the prosecution to establish facts specified by the relevant statutes, where there was no uncertainty as to the statutes' requirements.

In United States v. Leonzo, 50 F.3d 1086, 1088 (D.C.Cir.1995), the government did not introduce relevant evidence of the loss caused by the defendant's bank fraud. In United States v. Parker, 30 F.3d 542, 551-53 (4th Cir.1994), the government sought to enhance the defendant's sentence by charging him with distribution of drugs within 1000 feet of a playground, but failed to prove that the property met the statute's definition of "playground."

The majority in this case, having oversimplified matters greatly, may regard the principles governing application of the ACC enhancement as "clearly stated" by prior case law, but more careful examination of the issue discloses that these principles are quite complex, have spawned a great deal of litigation in the lower courts, and are far from "clearly stated." Accordingly, I see no reason to punish the government by prohibiting it from completing its showing on remand to establish the applicability of the ACC enhancement with even greater certainty.

The majority's new exception to its new rule will provide little guidance to future panels, and little comfort to those of us who seek predictability and consistency in sentencing. This case by case approach contradicts the goals of both the ACC enhancement and the Sentencing Guidelines: The ACC enhancement was enacted in order to provide mandatory minimum sentences for armed career criminals. See Sweeten, 933 F.2d at 770. The Sentencing Guidelines were established in large part to reduce unwarranted sentencing disparities. See United States v. Banuelos-Rodriguez, 215 F.3d 969, 976 (9th Cir.2000) (en banc). In allowing Matthews to escape imposition of the ACC enhancement simply because of the fortuity (from Matthews's perspective) that his probation officer prepared a less-than-complete PSR, the majority flouts congressional intent with respect to both the ACC enhancement and the Sentencing Guidelines.

The process of criminal sentencing is not a game between the government and criminal defendants, in which one side or the other gets penalized for unskillful play. The goal of sentencing is to determine the most appropriate sentence in light of the characteristics of the crime and the defendant. If Matthews is an "armed career criminal" under the ACC statute (and the record makes clear that he is), then he should be sentenced as one. Because I cannot agree to bestowing a sentencing windfall upon a defendant with a long and extensive history of committing violent crimes, especially when equally culpable but less fortunate defendants have been subjected to the enhancement, I must respectfully dissent.

Judge O'Scannlain's dissent in Barnett v. US Air, Inc. (Oct 4, 2000)

O'SCANNLAIN, Circuit Judge, with whom Circuit Judges TROTT and KLEINFELD join, dissenting:

The sweeping language and exalted tone of the court's wide-ranging opinion make clear that it aspires to offer a definitive interpretation of the Americans with Disabilities Act (ADA). This might be less disturbing if this case actually involved an American with a disability. Because the court reaches out to decide several important issues of first impression in a case without a proper plaintiff, I must respectfully dissent.

I

Robert Barnett suffers from back problems. Barnett's doctor has imposed upon him permanent restrictions that prohibit him from excessive bending, twisting, and turning; prolonged standing or sitting; and lifting twenty-five pounds or more. Barnett claims that these restrictions prevent him from serving in the cargo position but do not prevent him from working in the swing-shift mailroom position. The functions of the mailroom position include occasional bending and frequent twisting and turning; occasional standing or sitting; and some lifting. The crucial limitation imposed upon Barnett, then, is the twenty-five pound lifting restriction, because it is the only restriction that would prevent him from handling cargo, but would not prevent him from working in the mailroom.

The record evidence in this case clearly establishes that Barnett is not disabled within the meaning of the ADA. In Thompson v. Holy Family Hospital, 121 F.3d 537 (9th Cir.1997), we affirmed the summary judgment dismissal of an ADA case on the ground that the plaintiff failed to create a genuine issue of material fact as to her disability. Cynthia Thompson, like Robert Barnett, suffered from back problems, and her doctor, like Barnett's doctor, prohibited her from lifting more than twenty-five pounds. See id. at 539. The Thompson court found this limitation inadequate to establish a triable issue as to the plaintiff's disability. Although it acknowledged that lifting and working constitute "major life activities" for purposes of the ADA's implementing regulations, Thompson's twenty-five-pound lifting restriction did not constitute "the requisite evidence that she is substantially limited with respect to these activities." Id. at 539-40 (expressing agreement with "[a] number of courts [that] have held that lifting restrictions similar to Thompson's are not substantially limiting" (citing cases)). Although Thompson's lifting restriction prevented her from serving as a nurse performing "total patient care" duties, just as Barnett's identical lifting restriction prevented him from serving in the cargo position, the panel held that "[t]he inability to perform one particular job does not constitute [a substantial] limitation" on the general ability to work. Id. at 540.

The similarities between Thompson and the instant case, in terms of both the plaintiff's claimed disabilities and the employer's responses thereto, are striking. Under Thompson, it is clear that no genuine issue of material fact exists as to Barnett's disability. The district court's grant of summary judgment should be affirmed.

II

The court addresses (or dodges) the question whether Barnett is "disabled" under the ADA in a footnote, noting in passing that the district court concluded that Barnett was "disabled" under the ADA and that U.S. Air did not raise the issue of Barnett's disability on appeal. Maj. op. at 1110 n. 1. The failure of U.S. Air to file a cross-appeal, however, in no way precludes us from affirming based on Barnett's failure to establish that he is disabled. Contrary to the suggestion in that footnote, it is well-settled that we may affirm a grant of summary judgment based on any ground supported by the record. See, e.g., Albertson's, Inc. v. United Food and Commercial Workers Union, 157 F.3d 758, 760 n. 2 (9th Cir.1998); Intel Corp. v. Hartford Accident and Indem. Co., 952 F.2d 1551, 1556 (9th Cir.1991). In Intel, the district court granted Intel's motion for summary judgment, holding, in part, that Hartford, which had issued an insurance policy to Intel, waived its reliance on one of the policy's exclusions. We affirmed the grant of summary judgment, but on a different ground. We examined the policy's exclusion, and held that there was no material issue of fact as to the exclusion's application. See id. at 1561.

Although U.S. Air did not present the issue of Barnett's disability (or lack thereof) in a separate appeal, the parties have had more than ample opportunity to brief and to argue the issue in both the district court and this court. Before the district court, U.S. Air argued that Barnett's lifting restrictions did not render him disabled under the ADA; Barnett opposed granting summary judgment on that basis. In a fairly brief discussion, the district court determined that summary judgment could not be properly granted on the issue because of evidence showing Barnett's back injury to be "serious and permanent."

On August 26, 1996, Barnett filed his notice of appeal in our court; U.S. Air did not file a cross-appeal.[1] One year later, on August 8, 1997, we decided Thompson. In our order filed September 16, 1997, we specifically directed the parties to file supplemental briefs discussing Thompson. These briefs were filed in advance of oral argument before the three-judge panel, held on October 8, 1997.

In both the district court and this court, the parties have had the opportunity to develop, and have actually developed, the issue of Barnett's disability, both before, and in light of, Thompson. As a result, nothing bars us from taking the prudential path and refraining from deciding weighty issues in a weightless case. Cf. Bellotti v. Baird, 428 U.S. 132, 143-44, 96 S.Ct. 2857, 49 L.Ed.2d 844 (1976). In Bellotti, the Court held that the district court should have abstained from deciding a constitutional issue, stating that, "It is not entirely clear that appellants suggested the same interpretation in the District Court as they suggest here. Nevertheless, the fact that full arguments in favor of abstention may not have been asserted in the District Court does not bar this Court's consideration of the issue." Id. at 143 n. 10, 96 S.Ct. 2857 (internal citation omitted). Cf. Delange v. Dutra

Const. Co., 183 F.3d 916, 919 n. 3 (9th Cir.1999) (recognizing that this circuit may exercise its discretion to review issues raised for the first time on appeal).

III

Barnett's case simply cannot bear the weight that the court seeks to place upon it. A case so transparently lacking in merit is an inappropriate vehicle for deciding multiple questions of first impression concerning the proper construction of an important statute (and creating a circuit split in the process, see maj. op. at 1118 n. 8). The court has issued what in effect amounts to a lengthy advisory opinion on the ADA; when this case returns to the district court, the only appropriate course of action will be to dispose of it under Thompson.

Because Barnett is simply not disabled under the ADA, the district court's grant of summary judgment was proper and should be affirmed. I respectfully dissent.

Notes

[1] The fact that Thompson was decided well after the time for U.S. Air to file a notice of appeal had passed may explain in part U.S. Air's failure to take a cross-appeal.

Judge O'Scannlain's dissent in Gafoor v. INS (Nov 3, 2000)

O'SCANNLAIN, Circuit Judge, dissenting:

Under the Immigration and Nationality Act, Gafoor and his family are eligible for asylum only if he has at least a "well-founded fear" that returning to Fiji would result in his "persecution on account of race, religion, nationality, membership in a particular social group, or political opinion." 8 U.S.C. § 1101(a)(42)(A). Because the motive of Gafoor's potential tormentors is "critical" under the terms of the Act, "he must provide some evidence of it, direct or circumstantial," in his asylum application. INS v. Elias-Zacarias, 502 U.S. 478, 112 S.Ct. 812, 817, 117 L.Ed.2d 38 (1992). Indeed, as the Supreme Court has taken pains to remind us, because Gafoor "seeks to obtain judicial reversal of the ... determination" of the Board of Immigration Appeals ("BIA") that he has failed to show that he would risk persecution on account of one of the five grounds enumerated in the Act, he now "must show that the evidence he presented [to the BIA] was so compelling that no reasonable factfinder could fail to find" otherwise. Id. (emphasis added).

After a hasty acknowledgment of the formidable barriers to granting Gafoor relief, the majority grants it nevertheless. In doing so, the majority over-reads our decision in Borja v. INS, 175 F.3d 732 (9th Cir.1999) (en banc), to effect exactly the sort of judicial usurpation which the Supreme Court intended to forestall in Elias-Zacarias. As if this did not constitute sufficient arrogation of the Attorney General's province, the majority also declares that this court can compel, sua sponte, a reopening of an asylee's case whenever it concludes that conditions in his home country may have changed subsequent to the BIA's adverse decision. This novel assertion conflicts with a plain holding of our court sitting en banc. I respectfully dissent.

I

Gafoor is a police officer who arrested a man he caught in the act of attempting to rape a thirteen-year-old-girl. The man turned out to be a high-ranking officer in the Fijian army who was, apparently as a result, promptly released. The next night, the same officer invaded Gafoor's house with seven or eight uniformed men. The men beat Gafoor and took him to a military compound where they questioned him over the ensuing week about the arrest of the army officer and warned him not to testify against the officer or tell anyone else about the attempted rape. At some point in his incarceration, the army officer's confederates also accused Gafoor of being "against the army." Some time after Gafoor had recovered from his beating and incarceration, the army officer whom he had arrested led several men in another assault on Gafoor as he patrolled a public street. During the assault, one of the men told Gafoor that he "should go back to India."

This course of events, which represents the sum of Gafoor's factual testimony, establishes fairly plainly that the army officer orchestrated the attacks on Gafoor purely as reprisals for his arrest and vivid warnings of what would befall Gafoor if he ever disclosed the facts surrounding it. This is, appropriately enough, precisely what the immigration judge ("IJ") and the BIA concluded. There is no dispute that this conclusion renders Gafoor ineligible for asylum under the Act, for reprisal and intimidation are not among the five cognizable grounds for persecution.

In granting Gafoor's petition for review, however, the majority contends that these events establish that Gafoor's assailants had motives other than reprisal and intimidation. In particular, the majority asserts that the vague accusation that Gafoor "oppos[ed] the army" and the slur to the effect that Gafoor "should go back to India" "compel[] a conclusion that he was persecuted not solely because he arrested a high-ranking army officer, but also because of his race and the political opinion imputed to him by the soldiers." Supra at 651. Given that the evidence fails on the whole to do anything more than suggest that Gafoor's imputed political opinion and race actually animated his assailants' attacks, I think preposterous the majority's implicit contention that "a reasonable factfinder would have to conclude" that the evidence established as much. Elias-Zacarias, 502 U.S. at 481, 112 S.Ct. 812 (emphasis added).

A

The majority argues that the off-the-cuff accusation and slur emitted by Gafoor's assailants amount to proof of enumerated motives by analogizing Gafoor's case to those of the successful petitioners in Surita v. INS, 95 F.3d 814 (9th Cir.1996), and Prasad (Gaya) v. INS, 101 F.3d 614 (9th Cir.1996). See supra at 651. There are, however, important distinctions between those cases and Gafoor's.

In Surita, the petitioner, an Indo-Fijian woman, was robbed twice daily by ethnic Fijians as she went to and from work. Her house was also looted by ethnic Fijian soldiers who "stated that they were looting the family's home because the family was of Indian descent" and "told Surita that the family's possessions belonged to ethnic Fijians." Surita, 95 F.3d at 818, 819. On another occasion, the petitioner's Hindu temple was desecrated and she and her mother were robbed attempting to worship at another place. Under these circumstances, we concluded that a reasonable factfinder would have had to conclude that the petitioner had "suffered past persecution on account of race." Id. at 820.

Our holding in Surita cannot compel the conclusion that Gafoor was persecuted on account of race. Unlike the petitioner's case in Surita, Gafoor's assailants never declared that Gafoor was being assaulted because he was Indo-Fijian-they simply belittled him as an Indo-Fijian during their attack. The majority holds that this difference is "insufficient to distinguish the two cases," because, with their derision, "[t]he soldiers made clear to Gafoor that his race and imputed political opinion contributed to their hatred of him and provided them with additional motive for their actions." Supra at 651. According to the majority, the fact that the soldiers "did not tell him specifically that they were motivated by these factors is unimportant." Surita differs from the present case, the majority contends, merely because the petitioner in Surita presented direct evidence of her persecutors' motivations, whereas Gafoor presented circumstantial evidence. See supra at 651-52.

The majority is simply wrong. The two cases fundamentally differ with respect to the ultimate issue that the evidence in question proves. In Surita, the petitioner presented unrefuted evidence of an actual causal connection between her race and her persecution. But for her race, her attackers would have left her alone. Here, Gafoor has made no such showing. He has merely presented evidence that the soldiers taunted him with a racial slur during the course of an attack prompted by a personal vendetta. Taunting or degrading an opponent by referring to one or another of his traits hardly makes "clear" that the trait has any causal significance — indeed, the trait may be wholly irrelevant to any actual difference of opinion.[1] The majority cannot be serious in holding that the utterance of such a racial slur not only suggests that a contemporaneous assault is racially motivated but compels that conclusion.

Nor does our decision in Prasad establish that a reasonable factfinder would have to conclude that Gafoor was persecuted on account of a political opinion imputed to him. The petitioner in Prasad was a local delegate of the Hindu-dominated Labor Party who was dogged by native Fijian military officers following the 1987 coup. See id. at 616. He was twice incarcerated and, "during his detention[,] ... was questioned about his involvement with the ousted Labour Party." Id. The military also attempted to prevent the petitioner "from meeting in groups" with other Hindus. Id. We concluded that the petitioner had "established past persecution on account of his political activity." Id. at 617.

Compared to the petitioner in Prasad, Gafoor has presented scant evidence that his political opinion (imputed or otherwise) actually motivated his tormentors. The majority implicitly relies on the fact that at least one of Gafoor's jailers accused him of being "against the army." See supra at 651 ("In his testimony before the IJ, Gafoor stated that when he was locked up at Nambala, the soldiers asked him why he had arrested an army officer and accused him of opposing the army."). This fact is certainly suggestive, but taken alone — as it must be, for in this regard it is alone — it can compel at most the uninteresting conclusion that the accuser believed Gafoor to be opposed to the army. This is particularly so because the role of the unnamed accuser in the assaults on Gafoor is unknown and may well have been entirely peripheral.

Simply put, the facts that Gafoor's assailants told him to go back to India and that an officer in the jail accused him of opposing the army do not compel the conclusion that Gafoor's assailants were motivated by Gafoor's race or political opinion. Nor would they be compelling even if we were to interpret these facts, as the majority insists, within the political "context" that the majority develops from sources wholly outside the administrative record, a "context" that Fisher v. INS, 79 F.3d 955, 964 (9th Cir.1996) (en banc), in fact prohibits us from considering. No decision of this court suggests otherwise. The majority thus oversteps its bounds in reversing the BIA's decision.

B

Reality is that policeman Gafoor was persecuted because he caught a powerful military figure in flagrante delicto and dared to arrest the officer whom he witnessed in the criminal act of attempting to rape a young girl. No one thinks otherwise, not even the majority, which concedes that the soldiers were "activated" by the arrest. The fundamental problem, therefore, with the majority's conclusion that Gafoor was indubitably persecuted "on account of" his race and imputed political opinions is not really that the facts pointing thereto are less informative in this case than they were in Surita and Prasad. Indeed, at his hearing Gafoor himself unfailingly attributed his persecution, in the final calculus, to his arrest of the officer:

IJ: Did they tell you why they were beating you up?

Gafoor: They thought, they thought that I had sent some kind of enemy with them.

IJ: Some kind of what?

Gafoor: Enemy. Uh, they said that they were going to kill me and, and they were going to kill my family.

IJ: Why?

Gafoor: Because I arrested them.

* * *

IJ: Why? Wait a minute. Why did you think they took you to the military camp? Why do you think you were arrested?

Gafoor: They said that we have some kind of enmity with each other but I — They said that we police officers, we don't like the army but it was — they said they were going to kill me and destroy us and he beat me.

IJ: Did he tell you why they thought you, there was some kind of enmity between the Army and the police?

Gafoor: He said why I was arresting the Army officer. I didn't know.

* * *

Hiester:[2] As far as you know, he was never charged with the crime?

Gafoor: If they would have charged him with the crime, then nothing would have — then they wouldn't have done to me what, what they did to me.

      Hiester: If he was not charged with the crime, why was the military so interested in you?

      Gafoor: They were angry with me.

      Hiester: About what?

      Gafoor: Because I arrested an Army officer.

      The majority implies that the undisputed fact that Gafoor's arrest of the army officer caused his persecution is irrelevant because we held in Borja "that asylum may be granted if the persecution `was motivated, at least in part, by an actual or implied protected ground.'" Supra at 652 (quoting Borja, 175 F.3d at 736). The majority is mistaken. The fact that an act of abuse may be "motivated" by two or more distinct considerations does not dispense with the logical requirement that any single factor actually "motivated" the conduct.

      This requirement, I would be the first to acknowledge, is not easily satisfied. Concluding that something actually "motivated" a human being to act is often not only speculative but conceptually challenging. Is a situational factor that makes a person's action more likely to occur than it otherwise would be a "motive"? What if only infinitesimally more likely? Is a factor a "motive" when it is sufficient to incite an action but does not make that action more likely to occur at all (because the action will certainly occur anyway)?

      Answering these questions and marshaling evidence to categorize situational factors as precisely as the resulting answers may demand requires a degree of inferential hair-splitting that the majority in Borja did not, and indeed did not need to, address. The majority concluded that there could be little doubt that the petitioner's announced opposition to the New People's Army ("NPA") was the sufficient and primary cause that "triggered" the NPA agents' extortion and ensuing attack on her. See Borja, 175 F.3d at 736, 737 ("Had she not interjected her willingness to pay, the evidence strongly suggests that the NPA would have taken her life as a response to her political statement.").

      Unlike the facts of Borja, the facts of this case plainly indicate that the petitioner would not have been persecuted absent a motive that is not enumerated in the Act — that is, Gafoor would never have been persecuted if he had not arrested the army officer. This case thus requires us to determine just how causally significant a factor must be for us to conclude that it is a "motive" for purposes of the Act. It is apparent that for the majority, a motivating factor need not have any causal significance at all. The majority claims that persecution may be "on account of" a protected ground even if the protected ground is neither a sufficient nor even a necessary cause of the persecution. See supra at 653 ("It is unreasonable, therefore, to require asylum applicants to show that a protected ground, standing alone, would have led to their persecution, or even to require a showing that the persecution would not have occurred in the absence of a protected ground."). The majority's definition of "motive" remains elusive, but it is apparent that it does not comprehend the concept of causation.

In dispensing with a causation requirement, the majority wilfully disregards the well-settled law of this court. We have regularly rejected the proposition that persecutory conduct is "on account of" a statutorily protected characteristic just because the presence of that characteristic enhanced the probability that the persecutory conduct would occur. See, e.g., Singh v. INS, 134 F.3d 962, 970 (9th Cir.1998) (acknowledging that ethnic Fijians were known to commit crimes against Indo-Fijians because of their race but rejecting the petitioner's allegation that crimes committed against her by persons who may have been ethnic Fijians were "on account of" her race); Sangha v. INS, 103 F.3d 1482, 1490 (9th Cir.1997) (noting that, even if guerrillas had imputed opposing political opinion to petitioner, there was "no evidence" that the guerrillas' persecution of him was "`on account of' [his] political views").

The majority seemingly feels that it would be unfair to require asylum applicants actually to demonstrate that they were persecuted "on account of" a protected ground. Causation, after all, is a tricky business and can raise difficult evidentiary obstacles. Congress has lowered the burden for Title VII plaintiffs; why shouldn't we, the majority asks, lower the burden for asylum applicants? In the face of the extravagance and impertinence of this argument, is it too pedestrian to explain that Congress has already weighed the relevant policy choices and decided to require asylees to demonstrate that they suffered persecution "on account of" a protected ground? Of course, it is for Congress alone to decide whether to lower the burden as it has done for Title VII plaintiffs, in contrast to asylum applicants.

The evidence in this case and the history of Fiji developed outside the record do nothing to suggest — much less conclusively establish — that Gafoor's race had anything to do with the violence he suffered. The majority does not, and indeed cannot, contend that he would have been treated any differently were he an ethnic Fijian. He has plainly failed to show that his persecution was "on account of" his race or imputed political opinion, as that term has been interpreted time and again by this court.

II

In addition to reversing the BIA's determination that Gafoor has not demonstrated past persecution on account of a statutorily enumerated ground, the majority proceeds to reject the BIA's determination that a change in country conditions refutes any supposition that Gafoor has a well-founded fear of persecution in the future. The majority observes that country conditions have changed yet again since the BIA made its determination, see supra at 654 ("Since that time, all progress made in Fiji toward eliminating racial conflict has been undone."), and remands for the BIA to consider changes in country conditions as of, one is left to imagine, right now. The majority bases its disregard for the BIA's determination not on anything in the record (because there is no support there) but on post-hearing magazine articles. The majority acknowledges but essentially disregards the fact that we have held explicitly that "we are limited to reviewing the facts considered by the Board" and "are statutorily prevented from taking judicial notice" of evidence from outside the administrative record in reviewing asylum claims.

Fisher v. INS, 79 F.3d 955, 963 (9th Cir.1996) (en banc) (emphasis added).

The majority attempts to skirt our plainly controlling decision in Fisher by relying on a particularly broad dictum from Lising v. INS, 124 F.3d 996 (9th Cir.1997). See supra at 655 ("In particular, Fisher related to evidentiary material that could have been, but was not, presented to the BIA.") (citing Lising, 124 F.3d at 998). Lising, given a fair reading, stands only for the proposition that we may take judicial notice of extra-record INS forms that rest in official INS files. See 124 F.3d at 998 ("Fisher does not treat the issue of a court's taking judicial notice of the agency's own records — and particularly of an official INS form that serves as the very basis of the BIA's decision."); cf. id. at 999 (Boochever, J., concurring) ("While I agree that almost all rules may be subject to exceptions for unforeseen contingencies, I do not believe that it is necessary in this case to carve even the narrow exception to Fisher v. INS proposed by the majority." (citation omitted) (emphasis added)). Whatever the merit of Lising,[3] it hardly supports the majority's claim that any perceived change in country conditions nullifies the BIA's otherwise valid determination.

In taking judicial notice of recent developments in Fiji as reported in several magazine articles, matters entirely outside the record, the majority has plainly exceeded the bounds of this court's authority as a reviewing court under the law of this circuit. See Fisher, 79 F.3d at 963; see also Gomez-Vigil v. INS, 990 F.2d 1111, 1113 (9th Cir.1993) (because "'this court does not sit as an administrative agency for the purpose of fact-finding in the first instance'," it "must reject petitioners' implied request that we consider news articles and other materials appended to the briefs that were not part of the administrative record.") (quoting Tejeda-Mata v. INS, 626 F.2d 721, 726 (9th Cir.1980)). But the majority does not stop there. The majority relies upon articles that appeared six months after this case was argued and submitted, let alone almost two years after the BIA's decision was filed. Federal Rule of Evidence 201(e), which governs judicial notice, provides that a party must be afforded "an opportunity to be heard as to the propriety of taking judicial notice and the tenor of the matter noticed." See also Gomez-Vigil, 990 F.2d at 1115 (Aldisert, J., concurring) ("A court may take judicial notice of facts without prior notification to the parties, so long as the court subsequently provides an opportunity to rebut the noticed facts....") The majority deprives the INS of any opportunity to respond, before this court, to its unwelcome excursus on recent developments in Fijian politics.

Even if one were to acknowledge the lawfulness of the majority's proposed "recent events" new exception to the rule in Fisher and the lawfulness of the majority's manner of taking judicial notice, one would nevertheless expect such "recent events" to be at least facially relevant to the issue the BIA was deciding — otherwise, there would be a new reason to remand with every new day (or at least with every new issue of The Economist). And yet, we are left disappointed. Here, the majority makes almost no effort to evaluate the relevance of the "recent events" to the issue of whether Gafoor is more likely than he was in 1992 to face renewed persecution at the hands of the army officer and his personal posse, who were the only Fijians who ever molested Gafoor, even at the height of the 1987 coup. The "recent events," as it turns out, are not terribly germane.

I regret that I cannot endorse the majority's proposed "recent events" exception to Fisher. It is plainly contrary to that decision, and it invites precisely the sort of misapplication that the majority has engaged in here. The net effect will inevitably be to frustrate and to obstruct the enforcement of our immigration laws as judges of this court persist in attempting to grant relief that Congress has delegated exclusively to the Attorney General to grant.

III

The BIA's dismissal of Gafoor's appeal was supported by substantial evidence and perfectly justified. Gafoor has endured dreadful misfortune, but he has not been persecuted on account of any statutorily enumerated ground. Even if he had been, nothing in the record undermines the BIA's conclusion that conditions in Fiji are now such that Gafoor need no longer fear persecution at the untrammeled hands of a vengeful army officer or any of his soulmates.

I respectfully dissent.

Notes

[1] This principle is so self-evident and intuitive that Hollywood routinely applies it for mass amusement: Sarcastic derision is frequently deployed in the dialogue of action movies to insinuate comic relief into even the most violent of confrontations between mortal enemies. For example, in the opening scene of Tomorrow Never Dies, super-agent James Bond is infiltrating a terrorist arms bazaar. He incapacitates a cigarette-smoking henchman while superciliously muttering the line: "Filthy habit." Tomorrow Never Dies (United Artists 1997). Despite the pointed reference, only the hopelessly obtuse would maintain that Bond dispatched the gun-toting smoker "on account of" his tobacco use.

[2] Thomas L. Hiester was the attorney of record for Gafoor.

[3] This is slight, given that the analysis rested on the hoary jurisprudential proposition that a precedent of this court is only as applicable as a later panel cares to allow.

Judge O'Scannlain's dissent in In re Smith (Dec 19, 2000)

O'SCANNLAIN, Circuit Judge, dissenting:

I respectfully disagree with the majority's conclusion that a bankruptcy trustee is prohibited from adjourning a meeting of creditors "until further notice." Rather, I would hold that the creditors objected in a timely manner in this case. Consequently, I would also reach the merits of whether the Bellwood holdings constitute a "private retirement plan" under California law and I conclude that it decidedly does not.

I

According to Federal Rule of Bankruptcy Procedure 2003(e), a meeting of creditors under 11 U.S.C. § 341(a) "may be adjourned from time to time by announcement at the meeting of the adjourned date and time without further notice." Fed. Rule Bkrtcy.

Proc.2003(e) (emphasis added). The majority argues that the meeting of creditors was concluded rather than adjourned on October 27, 1995, because the trustee adjourned the meeting until further notice without specifying a new meeting date.

This contention is not persuasive. In In re Bernard, 40 F.3d 1028 (9th Cir.1994), we stated that a trustee "has broad discretion whether to adjourn or conclude the meeting," which depends on the degree to which the debtor has furnished satisfactory information relating to the bankruptcy. Id. at 1031 n. 4. "The scant available authority agrees that `may' in Rule 2003(e) is permissive and not mandatory." In re Flynn, 200 B.R. 481, 483 (Bankr.D.Mass. 1996); see also In re DiGregorio, 187 B.R. 273, 275 (Bankr.N.D.Ill.1995); In re Havanec, 175 B.R. 920, 922 (Bankr.N.D.Ohio 1994) (finding that limiting adjournments to a specific date is "unduly constrictive"). The meeting is not concluded until the trustee so declares or the court so orders. See In re Flynn, 200 B.R. at 484; In re DiGregorio, 187 B.R. at 276. But see In re Levitt, 137 B.R. 881, 883 (Bankr.D.Mass.1992) ("[W]here the trustee fails to announce an adjourned date and time within thirty days of the date on which the meeting of creditors was last held, the meeting will be deemed to have concluded on the last meeting date."). I would decline to follow Levitt in favor of the more recent pronouncements in Flynn, DiGregorio, and Havanec, and hold that an adjournment of a § 341(a) hearing does not conclude the hearing merely due to the absence of a future specified date.

There are two good reasons to allow adjournments "until further notice." First, "[s]ince the debtor has the greatest interest in concluding the meeting so as to trigger the 30-day objection period, this Court deems it appropriate to place the burden on the debtor to move for a court order concluding the § 341 meeting." In re DiGregorio, 187 B.R. at 276; see also In re Bernard, 40 F.3d at 1031 n. 4. Second, a court allowing an adjournment until an unspecified date retains control and may cut off the time for objections in the case of unreasonable delay. See In re Flynn, 200 B.R. at 484.

The permissibility of such adjournments, of course, does not mean that they are to be commended or that the bankruptcy court should allow them in all cases. Often, a trustee can easily adjourn the meeting to a time certain, as provided in Rule 2003(e). A case-by-case analysis is appropriate. Trustees cannot keep these meetings open indefinitely without "legitimate grounds for believing that further investigation will prove fruitful." In re Bernard, 40 F.3d at 1031 n. 4.

> 28 U.S.C. § 586 may commit to UST discretion [to choose] among otherwise available means; but it does not give the UST "discretion" to use any means she fancies in any way she pleases. No part of 28 U.S.C. § 586 authorizes the UST to act in an otherwise unlawful or abusive manner and excuse herself by pleading "discretion."

In re Vance, 120 B.R. 181, 194 (Bankr. N.D.Okla.1990).

In this case, an adjournment "until further notice" was appropriate. As the district court stated,

> [a]t the end of the October 27, 1995 creditors' meeting, several issues were left open for later resolution. Further, Smith represented that he would amend his schedules

to correct errors and omissions. At the conclusion of the meeting, the trustee stated "this 341(a) hearing in John Douglas Smith is hereby adjourned until further notice." Given the context, the Court finds that the trustee's initial decision to leave the date of the next meeting open until the requested information was available was both clearly stated and reasonable.

Smith v. Kennedy, No. CV-97-7173 at 10. (There is no indication that Smith objected to the length of the continuance, nor did he move to conclude the § 341(a) hearing. Indeed, on appeal, Smith has not even attempted to rebut the district court's factual findings. Thus, I agree with the district court that the Trustee did not err by granting an adjournment to an unspecified date and that the thirty-day objections period had not yet begun to run.

II

Consequently, I would reach Smith's substantive argument that his Bellwood holdings constitute a "private retirement plan" under California law. Pursuant to 11 U.S.C. § 522(b), a debtor may exempt from the bankruptcy estate any assets that are exempted under the law of the debtor's state. 11 U.S.C. § 522(b)(2)(A); see In re MacIntyre, 74 F.3d 186, 187 (9th Cir.1996). California law provides for the exemption of "private retirement plans" from bankruptcy estates. See § Cal.Code Civ. P. § 704.115(a).

We have explored the definition of such a plan before, concluding that the appropriate analysis is whether the retirement plan at issue was "designed and used for a retirement purpose." In re Bloom, 839 F.2d 1376, 1379-80 (9th Cir.1988). Of course, this "designed and used" inquiry presumes that the entity at issue is in fact a retirement plan. Before proceeding to the issue of whether this plan was of the retirement variety, it is necessary to decide the liminal question of whether it was a plan at all.

Smith points to Webster's to ground his conclusion that the Bellwood property constituted a plan. Alas, the task of adjudication is not always as simple as looking up words in the dictionary. Often we must turn instead to judicial precedent and the reasoning of our fellow jurists. In In re Phillips, 206 B.R. 196 (Bankr.N.D.Cal. 1997), the court declined to consider a plan the debtors' informal and unwritten sentiments. Subjective intent alone, the court concluded, does not constitute a plan. See id.

Similarly, in In re Rogers, 222 B.R. 348 (Bankr.S.D.Cal.1998), the court concluded that the annuity at issue was not a private retirement plan. The court reasoned that the language of § 704.115 "does not extend to protect anything a debtor unilaterally chooses to claim as intended for retirement purposes." Id. at 351.

I agree with these precedents and with the bankruptcy court in concluding that Smith needed to offer more than merely his illusory intentions and dictionary definitions to satisfy the courts that the property was acquired as part of his private retirement plan. Such an instantiation of the purported plan is required to prevent an abuse of this exemption. Finding none, I would reject Smith's appeal and uphold the bankruptcy court's decision.

Judge O'Scannlain's dissent in Cramer v. Consolidated Freightways Inc. (June 15, 2001)

O'SCANNLAIN, Circuit Judge, dissenting:

I respectfully dissent from the Court's opinion in this very sensitive application of the federal Labor Management Relations Act ("Act") to a freely negotiated collective bargaining agreement ("CBA") between Consolidated Freightways ("Consolidated") and its union-member employees.

No doubt, the majority is correct in the formulation of the rule we should apply in this case: the plaintiffs' state law claim is preempted under Section 301 of the Act if Consolidated can assert a "reasonable" invocation of a provision of the CBA which makes the resolution of the plaintiffs' claim depend on its interpretation. Majority Opinion at 688. Such formulation is familiar and is substantially similar to that used in other Circuits. E.g., Martin v. Shaw's Supermarkets, Inc., 105 F.3d 40, 42 (1st Cir.1997) ("[S]ection 301 preempts a state-law claim wherever a court, in passing upon the asserted state-law claim, would be required to interpret a plausibly disputed provision of the collective bargaining agreement." (emphasis added)); Brazinski v. Amoco Petroleum Additives Co., 6 F.3d 1176, 1181 (7th Cir.1993) (noting that state law privacy claim was preempted because "it was arguably within the scope of the [collective bargaining] agreement" (emphasis added)). Regrettably, the majority fails in its application of the rule to the CBA at issue in this case.

Because the CBA expressly provides for video surveillance of its covered employees, it cannot be so cavalierly ignored as the majority holds. Because the CBA can be reasonably interpreted to affect materially the resolution of the plaintiffs' state law claim here, their state law claim is preempted under federal law and therefore I must dissent.

I

Remarkably, the majority chooses to reach alternative holdings. In Part III, it concludes, with little elaboration, that Consolidated cannot assert even a reasonable interpretation of the CBA that makes its interpretation necessary to resolve the plaintiffs' claim. Majority Opinion at 694. ("[A] cursory examination of those provisions makes clear they apply to a completely different context and set of circumstances."). In Part IV, the majority holds that, even if Consolidated could make such an argument, the California Penal Code trumps. Majority Opinion at 695 ("Even if the CBA did expressly contemplate the use of two-way mirrors to facilitate detection of drug users, such a provision would be illegal under California law...."). Neither holding is compelling.

1

As to the analysis in Part III, the elements of a right to privacy cause of action under California law require these plaintiffs to show, among other things, 1) that they had a subjective expectation of privacy in the restroom, and 2) that their subjective expectation of privacy was reasonable. Alarcon v. Murphy, 201 Cal.App.3d 1, 248 Cal.Rptr. 26, 29 (1988) ("To determine whether there has been a violation of Alarcon's constitutional right of privacy, we determine whether his personal and objectively reasonable expectation of privacy has been infringed...." (emphasis added)).

To what sources of information must we look in order to determine, under California law, whether an employee has a subjective and objectively reasonable expectation of privacy? The California Supreme Court tells us this much: "[T]he presence or absence of opportunities to consent voluntarily to activities impacting privacy interests obviously affects the expectations of the participant." Hill v. NCAA, 7 Cal.4th 1, 26 Cal.Rptr.2d 834, 865 P.2d 633, 655 (1994). And where might have the plaintiffs here had the "opportunit[y] to consent voluntarily" to the videotaping of which they complain? They had such an opportunity every time they entered the terminal in which they were videotaped. The record shows that Consolidated placed no fewer than six signs in and around the terminal housing the restroom which read: "NOTICE! 24 Hour Surveillance Recorded on Videotape." This is hardly irrelevant to their objective and subjective expectations of privacy.[1]

But more important to the purposes of preemption, the plaintiffs had an "opportunit[y] to consent voluntarily" to the videotaping in the CBA they signed with their employer. In the section entitled "Use of Video Cameras for Discipline and Discharge," the CBA provides:

The Employer may not use video cameras to discipline or discharge an employee for reasons other than theft of property or dishonesty. If the information on the video tape is to be used to discipline or discharge an employee, the Employer must provide the Local Union, prior to the hearing, an opportunity to review the video tape used by the Employer to support the discipline or discharge. Where a Supplement imposes more restrictive conditions upon the use of video cameras for discipline or discharge, such restrictions shall prevail.

This provision of the CBA makes explicit two things. First, the plaintiffs consented to be videotaped by Consolidated, subject to the restriction that the videotaping was for the purpose of "discipline or discharge" related to "theft of property or dishonesty." Second, the plaintiffs contemplated that they might want to place additional restrictions on Consolidated's use of video cameras through the mechanism of a "Supplement."[2] A number of "Supplements" were agreed to between the plaintiffs and Consolidated. None of the terms in these "Supplements," however, placed any additional restrictions on Consolidated's use of video cameras.

What this provision of the CBA does not make explicit is whether Consolidated may use video cameras in the restroom, or whether Consolidated may use video cameras behind a two-way mirror. Of course, nor does it make explicit whether Consolidated may use video cameras in the hallway, or whether Consolidated may use video cameras on a tripod. I do not understand the majority to suggest, however, that a "cursory examination" of the CBA "makes clear" that Consolidated is barred from putting cameras in the hallway or from putting cameras on tripods. This, no doubt, is the case because, although the CBA does not explicitly say that Consolidated may do such things, nor does it explicitly say that

Consolidated may not do such things.

Thus, the contract is silent, as contracts often are, on whether Consolidated's precise behavior is allowed. And, using traditional principles of contract interpretation, one could very easily make a reasonable argument that this silence should be interpreted to mean that the plaintiffs consented to Consolidated's behavior. Such an argument might take the following form: 1) the CBA explicitly places but one restriction upon Consolidated's use of video cameras; 2) the CBA contemplates that additional explicit restrictions might be placed thereupon; 3) no such additional explicit restrictions were ultimately imposed; 4) thus, one could reasonably conclude that the only restriction the CBA imposes on Consolidated's use of video cameras is the one explicitly set forth.[3] Because the contract does not restrict the use of video cameras to areas other than the restroom, or to positions other than behind a two-way mirror, one could reasonably conclude that the plaintiffs in this case consented to the very videotaping on which their state law privacy claim is based. Accordingly, in order to resolve the plaintiffs' state law privacy claim, the Court must resort to interpretation of the CBA to determine whether this reasonable argument is a winning one.[4]

Not only is there a reasonable argument that the plaintiffs consented in the CBA to the videotaping, but Consolidated's argument in this regard is much stronger than arguments other courts have accepted for the purposes of finding preemption. For example, in a case remarkably similar to this one, the Seventh Circuit held that a suit which alleged that a company had violated state law privacy rights by installing video cameras in a restroom was preempted because the CBA may have authorized the practice, even though there was "not one word in the compact about cameras, locker rooms, or surveillance in general." In re Amoco Petroleum Additives Co., 964 F.2d 706, 709-10 (7th Cir. 1992). The court based preemption on a "management-rights" clause that the company argued left everything "neither regulated nor forbidden" to "its discretion." Id. at 709. The court further noted that several courts had held state law privacy suits over employee drug tests preempted "whether or not the collective bargaining agreement expressly mention[ed] drug tests." Id. at 710. Needless to say, Consolidated's argument regarding the interpretation of the CBA in this case, which does expressly authorize videotaping, is far more plausible than these.[5]

2

In Part IV, the majority relies on the California Penal Code to conclude that, even if one could reasonably argue that the employees consented in the CBA to Consolidated's videotaping, such consent does not matter. In order to reach this conclusion, the majority must rewrite California law.

To repeat: the elements of a right to privacy cause of action under California law require these plaintiffs to show two things: 1) that they had a subjective expectation of privacy in the restroom, and 2) that their subjective expectation of privacy was reasonable.[6] Alarcon, 248 Cal.Rptr. at 29. The majority concludes that, because Consolidated's videotaping is presumably a misdemeanor under California Penal Code §

653n,[7] any expectation of privacy the plaintiffs had in the restroom was reasonable as a matter of law. Fair enough. But this only establishes the second prong of the required showing; it does not establish the first prong, whether the plaintiffs had a subjective expectation of privacy in the restroom. Before the plaintiffs can establish that, the Court must resort to interpretation of the CBA to determine whether they consented to the videotaping.

Astonishingly, the majority ignores this first prong altogether. Which perhaps is unsurprising because there simply is no decision of the California Supreme Court which holds as a matter of law that one has a subjective expectation of privacy from illegal intrusions to which one has consented. Moreover, I doubt that there will ever be such a holding of the California Supreme Court. This is likely because, if the California Supreme Court did make such a holding, it would lead to the ridiculous situation in which I could invite someone to videotape me behind a two-way mirror, only to then turn around and sue that person for violating my right to "privacy."

Nonetheless, this is the interpretation of California law urged upon us by the majority in this case. As support, the majority can only muster the following assertion: "Nothing in Hill suggests that all privacy determinations turn on issues of consent." Majority Opinion at 696. This is true. Hill never used the word "all." Instead, it used the word "obviously": "[T]he presence or absence of opportunities to consent voluntarily to activities impacting privacy interests obviously affects the expectations of the participant." Hill, 26 Cal.Rptr.2d 834, 865 P.2d at 655 (emphasis added). What was "obvious" to the California Supreme Court in Hill should be obvious to everyone else who considers the question: a person's subjective expectation of privacy from an intrusion turns on whether he consented to the intrusion. The majority's conclusion otherwise can only be explained as an attempt to rewrite California law.

II

It is clear that the plaintiffs consented in the CBA to video surveillance. It is at least a "reasonable" interpretation of the CBA that the plaintiffs additionally consented therein to video surveillance behind two-way mirrors. Whether this reasonable interpretation is a winning one is a question that can be answered only by interpreting the CBA in the appropriate forum. Therefore, the plaintiffs' state law claim is preempted. This does not mean, of course, that the plaintiffs in this case have no remedy at all. It simply means that the plaintiffs must pursue their remedies under federal rather than state law. Indeed, the plaintiffs in this case submitted their claim to the grievance process provided for in the CBA, and they prevailed. Thus, not only are the majority's efforts misguided, but unnecessary as well. For these reasons, I respectfully dissent.[8] [*]

Notes

[1] In addition, the record indicates that the Riverside County Sheriff's Department investigated the use of video cameras in the men's restroom of Consolidated's facilities and found two additional video cameras in the ceiling in a different men's

employees restroom which were not behind two-way mirrors and which were presumably visible. This served to put the plaintiffs further on notice that they may have been subject to videotaping in the restrooms of Consolidated's facilities.

Curiously, Consolidated's Supplemental Brief asserts that there was a second video camera in the ceiling of the restroom in which the two-way mirror and hidden camera were discovered. Such assertion is belied by the Sheriff's investigation report.

[2] The term "Supplement" in this provision means a "Supplemental Agreement" setting forth additional terms to "each of the specific types of work performed by the various classifications of employees controlled by this Master Agreement."

[3] The reporters are replete with cases employing such an interpretative method. E.g., Republic Pictures Corp. v. Rogers, 213 F.2d 662, 665 (9th Cir.1954) ("[C]ourts are loathe to impose limitations or restrictions upon the parties which are not expressly contained in their agreement or which do not arise by necessary implication, and without such implied restrictions the contract could not be effectively performed...."); see also Margaret N. Kniffin, 5 Corbin on Contracts § 24.28 (Revised Ed.1998) ("If the parties in their contract have specifically named one item ... a reasonable interpretation is that they did not intend to include other, similar items not listed.").

[4] The majority apparently feels that this legal effort to determine whether there is a reasonable argument that the plaintiffs consented in the CBA to the videotaping is beside the point because it instead relies on the surmise that "the surreptitious nature of the violation of plaintiffs' privacy belies any notion of bargaining or consent to hidden cameras behind two-way mirrors." Majority Opinion at 694. By this statement, I understand the majority to be surmising that Consolidated would not need to hide cameras behind a two-way mirror if it truly thought that the plaintiffs had consented to the videotaping. With all due respect to the majority, our job is not to engage in dubious surmises about the thoughts of the parties, but, rather, to engage in the traditional legal analysis to be followed in section 301 preemption cases like the one before us.

At another point, the majority also appears to argue that the plaintiffs' state law rights can be preempted only by a "clear and unmistakable" waiver, rather than a "reasonable" argument regarding waiver, in the CBA. Majority Opinion at 692, 695 n.7. This would be the case, however, only if the plaintiffs' state law rights were "nonnegotiable." The Supreme Court made this clear in Lingle v. Norge Division of Magic Chef, Inc., 486 U.S. 399, 108 S.Ct. 1877, 100 L.Ed.2d 410 (1988). The state law right at issue in Lingle, freedom from retaliatory discharge, was "nonnegotiable," id. at 407 n. 7, 108 S.Ct. 1877, because "under [state] law, the parties to a collective bargaining agreement may not waive the prohibition against retaliatory discharge," id. at 409 n. 9, 108 S.Ct. 1877. Thus, "[b]efore deciding whether such a state-law bar to waiver could be pre-empted under federal law by the parties to a collective-bargaining agreement, we would require `clear and unmistakable' evidence in order to conclude that such a waiver had been intended." Id. at 409 n. 9, 108 S.Ct. 1877 (citations omitted). There is no "state-law bar to waiver" of the right to privacy in California. To the contrary, the California Supreme Court has held that the right to privacy can be extinguished by consent: "[T]he presence or absence of opportunities to consent voluntarily to activities impacting privacy interests obviously affects the expectations of the participant." Hill, 26 Cal. Rptr.2d 834, 865 P.2d at 655.

[5] The majority's attempt to distinguish these cases is non-responsive. Majority Opinion at 694 n.6. The fact that the videotaping in these cases was not done, as far as we know, in violation of state criminal laws cannot save the majority's holding in Part III of its opinion. As I understand Part III, the majority holds that, without even considering the California criminal law, Consolidated cannot make a reasonable argument that the plaintiffs consented in the CBA to its videotaping. The majority does not invoke the California criminal law until its holding in Part IV of its opinion, which, as explained below, is deficient for separate reasons.

[6] The majority appears to argue that the elements of a right to privacy cause of action under California law do not require the plaintiffs to show that they had a subjective expectation of privacy in the restroom. Majority Opinion at 696-97 n. 10. The majority appears to suggest that this is the case because Hill altered the elements recited in Alarcon. Id. I respectfully disagree. Nowhere in Hill did the Supreme Court state that it was overruling the understanding in Alarcon. Moreover, although Hill did not use the phrase "subjective expectation of privacy," it included as the second element of the cause of action "a reasonable expectation of privacy on the plaintiff's part." Hill, 26 Cal.Rptr.2d 834, 865 P.2d at 655. I take this to mean that the plaintiff must show both that he had an expectation of privacy and that it was reasonable. This view is confirmed by the fact that the Court explained this element by noting that "the presence or absence of opportunities to consent voluntarily to activities impacting privacy interests obviously affects the expectations of the participant." Id. Indeed, in fashioning the elements of the right to privacy under the California Constitution, the Supreme Court drew upon both the California common law right to privacy and the federal constitutional right to privacy, id., 26 Cal. Rptr.2d at 848-53, 865 P.2d 633, both of which include a subjective expectation of privacy as one of their elements. Id., 26 Cal. Rptr.2d at 849-50, 865 P.2d 633 ("The plaintiff in an invasion of privacy case must have conducted himself or herself in a manner consistent with an actual expectation of privacy, i.e., he or she must not have manifested by his or her conduct a voluntary consent to the invasive actions of the defendant."); California v. Greenwood, 486 U.S. 35, 39, 108 S.Ct. 1625, 100 L.Ed.2d 30 (1988) ("[T]he Fourth Amendment [is violated] only if respondents manifested a subjective expectation of privacy ... that society accepts as objectively reasonable.").

[7] It is far from clear whether Consolidated's videotaping violated § 653n. The majority assumes arguendo in Part IV that there is a reasonable argument that the plaintiffs consented in the CBA to the videotaping, but it nonetheless holds that the videotaping was illegal. In doing so, the majority extends California law in a manner that appears to contradict decisions by the California Supreme Court. Although the text of § 653n does not limit liability to "non-consensual" viewing, the California Supreme Court

has appeared to do just that. In People v. Triggs, 8 Cal.3d 884, 106 Cal.Rptr. 408, 506 P.2d 232 (1973), the Supreme Court held that a criminal defendant had a reasonable expectation of privacy in a restroom on account of § 653n. Id., 106 Cal.Rptr. 408, 506 P.2d at 238. In a subsequent decision, however, the Supreme Court clarified that Triggs extended only to "clandestine, unexpected" viewing. In re Deborah C., 30 Cal.3d 125, 177 Cal.Rptr. 852, 635 P.2d 446, 452 (1981) (emphasis added). The Court based this clarification on the fact that "section 653n is limited to a method of ... clandestine observation" and "implies no belief that restrooms and fitting rooms are immune from all observation." Id., 177 Cal. Rptr. 852, 635 P.2d at 452 n. 9 (internal quotation marks omitted). Thus, it appears that one of the modes of "observation" from which § 653n does not make the plaintiffs "immune" is an "expected" viewing from behind a two-way mirror. Such a viewing would be "expected" if the plaintiffs consented to it in the CBA. Indeed, to interpret § 653n otherwise (i.e., in the manner advanced by the majority) would allow the State to prosecute criminally someone who erects a two-way mirror at the invitation of the person he is videotaping!

In addition to the reasonable argument that the plaintiffs consented in the CBA to Consolidated's viewing, there are other facts which suggest that Consolidated's viewing was not "unexpected" to the plaintiffs, and, therefore, not in violation of § 653n. As already noted, Consolidated placed no fewer than six signs in and around the terminal in which the plaintiffs were videotaped that read: "NOTICE! 24 Hour Surveillance Recorded on Videotape." Moreover, there were two other video cameras in another restroom which were not behind two-way mirrors and which were presumably visible.

Finally, it is not surprising that following the Sheriff's investigation referred to in footnote 1, the Riverside Country District Attorney decided not to file any criminal charges against Consolidated, stating that "the conduct involved was not motivated by an intent that would warrant criminal prosecution."

[8] I also dissent from Part V of the Court's opinion. The majority rests its conclusion in this Part on our decision in Miller v. AT & T Network Systems, 850 F.2d 543 (9th Cir.1988). But, in Miller, regarding the tort of intentional infliction of emotion distress, we said: "Because the tort requires inquiry into the appropriateness of the defendant's behavior, the terms of the CBA can become relevant in evaluating whether the defendant's behavior was reasonable. Actions that the collective bargaining agreement permits might be deemed reasonable in virtue of the fact that the CBA permits them." Id. at 550. Only if "the particular CBA does not govern the offending behavior ... [will] an emotional distress claim [not be] preempted." Id. at 550 n. 5.

[*] As explained above, there is a reasonable argument that the CBA governs Consolidated's behavior in this case, and, therefore, the plaintiffs' intentional infliction of emotional distress claim is preempted as well. Moreover, even if Consolidated's behavior constituted a misdemeanor under California law, which, as I noted above, is doubtful, it would not foreclose preemption: "we cannot assume that the employer's behavior was outrageous for purposes of an emotional distress claim just because the employer may

have violated a statutory prohibition...." Id. at 551.

Judge O'Scannlain's dissent in Lal v. INS (July 3, 2001) [Notes omitted]

O'SCANNLAIN, Circuit Judge, dissenting:

With respect, I cannot join the court's opinion. Regrettably, the court ignores the teaching of the Supreme Court by failing to defer to the BIA's permissible construction of its own asylum regulation. Further, the court simply misconstrues the record in arriving at its conclusion that the BIA's decision to deny asylum is not supported by substantial evidence. Finally, the court misapplies our precedents in rejecting the State Department's opinion, and BIA's reliance on it, that circumstances in Fiji have changed. For these reasons, I must dissent.

I

Congress has authorized the Attorney General to grant asylum to "refugees." 8 U.S.C. § 1158(b)(1). To be considered a "refugee" and thus be eligible for asylum, an applicant must demonstrate that he is unable or unwilling to return to his country of nationality "because of persecution or a well-founded fear of persecution on account of race, religion, nationality, membership in a particular social group, or political opinion." 8 U.S.C. § 1101(a)(42)(A). The applicant's credible account of past persecution raises a presumption that his fear of future persecution is well-founded. See 8 C.F.R. § 208.13(b)(1)(i). The INS can then rebut this presumption by demonstrating, "by a preponderance of the evidence, that conditions `have changed to such an extent that the applicant no longer has a well-founded fear of being persecuted if he or she were to return.'" Marcu v. INS, 147 F.3d 1078, 1081 (9th Cir.1998) (quoting 8 C.F.R. § 208.13(b)(1)(i)). In Lal's case, the BIA found that the INS successfully rebutted the presumption that his fear of future persecution was well-founded by demonstrating that conditions in Fiji have improved significantly since the tumultuous 1987 coup.[1] Unless Lal could benefit from some other applicable rule, the BIA had no choice but to affirm denial of asylum.

A

But the BIA has developed a humanitarian exception to the general rule. See Matter of Chen, 20 I. & N. Dec. 16 (BIA 1989). Where he cannot demonstrate a well-founded fear of future persecution (because, for example, country conditions have changed), asylum shall be granted if "it is determined that the applicant has demonstrated compelling reasons for being unwilling to return to his or her country of nationality ... arising out of the severity of the past persecution." 8 C.F.R. § 208.13(b)(1)(ii). This regulation grows out of Chen, which remains the touchstone for determining the applicability of this exception. See Kumar v. INS, 204 F.3d 931, 935 (9th Cir.2000); Vongsakdy v. INS, 171 F.3d 1203, 1207 (9th Cir.1999). In Chen, the BIA explained that where a petitioner has suffered from "atrocious" persecution, changed country conditions "may not always produce a complete change..., in view of his past experiences, in the mind of the refugee." 20 I. & N. Dec. at 20.

In Lal's case, the BIA appears to have considered Chen's humanitarian exception[2] and, in concluding that it did not apply, stated, "a preponderance of the evidence establishes ... that there are not compelling reasons for being unwilling to return to Fiji arising out of the severity of the past persecution of the lead respondent. In this regard we observe that [Lal] does not claim to suffer from lasting physical or emotional disability as a result of past mistreatment." The majority takes issue with this conclusion, interpreting the latter sentence as requiring that the applicant must demonstrate an on-going disability to qualify for asylum under Chen. The majority reverses the BIA's determination because it concludes that a requirement of "lasting... disability" (sometimes referred to as "ongoing disability") is inconsistent with the plain language and intent of the regulation and because neither Chen, nor other BIA cases nor our own cases applying the humanitarian exception require the applicant to establish lasting disability.[3]

With respect, the majority errs because it does not defer to the BIA's permissible construction of its own regulation. In so doing it repeats the error we made in Aguirre-Aguirre v. INS, 121 F.3d 521 (9th Cir.1997) ("Aguirre I"), reversed, 526 U.S. 415, 119 S.Ct. 1439, 143 L.Ed.2d 590 (1999) ("Aguirre II"). "In the course of its analysis, [the Ninth Circuit] fail[s] to accord the required level of deference to the interpretation of the [BIA] ... it should have applied the principles of deference described in Chevron U.S.A. Inc. v. Natural Resources Defense Council, Inc., 467 U.S. 837, 842, 104 S.Ct. 2778, 81 L.Ed.2d 694 (1984)." Aguirre II, 526 U.S. at 424, 119 S.Ct. 1439. Although the majority correctly states that substantial deference is owed to the legal decisions of the BIA, it misapplies this broad standard and substitutes its own judgments for that of the agency. The Supreme Court corrected us for making similar errors two years ago in Aguirre I. We should not repeat such errors now.

1

The BIA's interpretation of its own regulation is owed "substantial deference." Thomas Jefferson University v. Shalala, 512 U.S. 504, 512, 114 S.Ct. 2381, 129 L.Ed.2d 405 (1994). This broad deference is especially warranted because the BIA's significant expertise makes it well suited to interpret its own regulations in this complex regulatory scheme. See id; Department of Health & Human Servs. v. Chater, 163 F.3d 1129 (9th Cir.1998). The BIA's interpretation "must be given `controlling weight unless it is plainly erroneous or inconsistent with the regulation.'" Thomas Jefferson, 512 U.S. at 512, 114 S.Ct. 2381 (quoting Udall v. Tallman, 380 U.S. 1, 16, 85 S.Ct. 792, 13 L.Ed.2d 616 (1965)). The Supreme Court has cautioned that we must defer to the agency's interpretation "unless an `alternative reading is compelled by the regulation's plain language or by other indications of the Secretary's intent at the time of the regulation's promulgation." Id. (quoting Gardebring v. Jenkins, 485 U.S. 415, 430, 108 S.Ct. 1306, 99 L.Ed.2d 515 (1988)).

The majority, however, concludes that a requirement of on-going disability is contrary to both the plain language and the intent of the agency in promulgating the regulation. Yet, it fails to demonstrate how the plain language of the regulation or its intent compels an interpretation that does not allow for the imposition of an on-going disability requirement.

2

Under BIA's regulations, an applicant is eligible for asylum if he or she "has demonstrated compelling reasons for being unwilling to return to his or her country of nationality ... arising out of the severity of the past persecution." 8 C.F.R. § 208.13(b)(1)(ii) (emphasis added). I respectfully disagree with the majority's assertion that demonstrating severe past persecution is sufficient. See supra 1006-07. The BIA has stated: "the applicant must also show that he belongs to the smaller group of persecution victims whose persecution (including the aftermath) is so severe that the `compelling reasons' standard has been met." Matter of N-M-A-, Interim Decision 3368, at 35 1998 WL 744095 (BIA 1998). In N-M-A-, the BIA concluded that the applicant did not qualify for the "humanitarian exception" because the applicant had not demonstrated "the severe harm and the long-lasting effects of that harm." Id. (emphasis added). In other words, the applicant had not shown severe past persecution and compelling reasons arising from that persecution. Here, regardless of whether Lal has demonstrated severe past persecution, he has clearly not demonstrated compelling reasons based on this persecution for not being willing to return to his country. The majority erroneously concludes that Lal has satisfied the requirements of 8 C.F.R. § 208.13(b)(1)(ii) without even mentioning a single compelling reason.

Because "compelling reasons" is not defined in regulation or statute, we must give substantial deference to the BIA's interpretation so long as it is not plainly erroneous or inconsistent with the regulation. Even the majority would agree that an on-going physical impairment and an on-going mental impairment caused by the past persecution are compelling reasons for an applicant's unwillingness to return to his country. Certainly, requiring such an on-going impairment to satisfy the compelling reasons standard is not contrary to the plain language of the regulation. Absent an express definition, the BIA's interpretation to restrict "compelling reasons" to on-going impairments is reasonable and is thus owed substantial deference. Thomas Jefferson, 512 U.S. at 512, 114 S.Ct. 2381 (Court must defer to agency's interpretation unless alternative interpretation compelled by plain language or intent). At the very least, the plain language does not foreclose such a requirement. An alternative reading is not, therefore, compelled by the plain language and the majority erred in so holding.

3

Nor does the intent of the regulation compel an alternative interpretation rejecting the requirement of on-going disability. As the majority notes, Chen is the case the regulation was intended to codify and is a useful guide to determining agency intent. See supra 1005. In no way does Chen foreclose the INS's requiring on-going disability. Indeed, that case specifically declines "to delineate the circumstances under which past persecution may or may not be the basis for a successful asylum claim." 20 I. & N. Dec. 16, 22 (BIA 1989).

Moreover, Chen actually supports a requirement of an on-going disability. There, the BIA focused not only on the past persecution but also on how such persecution currently affected Chen. The BIA made careful note that Chen was "physically debilitated, must wear a hearing aid ..., is always anxious and fearful, and is often suicidal." Id. at 20. The Board also noted that Chen had vowed suicide if he were forced to return to China. See id. These findings by the Board demonstrate that Chen was both physically and emotionally disabled. In explaining the rationale behind the exception, the Board highlights the importance of examining the connection between the past persecution and the present day: "It is frequently recognized that a person who — or whose family — has suffered under atrocious forms of persecution should not be expected to repatriate. Even though there may have been a change of regime in his country, this may not always produce a complete change in the attitude of the population, nor, in view of his past experiences, in the mind of the refugee." Id. at 18-19. The board's reference to the applicant's present mind-set in light of the past persecution appears to speak directly to whether the applicant is "emotionally disabled." The intent of the agency in promulgating the regulation, as amplified by Chen, supports a requirement that the applicant demonstrate an emotional or physical ailment that makes him unwilling to return to his country.[4]

B

The majority attacks the BIA's interpretation of its own humanitarian rule on several fronts, each of which fails to survive careful scrutiny.

1

The majority states repeatedly that a requirement of on-going disability is unreasonable "because it treats two applicants who are tortured alike differently if one has the good fortune to fully recover from his injuries and the other does not." Supra at 1004. But such observation highlights the majority's fundamental miscomprehension of the humanitarian exception. Based solely on the fact of their past torture, the two hypothetical applicants have only demonstrated that they have suffered past persecution. Nevertheless, the regulation requires that the applicant also demonstrate compelling reasons arising out of the past persecution for not being willing to return to his country.

Treating two similarly tortured applicants differently is amply supported by the policies of this regulation and of asylum generally. Virtually all victims of persecution carry with them the memories of their persecution. Our asylum law, however, seeks only to help those who cannot, by repatriation, get a fresh start in their country, whether it be from an objective fear of future persecution or for compelling reasons based on severe past persecution. "Asylum is a prophylactic protection ... [and] is designed not to remedy the past." N-M-A-, Interim Decision 3368, at 29 (citing Marquez v. INS, 105 F.3d 374 (7th Cir.1997)) (internal citations omitted). The regulation is aimed at helping those who, like Mr. Chen, suffer from the long-lasting effects of persecution to the extent of being physically debilitated, always anxious and fearful, and suicidal at the prospect of returning to the country of his persecution. Chen, 20 I. & N. Dec. 16, 20.

The majority would restrict the application of the regulation to treating all similarly tortured applicants alike regardless of changed conditions. But this oversteps the judicial role. While the BIA may, in the exercise of its discretion, interpret the regulation in such manner it is simply not compelled to do so either by the plain language or intent. Based on the majority's confined interpretation of the regulation, two applicants who have suffered identical past persecution would be treated the same regardless of whether one applicant has no memory nor physical reminder of his past persecution. To such applicant, asylum would only be a remedy for a past persecution he does not even remember; it would serve no prophylactic function in having the applicant avoid repatriation to relive the horrors of his memories amidst his persecutors and the surroundings of his persecution. Yes, the applicant who has had the good fortune of recovering from his physical and emotional wounds has no right, under the regulation, to asylum from a country in which the conditions which wrought the persecution no longer exist.

2

The majority further contends that the BIA's interpretation is owed less deference because it is arbitrary and capricious and represents an irrational departure from a settled course of adjudication. See Supra at 1006-07. The BIA's application of the Chen exception, however, demonstrates that a requirement of an on-going disability is a logical extension of a consistent policy. Indeed, virtually all decisions applying the Chen exception have discussed the presence or absence of the long-term effects of the past persecution.

In Chen itself, the BIA carefully detailed emotional and physical scars from his past persecution in granting him asylum. Without expressly referring to "lasting... disability," Chen specifically declined to prescribe the requirements for asylum under this exception. Chen, 20 I. & N. Dec. 16, 22. Applying such a disability requirement here is fully consistent with Chen.

In N-M-A-, the BIA noted that to meet the "compelling reasons" standard of the regulation the focus is appropriately on the "aftermath" of the persecution and "the long-lasting effects of [the] harm." N-M-A, Interim Decision 3368, at 35. In finding that he did not qualify for asylum, the board noted that the applicant had not testified to any "long-lasting effects" from the persecution and that there was a lack of "evidence of severe psychological trauma stemming from the harm." Id.

In Matter of H-, where the Board granted asylum to the applicant based on the Chen exception, the Board noted that the applicant had been "badly beaten on his head, back, and forearm with a rifle butt and a bayonet, resulting in scars to his body which remain to the present." Matter of H-, Interim Decision 3276, at 14 1996 WL 291910 (BIA 1996). The Board clearly found that the applicant had an on-going physical disability. Requiring such a disability there was not an irrational departure from Chen.

Matter of B-, contrary to the majority's assertion, is not inconsistent with a requirement of on-going disability. While the Board did not make a specific finding of on-going physical or emotional disability, the Board did note that the applicant had suffered "electric shocks" and thirteen months in detention and prison receiving "various forms of physical torture and psychological abuse." Matter of B-, Interim Decision 3251, at 2, 6 1995 WL 326740 (BIA 1995). It is highly probable that the applicant suffered permanent physical and emotional scars from this atrocious persecution. A person who suffers electric shocks will likely be permanently scarred. Equally probable is that a person who receives 13 months of various forms of psychological abuse will be emotionally scarred. Where it is likely that Bhad either emotional or physical scarring, a requirement of such a disability cannot be said to be inconsistent with this decision. Even if Bdid not suffer from an on-going disability, one BIA decision granting asylum without requiring such a disability would not render the general requirement an irrational departure from BIA policy.

A requirement of on-going disability is clearly consistent with the BIA's past application of the Chen exception. In N-M-A-, the Board made an explicit finding that the applicant had not testified to the long-lasting effects of the persecution. In Chen and B-, the Board specifically noted the physical scars of the applicants. In H-, it is highly likely that the applicant suffered both physical and emotional disabilities from his electric shock torture and the many months of psychological abuse. To require an explicit on-going disability now is not contrary to these previous BIA decisions that relied heavily on the presence and absence of such a disability.

At worst, the "lasting ... disability" requirement is a narrow view of what constitutes compelling reasons. In INS. v. Yueh-Shaio Yang, 519 U.S. 26, 32, 117 S.Ct. 350, 136 L.Ed.2d 288 (1996), the Supreme Court reasoned that since "entry fraud" was "a rule of the INS's own invention, the INS is entitled, within reason, to define that exception as it pleases." Id. Similarly, a narrow view of "compelling reasons" is not a disregard of the BIA's general policy of considering the long-lasting effects of the persecution. After all, the Chen exception is a regulation created by the BIA, and, as such, it is entitled to define it as it pleases.

3

Sadly, the majority repeats the errors of Aguirre I, which was reversed by Aguirre II, in which the Supreme Court admonished this court for having failed to accord the BIA's interpretations the deference they are owed and for simply imposing our own construction of the statute.

Aguirre II involved the definition of a "serious nonpolitical crime," a provision of asylum law that prevents an applicant, otherwise eligible for withholding of deportation, from remaining in the United States because of crimes committed in his country of origin. See 526 U.S. at 419, 119 S.Ct. 1439; 8 U.S.C. § 1253(h)(2)(C). Applying the definition of a "serious nonpolitical crime" adopted in one of its earlier decisions, the BIA had concluded that the applicant committed serious nonpolitical crimes. See Aguirre II, 526 U.S. at 422-23, 119 S.Ct. 1439. We reversed, concluding that the BIA had incorrectly interpreted the provision. See Aguirre I, 121 F.3d at 524. We held that the BIA had erred because it failed to consider the United Nations High Commissioner for Refugees, Handbook on Procedures and Criteria for Determining Refugee Status ("UN Handbook") and did not heed our precedent when it applied the serious nonpolitical crime provision. See id. We held that following the UN Handbook and our cases, the BIA should have considered the persecution the petitioner might suffer if he returned, whether his crimes were grossly disproportionate to their alleged objectives, and whether his actions were "atrocious" as defined by our cases. See id. Judge Kleinfeld dissented. See id. at 524-25. In turn, the Supreme Court reversed and held that we had not appropriately deferred to the BIA as the agency charged with administering the statute. See Aguirre II, 526 U.S. at 425, 119 S.Ct. 1439. In analyzing the present case, the majority fails to follow the principles and path laid out in Aguirre II.

In Lal's case, the BIA interpreted its own decision (Chen) as codified in the regulations (8 C.F.R. § 208.13(b)(1)(ii)). Such an interpretation must be given "controlling weight unless it is plainly erroneous or inconsistent with the regulation." Udall v. Tallman, 380 U.S. 1, 16, 85 S.Ct. 792, 13 L.Ed.2d 616 (1965). Thus, the issue before us, of course, is whether the BIA's requirement that an applicant show "lasting ... disability" in order to avoid the well-founded fear of future persecution element of asylum eligibility is a "permissible construction" of the regulation. Id. The question becomes whether an alternative interpretation is compelled by the plain language of the regulation or the intent in promulgating it. Thomas Jefferson, 512 U.S. at 512, 114 S.Ct. 2381. In rejecting the BIA's decision, the majority never states how the plain language or intent of the regulation compels an alternative interpretation that disallows a requirement of on-going disability.

Applying the lessons of Aguirre II here, the majority's interpretation of the Chen exception, "is not obvious" "[a]s a matter of plain language." Aguirre II, 526 U.S. at 426, 119 S.Ct. 1439. Nowhere in the regulation is the meaning or scope of "compelling reasons" defined. It is not at all obvious that "compelling reasons" should be based on anything more than physical and emotional disabilities. Although the majority's interpretation may well be reasonable, the BIA is not compelled to follow it. Because of the BIA's expertise, we defer to it to choose among all of the competing reasonable interpretations the one interpretation which it believes best comports with its policy goals. By not deferring to the BIA and, instead, substituting its own judgment, the majority has repeated our errors from Aguirre I.

4

Finally, the majority faults the BIA for failing to follow our previous cases applying the Chen exception, in particular Vongsakdy and Lopez-Galarza. None of our cases forecloses the requirement that a petitioner claim an on-going disability in order to qualify for asylum under Chen, and the facts of those cases indicate that the existence of a continuing disability is an important consideration. In Vongsakdy, we compared the persecution suffered by the petitioner to that suffered by Chen. We noted specifically that "[b]oth suffered serious physical injuries and were denied medical care, resulting in permanent impairment." 171 F.3d at 1207 (emphasis added). In Lopez-Galarza, where the petitioner was raped, abused, deprived of food and imprisoned, there is no indication of whether she suffered an on-going disability. But we did not hold in that case that the persecution satisfied the requirements of humanitarian asylum; instead, we remanded the case to the BIA so that it could consider the possibility. See 99 F.3d at 963. Thus the best that can be said for the majority's position is that none of our cases explicitly state that on-going disability is a requirement. But the BIA's imposition of such a requirement certainly does not contradict our case law.[5] According to the majority's analysis, an agency is foreclosed from altering its interpretation of a statute or regulation unless that interpretation has been specifically acknowledged and approved by our case law. This standard does not accord the deference embodied in Chevron that is necessary for an agency to "give[] ambiguous statutory terms `concrete meaning through a process of case-by-case adjudication.'" Aguirre II, 526 U.S. at 425, 119 S.Ct. 1439 (citing INS v. Cardoza-Fonseca, 480 U.S. 421, 448-49, 107 S.Ct. 1207, 94 L.Ed.2d 434 (1987)).

C

Neither the humanitarian exception, nor the majority's reinterpretation of it, can overcome the deference Aguirre II requires us to give to the BIA in the disposition of its regulations. For the foregoing reasons, the BIA's decision to deny Lal asylum is based on a permissible construction of the asylum statute, is consistent with Chen and our cases, and should be upheld.

II

Notwithstanding the discussion in Part I, it is entirely possible that the majority has over-interpreted the BIA's decision; that is, the BIA may never have intended to establish a new "lasting ... disability" requirement as a matter of law. After laying out the facts of Lal's persecution, the BIA concluded:

a preponderance of the evidence establishes ... that there are not compelling reasons for being unwilling to return to Fiji arising out of the severity of the past persecution of the lead respondent. In this regard we observe that the principal respondent does not claim to suffer from lasting physical or emotional disability as a result of past mistreatment.

Rather than establishing a new legal requirement, the BIA may have been simply supporting its conclusion that the totality of the facts of this case does not support asylum under Chen by noting that Lal did not claim ongoing disability. If this interpretation of the BIA's opinion is correct then, the majority should have reviewed the BIA's decision under the substantial evidence standard. See INS v. Elias-Zacarias, 502 U.S. 478, 483-84, 112 S.Ct. 812, 117 L.Ed.2d 38 (1992); Kumar, 204 F.3d at 934-35 (applying the substantial evidence standard to our review of the BIA's decision that the petitioner did not qualify for asylum under Chen). On the facts of this case, the BIA's decision that the severity of the persecution suffered did not rise to the level of "atrocity" is clearly supported by substantial evidence and the majority errs in concluding otherwise.

We have held that in considering the humanitarian exception, the BIA should compare the severity of the persecution endured by the applicant with that suffered by the petitioner in Chen. See Lopez-Galarza, 99 F.3d at 963. As the majority recognizes, the BIA here did just that. After describing extensively the persecution that Lal suffered, the BIA's conclusion, citing Chen, was sufficient and does not lack substantial evidence to support it. See Marcu, 147 F.3d at 1082-83. In Marcu, we stated:

> With regard to [the claim for humanitarian asylum], the BIA held: "[B]ased on the evidence on hand, we do not find sufficient humanitarian grounds to grant the respondent asylum as a matter of discretion. The actions were not so severe or atrocious in nature to warrant asylum for humanitarian reasons." Although we require more than a mere comment from the BIA, all that is necessary is a decision that sets out terms sufficient to enable us as a reviewing court to see that the Board has heard, considered and decided.

Id. at 1082. As in Lal's case, in Marcu, "[t]he BIA set forth in its opinion an extensive description of the harassment and abuse [the petitioner] endured.... In the BIA's judgment, however, that harassment and abuse did not rise to the necessary level of severity or atrociousness to warrant asylum on humanitarian grounds. The BIA's opinion demonstrates that it heard the claim, considered the evidence, and decided against [the petitioner]." Id. at 1083. That is precisely what occurred here. As we concluded in Marcu, "No more was required." Id. See also Kazlauskas, 46 F.3d at 906-07 (holding that the IJ did not abuse his discretion where he considered the severity of the petitioner's and his family's persecution, the likelihood of future persecution, the circumstances surrounding the petitioner's departure and entry into the United States).

The two cases cited by the majority — Lopez-Galarza and Vongsakdy — do not teach otherwise. In Lopez-Galaraza, the BIA erred because it "simply failed to consider the level of atrocity of past persecution." 99 F.3d at 963. In that case, the BIA did not "provide an explanation sufficient to enable us as a reviewing court to see that the Board has heard, considered, and decided." Id. (quotations omitted). Here, the BIA made it clear that it had considered the severity of the past persecution, but did not consider it to rise to the level of "atrocity." It fulfilled all the requirements of Marcu.

In Vongsakdy, the petitioner suffered permanent impairment resulting from his two-year ordeal at a forced labor camp. There, he was deprived of food and water, beaten and tortured, had his fingers broken, denied medical care, compelled to witness the killing of his friend, and had his thumb severed by a rifle blow. See 171 F.3d at 1205-06. Lal's experience, though brutal, was simply not as serious. Lal was beaten and tortured and deprived of adequate food and water for three days, not two years. His home and temple were robbed. He was forced to watch as soldiers fondled his wife. He was detained an additional three times. He was prevented from leaving the country. One should not minimize in any way the severity of the brutality suffered by the Lal family, but the standard, as established by Chen and our own cases is one of "atrociousness." This standard must be kept high to prevent the exception from destroying the carefully calibrated statutory and regulatory scheme.

Let us remember, our standard of review is substantial evidence; that is, the evidence in the record must compel the opposite conclusion reached by the BIA before we are at liberty to overturn its judgment. See Vongsakdy, 171 F.3d at 1206. Given the definition of "atrocity" endorsed by the Supreme Court, the appropriate standard of review, and the need to take care that the exception does not swallow the rule, I cannot say that the BIA's conclusion that the persecution was not serious enough is not supported by substantial evidence.

Finally, the majority's conclusion cannot be reconciled with our recent decision in Kumar. In that case, the petitioner, like Lal, a Fijian of Indian descent and supporter of the Labour Party, suffered from extensive persecution. The soldiers entered the Kumar's home, beat and tied up Kumar's parents and then forced them to watch as they stripped Kumar of her clothes and sexually assaulted her. See 204 F.3d at 932-33. The soldiers threatened Kumar's life and took her father into custody where they beat him for two weeks. See id. Later that same year, soldiers destroyed the temple where Kumar was worshiping, dragged her out by her hair and punched and kicked her until she agreed to convert from Hinduism. See id. at 933. They also knocked her mother unconscious when she tried to intervene. Still later, a group of soldiers caught up with Kumar while she was at school and beat her until she was unconscious. See id. Despite the ferocity of the persecution Kumar suffered, we held that the record did not compel us to conclude that the BIA erred when it decided that the severity of the persecution did not rise to the level required for humanitarian asylum. See id. at 935.

The majority does not even attempt to reconcile these cases, and I believe it cannot. On the facts, Kumar and Lal suffered from very similar experiences of persecution. I find it improbable that the facts of Lal could compel us to conclude that no reasonable person could fail to find that the severity of Lal's persecution rose to the level of "atrocity" required for humanitarian asylum, while those of Kumar do not.

Substantial evidence supports the BIA's conclusion that Lal is not eligible for asylum because he failed to demonstrate compelling reasons arising out of severe past persecution for not being willing to return to his country. If the BIA did require a showing of permanent impairment before granting asylum based on the "compelling reasons" standard of 8 C.F.R. § 208.13(b)(1)(ii), we should defer to its decision as a permissible construction of its regulation.

III

In light of the discussion in Parts I and II, one must reach the question whether substantial evidence also supports the BIA's conclusion that changed country conditions have obviated Lal's well-founded fear of future persecution.

A

The BIA found by a preponderance of the evidence that since the 1987 coup, "country conditions in Fiji have changed to such an extent that [Lal] no longer has a well-founded fear of being persecuted...." The BIA noted that the State Department report, issued in 1994, stated that there was no evidence of widespread human rights violations in Fiji against ethnic Indians and that Indo-Fijians engage in business and professional activities. It noted that both ethnic Fijians and ethnic Indians lead "`tranquil and productive lives' throughout Fiji."[6] Thus the BIA ordered the Lals deported if they did not depart voluntarily within 30 days.

We review the BIA's conclusion regarding changed country conditions for substantial evidence. See Marcu, 147 F.3d at 1081. Lal's past persecution establishes a presumption of a well-founded fear of future persecution. See 8 C.F.R. § 208.13(b)(1)(i). The INS then rebutted this presumption by demonstrating, "by a preponderance of the evidence, that conditions have changed to such an extent that the applicant no longer has a well-founded fear of being persecuted if he or she were to return." Marcu, 147 F.3d at 1081 (quotations omitted). The State Department country reports are "the most appropriate and perhaps the best resource for information on political situations in foreign nations." Kazlauskas, 46 F.3d at 906 (quotations omitted).

The events which Lal alleges took place primarily from 1987 to 1988, the year following the coups, with one isolated incident in 1991. Despite Lal's credible accounts of severe past persecution, the Report provides substantial support for the BIA's conclusion that the situation in Fiji has changed so significantly that Lal may return without fear of future persecution. cf. Marcu, 147 F.3d at 1081-83. In Marcu, an applicant who had been persecuted for more than twenty-five years in Romania on account of his pro-American views was denied asylum because of the changes that occurred in that country after the fall of the Ceausescu regime. This was so despite the fact that Marcu had been beaten in the year following the change in leadership. See Marcu, 147 F.3d at 1081. As in Marcu, almost all of the incidents Lal alleges here occurred in that "chaotic" first year following the coup. Unlike the petitioner in Marcu, here Lal suffered one additional instance of persecution after that time in 1991. Mindful of the Supreme Court's admonishment that we are not to overturn the decision of the BIA unless the evidence "compels" us to do so, we cannot say that this one later event compels us to conclude "that no reasonable factfinder could fail to find the requisite fear of persecution." Elias-Zacarias, 502 U.S. at 483-84, 112 S.Ct. 812 (emphasis added).

Despite the targeted and protracted nature of the persecution Lal suffered, the record provides substantial evidence to support the BIA's conclusion. Lal was persecuted on account of his political views, his ethnicity and his religion. The 1994 country report indicates that the previous two elections (both taking place after Lal's last instance of persecution) were fair and free; the Indo-Fijian parties participated without interference on the part of the government. In the 1992 elections four of the twelve parties were Indo-Fijian. Although prevented by the Constitution from gaining control of the government, the record shows that the non-ethnic Fijian parties controlled 33 (in contrast to the ethnic Fijians' 37) of the seats in the lower house of Parliament. Thus the Report provides substantial support for the BIA's conclusion that if Lal were to return, he would not face persecution on account of his political participation.

With respect to the persecution Lal suffered on account of his ethnicity and religion, the State Department report concludes that Fijians of all faiths and ethnicities lead tranquil and active business and personal lives. The Indian community dominates the business and the professions, and is well-represented in public service. It is true that the report and several newspaper articles in the record indicate some continued ethnic tension, and that the police are at times slow to prevent harassment of Indo-Fijians. The report concludes, however, that overall Fijians of both ethnicities "are leading tranquil and productive lives throughout Fiji," and there is no widespread violation of human rights against Indo-Fijians on the part of the military or the police.[7]

As the court held in Marcu, we need not resolve the factual dispute over the current conditions in Fiji. See id. at 1082. "Our task is to determine whether there is substantial evidence to support the BIA's finding, not to substitute an analysis of which side in the factual dispute we find more persuasive." Id. Our case law well establishes "that the country report from our Department of State is the `most appropriate' and `perhaps best resource,'" for determining country conditions. Id.; Kazlauskas, 46 F.3d at 906. As such, the State Department report "provide[s] substantial evidence for the BIA's determination that the INS successfully rebutted the presumption of future prosecution." Marcu, 147 F.3d at 1082.[8] The record simply does not compel a reasonable factfinder to reach the opposite conclusion.

B

Lal and the majority assert that the State Department reports are insufficiently individualized to be helpful is assessing the reasonableness of Lal's fear of future persecution. As noted above, however, the State Department reports are the best source of information regarding country conditions, and we have held that the BIA may rely on them to determine whether an applicant has a well-founded fear of future persecution. See, e.g., Kazlauskus, 46 F.3d at 906.

Nor is the BIA's conclusion that Lal need no longer fear persecution based on an insufficiently individualized assessment of the Report as it applies to his case. See Garrovillas v. INS, 156 F.3d 1010 (9th Cir.1998). In Garrovillas, this court held the BIA's analysis of changed country conditions to be insufficiently specific. But the context of that determination differed significantly from the case at hand. In Garrovillas, the BIA had found that the petitioner did not establish past persecution and it did not afford him the presumption of well-founded fear of future persecution. See id. at 1017. Nor did it analyze the facts to assess whether the presumption had been rebutted by the changed country conditions. All the BIA did was quote two paragraphs of the State Department report without mentioning its applicability to the case. See id. "Thus it [was] not clear whether this quotation was intended to serve as a means of rebutting the presumption of a well-founded fear of future persecution." Id.

In contrast, the BIA here afforded Lal the presumption of a well-founded fear of future persecution, and then found that the country report "establishes that since that persecution occurred, country conditions in Fiji have changed to such an extent that the lead respondent no longer has a well-founded fear of being persecuted...." Lal claims persecution on account of political opinion, religion, and ethnic origin; the portions of the report cited by the BIA referred specifically to the decreased political and ethnic tension between ethnic Fijians and Indians and the "tranquil and productive lives" of Fijians of all faiths. Unlike in Garrovillas, the BIA here made it clear that it considered the appropriate presumption, found it rebutted, and discussed those sections of the report that dealt specifically with the reasons for which Lal was persecuted. In sum, the requirement that the changed country conditions analysis be individualized to the petitioner is met in this case.[9]

IV

The majority rejects a reasonable interpretation by the BIA of its own regulation and misinterprets it as adding a new requirement. It then compounds its error by failing to apply the correct standard of review. Finally it misconstrues the law on "changed country conditions." In my view, the BIA's construction of the statute is a permissible one. As sympathetic as the Lals' application is, nothing in the record legally compels a result different from that reached by the BIA.

Accordingly, Lal's petition for review of the BIA decision should be denied and, I, therefore, respectfully dissent.

Judge O'Scannlain's dissent in Socop-Gonzalez v. INS (Dec 5, 2001)

O'SCANNLAIN, Circuit Judge, with whom Circuit Judge SILVERMAN joins, dissenting:

With respect, and with regret, I must dissent from the court's opinion; we simply don't have jurisdiction under any of the theories advanced by the majority.

Socop-Gonzalez ("Socop") first raised the issue of equitable tolling at oral argument before the en banc court; we have jurisdiction only over issues raised before the Board of Immigration Appeals ("BIA"). While Socop's plight may be sympathetic, nothing, not even forty-four pages of energetic legal massage by the majority, can cure the jurisdictional defect in this case. Socop's petition for review challenging the BIA's denial of his motion to reopen should have been dismissed for lack of jurisdiction.

I

In April 1996, Socop filed a timely appeal with the BIA seeking review of the Immigration Judge's decision denying his request for asylum and withholding of deportation. Socop, indeed acting on poor advice given to him by an INS officer, sought to withdraw his pending appeal with the BIA in April 1997. On May 5, 1997, the BIA granted his request, which constituted a final administrative determination in his case. Socop thereafter decided that he never should have withdrawn his appeal and filed a motion to reopen with the BIA. However, Socop's motion was seven days late: a petitioner must file a motion to reopen within ninety days of the final administrative determination. See 8 C.F.R. § 3.2(c)(2).

Socop dealt with his legal hurdle by vigorously arguing to the BIA that the INS was equitably estopped from enforcing the ninety-day limitations period. In particular, he relied upon In re Petition of LaVoie, 349 F.Supp. 68, 72 (D.Vi.1972), in which a district court held that the INS was equitably estopped from enforcing a provision of the

Immigration and Naturalization Act. The BIA, however, was unpersuaded by Socop's equitable estoppel argument, and denied his motion as untimely.

Socop then petitioned for review by this court. Socop reasserted his equitable estoppel argument, which the panel rejected. Socop-Gonzalez v. INS, 208 F.3d 838, 840 (9th Cir.2000) ("We hold that the doctrine of equitable estoppel does not apply in this case...."). After we agreed to hear the case en banc, Socop continued to press his equitable estoppel argument in his briefs.

At the en banc oral argument, however, Socop suddenly changed course. Socop now argues that the ninety-day period was equitably tolled. As we have repeatedly explained, equitable estoppel and equitable tolling are two distinct doctrines. See, e.g., Santa Maria v. Pacific Bell, 202 F.3d 1170, 1176 (9th Cir.2000) (discussing differences between the two doctrines); Lehman v. United States, 154 F.3d 1010, 1015-17 (9th Cir.1998) (same); Naton v. Bank of Cal., 649 F.2d 691, 696 (9th Cir. 1981) (same). Equitable estoppel holds that a party may be precluded from taking a position because of his affirmative misconduct. See, e.g., Lehman, 154 F.3d at 1016-17. Equitable tolling provides that a party's excusable ignorance may toll the limitations period. See, e.g., Lehman, 154 F.3d at 1015. Under equitable estoppel, the primary focus is the nature of the INS's conduct. Under equitable tolling, the primary focus is whether Socop's ignorance of the limitations period is excusable. Each issue is distinct and separate. Socop only raised estoppel before the BIA; he now raises tolling for the first time.

Congress has confined our jurisdiction to only those issues that the petitioner raised before the BIA. See 8 U.S.C. § 1105a(c) (repealed 1996);[1] see also Vargas v. U.S. Dept. of Immigration and Naturalization, 831 F.2d 906, 907-08 (9th Cir. 1987) ("Failure to raise an issue in an appeal to the BIA ... deprives this court of jurisdiction to hear the matter."). Because Socop failed to raise the issue of equitable tolling with the BIA, we are without jurisdiction.

II

The majority advances three unconvincing arguments in its strain to find jurisdiction under equitable tolling. First, the majority relies upon Honda v. Clark, 386 U.S. 484, 87 S.Ct. 1188, 18 L.Ed.2d 244 (1967). In Honda, depositors of the Yokohama Specie Bank filed claims against the United States under the Trading with the Enemy Act. The Court of Appeals had held that the depositors' claims were time-barred. See Kondo v. Katzenbach, 356 F.2d 351, 359 (D.C.Cir.1966). The Supreme Court reversed, concluding that the limitations period was equitably tolled. Honda, 386 U.S. at 486, 87 S.Ct. 1188. The majority concedes that the depositors raised equitable tolling, as distinguished from equitable estoppel, with the Supreme Court. Nonetheless, the majority remarkably concludes that Honda stands for the proposition that if a party raises only equitable estoppel, the court may still consider whether equitable tolling applies. The fact that the depositors in Honda did not argue equitable tolling, apart from equitable estoppel, in their opening Court of Appeals brief, is irrelevant. The majority overlooks the fact that the Supreme Court never suggested that the depositors failed to raise equitable tolling with the lower courts.[2] This omission is unsurprising given that the government did not argue that the depositors had waived equitable tolling. We cannot assume that the Supreme Court independently discovered that the depositors failed to raise the issue in its opening brief with the Court of Appeals.

In any event, the majority's reliance upon Honda is misplaced. The majority overlooks a critical distinction between Honda and this case: unlike the Immigration and Nationality Act, under the Trading with the Enemy Act there is no jurisdictional bar to consider issues that were not properly raised below. Honda cannot support the majority's excusal of Socop's belated attempt to raise equitable tolling.

III

The majority next claims that we should assert jurisdiction to avoid "penaliz[ing] Socop for his lawyer's failure to seize on equitable tolling." Majority Opinion at 1185. In essence, the majority claims that we should excuse Socop's failure to raise equitable tolling because the doctrines of equitable estoppel and equitable tolling are easily confused with one another. While the subtleties between the doctrines may help explain Socop's lawyer's poor performance, it cannot cure the jurisdictional defect in this case. "Failure to raise an issue in an appeal to the BIA ... deprives this court of jurisdiction to hear the matter." Vargas, 831 F.2d at 907-08. Scoop's lawyer's poor performance is simply irrelevant to the jurisdictional question.

IV

Finally, the majority incredulously claims that the BIA considered whether the limitations period should be equitably tolled. The fact that the majority makes this argument last is telling. There is not even a hint anywhere in the BIA's decision that it considered equitable tolling, as opposed to equitable estoppel. Of course, this is not at all surprising given the fact that Socop only argued equitable estoppel in front of the BIA. Even if the BIA had addressed equitable tolling in its decision, it would merely be relevant to whether Socop raised the issue with the BIA. We only have jurisdiction over issues that were actually raised by the petitioner below; we cannot acquire jurisdiction simply because the BIA decides to review an issue sua sponte. See Singh-Bhathal v. INS, 170 F.3d 943, 947 (9th Cir.1999) (holding that court lacked jurisdiction over an issue not raised in front of the BIA even though a BIA dissenter expressly considered the issue). In any event, because Socop's BIA filings unambiguously show that he was only arguing equitable estoppel, the fact that the BIA might have considered the issue is irrelevant to the jurisdictional question.

The underlying circumstances of this case are unfortunate. But "bad facts" cannot create jurisdiction where none exists. I respectfully dissent from the majority's grant of Socop's petition for review.

Notes

[1] Congress repealed § 1105(a). See Illegal Immigration Reform and Immigrant Responsibility Act of 1996 (IIRIRA), § 306(b), 110 Stat. 3009-546, 3009-612. Nonetheless,

as the majority concedes, ante at 1183, because Socop is subject to IIRIRA's transitional rules, it remains applicable to his case. See § 309(c)(1)(B), 110 Stat. at 3009-625.

[2] The Supreme Court did note that the depositors "largely" argued equitable estoppel with the Court, and that the lower courts had limited its discussion to equitable estoppel. Honda, 386 U.S. at 486, 87 S.Ct. 1188.

Judge O'Scannlain's specially concurring in the denial of full court en banc rehearing in US v. Orso (Dec 28, 2001)

O'SCANNLAIN, Circuit Judge, with whom Circuit Judges KOZINSKI, KLEINFELD, and GOULD join, specially concurring in the denial of full court en banc rehearing:

Judge Trott's impassioned dissent from our denial of full court en banc rehearing in this case makes clear that he disapproves of the methods that the police employed which produced Jody Orso's Mirandized confession in this case. His views are perfectly reasonable. And who knows — if this court were free to rewrite Fifth Amendment law I might well agree with him. But we are not free to rewrite the law. And that is where I part company with Judge Trott and his merry band of dissenters.[1]

To begin, let us remember that this court does not sit as a kind of super-Citizens' Police Review Board, creating some set of federal common-law police regulations for local law enforcement officers in this circuit by distinguishing, on a case-by-case basis, "good" police conduct from "bad." Instead, our only proper role in this context is to determine whether police conduct has in some way rendered the admission of evidence at a criminal trial violative of a defendant's constitutional rights. In short, not everything that this court might consider "bad" (or "improper") is accordingly unconstitutional. Cf. Pittsley v. Warish, 927 F.2d 3, 7 (1st Cir.1991) (recognizing that even though "state officials may have misused their authority," and that the court "certainly [did] not condone the acts of the police in this instance," "[t]he plaintiffs, however, have not established a violation of any constitutionally recognized right").

Turning to the constitutional issue we review in this case, I respectfully suggest that, to the extent that Judge Trott is concerned that a Miranda violation does not require a "fruit-of-the-poisonous-tree" analysis when it leads to a second, voluntary, warned confession, his quarrel is not with Orso, but with the Supreme Court's decision in Elstad. In Elstad, the Court held that it simply does not matter that a statement is procured because an earlier statement was elicited from a suspect in violation of Miranda. So long as the earlier statement was not involuntary due to unconstitutional coercion, the subsequent, voluntary, warned statement is still admissible — without regard to whether the subsequent statement was "tainted" by the earlier statement. Elstad, 470 U.S. at 309, 105 S.Ct. 1285. True, Elstad's rationale relied heavily on the fact that, when Elstad was decided, Miranda was not understood to be a constitutional rule. Id. at 305, 105 S.Ct. 1285("Respondent's contention that his confession was tainted by the earlier failure of the police to provide Miranda warnings and must be excluded as `fruit of the poisonous tree' assumes the existence of a constitutional violation"). And true, the Court's recent decision in Dickerson v. United States, 530 U.S. 428, 120 S.Ct. 2326, 147 L.Ed.2d 405 (2000), calls this premise into question. See id. at 444, 120 S.Ct. 2326("[W]e conclude that Miranda announced a constitutional rule...."). I can therefore understand Judge Trott's desire to take this opportunity to tease out of Elstad an entirely new category of police activity, "improper tactics," that gives rise to a fruit-of-the-poisonous-tree analysis.[2] Indeed, he was disposed to do so long before Dickerson. See Pope v. Zenon, 69 F.3d 1018, 1024 (9th Cir.1996) (Trott, J.) (hypothesizing that "the tactic of using pre-advice interrogation to open up a suspect" is "precisely what the Supreme Court had in mind in [Elstad] when it exempted `deliberately coercive or improper tactics in obtaining the initial statement' from the ordinary rule that subsequent statements are not to be measured by a `tainted fruit' standard, but by whether they are voluntary") (emphasis added), overruled by United States v. Orso, 266 F.3d 1030 (9th Cir.2001) (en banc).

Perhaps the most crucial point that Judge Trott makes in his dissent, though, is that "[w]hat emerges from Dickerson is unmistakable." Infra, Dissent from Denial at 17408. Quite so — but not what Judge Trott envisions. What emerges from Dickerson is that Elstad, as explicated in the limited en banc panel's opinion, is good law; unless a first-obtained, un-Mirandized confession is involuntary, a later-obtained, Mirandized confession is not subject to a fruit-of-the-poisonous-tree analysis. See Dickerson, 530 U.S. at 441, 120 S.Ct. 2326("Our decision in [Elstad] ... simply recognizes the fact that unreasonable searches under the Fourth Amendment are different from unwarned interrogation under the Fifth Amendment."). Admittedly, the Court's analysis of this point in Dickerson (all one sentence of it) is less than fully satisfying. But faced with a clear statement of the law from the Supreme Court, our duty is clear: our court must follow. See State Oil Co. v. Khan, 522 U.S. 3, 20, 118 S.Ct. 275, 139 L.Ed.2d 199 (1997) ("Despite what Chief Judge Posner aptly described as Albrecht's `infirmities, [and] its increasingly wobbly, motheaten foundations,' ... [t]he Court of Appeals was correct in applying [it] despite disagreement with Albrecht, for it is this Court's prerogative alone to overrule one of its precedents."); Rodriguez de Quijas v. Shearson/American Express, Inc., 490 U.S. 477, 484, 109 S.Ct. 1917, 104 L.Ed.2d 526 (1989) ("If a precedent of this Court has direct application in a case, yet appears to rest on reasons rejected in some other line of decisions, the Court of Appeals should follow the case which directly controls, leaving to this Court the prerogative of overruling its own decisions."); see also Spector Motor Serv., Inc. v. Walsh, 139 F.2d 809, 823 (2d Cir.) (L. Hand, J., dissenting) ("Nor is it desirable for a lower court to embrace the exhilarating opportunity of anticipating a doctrine which may be in the womb of time, but whose birth is distant; on the contrary I conceive that the measure of its duty is to divine, as best it can, what would be the event of an appeal in the case before us."), vacated sub nom. Spector Motor Serv., Inc. v. McLaughlin, 323 U.S. 101, 65 S.Ct. 152, 89 L.Ed. 101 (1944).

The constitution neither ordains nor establishes this Inferior court as an oracle of future Supreme Court holdings. Instead, the role that the Founders assigned us is a more humble one, that of simply following the Supreme Court's dictates and applying them to the inhabitants of the Nine Western States. Because that is precisely what our limited en banc opinion in Orso does, I concur in the order by which my colleagues decide to follow and to apply Elstad, and to refuse full court en banc rehearing in this case.

Notes

[1] It is telling that not even a single member of our limited en banc court thought that we could ignore controlling Supreme Court precedent; even those joining in the concurrence recognized that Oregon v. Elstad, 470 U.S. 298, 105 S.Ct. 1285, 84 L.Ed.2d 222 (1985) controls. See United States v. Orso, 266 F.3d 1030, 1040 (9th Cir.2001) (en banc) (Paez, J., concurring) ("With some reluctance, I ... concur in the conclusion that, under [Oregon v. Elstad], the district court need not suppress the confession Orso made after she was read, then waived, her Miranda rights."). Thus, at least on its face, the limited en banc decision reflects an 11-0 vote on the merits. (It may no longer, in fact, reflect an 11-0 vote, given that Judge Hawkins, who joined Judge Paez's concurrence, has subsequently joined in Judge Trott's dissent from denial of full court en banc rehearing.)

[2] It seems that, at least for now, Judge Trott is content to give content to his newfound category by defining it as "wittingly and purposefully" asking questions before giving Miranda warnings. See infra, Dissent from Denial at 17408. Fine for today, but why stop there? Why not make "improper tactics" coextensive with "anything that two out of three judges on a panel don't like," effectively converting this Article III court into the aforementioned super-Citizens' Police Review Board? Regrettably, I see no principled limit to the unwarranted judicial foray into the propriety of law enforcement tactics that Judge Trott's dissent advocates.

Judge O'Scannlain's dissent in Greene v. Lambert (March 26, 2002)

O'SCANNLAIN, Circuit Judge, dissenting.

I respectfully dissent from the court's determination that Greene's claim is properly exhausted. I place more reliance than does the majority on the Washington Supreme Court's explicit statement that it did not reach Greene's claim, and I am simply not persuaded that the majority's construction of the state court's explanatory language justifies the contrary conclusion at which it arrives.

Because I conclude that Greene did not fairly present his federal claim to the Washington courts, I express no view on the merits of that claim.

I

I largely agree with the majority's discussion of the legal standard by which we must determine whether Greene properly exhausted the federal claim in his habeas petition.[1] Specifically, I agree that "[o]ur decision hinges on what happened to [Greene's] motion [for reconsideration]," and that "[i]f the Washington Supreme Court ...

adjudicated the claim on the merits, then the claim may proceed" in federal court. Supra at 1087. The reason, as the majority recognizes, see id. at 1087 & n. 2, is that the constitutional claim was "presented for the first and only time in a procedural context in which its merits will not be considered" as of right, but reviewed only at the state court's discretion. Castille v. Peoples, 489 U.S. 346, 351, 109 S.Ct. 1056, 103 L.Ed.2d 380 (1989). Raising a claim in that manner does not satisfy the exhaustion requirement unless the state court "actually pass[es]" upon the claim." Id.

Thus, the majority and I frame our analyses largely the same way. I note, however, that the majority's invocation of Harris v. Superior Court, 500 F.2d 1124 (9th Cir.1974) (en banc), may be misplaced. Like Hunter v. Aispuro, 982 F.2d 344 (9th Cir.1992), which the majority also cites, Harris turned on the practices and procedures by which the California appellate courts considered state habeas corpus petitions. I do not think that Harris creates a presumption in favor of finding a claim exhausted, for two reasons: First, the Harris court considered the exhaustion requirement in the context of California's system of postconviction relief, which permits prisoners to bring original habeas corpus petitions in the state Supreme Court, rather than require them first to file in a lower court and then to seek discretionary review of that court's denial of relief. See Harris, 500 F.2d at 1127-28 & nn. 5-6. In that context, the Harrises' original petitions to the California Supreme Court more closely resemble the appeal as of right considered in Smith v. Digmon, 434 U.S. 332, 333, 98 S.Ct. 597, 54 L.Ed.2d 582 (1978) (per curiam), and distinguished in Castille, 489 U.S. at 350-51, 109 S.Ct. 1056, than the more discretionarily decided motion for reconsideration that is at issue in this case.[2] Cf. Nino v. Galaza, 183 F.3d 1003, 1006 & nn. 2-3 (9th Cir.1999) (treating three original habeas petitions to the three levels of the California court system as a single "pending" proceeding). Second, Harris relied specifically on the California Supreme Court's practice of making its intentions explicit when denying original habeas petitions on procedural grounds, a procedure that justified our presumption that unexplained denials from that court rested on the merits. See Harris, 500 F.2d at 1128-29. Harris did not indicate that state courts must adopt such a clear-statement rule, only that state courts that do adopt such a "beneficial" practice, id. at 1128, may rely on this court to apply it faithfully.[3]

Notwithstanding our differing readings of Harris, the majority and I agree that if the Washington Supreme Court declined to reach the claim presented in Greene's motion for reconsideration, then that motion was inadequate to exhaust the claim. Although in that case Greene still could have brought his claim in an application for state postconviction relief, a "personal restraint petition" (PRP) to the Washington appellate courts, see Wash. R.App. P. 16.3.4; see also In re Gentry, 137 Wash.2d 378, 972 P.2d 1250, 1256 (1999) (en banc) (indicating that failure to raise a claim on direct review does not preclude raising it in a PRP), Greene filed no such petition, and he cannot now do so. See Wash. Rev.Code Ann. § 10.73.090(1) (West 1990) (imposing a one-year time limit on most petitions for postconviction relief). Thus, if the Washington Supreme Court did not address the merits of the constitutional claim in denying the motion for reconsideration,

Greene's claim is now procedurally defaulted. See, e.g., Shumway v. Payne, 223 F.3d 982, 988-89 (9th Cir.2000) (reaffirming that Washington's one-year limitations period is an adequate and independent state ground that bars habeas review of an unexhausted claim, absent a showing of cause and prejudice or actual innocence).

II

I next turn to the dispositive question: whether the Washington Supreme Court considered the merits of Greene's claim. Here I must part company with the majority.

As the court's opinion recognizes, we certainly would have concluded that Greene's claim was unexhausted had the Washington Supreme Court merely denied his motion for reconsideration without comment. Supra at 1087 & n. 2. The only evidence pointing to an even possibly contrary conclusion is the footnote that the state court added to its opinion at the same time it denied the motion. However, on my reading, the text of that footnote evinces little more consideration of the merits than would the denial of the motion standing alone.

For me, the starting point is the court's explicit statement that it "d[id] not reach this issue." Indeed, this pronouncement standing alone would likely be enough to satisfy even a clear-statement rule like the one that applies in the procedural default context. Where, as here, the bar is lower and the question is only whether the state court exercised its discretion to consider the claim at issue, the court's own announcement that it chose not to exercise that discretion ought to be virtually dispositive.

Of course, the state court did add a few more words, specifically the subordinate clause "Since we decide this case on more narrow grounds." And as the majority states, this verbiage did render the added footnote somewhat "cryptic." Supra at 1087. However, I believe that the only reading of that footnote that gives full effect to the court's own words leads directly to the conclusion that the court did not consider Greene's claim on the merits.

The majority divines in the opening dependent clause's language an anticipatory repudiation of the succeeding independent clause's plain statement that the court was not addressing the constitutional issue. In the majority's view, see id., the reference to "more narrow grounds" encapsulates the court's decision on the merits of Greene's claim: the state evidentiary rule is legitimate, so its application to keep the testimony out does not violate the Sixth Amendment. But if the state court reasoned as the majority thinks it did, it collapsed into one the separate inquiries into the state rules of evidence and the U.S. Constitution. I cannot see why a court that based its rejection of a constitutional claim on its reading of state law would then turn around and describe the state law as "more narrow grounds" that justify its decision not to reach the federal issue.

There is a more natural interpretation of the qualifying clause "Since we decide this case on more narrow grounds," one that does not negate the independent clause it modifies.[4]

I read the Washington Supreme Court's amendment to indicate that the court did not feel free to consider the constitutional claim because the state law issue was the only issue properly before it. This is the only construction that gives effect to the entire text of the state court's amendment — the word "Since"; the phrase "more narrow"; and, of course, the operative clause "we do not reach."[5] And it makes eminent sense in light of the Washington Rules of Appellate Procedure, under which the Washington Supreme Court considers only issues raised in the petition for review, the answer, or the order granting review, see Wash. R.App. P. 13.7(b), or (in exceptional cases) in a supplemental brief filed before the decision, see Wash. R.App. P. 12.1(a), 13.7(d); Douglas v. Freeman, 117 Wash.2d 242, 814 P.2d 1160, 1168 (1991) (en banc).

In at least one recent case, the Washington Court of Appeals took a similar course in a comparable situation. Rule 12.1(a)'s restrictions on the issues properly before an appellate court and Rule 12.4(c)'s strictures on the points appropriate to a motion for reconsideration apply equally to both Washington appellate courts, see Wash. R.App. P. 1.1(d), so the interpretation of those rules by the Court of Appeals is instructive. Just as in this case, in response to a motion for reconsideration that raised an argument not argued in the briefs, the court added a footnote to its published decision declining to reach the late-raised contentions. 1515-1519 Lakeview Boulevard Condo. Ass'n v. Apartment Sales Corp., 17 P.3d 639, 640 (Wash. Ct.App.) (stating that "[b]ecause the parties did not argue public policy in their briefs, we do not reach this issue," and citing Rule 12.1(a)), modifying 102 Wash. App. 599, 9 P.3d 879, 883 (2000). And unlike Greene, the civil litigant in Lakeview Boulevard lacked the guaranteed opportunity to present its claim on collateral review.

Thus, reading the Supreme Court's added footnote in context — in light of the restrictions on presenting issues to that court and Greene's complete failure to comply with them — leads me back to the same conclusion to which the text of the footnote pointed: that the Washington Supreme Court declined to consider Greene's claim, for the entirely legitimate reason that Greene had presented it belatedly, in a pleading to which the State lacked the right to respond,[6] when he still had available the more appropriate option of filing a PRP. And the court's decision not to reach the constitutional issue left that issue unexhausted — notwithstanding the court's addition of a few explanatory words. All the court did was to consider whether to consider the constitutional claim and decide that it "need not" do so (not that the claim was meritless); that degree of examination simply is not enough to satisfy the exhaustion requirement where an avenue of state court review (here, a PRP) remains open. See Castille, 489 U.S. at 351, 109 S.Ct. 1056 (concluding that a claim remained unexhausted when it was raised only in a petition for allocatur, a certiorarilike form of discretionary review by the Pennsylvania Supreme Court, and that petition was denied). Although a court necessarily "ha[s] thought about[a] new federal claim" when it chooses not to reach it, supra at 1087, that thought does not focus and that choice does not rest squarely on the merits. Cf., e.g., Sup.Ct. R. 10; United States v. Carver, 260 U.S. 482, 490, 43 S.Ct. 181, 67 L.Ed. 361 (1923) ("The denial of a writ of certiorari imports no expression of opinion upon the merits of the case, as the bar has been told many times.").

A decision not to decide an issue, even when accompanied by a few explanatory sentences, does not mean that the court "actually passes" on that issue; it means instead that it "takes a pass." And where, as here, the defendant retains the right to place his claim unambiguously before a state court simply by filing a petition for state postconviction relief, the exhaustion requirement demands that he do precisely that before coming to federal court. To hold otherwise is to "blue-pencil[] ... from the text of the statute" the requirement that the petitioner present his claim to the state courts by "any available procedure." Castille, 489 U.S. at 351, 109 S.Ct. 1056; 28 U.S.C. § 2254(c).

III

Far from a mere formality, the exhaustion requirement represents Congress's decision, rooted in respect for our federal system, that state judiciaries must be given the first opportunity to correct their own errors — even errors of federal law — and that federal habeas courts are to step in only if the state courts fail to do so.[7] In concluding that Greene complied with this requirement, the majority lowers the bar and undermines Congress's policy judgment.

I respectfully dissent.

Notes

[1] Although Greene's federal habeas petition presented his constitutional claim under three separate headings, see supra at 1085, his motion for reconsideration in the state court listed it under a single heading and with a single rationale. Thus, like the majority, I refer to Greene's claim in the singular.

[2] A related distinction between that case and this one is that Harris's habeas petition was his last opportunity to exhaust his claims before his state's court of last resort, whereas Greene still had open the option of filing a PRP. Cf. Castille, 489 U.S. at 350-51, 109 S.Ct. 1056 (noting that federal courts "infer an exception" to the plain language of 28 U.S.C. § 2254(c), which "appears to preclude a finding of exhaustion if there exists any possibility of further state-court review," when the state courts have "actually passed on the claim").

[3] In the separate but closely related context of procedural default, the Supreme Court has cautioned us that this presumption is not absolute even when considering the California Supreme Court's denials of habeas petitions. Where the petitioner files in the lower courts, rather than proceeding straight to the California Supreme Court, and where the "last reasoned decision" before the petition reaches the state's high court "explicitly imposes a procedural default," the Supreme Court has stated that an unexplained denial from the California Supreme Court presumptively does not represent a decision on the merits that lifts that default. Ylst v. Nunnemaker, 501 U.S. 797, 803, 111 S.Ct. 2590, 115 L.Ed.2d 706 (1991), rev'g 904 F.2d 473 (9th Cir.1990).

[4] Cf. United States v. Emerson, 270 F.3d 203, 233 n. 32 (5th Cir.2001) (discussing principles by which courts construe introductory clauses in relation to the independent clauses they modify and justify).

[5] The existence of "more narrow" state law grounds would also explain a decision not to reach a broader constitutional issue if upholding the federal claim would lead to the same result. E.g., Skagit Surveyors and Engineers, LLC v. Friends of Skagit County, 135 Wash.2d 542, 958 P.2d 962, 964 (1998) (en banc) ("Because we decide this appeal on statutory grounds, we do not reach the constitutional issues."). That is not the case here; state law led the Washington Supreme Court to reverse, and accepting Greene's constitutional argument would have required it to affirm (on other grounds).

[6] Wash. R.App. P. 12.4(d); see State v. Thomson, 123 Wash.2d 877, 872 P.2d 1097, 1101 (1994) (en banc) ("This court will not consider a constitutional issue when it is not timely filed. As the defense counsel conceded at oral argument, he first raised the issue in a supplemental brief belatedly filed on January 3. The issue was not raised in the courts below or in prior briefs, and the State did not have an adequate opportunity to respond to the argument. Because the Defendant did not timely raise the state constitutional issue, we do not reach it."). By contrast, the State has not only the opportunity but the obligation to respond to a PRP. Wash. R.App. P. 16.9.

[7] See, e.g., Duncan v. Walker, 533 U.S. 167, 121 S.Ct. 2120, 2127-28, 150 L.Ed.2d 251 (2001) (citing cases); Tillema v. Long, 253 F.3d 494, 501 (9th Cir.2001).

Judge O'Scannlain's dissent from the denial of rehering en banc in Douglas v. California Dep't of Youth Auth. (April 12, 2002)

O'SCANNLAIN, Circuit Judge, with whom KOZINSKI, KLEINFELD, and RONALD M. GOULD, Circuit Judge, join, dissenting from the denial of rehering en banc:

By failing to rehear Douglas v. Cal. Dep't of Youth Auth., 271 F.3d 812 (9th Cir.2001), en banc, we also fail to resolve the conflict between two competing constitutional provisions implicated in this case — namely, the Spending Clause and the Eleventh Amendment. Because I believe that had this important issue received the thoughtful consideration it deserved Douglas would have reached a different result, I respectfully dissent from the order denying rehearing en banc.

I

Courts which must decide whether a State retains its sovereign immunity after accepting conditioned federal funds are caught between two competing lines of jurisprudence. Under the Supreme Court's approach to the Spending Clause of Article I,[1] Congress has great leeway to place conditions on the funding it gives to the States. See South Dakota v. Dole, 483 U.S. 203, 107 S.Ct. 2793, 97 L.Ed.2d 171 (1987). Yet, under the Supreme Court's Eleventh Amendment sovereign immunity jurisprudence, Congress's ability to place affirmative obligations on the States using its Fourteenth Amendment enforcement power is rapidly diminishing. See, e.g, Bd. of Trustees of the Univ. of Ala. v. Garrett, 531 U.S. 356, 374, 121 S.Ct. 955, 148 L.Ed.2d 866 (2001) (holding that Title I of the ADA did not validly abrogate States's sovereign immunity); Kimel v. Fla. Bd. of Regents, 528 U.S. 62, 91, 120 S.Ct. 631, 145 L.Ed.2d 522 (2000) (holding that the ADEA did not validly abrogate States's sovereign immunity). Each doctrine pulls us in an opposite direction.

Douglas, following our precedent Clark v. California, 123 F.3d 1267 (9th Cir.1997), holds that by accepting federal funds, California waived its sovereign immunity from suits by individuals under § 504 of the Rehabilitation Act. With respect, I believe that Clark is now outdated — and Douglas wrong — for failing to recognize the change in the legal landscape of sovereign immunity and, as I explain below, how that might impact Spending Clause jurisprudence. Furthermore, Douglas notably — and regrettably — fails to cite Garcia v. S.U.N.Y. Health Sciences Ctr., 280 F.3d 98 (2d Cir.2001), a significant post-Kimel and Garrett case holding that a waiver of sovereign immunity cannot be inferred by mere acceptance of federal funds. In my view, we should have reheard Douglas en banc to consider the important constitutional protections embodied in the Eleventh Amendment — especially in light of recent Supreme Court developments.

II

The California Department of Youth Authority ("CYA") denied Mr. Dossey Douglas employment as a group supervisor because he is color-blind. Mr. Douglas brought a discrimination suit against CYA, claiming that the color vision test violated the Americans with Disabilities Act ("ADA"), 42 U.S.C. § 12101 et seq., and § 504 of the Rehabilitation Act, 29 U.S.C. § 794. The district court granted summary judgment to CYA on the grounds that Douglas failed to exhaust his administrative remedies and that his § 504 claim was filed after the statute of limitations expired.

Before addressing the timeliness of Mr. Douglas's claims, however, our court held that California, by accepting federal funds, waived its sovereign immunity from suits by individuals under § 504 of the Rehabilitation Act. Douglas, 271 F.3d at 820. This allowed Mr. Douglas to proceed with his claim in federal court. Had Douglas not reached this conclusion, Mr. Douglas would have had no discrimination claim against California because Garrett squarely held that Title I of the ADA did not validly abrogate States's sovereign immunity.

The same analysis would apply to § 504 as well. See Kilcullen v. N.Y. State Dep't of Labor, 205 F.3d 77, 82 (2d Cir.2000) ("[T]he validity of abrogation under the twin statutes [ADA and Rehabilitation Act] presents a single question for judicial review."); see also Reickenbacker v. Foster, 274 F.3d 974, 983 (5th Cir.2001) (holding that § 504 did not validly abrogate States's sovereign immunity).

Douglas reaffirmed Clark, which, in an alternative holding spanning only three paragraphs of analysis,[2] held that by accepting federal funds a State waives its immunity from suit in federal court. Clark stated that since the Rehabilitation Act "manifests a clear intent to condition a state's participation on its consent to waive its Eleventh Amendment immunity" — and California had accepted federal funds — the State had waived its immunity. Id. at 1271. Douglas, without recognizing the competing commands of the constitutional provisions at issue, simply "adhere[d] to our decision Clark." 271 F.3d at 820.

III

I respectfully suggest that Douglas did not give adequate consideration to the question of whether California waived its sovereign immunity. To establish waiver, Congress must first make it clear that amenability to suit in federal court is a condition of a State accepting federal funds, and, second, the State must make a "clear declaration" that it intends to waive its immunity. College Sav. Bank v. Fla. Prepaid Postsecondary Educ. Expense Bd., 527 U.S. 666, 676, 119 S.Ct. 2219, 144 L.Ed.2d 605 (1999). As Clark and Douglas recognized, § 504 meets the first requirement. Congress explicitly provided: "[a] state shall not be immune under the Eleventh Amendment ... from suit in Federal court for a violation of section 504 of the Rehabilitation Act of 1973." 42 U.S.C. § 2000d-7(a)(1). See also Lane v. Pena, 518 U.S. 187, 200, 116 S.Ct. 2092, 135 L.Ed.2d 486 (1996) (characterizing the language of § 504 as "an unambiguous waiver" of States's sovereign immunity).

Whether Congress clearly required that a State waive its immunity before accepting federal funds (the first inquiry) is not the same thing, however, as whether the State clearly declared its knowing waiver (the second inquiry). Clark and Douglas fail adequately to address the second requirement, which is a key component of ensuring proper respect for a State's constitutional rights.

A

A State may waive its sovereign immunity by making a "`clear declaration' that it intends to submit itself" to federal court jurisdiction. College Sav., 527 U.S. at 676, 119 S.Ct. 2219 (quoting Great N. Life Ins. v. Read, 322 U.S. 47, 54, 64 S.Ct. 873, 88 L.Ed. 1121 (1944)); see also Pennhurst State Hosp. v. Halderman, 465 U.S. 89, 99, 104 S.Ct. 900, 79 L.Ed.2d 67 (1984) (a State's consent to suit must be "unequivocally expressed"). Because a State's decision to waive its immunity must be "altogether voluntary," the "test for determining whether a State has waived its immunity from federal-court jurisdiction is a stringent one." College Sav., 527 U.S. at 675, 119 S.Ct. 2219 (internal quotation marks omitted).

College Savings overruled the doctrine of "constructive waiver" found in Parden v. Terminal Ry., 377 U.S. 184, 84 S.Ct. 1207, 12 L.Ed.2d 233 (1964), which allowed waiver of sovereign immunity "based upon the State's mere presence in a field subject to congressional regulation." College Sav., 527 U.S. at 680, 119 S.Ct. 2219. The "constructive waiver" doctrine is not at issue here, but the Court's recent teachings on how explicit a State's waiver must be are instructive:

There is a fundamental difference between a State's expressing unequivocally that it waives its immunity and Congress's expressing unequivocally its intention that if the State takes certain action it shall be deemed to have waived that immunity. In the latter situation, the most that can be said with certainty is that the State has been put on notice that Congress intends to subject it to suits brought by individuals. That is very far from concluding that the State made an "altogether voluntary" decision to waive its immunity.

Id. at 680-81, 119 S.Ct. 2219 (quoting Beers v. Arkansas, 61 U.S. (20 How.) 527, 529, 15 L.Ed. 991 (1858)) (emphasis added). As with the waiver of any constitutionally protected right, a State must make an "`intentional relinquishment or abandonment of a known right or privilege.'" Id. at 682, 119 S.Ct. 2219 (quoting Johnson v. Zerbst, 304 U.S. 458, 464, 58 S.Ct. 1019, 82 L.Ed. 1461 (1938)). Finally, courts must "`indulge every reasonable presumption against waiver' of fundamental constitutional rights." Id. (quoting Aetna Ins. v. Kennedy ex rel. Bogash, 301 U.S. 389, 393, 57 S.Ct. 809, 81 L.Ed. 1177 (1937)) (emphasis added).

Having set forth the standards that guide one portion of the analysis — waiver of sovereign immunity — let us turn to the competing standards that govern the other — the Spending Clause.

B

When exercising its Article I spending power, Congress may condition its grant of funds to the States, even by requiring States to take actions that Congress could not directly require them to take, such as waiving their sovereign immunity. College Sav., 527 U.S. at 685, 119 S.Ct. 2219; Dole, 483 U.S. at 207, 107 S.Ct. 2793 (Congress may accomplish "objectives not thought to be within Article I's enumerated legislative fields ... through the use of the spending power and the conditional grant of federal funds.") (internal quotation marks and citation omitted). Indeed, "such funds are gifts." College Sav., 527 at 686-87, 119 S.Ct. 2219. Thus, Congress's power to control States's actions through the tightening and/or loosening of the purse strings is great. However, "the financial inducement offered by Congress [cannot] be so coercive as to pass the point at which `pressure turns into compulsion.'" Dole, 483 U.S. at 211, 107 S.Ct. 2793 (quoting Steward Mach. Co. v. Davis, 301 U.S. 548, 590, 57 S.Ct. 883, 81 L.Ed. 1279 (1937)).

Douglas held that by the mere acceptance of Rehabilitation Act funds, California agreed to subject itself to the jurisdiction of the federal courts. Indeed, "acceptance of the funds entails an agreement to the actions [that Congress could not otherwise force the States to take]." College Sav. 527 U.S. at 686, 119 S.Ct. 2219. But, is accepting conditioned federal funds a clear and unequivocal waiver of sovereign immunity? After engaging in every reasonable presumption against waiver, as we must, can we say that California was making an "`intentional relinquishment or abandonment of a known right or privilege,'" id. at 682, 119 S.Ct. 2219 (quoting Johnson, 304 U.S. at 464, 58 S.Ct. 1019), by accepting conditioned funds? Douglas ducks this question; had it not done so the result would likely be different.

As I explain below, at the time California allegedly engaged in discriminatory hiring practices and also accepted Rehabilitation Act funds, it did not know it possessed the right to resist federal court jurisdiction. Without this knowledge, gleaned only after the Supreme Court decided Garrett, California's acceptance of funds simply could not constitute an unequivocal or intentional abandonment of its Eleventh Amendment rights.

IV

What makes this case interesting, and what Douglas and cases in other circuits (except one) overlook, is the interplay of a § 504 waiver with the ADA's abrogation of States's sovereign immunity. Until the Supreme Court decided Garrett in February 2001, California operated under the reasonable assumption that Title I of the ADA, which provides essentially the same protections for people with disabilities as § 504,[3] effectively abrogated its immunity from suits by individuals claiming disability discrimination in state employment.[4]

Indeed, in this Circuit, we have repeatedly held that Title II of the ADA was a permissible exercise of Congress's Fourteenth Amendment enforcement power.[5] See Hason v. Med. Bd., 279 F.3d 1167, 1170-71 (9th Cir.2002); Dare v. California, 191 F.3d 1167, 1173 (9th Cir.1999); Clark, 123 F.3d at 1270. We have also found that the Rehabilitation Act itself abrogates States's sovereign immunity. Clark, 123 F.3d at 1270.[6]

Other circuits, pre-Garrett, found Title I of the ADA to constitute a valid abrogation. See, e.g., Cisneros v. Wilson 226 F.3d 1113, 1124 (10th Cir.2000) (upholding Title I as applied to the States); Kilcullen v. New York State Dep't of Labor, 205 F.3d 77, 81 (2d Cir.2000) (same); Garrett v. Univ. of Ala. at Birmingham Bd. of Trustees, 193 F.3d 1214, 1218 (11th Cir.1999) (same). When California accepted Rehabilitation Act funds, it could not know it was giving up anything; any immunity it had to surrender was already abrogated by the ADA or Rehabilitation Act itself.

Were this just a question of whether Congress may condition delivery of federal funds upon the waiver of sovereign immunity, there might not be sufficient compulsion to invalidate § 504 as an impermissible exercise of the Spending Clause. See Bell Atlantic Maryland, Inc. v. MCI Worldcom, Inc., 240 F.3d 279, 292 (4th Cir.) (stating that by accepting Rehabilitation Act funds a State "would clearly understand that ... it was consenting to resolve disputes ... in federal court"), cert. granted, 533 U.S. 928, 121 S.Ct. 2548, 150 L.Ed.2d 715 (2001); Nihiser v. Ohio Envtl. Prot. Agency, 269 F.3d 626, 628 (6th Cir.2001) (same); Jim C. v. United States, 235 F.3d 1079, 1082 (8th Cir.2000) (en banc) (holding that the conditions imposed on § 504 federal funds did not reach the level of compulsion required by Dole), cert. denied, 533 U.S. 949, 121 S.Ct. 2591, 150 L.Ed.2d 750 (2001); Stanley v. Litscher, 213 F.3d 340, 344 (7th Cir.2000) (finding the Rehabilitation Act "enforceable in federal court against recipients of federal largess"); Sandoval v. Hagan, 197 F.3d 484, 494 (11th Cir.1999) (same), overruled on other grounds, 532 U.S. 275, 121 S.Ct. 1511, 149 L.Ed.2d 517 (2001); see also Pederson v. La. State Univ., 213 F.3d 858, 875-76 (5th Cir.2000) (holding that by accepting federal funds a State waives its sovereign immunity defense to Title IX actions); Litman v. George Mason Univ., 186 F.3d 544, 554-55 (4th Cir.1999) (same); but see Jim C., 235 F.3d at 1085 (Bowman, J., dissenting) ("The [Supreme] Court's holdings in [recent Eleventh Amendment] cases reflect the rock-solid principle that Eleventh Amendment immunity trumps any exercise of the powers of Congress enumerated in the original Constitution; controlling weight must be given to the provision that became part of the Constitution later in time.").

Indeed, if it does not like the strings attached, a State need not accept Congress's funds. Even where there is no showing of compulsion, there still remains the requirement that a State unequivocally abandon a known right. Until Garrett was decided, however, California could not have known that its sovereign right to resist federal court jurisdiction still existed. How could a State waive that which has already been abrogated by Congress?

V

Recently, the Second Circuit in Garcia spotted this problem and dealt with it, as we should have, consistent with the post-Garrett legal landscape. Noting that the proscriptions of the ADA and § 504 are virtually identical, it held that "a state accepting conditioned federal funds could not have understood that in doing so it was actually abandoning its sovereign immunity from private damages suits, since by all reasonable appearances state sovereign immunity had already been lost." 280 F.3d at 114 (internal citations omitted). Garcia dismissed the § 504 claim on sovereign immunity grounds.

Unlike Garcia, other circuits' decisions, cited above, do not reconcile the tension between Spending Clause and sovereign immunity jurisprudence. Garcia's approach is faithful to both constitutional provisions and recognizes that Congress may condition delivery of funds upon a waiver of sovereign immunity, yet respects the Supreme Court's teachings, recently articulated in College Savings, that a waiver of a constitutional right must be intentional and knowing.

Unfortunately, Douglas did not cite Garcia and failed to recognize that what might now be a known right did not exist in any meaningful sense until quite recently. Blind adherence to our 1997 decision in Clark is misguided. Douglas's failure to give proper weight to the requirement that a waiver of a constitutional right be intentional and knowing, renders the decision incomplete, incorrect, and in need of reconsideration en banc.

VI

This issue — in the cross-hairs of two constitutional provisions and squarely presented in Douglas — deserved close and careful reconsideration in light of recent Supreme Court precedent. I respectfully dissent from this unfortunate order denying rehearing en banc.

Notes

[1] The Spending Clause empowers Congress to "lay and collect Taxes, Duties, Imposts, and Excises, to pay the Debts, and to provide for a common Defense and general welfare of the United States." U.S. CONST. art. I, § 8, cl. 1.

[2] Clark's main holding was that Congress validly abrogated States's sovereign immunity when it passed § 504 pursuant to its Fourteenth Amendment enforcement powers. Kimel and Garrett call this holding into serious doubt. Clark went on to "note" that by accepting federal funds a State waives its sovereign immunity. 123 F.3d at 1271.

[3] The ADA has no federal funding requirement, but it is otherwise similar in substance to the Rehabilitation Act, and "cases interpreting either are applicable and interchangeable." Allison v. Dep't of Corrections, 94 F.3d 494, 497 (8th Cir.1996). The statute itself states that "[t]he remedies, procedures, and rights" under § 504 are also

available under the ADA. 42 U.S.C. § 12133. Furthermore, Congress amended § 504 to expressly incorporate the liability standards of the ADA. See Rehabilitation Act Amendments of 1992, Pub.L. No. 102-569, § 506, 106 Stat. 4344, 4428 (1992) (codified at 29 U.S.C. § 794(d)) ("The standards used to determine whether this section has been violated in a complaint alleging employment discrimination under this section shall be the standards applied under title I of the Americans with Disabilities Act.").

[4] The ADA explicitly provided that "[a] State shall not be immune under the eleventh amendment ... from an action in [a] Federal or State court of competent jurisdiction for a violation." 42 U.S.C. § 12202.

[5] Title I prohibits employment discrimination against qualified individuals on the basis of their disability, 42 U.S.C. § 12112, and Title II prohibits discrimination in the provision of public services and programs, 42 U.S.C. § 12132.

[6] Garrett's reasoning undoubtedly undercuts the Rehabilitation Act's attempt to abrogate sovereign immunity. See Reickenbacker, 274 F.3d at 983; Kilcullen, 205 F.3d at 82 (suggesting that the Rehabilitation Act's legislative history is less compelling than that of the ADA); see also Armstrong v. Davis, 275 F.3d 849, 862 n. 17 (9th Cir.2001); Roger C. Hartley, Enforcing Federal Civil Rights Against Public Entities After Garrett, 28 J.C. & U.L. 41, 89 n. 272 (2001) ("There is no reason to believe that the Rehabilitation Act's legislative history better supports a pattern of state employment discrimination than does that of the ADA Title I.").

Judge O'Scannlain's dissent in Vinson v. Thomas (May 3, 2002) [Notes omitted]

O'SCANNLAIN, Circuit Judge, dissenting:

I respectfully dissent from Part III of the majority's determination that Brian Vinson's claim of disability discrimination against Hawai'i should survive summary judgment. Indeed, if I were writing on a clean slate, I would not even reach the merits of his claim because I believe Hawai'i enjoys a constitutionally protected right of sovereign immunity from these suits that was neither waived nor validly abrogated by Congress.

I

For over a century, the Supreme Court has taught us that federal jurisdiction over suits against unconsenting States "was not contemplated by the Constitution when establishing the judicial power of the United States." Hans v. Louisiana, 134 U.S. 1, 15, 10 S.Ct. 504, 33 L.Ed. 842 (1890). Indeed, the Eleventh Amendment's "ultimate guarantee" is "that nonconsenting States may not be sued by private individuals in federal court." Bd. of Trustees of the Univ. of Ala. v. Garrett, 531 U.S. 356, 363, 121 S.Ct. 955, 148 L.Ed.2d 866 (2001). We have seen the Supreme Court strike down statutes passed pursuant to Congress's Article I power that purported to abrogate state sovereign immunity, Seminole Tribe of Fla. v. Fla., 517 U.S. 44, 72-73, 116 S.Ct. 1114, 134 L.Ed.2d 252 (1996); see also Alden v. Maine, 527 U.S. 706, 759-60, 119 S.Ct. 2240, 144 L.Ed.2d 636 (1999) (holding that Article I does not permit Congress to subject nonconsenting States to private suits in their own courts), limit the reach of Congress's power to enforce against the States the rights guaranteed by the Fourteenth Amendment, Garrett, 531 U.S. at 374, 121 S.Ct. 955 (holding Title I of the ADA did not validly abrogate sovereign immunity); Kimel v. Fla. Bd. of Regents, 528 U.S. 62, 91, 120 S.Ct. 631, 145 L.Ed.2d 522 (2000) (holding that the Age Discrimination in Employment Act did not validly abrogate sovereign immunity); United States v. Morrison, 529 U.S. 598, 625-26, 120 S.Ct. 1740, 146 L.Ed.2d 658 (2000) (holding that Congress lacked the authority to create the civil remedy provision of the Violence Against Women Act), and allow States to participate in a field subject to congressional regulation without waiving their constitutionally guaranteed sovereign immunity, College Sav. Bank v. Fla. Prepaid Postsecondary Educ. Expense Bd., 527 U.S. 666, 680, 119 S.Ct. 2219, 144 L.Ed.2d 605 (1999). It cannot be more clear that the States retain "a residuary and inviolable sovereignty. They are not relegated to the role of mere provinces or political corporations, but retain the dignity, though not the full authority, of sovereignty." Alden, 527 U.S. at 715, 119 S.Ct. 2240 (internal citation and quotations marks omitted).

A

I recognize, however, that we have recently reaffirmed that by accepting federal funds under the Rehabilitation Act, 29 U.S.C. § 794, a State waives its sovereign immunity from suits by individuals in federal court. Douglas v. Cal. Dep't of Youth Auth., 271 F.3d 812, as amended, 271 F.3d 910 (9th Cir.2001); see also Armstrong v. Davis, 275 F.3d 849, 878 (9th Cir.2001); Clark v. Cal., 123 F.3d 1267 (9th Cir.1997). My dissent from the order denying Douglas en banc rehearing fully explains my disagreement with our approach to the question of sovereign immunity waiver. Douglas v. Cal. Dep't of Youth Auth., No. 99-17140, 2002 WL 538806 (9th Cir. April 12, 2002) (O'Scannlain, J., dissenting); see also Garcia v. S.U.N.Y. Health Sciences Ctr., 280 F.3d 98 (2d Cir.2001). I will not belabor the point here, but reluctantly acquiesce in Part II of the opinion.

B

Vinson waived reliance on Title II of the Americans with Disabilities Act ("ADA"), 42 U.S.C. § 12101 et seq., at oral argument. While I agree that this was a wise choice considering the clear holding and import of Garrett, 531 U.S. at 374, 121 S.Ct. 955 (holding Title I of the ADA did not validly abrogate state sovereign immunity),[1] we have recently upheld Title II as a valid abrogation of state sovereign immunity. Hason v. Med. Bd. of Cal., 279 F.3d 1167, 1171 (9th Cir.2002); see also Dare v. Cal., 191 F.3d 1167, 1175 (9th Cir.1999), cert. denied, 531 U.S. 1190, 121 S.Ct. 1187, 149 L.Ed.2d 103 (2001).

Since Title II is no longer an issue in Vinson's appeal, I simply note that Hason's holding conflicts with no fewer than five of our sister circuits who have reconsidered the issue in light of Garrett. See Reickenbacker v. Foster, 274 F.3d 974, 983 (5th Cir.2001); Thompson v. Colorado, 278 F.3d 1020, 1034 (10th Cir.2001), petition for cert. filed, 70 U.S.L.W. 3464 (U.S. Jan. 7, 2002) (No. 01-1024); Erickson v. Bd. of Governors of State Colleges and Univ., 207 F.3d 945, 948 (7th Cir.2000) (questioning the continued authority of Crawford v. Ind. Dep't of Corrections, 115 F.3d 481, 487 (7th Cir.1997), which upheld

Title II as a valid abrogation of state sovereign immunity), cert. denied, 531 U.S. 1190, 121 S.Ct. 1187, 149 L.Ed.2d 104 (2001); Alsbrook v. City of Maumelle, 184 F.3d 999, 1009-10 (8th Cir.1999) (en banc); cf. Brown v. N.C. Div. of Motor Vehicles, 166 F.3d 698, 707 (4th Cir.1999) (holding regulation enacted pursuant to Title II did not validly abrogate state sovereign immunity); but see Garcia, 280 F.3d at 111-12 (holding that Title II actions may be brought against States if the plaintiff can establish that the "violation was motivated by discriminatory animus or ill will based on the plaintiff's disability"); but cf. Popovich v. Cuyahoga County Court of Common Pleas, 276 F.3d 808, 812, 815 (6th Cir.2002) (en banc) (agreeing that Title II is not a valid abrogation of sovereign immunity when Congress is enforcing the Equal Protection Clause, but holding it is permissible when enforcing the Due Process Clause).[2]

II

Of course, if Hawai'i's sovereign immunity prevents it from being haled into federal court for an alleged violation of the ADA or Rehabilitation Act, we would have no occasion to reach the merits of Vinson's claim. Accepting the majority's recital of our current law of sovereign immunity in Part II, however, the majority still errs in Part III by reversing the district court's grant of summary judgment.

A

To qualify as a disabled individual under the Rehabilitation Act, Vinson must establish that he has an impairment that substantially limits at least one of his major life activities. 42 U.S.C. § 12102(2); 29 U.S.C. § 791(g).[3] Certainly dyslexia can constitute an "impairment," 29 C.F.R. § 1630.2(h)(2) (defining impairment to include "specific learning disabilities"); however, I am not persuaded that Vinson presented evidence sufficient to survive summary judgment on whether he had an impairment — particularly one that substantially limited a major life activity.

While interpretative regulations include "learning" as a major life activity, 29 C.F.R. § 1630.2(i),[4] Vinson must demonstrate that his dyslexia substantially limits his ability to learn. The phrase "substantially limits" requires that "a person be presently — not potentially or hypothetically — substantially limited in order to demonstrate a disability." Sutton v. United Air Lines, Inc., 527 U.S. 471, 482, 119 S.Ct. 2139, 144 L.Ed.2d 450 (1999) (emphasis added). This is an individualized inquiry. Id. at 483, 119 S.Ct. 2139. More specifically, "substantially limited" refers to the inability to perform a major life activity as compared to the average person in the general population, or a significant restriction as to the condition, manner, or duration under which an individual can perform the particular activity. Toyota Motor Mfg. v. Williams, 534 U.S. 184, 122 S.Ct. 681, 690, 151 L.Ed.2d 615 (2002) (citing 29 C.F.R. § 1630.2(j)).

In short, dyslexia does not render an individual disabled per se for purposes of the Rehabilitation Act.

B

It is not enough for Vinson to establish post hoc that he has an impairment that substantially limits the major life activity of learning. Rather, because his suit is based upon the Department of Labor and Industrial Relations's ("the Department") initial failure to accommodate his disability, he must establish that he presented sufficient proof of his disability to the Department. Indeed, a public entity does not violate the law by refusing to accommodate individuals who cannot establish that they have disability that qualifies them for an accommodation.

Thus, it is important to focus on the information that the Department — particularly Alice Thomas, Director of the Vocational Rehabilitation Branch — had at the time it decided to close Vinson's file in October 1996. For that reason, the sworn statement of Vinson's learning disabilities expert, Barbara Bateman, cited by the majority, supra at ____, is immaterial to the question of what the Department knew; she prepared her statement well after the department closed Vinson's file. The Department did have a September 26, 1996 letter from C. Lynne Douglas, a learning disability specialist, that Vinson argues is the definitive letter that should have satisfied the Department that his dyslexia substantially limited his ability to learn.

However, Douglas herself admitted that her letter was not meant to be a diagnostic report. When asked in her deposition whether her letter was a "diagnosis of a learning disability," she replied, "It was not, and it was never intended to be one." Indeed, she did not complete her diagnostic tests until February 1997, months after Vinson's file had been closed. Later in her deposition, Douglas testified that her report was not intended to meet the "diagnostic criteria outlined in [her own] attached guidelines." However, she asserted that "most specialists in the field" would, "without a doubt," believe that her letter demonstrated "overwhelming and convincing evidence that [Vinson] would or did have a diagnosis of dyslexia." (emphasis added).

How can an assertion that Vinson would have a diagnosis of dyslexia — if he ever was diagnosed — constitute sufficient evidence of a disability? Second, even if a specialist might be able to decipher from Douglas's 19 page letter that Vinson had a diagnosis of dyslexia, it is unreasonable to ask an untrained person to connect those same dots. Vinson's own expert witness, Bateman, accused Thomas of lacking "the knowledge or expertise to determine whether or not" Douglas's letter established that Vinson had a disability. I agree, which makes it all the more important that Vinson submit a specialist's actual diagnosis. If, in fact, a specialist could have made the diagnosis, she should have. Then, Vinson should have submitted that diagnosis to the Department.

Vinson argues that the Department was requesting information that did not exist. However, Douglas herself eventually did complete diagnostic tests, and she also asserted that a specialist could have diagnosed Vinson's dyslexia from her November 1996 letter. Indeed, a specialist in connection with this litigation — namely, Bateman — did in fact review Douglas's letter and conclude that Vinson was dyslexic. This is precisely the information the Department sought, and Douglas's and Bateman's own sworn statements prove that it was readily available.

While acknowledging that the Department is entitled to ask an individual for more information regarding his disability, Weinreich v. Los Angeles County Metro. Transp.

Auth., 114 F.3d 976, 979 (9th Cir. 1997), the court holds that a public agency cannot request information beyond that which would satisfy a reasonable expert in the field, supra at 1153. This seems reasonable enough, see Grenier v. Cyanamid Plastics, Inc., 70 F.3d 667, 674 (1st Cir. 1995) ("When an applicant requests reasonable accommodation, an employer may request documentation from an appropriate professional (e.g., a doctor, rehabilitation counselor, etc.), stating that s/he has a disability.") (quotation marks omitted), but I do not agree that the Department was making an unreasonable demand of Vinson. Not only must Vinson supply evidence showing that he is dyslexic, he must also show how that impairment currently limits a major life activity. As detailed above, apparently such a diagnosis was obtainable, and it is unrealistic to require Thomas, who is not a learning disabilities specialist, to glean a diagnosis from Douglas's letter and how that diagnosis might substantially limit Vinson's present ability to learn.

Denying public agencies who provide important, but finite, services the ability to request specific documentary support of an individual's disability risks creating a system ripe for abuse. Therefore, I cannot fault the Department for seeking an actual diagnosis of dyslexia before the State expended funds on Vinson's behalf.

C

In any event, even if Vinson had established that he is disabled, he must show that the Department closed his file solely because of his disability. Zukle v. Regents of the Univ. of Cal., 166 F.3d 1041, 1045 (9th Cir.1999). This is well-established law. E.g., Wong v. Regents of the Univ. of Cal., 192 F.3d 807, 816 (9th Cir.1999). Thus, the majority's assertion that the district court erred by requiring Vinson to show that his file was closed because he was disabled befuddles me, supra at 1154 n. 9. The Department asserted three non-discriminatory reasons for closing his file: (1) Gina Eustaquio, Senior Rehabilitative Specialist at Intracorp and Vinson's counselor, no longer had his trust;[5] (2) Vinson demonstrated proficiency in obtaining schooling and employment on his own; and (3) he evinced a preference to rely on resources and individuals outside the program. I would add one more: Vinson failed to produce adequate information regarding his impairment.

In Zukle, we applied the familiar burden-shifting analysis of McDonnell Douglas Corp. v. Green, 411 U.S. 792, 93 S.Ct. 1817, 36 L.Ed.2d 668 (1973), to the disability discrimination context. Zukle, 166 F.3d at 1047; see also Snead v. Metro. Prop. & Cas. Ins., 237 F.3d 1080, 1092-93 (9th Cir. 2001); Mustafa v. Clark County Sch. Dist., 157 F.3d 1169, 1175-76 (9th Cir.1998). After the Department puts forth legitimate, non-discriminatory reasons for closing Vinson's file, he must demonstrate that the Department's proffered reasons were a pretext for disability discrimination. See Snead, 237 F.3d at 1093.

In Weinreich, we held that Los Angeles's transit system did not discriminate on the basis of disability by requiring updated certification of a rider's disability before he qualified for its Reduced Fare Program. 114 F.3d at 979. The transit system denied plaintiff access to the program because he could not submit an update due to financial limitations. We held that this denial was due not to his medical disability, but rather due to his own failure to satisfy a condition of eligibility. Id. I see little to distinguish this case from Weinreich. Here, Vinson was not denied a reduced course load because of his disability, rather, it was due to his failure to provide a specialist's diagnosis of dyslexia. Furthermore, like Weinreich, the Department's criteria were valid; there is no evidence that the Department made unreasonable demands with the discriminatory purpose to screen out disabled individuals from its programs.

Thus, I agree with the district court that even if Vinson established his disability, he failed to show that the Department closed his file because of it.

III

I cannot agree that the district court erred by granting summary judgment on Vinson's disability discrimination claim. Despite the opportunity and repeated requests for clarification, Vinson did not submit a clear diagnosis of dyslexia. Of course, if our caselaw were consistent with the Supreme Court's teachings, the merits of Vinson's claim would present a question without need of an answer because the constitutional sovereignty and dignity Hawai'i enjoys as a State would bar Vinson's suit against it.

I respectfully dissent.

Judge O'Scannlain's dissent in Island Ins. Co. v. Hawaiian Foliage & Landscape (May 3, 2002)

O'SCANNLAIN, Circuit Judge, dissenting.

I respectfully dissent from the court's determination that the state and federal governments were intended beneficiaries of the surety bond insuring Hawaiian Foliage and Landscape's ("Hawaiian") performance. The purpose and language of the surety bond nowhere evinces an intent that Island Insurance Co. ("Island") be held liable for Hawaiian's unpaid taxes. Indeed, as I explain below, it would have made little sense for the parties to enter into the agreement described by the majority.

I

I do not dispute the majority's recital of the facts or the relevant language of the bond and subcontract. I part company, however, with its conclusion that the surety bond, which is clearly meant to protect Oahu Construction Co. ("Oahu") from Hawaiian's failure to perform and nowhere mentions the state or federal government as beneficiaries, requires Island to pay Hawaiian's taxes.

The bond provides that Island is liable if Hawaiian fails: (1) to duly and truly perform and to complete the subcontract, (2) to pay for all materials used in performance of the subcontract, and (3) to hold Oahu harmless from all claims for any labor and materials used in the performance of the subcontract. Because, in a litany of other provisions, Article XIV of the subcontract mentions Hawaiian's responsibility to pay its own taxes, the majority divines that Hawaiian's failure to pay such taxes is a failure to "duly and truly perform and complete the subcontract" that triggers Island's obligation under the bond. Even more problematic, instead of being obligated to Oahu — the entity the surety bond was meant to protect — the majority holds that Island must directly reimburse the state and federal governments.

However, it is hornbook law that only if the governments are intended beneficiaries of the surety bond — not just incidental beneficiaries — is Island obligated to pay the taxes owed by Hawaiian. See Pancakes of Hawaii, Inc. v. Pomare Prop. Corp., 85 Hawai'i 300, 944 P.2d 97, 106 (App.1997) (stating the general rule that a third party does not have enforceable contract rights unless it is an intended beneficiary). The contracting parties must have intended directly to benefit the third party. Wright v. Associated Ins. Cos., 29 F.3d 1244, 1249 (7th Cir.1994).

As the majority recognizes, the governments may be intended beneficiaries of the bond if "recognition of a right to performance in [the governments] is appropriate to effectuate the intention of the parties and ... the performance of the promise will satisfy an obligation of [Island] to pay money to the beneficiary." Restatement (Second) of Contracts § 302(1)(a) (1979) [hereinafter "Restatement"]. The bond's reference to the subcontract, which includes a provision requiring Hawaiian to pay its own taxes, seems to satisfy the majority that Island bound itself to pay those taxes should Hawaiian fail to do so. I am not persuaded.

True, the surety bond references the subcontract, which, in turn, required Hawaiian to pay its own taxes. However, that fact alone does not make the governments intended beneficiaries of the bond. We presume that parties contract for themselves alone, see United States v. Seaboard Surety Co., 201 F.Supp. 630, 636 (N.D.Tex.1961), so a party claiming intended beneficiary status bears the burden of showing that the contracting parties intended to confer a direct benefit on it, United States v. Md. Cas. Co., 323 F.2d 473, 476 (5th Cir.1963). "An intent to benefit the third party must be apparent from the construction of the contract in light of all surrounding circumstances to qualify that party as a third party beneficiary." O'Connor v. R.F. Lafferty & Co., 965 F.2d 893, 901 (10th Cir.1992).

II

The language of the bond indicates that the only identified and intended beneficiary of the bond is Oahu; it does not name the governments. The governments seize upon the fact that the bond and subcontract do not explicitly exclude them. However, to qualify as third party beneficiaries, the governments must show more than just that the original contracting parties did not consciously exclude them; rather, they must demonstrate that those parties intended to include them. Of course, the bond benefits entities to whom Oahu could be held liable in the event of a default by Hawaiian, such as those to whom Hawaiian might owe funds for materials and supplies, and for which Oahu, as the primary contractor, could be liable under state law. These suppliers are intended beneficiaries of the surety bond because they were clearly contemplated by the parties — the bond requires that Hawaiian "hold Oahu harmless from all claims for any labor and materials used in the performance of the subcontract." The governments are not so named.

Furthermore, the purpose of a performance bond is to guarantee to an obligee, such as Oahu, that its contract will be completed even if the subcontractor defaults. This generally involves the surety, here Island, agreeing to complete the construction or pay the obligee the reasonable costs of completing it. E.g., Aetna Cas. & Sur. Co. v. United States, 845 F.2d 971, 973-74 (Fed.Cir.1988). The primary and obvious reason to reference the subcontract in the bond is to establish the limits of and to aid in measuring Island's obligation to Oahu under the bond.[1] Indeed, virtually all of the provisions in the subcontract consist of obligations that Hawaiian undertakes for the benefit of Oahu: performance in a timely manner, obtaining insurance, providing qualified personnel, and indemnifying and defending Oahu against claims.

In construing contracts, we should adopt the interpretation that, under all circumstances, "ascribes the most reasonable, probable, and natural conduct of the parties, bearing in mind the objects to be accomplished." Alliance Metals, Inc. v. Hinely Indus., 222 F.3d 895, 901 (11th Cir.2000) (quotations omitted); see also Am. Home Assurance v. Larkin Gen. Hosp., 593 So.2d 195, 197 (Fla.1992) ("To determine the intent of the parties, a court should consider the language in the contract, the subject matter of the contract, and the object and purpose of the contract."). The purpose of this bond was to ensure to Oahu that Hawaiian's portion of the project was completed, i.e., to protect Oahu from actual damages it could suffer if Hawaiian failed to perform.

Paying Hawaiian's taxes has nothing to do with completing the actual construction of the project, particularly considering that Oahu needs no protection from Hawaiian's tax liability since a general contractor is not liable for a subcontractor's failure to pay its taxes. United States Fid. & Guar. Co. v. United States, 201 F.2d 118, 120 (10th Cir.1952) (employer's duty to pay state and federal employment taxes "is a tax liability for which [it] alone is liable to the Government"). Hawaiian's liability for its unpaid taxes could not have been imposed on Oahu, an innocent third party, because that duty inhered solely in Hawaiian.[2] Thus, the bond, which was intended only to protect Oahu (who needed no protection from Hawaiian's tax liability), should not be read to protect the governments.[3]

The bond's purpose becomes even more evident when one considers the result of the majority's holding, which essentially ascribes to Oahu the intent to seek protection in a bond that harms, not guards, its interests. Allowing the governments to collect taxes from performance bonds reduces the amount of funds available to Oahu for completion of the project, payment to laborers, and payment of other damages that Oahu could incur as a result of Hawaiian's default. For example, the owner of the golf course indicated that it might file a claim for alleged defects in Hawaiian's work, involving almost $200,000 per hole of the golf course. The governments' tax claims, not including interest and penalties, total almost $600,000. The sum of the bond is $2,698,787, of which $297,303 has already been expended for claims. When one considers the amount of the golf course's potential claim, it becomes clear why Oahu would want the full amount of the bond available to cover claims against it. I cannot believe that the parties intended that this bond, which was meant to protect Oahu, would cover payments to taxing authorities, thereby reducing the bond's value to Oahu by over 20 percent.[4]

Both Oahu and Hawaiian admit that they had no intention for the bond to cover Hawaiian's tax obligations. See McCarthy v. Azure, 22 F.3d 351, 362 (1st Cir.1999) ("As is generally the case in matters of contract interpretation, `[t]he crux in third-party beneficiary analysis ... is the intent of the parties.'") (quoting Mowbray v. Moseley, Hallgarten, Estabrook & Weeden, 795 F.2d 1111, 1117 (1st Cir.1986)). Indeed, as discussed above, it would make little sense for a general contractor like Oahu to seek such an arrangement. Neither the language nor the purpose of the bond lead me to conclude that the governments were intended beneficiaries of it.

III

The majority lists two instances in which a general contractor like Oahu might be affected if its subcontractor did not pay its taxes, supra at 1166. However, the fact that Oahu may have self-protective reasons for requiring Hawaiian to pay its taxes does not establish that the governments are intended beneficiaries of Oahu's subcontract and bond. Rather, as Island argues, it demonstrates that the subcontract's tax provisions are for the primary benefit of the general contractor and only incidentally for the benefit of any taxing authority. See Seaboard Surety Co., 201 F.Supp. at 635 (holding that a provision requiring subcontractor to pay taxes did not evidence an intent to benefit the United States, but showed instead that the general contractor was primarily concerned with its own position). One should remember that incidental beneficiaries have no legal right to enforce a contract. Eastman v. McGowan, 86 Hawai'i 21, 946 P.2d 1317, 1324 (1997). If Hawaiian's failure to pay its taxes did affect Oahu in the form imagined by the majority, the bond would mitigate Oahu's actual loss stemming from Hawaiian's failure.[5] It is quite a leap for the majority to conclude that by contracting to protect itself from Hawaiian's failure to pay its taxes, Oahu also contracted to cover losses sustained by the taxing authorities.

As the majority correctly recognizes, I am not refuting the possibility that a contractor, in some rare cases, could be held liable for a subcontractor's unpaid taxes, supra at 1165 n. 4. My point is simply that the parties provided for that possibility not by payment to the taxing authorities of the entire amount owed by Hawaiian, but rather by payment of the amount that would actually be owed by Oahu. That is why the subcontract requires Hawaiian to "save Oahu harmless from the payment of any and all" taxes. The parties' intent extended no further.

Finally, as the district court noted, despite the subcontract's provision that Hawaiian pay its taxes, its duty to do so arose not from its contractual relationship with Oahu, but rather by virtue of law. See Central Bank v. United States, 345 U.S. 639, 645-46, 73 S.Ct. 917, 97 L.Ed. 1312 (1953). The provision in the subcontract did not create Hawaiian's tax obligation, but was merely declaratory of its existing legal duty. Md. Cas., 323 F.2d at 475; United States Fid., 201 F.2d at 119. Thus, because the duty arose not under the subcontract, but by operation of law, the fact that the bond incorporates the duties imposed by the subcontract is immaterial.

IV

Even conceding that the majority's reading of the surety bond's reference to the subcontract could be plausible, "[w]here the language of a contract `is susceptible of two constructions, one of which makes it fair, customary and such as prudent men would naturally execute, while the other makes it inequitable, unusual, or such as reasonable men would not likely enter into, the interpretation which makes a fair, rational and probable contract must be preferred.'" Amfac, Inc. v. Waikiki Beachcomber Inv. Co., 74 Haw. 85, 839 P.2d 10, 25 (1992) (quoting Mgmt. Sys. Assoc. v. McDonnell Douglas Corp., 762 F.2d 1161, 1172 (4th Cir.1985)). Here, the majority's interpretation is inequitable and unusual, and it certainly does not describe a contract into which reasonable men and women would likely enter.

I respectfully dissent.

Notes

[1] Thus, I read the bond's condition that Hawaiian "perform and complete" the subcontract as referring to Island's obligation to complete or pay for completion of Hawaiian's work under the subcontract in the event of a default. This does not mean completing each and every recital in the subcontract for the benefit of persons other than Oahu.

It is hard to divine a limiting principle in the majority's approach to third-party beneficiary status. Consider, for example, that the subcontract also requires Hawaiian to "maintain a qualified and skilled Superintendent or Foreman at the site." Article XXI. If Hawaiian fails to do so, is the individual who might have been employed in that position an intended beneficiary of the bond? Just as requiring payment of taxes, the subcontract required Hawaiian to hire a skilled Superintendent to monitor the worksite; Hawaiian's failure to do so would be a breach of the subcontract, which, in turn, is incorporated by the bond. Would not Island be required to pay lost wages to the person who should have been Superintendent under the majority's theory?

[2] Neither 26 U.S.C. §§ 3505(a), (b) or Haw. Rev.Stat. § 235-61(a)(3)(B), which provide narrow circumstances in which third parties may be held liable for unpaid taxes, apply to this situation because Hawaiian's unpaid taxes accrued when it had control over its payment of wages. Nor was Oahu paying those wages or supplying funds for the specific purpose of paying the employees' wages.

[3] The United States and Hawaii already have a full arsenal of statutory powers to collect taxes from Hawaiian (e.g., liens and seizures). They do not need the additional firepower that the majority gives them today.

[4] The majority takes issue with my "economic reasoning," supra at 1166 n. 5, but reads too much into the fact that the amounts of the bond and subcontract are equal. Certainly a subcontractor "normally calculates its charge to the contractor on the assumption that its work would be completed properly," supra at 1166 n. 5; however, the very purpose of a surety bond is to protect a general contractor in case the work is done improperly or incompletely. Usually when that happens, the cost of repairing the

unacceptable work, or hiring someone else on short notice to complete the project, is more than the original contract price. Or, as demonstrated by this case, Hawaiian surely did not budget into its subcontract price the possibility that it would owe fines and interest on unpaid taxes.

[5] For example, under the majority's hypothetical, if Oahu assisted Hawaiian with the payment of wages, thus potentially making itself liable for unpaid withholding taxes under state and federal law, supra at 1166, Oahu's remedy would be to seek the bond's coverage for the actual amount it might have owed the taxing authorities.

Judge O'Scannlain's dissent in US v. Kim (June 6, 2002)

O'SCANNLAIN, Circuit Judge, dissenting:

I respectfully dissent from the court's determination that Insook Kim was "in custody" for Fifth Amendment purposes when police officers questioned her. While paying lip service to the factors that properly guide our determination, the majority fails, in my view, to apply them faithfully to the facts before us.

I

As the majority correctly states, an officer's obligation to give the traditional Miranda warning to a suspect applies only to custodial interrogation. "In determining whether an individual was in custody, a court must examine all of the circumstances surrounding the interrogation, but the ultimate inquiry is simply whether there was a formal arrest or restraint on freedom of movement of the degree associated with a formal arrest." Stansbury v. Cal., 511 U.S. 318, 322, 114 S.Ct. 1526, 128 L.Ed.2d 293 (1994) (quotation marks and brackets omitted). The inquiry should focus on the objective circumstances of the interrogation, not the subjective views of the officers or the individual being questioned. Id. at 323, 114 S.Ct. 1526. "An objective standard avoids imposing upon police officers the often impossible burden of predicting whether the person they question, because of characteristics peculiar to him, believes himself to be restrained." United States v. Beraun-Panez, 812 F.2d 578, 581 (9th Cir.), modified, 830 F.2d 127 (9th Cir.1987).

We ask whether, based upon a review of all the pertinent facts, "a reasonable innocent person in such circumstances would conclude that after brief questioning [she] would not be free to leave." United States v. Booth, 669 F.2d 1231, 1235 (9th Cir.1981); see also United States v. Mendenhall, 446 U.S. 544, 554, 100 S.Ct. 1870, 64 L.Ed.2d 497 (1980) (plurality). Factors that we should consider in determining whether a person was in custody include: (1) the language used to summon the individual, (2) the extent to which the defendant is confronted with evidence of guilt, 8151(3) the physical surroundings of the interrogation, (4) the duration of the detention, and (5) the degree of pressure applied to detain the individual. United States v. Hayden, 260 F.3d 1062, 1066 (9th Cir.2001), cert. denied, ___ U.S. ___, 122 S.Ct. 1117, 151 L.Ed.2d 1011 (2002).

A

As to the first factor, the police did not summon Kim; rather, she came to her store voluntarily. Indeed, the officers allowed her inside only after she knocked and shook the door. The Supreme Court has consistently found that a suspect is not in custody if she voluntarily approaches or accompanies law enforcement. See Cal. v. Beheler, 463 U.S. 1121, 1125, 103 S.Ct. 3517, 77 L.Ed.2d 1275 (1983) (per curiam) (holding defendant was not in custody when he voluntarily accompanied police to the station for questioning and was allowed to leave after the interview); Oregon v. Mathiason, 429 U.S. 492, 495, 97 S.Ct. 711, 50 L.Ed.2d 714 (1977) (holding defendant was not "clearly" in custody when he came to the station voluntarily and left "without hindrance" after a 30-minute interview); see also Hayden, 260 F.3d at 1066-67 (holding defendant was not in custody when she voluntarily appeared at FBI building for questioning and was told that she was free to leave); People v. Palomo, 35 F.3d 368, 375 (9th Cir.1994) (holding defendant was not in custody despite "the duration of the interview and the nature of the interrogation room" when he went to the police station voluntarily and "left of his own accord"); United States v. Hudgens, 798 F.2d 1234, 1236-37 (9th Cir.1986) (holding defendant was not in custody when he initiated contact with police, was not physically restrained, and was questioned for 45 minutes).[1]

The majority distinguishes between a person voluntarily approaching the police with the expectation that she will be asked questions and Kim's voluntarily entering her store. Supra at 976-77. To the majority, the fact that she voluntarily entered her store for the purpose of checking on her son does not suggest that she voluntarily subjected herself to the possibility of a police interview. Yet, we rejected a similar distinction in Palomo, where the defendant went to the police station because his relatives had been taken there — not to speak to the police. We held that the defendant's "assertion that he went to the station only because his relatives had been taken there does not, without more, indicate that he did not initiate contact with the police." Palomo, 35 F.3d at 375. The same must be said regarding Kim.[2]

Furthermore, it seems somewhat disingenuous to say that when Kim approached her store with police cars parked in front, found the front door locked, and then had to knock and gain entrance from an officer, that she had no expectation that maybe, just maybe, she might be called upon to answer questions.[3] While her purpose for coming to her store was to check on her son, once she saw the police presence and sought access to a premise that was being searched by law enforcement, it would be utterly naive to suggest that she did not consent to an encounter with the police.

B

The second factor — the extent to which the defendant is confronted with evidence of guilt — is not implicated here. The record does not indicate that the officers confronted Kim with evidence of her guilt.

C

The third factor looks to the physical surroundings of the interrogation. Here, Kim was in familiar surroundings — her own store — during the interview, which stands in direct contrast to the more coercive environment of a police station. However, the Supreme Court has found that even when questioning occurs at a police station there is not custody per se. Beheler, 463 U.S. at 1125, 103 S.Ct. 3517 ("[W]e have explicitly recognized that Miranda warnings are not required `simply because the questioning takes place in the station house, or because the questioned person is one whom the police suspect.'" (quoting Mathiason, 429 U.S. at 495, 97 S.Ct. 711)). Here, of course, the familiar surroundings of Kim's store would be much less coercive than an interrogation room at the police station. Cf. Michigan v. Summers, 452 U.S. 692, 702, 101 S.Ct. 2587, 69 L.Ed.2d 340 (1981) (finding detention of an individual at his home during the execution of a search warrant is permissible because it is "substantially less intrusive" than an arrest and involves "neither the inconvenience nor the indignity associated with a compelled visit to the police station"); United States v. Eide, 875 F.2d 1429, 1437 (9th Cir.1989) (holding defendant was not in custody "[p]articularly because the FBI agents interviewed [him] at his home.").

D

The fourth factor we consider is the duration of the detention. The district court found that she was questioned for approximately 45-50 minutes, but had been detained for "some time" before the interview began. The government states that the entire detention lasted about 90 minutes, which admittedly seems on the high end of our precedent.

E

Finally, we must consider the degree of pressure applied to detain the individual. Here, Kim was neither handcuffed nor 8155 told that she was under arrest. It also appears that, at least until the interpreter arrived, Kim had a clear path of egress during the interview. While the front door was locked, it is a reasonable police procedure to control access to a scene during the execution of a search warrant. See Booth, 669 F.2d at 1236 ("Strong but reasonable measures to insure the safety of the officers or the public can be taken without necessarily compelling a finding that the suspect was in custody.");[4] see also Summers, 452 U.S. at 702-03, 101 S.Ct. 2587 ("The risk of harm to both the police and the occupants is minimized if the officers routinely exercise unquestioned command of the situation.").

Furthermore, the presence of many officers conducting a search cannot alone establish a custodial situation:

Such a noncustodial situation is not converted to one in which Miranda applies simply because a reviewing court concludes that, even in the absence of any formal arrest or restraint on freedom of movement, the questioning took place in a "coercive environment." Any interview of one suspected of a crime by a police officer will have coercive aspects to it, simply by virtue of the fact that the police officer is part of a law enforcement system which may ultimately cause the suspect to be charged with a crime.

Mathiason, 429 U.S. at 495, 97 S.Ct. 711 (emphasis added). Other than the mere presence of officers, there was no pressure applied to detain Kim, even taking as true the district court's determination that no officer told her that she was free to leave.

Finally, it is significant that when the officers finished searching the store, they left without arresting Kim or her son. See Palomo, 35 F.3d at 375 (weighing as an important factor that the defendant "left of his own accord").

II

I recognize that Kim was justifiably concerned about her son and worried about the presence of officers in her store. However, under the five Hayden factors that guide our analysis, I cannot agree that there was a "restraint on [Kim's] freedom of movement of the degree associated with a formal arrest." Stansbury, 511 U.S. at 322, 114 S.Ct. 1526. While the interview lasted about 90 minutes, the police did not summon Kim, she was not confronted with evidence of her guilt, she was in familiar surroundings, and the degree of pressure applied to detain her was minimal. See Palomo, 35 F.3d at 375 ("Although the duration of the interview and the nature of the interrogation room support Palomo's position, the remaining factors strongly support the government's contention that Palomo was not in custody."). Because I would conclude that Kim was not in custody during her presence at her store, I respectfully dissent.

Notes

[1] The majority's characterization of United States v. Crawford, 52 F.3d 1303 (5th Cir.1995), as having "significant factual differences" from this case is, with respect, inaccurate. See supra at 977. In Crawford, the Fifth Circuit held that defendants were not in custody when they made incriminating statements during the execution of a search warrant at their electronics store. Id. at 1309. There, officers did not tell defendants that they were or were not free to leave, the defendants (who are husband and wife) could not move around the store without being accompanied by an agent and could not be in each other's presence, and one defendant came to the shop voluntarily after the search was underway, but was then "sandwiched between two men at all times." Id. at 1307-09. Like Kim, who was probably more worried about her son and having her store disrupted than about being questioned, the Crawford defendants were "more worried about their electronic equipment [and] not having their store disrupted than about being held in custody." Id. at 1308. Furthermore, the defendants knew that the officers had found a small quantity of marijuana — evidence of their guilt — during the search. Id. at 1308. Thus, Crawford's "factual differences" from this case actually make the situation there more coercive. Despite Crawford's coercive aspects, however, the Fifth Circuit held that they did not constitute a custodial situation for Miranda purposes.

The majority attempts to distinguish Crawford primarily by relying on the standard of review exercised by the Fifth Circuit. First, it is not entirely clear what standard of review Crawford employed, as the court simply stated "[w]e review the district court's finding that the Appellants were not in custody at the time of the statements." Id. at 1307. Second, assuming Crawford did review for clear error, the more deferential standard of review did not appear to be the decisive factor in the court's decision, i.e., the court was not torn between two equally meritorious arguments as the majority makes it seem. Id. at 1308-09.

[2] The majority again attempts to distinguish a case that undermines its analysis — this time, Palomo — based on the fact that in Palomo we reviewed the district court's "in custody" determination for clear error. Supra at 976 n. 3. Again, to respond: the more deferential standard of review did not appear to be the decisive factor in our decision. Palomo, 35 F.3d at 375. Reliance on the standard of review in this situation is nothing more than a makeweight.

Furthermore, nothing in the majority's characterization of Palomo undermines our clear rejection of the distinction between voluntarily subjecting oneself to be interviewed and voluntarily subjecting oneself for some other reason. The "without more" language in Palomo, 35 F.3d at 375, does not refer to other coercive elements that make a situation custodial, as the majority seems to suggest. Rather, Palomo simply rejected the defendant's argument that because he went to the police station to visit relatives — not to subject himself to an interview — he did not initiate contact with the police. Or, in other words, it takes more than approaching the police for a purpose other than speaking to them to make one's encounter with the police involuntary.

[3] This is all the more demonstrated by the fact that months prior to the search she had received an explicit warning from DEA officers, in Korean, about the connection between sales of large quantities of pseudoephedrine and methamphetamine production. Thus, she should have had some idea as to why the police were there and that they might be interested in talking to her. Kim's status as a suspect, of course, is irrelevant to whether she was in custody. Palomo, 35 F.3d at 375.

[4] I note that the Booth court found this factor important in determining whether defendant was in custody for Fifth Amendment purposes. Thus, the majority cannot simply relegate reasonable police measures designed to insure safety to the Fourth Amendment context. Supra at 978.

Judge O'Scannlain's dissent from denial of rehearing en banc in Hason v. Medical Bd. of California (June 26, 2002) [Notes omitted]

O'SCANNLAIN, Circuit Judge, with whom Circuit Judges KOZINSKI, T.G. NELSON, and KLEINFELD join, dissenting from denial of rehearing en banc.

Stubbornly extending enforcement of Title II of the Americans with Disabilities Act ("ADA") against the Nine Western States, today's opinion blithely ignores recent Supreme Court precedent and follows superseded cases of our court instead. It bears repeating: This decision cannot possibly be right. See Vinson v. Thomas, 288 F.3d 1145, 1157-58 (9th Cir.2002) (O'Scannlain, J., dissenting); see also Douglas v. Cal. Dep't of Youth Auth., 285 F.3d 1226, 1226-27 (9th Cir.2002) (O'Scannlain, J., dissenting from denial of rehearing en banc). Because Hason all but invites a grant of certiorari and reversal for putting us out of step with the Supreme Court and creating a split with every other circuit to have considered the issue, I must dissent from the order denying en banc rehearing.

I

This opinion reaffirms two prior decisions of this court — Dare v. California, 191 F.3d 1167 (9th Cir.1999), and Clark v. California, 123 F.3d 1267 (9th Cir.1997) — which concluded that Title II validly abrogated the sovereign immunity of the several States. See Hason v. Med. Bd., 279 F.3d 1167, 1170-71 (9th Cir.2002). In so doing, however, it refuses to deal in a meaningful way with intervening Supreme Court precedent, specifically Board of Trustees of the University of Alabama v. Garrett, 531 U.S. 356, 121 S.Ct. 955, 148 L.Ed.2d 866 (2001). This, in a nutshell, is where Hason goes astray.

A bit of history is required to see clearly the misstep that this opinion takes.

A

It is beyond dispute that recent decisions of the Supreme Court, including Garrett, have fundamentally changed the landscape of Eleventh Amendment jurisprudence. See, e.g., William A. Fletcher, The Eleventh Amendment: Unfinished Business, 75 Notre Dame L. Rev. 843, 843-44 (2000). Garrett in particular clarified, in extensive detail, the approach that a court must take when addressing a claim that the ADA validly abrogated State sovereign immunity pursuant to section 5 of the Fourteenth Amendment.[1] Garrett drew on City of Boerne v. Flores, 521 U.S. 507, 117 S.Ct. 2157, 138 L.Ed.2d 624 (1997), which made clear that it was up to the courts to "define the substance of [the] constitutional guarantee[]" that Congress purported to enforce, Garrett, 531 U.S. at 365, 121 S.Ct. 955 (citing Boerne, 521 U.S. at 519-24, 117 S.Ct. 2157), and that "§ 5 legislation reaching beyond the scope of § 1's actual guarantees must exhibit `congruence and proportionality between the injury to be prevented or remedied and the means adopted to that end,'" id. (citing Boerne, 521 U.S. at 520, 117 S.Ct. 2157). But Garrett also elaborated on the Boerne analysis. For instance, Garrett made clear that once a court has "determined the metes and bounds of the constitutional right in question," it must examine "whether Congress identified a history and pattern of unconstitutional ... discrimination by the States against the disabled." Garrett, 531 U.S. at 368, 121 S.Ct. 955 (emphasis added). A showing of discrimination against the disabled in general, or discrimination by local governments rather than the States themselves, will not do. Id. at 368, 121 S.Ct. 955 ("Just as § 1 of the Fourteenth Amendment applies only to actions committed `under color of state law,' Congress' § 5 authority is appropriately exercised only in response to state transgressions."); id. at 368-69, 121 S.Ct. 955 (explaining that "[i]t would make no sense to consider constitutional violations on" the part of local governments "when only the States are the beneficiaries of the Eleventh Amendment").

Moreover, Garrett makes clear that generalizations about disability discrimination and how the ADA is designed to remedy it are inadequate; instead, a court must "dissect[] the statutory regime in question and carefully compare[] it to the baseline definition of constitutional action under the Fourteenth Amendment." Reickenbacker v. Foster, 274 F.3d 974, 981 (5th Cir.2001). Indeed, "Garrett specifically focused on the burdens of proof, exceptions, and defenses available in Title I of the ADA in order to find that `the rights and remedies created by the ADA against the States raise the same sort of concerns as to congruence and proportionality as were found in [Boerne].'" Id.

B

Garrett, then, refined the abrogation inquiry set out in Boerne. Regrettably, however, both cases on which Hason relies — Clark and Dare — were handed down before Garrett was decided. Accordingly, they do not undertake the searching inquiry that Garrett requires.

1

In Clark, we concluded that the ADA, as a whole, validly abrogated the States' sovereign immunity.[2] We first recognized, correctly, that in Cleburne v. Cleburne Living Center, Inc., 473 U.S. 432, 105 S.Ct. 3249, 87 L.Ed.2d 313 (1985), the Supreme Court "held that the disabled are protected against discrimination by the Equal Protection Clause." Clark, 123 F.3d at 1270. But from there the analysis went astray, at least as seen in hindsight through the lens of Garrett. Reading the ADA at its most general level, we next observed that the purpose of the ADA was "to prohibit discrimination against the disabled," id., and that "Congress explicitly found that persons with disabilities have suffered discrimination," id. Consequently, we decided that the ADA was "within the scope of appropriate legislation under the Equal Protection Clause as defined by the Supreme Court," id., and added as a general afterthought that the Act does not "provide[] remedies so sweeping that they exceed the harms that they are designed to redress." Id. We therefore concluded that the ADA was "validly enacted under the Fourteenth Amendment." Id.

This minimalist analysis is a far cry from the detailed approach mandated by Garrett; its infirmities are manifest. It is devoid of any discussion whatsoever of legislative findings of discrimination by States — and specifically, by States rather than by local governments. Nor does it analyze any of the specific provisions of Title II to arrive at its sweeping conclusion that Title II does not provide remedies so sweeping that they exceed the harms that they are designed to redress — let alone does it "lay them next to the baseline of what defines constitutional state action under the Fourteenth Amendment," Reickenbacker, 274 F.3d at 981, or "dissect[] the statutory regime in question and carefully compare[] it to the baseline definition of constitutional action under the Fourteenth Amendment," id., as Garrett requires.[3]

2

In Dare, we attempted to square Clark's result with the Supreme Court's intervening decision in Florida Prepaid Postsecondary Education Expense Board v. College Savings Bank, 527 U.S. 627, 119 S.Ct. 2199, 144 L.Ed.2d 575 (1999). But Dare's approach is no more sound than Clark's. Like Clark's, Dare's congruence analysis deals with legislative findings only of discrimination generally — not of discrimination by States. See Dare, 191 F.3d at 1174 ("When it enacted the ADA, Congress made specific factual findings of arbitrary and invidious discrimination against the disabled. On the basis of these findings, Congress concluded that the ADA was a necessary legislative response to a long history of arbitrary and irrational discrimination against people with disabilities.")

(citation omitted). Dare's proportionality analysis is even less tenable, if one can call it an analysis at all:

> Having established the ADA's congruence with Congress's power to enforce the Equal Protection Clause, we turn to proportionality. In so doing, we reiterate the importance of deference to Congress in this analysis. The Supreme Court has specifically found protections for people with disabilities to be an area in which Congressional judgment should be given great deference. See [Cleburne, 473 U.S. at 442-43, 105 S.Ct. 3249]. The ADA is thus an appropriate exercise of § 5 powers if Congress enacted it in response to a widespread problem of unconstitutional discrimination that includes state programs and services and if the ADA's provisions are proportional to the scope of that discrimination.
>
> As noted above, Congress made extensive factual findings regarding the widespread arbitrary and invidious discrimination which disabled people face. See 42 U.S.C. § 12101(a). The ADA's particular provisions for each sector then indicate specifically the discrimination which is forbidden and the conduct needed to remedy the discrimination. See 42 U.S.C. § 12101 et seq. Although Title II's provisions may prohibit some State conduct which would pass muster under rational basis review, the Title's focus is on eliminating the discrimination outlined in the factual findings.

Id. at 1175 (footnotes omitted). Again, this sort of blanket generalization, coupled this time with a generous helping of deference to Congress, stands in stark contrast to the provision-by-provision comparison with the constitutional baseline that Garrett requires.

II.

In light of Garrett, then, it is clear that our pre-Garrett Title II precedents are outdated. Yet Hason refuses to acknowledge this. The discussion in the opinion dealing with abrogation is short; indeed, it comprises all of two paragraphs. See Hason, 279 F.3d at 1170-71. It can be summarized as follows: (1) Clark and Dare held Title II validly abrogated sovereign immunity; (2) Garrett did not expressly deal with Title II; it dealt only with Title I, and reserved judgment on Title II; ergo (3) Clark and Dare are good law.

This logic breaks down between steps (2) and (3). To be sure, in Garrett the Court expressly declined to decide whether Congress validly abrogated state sovereign immunity in enacting Title II of the ADA. See Garrett, 531 U.S. at 360 n. 1, 121 S.Ct. 955. But it does not follow that because Garrett did not invalidate Title II, our prior case law upholding it remains relevant. For it is not just the holding of Garrett that matters; we must also be mindful of the approach the Court set forth there. As the foregoing analysis makes clear, the blunt approach taken in Clark and Dare has now been supplanted with a new, more nuanced inquiry. If we are to follow Garrett faithfully, we must re-analyze our prior precedents accordingly.

Two of our sister circuits have already recognized as much, and have re-analyzed their pre-Garrett precedents holding that Title II validly abrogated States' sovereign immunity. Each has concluded that Title II did not abrogate sovereign immunity — old circuit precedents to the contrary notwithstanding. See Reickenbacker, 274 F.3d at 981 (concluding that Garrett "effectively overruled" prior circuit precedent holding that Title II validly abrogated State sovereign immunity); Thompson v. Colorado, 278 F.3d 1020, 1034 (10th Cir. 2001), cert. denied, ____ U.S. ____, 122 S.Ct. 1960, 152 L.Ed.2d 1021 (2002).

Indeed, Hason's holding, that Title II validly abrogated States' sovereign immunity, period, splits us from seven of our peers that have considered the issue in the post-Garrett world. Every one, besides us, has gotten the message that something more nuanced is required; we now stand alone. See Klingler v. Dir., Dep't of Revenue, 281 F.3d 776, 777 (8th Cir.2002) (affirming pre-Garrett decision holding that Title II did not validly abrogate State sovereign immunity); Reickenbacker, 274 F.3d at 983; Thompson, 278 F.3d at 1034; Erickson v. Bd. of Governors of State Colls. and Univs., 207 F.3d 945, 948 (7th Cir.2000) (questioning the continued authority of Crawford v. Indiana Department of Corrections, 115 F.3d 481, 487 (7th Cir.1997), which upheld Title II as a valid abrogation of State sovereign immunity), cert. denied, 531 U.S. 1190, 121 S.Ct. 1187, 149 L.Ed.2d 104 (2001); see also Popovich v. Cuyahoga County Court of Common Pleas, 276 F.3d 808, 812, 815-16 (6th Cir. 2002) (en banc) (agreeing that Title II is not a valid abrogation of sovereign immunity when Congress is enforcing the Equal Protection Clause, but holding that it is permissible when enforcing the Due Process Clause); Garcia v. S.U.N.Y. Health Scis. Center, 280 F.3d 98, 110-12 (2d Cir. 2001) (holding that Title II actions may only be brought against States if the plaintiff can establish that the "violation was motivated by discriminatory animus or ill will based on the plaintiff's disability"); cf. Brown v. N.C. Div. of Motor Vehicles, 166 F.3d 698, 707 (4th Cir.1999) (holding that a regulation enacted pursuant to Title II did not validly abrogate State sovereign immunity).

III

Clark and Dare have gone the way of the dodo bird and the wooly mammoth, overtaken and relegated to extinction by the course of events. "Clark is now outdated — and Douglas wrong — for failing to recognize the change in the legal landscape of sovereign immunity." Douglas, 285 F.3d at 1226-27 (O'Scannlain, J., dissenting from denial of rehearing en banc). As every circuit to have analyzed the issue now agrees (except, of course, ours), in light of Garrett, Title II did not abrogate the Eleventh Amendment immunity of the several States.

We should have taken Hason en banc to reconsider, and to overrule, Clark and Dare. I respectfully dissent.

Judge O'Scannlain's concurrence and dissent in Dazo v. Globe Airport Security Services (July 1, 2002)

O'SCANNLAIN, Circuit Judge, concurring in part and dissenting in part.

I concur in the court's affirmance of Dazo's wilful misconduct claim, but I must respectfully dissent from its holding that Globe, as agent of TWA, is not entitled to the protection of the Warsaw Convention.

At the time of Dazo's flight, airlines were charged by federal statute with the responsibility to screen all passengers and property. See 49 U.S.C. § 44901 (2000).[1]

TWA, which provided Dazo carriage to Toronto, delegated its screening responsibility to Globe.[2] Thus, Dazo concedes, as she must, that Globe acted as TWA's agent when she passed through the security checkpoint. The Warsaw Convention extends to an airline's agents and employees, a premise not challenged by the majority. See, e.g., Reed v. Wiser, 555 F.2d 1079, 1089-92 (2d Cir.1977); Kabbani v. Int'l Total Servs., 805 F.Supp. 1033, 1039-40 (D.D.C.1992); In re Air Disaster at Lockerbie, Scotland on Dec. 21, 1988, 776 F.Supp. 710, 712-14 (E.D.N.Y.1991); Baker v. Lansdell Protective Agency, Inc., 590 F.Supp. 165, 170-71 (S.D.N.Y.1984). Hence, to the extent that Globe acts as agent of TWA, it must be afforded the protection of the Warsaw Convention. See, e.g., In re Air Disaster, 776 F.Supp. at 714 (holding airport security company protected by the Convention).

The majority implies that if Globe provided screening only for TWA, Globe would indeed fall within the Convention. Supra at 939.[3] Nevertheless, it claims the fact that Globe also provides screening for two other airlines at the checkpoint somehow destroys its Convention status. According to the majority, an agent of multiple airlines can never fall within the Convention because the agent performs services for airlines other than the one that provided international carriage.

The majority's approach suffers from a fundamental misunderstanding of agency principles. An agent may serve two masters at once, as long as service to one does not involve abandonment of service to the other. See Restatement (Second) of Agency § 226 (1958); see also Ward v. Gordon, 999 F.2d 1399, 1404 (9th Cir.1993). Globe served multiple masters; TWA, America West Airlines, and Continental Airlines each arranged for Globe to provide screening at Terminal C of the airport. However, Globe's service to one airline in no way involved an abandonment to the others. Globe was fulfilling its duty to TWA when Dazo passed through security. In short, Globe's association with America West and Continental does not destroy its agency relationship with TWA.

Apart from proper application of agency principles, common sense dictates that the majority's approach is misguided. Under that approach, a security company serving one airline is entitled to the protection of the Convention, but a security company serving multiple airlines is not. Why should the arbitrary happenstance of whether a security service contracts with multiple partners determine whether a person's claims are preempted by the Warsaw Convention?[4]

Of course, the majority is correct in saying that the protections of the Warsaw Convention do not extend to America West and Continental. The Warsaw Convention is limited to airlines and its agents that actually provide international carriage, and neither America West nor Continental provided any carriage to Dazo whatsoever. Accordingly, while TWA and Globe are entitled to Warsaw Convention status, America West and Continental are not.

Nonetheless, I disagree with the majority's decision to reinstate Dazo's claims against America West and Continental. Dazo has made no attempt to distinguish among the three airlines she has sued. Indeed, she waited until her petitions for rehearing to even identify which airline provided her carriage to Toronto. In these circumstances, Dazo has waived any claim against America West and Continental. See, e.g., Greenwood v. FAA, 28 F.3d 971, 977 (9th Cir.1994) ("We review only issues which are argued specifically and distinctly in a party's opening brief.").

I appreciate the fact that the tragic events of September 11, 2001 have cast this case in a different light from when it was first taken under submission. To some, the experience of September 11 undoubtedly makes it far less palatable to shroud airport security companies within the liability caps of the Warsaw Convention. Globe's parent, after all, screened passengers for American Airlines Flight 11, which was used to destroy the north tower of the World Trade Center. See, e.g., Milo Geyelin, Judge Wants Victims of Sept. 11 Who Sue to Know Risks of Action, Wall St. J., Apr. 12, 2002, at B2; Patricia Hurtado, Victim's Kin Sues Airline, Newsday (New York), Apr. 9, 2002, at A3. But this nation's recent tragedy simply does not bear on the legal question presented in this case, and does not justify a panel majority reversing course. Our judicial charge is to stand above the inflamed passions of the public, however much we may share them; we must apply the law faithfully and evenhandedly. See LaVine v. Blaine Sch. Dist., 279 F.3d 719, 728 (9th Cir.2002) (Kleinfeld, J., dissenting from denial of rehearing en banc) ("[The] ... law ought to be based on neutral principles, and should not easily sway in the winds of popular concerns, for that would make our liberty a weak reed that swayed in the winds.").

I respectfully dissent.

Notes

[1] In the wake of September 11, 2001, Congress enacted the Aviation and Transportation Security Act, Pub.L. No. 107-71, 115 Stat. 597 (2001) (codified in scattered sections of 49 U.S.C.). The Act shifts the responsibility for screening from the airlines to the federal government effective November 19, 2001.

[2] While the record does not reveal which airline provided international carriage, Dazo identified TWA as the airline in her petitions for rehearing. Thus, for ease of discussion, I refer to TWA as the airline that provided carriage to Toronto. Of course, Globe's Convention status is not affected by the absence of the airline's identity in the record. It is undisputed that Globe acted as the agent for the airline (whichever one it was) that provided international carriage.

[3] I recognize that the majority does not explicitly concede this point. However, the majority distinguishes several cases extending Convention status to an airline's agent solely on the ground that in those cases the agent served one airline exclusively. Supra at 939. Thus, the majority implicitly concedes that the result in this case would be different if Globe served only TWA.

[4] Apparently, even Dazo appreciates the deficiency of the majority's approach. Judge Tashima articulated this approach in his dissent to the original panel decision. In her twelve page petition for rehearing, Dazo afforded merely a single sentence in support,

under the heading "Miscellaneous."

Judge O'Scannlain's concurrence in In re Watts (Aug 6, 2002)

O'SCANNLAIN, Circuit Judge, concurring in the judgment:

I find myself in the perplexing position of being bound by a precedent counseling that I need not be bound by a precedent.

Although there is much in the court's fine opinion with which I agree entirely — I would have no quarrel with its analysis of California law were the issue one of first impression — I am profoundly troubled by the notion of reaching this result by our "overruling," as a three-judge panel, the precedent set by an earlier panel in Jones v. Heskett (In re Jones), 106 F.3d 923 (9th Cir.1997).

I

It is a bedrock principle of our court that the published decision of one three-judge panel binds every other panel,[1] from that day forward.[2] Put another way, one panel may not overrule another; the power to overrule is confided to the en banc court, and the en banc court alone.[3] Panels may distinguish; they may question; they may deploy virtually any of the other verbs in the Shepard's vocabulary. But they may not overrule.

There are exceptions. We need not convene the en banc court when the Supreme Court reverses us directly. Nor must we do so when that Court, in reviewing a case from another circuit, knocks the props out from under one of our decisions. See, e.g., Le Vick v. Skaggs Cos., Inc., 701 F.2d 777, 778 (9th Cir.1983); Piedmont Label Co. v. Sun Garden Packing Co., 598 F.2d 491, 495 (9th Cir.1979); see also, e.g., Circuit City Stores, Inc. v. Najd, 294 F.3d 1104 (9th Cir.2002) (noting that Duffield v. Robertson Stephens & Co., 144 F.3d 1182 (9th Cir.1998), has likely been implicitly overruled). This practice represents our confidence, as a court, that our three-judge panels are able to tell the difference between a Supreme Court ruling that rips one of our decisions from the Federal Reporter altogether and one that leaves at least a hanging chad behind. But it also represents our confidence that the Supreme Court stands ready to review and to reverse us when necessary (a proposition for which, I think, no citation is required).

We also permit our panels to use the big eraser when the earlier decision is based on state law that has demonstrably changed in the intervening period. Herein lies the rub. A proposition's demonstrability depends on the audience's receptivity. How skeptical must we ask our panels to be when they are urged to exercise the power to overrule in light of a supervening change in the underlying law?

To my mind, a panel must not act in contravention of our precedent without being highly certain of its authority to do so. And that certainty is not easily obtained when, as here, the alleged change in state law comes from case law rather than statutory law.

When it is a state statute that has changed, the question is much simpler, particularly in this age of formal codification.[4]

In most cases, we need no longer hunt through yellowing volumes of the

California state session laws; either the state legislature has altered the statutory section relied upon in the prior decision, or it has not.

But with case law, whether pure common law or judicial glosses on statutory law, the question is more difficult. We can be certain that state case law is an authoritative expression of state law only when it comes from the state's court of last resort.[5]

Anything less leaves room for doubt — including a decision by an intermediate state appellate court, which, though perhaps weightier authority than a trial court's ruling, an attorney general's opinion, or a learned commentator's pronouncement, is inevitably less than conclusive. And it seems to me that where there is room for doubt, we must stay our erasers.

II

For the contrary position, the court's opinion relies primarily on Owen ex rel. Owen v. United States, 713 F.2d 1461 (9th Cir.1983). Supra, at 1082-83. I do not disagree with the court's discussion of Owen, but I find the reasoning of that case troubling. Owen relied on our cases requiring that we "follow the decision of the intermediate appellate courts of the state unless there is `compelling evidence that the highest court of the state would decide differently.'" Owen, 713 F.2d at 1464 (quoting Andrade v. City of Phoenix, 692 F.2d 557, 559 (9th Cir.1982) (per curiam)) (internal quotation marks omitted). The Owen court reasoned that because we must presumptively follow the decisions of state intermediate appellate courts when we decide questions of first impression, we must also revisit our decisions on the same basis. I do not think that the one proposition follows from the other.

Consider a state with an intermediate appeals court whose two divisions do not bind one another with their decisions. Suppose the two divisions simultaneously reach opposite conclusions on the identical question of law. Suppose further that the issue is so thorny and the two decisions so well-reasoned that, despite the diametrically opposed outcomes, the impartial observer can find one more persuasive than the other only by a hairsbreadth — the winner by a preponderance, but not by clear and convincing evidence. Yet we require "convincing evidence" before disregarding the decision of an intermediate appellate court. Owen, 713 F.2d at 1465. In this example, neither decision is weighty enough to justify disregarding the other. A panel of this court confronted with this situation, but blessed with a prior, on-point Ninth Circuit precedent, would likely sigh with relief and apply the law of the circuit, even if one or both of the state cases postdated the earlier panel's decision. The law in our court and those bound by our rulings remains unchanged, predictable, reliable until the state's highest court tells us otherwise.

I believe this salutary predictability justifies following circuit precedent even when a state intermediate appellate court subsequently issues a contrary opinion. One never knows, after all, when the other shoe will drop and another state court will take the opposite position. California maintains a dispersed intermediate appellate court, with six independent districts. Cal. Gov't Code § 69100. Are we to revisit our rulings each time the weight of authority shifts? (If the First District decides on holding A, the Second and Third hand down holding not-A the next year, and the Fourth, Fifth, and Sixth weigh in with holding A the following year, will we have to undertake three overrulings, with a fourth when the California Supreme Court finally settles on outcome not-A?) I would prefer to keep to a minimum the frequency with which we receive a new datum, revise our view of state law accordingly, and reverse ourselves.

But can we not ascertain from our own reading of the law how likely it is that this parade of horribles will actually march in any given case? To do so here, we would have to evaluate whether the Jones panel's decision is so out of line with California law that no other Court of Appeal is likely to adopt it. And it is precisely that sort of on-the-merits reexamination of prior precedent that we are supposed to leave to the en banc court.[6]

III

One could certainly argue that the mere fact of a panel opinion should not be given this near-conclusive weight. After all, the three judges (or two) who arrived at the precedential holding in question may or may not have had the benefit of thorough briefing, immersion in the pertinent state law, or a nutritious and balanced breakfast. Cf. Payne v. Tennessee, 501 U.S. 808, 834, 111 S.Ct. 2597, 115 L.Ed.2d 720 (1991) (Scalia, J., concurring) ("[W]hat would enshrine power as the governing principle of this Court is the notion that an important constitutional decision with plainly inadequate rational support must be left in place for the sole reason that it once attracted five votes.").

But that is not our usual rule — and for good reason. Stare decisis is of particular importance in federal courts. We are, after all, courts of limited jurisdiction that do not enjoy the general common lawmaking authority that many state courts do. And the fact that federal judges are not lawmakers is inextricable from the fact that we enjoy the constitutional armoring that secures our independence — appointment (rather than election), life tenure, and salary protection. Cf. Chisom v. Roemer, 501 U.S. 380, 400, 111 S.Ct. 2354, 115 L.Ed.2d 348 (1991); Northern Pipeline Constr. Co. v. Marathon Pipe Line Co., 458 U.S. 50, 59 n. 10, 102 S.Ct. 2858, 73 L.Ed.2d 598 (1982) (plurality opinion). Our status ill suits us to lawmaking; indeed, the Framers' expectation that we would not be making law secured us our judicial independence in the first place.

Stare decisis provides crucial reassurance on the latter point: it demonstrates that our decisions represent more than the subjective preferences of the concurring judges. The Federalist No. 78, at 471 (Alexander Hamilton) (Clinton Rossiter ed. 1961) ("To avoid an arbitrary discretion in the courts, it is indispensable that they should be bound down by strict rules and precedents which serve to define and point out their duty in every particular case that comes before them...."); see also, e.g., Pollock v. Farmers' Loan & Trust Co., 157 U.S. 429, 652, 15 S.Ct. 673, 39 L.Ed. 759 (1895) (White, J., dissenting) ("The fundamental conception of a judicial body is that of one hedged about by precedents which are binding on the court without regard to the personality of its members."). In the courts of appeals, we three-judge panels bind ourselves rigorously to this mast and allow only the en banc court to release us. I find it unfortunate that Owen and Stephan v. Dowdle, 733 F.2d 642 (9th Cir. 1984), have departed from this rule. See supra at 1083.

But depart they have, and I must respect those holdings, for they cannot be dismissed as dicta. See, e.g., Spears v. Stewart, 283 F.3d 992, 1006 (9th Cir.2002) (Kozinski, J., statement concerning the denial of the petitions for rehearing en banc) ("[S]o long as the issue is presented in the case and expressly addressed in the opinion, that holding is binding and cannot be overlooked or ignored by later panels of this court or by other courts of the circuit."). Nor have they been overruled.

Thus, reluctantly applying the Owen rule, I agree with the majority's conclusion that Jones is no longer viable and must be rejected — although, for the reasons detailed above, I decline to use the term "overruled." Accordingly, I concur in the judgment.

Notes

[1] Indeed, our three-judge panels are bound even before the litigants themselves are bound. Even when a judgment is not yet enforceable, the opinion remains circuit precedent unless and until a majority of judges vote to take it en banc, at which point it may not be cited. 9th Cir. Gen. Order 5.5(d); see, e.g., Newdow v. U.S. Cong., 292 F.3d 597 (9th Cir.2002), judgment purportedly "stayed" by one-judge order (9th Cir. June 27, 2002) (No. 00-16423).

[2] And occasionally backward: because a panel's decision in any given case is controlling over others submitted for decision afterward, occasionally a case is submitted first but decided second, necessitating the amendment or withdrawal of the case submitted second but decided first. See 9th Cir. Gen. Order 4.1(a).

[3] Although, in this circuit, the en banc court that exercises that authority in the first instance is a limited, eleven-judge panel rather than the full court, see 9th Cir. R. 35-3, the decision to convene the en banc court is made by a majority of the court's active, nonrecused circuit judges, as the governing statute mandates. 28 U.S.C. § 46(c); Fed. R.App. P. 35. And participation on the en banc court is specifically restricted to judges of this court (and, with one exception, see 28 U.S.C. § 26(c)(1), to judges in regular active service).

[4] "Formal codification" refers to the consolidation of legislative enactments under readily indexed subject headings, rather than an attempt to reduce all substantive law to the form of code law to the exclusion of common law. Gunther A. Weiss, The Enchantment of Codification in the Common Law World, 25 Yale J. Int'l L. 435, 517 & n. 418 (2000).

[5] Certainty that state case law is an authoritative and enduring expression of state law is at its highest when a state court of last resort construes a statute, rather than the state constitution or the common law, due to the customary rule that stare decisis is most strongly applicable in statutory construction cases, see, e.g., Patterson v. McLean Credit Union, 491 U.S. 164, 172-73, 109 S.Ct. 2363, 105 L.Ed.2d 132 (1989). But the possibility that the state's highest court will one day overrule itself does not make its extant rulings any less authoritative for our purposes, if not the historians'.

[6] I should add that one way to reduce the incidence of this difficult situation is to

exercise the utmost restraint in publishing precedential decisions in diversity cases. However, that tool is not available to us in cases like this one, where federal law incorporates or intersects with state law. We must apply the same Erie-derived principles to ascertain the state law, but we must also give precedential effect to our application of the federal law in some cases, thus creating federal court precedent on state law that Erie principles may later undermine.

Judge O'Scannlain's dissent from the denial of rehearing en banc in Newdow v. US Congress (Feb 28, 2003) [Notes omitted]

O'SCANNLAIN, Circuit Judge, with whom KLEINFELD, GOULD, TALLMAN, RAWLINSON, and CLIFTON, Circuit Judges, join, dissenting from the denial of rehearing en banc.

Last June, a two-judge majority of a three-judge panel of this court ruled that the Pledge of Allegiance was unconstitutional simply because of the presence of two offending words: "under God." It was an exercise in judicial legerdemain which, not surprisingly, produced a public outcry across the nation. Since that time we, as a court, have had the opportunity to order reconsideration of that decision en banc, yet a majority of the 24 active judges eligible to vote has decided not to do so. While there are, no doubt, varied and plausible reasons why this result occurred, I respectfully conclude that our court has made a serious mistake and thus must dissent from its order denying reconsideration.

I

While I cannot say that a randomly selected 11-judge panel would have ruled differently, I believe that neither the June 2002 version, Newdow v. United States Congress, 292 F.3d 597 (9th Cir.2002) ("Newdow I"), nor today's slightly revised version, 328 F.3d 466 ("Newdow II") to essentially the same effect, is defensible. We should have reheard Newdow I en banc, not because it was controversial, but because it was wrong, very wrong — wrong because reciting the Pledge of Allegiance is simply not "a religious act" as the two-judge majority asserts, wrong as a matter of Supreme Court precedent properly understood, wrong because it set up a direct conflict with the law of another circuit, and wrong as a matter of common sense.[1] We should have given 11 judges a chance to determine whether the two-judge majority opinion truly reflects the law of the Ninth Circuit.[2] Reciting the Pledge of Allegiance cannot possibly be an "establishment of religion" under any reasonable interpretation of the Constitution.[3]

Perhaps in an effort to avoid ultimate Supreme Court review, Newdow II which replaces it, avoids expressly reaching the technical question of the constitutionality of the 1954 Act. Fundamentally, however, the amended decision is every bit as bold as its predecessor. It bans the voluntary recitation of the Pledge of Allegiance in the public schools of the nine western states thereby directly affecting over 9.6 million students,[4] necessarily implies that both an Act of Congress[5] and a California law[6] are unconstitutional, clearly conflicts with the Seventh Circuit's decision in Sherman v. Cmty.

Consol. Sch. Dist. 21 of Wheeling Township, 980 F.2d 437 (7th Cir. 1992), and threatens cash-strapped school districts and underpaid teachers with the specter of civil actions for money damages pursuant to 42 U.S.C. § 1983.

Newdow I, the subject of our en banc vote, no longer exists; it was withdrawn after the en banc call failed. The panel majority has evolved to this extent: in Newdow I the Pledge was unconstitutional for everybody; in Newdow II the Pledge is only unconstitutional for public school children and teachers. The remainder of this dissent is directed entirely to Newdow II, which, as shall be demonstrated, differs little from Newdow I in its central holding. With grim insistence, the majority in Newdow II continues to stand by its original error — that voluntary recitation of the Pledge of Allegiance in public school violates the Establishment Clause because, according to the two-judge panel majority, it is "a religious act." Newdow II, 328 F.3d at 490. Common sense would seem to dictate otherwise, as the public and political reaction should by now have made clear. If reciting the Pledge is truly "a religious act" in violation of the Establishment Clause, then so is the recitation of the Constitution[7] itself, the Declaration of Independence,[8] the Gettysburg Address,[9] the National Motto,[10] or the singing of the National Anthem.[11] Such an assertion would make hypocrites out of the Founders, and would have the effect of driving any and all references to our religious heritage out of our schools, and eventually out of our public life.

II

The Newdow II majority's primary legal argument is that the Supreme Court's decision in Lee v. Weisman, 505 U.S. 577, 112 S.Ct. 2649, 120 L.Ed.2d 467 (1992), a school prayer case, controls the outcome of this case. In fact, rather than merely following Lee and its predecessors, the two-judge panel majority makes a radical departure from Lee and the cases it purports to apply. To understand why this is so, an examination of the Supreme Court's school prayer decisions which culminate in Lee is in order.

A

1

The fountainhead of all school prayer cases is Engel v. Vitale, 370 U.S. 421, 82 S.Ct. 1261, 8 L.Ed.2d 601 (1962). In Engel the Court considered a school policy whereby children were directed to say aloud a prayer composed by state officials. The Court found that this practice was inconsistent with the Establishment Clause, reasoning that "[the] program of daily classroom invocation of God's blessings as prescribed in the Regents' prayer is a religious activity. It is a solemn avowal of divine faith and supplication for the blessings of the Almighty. The nature of such a prayer has always been religious." Id. at 424-25, 82 S.Ct. 1261. The Court concluded by stating that the state should leave prayer, "that purely religious function, to the people themselves." Id. at 435, 82 S.Ct. 1261. In a footnote, it reasoned as follows:

There is of course nothing in the decision reached here that is inconsistent with the fact that school children and others are officially encouraged to express love for our country by reciting historical documents such as the Declaration of Independence which contain references to the Deity or by singing officially espoused anthems which include the composer's professions of faith in a Supreme Being, or with the fact that there are many manifestations in our public life of belief in God. Such patriotic or ceremonial occasions bear no true resemblance to the unquestioned religious exercise that the State of New York has sponsored in this instance.

Id. at 435 n. 21, 82 S.Ct. 1261. The Court drew an explicit distinction between patriotic invocations of God on the one hand, and prayer, an "unquestioned religious exercise," on the other. Concurring, Justice Douglas wrote that the narrow question presented was whether the state "oversteps the bounds when it finances a religious exercise." Id. at 439, 82 S.Ct. 1261 (Douglas, J., concurring). Justice Douglas noted that the Pledge of Allegiance, "like ... prayer, recognizes the existence of a Supreme Being." Id. at 440 n. 5, 82 S.Ct. 1261. However, he noted that the House Report recommending the addition of the words "under God" to the Pledge stated that those words "in no way run contrary to the First Amendment but recognize `only the guidance of God in our national affairs.'" Id. (quoting H.R.Rep. No. 1693, 83d Cong., 2d Sess., p. 3).

2

The following year, the Supreme Court decided Abington School Dist. v. Schempp, 374 U.S. 203, 83 S.Ct. 1560, 10 L.Ed.2d 844 (1963). In that case, the Court considered the constitutionality of a Pennsylvania statute requiring that "[a]t least ten verses from the Holy Bible shall be read, without comment, at the opening of each public school on each school day." Id. at 205, 83 S.Ct. 1560. The practice in public schools was for a teacher or student volunteer to read the required Bible verses each morning. This in turn was followed by a recitation of the Lord's prayer. Finally, the class would recite the Pledge of Allegiance to the Flag. Id. at 207-08, 83 S.Ct. 1560. The Court struck down the Bible reading and the practice of reciting the Lord's prayer as a state prescribed "religious ceremony," id. at 223, 83 S.Ct. 1560, but said nothing about the practice of reciting the Pledge.

As in Engel, the Court took pains to point to the character of the exercises it found wanting. The Court reasoned that "reading ... the verses ... possesses a devotional and religious character and constitutes in effect a religious observance. The devotional and religious nature of the morning exercises is made all the more apparent by the fact that the Bible reading is followed immediately by a recital in unison by the pupils of the Lord's prayer." Id. at 210, 83 S.Ct. 1560. "The pervading religious character of the ceremony," wrote Justice Clark, "cannot be gainsaid," and led to the conclusion that the exercises violated the Establishment Clause. Id. at 224, 83 S.Ct. 1560.

The concurring opinions in Schempp were all to the same effect. Justice Douglas agreed with the majority's conclusion that the practices at issue violated the Establishment Clause because "the State is conducting a religious exercise." Id. at 229, 83 S.Ct. 1560 (Douglas, J., concurring). In a lengthy concurrence, Justice Brennan wrote that "[t]he religious nature of the exercises here challenged seems plain." Id. at 266, 83 S.Ct. 1560 (Brennan, J., concurring). After surveying the history of devotional exercises in American public schools, Justice Brennan stated that "the panorama of history permits no other conclusion than that daily prayers and Bible readings in the public schools have always been designed to be, and have been regarded as, essentially religious exercises." Id. at 277-78, 83 S.Ct. 1560. For Justice Brennan, "religious exercises in the public schools present a unique problem" but "not every involvement of religion in public life violates the Establishment Clause." Id. at 294, 83 S.Ct. 1560. He warned that "[a]ny attempt to impose rigid limits upon the mention of God ... in the classroom would be fraught with dangers." Id. at 301, 83 S.Ct. 1560. Specifically, he wrote that "[t]he reference to divinity in the revised pledge of allegiance ... may merely recognize the historical fact that our Nation was believed to have been founded `under God.' Thus reciting the pledge may be no more of a religious exercise than the reading aloud of Lincoln's Gettysburg Address, which contains an allusion to the same historical fact." Id. at 304, 83 S.Ct. 1560.

Justice Goldberg also wrote separately, stating that "the clearly religious practices presented in these cases are ... wholly compelling." Id. at 305, 83 S.Ct. 1560 (Goldberg, J., concurring). He reasoned that "[t]he pervasive religiosity and direct governmental involvement inhering in the prescription of prayer and Bible reading in the public schools... cannot realistically be termed simply accommodation." Id. at 307, 83 S.Ct. 1560. Like Justice Brennan, Justice Goldberg cautioned that the decision "does not mean that all incidents of government which import of the religious are therefore and without more banned by the strictures of the Establishment Clause." Id. at 307-08, 83 S.Ct. 1560. He then quoted in full the passage from Engel which drew a distinction between patriotic invocations of God, and unquestioned religious exercises that give rise to Establishment Clause violations. Id.

3

The next case in this line is Wallace v. Jaffree, 472 U.S. 38, 105 S.Ct. 2479, 86 L.Ed.2d 29 (1985). That case considered the constitutionality of an Alabama statute authorizing a 1-minute period of silence in public schools "for meditation or voluntary prayer." Id. at 40, 105 S.Ct. 2479. The Court found that "[t]he wholly religious character" of the challenged law was "plainly evident from its text." Id. at 58, 105 S.Ct. 2479. The legislature's one and only purpose in enacting the law was "to return prayer to the public schools." Id. at 59-60, 105 S.Ct. 2479. Justice Powell's separate concurrence was "prompted by Alabama's persistence in attempting to institute state-sponsored prayer in the public schools." Id. at 62, 105 S.Ct. 2479 (Powell, J., concurring). Justice O'Connor wrote separately to suggest that moment-of-silence statutes were not "a religious exercise," and therefore were constitutional. Id. at 72, 105 S.Ct. 2479 (O'Connor, J., concurring). Justice O'Connor wrote further that "the words `under God' in the Pledge ... serve as an acknowledgment of religion with `the legitimate secular purposes of solemnizing public occasions, [and] expressing confidence in the future.'" Id. at 78 n. 5, 105 S.Ct. 2479 (quoting Lynch v. Donnelly, 465 U.S. 668, 693, 104 S.Ct. 1355, 79 L.Ed.2d 604 (1984) (O'Connor, J., concurring)) (alterations in original). In contrast, the Alabama statute at issue was very different from the Pledge—the state had "intentionally crossed the line [by] affirmatively endorsing the particular religious practice of prayer." Id. at 84, 105 S.Ct. 2479.

4

Finally, there is the Supreme Court's decision in Lee v. Weisman. The issue presented was "whether including clerical members who offer prayers as part of the official school graduation ceremony" is consistent with the Establishment Clause. 505 U.S. at 580, 112 S.Ct. 2649. The graduating students entered as a group in a processional, after which "the students stood for the Pledge of Allegiance and remained standing during the rabbi's prayers." Id. at 583, 112 S.Ct. 2649. Justice Kennedy wrote that "the significance of the prayers lies ... at the heart of [the] case." Id. He framed the inquiry as follows:

These dominant facts mark and control the confines of our decision: State officials direct the performance of a formal religious exercise at promotional and graduation ceremonies for secondary schools. Even for those students who object to the religious exercise their attendance and participation in the state-sponsored religious activity are in a fair and real sense obligatory, though the school district does not require attendance as a condition for receipt of the diploma.

Id. at 586, 112 S.Ct. 2649.

The Court in Lee concluded that Engel and its progeny controlled the outcome, writing that "[c]onducting this formal religious observance conflicts with settled rules pertaining to prayer exercises for students." Id. at 587, 112 S.Ct. 2649. As in Engel, Schempp, and Wallace, the crucial factor was the nature of the exercise in which the students were asked to participate. Time and again the Court went out of its way to stress the nature of the exercise, writing that prayer was "an overt religious exercise," id. at 588, 112 S.Ct. 2649, and that "prayer exercises in public schools carry a particular risk of indirect coercion." Id. at 592, 112 S.Ct. 2649. The practice was unconstitutional because "the State has in every practical sense compelled attendance and participation in an explicit religious exercise at an event of singular importance to every student." Id. at 598, 112 S.Ct. 2649. Just like the decisions in Engel and Schempp, the Court in Lee took pains to stress the confines of its holding, concluding that "[w]e do not hold that every state action implicating religion is invalid if one or a few citizens find it offensive," id. at 597, 112 S.Ct. 2649, and that "[a] relentless and all-pervasive attempt to exclude religion from every aspect of public life could itself become inconsistent with the Constitution." Id. at 598, 112 S.Ct. 2649.

B

Two fundamental principles may therefore be derived from the school prayer cases culminating in Lee.

1

Formal religious observances are prohibited in public schools because of the danger that they may effect an establishment of religion. See Engel, 370 U.S. at 424-25, 82 S.Ct. 1261 ("[D]aily classroom invocation of God's blessings ... is a religious activity."); Schempp, 374 U.S. at 210, 83 S.Ct. 1560 (Bible reading followed by the Lord's prayer "possesses a devotional and religious character and constitutes in effect a religious observance."); Wallace, 472 U.S. at 58, 105 S.Ct. 2479 (Prayer is of a "wholly religious character."); Lee, 505 U.S. at 586, 112 S.Ct. 2649 (Prayer written by state officials constitutes a "formal religious exercise"). In each of these cases, the Court took pains to stress that not every reference to God in public schools was prohibited. See Engel, 370 U.S. at 435 n. 21, 82 S.Ct. 1261 ("patriotic or ceremonial occasions" which contain "references to the Deity" bear "no true resemblance to the unquestioned religious exercise" of prayer); Schempp, 374 U.S. at 301, 83 S.Ct. 1560 (Brennan, J., concurring) ("Any attempt to impose rigid limits upon the mention of God ... in the classroom would be fraught with dangers."); Wallace, 472 U.S. at 78 n. 5, 105 S.Ct. 2479 (O'Connor, J., concurring) ("the words `under God' in the Pledge" are not unconstitutional); Lee, 505 U.S. at 598, 112 S.Ct. 2649 ("A relentless and all-pervasive attempt to exclude religion ... could itself become inconsistent with the Constitution.").

2

Once it is established that the state is sanctioning a formal religious exercise, then the fact that the students are not required to participate in the formal devotional exercises does not prevent those exercises from being unconstitutional. See Engel, 370 U.S. at 431, 82 S.Ct. 1261 ("[T]he indirect coercive pressure upon religious minorities to conform" to the prayer exercises "is plain."); Schempp, 374 U.S. at 210-11, 83 S.Ct. 1560 ("The fact that some pupils, or theoretically all pupils, might be excused from attendance at the exercises does not mitigate the obligatory nature of the ceremony."); Wallace, 472 U.S. at 57, 105 S.Ct. 2479 (State-sanctioned voluntary prayer in public schools violates Establishment Clause); Lee, 505 U.S. at 592, 112 S.Ct. 2649 ("[P]rayer exercises in public schools carry a particular risk of indirect coercion."). To be sure, Lee is the Court's most elaborate pronouncement with respect to indirect coercion. It identifies the circumstances in which indirect coercion may be said to be unconstitutional: when the government directs "the performance of a formal religious exercise" in such a way as to oblige the participation of objectors. Lee, 505 U.S. at 586, 112 S.Ct. 2649.

III

No court, state or federal, has ever held, even now, that the Supreme Court's school prayer cases apply outside a context of state-sanctioned formal religious observances. But Newdow II finesses all that, and the sleight of hand the majority uses becomes immediately apparent: obfuscate the nature of the exercise at issue and emphasize indirect coercion. The panel majority simply ignores, because they are inconvenient, the "dominant and controlling facts" in Lee and its predecessors: that Establishment Clause violations in public schools are triggered only when "State officials direct the performance of a formal religious exercise." 505 U.S. at 586, 112 S.Ct. 2649 (emphasis added); see also Schempp, 374 U.S. at 210, 83 S.Ct. 1560 ("devotional ... religious observance" prohibited); Wallace, 472 U.S. at 58, 105 S.Ct. 2479 (activities of a "wholly religious character" prohibited).

A

To avoid a flagrant inconsistency with Lee, and with 40 years of Supreme Court precedent, the two-judge panel majority must first examine whether the act of pledging allegiance is "a religious act." As the Seventh Circuit in Sherman framed it, "Does `under God' make the Pledge a prayer, whose recitation violates the establishment clause of the first amendment?" 980 F.2d at 445. That court answered the question in the negative; the Newdow II majority, in conclusory fashion, simply assumes the affirmative. 328 F.3d at 487 ("[W]e conclude that the school district policy impermissibly coerces a religious act.") (emphasis added).

This assertion belies common sense. Most assuredly, to pledge allegiance to flag and country is a patriotic act. After the public and political reaction last summer, it is difficult to believe that anyone can continue to think otherwise. The fact the Pledge is infused with an undoubtedly religious reference does not change the nature of the act itself. The California statute under which the school district promulgated its policy is entitled "[d]aily performance of patriotic exercises in public schools." Cal. Educ.Code § 52720 (emphasis added). The Pledge is recited not just in schools but also at various official events and public ceremonies, including perhaps the most patriotic of occasions — naturalization ceremonies. Generally, the Pledge is recited while standing, facing a United States flag, with the right hand held over the heart, much like the National Anthem. See 4 U.S.C. § 4 (articulating proper procedure for reciting Pledge); 36 U.S.C. § 301 (during anthem "all present ... should stand at attention facing the flag with the right hand over the heart."). Whatever one thinks of the normative values underlying the Pledge, they are unquestionably patriotic in nature. Indeed, it is precisely because of the Pledge's explicitly patriotic nature that in 1943 the Supreme Court ruled that no one is required to Pledge allegiance against their will. West Virginia v. Barnette, 319 U.S. 624, 642, 63 S.Ct. 1178, 87 L.Ed. 1628 (1943).

In contrast, to pray is to speak directly to God, with bowed head, on bended knee, or some other reverent disposition. It is a solemn and humble approach to the divine in order to give thanks, to petition, to praise, to supplicate, or to ask for guidance. Communal prayer, by definition, is an even more forceful and profound experience for those present. Little wonder that the Supreme Court has recognized the "unique problem" and "particular risk" posed by school prayer to nonparticipating students. Lee, 505 U.S. at 592, 112 S.Ct. 2649 ("[P]rayer exercises in public schools carry a particular risk of indirect coercion."); Schempp, 374 U.S. at 294, 83 S.Ct. 1560 (Brennan, J., concurring) (noting that prayers in public schools "present a unique problem").

Not only does the panel majority's conclusion that pledging allegiance is "a religious act" defy common sense, it contradicts our 200-year history and tradition of patriotic references to God. The Supreme Court has insisted that interpretations of the Establishment Clause must comport "with what history reveals was the contemporaneous understanding of its guarantees." Lynch, 465 U.S. at 673, 104 S.Ct. 1355; see also Schempp, 374 U.S. at 294, 83 S.Ct. 1560 ("[T]he line we must draw between the permissible and the impermissible is one which accords with history and faithfully reflects the understanding of the Founding Fathers.") (Brennan, J., concurring).

The majority's unpersuasive and problematic disclaimers notwithstanding, Newdow II precipitates a "war with our national tradition," McCollum v. Bd. of Ed., 333 U.S. 203, 211, 68 S.Ct. 461, 92 L.Ed. 649 (1948), and as Judge Fernandez so eloquently points out in dissent, only the purest exercise in sophistry could save multiple references to our religious heritage in our national life from Newdow II's axe. Of course, the Constitution itself explicitly mentions God, as does the Declaration of Independence, the document which marked us as a separate people. The Gettysburg Address, inconveniently for the majority, contains the same precise phrase — "under God" — found to constitute an Establishment Clause violation in the Pledge.[12] After Newdow II, are we to suppose that, were a school to permit — not require — the recitation of the Constitution, the Declaration of Independence, or the Gettysburg Address in public schools, that too would violate the Constitution? Were the "founders of the United States ... unable to understand their own handiwork[?]" Sherman, 980 F.2d at 445. Indeed, the recitation of the Declaration of Independence would seem to be the better candidate for the chopping block than the Pledge, since the Pledge does not require anyone to acknowledge the personal relationship with God to which the Declaration speaks.[13] So too with our National Anthem and our National Motto.

Our national celebration of Thanksgiving dates back to President Washington, which Congress stated was "to be observed by acknowledgment with grateful hearts, the many and signal favours of Almighty God." Lynch, 465 U.S. at 675 n. 2, 104 S.Ct. 1355. Congress made Thanksgiving a permanent holiday in 1941,[14] and Christmas has been a national holiday since 1894.[15] Are pere Newdow's constitutional rights violated when his daughter is told not to attend school on Thanksgiving? On Christmas day? Must school outings to federal courts be prohibited, lest the children be unduly influenced by the dreaded intonation "God save these United States and this honorable Court"?[16] A theory of the Establishment Clause that would have the effect of driving out of our public life the multiple references to the Divine that run through our laws, our rituals, and our ceremonies is no theory at all.

B

As if all of this were not enough, the Supreme Court has gone out of its way to make it plain that the Pledge itself passes constitutional muster. In two of the school prayer cases, the Court noted without so much as a hint of disapproval the fact that the students, in addition to being subject to formal religious observances, also recited the Pledge of Allegiance. See Schempp, 374 U.S. at 207-08, 83 S.Ct. 1560 (noting that the practice in public schools consisted of Bible reading and recitation of the Lord's prayer, followed by recitation of the Pledge); Lee, 505 U.S. at 583, 112 S.Ct. 2649 (noting that "the students stood for the Pledge of Allegiance and remained standing during the rabbi's prayers.").

Several other Supreme Court cases contain explicit references to the constitutionality of the Pledge. See Engel, 370 U.S. at 440 n. 5, 82 S.Ct. 1261 (Douglas, J., concurring) ("[The Pledge] in no way run[s] contrary to the First Amendment") (quoting H.R. Rep. No. 1693, 83d Cong., 2d Sess., p. 3); Schempp, 374 U.S. at 304, 83 S.Ct. 1560 (Brennan, J., concurring) ("[R]eciting the pledge may be no more of a religious exercise than the reading aloud of Lincolns' Gettysburg Address."); Wallace, 472 U.S. at 78 n. 5, 105 S.Ct. 2479 (O'Connor, J., concurring) ("[T]he words `under God' in the Pledge ... serve as an acknowledgment of religion."); Co. of Allegheny v. ACLU, 492 U.S. 573, 602-03, 109 S.Ct. 3086, 106 L.Ed.2d 472 (Blackmun, J., for the court) ("Our previous opinions have considered in dicta ... the pledge, characterizing [it] as consistent with the proposition that government may not communicate an endorsement of religious belief."); Lynch v. Donnelly, 465 U.S. 668, 676, 104 S.Ct. 1355, 79 L.Ed.2d 604 (1984) (Burger, C.J., for the court) ("Other examples of reference to our religious heritage are found ... in the language `One nation under God,' as part of the Pledge of Allegiance to the American flag. That pledge is recited by many thousands of public school children — and adults — every year.").

The panel majority's answer to these myriad statements from our high court is summarily to dismiss them as dicta. However, "dicta of the Supreme Court have a weight that is greater than ordinary judicial dicta as prophecy of what that Court might hold. We should not blandly shrug them off because they were not a holding." Zal v. Steppe, 968 F.2d 924, 935 (9th Cir. 1992) (Noonan, J., concurring and dissenting in part); see also United States v. Baird, 85 F.3d 450, 453 (9th Cir.1996) ("[W]e treat Supreme Court dicta with due deference.").[17]

C

The Newdow II majority, then, finds itself caught between a rock and a hard place — the recitation of the Pledge is not a formal religious act, while patriotic invocations of God do not give rise to Establishment Clause violations. It nonetheless manages to skirt these obstacles to reach its indirect coercion analysis. Newdow II's conclusory foray into the social sciences is a case study, an advertisement, for why it is that the Supreme Court has anchored coercion analysis only to those situations where "formal religious exercises" take place in our public schools. The panel majority seeks to protect dissenters at the risk of courting some unpopularity, but this is not the test. "[O]ffense alone does not in every case show a violation .... and sometimes to endure social isolation or even anger may be the price of conscience or nonconformity." Lee, 505 U.S. at 597-98, 112 S.Ct. 2649. The Newdow II majority's expansive application of the coercion test is ill-suited to a society as diverse as ours, since almost every cultural practice is bound to offend someone's sensibilities. In affording Michael Newdow the right to impose his views on others, Newdow II affords him a right to be fastidiously intolerant and self-indulgent. In granting him this supposed right, moreover, the two-judge panel majority has not eliminated feelings of discomfort and isolation, it has simply shifted them from one group to another.

Newdow II's psychological ipse dixit is also delivered without reference or regard to our collective experience in the half-century since the passage of the offending statute. In that time, generations of Americans have grown up reciting the Pledge, religious tolerance and diversity has flourished in this country, and we have become a beacon for other nations in this regard. As Judge Fernandez observes, "it is difficult to detect any signs of incipient theocracy springing up since the Pledge was amended in 1954." Newdow I, 292 F.3d at 614 n. 4 (Fernandez, J., dissenting).

IV

In fairness to the Newdow II panel majority, its professed "neutrality" does have some plausible basis in the case law of the Supreme Court, which has undoubtedly constructed a "fractured and incoherent doctrinal path" in the Establishment Clause area, broadly speaking. Sep. of Church and State Comm. v. City of Eugene, 93 F.3d 617, 622 (9th Cir.1996) (O'Scannlain, J., concurring). Indeed, its Establishment Clause cases sometimes "more closely resemble ad hoc Delphic pronouncements than models of guiding legal principles." Ingebretsen v. Jackson Pub. Sch. Dist., 88 F.3d 274, 282 (5th Cir.1996) (Jones, J., dissenting from denial of rehearing en banc). Supreme Court Justices themselves have recognized that if some of its reasoning "were to be applied logically, it would lead to the elimination" of many cherished, long-standing practices. Co. of Allegheny, 492 U.S. at 674 n. 10, 109 S.Ct. 3086 (Kennedy, J., dissenting).

With respect to the issue presented in this case, however, the Supreme Court has displayed remarkable consistency — patriotic invocations of God simply have no tendency to establish a state religion. Even Justice Brennan, that most stalwart of separationists, recognized that some official acknowledgment of God is appropriate "if the government is not to adopt a stilted indifference to the religious life of the people." Lynch, 465 U.S. at 714, 104 S.Ct. 1355 (Brennan, J., dissenting). The decision reached in Newdow II does precisely that: it adopts a stilted indifference to our past and present realities as a predominantly religious people.

But Newdow II goes further, and confers a favored status on atheism in our public life. In a society with a pervasive public sector, our public schools are a most important means for transmitting ideas and values to future generations. The silence the majority commands is not neutral — it itself conveys a powerful message, and creates a distorted impression about the place of religion in our national life.[18] The absolute prohibition on any mention of God in our schools creates a bias against religion. The panel majority cannot credibly advance the notion that Newdow II is neutral with respect to belief versus non-belief; it affirmatively favors the latter to the former. One wonders, then, does atheism become the default religion protected by the Establishment Clause?

In short, a lack of clarity in the Supreme Court's Establishment Clause cases generally does not help to explain or to justify the panel majority's decision with respect to this particular issue. Put simply, the panel was asked to decide whether the recitation of the Pledge of Allegiance in public schools amounted to a government establishment of religion. The answer to that question is clearly, obviously, no. We made a grave error in failing to take Newdow I en banc, and we have failed to correct that error ourselves. Now we have Newdow II. Perhaps the Supreme Court will have the opportunity to correct the error for us. I must respectfully dissent from the order denying reconsideration en banc.

Judge O'Scannlain's concurrence and dissent in McEuin v. Crown Equipment Corp. (April 24, 2003)

O'SCANNLAIN, Circuit Judge, concurring in part and dissenting in part.

Because I readily agree with my colleagues that the military specifications were properly excluded, I join Parts I, II, and III.A.1 of the majority opinion. I believe the district court abused its discretion in refusing to admit the engineering reports, however, and therefore I must respectfully dissent from Part III.A.2.

To recover punitive damages, the plaintiff had to prove by clear and convincing evidence that the defendant acted with wanton disregard for the health, safety, and welfare of others. See O.R.S. §§ 18.537, 30.925. The plaintiff built his case for punitives on evidence tending to show that the defendant had wilfully disregarded its own accident data, ignored applicable safety standards, and lied to purchasers of its equipment, all as a part of an overall strategy to stave off product liability litigation. In response to these charges of bad faith, the defendant offered evidence that it had commissioned two independent engineering reports. These reports recommended against the installation of doors because the addition of doors would cause more injuries, and more serious injuries. The district court excluded the reports, however, and the jury returned a punitive damages award of $1.25 million.

Federal Rule of Evidence 403 provides,

Although relevant, evidence may be excluded if its probative value is substantially outweighed by the danger of unfair prejudice, confusion of the issues, or misleading the jury, or by considerations of undue delay, waste of time, or needless presentation of cumulative evidence.[1]

The significance of the independent reports is obvious. The plaintiff argued that Crown acted with reckless indifference in failing to include a forklift door, and that Crown ignored its own accident data, which allegedly showed a clear need for a door. Crown's retention of multiple, independent consultants directly counters this theory of the case, and strongly supports its contention that it did not close its eyes to the need for a door. Rather, the reports tend to show that Crown went to the expense and trouble to solicit an independent assessment with regard to the wisdom of adding doors to its forklift design. The fact that both of the independent consultants, after detailed analysis, recommended against the addition of doors is strong evidence that Crown did not act in bad faith.

The only factor the district court pointed to in excluding the reports was that they were hearsay as to liability,[2] and that therefore the jury may consider them for an improper purpose. To be sure, this is a legitimate concern, but it is one that could have been negated by the issuance of a limiting instruction. See Fed.R.Evid. 105 ("When evidence is admissible ... for one purpose but not admissible ... for another purpose ..., the court, upon request, shall restrict the evidence to its proper scope and instruct the jury accordingly."). Indeed, the defendant urged to the district court to admit the reports with a proper limiting instruction. Given the unquestioned significance of the reports, the district court's failure to admit them with a proper limiting instruction was an error.

That error was prejudicial. See Freeman v. Allstate Life Ins. Co., 253 F.3d 533, 536 (9th Cir.2001) (reversal required where evidentiary rulings result in prejudice). While the district court allowed Crown's engineer to testify that he relied upon the views of outside consultants, the impact of the reports was lost because the jury was not allowed to review them directly. The jury was unable to observe that the reports were comprehensive and obviously prepared by experts in the field. Nor was the jury able to view the substance of the reports, which directly supports Crown's contention that it, in good faith, believed the addition of a door would make its forklifts more dangerous.

That the failure to admit the reports was prejudicial to the defendant is apparent when one considers the plaintiff's closing argument, where counsel argued that Crown did not "objectively reach a decision as to whether doors are a good thing or not." The reports Crown commissioned provide a direct and highly relevant counter-point to this argument, but because of their exclusion, Crown was left with no comeback. The jury might well have come to a different conclusion on the issue of punitive damages had the district court admitted the reports with a proper limiting instruction, and in my view, "the lower court's error tainted the verdict." Tennison v. Circus Circus Enters., Inc., 244 F.3d 684, 688 (9th Cir.2001).

I am not unmindful of the fact that the district court, as it should, is afforded a great deal of discretion in making Rule 403 determinations. But that discretion is not unfettered. See, e.g., United States v. Crosby, 75 F.3d 1343, 1349(9th Cir.1996) (district court abused discretion in refusing to admit evidence pursuant to Rule 403); United States v. Blaylock, 20 F.3d 1458, 1464 (9th Cir.1994) (same); Baker v. Delta Air Lines, Inc., 6 F.3d 632, 642 (9th Cir. 1993) (same); United States v. Armstrong, 621 F.2d 951, 953 (9th Cir.1980) (same). Where, as here, the probative value of the excluded evidence is great, and the danger that the evidence will be considered for an improper purpose is slight, and easily mitigated by the issuance of a proper instruction, Rule 403 requires that the evidence should be admitted. See 2 James B. Weinstein et al., Weinstein's Federal Evidence § 403.02[2][c] (2d ed.2003) (discussing the preference under Rule 403 for admissibility).

In sum, I respectfully dissent from the decision to exclude the independent engineering reports. Because I would reverse for a new trial, I would not reach the issue as to whether the district court correctly denied the motion for a new trial on the issue of punitive damages.

Notes

[1] In excluding the independent reports, the district court misstated the standard for admissibility, stating that "it's a question, under Rule 403, whether the relevancy of those documents outweighs its potential prejudicial value." In doing so, the district court impermissibly placed the burden on Crown to show that the reports' probative value

outweighed any potential for prejudice. While we have held that a district court abuses its discretion when it fails to apply the correct legal standard, see Bateman v. U.S. Postal Serv., 231 F.3d 1220, 1223-24 (9th Cir.2000), it may well be the case that the district court simply misspoke, and that it understood and applied the correct governing standard. It is not necessary to reverse on that ground because, even if the district court got the standard right, it gave insufficient weight to the high probative value of the reports, and its decision to exclude the reports tainted the jury's verdict.

[2] The majority suggests that because the reports are hearsay as to liability, they are only admissible because they come within Rule 803's `state of mind' exception. With respect, this is wrong. Whether an item of evidence is hearsay depends on the purpose for which it is offered. See Fed.R.Evid. 801(c). The reports may be hearsay as to liability, but they are not hearsay as to the claim for punitive damages. This is so because the purpose of the offer is not to prove the truth of the matter asserted in the reports, but to show that Crown engaged in a good faith decision-making process. See Keisling v. SER-Jobs for Progress, Inc., 19 F.3d 755, 762 (1st Cir.1994) (affirming district court's decision to admit out-of-court statements because not being offered to prove truth of matter asserted, but to negate allegations of bad faith); Worsham v. A.H. Robins Co., 734 F.2d 676, 686 (11th Cir.1984) (affirming district court's decision to admit reports in a products liability action because reports offered only for purpose of showing notice, and not to prove truth of matters asserted in the reports). Therefore, for the purpose of showing Crown's good faith, the reports do not come within the definition of hearsay, and the majority's reliance on Rule 803 is misplaced.

Judge O'Scannlain's concurrence and dissent in Ostad v. Oregon Health Sciences University (April 28, 2003)

O'SCANNLAIN, Circuit Judge, concurring in part and dissenting in part:

I agree that the district court did not err in denying the motion for judgment as a matter of law (and that OHSU has waived any right to have its liability considered separate from that of Seyfer's). Furthermore, I agree that the district court did not abuse its discretion in any of the contested evidentiary rulings. Accordingly, I concur in Parts I, II-A, II-B.2, and II-C of the opinion. However, because I would hold that Seyfer and OHSU are entitled to a new trial on the basis of an improper jury instruction, I must dissent from Part II-B.1.

"Under the dual motive test, a plaintiff must show that her protected activities were a `substantial factor' in the complained of adverse employment action. Protected activities are a `substantial factor' where the adverse actions would not have been taken `but for' the protected activities." Knickerbocker v. City of Stockton, 81 F.3d 907, 911 (9th Cir.1996). Our decision in Gilbrook v. City of Westminster, 177 F.3d 839 (9th Cir.1999), reaches a similar conclusion: "[A] subordinate cannot use the nonretaliatory motive of a superior as a shield against liability if that superior never would have considered a dismissal but for the subordinate's retaliatory conduct." Id. at 855 (emphasis added). Seyfer and OHSU requested a jury instruction to this effect,[1] which the district court denied. As it was a correct statement of the law, the district court's failure to give it was an abuse of discretion that was not harmless.

The district court did properly instruct the jury that in order to prevail on the retaliation claim, Ostad's protected activities had to be a "substantial or motivating factor" in his termination. Unfortunately, in response to a query from the jury concerning the definitions of "substantial" and "motivating," the court erred in subsequently instructing the jurors that the protected conduct needed only to be a "significant factor" in the termination. This latter instruction sets the bar too low as a matter of law.

Failure to require that the subordinate's retaliatory conduct have played a substantial role in the unbiased decisionmaker's deliberations runs the risk of immunizing a plaintiff who rightfully should be terminated. If a malevolent subordinate brings genuine misconduct to the attention of an unbiased decisionmaker, that decisionmaker should still be able to terminate the plaintiff for the unrelated malevolence. It is precisely for such circumstances that the burden of establishing liability is considerably higher than a finding that the protected activities were only "a significant factor."

Therefore, I would reverse the district court and remand for a new trial so that a jury could evaluate Seyfer's and OHSU's conduct under the proper legal standard.

Notes

[1] The defendants requested the following jury instruction: "An improper motive is a `substantial or motivating' factor in the termination if the termination would not have occurred except for the improper motive." Supra at 884.

Judge O'Scannlain's dissent in Jenkins v. Johnson (May 20, 2003)

O'SCANNLAIN, Circuit Judge, dissenting:

The court holds that Jenkins's state post-conviction petition was "properly filed" within the meaning of 28 U.S.C. § 2244(d)(2) on the basis of a purported ambiguity in Oregon law that existed at the time of filing of his petition for relief but has since been clarified. I respectfully disagree. The plain meaning of Oregon statutory law was perfectly clear, and we are bound to follow it. Accordingly, I would affirm the district court, and hold that Jenkins was not entitled to statutory tolling and that his federal petition was therefore untimely under AEDPA.

I

At issue, of course, is whether Jenkins is entitled to statutory tolling under § 2244(d)(2), thereby rendering his writ of federal habeas corpus timely. Statutory tolling applies to "[t]he time during which a properly filed application for State post-conviction or other collateral review with respect to the pertinent judgment or claim is pending." 28 U.S.C. § 2244(d)(2) (emphasis added). A petition is "properly filed" within the meaning of

§ 2244(d)(2) if it satisfies certain procedural requirements known as "conditions to filing." Artuz v. Bennett, 531 U.S. 4, 11, 121 S.Ct. 361, 148 L.Ed.2d 213 (2000). Other requirements, which incorporate some aspect of the merits of the petition, are termed "conditions to obtaining relief." Id. Failure to comply with this latter set of requirements does not render the petition improperly filed for purposes of § 2244(d)(2). Id.

In the context of Jenkins's petition for relief, we are thus confronted with the issue of whether a statute of limitations for the filing of a state petition is properly classified as a "condition to filing" or a "condition to obtaining relief." If compliance with the timeliness requirement is a "condition to filing," then Jenkins is not entitled to statutory tolling for the pendency of his state petition for relief because it was not "properly filed" pursuant to § 2244(d)(2).

In Dictado v. Ducharme, 244 F.3d 724, 728 (9th Cir.2001), we held that a state statute prescribing a timely filing requirement constituted a "condition to obtaining relief" if it "contain[ed] exceptions [requiring] a state court to examine the merits of a petition before it is dismissed." Accordingly, under Dictado, a statute of limitations is ordinarily a "condition to filing," which does not warrant statutory tolling, unless it contains a good cause exception or some similar provision that entails a review of the merits.

II

Turning to the case at hand, the Oregon statute of limitations for post-conviction petitions has two pertinent subsections. See Or.Rev.Stat. § 138.510. Subsection (2), applicable to would-be petitioners whose convictions became final after a certain date, provides for a good cause exception. Subsection (3), which applies to would-be petitioners (including Jenkins) convicted before the specified date, contains no such exception; it is a flat one-year time bar.

In 1992, before subsection (3) was enacted, the Oregon Supreme Court upheld the constitutionality of subsection (2). See Bartz v. State, 314 Or. 353, 839 P.2d 217 (1992) (en banc). In a unanimous opinion, the court stated that the limitations period for filing petitions (then 120 days, now two years) was constitutionally permissible. The court found "that the 120 day period of limitation[,] ... which incorporates an exception in certain circumstances, does not prevent the available procedure from being reasonable for persons who seek redress." Id. at 225.

Extending the Oregon Supreme Court's pronouncement in Bartz to this case, the majority remarkably recites that it was unclear whether a good cause exception also applied to subsection (3). The majority divines that an ambiguity existed until the Oregon Court of Appeals in Wallis v. Baldwin, 152 Or.App. 295, 954 P.2d 192 (1998) explicitly rejected the idea that subsection (3) impliedly contains a good-cause exception like the one expressly contained in subsection (2). Because Wallis was decided after Jenkins's untimely petition to the Oregon courts (filed in 1996), the majority bootstraps the claim that the "clarity" that Wallis brought to the law does not bar Jenkins's untimely petition.

This argument might conceivably have some merit in some other circumstance, as where there was a genuine ambiguity in the state procedural rule and the record indicated that, before the clarifying decision, the state courts treated the rule as a "condition to obtaining relief" rather than a "condition to filing." However, there simply is no such ambiguity in this case. Subsection (3) required those convicted before August 5, 1989, who had not previously filed a petition for post-conviction relief, to file their petitions before November 4, 1994. That gave the petitioners over five years, which is ample for constitutional purposes, as the Wallis court duly recognized.

In evaluating the constitutionality of old subsection (2), the Oregon Supreme Court stated that "a reasonable time limitation may be placed on the assertion of a state constitutional claim." Bartz, 839 P.2d at 225. The court further stated, "The 120-day limit, when combined with the exception, provides a reasonable opportunity to seek post-conviction relief." Id. Accordingly, the court in Bartz merely decided the reasonableness of subsection (2), a legislatively enacted 120-day limit which contained a good cause exception.

Nevertheless, the majority interprets the Oregon Supreme Court's holding in Bartz as injecting an ambiguity into the statutory scheme such that the plain meaning of subsection (3) is to be ignored. The majority infers from Bartz that any time limit without an express good cause exception would be unconstitutional. Accordingly, the majority reasons that until Wallis was handed down subsection (3) must be read to include such an exception, even though its text contains no such thing. This interpretation of Bartz stretches far beyond a reasonable limit and constitutes a stunning departure from the scheme enacted by the Oregon legislature. Indeed, since subsection (3) was enacted after Bartz, the Oregon Legislature knew of the holding in that case and understood, presumably better than we do, the import of Bartz.

III

Therefore, I must dissent from the conclusion that subsection (3) "was not an adequate state ground of decision for procedural bar purposes prior to Wallis." Supra at 1153.[1] The text of subsection (3) is clear on its face and does not allow us to insinuate an ambiguity where none exists.

Notes

[1] It also seems to me that the bar contained in the second sentence of § 138.510(3) posed a "condition to filing" and would deny Jenkins's claim for statutory tolling. The clear import of the statutory text is that second or successive petitions by prisoners convicted before 1989 are absolutely barred. See Or. Rev.Stat. § 138.510(3) ("A person whose post-conviction petition was dismissed prior to November 4, 1993, cannot file another post-conviction petition involving the same case."). Nevertheless, I agree with the majority that this argument has been waived because the State disclaimed reliance — for reasons that are beyond me — on this provision at oral argument.

Judge O'Scannlain's dissent in Alvarez-Machain v. US (June 3, 2003)

O'SCANNLAIN, Circuit Judge, with whom Circuit Judges RYMER, KLEINFELD, and TALLMAN join, dissenting:

We are now in the midst of a global war on terrorism, a mission that our political branches have deemed necessary to conduct throughout the world, sometimes with tepid or even non-existent cooperation from foreign nations. With this context in mind, our court today commands that a foreign-national criminal who was apprehended abroad pursuant to a legally valid indictment is entitled to sue our government for money damages. In so doing, and despite its protestations to the contrary, the majority has left the door open for the objects of our international war on terrorism to do the same.[1]

What makes this astounding pronouncement even more perverse is that our court divines the entitlement to recovery from the Alien Tort Claims Act ("ATCA"), 28 U.S.C. § 1350, a statute first enacted over 200 years ago by members of the First Congress, many of whom were Framers of our nation's Constitution. With utmost respect to the majority, there is simply no basis in our nation's law for this bewildering result, and the implications for our national security are so ominous that I must dissent.

I

Notwithstanding the majority's lengthy disquisitions concerning various theories and sources of international law, the central issue in this case is very simple: Do American law enforcement agents violate well-established principles of American jurisprudence when they apprehend a duly-indicted suspect outside the confines of our nation's borders?[2] The answer is clearly no; the United States has neither now nor ever agreed to an asserted international law principle prohibiting the practice of transborder abduction.[3]

The majority, perhaps overlooking the grandeur of the forest while gazing with much admiration at the trees, meanders through various sources which suggest how pleasant it would be if transborder abduction were actionable. However, the majority's searching inquiry into the scope of international law is simply unnecessary. The ATCA is a congressionally enacted statute; accordingly, international law in this context must first and foremost comport with American case law and congressional intent, rather than be defined by the amorphous expressions of other countries or international experts. In other words, no claim can be actionable under the ATCA based on a norm to which the United States itself does not subscribe.

I do not suggest that the majority's inquiry into the status of transborder arrest in the broader international community — which Congress, by enacting the ATCA, has directed us to perform in appropriate cases — is one beyond the federal courts' ability to undertake. Indeed, some areas of substantial international unanimity are easily recognized. See, e.g., Trajano v. Marcos (In re Estate of Ferdinand E. Marcos Human Rights Litig.) ("Marcos I"), 978 F.2d 493, 500 (9th Cir.1992). Nevertheless, I believe that in many cases, as in this one, it will be far easier to determine whether the United States subscribes to a given norm than whether other countries do, and accordingly the former inquiry should appropriately precede the latter.

II

I respectfully suggest that the majority has imprudently ignored the relevant underpinnings of the ATCA. As demonstrated below, a proper historical understanding of the ATCA compels the conclusion that no claim can prevail where the United States, through its political branches, does not acquiesce in an international norm.

A

First enacted as part of the Judiciary Act of 1789, the ATCA still reads today almost exactly as the First Congress drafted it; the version currently enshrined in Title 28 provides: "The district courts shall have original jurisdiction of any civil action by an alien for a tort only, committed in violation of the law of nations or a treaty of the United States." 28 U.S.C. § 1350 (1994); see Judiciary Act of Sept. 24, 1789, ch. 20, § 9(b), 1 Stat. 73, 77.

The ATCA was, from the beginning, a curious provision. As one eminent scholar of both federal jurisdiction and American legal history notes, the ATCA was one of only two provisions of the Judiciary Act that "arguably g[a]ve federal courts jurisdiction over judicial matters outside the enumeration of Article III." David P. Currie, The Constitution in Congress: The Federalist Period 1789-1801, at 51-52 (1997).[4] Perhaps because of the singular nature of its jurisdictional grant, the ATCA was infrequently used for almost two hundred years, until fairly recently when courts have eagerly exploited the opportunity to revivify it.

In the course of this resurgence of a statutory provision that lay largely dormant since our nation's founding, our court has determined that certain international law principles may be incorporated into federal common law, and thereby into the ATCA as well. See Hilao v. Estate of Marcos (In re Estate of Ferdinand Marcos, Human Rights Litig.) ("Marcos II"), 25 F.3d 1467, 1475 (9th Cir.1994). The Marcos II court set out the standard for evaluating whether an ATCA plaintiff states a claim: "Actionable violations of international law must be of a norm that is specific, universal, and obligatory." Id; accord, e.g., Papa v. United States, 281 F.3d 1004, 1013 (9th Cir.2002); Martinez v. City of Los Angeles, 141 F.3d 1373, 1383-84 (9th Cir.1998).

B

The requirement of "universality" constitutes an insurmountable bar to recovery for transborder arrest.[5] I focus in particular on the corollary of this requirement: a norm of international law not recognized by the United States cannot be deemed a universal one, actionable in this nation's courts.

We have previously noted the importance of determining whether a norm of international law is recognized by the United States. See Martinez, 141 F.3d at 1383 ("To determine whether this tort satisfies the requirement for a tort claim under the Alien Tort Act, we must decide `[1] whether there is an applicable norm of international law [proscribing such a tort] ... recognized by the United States ... and [2] whether [that tort] was violated in [this] particular case.'" (quoting Marcos I, 978 F.2d at 502 (alterations in original) (emphasis added))). Marcos I did not state this requirement explicitly, but the exposition of the constitutional basis for the ATCA, see supra at 612, makes clear that the Martinez court correctly recognized that ATCA jurisdiction subsumes it.

Federal common law is a means of preserving a uniform national construction of rights and obligations within a given area of the law even in the absence of a detailed statutory scheme. See, e.g., Tex. Indus., Inc. v. Radcliff Materials, Inc., 451 U.S. 630, 640-41, 101 S.Ct. 2061, 68 L.Ed.2d 500 (1981). This consideration carries particular force in the foreign policy context in which the ATCA lies; it was passed, let us remember, in 1789, only months after the First Congress convened. The Framers, and presumably those who went on to serve the new government, were acutely conscious of the need for the national government's interpretation of the law of nations to be controlling. See, e.g., The Federalist No. 3, at 43 (John Jay), No. 80, at 476-77, 478 (Alexander Hamilton) (Clinton Rossiter ed., 1961). Yet one equally basic characteristic of federal common law is that Congress may supplant it as the rule of decision, because the power to legislate rests most properly with the elected representatives who possess both the greater competence and the greater authority, conferred by the people, to wield it. And the same is no less true with regard to the law of nations as federal common law; indeed, foreign policymaking is essentially confided not merely to the national government writ large, but to its political branches in particular.[6] E.g., Chi. & S. Air Lines, Inc. v. Waterman S.S. Corp., 333 U.S. 103, 111, 68 S.Ct. 431, 92 L.Ed. 568 (1948); Oetjen v. Cent. Leather Co., 246 U.S. 297, 302, 38 S.Ct. 309, 62 L.Ed. 726 (1918); see Banco Nacional de Cuba v. Sabbatino, 376 U.S. 398, 423, 84 S.Ct. 923, 11 L.Ed.2d 804 (1964).

The Framers and the First Congress viewed the United States's substantial adoption of the law of nations as furthering their intention that the new nation take its place among the civilized nations of the world. E.g., Chisholm v. Georgia, 2 U.S. (2 Dall.) 419, 474, 1 L.Ed. 440 (1793) (opinion of Jay, C.J.). Yet they clearly did not mean for the law of nations to act as an irrevocably binding constraint on the law and policy-making authority of the national government. In his last contribution as Publius, John Jay famously recognized the binding nature of treaties, and a number of the Framers shared his view that treaties created a binding obligation on the contracting parties under the law of nations. The Federalist No. 64, at 394 (John Jay); see, e.g., Note, Restructuring the Modern Treaty Power, 114 Harv. L. Rev. 2478, 2484-90 (2001) (discussing the Framers' views). But the law of nations imposed constraints "in point of moral obligation," not restrictions on national policymakers' power to breach. Ware v. Hylton, 3 U.S. (3 Dall.) 199, 272, 1 L.Ed. 568 (1796) (opinion of Iredell, J.). The Framers intended that the United States would have the power, if not necessarily the right under the law of nations, to violate or even to repudiate aspects of the law of nations, provided it were willing to face the consequences of its breach, possibly including war.[7] And it was for this reason that the power to violate or to repudiate, like the power over foreign affairs generally, was confided to the national government. See The Federalist No. 80, supra, at 476 ("[T]he peace of the WHOLE ought not to be left at the disposal of a PART. The Union will undoubtedly be answerable to foreign powers for the conduct of its members. And the responsibility for an injury ought ever to be accompanied with the faculty of preventing it."). The federal common law's incorporation of the law of nations, in short, is not beyond the political branches' power to alter. And this fact is entirely consonant with the principle, expressed in our cases as elsewhere, that "[c]ustomary international law, like international law defined by treaties and other international agreements, rests on the consent of states." Siderman de Blake v. Republic of Argentina, 965 F.2d 699, 715 (9th Cir.1992); see id. ("A state that persistently objects to a norm of customary international law that other states accept is not bound by that norm ...." (citing Restatement (Third) of the Foreign Relations Law of the United States [hereinafter Restatement] § 102 cmt. d)).

Therefore, where the political branches have exercised their power to diverge from the course that others see the law of nations as setting, ATCA liability cannot lie. The ATCA's conformity with Article III rests on the incorporation of the law of nations as federal common law — particularly in a case like this one, where neither alienage, nor admiralty, nor any of the other headings of Article III provides a basis for federal jurisdiction. It is for this reason that an ATCA plaintiff relying on the law of nations (as opposed to a treaty) must allege a tort that violates some norm of international law recognized by the United States.

At least one of the few Supreme Court opinions to consider the ATCA directly appears to have recognized as much. In O'Reilly De Camara v. Brooke, 209 U.S. 45, 28 S.Ct. 439, 52 L.Ed. 676 (1908), Justice Holmes wrote for a unanimous Court in affirming the dismissal of an ATCA complaint that alleged the tortious destruction of a hereditary title during the Spanish-American War. Id. at 48-49, 28 S.Ct. 439. Although the Court did not directly decide whether the plaintiff had alleged a tort cognizable under the ATCA, see id. at 52-53, 28 S.Ct. 439, it did make the following comment on that question: "[W]e think it plain that where, as here, the jurisdiction of the case depends upon the establishment of a `tort only in violation of the law of nations, or of a treaty of the United States,' it is impossible for the courts to declare an act a tort of that kind when the Executive, Congress, and the treaty-making power all have adopted the act." Id. at 52, 28 S.Ct. 439.

Such analysis fits with our case law's incorporation of the requirement that an actionable norm of international law be "universal." The case at hand does not require us to delineate the bare minimum level of acceptance that would constitute "universality"; instead, it invokes the simple proposition, stated explicitly in Martinez and implicitly in other cases, that in determining whether a norm is "universal," the United States is to be counted as a part of the universe. A norm to which the political branches of our government have refused to assent is not a universal norm. It is not the judiciary's place to enforce such a norm contrary to their will.[8]

C

The majority fails to take into account these fundamental principles, which invoke the historical understanding in which the ATCA was passed and the proper role of the political branches in determining our nation's actions as they relate to national security.

As a result, the majority's analysis of the status of transborder arrest as an instrument of law enforcement — which has great bearing on its treatment of Alvarez's alternative claim for relief for arbitrary arrest — is seriously flawed because it ignores the baseline proposition that it is easier for this court to determine whether the United States agrees with a norm than to determine whether a preponderance of the world's other nations does.

Let us recall the particular circumstances of the case at hand. Alvarez was charged in 1990 with, among other offenses, the kidnaping[9] and felony murder of a federal agent in violation of 18 U.S.C. §§ 1114(1) and 1201(a)(5). See, e.g., Alvarez-Machain II, 504 U.S. at 657 n. 1, 112 S.Ct. 2188. The kidnaping statute appears to contemplate the exercise of federal criminal jurisdiction over certain defendants who are neither Americans nor found in the United States. See 18 U.S.C. § 1201(e) (2000) (authorizing the exercise of jurisdiction over defendants if they are American nationals, if they are found in the United States, or "if the victim is a representative, officer, employee, or agent of the United States"). Notwithstanding the majority's assertions to the contrary, the general statutes governing the operation of the Drug Enforcement Administration confer on DEA agents the authority to "make arrests without warrant ... for any felony, cognizable under the laws of the United States, if [an agent] has probable cause to believe that the person to be arrested has committed or is committing a felony." 21 U.S.C. § 878(a)(3) (2000). DEA agents may also "perform such other law enforcement duties as the Attorney General may designate." Id. § 878(a)(5).

This statutory framework confers on the DEA agents the same degree of authority to act extraterritorially that we have previously held INS agents to possess. See United States v. Chen, 2 F.3d 330 (9th Cir.1993). In Chen, we considered whether the INS was authorized to conduct criminal law enforcement activity outside the United States. We held that "Congress need not confer such authority explicitly and directly on the INS agents themselves." Id. at 333. We inferred from Congress's broad grant of authority to the Attorney General to enforce the immigration laws,[10] and from the extraterritorial applicability of those laws, that the enforcement power extended where the laws themselves extended. See id. at 333-34.

Faced with our holding in Chen, Alvarez argues, and the majority erroneously agrees, that the criminal context presented in this case is distinguishable from the unique context of border security at issue in Chen. Yet the statutes at issue here bear just as directly on national security, particularly insofar as they relate to and promote the federal government's ability to enforce the drug laws, and to protect the agents who carry out that enforcement, no matter on which side of the border they may be threatened. And so our cases have recognized. "Our circuit has repeatedly approved extraterritorial application of statutes that prohibit the importation and distribution of controlled substances in the United States because these activities implicate national security interests and create a detrimental effect in the United States." United States v. Vasquez-Velasco, 15 F.3d 833, 841 (9th Cir. 1994). As we stated in another prosecution arising from the Camarena abduction and murder: "We have no doubt that whether the kidnapping and murder of

[DEA] agents constitutes an offense against the United States is not dependent upon the locus of the act. We think it clear that Congress intended to apply statutes proscribing the kidnapping and murder of DEA agents extraterritorially." United States v. Felix-Gutierrez, 940 F.2d 1200, 1204 (9th Cir.1991).

Applying the reasoning of Chen to the statutes that protect American drug enforcement personnel leads to the inescapable conclusion that Congress has authorized federal agents enforcing those statutes to make warrantless arrests beyond our borders — a conclusion at odds with the argument that the United States respects a norm prohibiting transborder arrests.

Moreover, such a norm, which would render a transborder arrest violative of the law of nations absent the host country's consent, does not seem tenable either as a matter of statutory construction or as a reflection of Congress' likely goal. I can conceive of a number of situations in which the nature of the host country's government, or even the utter nonexistence of a functioning government, precludes obtaining the formal sanction of the local judiciary or of the host country. Indeed, in the months since September 11, 2001, the United States government has retrieved a number of individuals from lawless locales of this sort. See, e.g., Al Odah v. United States, 321 F.3d 1134 (D.C.Cir.2003). Therefore, the statutory authorization to make arrests overseas for violations of extraterritorially applicable law runs contrary to an alleged prohibition on transborder arrests.

It is true that in a number of other cases dealing with transborder arrests, the nation in which the arrest occurred did not object, even if it did not cooperate. While Mexico, by contrast, clearly and consistently protested Alvarez's seizure, it does not follow that the United States was obliged to comply with the processes of Mexico's judicial system.

One highly visible abduction, that like the case at hand also involved the extraterritorial enforcement of our nation's drug laws, refutes the notion that the United States has somehow divested itself of the authority to engage in transborder arrest without the consent of the host country. United States v. Noriega, 117 F.3d 1206 (11th Cir.1997), of course, dealt with the arrest of Panama's former strongman on drug-related charges. Id. at 1209-10.[11] Noriega was functioning "as the de facto, if not the de jure, leader of Panama" when the American military incursion to seize him occurred. Id. at 1211. Surely any protest from a Panamanian government controlled by Noriega himself could be disregarded, could it not, particularly if, as a matter of law, Noriega had forfeited his head-of-state immunity? See id. at 1212. Moreover — and herein lies the rub — the United States had consistently refused to acknowledge the legitimacy of Noriega's rule from its inception, which was after his indictment but well before the effort to retrieve him was ordered. Id. at 1209-10.

Therefore, irrespective of what various international law scholars and others may deem as advisable policy, these ruminations are of little consequence under the ATCA when the political branches of the United States have firmly decided on a course of action.

Examining the relevant statutes, the actions of the political branches in other circumstances, and as discussed by the majority, the manner in which the President and the Senate have exercised the treaty power in this area, see supra at 618-619, leads to only one conclusion: The United States does not, as a matter of law, consider itself forbidden by the law of nations to engage in extraterritorial arrest, but reserves the right to use this practice when necessary to enforce its criminal laws.[12]

III

If the majority had merely denied Alvarez's claims based on its exposition of international mores, I would be troubled by its failure to engage in a review of both the history behind the ATCA and the manner in which the political branches have exercised the option of transborder arrest in varied circumstances. But at least I would feel secure that we as judges had not improperly encroached upon the duties reserved for the political branches in formulating our nation's foreign policy. Most regrettably, by providing relief to Alvarez on his claim of prolonged arbitrary arrest, our court has in effect restricted the authority of our political branches, and it has done so in a way that finds no basis in our law.

A

The parties do not dispute that the prohibition on prolonged arbitrary detention is actionable under the ATCA. See Martinez, 141 F.3d at 1383-84. Nevertheless, the question remains whether the prohibition was violated in this case.

B

Notwithstanding its express recognition that the criminal statutes covering kidnaping, felony murder, and the other crimes involved in this case extend to conduct outside of the borders of the United States, the majority deems the government's action as "arbitrary."

The majority, although not expressly stating it as such, seems most troubled by the lack of Mexican authority for Alvarez's arrest. Indeed, imagine that the DEA had communicated with the Mexican government prior to seizing Alvarez and that such dialogue led to Mexican authorities assisting in the arrest, or acknowledging consent to the DEA's actions in some other manner. Under the majority's proffered approach the United States would be forced to compensate an alleged foreign-national criminal for "arbitrary arrest" within the meaning of the law of nations merely because the "wrong" Executive agency spearheaded the operation.

If Mexico had indeed sanctioned its actions, our court would not be subjecting the DEA to liability for successfully negotiating via diplomatic means the capture of a wanted criminal. Or would it? This simple hypothetical, however, underscores the fallacy of the majority's approach. Whether the United States procured an arrest warrant through the Mexican judiciary should not affect our analysis, because the availability of local process is extremely sensitive, bound up with important foreign policy considerations that are confided to the political branches in general and to the Executive in particular. Indeed, the majority elsewhere recognizes that "an individual's right to be free from transborder abductions has not reached a status of international accord sufficiently to render it `obligatory' or `universal,' [and therefore] cannot qualify as an actionable norm under the ATCA." Supra at 620.

Nevertheless, seemingly under the majority's approach, such extraterritorial arrest authority may still be subject to a requirement that any agents exercising it on foreign soil — as opposed to the high seas, as was the case in Chen, 2 F.3d at 332 — obtain the consent or assistance of the host country. The majority, in a rare moment of restraint, does recognize the "powers of the political branches to override the principles of sovereignty in some circumstances, should the need arise." Supra at 629 (emphasis added). However, the "need" to engage in transborder arrest without the prior consent of a foreign nation should appropriately be left to the discretion of the political branches.

Indeed, the federal courts are not charged with determining the legitimacy of another nation's government. Yet this is essentially what the majority would have us do. Under its approach, the United States would have departed from the ostensibly black-and-white approach that sanctions transborder arrests when employed by our nation's political branches. In its place, a decision to make a transborder arrest would only be permissible when the host country's system of government absolutely requires it, as determined by this country's courts through the medium of ATCA litigation. As judges, we would have to determine whether a nation's courts are open and functioning; whether it has a legitimate government that can be consulted for permission to seize a suspect; if there are multiple contenders, see, e.g., Noriega, 117 F.3d at 1209-10, to which one such a request must be addressed; and so on. Courts are quite unsuited to undertake such analyses, and, indeed, to do so would bring us perilously close to trenching on the power of diplomatic recognition that Article II, Section 3 places at the core of the Executive's foreign affairs authority. See, e.g., Guaranty Trust Co. v. United States, 304 U.S. 126, 137-38, 58 S.Ct. 785, 82 L.Ed. 1224 (1938); Oetjen, 246 U.S. at 302-03, 38 S.Ct. 309.

I am simply not prepared to declare that Congress intended that any alien charged with a crime, under extraterritorially applicable U.S. criminal law, could remain in a country that refuses extradition. Congress has authorized the arrest, without warrant, of aliens for whom there is probable cause to suspect violation of an extraterritorially applicable statute. In so doing, Congress has left to the Executive, which already possesses the general responsibility for deciding both when and whether to arrest and to prosecute and how best to conduct the nation's foreign relations, the burden of determining when the national interest requires bypassing diplomatic channels to secure such arrest. As the Supreme Court has held in another context, "Situations threatening to important American interests may arise half-way around the globe, situations which in the view of the political branches of our Government require an American response with armed force. If there are to be restrictions on searches and seizures which occur incident to such American action, they must be imposed by the political branches through diplomatic understanding, treaty, or legislation." United States v. Verdugo-Urquidez, 494 U.S. 259, 275, 110 S.Ct. 1056, 108 L.Ed.2d 222 (1990).

C

Turning now to its proffered reason for granting Alvarez redress under the ATCA, the majority claims there was "no basis [under United States] law for the DEA's actions." Supra at 631.

1

The majority reaches this extraordinary result even though it concedes that the United States has reserved for itself the authority to arrest criminals and terrorists abroad as a valid law enforcement technique, and that Congress has explicitly extended the reach of criminal statutes for which Alvarez was charged to apply to conduct outside of the nation's borders. Even more astonishing is that the majority bases its holding on the premise that the DEA's actions were "arbitrary" within the meaning of the law of nations because they were beyond the scope of authority conferred by Congress.

In this case, Alvarez was arrested pursuant to an American warrant, issued following his indictment by a federal grand jury on felony charges. He was held overnight and then brought to the United States, where he was promptly placed in federal custody and was arraigned as soon as his medical condition permitted. The majority fails to explain adequately how an arrest supported by probable cause and ordered by a warrant, leading to a brief period of confinement before transfer to custody on American soil with all its attendant legal process, rises to the level of arbitrary detention merely because a parallel warrant was not obtained from the harboring state.

This view does not necessarily render such a seizure legal in every respect; we are limited here to the question whether the arrestee can recover in tort under the Alien Tort Claims Act, which presupposes a violation of the law of nations.[13] Whatever false arrest claim Alvarez might have, he has not stated a violation of the law of nations to which we adhere.

2

In any event, contrary to the majority's surmise, the DEA was well within its delegated powers when arresting Alvarez. The relevant statutory provisions confer on DEA agents the authority to "make arrests ... for any felony, cognizable under the laws of United States" and the added authority to "perform such other law enforcement duties as the Attorney General may designate." 21 U.S.C. § 878(a) (emphasis added). Because it is undisputed that Congress has authorized the extraterritorial application of the criminal statutes for which Alvarez was charged, see supra at 624, this broad legislative delegation of enforcement powers to the DEA would seemingly sanction the extraterritorial arrests at issue in this case.

Nevertheless the majority would narrow this broad delegation of enforcement power and restrict the DEA's authority to engage in transborder arrests because it concludes that it would be "anomalous" for Congress to confer a similar degree of authority to "any State or local law enforcement officer designated by the Attorney General." Supra at 626-627. However, there is nothing "anomalous" about the legislative branch delegating to the Attorney General to determine in his best judgment whether non-federal law enforcement agents can aid in the application and enforcement of this nation's criminal laws extraterritorially. Instead, Congress engaged in such a broad delegation of law enforcement authority to the DEA and to the Attorney General in order to allow the Executive branch to have the widest array of enforcement options at its disposal.

In addition to the clear language of 21 U.S.C. § 878(a), this court's statutory interpretation is guided by the Supreme Court's recognition that "Congress simply cannot do its job absent an ability to delegate power under broad general directives." Mistretta v. United States, 488 U.S. 361, 372, 109 S.Ct. 647, 102 L.Ed.2d 714 (1989). Furthermore, "[d]elegation of foreign affairs authority is given even broader deference than in the domestic area." Freedom to Travel Campaign v. Newcomb, 82 F.3d 1431, 1438 (9th Cir. 1996). "Congress — in giving the Executive authority over matters of foreign affairs — must of necessity paint with a brush broader than it customarily wields in domestic areas." Id. (quoting Zemel v. Rusk, 381 U.S. 1, 17, 85 S.Ct. 1271, 14 L.Ed.2d 179 (1965)).

Nevertheless, the majority claims there is an utter void of authority for the DEA's actions. The majority is undeterred by the fact that Congress has authorized the extraterritorial application of the criminal statutes involved in this case and has delegated broad powers of enforcement to the DEA "for any felony, cognizable under the laws of the United States." The majority's holding flies in the face of the clear statutory language enacted by Congress as well as the principle of statutory construction that delegations to the Executive branch are entitled to greater judicial deference in matters involving politically sensitive foreign affairs.

Furthermore the majority's approach leads unavoidably to the following question: if Congress through enactment of 21 U.S.C. § 878(a) has not in fact authorized the DEA and Attorney General to enforce extraterritorially the criminal laws for which Alvarez was charged, to whom exactly has Congress delegated this enforcement authority? By extending the reach of our criminal laws to apply to conduct outside of the nation's borders, Congress must have intended to have the laws enforced by some member of the Executive branch.[14]

Under the majority's approach, this nation would be left to the whims of foreign countries in enforcing its laws because Congress, in delegating broad law enforcement powers to the Executive branch, did not redundantly recite that extraterritorial enforcement is to be included.[15]

3

Both the statutory structure and our own precedent indicate that the criminal provisions in question apply extraterritorially. Correspondingly, the statutes and precedent also indicate that Congress has authorized their extraterritorial enforcement. Under such circumstances, we are not free to conclude that the political branches have bound themselves — or, to be more precise, have bound the Executive — to the mast. And the prospect of international opprobrium is not sufficient for us as judges to impose a constraint the political branches have not.[16]

IV

Dr. Alvarez's capture and delivery to the United States may have offended the sensibilities of some members of our court. As a matter of public policy, such actions may even be worthy of the condemnation that certain pundits and foreign countries, as cited by the majority, have bestowed. But we are not asked in this case to condemn or to condone the federal government's actions; we are asked to compensate Dr. Alvarez in tort under the law of nations. The decision to exercise the option of transborder arrest as a tool of national security and federal law enforcement is for the political branches to make. They, unlike the courts, may be held accountable for any whirlwind that they, and the nation, may reap because of their actions. By its judicial overreaching, the majority has needlessly shackled the efforts of our political branches in dealing with complex and sensitive issues of national security. After today's ruling, if the political branches are intent on protecting the security interests of our nation by arresting and prosecuting those who would do the country harm, Congress and the President should also ensure that the United States Treasury is well-stocked to compensate the captured miscreants.

Notes

[1] Perhaps cognizant that its analysis cannot bear its own weight if applied more broadly, the majority recites that we need not worry because its holding "is a limited one." Supra at 608. Count me, however, among those unassuaged by the majority's assurances. I believe that impermissibly encroaching upon the duties rightfully reserved to the political branches is of serious consequence, and unfortunately such encroachment establishes a very troubling precedent which we will regret. [. . .]

Judge O'Scannlain's partial concurrence in Miller v. Gammie (July 9, 2003)

O'SCANNLAIN, Circuit Judge, with whom Circuit Judge TALLMAN joins, concurring in part:

While I concur in the outcome reached by the majority today, I write separately to note my firm conviction that such an outcome was reachable only by way of en banc review. Thus, I cannot join the majority's pronouncement in Part V.B, "Whether En Banc Review Was Required," implying as it does that the three-judge panel in this case was free to disregard prior Ninth Circuit precedent.

We took this case en banc to determine whether our court's holding in Babcock was still good law. We have properly concluded that it is not. I am as comfortable with this court's conclusion as I was uncomfortable when writing for the three-judge panel, see Miller, 292 F.3d at 990 ("Indeed, we are profoundly disturbed that persons acting in the name of the State of Nevada would place a known sexual predator into a home with two small children ...") (emphasis in original), but my conviction as to the ultimate rectitude of each decision flows from the same source: the clear authority of the en banc court to do what three-judge panels normally cannot — namely, overrule prior decisions of three-judge panels.

I do not believe that the Supreme Court's intervening precedent — as set forth in cases such as Antoine and Kalina — had so clearly undermined Babcock as to allow a three-judge panel to overrule it. The en banc court, however, is unencumbered by any obligation to follow the decision of a three-judge panel, and therefore is free to do what, in my view, the panel could not. I agree that recent Supreme Court precedent indicates that Babcock's central holding had, at best, an uncertain future. Accordingly, I concur in all but Part V.B of the Court's opinion.

Judge O'Scannlain's dissent in US v. Kincade (Oct 2, 2003)

O'SCANNLAIN, Circuit Judge, dissenting:

Binding Ninth Circuit authority compels the conclusion that the DNA Act passes muster under the Fourth Amendment. The court now blithely holds that our decision in Rise v. Oregon, 59 F.3d 1556 (9th Cir.1995), has been overruled. I respectfully disagree. In reaching its conclusion, the majority relies on the Supreme Court's "special needs" decisions in Indianapolis v. Edmond, 531 U.S. 32, 121 S.Ct. 447, 148 L.Ed.2d 333 (2000), and Ferguson v. City of Charleston, 532 U.S. 67, 121 S.Ct. 1281, 149 L.Ed.2d 205 (2001). This reliance, however, is misplaced because it merely begs the question we really need to be asking: whether the Supreme Court's "special needs" jurisprudence is at all applicable to suspicionless searches of probationers conducted for the purposes of preventing crime. And even if one concedes the contention—voiced by the appellant and adopted by the majority—that Edmond and Ferguson cast doubt on our holding in Rise, it is clear that they have not done so to such a degree as to allow one three-judge panel of this court to overrule the holding of another three-judge panel. Accordingly, I must dissent.

In Rise, this court held that an Oregon statute requiring convicted murderers and sex offenders to submit a blood sample for inclusion in a DNA database did not violate the Fourth Amendment. We based our holding on a series of factors, including

the reduced expectations of privacy held by persons convicted of one of the felonies to which [the statute] applies, the blood extractions' relatively minimal intrusion into these persons' privacy interests, the public's incontestable interest in preventing recidivism and identifying and prosecuting murderers and sexual offenders, and the likelihood that a DNA data bank will advance this interest.

Rise, 59 F.3d at 1562. Our analysis in Rise therefore employed the "general Fourth Amendment approach of examining the totality of the circumstances." United States v. Knights, 534 U.S. 112, 118, 122 S.Ct. 587, 151 L.Ed.2d 497 (2001) (citing Ohio v. Robinette, 519 U.S. 33, 39, 117 S.Ct. 417, 136 L.Ed.2d 347 (1996)) (internal quotation marks omitted). Indeed, we explicitly rejected at the outset of our opinion in Rise the contention that special needs analysis was applicable:

The plaintiffs maintain that the "special needs" doctrine and the so-called "prison inmate" exception to the warrant and probable cause requirements do not apply because [the statute's] sole purpose is to assist in the arrest and prosecution of suspected criminals. We need not determine whether [the statute] also serves legitimate penal interests, as the defendants argue, because we find that the statute is constitutional even if its only objective is law enforcement.

See Rise, 59 F.3d at 1559 (emphasis added).

Despite clear evidence to the contrary, the majority insists that Rise should be interpreted as applying the narrow special needs exception. The majority's basis for treating it as such appears to be the Rise court's citation, near the start of its analysis, to the Supreme Court's holding in Michigan Department State Police v. Sitz, 496 U.S. 444, 110 S.Ct. 2481, 110 L.Ed.2d 412 (1990),[1] in support of the proposition that "[e]ven in the law enforcement context, the State may interfere with an individual's Fourth Amendment interests with less than probable cause and without a warrant if the intrusion is only minimal and is justified by law enforcement purposes." Rise, 59 F.3d at 1559.

Sitz, it must be conceded, is a special needs case. But the Rise court did not cite just to Sitz to establish the pedigree of its "totality of the circumstances" approach—it also cited to a more time-tested "totality of the circumstances" case: Terry v. Ohio, 392 U.S. 1, 20, 88 S.Ct. 1868, 20 L.Ed.2d 889 (1968). Thus, it simply does not suffice to point out the Rise court's citation to Sitz and conclude on that basis alone that the former is a "special needs" case—yet this is precisely what the majority appears to do. See Majority Op. at 1108 n. 25.[2] How else to read the majority's conclusory assertion that "Rise relied on an interpretation of Supreme Court precedent that has since been wholly discredited by Edmond and further undermined by Ferguson"? Maj. Op. at 1107 (citations omitted).

The reason for the majority's insistence that Rise was, in fact, a "special needs" case is simple: The Supreme Court's holdings in Edmond and Ferguson have held that no "special needs" exception exists where the searches at issue evince a purpose "`ultimately indistinguishable from the general interest in crime control.'" Ferguson, 532 U.S. at 82, 121 S.Ct. 1281 (quoting Edmond, 531 U.S at 44, 121 S.Ct. 447). Thus, to the extent that Rise and the present case are cast as "special needs" cases, or analogues thereof, Edmond and Ferguson would appear to dictate the fate of each: Because the parolee's DNA is sought primarily for the purpose of "detect[ing] evidence of ordinary criminal wrongdoing," Edmond, 531 U.S. at 41, 121 S.Ct. 447, such searches cannot be justified by reference to any other special purposes they might happen to further.

Edmond and Ferguson, then, cast their shadows over Rise only insofar as Rise itself can be classified as a "special needs" case. But Rise specifically eschewed "special needs" analysis in favor of the traditional "totality of the circumstances" approach. Indeed, our decision in Rise to employ a "totality of the circumstances" approach when analyzing searches of probationers conducted for a law enforcement purpose received at least the tacit approval of the Supreme Court in Knights, a case that was handed down after Edmond and Ferguson. In Knights, the Supreme Court reversed our holding that a warrantless search of a probationer's apartment violated the Fourth Amendment. The Court noted that its holding in Griffin v. Wisconsin, 483 U.S. 868, 107 S.Ct. 3164, 97 L.Ed.2d 709 (1987), had applied special needs analysis to a Wisconsin regulation that authorized warrantless searches of probationers, but rejected the assertion that Griffin required the use of "special needs" analysis in cases involving warrantless searches of probationers:

> In [Appellant's] view, apparently shared by the Court of Appeals, a warrantless search of a probationer satisfies the Fourth Amendment only if it is just like the search at issue in Griffin—i.e., a "special needs" search conducted by a probation officer monitoring whether the probationer is complying with probation restrictions. This dubious logic—that an opinion upholding the constitutionality of a particular search implicitly holds unconstitutional any search that is not like it—runs contrary to Griffin's express statement that its "special needs" holding made it "unnecessary to consider whether" warrantless searches of probationers were otherwise reasonable within the meaning of the Fourth Amendment.

Knights, 534 U.S. at 117-18, 122 S.Ct. 587.

The Court then proceeded to apply what it described as the "general Fourth Amendment approach of examining the totality of the circumstances," id. at 118, 122 S.Ct. 587 (internal quotation marks omitted), and concluded that the challenged search was constitutional. In reaching its conclusion, the Court noted first that the regulation that imposed the warrantless search requirement as a condition to probation furthered the two primary goals of probation—"rehabilitation and protecting society from future criminal violations," id.—and that because "[t]he probation order clearly expressed the search condition and [Appellant] was unambiguously informed of it," the condition "significantly diminished[Appellant's] reasonable expectation of privacy." Id. at 120, 122 S.Ct. 587. Second, the Court noted that, given this lowered expectation of privacy, the reasonable suspicion which both sides in the case admitted was present could be deemed sufficient to satisfy the Fourth Amendment.[3]

While distinguishable on its facts from the present case, Knights remains vitally important for two principal reasons. First, as set forth above, it is far from settled that "special needs" analysis remains applicable to searches involving probationers that, like this one, are conducted for a law-enforcement purpose. Indeed, Ferguson's admission that "probationers have a lesser expectation of privacy," Ferguson 532 U.S. at 79 n. 15, 121 S.Ct. 1281, when read alongside Knights' rejection of the argument that warrantless searches of probationers must be limited to the "special need" of ensuring compliance with probation restrictions, see Knights 534 U.S. at 117-18, 122 S.Ct. 587, renders the Edmond-Ferguson line's applicability to the probation context sketchy at best.

If the latter observation is true, and I believe it is, our panel must decide which analysis to apply. And Knights appears to answer that question for us by looking to the "totality of the circumstances." See Knights 534 U.S. at 118-19, 122 S.Ct. 587 ("The touchstone of the Fourth Amendment is reasonableness, and the reasonableness of a search is determined `by assessing, on the one hand, the degree to which it intrudes upon an individual's privacy and, on the other, the degree to which it is needed for the promotion of legitimate government interests.") (citations and internal quotations omitted).

This leads to the second reason for Knights' significance here. Not only is Knights' analytical framework very similar to that employed by this court in Rise; the Knights Court expressly reserved the question whether "a search by a law enforcement officer without any individualized suspicion would have satisfied the reasonableness requirement of the Fourth Amendment." Knights, 534 U.S. at 120 n. 6, 122 S.Ct. 587. The only possible inference to be drawn from the Court's refusal to address the constitutionality of suspicionless searches of probationers is obvious: It is an open question. If Rise did not rely on special needs analysis, and the constitutionality of suspicionless searches of probationers remains an open question, then—quite clearly—the majority cannot legitimately contend that the Edmond-Ferguson line of cases has overruled Rise. Indeed, the Supreme Court's own application of a Rise-style totality of the circumstances approach counsels that Rise is still good law. At the very least, it cannot be said that intervening Supreme Court decisions have so undermined this court's holding in Rise that it can be overruled by a three-judge panel of the court.

The majority tries to skirt this reality by simply reclassifying Rise as a special needs case and then leaping to the conclusion that it has necessarily been overruled by Edmond and Ferguson. But if Rise is not a special needs case—and I take the Rise court at its word, see Rise, 59 F.3d at 1559—the majority has no sanction whatever for its conclusion that Rise is no longer good law. Rise has already confronted the type of search we are presented with here and, applying the totality of the circumstances analysis endorsed by the Supreme Court in Knights, concluded that the extraction of a probationer's blood for inclusion in a database designed to aid in swifter and more accurate resolution of crimes "is reasonable and therefore constitutional under the Fourth Amendment." Rise, 59 F.3d at 1562.

Because in my view we are bound by our holding in Rise, I would affirm the judgment of the district court. Accordingly, I must respectfully dissent.

Notes

[1] In Sitz, the Supreme Court held that a roadblock designed to detect and remove from the road drunk drivers did not violate the Fourth Amendment because its principal purpose was to make the roads safer, even though it would result in some criminal prosecutions for those caught driving under the influence.

[2] Admittedly, the majority is not alone in erroneously reading Rise as a special needs case that has been undermined by the Supreme Court's holdings in Edmond and Ferguson. Both of the recent district court cases considering the constitutionality of this statute conclude that Rise is essentially a special needs case. See United States v. Miles, 228 F.Supp.2d 1130, 1135 (E.D.Cal.2002); United States v. Reynard, 220 F.Supp.2d 1142, 1166 n. 29 (S.D.Cal.2002).

[3] In reaching this conclusion the Court went out of its way to note: "We do not decide whether the probation condition so diminished, or completely eliminated, Knights' reasonable expectation of privacy . . . that a search by a law enforcement officer without

any individualized suspicion would have satisfied the reasonableness requirement of the Fourth Amendment." Id. at 120 n. 6, 122 S.Ct. 587.

Judge O'Scannlain's dissent in McGinest v. GTE Service Corp (March 11, 2004) [Notes omitted]

O'SCANNLAIN, Circuit Judge, concurring in part and dissenting in part.

I agree that the court must reverse the grant of GTE's motion for summary judgment and remand for further proceedings on McGinest's hostile work environment; regrettably, however, I cannot concur in the majority's analysis, and thus dissent from the reasoning of Part III. I disagree with the court's reversal of the dismissal on summary judgment of McGinest's discriminatory failure to promote claim and thus dissent from Part IV.A.; I would affirm. But I do agree that we must affirm dismissal on summary judgment of McGinest's retaliatory failure to promote claim, and thus concur in Part IV.B. of the court's opinion as to result and analysis.

Because I believe the majority's opinion sidesteps Raytheon Co. v. Hernandez, ____ U.S. ____, 124 S.Ct. 513, 157 L.Ed.2d 357 (2003), essentially abandons Nat'l R.R. Passenger Corp. v. Morgan, 536 U.S. 101, 122 S.Ct. 2061, 153 L.Ed.2d 106 (2002), and creates an unreasonable expansion of Title VII liability in the workplace, I must respectfully dissent from the opinion of the court to the foregoing extent.

I

Title VII prevents the establishment of a "hostile work environment" that becomes "sufficiently severe or pervasive to alter the conditions of [one's] employment." Meritor Sav. Bank, FSB v. Vinson, 477 U.S. 57, 67, 106 S.Ct. 2399, 91 L.Ed.2d 49 (1986); see 42 U.S.C. § 2000e-2(a)(1).

Our evaluation of such claims requires an examination of the totality of the circumstances. Harris v. Forklift Systems, Inc., 510 U.S. 17, 23, 114 S.Ct. 367, 126 L.Ed.2d 295 (1993) ("[W]hether an environment is `hostile' or `abusive' can be determined only by looking at all the circumstances."); Fuller v. City of Oakland, 47 F.3d 1522, 1527 (9th Cir.1995) ("Hostility [under Title VII] must be measured based on the totality of the circumstances."). This appraisal includes consideration of "the frequency of the discriminatory conduct; its severity; whether it is physically threatening or humiliating, or a mere offensive utterance; and whether it unreasonably interferes with an employee's work performance." Harris, 510 U.S. at 23, 114 S.Ct. 367.

A

However, before considering the totality of the circumstances, we must first determine exactly which of the plaintiff's claims properly form a part of that inquiry. Because the district court dismissed this case on summary judgment, we must review the evidence in the light most favorable to the plaintiff. T.W. Elec. Serv., Inc. v. Pac. Elec. Contr. Ass'n, 809 F.2d 626, 630-31 (9th Cir.1987). Yet even under this deferential standard, not every allegation must be taken at face value, nor is every factual claim necessarily available to impose potential liability. The majority, regrettably, appears to assume the opposite, for its analysis hardly considers the suitability of McGinest's allegations. The court's opinion appears not only to presume that all facts are true, but that every allegation is admissible evidence of a hostile work environment upon which liability may be based. There is no recognizable legal support for this approach.

Specifically, my review of our precedent indicates that there are at least two kinds of allegations that may not be considered at summary judgment as evidence of liability for a particular hostile work environment claim: First, if any distant act "was no longer part of the same hostile environment claim, then the employee cannot recover for the previous act[]." Nat'l R.R. Passenger Corp. v. Morgan, 536 U.S. 101, 118, 122 S.Ct. 2061, 153 L.Ed.2d 106 (2002). Second, claims that amount to mere "conclusory allegations" are insufficient to merit consideration. Hernandez v. Spacelabs Med., Inc., 343 F.3d 1107, 1116 (9th Cir.2003). With these principles in mind, I believe it is necessary to undertake a careful review of McGinest's numerous allegations before one may fairly judge the strength of his Title VII claim.

1

GTE urges that the events involving supervisor Noson must be excluded as distant acts beyond the statutory scope of the rest of McGinest's hostile work environment claim. Title VII does indeed require that a "charge under this section shall be filed within one hundred and eighty days after the alleged unlawful employment practice occurred."[1] 42 U.S.C. § 2000e-5(e)(1). Of course, we must not engage in overly literal interpretations of this statute of limitations. See Morgan, 536 U.S. at 115-21, 122 S.Ct. 2061. So the simple fact that some of the alleged discriminatory acts occurred outside the limitations period does not automatically preclude their admission. Rather, "consideration of the entire scope of a hostile work environment claim, including behavior alleged outside the statutory time period, is permissible for the purposes of assessing liability, so long as an act contributing to that hostile environment takes place within the statutory time period." Id. at 105, 122 S.Ct. 2061.

a

The majority, however, appears to take this concept to an extreme, implying that so long as any single act occurs within the statute of limitations, all alleged acts — no matter how far in the past — become part of the same hostile work environment claim. It dismisses the statute of limitations argument in a footnote, and explicitly considers Noson's conduct because it is merely "possible" that it functioned as part of the same claim. Maj. Op. at 1114 n. 6. It is our duty faithfully to apply controlling precedent, and I do not believe that Morgan's threshold can be so pitifully low. Indeed, I believe the majority's "possibly part of the same claim" standard eviscerates Morgan's limitation.

To the contrary, I believe Morgan establishes a workable and relatively stringent standard: "if a [distant] act ... had no relation to the [recent] acts ..., or for some other reason, such as certain intervening action by the employer, was no longer part of the same hostile environment claim, then the employee cannot recover for the previous acts."[2]

Morgan, 536 U.S. at 118, 122 S.Ct. 2061. Employers retain additional protections beyond even this principle because distant acts alleged as part of a single hostile work environment claim also remain "subject to waiver, estoppel, and equitable tolling when equity so requires." Id. at 121, 122 S.Ct. 2061 (internal quotation omitted).

With respect, while the court's opinion formally recognizes this language, it fails to apply it. The majority appears to argue that we need not take Morgan seriously because "neither the district court nor the parties had the benefit of" that decision. Maj. Op. at 1114 n. 6. This is irrelevant. Morgan imposes a rule of law establishing when a particular fact may support a legal claim. And, of course, "[o]ur duty is to interpret the law." Seaman v. Comm'r of Internal Revenue, 479 F.2d 336, 338 (9th Cir.1973).

The majority also emphasizes that Morgan deals with an employer's "liability." Maj. Op. at 1114 n. 6 (emphasis in original). I am unable to recognize the significance of such a distinction, or why it would counsel for application of the majority's nearly nonexistent threshold. The district court's summary judgment order, which we now review on appeal, determined precisely the issue of GTE's potential liability. Morgan is thus directly relevant, and I respectfully believe that we must determine which of McGinest's assertions are properly encompassed in his hostile work environment claim before determining whether that claim properly survives summary adjudication. For it is clearly incorrect to consider every claim a plaintiff makes—no matter how stale or unsupported — in adjudicating a motion for summary judgment. See Morgan, 536 U.S. at 118, 122 S.Ct. 2061; Hernandez, 343 F.3d at 1116.

Of course, determining the scope of events that may be considered for purposes of establishing liability does not affect Federal Rule of Civil Procedure 16 and the admissibility of stale evidence for other purposes. For example, an utterance, though time barred for purposes of liability, may be admissible to challenge the credibility of a witness as a prior inconsistent statement. See Fed.R.Evid. 613.

But summary judgment is about establishing liability. Thus, I must respectfully disagree with the majority's implication that both Morgan and Lyons v. England, 307 F.3d 1092 (9th Cir.2002) might be extended to allow time-barred evidence to be used at summary judgment as "background evidence" of a hostile work environment claim. See Maj. Op. at 1114 n. 6. The quoted language from Morgan, and the entire Lyons opinion, dealt only with discrete act claims. In such cases, a plaintiff may rely on time-barred evidence as a "background" to help establish that an adverse employment decision was actually based on discriminatory animus. See Lyons, 307 F.3d at 1110 ("In the context of a racial disparate treatment claim, admissible background evidence must be relevant to determine the ultimate question: whether the defendant intentionally discriminated against the plaintiff because of his race." (internal quotations and edit marks omitted)).

However, "[h]ostile environment claims are different in kind from discrete acts." Morgan, 536 U.S. at 115, 122 S.Ct. 2061.

Under Morgan, evidence of a hostile work environment may extend beyond the statute of limitations period if it is related. See id. at 118, 122 S.Ct. 2061. But if evidence is un related to a claim, it must necessarily be irrelevant to that same claim. See, e.g., Eclipse Assocs. v. Data General Corp., 894 F.2d 1114, 1119 (9th Cir.1990) (equating "unrelated" with "irrelevant"). So evidence that is time-barred under the Morgan standard cannot be considered at summary judgment because it is simply not relevant to the question of whether wholly unrelated conduct amounts to a hostile work environment. The very term "background evidence" makes little sense in this context because no "background" of discriminatory animus can be established from unrelated, irrelevant activity. Such evidence may well have triggered liability in the past, but that was liability upon which the plaintiff declined to act. Allowing consideration of stale, unrelated events as "background evidence" at summary judgment guts the concept of a statute of limitations in the hostile work environment context, and only serves as a backdoor method by which to introduce time-barred statements to avoid summary dismissal.

 I also find no basis for the assertion that we lack facts necessary properly to interpret Morgan. Maj. Op. at 1114 n. 6. The record includes detailed information regarding Noson's actions, as amply related by the majority's opinion. The district court made specific findings regarding GTE's response, and when and where the alleged conduct occurred, including the fact that it "took place seven years before McGinest filed his EEOC complaint." Thus, unlike the majority, I feel obligated to determine whether McGinest's claims regarding Noson are time-barred under a standard stringent enough to comply with Morgan's dictates.

 b

 McGinest's claims involving Noson occurred in the late 1980s culminating in Noson's dual apologies, as requested by GTE, in 1990. McGinest makes no further allegation of objectionable conduct by Noson since those apologies. The next formal notice of discriminatory conduct occurred after McGinest filed his EEOC complaint in 1997. In fact, McGinest himself alleges no discrimination of any kind between 1990 and 1995, when he claims to have been denied equal bonus pay. Construed as liberally as possible,[3] no less than 1,500 days elapsed between the successful resolution of Noson's behavior and all other alleged misconduct. Strikingly, 1,500 days amounts to more than eight full, consecutive Title VII statutory limitations periods. See 42 U.S.C. § 2000e-5(e)(1). Each of the exclusions set forth in Morgan, therefore, apply.

 First, the acts involving Noson cannot reasonably be understood to have any "relation to" the subsequent allegations setting forth a hostile work environment claim. During the intervening several years, McGinest received at least one change in job title and at least one transfer, such that he no longer worked with or for Noson, and no longer worked at the same GTE location. In fact, the only relationship between these distant acts and all the other alleged conduct is that (1) they were discriminatory; and (2) GTE employed McGinest throughout.

 Contrary to the majority's implication, I do not believe these facts alone can establish a sufficient "relation" as that term has been defined by the Supreme Court. See Morgan, 536 U.S. at 118, 122 S.Ct. 2061. This is because every hostile work environment claim is by definition asserted against a single employer for discriminatory conduct. Thus, the majority's version of "relation" would be satisfied even if a plaintiff alleged only two instances of differing forms of offensive conduct, perpetrated by different people, in different locations, separated by twenty-five years.

The Supreme Court has not yet given us specific guidance on the precise contours of a sufficient relation, so, for now, this is our job. Perhaps evidence of adequate relation might consist of the following:[4] an identity of offenders, an identity of location, an identity of a sufficiently distinct mode of harassment, or a reasonable identity of time in relation to the applicable statute of limitations. McGinest failed to submit any such evidence. The offenders differed, the place of the offense differed, and, even if all the alleged conduct was discriminatory by nature, the particular form of abuse differed. And, taken in the light most favorable to McGinest, there is no reasonable identity of time. Morgan itself provides a guiding example. Based on a 300 day statute of limitations, the Court concluded that conduct extending over a 400-day period — even if separated by 300 days within that time — reasonably could be construed as part of the same claim. Id. at 118, 122 S.Ct. 2061. In McGinest's case, discriminatory conduct separated by at least 1,500 days cannot be understood to present a reasonable identity of time in relation to the 180-day statute of limitations.

Second, it is conceded that GTE engaged in "certain intervening action" to prevent Noson's conduct from reoccurring. Id. For, while GTE concluded that there was no racial discrimination, it nonetheless required Noson to apologize. Perhaps McGinest may have preferred a stronger response from GTE. But the fact that there are no allegations of harmful conduct by Noson — or by anyone else for several years — necessarily establishes that GTE's intervening response was at least sufficient to maintain an acceptable work environment for eight full, consecutive exhaustions of the statute of limitations.[5]

Finally, if Noson's conduct created a hostile work environment in 1990, even despite GTE's response, McGinest had by 1995 waived his right to bring any resulting Title VII claim many times over. It is contrary to the principles of equity to allow McGinest to include these allegations as part of a hostile work environment claim arguably "redeveloping" nearly five years later. For, "when [a] delay is caused by the employee, ... the federal courts have the discretionary power to locate `a just result' in light of the circumstances peculiar to the case." Id. at 121, 122 S.Ct. 2061 (internal citations and quotations omitted). It might be one thing if discrete acts making up the hostile work environment claim continued at regular intervals for a period significantly longer than the 180-day limitation. Yet we should not countenance McGinest's attempts to revive the Noson allegations when, after at least 1,500 days of experiencing acceptable working conditions, he failed to alert the EEOC and failed to file suit. He should not now retroactively invoke these claims after so long a period of apparent calm.

For these reasons, I respectfully disagree with the majority's conclusion that Noson's conduct may form the basis for McGinest's present hostile work environment claim. Instead, I believe they are excluded by § 2000e-5(e)(1).

2

GTE would also exclude certain factual claims as mere "conclusory allegations." Hernandez, 343 F.3d at 1116. The majority briefly dispenses with this argument. See Maj. Op. at 1113 n. 5 (accepting McGinest's testimony because it "would suffice to enable a reasonable trier of fact to conclude that discrimination had occurred, without the need for further corroborating evidence"). The majority apparently concludes that McGinest set forth sufficient factual detail in his allegations so as to survive summary judgment. See id. (relying on United States v. One Parcel of Real Prop., 904 F.2d 487, 491-92 (9th Cir.1990) (denying summary judgment for the government in a land forfeiture case)). However, One Parcel is not a Title VII case, where the analysis is somewhat more nuanced. For, in the hostile work environment context, McGinest must demonstrate something more than evidence suggesting that he experienced hostility. He must also sufficiently demonstrate that any hostility arose "because of [his] race." 42 U.S.C. § 2000e-2(a)(1); see Holly D. v. Cal. Inst. of Tech., 339 F.3d 1158, 1174 (9th Cir.2003) (holding, in workplace sexual harassment context, that even if supervisor-employee sexual relations occurred, "we require more than conclusory allegations that the supervisor proposed a sexual liaison and the employee responded to the overtures in order to protect her employment interests"). A plaintiff might allege sufficient detail to suggest that a hostile event occurred, but fail to provide anything more than the unsupported conclusion that race motivated it. I am not certain whether the majority fully considered this latter requirement. For, in my view, two of McGinest's claims appear to fail under this standard.

a

First is the incident involving McGinest's truck tire. No one disputes that he was involved in a serious automobile accident due to a blown-out tire. McGinest alleges that not long before the accident, he requested and was denied new tires by GTE mechanics — even though at least one supervisor agreed that they looked bald. McGinest arguably produced sufficient evidence to suggest that such a denial occurred.

Yet McGinest includes this incident in his hostile work environment claim not because an alleged denial occurred, but because such a denial was based on his race. Unfortunately, however, McGinest submitted no evidence to substantiate this charge. He does not claim, for instance, that the mechanics directly said or did anything to him to suggest that there was a racial component to such a denial. Nor does he present any circumstantial evidence that GTE provided mechanical services in a discriminatory manner.

Rather, McGinest relies only on the deposition testimony of Brand, which offers no support for his claim. Brand, who is white, did agree that sometimes it "seem[ed]" that vehicles driven by African-Americans were not "given the same level of maintenance as vehicles driven by white employees." However, he explicitly noted that this was only one possible interpretation of the mechanic's behavior — one that even he acknowledged was not necessarily supported by the facts. For Brand conceded that some of the same mechanics treated him poorly also, while they treated at least one other African-American employee "pretty well." Ultimately, the best that Brand could conclude was that "it could have been racial. It could have been just personality." By Brand's own admission, then, his direct experience and resulting testimony could not form a sufficient supporting basis for McGinest's allegations.

McGinest's accident was undoubtedly a traumatic experience. And given some of his experiences at GTE in other contexts, he might understandably suspect wide-ranging racial discrimination. Nevertheless, our precedent makes clear that individual claims of discriminatory treatment must be "supported by facts." Id. With respect to this allegation, at least, McGinest has failed to provide such evidence, and I do not believe we may consider it as part of his overall hostile work environment claim.

b

McGinest's claim of differential bonus overtime pay presents a similar problem. McGinest submitted time sheets showing that several white employees received more overtime pay than McGinest did over a (roughly) six-month time period in 1996.[6] Nevertheless, as noted above, McGinest must demonstrate not only that this differential existed, but that it arose on account of his race. See 42 U.S.C. § 2000e-2(a)(1) (prohibiting discrimination "because of such individual's race").

Here, McGinest claims that there was an "unwritten rule" regarding the payment of "relief supervisor pay," whereby arriving even five minutes early would earn employees a full hour of wages. While his immediate supervisor, Roberts, allowed others to claim this bonus, he is alleged to have prevented McGinest from doing so because of McGinest's race.[7] On the occasions McGinest attempted to note the bonus overtime on his time sheets, he alleges that Roberts erased it. While this additional information may provide context for McGinest's claims, they still rest on the conclusory allegation that the wage differential arose on account of race.

Nevertheless, the record does not support McGinest's version of events. First, McGinest admitted in a deposition that the time sheets he submitted show no evidence of any relevant erasures.[8] Most damagingly, McGinest's own time sheets conclusively demonstrate that he actually received both overtime pay and "relief supervisor" pay. This clearly contradicts his assertion that he was completely barred from receiving such pay.

McGinest attempts to find support in Begg's admission that GTE may have allowed the bonus overtime practice sometime prior to 1993. However, McGinest appears selectively to read Begg's testimony. While Begg may have known of this practice in the past, he stopped it in 1993 when he became manager. And McGinest specifically alleged that his denials occurred from 1995 to 1997, well after Begg testified that the practice ended. In other words, McGinest's allegations find no support in Begg's testimony.

Notably, the EEOC investigated this complaint and determined that McGinest "had in fact been paid his due relief pay." The district court, as well, specifically found that there was "no credible evidence of a differential application of any `unwritten rule' regarding relief supervisor overtime" — much less that the differential application arose on account of race. A careful review of the evidence compels the same conclusion:

McGinest's allegations involving the "unwritten" relief supervisor rule are unsupported by Begg's testimony, and directly contradicted by McGinest's own time sheets. And to the extent that McGinest's time sheets show that he received less overtime than four other white employees, he presented neither direct nor circumstantial evidence that the wage differential arose on account of race. Therefore, I believe this allegation must be excluded from our review of the totality of the circumstances, and I must dissent from the majority's use of it.

3

On the other hand, GTE's other contentions are unavailing. McGinest's remaining claims must be included as part of the "totality of the circumstances" we properly may consider. For example, at least some portion of the bathroom graffiti ("n____,"[9] "P.O.N.T.I.A.C."), the banner graffiti ("n____ History Month"), Hughes's comments (referring to McGinest as "a stupid n____"), Ledbetter's comments (criticizing McGinest while comparing him to "the other colored guy who used to work here"), DeLeon's comments (referring to McGinest as "mammy"), and Talmadge's comments (saying to McGinest, "I'll retire before I work for a black man") may all reasonably be understood as explicitly, racially hostile.

DeLeon's use of the term "Aunt Jemima" may also serve as evidence of racial hostility sufficient to survive summary judgment. DeLeon did not direct the phrase at McGinest himself, but rather to a white coworker and friend of McGinest's. Perhaps DeLeon truly did lack a racially hostile motive in his use of the nickname. However, a reasonable factfinder could conclude that it was meant to isolate McGinest by referring disparagingly, in his presence, to his friend as an African-American woman. Moreover, use of the term itself may reasonably be construed as racially hostile, whether directed at McGinest or not. See, e.g., Woods v. Graphic Communications, 925 F.2d 1195, 1202 (9th Cir.1991) (upholding hostile work environment judgment where prevailing plaintiff "was surrounded by racial hostility, and subjected directly to some of it"). Roberts's comments upon learning of the removal of the racist bathroom graffiti ("Oh well, I guess I'll have to write it again. Ah, why can't we all just get along?") arguably exhibited racial hostility as well. While GTE claims that Roberts did not know that the graffiti was racist in nature, this only creates a material factual dispute precluding summary judgment.

Finally, McGinest offered sufficient supporting evidence, including an affidavit from coworker Brand, from which a reasonable factfinder could conclude that at least some employees, including Talmadge and Frick ("I refuse to work for that dumb son of a bitch"), may have refused to work with McGinest because of his race.

B

Once identifying which assertions are relevant and properly supported, we must consider whether McGinest presented sufficient evidence to survive summary judgment on his hostile work environment claim. Because the set of facts I review differs from that of the majority, I must conduct an independent analysis.

Three important principles bear upon the inquiry. First, because McGinest appeals from summary judgment dismissal, we must review the evidence in the light most favorable to him. T.W. Elec., 809 F.2d at 630-31. Second, "the objective severity of harassment should be judged from the perspective of a reasonable person in the plaintiff's position, considering all the circumstances." Oncale v. Sundowner Offshore Servs., Inc., 523 U.S. 75, 81, 118 S.Ct. 998, 140 L.Ed.2d 201 (1998) (internal quotation omitted).[10] Finally, McGinest's evidence must "prove that the conduct at issue was not merely tinged with offensive ... connotations, but actually constituted discrimina[tion] ... because of ... [race]." Id. at 81, 118 S.Ct. 998 (emphasis in original, internal quotation omitted).

1

With these principles in mind, I agree with the district court that this case presents a "close question" of whether a proper review of McGinest's admissible evidence suggests that GTE may be held liable in this case. Ultimately, however, I am satisfied that McGinest presented a triable issue of material fact on whether he was subjected to a hostile work environment. First, the opprobriousness of most of the comments, and the frequency with which they arose, could lead a reasonable fact-finder to conclude that together they amounted to more than "a mere offensive utterance." Harris, 510 U.S. at 23, 114 S.Ct. 367; Swinton v. Potomac Corp., 270 F.3d 794, 817 (9th Cir.2001) (describing "n____" as "perhaps the most offensive and inflammatory racial slur in English"). Here, the repeated invocation of highly offensive language in a variety of contexts may be understood to have created a humiliating atmosphere as seen from the objective perspective of a reasonable African-American.

Oncale, 523 U.S. at 81, 118 S.Ct. 998; Harris, 510 U.S. at 21 114 S.Ct. 367 (requiring a hostile work environment to be "severe or pervasive enough to create an objectively hostile or abusive work environment"). Further, at least the stated refusal of certain colleagues to work with McGinest because of his race may have "unreasonably interfere[d] with [McGinest's] work performance." Harris, 510 U.S. at 23, 114 S.Ct. 367. Finally, McGinest's frequent complaints, both formal and informal, reasonably allow the conclusion that he "subjectively perceive[d] the environment to be abusive." Id. at 21, 114 S.Ct. 367.

Even if a hostile working environment exists, "an employer is only liable for failing to remedy harassment of which it knows or should know." Fuller, 47 F.3d at 1527. As the majority correctly notes, when a supervisor engages in harassing conduct, the employer generally may be held "vicariously liable for a hostile environment created by a supervisor." Nichols v. Azteca Rest. Enters., Inc., 256 F.3d 864, 877 (9th Cir.2001). In supervisor-harassment circumstances, then, GTE may not defend for lack of knowledge of the conduct. Therefore, no notice is required for the comments made by supervisors Ledbetter and Roberts. Hughes is a somewhat more complicated case. Both McGinest and the EEOC describe Hughes as "[McGinest]'s Manager," but GTE challenges whether he was McGinest's manager or just a manager. This only demonstrates that there is genuine factual dispute on the issue. At this stage of the proceedings, then, I agree that we must accept McGinest's allegations as true and that GTE would be vicariously liable for

Hughes's comments as well. Still, comments by these three men make up a relatively small portion of McGinest's allegations.

2

Employers are not necessarily vicariously liable for coworker harassment, however, in which case lack of notice can defeat hostile work environment claims. Swinton, 270 F.3d at 803. McGinest alleges that he notified his immediate supervisors of at least one instance of offensive bathroom graffiti, of DeLeon's comments, of Talmadge's comments, and of the stated refusal of some employees to work with him. GTE notes that many of these incidents were not formally reported to "management." I need not determine whether this distinction generally makes a difference because in this case, GTE's own anti-discrimination policy specifically directs employees to discuss discrimination concerns "with your supervisor or human resources representative" (emphasis added). In general, employers "are liable for failing to remedy or prevent a hostile work environment of which management-level employees knew, or in the exercise of reasonable care should have known." Swenson v. Potter, 271 F.3d 1184, 1202 (9th Cir.2001) (emphasis in original, internal quotations omitted). Because McGinest followed GTE's own instructions for reporting discrimination, at least management reasonably "should have known" of the existence of the complaints.

Allegations involving the additional bathroom graffiti and the banner graffiti were not specifically reported by McGinest. But in each case, McGinest alleges that the offensive markings appeared in areas used by, and accessible to, supervisory employees, which GTE does not dispute. Therefore, a reasonable factfinder could conclude that GTE "in the exercise of reasonable care should have known" of the existence of the graffiti. Id. (emphasis omitted). This is particularly true for graffiti that appeared after McGinest filed his complaint. Thus, I would conclude that GTE may not claim lack of notice for any of McGinest's admissible allegations.

3

There remains one additional ground upon which GTE might succeed on summary judgment. Where, as here, there is evidence suggesting that a company had sufficient notice of discriminatory conduct, it generally may avoid liability if it adequately responded to the situation. Fuller, 47 F.3d at 1527. This may be so whether the offending employee is a coworker or a manager, although the burdens of proof differ. See Swinton, 270 F.3d at 803 (holding, in coworker harassment context, that plaintiff must prove "that the employer knew or should have known of the harassment but did not take adequate steps to address it"); Nichols, 256 F.3d at 877 (holding, in supervisor harassment context, that an employer can partially defend by proving that it "exercised reasonable care to prevent and correct promptly any ... harassing behavior").[11]

In considering adequacy, we examine a company's response in its ability to "stop harassment by the person who engaged in harassment." We must also consider whether that response might "persuade potential harassers to refrain from unlawful conduct." Ellison v. Brady, 924 F.2d 872, 882 (9th Cir.1991).

In this case, GTE did formally respond to some of McGinest's complaints. And when GTE acted to address McGinest's specific allegations, discriminatory conduct from that particular employee appears to have ceased. For example, when GTE eventually learned the identity of a witness to Hughes's comments, it immediately reprimanded him, and there are no further allegations of misconduct against him. Likewise, when GTE spoke to DeLeon about the nicknames he used, DeLeon, too, ceased the offensive conduct. Finally, when McGinest complained to management about the bathroom graffiti, GTE promptly removed it.

Taken individually, GTE's responses might perhaps appear reasonable.[12] Indeed, there is no question that they worked to cease any additional actionable conduct by the offending employee. Nevertheless, despite GTE's efforts, opprobrious comments and behavior continued with some regularity from 1995 through 2000. And considering the totality of the circumstances, as we must, a reasonable factfinder could conclude that GTE's corrective measures were inadequate for failing "to impose sufficient penalties to assure a workplace free from ... harassment." Id.

In other words, the totality of the circumstances may suggest that the discriminatory conduct still occurred with sufficient frequency and severity such that GTE's remedies did not reasonably "persuade potential harassers to refrain from unlawful conduct." Id. This precludes summary judgment for GTE on these grounds. Harris, 510 U.S. at 23, 114 S.Ct. 367.

C

Ultimately, my review of McGinest's admissible evidence, considering the totality of the circumstances, reveals a "close case" indeed. GTE made efforts to respond to McGinest's complaints, after which no one particular aggressor continued harassing McGinest. But considering the claim as a whole, McGinest's allegations present evidence of an overall work environment that may have been sufficiently hostile to trigger Title VII's protections.

Because I believe that we must exclude some of McGinest's allegations either as time barred or as merely conclusory, I am regrettably unable to concur in the majority's analysis. While I do agree that McGinest's claims may go forward, I must nonetheless dissent from the majority's unwillingness properly to examine the scope of that inquiry. The majority's opinion sets a dangerous precedent whereby plaintiffs who present a kitchen sink's worth of unsupported and time-barred allegations can survive summary judgment because "taken all together" they somehow mesh with each other so as to deny an employer's efforts to avoid liability without a trial. Nevertheless, even upon a more soundly based analysis, triable issues of material fact remain in this case, and I therefore concur in the majority's decision to reverse the district court's summary judgment dismissal of the hostile work environment claim.

II

McGinest also claims that GTE failed to promote him to the position of Outside Plant Construction Installer Supervisor on account of his race, a Title VII disparate treatment claim. See 42 U.S.C. § 2000e-2(a); Jauregui v. City of Glendale, 852 F.2d 1128, 1134 (9th Cir.1988) (describing disparate treatment as being "singled out and treated less favorably than others similarly situated on account of race" (internal quotation omitted)).

In support of this claim, McGinest invoked the familiar McDonnell Douglas presumption. See McDonnell Douglas Corp. v. Green, 411 U.S. 792, 93 S.Ct. 1817, 36 L.Ed.2d 668 (1973). I agree with the majority that the litigants appear somewhat confused about the use of the McDonnell Douglas presumption and how it relates to other evidence of discrimination. And because these burden-shifting issues are somewhat complicated, like the majority, I, too, engage in a complete analysis of the issue, but reach a different conclusion.[13]

A

There is no question that McGinest is a member of a protected class, that he applied to and was qualified for the supervisor position, and that he was rejected from that position.

GTE disputes whether McGinest satisfied the fourth factor, "that, after his rejection, the position remained open and the employer continued to seek applicants from persons of complainant's qualifications." Id. at 802, 93 S.Ct. 1817. For, while a white supervisor received the job, GTE claims that because it was only a lateral transfer, the supervisor was not "treated more favorably." Chuang v. Univ. of Cal., Davis Bd. of Trustees, 225 F.3d 1115, 1123 (9th Cir.2000).

GTE takes an overly literal approach to the question. The Supreme Court in McDonnell Douglas itself indicated that the test must be practically applied. McDonnell Douglas, 411 U.S. at 802 n. 13, 93 S.Ct. 1817. And here, GTE does not contest that McGinest qualified for a favorable promotion, and that the same job went to a white candidate instead. Therefore, I agree that McGinest successfully invoked the presumption.

GTE may rebut, however, by setting forth "some legitimate, nondiscriminatory reason for the challenged action." Chuang, 225 F.3d at 1123-24. GTE presented evidence that a "salary/hiring freeze" was in effect at the time, prohibiting outside hiring and internal promotions accompanied by increased pay. Salary and hiring freezes, of course, are common in the business world. On its face, then, this is a legitimate, nondiscriminatory reason for failing to promote McGinest. See Maj. Op. at 1123 (concluding that McGinest "must counter GTE's explanation that a hiring freeze accounted for its failure to promote him"); see also, e.g., Jones v. Fla. Power Corp., 825 F.2d 1488, 1492 (11th Cir.1987) (upholding factual finding that plaintiff's job denial "was not the result of racial discrimination but was justified due to a company hiring freeze"). Consequently, we are presented with an explanation that is "legally sufficient to justify a judgment for the defendant," Tex. Dept. of Cmty. Affairs v. Burdine, 450 U.S. 248, 255, 101 S.Ct. 1089, 67 L.Ed.2d 207 (1981), so the McDonnell Douglas "presumption of discrimination drops out of the picture." Reeves v. Sanderson Plumbing Prods., Inc., 530 U.S. 133, 143, 120 S.Ct. 2097, 147 L.Ed.2d 105 (2000) (internal quotation omitted).

B

In the absence of the McDonnell Douglas presumption, McGinest's "burden now merges with the ultimate burden of persuading the court that []he has been the victim of intentional discrimination. [H]e may succeed in this either [(1)] directly by persuading the court that a discriminatory reason more likely motivated the employer or [(2)] indirectly by showing that the employer's proffered explanation is unworthy of credence." Burdine, 450 U.S. at 256, 101 S.Ct. 1089. As to the first method, the majority correctly concludes that McGinest may present either direct or circumstantial evidence of discrimination, so long as it is sufficient to satisfy his ultimate burden. See Desert Palace, Inc. v. Costa, 539 U.S. 90, 123 S.Ct. 2148, 156 L.Ed.2d 84 (2003).

1

McGinest offers two pieces of evidence directly to prove discrimination.[14] First, he points to the offensive comments and other evidence that make up his hostile work environment claim. The majority specifically relies on this evidence — or at least on GTE's "permissive" response to it — to conclude that McGinest meets his burden. However, Ninth Circuit cases involving discriminatory failure to promote have always involved evidence of discrimination among decisionmakers. See, e.g., Lam v. University of Hawaii, 40 F.3d 1551 (9th Cir.1994) (finding evidence that professor who headed appointments committee was biased). Indeed, in the absence of additional evidence, "statements by nondecisionmakers, nor statements by decisionmakers unrelated to the decisional process itself, [cannot alone] suffice to satisfy the plaintiff's burden in this regard." Price Waterhouse v. Hopkins, 490 U.S. 228, 277, 109 S.Ct. 1775, 104 L.Ed.2d 268 (1989) (O'Connor, J., concurring); see, e.g., DeHorney v. Bank of Am. Nat'l Trust & Sav. Ass'n, 879 F.2d 459, 467 (9th Cir.1989) (holding that the plaintiff failed to make out a prima facie case of race discrimination when there was no evidence to establish a nexus between the subordinate's racial slur and the superior's decision to terminate).

Here, the immediate decisionmaker, Begg, actually recommended hiring McGinest, and there are no allegations that he engaged in any discriminatory conduct either before, during, or after he declined to hire him. The salary/hiring freeze decision itself came from upper management, and evidence of harassment among co-workers and supervisors at McGinest's yard simply does not establish discrimination extending to those higher levels. See DeHorney, 879 F.2d at 467. Neither has McGinest produced any other evidence connecting these decisionmakers to the discriminatory conduct of Hughes, Ledbetter, and others, nor has he suggested that GTE's upper management intended to discriminate against him by instituting the freeze. There may be a triable issue of fact as to whether GTE's responses to the allegedly hostile work environment were insufficient for purposes of summary judgment. But this does nothing to establish that GTE upper management had any discriminatory motive for failing to promote McGinest.

Indeed, the evidence suggests the contrary in this case. GTE management responded to — and remedied — each individual instance of discrimination of which it formally became aware, including Hughes's comments, DeLeon's comments, and even Noson's behavior. While these responses may have been insufficient to rebut an overall hostile work environment claim, they certainly do not suggest that GTE management acted with any kind of discriminatory intent. Therefore, unlike the majority, I do not believe that McGinest may rely on his admissible evidence of a hostile work environment to bootstrap his disparate treatment claim.

Both McGinest and the majority also rely on evidence that GTE may have employed a disproportionately small number of African Americans. The majority accepts this allegation. Maj. Op. at 1124. But I, respectfully, cannot. First, there is no such statistical evidence in the record, even though McGinest presumably had an opportunity to develop it during discovery. Indeed, the district court denied McGinest's request at summary judgment to take judicial notice of such information. This ruling was clearly correct, as the information was both reasonably disputed by GTE and was not readily verifiable. Fed.R.Evid. 201(b). The district court further concluded that McGinest's statistics were irrelevant because they were not accompanied by any analysis and because they involved a different county than where he actually worked. Such an evidentiary ruling is reviewed for abuse of discretion, of which I find none. See Domingo v. T.K., 289 F.3d 600, 605 (9th Cir.2002) (noting limited review "even when the rulings determine the outcome of a motion for summary judgment").

Moreover, this kind of data would shed little light on McGinest's disparate treatment claim because it says next to nothing about whether GTE used its neutrally applicable salary/hiring freeze in an effort to discriminate against him. Rather, it is more properly understood as evidence of disparate impact, tending to show that the effects of GTE's employment practice fell more harshly on him. See Raytheon Co. v. Hernandez, ____ U.S. ____, ____, 124 S.Ct. 513, 519, 157 L.Ed.2d 357 (2003) ("This Court has consistently recognized a distinction between claims of discrimination based on disparate treatment and claims of discrimination based on disparate impact.").

Unfortunately, McGinest raised the issue of disparate impact for the first time on summary judgment, when he asked the court to take judicial notice of the statistics. Because McGinest failed to "plead the additional disparate impact theory in [his] complaint[], or ... to make known during discovery [his] intention to pursue recovery on the disparate impact theory," he may not now rely on it. Coleman v. Quaker Oats Co., 232 F.3d 1271, 1294 (9th Cir.2001). In light of this failure, and because GTE has "offered a legitimate, non-discriminatory reason for its actions so as to demonstrate that its actions were not motivated by [McGinest's race]," consideration of this evidence would require us to "stray[] from [our] task by considering not only discriminatory intent but also discriminatory impact." Raytheon, ____ U.S. at ____, 124 S.Ct. at 521. This, the Supreme Court has told us we cannot do. See id.

2

Alternatively, McGinest attempts to meet his burden "indirectly by showing that the employer's proffered explanation is unworthy of credence." Burdine, 450 U.S. at 256, 101 S.Ct. 1089. McGinest first asks us to take judicial notice of reports of GTE's financial health around the time of the salary/hiring freeze. I agree with the majority that we must deny this motion, as these reports are not "capable of accurate and ready determination" as required by Fed.R.Evid. 201(b).[15]

McGinest is then left with a simple attack on the credibility of GTE's witnesses, arguing that the lack of documentary evidence of a freeze suggests that its explanation is "unworthy of credence." Burdine, 450 U.S. at 256, 101 S.Ct. 1089. In reversing the district court, the majority, too, relies heavily on "the absence of any documentation confirming that a hiring freeze was in place during the relevant time period." Maj. Op. at 1123.

This, of course, is not even evidence at all. See Saint Mary's Honor Ctr. v. Hicks, 509 U.S. 502, 519, 113 S.Ct. 2742, 125 L.Ed.2d 407 (1993) ("It is not enough, in other words, to disbelieve the employer...." (emphasis in original)). Rather, it is simply an attack on the form of the admissible evidence GTE submitted. It is axiomatic that adjudicators "must follow the same rules regarding documentary evidence as [those] regarding testimonial evidence." Zahedi v. INS, 222 F.3d 1157, 1165 (9th Cir.2000); see also, e.g., Vera-Villegas v. INS, 330 F.3d 1222, 1233 (9th Cir.2003) (holding that "documentary evidence is judged by the same credibility standards that apply to testimonial evidence").[16]

But the majority appears somehow to have transformed its disparagement of GTE's testimonial evidence into McGinest's "[p]roof" that is sufficient to carry his burden of persuasion. See Maj. Op. at 1124 (describing the testimonial nature of GTE's evidence as "[p]roof that the defendant's explanation is unworthy of credence" (internal quotation omitted)). This may be a neat trick, but it is directly contrary to Supreme Court precedent, for it clearly "disregards the fundamental principle ... that a presumption does not shift the burden of proof, and ignores [the Supreme Court's] repeated admonition that the Title VII plaintiff at all times bears the ultimate burden of persuasion." Hicks, 509 U.S. at 511, 113 S.Ct. 2742 (internal quotation omitted).

Indeed, the majority's rejection of GTE's explanation can only be described as an independent credibility determination.[17] But again, direct Supreme Court authority stands in the way. Because GTE's burden of submitting a neutral hiring justification "is one of production, not persuasion[,] it `can involve no credibility assessment.'" Reeves, 530 U.S. at 142, 120 S.Ct. 2097 (quoting Hicks, 509 U.S. at 509, 113 S.Ct. 2742). Neither McGinest nor the majority may simply cast aspersions on GTE's non-discriminatory explanation. Id. Rather, McGinest must present evidence that it is untrue, and this he has not done.

Even if an examination of GTE's "trustworthiness" were proper, I would find no fault. Two GTE employees, Begg and Nakamura, testified that they had direct knowledge of the freeze, while two other employees, Brand and Valle, were familiar with it. Corroborating this testimony is the undisputed fact that the man hired in McGinest's place did not receive a promotion or a pay increase. McGinest was unwilling or unable even to produce evidence, circumstantial or otherwise, that GTE hired or promoted anyone else during the relevant time period.

3

Once the McDonnell Douglas presumption vanished in the face of GTE's neutral hiring justification, McGinest failed to produce any admissible, relevant evidence of a discriminatory failure to promote him. Neither did he present any evidence suggesting that GTE's neutral explanation was "unworthy of credence." Burdine, 450 U.S. at 256, 101 S.Ct. 1089. Therefore, I must respectfully dissent from the majority's decision to reverse the district court's dismissal of this claim.

III

Finally, McGinest also brings suit for retaliatory failure to promote. See 42 U.S.C. § 2000e-3(a) ("It shall be an unlawful employment practice for an employer to discriminate against any of [its] employees ... because he has opposed any [discriminatory] practice."). I agree with the majority's reasoning and conclusion that we must uphold the district court's dismissal of this claim.

IV

In conclusion, I agree that we must reverse on the hostile work environment claim, but for reasons different from the majority. I respectfully disagree with the majority on the disparate treatment claim, and would affirm. Finally, I concur in the court's decision to affirm summary judgment dismissal on the retaliatory failure to promote claim.

Judge O'Scannlain's concurrence and dissent in Gwaduri v. INS (March 18, 2004) [Notes omitted]

O'SCANNLAIN, Circuit Judge, concurring in part and dissenting in part:

I join my colleagues in voting to deny the Government's motion for late filing of an objection to the Gwaduris' request for fees under the Equal Access to Justice Act ("EAJA"), 28 U.S.C. § 2412 (2003). Although I certainly understand what it is like to have to handle a "high volume of work,"[1] and even to have to "prepare much of [my] own correspondence," these excuses offered by the Government's attorney are simply inadequate to forgive its having missed—by nearly six weeks —our court's 14-day deadline for filing such a response. See Ninth Cir. R. 39-1.7 ("Any party from whom attorneys fees are requested may file an objection to the request . . . within 14 days after service of the request.").

I must dissent, however, from the court's grant of attorneys' fees. I certainly recognize that, absent the peculiar combination of the court's administrative oversight and the Government's belated motion for late filing of its objection, the Gwaduris' otherwise unopposed motion for fees apparently long ago would have been granted by a staff attorney. Yet now that this application has come formally before the panel, I believe a fee award in this case to be statutorily unauthorized.

I

It is well-settled that fees under the EAJA may be awarded against the Government only if its litigating position in the case from which the prevailing party's request arises lacked "a reasonable basis in law and fact." Pierce v. Underwood, 487 U.S. 552, 566 n.2 (1988); see also 28 U.S.C. § 2412(d)(1)(A). That simply cannot be said of the position taken by the Government in response to the Gwaduris' assertion that their due process rights were violated by having received ineffective assistance of counsel before the INS. Cf. Lopez v. INS, 775 F.2d 1015, 1017 (9th Cir. 1985) ("Ineffective assistance of counsel in a deportation proceeding is a denial of due process under the Fifth Amendment if the proceeding was so fundamentally unfair that the alien was prevented from reasonably presenting his case.").

In its disposition awarding relief, the majority conceded that the Gwaduris had not complied with the BIA's procedural requirements for the presentation of an ineffectiveness claim, as established in Matter of Lozada, 19 I & N Dec. 637, 639 (BIA 1988). See Gwaduri v. INS, 69 Fed. Appx. 878, 880 (2003) (unpublished disposition).[2] Our prior caselaw had held that those requirements generally are waivable only when the court is presented with what the record reveals to be "a clear and obvious case of ineffective assistance." See Rodriguez-Lariz v. INS, 282 F.3d 1218, 1227 (9th Cir. 2002). As explained in greater detail in my dissenting opinion, I believe neither that that standard was met here, nor that the Gwaduris even received constitutionally ineffective assistance at all. See Gwaduri, 69 Fed. Appx. at 884 (O'Scannlain, J., dissenting). I therefore believe the Government's position that the BIA did not err in denying the Gwaduris' motion to remand was at least reasonable—even if it ultimately failed to garner a majority vote of this court. See Pierce, 487 U.S. at 552 ("[T]he Government could take a position that is not substantially justified, yet win; even more likely, it could take a position that is substantially justified, yet lose.").

Notably, the court's decision to grant fees does not suggest otherwise. Instead, my colleagues seem merely to follow a practice of routinely granting EAJA fee requests whenever the government fails to oppose their award. That custom is understandable in light of the uniquely demanding burdens generated by our court's gargantuan caseload, and in view of the adversary nature of our system of justice. Cf. Order at 3331.

But while I do not think it impermissible, I also do not believe it to be required. Therefore, I must disagree with my colleagues' apparent suggestion that, in these circumstances, the court has but two alternatives. See id. ("[The court may] determine that the government's lack of timely opposition is tantamount to a concession that its position . . . was not substantially justified. Alternatively, we may treat the government's non-opposition as . . . a failure to carry its burden of proof.") (citations omitted). Indeed, there is an obvious but overlooked third alternative: At least two of our sister circuits have recognized that a court properly may reach the merits of, and in the end may even deny, an unopposed fee request under the EAJA. See Libas, Ltd. v. U.S., 314 F.3d 1362, 1366 (Fed. Cir. 2003) (holding that a court may deny an unopposed request for fees pursuant to the EAJA so long as it provides a reasoned explanation for its decision); United States v. Eleven Vehicles, Their Equipment, and Accessories, 200 F.3d 203, 212 (3rd Cir. 2000) (explaining that, although a court generally may not reduce EAJA fees in the absence of a

Government objection, that limitation on sua sponte court action applies only to the amount of fees—not to whether those fees are available in the first instance).[3]

Most surprising, given the curious mordancy of their order awarding fees, is the fact that my colleagues appear entirely to agree with the eminently moderate position I have advanced. Though they decline to reach the issue whether the Government's position was "substantially justified," they have opted to award fees at a rate lower than requested by the Gwaduris—apparently on the theory that no special legal expertise was required to prosecute the Gwaduris' ineffectiveness claim. See Order at 3332-33; cf. Ramon-Sepulveda v. INS, 863 F.2d 1458, 1463 (9th Cir. 1988) ("[E]ven if immigration law can be classified as a practice specialty, the legal problem posed in [this case] requires no `distinctive knowledge' or `specialized skill' . . . . On the contrary, [petitioner's] legal claim against the INS involves established principles of res judicata—principles with which the majority of attorneys are, or should be, familiar.") (quoting Pierce, 487 U.S. at 572). The majority's colorful talk of "concession" and of "the government's failure to carry its burden of proof," Order at 3331, thus rings hollow—for, by reaching the merits of an unopposed motion in this fashion, the majority engages in precisely the analysis it suggests we ought now to eschew.[4]

II

One further observation might be appropriate. Had an administrative oversight not resulted in the Gwaduris' fee request coming before this panel in such peculiar fashion, and had a motions attorney simply granted the Gwaduris' request for fees pursuant to what appears to be the prevailing practice, the Government would have had 14 days within which to contest such award. See Ninth Cir. R. 27-7; Ninth Cir. Gen. Order App. A. One wonders whether such an adverse disposition would not have at last prompted the Government timely to respond to the Gwaduris' request, in which case the motions attorney's decision then would have been reconsidered on the merits by our court's Appellate Commissioner or by a single judge of this court. See id.[5]

By contrast, today's order denies the Government that critical opportunity, leaving as its only possible path to redress the filing of a petition for rehearing en banc. Now, to garner what otherwise would be an automatic reconsideration of this award in response to an objection, the Government will have to obtain the votes of some 14 of our present complement of 26 active judges. Thus, even though today's award of fees appears merely to achieve the same result that our administrative practice otherwise would have reached, the panel's decision to mimic that custom here sets the Gwaduris' motion on a distinct procedural course—and one that appears far more likely to result in the needless expenditure of taxpayer dollars.

III

For the foregoing reasons, I respectfully dissent from the court's discretionary decision to award attorneys' fees.

Judge O'Scannlain's dissent in Kennedy v. Lockyer (June 14, 2004)

O'SCANNLAIN, Circuit Judge, dissenting:

This case represents a triumph of lawyering from the bench. While I share some of the court's evident sympathy for the defendant — whose third strike resulted from the sale of less than one-tenth of one gram of a legal substance to an undercover officer [1] — I respectfully dissent from its decision to step into counsel's shoes and tango its way around the deference we owe to state courts as coordinate expositors of federal law.

I

There is no dispute that Kennedy was entitled to some portion of the transcript from his first trial on these charges. See generally Britt v. North Carolina, 404 U.S. 226, 92 S.Ct. 431, 30 L.Ed.2d 400 (1971). The only issue before the court is whether clearly established Supreme Court precedent requires the State to have provided him with a complete transcript, including opening and closing arguments and a recounting of any preliminary trial motions. The majority cites no Supreme Court case that extends Britt beyond a requirement that a transcript of all testimonial evidence adduced in prior proceedings be made available to indigent defendants; it finds its clearly established Supreme Court precedent not in the U.S. Reports, but in Black's Law Dictionary. Opinion at 1046-47, 1048.

If this were a direct criminal appeal, I might not necessarily disagree with the court's interpretation of Britt. But on collateral review, our job is not to divine the best interpretation of an admittedly vague Supreme Court precedent, see United States v. Kirk, 844 F.2d 660, 662 (9th Cir.1988) ("[T]he right to free transcripts is not absolute. The Court in Britt recognized that the `outer limits of that principle are not clear.'") (quoting Britt, 404 U.S. at 227, 92 S.Ct. 431),[2] but to determine whether the state court's result in this case reflected an objectively reasonable interpretation of an unmistakably clear Supreme Court decision. At least one court has held that the relevant Supreme Court case law does not extend so far as the majority would take it, and given our acknowledgment of Britt's fuzzy contours, I have difficulty concluding that the state court's decision unreasonably interpreted clearly established federal law within the meaning of AEDPA. See Williams v. Leeke, 444 F.Supp. 229, 232 (D.S.C.1976), aff'd per unpublished memorandum 571 F.2d 579 (4th Cir.1978) ("[T]he authorities cited by petitioners to support their contention that the Constitution requires them to obtain a transcript of closing arguments do not recognize such a requirement. A transcript of arguments to a jury is omitted from the requirements set out in Hardy v. United States, 375 U.S. 277, 84 S.Ct. 424, 11 L.Ed.2d 331 (1964), and Britt v. North Carolina, 404 U.S. 226, 92 S.Ct. 431, 30 L.Ed.2d 400 (1971), and Herring v. New York, 422 U.S. 853, 95 S.Ct. 2550, 45 L.Ed.2d 593 (1975), make no reference to the reduction of argument to the jury into transcript form.") (citations edited); see also Price v. Vincent, 538 U.S. 634, 643, 123 S.Ct. 1848, 155 L.Ed.2d 877 (2003) ("This was not an objectively unreasonable application of clearly established law as defined by this Court. Indeed, numerous other courts have refused to find [constitutional] violations under similar circumstances.") (emphasis in original).

The court's castigation of the state tribunal for its creation of a "doctrine of `substantial compliance'" presents a red herring. See Opinion at 1050. Britt itself fails to set forth a rigid requirement that defendants be provided with a transcript in every case, but rather establishes its own rule of substantial compliance — demanding delivery of a free transcript only when doing so "is necessary for an effective defense," Britt, 404 U.S. at 227, 92 S.Ct. 431, and failing to find a constitutional violation where a "substantially equivalent" device is available. Id. at 230, 92 S.Ct. 431. Read in the charitable light demanded by AEDPA, see Himes v. Thompson, 336 F.3d 848, 854 (9th Cir.2003) (noting AEDPA's demand that courts must "presume... that state courts know and follow the law and give state court decisions the benefit of the doubt.") (citation and quotations omitted), the state court's reference to "substantial compli[ance]" hardly "created a new and additional ... exception" to established Supreme Court doctrine. Contra Opinion at 1052. It simply represents the Court of Appeal's eminently reasonable conclusion that the partial transcript delivered to Kennedy satisfied Britt's requirement that indigent defendants be given free access to only those portions of a transcript which are necessary to ground a constitutionally competent defense.

Indeed, the following two sentences of the Court of Appeal's opinion confirm that is precisely what was meant by its allusion to substantial compliance: "Kennedy was afforded a free transcript of all the testimony.

He thus had available those crucial portions which might be necessary ... for the purposes of impeaching witnesses and rebutting evidence." Kennedy v. Terhune, No. D027718 at 6 (Cal. Ct.App. filed Sep. 8, 1998). Nonetheless, the majority once again faults the state appellate court's reaching the same conclusion that at least one of our sister circuits has suggested. See Phegley v. Greer, 691 F.2d 306, 309 (7th Cir.1982) ("Due process does not always require the state to provide a full transcript to an indigent defendant if a partial transcript or appropriate substitute is made available.") (emphasis added), cert. denied 459 U.S. 946, 103 S.Ct. 262, 74 L.Ed.2d 204 (1982); see also Lindsey v. Smith, 820 F.2d 1137, 1148 (11th Cir.1987), cert. denied 489 U.S. 1059, 109 S.Ct. 1327, 103 L.Ed.2d 595 (1989) ("Moreover, in contrast to Britt, appellant's attorneys had access to portions of the actual transcripts of the first trial.").

The majority's only cogent critique of the Court of Appeal's conclusion that Kennedy had all he needed to prepare a constitutionally effective defense is its vague assertion that "motions to suppress or exclude often reveal, as here, information regarding damaging and prejudicial evidence that the state plans to introduce, and the rulings thereon may sometimes be case-dispositive." Opinion at 1048. But there are two serious problems with this conclusory reasoning. First, the majority utterly fails to explain why such evidence cannot be adequately and effectively dealt with by contemporaneous objection when it is encountered in the courtroom.[3] For a complete transcript truly to be "necessary to an effective defense," Britt, 404 U.S. at 227, 92 S.Ct. 431 (emphasis added), it must be more than merely helpful. See Webster's Third New Int'l Dictionary 1510-11 (1986) (defining necessary as "of, relating to, or having the character of something that is logically required ... that cannot be done without; that must be done or had; absolutely required; essential, indispensable."); cf. Opinion at 1047 ("In asking this court to limit the meaning of `prior proceedings' to a transcript of witness testimony, the state would have us construe the term so as to violate its ordinary and plain meaning. We are not free to do so."). At bottom, the majority offers only a thinly-reasoned justification to support its extension of precedent beyond that clearly established by the Supreme Court.[4]

Second, the majority entirely overlooks the fact that — as a constitutional matter — the admission of prejudicial evidence generates reversible error only when it "renders the trial fundamentally unfair." Payne v. Tennessee, 501 U.S. 808, 825, 111 S.Ct. 2597, 115 L.Ed.2d 720 (1991) (citing Darden v. Wainwright, 477 U.S. 168, 179-183, 106 S.Ct. 2464, 91 L.Ed.2d 144 (1986)). Thus, whatever value there may be in securing the exclusion of potentially prejudicial evidence from the courtroom prior to the commencement of trial, the fact that the courts subject the ultimate admission of prejudicial evidence to such a stringent standard of review evinces a constitutionalized conclusion that excluding such evidence by pre-trial motion is hardly necessary to securing a fair trial or guaranteeing a constitutionally effective defense. Otherwise, the courts long ago would have established a per se rule of ineffectiveness for failure to object to the admission of prejudicial statements at trial. Yet we have soundly rejected that proposition. See, e.g., Phyle v. Leapley, 66 F.3d 154 (8th Cir.1995) ("[Due to] the kinds of broad, highly subjective factors that trial lawyers must take into account as they make repeated, instantaneous decisions whether to object to a question, whether to move to strike a damaging unresponsive answer, or whether to move for a mistrial when a witness has delivered an unexpected low blow[,][w]hen we review such trial decisions, the ineffective assistance standard is high — they are `virtually unchallengeable' — in part because appellate judges cannot recreate from a cold transcript the courtroom dynamics that are an essential part of evaluating the effectiveness of counsel's performance.") (quoting 2 Wayne R. LaFave & Jerold H. Israel, Criminal Procedure § 11.10, at 95 (1984)).

Viewed in this light, the state court's decision rejecting Kennedy's assertion of Britt error was neither contrary to, nor an unreasonable application of, clearly established federal law as set forth by the Supreme Court.

II

Even if it were objectively unreasonable for the state Court of Appeal to have concluded that a transcript of prior pretrial motions was not "needed for an effective defense" — which is was not — it was not objectively unreasonable for the Court of Appeal to have concluded that any resulting constitutional error was harmless.

A

Notwithstanding more than twenty years of Ninth Circuit jurisprudence making clear that Britt errors are subject to harmless error review, see, e.g., United States v. Rosales-Lopez, 617 F.2d 1349, 1355-56 (9th Cir.1980), and despite the fact that the Certificate of Appealability issued by the district court directed Kennedy to address "whether denial of a transcript of pretrial proceedings and motions in limine was a denial

of Petitioner's rights and whether it was harmless error," petitioner's opening brief failed
to allege that any prejudice stemmed from the trial court's refusal to provide him a
complete transcript, asserting instead that no such showing was necessary. See Alaska Ctr.
for the Env't v. United States Forest Serv., 189 F.3d 851, 858 n. 4 (9th Cir.1999)
("Arguments not raised in opening brief are waived.").

Even after the state's responsive brief conclusively demonstrated that his claim
was subject to harmlessness review, Kennedy did not suggest that he was in any way
prejudiced until the final sentence of his reply brief. See Bazuaye v. INS, 79 F.3d 118, 120
(9th Cir.1996) ("Issues raised for the first time in the reply brief are waived."); see also
Sophanthavong v. Palmateer, 365 F.3d 726, 737 (9th Cir.2004) (noting the "obvious"
prejudice wrought by allowing litigants to raise arguments for the first time in reply: doing
so deprives opposing counsel of "the opportunity to point to the record to show that the
new theory lacks legal or factual support").[5] Yet even then he was unable to identify any
specific reason why counsel's lack of access to a complete transcript affected the outcome
of his second trial. Cf. United States v. Anzalone, 886 F.2d 229, 232 (9th Cir.1989) ("The
second reason that appellant's claim fails is that [he] has not pointed to any specific
prejudice he has suffered from the alleged errors in the transcripts.... [E]ven assuming
there were omissions in the transcripts, appellant cannot prevail without a showing of
specific prejudice.").

It is particularly curious that the majority seeks to escape Kennedy's waiver by
pointing to the state's alleged factual concessions at oral argument. See Opinion at 1055.
Let's have a look at what actually happened at the oral argument. Recognizing that we long
have held Britt error subject to harmlessness review, the court had repeatedly prodded
petitioner's counsel to identify some plausible instance of actual prejudice stemming from
the trial court's failure to furnish his client a transcript of the pre-mistrial motions. The
majority's final exchange with Kennedy's counsel during his opening argument is most
illuminating:

[Counsel for Kennedy]: ... If the new counsel had had [a complete transcript], he
would be much-better equipped.

[Court]: Well, that's true. I mean, I think one can assume that the — more
information is better than no information, or some information. So let's accept that
premise. Is there anything you can point to that occurred in the second trial — there was a
mistrial on the first one, right?

[Counsel for Kennedy]: Yes.

[Court]: Okay. So in the second trial, was there something that you can point to
where it's clear that, had [petitioner] had the full trial transcript, he would have avoided
some prejudicial episode?

[Counsel for Kennedy]: Not as I stand here. But I will say —

[Court]: Well then maybe you should sit down for a while, and on rebuttal
maybe you can figure out your case.

That highlighted admission — following a ten second silence during which counsel searched in vain for some answer to the court's question — should have ended this matter. Aware that, beyond having waived it in the briefs, Kennedy's counsel had thus conceded the critical argument in this litigation, counsel for the State rose with the intention of only briefly addressing the court. In remarks lasting just 30 seconds, counsel noted that we long have held that Britt error is subject to harmless error review, and that petitioner had failed to identify any prejudice. The following exchange with the majority ensued:

[Counsel for the State]: Unless the court has any questions, I — I believe that there's ...

[Court]: Yes. I have a question.

[Counsel for the State]: Yes, your honor.

[Court]: Umm ... There was gang testimony at the second trial and not at the first. Right?

[Counsel for the State]: I believe that's correct, your honor.

[Court]: And at the first trial, the district court excluded references to his membership in a gang. Right?

[Counsel for the State]: I believe that is correct, your honor, yes.

[Court]: And that was done at a pre-trial hearing with a motion. And that part of the transcript was not furnished for the second trial. Right?

[Counsel for the State]: I believe that's correct, your honor.

[Court]: And, as a result, the lawyer was not aware of the issue, and didn't object. And the evidence was admitted. Right?

[Counsel for the State]: Yes, your honor.

[Court]: And we have a number of cases that establish how prejudicial the introduction of gang testimony is. Right?

[Counsel for the State]: Yes, your honor, depending on the nature and the circumstances of gang testimony that is introduced.

[Court]: Well, in this case, it was introduced gratuitously, by the deputy district attorney asking for an elaboration on what "cuz" meant. Right?

[Counsel for the State]: Yes, your honor, but I believe it was limited to the definition of what "cuz" meant, or could have meant.

[Court]: Well, what was it relevant to?

[Counsel for the State]: Umm ...I — I believe it was, it may have been relevant to the area and the, the drug deal, the drug transaction.

[Court]: The fact that he was part of a gang. Right?

[Counsel for the State]: That's right.

[Court]: There's a minute order which was entered in the first case that said there will be no mention of gangs or gang affiliation unless clearly — unless cleared by the court out of the presence of the jury. That one came after the hearing on which it was made clear of the prejudicial nature of gang testimony. Did the same district attorney, deputy D.A. Clabby, try the second trial?

[Counsel for the State]: I am not sure.

[Court]: Well if the first judge thought it was prejudicial, why shouldn't we just assume, therefore, that prejudice is established in the second trial. Counsel (a) didn't know about the issue, didn't know about the prior ruling, and presumably the state did. And yet in the face of that prior minute order, the state went ahead and let its witness — in fact, invited its witness — to go ahead and inject the issue of gangs. Why isn't that sufficient to establish error? ...

By the time the State's argument time had expired, Kennedy's counsel had been so embarrassed by the court's relentless interrogation of counsel for the State — and by its viscerally derisive display of frustration at the close of his opening argument — that he began his rebuttal with an offer of atonement:

[Counsel for Kennedy]: I apologize to the court for missing that clear argument about the gang testimony.

Now, I have nothing but the greatest respect for my panel colleagues' lawyerly acumen. But I do not find its exercise compatible with the basic obligations of the office we share. As judges, the essence of our role is restrained service as impartial arbiters of disputes framed by litigants. It is not, I respectfully suggest, to act as backup counsel when litigants make poor arguments, or when they come into court without first having "figure[d] out" their cases [6] — even when doing so is motivated by a well-intentioned, but unavoidably standardless "philosophy of law ... infused by concepts like... social justice." [7]

Indeed, it was just a few months ago that today's majority offered almost precisely that admonition. In proceedings arising out of a case we resolved following an oral argument held the very same morning we heard this appeal, an order signed by Judges Reinhardt and Fisher instructed: "Given the overwhelming volume of work which today confronts our courts, we do not generally favor requiring judges ... to search out and research arguments that the other side does not make...." Gwaduri v. INS, 362 F.3d 1144, 1146 (9th Cir.2004). But what's sauce for the goose is supposed to be sauce for the gander. "Right?"

Events transpiring after initial publication of the majority's opinion granting Kennedy relief make clear the dangers inherent in my colleagues' eagerness to overreach from the bench. In their prior opinion — helping prove the wisdom of the age-old adage that "bad facts make bad law" — the majority repeatedly emphasized the bad "fact" that a single prosecutor was responsible for both of Kennedy's trials. For instance, the court noted in now-deleted language developing the factual basis for its decision that "[t]he prosecutor remained the same for both trials; he, thus, had personal knowledge of all that transpired during the prior proceedings," Kennedy, 372 F.3d 1013, 1016-17 (9th Cir.2004), and it emphasized that "[d]uring the second trial, the prosecutor, who was aware that the prior trial judge had excluded any mention of Kennedy's alleged gang involvement, proceeded, deliberately, to elicit testimony from Detective McDowell on the subject of gangs." Id. at 1017. Ultimately, the court concluded,

In hindsight, it is difficult to conclude that the omitted portions of the transcript would not have been important to Kennedy in preparing an effective defense, particularly where, as here, the prosecutor had a distinct advantage in presenting the government's case, having been present when the defense delivered its opening and closing arguments and throughout all of the proceedings both before and during the first trial.

    Id. at 1029-30.

    From such factual characterizations, one would have thought this case is, at bottom, about an overzealous prosecutor's nefarious plot to railroad a hapless defendant. How ... socially unjust! There is only one problem: The State's petition for rehearing en banc — which, by the way, is the first opportunity the State has had to respond to the majority's lawyering at the oral argument — reveals that different prosecutors handled Kennedy's two trials. The majority's factual predicate was utterly baseless.

    In the end, one would be hard-pressed to find a better illustration of what Sophanthavong had in mind when it identified how clearly prejudicial it can be for a court to overlook a party's clear waiver (not to mention a party's outright concession, as in this case): "The unfairness of such a tactic is obvious. Opposing counsel is denied the opportunity to point to the record to show that the new theory lacks legal or factual support." Sophanthavong, 365 F.3d at 737 (emphasis added).

    B

    Kennedy's personal failure to present any cogent basis for thinking he was prejudiced by the state trial court's alleged Britt error aside, the thin reed relied upon by the majority hardly suffices to demonstrate that the Court of Appeal's finding of harmlessness was objectively unreasonable. In its decision on direct appeal, the Court of Appeal noted that beyond Detective McDowell's statement that "a lot of people use [`cuz']," the prosecution elicited an acknowledgment from McDowell that the term often is used simply to refer to people from one's own neighborhood. See Kennedy v. Terhune, No. D027718 at 7. It is perhaps for that reason that the defense never objected to McDowell's testimony regarding gang affiliation: Considered in context, McDowell's "allusion to gang membership was not significant." Id. & id. at 17. Indeed, it was laughable — as the Court of Appeal quite reasonably concluded.

    Defense counsel's failure to object to the testimony has an additional significance: It undermines the chain of causation the majority uses to connect the trial court's failure to provide Kennedy a complete transcript to some meaningful error on retrial. The court speculates that, on notice of the need to object to McDowell's potentially prejudicial testimony concerning Kennedy's possible gang affiliation, there is "little doubt that Kennedy's counsel in the second trial would have presented a similar motion with a substantial likelihood of success." Opinion at 1054. Indeed, the majority tells us that counsel "would undoubtedly have based a motion to exclude on the arguments already presented." Id. at 1055 n. 16. Yet, confronted in court with McDowell's etymological testimony, counsel did not even seek to exclude it from the record as irrelevant or prejudicial. The majority's confidence that counsel would have acted differently prior to trial thus defies sound reason.

At the same time it undermines the majority's speculative chain of causation, counsel's failure to object to McDowell's testimony breaks it. For, in a variety of contexts, we have repeatedly recognized that contemporaneous objections can prevent reversible error stemming from the improper admission of prejudicial remarks by providing an opportunity for the court to purge the record or offer a curative instruction. See, e.g., Davis v. Woodford, 333 F.3d 982, 997(9th Cir.2003) (prosecutorial misconduct/documentary vouching); Bird v. Glacier Elec. Coop., Inc., 255 F.3d 1136, 1148(9th Cir.2001) ("Doubtless, contemporaneous objections at trial are to be encouraged. Where objections are made, there may be an opportunity for the trial judge to foreclose further error or to provide a curative instruction.") (civil litigation/appeal to racial prejudice); Dubria v. Smith, 224 F.3d 995, 1002 (9th Cir.2000) (improper admission of pre-trial law enforcement officer statements); Nevius v. Sumner, 852 F.2d 463, 470 (9th Cir.1988) ("Although the prosecutor's behavior at trial might have approached misconduct, any error could have been cured by contemporaneous objections.") (prosecutorial misconduct/argumentative vouching); Jeffries v. Blodgett, 5 F.3d 1180, 1192 (9th Cir.1993) (prosecutorial misconduct/commenting on defendant's refusal to testify); U.S. v. Schuler, 813 F.2d 978, 982 (9th Cir.1987) (prosecutorial misconduct/referencing a non-testifying defendant's out-of-court behavior); U.S. v. Stephens, 486 F.2d 915, 918 (judicial misconduct/instructing jury on how to weigh evidence); see also supra at 6, n. 3. Thus, whatever impact McDowell's gang testimony may have had on Kennedy's trial — and again it was not unreasonable to conclude that it had none — it cannot be attributed to the trial court's refusal to deliver Kennedy a complete transcript of his initial trial.

Were this not enough, the State's petition for rehearing en banc drives yet another nail through the heart of the court's opinion. Perhaps the most important step in the majority's logic was its assertion that the court on retrial would have been bound by the previous decision to exclude any gang testimony from Kennedy's mistrial, such that any motion by Kennedy to exclude such testimony would have had "a substantial likelihood of success," Kennedy, 372 F.3d at 1027:

Although we have found no California cases addressing the exact issue presented here, generally "under the law of the case doctrine and general principles of comity, a successor judge has the same discretion to reconsider an order as would the first judge, but should not overrule the earlier judge's order or judgment merely because the later judge might have decided matters differently." United States v. O'Keefe, 128 F.3d 885, 891 (5th Cir.1997). A second judge will generally follow a ruling made by an earlier judge unless the prior decision was erroneous, is no longer sound, or would create an injustice. Id. None of the exceptions to the application of this basic doctrine exists here.

Id. at 1027 n. 16.

Not so fast. Like its unsupported (and, until the State's petition for rehearing en banc, unrebutted) assertion that a single prosecutor was responsible for both Kennedy's mistrial and retrial, the majority's resort to generic law of the case principles turns out, again, to have been utterly baseless. For as the State points out in its petition for rehearing en banc — again taking advantage of its first real opportunity to respond to arguments developed and deployed by the majority at oral argument — law of the case doctrine actually does not apply to trial court decisions in California. See 9 Bernard E. Witkin, California Procedure § 896 at 930-31 (4th ed.1997) (collecting cases). Poof! Gone is the premise for the majority's speculative prediction that a motion to exclude gang testimony would almost certainly have been granted at retrial; in reality, the majority has absolutely no idea whether a motion to exclude would have been successful or not. At bottom, given the (new) prosecutor's efforts to minimize the impact of the already laughable gang testimony, and in light of the severe gaps in the majority's speculative chain of causation between any alleged Britt error and the introduction of gang testimony on retrial, no fair-minded jurist could conclude that it was objectively unreasonable for the Court of Appeal to have determined that any constitutional error was harmless.

Finally, I observe that there were ample additional reasons to believe that McDowell's allegedly prejudicial statements did not impact the jury's determination that Kennedy had committed the offense charged. In addition to the detective's persuasive testimony concerning the circumstances of petitioner's sale of a non-controlled substance in lieu of a controlled substance, Kennedy's "cousin," Randall Tucker, testified to delivering McDowell the paper bag containing the non-controlled substance (though he denied his own intent and any misrepresentation of its contents). As a result of that denial, the prosecution then lawfully impeached Tucker with evidence that he had pled guilty to the very offense at issue in Kennedy's trial. Given such powerful trial testimony to the jury suggesting petitioner's guilt, it seems something of a stretch to think that the jury's verdict would have been different had McDowell not been allowed to intimate that, among other completely innocuous meanings, the lingo "cuz" had gang significance.[8]

III

Apparently in search of a result, the majority yet again runs roughshod over the principles of comity and federalism underlying the Antiterrorism and Effective Death Penalty Act. "[P]remised on the fact that the state courts, as part of a coequal judiciary, are competent interpreters of federal law deserving of our full respect," Clark v. Murphy, 331 F.3d 1062, 1067 (9th Cir.2003), AEDPA mandates a "highly deferential standard for evaluating state-court rulings," Lindh v. Murphy, 521 U.S. 320, 333 n. 7, 117 S.Ct. 2059, 138 L.Ed.2d 481 (1997), and adamantly "demands that state court decisions be given the benefit of the doubt." Brodit v. Cambra, 350 F.3d 985, 987 (9th Cir.2003) (quotation and citation omitted). Notwithstanding the eminent reasonableness of their colleagues' analysis, two judges today inform seven others — a state trial judge, three state appellate judges, a federal magistrate judge, a federal district court judge, and a federal appellate judge (and that's not to mention the seven Justices of the California Supreme Court who summarily denied Kennedy's state petition for review) — that their understanding of the law is contrary to clearly established Supreme Court precedent. Again, one is tempted to ask: "Objectively, who is being unreasonable?" Payton v. Woodford, 346 F.3d 1204, 1225 (9th Cir.2003) (en banc) (Tallman, J., joined by Kozinski, Trott, Fernandez, and T.G.

Nelson, JJ., dissenting), cert. granted sub nom. Goughnour v. Payton, 541 U.S. ___, 124 S.Ct. 2388, 158 L.Ed.2d 962, 2004 WL 102831 (May 24, 2004).

Our apparent inability to internalize AEDPA's strict standard of review has become a source of repeated public embarrassment. During the past two terms alone, we have been summarily reversed by a unanimous Supreme Court no fewer than four times for disregarding AEDPA's strict limitations on the scope of our collateral review of state court constitutional adjudications. Middleton v. McNeil, 541 U.S. ___, 124 S.Ct. 1830, 158 L.Ed.2d 701 (2004) (per curiam), rev'g 344 F.3d 988 (9th Cir.2003); Yarborough v. Gentry, 540 U.S. 1, 124 S.Ct. 1, 157 L.Ed.2d 1 (2003) (per curiam), rev'g Gentry v. Roe, 320 F.3d 891 (9th Cir.2002); Woodford v. Visciotti, 537 U.S. 19, 123 S.Ct. 357, 154 L.Ed.2d 279 (2002) (per curiam), rev'g 288 F.3d 1097 (9th Cir.2002); Early v. Packer, 537 U.S. 3, 123 S.Ct. 362, 154 L.Ed.2d 263 (2002) (per curiam), rev'g Packer v. Hill, 291 F.3d 569 (9th Cir.2002). Because we are once again "nowhere close to the mark," Yarborough v. Alvarado, 541 U.S. ___, 124 S.Ct. 2140, 158 L.Ed.2d 938, 2004 WL 1190042 (June 1, 2004), rev'g Alvarado v. Hickman, 316 F.3d 841 (9th Cir.2002), I lamentably, yet respectfully, dissent.

Notes

[1] Pursuant to California Health and Safety Code § 11355, "Every person who ... offers, arranges, or negotiates to have sold, delivered, transported, furnished, administered, or given to any person any ... liquid, substance, or material in lieu of a[ ] controlled substance shall be punished by imprisonment in the county jail for not more than one year, or in the state prison." As a "wobbler" — an offense that can be punished as either a felony or misdemeanor, see Lockyer v. Andrade, 538 U.S. 63, 67, 123 S.Ct. 1166, 155 L.Ed.2d 144 (2003) — sale of a substance in lieu of a controlled substance can (as in this case) lead a recidivist to be sentenced to twenty-five years to life under California's Three Strikes Law, Cal.Penal Code §§ 667(e) & 1170.12(c)(2).

Kennedy's prior offenses included disorderly conduct, theft, burglary, battery, and forcible rape; numerous parole violations followed his nine-year incarceration in state prison for the latter offense. Cf. Ramirez v. Castro, 365 F.3d 755, 767-69 (9th Cir.2004) (declaring unconstitutional the imposition of a three-strikes twenty-five-to-life sentence on a recidivist whose prior history consisted only of three non-violent shoplifting offenses and who previously had served just six months and 20 days in county jail).

[2] The majority suggests that Kirk's reference to Britt's own recognition of its ambiguity is limited to the facts of Kirk. Opinion at 1048 n.8. Aside from the weakness of such a proposition, I note that while Kirk surely addressed a distinguishable factual scenario, no fair reading of the quoted passage — which opened the court's analysis of Britt and its progeny — supports such a limited interpretation. For the sake of ease, I here quote the Kirk passage in full:

The Supreme Court has held that a state `must, as a matter of equal protection, provide indigent prisoners with the basic tools of an adequate defense or appeal, when those tools are available for a price to other prisoners.' Britt v. North Carolina, 404 U.S. 226, 227, 92 S.Ct. 431, 30 L.Ed.2d 400 (1971) (emphasis added). However, the right to free transcripts is not absolute. The Court in Britt recognized that the `outer limits of that principle are not clear.' Id.

The Court, quite simply, has never clearly held that a transcript of premistrial motions are "basic tools of an adequate defense" — that is, that they fall within the admittedly "not clear ... outer limits" of its doctrine.

[3] The majority's suggestion that an objection would have been ineffectual because it may not have removed the prejudicial testimony from the jurors' minds, Opinion at 1056-57 n.19, not only contradicts case law establishing that jurors are generally presumed to follow the instructions of the court, see, e.g., United States v. Griffith, 301 F.3d 880, 884 n. 3 (8th Cir.2002) ("[T]he district court instructed the jury that the statements and comments of the prosecutor are not evidence. Because jurors are presumed to follow their instructions, this provides further evidence that Griffith suffered no prejudice as a result of the prosecutor's allegedly improper remarks.") (citation omitted); United States v. Magana, 127 F.3d 1, 6 (1st Cir.1997) ("Within wide margins, the potential for prejudice stemming from improper testimony can be satisfactorily dispelled by appropriate curative instructions. Jurors are presumed to follow such instructions, except in extreme cases.") (citations, quotations, and alterations omitted); United States v. Bullock, 71 F.3d 171, 175 (5th Cir.1995) ("[T]he court admonished the jury that it could consider Bullock's prior felony conviction only in connection with the firearm count. Any possible prejudice could be cured with proper instructions and juries are presumed to follow their instructions. Therefore, the jury instructions were sufficient to cure any possible prejudice."), but also case law demonstrating precisely how effective objections and instructions can be. See infra at 7890 (collecting cases).

[4] Contrary to the majority's assertion, I do not "put the burden on the defendant to prove that there is a `need' for the transcript" tailored to the particular facts of his case. Opinion at 1051. That might indeed create tension with Britt's holding that a trial court may not base its denial of a petitioner's request for a transcript on his failure to show "particularized need." Britt, 404 U.S. at 228, 92 S.Ct. 431 (emphasis added). Instead, I place the burden on the majority to justify its novel articulation of a thin rationale supporting the extension of prior precedent in order to impose a general requirement that indigents must be given a transcript of all non-testimonial preliminary proceedings; and to demonstrate that the state court objectively unreasonably concluded that, as a general matter, delivery of a partial transcript recording all testimony enables a constitutionally-effective defense.

[5] The majority's suggestion that no one could "have been prejudiced in any way by defense counsel's failure to address the prejudice question more directly," Opinion at 1054-55 n. 15, thus flatly contradicts our court's well-established — and just recently restated — understanding of how a party's failure adequately to brief an issue prejudices the opposing party.

[6] The majority's novel assertion that the habeas petitioner himself need neither argue nor identify prejudice because we must gauge the existence of prejudice in light of the record as a whole merely begs the question. Opinion at 1054-55 n.15. For who could deny that when we assess prejudice we must do so based on the complete record, as opposed to a fragmentary image of proceedings below? The real question, which the majority fails to answer, is what triggers such an assessment in the first instance. I submit that — as with any other claim courts are called upon to address — we only assess prejudice once the petitioner argues that he has been harmed in some specific way by an alleged constitutional error. The majority simply confuses a statement of how we must analyze well-preserved claims of prejudice with the untenable conclusion that such arguments can never be waived.

[7] Stephen Reinhardt and Howard Bashman, 20 Questions for Circuit Judge Stephen Reinhardt of the U.S. Court of Appeals for the Ninth Circuit, available at http://legalaffairs.org/howappealing/20q/ XXXX_XX_XX_XXq-appellateblog — archive.html (quotation marks omitted); see also Stephen Reinhardt, The Role of Social Justice in Judging Cases, Keynote Speech at the University of St. Thomas Law Journal Symposium Honoring Judge John T. Noonan, Jr. (Oct. 18, 2003) ("[S]ocial justice is a substantive legal principle that pervades all aspects of the law from torts to Social Security claims. The purpose of our legal system is not to provide an abstract code of rigid rules; rather it is to promote values that are compatible with the vision of a just existence for all individuals.").

[8] Though superficially plausible, we have previously declined to adopt the majority's theory that lengthy deliberations necessarily support a finding of prejudicial error. See Opinion at 1056 & n.18. Indeed, in United States v. Galindo, 913 F.2d 777, 779 (9th Cir.1990), we drew precisely the opposite inference. There, we addressed two criminal defendants' claims that they were incurably prejudiced by the judge's reference to ongoing plea negotiations. Rejecting the assertion, "we note [d] that the jury deliberated approximately three full days after a trial that lasted about that same length of time. Although this is a circumstance which in a given case can indicate a confused jury, here it negates any suggestion that the jury was stampeded to a verdict against the [defendants] out of prejudice resulting from the district court's statement at trial about plea negotiations." Id. at 779.

I do not mean to suggest that Galindo rules out the majority's argument. Indeed, we have reached such a conclusion in other cases. See, e.g., Dyas v. Poole, 317 F.3d 934, 937 (9th Cir.2003) (per curiam); Jennings v. Woodford, 290 F.3d 1006, 1019 (9th Cir.2002). But the majority's opinion in this case hinges on the introduction of prejudicial testimony — precisely the kind of occurrence that, like a judge's indication to the jury that a defendant is considering pleading guilty, could lead a jury to "stampede[ ] to a verdict." As in Galindo, that did not happen here. And the fact that we have refused to draw the majority's inference on direct appeal in closely analogous circumstances in turn supports the reasonableness of the state court's decision not to draw the inference below. For if a "difference of opinion among the courts of appeal [means] we cannot say that the state court unreasonably applied clearly established Federal law," Bailey v. Newland, 263 F.3d 1022, 1032 (9th Cir.2001), then a difference of opinion within this court of appeals would seem to suggest that we may not conclude that the state court's harmlessness determination was objectively unreasonable.

Judge O'Scannlain's dissent in Chein v. Shumsky (June 25, 2004)

O'SCANNLAIN, Circuit Judge, dissenting, with whom RYMER, T.G. NELSON, RAWLINSON, and CLIFTON, Circuit Judges, join.

I respectfully dissent from the court's decision to grant Edmund Chein's habeas corpus petition based on its conclusion that there was insufficient evidence to convict him of perjury in state court. I do not believe that the State of California deprived Chein of his constitutional rights on these grounds.[1]

I

Chein was convicted of three separate counts of perjury, the "specialist" count, the "office" count, and the "university" count. I discuss the constitutional sufficiency of the evidence for each conviction in turn.

A

As an expert medical witness at a personal injury trial, Chein was asked the following under oath: "And your specialty, what would be the correct designation?" He answered, "Physical medicine and orthopedic surgery." While Chein's residency included some rudimentary training in orthopedic surgery, the actual title of his residency program and consequent speciality designation was "physical medicine and rehabilitation" — not orthopedic surgery. Under California law, a perjurious statement must be both false and material. Cal.Penal Code § 118 (defining perjury as when a person, under oath, "states as true any material matter which he or she knows to be false"). As to the falsity of this statement, the majority ultimately assumes what I believe to be self-evident: that a rational jury could conclude that Chein lied under oath by claiming such a nonexistent credential. See Maj. Op. 985-86.

I disagree with the majority's conclusion as to the materiality of that lie; specifically, whether a jury in a personal injury case might have been influenced by Chein's made-up speciality in orthopedic surgery when he "testified as an expert witness [to establish] that the plaintiffs would require orthopedic surgery." Maj. Op. 986. The majority says no. But if two doctors gave me conflicting diagnoses about my need for invasive orthopedic surgery, I know I would be more inclined to trust the opinion of the actual orthopedic surgery specialist over the doctor who practiced physical medicine and rehabilitation. I believe that a rational jury could come to the same conclusion.

Under California law, the materiality of an allegedly perjurious statement is a question for the jury. People v. Kobrin, 11 Cal.4th 416, 425-29, 45 Cal.Rptr.2d 895, 901-02, 903 P.2d 1027, 1033-34 (1995). California's penal code provides specific detail about this requirement in § 123:

It is no defense to a prosecution for perjury that the accused did not know the materiality of the false statement made by him; or that it did not, in fact, affect the proceeding in or for which it was made. It is sufficient that it was material, and might have been used to affect such proceeding.[2]

According to California law, a "person is qualified to testify as an expert if he has special knowledge, skill, experience, training, or education sufficient to qualify him as an expert on the subject to which his testimony relates." Cal. Evid.Code § 720(a). Indeed, when challenged,"such special knowledge, skill, experience, training, or education must be shown before the witness may testify as an expert." § 720(a). Thus, Chein's qualifications, including the correct designation of his specialty, are threshold inquiries that must be established in order for him to testify. In other words, under California law, an expert witness's credentials are inherently material to his or her testimony.

This is not some "novel per se rule." Maj. Op. 987 n. 3. Rather, it simply reflects the nature of perjury, under California law, in the context of courtroom testimony. California is generally free to enact rules of evidence establishing when and how witnesses are qualified to testify at trial, and to bar them from testifying otherwise. For example, if a witness is required to have personal knowledge of events in order to testify about them, the fact that he or she did not witness an entire conversation would be grounds for excluding some portion of his or her testimony about it. Likewise, California law required Chein to possess medical credentials in order to offer his expert opinion in the first place — but he lied about the extent of those credentials, and hence about his very ability to testify at all.[3] See Cal. Evid.Code § 720.

Indeed, under California law, Chein would have been precluded from offering his opinion if he refused to specify his qualifications, so a rational jury should be able to conclude that lying about those same qualifications was material. See Law Revision Commission Comment to Cal. Evid.Code § 802 (1995)

Under existing law, where a witness testifies in the form of opinion not based upon his personal observation, the assumed facts upon which his opinion is based must be stated in order to show that the witness has some basis for forming an intelligent opinion and to permit the trier of fact to determine the applicability of the opinion in light of the existence or nonexistence of such facts.

(citing Eisenmayer v. Leonardt, 148 Cal. 596, 84 P. 43 (1906) and Lemley v. Doak Gas Engine Co., 40 Cal.App. 146, 180 P. 671 (1919)). The asserted "fact" that Chein was a specialist in "orthopedic surgery" must have been at least one of his "bas[e]s for forming an intelligent opinion," id., of the orthopedic injuries sustained by the Lopez plaintiffs. Accordingly, the jury was entitled to make its determination "in light of the existence or nonexistence" of that asserted specialty.

Id. California law also extends the scope of cross-examination in this context to allow an expert to "be fully cross-examined as to ... his or her qualifications." Cal. Evid.Code § 721(a). Thus, Chein's lie prevented both the jury and the opposing party from determining a fact that each had the statutory right to consider.

Furthermore, as I understand it, the majority's interpretation of California perjury law would seem to allow Chein, with impunity, also to have falsely testified that he was a recipient of the Nobel Prize in Medicine for his work in orthopedic surgery.[4] For this false, though hugely persuasive credential would only have conferred an enhanced ability to determine "the precise type of surgical procedure" that would be necessary, and would not be squarely relevant to the majority's critically narrow question of who was better qualified to determine whether the plaintiffs might have "a need for future [orthopedic] surgery." Maj. Op. 987. This is difficult to accept.

Perhaps, then, this is why the majority is willing to concede that a falsely claimed Nobel Prize in orthopedic surgery "could have been material." Maj. Op. 987 n. 4 (emphasis in original). But if that is true, it is for a state court jury — not a federal appellate court in a habeas corpus case — to determine whether Chein's false advanced credential was material. We have no businesses determining, as a matter of state law, that a physician with a Nobel Prize in orthopedic surgery possesses a material expert qualification, while a physician with a recognized specialty in orthopedic surgery plainly does not. In other words, the majority has simply chosen the kind of advanced orthopedic credential it — rather than the jury — finds impressive. I believe such an approach is unwarranted.

This is particularly true given that the expert witnesses at Chein's perjury trial emphasized the hard work, dedication, and years of advanced training and education it takes to become a "normal, albeit specialist doctor" in orthopedic surgery, as the majority somewhat cavalierly puts it. Id. If nothing else, these witnesses demonstrated that achieving such an advanced credential means a whole lot to them, and that it is certainly an accomplishment worthy of true "recognition ... in a career in medicine." Id. Nevertheless, the majority says no reasonable person could conclude that such training could potentially have any persuasive value in the Lopez case. With respect, I do not believe California has set so high a bar for perjury convictions.

The majority heavily emphasizes that the defendants in the Lopez case argued that the plaintiffs never suffered any injury at all. See Maj. Op. 988. But that has no bearing in this context. Whatever the defense's legal theory of the case, the Lopez plaintiffs had to establish the fact of their injuries to recover for them in their tort suit. One of the particular injuries they claimed was orthopedic in nature. Maj. Op. 986 ("Chein testified as an expert witness that the plaintiffs would require orthopedic surgery."). So if the jury did not believe Chein's assessment that the plaintiffs had actually suffered those injuries, their recovery would have been reduced accordingly. In other words, regardless of the defense's position, the plaintiffs had to establish that they actually suffered the orthopedic injuries they claimed in order to receive all of the compensation they sought, and any change in the amount of compensation they may have recovered necessarily affects the outcome of the proceeding.

Chein may have lied believing that his testimony would be excluded if he were not an orthopedic surgeon. Or, he may simply have presented a false credential (one that the opposing expert possessed) to bolster his medical opinion testimony. There is also a fair probability that reasonable jurors might specifically consider Chein's uncorrected lie in making their ultimate determination, at least as to compensation. In any case, a reasonable person could conclude that Chein's false statement "might have been used to affect[the Lopez] proceeding." Cal.Penal Code § 123.

Therefore, I must respectfully dissent from the majority's conclusion that no rational trier of fact could believe that Chein's "specialist" testimony was material under California law.

B

The majority also concludes that the jury did not have sufficient evidence upon which to convict Chein of "the office count." Chein testified that he had only one office, when in fact he had several. Here, the majority clearly concedes that a rational trier of fact could determine that the testimony was false, see Maj. Op. 988-89, but mistakenly holds that no rational jury could have found the essential element of materiality beyond a reasonable doubt.

California courts have interpreted the materiality provision of perjury broadly. For example, "[f]alse testimony even unrelated to an issue but which has the tendency to impeach the credibility of a witness who testified on a material issue may be perjurious" under the materiality requirement. People v. Gamble, 8 Cal.App.3d 142, 87 Cal.Rptr. 333, 335 (1970) (emphasis added). Additionally, false "statements not directly related to an issue may also be material where they have a tendency to influence the trier of fact on an issue."[5] Id.

At least one witness at Chein's trial, Judge Robert Altman, testified that the maintenance of multiple offices could negatively affect the persuasiveness of Chein's qualifications because it could lead to the inference that Chein ran "a [personal injury] mill and that the doctor isn't just in medicine just making money and that the doctor is handling all personal injuries and workmen's compensation and then churning cases through the courtroom." This is a simple credibility inference that need not be established by an expert witness, so the fact that Judge Altman was not a medical doctor does not affect the admissibility of his testimony. Judge Altman was a trial judge who presumably adjudicated many personal injury cases involving numerous medical experts and their relative credibility as ultimately evidenced by verdicts. Therefore, his lay opinion testimony was admissible under California law as "[r]ationally based on the perception of the witness." Cal. Evid.Code § 800(a).

I sincerely doubt that Judge Altman's "personal injury mill" inference would "in fact, affect the proceeding in or for which it was made." Cal.Penal Code § 123. Nevertheless, a rational jury could believe that the false statement "might have been used to affect [the Lopez] proceeding," § 123, because I believe that a rational juror could conclude that Chein's false testimony, though perhaps "unrelated to an issue ... ha[d] the tendency to impeach the credibility of a witness who testified on a material issue."[6] Gamble, 87 Cal.Rptr. at 335. Chein's false testimony also may rationally be understood at least to have had a "tendency to influence the trier of fact on [the] issue" of Chein's qualification as a credible medical expert. Id. Therefore, I must respectfully dissent from the majority's conclusion that no reasonable jury could have found Chein's lie about his offices material beyond a reasonable doubt under California law.

C

Chein's interrogatory testimony regarding the medical school he attended presents a more difficult question, and one that may hinge on whether or not AEDPA deference applies. Nevertheless, for purposes of this dissent, I need not address it: Because I believe that there were at least two clearly sustainable perjury convictions, and because there is no suggestion that Chein's sentence would have been different if he had been convicted only of these two perjury counts, Chein's incarceration remains constitutionally valid. See United States v. Barron, 172 F.3d 1153, 1160 (9th Cir.1999) (en banc).

II

For the foregoing reasons, I must respectfully dissent.[7]

Notes

[1] Because I believe the standard of review in this case does not affect the outcome, I, too, express no opinion regarding the interplay between AEDPA and Jackson v. Virginia, 443 U.S. 307, 99 S.Ct. 2781, 61 L.Ed.2d 560 (1979). See Maj. Op. 982.

[2] The majority asserts that the last part of § 123, "might have been used to affect such proceeding," "seems not to be a definition of materiality but an additional requirement." Maj. Op. 985 n. 2 (emphasis in original). We have no power to decide how California should best interpret its own law, so such a contention is plainly inappropriate given that the two most recent California cases on the subject specifically define the "materiality" element of perjury as "whether the statement or testimony `might have been used to affect [the proceeding in or for which it was made].'" Kobrin, 11 Cal.4th at 420, 45 Cal.Rptr.2d at 896, 903 P.2d at 1028 (quoting § 123) (brackets in original); People v. Feinberg, 51 Cal.App.4th 1566, 60 Cal.Rptr.2d 323, 329 (1997). Indeed, in the very case at bar, the California Court of Appeal invoked this standard in rejecting Chein's sufficiency of the evidence claim.

The majority claims that Kobrin's formulation is dicta. This is plainly untrue: Kobrin established that the question of materiality must be submitted to the jury, and the specific formulation of that requirement is clearly a valid holding of the court. Indeed, People v. Wade, 39 Cal.App.4th 1487, 46 Cal.Rptr.2d 645 (1995), which the majority relies on to establish the "correct" materiality standard, is not even a perjury case at all, but a second degree murder case that distinguished California perjury jurisprudence. See Maj. Op. 984. Now there's real dicta.

More importantly, the majority's analysis suggests that there is some material difference between the "could probably" and the "might" standard, and that only one or the other can apply to this case. See Maj. Op. 984 (arguing that Kobrin did not "overrule earlier formulations of the materiality standard"). I do not believe this to be true, at least under California law. See Feinberg, 60 Cal.Rptr.2d at 329 (stating that "[t]he test for whether a statement is material has been stated as whether the statement or testimony might have been used to affect the proceeding in or for which it was made or whether the statement could probably have influenced the outcome of the proceedings" (internal citations, alterations, and quotation marks omitted)).

Even if they are materially different standards, a "could probably" formulation must be more favorable to Chein than a "might" standard, and the jury's determination under the higher burden necessarily encompassed the lesser finding. In other words, when the jurors specifically found beyond a reasonable doubt that Chein's false statements could probably have affected the outcome, they perforce found that Chein's lies might have been used to such effect. Longstanding precedent establishes that when criminal "defendants [are] convicted under [a] heavier standard, they have no cause for complaint. The error [can] only work in their favor and [is] therefore, harmless." United States v. Pheaster, 544 F.2d 353, 362 n. 3 (9th Cir.1976); see also United States v. Rea, 532 F.2d 147, 149 (9th Cir.1976) (refusing to find error in a case where "[a]ny ambiguity in the instructions could only have benefitted the defendant, because some jurors might have had an erroneous, but more stringent, view of the government's burden of proof").

For these reasons, I must reject the majority's implication that the "might" standard is not an equally valid formulation of materiality under California law. And to the extent it makes any difference at all, I generally employ this baseline materiality standard enunciated in § 123 and reiterated in Kobrin and Feinberg.

[3] It is undisputed that "Chein testified as an expert witness [to establish] that the plaintiffs would require orthopedic surgery." Maj. Op. 986. At the very least, then, if Chein admitted that he had not received sufficient training to qualify as an orthopedic surgery specialist, the trial court probably would not have abused its discretion if it determined that he could not testify at least as to that issue. The majority counters that "[t]here is no basis" to conclude that Chein would have been barred from testifying had the trial court known his actual credentials. Maj. Op. 987 n. 3. But this only demonstrates a fundamental misunderstanding of California perjury law, for whether there is any evidence to suggest that a false statement actually may have affected the outcome of a case is irrelevant. Cal.Penal Code § 123 ("It is no defense to a prosecution for perjury that the ... false statement ... did not, in fact, affect the proceeding in or for which it was made.").

[4] The simple fact that such a lie would be so easy to detect would have no bearing on a later perjury charge under California law. See Cal.Penal Code § 118.

[5] Because these statements demonstrate that California law does not confine materiality to any one specific issue in a case, I must reject the majority's attempt to limit our inquiry to the very narrow question of whether the "number of offices out of which a physician practices [is] material to the question of whether he actually examined the patients about whom he testified." Maj. Op. 991. The jury was free to frame the issues its own way. It could even determine that Chein's lie about his multiple offices was not "directly related to an issue" in the case at all, but merely had "a tendency to influence the

trier of fact" in any aspect of its decision. Gamble, 87 Cal.Rptr. at 335.

[6] While this statement may generally refer to one witness falsely disparaging the credibility of another, I do not believe this is distinguishable from a witness falsely bolstering his or her own credibility. And there is no doubt that Chein testified on a material issue.

[7] Aside from a sufficiency of the evidence challenge, Chein presented additional arguments to support his petition. Given the court's disposition, however, I do not address them.

Judge O'Scannlain's dissent in Campbell v. Allied Van Lines (June 7, 2005)

O'SCANNLAIN, Circuit Judge, dissenting.

This exercise in statutory interpretation forces us to confront the fact that the most literal interpretation of a phrase is not always the most natural and reasonable one. For that reason, I cannot agree with the majority's interpretation of 49 U.S.C. § 14708(d).

That subsection awards attorney fees to a shipper prevailing in a lawsuit against a carrier only if

(A) a decision resolving the dispute was not rendered through arbitration under this section within the period provided ... or

(B) the court proceeding is to enforce a decision rendered through arbitration under this section and is instituted after the period for performance under such decision has elapsed.

49 U.S.C. § 14708(d)(3)(A)-(B). On the majority's reading, § 14708(d)(3)(A) applies even when no arbitration occurs at all because the shipper elects to head straight into court. In its insistence that this reading of § 14708(d)(3)(A) is not only preferable but unambiguously correct, the majority adheres to a decontextualized literalism that even the staunchest defenders of textualism eschew. See Antonin Scalia, A Matter of Interpretation 24 (1997) ("[T]he good textualist is not a literalist...."); Smith v. United States, 508 U.S. 223, 242, 113 S.Ct. 2050, 124 L.Ed.2d 138 (1993) (Scalia, J., dissenting) ("When someone asks, `Do you use a cane?,' he is not inquiring whether you have your grandfather's silver-handled walking stick on display in the hall.").

I do not deny that it is possible to read the words of subsection (A) as the majority does, but our task is to find the most ordinary, natural, and reasonable interpretation of the provision's language. See Bailey, 516 U.S. at 145, 116 S.Ct. 501. The provision appears in the midst of a statute designed to promote and to facilitate arbitration of claims under the Carmack Amendment. Yet the majority's interpretation of the attorney-fee provision turns it into a powerful incentive for shippers not to pursue arbitration. A shipper who takes his claim straight to court and wins has his legal costs paid by the carrier, while a shipper who submits the claim for arbitration must pay not only his own legal fees but part of the cost of the arbitration as well. See 49 U.S.C. § 14708(b)(5).

Only an unnatural literalism permits the majority to conclude that the statute's text compels this counterintuitive result. Imagine that, one summer's afternoon, a father turns to his son and says, "If you'd like to, we'll go to the ballpark this afternoon and hit some balls. And I'll tell you what—if your old Dad doesn't hit a baseball over the fences, he promises to buy you some ice cream." "Great, Dad," says the son, "but I don't want to play baseball this afternoon. Let's play football in the yard instead."

The father agrees, and after a few spirited hours of play, the two head back to the house for dinner. As they brush the dirt out of their clothes, the son says, "Well, Dad, you owe me an ice cream. You didn't hit a single baseball over the fences."

Were the majority present at this scene and called upon to adjudicate the conflict, the father would protest in vain that his conditional promise of ice cream depended on the son's acceptance of his invitation to play baseball. After all, the majority would insist, the father's words were unambiguous: "If I don't hit a baseball over the fences, I promise to buy you some ice cream." And the majority would conclude that—to paraphrase its own reasoning— "given the ease with which the father expressly listed one eligibility criterion (his failure to hit a home run)," there was "no reason why he would bury a second (the son's acceptance of the invitation to play baseball) implicitly within" his proposal. See Majority op., supra at 622.

But that is not how language works, either in conversation or in statutory interpretation. We begin with a statute's plain meaning, of course, but plain meaning is not meaning divorced from context. See Verizon Communications, Inc. v. FCC, 535 U.S. 467, 499-500, 122 S.Ct. 1646, 152 L.Ed.2d 701 (2002) (rejecting a "plain-meaning argument [that] ignores the statutory setting in which [the provision at issue] occurs"); Bailey v. United States, 516 U.S. 137, 145, 116 S.Ct. 501, 133 L.Ed.2d 472 ("[T]he meaning of statutory language, plain or not, depends on context." (alteration in original)). A reasonable person would understand the father to be promising ice cream only if the son agrees to play baseball and the father hits no home runs. Similarly, in my view, the most reasonable interpretation of § 14708(d)(3)(A) is that it makes attorney fees available if the shipper takes advantage of the opportunity for arbitration that the carrier is statutorily bound to provide and no decision is rendered within the sixty-day period provided.

Turning to extrinsic sources—as we may when statutes are ambiguous, see Int'l Ass'n of Machinists & Aerospace Workers, Local Lodge 964 v. BF Goodrich Aerospace Aerostructures Group, 387 F.3d 1046, 1051-52 (9th Cir.2004)—only strengthens the case against the majority's interpretation. The current § 14708 is the result of Congress's 1995 amendments to the dispute-settlement provisions of the Carmack Amendment. The earlier statute allowed, but did not require, carriers to offer arbitration. See 49 U.S.C. § 11711 (1995) (repealed 1995). It provided in relevant part:

(d) In any court action to resolve a dispute between a shipper of household goods and a motor common carrier providing transportation subject to the jurisdiction of the Commission under subchapter II of chapter 105 of this title concerning the transportation of household goods by such carrier, the shipper shall be awarded reasonable attorney's fees if—

(1) the shipper submits a claim to the carrier within 120 days after the date the shipment is delivered or the date the delivery is scheduled, whichever is later;

(2) the shipper prevails in such court action; and

(3) (A) no dispute settlement program approved under this section was available for use by the shipper to resolve the dispute; or

(B) a decision resolving the dispute was not rendered under a dispute settlement program approved under this section within the period provided under subsection (b)(8) of this section or an extension of such period under such subsection; or

(C) the court proceeding is to enforce a decision rendered under a dispute settlement program approved under this section and is instituted after the period for performance under such decision has elapsed.

49 U.S.C. § 11711(d) (1995) (repealed 1995).

Notably, former § 11711(d)(3)(B) is identical for all relevant purposes to current § 14708(d)(3)(A), the provision at issue in this case: each grants attorney fees when "a decision resolving the dispute was not rendered [in arbitration] within the period provided."[1] It would be extremely odd if the two provisions, whose text is essentially the same, meant two sharply different things. Yet that is what the majority's holding implies; for the former § 11711(d)(3)(B) cannot reasonably bear the interpretation the majority would place upon current § 14708(d)(3)(A). That interpretation would render subsection (A) of the earlier statute wholly redundant and unnecessary, because whenever "no dispute settlement program approved under [§ 11711] was available for use by the shipper to resolve the dispute," it would necessarily have been true that "a decision resolving the dispute was not rendered under a dispute settlement program approved under this section within the period provided."

Because I believe that the plain meaning of the language of § 14708(d)(3)(A) in its context[2] is that attorney fees are available only when shippers attempt arbitration but cannot obtain a decision within the allotted time—and because that interpretation, unlike the majority's, is consonant with the statute's history—I respectfully dissent.

Notes

[1] The only difference is that the phrase "under a dispute settlement program approved under this section" has been replaced with "through arbitration under this section," a change that merely reflects the fact that arbitration programs need no longer be "approved" by the Commission.

[2] Part of the relevant context is the title of § 14708: "Dispute settlement program for household carriers." The majority's interpretation turns § 14708(d)(3)(A) into a general attorney-fee provision whose scope extends well beyond cases in which a dispute-settlement program is involved. The "title of a statute and the heading of a section are tools available for the resolution of a doubt" about the meaning of a statutory provision. Almendarez-Torres v. United States, 523 U.S. 224, 234, 118 S.Ct. 1219, 140 L.Ed.2d 350 (1998) (internal quotation marks omitted).

Judge O'Scannlain's dissent in Quan v. Gonzales (Nov 7, 2005)

O'SCANNLAIN, Circuit Judge, dissenting.

I respectfully submit that the court has substituted its independent analysis of the record for that of the Immigration Judge (the "IJ"), and, in so doing, has exceeded its authority and intruded upon the proper role of the fact finder. Because I conclude that the IJ's findings deserve greater deference than the majority accords them, I respectfully dissent from the decision to grant Lin Quan's petition.

I

Where the BIA has summarily affirmed the decision of an IJ, we review the IJ's decision as though it were the opinion of the BIA, see Falcon Carriche v. Ashcroft, 350 F.3d 845, 849 (9th Cir.2003), and we must accept the IJ's finding of fact unless the evidence compels a contrary conclusion. See INS v. Elias-Zacarias, 502 U.S. 478, 481 n. 1, 112 S.Ct. 812, 117 L.Ed.2d 38 (1992). This is an extremely deferential standard of review: it is not enough that the evidence supports a contrary conclusion, that the panel would have weighed the evidence differently, id., or even that the panel is persuaded that the finding is incorrect; the evidence must be so over-whelming that not just the panel in question but "any reasonable adjudicator would be compelled to conclude the contrary." 8 U.S.C. § 1252(b)(4)(B) (emphases added). The law and the Supreme Court are unequivocal on this point. See id.; Elias-Zacarias, 502 U.S. at 481 n. 1, 112 S.Ct. 812 ("To reverse the BIA finding we must find that the evidence not only supports that conclusion, but compels it.").

A

The majority discusses some of the implausibilities and inconsistencies on which the IJ based his adverse credibility finding and purports to show how the implausibilities are conjectural and how the inconsistencies can be explained. On some points the majority is persuasive, but, given the extremely deferential standard of review that we must apply, enough evidence remains, in my view, to support the IJ's finding.

In particular, Quan's account of how her mother was able to obtain 3,000 RMB to procure her release from detention is accepted at face value by the majority despite contrary evidence in the record. Quan testified that her mother was able to withdraw the money from her savings bank on a Sunday, but Quan's husband repeatedly testified that such banks are closed on Sundays. It is not accurate, therefore, to say that "[i]n order for the IJ to come to [his] conclusion, he had to assume facts not in evidence," maj. op. at 888.[1] The IJ explicitly found that the contradictory testimony of the husband — who had every reason to corroborate his wife's story and no reason to undermine it — cast substantial doubt on Quan's credibility. This sort of weighing of evidence is emphatically the prerogative of an IJ and the fact that the apparent inconsistency affects a key aspect of Quan's allegation of persecution should make it an unassailable basis for an adverse credibility finding.

Quan's testimony was also confused and incomplete with respect to the number and dates of the prayer meetings that she attended, and the timing of her confession of her belief in Jesus Christ to her husband. The majority attempts to down-play the significance of the latter point by labeling it as a minor discrepancy in dates. As the majority characterizes it, the one month difference between the date when Quan claims to have told her husband about her Christian practice and the date that her husband claims to have learned of it is of no import, but the IJ had good reason to view it otherwise. What concerned the IJ was the fact that, although Quan attributed her mother's recovery from illness to her new practice of Christianity, she appears to have withheld this information from her husband — who was sympathetic to Christianity — throughout the course of his own father's illness. The time between July and August, 1996, therefore, was not insignificant. That month marks an important change in circumstances: it is the difference between Quan informing her husband of her newfound faith in the healing power of Christian prayer while her husband's father was still alive and telling him at his father's funeral. In the case of a meaningful inconsistency such as this, it is the IJ's duty to consider the first-person testimony before him and to resolve the evidentiary confusion either for or against the petitioner. This the IJ did, and, because his conclusion is reasonably supported by evidence in the record—namely, the testimony of Quan's husband—we are not entitled to disturb it.

The majority's justifications of its own interpretations of this and other inconsistencies are reasonable, but so too is the IJ's scepticism, which should not be supplanted unless it is wholly conjectural or has no basis in the record. Because there is genuine confusion and inconsistency in the record on these points, and because the IJ's conclusions are supported by evidence in the record, it simply cannot be said that the evidence compels reversal. I would, therefore, affirm the IJ's adverse credibility finding and deny the petition.

II

The IJ also found that a single detention, for less than one day, during which Quan had her hair pulled, was shaken, and was poked once with an electric prod in her shoulder/neck area did not rise to the level of persecution.

Given the inconsistent thresholds for finding persecution applied by different panels of this court, it is not surprising that the majority is able to cite a case in which we held that similar facts amounted to persecution. See Guo v. Ashcroft, 361 F.3d 1194 (9th Cir.). In that case, however, the petitioner was detained for a day and half (more than 50% longer than in this case), was struck twice in the face, kicked in the stomach, and ordered to do push-ups until he collapsed. By contrast, in other cases we have held that a single detention, during which the petitioner was beaten, did not compel a finding of persecution because the petitioner did not require medical attention. See, e.g., Prasad v. INS, 47 F.3d 336, 339 (9th Cir.1995).

The majority argues that the lingering physical and mental symptoms about which Quan testified and the fact that she lost her job because the police visited her workplace support a finding of persecution. That may be so, but the fact that Quan did not testify that she required medical treatment, which was an important factor in our holding in Prasad, that she claims to have heard, second-hand, that she had lost her job but never bothered to confirm the report, and that, although her husband worked at the same company, nobody ever told him that she had been fired. On the basis of this evidence it was reasonable for the IJ to find that Quan had not been persecuted.

Because I do not believe that an IJ's decision should be overturned merely because the reviewing panel disagrees with it or can point to a plausibly analogous case from our abundant and inconsistent precedent, and because the evidence in this case does not compel a finding of persecution, I would affirm the IJ's decision and deny the petition.

III

Finally, Quan and her counsel, Mr. Douglas Ingraham, are fortunate that this petition was not dismissed for failure to abide by Fed. R.App. P. 28(a)(9)(A), which requires a brief to contain "citations to the ... part of the record on which the appellant relies." See also Ninth Circuit Rule No. 28-2.8. Given the limited resources of both the government and this court, it was irresponsible of Quan's counsel to shift the burden of sifting through almost 900 pages of administrative record onto the government and this court to find the facts on which Quan bases her argument. In De la Rosa v. Scottsdale Memorial Health Systems, Inc., 136 F.3d 1241, 1243 (9th Cir. 1998), we "declare[d] that this habit of noncompliance must end" and we have, on at least two occasions, struck briefs and dismissed appeals for failure to comply with this basic requirement. See Mitchel v. General Electric Company, 689 F.2d 877, 878 (9th Cir.1982); N/S Corporation v. Liberty Mutual Insurance Company, 127 F.3d 1145, 1146 (9th Cir.1997).

The majority concedes the technical deficiencies of the brief and admits that it is "sympathetic to the Respondent's argument [that the brief be struck and the case dismissed]," maj. op. at 886, but concludes that dismissal is not necessary "[b]ecause we have conducted our own independent review of the administrative record." Id. at 886. With all due respect to the majority's commendable diligence, that is beside the point. Opposing counsel, or, as in this case, the court, will often be able to compensate for a party's shortcomings, but doing so involves a waste of limited time and resources. The rules governing the form and content of appellate briefs are not merely hortatory; they must be obeyed, and, when they are not, the consequences should be real. Mr. Ingraham should consider himself exceedingly fortunate that the only consequence of his inadequate performance in this case is a verbal admonishment. He should not expect to escape so lightly in the future.

Notes

[1] Ironically, it is the majority's analysis which relies on facts not in evidence. The majority's reliance on a website of unknown reliability to establish that "banks in China are typically open on Sundays," maj. op. at 888 (emphasis added), is a novel — and, I would respectfully suggest. misguided — application of the doctrine of judicial notice. See

Fed.R.Evid. 201 (b) ("A judicially noticed fact must be one not subject to reasonable dispute in that it is either (1) generally known within the territorial jurisdiction of the trial court or (2) capable of accurate and ready determination by resort to sources whose accuracy cannot reasonably be questioned.").

More importantly, this "evidence" fails to undermine the IJ's adverse credibility determination. Even assuming these dubious sources establish the veracity of the petitioner's statement, the IJ relied on inconsistencies between the petitioner's testimony and her husband's in making a credibility determination — a fact independent of the bank's actual operating hours. The IJ needed to consider only the petitioner's testimony — not facts outside the record — to support this conclusion.

Judge O'Scannlain's concurrence in Yahoo! Inc. v. La Ligue Contre Le Racisme (Jan 12, 2006)

O'SCANNLAIN, Circuit Judge, with whom FERGUSON and TASHIMA, Circuit Judges, join, concurring only in the judgment:

Our requirement that a defendant have "purposefully availed" himself of the protections and benefits of the forum state, or have "purposefully directed" his activities into the forum state, must be read in light of the Supreme Court's admonition in Milliken v. Meyer, 311 U.S. 457, 61 S.Ct. 339, 85 L.Ed. 278 (1940), that the exercise of personal jurisdiction must comport with "traditional notions of fair play and substantial justice." Id. at 463, 61 S.Ct. 339. Because I cannot agree that California's exercise of personal jurisdiction over La Ligue Contre Le Racisme et L'Antisemitisme ("LICRA") and L'Union des Etudiants Juifs de France ("UEJF") comports with those basic principles, I respectfully dissent from the majority's opinion while concurring in its conclusion that Yahoo!'s suit must be dismissed. For similar reasons, I concur in Judge Tashima's concurrence and in Part I of Judge Ferguson's concurrence.

I

A State's jurisdiction is defined not by force or influence but by physical territory and its judicial power traditionally extended over only those persons and property within its borders. See Pennoyer v. Neff, 95 U.S. 714, 720-22, 24 L.Ed. 565 (1878). The idea of "minimum contacts" developed as a surrogate for actual presence in a State but did not alter the essentially territorial nature of jurisdiction. The question in every personal jurisdiction case, then, is whether an individual's contacts with the forum State are so substantial that they render the extension of sovereign power just, notwithstanding his lack of physical presence there.

A

The personal jurisdiction requirement is not merely a rule of civil procedure; it is a constitutional constraint on the powers of a State, as exercised by its courts, in favor of the due process rights of the individual. See Omni Capital Int'l v. Rudolf Wolff & Co., 484 U.S. 97, 104, 108 S.Ct. 404, 98 L.Ed.2d 415 (1987) ("The requirement that a court have personal jurisdiction flows not from [Article] III, but from the Due Process Clause. It represents a restriction on judicial power not as a matter of sovereignty, but as a matter of individual liberty."). Grounded in the Fourteenth Amendment's protection of the processes necessary to ensure basic fairness in the application of the law, the requirement that an individual have "certain minimum contacts" with the relevant forum "such that the maintenance of the suit does not offend `traditional notions of fair play and substantial justice,'" International Shoe v. Washington, 326 U.S. 310, 316, 66 S.Ct. 154, 90 L.Ed. 95 (1945) (quoting Milliken, 311 U.S. at 463, 61 S.Ct. 339), protects him from the unpredictable and burdensome exercise of authority by foreign courts. It follows from this that the rights and interests of Yahoo! and the interests of the State of California, if not irrelevant to the inquiry, are clearly subordinate to the rights of LICRA and UEJF, the parties against whom jurisdiction is asserted and whose rights are protected by the Due Process Clause.

The Supreme Court has advised that

the constitutional touchstone remains whether the defendant purposefully established "minimum contacts" in the forum State. Although it has been argued that foreseeability of causing injury in another State should be sufficient to establish such contacts there when policy considerations so require, the Court has consistently held that this kind of foreseeability is not a "sufficient benchmark" for exercising personal jurisdiction. Instead, the foreseeability that is critical to due process analysis is that the defendant's conduct and connection with the forum State are such that he should reasonably anticipate being haled into court there.

Burger King v. Rudzewicz, 471 U.S. 462, 474, 105 S.Ct. 2174, 85 L.Ed.2d 528 (1985) (emphases added). By requiring that individuals have "fair warning that a particular activity may subject [them] to the jurisdiction of a foreign sovereign," Shaffer v. Heitner, 433 U.S. 186, 218, 97 S.Ct. 2569, 53 L.Ed.2d 683 (1977) (STEVENS, J., concurring in judgment), the Due Process Clause "gives a degree of predictability to the legal system that allows potential defendants to structure their primary conduct with some minimum assurance as to where that conduct will and will not render them liable to suit." World-Wide Volkswagen Corp. v. Woodson, 444 U.S. 286, 297, 100 S.Ct. 559, 62 L.Ed.2d 490 (1980).

B

The Supreme Court has never approved such a radical extension of personal jurisdiction as would sanction the majority's holding that, by litigating a bona fide claim in a foreign court and receiving a favorable judgment, a foreign party automatically assents to being haled into court in the other litigant's home forum. Such a result cannot be reconciled with the "constitutional touchstone" of foreseeability: that the defendant "should reasonably anticipate being haled into court" in the forum. Burger King, 471 U.S. at 474, 105 S.Ct. 2174, 85 L.Ed.2d 528.

In Calder v. Jones, 465 U.S. 783, 104 S.Ct. 1482, 79 L.Ed.2d 804 (1984), the defendants should reasonably have expected that, by circulating a libelous story in

California about a California celebrity, they would be haled into court in California to answer for their tortious behavior. And in Burger King, because the defendants' business ties with the State of Florida were "shielded by the `benefits and protections'" of Florida's laws, it was "presumptively not unreasonable to require [them] to submit to the burdens of litigation [there] as well." 471 U.S. at 543, 105 S.Ct. 2218. These cases stake out the limits of personal jurisdiction as approved by the Supreme Court.

LICRA's and UEJF's actions lie beyond that limit. Neither party has ever carried on business or any other activity through which they have availed themselves of the benefits and protections of California's laws,[1] nor should either party have reasonably anticipated that it would be haled into court in California to answer for the legitimate exercise of its rights in France.

II

This case was reheard en banc primarily for the purpose of answering the question of whether the underlying action in a non-contract case must be tortious or otherwise wrongful to justify the exercise of personal jurisdiction, or whether the "express aiming" of any action, regardless of culpability, will suffice.[2] Although the resolution of that question does not affect my conclusion that California cannot exercise personal jurisdiction over LICRA or UEJF, I respectfully disagree with the majority's interpretation of Calder on this point.

A

Under the majority's reading of Calder, acts giving rise to personal jurisdiction in a non-contract case need not be wrongful. Maj. op. at 1208 ("[W]e do not read Calder necessarily to require in purposeful direction cases that all (or even any) jurisdictionally relevant effects have been caused by wrongful acts."). That conclusion is undermined by the language of Calder itself and requires the majority to divorce that case's holding from its fact — always a dubious exercise. In Calder, the Supreme Court affirmed a decision that had "concluded that a valid basis for jurisdiction existed on the theory that petitioners intended to, and did, cause tortious injury to respondent in California." Calder, 104 S.Ct. at 1485 (emphasis added). The Court itself held that "[i]n this case, petitioners are primary participants in an alleged wrongdoing intentionally directed at a California resident, and jurisdiction is proper on that basis." Id. at 1487 (emphasis added). The wrongfulness of the defendants' acts was, therefore, a key element in the jurisdictional calculus, possibly because a person who has committed a wrongful act should expect to be haled into court by his victim in the victim's home State. Although the Court might have reached the same result if the act in question had not been wrongful — as the majority apparently presumes it would — it is reckless of us to proceed on the basis of such speculation beyond what is currently the farthest reach of personal jurisdiction approved by the Court.

B

The majority's jurisdictional legerdemain is nimble but, like any trick, does not stand up to close scrutiny. It begins innocuously enough by noting that the traditional analysis of minimum contacts depends on whether the disputed act sounds in tort or in contract. In tort cases, "we typically inquire whether a defendant `purposefully direct[s]` his activities' at the forum state," maj. op. at 1206. And in commercial and contract cases, "we typically inquire whether a defendant `purposefully avails itself [sic] of the privilege of conducting activities' or `consummate[s][a] transaction' in the forum." Id. and do not require that the defendants actions be wrongful. However, that traditional distinction is abruptly jettisoned when the majority next asserts that "in any personal jurisdiction case we must evaluate all of a defendant's contacts with the forum state, whether or not those contacts involve wrongful activity by the defendant." Id. at 1207 (emphases added).

The majority's statement is, quite literally, unprecedented. With a stroke of its pen, the majority extends the analysis previously applied only to commercial and contract cases to all assertions of personal jurisdiction. Tellingly, the only cases that the majority musters in support of its novel assertion are commercial or contract-related "purposeful availment" cases. In Quill Corp. v. North Dakota, 504 U.S. 298, 112 S.Ct. 1904, 119 L.Ed.2d 91 (1992), the Supreme Court held that when an out-of-state mail order company "purposefully avails itself of the benefits of an economic market in the forum State, it may subject itself to the State's in personam jurisdiction even if it has no physical presence in the State." 504 U.S. at 302, 112 S.Ct. 1904. And, in Burger King, the Court held that jurisdiction was proper on the grounds that defendants' business ties with the State of Florida were "shielded by the `benefits and protections'" of Florida's laws. 471 U.S. at 543, 105 S.Ct. 2218. In sharp contrast, every "purposeful direction" case that the majority cites in its opinion involved tortious or otherwise wrongful acts by the defendants.

Given our long line of precedent applying the "purposeful availment" test only in contract and commercial cases, and the majority's concession that this case should be analyzed under Calder's "purposeful direction" test, see maj. op. at 1208, the majority's conflation of the elements of these two tests is an unseemly act of judicial slight of hand. LICRA and UEJF are, indisputably, non-commercial actors who have never purposefully availed themselves of the benefits or protections of California's laws. Therefore, neither Calder nor any other Supreme Court precedent justifies California's assertion of personal jurisdiction over them.

III

LICRA's and UEJF's actions and contacts with the State of California were, at most, incidental to the legitimate exercise of their rights under French law. They should not have reasonably anticipated being haled into court in California to answer for their prosecution of a lawsuit in France. Because California's exercise of personal jurisdiction over them on that basis would violate traditional notions of fair play and substantial justice and, therefore, the procedural guarantees of the Due Process Clause, I would remand the case with instructions to dismiss for want of personal jurisdiction and not reach the issue of ripeness.

Thus, while I must dissent from its rationale, I concur in the majority's conclusion that the district court's opinion must be reversed.

Notes

[1] I agree with the majority that the mailing in good faith of cease and desist letters and the use of the United States Marshal's Office to effect service of process of documents related to the French legal proceedings are not sufficient bases for jurisdiction. Maj. op. at 1208-1209.

[2] Although the fact is ignored by the majority, this question was settled law in our circuit prior this appeal being reheard en banc. In Bancroft & Masters, Inc. v. Augusta Nat'l Inc., 223 F.3d 1082, 1086 (9th Cir.2000), the panel made it clear that its decision relied on the assumption that the defendant had engaged in tortious conduct. Judge Sneed, writing for a majority of the panel, further held that "[j]urisdiction in California would be ripe for challenge if following the development of trial it should appear that ANI acted reasonably and in good faith to protect its trademark against an infringer." Id. at 1089 (Sneed, J., concurring).

Judge O'Scannlain's concurrence and dissent in Maharaj v. Gonzales (June 9, 2006) [Notes omitted]

O'SCANNLAIN, Circuit Judge, with whom KLEINFELD, RAWLINSON, and CALLAHAN, Circuit Judges, join, concurring in part and dissenting in part:

While I agree that a remand to consider changed circumstances in Fiji is warranted with respect to the Maharajs' request for withholding of removal, I must respectfully dissent from the court's holding with respect to the merits of the Maharajs' asylum petition. I believe the Immigration Judge ("IJ") properly concluded that the Maharajs had been firmly resettled in Canada. In my view, the opinion of the court misconstrues the law of resettlement, opens our asylum process to an alien who is not fleeing from persecution, and invites abusive country-shopping.

I

The Maharajs fled Fiji in 1987, having experienced substantial persecution, see Maj. Op. at 964-65, on account of their Indo-Fijian ethnicity. The family settled in Canada, where it sought refugee status and applied for asylum. The Maharajs lived undisturbed, legally and openly, in Canada for four years, during which time Mr. Maharaj worked as a fulltime janitor and bakery deliveryman, while Mrs. Maharaj received training to become a nurse's assistant and worked full-time caring for the elderly. The Maharajs rented an apartment, sent their children to free public school, and received free government-provided health care. Both Mr. and Mrs. Maharaj received Social Insurance Numbers and work authorization. Though the Maharajs disliked working menial jobs and felt that there was stigma attached to their status as refugees, they worshiped freely at a Hindu temple and developed friendships with non-Indians and non-Fijians in Canada.

The Immigration Judge ("IJ") concluded that the Maharajs lived free from persecution in Canada; indeed, it is undisputed that while living there, the Maharajs enjoyed the stability, freedom, and safety offered to Canadian immigrants. Yet the

Maharajs, dissatisfied with the vocational opportunities in Canada, crossed the border into the United States. Mr. Maharaj explained that he "wanted to move to United States because, uh, [he] wanted to see what United States looks like" and that the "main thing was job. We never had a good job." Mrs. Maharaj testified that "we were not getting good job. . . . We wanted to, you know, go up and have more money and build ourself. So, that's the time when we thought we don't like Canada." When they arrived, they "liked this place much better than Canada, so [they] decided to stay here."

Once in the United States, the Maharajs overstayed the six month window permitted to visitors, and were served with Orders to Show Cause, charging them with deportability. The family conceded deportability, but requested asylum and withholding of removal. After hearing Mr. and Mrs. Maharajs' testimony, the IJ concluded that although Canada has a refugee program similar to that of the United States, the Maharajs voluntarily chose to leave Canada before Canadian authorities reviewed their petition. Indeed, when asked whether "it's possible that you could have refugee status in Canada and not even know it," Mr. Maharaj answered, "Could be."[1]

The IJ concluded that the Maharajs "never were actually granted refugee status, but it clearly was offered them. They just chose not to take advantage of it, or not wait until it was offered them, or until there was a final resolution of the problem." Because the IJ concluded that the Maharajs had been firmly resettled in Canada, the IJ, in my view quite properly, denied asylum because of statutory ineligibility. See 8 C.F.R. §§ 208.13(c)(2)(i)(B), 208.15. The IJ also denied the Maharajs' request for withholding of removal on the grounds of changed circumstances in Fiji, which we are, quite properly, remanding to the IJ.

II

Here the IJ concluded that—given the circumstances of the Maharajs' four-year sojourn in Canada—the Maharajs had been firmly resettled despite a concession by the government that the Maharajs' pending application for asylum there had not yet been authoritatively resolved. I suggest that in reversing the IJ's legal conclusion, the majority misreads the firm resettlement regulation in two respects. First, it too narrowly construes the catch-all provision. Second, it ignores the history and purpose of the regulation by improperly reading the list of factors which the IJ can apply in determining "firm resettlement" as exhaustive.

A

The plain text of §§ 208.15 and 208.13 allow the IJ significant latitude for finding that an alien "has been firmly resettled" based not only on "offers" of permanent resident status or citizenship, but also on the basis of "some other type of permanent resettlement." The phrase "some other type of permanent resettlement" must be read in the context of the preceding examples. See, e.g., Circuit City Stores v. Adams, 532 U.S. 105, 114-115, 121 S.Ct. 1302, 149 L.Ed.2d 234 (2001) ("`[W]here general words follow specific words in a statutory enumeration, the general words are construed to embrace only objects similar in nature to those objects enumerated by the preceding specific words.'" (quoting 2A N.

Singer, Sutherland on Statutes and Statutory Construction § 47.17 (1991))). Here the preceding objects—"permanent resident status" and "citizenship"—are non-temporary classifications which, if granted by a third country, relieve the fear of persecution in the native country. Similarly, "some other type of permanent resettlement" can include informal understandings, as might be seen in less developed immigration systems, as the majority concedes, but need not necessarily be so limited. Rather, the phrase could also encompass others types of "permanent resettlement" short of full citizenship, so long as circumstances of the arrangement are such that the alien is not at risk of being deported back to his native country.

Moreover, the regulation by its plain text does not require that the alien actually receive permanent resident status, citizenship, or some other type of permanent resettlement; rather, it only requires an "offer" of such. Thus, while "some other type of permanent resettlement" is a minimal requirement in itself, the regulations require even less: only a mere offer. The regulation's focus on an "offer" rather than on receipt of "some other type of permanent resettlement" underscores that the resettlement question turns on whether the alien remains in fear of being returned to persecution in his native country.

The text of the regulation clearly empowers the IJ to make just such an inquiry.

Under these circumstances, I would conclude that the Maharajs fall into such category: they were offered, and had accepted, the ongoing protection of the Canadian government while it processed their asylum application. Though that protection may at some point culminate in a formal "offer" of citizenship or other status, when the IJ evaluated the Maharajs' claim there was nothing to indicate that they would not be allowed permanently to resettle in Canada. Indeed, the IJ reasonably determined that the Maharajs were not just offered temporary resident status; rather, they were offered, and accepted, indefinite resettlement. The difference is crucial. While temporary status, by definition, entails a definitive ending point—and therefore necessarily means that the immigrant will be in flight again—indefinite resettlement does not create such worries. Here, the Maharajs' asylum and refugee applications were pending with the Canadian government. Until such time as the Canadian government acted on the applications, the Maharajs were free to remain in Canada. This arrangement, which is not temporary, qualifies under the regulatory definition and the IJ could properly so find. Simply, the lack of a formal "offer" is not dispositive where the conditions of the aliens' stay are such that there was no risk of deportation when they chose to leave.[2]

B

1

To parse the regulation in more detail, § 208.15 states that "An alien is considered to be firmly resettled if . . . [he or she has] received, an offer of permanent resident status, citizenship, or some other type of permanent resettlement." While the regulation plainly provides that a finding of an "offer" of permanent resident status, citizenship, or some other type of permanent resettlement automatically and conclusively bars the alien from applying for asylum, the regulation does not state that only such a showing establishes firm resettlement. Rather, because the regulation is not limited, other factors—for example, the length of the alien's stay in the safe third country, the alien's work history in the safe third country, or the alien's ability to take advantage of the safe third country's social services—may inform the IJ's firm resettlement analysis.[3] These factors, however, are discretionary and do not necessarily disqualify the asylum applicant.[4]

This interpretation fits with the purpose of the Refugee Act: to help those fleeing persecution. As the facts of this case show, it is not only those who have been offered permanent resettlement that are no longer fleeing persecution. The Maharajs did not receive a formal "offer" of permanent resettlement; yet, considering the circumstances of their stay, it is clear that they were not fleeing persecution. Over the course of four years, Mr. and Mrs. Maharaj were employed and received social services in the form of health care and education. On the basis of these factors, the IJ rightly determined that the Maharajs had firmly resettled in Canada.

2

The focus of the firm resettlement analysis has always been—and remains—whether the refugee remains in flight. Thus, the regulation requires that the adjudicator consider whether there is an "offer" of permanent resettlement as a means of determining whether the refugee remains in flight; however, the regulation still entertains other means of determining whether the refugee is fleeing persecution.

Such interpretation is the only one consistent with the Supreme Court's sole discussion of firm resettlement. In 1971, the Court considered the case of Yee Chien Woo, a native of Red China who had fled for Hong Kong in 1953, where he lived until 1960, when he moved to the United States. See Rosenberg v. Yee Chien Woo, 402 U.S. 49, 50, 91 S.Ct. 1312, 28 L.Ed.2d 592 (1971). Considering the 1957 extension of the Refugee Relief Act, which omitted reference to "firm resettlement," the Court held that the firm resettlement doctrine still persisted in the new definition of "refugee" because "both the terms `firmly resettled' and `fled' are closely related to the central theme of all 23 years of refugee legislation—the creation of a haven for the world's homeless people." Id. at 55, 91 S.Ct. 1312. The Court explained that:

[The act] was never intended to open the United States to refugees who had found shelter in another nation and had begun to build new lives. Nor could Congress have intended to make refugees in flight from persecution compete with all of the world's resettled refugees for the 10,200 entries and permits afforded each year under [the statute]. Such an interpretation would subvert the lofty goals embodied in the whole pattern of our refugee legislation.

Id. at 56, 91 S.Ct. 1312. The Court also announced that "the correct legal standard" to apply in cases where a petitioner has fled persecution is that the petitioner's "physical presence [in the United States] must be one which is reasonably proximate to the flight and not one following a flight remote in point of time or interrupted by intervening residence in a third country reasonably constituting a termination of the original flight in search of refuge." Id. at 56-57, 91 S.Ct. 1312 (internal quotation marks omitted and emphasis added).

In adopting the 1990 amendments, the INS intended to recognize the importance of the existence of an "offer" to analyzing firm resettlement.[5] I would not, however, take an unwarranted additional step and conclude that the INS intended to make the existence vel non of an "offer" for permanent resettlement the exclusive sine qua non of the refugee analysis. The Supreme Court's guidance in Woo should not be ignored; "firm resettlement" must still be understood with an eye towards overall refugee policy, whose "central theme" is related to the concepts "firmly resettled" and "fled." Id. at 55, 91 S.Ct. 1312.

The Supreme Court's exegesis of "firm resettlement" in Woo is consistent with both the origins of, and the continuing rationale supporting, our refugee and asylum laws. The original congressional declaration of policies and objectives for the Refugee Act of 1980, Pub.L. No. 96-212, 94 Stat. 102 (codified as amended in scattered sections of 8 U.S.C.), recognized that

it is the historic policy of the United States to respond to the urgent needs of persons subject to persecution in their homelands. . . . The Congress further declares that it is the policy of the United States to encourage all nations to provide assistance and resettlement opportunities to refugees to the fullest extent possible.

Refugee Act § 101.

Of course, a consequence of the international and cooperative nature of our obligations under the Refugee Act is that our obligations, by practical necessity, became limited. The most obvious limitations are the discretion bestowed on the Attorney General to accept or to reject the asylum application of a qualified refugee, see 8 U.S.C. § 1158(b)(1), and the numerical ceiling on the number of refugees that may be admitted into the United States each year, see 8 U.S.C. § 1157(a). These limitations are consistent with the Court's observation in Woo that "refugees in flight from persecution" should not be forced to compete with "the world's settled refugees," 402 U.S. at 56, 91 S.Ct. 1312, for the finite number of places available in the United States each year. Further, these limitations underscore the importance of our task: Our refugee system is intended for those in flight, and in need of a safe harbor; in contrast, immigrants who voluntarily choose to abandon a perfectly safe haven may be abusing the generosity of the Refugee Act.[6]

We must consider these policy goals and limitations as part of a proper interpretation of § 208.15. I cannot support an interpretation of the regulations which constricts the analysis to only a single element, when the text of the regulations, their purpose, and Supreme Court precedent point to a broader construction.

3

Under our own case law, we long ago jettisoned the notion that § 208.15 requires an analysis exclusively aimed at the existence of an "offer." In our seminal case on the subject, Cheo v. INS, 162 F.3d 1227 (9th Cir.1998), Meng Ly Cheo and Meng Heng Cheo, Cambodian nationals, fled to Vietnam and thence to Thailand, where they stayed for three years before entering the United States through Mexico. Id. at 1228. We concluded, however, that:

Three years of peaceful residence established that the ground of "firm resettlement" in Malaysia might apply, so the Cheos had the burden of proving that they were not firmly resettled. That was enough time so that, in the absence of evidence to the contrary, it would be a reasonable inference from the duration that Malaysia allowed the Cheos to stay indefinitely. A duration of residence in a third country sufficient to support an inference of permanent resettlement in the absence of evidence to the contrary shifts the burden of proving absence of firm resettlement to the applicant.

Id. at 1229 (emphasis added) (citing Abdalla v. INS, 43 F.3d 1397, 1399 (10th Cir. 1994), and Chinese Am. Civic Council v. Attorney General, 185 U.S.App. D.C. 1, 566 F.2d 321, 328 n. 18 (D.C.Cir.1977)). We did not state that the Cheo presumption requires an immigrant prove that he or she has "not received an offer," but rightly required the immigrant prove that he or she is "not firmly resettled." Critically, therefore, Cheo concluded that other facts besides the existence of an "offer" can show firm resettlement.[7]

Our later case law applying Cheo is consistent with a broader reading of the regulation. In Andriasian v. INS, 180 F.3d 1033 (9th Cir.1999), the petitioner fled Azerbaijan with his family, escaping to Armenia. Id. at 1036. The family moved between Russia, Armenia, and the Ukraine, nine times over the next forty-four months, though the petitioner testified that the family did not report any substantial problems living in Armenia. Id. at 1039. On this basis, the IJ concluded that the petitioner firmly resettled in Armenia. We reversed, concluding that firm resettlement "precludes asylum, unless the application can demonstrate that his stay in the third country lasted only until he could arrange for further travel or that the conditions of life in that country would be unduly restrictive." Id. at 1043. This in no way precludes the consideration of additional factors to determine whether the petitioner has firmly resettled. Indeed, Andriasian is consistent with Woo's explanation that:

many refugees make their escape to freedom from persecution in successive stages and come to this country only after stops along the way. Such stops do not necessarily mean that the refugee's aim to reach these shores has in any sense been abandoned. . . . The presence of such persons in this country is not "one which is reasonably proximate to the flight" or is "remote in point of time or interrupted by intervening residence in a third country."

402 U.S. at 57 n. 6, 91 S.Ct. 1312. Unlike the Supreme Court's warning in Woo, or the meanderings in Andriasian itself, the Maharajs stayed in Canada—and Canada alone—for four years. It is clear from these facts that Canada was not a mere stopover; it was the destination in which they first intended to resettle and did so.[8]

In sum, our prior case law, in accordance with the language of the regulation, allowed consideration of a variety of factors to show firm resettlement. Cheo properly put the focus of the analysis on "firm resettlement," rather than on the existence vel non of an "offer" for permanent resettlement. Again, based on our precedent, the history, text, and structure of the regulation, and Supreme Court precedent, I cannot agree that the regulation requires exclusive focus on one factor; rather, the existence of an "offer" is one means of proving firm resettlement—and is determinative if shown—but it is not the exclusive means of proving firm resettlement.

C

Under a proper reading of the regulations, a variety of factors may be considered as part of the analysis of firm resettlement. If the petitioner has been offered permanent resident status, citizenship, or another type of permanent resettlement, then "firm resettlement" is established and the asylum petition must be denied, unless the petitioner establishes that one of the two exceptions provided at § 208.15(a)-(b) apply. However, if no "offer" of permanent resident status, citizenship, or other type of permanent resettlement is made, the IJ may still consider the facts of the case to determine whether the totality of the circumstances indicate that the petitioner had firmly resettled in the third country. This interpretation fits with the broader asylum policy, and the concept that asylum is for those in need. See Sall v. Gonzales, 437 F.3d 229, 233 (2d Cir. 2006) (per curiam) (noting that "the underlying purpose of asylum regulations—to provide refuge to desperate refugees who reach our shores with nowhere else to turn—accords with reserving the grant of asylum for those applicants without alternative places of refuge abroad"); see also id. (noting that while aliens physically present in the United States are generally allowed to apply for asylum, 8 U.S.C. § 1158(a)(2)(A) exempts any alien who could be removed to a "[s]afe third country").

Applying such construct to the facts of this case, the IJ rightly denied the asylum petition. The facts overwhelmingly indicate that the petitioners had firmly resettled in Canada: the Maharajs had jobs and received job training, enjoyed free health care and education, experienced no substantial discrimination, and appeared to enjoy a relatively peaceful existence. Thus, the IJ had the authority to conclude that the Maharajs had been firmly resettled in Canada. Having so concluded, the IJ rightly determined that neither of the exceptions in § 208.15(a)-(b) applied, and therefore the firm resettlement bar required the denial of the asylum petition. Simply, "[t]he United States offers asylum to refugees not to provide them with a broader choice of safe homelands, but rather, to protect those arrivals with nowhere else to turn." Id. I would, therefore, deny the petition for review.

III

I agree with the majority that there is a split of authority among the circuit courts of appeals; regrettably, the majority follows the weaker line of the Third and Seventh Circuits, rather than the more persuasive view of the Second, Fourth, Eighth, and D.C. Circuits. In Second Circuit's opinion in Sall v. Gonzales—the most recent discussion of this issue—the petitioner was a native and citizen of Mauritania who fled to Senegal. 437 F.3d at 231. Sall stayed in a Red Cross camp for four-and-one-half years, then moved to the capital of Senegal, Dakar, where he stayed for another nine months before paying for transportation to the United States. Id. The IJ concluded that Sall was ineligible for asylum because he had firmly resettled in Senegal, having lived there for approximately five years with no impediments to work or travel. Id. at 232. On review, the Second Circuit reviewed the IJ's conclusion with an eye toward the purpose of the asylum regulations: "to provide refuge to desperate refugees who reach our shores with nowhere else to turn." Id. at 233. Thus, it was proper to "reserv[e] the grant of asylum for those applicants without alternative places of refuge abroad, regardless of whether a formal `offer' of permanent settlement has been received." Id. (emphasis added).

Turning to the text of the regulations, the Second Circuit rightly noted that while "the regulation places particular importance on the presence vel non of an actual "offer" of permanent resident status," the "language of the regulation . . . requires an IJ to examine the specific circumstances of an applicant's case to decide whether he has firmly resettled in a third country." Id. Thus, Sall instructed the IJ to

consider the totality of the circumstances, including whether Sall intended to settle in Senegal when he arrived there, whether he has family ties there, whether he has business or property connections that connote permanence, and whether he enjoyed the legal rights—such as the right to work and to enter and leave the country at will—that permanently settled persons can expect to have. Of particular importance is whether he received an offer of permanent resident status.

Id. at 235.

Here, the facts show that the Maharajs intended to settle in Canada, that they have family ties to Canada, that they were employed in Canada, that they have permanent (or at least non-temporary) housing in Canada, and that they enjoyed rights and privileges commensurate with Canadian citizens. I agree with Sall's statement that an "offer" of permanent resident status is "of particular importance"; however, the Second Circuit is also correct that this inquiry is not a sine qua non of a firm resettlement analysis.

Under facts virtually indistinguishable from those presented here, the Eighth Circuit considered the case of an Iranian native and citizen who fled to Spain. Farbakhsh v. INS, 20 F.3d 877 (8th Cir.1994). Shortly after arriving in Spain, the petitioner "filed an application for refugee status in Spain." Id. at 880. Farbakhsh stayed in Spain for almost four years, though he "did not have official permission to work or study in Spain." Id. When the petitioner left, his application for refugee status was still pending. Id. Nevertheless, the IJ concluded, and the BIA agreed, that the petitioner "had `firmly resettled' in Spain and was no longer fleeing persecution when he entered the United States." Id.

On review, the Eighth Circuit concluded:

We hold the record supports the Board's finding that petitioner had firmly resettled in Spain. Petitioner had lived more than four years in Spain without fear of being returned to Iran; he initially intended to remain in Spain because he filed an application for refugee status there; his application for refugee status was pending; his younger brother and younger sister were living in Spain. Moreover, petitioner's travels do not suggest that his arrival in the United States in 1987 was reasonably proximate to his flight from persecution in Iran in 1982.

20 F.3d at 882.

In short, the "firm resettlement" bar prohibited consideration of Farbakhsh's asylum application, even though he had not received an "offer" of permanent resettlement from Spain. The Eighth Circuit rightly concluded that an asylum application, coupled with an undisturbed and lengthy stay in the third country, was sufficient to bar the application at the IJ's discretion (as opposed to a finding of firm resettlement, which mandates denial of the application). See also Chinese American Civic Council v. Attorney General, 566 F.2d 321 (D.C.Cir.1977) (noting that "[a]ppellants did not present any facts to rebut the normal conclusion from such extended residence that appellants were firmly resettled and no longer in flight" and citing Woo, 402 U.S. at 49, 91 S.Ct. 1312, for support).

The Eighth Circuit recently reiterated this view in Rife v. Ashcroft, 374 F.3d 606 (8th Cir.2004):

>   We agree with the Third Circuit in Abdille that the text of 8 C.F.R. § 208.15 makes [an offer of permanent resettlement] an important factor and, indeed, the proper place to begin the firm resettlement analysis. But in some cases it will not be dispositive. For example, in our only decision resolving a firm resettlement issue, we affirmed the BIA's determination that the alien's four-year stay in Spain constituted firm resettlement even though his application for refugee status in Spain was still pending when he came to the United States.[9]

Id. at 611. I agree, along with the Eighth Circuit, that an "offer" of permanent resettlement is "the proper place to begin the firm resettlement analysis"; the majority here errs by claiming that an "offer" of permanent resettlement is the proper place to end the firm resettlement analysis.

The Fourth Circuit adopted a similar approach. In Mussie v. INS, 172 F.3d 329 (4th Cir.1999), the petitioner was a native and citizen of Ethiopia who fled to Germany. Id. at 330. Mussie applied for, and was granted, asylum in Germany, though the record did not disclose whether she received permanent resident status. Id. Mussie received government-paid language schooling, and monetary assistance for transportation, rent, and food. Id. at 330-31. With some relatively minor exceptions, Mussie lived peacefully in Germany for approximately six years. Id. at 331.

On review, the Fourth Circuit noted that although "the record is silent as to whether Mussie actually received a formal "offer" of permanent residency in Germany, the INS introduced sufficient `evidence indicating' that Mussie had received at least an offer of `some other type of permanent resettlement' in Germany, thereby meeting its evidentiary burden." Id. at 331 (quoting § 208.15). Supporting this conclusion, Mussie noted that the petitioner "received government assistance for language schooling, transportation, rent, and food; held a job; paid taxes; and rented her own apartment." Id. at 332.

Similarly here, the Maharajs received a variety of government benefits, including free health care and schooling, held jobs, and rented an apartment. Unlike Mussie, the Maharajs' asylum petition was still pending when they chose to leave Canada; yet, the evidence indicated that the Maharajs and the Canadian government were in stasis, much like the relationship between Mussie and the German government. While both the Maharajs and Mussie had something less than an explicit "offer" of permanent resettlement, the facts and circumstances surrounding their lives in Canada and Germany, respectively, indicate that an IJ could have reasonably concluded that both had established an "other type of permanent resettlement."

In sum, other Circuits have rejected the improperly narrow reading of the regulations promulgated by the majority. Moreover, several Circuits have done so recently, belying the majority's claim that the 1990 amendments to the regulations dramatically altered the "firm resettlement" analysis.

IV

I am also persuaded that public policy concerns reinforce the IJ's interpretation here. The majority's analysis will open the door to rampant country-shopping, a result that our immigration laws have long sought to avoid. See, e.g., Kalubi v. Ashcroft, 364 F.3d 1134, 1140 (9th Cir.2004) (noting that "[i]n an appropriate case, `forum shopping' might conceivably be part of the totality of circumstances that sheds light on a request for asylum in this country"); Susan F. Martin and Andrew I. Schoenholtz, Asylum in Practice: Successes, Failures, and the Challenges Ahead, 14 GEO. IMMIGR. L.J. 589, 606 (noting that "[m]ost advanced Western nations have adopted the principle in their asylum laws that the first safe haven country to which a refugee flees should be the one in which he or she seeks asylum" in order to reduce "asylum-shopping"). Indeed, the facts of this case demonstrate the likely effect of the majority's narrow reading of § 208.15. The Maharajs lived peacefully in Canada for four years, enjoying that country's social and economic benefits. Dissatisfied with life in Canada—rather than with life in Fiji—the Maharajs decided to move to the United States. What a blatant abuse of the refugee and asylum system! It is undisputed that the Maharajs were no longer fleeing from persecution when they came to the United States. By their own admission, they were merely dissatisfied with their job prospects in Canada. While the desire to enjoy improved economic circumstances may motivate many immigrants, it is emphatically not a reasonable or a proper basis for granting an asylum petition.

Indeed, the Maharajs—who apparently immigrated for economic gain—may not be the worst example. Nothing in the majority opinion prevents an immigrant who flees his native country, settles into a new third country, lives there legally (under any status short of a formal "offer" of permanent resettlement), enjoys peace and prosperity in the third country for many years, then, having decided that the grass is greener in the United States, immigrates here. Such a hypothetical immigrant could apply for asylum—a system intended "to respond to the urgent needs of persons subject to persecution in their homelands," Refugee Act § 101 (emphasis added)—and the firm resettlement bar, amazingly, would not apply. Considering our hypothetical immigrant, who could be further from the platonic refugee? This immigrant enjoys safety, prosperity, and security offered by the third country, and the immigrant's move is motivated by economics rather than fear. Yet the majority is willing to reward him by allowing the asylum petition to proceed.

I would add that country-shopping is particularly egregious where, as here, the petitioner has an asylum petition pending in another safe third country when he arrives here. These petitioners may be seeking better economic opportunities or may be attempting to game the immigration law system, but what is certain, is that these petitioners do not need the asylum in the United States to protect them from persecution. Given that the Refugee Act allows the granting of only a limited number of asylum petitions, and is intended to respond to the dire and urgent needs of a deserving group of people, the effect of the majority's unnecessarily narrow reading of § 208.15 is most problematic.

What's more, let's not lose sight of the forest for the trees. The likely effect of the majority opinion will be to increase greatly the government's burden in asylum cases. Once the alien denies having received a formal offer, the burden shifts to the government to prove that the alien did receive some sort of offer. However, the circumstantial evidence which the Department of Homeland Security ("DHS") typically uses to prove an asylum case will be largely useless. This case is a perfect example of the difficulty DHS will face in future asylum proceedings: During their hearing, the Maharajs admitted to living a perfectly happy life in Canada; yet the circumstances of their stay, under the majority construct, may only be used to show whether or not the Maharajs received an "offer." If the evidence shows that they did not receive an offer, any other evidence—even if patently and obviously probative—is automatically disregarded. Simply, the majority's construct will hamstring DHS to an intolerable and unreasonable degree in future asylum proceedings.

V

The Maharajs emigrated from Canada, where they had lived peacefully for four years, not from Fiji, where they were persecuted. The majority's unnecessarily narrow reading of "firm resettlement"—focusing exclusively on an "offer"—ignores the Supreme Court's guidance on how to interpret our asylum laws. As a result, the majority opinion puts us on the wrong side of a circuit split and invites blatant country-shopping. I respectfully dissent.

Judge O'Scannlain's dissent in Stout v. Social Sec. Admin. Comm'r (July 25, 2006)

O'SCANNLAIN, Circuit Judge, dissenting:

I respectfully dissent from the majority's conclusion that the ALJ's failure to comment properly on the lay witness testimony of Stout's sister and brother-in-law was not harmless error. I am persuaded, as was the District Court, that even if the lay witness testimony is credited, all the evidence taken as a whole overwhelmingly supports denial of Stout's application for Disability Insurance Benefits and Supplemental Security Income.

"A decision of the ALJ will not be reversed for errors that are harmless." Burch v.

Barnhart, 400 F.3d 676, 679 (9th Cir.2005). Here, the lay testimony, when viewed in conjunction with the evidence the ALJ properly considered, does not undermine the ALJ's finding that Stout can engage in his prior work as a vine pruner.

The thrust of the lay testimony was that, in his past work as a roofer, Stout had difficulty working with other people without supervision. Although the letter from Stout's brother-in-law, Jay Vasquez, used the term "constant supervision" to describe the assistance Stout requires, the remainder of Vasquez's letter indicates that Vasquez did not provide Stout literal, constant supervision during the ten years Stout worked in his construction company. It also indicates that after Vasquez closed his construction company, Stout worked as a roofer for another company without supervision and support from a family member. Similarly, the testimony of Stout's sister, Udena Stout, does not stand for the proposition that Stout requires constant supervision. In fact, Udena testified that Stout's need for supervision would vary in relationship to the complexity of the task. She indicated that Stout could handle simple tasks that require minimal interaction with others, although he would have a tendency to become bored or lose focus.

All the limitations reasonably supported by the lay testimony appeared in the ALJ's RFC finding. The ALJ noted that Stout has "mild to moderate" difficulties in social functioning and in concentration, persistence, or pace. This information appeared in the ALJ's RFC, which noted that Stout "has a limited capacity for teamwork and needs to minimize repetitive public contact. . . . has a limited capacity for multitasking with complex instructions. . . . [and] . . ." needs two to three step tasks which are fairly repetitive."

As the district court observed, Stout has engaged in substantial work activity in the past and there is no evidence, in the lay testimony or elsewhere, that his mental capabilities have changed. I accordingly agree with the district court's determination that the ALJ's failure to comment properly on the lay testimony is harmless error.

Judge O'Scannlain's dissent from denial of rehearing en banc in Harper v. Poway Unified School Dist. (July 31, 2006)

O'SCANNLAIN, Circuit Judge, with whom KLEINFELD, TALLMAN, BYBEE, and BEA, Circuit Judges, join, dissenting from denial of rehearing en banc:

Judge Kozinski's powerful dissent explains why the court errs in permitting school administrators to engage in viewpoint discrimination on the basis of a student's newly promulgated right to be free from certain offensive speech. I write only to emphasize why it was a mistake to fail to rehear this case en banc.

I

The Supreme Court has clearly stated that

[i]n order for the State in the person of school officials to justify prohibition of a particular expression of opinion, it must be able to show that its action was caused by something more than a mere desire to avoid the discomfort and unpleasantness that

always accompany an unpopular viewpoint.

Tinker v. Des Moines Indep. Cmty. Sch. Dist., 393 U.S. 503, 509, 89 S.Ct. 733, 21 L.Ed.2d 731 (1969). Tyler Harper wore a T-shirt to his high school with the words "Be Ashamed, Our School Embraced What God Has Condemned" on the front and "Homosexuality Is Shameful `Romans 1:27'" on the back. Harper v. Poway Unified Sch. Dist., 445 F.3d 1166, 1171 (9th Cir.2006). Harper's shirt was undoubtedly unpleasant and offensive to some students, but Tinker does not permit school administrators to ban speech on the basis of "a mere desire to avoid the discomfort and unpleasantness that always accompany an unpopular viewpoint." 393 U.S. at 509, 89 S.Ct. 733.

Nevertheless, the panel majority stretches mightily to characterize Harper's message as a psychological attack that might "cause young people to question their self-worth and their rightful place in society." Harper, 445 F.3d at 1178.

According to the panel majority, a student's "right to be let alone" now includes a right to be free from "verbal assaults on the basis of a core identifying characteristic such as race, religion, or sexual orientation." Id. But if displaying a distasteful opinion on a T-shirt qualifies as a psychological or verbal assault, school administrators have virtually unfettered discretion to ban any student speech they deem offensive or intolerant.

In my view, this unprecedented—and unsupportable—expansion of the right to be let alone as including a right not to be offended has no basis in Tinker or its progeny, and we neglect our duty by failing to reexamine the majority's decision.

II

In reality, the panel majority's decision amounts to approval of blatant viewpoint discrimination. Harper wore his T-shirt after students involved in the Gay-Straight Alliance organized a "Day of Silence" in support of those of a different sexual orientation. School administrators permitted the "Day of Silence" but prohibited Harper from offering a different view—a decision now upheld by this court.

Such action is directly contrary to the "prohibition on viewpoint discrimination [that] serves . . . to bar the government from skewing public debate." Rosenberger v. Rector & Visitors of Univ. of Va., 515 U.S. 819, 894, 115 S.Ct. 2510, 132 L.Ed.2d 700 (1995). We normally subject this type of viewpoint discrimination "to the most exacting First Amendment scrutiny," Saxe v. State Coll. Area Sch. Dist., 240 F.3d 200, 207 (3d Cir.2001), because it "suggests an attempt to give one side of a debatable public question an advantage in expressing its views," First Nat. Bank of Boston v. Bellotti, 435 U.S. 765, 785, 98 S.Ct. 1407, 55 L.Ed.2d 707 (1978). The panel majority failed to do so in this case.

Instead, under the panel majority's decision, school administrators are now free to give one side of debatable public questions a free pass while muzzling voices raised in opposition. A respected First Amendment scholar notes that the panel majority's decision constitutes

a dangerous retreat from our tradition that the First Amendment is viewpoint-neutral. It's an opening to a First Amendment limited by rights to be free from offensive viewpoints. It's a tool for suppression of one side of public debates (about same-sex marriage, about Islam, quite likely about illegal immigration, and more) while the other side remains constitutionally protected and even encouraged by the government.

Eugene Volokh, Sorry, Your Viewpoint Is Excluded from First Amendment Protection, April 20, 2006, http://volokh.com/ posts/XXXXXXXXXX.shtml. No Supreme Court decision empowers our public schools to engage in such censorship nor has gone so far in favoring one viewpoint over another.

III

I regret that we have failed to avail ourselves of the opportunity to reconsider a decision that departs so sharply from long-accepted First Amendment principles. I therefore respectfully dissent from our order denying rehearing en banc.

Judge O'Scannlain's dissent in Ornelas-Chavez v. Gonzales (Aug 21, 2006) [Notes omitted]

O'SCANNLAIN, Circuit Judge, dissenting.

In this case our modest task is to decide whether the Board of Immigration Appeals' ("BIA") decision to deny Petitioner Ornelas-Chavez's claims was free of legal error and supported by substantial evidence. Because neither sympathy for the petitioner nor distrust of the BIA or the Immigration Judge ("IJ") should compromise a careful assessment of the administrative decisions and record evidence, I respectfully dissent.

I

First, the court holds that the BIA applied the wrong legal standard to Ornelas-Chavez's claim to withholding of removal under 8 U.S.C. § 1231(b)(3) because it imposed a strict "reporting requirement" to establish government persecution. Maj. Op. at 1056-58. With respect, it did no such thing.

A

Any fair reading of the BIA's decision demonstrates that it applied the proper legal standard. In relevant part, the BIA stated:

The respondent suffered an incident of harm, a detention of several hours apparently at this [sic] request of his father, at the hands of government agents. This single incident does not rise to the level of persecution. All of the other harm suffered by the respondent occurred at the hands of private citizens. The respondent did not report any of these incidents to government authorities.

. . . Accordingly, where the respondent never reported his incidents of harm to government authorities, and where the background evidence in the record is inconclusive, the Immigration Judge properly found that the respondent did not prove that the Mexican government is unwilling or unable to control those who harmed or may harm him.

(Emphasis added.) The majority, adopting Ornelas-Chavez's argument wholesale, seems to fixate on the last sentence of the first quoted paragraph: "The respondent did not report any of these incidents to government authorities." Indeed, with only a passing nod to the sentence's context, the majority distorts entirely the BIA's reasoning.

The BIA did not apply nor did it adopt a strict "reporting requirement." True, it observed that there was no evidence that Ornelas-Chavez reported the alleged incidents. However, as the majority concedes, it then considered this dearth of evidence in combination with the background country conditions evidence, which failed to demonstrate a pattern of indifference by the government. The BIA concluded, in light of these categories of evidence, that the IJ could appropriately find "that the respondent did not prove that the Mexican government is unwilling or unable to control those who harmed or may harm him."

Under our circuit's case law, this is an entirely proper mode of analysis. The persecution of which Ornelas-Chavez complains must be shown to have been perpetrated by the government, or else Ornelas-Chavez must show that the government "is unwilling or unable to control those elements of its society responsible for targeting a particular class of individuals." Avetova-Elisseva v. INS, 213 F.3d 1192, 1196 (9th Cir.2000) (citation and internal quotation marks omitted). Accordingly, whether the petitioner has reported the incidents to the authorities is clearly relevant to, even if not dispositive of, the ultimate question of whether the government was "unwilling or unable to control" the persecutors. See, e.g., Baballah v. Ashcroft, 367 F.3d 1067, 1078 (9th Cir.2004) (citations omitted).

In this light, it is clear that the BIA's consideration of general country conditions stood to confirm its conclusion that Ornelas-Chavez did not meet his burden. That the BIA considered such background evidence itself conclusively demonstrates that the inquiry was not terminated by any rigid reporting requirement. Ultimately, I think it clear that the BIA asked and answered the right question: whether Ornelas-Chavez's alleged persecutors were parties whom the Mexican authorities were unwilling or unable to control. The BIA was correct to treat Ornelas-Chavez's failure to report the alleged persecution as relevant to that question.

In arriving at its errant conclusion, the majority observes that the BIA "cited only two pieces of evidence," and since one of them was inconclusive, it must have been improper that the other—the alleged "reporting requirement"—was "a sine qua non for the success of Ornelas-Chavez's withholding of removal claim." Maj. Op. at 1057, 1058. But where, I wonder, is the flaw in the BIA's analysis?

Presumably Ornelas-Chavez had two options: to prove that the government was unwilling or unable to control such persecution generally, or to prove that it was unwilling or unable to control his persecutors specifically. See, e.g., Castro-Perez v. Gonzales, 409 F.3d 1069, 1072 (9th Cir. 2005) (considering country reports to determine whether the Honduran government was willing or able to control rape generally, and considering the petitioner's specific situation). Since Ornelas-Chavez failed to do the former, to meet his burden it was necessary that he have done the latter. And because there is little other evidence in the record to suggest the government's disposition towards Ornelas-Chavez's particular troubles, the BIA properly deemed rather important in this case—"a sine qua non," even!—that Ornelas-Chavez failed to report the alleged abuse to government authorities.[1] So, the majority concedes that reporting vel non may be relevant, see Maj.

Op. at 1057-58; yet it grants the petition because in this particular case the failure to report is too relevant.

The BIA did not, as the majority seems to suggest, improperly consider background country conditions as "establish[ing] that specific acts of persecution occurred or did not occur." Maj. Op. at 1056. Although the BIA, having made no adverse credibility determination, was required to accept Ornelas-Chavez's testimony as factually true, it was not required to adopt his preferred legal conclusion: that the authorities would not have acted to curb the persecution he alleges took place. The background evidence in the record was obviously relevant to the merits of that issue, and the BIA was entitled, if not obligated, to consider it. See Castro-Perez, 409 F.3d at 1072; Avetova-Elisseva, 213 F.3d at 1198-99; Andriasian v. INS, 180 F.3d 1033, 1042-43 (9th Cir.1999).[2]

The testimony provided by Ornelas-Chavez, while also relevant, was evidence of an anecdotal, subjective variety and thus not particularly probative. Indeed, the background evidence substantially negates Ornelas-Chavez's perception. See infra section I.B.1.

Our standard of review in immigration cases is well-established: we must affirm the BIA if the record contains substantial evidence for its decision; we cannot justify granting the petition for review merely by pointing to other record evidence which, in our own view, supports the alien's claim. See INS v. Elias-Zacarias, 502 U.S. 478, 481 & n. 1, 112 S.Ct. 812, 117 L.Ed.2d 38 (1992). The majority cannot say that Ornelas-Chavez's testimony compels a rational fact finder to conclude that the government was unwilling or unable to control his alleged persecutors. Thus, the majority opts for another, more innovative approach: it holds that the BIA applied the wrong legal standard—simply because there exists supportive evidence that the BIA failed explicitly to discuss. See Maj. Op. at 1057-58. But Ornelas-Chavez's testimony was not somehow legally distinct from the balance of the record; it was merely additional evidence on the same "unwilling or unable to control" question. Accordingly, the majority's holding seems little more than a willful circumvention of the Supreme Court's prescribed standard of review.

In short, the majority goes to great lengths to divine in the BIA's analysis some kind of per se rule, which it can then merrily reject. As I have sought to demonstrate, such "reporting requirement" is of the majority's own imagining. Surely one may infer much from the typically brief text of an administrative decision-especially when one is all too eager to conjure a meaning that will justify granting the petition for review. Cf. Kumar v. Gonzales, 435 F.3d 1019, 1037 (9th Cir. 2006) (Kozinski, J., dissenting) ("[T]he majority picks apart the [BIA's] findings piece by piece, scrutinizing [its] every sentence as if it is completely unconnected to the rest of the opinion."). Such creative invention, however, is not appropriate to our role in reviewing the lawful adjudication of an administrative body.

B

Had the majority given the BIA's decision a fair reading, it could not then hold that Ornelas-Chavez met his burden of showing that the evidence would compel any reasonable fact finder to conclude that he was more likely than not to suffer persecution upon his return to Mexico. Singh v. INS, 134 F.3d 962, 966 (9th Cir. 1998).

1

There is no evidence of past persecution, as defined by the regulations, in this case. The Mexican government was not involved in any persecution of Ornelas-Chavez; the single, six-hour detention by a reluctant local police chief, at the request of Ornelas-Chavez's father, does not rise to that level. See, e.g., Prasad v. INS, 47 F.3d 336, 339-40 (9th Cir.1995).

Critically, the evidence also falls short of compelling a finding that any past private "persecution" at issue was perpetrated by parties whom the government was unwilling or unable to control. Ornelas-Chavez has not "convincingly established"—or proven by any standard—that his resort to government authorities would have been futile. Cf. Korablina v. INS, 158 F.3d 1038, 1045 (9th Cir.1998). As the BIA found, the relevant background evidence is, at best, inconclusive. Ornelas-Chavez relies on little more than a bare assumption that the police would have done nothing had he reported the abuse—a showing that we have previously deemed insufficient. See Castro-Perez, 409 F.3d at 1072.

The administrative record provides little support for Ornelas-Chavez's claim of past persecution. The evidence regarding general country conditions, while perhaps revealing societal disfavor of homosexuals, does not demonstrate that the authorities would have been inattentive to the primary incidents of persecution alleged here: the rape and physical abuse of a young child. Even if the majority were willing to overlook the relevance of Ornelas-Chavez's age—allowing him to gild his allegations in the armor of sexual orientation and gender identity—there is no evidence in the record that the Mexican authorities would have viewed the incidents in similar terms and thus permitted the abuse.

Even assuming that a few individual police officers were beholden to Ornelas-Chavez's father because they rented a house on his land, Ornelas-Chavez makes no allegation that this potential bias somehow seeped into all (or even most) persons holding Mexican authority. It is true that Ornelas-Chavez's teacher failed to take any action in response to his allegations of sexual contact. But at best, this testimony establishes one teacher's ineptitude; it does not compel a finding that the Mexican authorities generally would have been indifferent to the rape of a young child.[3] Lastly, I note that when, at the prison at which he worked, Ornelas-Chavez informed his supervisor of the abuse by his coworkers, the supervisor exhibited a willingness to control the alleged conduct by offering to adjust Ornelas-Chavez's shift so that he could avoid his would-be persecutors. Ornelas-Chavez cannot prove that this measure would have been inadequate because he chose to resign his employment. That the supervisor "took no action against the co-workers," Maj. Op. at 1054, is of little relevance.

The various items of evidence Ornelas-Chavez put forth fail to support his claim because his subjective perceptions of government officials are not relevant—much less dispositive. The critical inquiry as to government responsiveness is objective, and we have always considered the "unwilling or unable to control" requirement in that context. See, e.g., Malty v. Ashcroft, 381 F.3d 942, 948 (9th Cir.2004). Ornelas-Chavez's personal belief that the relevant Mexican authorities would have been unwilling to shield him from persecution is grossly insufficient.

In sum, while I do not discount nor make light of the harms Ornelas-Chavez has apparently suffered, I must also conclude that the evidence does not compel a finding—as it must do under our limited standard of review—that the harms were occasioned by persons whom the government was unwilling or unable to control.

2

Having failed to produce compelling evidence of past persecution by actors whom the government was unwilling or unable to control, Ornelas-Chavez would not be entitled to a presumption of future persecution. See 8 C.F.R. § 1208.13(b)(1). His claim to withholding of removal would then fail if he also falls short of independently establishing a clear probability of future persecution. See Lim v. INS, 224 F.3d 929, 938 (9th Cir.2000).

a

On this record, there simply is insufficient showing that homosexuals are currently subject to official persecution in Mexico. The U.S. Department of State's June 1997 country report documented "no evidence of systematic official persecution of homosexuals," and Ornelas-Chavez's other evidence was not to the contrary. A report from a private group, dated May 2000, stated that "repression by . . . authorities is now the exception, not the rule," and noted that societal attitudes are trending towards tolerance.

The record evidence further demonstrates extensive legal, political, and cultural advances by homosexuals in Mexico, including the enactment of legislation prohibiting discrimination on the basis of sexual orientation, wide acceptance of participation by homosexuals in two of the three major political parties, and the election of openly homosexual government representatives. To the extent private persecution occurs, the record suggests that the government's response has changed. One news report in the record, for example, notes that the Mexico City police "have set up a unit specializing in dealing with homophobic crimes, and are to get sensitivity training."

b

Nor was the evidence so compelling that any rational fact finder must conclude that Ornelas-Chavez, individually, would more likely than not be subject to persecution by actors whom the government was unwilling or unable to control. 8 C.F.R. § 1208.16(b)(1)-(2); see Sael v. Ashcroft, 386 F.3d 922, 925 (9th Cir.2004); Hoxha v. Ashcroft, 319 F.3d 1179, 1185 (9th Cir. 2003). While the record reveals societal disfavor of homosexuality generally, it exposes few incidents of actual persecution. These general country conditions do not compel reversal of the BIA. More directly, there is simply no evidence that Ornelas-Chavez is likely to be singled out by the government or by private forces whom the government is unwilling or unable to control.[4]

Read as a whole, the record is not such that a reasonable fact finder must conclude that Ornelas-Chavez is more likely than not to be persecuted in the future if he is returned to Mexico.[5] I would affirm the BIA's decision because it is supported by substantial evidence.

II

I must also dissent from the majority's holding that the BIA applied an incorrect legal standard as to the level of government involvement required for relief under the Convention Against Torture ("CAT"). Maj. Op. at 1058-61. Again, the majority's reading of the relevant administrative decision is partisan and inaccurate. Further, there is absolutely no evidence of torture of homosexuals by the Mexican government (or by private parties with the government's consent or acquiescence) in this record. Random incidents of private violence simply cannot support the notion that official torture of homosexuals is systematic or even common. As such, the IJ's decision on the CAT claim is supported by substantial evidence.

A

The applicable regulations define "torture" as "severe pain or suffering, whether physical or mental" when intentionally inflicted "with the consent or acquiescence of a public official or other person acting in an official capacity." 8 C.F.R. § 208.18(a)(1) (emphasis added). In this case, the IJ found that Ornelas-Chavez had "provided no evidence of past torture or any mental or physical intentionally inflicted severe pain or suffering that is sanctioned by a public official." (Emphasis added.) The majority seizes upon the word "sanctioned" to assert an erroneous application by the IJ of a legal standard "higher" than that prescribed in the regulations. Maj. Op. at 1058.

While the IJ may have employed imprecise diction in that passage, the majority is again too keen to find fault in the agency decision we now review. Earlier in its order, the IJ explained, in part, that "[t]he Respondent presented no evidence that the authorities refused to protect him or that the authorities did not protect him, since he never reported any of these incidents to the authorities." Id. at 1059. This phraseology indicates that the IJ considered whether the authorities were aware of the alleged abuses such that they could possibly "consent or acquiesce." Thus, the IJ necessarily found that Ornelas-Chavez's evidence fell short of even the proper "consent or acquiescence" standard. Although the word "sanctioned" arguably suggests affirmative approval by the government, there is no indication in the opinion that the IJ actually reviewed the evidence for conduct beyond the government's "tacit or passive acceptance" or "implied consent to an act." I also find it significant that the IJ's errant word choice was simply part of its summary declaration at the end of the opinion, not in any way enmeshed in the actual analysis of the facts.

There was not, as the majority suggests, implicit in the IJ's finding a standard "also higher than that dictated by CAT." Maj. Op. at 1059. In so asserting, the majority again lays bare the analytical flaw that infects its entire opinion: it posits that "the IJ's decision rests on the unwarranted premise that the only way a public official can have such awareness . . . is if the applicant reports the alleged torture to him." Id. at 1060. Reporting is not the only way a public official can have such awareness, but in this case there was absolutely no suggestion of an alternative. No government agent witnessed the alleged torture; there was no suggestion that someone else may have told the government about it; and there was insufficient evidence that the government is willfully blind to such torture generally. The IJ's statement, read in context, was clearly an assessment of the facts of this particular case. It was not an erroneous, general statement of law upon which we could grant the petition for review.

In sum, a fair reading of the decision leads to the conclusion that the word "sanctioned" was inconsequential to the analysis and ultimately harmless.[6] Yet the majority excitedly reverses the IJ on the CAT claim as if one errant word choice, bereft of context and contained in a summary sentence, constituted the smoking gun for which it was searching. See Kumar, 435 F.3d at 1035 (Kozinski, J., dissenting) ("This is the nub of the IJ's reasoning, which the majority ignores, preferring to nitpick the IJ's isolated statements."). Rather than condemn the IJ solely on the authority of Black's Law Dictionary and Merriam-Webster's Collegiate, I would look to the mode of analysis it actually employed. The IJ applied the correct standard and committed no error of any consequence to this case.

B

Because, in my view, the IJ did not apply an erroneous standard to his CAT claim, the final step in our review is to consider whether the record evidence is so compelling that any rational finder of fact would conclude that Ornelas-Chavez more likely than not would be tortured, with the consent or acquiescence of the government, upon his return to Mexico. Ochoa v. Gonzales, 406 F.3d 1166, 1172 (9th Cir. 2005). Clearly, the record evidence does not even come close to meeting this stringent standard.

1

The majority seeks to curtail such inquiry by suggesting that "the IJ concluded simply that Ornelas-Chavez failed to show that the authorities `sanctioned' his alleged torture because he did not report it," and that we therefore cannot affirm the IJ's decision on any other ground even if supported by substantial evidence. Maj. Op. at 1060.

But the IJ's decision was not so cabined. She found no past torture because, in part, Ornelas-Chavez did not report any abuse. But the majority ignores at least four paragraphs in which the IJ discussed the facts that she felt undermined Ornelas-Chavez's claims of future harm. She considered "[Petitioner's] testimony and evidence offered by the[Petitioner]," and concluded that Ornelas-Chavez had "not shown that he is more likely than not to be tortured if he were to be removed to Mexico."

Given that conclusion, the IJ necessarily found many of the facts the majority claims it did not find.[7]

As such, we should consider any record evidence that supports the IJ's finding that Ornelas-Chavez failed to meet his burden of showing a likelihood of torture upon his return to Mexico. See Turcios v. INS, 821 F.2d 1396, 1398 (9th Cir.1987) ("The substantial evidence test is essentially a case-by-case analysis requiring review of the whole record.").[8]

2

As already noted, the regulations define torture for CAT purposes as severe pain or suffering "inflicted by or at the instigation of or with the consent or acquiescence of a public official or other person acting in an official capacity." 8 C.F.R. § 208.18(a)(1) (emphasis added). In turn, "[a]cquiescence of a public official requires that the public official, prior to the activity constituting torture, have awareness of such activity and thereafter breach his or her legal responsibility to intervene to prevent such activity." Id. § 208.18(a)(7) (emphasis added); see Kamalthas v. INS, 251 F.3d 1279, 1282 (9th Cir.2001). In short, the "consent or acquiescence" requirement means that the government must be aware of the allegedly tortuous conduct, or at least willfully blind to it. Zheng v. Ashcroft, 332 F.3d 1186, 1188-89 (9th Cir.2003) (citation omitted).

Past torture does not create a presumption of entitlement to CAT relief, although it is relevant to the ultimate inquiry: whether "it is more likely than not that [the petitioner] would be tortured if removed to the proposed country of removal." 8 C.F.R. § 208.16(c)(2); see Mohammed v. Gonzales, 400 F.3d 785, 802 (9th Cir.2005) (citing 8 C.F.R. § 1208.16(c)(3)). There is no evidence on this record that the Mexican authorities were aware of or willfully blind to the past abuses perpetrated by Ornelas-Chavez's father, cousins, or others.[9] By his own admission, Ornelas-Chavez never told anyone about the rapes he endured as a child. The lone exception was his confession to a school teacher that he had been sexually abused. However, the teacher was not informed of the alleged torture "prior to" its occurrence such that she could breach a legal duty to prevent it. See 8 C.F.R. § 208.18(a)(7).[10] The allegation of an attempt by Ornelas-Chavez's co-workers to smother him with a pillow—which, if anything, constitutes only attempted torture-suffers from the same flaw: the supervisor was not aware of the incident until after its occurrence. Moreover, as suggested above, the record does not compellingly demonstrate that the authorities were willfully blind to such conduct. As such, I must conclude that on this record there is no evidence of past torture, as defined by the regulations, to be considered under Ornelas-Chavez's CAT claim.

As to the ultimate question, the likelihood that Ornelas-Chavez will be tortured in the future if removed to Mexico, the evidence utterly falls short. It is first worth noting that the sexual abuse took place during Ornelas-Chavez's youth, specifically between the ages of six and twelve. Circumstances have so fundamentally changed—he is now an adult—that Ornelas-Chavez is rather unlikely to be subjected to future injury in the form of rape. As noted, the same conclusion applies to the beatings to which Ornelas-Chavez was subjected by his father. And as to the attempted assault by Ornelas-Chavez's co-workers at the state prison, there is simply no indication that these would-be torturers have singled out Ornelas-Chavez such that he would again be a target.

The evidence of general country conditions as it pertains to Mexican homosexuals does not paint a picture so dire as to compel reversal of the BIA decision. See 8 C.F.R. § 1208.16(c)(3)(iii)-(iv). Quite the contrary, the record contains numerous references to an ever-improving situation. And although there have been some homosexuality-related murders documented over five years, there are, according to this record, as many as

12,600,000 Mexicans of homosexual orientation.[11] Thus, it is impossible to conclude that "more likely than not" Ornelas-Chavez would suffer this fate. Harassment and arbitrary detentions by police officers, to the extent they occur, do not constitute torture. More generally, the evidence does not rise to the level that has compelled us to grant a petition for review in prior cases. There is no record evidence alleging that "torture [is] routinely administered" to any group in Mexico, see Al-Saher, 268 F.3d at 1147; nor is there evidence that torture is "an institution," or otherwise so pervasive against homosexuals that we must conclude more likely than not Ornelas-Chavez would fall prey to it, see Khup v. Ashcroft, 376 F.3d 898, 907 (9th Cir.2004).

I would affirm the determination that Ornelas-Chavez failed to meet his burden of showing that he was more likely than not to be tortured, as specifically defined by the regulations, if returned to Mexico.

III

For all of the foregoing reasons, I respectfully dissent.

Judge O'Scannlain's concurrence and dissent in Clark v. Capital Credit & Collection Serv. (Aug 24, 2006)

O'SCANNLAIN, Circuit Judge, concurring in part, dissenting in part.

While I agree generally with the Court's desire "to reinforce that the broad remedial purpose of the [Fair Debt Collection Practices Act] is concerned primarily with the likely effect of various collection practices on the minds of unsophisticated debtors," and while I specifically join parts I.B., I.C., and II. of the majority's opinion, I must respectfully dissent from part I.A. I cannot agree that Mrs. Clark's waiver of § 1692c(c)'s protections did not extend to Janine Brumley ("Brumley") or Capital Credit & Collection Service ("Capital"); the trial court properly concluded that Brumley did not violate § 1692c(c) by returning Mrs. Clark's call. For that reason, I must dissent to that extent.

I

The majority properly holds that a debtor may waive the protections of 15 U.S.C. § 1692c(c), which requires a debt collector to cease communication with the debtor upon written request. Here, Mrs. Clark did so by initiating a communication with Jeffrey Hasson ("Hasson") to obtain information. The majority extends her waiver only to Hasson, but in my view, the waiver should also apply to Brumley and Capital.

A

Congress enacted the Fair Debt Collection Practices Act ("FDCPA"), 15 U.S.C. §§ 1692-16920, in order to eliminate "abusive debt collection practices by debt collectors [and] to insure that those debt collectors who refrain from using abusive debt collection practices are not competitively disadvantaged." 15 U.S.C. § 1692(e). As the majority acknowledges, "there is nothing inherently abusive, harassing, deceptive or unfair about a return phone call." Maj. Op. at 1170. This is so regardless of who makes the call. The fact that Brumley returned Mrs. Clark's call instead of Hasson does not suddenly transform the

call into an abusive practice. The majority recognizes the possibility of waiver of §
1692c(c)'s protections because failure to do so would be inconsistent with the purposes of
the FDCPA. Refusing to extend Mrs. Clark's waiver to Brumley and Capital is similarly
inconsistent.

B

The majority argues that a waiver of § 1692c(c)'s protections must be knowing and
intelligent, Maj. Op. at 1170, and I do not disagree. But, in any conceivable case, a debtor
who phones a debt collector to request information must be said to have "sufficient
awareness of the relevant circumstances and likely consequences" of her action, United
States v. Larson, 302 F.3d 1016, 1021 (9th Cir.2002), namely that someone will return the
call with the requested information. In fact, one would almost certainly expect the person
with the information to be the one to place the return call. But the majority concludes that
the "least sophisticated debtor" would not have expected Brumley, or anyone at Capital, to
return Mrs. Clark's call. In my view, the majority errs in applying such standard.

Use of the "least sophisticated debtor" standard here, to determine the meaning a
debtor would ascribe to her own actions, is unique. Previously, we have employed it only
to determine whether a debt collector's communications to a debtor violate the FDCPA.
See Dunlap v. Credit Prot. Ass'n., L.P., 419 F.3d 1011, 1012 (9th Cir. 2005) (judging "[t]he
impact of language alleged to violate the FDCPA"). To that end, we examine
communications with an eye towards the "tendency of language to deceive" the "least
sophisticated debtor." Baker v. G.C. Servs. Corp., 677 F.2d 775, 778(9th Cir.1982); see also
Renick v. Dun & Bradstreet Receivable Mgmt. Servs., 290 F.3d 1055, 1057 (9th Cir.2002)
(holding that a communication "was not misleading even to the least sophisticated
debtor"); Terran v. Kaplan, 109 F.3d 1428, 1431 (9th Cir.1997) (stating that "whether the
initial communication violates the FDCPA depends on whether it is likely to deceive or
mislead a hypothetical `least sophisticated debtor'" (internal quotation marks and citation
omitted)); Wade v. Reg'l Credit Ass'n, 87 F.3d 1098, 1100 (9th Cir.1996) (stating that a
communication violates the FDCPA if "likely to deceive or mislead a hypothetical `least
sophisticated debtor'"). We have also used it to determine whether such a debtor would
understand a debt collector's communication as a threat. See Swanson v. S. Or. Credit
Serv., Inc., 869 F.2d 1222, 1227 (9th Cir.1988).

Significantly, Clomon v. Jackson, 988 F.2d 1314, 1320(2d Cir.1993), cited by the
majority, notes that the "least sophisticated consumer" standard serves a dual purpose.
"[I]t (1) ensures the protection of all consumers, even the naive and the trusting, against
deceptive debt collection practices, and (2) protects debt collectors against liability for
bizarre or idiosyncratic interpretations of collection notices." Id. When used to determine
whether a debtor "would understand that he or she was waiving his or her rights under §
1692c(c)," the standard serves neither of these purposes. Maj. Op. at 1170-1171. Because
returning a debtor's call is not a deceptive practice, I see no reason for the majority's novel
application of the "least sophisticated debtor" standard here.[1]

C

Indeed, I see no reason to use any standard other than common sense. Mrs. Clark called Hasson's office seeking information concerning a specific debt, despite her earlier cease communication instruction. In my view, by doing so, Mrs. Clark waived her right to avoid a return communication—albeit one specifically limited to providing the information requested. Although Hasson and Brumley's employer, Capital, are different entities, they were working together to collect the specific debt about which Mrs. Clark inquired. Allowing one of the parties to return the call while preventing the others from doing so is nonsensical, particularly where one party has better access to the information. Here, Capital, and Brumley specifically, had the information Mrs. Clark requested; thus, Mrs. Clark's waiver should, as a matter of common sense, apply to both Capital and Brumley.[2]

In my view, then, Capital and Brumley did not violate § 1692c(c) of the FDCPA by returning Mrs. Clark's call, and the district court's grant of summary judgment on the issue was proper.

II

Because Mrs. Clark waived her cease-communication directive as to both Hasson and Brumley, I would affirm the district court's grant of summary judgment to all parties on the Clarks' § 1692c(c) claim.

Notes

[1] Even were the "least sophisticated debtor" standard appropriate, the majority errs by injecting a subjective element into what is, by its own admission, an "objective" standard. Majority Op. at 10151. Mrs. Clark's subjective intentions and expectations are not relevant; nor is her characterization of her previous interactions with Brumley. Mrs. Clark may have been upset by Brumley's collection efforts; however, § 1692c(c), and the FDCPA generally, prohibits only deceptive and abusive practices, not any and all actions that upset debtors. Thus, Mrs. Clark's alleged need for therapy is relevant only on the issue of damages flowing from actual violations of the FDCPA. Her unhappiness with the collection process generally is not relevant to the issue of whether her limited waiver of § 1692c(c) should extend to Brumley and Capital.

[2] A debtor might claim that a debt collector exceeded the scope of the waiver or was abusive. Abusive conduct violates § 1692d of the FDCPA, and a debt collector who exceeds the scope of a waiver might still violate § 1692c(c). However, it is unnecessary to reach that question because, although the majority states that the parties dispute the substance of Brumley's return call, this specific issue was tried to a jury following the district court's partial grant of summary judgment. The jury found that Brumley was not abusive and did not exceed the scope of Mrs. Clark's information request.

Judge O'Scannlain's dissent in Robbins v. Social Security Administration (Oct 27, 2006)

O'SCANNLAIN, Circuit Judge, dissenting.

I respectfully dissent from the court's holding that reversal and remand are required in this case. The administrative law judge's ("ALJ") analysis is thorough and cogent, and it should be affirmed.

I

First, the majority overturns the ALJ's adverse credibility determination. Maj. Op. at 882-85. I disagree with its analysis, and I would instead hold that the ALJ satisfied the requirement of providing "clear and convincing" reasons for its finding, which is supported by substantial evidence in the record as a whole. See Reddick v. Chater, 157 F.3d 715, 722 (9th Cir.1998); Johnson v. Shalala, 60 F.3d 1428, 1433 (9th Cir.1995).

A

As the majority suggests, we have held previously that "[t]he claimant need not produce objective medical evidence of the pain or fatigue itself, or the severity thereof." Smolen v. Chater, 80 F.3d 1273, 1282 (9th Cir.1996). In other words, an ALJ "may not discredit the claimant's allegations of the severity of pain solely on the ground that the allegations are unsupported by objective medical evidence." Bunnell v. Sullivan, 947 F.2d 341, 343 (9th Cir.1991) (en banc) (emphasis added); accord 20 C.F.R. § 416.929(c)(2). That point of law is well-established.

The applicable regulations, however, make clear to claimants that in "[e]valuating the intensity and persistence of your symptoms, such as pain, and determining the extent to which your symptoms limit your capacity for work," the agency will "consider all of the available evidence, including your history, the signs and laboratory findings, and statements from you, your treating or nontreating source, or other persons about how your symptoms affect you." 20 C.F.R. § 416.929(c)(1). They specifically state that the agency will

"also consider the medical opinions of your treating source and other medical opinions." Id. The regulations continue:

Objective medical evidence of this type is a useful indicator to assist us in making reasonable conclusions about the intensity and persistence of your symptoms and the effect those symptoms, such as pain, may have on your ability to work....

. . . .

.... We will consider your statements about the intensity, persistence, and limiting effects of your symptoms, and we will evaluate your statements in relation to the objective medical evidence and other evidence, in reaching a conclusion as to whether you are disabled. We will consider whether there are any inconsistencies in the evidence and the extent to which there are any conflicts between your statements and the rest of the evidence, including your history, the signs and laboratory findings, and statements by your treating or nontreating source or other persons about how your symptoms affect you.

Id. § 416.929(c)(2), (4) (emphases added); accord id. § 404.1529(c). We have also recognized that an ALJ may consider, as a factor in discrediting a claimant's subjective complaints, "`testimony from physicians and third parties concerning the nature, severity, and effect of the symptoms of which [claimant] complains.'" Thomas v. Barnhart, 278 F.3d

947, 959 (9th Cir. 2002) (quoting Light v. Soc. Sec. Admin., 119 F.3d 789, 792 (9th Cir.1997)); accord Smolen, 80 F.3d at 1284 & n. 8 (stating that the ALJ shall consider the "observations of treating and examining physicians" regarding, inter alia, any "functional restrictions caused by the symptoms"). The applicable Social Security Ruling states likewise. It instructs that the adjudicator's credibility finding must be based on the available "medical signs and laboratory findings," as well as on "any statements and other information provided by treating or examining physicians or psychologists and other persons about the symptoms and how they affect the individual." See SSR 96-7p, 1996 WL 374186, at *2.

In short, while the claimant is not required to provide objective medical evidence affirmatively proving the severity of his pain, Bunnell, 947 F.2d at 343, the foregoing authority makes clear that an ALJ may reject a claimant's statements about the severity of his symptoms and how they affect him if those statements are inconsistent with or contradicted by the objective medical evidence. See, e.g., Johnson, 60 F.3d at 1434 (noting that "[t]he ALJ also identified several contradictions between claimant's testimony and the relevant medical evidence"). The majority's confusion on this fundamental issue is patent.

The ALJ's assessment of Appellant Leroy Robbins's testimony, which I would hold entirely proper, began with the following correct statement of law:

In establishing the residual functional capacity, I must determine whether claimant's complaints of symptoms can reasonably be accepted as consistent with the objective medical evidence and other evidence based on the requirements of 20 C.F.R. § 416.929 and Social Security Ruling 96-7. I must also consider any medical opinions from acceptable medical sources which reflect judgments about the nature and severity of the impairments and resulting limitations on claimant's residual functional capacity.

(Citations omitted.) The ALJ then noted Robbins's testimony regarding his past work, which was that he was no longer able to even carry a can of paint upstairs.

Robbins had further testified "that his typical day consist[ed] of sitting and watching television, because of his pain."

The ALJ found these allegations regarding Robbins's functional limitations "not entirely credible," noting that they were not "consistent with or supported by the overall medical evidence of record which reflects no serious physical or mental functional limitations." In making that finding, the ALJ permissibly relied on the opinion of Dr. Victoria Carvalho, which was that Robbins was "consistently assessed as capable of `Medium' exertion, with the accommodation [due to Robbins's `perceived pain'] of being able to `change position every 2 hours, for 10-to-15 minutes.'" Aside from a "slight deviation in the claimant's knees, ankles and toes," Dr. Carvalho had assessed Robbins as having "no functional impairment in the upper or lower extremities; good strength and no difficulties ambulating."[1] It was also proper for the ALJ to rely on the opinion of the impartial medical examiner, Dr. Orin H. Bruton, who agreed that Robbins could perform duties involving "Medium" exertion. Further, Dr. Julie Isaacson opined that Robbins's knee pain had improved following knee-replacement surgery and that he should "get back in the work force." As for Robbins's psychological state, Dr. Paul Stoltzfus's view, even as late as 2002, was that he had only "`slight'-or-`mild' socialization limitations in a work environment and `no' cognitive functional limitations." See SSR 96-7p, at *5 (stating that the ALJ's credibility determination should take into account any "[d]iagnosis, prognosis, and other medical opinions provided by treating or examining physicians or psychologists and other medical sources").

These medical opinions simply were not consistent with Robbins's claim that his pain resigned him to a sedentary life of watching television. Thus, the ALJ did not, as the majority erroneously holds, disregard Robbins's testimony solely because he did not prove the severity of his pain by objective medical evidence. Rather, in the phrasing of the Social Security Administration, the ALJ properly found that Robbins's "alleged functional limitations and restrictions due to symptoms [could not] reasonably be accepted as consistent with the objective medical evidence and other evidence in the case record." SSR 96-7p, at *2.

The majority's approach is one I hope we will not repeat. Its conflating of the two relevant categories — a lack of affirmative support versus the presence of contradictory medical evidence — would absolutely bar adjudicators from making adverse credibility determinations so long as the claimants are able to keep their stories straight. The applicable regulations, agency ruling, and case law all counsel strongly against such an approach.

B

Additionally, a claimant's inconsistent statements about the use of alcohol can contribute to a determination regarding that claimant's credibility. See Thomas, 278 F.3d at 959; Verduzco v. Apfel, 188 F.3d 1087, 1090 (9th Cir.1999).

The ALJ made such a finding in this case, stating that Robbins presented "conflicting testimony and reports to doctors of maintaining sobriety, versus continuing to drink in lesser amounts." The ALJ noted that "[d]uring his initial screening on April 4, 1989, [Robbins] specifically denied having a problem with alcohol." Yet during that same period, Dr. Charles Reagan observed, "The claimant has been drinking up to a case a day. This drinking escalated beginning in 1988." Then on November 12, 1996, as the ALJ further noted, Robbins reported to Dr. Carvalho "that he continues to `occasionally drink' but admitted `he did have a problem with alcohol.'"[2]

C

The majority's fallback argument is that the ALJ's decision is characterized by a "complete lack of meaningful explanation [which] gives this court nothing with which to assess its legitimacy." Maj. Op. at 884. It asserts that the same error infects the ALJ's finding regarding Robbins's conflicting testimony as to his alcohol abuse. See Maj. Op. at 884 n. 2.

It is unclear to me why the majority chooses simply to disregard the many pages preceding (as well as the few pages following) the paragraph in which the ALJ made the credibility determination explicit. As the Commissioner suggests, after discussing in great detail the reasons supporting its ultimate findings, the ALJ was not required explicitly to link his determination to those reasons. See, e.g., Lewis v. Apfel, 236 F.3d 503, 512 (9th Cir.2001) ("In all, the ALJ at least noted arguably germane reasons for dismissing the family members' testimony, even if he did not clearly link his determination to those reasons.").

Indeed, all of the reasons discussed above constitute "grounds invoked by the agency," SEC v. Chenery Corp., 332 U.S. 194, 196, 67 S.Ct. 1575, 91 L.Ed. 1995 (1947), or "reasons the ALJ assert[ed]," Connett v. Barnhart, 340 F.3d 871, 874 (9th Cir.2003). The majority is utterly wrong to suggest otherwise.

D

In sum, the ALJ properly supported and adequately explained his adverse credibility determination. The finding is supported by specific, clear, and convincing reasons, and it should be affirmed.

II

I also disagree with the majority's view that a remand is required because the ALJ failed explicitly to comment on the lay opinion testimony of Rodney Robbins, the claimant's son. See Maj. Op. at 884.

A

The application of harmless error doctrine in our review of the denial of Social Security disability benefits is well-established. See, e.g., Booz v. Sec'y of Health & Human Servs., 734 F.2d 1378, 1380 (9th Cir.1983). In Batson v. Comm'r of Soc. Sec. Admin., 359 F.3d 1190 (9th Cir.2004), for example, we simply asked whether there remained "substantial evidence supporting the ALJ's decision," or whether the error in any way "negate[d] the validity of the ALJ's ultimate conclusion." Id. at 1197. A similar analysis would have been proper in this case.

But, as the majority says, "[w]e recently clarified the proper application of the harmless error standard in Social Security cases." Maj. Op. at 885. I did not agree with this same majority's formulation in Stout v. Commissioner, 454 F.3d 1050 (9th Cir.2006), and I do not endorse it here. Stout's "no reasonable ALJ" standard unduly curtails the latitude we have always accorded to the administrative bodies we review.

B

Regardless, I would hold that the ALJ's error in this case was harmless — even under Stout's exacting test. In Stout, as in each of the cases upon which the majority there relied, the ALJ failed to consider all available lay witness testimony. See 454 F.3d at 1056 (citing various in-and out-of-circuit cases). This case is quite different. Although the ALJ failed to comment on the testimony of the claimant's son, he considered at length the strikingly similar testimony of the claimant's wife and daughter. Given that aspect of the case, as well as the nature of the ALJ's ultimate determination, we "can confidently conclude that no reasonable ALJ, [even] fully crediting the [omitted] testimony, could have reached a different disability determination." Id.

1

As noted, the majority reverses because the ALJ erred in failing to mention the substance of roughly four pages of Rodney Robbins's unsworn testimony, dated August 28, 1998. Rodney testified that in August 1993 his father had trouble walking, i.e., a "slight limp that become more pronounced ... on some days than others." He explained that given his father's high level of pain tolerance, his verbalizing his pain was "noteworthy." Rodney recalled his father having "some difficulty" using his arms and hands. He further testified that his father was in pain on approximately half of the occasions on which Rodney saw him, and that his father would become "worn out" easily. Rodney also noticed "marked depression" and some irritability. According to Rodney's testimony, his father's condition had only worsened since August 1993.

Though the ALJ did not mention this testimony in his decision, he did explicitly consider the testimony of Rhonda Heaps, Robbins's daughter. Heaps testified that she had seen her father two to three times per week since August 1993. She testified that he had difficulty walking because of swollen knees, a condition she noticed perhaps once every month. Heaps also discussed her father's pain, explaining that he engaged in uncharacteristic behaviors such as "sitting in [a] chair with his leg up." She testified that her father was depressed and irritable, and that his condition made it difficult to engage in physical tasks associated with managing apartments. The ALJ found her testimony "generally credible, at least to the extent of her reported first-hand observations of her father."

The ALJ also discussed the testimony of Gloria Jean Robbins, the appellant's wife. Ms. Robbins similarly testified to the difficulty Robbins experienced with the physical duties — such as painting, cleaning, and moving heavy items — of his past work as an apartment manager. Even paperwork became a problem, according to Ms. Robbins, because of lapses in memory and an inability to concentrate.

The lay witness testimony from the foregoing individuals stood in the record alongside various items of medical evidence and the expert opinions of multiple medical professionals. The ALJ agreed with Robbins's claim that his impairments were "severe," within the meaning of the regulations. The judge found that Robbins suffered from "severe" impairments of left rotator cuff tendinitis; pseudo-gout of the knees, bilaterally; degenerative disc disease of the lumbar spine and history of alcoholism, in partial remission." In assessing the impact of these impairments, the ALJ considered the opinion of Dr. Richard Guidry, who examined Robbins in May and June of 1995. Dr. Guidry noted that Robbins exhibited "no discomfort" during range-of-motion testing and that Robbins gave "poor effort" during portions of the test. The ALJ also assessed x-ray and MRI findings from May 1995, which showed "moderately severe degenerative changes" in Robbins's spine, but no "signs of disc herniation." Dr. Guidry placed Robbins on "light" duty status.

The ALJ next considered a November 1996 consultative orthopedic evaluation by Dr. Carvalho, which revealed "a slightly decreased radial deviation (i.e., movement through normal range incurring slight pain or numbness), bilaterally in the ankles, with vibratory sensation absent in the knees, ankles and toes, bilaterally." The ALJ noted that Dr. Carvalho otherwise "found no functional impairment in the upper or lower extremities; good strength and no difficulties ambulating." Dr. Carvalho's assessment of Robbins's residual functional capacity ("RFC") was that he could perform "medium" exertion, and was able to carry up to 25 pounds "frequently" and up to 50 pounds "occasionally." The doctor noted that because of his "perceived pain," Robbins should be permitted to "change position every two hours for 10 to 15 minutes."

From February through November of 1997, Dr. Sean Stadtlander treated Robbins for pain in his back, left shoulder, right knee, right wrist and elbow, and neck. Spinal x-rays revealed "moderate" or "mild" degenerative disc disease, but "no evidence of acute bony trauma." The doctor prescribed pain medication. With respect to Robbins's knees, x-rays showed "prominent cartilage calcification" of the left knee and softening of the cartilage in the right knee. Robbins was referred to Dr. Julie Isaacson, an orthopedic surgeon, who aspirated Robbins's right knee and thereafter noted "significant improvement."

In June 1998, upon finding evidence of a meniscal tear and complaints of pain, swelling, and tenderness, Dr. Isaacson performed a total right knee replacement surgery. Thereafter Robbins underwent a course of physical therapy and received pain medication. The ALJ noted that by August 11, 1998, Robbins reported no longer using the pain medication. The ALJ further noted Dr. Isaacson's opinion "that she would like to see [Robbins] in the work force."

Turning to Robbins's RFC, the ALJ considered Robbins's past work experience; the impact of alcoholism, which the ALJ found minimal; Robbins's own testimony of pain and anxiety, which the ALJ found "not entirely credible"; and the testimony of Robbins's wife and daughter, which primarily concerned Robbins's inability to perform work as an apartment manager. The ALJ reviewed the RFC assessment made by "the State agency non-examining medical consultants," which stated that Robbins was capable of "medium" exertion but should be allowed to "change position every 2-hours, for 10-to-15 minutes." Dr. Bruton, as the "impartial medical expert," reviewed all of the medical evidence and testified that he concurred with the opinion of the State agency consultants. Ultimately, then, the ALJ concluded that Robbins's pre-1998 RFC was "at the level of `less than a wide or full range of Medium' exertion with Postural and Manipulative non-exertional limitations."[3]

Next, the ALJ agreed with Robbins's claim (which was supported by the testimony of an impartial vocational expert) that he could no longer perform any of his past work, including the management of apartment buildings. However, the ALJ then held that the Social Security Administration had met its burden of showing other jobs, "existing in significant numbers in the regional or national economy," that Robbins could have performed from 1993 to 1998. Although Robbins was without transferable skills, the vocational expert testified that he could perform other jobs which required "less than a wide or full range of Medium" exertion. Namely, Robbins could have worked as a "general clerk" or a "security or gate guard." Those jobs required only "Light exertion, at a semi-skilled level," and would be available even with Robbins's limitations. The ALJ concurred, and he thus found Robbins "not disabled" from August 20, 1993, though September 7, 1998.

2

I think it clear that the ALJ made a careful assessment of the available medical evidence and found that notwithstanding various postural and manipulative limitations, Robbins could perform work involving something less than a medium range of exertion. The ALJ's reasoned conclusion, in other words, was that the "overall medical evidence of record [] reflect[ed] no serious physical or mental functional limitations."

Taking Rodney Robbins's testimony into account, the record hardly looks different. Rodney's testimony covered no ground not also covered by the appellant's daughter and wife. Rodney discussed the pain in his father's knees; testified to uncharacteristic behavior that indicated the extent of his father's pain; said that his father had difficulty using his arms; and noted depression and irritability. Rhonda Heaps also discussed each of these issues, in very similar terms, and the ALJ found her credible. It defies reason to conclude that the ALJ's determination of Robbins's RFC may have been different had he only considered a second recitation of the very same observations.

I am also confident in the harmlessness of the error at issue because of the nature of the ALJ's decision. The ALJ did not doubt that Robbins experienced significant pain; he accepted Rhonda Heaps's testimony as credible, and thus accounted for every limitation to which Rodney Robbins testified. The ALJ further agreed that some impairments were "severe," and his findings accommodated Robbins's need to change positions regularly and take breaks. He also agreed that Robbins could no longer perform work as an apartment manager, which was the subject with which the lay opinion testimony was primarily concerned.

As such, and in light of the proper credibility determination as to Robbins, the ALJ could then reasonably rely on the medical evidence in determining the impact the perceived pain would have had on Robbins's ability to work in other jobs. That medical evidence showed, without equivocation, that prior to September 7, 1998, Robbins had no functional limitation that would have prevented his employment. As detailed above, he had little discomfort during range of motion testing in 1995; x-rays showed only "moderate" degeneration in his spine; he responded well to pain medication, even after the knee replacement; and he had "good strength and no difficulties ambulating." Every medical professional who offered an opinion on the subject — including Drs. Guidry, Carvalho, and Isaacson, as well as the State agency medical consultants and Dr. Bruton, the independent medical expert — suggested in clear terms that Robbins could re-enter the workforce. The ALJ determined that Robbins could do so in a capacity requiring "less than a wide or full range of Medium" exertion. The testimony of Rodney Robbins, which concerned the pain his father experienced while walking or working as an apartment manager, in no way could have undermined this determination so as to deprive it of support by substantial evidence.

C

Because the lay witness testimony did not actually touch on Robbins's ability to perform work as a "general clerk" or "security or gate guard," the "weight" it may have added — while hardly "substantial" — is entirely beside the point. In determining whether the ALJ's failure to address Rodney Robbins's testimony was harmless error, after Stout we ask whether a reasonable ALJ could have arrived at a different conclusion. Rodney Robbins provided no information not already provided by Rhonda Heaps, and he spoke to no limitations not already accounted for by the ALJ. For those reasons, I think it utterly apparent that there is no such possibility here.[4]

III

Because the majority's opinion suffers from fundamental errors and fails fairly to apply its own harmless-error standard, I respectfully dissent.

Notes

[1] As the relevant Social Security Ruling notes, the "effects [of symptoms such as pain] can often be clinically observed." SSR 96-7p, at *6.

[2] That the ALJ uttered the word "equivocal" is of no importance. See Maj. Op. at 883-84. The opinion states that Robbins's "testimony regarding his alcohol dependence and abuse problem remains equivocal" because of "his conflicting testimony." Robbins's testimony was clearly "conflicting"; it was the relevance of such testimony that the ALJ considered to be equivocal. This view is perfectly consistent with the finding that Robbins was "not entirely credible."

[3] Specifically, the ALJ found that Robbins could lift and carry up to 50 pounds "occasionally" and up to 25 pounds "frequently"; could stand and walk up to six hours in an eight-hour work day with normal breaks; could sit about two hours in an eight-hour work day with normal breaks; and had "push/pull abilities" limited to the amount of weight he could lift and carry. The ALJ also agreed that Robbins had "postural and manipulative non-exertional limitations;" he was "precluded from any kneeling, squatting, crawling or crouching, because of his bilateral knee condition." Robbins was also limited to "only `occasional' overhead reaching with his non-dominant left arm and shoulder."

[4] Moreover, the ALJ's assessment of Robbins's RFC was complete, specific, and supported by substantial evidence. See Bayliss v. Barnhart, 427 F.3d 1211, 1217 (9th Cir.2005) ("In making his RFC determination, the ALJ took into account those limitations for which there was record support that did not depend on [the claimant's] subjective complaints."). As a result, the hypothetical posed to the vocational expert was without error. Id. at 1217-18 ("The hypothetical that the ALJ posed to the VE contained all of the limitations that the ALJ found credible and supported by substantial evidence in the record." (citing Magallanes v. Bowen, 881 F.2d 747, 756-57 (9th Cir.1989))).

Judge O'Scannlain's dissent in Phillips v. Hust (Feb 13, 2007)

O'SCANNLAIN, Circuit Judge, dissenting:

I respectfully dissent from the court's holding that prison librarian Hust's refusal to allow inmate Phillips access to the prison comb-binding machine hindered his ability to file his petition for certiorari timely in the Supreme Court. I must also dissent from the court's holding that Hust is not entitled to qualified immunity.

I

In Bounds v. Smith, 430 U.S. 817, 97 S.Ct. 1491, 52 L.Ed.2d 72 (1977), the Supreme Court held that "the fundamental constitutional right of access to the courts requires prison authorities to assist inmates in the preparation and filing of meaningful legal papers by providing prisoners with adequate law libraries or adequate assistance from persons trained in the law." Id. at 828, 97 S.Ct. 1491. In Lewis v. Casey, 518 U.S. 343, 116 S.Ct. 2174, 135 L.Ed.2d 606 (1996), the Court subsequently recognized the limits of Bounds when it held that an inmate must demonstrate that official acts or omissions "hindered his efforts to pursue a [non-frivolous] legal claim." Id. at 351, 116 S.Ct. 2174; see also id. at 365, 116 S.Ct. 2174 (Thomas, J., concurring) ("[T]he majority opinion ... places sensible and much-needed limitations on the seemingly limitless right to assistance created in Bounds ...."). While Lewis recognized that the tools of litigation must be made available when necessary to ensure "meaningful access" to the courts, the majority opinion goes beyond that to require prison officials to provide inmates with whatever tools seem reasonable in a given situation, even if not necessary to vindicate the inmate's right of action. In so doing, today's decision ignores the sensible limitations recognized by the Supreme Court in Lewis.

A

At the outset, I note several points of agreement with the majority. First, the court correctly recognizes that in order to prevail on a motion for summary judgment and to merit a remedy for a lost opportunity to present a legal claim, Phillips must affirmatively establish three elements: (1) actual injury in the form of a loss of a non-frivolous underlying legal claim; (2) that official acts hindered his pursuit of the legal claim; and (3) that he is pursuing a remedy that may be awarded as recompense but that is not otherwise available in a future suit. Maj. Op. at 1075-76 (citing Christopher v. Harbury, 536 U.S. 403, 413-14, 122 S.Ct. 2179, 153 L.Ed.2d 413 (2002)).

I also agree with the majority that it is "arguable," Lewis, 518 U.S. at 351, 116 S.Ct. 2174, that at least one of Phillips's claim was non-frivolous. Maj. Op. at 1076. Specifically, I accept as non-frivolous Phillips's claim that the state court applied a standard that differed from that set forth in Strickland v. Washington, 466 U.S. 668, 104 S.Ct. 2052, 80 L.Ed.2d 674 (1984). Finally, I agree with the court that Phillips is able to point to a "specific instance" in which he was denied access to the courts: his petition for a writ of certiorari was denied as untimely by the Supreme Court. See Lewis, 518 U.S. at 356, 116 S.Ct. 2174 (describing the loss of an actionable claim).

B

Despite these points of agreement, I cannot agree with the majority's resolution of this case. Simply stated, Phillips has failed to establish, at the summary judgment stage, that the official actions of the prison librarian were the proximate cause of his loss. See Arnold v. IBM Corp., 637 F.2d 1350 (9th Cir.1981) ("The causation requirement of Section 1983 is not satisfied by showing of mere causation in fact. Rather the plaintiff must establish proximate causation.") (internal citations omitted); Stevenson v. Koskey, 877 F.2d 1435, 1438-39 (9th Cir.1989).

1

In Lewis, the Supreme Court made clear that Bounds "guarantee[d] no particular methodology but rather the conferral of a capability — the capability of bringing challenges to sentences or conditions of confinement before the courts." 518 U.S. at 356, 116 S.Ct. 2174 (emphasis added). Capability is defined as the "quality or state of ability; having the physical, mental or legal power to perform." WEBSTER'S NINTH NEW COLLEGIATE DICTIONARY 203 (1986). The conferral of a capability to bring a non-frivolous legal action does not, however, require states to turn prisoners into litigation machines. As the Supreme Court stated in Lewis,

[Bounds] does not guarantee inmates the wherewithal to transform themselves into litigating engines ... The tools it requires to be provided are those that the inmates need in order to attack their sentences, directly or collaterally, and in order to challenge the conditions of their confinement. Impairment of any other litigating capacity is simply one of the incidental (and perfectly constitutional) consequences of conviction and incarceration.

518 U.S. at 355, 116 S.Ct. 2174 (emphasis in original).

Thus, in Lindquist v. Idaho State Bd. of Corrections, 776 F.2d 851, 856 (9th Cir. 1985), we rejected the contention of inmates that a prison library must contain the Pacific Reporter 2d, Shepard's Citations and a number of other reference books. We noted that Bounds did not require a prison to provide its inmates with "a library that results in the best possible access to the courts." Id. (emphasis added). Instead, what Bounds required was that the resources meet minimum constitutional standards sufficient to provide meaningful, though perhaps not "ideal," access to the courts. Id. We thus had no trouble also concluding that inmates had no right to a typewriter to prepare their legal documents where the court rules permit pro se litigants to hand-write their pleadings.

The situation in Lindquist may be contrasted with that with which we were presented in Allen v. Sakai, 40 F.3d 1001 (9th Cir.1994). In that case, Allen's notice of appeal to the Hawaii Circuit Court was rejected because it was written in pencil and not ink. Allen claimed that the outright denial of a pen deprived him of access to the courts. We held:

Hawaii's Circuit Court Rule 3(a) requires that all "handwritten entries on papers shall be in black ink," and defendants concede that this mandate was "clear and explicit" and provided no exceptions. In light of the clarity of the pre-existing law, it should have been apparent to the defendants that a ban on the use of pens would seriously hamper an inmate's access to the courts and therefore constitute a violation of his rights under Bounds.

40 F.3d at 1006. Allen presented a stark example of how the complete denial of a "clear[ly]" necessary writing utensil — specifically mentioned as a required tool by the Bounds court — could effectively deprive an inmate of their right of access to the courts. The result in Allen is thus unremarkable. See also Sands v. Lewis, 886 F.2d 1166, 1169 (9th Cir.1989) ("[We] have considered claims based on Bounds's teaching that the State must provide `indigent' prisoners with basic supplies which ensure that their access is `meaningful.' In evaluating this latter type of claim, we have declined to read into the Constitution any specific minimum requirements beyond those mentioned in Bounds itself.") (emphasis added); OR. ADMIN. R. XXX-XXX-XXXX (requiring prison officials to make available "necessary supplies for the preparation and filing of legal documents") (emphasis added).

Our precedents, therefore, require that for Phillips to prevail on summary judgment, he must make a showing that use of the comb-binding machine was a necessary pre-requisite to allowing him "meaningful access" to the courts.

2

The majority opinion appears to acknowledge that what is required is the provision of tools sufficient to afford a "capability" of litigation, but then, with a magician's sleight of hand, the focus of the inquiry is shifted to the apparent "arbitrary" nature of Hust's denial. The majority gets it mostly correct, however, in its initial statement that "[n]evertheless, it remains true that some means of preparing legal documents, including a means of binding them where required, must be made available." Maj. Op. at 1077 (emphasis added). Unfortunately, rather than adhering to the clear limits established by Supreme Court precedent, the majority here mandates prison employees to anticipate when the denial of unnecessary services will so fluster an inmate that his filing, though in no way actually frustrated, might be delayed. Such a rule amounts to an unreasonable demand that prison librarians be not only experts on their actual duties, but also clairvoyant.

Supreme Court Rule 33.2 governs the form of documents to be filed with the Court. It provides that every document "shall be stapled or bound at the upper left-hand corner." In turn, Supreme Court Rule 39.3 governs proceedings in forma pauperis and requires every document presented by a party to be "prepared as required by Rule 33.2 (unless such preparation is impossible)." (emphasis added) It further requires that the petition be legible, obviously expecting most filings to be handwritten. Finally, the rule directs the Clerk to "mak[e] due allowance for any case presented under this Rule by a person appearing pro se."

Three simple points may be made. First, while an initial reading suggests that stapling or binding is affirmatively required, Rule 39.3 provides an exception when such methods are not possible. Second, Rule 33 requires the staple or binding to be at the upper left-hand corner. A comb-binding machine, in contrast, binds an entire side of a petition, and thus does not even come within the rule. Finally, the rule specifically mandates leniency for pro se litigants, many of whom the Court is fully aware are indigent prisoners.

The district court's grant of summary judgment, however, did not take into account the flexible — or at least disputed — nature of these rules. The district court ruled:

[Hust's] actions caused him to face the difficult choice of violating a Supreme Court Rule by submitting a partially bound brief, or missing his deadline. Plaintiff chose to comply with the Supreme Court Rule, and missed the filing deadline; his petition was subsequently denied as untimely by the Supreme Court. Viewing the facts in a light most favorable to plaintiff, it appears from the factual allegations and from the record on summary judgment that defendant violated plaintiff's constitutional right to access the courts.

The district judge's conclusion is incorrect.[1] The applicable Supreme Court rule neither requires nor allows comb-binding. The only way a comb-bound petition would be compliant with the clear text of this rule is by virtue of the impossibility clause in Rule 39.3. Reference to that rule, however, would defeat Phillips's claim that the rule is clear and provides for no exceptions. See Allen, 40 F.3d at 1006. Thus, there is no nexus between the denial of access to the comb-binding machine and the late filing of Phillips's petition. It was only Phillips's dogged insistence on this particular means of binding that caused his petition to be filed late and therefore rejected.[2] The district court's erroneous conclusion that Phillips was attempting to bind his petition in accordance with Supreme Court Rules finds no support in the record or in the text of the provisions. Accordingly, Hust's actions cannot be the proximate cause of Phillips's alleged loss.

Second, the record also reflects that the district court's analysis of the merits of the issue was permeated with incorrect presumptions for the summary judgment stage of this case. While the above-quoted analysis was performed as the first step of the Saucier qualified-immunity analysis, see Saucier v. Katz, 533 U.S. 194, 121 S.Ct. 2151, 150 L.Ed.2d 272 (2001), the district court expressly referred back to it with a supra citation in concluding that summary judgment for Phillips was warranted. On the merits of plaintiff's summary judgment motion, however, it is well-established that the evidence must be viewed in a light most favorable to the non-moving party, in this case Hust. See T.W. Electric Service, Inc. v. Pacific Elec. Contractors Ass'n, 809 F.2d 626, 630-31 (9th Cir.1987) ("[A]t the summary judgment, the judge must view the evidence in the light most favorable to the nonmoving party ... [I]f a rational trier of fact might resolve the issue in favor of the nonmoving party, summary judgment must be denied. Inferences must also be drawn in the light most favorable to the nonmoving party."). The court's analysis of the merits of the issue, however, which expressly incorporated its earlier analysis and not much more, viewed the facts in a light most favorable to plaintiff.

A de novo review of the record shows that Phillips failed to establish there were no disputed material issues of fact. There was not "but one reasonable conclusion as to the verdict" in this case, Anderson v. Liberty Lobby, Inc., 477 U.S. 242, 250, 106 S.Ct. 2505, 91 L.Ed.2d 202 (1986), and thus summary judgment was not appropriate.

3

The majority's focus on the allegedly arbitrary manner in which the prison enforced its policy against allowing inmates to use the comb-punch is thus beside the point. Under Christopher v. Harbury, 536 U.S. at 413-14, 122 S.Ct. 2179, Phillips must show that even an unreasonable prison policy was the cause of his loss. Our decision in Gluth v. Kangas, 951 F.2d 1504, 1508 (9th Cir.1991), cited by the majority, does not counsel differently. There, we simply recited the unremarkable conclusion that the existence of a law library does not provide for meaningful access when inmates are not afforded, in part because of arbitrary denials, a reasonable amount of time to use the facility. Id. Moreover, Gluth was a case decided before Lewis, when our circuit law did not require inmates alleging "core" Bounds violations to establish actual injury. Id. at 1509 n. 2; see also Sands, 886 F.2d at 1171.

C

Today's holding may seem eminently reasonable to some. As the court notes, "[W]e simply reach the unexceptional conclusion that otherwise valid prison policies may not be selectively or arbitrarily enforced in such a way as to interfere with prisoners' access to the courts to pursue litigation arising from their incarceration." Maj. Op. at 1078 n. 2 (emphasis added). In applying such an approach, however, the majority focuses only on the apparent arbitrary nature of Hust's denial to the detriment of the causation analysis. Because I am persuaded that the majority errs in applying its own rule, and because I believe the record does not establish, at the summary judgement stage, that Hust's actions were the proximate cause of Phillips's injury, I would reverse the grant of summary judgment and remand for trial.

II

Nor am I persuaded by the majority's view of Hust's qualified immunity claim.

A

A state officer is not protected by qualified immunity where he or she has violated a clearly established constitutional right. Under Saucier v. Katz, 533 U.S. 194, 121 S.Ct. 2151, 150 L.Ed.2d 272 (2001), "[t]he relevant, dispositive inquiry in determining whether a right is clearly established is whether it would be clear to a reasonable officer his conduct was unlawful in the situation he confronted." Id. at 201, 121 S.Ct. 2151; see also Anderson v. Creighton, 483 U.S. 635, 640, 107 S.Ct. 3034, 97 L.Ed.2d 523 (1987) ("The contours of the right must be sufficiently clear that a reasonable official would understand that what he is doing violates that right."). Although the author's subjective intent is irrelevant, id. at 641, 107 S.Ct. 3034, the information actually possessed by the officer is relevant to this determination. Hunter v. Bryant, 502 U.S. 224, 227, 112 S.Ct. 534, 116 L.Ed.2d 589 (1991) (per curiam).

The Lewis court made clear that the right at issue in a case such as this is not "an abstract, freestanding right to a law library or legal assistance." 518 U.S. at 351, 116 S.Ct. 2174. Instead, the right vindicated by Bounds was a right of "meaningful access to the courts." Id. Thus, the question before us is whether a reasonable prison official would believe that denying access to the prison combbinding machine would violate an inmate's right of access to file a brief for a writ of certiorari in the Supreme Court of the United States.

B

There are three key facts that establish Hust's entitlement to qualified immunity. First, despite her unfamiliarity with the explicit holding of Lewis v. Casey, she was clearly aware of her affirmative duty to aid inmates in the filing of legal documents.[3]

She stated that her job was not to provide legal assistance to inmates, but instead to supervise inmates in accord with ODOC Administrative Rules. Those rules provide:

Policy: "Within the inherent limitations of resources and the need for facility security, safety, health and order, it is the policy of the Department of Corrections to satisfy its legal obligation to provide inmates meaningful access to the courts by affording inmates reasonable access to a law library or contract legal services, and to necessary supplies for the preparation and filing of legal documents...."

OR. ADMIN. R. XXX-XXX-XXXX. That Hust was aware of this policy requiring her to aid in the preparation of legal materials is not disputed in the record.

Second, the delay in time responding to Phillips's request was not unreasonable based upon the information known to Hust at the time. See Anderson, 483 U.S. at 641, 107 S.Ct. 3034 (noting that the determination of whether official action is objectively legally reasonable "will often require examination of the information possessed by" the state actor). Here, the undisputed record shows that the June 13 request which Phillips sent to Hust did not indicate the date which his petition was due.

Finally, the record establishes that Hust was knowledgeable about filing requirements in courts. Hust stated in her affidavit that in her experience as a prison law librarian the courts accept pro se briefs without comb-binding. Her view that comb-binding was not required was reasonable, as the majority opinion itself recognizes before ultimately dismissing her interpretation of the rules as "not the only reasonable interpretation." Maj. Op. at 1078. Furthermore, it is not disputed that Hust "even contacted Trent Axen, Law Librarian at the Oregon State Penitentiary (OSP) in Salem, Oregon, who has experience with this matter to confirm what [she] already knew. Mr. Axen confirmed that he does not bind inmate briefs and the court has accepted unbound inmate briefs." This type of reference to an outside, knowledgeable source is ample proof of the reasonableness of Hust's actions.

The "unlawfulness" of Hust's actions is simply not apparent. Anderson, 483 U.S. at 640, 107 S.Ct. 3034. It was not an unreasonable reading of the rules of the Supreme Court to conclude that they do not require, nor even allow, the combbinding of petitions. Furthermore, in light of the general tenor of Lewis v. Casey and our previous cases which have held that only basic legal supplies, and not unnecessary amenities, are to be provided to inmates, see Sands v. Lewis, 886 F.2d at 1170, Hust's denial of access was not "willfully blind" to the requirements of law. Accordingly, it was "objectively legally reasonable," even if ultimately mistaken, Anderson, 483 U.S. at 641, 107 S.Ct. 3034; Act Up!/Portland v.

Bagley, 988 F.2d 868, 872 (9th Cir.1993), for Hust to conclude that her denial of access to the combbinding machine would not hinder Phillips's "capability" to file his petition. She is therefore entitled to qualified immunity.

I respectfully dissent from the court's holding otherwise.

Notes

[1] We review the grant of summary judgment de novo, Messick v. Horizon Industries, Inc., 62 F.3d 1227, 1229 (9th Cir.1995).

[2] The majority contends, "Hust's refusal to allow Phillips to use the comb-binder placed him in the untenable position of having to decide whether to file the petition on the date it was due in the hopes that it would be accepted unbound or partially bound, or to wait until he could bind the petition in the hopes that it would be accepted late." Maj. Op. at 1078. While this is literally true because the rules do not guarantee under what circumstances the clerk will deem proper presentation to have been "impossible," this is simply the nature of a general standard and cannot be grounds for finding the denial of access to the courts. To do so would be to directly countermand the two explicit provisions in the Supreme Court rules that suggest leniency for pro se litigants. The argument also ignores that Phillips would have assumed an even greater risk in filing a comb-bound cert. petition when the rules explicitly require binding at the upper left-hand corner of the document.

[3] The district court's reading of Hust's response to Phillips's interrogatory about Lewis v. Casey is clearly erroneous. The court found Hust to be "willfully blind" to the applicable law when she "denied" the statement that she was "somewhat familiar with Lewis v. Casey, 518 U.S. 343, 116 S.Ct. 2174, 135 L.Ed.2d 606 (1996)." That statement, when read in context, merely denies a precise knowledge of the Lewis case. It in no way suggests that Hust was "willfully blind" to the requirement that the basic supplies of litigation be afforded to inmates. Indeed, in the very same affidavit, Hust asserts that part of her position is to supervise inmates "in accordance" with the ODOC Administrative Rules governing "Legal Affairs (Inmate)," which requires prison officials to make available "necessary supplies." The district court's reading is akin to requiring a state official, even one not required to be trained in the law, to be intimately familiar with the names and holdings of decided cases. We have never required as much. See Cox v. Roskelley, 359 F.3d 1105, 1115 n. 1 (citing McCullough v. Wyandanch Union Free Sch. Dist., 187 F.3d 272, 278 (2d Cir.1999)) ("The question is not what a lawyer would learn or intuit from researching case law, but what a reasonable person in the defendant's position should know about the constitutionality of the conduct. The unlawfulness must be apparent."). The context of Hust's statements makes clear that she was generally knowledgeable about what was required of her as a law librarian. Nothing more is required.

Judge O'Scannlain's dissent from the denial of rehearing en banc in US v. Ressam (June 6, 2007) [Notes omitted]

O'SCANNLAIN, Circuit Judge, dissenting from the denial of rehearing en banc, joined by KLEINFELD, GOULD, BYBEE, CALLAHAN and BEA, Circuit Judges:

With all due respect to my colleagues, this high-profile case, involving an individual trained in Afghanistan by al-Qaeda and convicted of conspiring to detonate explosives at Los Angeles International Airport as part of a terrorist attack, is an ideal candidate for rehearing en banc. In United States v. Ressam, 474 F.3d 597 (9th Cir.2007), a panel majority concluded that a conviction under 18 U.S.C. § 844(h)(2) requires that explosives be carried not only during a felony, as the statute says, but also in relation to that felony, which the statute does not say. The panel thus reversed one count of conviction of "Millenium Bomber" Ahmed Ressam. I dissent from the denial of rehearing en banc because United States v. Stewart, 779 F.2d 538, 539-40 (9th Cir.1985), the two-decade old decision of our court upon which the panel relied, does not compel the result reached, and, further, by extending Stewart and reading the "in relation to" language into § 844(h)(2), we have not only usurped the congressional function, but have also created a split of authority with every other United States Court of Appeals that has addressed this question. See Fed. R.App. P. 35(b)(1)(B).

I

The facts and circumstances surrounding al-Qaeda trainee Ahmed Ressam's plot to detonate explosives at Los Angeles International Airport and his capture as he entered the United States are well-detailed in the panel opinion. Ressam, 474 F.3d at 599-601. In brief, Ressam and an associate loaded the trunk of a rental car with explosives, electronic timing devices, detonators, fertilizer, and aluminum sulfate, and drove to a ferry terminal at Twassen, British Columbia. Id. at 600. Ressam drove the rental car aboard the ferry, which later that day docked in Port Angeles, Washington. When Ressam attempted to drive his car off, a customs inspector stopped him for inspection. Id. After the customs officer became suspicious and subjected Ressam's vehicle to a more intrusive search, inspectors discovered some of the bomb's component parts. Once the car and all its contents were inventoried and tested, authorities realized that Ressam had all the materials for a full scale terrorist attack. Id. Ressam was indicted and convicted on nine counts, including one count of carrying an explosive during the commission of a felony, in violation of 18 U.S.C. § 844(h)(2). Id. at 600-01.

II

The critical legal issue in this appeal is whether Ressam's conviction for carrying an explosive during the commission of a felony must be reversed because the government did not also prove that Ressam was carrying the explosives in relation to the underlying felony (the "relational element"), which in this case the government designated as making a false statement in a customs declaration. See 18 U.S.C. § 844(h) ("Whoever ... carries an explosive during the commission of any felony which may be prosecuted in a court of the United States ... shall, in addition to the punishment provided for such felony, be sentenced to imprisonment for 10 years.").

The panel reasoned that our decision in Stewart, 779 F.2d at 539-40 compelled it to conclude that 18 U.S.C. § 844(h)(2) contains a relational element. I respectfully disagree. Then-Judge Kennedy's majority opinion in Stewart construed 18 U.S.C. § 924(c), which made unlawful the carrying of a firearm during the commission of a felony. At the time of Mr. Stewart's conviction, § 924(c) did not include an explicit relational element. See Stewart, 779 F.2d at 539. But by the time his case reached our court on appeal, "Congress [had] revised section 924(c), combining former subsections 924(c)(1) and 924(c)(2). The 1984 amendment substituted for the word `during' the phrase `during and in relation to.'" Id.

In determining whether the jury was properly instructed at Mr. Stewart's trial, our court focused almost entirely upon the legislative history of the 1984 amendment. The court's reading of the legislative history "indicate[d] the `in relation to' language was not intended to create an element of the crime that did not previously exist, but rather was intended to make clear a condition already implicit in the statute." Id. Thus, it concluded, because the relational element existed at the time of Stewart's trial, his jury instruction was in error.

But critically, there is no similar legislative history as to § 844(h)(2) because Congress never amended that statute to include the language that it added to § 924(c).[1] As the Third Circuit reasoned in reaching a conflicting conclusion than that of our Ressam panel, "even if the Stewart court was correct in its analysis of why Congress amended § 924(c), Congress has not seen fit to modify § 844(h) in the same manner." United States v. Rosenberg, 806 F.2d 1169, 1178 (3d Cir.1986).

Indeed, it is telling that when Congress did amend § 844(h)(2) in 1988, it did not add the relational language. At that time, Congress had before it our circuit's decision in Stewart, 779 F.2d at 539-40, and the Third Circuit's decision in Rosenberg, 806 F.2d at 1179. Rosenberg had rejected Stewart's general reasoning and its reasoning as specifically applied to § 844(h)(2), instead relying upon the plain, unambiguous language of that section. With these divergent decisions before it, Congress chose in 1988 not to add the "in relation to" language to § 844(h)(2). As the Supreme Court has explained, "where Congress includes particular language in one section of a statute but omits it in another section of the same Act, it is generally presumed that Congress acts intentionally and purposely in the disparate inclusion or exclusion." Russello v. United States, 464 U.S. 16, 23, 104 S.Ct. 296, 78 L.Ed.2d 17 (1983). This presumption of a knowing and intentional Congress in my view compels us to recognize that we are not "constrained" by Stewart's reasoning in deciding the proper interpretation of § 844(h)(2).

III

But even were the panel constrained by Stewart, I think it appropriate to rehear this case en banc because our holding that § 844(h)(2) includes a relational element is in conflict with every other circuit which has had occasion to consider the question. See Rosenberg, 806 F.2d at 1178; United States v. Ivy, 929 F.2d 147 (5th Cir.1991); United States v. Jenkins, 229 Fed.Appx. 362, 365-68, 2005 WL 3440416, **3-5 (6th Cir.2005) (unpublished).[2]

The main thrust of our sister circuits' decisions is that the plain language of § 844(h)(2) says nothing about a relational element, but only requires carrying the explosives during the commission of a felony. As Rosenberg stated:

> Section 844(h)(2) by its terms only requires that the government show that the defendant unlawfully carried an explosive "during the commission of any felony." The plain everyday meaning of "during" is "at the same time" or "at a point in the course of." See, Webster's Third New International Dictionary 703 (1961). It does not normally mean "at the same time and in connection with...." It is not fitting for this court to declare that the crime defined by § 844(h)(2) has more elements than those enumerated on the face of the statute. If Congress sees fit to add a relational element to § 844(h)(2), it is certainly free to do so, in the same manner that it added a relational element to § 924(c).

806 F.2d at 1178-79.

Further, as the Supreme Court more recently explained, when interpreting a statute "[w]ith a plain, nonabsurd meaning in view," we should not undertake to add missing words or elements, or to soften the impact of Congress' enactments. Lamie v. United States Trustee, 540 U.S. 526, 538, 124 S.Ct. 1023, 157 L.Ed.2d 1024 (2004). According to the Court, "[o]ur unwillingness to soften the import of Congress' chosen words even if we believe the words lead to a harsh outcome is longstanding. It results from `deference to the supremacy of the Legislature, as well as recognition that Congressmen typically vote on the language of a bill.'" Id. (quoting United States v. Locke, 471 U.S. 84, 95, 105 S.Ct. 1785, 85 L.Ed.2d 64 (1985) (internal citations omitted)). As Judge Alarcón stated in his dissent, "Mr. Ressam's proposed instruction would have required the District Court to add an element to § 844(h)(2) that does not appear in the statute enacted by Congress." Ressam, 474 F.3d at 606 (Alarcón, J., dissenting in part). It remains to be seen how, in practice, this additional requirement will impact the ability of prosecutors in this circuit to obtain convictions in explosives and terrorism cases. But in my view, Lamie confirms that the wisdom of such additions are firmly left to the determination of the legislative branch.

The reasoning and restraint of Lamie and of our sister circuits' decisions stand in stark contrast to Stewart and the panel decision in Ressam.[3] The great advantage of rehearing this appeal before our en banc court is that we could decide the proper interpretation of § 844(h)(2) and overrule Stewart, even if it is true that decision has left our circuit with something less than a "clean slate." Ressam, 474 F.3d at 602.

IV

Regardless of whether Stewart was correctly decided, I would quite simply not allow that decision to control the outcome of this case without en banc review. Because the panel's decision to vacate "Millenium Bomber" Ahmed Ressam's conviction under 18 U.S.C. § 844(h)(2) is in square conflict with the reasoning of our sister circuits and with the cautionary pronouncements of the Supreme Court, we should have reheard this case en banc. I respectfully dissent from the court's decision otherwise.

Judge O'Scannlain's dissent in Oregon Natural Resources Council Fund v. Brong (July 24, 2007) [Notes omitted]

O'SCANNLAIN, Circuit Judge, dissenting:

Both the district court and our court have now ruled that the Bureau of Land Management ("BLM") violated the Federal Land Policy and Management Act ("FLPMA") and the National Environmental Policy Act ("NEPA") in proposing the Timbered Rock Fire Salvage and Elk Creek Watershed Restoration Project ("Timbered Rock Project" or "Project") to salvage the remains of a disastrous fire in the Elk Creek Watershed.

With respect, I am unpersuaded that BLM violated either Act when the question is viewed under the proper standard of review. Because it appears that both courts have inappropriately substituted their own policy views for the BLM's, I cannot concur. The majority opinion recognizes that we must not invalidate agency action where the agency can present "a rational connection between the facts found and the conclusions made." Ante, at 1125. Unfortunately, because I can discern no rational connection between this extremely deferential standard of review and the majority's conclusions in this case, I must respectfully dissent.

I

FLPMA authorizes the BLM to "develop, maintain, and, when appropriate, revise land use plans which provide by tracts or areas for the use of the public lands." 43 U.S.C. § 1712(a). Once such plans are in place, FLPMA mandates that the BLM act "in accordance" with them. 43 U.S.C. § 1732(a). In the instant case, the governing land use plans are the Medford District Bureau of Resource Management Plan ("Medford RMP" or "RMP"), as amended by the Northwest Forest Plan ("NFP"). Our task is to determine whether the Timbered Rock Project is consistent with the Medford RMP and the NFP.

Our review must be deferential, because the BLM was interpreting its own guidelines. Forest Guardians v. U.S. Forest Service, 329 F.3d 1089, 1098 (9th Cir.2003) ("[F]ederal courts are required to defer to an agency's reasonable interpretation of its own guidelines."). Furthermore, we owe heightened deference where, as here, the agency's interpretation involves its own technical expertise and complex scientific methodologies. See, e.g., Envtl. Def. Ctr., Inc. v. EPA, 344 F.3d 832, 869 (9th Cir. 2003) ("We treat EPA's decision with great deference because we are reviewing the agency's technical analysis and judgments, based on an evaluation of complex scientific data within the agency's technical expertise.").

II

The majority mistakenly reads the NFP's requirement that the Forest Service ("Service") "focus on" snag retention as one that "expressly limits the removal" of snags. Ante, at 1128-29. One searches in vain for any such express limitation; a requirement to "focus on" retention, I suggest, more naturally reflects a presumption that snags will indeed need to be removed. The insistence upon its own best vision for silviculture, rather than upon the language of Congress or the professional expertise of the Service, pervades today's majority opinion, which far exceeds our limited role in reviewing agency action.

I concede that if the NFP posed an absolute bar to any and all snag removal, then the Forest Service has not made a showing that would overcome such a prohibition. But of course the NFP contains no such requirement, not by its plain language nor by any reasonable inference therefrom. The majority maintains that the BLM can "point to no part of the NFP to support its argument that using the some-is-enough standard satisfies the Plan." Ante, at 1129. On the contrary, the "some is enough" standard is implicit in the language the majority relies upon. It is the majority, rather, that can point to no language in the NFP stating that "some is never enough" — rather, it simply quotes "focus on" to divine an "express limitation."

Perhaps the majority has a better idea than the BLM about how many large snags to retain; our task, however, only requires — and only permits — us to review whether the BLM's determination is "arbitrary and capricious," and this the majority utterly fails to demonstrate. The majority derides the BLM's use of averaging in analyzing snag retention levels, ante, at 1129, though it acknowledges, ante, at 1129-30, that the BLM cites to two scientific studies supporting the practice. Rather than demonstrating, as it must but cannot, that the BLM has failed to establish a rational connection between the facts in the record and its conclusions, the majority constructs its own straw man example of an egregious abuse of averaging and quotes a Justice Brandeis aphorism to boot. Ante, at 1129 n. 13. Yet, the record demonstrates that 87% of snags on BLM land would still be present after the Timbered Rock Project, and that no salvage logging would occur on roughly 63% of the forest areas affected by the fires. Justice Brandeis was a wise man, but application of his aphorism to silviculture is surely inapposite.

The folly of the majority's analysis is also apparent in its discussion of the NFP's explicit allowance for non-beneficial recovery of timber volume after catastrophic events. See ante at 1129-30. Though the majority opinion repeatedly derides the principle that "some is enough," it does not seem to recognize that the only alternative to that truism is an absolute prohibition on snag removal. Yet it acknowledges that such a reading is untenable and that "salvage can occur in LSRs." Ante, at 1130. Therefore, it too believes that some, but not all, large snags must be maintained.

Further, the majority chides the BLM for purportedly failing to "claim or offer evidence" that the Timbered Rock fire killed more trees than are needed to maintain late successional conditions. Ante, at 1130-31. On the contrary, the Final Environmental Impact Study ("FEIS") provides multiple scientific references supporting its proposed level of snag retention — specifically relying upon the DecAID Wood Advisor, as well as upon separate 2002 studies by Rose, et al., and Ohmann.[1]

It follows, therefore, that the BLM has indeed argued, and to my mind demonstrated, that the Timberland Rock Fire killed more trees than are needed to maintain late successional conditions. It is baffling, and in any event demonstrably false, to contend that the BLM "does not claim or offer evidence to this end." The majority, so eager to lampoon the BLM's position as "some is enough," is apparently unwilling to concede that enough is enough.

Because the BLM has easily demonstrated its compliance with the NFP's general requirement to "focus on" snag retention, and because it has shown the requisite rational connection between the facts in the record and its conclusions about how many snags to retain, I cannot join the court's naked imposition of its own preference under the guise of a review for arbitrariness and capriciousness. With respect, I would reverse the district court.

III

The majority undertakes to reject the post-fire research logging proposed by the BLM under either of two tests permitting logging: first, that the activity is consistent with Late-Successional Reserve ("LSR") objectives, or second, if the proposal meets any of a series of alternate criteria and no equivalent opportunities outside of the LSR exist. The majority contends that the BLM's proposal fails the first test "for the same reasons the Project falls short with regard to snag retention." Ante, at 1131. As I have already shown, only by ignoring the studies relied upon by the BLM and by distorting the instruction to "focus upon" snag retention into an "express limitation" upon snag removal does the majority reach its erroneous conclusion concerning snag retention. Thus, I cannot agree that the proposed research logging is inconsistent with LSR objectives.

Although it is not necessary to my dissent on this score, let me add that the BLM has also demonstrated that the research logging would be permissible under the NFP even if inconsistent with LSR objectives. This is so first because the research logging would test critical assumptions concerning salvage of fire-killed trees and second because the BLM demonstrated that there were no "equivalent opportunities outside Late-Successional Reserves." Specifically, the BLM stated that while there are other recently burned areas in southwest Oregon, the Medford District was the only recently burned LSR. The BLM stated that research in an LSR is critical because of the manner in which LSR land is treated. These types of scientific and technical decisions are owed our deference. See Envtl. Def. Ctr., Inc. v. EPA, 344 F.3d 832, 869 (9th Cir.2003) ("We treat [this] decision with great deference because we are reviewing the agency's technical analysis and judgments, based on an evaluation of complex scientific data within the agency's technical expertise.").

IV

Because the majority agrees with the district court's finding of FLPMA violations with respect to snag removal and research logging, it does not reach the district court's further finding of a violation in the BLM's decision not to designate 92 acres as "riparian reserves." I would reverse the district court's decision here as well, as the BLM persuasively argues that the district court erroneously assumed that all "unstable or potentially unstable areas" must be designated as riparian reserves, whereas the NFP indicates that the BLM should decide if an area is a riparian reserve by focusing on "when watershed analysis determines that present and future coarse woody debris needs are met." The NFP also discusses riparian reserves in terms of their proximity to streams and rivers, not simply their stability. Because the BLM determined that the 92 acres in question were not adjacent to or related to streams or rivers, I would hold that the BLM was not in error in deciding not to designate them as riparian reserves.

Finally, the district court agreed with ONRC's contention that the project violates the Medford RMP by providing for salvage logging on lands that might be designated "nonsuitable woodlands." Although the RMP does state that nonsuitable woodlands "are not suitable for timber harvest," elsewhere it permits such logging for various purposes, including "reduc[ing] road construction," improving the "safety of forest users," and for "research studies." Thus, the RMP's discouragement of logging is not absolute, and the BLM's proposed logging here would be consistent with the RMP's discussion of permissible logging.

In sum, the district court erroneously found that the Project violated the FLPMA with respect to the removal of large snags, research logging, timber removal from nonsuitable woodlands, and the non-designation of riparian reserves, and I would reverse as to each.

V

The majority faults the BLM's FEIS and holds that it violated NEPA. But the BLM's FEIS is entitled to a "presumption of regularity." Citizens to Preserve Overton Park, Inc. v. Volpe, 401 U.S. 402, 415, 91 S.Ct. 814, 28 L.Ed.2d 136 (1971). Contrary to the majority's analysis, we ask only "whether the ... decision was based on a consideration of the relevant factors and whether there has been a clear error of judgment." Akiak Native Cmty. v. U.S. Postal Serv., 213 F.3d 1140, 1146 (9th Cir. 2000).

The majority relies principally on two cases to support its view that the Timbered Rock Project violates NEPA. First, it cites Klamath-Siskiyou Wildlands Center v. BLM, 387 F.3d 989, 993-94 (9th Cir.2004), where this court concluded that the BLM's Environmental Impact Statement ("EIS") was insufficient. However, the EIS in Klamath-Siskiyou neglected all discussion of cumulative effects. Rather than specifically analyzing environmental impacts, the BLM merely listed possible environmental concerns in generic terms. From this, the Klamath-Siskiyou court had no difficulty concluding that in a cumulative impact statement, "[g]eneral statements about possible effects and some risk do not constitute a hard look absent a justification regarding why more definitive information could not be provided." Id. at 993-94 (citation and quotation marks omitted); see also id. at 996 ("In sum, the only mention of cumulative effects in the two EAs comes in the form of generalized conclusory statements that the effects are not significant or will be effectively mitigated.").

Second, the majority points to Lands Council v. Powell, 379 F.3d 738, 745 (9th Cir.2004). Lands Council found insufficient an EIS that referenced pertinent facts, but did not contain analysis that "set forth in sufficient detail to promote an informed assessment of environmental considerations and policy choices by the public and agency personnel upon review of the [EIS]." Id. at 745.

The FEIS in this case violates neither Klamath-Siskiyou nor Lands Council. The discussion of the cumulative impacts runs 13 lengthy and detailed paragraphs. The FEIS states, for example, that:

- the fire suppression activities "increased the amount of erosion and subsequent sedimentation";
- "[a]nother area that could potentially deliver sediment would be roads in moderate to high burn severity areas hydrologically-connected to streams";
- "[particular fire suppression activities] aid in reducing the amount of erodible sediment by keeping water from channeling on the firelines";
- "[t]he potential for sediment delivery from roads paralleling streams would be greatest where cross drain spacing is insufficient ... [which] is common in the watershed";
- "[s]ediment would also be delivered to streams from salvage logging through hauling on natural surface roads".

The second set of cumulative effects analysis is similarly detailed, spanning 12 paragraphs.

The question, indeed, is whether the FEIS shows that the agency took a "hard look" at the environmental consequences and provided sufficient analysis such that it "foster[s] both informed decision-making and informed public participation." Native Ecosystems Council v. U.S. Forest Serv., 418 F.3d 953, 960 (9th Cir.2005) (citations omitted). But the FEIS satisfies those requirements here — the agency provided a sufficient analysis such that a reader could understand the likely environmental impact of the activities under consideration.

Finally, the majority holds, as did the district court, that deferred watersheds "present a distinct problem." Ante, at 1134. The FEIS did not separately discuss the cumulative impact of logging activities on deferred watersheds, which the district court concluded was error. The majority's analysis is logically faulty: an EIS discusses the cumulative impacts of agency sponsored activities, not the effects on particular geographic areas. For example, the FEIS discusses the cumulative impact on the environment of fire suppression and private logging. There is no further requirement that an EIS separately detail the impact of activities on areas classified as deferred watersheds. In any event, the FEIS did address the background facts related to deferred watersheds, and also discussed mass wasting, sedimentation, fisheries, soil, hydrology, vegetation, and special habitats. There is ample evidence that the BLM's decisions in the Timbered Rock Project were indeed based on a consideration of the relevant factors, and that no clear error of judgment has been shown. Akiak, 213 F.3d at 1146. NEPA requires no more. Accordingly, I disagree with the conclusion that the BLM violated NEPA in this case, and would reverse the district court as to the alleged NEPA violations as well.

VI

For the foregoing reasons, I am convinced that the BLM has made an ample showing to demonstrate a rational connection between the facts found and the conclusions made in formulating its Timbered Rock Project. Therefore, I respectfully dissent.

Judge O'Scannlain's dissent in Hulteen v. AT&T (Aug 17, 2007) [Notes omitted]

O'SCANNLAIN, Circuit Judge, with whom Judges RYMER, BYBEE, and CALLAHAN join, dissenting:

By concluding that Pallas v. Pacific Bell, 940 F.2d 1324 (9th Cir.1991), cert. denied, 502 U.S. 1050, 112 S.Ct. 916, 116 L.Ed.2d 815 (1992), remains good law, the majority erroneously perpetuates a circuit split with the Sixth and the Seventh Circuits.[1] I believe that Pallas was wrong then and is wrong now. Because this en banc court can and should overrule Pallas and follow the Seventh Circuit's well-reasoned decision in Ameritech Benefit Plan Committee v. Communication Workers of America, 220 F.3d 814 (7th Cir.), cert. denied, 531 U.S. 1127, 121 S.Ct. 883, 148 L.Ed.2d 791 (2001), I must respectfully dissent from the majority's conclusion that the sex discrimination claims in this case are timely.[2]

I

At the core of this dispute is AT & T Corporation's ("AT & T")[3] Net Credit Service ("NCS") seniority system, a concept which is not defined in Title VII. See Cal. Brewers Ass'n v. Bryant, 444 U.S. 598, 605, 100 S.Ct. 814, 63 L.Ed.2d 55 (1980). The term "seniority" connotes length of employment. Id. "A `seniority system' is a scheme that, alone or in tandem with non-`seniority' criteria, allots to employees ever improving employment rights and benefits as their relative lengths of pertinent employment increase." Id. at 605-06, 100 S.Ct. 814 (footnotes omitted). "[T]he principal feature of any and every `seniority system' is that preferential treatment is dispensed on the basis of some measure of time served in employment." Id. at 606, 100 S.Ct. 814. "In order for any seniority system to operate at all, it has to contain ancillary rules that accomplish certain necessary functions." Id. at 607, 100 S.Ct. 814. "[E]very seniority system must include ancillary rules that delineate how and when the seniority time clock begins ticking," as well as other provisions that "define which passage of time will `count' towards the accrual of seniority and which will not." Id.

AT & T has such a seniority system. Pursuant to that system, AT & T maintains an NCS date for each employee (from the initial date of hire until the date of termination) that consists of that employee's original hire date and any adjustments for periods during which no service credit is accrued pursuant to ancillary rules. AT & T moves the NCS date forward to "squeeze out" the periods of leave or breaks in service that are not credited, resulting in a later NCS date. AT & T uses the NCS date that it maintains for each employee for purposes of determining retirement benefits and other employment benefits. An earlier NCS date places an employee in a comparatively better position for employment-related determinations, including job bidding, layoffs, and eligibility for and calculation of certain retirement benefits.

Prior to August 7, 1977, AT & T's seniority system included two ancillary rules important to this case. The first provided that an employee received only 30 days of NCS credit for personal leave, but received full credit for temporary disability leave. The second specified that pregnancy leave would be treated as personal leave. AT & T applied these two rules to calculate NCS dates for all employees who became pregnant prior to that date. At no time did AT & T apply the pregnancy leave rule to any employee who became pregnant on or after August 7, 1977. With one exception,[4] the record fails to establish that on or after August 7, 1977, AT & T applied the pregnancy leave rule in effect before that date to adjust or to recalculate any employee's NCS date.

On August 7, 1977, AT & T adopted the Maternity Payment Plan ("MPP"), which supplanted the prior pregnancy leave rule. According to the MPP's new rule, up to six months of pregnancy leave would be treated as disability leave with full NCS credit, and any pregnancy leave in excess of six months would be treated as personal leave with a maximum of 30 days of NCS credit. Employees on non-pregnancy related disability leave continued to receive full NCS credit. AT & T applied the MPP pregnancy leave rule to adjust the NCS dates for all employees who became pregnant before April 29, 1979; AT & T did not retroactively apply the MPP pregnancy leave rule to adjust the NCS dates for any employees who became pregnant before August 7, 1977. The record fails to demonstrate that AT & T applied the MPP pregnancy leave rule to adjust or to recalculate any employee's NCS date on or after April 29, 1979.

In response to the Pregnancy Discrimination Act of 1978 ("PDA"), Pub.L. No. 95-555, 92 Stat. 2076, on April 29, 1979 (the effective date of the PDA), AT & T adopted the Anticipated Disability Plan ("ADP"), which superseded the MPP pregnancy leave rule. The ADP provided that pregnancy leave would be treated as disability leave with full NCS credit for the entire period of pregnancy. The ADP pregnancy leave rule remains in effect in AT & T's current NCS seniority system.

AT & T applies the new ADP pregnancy leave rule to adjust the NCS dates for all employees who become pregnant on or after April 29, 1979. AT & T, however, made no adjustment to the NCS dates for employees who had been subject to the MPP pregnancy leave rule or the pre-1977 pregnancy leave rule. Thus, for example, an employee who took pregnancy leave in 1980, after the effective date of the PDA, would receive full NCS seniority credit for that period of leave, but no adjustments were made to the NCS date of an employee who took pregnancy leave in 1976 and received a maximum of 30 days NCS seniority credit, or who took pregnancy leave in 1977 and received a maximum of six months and 30 days of credit.

Noreen Hulteen, Eleanora Collect, Linda Porter, and Elizabeth Snyder are all female employees of AT & T who took pregnancy leaves between 1968 and 1976, before the enactment of the PDA.[5] Under AT & T's NCS seniority system in effect at that time, Hulteen, Collect, Porter, and Snyder received only partial NCS credit for their pregnancy leaves, resulting in a later NCS date. AT & T's subsequent calculation of their benefits or the dates of their retirement eligibility between 1994 and 2000, would have been more favorable had AT & T retroactively credited their NCS dates for the previously uncredited periods of pregnancy leave before the enactment of the PDA. They contend that AT & T discriminated on the basis of sex in violation of Title VII when AT & T determined their benefits based on the NCS dates that were unadjusted to account for uncredited pre-PDA pregnancy leave.

II

A

Title VII of the Civil Rights Act of 1964, Pub.L. No. 88-352, 78 Stat. 241, makes it an "unlawful employment practice" for any employer "to discriminate against any individual with respect to his compensation, terms, conditions, or privileges or employment, because of such individual's ... sex." 42 U.S.C. § 2000e-2(a)(1).

In General Electric Co. v. Gilbert, 429 U.S. 125, 97 S.Ct. 401, 50 L.Ed.2d 343 (1976), the Supreme Court held that discrimination based on pregnancy was not discrimination within the meaning of Title VII. Id. at 145-46, 97 S.Ct. 401. There, General Electric adopted an employee disability benefit plan that paid weekly nonoccupational sickness and accident benefits. Id. at 127, 97 S.Ct. 401. However, General Electric excluded from that plan's coverage disabilities arising from pregnancy. Id. The specific issue before the Court was whether Title VII prohibited excluding pregnancy-related disabilities from an employer's disability benefit plan. The Supreme Court recognized that pregnancy is confined to women, but reasoned that the disability benefit plan did not discriminate in violation of Title VII by excluding pregnancy-related disabilities from its coverage:

The Plan, in effect (and for all that appears), is nothing more than an insurance package, which covers some risks but excludes others. The "package" going to relevant identifiable groups we are presently concerned with — General Electric's male and female employees — covers exactly the same categories of risk, and is facially nondiscriminatory in the sense that "there is no risk from which men are protected and women are not. Likewise, there is no risk from which women are protected and men are not." As there is no proof that the package is in fact worth more to men than to women, it is impossible to find any gender-based discriminatory effect in this scheme simply because women disabled as a result of pregnancy do not receive benefits; that is to say, gender-based discrimination does not result simply because an employer's disability-benefits plan is less than all-inclusive.

Id. at 138-39, 97 S.Ct. 401 (internal citations and footnote omitted).

In 1978, in response to Gilbert, Congress passed the Pregnancy Discrimination Act of 1978, Pub.L. No. 95-555, 92 Stat. 2076, which became effective on April 29, 1979,[6] and amended Title VII to define "because of sex" or "on the basis of sex" to include discrimination based on pregnancy. 42 U.S.C. § 2000e(k). The PDA states in relevant part:

The terms "because of sex" or "on the basis of sex" include, but are not limited to, because of or on the basis of pregnancy, childbirth, or related medical conditions; and women affected by pregnancy, childbirth, or related medical conditions shall be treated the same for all employment-related purposes, including receipt of benefits under fringe benefit programs, as other persons not so affected but similar in their ability or inability to work, and nothing in section 2000e-2(h) of this title shall be interpreted to permit otherwise....

Id.

An individual must file charges of discrimination under Title VII within 180 days "after the alleged unlawful employment practice occurred," unless the employee has first instituted proceedings with a state or local agency, in which case the period is extended to 300 days. 42 U.S.C. § 2000e-5(e)(1). The dispositive issue in this case is whether Hulteen timely filed a sex discrimination action within the specified period of limitations.

As the Supreme Court has repeatedly stressed, we must "identify with care the specific employment practice that is at issue" when determining whether the sex-discrimination action is timely. Ledbetter v. Goodyear Tire & Rubber Co., ____ U.S. ____, 127 S.Ct. 2162, 2167, 167 L.Ed.2d 982 (2007) (citing Nat'l Railroad Passenger Corp. v. Morgan, 536 U.S. 101, 110-11, 122 S.Ct. 2061, 153 L.Ed.2d 106 (2002)); see also Delaware State College v. Ricks, 449 U.S. 250, 257, 101 S.Ct. 498, 66 L.Ed.2d 431 (1980). There are three possible candidates in this case: (1) AT & T's adoption of its pregnancy leave rules before the enactment of the PDA; (2) AT & T's application of those leave rules to adjust Hulteen's NCS date before the enactment of the PDA; and (3) AT & T's calculation of Hulteen's retirement benefits in 1994 based, in part, on the NCS date it consistently maintained for her without retroactively adjusting that date for pre-PDA pregnancy leave. The time to challenge the first and second possible employment practices, however, has long since expired. Accordingly, relying on our prior decision in Pallas, Hulteen points us to the third alternative employment practice in 1994 when AT & T declined to grant retroactive NCS credit for pre-PDA pregnancy leave before it calculated her retirement benefits.

Accepting Hulteen's argument that such calculation in 1994 constituted a new and current violation of Title VII, the majority holds that her Title VII action is timely. In so concluding, the majority perpetuates Pallas's error by breathing new life into an expired sex discrimination claim. On virtually identical facts, the Seventh Circuit reached the opposite conclusion in Ameritech.[7] Because I believe the Seventh Circuit's decision faithfully applies controlling Supreme Court precedents and the relevant provisions of Title VII, I would follow that court's reasoning.

III

"The outcome of this case," as the Seventh Circuit recognized, "turns on which of two competing lines of authority provide a better `fit' here." Ameritech, 220 F.3d at 822. The Seventh Circuit followed United Air Lines v. Evans, 431 U.S. 553, 97 S.Ct. 1885, 52 L.Ed.2d 571 (1977), and its progeny. In Pallas, on the other hand, this court followed Bazemore v. Friday, 478 U.S. 385, 106 S.Ct. 3000, 92 L.Ed.2d 315 (1986) (per curiam). Because the majority follows Pallas today, the Bazemore and Evans line of cases deserve careful attention.

A

In Bazemore, the North Carolina Agricultural Extension Service ("Service") maintained two separate, racially segregated work forces and paid black employees less than white employees prior to the enactment of Title VII. 478 U.S. at 390-91, 106 S.Ct. 3000 (Brennan, J., joined by all other Members of the Court, concurring in part). After the enactment of Title VII, the Service integrated the workforce, but the pay disparity between black employees and white employees in the same positions remained. Id. The Supreme Court held that the Service was not liable for the discriminatory acts that occurred prior to the enactment of Title VII and therefore "recovery may not be permitted for [pre-Title VII] acts of discrimination." Id. at 395, 106 S.Ct. 3000. However, the Supreme Court concluded that the pay disparity that remained after the enactment of Title VII was unlawful because "[e]ach week's paycheck that delivers less to a black than to a similarly situated white is a wrong actionable under Title VII, regardless of the fact that this pattern was begun prior to the effective date of Title VII." Id. at 395-96, 106 S.Ct. 3000.

B

1

The Supreme Court's decision in Evans represents the fountainhead for the competing line of authority. In Evans, United Air Lines ("United") maintained a policy of refusing to allow its female flight attendants to be married. 431 U.S. at 554, 97 S.Ct. 1885. Evans married in 1968 and therefore was forced to resign pursuant to United's no-marriage policy. Id. Previously, the Seventh Circuit held that United's policy violated Title VII. Sprogis v. United Air Lines, 444 F.2d 1194(7th Cir.), cert. denied, 404 U.S. 991, 92 S.Ct. 536, 30 L.Ed.2d 543 (1971). Evans, however, was not a party to Sprogis and failed to initiate any proceedings against United within the period of limitation for that past act of discrimination. Evans, 431 U.S. at 555, 97 S.Ct. 1885. After United ended the no-marriage policy, United rehired Evans in 1972 as a new employee, but refused to give her seniority credit for any prior service with United. Id. Evans conceded that it was too late to bring an action for her forced termination, but asserted that "United [was] guilty of a present, continuing violation of Title VII and therefore that her claim is timely." Id. at 557, 97 S.Ct. 1885.

Evans argued that "the seniority system gives present effect to the past illegal act and therefore perpetuates the consequences of forbidden discrimination." Id. at 557, 97 S.Ct. 1885. Rejecting that argument, the Court emphasized that "United's seniority system does indeed have a continuing impact on her pay and fringe benefits. But the emphasis should not be placed on mere continuity; the critical question is whether any present violation exists." Id. at 558, 97 S.Ct. 1885 (first emphasis added). Concluding that none did, the Court explained that "[a] discriminatory act which is not made the basis for a timely charge is the legal equivalent of a discriminatory act which occurred before the statute was passed..... [I]t is merely an unfortunate event in history which has no present legal consequences." Id. at 558, 97 S.Ct. 1885.

2

The Supreme Court again embraced Evans's reasoning in Delaware State College v. Ricks, 449 U.S. 250, 101 S.Ct. 498, 66 L.Ed.2d 431. In that case, Delaware State College denied Ricks, an African American librarian, academic tenure in March 1974. Id. at 252, 101 S.Ct. 498. Adhering to its policy of not discharging immediately a junior faculty member who did not receive tenure, the College offered Ricks a nonrenewable one-year "terminal" contract that would expire on June 30, 1975, with explicit notice that his employment would end on that date. Id. at 253. Ricks filed an employment discrimination charge against the College in April 1975, alleging, inter alia, that the College unlawfully discriminated against him on the basis of race in violation of Title VII. Id. at 255, 101 S.Ct. 498.

Ricks argued that the period of limitations ran from the date that his one-year terminal contract expired rather than the date when the College denied tenure. Id. at 257, 101 S.Ct. 498. Rejecting Ricks's argument, the Supreme Court held that his claim for discrimination in violation of Title VII was untimely. Id. at 256, 101 S.Ct. 498. The Court concluded that "the only alleged discrimination occurred — and the filing limitations period therefore commenced — at the time the tenure decision was made and communicated to Ricks.... even though one of the effects of the denial of tenure — the eventual loss of a teaching position — did not occur until later."[8] Id. at 258, 101 S.Ct. 498. The Supreme Court emphasized that "[i]t is simply insufficient for Ricks to allege that his termination `gives present effect to the past act and therefore perpetuates the consequences of forbidden discrimination.'" Id. (quoting Evans, 431 U.S. at 557, 97 S.Ct. 1885).

      3

The Supreme Court's recent decision in Ledbetter v. Goodyear Tire & Rubber Co., ____ U.S. ____, 127 S.Ct. 2162, 167 L.Ed.2d 982, confirms this understanding of the Evans line of authority. Ledbetter worked for Goodyear Tire and Rubber Company ("Goodyear") from 1979 until 1998. Id. at 2165. Goodyear maintained a policy during that time of granting or denying raises for salaried employees based on their supervisors' evaluations of their performance. Id. In 1998 Ledbetter brought an action against Goodyear, asserting, among other claims, a Title VII pay discrimination claim. Id. At trial, she "introduced evidence that during the course of her employment several supervisors had given her poor evaluations because of her sex, that as a result of these evaluations her pay was not increased as much as it would have been if she had been evaluated fairly, and that these past pay decisions continued to affect the amount of her pay throughout her employment." Id. at 2165-66. The evidence also established that Ledbetter was earning significantly less than her male counterparts at the end of her career. Id. at 2166.

Ledbetter argued that her action was timely, pointing to two different employment practices during the applicable period of limitation as possible candidates. Id. at 2167. First, she argued that each paycheck issued during the period of limitations was a separate act of discrimination. Id. Alternatively, she argued that the 1998 decision denying her a raise "was `unlawful because it carried forward intentionally discriminatory disparities from prior years.'" Id. "In essence, she suggests that it is sufficient that discriminatory acts that occurred prior to the charging period had continuing effects during that period." Id.

The Supreme Court rejected Ledbetter's first argument because she failed to allege actual discriminatory intent by the relevant Goodyear decisionmakers when they issued her checks or denied her a raise in 1998. Id. Furthermore, the Court rejected Ledbetter's alternative argument, concluding that it was squarely foreclosed by the Evans line of authority. Id. The Court emphasized that the instruction from that line of authority is clear: "The EEOC charging period is triggered when a discrete unlawful practice takes place. A new violation does not occur, and a new charging period does not commence, upon the occurrence of subsequent non-discriminatory acts that entail adverse effects resulting from the past discrimination." Id. at 2169. The Court specifically rejected as unsound Ledbetter's attempt to shift the intent from the prior discriminatory employment practice to the 1998 pay decision denying her raise. Id. at 2170. Accordingly, the Supreme Court held that Ledbetter's claim was untimely. Id. at 2172.

C

Bazemore stands for the general proposition that an employment practice coupled with discriminatory intent within the charging period gives rise to a current violation of Title VII, even if related to past, uncharged discriminatory acts. See Ledbetter, 127 S.Ct. at 2174. The Evans-Ricks-Ledbetter line of authority stands for the proposition that an act within the charging period that gives present effect to past discriminatory acts, without more, does not give rise to a current violation. Hulteen's case turns on whether AT & T calculated her benefits in 1994 with the requisite discriminatory intent (Bazemore) or whether that calculation simply gave effect through the NCS date of past, uncharged discriminatory acts (Evans-Ricks-Ledbetter).

In Ameritech, the Seventh Circuit found the Evans line of authority controlling because of the "fact, simplistic as it may seem, that [the] case involves computation of time in service — seniority by another name — followed by a neutral application of a benefit package to all employees with the same amount of time." Ameritech, 220 F.3d at 823. Pallas and the majority today, on the other hand, reached the contrary conclusion, finding that Bazemore was the "controlling Supreme Court precedent" for two reasons: "First, the discriminatory program which gave rise to this suit, the Early Retirement Opportunity, was instituted in 1987.... Pallas challenges the criteria adopted in 1987 to determine eligibility for the new benefit program.... Second, the net credit system used to calculate eligibility under the Early Retirement Opportunity is not facially neutral. The system used to determine eligibility facially discriminates against pregnant women." 940 F.2d at 1327. With respect, Pallas was clearly wrong. The Supreme Court's logic in Evans, Ricks, and Ledbetter dictates the outcome of the case before us today.

1

The Supreme Court's most recent decision in Ledbetter confirms that under Evans "current effects alone cannot breathe life into prior, uncharged discrimination." Ledbetter, 127 S.Ct. at 2169. The charging period (here, the 180 days during which Hulteen was required to file a charge with the EEOC), "is triggered when a discrete unlawful practice takes place." Id. Such a discrete unlawful practice requires the coalescence of two elements: (1) an employment practice (defined as "a discrete act or single `occurrence' that takes place at a particular point in time"); and (2) discriminatory intent. Id. at 2169, 2171. Here, the majority concludes that the AT & T's denial of benefits under the retirement plan in 1994 is an "employment practice." Ante, at 1009-10. But that alone is insufficient. Ledbetter requires concurrent discriminatory intent.

a

Pallas concluded that the "NCS [seniority] system used to calculate eligibility under the [retirement plans] is not facially neutral. The system used to determine eligibility facially discriminates against pregnant women." 940 F.2d at 1327. Today, the majority locates discriminatory intent at the point AT & T calculated Hulteen's benefits in 1994 by embracing Pallas's erroneous determination that the NCS seniority system is facially discriminatory and concluding that "[f]acial discrimination is `by its very terms' intentional discrimination." Ante, at 1012 (citation omitted). The majority's position is erroneous.

AT & T's current NCS seniority system includes a facially nondiscriminatory and neutrally applied pregnancy leave rule that grants female employees who become pregnant after the enactment of the PDA full NCS seniority credit on the same terms as employees who become temporarily disabled. The retirement benefit plan under which Hulteen received retirement benefits is also facially nondiscriminatory and neutrally applied: calculation of eligibility and benefits under that plan are determined based on an NCS date maintained for each employee. That NCS date is also facially nondiscriminatory. But the majority asserts facial discrimination by looking long ago to the pre-PDA pregnancy leave rules that AT & T lawfully applied before the enactment of the PDA to adjust the NCS dates to grant only partial seniority credit for pre-PDA pregnancy leave. The majority's conclusion reaches too far.

The problem with the majority's conclusion that the NCS seniority system is facially discriminatory because the NCS date reflects AT & T's pre-PDA pregnancy leave rules is that it necessarily depends on a retroactive application of the PDA. Before the enactment of the PDA, the Supreme Court had concluded in Gilbert, 429 U.S. 125, 97 S.Ct. 401, 50 L.Ed.2d 343, that classifications based on pregnancy involved no facial gender-based discrimination. Id. at 134-36, 138, 97 S.Ct. 401; see also Nashville Gas Co. v. Satty, 434 U.S. 136, 140, 98 S.Ct. 347, 54 L.Ed.2d 356 (1977) ("Petitioner's decision not to treat pregnancy as a disease or disability for purpose of seniority retention is not on its face a discriminatory policy."). Pallas concluded that the NCS seniority system was facially discriminatory because it "distinguishes between similarly situated employees: female employees who took leave prior to 1979 due to a pregnancy-related disability and employees who took leave prior to 1979 for other temporary disabilities." 940 F.2d at 1327. This conclusion therefore rests on a silent premise that gives impermissible retroactive effect to the PDA.

A system is facially discriminatory, of course, if it treats similarly situated employees differently. Hulteen asserts that, as a female employee who took pregnancy leave prior to the enactment of the PDA, she was treated differently from employees who took leave for other temporary disabilities during that same period. But these two groups are not similarly situated. Temporarily disabled employees were not female employees who took pregnancy leaves, but were female and male employees who took other types of disability leaves and, under the lawful seniority rules then in effect, were entitled to accrue seniority credit for the full duration of their leaves. And female employees who took pre-PDA pregnancy leaves under AT & T's then lawful pre-PDA pregnancy leave rules accrued seniority credit only for a portion of their leaves. While this may be regrettable in hindsight, because it was then lawful to distinguish between the two reasons for leaves prior to the PDA, the two groups were not similarly situated. AT & T's failure to award full seniority credit for pre-PDA pregnancy leaves could be labeled facially discriminatory only if employees in both groups were similarly situated. That would be true, however, only if the PDA were given impermissible retroactive effect. Because the PDA is not retroactive,[9] Pallas is wrong and the majority today is mistaken in concluding that AT & T's pre-PDA pregnancy leave rules were facially discriminatory in violation of Title VII. Accordingly, because the majority errs in concluding that the NCS seniority system is facially discriminatory in violation of Title VII, it necessarily errs in finding current discriminatory intent based on the 1994 calculation.

     b

     Straining to find discriminatory intent when AT & T calculated Hulteen's retirement benefits in 1994 based on the NCS date, the majority also asserts that Hulteen satisfies that burden by pointing to a single act by AT & T in crediting another employee's NCS date based on the pre-PDA pregnancy leave rules. Ante, at 1012. In 2000, AT & T credited Snyder's NCS seniority date for 30 days because previously her NCS date mistakenly had not been credited at all for her pregnancy leave in 1974. The majority extrapolates from this retroactive credit that "in the determination of benefits, AT & T does not simply rely on pre-PDA NCS calculations," but "reviews an employee's entire work history and affirmatively chooses to apply `the policy at the time' that the leave occurred." Ante, at 1012. Any contrary assertion, the majority contends, "is belied by this record." Ante, at 1012. But it is the majority's perception of discriminatory intent based on this isolated response to an error that is belied by the applicable standard of review.

     While previously recognizing that "`[w]e must determine, viewing the evidence in the light most favorable to[AT & T], the non-moving party, whether [there are any genuine issues of material fact and whether] the district court correctly applied the substantive law,'" ante, at 1005 (second alteration in original) (quoting Olsen v. Idaho State Bd. of Med., 363 F.3d 916, 922 (9th Cir.2004)), the majority fails to apply that standard here. Viewing the evidence in the light most favorable to AT & T, as we must, the letters evidencing AT & T's crediting of Snyder's NCS date fail to demonstrate that, "when AT & T determines benefits eligibility, it reviews an employee's entire work history and affirmatively chooses to apply `the policy at the time' that the leave occurred." Ante, at 1012. Rather, in the light most favorable to AT & T, that evidence suggests that AT & T relies on the pre-PDA NCS calculations, but in this one case an error came to light that required it to review Snyder's entire work history and to adjust her NCS date for a previously uncredited pre-PDA pregnancy leave. That evidence further suggests that AT & T reviewed Snyder's service record and adjusted her NCS date in response to her request, not as a matter of course for all employees: "In preparing your claim for service credit for the period of your maternity leave of absence for review by the Employees' Benefit Committee, it was determined that you were not given service credit for the first 30 calendar days of your leave (as was the policy at the time)." Moreover, the parties stipulated that "whether or not Snyder's NCS date was adjusted in the year 2000 does not affect the outcome of this [stage of the] proceeding."

The only thing that is "`too obvious to warrant extended discussion,'" ante, at 1012(quoting Ledbetter, 127 S.Ct. at 2173), is the majority's far-reaching efforts to infer the requisite discriminatory intent at the time AT & T calculated and/or denied retirement benefits. Simply put, the record fails to demonstrate that AT & T acted with discriminatory intent during the charging period.

2

There is no meaningful basis for distinguishing Evans and this case, which becomes abundantly evident when the key aspects of each case are compared. In both Evans and here, the employers maintained a host of employment programs[10] that determined eligibility based on a seniority system. Those benefit programs were facially nondiscriminatory and neutrally applied, but gave effect through the seniority system to past discriminatory acts. Evans's seniority was less because in early 1968 United maintained a policy that forced her to resign because she was female and because she married. Hulteen's seniority was less because AT & T maintained a pre-PDA pregnancy leave rule that forced her to take personal leave with only partial NCS seniority credit because she was female and because she became pregnant. Because of the past acts of discrimination, Evans and Hulteen had less seniority,[11] and, not surprisingly, the determinations of their benefits under those programs were adversely affected

Faced with "the question ... whether the employer is committing a second violation of Title VII by refusing to credit her with seniority for any [prior] period," the Supreme Court concluded in Evans that "such a challenge to a neutral system may not be predicated on the mere fact that a past event which has no present legal significance has affected the calculation of seniority credit, even if the past event might at one time have justified a valid claim against the employer." 431 U.S. at 554, 560, 97 S.Ct. 1885. Thinking itself the wiser, the majority adopts Pallas's "contrary view," which, with respect, should be rejected because it "substitute[s] a claim for seniority credit for almost every claim which is barred by limitations." Id. at 560, 97 S.Ct. 1885.

3

The majority repeats Pallas's error by invoking Bazemore in this case. See ante, at 1006-07. Bazemore is simply inapposite. First, as the Supreme Court recently emphasized in Ledbetter, "Bazemore stands for the proposition that an employer violates Title VII and triggers a new EEOC charging period whenever the employer issues a paycheck using a discriminatory pay structure. But a new Title VII violation does not occur and a new charging period is not triggered when an employer issues paychecks pursuant to a system that is `facially nondiscriminatory and neutrally applied.'" Ledbetter, 127 S.Ct. at 2174(quoting Lorance v. AT & T Technologies, Inc., 490 U.S. 900, 911, 109 S.Ct. 2261, 104 L.Ed.2d 961 (1989)). As discussed above, Hulteen's retirement benefits were calculated pursuant to a facially nondiscriminatory and neutrally applied benefits plan, which relies upon the NCS date. That date, which is the product of the NCS seniority system, gives effect to the then lawful pre-PDA pregnancy leave rules that granted only partial NCS credit for pre-PDA pregnancy leave. However, without having established discriminatory intent in 1994 when AT & T calculated benefits, Bazemore is of no help to Hulteen. As the Supreme Court emphasized in Ledbetter, "[t]he fact that precharging period discrimination adversely affects the calculation of a neutral factor (like seniority) that is used in determining future pay does not mean that each new paycheck constitutes a new violation and restarts the EEOC charging period." 127 S.Ct. at 2174 (emphasis added).

Second, in Bazemore the post-Title VII salary structure resulted in a fresh violation of Title VII because it was a "`mere continuation'" of the pre-Title VII discriminatory pay structure. Ledbetter, 127 S.Ct. at 2173(quoting Bazemore, 478 U.S. at 397 n. 6, 106 S.Ct. 3000 (Brennan, J., joined by all other Members of the Court, concurring in part)). But in this case, AT & T's NCS seniority system is not the "mere continuation" of the pre-PDA pregnancy leave rules; indeed it was expressly amended to give full effect to pregnancy leave post-PDA. In Bazemore, a current violation existed because the Service paid black employees less than white employees for each new hour (week, month, or year) of work after the enactment of Title VII. In this case, no current violation exists: AT & T grants NCS seniority credit for each period of pregnancy leave after the enactment of the PDA, on the same terms as disability-related leave. Simply put, unlike in Bazemore, AT & T's pre-PDA pregnancy leave rules no longer apply to female employees who took pregnancy leave after the enactment of the PDA, which made such distinction based on pregnancy a violation of Title VII. Bazemore would only be analogous in this case if AT & T had continued to deny full NCS seniority credit to female employees who had taken pregnancy leave after the enactment of the PDA and attempted to defend that practice on the ground that it began before the enactment of that Act.[12] But AT & T did no such thing.

Finally, the majority's strained interpretation of Bazemore effectively imposes an unjustified burden on AT & T to remedy all acts of discrimination on the basis of pregnancy before the enactment of the PDA. Because the PDA is not retroactive,[13] that is more than Congress required with the PDA. That is also more than the Supreme Court required in Bazemore. There, the Court held that "recovery may not be permitted for pre-[Title VII] acts of discrimination"; thus the Service was not required to pay retroactively the salary disparity for pre-Title VII discrimination. Bazemore, 478 U.S. at 395, 106 S.Ct. 3000(Brennan, J., joined by all other Members of the Court, concurring in part) (emphasis added). Indeed, the Supreme Court emphasized that its decision in Bazemore "in no sense gives legal effect to the pre-1972 actions, but, consistent with Evans ... , focuses on the present salary structure, which is illegal if it is a mere continuation of the [pre-Title VII] discriminatory pay structure." Id. at 396 n. 6, 106 S.Ct. 3000. By requiring AT & T now to grant retroactive NCS seniority credit for pregnancy leave prior to the effective date of the PDA, the majority impose an entirely gratuitous burden upon AT & T to remedy the NCS seniority system with respect to all classifications based on pregnancy occurring before the enactment of the PDA. Bazemore provides no support for such arbitrary result.

D

In sum, because there is no evidence that AT & T acted with the requisite discriminatory intent in 1994 when it calculated Hulteen's retirement benefits based in part on the NCS seniority system, Bazemore is inapposite. Without more, the NCS seniority system simply gives present effect to a past pre-PDA incident. Under Evans that pre-PDA incident is "merely an unfortunate event in history [with] no present legal consequences." 431 U.S. at 558, 97 S.Ct. 1885. For this reason, the Supreme Court's logic in the Evans line of authority, reinforced weeks ago in Ledbetter, controls the outcome of this case. Under that line, "[a] new violation does not occur, and a new charging period does not commence, upon the occurrence of subsequent nondiscriminatory acts that entail adverse effects resulting from the past discrimination." Ledbetter, 127 S.Ct. at 2169 (emphasis added). The time for Hulteen to have challenged AT & T's pre-PDA pregnancy leave rules has long since expired.

IV

A

As the Seventh Circuit recognized in Ameritech, 42 U.S.C. § 2000e-2(h) "offers good reason to treat seniority systems with special care, because it specifically exempts discriminatory effects that flow from bona fide seniority systems from the definition of unlawful employment practices, as long as the differences are not the result of an intention to discriminate." Ameritech, 220 F.3d at 823; see also Trans World Airlines, Inc. v. Hardison, 432 U.S. 63, 81, 97 S.Ct. 2264, 53 L.Ed.2d 113 (1977) ("Seniority systems ... are afforded special treatment under Title VII."). That section states:

Notwithstanding any other provision of this subchapter, it shall not be an unlawful employment practice for an employer to apply different standards of compensation, or different terms, conditions, or privileges of employment pursuant to a bona fide seniority or merit system, or a system which measures earnings by quantity or quality of production or to employees who work in different locations, provided that such differences are not the result of an intention to discriminate because of race, color, religion, sex, or national origin, nor shall it be an unlawful employment practice for an employer to give and to act upon the results of any professionally developed ability test provided that such test, its administration or action upon the results is not designed, intended or used to discriminate because of race, color, religion, sex or national origin. It shall not be an unlawful employment practice under this subchapter for any employer to differentiate upon the basis of sex in determining the amount of the wages or compensation paid or to be paid to employees of such employer if such differentiation is authorized by the provisions of section 206(d) of Title 29.

42 U.S.C. § 2000e-2(h).

Section 2000e-2(h) provides AT & T no protection in this case if (1) AT & T's NCS seniority system is not a "bona fide" seniority system; or (2) the differences are a result of an intention to discriminate. Neither exception bars protection of AT & T's NCS seniority system here.

First, the Supreme Court held in International Brotherhood of Teamsters v. United States, 431 U.S. 324, 97 S.Ct. 1843, 52 L.Ed.2d 396 (1977), that an otherwise valid seniority system did not lose its bona fide character simply because its operation may perpetuate past discrimination. Id. at 353-54, 97 S.Ct. 1843. In Teamsters, the Supreme Court considered a seniority system that allegedly perpetuated the effects of pre-Title VII discrimination. Id. at 348, 97 S.Ct. 1843. The employer's seniority system unmistakably advantaged white employees who had accumulated longer tenure because of the "employer's prior intentional discrimination" against "Negro and Spanish-surnamed employees" before the enactment of Title VII. Id. at 349-50, 97 S.Ct. 1843. The Court stated that it "must decide, in short, whether [§ 2000e-2(h)] validates otherwise bona fide seniority systems that afford no constructive seniority to victims discriminated against prior to the effective date of Title VII." Id. at 349, 97 S.Ct. 1843. And the Court concluded that, "[a]lthough a seniority system inevitably tends to perpetuate the effects of pre-Act discrimination in such cases, the congressional judgment [through § 2000e-2(h)] was that Title VII should not outlaw the use of existing seniority lists and thereby destroy or water down the vested seniority rights of employees simply because their employer had engaged in discrimination prior to the passage of the Act." 431 U.S. at 352-53, 97 S.Ct. 1843. Thus, AT & T's NCS seniority system does not lose its bona fide characteristic simply because it gives effect to the pre-PDA pregnancy leave rules that granted only partial NCS credit for pre-PDA pregnancy leave.

Second, under § 2000e-2(h), "[t]o be cognizable, a claim that a seniority system has a discriminatory impact must be accompanied by proof of a discriminatory purpose." Am. Tobacco Co. v. Patterson, 456 U.S. 63, 69, 102 S.Ct. 1534, 71 L.Ed.2d 748 (1982). But, as the Seventh Circuit held in Ameritech, "these employees cannot show the kind of intentional discrimination that would trigger the exception to the statutory protection afforded to seniority systems" because "prior to the adoption of the PDA an authoritative Supreme Court decision had held that Title VII did not prohibit distinctions based on pregnancy." 220 F.3d at 823 (citing Gilbert, 429 U.S. 125, 97 S.Ct. 401, 50 L.Ed.2d 343). Moreover, because the PDA is not retroactive, see supra n. 9, AT & T "would have no reason to think it had to reshuffle its NCS list after the Act was passed," Ameritech, 220 F.3d at 823, and therefore the continued reliance on the unadjusted NCS date cannot constitute intentional discrimination.

B

In an effort to frustrate reliance on § 2000e-2(h), the majority simply reads that provision out of the statute in all pregnancy discrimination cases. Ante, at 1013-15. The majority points to the PDA, which states that "women affected by pregnancy, ... shall be treated the same for all employment related purposes, ... as other persons not so affected but similar in their ability or inability to work, and nothing in section § 2000e-2(h) of this title shall be interpreted to permit otherwise" (the "§ 2000e-(2)(h) proviso"). 42 U.S.C. § 2000e(k) (emphasis added). While the majority's argument has surface appeal, that proviso cannot bear the burden it attempts to place upon it.

First, the majority's interpretation of that section completely removes the application of § 2000e-2(h) in all pregnancy discrimination suits under Title VII. Ante, at 1013-15. But Congress did not go so far. If Congress had intended wholly to prohibit the application of § 2000e-2(h) in all pregnancy discrimination cases, Congress would have expressed this intent more clearly, as it did with other provisions in the Civil Rights Act. Compare, e.g., 42 U.S.C. § 2000a(e)("The provisions of this subchapter shall not apply to a private club or other establishment not in fact open to the public, except to the extent that the facilities of such establishment are made available to the customers or patrons of an establishment within the scope of subsection (b) of this section."); id. § 2000e-1(c)(2) ("Sections 2000e-2 and 2000e-3 of this title shall not apply with respect to the foreign operations of an employer that is a foreign person not controlled by an American employer.").

Second, the conclusion that Congress did not intend that proviso to remove § 2000e-2(h)'s protection for bona fide seniority systems in all pregnancy discrimination cases draws further support from the context in which Congress passed the PDA. "Congress enacted the Pregnancy Discrimination Act of 1978, amending Title VII to include pregnancy classifications within the statutory definition of sex discrimination," in response to the Supreme Court's decision in Gilbert. See Toomey v. Clark, 876 F.2d 1433, 1437 (9th Cir.1989). By amending Title VII to define "because of sex" to include on the basis of pregnancy, the PDA "in effect overruled" Gilbert's general holding that an employer's disability benefit plan did not violate Title VII because it excluded pregnancy-related disabilities. Toomey, 876 F.2d at 1437. By adding the § 2000e-2(h) proviso to the PDA, Congress did not intend to remove that section's protection of bone fide seniority systems in all pregnancy discrimination actions as the majority argues, but rather to address a specific anomaly suggested in Gilbert.

In Gilbert, the Supreme Court refused to defer to the EEOC's interpretation of Title VII to prohibit discrimination on the basis of pregnancy, because it appeared to conflict with another agency's interpretation of the Equal Pay Act. 429 U.S. at 144-45, 97 S.Ct. 401. The last sentence of § 2000e-2(h), the so-called Bennett Amendment, was the source of the apparent conflict in Gilbert. The Bennett Amendment provides that "[i]t shall not be an unlawful employment practice under this subchapter for any employer to differentiate upon the basis of sex in determining the amount of the wages or compensation paid or to be paid to employees of such employer if such differentiation is authorized by the provisions of[the Equal Pact Act, 29 U.S.C. § 206(d)]." 42 U.S.C. § 2000e-2(h). The Equal Pay Act, in turn, generally authorizes the payment of wages to employees at a lesser rate than the opposite sex "where such payment is made pursuant to (i) a seniority system; (ii) a merit system; (iii) a system which measures earnings by quantity or quality or production; or (iv) a deferential based on any other factor other than sex" 29 U.S.C. § 206(d)(1), quoted in Gilbert, 429 U.S. at 144 n. 21, 97 S.Ct. 401.[14] In Gilbert the Supreme Court interpreted the Bennett Amendment, in conjunction with an agency regulation under the Equal Pay Act, to permit under Title VII the exclusion of benefits under Title VII for pregnancy-related disabilities under an employer's disability plan. Id. 144-45, 97 S.Ct. 401. Considering itself "pointed in diametrically opposite directions by the conflicting regulations," the Supreme Court declined to grant deference to the EEOC's interpretation of Title VII to prohibit discrimination on the basis of pregnancy. Id. 145-46, 97 S.Ct. 401. For these reasons, Congress added the § 2000e-2(h) proviso to foreclose the possibility raised in Gilbert that the Bennett Amendment would permit wage discrimination under Title VII on the basis of pregnancy.

In sum, contrary to the majority's conclusion, the plain meaning of the § 2000e-2(h) proviso in the PDA and the accompanying context establish that Congress did not intend to remove the protections of § 2000e-2(h) for bona fide seniority systems in all pregnancy discrimination actions. Congress, of course, was free to excise § 2000e-2(h) with respect to pregnancy discrimination actions. But the majority reads far too much into the § 2000e-2(h) proviso in the PDA, and therefore it is the majority, and not Congress, that renders that section wholly inapplicable in such actions.

V

The majority also relies on 42 U.S.C. § 2000-5(e)(2) to shore up its conclusion that Hulteen's sex discrimination claim is timely. Congress added § 2000-5(e)(2) to Title VII with the Civil Rights Act of 1991, Pub.L. No. 102-166, 105 Stat. 1071, 1078-79 (Nov. 21, 1991).[15] That section states in relevant part that an unlawful employment practice occurs, with respect to a seniority system that has been adopted for an intentionally discriminatory purpose in violation of this subchapter (whether or not that discriminatory purpose is apparent on the face of the seniority provision), when the seniority system is adopted, when an individual becomes subject to the seniority system, or when a person aggrieved is injured by the application of the seniority system or provision of the system.

42 U.S.C. § 2000e-5(e)(2). As the Seventh Circuit succinctly put it in Ameritech, under § 2000e-5(e)(2) "[i]f the employees are able to show intentional discrimination, their action accrues at the time they are injured by the seniority system — that is, when they are denied benefits."[16] Ameritech, 220 F.3d at 823 (emphasis added).

If that section were to apply here, Hulteen's sex discrimination action, of course, would have been timely. For § 2000e-5(e)(2) to apply, however, Hulteen would have to establish that AT & T adopted its NCS seniority system "for an intentionally discriminatory purpose in violation of" Title VII. The majority boldly asserts that AT & T's seniority system intentionally discriminates against pregnant women because the NCS system "`facially discriminates against pregnant women [because it] distinguishes between similarly situated employees'" and "[f]acial discrimination is `by its very terms' intentional discrimination." Ante, at 1012 (quoting Pallas, 940 F.2d at 1327, and Lovell v. Chandler, 303 F.3d 1039, 1057 (9th Cir.2002)). But the majority simply ignores the statutory requirement that Hulteen must show such intentional discrimination at the time the seniority system was adopted.

Contrary to the majority's assertion, § 2000-5(e)(2) cannot serve to revive Hulteen's sex discrimination charge in this case. Hulteen cannot show that AT & T adopted the pre-PDA pregnancy leave rules at the heart of this case with an intentionally discriminatory purpose. See also Ameritech, 220 F.3d at 823 (holding that the "employees cannot show the kind of intentional discrimination that would trigger the exception to the statutory protection afforded to seniority systems"). First, the Supreme Court held in Gilbert that Title VII did not necessarily prohibit distinctions based on pregnancy before the enactment of the PDA. 429 U.S. at 145-56, 97 S.Ct. 401. There, the Supreme Court concluded that an employer's disability benefits plan did not violate Title VII because it failed to cover pregnancy-related disabilities. Id.[17] Second, the Supreme Court expressly held in Gilbert that classifications based on pregnancy were not facially discriminatory. Id. at 134-36, 138, 97 S.Ct. 401; see also Satty, 434 U.S. at 140, 98 S.Ct. 347("Petitioner's decision not to treat pregnancy as a disease or disability for purposes of seniority retention is not on its face a discriminatory policy."); supra pp. 1022-24. AT & T adopted the pregnancy leave rules at the core of this case before the PDA and changed those rules prospectively upon the enactment of the PDA in full compliance with the statute that changed the operative playing field previously defined by the Supreme Court. Accordingly, in light of these authoritative Supreme Court precedents, Hulteen cannot establish that AT & T adopted those pre-PDA pregnancy leave rules for an intentionally discriminatory purpose in violation of Title VII. See Ameritech, 220 F.3d at 823. Absent a showing of discriminatory intent at that time, § 2000e-5(e)(2) does not apply in this case.

VI

As Judge Dumbauld lamented in his dissent to Pallas, we consider "`a melancholy tale [o]f things done long ago, and ill-done.'" 940 F.2d at 1327 (Dumbauld, J., dissenting) (quoting John Ford, The Lover's Melancholy). Because Pallas invented a timely Title VII violation where the determination of benefits simply gave present effect to past, unchallenged acts, contrary to Supreme Court authority, it must be overruled. Because the majority today erroneously embraces Pallas and perpetuates a circuit split with the Sixth and Seventh Circuits, I must respectfully dissent.

Judge O'Scannlain's dissent in US v. Richard (Oct 12, 2007) [Notes omitted]

O'SCANNLAIN, Circuit Judge, dissenting:
I begin with what one would think an unassailable proposition: An abuse of

discretion standard of review presupposes that the district court has some amount of discretion. Apparently, however, that proposition is no longer true in this circuit in the context of whether and how to permit a replay of trial testimony in a criminal case. For under the court's reasoning, if a district judge is to allow a replay at all without inviting reversible error, three requirements must be met. First, the district court must replay the testimony in open court with all parties present. Second, if the district court decides to allow a replay, it must replay the witness's entire testimony, including cross-examination. Finally, the district court must give a limiting instruction, sua sponte, counseling the jury not to place undue emphasis on such testimony.

Although district courts might be well advised to observe these precautions, the majority's rigid, rule-based approach effectively usurps the trial court's function, transforming our abuse of discretion standard into a de novo review. Since I cannot conclude that the district court in this case abused its discretion by allowing an audio replay in open court of the specific portion of testimony requested by the jury, I respectfully dissent.

I

During deliberations, the jury requested to "have Nikole Reeder's testimony and cross examination." Since no transcript was yet available, the judge informed the jury that "[i]f you want to hear a readback of somebody's testimony you have to let us know what part you want to hear" and sent the jury back to the jury room for five minutes to decide. When the jury returned, it requested the portion of Reeder's testimony "from after the side bar until right after — or right toward the beginning of cross-examination." Later, outside the presence of the jury, Richard's counsel objected to playing only the excerpt selected by the jury and moved "that the court play the entire testimony of Nikole Reeder." The judge overruled the objection as untimely.

The court then replayed the requested excerpt, which comprised 10 pages of the 42-page testimony. Prior to the excerpted testimony, Reeder had testified twice that she did not recognize anyone in the courtroom as the person sitting behind her in the car when it was pulled over. During the excerpted testimony, the government produced a photograph, which Reeder had identified as Richard during the grand jury proceedings, and asked her if she saw the person in the photograph in the courtroom. Reeder testified that she did not. Then the government directed her to look at the "person sitting at the defense counsel table as the defendant," and Reeder replied, "I don't think he's in here." After another round of prompting by the government, Reeder replied that the picture looked like the defendant, but his weight and hairstyle had changed. Three pages into the replayed excerpt, Reeder finally identified the defendant.

Reeder then established that she had met Richard for the first time that night through her "man" Martin, the driver of the car. She proceeded to describe what happened while the police pulled over the car, including hearing Richard say that "he had to run, he had warrants, and he had a gun," and witnessing Richard pull a black handgun from his pants and put it in or under the seat.

After replaying the excerpt for the jury, the judge asked, "Was that sufficient for the jury then?" The foreman answered, "I think so, your honor."

II

Our cases establish that when an objection is raised at trial, we review a district court's decision to replay testimony for an abuse of discretion. United States v. Binder, 769 F.2d 595, 600 (9th Cir.1985) ("A decision to replay testimony during jury deliberations will not be reversed absent an abuse of discretion.").[1] Under the abuse of discretion standard, "we will not reverse unless we have a definite and firm conviction that the district court committed a clear error in judgment." United States v. Plainbull, 957 F.2d 724, 725 (9th Cir.1992). Moreover, in this specific context, we have noted that the trial court has "`great latitude' over whether to allow rereading or replaying of testimony." United States v. Sacco, 869 F.2d 499, 501 (9th Cir.1989) (quoting United States v. Nolan, 700 F.2d 479, 486 (9th Cir.1983)).

Applying this deferential standard of review, I would affirm Judge Mahan's ruling.

A

Although the court performed the replay in open court, as we have preferred, see United States v. Hernandez, 27 F.3d 1403, 1408 (9th Cir.1994), it failed either to give a limiting instruction or to replay Reeder's testimony in its entirety. Nevertheless, because I find no support in our case law for blanket rules requiring such precautions sua sponte, the district judge's failure to adhere to the rules newly imposed by the majority does not compel the conclusion that the replay was unduly prejudicial.

1

The "facts and circumstances of the case" dictate whether the district judge should allow a replay and if so, which precautions are necessary to avoid "[u]ndue emphasis of particular testimony." Binder, 769 F.2d at 600.[2] In our previous cases, we have noted that providing the jury with "both the direct and cross-examination" of a witness's testimony can serve as a "precaution" against undue emphasis. Hernandez, 27 F.3d at 1409; see also United States v. Barker, 988 F.2d 77, 80 (9th Cir.1993) (approving of the replay of "both the entire direct and the entire cross examination"); United States v. Sacco, 869 F.2d 499, 502 (same). But the majority today converts this precaution into what can only be described as a prerequisite. See Maj. Op. at 1114. There is no support in our case law, until now, for such an affirmative requirement; indeed, our cases have noted that the district court may permit portions of certain testimony to be reread, United States v. King, 552 F.2d 833, 850 (9th Cir.1977), and it "is not required to reread all of a particular witness' testimony." Binder, 769 F.2d at 604 (Wallace, J., dissenting) (citing King for the proposition).

The lack of a rigid rule requiring all testimony of a given witness to be read or played back finds support in cases decided by our sister circuits, which have emphasized the great discretion that a district court is given in rereading or replaying testimony, especially when the jury does not request it. See, e.g., United States v. Bennett, 75 F.3d 40, 46 (1st Cir.1996) (Boudin, J.) (citing United States v. Wright-Barker, 784 F.2d 161, 174 (3d

Cir. 1986)) (noting that "no inflexible rule exists that the cross must always be read"); United States v. McElroy, 910 F.2d 1016, 1026 (2d Cir.1990) (finding the court "well within the bounds of discretion in declining to have more [than the cross-examination] reread").[3]

While there admittedly is a danger that a partial replay may cause the jury to overemphasize certain testimony, I disagree with the majority's assertion that the trial court "crystallize[d]" the risk of undue emphasis when it asked the jury to select what portions to hear. Maj. Op. at 1116; see also Hernandez, 27 F.3d at 1409 (inferring the "jury's obvious intent to emphasize a specific portion of the transcript" after naming what part of the testimony it wanted excerpted). If the very act of naming which portions to rehear creates the risk of undue emphasis, then by that logic any replay request that fails to encompass the entire trial should be denied. We have already recognized the absurdity of such a proposition in United States v. De Palma, 414 F.2d 394, 396 (9th Cir.1969) ("Perhaps if any evidence is read, all should be read. Any trial could thus be almost endless.").

The trial court must balance the danger of undue emphasis created by partial replays against the delays caused by replaying a witness's testimony in its entirety. United States v. Zarintash, 736 F.2d 66, 69-70 (3d Cir.1984). Here the portions requested by the jury encompassed about a quarter of the roughly hour-long testimony given by Reeder. While Richard argues that replaying the rest of the testimony would not have unduly delayed the proceedings, I see no reason that the jury should be forced to listen to "additional, related testimony that the jury made clear it did not need to rehear." Bennett, 75 F.3d at 46.

Here the trial judge asked after replaying the excerpt whether it had been "sufficient for the jury," and the foreman responded that it was. Having afforded the jury the opportunity to request additional testimony, which the jury declined,[4] the court did not abuse its discretion when it failed to provide the remaining 45 minutes of the Reeder testimony. See Wright-Barker, 784 F.2d at 174 (finding no abuse of discretion even when the "[a]dditional testimony cited by defendants [was] only 4-5 pages long," since "it was not within the jury's description" and the "jury did not request any additional testimony" when prompted); see also McElroy, 910 F.2d at 1026 (finding no abuse of discretion when the court refused to allow additional testimony reread, since the court asked the jury whether the reread portion was "what [it] requested" and the jury answered in the affirmative); United States v. Rosenberg, 195 F.2d 583, 598-99 (2d Cir.1952) (same).

2

The majority also faults the district judge for failing to include a limiting instruction to minimize the risk of undue emphasis. While I agree that providing a limiting instruction might have been prudent, see United States v. Lujan, 936 F.2d 406, 411 (9th Cir.1991), I cannot say on this record that the failure to do so warrants reversal of Richard's conviction. First, Richard failed to request such an instruction. See Bennett, 75 F.3d at 46 (dismissing a claim of error for failure to provide a limiting instruction that the defense did not request). Further, in asking for a portion of the testimony and failing to request more when prompted, the jury may have "merely desired a confirming clarification on one point" in reaching "a verdict properly based on the totality of the evidence." King, 552 F.2d at 850.

B

The majority opinion takes issue not only with the form of the replay but also with the substance of the testimony that was replayed. As we noted in United States v. Sacco, 869 F.2d at 502, "the quantum of other evidence against the defendant" and "the importance of the [replayed] testimony in relation to the other evidence" also factor into the abuse of discretion analysis.

According to the majority, the district court committed clear error by "`effectively repeat[ing] the entirety of the government's case' against Richard," given that "Reeder was the only witness to directly testify to Richard's possession of the gun — the only issue before the jury — and there was no physical evidence linking the gun to Richard." Maj. Op. at 1115 (quoting Sacco, 869 F.2d at 502). The majority analogizes this case to Binder, in which the government's entire case hinged on witness credibility, and distinguishes it from Sacco, in which ample additional evidence supported the replayed testimony.

In Binder, the defendant was accused of child molestation, and the parties agreed to substitute the children's videotaped testimony to relieve their apprehension about testifying in open court. "None of the other witnesses corroborated the specific allegations of the children," making their credibility "a crucial issue." 769 F.2d at 598, 601. Consequently, replaying the videotaped testimony indeed "allowed the repetition of the government's case against Binder." Id. at 601.

In Sacco, the key issue was whether Sacco knew that a large quantity of money was hidden in the trunk of his car. Since customs officials testified they had seen Sacco "do[ing] something with his hands inside the trunk" and his hands showed traces of fluorescent powder used to mark the money, replaying one witness's deposition "did not, therefore, effectively repeat the entirety of the government's case against Sacco." 869 F.2d at 502.

Here, while Reeder's testimony was undoubtedly important, it did not comprise the "entirety" of the government's case against Richard. Indeed, the government presented other strong circumstantial evidence corroborating Reeder's testimony. First, the police recovered the weapon from inside the seat where Richard had been sitting in the car. He does not dispute the relative positions of the car's occupants, nor does he dispute that the gun was found in his seat. Second, Detective Stanton testified that the other backseat passenger, Schneider, had seen Richard with the weapon. In addition, Detective Stanton testified that Schneider was the one who initially tipped off the police that Richard had a gun in the car and that Schneider led police to the car in the impound lot and pointed out the specific position of the gun and how it had been wedged into the seat. Relatedly, there was no dispute that the car took at least a minute to stop, even though it could have pulled over immediately, giving Richard the opportunity to hide the weapon. Detective Stanton testified that in his experience, such delays usually mean an occupant of the car is attempting to hide contraband. Finally, Richard admitted to police that he may have touched the weapon.

Given the quantum of corroborating evidence against Richard, the majority's analogy to Binder seems strained at best. The replayed testimony was far from the only evidence implicating Richard, and the government's case did not hinge entirely on the credibility of Reeder's account of the events.[5] In my view, the facts of this case and the quantum of evidence set forth by the government are more akin to Sacco, where we affirmed the district court's discretionary decision to allow a partial replay of testimony.

C

The majority also contends that the "portion replayed contained only the core of the government's case against Richard, entirely omitting large portions of Reeder's testimony ... that may have impeached her credibility." Maj. Op. at 1115. Specifically, the majority contends that the replay omitted "(1) portions of Reeder's testimony that [the driver] was her boyfriend at the time; (2) Reeder's extraordinary difficulty in identifying the backseat passenger she claimed to have seen with the gun; and (3) Reeder's entire cross-examination." Id. at 1115-16. Consequently, in the majority's view, "the clearly one-sided nature" of the replayed excerpt warranted additional precautions.

However, as the majority reluctantly acknowledges in a footnote, Maj. Op. at 1115 n. 8, the replayed portion of Reeder's testimony was not uniformly damaging to the defense, since it included several pages' worth of Reeder's failed attempts to identify Richard,[6] and also noted the nature of her relationship with the driver Martin (whom she repeatedly referred to as "my man").[7] Thus, the excerpt captured key credibility issues raised by Richard on appeal, including "her extreme difficulty in identifying Richard at trial and fuzziness on other details, which created doubt as to her memory and capacity to observe Richard in the vehicle,"[8] as well as her potential bias. Since the replayed excerpt itself impeaches the witness's credibility,[9] I cannot agree that the district court was required to direct the jury to listen to more than it had specifically requested.

III

There can be little doubt that "[t]he district judge is in a better position than we are to determine whether the benefits of allowing the jury to review the ... testimony outweigh[] the risk that the jury would give undue weight to that portion of the evidence." Binder, 769 F.2d at 603 (Wallace, J., dissenting). I am therefore deeply troubled by the majority's substitution of rigid rules for the sound discretion of our many able district judges. Moreover, in this particular case, while the conditions of the playback were not ideal, the additional corroborating evidence, the jury's determination that the replayed portion was sufficient, and the mixed nature of the testimony significantly reduced the risk of undue emphasis by the jury. In short, I cannot say that the replay of a portion of Reeder's testimony in this case warrants reversal of Richard's conviction.

Accordingly, I must respectfully dissent.

Judge O'Scannlain's dissent from the denial of rehearing en banc in US v. Jenkins (March 4, 2008)

O'SCANNLAIN, Circuit Judge, dissenting from the denial of rehearing en banc, joined by KOZINSKI, Chief Judge, and KLEINFELD, TALLMAN, CALLAHAN, BEA, M. SMITH, Circuit Judges:

The opinion in this case holds that the Fifth Amendment bars prosecutors from charging a crime to which a defendant unequivocally admits in the course of a trial for an unrelated offense. Because it contradicts our precedent and creates a split with our sister circuits, I respectfully dissent from our order rejecting rehearing en banc.

I

On October 19, 2004, Sharon Ann Jenkins drove a car holding two undocumented aliens into the United States from Mexico. United States v. Jenkins, 504 F.3d 694, 697-98 (9th Cir.2007). Upon being questioned at the border, and before any Miranda warnings apparently were provided to her, Jenkins admitted that the passengers in the car were undocumented aliens, and that she had been hired to bring them into the United States. Id. at 697-98, 700 n. 2. She was thereupon released. Id. at 702. The next day, Jenkins once again attempted to drive into the United States from Mexico with two undocumented aliens. Id. at 698. Again she was stopped at the border and, this time after Miranda warnings were issued, she admitted that she had been hired to smuggle the two aliens into the United States. Id. at 698, 700 n. 2. Jenkins again was released that day. Id. at 702. She was not immediately prosecuted for either offense. Id. at 698.

Three months later, Jenkins attempted to cross the border, only this time in a van loaded with 118.20 kilograms of marijuana. Id. Upon being stopped at the border, Jenkins stated that she believed the van contained an undocumented alien and had no knowledge of the presence of marijuana. Id. Jenkins was charged with the illegal importation of marijuana. Id. At trial, Jenkins testified in her own defense that she believed the van contained undocumented aliens, specifically citing her two prior attempts to smuggle aliens. Id. Before the jury completed its deliberations, federal prosecutors charged Jenkins with one count of alien smuggling, to which three other counts were subsequently added; she was later indicted on the charges. Id.

Jenkins sought to dismiss the alien smuggling indictment on the ground that the government was retaliating against her for taking the stand in her own defense. Id. The government argued that the charges were filed because of the content of Jenkins' testimony rather than the fact that she took the stand, as her admission under oath to alien smuggling provided the government with the smoking gun it needed to prosecute her for the offenses. Id. The government acknowledged that it "had enough [evidence] to go forward" on the alien smuggling charges before Jenkins admitted to those crimes on the stand. Id. at 698, 700. Her statements at the border were arguably tainted by the Miranda violation at the first stop;[1] with Jenkins' admission now on the record, the government contends that it now has a winnable case. Id. at 698.

The district court credited the government's stated reasons for bringing the new charges, indicating that the "ruling should not in any way, shape or form be construed as casting doubt or indicating that I do not believe the government's counsel." Id. at 703. However, because the district court concluded that the timing of the charges failed the "smell test,"[2] the district court dismissed them as a "prophylactic" protection of Jenkins' right to testify on her own behalf that had "absolutely no relationship to reality." Id. at 703-04.

Holding that "the government had more than enough evidence to proceed with the alien smuggling charges prior to Jenkins's decision to testify," the opinion likewise presumed that the government's filing of the new charges was vindictive and affirmed their dismissal. Id. at 699-702.

Like Judge Conlon, who dissented on the grounds that there was an insufficient showing of prosecutorial vindictiveness and that acting on the defendant's testimony was within prosecutorial discretion, id. at 703-05, I believe the opinion errs.

II

It is a well-established principle that courts should tread upon prosecutorial charging decisions with hesitation. "[U]nder our system of separation of powers, the decision whether to prosecute, and the decision as to the charge to be filed, rests in the discretion of the Attorney General or his delegates, the United States Attorneys." United States v. Edmonson, 792 F.2d 1492, 1497 (9th Cir.1986). Accordingly, the Supreme Court has recognized that "the decision to prosecute is particularly ill-suited to judicial review" because courts are incapable of competently assessing "[s]uch factors as the strength of the case, the prosecution's general deterrence value, the Government's enforcement priorities, and the case's relationship to the Government's overall enforcement plan." Wayte v. United States, 470 U.S. 598, 607, 105 S.Ct. 1524, 84 L.Ed.2d 547 (1985); see also United States v. Armstrong, 517 U.S. 456, 465, 116 S.Ct. 1480, 134 L.Ed.2d 687 (1996) (noting that "[j]udicial deference to the decisions of [prosecutors] rests in part on an assessment of the relative competence of prosecutors and courts"). That is, because their perspectives are limited to those cases over which they preside, judges cannot feasibly determine how best to allocate prosecutorial resources, let alone weigh the strength of the prosecution's evidence against such consideration.

Yet that is precisely what the panel in Jenkins has done. Absent any evidence of actual prosecutorial vindictiveness, the opinion upholds the dismissal of the alien smuggling charges based upon its assertion that the government already had "more than enough evidence" to proceed with those charges prior to Jenkins' testimony, notwithstanding the government's adamant position that it did not have enough evidence to make the case worth pursuing. Jenkins, 504 F.3d at 700. By concluding that prosecutors should have sacrificed the resources necessary to pursue the charges before Jenkins admitted to the crimes under oath, the opinion oversteps our judicial function and flies in the face of the Supreme Court's caution against encroaching upon prosecutorial charging decisions by independently weighing the strength of the government's evidence.

III

A

The flaw in the opinion is that it broadens the doctrine of presumed prosecutorial vindictiveness well beyond its traditional bounds. Under that doctrine, of course, a court may dismiss charges filed against a defendant in retaliation for his exercise of a legal right. In the absence of sufficient evidence of actual retaliatory intent, a court may presume prosecutorial vindictiveness "where, as a practical matter, there is a realistic or reasonable likelihood of prosecutorial conduct that would not have occurred but for hostility or a punitive animus towards the defendant because he exercised a specific legal right." United States v. Gallegos-Curiel, 681 F.2d 1164, 1168-69 (9th Cir.1982).

Given the Supreme Court's admonition against judicial oversight of prosecutorial charging decisions, it is not surprising that the doctrine of presumed vindictiveness has been substantially curtailed by this and other courts. Under one such limitation, we have recognized that, "if the additional charge aris[es] out of the same nucleus of operative facts as the original charge, a presumption of vindictiveness is raised. If, however, the second charge is unrelated to the first, the presumption does not arise." United States v. Martinez, 785 F.2d 663, 669 (9th Cir.1986) (internal quotation marks and citations omitted); accord United States v. Groves, 571 F.2d 450, 454 (9th Cir.1978) (upholding a presumption of vindictiveness where new and old charges stemmed from the same investigation and thus "grew out of the same set of facts").[3]

B

Two of our sister circuits have affirmed that principle. In Williams v. Bartow, 481 F.3d 492 (7th Cir.2007), the defendant twice committed child molestation, once in 1990 and once in 1996. Prosecutors declined to pursue charges for the 1990 incident because they determined that there was insufficient evidence; however, they brought charges for the 1996 incident. Id. at 495. At the ensuing trial, the victim of the 1990 molestation testified to the facts of that incident. Id. at 496. After Williams successfully moved for a new trial based on ineffective assistance of counsel, prosecutors added a charge for the 1990 incident in reliance of the victim's testimony. Id.

The Seventh Circuit first noted that neither the Supreme Court's precedent nor its own had expressly addressed whether presumed vindictiveness may apply "to situations where the defendant is charged, post-appeal, on the basis of different criminal conduct, as opposed to a heightened charge on the basis of the same criminal conduct." Id. at 502 (emphasis in original). The court held that "when the prosecutorial conduct involves other criminal conduct, the defendant must demonstrate actual vindictiveness rather than relying on the presumption [of vindictiveness]." Id. at 502 (emphasis in original). Thus, the Williams court held that factual relatedness is dispositive in assessing a claim of presumed vindictiveness, a holding with which our opinion starkly conflicts. Id.

Moreover, one of the key factual considerations in Williams was that the prosecutor finally had the molestation victim's open court testimony, whereas "[p]reviously, he had only the police report statements of the two very young children." Id.

at 503. The facts of Williams and Jenkins are consistent. Both cases involve prosecutors who subsequently acquired enough evidence to proceed with a charge (or, in Jenkins, four charges) that previously had been insufficient to merit the sacrifice of prosecutorial resources. Just as the prosecutors in Williams obtained the testimony of the more mature victims, the prosecutors in Jenkins were handed an unchallengeable confession, which was what they lacked to make the charges worth pursuing.

For the same reason, Jenkins conflicts with the holding in Humphrey v. United States, 888 F.2d 1546 (11th Cir.1989). In Humphrey, while the defendant appealed a conviction of six counts of auto theft, prosecutors indicted him for an additional eleven counts of that offense stemming from "independent acts." Id. at 1547-49. He contested the second indictment in part on a claim of prosecutorial vindictiveness. Id. The Eleventh Circuit distinguished the Supreme Court's holding in Blackledge on the ground that it "addresse[d] the situation of state retaliation by substituting a more serious charge for the original charge." Id. at 1549 (emphasis in original). Rather, the court determined that in Humphrey, "[t]he charges in the second indictment are not a substitution; indeed, they are different charges based upon independent acts." Id. Thus, the court held that regardless of the "timing of the second indictment," the doctrine of presumed vindictiveness was inapplicable. Id.

IV

The Jenkins opinion is mistaken on another crucial point: it was not Jenkins' exercise of the right to testify that triggered the subsequent charges; it was the content of that testimony. We expressly held in United States v. Baker, 850 F.2d 1365, 1370 (9th Cir.1988), that the content of a defendant's testimony on his own behalf can be used as the basis for a new prosecution against him, because "a defendant can[not] expect to admit with impunity a crime for which he or she is liable." We therefore affirmed the principle that "encouraging a defendant to immunize oneself from other criminal conduct by testifying at a trial was never the intent of the fifth amendment." Id. By conferring upon Jenkins the right to testify about her past crimes with immunity from subsequent prosecution, the Jenkins opinion flatly contradicts our holding in Baker and creates the preposterous rule that a defendant can shield himself from future prosecution for unrelated crimes by openly admitting to them on the stand.

Indeed, while Jenkins would not have admitted to alien smuggling had she not testified, the same can be said for her having elected to plead not guilty or to have raised a defense in the first place. Accordingly, there is no limiting principle to the newly promulgated rule in Jenkins: so long as the prosecutors have "enough evidence" to bring charges before a trial is initiated for an unrelated crime, subsequent prosecution is barred if new evidence is acquired in the exercise of a constitutional right.[4] Such a broad "but for" test has no place in assessing whether to supplant prosecutorial charging discretion — our task is to assess only whether there is a "realistic likelihood" that the alien smuggling charges "would not have occurred but for hostility or a punitive animus" stemming from the exercise of a right. Under the rule properly created by Baker, prosecutors could feel overwhelming animus toward a defendant who admits to crimes on the stand, but filing unrelated charges in response does not give rise to a presumption of vindictiveness, as such is a legitimate prosecutorial consideration. Cf. Blackledge, 417 U.S. at 27, 94 S.Ct. 2098 ("[T]he Due Process Clause is not offended by all possibilities of increased punishment... but only by those that pose a realistic likelihood of vindictiveness.").[5]

V

The Jenkins opinion also creates a split with three of our sister circuits on a corollary rule. Just as presumed vindictiveness is improper where new and old charges stem from distinct factual nuclei, such presumption is available only where the severity of an indictment — i.e., the crimes charged for the same underlying conduct-is increased following a defendant's successful appeal. See United States v. Burt, 619 F.2d 831, 836 (9th Cir.1980) ("In most cases, [vindictive prosecution] involves a showing that the prosecutor has re-indicted the defendant and increased the severity of the charge, after the defendant has exercised a statutory or constitutional right").

That rule has been adopted by three of our sister circuits. See United States v. Peoples, 360 F.3d 892 (8th Cir.2004); United States v. Perry, 335 F.3d 316 (4th Cir.2003); United States v. Miller, 948 F.2d 631 (10th Cir.1991) (holding that Blackledge is generally limited to its facts); but cf. Johnson v. Vose, 927 F.2d 10 (1st Cir.1991). The Eighth Circuit has gone even further than us in holding that a "presumption of vindictiveness arises only when the prosecutor chooses to bring a more serious charge against a defendant in a second trial." Peoples, 360 F.3d at 896.

In Jenkins, the new charges were not filed following a successful appeal, nor did the prosecutors seek to increase the severity of the marijuana importation indictment. The opinion fails to provide any rationale for deviating from this general rule.

VI

In addition to the multiple splits created by the Jenkins opinion, rehearing of this case is necessary because of the dangerous precedent it has set. Jenkins will have the perverse result of compelling prosecutors to rely on ever-weaker evidence in bringing charges, lest they lose the opportunity ever to pursue those charges. That incentive is particularly strong when dealing with recidivist criminals, who are most likely to have committed unrelated offenses in the past, yet those are precisely the suspects for whom the government should have utmost discretion in investigating and prosecuting.

Such danger is precisely why we must not overstep the clear judicial boundary cautioning us against engaging in a judicial assessment of whether the government had "sufficient evidence" to pursue criminal charges on flimsier evidence. Thus, the rule propounded by our sister circuits in Williams and Humphrey, from which Jenkins has recklessly split, is a crucial prophylactic against tempting judges from supervising prosecutorial charging decisions.

VII

The opinion's holding that Jenkins can shield herself from prosecution by admitting to unrelated crimes during trial is unprecedented, creates multiple inter-circuit splits, and will disrupt the government's ability to manage its criminal caseload by impermissibly encroaching upon prosecutorial discretion.

For the foregoing reasons, I respectfully dissent from our unfortunate decision not to rehear this case en banc.

Notes

[1] Moreover, Judge Conlon's dissent aptly notes, with respect to the statements Jenkins made during the second stop, that "purported admissions to law enforcement officers may be denied or challenged on a number of grounds, including voluntariness and accuracy." Jenkins, 504 F.3d at 704.

[2] While we have great respect for the intuition of our district judges in many settings, here the so-called "smell test" has no roots in this or any court's precedent of which we are aware.

[3] Indeed, noting the "severity" of the doctrine of presumed vindictiveness, a plurality of the Supreme Court has implicitly affirmed the principle that the doctrine does not apply where the prior and new charges stem from distinct factual nuclei. See Wasman v. United States, 468 U.S. 559, 566, 104 S.Ct. 3217, 82 L.Ed.2d 424 (1984) ("[T]he Court has been chary about extending the [] presumption of vindictiveness when the likelihood of vindictiveness is not as pronounced as in ... Blackledge [v. Perry, 417 U.S. 21, 94 S.Ct. 2098, 40 L.Ed.2d 628 (1974)].").

In Blackledge, Perry was tried and convicted for a misdemeanor stemming from a prison altercation in which he was involved. 417 U.S. at 22, 94 S.Ct. 2098. When Perry obtained a new trial, the prosecutor indicted him for other offenses stemming from the same fight. Id. at 22-23, 94 S.Ct. 2098. After specifically noting that "the indictment covered the same conduct for which Perry had been tried and convicted," id. at 23, 94 S.Ct. 2098, the Supreme Court held that the charges were presumptively retaliatory against Perry's having pursued his right to a new trial. Id. at 28-29, 94 S.Ct. 2098.

While Blackledge expressly was predicated on the charges having stemmed from the same fight (and, hence, the same factual nucleus), the prosecutors here proffer a valid explanation for the alien smuggling charges; indeed, the district court credited their explanation. See Jenkins, 504 F.3d at 703 (noting that the government did not do "anything wrong").

[4] Cf. United States v. Bryser, 95 F.3d 182, 187 (2d Cir.1996) (rejecting the "absurd result that incriminating statements may not be used as evidence because they were made otherwise in aid, or under the umbrella, of a constitutional right").

[5] Similarly, the Court has held, "The possibility that a prosecutor would respond to a defendant's pretrial demand for a jury trial by bringing charges not in the public interest that could be explained only as a penalty imposed on the defendant is so unlikely that a presumption of vindictiveness certainly is not warranted." United States v. Goodwin, 457 U.S. 368, 384, 102 S.Ct. 2485, 73 L.Ed.2d 74 (1982) (emphasis in original). It is just as unlikely that prosecutors sought to punish Jenkins for testifying in her own

defense. Absent some other evidence, the only reasonable conclusion is that prosecutors responded not to the fact of her testifying but to the content of her testimony, which lies outside the scope of Fifth Amendment protection.

Judge O'Scannlain's dissent in US v. Lewis (March 13, 2008)

O'SCANNLAIN, Circuit Judge, dissenting:

After acknowledging that a Speedy Trial Act violation had occurred, the trial judge quite properly dismissed the indictment against Beau Lee Lewis without prejudice, weighing each factor the Act requires. Today, the court holds that the district court abused its discretion because it failed to calculate the precise number of days by which the Act was violated and that such failure "prevented it from accurately and carefully weighing the statutory factors provided by Congress." Maj. Op. at 2426. Because I do not believe that any such requirement is imposed by the Act or by any of our precedents I respectfully dissent.

I

The Speedy Trial Act requires that a defendant's trial begin within 70 days of his indictment, or the date of his first appearance before a judicial officer, whichever is later. 18 U.S.C. § 3161(c). Other provisions of the Act, however, provide exceptions under which certain delays may be excluded from this 70-day limit in appropriate circumstances. Id. § 3161(h). As the majority notes, in this case over two-and-a-half years elapsed between Lewis's indictment and the date of his first trial, in which he was convicted. Lewis appealed, and in United States v. Lewis, 349 F.3d 1116 (9th Cir. 2003) (per curiam) ("Lewis I"), we reversed his convictions, holding that the Speedy Trial Act had been violated because at least 117 days between Lewis's indictment and his trial were not excludable under the Act. We remanded to the district court to determine whether to dismiss Lewis's indictment with or without prejudice. Id. at 1121-22.

In Lewis I, Lewis had argued that the district court erred in finding that multiple portions of the delay between his indictment and trial were excludable under the Act. We held that the district court erred in finding at least one of these periods excludable—the 117 days between January 13, 2000 and May 9, 2000, when the government's pending motion to present a witness's testimony non-sequentially was the sole basis for delay. Id. at 1120. As a consequence, we declined to reach the question of whether any other periods were excludable because such period alone was sufficient to establish a Speedy Trial Act violation. Id. at 1122 n.9.

In this appeal, Lewis argues that on remand the district court was required to reach the other period contentions to determine whether to dismiss the indictment against him with or without prejudice under the guidance the Act provides, see 18 U.S.C. § 3162(a)(2), and the majority agrees. Such a conclusion not only contravenes the statute's plain text, I suggest it transforms the statutory standard of review from abuse of discretion to de novo.

II

When a Speedy Trial Act violation has occurred, the court must determine whether to dismiss the indictment against the defendant with or without prejudice by "consider[ing], among others, each of the following factors: the seriousness of the offense; the facts and circumstances of the case which led to dismissal; and the impact of a reprosecution on the administration of this chapter and on the administration of justice." 18 U.S.C. § 3162(a)(2). I agree with the majority that the Supreme Court has explained that Congress intended "the presence or absence of prejudice to the defendant" to be a fourth factor relevant to this determination. United States v. Taylor, 487 U.S. 326, 334 (1988). But the Act gives "neither remedy . . . priority," id. at 335, and Congress has left the decision to dismiss with or without prejudice "to the guided discretion of the district court," id. (emphasis added).

While § 3162(a)(2) provides a non-exclusive list of factors the district court may consider, it contains no express requirement that the court calculate the precise number of days that were or were not excludable under the Act before deciding whether to dismiss with or without prejudice, nor do our precedents set forth any such rule. The majority attempts to bridge this gap by noting that we have "recognized that 'the sheer length of the period involved' can weigh toward a dismissal with prejudice." Maj. Op. at 2426 (quoting United States v. Clymer, 25 F.3d 824, 831-32 (9th Cir. 1994)) (emphasis added). This observation is, of course, unassailable. A longer period of delay will weigh in favor of dismissal with prejudice in many, if not all cases. Yet § 3162(a)(2) enumerates other factors which a district court must consider, and our prior cases do not portend the rule the majority announces today, that a district court's "failure to consider all improperly excluded periods" is enough to constitute an abuse of discretion in applying § 3162(a)(2). Maj. Op. at 2426.

Indeed, in Clymer we referred to the total number of days (excludable and non-excludable) between the defendant's indictment and his trial in stating that the "sheer length" of this total period "weigh[ed] heavily in favor of a dismissal with prejudice." 25 F.3d at 831-32. But we expressly declined to make the distinction between excludable and non-excludable days which the majority now determines is required. Rather, after holding that the Speedy Trial Act had been violated, we simply remanded to the district court without unnecessary further calculations. 25 F.3d at 832 ("Even giving the government the benefit of every doubt, about five months of this period was not excludable under the Act. Were we forced to decide how much of the delay is actually excludable, we might conclude that the non-excludable delay is considerably more than that.") (emphasis added). Thus, our decision in Clymer firmly supports the conclusion that § 3162(a)(2) does not require a calculation of the total number of excludable and non-excludable days before a court may decide whether to dismiss with or without prejudice. As such, I believe the district court cannot abuse its discretion by failing to recite such calculations.

The majority notes that on remand, Lewis asked the district court to make specific findings as to whether each period of delay he challenged was excludable under the Act,

Maj. Op. at 2425, and labels the district court's failure to do so a "misconstruction of our mandate" in Lewis I, id. at 2426. But the trial judge made precisely such findings before Lewis's first trial, deeming all such periods excludable. In Lewis I, we held that the district court erred with respect to one 117-day period, but we never implied that this error tainted its findings with respect to the other periods. As such, I do not believe it was necessary for the trial judge to reconstruct its prior work on remand. Indeed, such an exercise would be redundant. When Lewis requested that the district court reissue specific findings on these other periods, the court acknowledged its previous conclusions and declined to revisit them. I find nothing in the Speedy Trial Act or our decision in Lewis I to prohibit such a course of action.

Since § 3162(a)(2) does not require the calculation the majority demands, the next question is whether the district court abused its discretion in weighing the statutory factors.

III

A

Section 3162(a)(2) lists three factors, "among others," which a court must consider in deciding whether to dismiss an indictment with or without prejudice, and the Supreme Court has held that prejudice is a fourth. Taylor, 487 U.S. at 334. As I view the record in this case, the district court considered each of these factors at length. It first acknowledged that Lewis was prejudiced as a result of the delay. Specifically, the district court explained that Lewis lost the opportunity to be represented by the counsel of his choice when his first attorney withdrew to accept a position with the International War Crimes Tribunal in the Netherlands after the 117-day non-excludable delay had occurred. The district court appropriately defined the right to one's counsel of choice as a "hallmark of our system of justice" and reasoned that Lewis's loss weighed in favor of dismissal with prejudice.

And then it considered the other § 3162(a)(2) factors. As such, the district court examined the severity of the offenses with which Lewis was charged: one count of money laundering in violation of 18 U.S.C. § 1956, two counts of conspiracy in violation of 18 U.S.C. § 371, six counts of smuggling merchandise into the United States in violation of 18 U.S.C. § 545, and nine counts of illegal importation and false labeling of wildlife in violation of 16 U.S.C. § 3372. Noting that a conspiracy requires the assistance of multiple parties, that the smuggling conduct with which Lewis was charged contravened international treaties, and that a high number of animals were involved in Lewis's scheme, the district court determined that this combination of offenses was "serious" and that their severity weighed in favor of dismissal without prejudice.

Finally, the district court considered the third factor: the impact of a reprosecution on the administration of the Speedy Trial Act and the administration of justice. In reasoning that such factor weighed in favor of dismissal without prejudice, the district court noted two important facts: First, Lewis was not incarcerated during the time of pretrial delay and, second, Lewis was charged with playing a central, rather than a peripheral, role in the crimes alleged.

B

The district court balanced the prejudice Lewis suffered against the consequences of reprosecution and the severity of his offenses and concluded that a dismissal without prejudice was the appropriate remedy. Based on the record before us, I cannot conclude that the district court abused its discretion in reaching such a decision. It considered each factor enumerated in § 3162(a)(2) with care. The offenses with which Lewis was charged, money laundering, conspiracy, smuggling, and illegal importation and false labeling of wildlife, are indeed serious offenses in their own right and are even more so when combined. In addition, it reasonably concluded that the consequences of reprosecution would not be severe. The district court was guided by Clymer, where we determined that the consequences of reprosecution weighed in favor of dismissal with prejudice where the defendant was "incarcerated for the entire pretrial period." 25 F.3d at 832. Lewis, on the other hand, has remained out of prison for the duration. The defendant in Clymer as a "relatively minor figure" in the criminal enterprise alleged in that case, id. at 826, whereas Lewis was charged as a central player here. In such circumstances, I believe the district court was well within its discretion to conclude that reprosecution would not conflict with the ends of justice.

Of course, the district court acknowledged that Lewis suffered prejudice from the loss of his counsel of choice and that this factor weighed in favor of dismissal with prejudice. Yet the majority seems to conclude that the district court's failure to quantify the precise number of days which were not excludable under the Act caused it to undervalue the degree of prejudice Lewis suffered. I simply cannot discern what relevance this calculation would have had in the district court's analysis. The prejudice Lewis suffered was a direct result of the 117-day delay. Whether or not other periods were also non-excludable would neither have added to nor subtracted from this harm. Without the 117-day delay, Lewis's trial would have begun before the date his counsel departed.

While the loss of his first attorney is not the only prejudice Lewis alleges (the general burden of an indictment looming over one's head is not to be discounted), it is certainly his greatest. Because the addition of other non-excludable periods would not have added to this harm, I cannot conclude that the district court abused its discretion in failing to perform additional calculations, nor can I conclude that it abused its discretion in finding that the prejudice Lewis suffered was not so great as to overwhelm the minimal consequences of reprosecution and the severity of Lewis's offenses.

Lewis was granted a continuance to allow his new counsel to prepare for trial. He was charged as a central figure in the commission of serious offenses, and was not incarcerated during the pre-trial delay. The district court explained as much in a reasoned decision, considering all factors required by § 3162(a)(2). In this area of the law, we do not engage in de novo review; I cannot conclude that the bounds of discretion were exceeded here.

Judge O'Scannlain's concurrence in Tualatin Valley Builders Supply, Inc. v.

US (April 10, 2008)

O'SCANNLAIN, Circuit Judge, specially concurring:

I join the court in its conclusion that Revenue Procedure 2002-40 is a valid exercise of the Internal Revenue Service's authority. Yet as the majority notes, there is tension in our case law as to whether the level of deference prescribed in Chevron U.S.A., Inc. v. Nat. Res. Def. Council, Inc., 467 U.S. 837, 104 S.Ct. 2778, 81 L.Ed.2d 694 (1984), or Skidmore v. Swift & Co., 323 U.S. 134, 65 S.Ct. 161, 89 L.Ed. 124 (1944), should apply to the agency's action in this case. Thus, while I agree with the majority that Revenue Procedure 2002-40 withstands scrutiny under either standard, I write separately because I believe this tension, left unresolved, could lead our court down a path that is inconsistent with Supreme Court authority and with common sense. As I explain, I believe that in this case, Chevron deference must apply.

I

Prior to 2002, the Internal Revenue Code allowed taxpayers to carry back the net operating loss accrued in a particular tax year by a maximum of two years. 26 U.S.C. § 172(b)(1)(A). In 2002, Congress enacted the Job Creation and Worker Assistance Act of 2002 ("JCWA Act"), Pub.L. No. 107-147, § 102(a), 116 Stat. 25-26, codified at 26 U.S.C. § 172(b)(1)(H), which temporarily extended the carryback period from two years to five years. Id. The new five-year carryback applied only to tax years ending in 2001 or 2002. In addition, the JCWA Act provided that taxpayers could opt out of the five-year carryback, stating that the taxpayer's "election shall be made in such manner as may be prescribed by the Secretary." 26 U.S.C. § 172(j). The Internal Revenue Service ("IRS") responded to this specific delegation of authority by promulgating Revenue Procedure 2002-40. Among other things, the Revenue Procedure required taxpayers wishing to opt out of the five-year carryback to make their election on or before October 31, 2002. In this appeal, we must decide whether the IRS exceeded its authority when it imposed this deadline.

II

As an initial matter, the JCWA Act states unequivocally that the Secretary shall prescribe the manner of elections. 26 U.S.C. § 172(j). Thus, because Congress has "directly spoken to the precise issue," Chevron, 467 U.S. at 842, 104 S.Ct. 2778, I would look no further than the statute's text in ascertaining the scope of the rulemaking authority Congress intended to delegate to the IRS. Accordingly, I do not believe the Congressional Letter discussed by the majority is relevant to our analysis. See Maj. Op. at 940-41 (citing Congressional Letter from Rep. Bill Thomas, Chair, Comm. on Ways and Means; Sen. Max Baucus, Chair, Comm. on Finance; Rep. Charles B. Rangel, Ranking Member, Comm. on Ways and Means; Sen. Charles E. Grassley, Ranking Member, Comm. on Finance, to Mark A. Weinberger, Assistant Sec'y (Tax Policy), Dep't of the Treasury (Apr. 15, 2002)). Although the Congressional Letter recites that Congress intended the Secretary to prescribe the manner of elections, such intent is made plain by § 172(j).

Where Congress unambiguously expresses its intent in the text of the statute, I believe it unnecessary to entertain correspondence signed by a handful of legislators to confirm that Congress meant what it said — a taxpayer's "election shall be made in such manner as may be prescribed by the Secretary." 26 U.S.C. § 172(j).

III

But just what level of deference should Revenue Procedure 2002-40 receive? In United States v. Mead Corp., 533 U.S. 218, 121 S.Ct. 2164, 150 L.Ed.2d 292 (2001), the Supreme Court explained that an agency's implementation of a statute will receive Chevron deference where it appears that Congress delegated authority to the agency to "make rules carrying the force of law," and where "the agency interpretation claiming deference was promulgated in the exercise of that authority." Id. at 226-27, 121 S.Ct. 2164. Agency action that does not meet this test is subjected to the less deferential analysis prescribed by Skidmore. See Mead, 533 U.S. at 234-35, 121 S.Ct. 2164.

A

In this case, the agency interpretation claiming deference is a revenue procedure. Revenue Procedure 2002-40 was published in the Internal Revenue Bulletin, which serves as "the authoritative instrument of the Commissioner for the announcement of official rulings, decisions, opinions, and procedures, and for the publication of Treasury decisions, ... and other items pertaining to internal revenue matters." Treas. Reg. § 601.601(d)(1). Importantly, however, revenue procedures are not produced through formal notice-and-comment rulemaking or formal adjudication.

The majority points out that our case law is unclear as to whether a revenue procedure should receive Chevron or Skidmore deference. Maj. Op. at 941-42 (citing Omohundro v. United States, 300 F.3d 1065 (9th Cir.2002) (applying Skidmore deference to an IRS revenue ruling) and Schuetz v. Banc One Mortgage Corp., 292 F.3d 1004 (9th Cir.2002) (applying Chevron deference to a Department of Housing and Urban Development policy statement)). The majority declines to resolve this tension, concluding instead that Revenue Procedure 2002-40 is valid even under the less deferential Skidmore analysis. Maj. Op. at 941-42. I agree with the majority that our precedents are inconsistent, but I believe the majority presents a question we are not required to ask. Mead does not instruct us to decide whether revenue procedures, as a class, are subject to one level of deference or another. Instead, the Supreme Court requires us only to determine whether this Revenue Procedure is entitled to deference under Skidmore or under Chevron.

In Mead, the Court explained that the formality of a particular agency action is an important factor in determining whether it receives Chevron or Skidmore deference, but not a determinative one. The Court noted that "[i]t is fair to assume generally that Congress contemplates administrative action with the effect of law when it provides for a relatively formal administrative procedure." Mead, 533 U.S. at 230, 121 S.Ct. 2164. And, as a consequence, the "the overwhelming number of[the Court's] cases applying Chevron deference have reviewed the fruits of notice-and-comment rulemaking or formal adjudication." Id. (citations omitted). Still, the Court emphasized that "[d]elegation of such authority may be shown in a variety of ways, as by an agency's power to engage in adjudication or notice-and-comment rulemaking, or by some other indication of a comparable congressional intent." Id. at 227, 121 S.Ct. 2164(emphasis added); see also Swallows Holding, Ltd. v. Comm'r, 515 F.3d 162, 169-71 (3d Cir.2008) (citing Mead for the proposition that "[w]hen determining whether Congress intends a particular agency action to carry the force of law, our inquiry does not hinge solely on the type of agency action involved.").

Yet on this point, our own cases are in conflict. In Schuetz, we applied Chevron deference to a Department of Housing and Urban Development ("HUD") Policy Statement, even though it was not the result of formal rulemaking or adjudication. 292 F.3d at 1012. In so doing, we directly quoted from the Supreme Court's decision in Barnhart v. Walton, 535 U.S. 212, 122 S.Ct. 1265, 152 L.Ed.2d 330 (2002), that "the fact that the Agency previously reached its interpretation through means less formal than notice and comment rulemaking does not automatically deprive the interpretation of the judicial deference otherwise due." Schuetz, 292 F.3d at 1012 (quoting Walton, 535 U.S. at 221, 122 S.Ct. 1265) (internal quotation marks omitted). But only a few months later in Omohundro, we applied Skidmore deference to an IRS revenue ruling which was not the product of formal rulemaking or adjudication, because we interpreted Mead as holding that "an administrative agency's interpretation of a statute contained in an informal rulemaking must be accorded the level of deference set forth in Skidmore." 300 F.3d at 1067-68(citations omitted) (emphasis added).

Our statements in Schuetz and Omohundro are irreconcilable. Moreover, our statement in Omohundro flatly contradicts the Supreme Court's instructions in Walton and Mead. See Walton, 535 U.S. at 221, 122 S.Ct. 1265; Mead, 533 U.S. at 230-31, 121 S.Ct. 2164. Indeed, the Court has emphasized that "as significant as notice-and-comment is in pointing to Chevron authority, the want of that procedure ... does not decide the case," for the Court has "sometimes found reasons for Chevron deference even when no such administrative formality was required and none was afforded." Mead, 533 U.S. at 230-31, 121 S.Ct. 2164(citing NationsBank of N.C., N.A. v. Variable Annuity Life Ins. Co., 513 U.S. 251, 256-57, 115 S.Ct. 810, 130 L.Ed.2d 740 (1995)).

I agree with the majority that Revenue Procedure 2002-40 would satisfy even Skidmore deference and, as such, I understand the majority's decision not to resolve the conflict between Schuetz and Omohundro in this case. Yet I am convinced that Omohundro's statement that all informal rulemaking must receive Skidmore deference cannot be reconciled with the Supreme Court's holdings in Walton and Mead.

Accordingly, I hope this court might one day confront Omohundro and clarify that the formality of a particular agency action, standing alone, does not determine the level of deference it receives. This was the path we followed in Schuetz and, in my view, this is the path that should be followed here. Under such framework, I believe Revenue Procedure 2002-40 is one example of informal rulemaking which is still entitled to Chevron deference.

B

When Congress has "explicitly left a gap" for an agency to fill, "there is an express delegation of authority to the agency to elucidate a specific provision of the statute by regulation," and "[s]uch legislative regulations are given controlling weight unless they are arbitrary, capricious, or manifestly contrary to the statute." Chevron, 467 U.S. at 843-44, 104 S.Ct. 2778. Congress has empowered the Secretary of the Treasury and, by his delegation, the IRS with the broad authority to "prescribe all needful rules and regulations" to enforce the Code, including "all rules and regulations as may be necessary by reason of any alteration of law in relation to internal revenue." 26 U.S.C. § 7805(a). Most revenue procedures are promulgated pursuant to this general delegation. Yet in § 172(j), Congress specifically delegated to the Secretary the authority to prescribe the manner of elections. Revenue Procedure 2002-40 is the product of that rulemaking authority. In my view, this specific delegation strongly indicates that the resulting IRS action would carry the force of law and, thus, receive Chevron deference. See Mead, 533 U.S. at 227-29, 121 S.Ct. 2164.

A comparison with Schuetz is instructive. In that case, we cited several reasons for applying Chevron deference to the HUD Policy Statement even though it was not formal action. First, the statute at issue authorized HUD to prescribe rules and regulations and to interpret the statute. 292 F.3d at 1012 (citing 12 U.S.C. § 2617(a)). Second, the Policy Statement was published in the Federal Register. Id. Finally, we noted that notice-and-comment rulemaking would have been impracticable because Congress issued a Conference Report which directed HUD to issue a policy statement within 90 days to resolve an ambiguity in the statute. Id. at 1009, 1012.

The same considerations counsel in favor of Chevron deference here. First, Revenue Procedure 2002-40 is supported by the Secretary's broad rulemaking authority under § 7805(a) and his specific authority under § 172(j). Second, the IRS published Revenue Procedure 2002-40 in the Internal Revenue Bulletin. Finally, notice-and-comment would have been impracticable in this case because time was of the essence for the IRS to exercise its power delegated by § 172(j) to establish the manner of elections out of the five-year carryback. As the majority explains, Congress enacted the JCWA Act on March 9, 2002. The Act created a five-year net operating loss carryback for tax years ending in 2001 and 2002. 26 U.S.C. § 172(b)(1)(H). It further provided that taxpayers could elect to opt out of the new carryback, but left the manner of election to the Secretary. Id. § 172(j). Yet by the time the Act became law, many taxpayers had already filed their tax returns of the tax years 2001 and 2002. Maj. Op. at 939-40. Such taxpayers were faced with an awkward problem — the Act allowed them to opt out of the carryback, but they had no way of doing so until the Secretary told them how. By April 2002, the ranking members of the House Ways and Means Committee and the Senate Finance Committee recognized the dilemma and sent a letter requesting that the Secretary "issue guidance under which taxpayers are given until November 1, 2002" to, among other things, make an election to opt out. Congressional Letter, supra at 944-45. In light of these factors, the

IRS's response in Revenue Procedure 2002-40 was entitled to Chevron deference.

Omohundro is distinguishable. In that case, we applied Skidmore deference to an IRS revenue ruling that interpreted 26 U.S.C. § 6511(a). 300 F.3d at 1067-68. While the revenue ruling was issued pursuant to the IRS's broad powers under § 7805(a), it was not the product of a specific delegation of rulemaking authority such as the one provided by § 172(j). In addition, there is no evidence that the revenue ruling in Omohundro was issued under a time constraint such as the one facing the IRS here. Thus, despite Omohundro's strained interpretation of Mead and its inconsistency with our earlier interpretation in Schuetz, several facts that counsel in favor of Chevron deference here were not before the court in that case.

IV

I concur in the result reached by the majority — Revenue Procedure 2002-40 was a valid and enforceable exercise of the IRS's authority. But while the majority declines to specify the necessary level of deference, I would apply Chevron deference to this particular agency action. The distinction between our positions is important because the Supreme Court has made clear that sometimes informal rulemaking may still lead to deference under Chevron. I believe this is such a case.

Judge O'Scannlain's concurrence and dissent in Cox v. Ocean View Hotel Corp. (July 23, 2008)

O'SCANNLAIN, Circuit Judge, concurring in part and dissenting in part:

While I concur in the court's decision that the motion to compel arbitration was erroneously denied by the district court, I respectfully disagree with its conclusion that the waiver issue was for the court to decide. In my view, arbitrability is a matter for the court; whether or not the agreement to arbitrate was properly invoked, by either side, at any time, is a matter for the arbitrator to decide. Thus I would reverse on the very narrow ground that a motion to compel must be granted because the arbitration clause is valid. I would leave all other issues to the arbitrator.

I

As the en banc opinion in Nagrampa v. Mailcoups, Inc., 469 F.3d 1257 (9th Cir. 2006) (en banc) has revealed, there are continued tensions in our arbitration jurisprudence which have failed to clarify this area. Very recently, the Supreme Court has renewed its commitment to support arbitration in Hall Street Associates, L.L.C. v. Mattel, ____ U.S. ____, 128 S.Ct. 1396, 1402, 170 L.Ed.2d 254 (2008). But Prima Paint Corp. v. Flood & Conklin Manufacturing Co., 388 U.S. 395, 400, 87 S.Ct. 1801, 18 L.Ed.2d 1270 (1967) (holding that a federal court must "order arbitration once it is satisfied that an agreement for arbitration has been made and has not been honored"), Howsam v. Dean Witter Reynolds, Inc., 537 U.S. 79, 85, 123 S.Ct. 588, 154 L.Ed.2d 491 (2002) (holding that "in the absence of an agreement to the contrary, issues of substantive arbitrability... are for a court to decide and issues of procedural arbitrability, i.e., whether prerequisites such as time limits, notice, laches, estoppel, and other conditions precedent to an obligation to arbitrate have been met, are for the arbitrators to decide" (quoting the Revised Uniform Arbitration Act of 2000 (RUAA) § 6(c) cmt. 2) (emphasis added and in the original)), Buckeye Check Cashing, Inc. v. Cardegna, 546 U.S. 440, 449, 126 S.Ct. 1204, 163 L.Ed.2d 1038 (2006) ("[A] challenge to the validity of the contract as a whole, and not specifically to the arbitration clause, must go to the arbitrator." (emphasis added)), and Nagrampa, 469 F.3d at 1293-94 (holding that an arbitration agreement that was invalid due to unconscionability was not enforceable), are absolutely clear that once the legal decision is made by the court that an arbitration clause is valid, all remaining issues are for the arbitrator.

The Supreme Court in Howsam could not be clearer: "the presumption is that the arbitrator should decide allegation[s] of waiver, delay, or a like defense to arbitrability." 537 U.S. at 84, 123 S.Ct. 588 (internal quotation marks and citation omitted). Thus, I find perplexing the majority's attempt to distinguish Howsam.

Here, I see no relevant distinction between Cox's attempt to avoid the arbitrability of his employment dispute based on whether or not he properly followed the procedures of the AAA and Dean Witter's challenge to arbitrability in Howsam based on the National Association of Securities Dealers (NASD) procedural rules. See Howsam, 537 U.S. at 81, 123 S.Ct. 588. In this case I would follow the reasoning of the Supreme Court in Howsam that "[b]ecause the parties would likely have committed interpretation of a[AAA] rule to a[AAA] arbitrator, that particular issue of procedure was left for the arbitrator to decide."[1] Opinion at 1121 (citing Howsam, 537 U.S. at 86, 123 S.Ct. 588).

Here, neither party disputes the existence nor validity of the arbitration agreement. Therefore, I concur in the majority's decision to compel arbitration. However, I would remand all other issues to the arbitrator, including the issues of whether the arbitration provision was waived or breached, and therefore dissent to the extent the court holds otherwise.[2]

See Howsam, 537 U.S. at 85, 123 S.Ct. 588.

II

Let me add that I find the majority's treatment of Brown v. Dillard's, Inc., 430 F.3d 1004 (9th Cir.2005), to be problematic and I would not reach it. If I, rather than the arbitrator, were to reach the question of whether or not arbitration was properly invoked, however, I would reluctantly conclude that Brown controls this case. In my view, there is simply no principled difference between the holding that Ms. Brown properly invoked arbitration in Brown and the district court's finding that Mr. Cox properly invoked arbitration here.

Notes

[1] Such approach is correct notwithstanding the majority's citation to out of circuit cases considering waiver based on extensive participation in litigation. See, e.g., Khan v. Parsons Global Servs., 521 F.3d 421, 428 (D.C.Cir.2008) (holding that Parsons

waived right to compel arbitration by "filing a motion for summary judgment based on matters outside of the pleadings"); In re Tyco Int'l Ltd. Sec. Litig., 422 F.3d 41, 43, 46 (1st Cir.2005) (considering question of waiver after the "AAA dismissed the Tyco demand for arbitration... for lack of written consent"); PPG Indus., Inc. v. Webster Auto Parts Inc., 128 F.3d 103, 107 (2d Cir.1997) (holding that "a party waives its right to arbitration when it engages in protracted litigation that prejudices the opposing party" (emphasis added)); Great W. Mortgage Corp. v. Peacock, 110 F.3d 222, 233 (3d Cir.1997) ("Indeed, a party waives the right to compel arbitration only in the following circumstances: when the parties have engaged in a lengthy course of litigation, when extensive discovery has occurred, and when prejudice to the party resisting arbitration can be shown." (emphasis added)).

[2] The majority opinion states that my approach leads to "a strange result: the arbitrator would get first crack at defenses to a motion to compel arbitration based on waiver or breach." Opinion at 1121 n. 5. However, the majority opinion's approach is no less strange; it would require a court to answer the question of waiver before deciding whether the question of waiver is one for the arbitrator to decide. See Opinion at 1120 n. 4, 1120-21. Such an approach leads to a waste of judicial resources should the court find that the arbitration clause was not breached or waived and it does take into account the FAA's policy favoring enforcement of arbitration agreements. Although not directly on point, Buckeye Check Cashing instructs us that when faced such a "conundrum" we must "resolve[] it in favor of the separate enforceability of arbitration provisions." 546 U.S. at 448-49, 126 S.Ct. 1204.

Judge O'Scannlain's concurrence and dissent in US v. Gomez-Leon (Sept 24, 2008)

O'SCANNLAIN, Circuit Judge, concurring in part and dissenting in part:

I concur in the court's holding in Part I that Gomez-Leon was "lawfully deported" under U.S.S.G. § 2L1.2(b), and in its conclusion in Part II that his state sentence for violating Cal. Health & Safety Code § 11379 did not exceed thirteen months, thus excluding him from a sentencing enhancement under U.S.S.G. § 2L1.2(b)(1)(A).

However, notwithstanding the government's concession to the contrary, I respectfully disagree with the court's articulation in Part III that Gomez-Leon's conviction for vehicular manslaughter without gross negligence under Cal.Penal Code § 192(c)(3) (1998) does not constitute a felony "crime of violence" pursuant to U.S.S.G. § 2L1.2(b)(1)(A)(ii). As engaging as I find the court's historical analysis of the requisite mens rea for a conviction of manslaughter and the court's exegesis of state law, the plain language of the Sentencing Guidelines speaks for itself. Section 2L1.2 cmt. 1(B)(iii) of the Guidelines unequivocally lists manslaughter as a "[c]rime of violence." "If the Guidelines writers had intended for manslaughter to be limited, they could easily have inserted the word `voluntary' in front of the word `manslaughter' or inserted a parenthetical, `involuntary manslaughter not included.'" United States v. Dominguez-Ochoa, 386 F.3d 639, 648 (5th Cir.2004) (Pickering, J., dissenting).

The government's concession that Gomez-Leon's conviction does not rise to the level of a "crime of violence" rests on its assertion that this case is controlled by Fernandez-Ruiz v. Gonzales, 466 F.3d 1121 (9th Cir.2006) (en banc). Fernandez-Ruiz, however, was not a sentencing case, nor did it involve a construction of the term "crime of violence" under U.S.S.G. § 2L1.2(b)(1)(A)(ii). Rather, there we construed the meaning of "crime of violence" under 18 U.S.C. § 16(a), see Fernandez-Ruiz, 466 F.3d at 1132, which does not include a similar provision listing enumerated qualifying offenses. Accordingly, Fernandez-Ruiz is irrelevant to an assessment of whether Gomez-Leon's conviction under Cal.Penal Code § 192(c)(3) (1998) constitutes an enumerated "crime of violence" under the Sentencing Guidelines.

Because the Guidelines writers did not make a distinction between types of manslaughter in U.S.S.G. § 2L1.2 cmt 1(B)(iii), even though they explicitly did so elsewhere in the Guidelines, see, e.g., U.S.S.G. § 2A1.4 (delineating between negligent and reckless involuntary manslaughter), I cannot join the court's decision to reverse the sentence imposed by the district court in this case.

Judge O'Scannlain's dissent in Vasquez v. Astrue (Nov 5, 2008, amended July 8, 2009)

O'SCANNLAIN Circuit Judge, dissenting:

Because I believe that this Circuit's precedents cannot be reconciled, I must respectfully dissent from that part of the court's opinion (slip op. at 593-94) that discusses the crediting-as-true rule. In my view, this issue can only be resolved by the court en banc. I do agree with the court's treatment of the remaining issues, including its conclusion that the Administrative Law Judge improperly rejected Vasquez's testimony and that the case should be remanded for consideration of Vasquez's ability to perform other work during steps four and five of the disability determination process.

Subsequent to our decision in this case, the government petitioned for rehearing en banc, arguing that the crediting-as-true rule is invalid because it is contrary to both statute and Supreme Court precedent. Vasquez did not respond to the government's arguments in detail, and so I do not opine whether the government is right. However, the case appears strong. The government asserts that under the Social Security Act, the Commissioner-not a federal court-is the fact-finder. See 42 U.S.C. § 405(g) (findings of Commissioner are conclusive so long as substantial evidence supports them). While the statute prohibits a claimant's testimony concerning pain or other symptoms alone from establishing a disability, this appears to be exactly what the crediting-as-true rule would require. Cf. 42 U.S.C. § 523(d)(5)(A) ("An individual's statement as to pain or other symptoms shall not alone be conclusive evidence of disability as defined in this section; there must be medical signs and findings ... which show the existence of a medical impairment... which could reasonably be expected to produce the pain or other symptoms alleged and which, when considered with all evidence ... would lead to a conclusion that the individual is under a disability." (emphasis added)). The government notes that the general rule (subject to "rare" exceptions) "is to remand to the agency for additional investigation or explanation." INS v. Ventura, 537 U.S. 12, 16, 123 S.Ct. 353, 154 L.Ed.2d 272 (2002) (per curiam). We do not credit-as-true in only "rare" cases; according to the government, we took some factfinding responsibility away from the Commissioner in at least twenty-two cases during 2007 and 2008.

The government finally notes that other circuits will remand for determination of benefits only in narrow circumstances. See, e.g., Faucher v. Sec'y of Health & Human Servs., 17 F.3d 171, 176 (7th Cir. 1994) ("If a court determines that substantial evidence does not support the Secretary's decision, the court can reverse the decision and immediately award benefits only if all essential factual issues have been resolved and the record adequately establishes a plaintiff's entitlement to benefits."); see also Miller v. Chater, 99 F.3d 972 (10th Cir.1996) (remanding for a fifth administrative hearing, but warning that "the Secretary is not entitled to adjudicate a case ad infinitum until [he] correctly applies the proper legal standard and gathers evidence to support [his] conclusion" (internal quotation marks omitted)). If, as the government argues, crediting-as-true is a de facto finding of disability, then our circuit's precedent is badly misaligned with that of other circuits.

Of course, because the crediting-as-true rule is part of our circuit's law, only an en banc court can change it. Although no judge has chosen to call for en banc rehearing in this case, I am hopeful that the en banc court will consider the argument when it is presented more directly in another case (e.g., one where there is an explicit remand for immediate payment of benefits based on the rule). Because the crediting-as-true rule applies in every case where a court finds no substantial evidence to support the Commissioner's decision, the issue is of exceptional importance. This is particularly so because the "Social Security hearing system is probably the largest adjudicative agency in the western world." Heckler v. Campbell, 461 U.S. 458, 461, 103 S.Ct. 1952, 76 L.Ed.2d 66 (1983) (noting that 2.3 million claims for disability benefits were filed in 1981).

I

When a panel is faced with an irreconcilable conflict in the law of the circuit, it is required to make a sua sponte call for en banc review. In Atonio v. Wards Cove Packing Co., Inc., the en banc court held that the three-judge panel facing conflicting circuit precedent erred in relying on one line of the court's authority on the basis that "it expressed the `correct view' or, alternatively, because it was the decision `first in line.'" 810 F.2d 1477, 1478 (9th Cir.1987) (en banc). Rather, the court stated that "the appropriate mechanism for resolving an irreconcilable conflict is an en banc decision. A panel faced with such a conflict must call for en banc review." Id. at 1478-79 (emphases added). The en banc court later affirmed this holding in United States v. Hardesty, 977 F.2d 1347, 1348 (9th Cir.1992) (en banc) (per curiam). In Hardesty, the court specifically rejected the view that "where there are two opposing lines of authority, a panel may, without calling for en banc review, follow the rule which has `successfully posed as the law of the circuit for long enough to be relied on.'" 977 F.2d at 1348 (overruling Greenhow v. Sec. of Health & Human Servs., 863 F.2d 633, 636 (9th Cir.1988)).

II

A

The crediting-as-true rule creates an irrebutable presumption that testimony before an administrative law judge and rejected by him for no adequate reason is true. "[I]f the Secretary fails to articulate reasons for refusing to credit ... testimony, then the Secretary, as a matter of law, has accepted that testimony as true."

Varney v. Sec. of Health and Human Servs. (Varney II), 859 F.2d 1396, 1398 (9th Cir.1988) (quoting Hale v. Bowen, 831 F.2d 1007, 1012 (11th Cir.1987)). The crediting-as-true rule is related to the decision on whether to remand for award of benefits; however, they are separate inquires.[1]

The court is correct to point out that the crediting-as-true rule was initially limited to cases "where there are no outstanding issues that must be resolved before a proper disability determination can be made, and where it is clear from the administrative record that the ALJ would be required to award benefits if the claimant's excess pain testimony were credited...." Id. at 1401. However, the court in Hammock v. Bowen, 879 F.2d 498 (9th Cir. 1989), extended the Varney II rule, holding it applicable where "the delay experienced by [claimant] has been severe and because of [her] advanced age."[2] Id. at 503.

B

Later decisions extend the crediting-as-true rule to all cases. As stated by the court in Lester v. Chater, 81 F.3d 821, (9th Cir.1995), "[w]here the Commissioner fails to provide adequate reasons for rejecting the opinion of a treating or examining physician, we credit that opinion `as a matter of law.'" Id. at 834; Harman v. Apfel, 211 F.3d 1172, 1178 (9th Cir.2000) (same); Benecke v. Barnhart, 379 F.3d 587 (9th Cir.2007) ("Because the ALJ failed to provide legally sufficient reasons for rejecting Benecke's testimony and her treating physicians' opinions, we credit the evidence as true."). The Lester, Harman, and Benecke courts did not require any other conditions to be fulfilled before the court credited testimony as true.[3] Rather, the Harman and Benecke courts followed the bright-line rule first set forth in Lester: that testimony which was improperly rejected will be credited as true as a matter of law.[4]

C

However, at least one other panel has explicitly held that the crediting-as-true rule is not mandatory. Connett v. Barnhart, 340 F.3d 871, 876 (9th Cir.2003) ("[W]e are not convinced that the `crediting as true' doctrine is mandatory in the Ninth Circuit.") The Connett court identifies several cases in which remands were made to allow the ALJ to make specific credibility findings:

In Dodrill, for example, our court specifically remanded for the ALJ to "articulat[e] specific findings for rejecting [the claimant's] pain testimony and the testimony of lay witnesses.". In Nguyen v. Chater, where the ALJ failed to consider the claimant's testimony with regard to his asthma, our court remanded with the specific proviso that "[i]t is not our intent... to preclude the ALJ from reopening the hearing to receive additional evidence," including, presumably, evidence regarding the claimant's credibility. See also Byrnes v. Shalala, 60 F.3d 639, 642 (9th Cir.1995) ("We therefore remand this case to the ALJ for further findings evaluating the credibility of [the claimant's] subjective complaints....").

Id. (alterations in original).

The Connett court concluded that the court has "some flexibility" in applying the crediting-as-true doctrine.[5] Id. None of the cases cited by the Connett court address the crediting-as-true doctrine, however. Furthermore, the court acknowledged the existence of "seemingly compulsory language" in other opinions of this court. Id. The Connett court decided to remand without crediting-as-true "[b]ecause there are insufficient findings as to whether Connett's testimony should be credited as true." Id.

D

The Connett court argued that "the propriety of remanding for reconsideration of credibility determinations was implicitly approved by our court en banc in Bunnell v. Sullivan, 947 F.2d 341, 348 (9th Cir. 1991)." Id. However, the en banc court never discussed the crediting-as-true rule. Thus, Bunnell is not particularly helpful in defining the scope of the rule. Furthermore, the decisions in Lester, Harman, and Benecke all came years after the Bunnell decision. While the Connett court's view that crediting-as-true is discretionary may draw support from Bunnell, it is hardly compelled by the en banc court's reasoning. Accordingly, I do not believe that we can ignore binding circuit precedent because of a case which merely suggests that crediting-as-true is discretionary. Indeed, even if Lester, Harman, and Benecke are inconsistent with Bunnell, we lack the authority as a three-judge panel to overturn those decisions.

III

Until the court sitting en banc resolves this conflict and clarifies how the crediting-as-true rule is to be applied in this circuit, three-judge panels will have to continue to pick among the competing lines of precedent, in violation of Atonio and Hardesty. District court judges and administrative law judges will be equally confused. Confusion is bad enough; but when panels can choose which rules apply, there is at least the perception that we do not dispense equal justice under law. Litigants will be concerned — perhaps not without cause — that sympathetic claimants will get the benefit of the crediting-as-true rule, while less sympathetic claimants are denied the benefit of the rule because the panel decides that the rule is discretionary and should not apply. This court and the district courts from which it hears appeals will be subject to litigation that would be unnecessary if the en banc court would clarify when the crediting-as-true rule applies. Of course, any step that could reduce the amount of unnecessary litigation in this Circuit would help speed up the process for other litigants — a most worthy goal indeed.

Because we lack authority to ignore either line of crediting-as-true cases, I must respectfully dissent from the court's attempt to wade through the morass that our crediting-as-true jurisprudence has become. I would stay the proceeding pending action by an en banc court.

Notes

[1] See Lester v. Chater, 81 F.3d 821, 834 (9th Cir.1995) (inquiries are "similar[ ]"); Harman v. Apfel, 211 F.3d 1172, 1178-80 (9th Cir. 2000) (applying the crediting-as-true rule but remanding for further consideration rather than immediately awarding benefits); Benecke v. Barnhart, 379 F.3d 587, 594 (9th Cir.2004) (applying the crediting-as-true rule and only then discussing whether there were "outstanding issues that must be resolved before a determination of disability [could] be made....").

[2] The Hammock claimant was fifty-seven at the time of her hearing, and the period between the ALJ hearing and the ruling by the court was about three years. Unfortunately, it is not uncommon for three years to transpire between an ALJ decision and a decision by this court. This is as true of cases where the crediting-as-true is applied as it is of cases in which it is not applied. See Nguyen v. Chater, 100 F.3d 1462 (9th Cir.1996) (seven-year delay between first ALJ decision and Ninth Circuit decision; no crediting-as-true); Byrnes v. Shalala, 60 F.3d 639 (9th Cir.2005) (over three years' delay; no crediting-as-true); Connett v. Barnhart, 340 F.3d 871 (9th Cir. 2003) (four-year delay; no crediting-as-true) Also, it is common knowledge that disabilities disproportionately affect older individuals. Accordingly, the court's attempt to dodge the split between the mandatory and discretionary crediting-as-true rules based on age and delay is unavailing. See slip op. at 8411-12. The court's opinion identifies the policy rationales behind the crediting-as-true rule, slip op. at 8411-12, but fails to identify why those rationales apply to the case at bar more than to cases in which the rule has not been applied.

[3] In Harman, the court justifies the use of the crediting-as-true rule with the policy rationales from Varney II. Id. at 1178-79. Such rationales — that the crediting-as-true rule encourages ALJs to reach a correct decision the first time, and that the rule minimizes the wait time for deserving claimants — are present in every case the crediting-as-true rule touches. The Harman court rejected the government's attempt to distinguish Lester on the basis that there actually was evidence to dispute the physician's testimony. Id. at 1178. Likewise, because the court remanded for further proceedings rather than for an award of benefits, Harman cannot be distinguished away by limiting the crediting-as-true rule to cases where remand for benefit calculation is appropriate. Id. at 1178-80.

[4] The concurrence states that Harman is inapplicable because the court held that the claimant was not eligible for her "evidence [to] be credited and an immediate award of benefits directed" made under our test in Smolen v. Chater, 80 F.3d 1273 (9th Cir.1996). Harman, 211 F.3d at 1178 (emphasis added). The dissent overlooks that the Harman court acknowledges the Lester rule, in fact stating that the Smolen rule is "built upon" it. Id. In Harman, the evidence before the ALJ, even if believed, was not enough to

direct payment of benefits. Instead, the case was remanded for consideration of further evidence that was not before the ALJ but was presented to the Appeals Council. On remand, "the ALJ [might] then consider, the Commissioner then [might] seek to rebut and the VE then [might] answer questions with respect to the additional evidence." Id. at 1180. Although admittedly the court could be clearer, it never states that the ALJ may reconsider evidence already presented to the ALJ — evidence which should be credited as true under Lester.

[5] The Connett court does not provide guidance on how this "flexibility" is to be employed, other than by explaining that there were "insufficient findings" to justify invoking the crediting-as-true rule. Presumably this does not mean that judges of this court are supposed to make factual findings concerning technical medical matters and without the benefit of being present at a hearing.

Judge O'Scannlain's dissent from the denial of rehearing en banc in Witt v. Department of Air Force (Dec 4, 2008) [Excerpt]

O'SCANNLAIN, Circuit Judge, dissenting from the denial of rehearing en banc, joined by BEA, M. SMITH, JR., and N.R. SMITH, Circuit Judges:
This is the first case in which a federal appellate court has allowed a member of the armed services to bring a substantive due process challenge to the congressionally enacted "Don't Ask, Don't Tell" homosexual personnel policy for the military. [. . .]
It is no secret that Lawrence pursues rational basis review with unusual vigor. But if the panel wished to identify cases analogous in this respect, it might have pointed either to City of Cleburne or to Romer v. Evans, 517 U.S. 620, 116 S.Ct. 1620, 134 L.Ed.2d 855 (1996), instead of to Sell. In both of those cases, as in Lawrence, the Supreme Court struck down, under the rational basis test, laws that on inspection seemed to reflect little more than "bare animus" and "irrationality." Compare Lawrence, 539 U.S. at 577, 123 S.Ct. 2472 (accepting as controlling the view that "the fact that the governing majority in a State has traditionally viewed a particular practice as immoral is not a sufficient reason for upholding a law prohibiting the practice"), with City of Cleburne, 473 U.S. at 450, 105 S.Ct. 3249 ("[T]he short of it is that [the statute] in this case appears to us to rest on an irrational prejudice against the mentally retarded ...."), and Romer, 517 U.S. at 634, 116 S.Ct. 1620 ("[A] bare ... desire to harm a politically unpopular group [is not a] legitimate governmental interest." (internal quotation marks omitted)). The same cannot be said of the "Don't Ask, Don't Tell" policy, which Congress enacted into law after an exhaustive review of the military's needs and the pros and cons of adopting the policy. See Cook, 528 F.3d at 58-60 (reviewing Congress' deliberations regarding "Don't Ask, Don't Tell").
Such observations dramatize the panel's mistake. A basic rule of substantive due process jurisprudence is that, barring subject-area-specific standards such as those the Court fashioned in the abortion cases or in Sell, fundamental rights get strict scrutiny, and everything else gets rational basis. [. . .]

IV

No matter how strongly some of us may feel about the underlying issues in this case, the Supreme Court's precedents in substantive due process law compel not only our usual obedience, but also our self-conscious restraint. We have no mandate to follow either our reasons or our convictions down paths the Constitution and the Court have left for Congress to chart. Lawrence did not change that, nor did it provide a forum for lower courts to measure the policy decisions of Congress against the circumstances of a particular litigant. [. . .]

Judge O'Scannlain's concurrence and dissent in Alaska v. EEOC (May 1, 2009)

O'SCANNLAIN, Circuit Judge, concurring in part and dissenting in part:

Although I agree with the court's determination that the allegations of sex discrimination, if true, would establish that the State of Alaska, through its Governor's Office, violated the Constitution's Equal Protection Clause, I do not think the same can be said for the allegation of retaliatory discharge in violation of the First Amendment. In my view, that claim does not state an actual constitutional violation. We must therefore analyze the statute under which the claim is made, the Government Employee Rights Act of 1991 ("GERA"), to determine whether it is valid prophylactic legislation under section 5 of the Fourteenth Amendment. See generally City of Boerne v. Flores, 521 U.S. 507, 117 S.Ct. 2157, 138 L.Ed.2d 624 (1997). I believe GERA fails such scrutiny. With respect, I must dissent from the court's opinion insofar as it holds that Alaska's sovereign immunity does not preclude the claim of retaliatory discharge.

I

Section 5 of the Fourteenth Amendment grants Congress the "power to enforce, by appropriate legislation, the provisions of [the Fourteenth Amendment]." U.S. Const. amend. XIV, § 5. As the majority correctly explains, in order for Congress to abrogate state sovereign immunity pursuant to this enforcement power, it must "unequivocally express[] its intent to abrogate that immunity" and "act[] pursuant to a valid grant of constitutional authority." Kimel v. Fla. Bd. of Regents, 528 U.S. 62, 73, 120 S.Ct. 631, 145 L.Ed.2d 522 (2000). Although I believe it to be a close question, and Judge Ikuta's conscientious dissent to the contrary notwithstanding, it seems to me that Congress did express its intent to abrogate sovereign immunity in the GERA. With respect to the second requirement, Congress acts pursuant to a valid grant of constitutional authority if it either passes so-called "prophylactic legislation" or enacts remedies for actual violations of the Constitution. For "purportedly prophylactic legislation [to] constitute[] appropriate remedial legislation, ... `there must be a congruence and proportionality between the injury to be prevented or remedied and the means adopted to that end.'" Kimel, 528 U.S. at 81, 120 S.Ct. 631 (quoting Boerne, 521 U.S. at 520, 117 S.Ct. 2157). Actual remedial laws, as the majority points out, do not have to meet this test. See United States v. Georgia, 546 U.S. 151, 158, 126 S.Ct. 877, 163 L.Ed.2d 650 (2006) ("[N]o one doubts that § 5 grants

Congress the power to enforce the provisions of the Amendment by creating private remedies against the States for actual violations of those provisions." (internal quotations marks and alteration omitted)).

A crucial threshold question, then, is whether a given claim against a state alleges conduct that would violate the Fourteenth Amendment to the Constitution. The allegations of pay discrimination state straightforward violations of the Equal Protection Clause, and I join the majority's opinion on that issue in its entirety. With respect to the claim of sex discrimination stemming from Jones' sexual harassment complaint, I concur in the result but remain wary of some of the majority's reasoning. Finally, I must disagree entirely with the majority's analysis of the purported First Amendment claim of retaliatory discharge, an analysis that wrongly enlarges the constitutional implications of employment decisions at the highest levels of state government.

A

While I agree with the majority's conclusion regarding the so-called sexual harassment issue, I wish to clarify that I read the majority opinion to hold no more than that it would violate the Equal Protection Clause if a state deliberately refused to protect its female employees from sexual harassment. In other words, it is not the sexual harassment that Jones allegedly suffered, as such, that generates her constitutional claim. After all, she does not claim that the State of Alaska, through the official acts of its agents, sexually harassed her. Rather, the constitutional claim properly rests on Jones's allegation that the Governor's Office, an arm of the State, responded to her formal complaint of sexual harassment by firing her.

It is worth pausing to consider this claim carefully, for it is not the ordinary instance of unconstitutional discrimination. In most suits against a state where sexual harassment is involved, it will make more sense to characterize the claim not as one for sexual harassment "but as a claim of failure to protect against such harassment." Bohen v. City of East Chicago, 799 F.2d, 1180, 1189 (7th Cir.1986) (Posner, J., concurring). This is because, although states can pass laws or adopt policies that treat women differently in hiring, pay, or other official emoluments of employment, they do not often pass laws or adopt policies to harass women sexually. However, "[i]f a state or city deliberately refused to provide police protection for women, it would be violating the equal protection clause" regardless of whether those who harassed them were state actors. Id. at 1190. In order for such a claim to succeed, there would have to be "a policy of nonresponse to complaints of harassment, or an authoritative decision not to respond." Id. In view of these considerations, I understand the majority to hold that Alaska's "authoritative decision not to respond" to Jones' formal complaint, but to fire her instead, if that is what happened, violated the Equal Protection Clause.

The logical corollary to this holding is that sexual harassment, as such, does not ordinarily violate the Equal Protection Clause.[1] This is because discrimination can only violate equal protection if it is intentional and done by the state. Cf. Washington v. Davis, 426 U.S. 229, 238-45, 96 S.Ct. 2040, 48 L.Ed.2d 597 (1976) (holding that evidence of discriminatory intent is necessary to make out an equal protection violation assuming the government action is neutral on its face). The actions of the Governor's aide in this case would not bring liability on Alaska unless the state officially sanctioned them. As the majority recognizes, the Constitution cannot support liability against the state for constitutional torts on the agency law theory of respondeat superior. Maj. Op. at 1070.

Thus, there is a crucial limitation to the majority's statement that sexual harassment can state a violation of the Equal Protection Clause, see Maj. Op. at 1069. This possibility is limited by the bedrock constitutional principle I have discussed: sexual harassment will state a violation only where there is intentional discrimination by the state.

I dwell on this caveat in order to emphasize that, without it, we would constitutionalize the type of claim employees might bring under Title VII. Such a result would be directly contrary to Supreme Court precedent. See Davis, 426 U.S. at 239, 96 S.Ct. 2040 ("We have never held that the constitutional standard for adjudicating claims of invidious racial discrimination is identical to the standards applicable under Title VII, and we decline to do so today."). And the cases from sister circuits on which the majority relies followed the Court's guidance. As the majority opinion stated in Bohen, "the ultimate inquiry," where someone alleges sexual harassment as a violation of equal protection, "is whether the sexual harassment constitutes intentional discrimination. This differs from the inquiry under Title VII as to whether or not the sexual harassment altered the condition of the victim's employment." Bohen, 799 F.2d at 1187.

Thus, I agree with the majority that Jones' claim — that the Governor's Office fired her rather than respond to her complaint of sexual harassment — states a violation of the Equal Protection Clause. But it is not the alleged sexual harassment but rather the "authoritative decision not to respond," Bohen, 799 F.2d at 1190, that justifies such conclusion.

B

Turning now to Ward's allegation of retaliatory discharge in violation of the First Amendment, as incorporated against the states through the Fourteenth, I note that, at oral argument, counsel for Ward admitted that his client's actual, First Amendment claim under the relevant case law was a "tough" one to make out. No wonder. This case, it seems to me, is a prototypical example of an employee's attempt to "constitutionalize [an] employee grievance," a practice that the Supreme Court has explicitly discouraged. See Connick v. Myers, 461 U.S. 138, 154, 103 S.Ct. 1684, 75 L.Ed.2d 708 (1983). But it goes farther even than that, for Ward attempts to constitutionalize a political spat over her loyalty to the administration of Alaska's Governor. With respect, the majority's approval of Ward's novel theory opens up a new frontier in this area of constitutional law, which, I believe, contravenes the spirit, if not the letter, of the Supreme Court's decisions on the subject.

1

In general, "[w]hen a citizen enters government service, the citizen by necessity must accept certain limitations on his or her freedom." Garcetti v. Ceballos, 547 U.S. 410, 418, 126 S.Ct. 1951, 164 L.Ed.2d 689 (2006). This is because the "government as employer indeed has far broader powers than does the government as sovereign." Id. (quoting Waters v. Churchill, 511 U.S. 661, 671, 114 S.Ct. 1878, 128 L.Ed.2d 686 (1994) (plurality opinion)). The reason the government would violate the First Amendment at all by firing one of its employees on account of what he or she said is that employees, as citizens, "retain the prospect of constitutional protection for their contributions to the civic discourse." Id. at 422, 126 S.Ct. 1951. It is thus necessarily within that context that we apply the doctrinal test for whether a public employee has alleged a First Amendment violation for retaliatory discharge.

Such test has two parts. First, unless "the employee spoke as a citizen on a matter of public concern[,].... the employee has no First Amendment cause of action based on his or her employer's reaction to the speech." Id. at 418, 126 S.Ct. 1951. Only if the employee passes this threshold does "the possibility of a First Amendment claim arise[]." Id. (emphasis added). A court must then evaluate that possibility under the balancing test of Pickering v. Board of Education of Township High School District 205. See 391 U.S. 563, 568, 88 S.Ct. 1731, 20 L.Ed.2d 811 (1968); Garcetti, 547 U.S. at 418, 126 S.Ct. 1951.

At the threshold stage, as Garcetti illustrated, First Amendment protection attaches only to speech analogous to that which an ordinary citizen would make as part of public discourse. 547 U.S. at 423, 126 S.Ct. 1951 ("Employees who make public statements outside the course of performing their official duties retain some possibility of First Amendment protection because that is the kind of activity engaged in by citizens who do not work for the government."). The First Amendment does not give more license to government employees than ordinary citizens. This is the meaning of the Supreme Court's admonition that the First Amendment neither "invest[s] [public employees] with a right to perform their jobs however they see fit," nor "empower[s] them to constitutionalize the employee grievance." Id. at 420, 422, 126 S.Ct. 1951 (internal quotation marks omitted).[2]

2

As I read the precedents, Ward has failed to state a claim under the First Amendment for retaliatory discharge.

To state a First Amendment claim, the employee must show that he or she spoke not as an employee, but as a private citizen in public discourse. See Garcetti, 547 U.S. at 418-25, 126 S.Ct. 1951. The majority's analysis on this point addresses the requirements of "speech as a citizen" and "matter of public concern" in rather narrow terms. To be sure, they are two distinct requirements for constitutional protection. Ceballos v. Garcetti, 361 F.3d 1168, 1186-87 (9th Cir.2004) (O'Scannlain, J., specially concurring) (insisting on both the "speech as a citizen" and "matter of public concern" prongs of the threshold inquiry), overruled by Garcetti, 547 U.S. at 426, 126 S.Ct. 1951. But the idea behind the caselaw is to ensure that public employees are still able to participate in public debate, not to provide them job security while they pursue their own ends. See, e.g., Pickering, 391

U.S. at 573, 88 S.Ct. 1731 (rejecting the school's attempt to "limit[] teachers' opportunities to contribute to public debate"); see also Garcetti, 547 U.S. at 419, 126 S.Ct. 1951 ("The Court has acknowledged the importance of promoting the public's interest in receiving the well-informed views of government employees engaging in civic discussion."). We must keep our eye on the ball here, for the case before us throws something of a curve.

The typical situation requires a court to determine whether speech was primarily an internal office matter or a contribution to the public debate. See, e.g., Connick, 461 U.S. at 140, 103 S.Ct. 1684 (considering "whether the First and Fourteenth Amendments prevent the discharge of a state employee for circulating a questionnaire concerning internal office affairs"). But this case involves policymaking staff in the office of the chief executive of the State of Alaska. Thus, the internal office politics are also the politics of the state. In this context, it contravenes the spirit of Garcetti and its predecessors to hold that, even though Ward criticized the Governor on a subject of public interest the Governor cannot constitutionally fire her for disloyalty.

The majority spends time illustrating that Ward's speech was not part of her official duties, which is surely correct. Garcetti does not squarely dictate the result in this case for that reason. Maj. Op. at ____-____; Garcetti, 547 U.S. at 421, 126 S.Ct. 1951 ("We hold that when public employees make statements pursuant to their official duties, the employees are not speaking as citizens for First Amendment purposes."). But the controlling ratio decidendi of Garcetti casts a longer shadow. The importance of the official nature of the speech in Garcetti lay in the distinction between speech that ordinary citizens make and speech that only occurs because of employment with the government. "Restricting speech that owes its existence to a public employee's professional responsibilities," the Court insisted, "does not infringe any liberties the employee might have enjoyed as a private citizen." Id. at 421-22. Garcetti explicitly contrasted such speech with "the expressions made by the speaker in Pickering, whose letter to the newspaper had no official significance and bore similarities to letters submitted by numerous citizens every day." Id. at 422, 126 S.Ct. 1951.

Thus, although Ward's press conference was not strictly part of her official duties, her importance in the Governor's administration necessarily means that more of her conduct came within the legitimate purview of her employer. The Supreme Court has emphasized the need to "afford[] governmental employers sufficient discretion to manage their operations." Id. at 422, 126 S.Ct. 1951. Nowhere is such discretion more important than at the highest levels of state government. At those levels, loyalty to the administration on matters of public concern is in a sense the price of employment. Ward chose to go public with one side of an internal struggle among the Governor's policy aides. The Governor's Office considered this to be disloyal and fired her. Especially in the context of a governor's office, this is a classic employment decision of the kind the Supreme Court has warned should not "bec[o]me a constitutional matter." Connick, 461 U.S. at 143, 103 S.Ct. 1684. We must remember that "a federal court is not the appropriate forum in which to review the wisdom of [such] a personnel decision." Id. at 147, 103 S.Ct. 1684.

It helps to consider analogies. Take the example of an aide to a governor who criticizes publically the governor's tax policy in a press conference. Such speech would be an undoubted contribution to the public debate, but would it violate the First Amendment if the governor fired the aide for disloyalty? I think not, and I imagine the majority would agree. And if the aide criticized not tax policy but the governor's policy regarding internal complaints of sexual harassment? The result is the same, even though the subject of the criticism is a potentially illegal practice (ignoring sexual assault on female employees).[3]

Such a result would only seem harsh from the myopic perspective of the conviction that the Constitution must provide remedies for all harms. We can, and should, take allegations like those Ward made very seriously without invoking the First Amendment. "As the [Supreme] Court noted in Connick, public employers should, `as a matter of good judgment,' be `receptive to constructive criticism offered by their employees.'" Garcetti, 547 U.S. at 425, 126 S.Ct. 1951 (quoting Connick, 461 U.S. at 149, 103 S.Ct. 1684). Indeed, "[t]he dictates of sound judgment are reinforced by the powerful network of legislative enactments — such as whistle-blower protection laws and labor codes — available to those who seek to expose wrongdoing."[4] Id. In the appropriate circumstances, we must rely on such customary and legislative protections if we are to avoid "constitutionaliz[ing] the employee grievance." Connick, 461 U.S. at 154, 103 S.Ct. 1684.

II

My conclusion that the allegation of retaliatory discharge does not state an actual violation of the Constitution compels me to address, insofar as the claim is remediable under the GERA, whether that statute constitutes valid "congruent and proportional" legislation under the Supreme Court's Boerne test.

A

Congress' power to enforce the Fourteenth Amendment under section 5 does not allow it "to decree the substance of the Fourteenth Amendment's restrictions on the States. Legislation which alters the meaning of the [Fourteenth Amendment] cannot be said to be enforcing [it]." Boerne, 521 U.S. at 519, 117 S.Ct. 2157. Boerne requires that for "purportedly prophylactic legislation [to] constitute[] appropriate remedial legislation, ... `there must be a congruence and proportionality between the injury to be prevented or remedied and the means adopted to that end.'" Kimel, 528 U.S. at 81, 120 S.Ct. 631 (quoting Boerne, 521 U.S. at 520, 117 S.Ct. 2157).

Because prophylactic legislation prohibits or regulates constitutional conduct that supposedly leads to unconstitutional conduct, Congress must explain its belief that regulating the former will help to prevent the latter. See Boerne, 521 U.S. at 519-20, 117 S.Ct. 2157. Such requirement responds to the Supreme Court's concern in Boerne that Congress not "decree the substance of the Fourteenth Amendment's restrictions" under the guise of enforcing them. Id. at 519, 117 S.Ct. 2157. The Supreme Court has outlined a three-step test for determining congruence and proportionality. "The first step ... is to identify with some precision the scope of the constitutional right at issue." Bd. of Trustees of the Univ. of Ala. v. Garrett, 531 U.S. 356, 365, 121 S.Ct. 955, 148 L.Ed.2d 866 (2001). Next, Congress must have identified a history and "pattern of constitutional violations" by the states. Fla. Prepaid Postsecondary Educ. Expense Bd. v. Coll. Sav. Bank, 527 U.S. 627, 639-640, 119 S.Ct. 2199, 144 L.Ed.2d 575 (1999); see also Garrett, 531 U.S. at 368, 121 S.Ct. 955. Finally, legislation must be in fact "congruent and proportional," in light of Congress' factual findings, "to the targeted violation." Garrett, 531 U.S. at 374, 121 S.Ct. 955. It seems to me that the crucial step in this case is the second one — the requirement that Congress identify a pattern of constitutional violations. One way courts pursue this inquiry is "by examining the legislative record containing the reasons for Congress' action." Kimel, 528 U.S. at 88, 120 S.Ct. 631.

The parties do not dispute that, when Congress enacted the GERA in 1991, it made no findings regarding discrimination against state employees at the policy-making level. When it passed the Equal Employment Opportunity Act in 1972, however, Congress did make extensive factual findings. H.R.Rep. No. 92-238, at 19 (1971), reprinted in 1972 U.S.C.C.A.N. 2137, 2152 (noting the existence of "widespread discrimination against minorities... in State and local government employment, and that the existence of this discrimination is perpetuated by the presence of both institutional and overt discriminatory practices"). The EEOC would like us to consider the latter findings in evaluating the former law for purposes of the Boerne test.

The EEOC's theory is that, with the GERA, Congress merely finished the job it started in 1972 when it amended Title VII to cover the States as employers. It cites extensive language from Supreme Court opinions and congressional records to show that gender discrimination persisted in state government as of 1991 the way it had existed in 1972.[5] But all of the passages the EEOC quotes speak of gender discrimination in general, not at the policymaking levels of state government to which the GERA applies. The EEOC argues that it need not present such particularized congressional findings. It cites for support Justice Powell's concurrence in Fullilove v. Klutznick, 448 U.S. 448, 100 S.Ct. 2758, 65 L.Ed.2d 902 (1980). But the question is what the more recent Boerne requires. A concurrence published seventeen years before Boerne is not probative of that question.

Furthermore, even if one could consider the 1972 findings, they do not pertain to the policymaking staff covered by the GERA. In 1972, Congress did find widespread discrimination in state and local government and it acted to prevent it, but it specifically excluded personal and policymaking staff. That is part of the background against which Congress legislated when it enacted the GERA. If one wants to impute congressional intent to that exclusion, the only responsible imputation is that Congress did not believe a remedy was necessary with respect to policy-making employees. That is to say, if there is any reason to believe what one reads in committee reports, the official position of the relevant House Committee belies the EEOC's position. In a section of the committee report entitled "Need for the Bill," it declared that the "time ha[d] come to bring an end to job discrimination once and for all," and that "[i]t is essential that... effective enforcement procedures be provided the [EEOC] to strengthen its efforts to reduce discrimination in employment." H.R.Rep. No. 92-238, at 2139-41. It would follow logically from this language that whatever levels of state and local employment Congress exempted from the 1972 Act's reach did not suffer from the job discrimination that so concerned the House Committee.

The background against which Congress enacted the GERA, therefore, does not illustrate that Congress had already found a pattern of unconstitutional discrimination at the policymaking level of state and local employment. Instead it shows that Congress had excluded employees at that level from protection. Because Congress explicitly excluded policymaking employees from Title VII's reach in 1972, I do not believe this court would be justified in using the findings Congress made in doing so to support its decision in 1991 to repeal that very exclusion.

Without the 1972 findings, the EEOC can point to no evidence that Congress identified, as the Supreme Court has required it to do, a history and pattern of violations of the constitutional rights of the states against high-level personal and policy-making employees. This compels me to conclude that the GERA is not "congruent and proportional" legislation within the meaning of Boerne. It therefore cannot constitute a valid abrogation of state sovereign immunity.

Neither the EEOC nor the federal courts are empowered to entertain the non-constitutional claim against the State of Alaska, which, as I have explained, is precisely Ward's retaliation claim. I must respectfully dissent from the majority's conclusion to the contrary.

Notes

[1] I hasten to add that the conduct Jones complained of is outrageous and unsavory; I do not mean to condone it in any way. At the same time, we should acknowledge that the State of Alaska has not conceded the truth of the allegations either of Jones or of Ward. Indeed, there seems to be vigorous dispute about the facts underlying their dismissal from the Governor's Office.

[2] We have also recently clarified that, at the second, balancing stage, "the plaintiff bears the burden of showing the state took adverse employment action and that the speech was a substantial or motivating factor in the adverse action." Eng v. Cooley, 552 F.3d 1062, 1071 (9th Cir.2009) (internal quotation marks and alterations omitted). If the plaintiff carries that burden, then the government must show that, under Pickering, its "legitimate administrative interests outweigh the employee's First Amendment rights" or that it would have made the same decision without the employee's protected speech. Id. at 1071-72 (internal quotation marks omitted). In my view, for the plaintiff to state a First Amendment claim, he or she must meet at least the initial burden under Eng.

[3] The majority conflates the supposed policy of ignoring illegality with the illegality itself, quoting back to me my observation that states sometimes adopt policies to treat women differently but not usually to harass them sexually. Maj. Op. 1070 n. 7. This

only confuses the issue. My point is that the scope of an employee grievance, as opposed to a contribution as a citizen to public debate, necessarily widens the higher one climbs up the ladder of government.

[4] Alaska, in fact, has such a whistle-blower protection law. Alaska Stat. 39.90.100-.150.

[5] There is no attempt to show congressional concern for the violation of First Amendment rights per se. The EEOC's and Intervenor Ward's argument seems to be that preventing retaliatory discharges against state employees for complaining about sexual harassment is part of Congress' prophylactic remedy for unconstitutional gender discrimination. It therefore stands or falls with the legitimacy of prophylactic remedies for employment discrimination.

Judge O'Scannlain's concurrence in Desai v. Deutsche Bank Securities Ltd. (July 29, 2009)

O'SCANNLAIN, Circuit Judge, concurring:

My colleagues and I agree that the district court did not err in rejecting the integrity of the market presumption that Investors proffered in this case. I therefore join the court's opinion affirming the district court's refusal to certify the class. Unfortunately, however, we are left to conclude abruptly with a declaration of the result, for we cannot agree on the correct approach. I believe that, because the validity of a presumption of reliance in securities class actions is a matter of law and because errors of law are per se abuses of discretion, we must explicitly decide whether Investors are entitled to this novel presumption as a matter of law. I write separately to explain my view.

I

We review class certification decisions for abuse of discretion, but errors of law constitute per se abuses of discretion. Cooter & Gell v. Hartmarx Corp., 496 U.S. 384, 405, 110 S.Ct. 2447, 110 L.Ed.2d 359 (1990) ("A district court would necessarily abuse its discretion if it based its ruling on an erroneous view of the law."). Here, Investors squarely raised and the district court forthrightly rejected a new legal theory—the "integrity of the market" presumption. This presumption, as described by Investors, would apply in this case. Therefore, if the presumption is legally valid, then Investors are entitled to plead it. If not, then they are not.

Consider the situation in reverse: suppose the district court had adopted the integrity of the market presumption and granted class certification. In such case, I believe we would be bound to reverse even if existing law did not squarely foreclose such a theory because we would have to decide whether the presumption was legally valid. The same is true here. The district court held that there is no integrity of the market presumption as a matter of law. We must decide whether that legal conclusion was correct.

In short, to reach the integrity of the market presumption on its merits is not a matter of choice. We must decide its validity. It was raised in the district court and addressed by the district court; it was raised and fully briefed on appeal. Where the district court "based its ruling on an erroneous view of the law," then it "necessarily abuse[d] its discretion." Id. I am at a loss as to how this case compels variation from this clear rule.

II

As explained, I would address the integrity of the market presumption on the merits. In my view, the presumption is legally unsupported and logically inadvisable. As presented to us, the integrity of the market presumption works in the following way. The average investor in securities typically relies on the "integrity of the market," that is, that no one has destroyed its efficiency by manipulation. This consideration justifies a presumption of reliance, according to Investors, when manipulation allegedly destroys the efficiency of the market, and with it the reliability of the market's price.

A

First, the cases from which Investors purport to have derived their theory do not support it.

Investors initially point to Gurary v. Winehouse, 190 F.3d 37 (2d Cir.1999), for support. But Gurary did not recognize any new presumption of reliance. It merely held that, to make out a manipulation claim, a plaintiff must show that he did not know "that the price was affected by the alleged manipulation." Id. at 45. To be sure, the Second Circuit also noted that "[t]he gravamen of manipulation is deception of investors into believing that prices at which they purchase and sell securities are determined by the natural interplay of supply and demand, not rigged by manipulators." Id. But this language merely summarizes the essence of a manipulation claim. It does not purport to go beyond the fraud on the market presumption.

Sticking with the Second Circuit, Investors also cite Schlick v. Penn-Dixie Cement Corp., 507 F.2d 374 (2d Cir.1974). Such case does indeed offer support, for the opinion held that "proof of transaction causation is unnecessary by virtue of the allegations as to the effectuation of a scheme to defraud which includes market manipulation." Id. at 381. This seems to say that there is no need to prove reliance to make out a manipulative conduct claim. But even Investors do not take that position. In any event, the Second Circuit has reversed itself on this point. See, e.g., ATSI Commc'ns, 493 F.3d at 101 (listing reliance as an element in a manipulative conduct claim). And In re Blech Securities Litigation, 961 F.Supp. 569 (S.D.N.Y. 1997), another case on which they rely, reiterated the reliance element, even to make out a claim for manipulative conduct. See id. at 585-86. Furthermore, Blech applied the fraud on the market presumption without recognizing any other presumption unique to manipulative conduct cases. Id.

Shores v. Sklar, 647 F.2d 462 (5th Cir. 1981) (en banc), does not help Investors either. In Shores, the Fifth Circuit concluded that, although the plaintiff could not show reliance on the specific misrepresentation, he could nonetheless show reliance because he was entitled to assume that an issued security was legally issued. See id. at 468. As the Fifth Circuit later described the case, Shores embraced a presumption of reliance where alleged fraud created the market for a security, insofar as "actors who introduced an otherwise unmarketable security into the market by means of fraud are deemed guilty of manipulation, and a plaintiff can plead that he relied on the integrity of the market rather than on individual fraudulent disclosures." Regents of Univ. of Calif. v. Credit Suisse First Boston (USA), Inc., 482 F.3d 372, 391 (5th Cir.2007).

This "fraud created the market" theory, even were it viable, would not help Investors. They do not allege that the manipulative scheme of Deutsche Bank and others created the market for GENI's stock. GENI's shares traded publicly before the date the scheme allegedly began. Furthermore, they did not purchase the unregistered shares that the GENI insiders had lent down the chain of broker-dealers. Thus the theory of Shores would not apply to this case.

B

Beside being virtually unknown, an integrity of the market presumption is inadvisable because it would swallow the reliance requirement. Most investors do, I think it fair to say, assume that the markets are not corrupt. Cf. Basic, 485 U.S. at 246-47, 108 S.Ct. 978 ("It has been noted that `it is hard to imagine that there ever is a buyer or seller who does not rely on market integrity. Who would knowingly roll the dice in a crooked crap game?'" (quoting Schlanger v. Four-Phase Sys. Inc., 555 F.Supp. 535, 538 (S.D.N.Y. 1982))). But if that hypothesis sufficed to presume reliance, then no plaintiff would ever have to prove reliance. That might not worry me if this novel presumption made "the requisite causal connection," which lies at the heart of the reliance element, "between a defendant's [bad act] and a plaintiff's injury." Basic, 485 U.S. at 243, 108 S.Ct. 978. But Investors' integrity of the market presumption only connects the buyer or seller of securities with the market price; it does not connect the price to the defendant's manipulative conduct. Unlike the fraud on the market presumption, this theory would permit a presumption of reliance no matter how unlikely it is that the market price in question would actually reflect the alleged manipulation.

The integrity of the market presumption that Investors proffer, then, would prove too much while doing too little. Prove too much, because it would obviate the need for plaintiffs in manipulative conduct cases to prove reliance; do too little, because it does not complete the causal connection between a plaintiff's transaction in securities and a defendant's manipulation. Therefore, I would reject the invitation to recognize this new presumption of reliance.

C

Investors make a final argument for a new presumption of reliance that deserves separate discussion. They contend that allegations of manipulative conduct warrant distinctive treatment because the fraud on the market presumption does not apply to them.

It is true that the fraud on the market theory is normally phrased in terms of misrepresentations or omissions. See, e.g., id. (explaining that the fraud on the market theory "provides the requisite causal connection between a defendant's misrepresentation and a plaintiff's injury." (emphasis added)); No. 84 Employer-Teamster Joint Council

Pension Trust Fund, 320 F.3d at 934 n. 12 (noting that the theory creates a "rebuttable presumption of investor reliance based on the theory that investors presumably rely on the market price, which typically reflects the misrepresentation or omission" (emphasis added)).

But these statements do not foreclose the application of the fraud on the market theory to manipulative conduct cases. They simply reflect the relative rarity of such cases. Indeed, courts have applied the fraud on the market theory in the context of manipulation. Peil, 806 F.2d at 1162-63 (concluding that the fraud on the market theory pertains to claims brought under clauses (a), (b), and (c) of Rule 10b-5); Scone Invs., L.P. v. Am. Third Market Corp., No. 97 CIV. 3802, 1998 WL 205338, *5 (S.D.N.Y. Apr.28, 1998) ("The fraud on the market theory is especially applicable in the market manipulation context. Market manipulation schemes which are intended to distort the price of a security, if successful, necessarily defraud investors who purchase the security in reliance on the market's integrity.").

As a matter of logic, too, the fraud on the market theory is not limited to cases of misrepresentation and omission. Recall that it is "based on the hypothesis that, in an open and developed securities market, the price of a company's stock is determined by the available material information regarding the company and its business." Basic, 485 U.S. at 241, 108 S.Ct. 978 (internal quotation marks omitted). The artificial market activity that constitutes manipulative conduct, no less than misrepresentations of, or misleadingly incomplete statements about, a company's earnings, is also information that the market price either does or does not reflect. The fraud on the market theory is one way courts can presume such a reflection, but Investors have chosen not to rely on it.[1]

They have also chosen not to argue for direct reliance. In other words, Investors have abandoned two well-worn paths to relief. There is no reason, then, to blaze a third, for the law does not let market manipulators off the hook.

III

In summary, it seems to me we must reach the validity of the integrity of the market presumption, for it is at the heart of the legal error Investors claim the district court made in the class certification ruling. I therefore concur in the court's opinion so far as it goes, but write separately to address the legal issue that, in my view, drives this appeal. Doing so, I would conclude that the integrity of the market presumption Investors proffered is not legally valid, so the district court did not err in refusing to recognize it. Thus, where a putative class alleges manipulative conduct as a violation of § 10(b), it must either prove reliance directly or invoke its presumption pursuant to the fraud on the market theory.

Notes

[1] I recognize the possibility that certain allegations of manipulative conduct might change the application of the fraud on the market theory. This is because the plaintiff in manipulation cases often alleges that a defendant directly manipulated the

price. Certainly, a plaintiff must still show that the market in question could absorb into the price the misinformation communicated by the alleged manipulation. But need a plaintiff show the same type of proof of an efficient market in a manipulation case as is required in a misrepresentation case? Although I note the doctrinal wrinkle, this is a question I would agree we actually do not need to reach, because Investors forsook the fraud on the market theory.

Judge O'Scannlain's dissent in Indergard v. Georgia-Pacific (Sept 28, 2009)

O'SCANNLAIN, Circuit Judge, dissenting:

The essential distinction between a medical examination and a physical fitness or agility test, for the purposes of the Americans with Disabilities Act ("ADA"), is that the former is designed to reveal disability, while the latter is designed to determine whether an employee can perform her job. I cannot conclude that the evaluation Kris Indergard underwent on her return to work at Georgia-Pacific was a medical examination under 42 U.S.C. § 12112(d)(4)(A), for it was not designed to reveal disability. Furthermore, even assuming that there were any "medical" aspects of the physical capacity evaluation ("PCE"), they were merely incidental to the physical agility aspects and did not in any way cause the harms that Indergard alleges. Therefore, I must respectfully dissent.

I

Indergard characterizes the PCE as "two days of testing, poking, palpating, and examining." However, over the course of those two days, no blood was drawn, no urine samples collected, no labwork performed, and no x-rays or scans taken. No doctor or nurse ever examined, diagnosed, or treated her. Instead, she went to an occupational therapy facility and performed various physical tasks designed to determine whether she could safely perform the duties of her old job. Such testing was unquestionably advisable given her own physician's permanent restrictions on climbing, kneeling, squatting, crawling, and lifting over thirty pounds. A common-sense reading of the term "medical examination" would not include this PCE.

Unfortunately, common sense plays no role in our ADA jurisprudence. Instead, the EEOC has muddied the jurisprudential waters by issuing "guidances" that appear to read the word "medical" right out of the statute. For example, the interpretive appendix to 29 C.F.R. § 1630.14(a) first states that "[p]hysical agility tests are not medical examinations" but then adds that "[i]f such tests screen out or tend to screen out individuals with disabilities, the employer would have to demonstrate that the test is job-related and consistent with business necessity...." Apparently, having a tendency to screen out disabled individuals automatically converts a physical agility test into a medical examination subject to the ADA. Given that physical agility tests by their very nature tend to screen out people with certain disabilities, I see no way for employers to conduct such tests without inviting ADA lawsuits from those who fail them.

In addition, an EEOC enforcement guidance defines a medical examination as "a procedure or test that seeks information about an individual's physical or mental impairments or health." EEOC Enforcement Guidance on Disability-Related Inquiries and Medical Evaluations, available at http://eeoc.gov/policy/docs/guidance-inquiries.html [hereinafter Enforcement Guidance]. Under this broad definition, any return-to-work test would necessarily qualify as a medical examination because it seeks to determine whether the employee is fit enough to resume her duties. Employers seeking to avoid ADA lawsuits would have to allow injured workers to return to the job without being able to verify their fitness for duty, creating the potential for re-injury.

The Enforcement Guidance also declares physical agility tests not to be medical examinations "as long as these tests do not include examinations that could be considered medical (e.g., measuring heart rate or blood pressure)." Hence, a single pulse measurement taken over the course of a two-day physical agility test would be sufficient to convert such test into a medical examination. If an employee taking a physical agility test shows obvious distress, the examiner would not be able to take her pulse or blood pressure as a precautionary measure without implicating the ADA. Employers seeking to ensure returning workers' safety must therefore navigate the precarious straits between the Scylla of ADA liability and the Charybdis of a negligence lawsuit. Fearing either form of liability, employers may very well decline to conduct any form of testing, thereby increasing the risk of returning worker injury.

The majority uncritically accepts these agency pronouncements as gospel, even though we owe them no deference when they subvert the plain text of the statute. See Gen. Dynamics Land Sys., Inc. v. Cline, 540 U.S. 581, 600, 124 S.Ct. 1236, 157 L.Ed.2d 1094 (2004). I decline to read the statute in such a way as to render a term entirely meaningless.

II

Turning to the PCE at issue in this case, I am not persuaded that it can be considered a medical examination merely by virtue of the "single factors" that the majority lists: range-of-motion and muscle strength tests, pulse measurement after a treadmill test, and observations about Indergard's breathing after the treadmill test. It is important to remember that the PCE was a two-day examination comprising numerous tests. While one or two of these measurements may arguably have been medical in nature, these were at most de minimis components that were incidental to the physical tasks that formed the bulk of the PCE.

Furthermore, application of the seven-factor test also does not convince me that the PCE as a whole was a medical examination. In particular, I disagree with the majority's conclusions regarding factors three, five, and seven. Factor three asks "whether the test is designed to reveal an impairment in physical or mental health." Enforcement Guidance. According to the majority, "although the PCE was ostensibly intended to determine whether Indergard could return to work, the broad reach of the test was capable of revealing impairments of her physical and mental health." Maj. op. at 1055. Here the majority appears to confuse intent with effect. Because the majority believes that the PCE could reveal an impairment, it assumes that Georgia-Pacific intended for it to do so. I do not read factor three so broadly. With respect to factors five and seven, any measurement of physiological response and use of medical equipment were de minimis in the overall context of the two-day PCE. On balance, the PCE looks overwhelmingly more like a physical agility test than a medical examination.

III

In my view, the PCE cannot be considered a single examination but rather a battery of individual tests. By its viewing of the PCE, the majority allows Indergard to proceed with her suit even though she has shown no injury resulting from the allegedly medical tests. However, it was unquestionably the lifting task that scuttled Indergard's return to work, not her pulse rate after the treadmill test or her knee flexion. Because she has suffered no injury from the parts of the test that allegedly were medical examinations, she cannot maintain a claim for a violation of § 12112(d).

Our sister circuits have agreed that a plaintiff seeking relief under 42 U.S.C. § 12112(d) must be able to show "something more than a mere violation of that provision. There must be some cognizable injury in fact of which the violation is a legal and proximate cause for damages to arise from a single violation." Armstrong v. Turner Indus., Inc., 141 F.3d 554, 562 (5th Cir.1998); see also Tice v. Centre Area Transp. Auth., 247 F.3d 506, 519 (3d Cir.2001); Cossette v. Minnesota Power & Light, 188 F.3d 964, 970 (8th Cir.1999); Griffin v. Steeltek, Inc., 160 F.3d 591, 594-95 (10th Cir.1998). In other words, "a technical violation" is not enough. Tice, 247 F.3d at 520. Here, even assuming that Georgia-Pacific technically violated § 12112(d)(4)(A) by measuring Indergard's pulse and range of motion, she has made no showing that such measurements have proximately caused her to lose her job. Therefore, any such measurements "presents no 'injury' capable of remedy, and thus affords no basis for suit." Id. at 519.

Armstrong is instructive because it presents a scenario analogous to this case, albeit in the context of preemployment medical inquiries.[1] Armstrong had applied for a position as a pipefitter and was asked questions in his application about prior injuries, his medical history, and worker's compensation claims. The questionnaire also asked whether he had "any injury or condition not mentioned on this form," and Armstrong answered "no." A background check later revealed that Armstrong had previously reported "possible asbestos exposure," and he was "rejected due to the provision of incorrect and/or incomplete information." 141 F.3d at 556-57. Because the failure to hire had not resulted directly from the prohibited medical inquiries, the court held that Armstrong lacked standing to sue for damages and injunctive relief under § 12112(d)(2)(A). Id. at 562-63. The court noted that the ADA was not intended to protect employees from adverse employment actions "incident to a prohibited section 12112(d)(2)(A) inquiry." Id. at 560 n. 15.

Similarly, Indergard's termination was merely incident to an alleged technical violation of § 12112(d)(4)(A). Had Georgia-Pacific administered only the treadmill exercise and range-of-motion tests, she would not have a cause of action under the ADA even assuming that they are medical examinations because she suffered no adverse employment action from these tests. Conversely, had Georgia-Pacific administered the lifting task alone, she also would not have a cause of action because the lifting task is not a medical examination. Only by yoking these tests together and attributing an injury from a permissible physical agility task to an allegedly improper medical examination can Indergard manufacture an ADA violation.

IV

Because the majority renders the term "medical" meaningless and allows a plaintiff to continue her $250,000 suit on the basis of a pulse measurement that caused her no harm, I respectfully dissent.

Notes

[1] Preemployment medical inquiries and examinations fall under 42 U.S.C. § 12112(d)(2) of the ADA. Although the majority attempts to distinguish Armstrong on this basis, see Maj. op. at 1057-58 n. 3, the same analysis applies to all of the medical inquiry and examination provisions under 42 U.S.C. § 12112(d). See Tice, 247 F.3d at 519 ("Other courts of appeal have addressed the question whether a plaintiff has a cause of action for a violation of § 12112(d) without demonstrating the existence of an injury-in-fact.... All have concluded that a violation of § 12112(d), without a showing, presents no `injury' capable of remedy, and thus affords no basis for suit.").

Judge O'Scannlain's dissent from the denial of rehearing en banc in Winn v. Arizona Christian School Tuition Org. (Oct 21, 2009) [Notes omitted]

O'SCANNLAIN, Circuit Judge, dissenting from the denial of rehearing en banc, joined by KOZINSKI, Chief Judge, KLEINFELD, GOULD, TALLMAN, BYBEE, BEA, and N.R. SMITH, Circuit Judges:

This case involves an Establishment Clause challenge to an Arizona educational tax credit program that provides scholarships to students wishing to attend private schools. This case is more notable, however, for what it does not involve: state action advancing religion. The government does not direct any aid to any religious school. Nor does the government encourage, promote, or otherwise incentivize private actors to direct aid to religious schools. Rather, "state aid reaches religious schools solely as a result of the numerous independent decisions of private individuals." Zelman v. Simmons-Harris, 536 U.S. 639, 655, 122 S.Ct. 2460, 153 L.Ed.2d 604 (2002).

Unable to find any forbidden state action, the district court correctly dismissed the case on the pleadings. Sadly, our three-judge panel reversed. See Winn v. Ariz. Christian Sch. Tuition Org., 562 F.3d 1002 (9th Cir.2009). Because a program of scrupulous "governmental neutrality between religion and religion, and between religion and nonreligion," Epperson v. Arkansas, 393 U.S. 97, 104, 89 S.Ct. 266, 21 L.Ed.2d 228 (1968), cannot violate the Establishment Clause, I respectfully dissent from our full court's regrettable denial of rehearing en banc.

I dissent not only because Winn cannot be squared with the Supreme Court's mandate in Zelman, but also because the panel's holding casts a pall over comparable educational tax-credit schemes in states across the nation and could derail legislative efforts in four states within our circuit to create similar programs.[1] In short, the panel's conclusion invalidates an increasingly popular method for providing school choice, jeopardizing the educational opportunities of hundreds of thousands of children nationwide.[2]

I

Arizona law ("Section 1089") allows individuals voluntarily to contribute money to private, nonprofit corporations known as "student tuition organizations" ("STOs"). Ariz.Rev.Stat. Ann. § 43-1089(A). Anyone can form an STO, and there are no constraints on a taxpayer's ability to donate to an STO of his choice. Should a taxpayer elect to direct funds to an STO, that contribution is refunded via tax credits of up to $500 for individual taxpayers and up to $1000 for married couples filing jointly.[3] Id.

STOs use these funds to provide scholarships and tuition grants to students attending schools within the state. Id. § 43-1089(G).

While essentially any private school is statutorily eligible to receive scholarship monies,[4] STOs may choose which institutions they will support, so long as they provide funds to more than one school. Id.[5] Parents then decide which private school they would like their child to attend, and apply for scholarships from appropriate STOs.

In sum, the state's involvement stops with authorizing the creation of STOs and making tax credits available. After that, the government takes its hands off the wheel. Anyone can create an STO. Anyone can contribute to any STO and receive identical tax benefits. Anyone can apply for any scholarship offered by any STO.

Shortly after Section 1089's enactment, the Arizona Supreme Court held that the statute, on its face, did not violate the Establishment Clause. See Kotterman v. Killian, 193 Ariz. 273, 972 P.2d 606 (1999). Taxpayer plaintiffs then brought this federal action, which was dismissed by the district court under the Tax Injunction Act. See Winn v. Killian, 307 F.3d 1011, 1013 (9th Cir.2002). After the suit was reinstated, see id. at 1020; see also Hibbs v. Winn, 542 U.S. 88, 124 S.Ct. 2276, 159 L.Ed.2d 172 (2004) (affirming our opinion reversing its dismissal), the district court again dismissed the action, this time on federal constitutional grounds, see Winn v. Hibbs, 361 F.Supp.2d 1117 (D.Ariz.2005).

Plaintiffs appealed. They allege (and no one disputes) that in practice, some STOs make their scholarships available only to students willing to attend religiously affiliated schools. Winn, 562 F.3d at 1006. While the majority of STOs do not so limit their scholarships,[6] plaintiffs maintain that those that do receive the overwhelming majority of taxpayer contributions. See id. Consequently, they assert that the pool of available scholarship money is diminished for parents wishing to send their children to secular schools. See id. Plaintiffs contend that this disparity means Section 1089, as applied, impermissibly favors religion over nonreligion. See id.

The three-judge panel agreed and reversed the district court's dismissal, holding that "if plaintiffs' allegations are accepted as true, Section 1089 violates the Establishment Clause." See id. at 1013. Concluding that the nature of the tax credit made taxpayer contributions tantamount to government funds, the panel found that Section 1089 potentially violated both the purpose and effects prongs of Lemon v. Kurtzman, 403 U.S. 602, 603, 91 S.Ct. 2105, 29 L.Ed.2d 745 (1971). See id. at 1011-23. The fact that taxpayers directed the majority of available funds to religious schools, the panel reasoned, deprived parents of a "genuinely independent and private choice[]" to send their children to secular private schools. Id. at 1013 (internal quotation marks and citation omitted). Accordingly, Section 1089 was not a "neutral program of private choice and a reasonable observer could ... conclude that the aid reaching religious schools ... carries with it the imprimatur of government endorsement." Id. at 1013-14 (internal quotation marks and citation omitted).[7]

II

I have no bone to pick with the manner in which the panel frames the basic constitutional inquiry. We all understand that the Establishment Clause "prevents a State from enacting laws that have the `purpose' or `effect' of advancing or inhibiting religion." Zelman, 536 U.S. at 648-49, 122 S.Ct. 2460. More often than not, the Court determines whether these commands have been violated by asking whether a "reasonable observer," who is "aware of the history and context underlying a challenged program," would conclude that the state has "endorsed" religion. Id. at 655, 122 S.Ct. 2460 (internal quotation marks and citation omitted).

The panel's heavy emphasis on Zelman is also warranted. In that case, the Supreme Court upheld an Ohio school voucher program that provided tuition aid to Cleveland families on the basis of need. Id. at 644-45, 122 S.Ct. 2460. The vouchers were distributed directly to parents, who could choose to use the scholarship money at any participating private, community, magnet, or public school. Id. at 645-46, 122 S.Ct. 2460. The Court ruled that a "neutral program of private choice, where state aid reaches religious schools solely as a result of the numerous independent decisions of private individuals" does not violate the Establishment Clause. Id. at 655, 122 S.Ct. 2460.

It is in the application of these standards, however, that the three-judge panel lost the forest for the trees. In doing so, it reached a result that simply cannot be reconciled with Zelman.[8]

III

The panel is correct that a law may not have the "forbidden `effect' of advancing... religion." Id. at 649, 122 S.Ct. 2460. What the panel seems to neglect, however, is that "[f]or a law to have forbidden `effects' under Lemon, it must be fair to say that the government itself has advanced religion through its own activities and influence." Corp. of Presiding Bishop of Church of Jesus Christ of Latter-Day Saints v. Amos, 483 U.S. 327, 337, 107 S.Ct. 2862, 97 L.Ed.2d 273 (1987).[9]

I must confess that I am at a loss to understand how a reasonable observer — one fully informed about all matters related to the program — could conclude that the "government itself" has endorsed religion in this case. Multiple layers of private, individual choice separate the state from any religious entanglement: the "government itself" is at least four times removed from any aid to religious organizations. First, an individual or group of individuals must choose to create an STO. Second, that STO must then decide to provide scholarships to religious schools. Third, taxpayers have to contribute to the STO in question. Finally, parents need to apply for a scholarship for their student. In every respect and at every level, these are purely private choices, not government policy. Under such circumstances, "government cannot, or at least cannot easily, grant special favors that might lead to a religious establishment." Zelman, 536 U.S. at 652-53, 122 S.Ct. 2460 (internal quotation marks and citation omitted). Only after passing through choice piled upon choice do government funds reach religious organizations. That is not government endorsement: that is government nonchalance.[10]

To illustrate my point, consider the following hypothetical. Assume the exact statutory scheme embodied in Section 1089: anyone can create an STO, anyone can donate to an STO, and STOs can limit their scholarships to particular types of schools. Now imagine that only agnostics decide to create STOs. Imagine further that every STO refuses to provide tuition assistance to religious schools. In short, assume there is absolutely no money available for parents who want to send their children to a religious school. Would the parents be justified in accusing the government of depriving their children of school funds? Of course not.

The foregoing example plainly shows that in this case, any "endorsement" of religion arising from the disbursement of state funds to religious entities turns wholly and completely on the independent, uncoerced choices of private individuals. The system Arizona created could just as easily have resulted in a total dearth of funding for religious organizations as opposed to the surfeit allegedly available. This feast or famine is utterly out of the state's hands. It simply cannot be, as the panel claims, that the "scholarship program ... skews aid in favor of religious schools." Winn, 562 F.3d at 1013 (emphasis added). The "program" does no such thing: any "skew[ing]" that occurs takes place because of private, not government action. It is axiomatic that such action cannot violate the Establishment Clause.

A

The panel however, believes that under this multi-tiered system, choice is the culprit, not the savior. After all, plaintiffs allege that it is "the choice delegated to taxpayers" which "channels a disproportionate amount of government aid to sectarian STOs [that] limit their scholarships to use at religious schools." Id. Zelman, the panel maintains, focused on parental choice. Id. at 1018. Here, however, that choice is purported impermissibly to be "constrained" by the decisions of taxpayers and STOs. Id. at 1016. In other words, the choices of others deprive parents of their own "independent and private choice[]." Id. at 1013 (internal quotation marks and citation omitted). They might want to send their children to secular private schools, but scholarships are not readily available for that purpose. Moreover, the panel claims the alleged abundance of funds from religious STOs creates an incentive for these parents to enroll their children in religious schools. Id. at 1017-18. The panel therefore holds that Section 1089 "fails to provide genuine opportunities for ... parents to select secular educational options for their school-age children." Id. at 1018 (internal quotation marks and citation omitted).

I admit that the panel's conclusion with respect to the purported lack of parental choice finds support in Zelman. The problem is, that support comes from Justice Souter's dissent, not the opinion of the Court. Several aspects of the majority's reasoning in that case make the Winn panel's conclusion infirm.

1

By focusing generally on the scope of parental choice, the Winn panel, like the Zelman dissent, is barking up the wrong tree. The question is not whether a parent's choice is somehow limited or constrained, the question is whether the government has somehow limited or constrained the choice.

In Zelman, Justice Souter accused the majority of allowing external factors to "influenc[e] choices in a way that aims the money in a religious direction." 536 U.S. at 703, 122 S.Ct. 2460 (Souter, J., dissenting). Of the fifty-six private schools that participated in the Cleveland voucher program, he noted, forty-six were religious. Id. In his mind, this lack of a "wide array of private nonreligious options" suggested that any "choice" was not genuine. See id. at 703-06, 122 S.Ct. 2460. Rather, he believed parents' decisionmaking process was skewed by "the fact that too few nonreligious school desks are available and few but religious schools can afford to accept more than a handful of voucher students." Id. at 707, 122 S.Ct. 2460. "For the overwhelming number of children in the voucher scheme," he concluded, "the only alternative to the public schools is religious." Id. He was not swayed by the fact that these constraints were unrelated to state action: "a Hobson's choice is not a choice, whatever the reason for being Hobsonian." Id. In sum, Justice Souter would have struck down the Ohio voucher program because parents' choice was influenced by factors beyond their control.

Obviously, Justice Souter's position did not carry the day. "That 46 of the 56 private schools now participating in the program are religious schools," the majority explained, "does not condemn it as a violation of the Establishment Clause." Id. at 655, 122 S.Ct. 2460 (majority opinion). For one thing, the Court noted that the imbalance was not a function of government action. See id. at 656-57, 122 S.Ct. 2460. Moreover, "[t]o attribute constitutional significance" to the availability of secular options, "would lead to the absurd result that a neutral school-choice program might be permissible in ... some states [with a high concentration of secular schools], but not in other States [where religious schools are plentiful]." Id. at 657, 122 S.Ct. 2460.[11] To avoid this absurdity, the majority held that "[t]he constitutionality of a neutral educational aid program simply does not turn on whether and why, in a particular area, at a particular time,[12] most private schools are run by religious organizations, or most recipients choose to use the aid at a religious school." Id. at 658, 122 S.Ct. 2460.[13]

I see no meaningful distinction between the situation in Zelman and the facts of this case. Both cases involve alleged "constraints" on access to a scarce secular resource — "nonreligious [private] school desks." In Zelman, only ten of the participating schools were secular. Id. at 656, 122 S.Ct. 2460. Parents were thus "constrained" by third-party decisions to fund religious, rather than secular schools. Here, while thirty out of fifty-five STOs offer scholarships to secular schools, the majority of program funds are allegedly concentrated in religious STOs. Parents are thus "constrained" by the decisions of some STOs to limit their scholarships to religious institutions, and taxpayer choices to direct their funds to those STOs. The key point is that in neither Zelman nor the case at hand are the purported "constraints" government-induced. There is simply no constitutionally significant distinction between a system where — for reasons unattributable to state action — money is available, but there are a limited number of schools to receive it, and a system where schools may be available, but there is a limited amount of money to spend. Under either scenario, as Justice Souter bemoaned, "[f]or the overwhelming number of children in the [program], the only alternative to the public schools is religious." Id. at 707, 122 S.Ct. 2460 (Souter, J., dissenting).

I can go on. In Zelman, voucher funds could be used at participating public schools in districts adjacent to Cleveland. Id. at 645, 122 S.Ct. 2460 (majority opinion). However, no such school "elected to participate." Id. at 647, 122 S.Ct. 2460. Parental choice was therefore "constrained" by the decisions of out-of-district public school administrators. Similarly, Ohio did not require private secular schools to accept vouchers: they chose to do so. See id. at 656 n. 4, 122 S.Ct. 2460. Citing overcrowding or a desire for independence from government funds, these schools could just as easily have decided to opt out of the program. Alternatively, they could have, for whatever reason, decided to close up shop. In either scenario, parents again would be left with a reduced "choice" to send their children to private, secular schools. Did the Zelman Court strike down the Ohio program for impermissibly "delegating" such decisions to school administrators? Was parental choice held to be unduly "constrained"? Of course not. Instead, the Court said that the availability of a private secular education, "in a particular area, at a particular time," was irrelevant to the constitutional inquiry. See Zelman, 536 U.S. at 656-60, 122 S.Ct. 2460; supra pp. 663-64.[14]

Ultimately, the panel seems to assume that parents must have the same access to "nonreligious [private] school desks" as they do to religious private school desks. But that was certainly not the case in Zelman, and the Ohio voucher program was upheld. Indeed, such result is unattainable in any program where the government is neutral with respect to religion and nonreligion. If the government takes the constitutionally required hands-off approach, external factors will define the playing field. Contrary to the panel's conclusion, the constitutional inquiry "simply does not turn" on whatever influence these factors might exert on parents. Zelman, 536 U.S. at 658, 122 S.Ct. 2460.

Again, provided there is "no evidence that the State deliberately skewed incentives toward religious schools," there is no Establishment Clause violation. Id. at 650, 122 S.Ct.

2460 (emphasis added); see supra pp. 661-62. As the Arizona tax credit program is just as much a program of "true private choice" as the program in Zelman, 536 U.S. at 649, 122 S.Ct. 2460, the panel erred in reinstating the constitutional challenge.[15]

2

In rejecting Justice Souter's position, the Zelman majority also emphasized that he was asking the wrong question. Rather than focusing narrowly on the challenged voucher program, the majority explained that the "Establishment Clause question is whether Ohio is coercing parents into sending their children to religious schools, and that question must be answered by evaluating all options Ohio provides Cleveland schoolchildren, only one of which is to obtain a[voucher]." Id. at 655-56, 122 S.Ct. 2460. Because the Winn panel adopts Justice Souter's overly restrictive approach, rather than assessing "all options" available to Arizona students, its result is similarly flawed.[16]

Indeed, the panel overtly limited its parental-choice inquiry to "the range of educational choices the STO-administered scholarship programs offer." Winn, 562 F.3d at 1018. It "reject[ed] the suggestion that the mere existence of the public school system guarantees that any scholarship program provides for genuine private choice." Id. While the latter statement may be true, it is also something of a non sequitur. No one claims the existence of a public school system grants a state license to ignore the Establishment Clause. The question, as Zelman instructs, is whether Arizona is "coercing parents into sending their children to religious schools," a question which must be answered by evaluating "all options" Arizona provides its schoolchildren. 536 U.S. at 655-56, 122 S.Ct. 2460.

The panel did not even engage in this inquiry. Had it done so, it would have discovered that Section 1089 is but one of a "range of educational choices" available to parents of school-aged children. Id. at 655, 122 S.Ct. 2460; see also Kotterman, 972 P.2d at 611 (noting that the "Arizona Legislature has, in recent years, expanded the options available in public education" and listing some of those options). Arizona's public schools must provide for open enrollment, allowing parents to send their children, tuition-free, to schools of their choice. Ariz.Rev.Stat. Ann. § 15-816.01(A). Tax credits are available for donations to public schools for "extracurricular activities or character education." Ariz.Rev.Stat. Ann. § 43-1089.01. An extensive system of charter schools "provide[s] additional academic choices for parents and pupils." Id. § 15-181.[17] Homeschooling is permitted and protected. Id. §§ 15-745, 802-03. Indeed, Section 1089 itself offers parents yet another alternative: they can create their own STO and solicit donations for use at secular private schools. These alternative educational opportunities mirror those the Court took into consideration in Zelman. See 536 U.S. at 655, 122 S.Ct. 2460 ("Cleveland schoolchildren enjoy a range of educational choices: They may remain in public school as before, remain in public school with publicly funded tutoring aid, obtain a scholarship and choose a religious school, obtain a scholarship and choose a nonreligious private school, enroll in a community school, or enroll in a magnet school.").[18]

This is no Hobson's choice. Far from "coercing" parents into sending their children to religious schools, Arizona provides a wide variety of secular alternatives. "Any objective observer familiar with the full history and context of [Section 1089] would reasonably view it as one aspect of a broader undertaking...." Id. at 655, 122 S.Ct. 2460. By shutting its eyes to the host of options available to Arizona parents, the panel's opinion directly conflicts with Zelman.[19]

B

As demonstrated by the foregoing arguments, the Arizona program provides parents with "true private choice." That established, the panel's discussion of taxpayer choice becomes surplusage. Indeed, is its curious focus on "taxpayer choice" an apt analogy at all? I suggest that Winn's reliance on Larkin v. Grendel's Den, Inc., 459 U.S. 116, 103 S.Ct. 505, 74 L.Ed.2d 297 (1982), is utterly mistaken.

The thrust of the panel's reasoning is that taxpayer choice is not a valid substitute for the parental choice allegedly at the core of Zelman. I am not certain, however, that parental choice was as central to the reasoning of Zelman as the panel would have it. While that opinion does repeatedly refer to aid "recipients," see Winn, 562 F.3d at 1018 (listing citations), at other times, it refers only to private, nongovernmental choice, see, e.g., Zelman, 536 U.S. at 649, 122 S.Ct. 2460 (describing programs where "government aid reaches religious schools only as a result of the genuine and independent choices of private individuals"); id. at 655, 122 S.Ct. 2460 (stating that "no reasonable observer" would find government endorsement where "state aid reaches religious schools solely as a result of the numerous independent decisions of private individuals"). Significantly, Zelman seems most concerned about preventing the state from reaching out to "grant special favors that might lead to a religious establishment." Id. at 652-53, 122 S.Ct. 2460 (internal quotation marks and citation omitted). So long as "favors" are doled out independent of state action, the Establishment Clause — which again, prohibits the "government itself" from endorsing religion — is not offended.

I further submit that under the endorsement test, any level of attenuation between government action and aid to religion necessarily reduces the likelihood that a "reasonable observer" will find impermissible government approbation. There can be no doubt that taxpayer choice contributes to that attenuation. Thus, the panel's analysis of whether the choice Section 1089 provides to taxpayers ensures that "'the circuit between government and religion was broken'" is beside the point. Winn, 562 F.3d at 1021 (quoting Zelman, 536 U.S. at 652, 122 S.Ct. 2460). The self-evident fact is that by "delegating" the choice to taxpayers, the government already broke the circuit.

Nonetheless, the panel contends a reasonable observer would consider two factors when deciding whether a program of individual choice violates the Establishment Clause: the "role the person making the choice occupies in the structure of the program," id. at 1020, and "whether the choice delegated ... has the effect of promoting, or hindering, the program's secular purpose," id. at 1021. Regarding the former, the panel determined there was "no 'effective means of guaranteeing'" that taxpayers would exercise their choice "'exclusively for secular, neutral, and nonideological purposes.'" Id. at 1020 (quoting

Larkin, 459 U.S. at 125, 103 S.Ct. 505). Parents, on the other hand, have "incentives to apply the program's aid based on their children's educational interests instead of on sectarian considerations." Id. at 1021. As for the latter, the panel concluded that taxpayers thwarted the secular purpose of the statute insofar as their contributions narrowed the range of available educational alternatives. Id. at 1022.

One could see how a reasonable observer in Larkin could perceive government endorsement of religion from the "role the [entity] making the choice" played in the scheme. Maybe I am stating the obvious, but a large part of that perception might rest on the fact that in Larkin, the state delegated legislative authority — the ability to veto liquor licenses — to churches. See 459 U.S. at 125, 103 S.Ct. 505. I say again: churches. Under such circumstances it is completely unsurprising that a reasonable observer would conclude that this "joint exercise of legislative authority by Church and State provides a significant symbolic benefit to religion in the minds of some." Id. at 125-26, 103 S.Ct. 505. To what pervasively sectarian organization has Arizona "delegated" the choice at issue in this case? The Arizona taxpayer.[20] When perceived endorsement of religion is at issue, state cooperation with churches is a far cry from state cooperation with taxpayers.[21]

Moreover, I disagree with the panel's conclusion that parents are somehow less motivated to promote religious objectives than taxpayers generally. As anyone who has grown up in a religious household will tell you, schooling decisions are as frequently made on the basis of religious considerations as they are on purely secular academic grounds. At the very least, sectarian considerations factor into the equation of what is in the child's best interests educationally. Thus, whether it resides with the taxpayer or the parent, once the choice is made available, the state has no "effective means of guaranteeing" that it will be exercised "exclusively for secular, neutral, and nonideological purposes." Id. at 125, 103 S.Ct. 505 (internal quotation marks and citation omitted). By contrast with engaging in pseudo-psychological inquires into motivation, under Zelman, we need only satisfy ourselves that the choice, whatever it is, is made by a private actor, not by the government.

With respect to taxpayers' ability to "thwart" the secular purpose of the statute, as discussed above, actors in any program of true private choice will have this ability. See supra pp. 663-65. In Zelman, for example, the purpose of providing a broad range of educational opportunities was "thwarted" by the decisions of neighboring public-school administrators to decline program vouchers. See supra pp. 664-65. The goal could be similarly "thwarted" if secular private school administrators decided to pull out of the program. See supra pp. 664-65. An inherent reality of true private choice programs cannot condemn Section 1089.

Ultimately, the panel appears to argue that Arizona's scheme is flawed because it essentially delegates to a private entity something the state could not constitutionally achieve by the exercise of its own powers; here, the promotion of religious education. See Winn, 562 F.3d at 1020; see also id. at 1021 (citing Norwood v. Harrison, 413 U.S. 455, 465, 93 S.Ct. 2804, 37 L.Ed.2d 723 (1973)). That may well be true, but as the panel's own citation indicates, for that to be the case, the state must somehow "induce, encourage or promote private persons to accomplish what it is constitutionally forbidden to accomplish." Norwood, 413 U.S. at 465, 93 S.Ct. 2804 (emphases added). At the risk of beating a dead horse, I repeat that the state here has done nothing to cajole parents, STOs, or taxpayers into supporting religious education. The state has simply said, if you donate to the STO of your choice, you get a tax credit. Such action in no way induces, encourages, or promotes private parties to aid religion.[22]

IV

The panel also holds that plaintiffs have alleged facts suggesting Section 1089 was not "enacted for ... [a] valid secular purpose." Winn, 562 F.3d at 1011 (internal quotation marks and citation omitted). The panel reaches this conclusion despite conceding that the statute is facially neutral with respect to religion. See id. at 1011-12. Nothing in the legislative history suggests that the driving force behind the bill was anything other than the desire to provide "equal access to a wide range of schooling options for students of every income level." Id.; see also Mueller, 463 U.S. at 395, 103 S.Ct. 3062 ("A state's decision to defray the cost of educational expenses incurred by parents — regardless of the type of schools their children attend — evidences a purpose that is both secular and understandable."). Nonetheless, the panel maintains that plaintiffs could prove, based on how Section 1089 operates in practice, that this "secular and valid" purpose is a sham. Winn, 562 F.3d at 1011-12.

From its citation to McCreary County v. ACLU, 545 U.S. 844, 125 S.Ct. 2722, 162 L.Ed.2d 729 (2005), the panel seems to argue that the very enactment of Section 1089 "bespoke" a religious purpose. Winn, 562 F.3d at 1012. But how can this be so? McCreary does say that government action can be so "patently religious" that its nonsecular nature is evident. 545 U.S. at 862, 125 S.Ct. 2722. The examples provided, however, are situations where the state mandated Bible study, the teaching of creationism, and prayer in schools. Id. at 862-63. Setting up a tax credit program to provide scholarships to children generally is hardly of the same ilk.

To the extent the panel claims that the manner in which Section 1089 has been implemented reveals the stated secular purpose to be a sham, their arguments are similarly unpersuasive. First, the Supreme Court has recognized that a "legislature's stated reasons will generally get deference," deference only abandoned in "those unusual cases where the claim was an apparent sham." Id. at 864-65, 125 S.Ct. 2722. Nothing in the plaintiffs allegations suggest this is one of those "unusual cases," and as setting up a tax credit program is not a "patently religious" act, there is nothing "apparent" about any purported sham. Second, the implementation inquiry centers on actions taken by the government. See id. at 862, 125 S.Ct. 2722 (stating that the inquiry turns on the "traditional external signs that show up in the text, legislative history, and implementation of the statute, or comparable official act") (internal quotation marks and citations omitted); id. at 870-74, 125 S.Ct. 2722 (questioning the government's newly proffered purposes after it altered a Ten Commandments display in an attempt to mitigate previously stated sectarian purposes). Here, the alleged impropriety arises from taxpayer, not government action. Third, the panel's holding turns on plaintiff's allegation that "in practice STOs are permitted to restrict the use of their scholarships to use at certain religious schools." Winn, 562 F.3d at 1012. But that result is apparent from the statute itself, which is satisfied so long as STOs provide scholarships to two or more schools, see supra note 5, a fact plaintiffs themselves recognize in their complaint. That an STO may independently decide to limit its scholarships does not make a religious purpose "apparent."[23]

Ultimately, the crux of the panel's purpose holding turns on matters previously discussed under the effects prong: a nonsecular purpose could be inferred from the fact that, at a given moment, the bulk of scholarship money is available only for use at religious schools. But as detailed above, money flows to religious institutions entirely at the whim of nongovernmental actors: taxpayers or STOs. The legislature could hardly have had the "purpose" of endorsing religion when it set up a plan that, for all it knew, could have resulted in absolutely no funding for religious entities. See supra pp. 661-62. This moving target is irrelevant to the Establishment Clause inquiry. See supra pp. 663-65.

V

The layer upon layer of private choice built into this program ensures that "the circuit between government and religion [is] broken." Zelman, 536 U.S. at 652, 122 S.Ct. 2460. Try as it may, the panel cannot complete such circuit. Ultimately, nothing in the panel opinion grapples with the fact that Arizona does nothing to encourage, to promote, or otherwise to incentivize private actors to direct aid to religious schools. Nothing explains how "the government itself has advanced religion through its own activities and influence." Amos, 483 U.S. at 337, 107 S.Ct. 2862. Nothing points to any "evidence that the State deliberately skewed incentives toward religious schools." Zelman, 536 U.S. at 650, 122 S.Ct. 2460 (emphasis added). Nothing shows how Section 1089 enables Arizona to "grant special favors that might lead to a religious establishment." Id. at 652-53, 122 S.Ct. 2460 (internal quotation marks and citation omitted).

But the three-judge panel can hardly be faulted for these omissions: it cannot manufacture what does not exist.[24] What does exist is a tax credit system that relies entirely on private choice. Individuals choose to create an STO. STOs choose to limit their funds to certain schools. Taxpayers choose to donate. Parents choose to apply for scholarships. In truth, every-one in Arizona has a choice — everyone except the government. No reasonable observer would think this lengthy chain of choice suggests the government has endorsed religion.

Because the three-judge panel's decision strays from established Supreme Court precedent, and because it jeopardizes the educational opportunities of thousands of children who enjoy the benefits of Section 1089 and related programs across the nation, I must respectfully dissent from our court's regrettable failure to rehear this case en banc.

Judge O'Scannlain's dissent in US v. Amezcua-Vasquez (Nov 10, 2009)

O'SCANNLAIN, Circuit Judge, dissenting from the denial of rehearing en banc, joined by KOZINSKI, Chief Judge, and GOULD, TALLMAN, CALLAHAN, BEA, and N.R. SMITH, Circuit Judges:

This is the first published opinion in this circuit reversing a within-Guidelines sentence as substantively unreasonable. The panel reaches this unprecedented result by casting aside Supreme Court and Ninth Circuit precedent in three ways: first, by failing to apply the appropriate standard of review; second, by recognizing a brand-new category of sentencing factors whose consideration by the district court warrants virtually no deference; and finally, by assuming a policymaking role properly reserved to the district court. I must respectfully dissent from our failure to rehear this case en banc.

I

Javier Amezcua-Vasquez ("Amezcua"), a Mexican national, became a lawful permanent resident of the United States in 1957, at the age of two. In 1981, he was convicted in state court of attempted voluntary manslaughter and assault with great bodily injury for stabbing someone with a knife in a gang-related bar fight. Based on his 1981 conviction, Amezcua was ordered removed to Mexico in 2006. Just two weeks after his removal, however, he was caught trying to reenter the United States. A grand jury returned an indictment charging him with attempted illegal reentry in violation of 8 U.S.C. § 1326. Amezcua pled guilty.

At sentencing, the district court determined that Amezcua's base offense level was 8 under U.S.S.G. § 2L1.2(a). The court then applied a sixteen-level increase under U.S.S.G. § 2L1.2(b)(1)(A)(ii) because Amezcua's 1981 conviction was for a felony that was a "crime of violence." After applying a two-level decrease for acceptance of responsibility, see U.S.S.G. § 3E1.1, the court arrived at a total offense level of 22. As for Amezcua's criminal history, the court placed him in category II based on a 1999 conviction for an offense involving a controlled substance. Significantly, Amezcua's 1981 conviction did not count toward his criminal history score because it fell outside the applicable time period under the Guidelines. See id. § 4A1.2(e). Six of Amezcua's other prior convictions also did not count.

Based on a total offense level of 22 and a criminal history category II, the district court calculated an advisory Guidelines range of 46 to 57 months' imprisonment. The court sentenced Amezcua to 52 months, in the middle of the range. It explained that it had "considered all" of the factors set forth in 18 U.S.C. § 3553(a), including "the defendant's prior record and the circumstances of the offense." Although the court did not think the circumstances of the offense were "particularly aggravating," it believed that 52 months was "the minimum sentence that would afford deterrence to criminal conduct," given "the defendant's prior criminal history and contacts with law enforcement." The court described those contacts as "significant," and noted that "a number" of them had not been scored under the Guidelines.

The panel reversed, holding that Amezcua's 52-month, within-Guidelines sentence was substantively unreasonable. The panel disapproved of "the unmitigated application of the Guidelines sentence with its 16-level enhancement" based on Amezcua's 1981 conviction for a "crime of violence." United States v. Amezcua-Vasquez, 567 F.3d 1050, 1055 (9th Cir.2009). The panel explained:

Although it may be reasonable to take some account of an aggravated felony, no matter how stale, in assessing the seriousness of an unlawful reentry into the country, it does not follow that it is inevitably reasonable to assume that a decades-old prior conviction is deserving of the same severe additional punishment as a recent one. The staleness of the conviction does not affect the Guidelines calculation, but it does affect the § 3553(a) analysis. We hold that the district court abused its discretion when it applied the Guidelines sentence to Amezcua without making allowances for the staleness of the prior conviction and his subsequent lack of any other convictions for violent crimes. The result was an unreasonable sentence.

Id. at 1055-56.

The panel maintained that its decision was "not inconsistent" with United States v. Whitehead, 532 F.3d 991 (9th Cir.2008), or United States v. Ruff, 535 F.3d 999 (9th Cir.2008), two cases in which we upheld sentences below the advisory Guidelines range. Amezcua-Vasquez, 567 F.3d at 1056. According to the panel, the sentences affirmed in Whitehead and Ruff were "the product of defendant-specific § 3553(a) mitigating (or aggravating) factors with respect to which the district court was in a superior position to find the relevant facts and to judge their import." Id. at 1057 (internal quotation marks omitted). By contrast, the panel suggested, Amezcua's sentence was the product of "offense-specific sentencing factors," which the district court was not in a superior position to evaluate. Id. Given this distinction, the panel concluded, "[n]either Whitehead nor Ruff requires us to affirm the sentence in the present circumstances." Id.

II

By now, we should all be familiar with the post-Booker standard governing appellate review of sentences for substantive reasonableness. As the Supreme Court reminded us in Gall v. United States, 552 U.S. 38, 128 S.Ct. 586, 169 L.Ed.2d 445 (2007), "courts of appeals must review all sentences — whether inside, just outside, or significantly outside the Guidelines range — under a deferential abuse-of-discretion standard." Id. at 591. "The fact that the appellate court might reasonably have concluded that a different sentence was appropriate is insufficient to justify reversal of the district court." Id. at 597.

The panel insists that it gave "due weight to these principles," Amezcua-Vasquez, 567 F.3d at 1055, but its analysis suggests otherwise. Despite quoting a few passages from Gall and other sentencing cases, see id., the panel pays no heed to the appropriate standard of review, giving little, if any, deference to the district court's conclusion that the § 3553(a) factors warranted a within-Guidelines sentence. Cf. Gall, 128 S.Ct. at 600.

The panel essentially concedes as much. It relies on a distinction between "defendant-specific" and "offense-specific" factors to justify giving virtually no weight to the district court's consideration of the seriousness of Amezcua's criminal history. But such a distinction finds no support in Supreme Court precedent. The Court has never said that a district court's decision with respect to some § 3553(a) factors deserves deference while a district court's decision with respect to other § 3553(a) factors does not. Instead, the Court has consistently referred to the § 3553(a) factors as a whole, without any indication that "defendant-specific" factors should be treated differently than "offense-specific" factors. See, e.g., Gall, 128 S.Ct. at 596-98.

In Ruff, moreover, we rejected the very notion that the level of deference we owe depends on the type of sentencing factors at issue. Although the panel attempts to portray Ruff as a case involving only "defendant-specific" factors, we expressly declined in Ruff to recognize any distinction among the factors set forth in § 3553(a). We explained:

> The clear message in Gall ... is that we must defer "to the District Court's reasoned and reasonable decision that the § 3553(a) factors, on the whole, justified the sentence." Gall happened to discuss postcrime maturation and self-rehabilitation because they were the basis of the district court's reasoned decision in that case, but it is the reasoned decision itself, not the specific reasons that are cited, that triggers our duty to defer.

535 F.3d at 1003 (emphasis added) (citation omitted) (quoting Gall, 128 S.Ct. at 602). Ruff makes plain that the deferential abuse-of-discretion standard applies regardless of which § 3553(a) factors form the basis of the district court's decision. By creating an exception to the deferential abuse-of-discretion standard for any sentence based on a district court's consideration of a defendant's criminal history (or other "offense-specific" factors), the panel's decision significantly distorts the law of this circuit.

To make matters worse, the panel's distinction between "defendant-specific" and "offense-specific" factors is hardly any distinction at all. Almost any "offense-specific" factor could also be characterized as a "defendant-specific" factor, and vice versa. The panel itself seems confused about the difference. For the most part, it seems to treat the seriousness of Amezcua's criminal history as an "offense-specific" factor, whose consideration by the district court is entitled to virtually no deference. But the panel also expressly refers to "the staleness of [Amezcua's] predicate prior conviction and its diminished import on the severity of [his] illegal reentry" as "defendant-specific facts." Amezcua-Vasquez, 567 F.3d at 1057 ("[T]he district court applied the Guidelines sentence without considering the defendant-specific facts that made the resulting sentence unreasonable under § 3553(a) — i.e., the staleness of the predicate prior conviction and its diminished import on the severity of the illegal reentry decades after the original conviction."). Even the panel can't seem to keep the two categories straight.

Although the panel assures us that the scope of its decision is "limited," id. at 1058, its novel distinction between "defendant-specific" and "offense-specific" factors will be a lasting source of confusion. In struggling to distinguish the two types of factors, future panels will be tempted to characterize the district court's considerations as involving either one or the other, depending on whether they agree or disagree with the defendant's sentence. From now on, any panel that disagrees with a defendant's sentence can justify giving the district court's considerations less weight by simply characterizing them as "offense-specific." No one will be the wiser, given the near-impossibility of telling the two types of factors apart.

III

The panel's failure to apply the appropriate standard of review is not the only reason we should have reheard this case en banc. By faulting the district court for not disagreeing with the sentencing policy reflected in U.S.S.G. § 2L1.2(b)(1)(A)(ii), the panel assumes a policymaking role inappropriate for an appellate court.

In Kimbrough v. United States, 552 U.S. 85, 128 S.Ct. 558, 169 L.Ed.2d 481 (2007), the district court imposed a sentence below the advisory Guidelines range based on a policy disagreement with the 100-to-1 crack/powder cocaine disparity under the Guidelines. See id. at 565. The Supreme Court held that the district court did not abuse its discretion, given that the crack cocaine Guidelines "do not exemplify the Commission's exercise of its characteristic institutional role." Id. at 575. But it is one thing to say that a district court may vary from the crack cocaine Guidelines on policy grounds; it is quite another to say that it must. Kimbrough does not "mean[] that a district court now acts unreasonably, abuses its discretion, or otherwise commits error if it does not consider the crack/powder sentencing disparity." United States v. Roberson, 517 F.3d 990, 995 (8th Cir.2008) (emphasis added).

Similarly, here, it is one thing to say that the district court could have varied from § 2L1.2(b)(1)(A)(ii); it is quite another to say that the district court had an obligation to vary. By requiring the district court to vary based on the panel's disagreement with the policy reflected in § 2L1.2(b)(1)(A)(ii), see Amezcua-Vasquez, 567 F.3d at 1056, the panel turns Kimbrough on its head. It converts the district court's discretion to vary from the Guidelines based on a policy disagreement into a mandate that it do so. But Kimbrough is a shield, not a sword. It protects the district court's discretion to make policy judgments; we are not supposed to pierce it. By taking issue with the "unmitigated application" of § 2L1.2(b)(1)(A)(ii), id. at 1055, the panel substitutes its own policy judgment for that of the district court as well as the Sentencing Commission.

In any event, the panel's policy disagreement with the Guidelines proceeds on a faulty premise. Contrary to the panel's view, the Guidelines do not "assume that a decades-old prior conviction is deserving of the same severe additional punishment as a recent one." Id. at 1055-56. The Guidelines do account for the staleness of a defendant's prior conviction — in the calculation of the defendant's criminal history score. Here, Amezcua's 1981 conviction did not count toward his criminal history score precisely because it was "decades-old." See U.S.S.G. § 4A1.2(e). To say that the Guidelines failed to account for the staleness of Amezcua's prior conviction is simply inaccurate.

IV

This is not just another sentencing case. Employing what amounts to a de novo standard of review, the panel becomes the first in our circuit to publish an opinion reversing a within-Guidelines sentence as substantively unreasonable. In the process, the panel recognizes a brand-new category of sentencing considerations purportedly undeserving of deference, and usurps the policymaking role of the district court as well as the Sentencing Commission. For these reasons, I respectfully dissent from the denial of rehearing en banc.

Judge O'Scannlain's dissent from the order denying rehearing en banc in US v. Alderman (Feb 3, 2010)

O'SCANNLAIN, Circuit Judge, dissenting from the order denying rehearing en banc, joined by PAEZ, BYBEE, and BEA, Circuit Judges:

The Supreme Court has told us with increasing fervor that there are limits to the power of Congress to federalize regulation of personal conduct. The Court told us in United States v. Lopez, 514 U.S. 549, 559, 115 S.Ct. 1624, 131 L.Ed.2d 626 (1995), that Congress has no power to make a federal crime of possession of a hand gun within 1,000 feet of a school, even if the gun traveled in inter-state commerce. The Court told us in United States v. Morrison, 529 U.S. 598, 610-12, 120 S.Ct. 1740, 146 L.Ed.2d 658 (2000), that Congress has no power to fashion a federal remedy for claims of violence against women. The Court told us in Jones v. United States, 529 U.S. 848, 120 S.Ct. 1904, 146 L.Ed.2d 902 (2000), that Congress has no power to make a federal crime of arson, even if the affected building is subject to a mortgage held by a bank in another state.

For the reasons articulated by our colleague, Judge Paez, in his eloquent dissent,[1] Congress has no power to make a federal crime of possession of body armor by a felon. Because the panel majority disagrees and fails to recognize the limits imposed on Congress by Lopez, Morrison, and Jones, because its opinion erroneously allows the federal government to legislate in a domain traditionally regulated by the states, and because its opinion now creates a split with seven other circuits, we should have reheard this case en banc.

I

The mischief this case creates is exceptionally troublesome.[2] The majority opinion allows Congress to punish possession offenses, as long as the enacting statute includes a mere recital purporting to limit its reach to goods sold or offered for sale in interstate commerce. The majority's opinion makes Lopez superfluous. Insert a jurisdictional recital, the majority in effect says, and Congress need not worry about whether the prohibited conduct has a "substantial relation to interstate commerce." Lopez, 514 U.S. at 559, 115 S.Ct. 1624. Seven circuits have expressly rejected this view of jurisdictional provisions. United States v. Maxwell, 446 F.3d 1210, 1218 (11th Cir. 2006); United States v. Patton, 451 F.3d 615, 632 (10th Cir.2006); United States v. Holston, 343 F.3d 83, 88 (2d Cir. 2003); United States v. McCoy, 323 F.3d 1114, 1118 (9th Cir.2003); United States v. Corp, 236 F.3d 325, 331 (6th Cir. 2001); United States v. Angle, 234 F.3d 326, 337 (7th Cir.2000); United States v. Rodia, 194 F.3d 465, 472-73 (3rd Cir.1999).

II

But the impact of the majority's opinion does not stop there. The majority's rationale, quite literally, "makes a federal case" out of numerous crimes previously punished only by the states. Cambridge Idioms Dictionary (2d ed.2006); see Andrew St. Laurent, Reconstituting United States v. Lopez: Another Look at Federal Criminal Law, 31 Colum. J.L. & Soc. Probs. 61, 113 (1998) ("A purely nominal jurisdictional requirement, that some entity or object involved in the crime be drawn from interstate commerce, does nothing to prevent the shifting of the [federal/state] balance in favor of the federal government [because] virtually all criminal actions in the United States involve the use of some object that has passed through interstate commerce.").

Such a view greatly empowers Congress to displace state legislatures with the full weight of the federal government, a result as undesirable as it is unconstitutional in the circumstances of this case. A federal statute may conflict with a state's policy judgment regarding the harshness of federal criminal punishments, Jones, 529 U.S. at 859, 120 S.Ct. 1904 (Stevens, J., concurring) (noting improper displacement of state choices with severe federal punishments), or discourage experimentation with different state policy approaches, see Lopez, 514 U.S. at 583, 115 S.Ct. 1624 (Kennedy, J., concurring) (suggesting that the gun statute improperly "foreclose[d] the States from experimenting"), or even intrude upon a traditional area of state concern, Lopez, 514 U.S. at 561, 115 S.Ct. 1624; Morrison, 529 U.S. at 615-17, 120 S.Ct. 1740. Such displacement has occurred here. At least thirty-one states regulated body armor, with a variety of approaches, until Congress overrode their choices. Patton, 451 F.3d at 631 & n. 7 (collecting state laws).

III

The majority opinion here failed to perceive the constitutional limits on Congress's power recognized by the Court in Lopez, Morrison, Jones, and Raich. In so doing, it "convert[s] congressional authority under the Commerce Clause to a general police power of the sort retained by the States," Lopez, 514 U.S. at 567, 115 S.Ct. 1624, contrary to Supreme Court doctrine. It is unfortunate that an en banc court will not have the opportunity to correct the error in this case. For these reasons, I must respectfully dissent from the order denying rehearing en banc.

Notes

[1] United States v. Alderman, 565 F.3d 641, 648-58 (9th Cir.2009) (Paez, J., dissenting).

[2] I will not repeat the well-reasoned analysis in Judge Paez's dissent nor the earlier decision by the Tenth Circuit as to why this statute does not survive the tests enunciated in Lopez, Morrison, Jones, and Gonzales v. Raich, 545 U.S. 1, 17-18, 125 S.Ct. 2195, 162 L.Ed.2d 1 (2005). See Alderman, 565 F.3d at 648 (Paez, J., dissenting); United States v. Patton, 451 F.3d 615, 632 (10th Cir.2006) (concluding that 18 U.S.C. § 931(a) fails Morrison). While it is true the Tenth Circuit in Patton ultimately upheld the statute, that was largely because of prior Tenth Circuit precedent interpreting Scarborough v. United States, 431 U.S. 563, 97 S.Ct. 1963, 52 L.Ed.2d 582 (1977), see Patton, 451 F.3d at 634, which the Tenth Circuit strongly suggested was inconsistent with Lopez and Morrison. Id.

at 636.

Judge O'Scannlain's dissent from the order denying rehearing en banc in Cooper v. FAA (Feb 22, 2010)

O'SCANNLAIN, Circuit Judge, dissenting from the order denying rehearing en banc, joined by KOZINSKI, Chief Judge, and GOULD, TALLMAN, BYBEE, CALLAHAN, BEA, and N.R. SMITH, Circuit Judges:

The Supreme Court has consistently held that the sovereign immunity of the United States may be waived only by an unequivocal expression in statutory text. Lane v. Pena, 518 U.S. 187, 192, 116 S.Ct. 2092, 135 L.Ed.2d 486 (1996). Today, our court neglects this principle by leaving in place a decision that the term "actual damages" in the Privacy Act, 5 U.S.C. § 552a(g)(4)(A), is sufficient to deem sovereign immunity waived for nonpecuniary damages, even though the opinion itself admits that the term is not defined in the statute, has no plain meaning, has no fixed legal meaning, and indeed, is a "chameleon." Cooper v. FAA, 596 F.3d 538, 544-45 (9th Cir.2010). Even more troubling, the opinion relies on abstract legislative intent and an interpretation of the Privacy Act that the Supreme Court recently rejected in Doe v. Chao, 540 U.S. 614, 124 S.Ct. 1204, 157 L.Ed.2d 1122 (2004). The effect of today's order is to open wide the United States Treasury to a whole new class of claims without warrant. In so doing, we exacerbate a circuit split that had been healing under the strong medicine of recent sovereign immunity jurisprudence.[1] Hence, it is most unfortunate that we did not rehear this case en banc.

I

"A waiver of the Federal Government's sovereign immunity must be unequivocally expressed in statutory text, and will not be implied. Moreover, a waiver of the Government's sovereign immunity will be strictly construed, in terms of its scope, in favor of the sovereign." Lane, 518 U.S. at 192, 116 S.Ct. 2092 (emphasis added) (internal citations omitted).[2] "[T]he `unequivocal expression' of elimination of sovereign immunity that we insist upon is an expression in statutory text." United States v. Nordic Village, Inc., 503 U.S. 30, 37, 112 S.Ct. 1011, 117 L.Ed.2d 181 (1992). "A statute's legislative history cannot supply a waiver that does not appear clearly in any statutory text...." Lane, 518 U.S. at 192, 116 S.Ct. 2092.

A

Here, the court all but admits that the statutory term "actual damages" does not unequivocally express a waiver for nonpecuniary damages. According to our court's opinion, "there is no ordinary or plain meaning of the term actual damages." Cooper, 596 F.3d at 544 (emphasis added). Indeed, definitional analysis "sheds little light on the type of injury or loss Congress intended plaintiffs to be able to prove." Id. (emphasis added). In addition, the court concedes that two other circuits "agree[] that the meaning of the term actual damages is ambiguous." Id. at 545 (emphasis added). It also states that "we have recognized the shifting sense we have attributed to the term." Id. (emphasis added). The term, the court concludes, is a "`chameleon,' as its meaning changes with the specific statute." Id. (emphasis added). Our court's own rationale, therefore, indicates that the statute does not waive sovereign immunity for nonpecuniary damages.

B

Notwithstanding such textual infirmities, the opinion resorts to the "clear purpose behind the [Privacy] Act" purportedly embodied in the Act's preamble, the way that Congress "signaled its intent" in the Act's recordkeeping provision, and the "presumption" that Congress intended the Act to mirror the Fair Credit Reporting Act. Id. at 545-48. But the proper conclusion to draw from the sources on which the court relies, if any can be drawn at all, is precisely the opposite of that drawn by the court. Assuming that recourse to a preamble is appropriate in the circumstances of this case, the Act's preamble uses the term "any damages," not the narrower term "actual damages." Privacy Act of 1974, Pub.L. No. 93-579, § 2(b)(6), 88 Stat. 1896. That the preamble differs from the operative provision indicates a difference in meaning, not, as the court concludes, an equivalence in meaning. Russello v. United States, 464 U.S. 16, 23, 104 S.Ct. 296, 78 L.Ed.2d 17 (1983). In addition, the recordkeeping provision requires agencies to prevent "embarrassment" but, notably, does not state that such harm is compensable. 5 U.S.C. § 552a(e)(10). Finally, the court's intuiting of congressional intent from our interpretation of the term "actual damages" in the Fair Credit Reporting Act, Cooper, 596 F.3d at 547-48, conflicts with the statement mere pages earlier that the meaning of the term "actual damages" varies from statute to statute. Id. at 545.

Although my colleague's concurrence insists that the majority opinion "correctly construed the waiver to allow the recovery of nonpecuniary damages," Concurrence at 1019, the opinion itself concedes that if the term "actual damages is susceptible of two plausible interpretations, then the sovereign immunity canon requires the court to construe the term narrowly in favor of the Government [and] hold[] that nonpecuniary damages are not covered." Id. at 549-50 (emphasis added). The language used in the preamble and recordkeeping provision, and the various ways the term is used in other statutes, make evident that it is indeed susceptible to an alternative plausible interpretation. By its own logic, the court should have construed the term narrowly.

C

But it is the court's recourse to the Privacy Act's standing provision that is the most troubling, because it conflicts with the Supreme Court's interpretation of the very provision of the Privacy Act at issue in this case. In Doe v. Chao, 540 U.S. 614, 124 S.Ct. 1204, 157 L.Ed.2d 1122 (2004), the Court distinguished standing to sue under the Privacy Act (which extends to all who suffer an "adverse effect") from the right to damages. The Court stated that the term "adverse effect" has the "limited but specific function" of "identifying a potential plaintiff who satisfies the injury-in-fact and causation requirements of Article III standing." Id. at 624, 124 S.Ct. 1204. "That is, an individual subjected to an adverse effect has injury enough to open the courthouse door, but without more has no cause of action for damages under the Privacy Act." Id. at 624-25, 124 S.Ct.

1204. Here, the court jumbles the two concepts, interpreting the term "actual damages" broadly with respect to the type of damages available simply because the term "adverse effect" is interpreted broadly with respect to standing. Cooper, 596 F.3d at 546-47. Not appropriate, said the Supreme Court quite clearly in Doe. 540 U.S. at 624-25, 124 S.Ct. 1204.

II

It is apparent that this case involves an important question of federal law. "It is inherent in the nature of sovereignty not to be amenable to the suit of an individual without its consent." The Federalist No. 81, at 548 (Alexander Hamilton) (Jacob E. Cooke ed., 1961). Sovereign immunity allows for majoritarian democracy, preventing the discouragement by courts of government action. See Harold J. Krent, Reconceptualizing Sovereign Immunity, 45 Vand. L.Rev. 1529, 1540 (1992). We ignore at our peril the well-established clear statement rule for waivers of sovereign immunity, which puts Congress, not the courts, in charge.

Concern over the impact of a waiver of sovereign immunity is particularly appropriate in this case. Even the dissent in Doe, which sought to expand damages under the Privacy Act, admitted that by its enactment "Congress did not want to saddle the Government with disproportionate liability." Doe, 540 U.S. at 637, 124 S.Ct. 1204 (Ginsburg, J., dissenting). Congress was prescient. Because more and more government records are accessible online through the Internet, they are easier to share. The proliferation of electronic records raises the stakes of a broader waiver of sovereign immunity, increasing the fiscal exposure of the United States to the tune of a $1000 minimum statutory award per claim. 5 U.S.C. § 552a(g)(4)(A). Only Congress has the keys to unlock our country's Treasury. The role of the courts is to ensure that Congress has used them in each case.

III

For these reasons, I must respectfully dissent from the order denying rehearing en banc.

Notes

[1] Compare Hudson v. Reno, 130 F.3d 1193, 1207 & n. 11 (6th Cir.1997) (holding Privacy Act does not waive sovereign immunity for nonpecuniary damages), and Fanin v. Dep't of Veterans Affairs, 572 F.3d 868, 872-75 (11th Cir.2009) (following Fitzpatrick v. IRS, 665 F.2d 327, 329-31 (11th Cir.1982)) (same), with Johnson v. IRS, 700 F.2d 971, 974-86 (5th Cir. 1983) (holding Privacy Act waives sovereign immunity for nonpecuniary damages), and Jacobs v. Nat'l Drug Intelligence Ctr., 548 F.3d 375, 378 (5th Cir.2008) (reluctantly following Johnson despite subsequent sovereign immunity jurisprudence).

[2] My colleague's concurrence in the denial of rehearing en banc agrees that the relevant issue is not the existence of a waiver, but the scope of the waiver. See Concurrence at 1019. However, since the meaning of the term "actual damages" is ambiguous, the court should have construed the waiver narrowly in "favor of the sovereign." Lane, 518 U.S. at

192, 116 S.Ct. 2092.

Judge O'Scannlain's dissent from the denial of rehearing en banc in Al-Kidd v. Ashcroft (March 18, 2010)

O'SCANNLAIN, Circuit Judge, joined by KOZINSKI, Chief Judge, and KLEINFELD, GOULD, TALLMAN, CALLAHAN, BEA and IKUTA, Circuit Judges, dissenting from the denial of rehearing en banc:

The majority holds that a former Attorney General of the United States may be personally liable for promulgating a policy under which his subordinates took actions expressly authorized by law. Judge Bea's dissent from the panel decision clearly and ably describes the several legal errors the panel makes in reaching this startling conclusion. See al-Kidd v. Ashcroft, 580 F.3d 949, 981-1000 (9th Cir.2009) (Bea, J., dissenting). For my part, I write to express my concern at the scope of this decision. First, the majority holds that al-Kidd's detention under a valid material witness warrant violated his clearly established constitutional rights — a conclusion that effectively declares the material witness statute unconstitutional as applied to al-Kidd. Second, the majority holds that a cabinet-level official may be personally liable for actions taken by his subordinates alone. Because of the gratuitous damage this decision inflicts upon orderly federal law enforcement, I must respectfully dissent from our refusal to rehear this case en banc.

I

On March 14, 2003, federal prosecutors sought a material witness warrant[1] to arrest Abdullah al-Kidd in connection with their prosecution of Sami Omar Al-Hussayen, whom a federal grand jury had indicted for visa fraud and making false statements to U.S. officials. According to a supporting affidavit submitted by prosecutors, al-Kidd had contacts with Al-Hussayen's suspected Jihadist organization, had received over $20,000 from Al-Hussayen, and, after returning from a trip to Yemen, had met with Al-Hussayen's associates. The affidavit also stated that al-Kidd had a plane ticket to fly to Saudi Arabia two days later, and that if he left the country, the government would "be unable to secure his presence at trial via subpoena." Based on this affidavit, a federal magistrate judge issued the warrant authorizing al-Kidd's arrest.

On March 16, federal agents arrested al-Kidd at the ticket counter at Dulles International Airport, outside Washington, D.C. After his arrest, the government detained al-Kidd for a total of sixteen days at several different federal facilities before releasing him on conditions that he surrender his passport, live with his wife at his in-laws' home in Nevada, limit his travel to Nevada and three other states, and regularly meet with a probation officer. The government did not ultimately call him to testify at Al-Hussayen's trial, and after the trial concluded, a judge granted al-Kidd's request that the restrictions on his travel be lifted.

Two years later, al-Kidd filed this lawsuit in the U.S. District Court for the District of Idaho. His first amended complaint alleges that Ashcroft violated the Fourth and Fifth

Amendments and the federal material witness statute by promulgating a policy directing federal prosecutors to seek material witness warrants to detain individuals whom they believed, but could not prove, were involved in criminal activities. After the district court denied Ashcroft's motion to dismiss al-Kidd's complaint, Ashcroft appealed to this court.[2] The panel majority then affirmed the pertinent part of the district court's ruling in an extraordinarily broad and unprecedented decision.[3]

II

By permitting al-Kidd's suit to proceed, the majority commits two distinct but equally troubling legal errors, each of which will have far-reaching implications for how government officials perform their duties. First, the majority strips Ashcroft of his official immunity, holding that it was clearly established at the time of al-Kidd's arrest that prosecutors violate the Fourth Amendment when they obtain and execute a material witness warrant as a pretext for other law-enforcement objectives. Second, by holding that Ashcroft may be personally liable if his subordinates swore false affidavits to obtain the warrant authorizing al-Kidd's arrest, the majority stretches beyond recognition the rule that a government official is liable only when he personally violates the constitution. See Ashcroft v. Iqbal, ____ U.S. ____, 129 S.Ct. 1937, 1949, 173 L.Ed.2d 868 (2009).

A

1

The majority begins by effectively declaring the material witness statute unconstitutional, at least as applied to al-Kidd. But al-Kidd does not appear to contest that he met the statutory requirements for arrest as a material witness. See al-Kidd, 580 F.3d at 957. Nor does he contend that the material witness statute is facially unconstitutional. Id. at 966. The majority nevertheless holds that because prosecutors used a material witness warrant to arrest al-Kidd as a pretext to a criminal investigation, his detention violated the Fourth Amendment. This conclusion — that the material witness statute authorized al-Kidd's arrest while the Fourth Amendment forbade it — can only mean that the material witness statute itself is unconstitutional in this circumstance.[4] With respect, such conclusion is preposterous.

The federal material witness statute has existed since 1789, Bacon v. United States, 449 F.2d 933, 938 (9th Cir.1971), every state has adopted a version of the statute, id. at 939, and (at least until now), "[t]he constitutionality of th[e] statute apparently has never been doubted," Barry v. United States ex rel Cunningham, 279 U.S. 597, 617, 49 S.Ct. 452, 73 L.Ed. 867 (1929). The majority's decision to invalidate a statute passed by the First Congress and retained by every subsequent Congress should have by itself prompted us to rehear this case.

The majority does not stop at declaring a 200-year-old statute unconstitutional, however. It also distorts the bedrock Fourth Amendment principle that an official's subjective reasons for making an arrest are constitutionally irrelevant. The majority holds that if prosecutors used the material witness warrant as a pretext to arrest al-Kidd "with the ulterior and ... unconstitutional purpose of investigating or preemptively detaining" him, they violated his Fourth Amendment rights. Al-Kidd, 580 F.3d at 957 (emphasis added). This holding is impossible to square with Supreme Court precedent, which has "flatly dismissed the idea that an ulterior motive might serve to strip the agents of their legal justification." Whren v. United States, 517 U.S. 806, 812, 116 S.Ct. 1769, 135 L.Ed.2d 89 (1996) (emphasis added). Given that al-Kidd has conceded that he met the facial requirements for arrest under the material witness statute, the prosecutor's purpose for arresting him is immaterial to the Fourth Amendment analysis because "[s]ubjective intent alone ... does not make otherwise lawful conduct illegal or unconstitutional." Scott v. United States, 436 U.S. 128, 136-37, 98 S.Ct. 1717, 56 L.Ed.2d 168 (1978); see also Devenpeck v. Alford, 543 U.S. 146, 153, 125 S.Ct. 588, 160 L.Ed.2d 537 (2004) ("[T]he Fourth Amendment's concern with `reasonableness' allows certain actions to be taken in certain circumstances, whatever the subjective intent[of the government official taking the action]." (internal quotation marks omitted)).

The majority, unfortunately, disagrees. Although it acknowledges that an officer's subjective intentions are irrelevant to "ordinary, probable-cause Fourth Amendment analysis," it holds that because al-Kidd's arrest was not supported by probable cause that al-Kidd had committed a crime, his detention was constitutionally infirm. Al-Kidd, 580 F.3d at 966. To reach this novel result, the majority relies on the Supreme Court's "programmatic purpose" test. Id. at 968-69. Contrary to the majority's analysis, that test is totally inapplicable here. The Supreme Court uses the programmatic purpose test to evaluate the constitutionality of warrantless searches. See Indianapolis v. Edmond, 531 U.S. 32, 121 S.Ct. 447, 148 L.Ed.2d 333 (2000). Because al-Kidd was arrested under a valid warrant, however, the programmatic purpose test, and its concern for the purpose of an arrest, is entirely inapplicable here. Thus, the majority concludes that the material witness warrant authorizing al-Kidd's arrest is unconstitutional only after examining the subjective reasons prosecutors sought the warrant, something the Supreme Court has repeatedly forbidden us to do. This error alone warranted en banc review.

2

The majority then compounds its error by holding that the right to be free from a detention under a pretextual material witness warrant was clearly established at the time of al-Kidd's arrest. The majority claims this result is compelled by three sources: the clearly established definition of probable cause, al-Kidd, 580 F.3d at 971, "the history and purposes of the Fourth Amendment," id., and a footnote in a district court opinion, id. at 972 (quoting United States v. Awadallah, 202 F.Supp.2d 55, 77 n. 28 (S.D.N.Y.2002), rev'd on other grounds, 349 F.3d 42 (2d Cir.2003)).

The majority's reliance on the first two sources proves too much, of course. All government officials are presumed to be aware of the definition of probable cause and the history and purposes of the Fourth Amendment. If this is sufficient clearly to establish how the Fourth Amendment applies in a particular setting, then how can any Fourth Amendment rule ever not be "clearly established"? See Anderson v. Creighton, 483 U.S. 635, 639-40, 107 S.Ct. 3034, 97 L.Ed.2d 523 (1987).

The majority's reliance on Awadallah is possibly even more troubling. The majority's assertion that three sentences of dicta in a footnote to a subsequently reversed district court opinion clearly establish a right that the majority expended nearly three-thousand words describing is truly astonishing.[5] Under the majority's reasoning, our government's officials may find themselves subject to suits for decisions that they did not — and, even if they spent their time doing nothing but reading reports of federal judicial decisions, could not — know contravened the Constitution. Indeed, the lack of support for the majority's conclusion is so glaring that even the editorial board of a distinguished newspaper remarked that "officials should not have to fear personal lawsuits for performing their duties in good faith and in violation of no established legal precedent." Editorial, Suing Mr. Ashcroft: Why a Court's Decision to Allow a Personal Lawsuit Against the Former Attorney General Should Not Stand, Wash. Post, Sept. 12, 2009, at A16 (emphasis added).

Thus, the majority has held that a former Attorney General might suffer personal liability solely for acting within the bounds of federal law. One shudders at the thought that this decision might deter the incumbent and future Attorneys General from exercising the full range of their lawful authority to protect the security of the United States.

B

The majority goes further still, however, by holding that Ashcroft may be held personally liable to al-Kidd if his subordinates provided false testimony in support of their application for a material witness warrant. Al-Kidd, 580 F.3d at 975-76. It cannot be contested that al-Kidd has a clearly established right to be free of an arrest based on fraudulent testimony. See Franks v. Delaware, 438 U.S. 154, 164-65, 98 S.Ct. 2674, 57 L.Ed.2d 667 (1978). Al-Kidd does not allege that Ashcroft personally swore any false testimony, however. Rather, it was Ashcroft's subordinates who provided the testimony that al-Kidd alleges was false. In light of Iqbal's holding that "each Government official, his or her title notwithstanding, is only liable for his or her own misconduct," 129 S.Ct. at 1949, al-Kidd's complaint fails to allege facts sufficient to establish a cause of action against Ashcroft.

As Judge Bea explains in detail, al-Kidd does not allege that Ashcroft encouraged federal prosecutors to lie in applications for material witness warrants. Al-Kidd, 580 F.3d at 992-93 (Bea, J., dissenting). Al-Kidd does not claim that Ashcroft even knew that his subordinates might be submitting false affidavits. At most, al-Kidd claims that Ashcroft's policies encouraged his subordinates to use material witness warrants to detain individuals within the maximum extent authorized by law. Id. at 993. By permitting al-Kidd's claim that Ashcroft has violated Franks to proceed, the majority permits al-Kidd to seek damages from Ashcroft for his subordinates' alleged misconduct, a result indisputably at odds with Iqbal. See 129 S.Ct. at 1949.

III

After this decision, a prosecutor who executes a perfectly valid material witness warrant must worry that he will find himself sued and liable in damages for violating the

Fourth Amendment. Moreover, any cabinet-level official must worry that he might be personally liable if his subordinates take an action perfectly consistent with then-existing federal law.[6]

Because these results are contrary to both logic and law, I respectfully dissent from our unfortunate rejection of the opportunity to correct these errors by rehearing this case en banc.

Notes

[1] The federal material witness statute, 18 U.S.C. § 3144, provides:

If it appears from an affidavit filed by a party that the testimony of a person is material in a criminal proceeding, and if it is shown that it may become impracticable to secure the presence of the person by subpoena, a judicial officer may order the arrest of the person and treat the person in accordance with the provisions of section 3142 of this title. No material witness may be detained because of inability to comply with any condition of release if the testimony of such witness can adequately be secured by deposition, and if further detention is not necessary to prevent a failure of justice. Release of a material witness may be delayed for a reasonable period of time until the deposition of the witness can be taken pursuant to the Federal Rules of Criminal Procedure.

[2] Al-Kidd's complaint also names several other federal officers and agencies as defendants. None of the other defendants appealed the district court's decision denying qualified immunity, and therefore al-Kidd's claims against them were not before the panel.

[3] In a portion of its opinion in which Judge Bea concurred, the majority reversed the district court's determination that Ashcroft was not immune from al-Kidd's claim arising from the conditions of al-Kidd's confinement. See al-Kidd, 580 F.3d at 977-79.

[4] I acknowledge that the majority does not say that it is declaring the material witness statute unconstitutional. Nevertheless, that is what it does. The majority acknowledges that individuals arrested under the allegedly unconstitutional policy "met the facial statutory requirements of [the material witness statute]." Al-Kidd, 580 F.3d at 957. Despite this, in a section of its opinion entitled "Al-Kidd's Fourth Amendment Rights Were Violated," id. at 965, it concludes that al-Kidd's arrest was impermissible. By concluding that the Constitution invalidates arrests authorized by the statute, the majority must conclude that the statute is unconstitutional to the extent it authorizes arrests such as the one in this case — put another way, that the statute is unconstitutional as applied to al-Kidd.

[5] In addition, the Chief Judge of the Southern District of New York has expressly declined to follow Awadallah. See In re Application of U.S. for a Material Witness Warrant, 213 F.Supp.2d 287, 288 (S.D.N.Y.2002).

[6] The possibility the federal government might reimburse Ashcroft for any judgment against him hardly removes the likelihood that this decision might deter the current or future Attorneys General from carrying out their duties. Anderson, 483 U.S. at 641 n. 3, 107 S.Ct. 3034 (noting that 28 C.F.R. § 50.15(c) "permit[s] reimbursement of

Department of Justice employees when the Attorney General finds reimbursement appropriate"). Claims for reimbursement have been denied on occasion. See Falkowski v. EEOC, 719 F.2d 470, 472-76 (D.C.Cir.1983) (arising after the government declined to represent a former employee in a lawsuit related to her employment), vacated sub nom. U.S. Dep't of Justice v. Falkowski, 471 U.S. 1001, 105 S.Ct. 1860, 85 L.Ed.2d 155 (1985); Turner v. Schultz, 187 F.Supp.2d 1288, 1290 (D.Colo.2002) (same). Moreover, the decision to provide or to deny such reimbursement is entirely within the discretion of the current Attorney General, and is not subject to judicial review. Falkowski v. EEOC, 764 F.2d 907, 911 (D.C.Cir.1985).

Judge O'Scannlain's dissent in US v. Burgum (Jan 25, 2011)

O'SCANNLAIN, Circuit Judge, dissenting:

Joseph Case Burgum pled guilty to two counts of bank robbery. As noted, in both robberies Burgum approached the bank manager and identified himself as an FBI agent. Burgum handcuffed both managers to a black box which Burgum claimed was a bomb. Burgum then displayed a remote control and said something to the effect of: "I've activated the bomb. This device is a remote control. If I press this button, it will blow you and half this building up."

At sentencing, the district court calculated a Guidelines range of 108-135 months, but, ultimately, departed upward to a sentence of 180 months. During a lengthy sentencing hearing, the district court noted that one aggravating factor, among many, was that Burgum was unlikely to repay the money that he stole from the banks. The majority concludes that such mention of Burgum's unlikeliness to pay restitution mandates that we vacate Burgum's sentence and remand for resentencing.

I agree that Ninth Circuit precedent prohibits the sentencing judge from treating Burgum's financial situation as an aggravating factor. But, as the majority concedes, because Burgum did not object to the district court's considering his inability to make restitution, our review is for plain error. We may vacate and remand only if there is "plain forfeited error affecting substantial rights that seriously affect the fairness, integrity or public reputation of judicial proceedings." United States v. Olano, 507 U.S. 725, 736, 113 S.Ct. 1770, 123 L.Ed.2d 508 (1993). For an error to affect a defendant's "substantial rights," the defendant typically must show that the error "affected the outcome of the district court proceedings." Id. at 734, 113 S.Ct. 1770. A review of the record here demonstrates that Burgum's sentence was driven by the violent method by which he accomplished the robberies and that Burgum's inability to make restitution for his crimes did not affect his sentence. Therefore, I respectfully dissent.

After calculating the Guidelines range and noting some mitigating factors, the sentencing judge said that he "found some very troubling, aggravating factors here, too." "The problem and issue that I am struggling with in this case," the judge continued, "and what was so upsetting to me was the nature of these bank robberies that [Burgum] did.

First and foremost I just find the infliction of emotional distress on the bank manager and the tellers to be incomprehensible. I can't imagine the terror that they must have fe[lt] and ... will continue to feel." The judge indicated that Burgum's robberies were "more terrifying" than most "because of the use of the hoax bomb," calling the robberies "cold and calculated," as well as "very cruel and tormenting to the victims." "And that's what troubles me the most about this case," he added.

After noting some other aggravating factors, the judge moved to his standard discussion of factors he considers at sentencing (drawn, of course, from 18 U.S.C. § 3553(a)). When the judge reached the need to provide restitution, section 3553(a)(7), he was reminded of another aggravating factor: "One additional aggravating factor that I didn't mention," the judge noted, is that "the chances of restitution in this case are probably slim, maybe even null," given that Burgum appeared unlikely to pay back the $258,280 he owed to the banks.

The judge revealed that he intended to depart upward to a sentence of fifteen years. He then noted that "what is ... driving me on the sentence is the nature of this offense. This is about as bad a bank robbery as I can imagine."

The sentencing judge echoed this statement several more times throughout the lengthy proceeding:

- "[A]gain, what is upsetting to me is the nature of the offense."
- "These offenses were two very, very serious robberies with hoax bombs; letting people [believe] that, at any moment, they could be blown to smithereens.... I have never seen anything like that. And, I'm actually surprised that everyone was saying [that a] seven and a half year[]" sentence was appropriate.
- "I can get past the criminal history.... But I just can't get over the cruel and unusual, violent nature of the robberies, to say that a seven-and-a-half year sentence is appropriate. I just can't do that."
- A seven-and-a-half year sentence "does not reflect the seriousness of what happened here."
- "[W]hen I look at this offense, it was terrifying to me. It was absolutely terrifying.... I would rather [have] a gun pointed at me than someone attaching" a bomb to my wrist. "I haven't seen ... anything as cruel as that."
- "There is a part of me that has compassion and mercy for Mr. Burgum.... But the thing that is upsetting to me, even as I speak, is I'm just envisioning handcuffs, attached to my wrist and telling me ... I could be blown up. That's just frightening. It's an act of terror. I can't get by the seriousness of the offense."

Viewed in the context of the sentencing as a whole, it is abundantly clear to me that the district judge upwardly departed because of the violent nature of the robberies, and that the judge's reference to unlikely restitution was an incidental observation that did not affect the sentence.

I respectfully dissent.

Judge O'Scannlain's dissent in Montz v. Pilgrim Films & TV (May 4, 2011)

O'SCANNLAIN, Circuit Judge, Joined by GOULD, TALLMAN and BEA, Circuit Judges, dissenting:

Montz does not claim to have sold his rights as a copyright owner. To the contrary, he alleges that he retained those rights, and that Pilgrim implicitly promised not to use or to disclose his ideas without his consent. As the district court properly held, an action to enforce a promise not to use or to disclose ideas embodied in copyrighted material without authorization asserts rights equivalent to those protected by the Copyright Act. Accordingly, the district court's determination that the Copyright Act preempts Montz's claims should be affirmed. I respectfully dissent from the Court's opinion to the contrary.

I

A state law claim is preempted if the rights asserted under state law "come within the subject matter of copyright," as described in 17 U.S.C. §§ 102 and 103, and are "equivalent" to the exclusive rights of copyright owners specified in 17 U.S.C. § 106. 17 U.S.C. § 301(a); see also Laws v. Sony Music Entm't, Inc., 448 F.3d 1134, 1137 (9th Cir.2006). The district court ruled that both of Montz's state law claims—which assert rights to ideas embodied in screenplays, videos, and other tangible media—come within the "subject matter of copyright." As the en banc court agrees with this ruling, I shall address only the second prong: whether Montz's claims are "equivalent" to the exclusive rights afforded to copyright owners by section 106.[1]

A

Montz's breach-of-implied-contract claim consists of the following allegations: (1) "[t]he Plaintiffs presented their ideas for the `Ghost Hunter' Concept to the Defendants[] in confidence, pursuant to the custom and practice of the entertainment industry, for the express purpose of offering to partner with the Defendants in the production, broadcast and distribution of the Concept," (2) "by accepting the Plaintiffs' disclosure of its concept," the defendants agreed that they "would not disclose, divulge or exploit the Plaintiffs' ideas and concepts without compensation and without obtaining the Plaintiffs' consent," (3) "the Plaintiffs justifiably expected to receive a share of any profits and credit that might be derived from the exploitation of [their] ideas and concepts," and (4) "by producing and broadcasting the Concept," "[t]he Defendants breached their implied agreement not to disclose, divulge or exploit the Plaintiffs' ideas and concepts without the express consent of the Plaintiffs, and to share with the Plaintiffs . . . the profits and credit for their idea and concepts." (emphasis added).

To distinguish itself from a copyright claim, a state law claim "must protect rights which are qualitatively different from the copyright rights." Laws, 448 F.3d at 1143 (internal quotation marks omitted). This requires that the state claim have an "extra element which transforms the nature of the action." Id. (internal quotation marks omitted). Montz's breach-of-implied-contract claim fails this test.

Under section 106, a copyright owner has the exclusive rights to reproduce, to distribute, and to display the copyrighted work, as well as to prepare derivative works based on the copyrighted work. 17 U.S.C. § 106. Section 106 also provides a copyright owner with the exclusive rights to authorize such reproduction, distribution, display, and preparation. Id. Montz alleges that "by producing and broadcasting" Ghost Hunters, "[t]he Defendants breached their implied agreement not to disclose, divulge or exploit the Plaintiffs' ideas and concepts without the[ir] express consent." In other words, Montz asserts that Pilgrim produced and broadcast a television program derived from Montz's screenplays, video, and other materials without authorization. These rights are equivalent to the rights of copyright owners under section 106—namely, the exclusive rights to authorize reproduction, distribution, and display of original works, and to authorize preparation of derivative works. See Del Madera Props. v. Rhodes & Gardner, Inc., 820 F.2d 973, 977 (9th Cir.1987), overruled on other grounds by Fogerty v. Fantasy, Inc., 510 U.S. 517, 114 S.Ct. 1023, 127 L.Ed.2d 455 (1994) ("[A]n implied promise not to use or copy materials within the subject matter of copyright is equivalent to the protection provided by section 106 of the Copyright Act.").

B

With respect, I suggest the majority does not appreciate the significance of Montz's refusal to authorize Pilgrim to use the ideas embodied in his materials.[2] This is not the same as authorizing Pilgrim to use his ideas so long as it pays him. A copyright is not just the right to receive money upon the use of a work; it is "the right to control the work, including the decision to make the work available to or withhold it from the public." Laws, 448 F.3d at 1137; see also eBay Inc. v. MercExchange, LLC, 547 U.S. 388, 392, 126 S.Ct. 1837, 164 L.Ed.2d 641 (2006) ("[A] copyright holder possesses the right to exclude others from using his property." (internal quotation marks omitted)). Indeed, because a copyright gives its owner a property right—not merely a liability right—injunctive relief for copyright infringement is provided for by Congress, and is routinely granted by courts. See 17 U.S.C. § 502; Elvis Presley Enters., Inc. v. Passport Video, 349 F.3d 622, 627 (9th Cir.2003).

To be sure, many copyright owners choose to sell the right to control their work. But a copyright holder may turn down money—or accept less money—in exchange for retaining more control over, and more involvement with, his work. For instance, Matt Damon and Ben Affleck famously refused to sell the rights to Good Will Hunting until they were promised starring roles in the film. See Bernard Weinraub, The Script is Modest, But Not the Buzz, N.Y. Times, Nov. 20, 1997, at E1. Such is the case here: Montz did not offer to sell his idea to Pilgrim; he offered "to partner" with Pilgrim in the show's "production and distribution." And when that offer was refused, Montz received an implied promise that Pilgrim would not use the ideas embodied in his materials without his consent.

Thus, Montz does not claim to have sold the rights to the ideas embodied in his materials, as did the plaintiff in Grosso v. Miramax Film Corp., 383 F.3d 965 (9th Cir.2004). Grosso involved a particular type of breach-of-implied-contract claim, the elements of which the California Supreme Court elucidated in Desny v. Wilder, 46 Cal.2d

715, 299 P.2d 257 (1956). To state a Desny claim, the plaintiff must plead that he "prepared the work, disclosed the work to the offeree for sale, and did so under circumstances from which it could be concluded that the offeree voluntarily accepted the disclosure knowing the conditions on which it was tendered and the reasonable value of the work." Grosso, 383 F.3d at 967.

"[M]irror[ing] the requirements of Desny," the complaint in Grosso alleged the plaintiff had submitted a movie script to the defendants "with the understanding and expectation . . . that [he] would be reasonably compensated for its use by Defendants." Id. (internal quotation marks omitted). We concluded that the defendants' "implied promise to pay" for use of the idea embodied in the script constituted "an `extra element' for preemption purposes." Id. at 968. The subject of the implied contract, then, was the sale of the plaintiff's idea. The plaintiff asserted that he had "disclosed [his] work to the offeree for sale," and that, by using the ideas embodied in his work, the offeree had implicitly agreed to pay for it. Id. at 967.

By contrast, Montz alleges that he retained his rights as a copyright owner. Montz "presented [his] ideas for the `Ghost Hunter' Concept to the Defendants[] . . . for the express purpose of offering to partner with the Defendants in the production, broadcast and distribution of the Concept." Pilgrim rejected the offer but allegedly promised implicitly not to use Montz's ideas "without [his] consent." Therefore, according to the complaint, Pilgrim did not promise to pay for the use of Montz's ideas. Rather, it promised (implicitly) to respect Montz's rights to the production, distribution, and broadcast of his work. Put differently, it promised to respect the rights afforded to Montz by the Copyright Act.

The majority asserts that there is "no meaningful difference between the conditioning of use on payment in Grosso and conditioning use in this case on the granting of a partnership interest in the proceeds of the production." Maj. Op. at 977. This was never the issue. The Montz panel did not rely on the difference between seeking compensation in the form of a lump sum versus a percentage of profits. Rather, it relied on the difference between authorizing the use of one's work in exchange for money, and not authorizing the use of one's work at all. See Montz v. Pilgrim Films & Television, Inc., 606 F.3d 1153, 1158 (9th Cir.2010) ("Whereas the breach of the alleged agreement in Grosso violated the plaintiff's right to payment on a sale, the breach of the alleged agreement in this case violated the plaintiffs' exclusive rights to use and to authorize use of their work. . . ."). I am mindful of Montz's allegation that he expected to receive compensation and credit if his ideas were ever used. But this fact alone is not sufficient to "transform the nature of the action." Laws, 448 F.3d at 1144. Montz expected to receive compensation and credit for use of his work only because he also expected—as any copyright owner would—that his work would not be used without authorization. Far from being "transformative," entitlement to compensation and credit under the implied contract was merely the result of the contract's prohibition against unauthorized use of Montz's work. There is thus nothing in the complaint that "qualitatively distinguish[es]" the breach-of-implied-contract claim from a copyright claim.[3] Id.

C

The majority insists that by limiting implied contract protection to those who authorize the use of their work in exchange for consideration, "the dissent misses the point." Maj. Op. at 981. But it is not clear just what point I am missing. If the point is to fill "the gap that would otherwise exist between state contract law and copyright law," id. at 981, then I suggest that a focus on authorization is entirely appropriate. Where a copyright owner authorizes the use of his work, but does not receive the consideration he was promised, he has a contract claim; where a copyright owner does not authorize the use of his work, but, nonetheless, someone uses it to produce a substantially similar work, he has a copyright claim.

If, however, "the point" is to provide greater protection against the unauthorized use of copyrighted material than is afforded under the Copyright Act, then it is a point I am glad to miss, as it is inconsistent with the objectives of Congress. The Copyright Act strikes a balance between the property rights of copyright owners, and the expressive rights of the rest of the creative community, by permitting copyright suits only where "there is substantial similarity between the protected elements" of the two works. Benay v. Warner Bros. Entm't, Inc., 607 F.3d 620, 624 (9th Cir.2010). Here, Montz attempts to use an implied contract claim to do what the Copyright Act does (i.e., to protect the unauthorized use of copyrighted materials). The only difference is that Montz's implied contract claim would protect those rights more broadly because California implied contract law does not require as strict a showing of substantial similarity as federal copyright law. See Benay, 607 F.3d at 631. But the "fact that the state-created right is . . . broader . . . than its federal counterpart will not save it from pre-emption." 1 Melville B. Nimmer & David Nimmer, Nimmer on Copyright § 1.01[B][1] (rev. ed. 2010).

II

Montz's breach-of-confidence claim also asserts rights equivalent to the rights protected by the Copyright Act. The complaint states that "the Plaintiffs' disclosure of their ideas and concepts [was] strictly confidential," and that "[b]y taking the Plaintiffs' novel ideas and concepts, exploiting those ideas and concepts, and profiting therefrom to the Plaintiffs' exclusion, the Defendants breached their confidential relationship with the Plaintiffs." Such claim simply echoes the allegations of the breach-of-implied-contract claim. Indeed, the alleged breach-of-confidence stems from the alleged violation of the very rights contained in section 106—the exclusive rights of copyright owners to use and to authorize use of their work.

The majority relies on two elements to distinguish the rights asserted in Montz's breach-of-confidence claim from the rights protected by the Copyright Act. First, the breach-of-confidence claim requires Montz to show that Pilgrim disclosed confidential material (i.e., the ideas embodied in Montz's materials) to third parties. Maj. op. at 981-82. But a copyright affords its owner the same right: the right against unauthorized disclosure of copyrighted work. See Laws, 448 F.3d at 1137. Second, the breach-of-confidence claim requires that Montz show Pilgrim breached a confidential relationship or entrustment. Maj. op. at 981-82. Yet a breach of a relationship of trust does not, by itself, transform the nature of an action. See Del Madera Props., 820 F.2d at 977 (noting that the breach of a fiduciary duty "does not add any `extra element' which changes the nature of the action"). The breach-of-confidence claim still asserts rights protected by the Copyright Act; the only difference is that the rights are asserted against a particular person (i.e., someone with whom the copyright holder had a confidential relationship). But the right against unauthorized disclosure of copyrighted work already applies against everyone, regardless of whether one had a confidential relationship with the copyright holder.

Because Montz's breach-of-confidence claim is not qualitatively different from a copyright claim, it is preempted.

III

Montz does not allege that he sold the ideas embodied in his Ghost Hunters materials to Pilgrim and that Pilgrim simply failed to make good on its promise to pay. Instead, he alleges that Pilgrim used the ideas embodied in Montz's copyrighted material without his permission. Because the Copyright Act protects such equivalent rights, I respectfully dissent.

Notes

[1] Although the allegations specific to Montz's breach-of-implied-contract claim refer only to "ideas" and "concepts"—which in the abstract are not subject to copyright protection, see 17 U.S.C. § 102(b)—it is clear from the complaint that Montz presented his "ideas" and "concepts" through television screenplay treatments, video, and other ancillary pre-production materials. Such materials qualify for copyright protection under section 102(a) as "original works of authorship fixed in [a] tangible medium of expression." Accordingly, the district court and the majority are correct that the rights asserted under Montz's breach-of-implied-contract claim "come within the subject matter of copyright" as described in section 102.

[2] Indeed, the majority apparently reads Montz's complaint as alleging that he authorized Pilgrim to use his idea so long as it paid him a share of the profits. See Maj. op. at 977 ("Montz . . . has alleged he revealed his concept to defendants reasonably expecting to be compensated, if his concept was used."); id. (stating that use of Montz's idea was conditioned "on the granting of a partnership interest in the proceeds of the production"); cf. id. at 977. (implying that Montz's idea was submitted "with the understanding that if the script is used, the producer must compensate" him). These statements overlook the fact that Montz did not just want money; he wanted to be involved in the show's production. And he presumably was not going to authorize Pilgrim to use his idea unless this condition was met.

[3] Montz argues that, at the very least, this Court should remand with instructions to grant leave to amend the complaint so that Montz can assert a breach-of-implied-contract claim that accords with Grosso. But the only way to cure the complaint

would be to allege that Montz authorized Pilgrim to use his work in exchange for a promise to pay for it. Such allegation would be inconsistent with the present complaint which states, emphatically, that Montz did not sell his work to Pilgrim, but rather that Pilgrim promised not to use Montz's ideas "without [his] express consent." Accordingly, it would be inappropriate to remand this case to allow for amendment. See Albrecht v. Lund, 845 F.2d 193, 195 (9th Cir.1988) (noting that dismissal without leave to amend is proper where the "allegation of other facts consistent with the challenged pleading could not possibly cure the deficiency" (internal quotation marks omitted)).

Judge O'Scannlain's dissent in Southeast Alaska Conservation Council v. Federal Highway Administration (May 4, 2011)

O'SCANNLAIN, Circuit Judge, dissenting:

The majority holds that the final environmental impact statement prepared by the State of Alaska and the Federal Highway Administration violates the National Environmental Policy Act, 42 U.S.C. § 4321 et seq., by failing to consider certain alternatives to the State's proposed plan to improve surface transportation to Juneau, Alaska. I respectfully dissent.

I

Under the National Environmental Policy Act ("NEPA"), a federal agency proposing a major action "significantly affecting the quality of the human environment" must prepare an environmental impact statement ("EIS") that includes a "detailed" account of the "alternatives to the proposed action." 42 U.S.C. § 4332(2)(C)(iii). The EIS must "[r]igorously explore and objectively evaluate all reasonable alternatives, and for alternatives which were eliminated from detailed study, briefly discuss the reasons for their having been eliminated." 40 C.F.R. § 1502.14(a).

"NEPA itself does not mandate particular results." Robertson v. Methow Valley Citizens Council, 490 U.S. 332, 350, 109 S.Ct. 1835, 104 L.Ed.2d 351 (1989). Rather, it "simply prescribes the necessary process" by which agencies must take a "hard look" at the environmental consequences of their proposed actions. Id. (internal quotation marks omitted). Accordingly, the question in this case is not whether the final EIS prefers the wrong alternative, but rather whether it considers a reasonable range of alternatives. As we explained in Headwaters, Inc. v. BLM, 914 F.2d 1174 (9th Cir.1990):

Section 4332 does not require the consideration of alternatives whose effect cannot be reasonably ascertained, and whose implementation is deemed remote and speculative. Nor must an agency consider alternatives which are infeasible, ineffective, or inconsistent with the basic policy objectives for the management of the area. Finally, NEPA does not require a separate analysis of alternatives which are not significantly distinguishable from alternatives actually considered, or which have substantially similar consequences. Thus, an agency's consideration of alternatives is sufficient if it considers an appropriate range of alternatives, even if it does not consider every available alternative.

Id. at 1180 (internal quotation marks and citations omitted).

II

The majority holds that the final EIS fails to consider certain alternatives for improving surface transportation to Juneau. According to the majority, the final EIS does not consider the possibility of improving ferry service by maximizing the use of existing infrastructure. Maj. Op. at 1053-54. In my view, however, the final EIS includes just such an alternative: the No Action Alternative.

As the final EIS explains, the No Action Alternative is based on the absence of capital improvements to ferry service in Lynn Canal. Thus, unlike the other alternatives considered in the final EIS, the No Action Alternative includes no new highways, terminals, or ferries. It is not the case, however, that the Alternative contemplates no new improvements at all. The final EIS makes clear that the No Action Alternative presumes the continued implementation of non-capital improvements, including measures designed to make the most of existing infrastructure. Indeed, the final EIS expressly considers "deploying different vessels," "changing schedules," and "experiment[ing] with different levels and types of service in Lynn Canal" as part of the No Action Alternative.

The majority asserts that the final EIS "expressly acknowledged that the No Action Alternative would provide reduced, not improved, ferry services." Maj. Op. at 1058. The suggestion is that the Alternative does not seriously contemplate improvements in ferry service if it anticipates that such a reduction would occur. The acknowledgment to which the majority refers, however, must be read in context. The relevant portion of the final EIS states: "The No Action Alternative is a reduction below the current level of service due to reduced mainliner frequency in Lynn Canal. Mainliner frequency would be reduced because of projected reduction in the number of mainliners operating in the [Alaska Marine Highway System or AMHS]." (emphases added). In short, the reduction in service would be caused by a lack of capital improvements, i.e., of new ferries servicing the canal. That the No Action Alternative presumes such a reduction says nothing about whether the Alternative contemplates the possibility of noncapital improvements. Just because there would be a reduction in service from the lack of new ferries does not mean that measures to maximize the efficiency of the existing infrastructure have been ignored.

The majority also faults the final EIS for not specifically considering the suggestion by the Southeast Alaska Conservation Council ("SEACC") to improve ferry transportation by reassigning two mainline vessels to service in Lynn Canal. NEPA, however, "does not require the consideration of alternatives ... whose implementation is deemed remote and speculative." Headwaters, 914 F.2d at 1180. Here, implementation of SEACC's suggestion is both. As explained in the final EIS, the No Action Alternative "is based on the most likely AMHS operations in the absence of any capital improvements specific to Lynn Canal," as reflected in the 2004 Southeast Alaska Transportation Plan ("SATP") developed by the Alaska Department of Transportation and Public Facilities (emphasis added). SEACC's proposal to reassign two mainline vessels to round-trip service in the canal is inconsistent with the SATP. Given that the SATP represents "a comprehensive, intermodal, long-range transportation plan" for the region, Alaska Stat. § 44.42.050(a), any possibility of implementing SEACC's proposal is remote and speculative.

Moreover, NEPA does not require the consideration of "alternatives which are infeasible, ineffective, or inconsistent with the basic policy objectives for the management of the area." Headwaters, 914 F.2d at 1180. As the final EIS notes, reassigning two mainline vessels to round-trip service in the Lynn Canal would come "at the expense of service elsewhere." Although it is true, as the majority points out, that the final EIS considers other alternatives that "would increase costs for the state and could have the ripple effect of reducing service elsewhere," Maj. Op. at 1057, the costs associated with SEACC's proposal are qualitatively different. By diverting vessels from one route to another in contravention of the SATP, the State would be directly depriving another area of committed resources. It was not arbitrary or capricious for the State to conclude that what amounts to robbing Peter to pay Paul would be "infeasible, ineffective, or inconsistent with the basic policy objectives of the area."

For these reasons, I believe the State reasonably concluded that SEACC's proposal to reassign mainline vessels did not require separate analysis. Because the final EIS considers a reasonable range of alternatives, it meets the requirements of NEPA. Accordingly, I would reverse the judgment of the district court.

Judge O'Scannlain's dissent in Singh v. Holder (June 17, 2011)

O'SCANNLAIN, Circuit Judge, joined by GOULD, RAWLINSON, CLIFTON, and CALLAHAN Circuit Judges, dissenting:

"Any alien who is physically present in the United States ... may apply for asylum," 8 U.S.C. § 1158(a)(1), but only if he "demonstrates by clear and convincing evidence that the application has been filed within 1 year after the date of the alien's arrival in the United States," id. § 1158(a)(2)(B). Here, the Immigration Judge ("IJ") was not convinced by Nirmal Singh's mere verbal assertions, credible as the petitioner may be, and thus required Singh to come forward with evidence corroborating his alleged date of entry. When Singh failed to do so, the IJ dismissed his application as time-barred, and the Board of Immigration Appeals ("BIA") affirmed, noting correctly that the burden of proof on granting asylum empowers an IJ to seek corroborating evidence from an otherwise credible witness.

Because the plain terms of the statutory scheme allow an IJ to seek corroboration from an applicant seeking to demonstrate his eligibility for asylum, and because the majority's reading would variegate an otherwise uniform statute, I respectfully dissent.

I

Our old rule that "the BIA may not require independent corroborative evidence from an asylum applicant who testifies credibly in support of his application," Kataria v.

INS, 232 F.3d 1107, 1113 (9th Cir.2000), has been formally extinguished. For asylum applications filed after May 11, 2005,[1] "Congress abrogated these holdings in the REAL ID Act of 2005." Aden v. Holder, 589 F.3d 1040, 1044 (9th Cir.2009). Instead, while credible testimony still can, in some circumstances, sustain the applicant's burden of proof, it does not automatically do so. See 8 U.S.C. § 1158(b)(1)(B)(ii) ("[T]he testimony of the applicant may be sufficient to sustain the applicant's burden without corroboration, but only if the applicant satisfies the trier of fact that the applicant's testimony is credible, is persuasive, and refers to specific facts sufficient to demonstrate that the applicant is a refugee." (emphasis added)). Now, "[w]here the trier of fact determines that the applicant should provide evidence that corroborates otherwise credible testimony, such evidence must be provided unless the applicant does not have the evidence and cannot reasonably obtain the evidence." Id. Thus, credible testimony may be sufficient to satisfy the applicant's burden of proof, but the Act also enables the trier of fact to require something more. To the extent our prior decisions hold to the contrary, they are superseded by the REAL ID Act. Aden, 589 F.3d at 1044.

That, more or less, should end the matter in this case. Although the IJ found Singh to be credible, the IJ concluded that Singh had not sustained his burden of demonstrating his date of entry into the United States through his testimony alone. The IJ thus required Singh to provide corroborating evidence of his alleged date of entry, which he failed to do. As the BIA concluded, such request was fully within the IJ's power, and there was no error in rejecting Singh's application as untimely.

II

The majority rejects all of this by concluding that 8 U.S.C. § 1158(b)(1)(B)(ii)—which explicitly provides for the IJ's authority to require corroborating evidence—applies to everything in an asylum applicant's burden except his duty to establish the timeliness of his application. As the majority would have it, no provision of the REAL ID Act explicates how an IJ may ensure that an immigrant has successfully demonstrated his date of entry by "clear and convincing evidence." In light of the statute taken as a whole, I cannot agree with the majority's conclusion.[2]

A

First, contrary to the majority's suggestion, the text of the section 1158(b)(1)(B)(ii) does not restrict the IJ's authority to seek corroborating evidence only to whether the applicant is a "refugee." Rather, this section speaks generally of "the applicant's burden" for demonstrating his eligibility for asylum, and states that, to sustain such burden, "[w]here the trier of fact determines that the applicant should provide evidence that corroborates otherwise credible testimony, such evidence must be provided unless the applicant does not have the evidence and cannot reasonably obtain the evidence." 8 U.S.C. § 1158(b)(1)(B)(ii). In order to demonstrate his eligibility for asylum, an asylum applicant must prove both that he has filed his application within one year after his entry into the United States and that he meets the statutory definition of a "refugee." See id. § 1158(a)-(b). In other words, an asylum applicant's "burden" for prevailing on his application necessarily includes the burden of establishing his date of entry.

Section 1158(b)(1)(B)(ii)'s discussion of the applicant's ability to sustain his "burden" thus refers to Singh's need to demonstrate his eligibility as a refugee meeting all statutory requirements for asylum. And because the text of such section nowhere limits its scope only to the determination of one portion of the applicant's statutory burden, as the majority suggests, the BIA did not err in consulting the section in affirming the IJ's decision.[3]

B

Moreover, although the majority suggests that structural elements of section 1158 leave some ambiguity as to the scope of subsection (b)(1)(B)(ii), I cannot conclude, as the majority does, that this structure was meant to frustrate the IJ's efforts to determine whether an applicant had provided clear and convincing evidence of his date of entry. As discussed, establishing both the timeliness of his application and his status as a "refugee" are necessary to an immigrant's successful asylum application. But under the majority's view, an IJ will be forced to evaluate the immigrant's testimony on these two questions under completely different standards. Under the majority opinion, an IJ will assess the question of an applicant's refugee status under section 1158(b)(1)(B)(ii), but will assess the timeliness of his application without regard to any provision explaining the applicant's standard for sustaining his burden. The text of the statute does not create such a divide, and there is no reason that we should.

Indeed, taking the statute as a whole, the analytical divide created by the majority's analysis goes far beyond the provisions dealing with asylum applications. The majority explains that the statute is divided into three general sections, each dealing with a different form of relief: section 1158 pertains to applications for asylum, section 1231(b)(3) pertains to withholding of removal, and section 1229a(c)(4) pertains to "other" requests for relief. See Majority Op. at 1166-68. But each of these sections contains a nearly identical provision that expressly permits an IJ to require corroborating evidence from an otherwise credible witness. See 8 U.S.C. §§ 1158(b)(1)(B)(ii); 1229a(c)(4)(B); 1231(b)(3)(C). Read together, these provisions set forth a single overarching corroboration standard for sustaining an immigrant's burden of proving his eligibility for any form of relief under the statute. Indeed, throughout the REAL ID Act, "Congress has installed a bias toward corroboration in the statute to provide greater reliability." Aden, 589 F.3d at 1045. And we treat the BIA's application of these corroboration provisions identically on review. See § 1252(b)(4)(D).

But the majority isolates Singh's testimony as to his date of entry from this uniform standard for assessing his credibility on all other matters relating to his requests for relief. This move is neither compelled by the statute's text, nor does it comply with the statute's general aim to "ma[ke] immigration litigation a little more like other litigation," where parties with the burden of proof ordinarily provide whatever corroboration they have when presenting their case.[4] Aden, 589 F.3d at 1045. In short, the majority has sidestepped the sweep of the statute's text to remove one of the most basic features of an asylum application from the statute's general corroboration standards.

III

In the case at hand, the IJ made no adverse credibility finding against Singh, but ultimately determined that he had not satisfied his burden of proving his date of entry by clear and convincing evidence. To meet that burden, the IJ sought corroborating evidence from Singh, which he failed to provide. As Singh admitted that he had no documents to corroborate his date of entry, it was his burden to explain its absence. In re J-Y-C-, 24 I. & N. Dec. 260, 263 (B.I.A.2007). Aside from his bald assertion that he "could not reasonably be expected to provide proof of when he entered the United States," the record is devoid of any indication from Singh as to why he was unable to corroborate a such a basic fact.

Without either evidence corroborating Singh's self-serving declaration of his date of entry or an explanation for the unavailability of such evidence, I have no choice but to conclude that the IJ did not err in barring Singh's application as untimely.[5]

Notes

[1] REAL ID Act of 2005, Pub.L. No. 109-13, § 101(h)(2), 119 Stat. 231, 305; Oyekunle v. Gonzales, 498 F.3d 715, 717 (7th Cir.2007) ("For aliens who applied for asylum after May 11, 2005[, the REAL ID Act] in effect codifies the [corroboration] rule....").

[2] The majority does not dispute that Singh's need to establish his date of entry by "clear and convincing evidence," 8 U.S.C. § 1158(a)(2)(B), may inherently empower the IJ to require corroborating evidence of such date. The only question enunciated by the majority, however, is whether the BIA erred in explicitly consulting section 1158(b)(1)(B)(ii) in affirming the IJ's actions.

[3] The majority suggests that its reading of the statute—which relies solely on the titles Congress ascribed to certain statutory subsections, many of which were not even codified in the United States Code—is compelled by the statute's text and through "[b]asic principles of statutory construction." Majority Op. at 1163. Yet, tellingly, the majority concludes that under a precedential order, the BIA's interpretation of the statute may be entitled to "some deference." Majority Op. at 1163 n. 4. Because administrative deference is applicable only where a statute is ambiguous, see Christopher v. SmithKline Beecham Corp., 635 F.3d 383, 392 (9th Cir.2011), I take this caveat to be an admission by the majority that its reading of the statute is indeed not compelled by the statute's text.

[4] This is a basic aspect of the REAL ID Act that the majority seems either to miss or to gloss over. Indeed, as we have previously recognized, with the REAL ID Act, Congress "changed the standard governing when a trier of fact may require corroborating evidence from where the evidence is `easily available' to where the evidence is `reasonably obtainable,' and imposed a heightened standard of review requiring that we reverse an agency's determination concerning the availability of corroborative evidence only if a reasonable trier of fact would be compelled to conclude that such corroborating evidence is unavailable." Shrestha v. Holder, 590 F.3d 1034, 1047-48 (9th Cir.2010) (citations

omitted).

[5] I note that the court lacks jurisdiction to consider Singh's claim that the REAL ID Act required the IJ to notify him of his need to present corroborating evidence and to provide him with an opportunity to bring forth such evidence, as Singh never exhausted this issue before the BIA. See 8 U.S.C. § 1252(d)(1); Barron v. Ashcroft, 358 F.3d 674, 677-78 (9th Cir.2004).

Judge O'Scannlain's dissent in US v. Hunt (Sept 1, 2011)

O'SCANNLAIN, Circuit Judge, dissenting:

The court orders Hunt's sentence effectively reduced from fifteen years to time served because the trial judge who took his guilty plea failed to seek an explicit admission that Hunt knew that the illegal drug he ordered, picked up, and possessed was cocaine. In my view, this error was harmless in light of the overwhelming and uncontroverted evidence that Hunt knew exactly what he was doing.

The majority does not really dispute this. Instead, it promulgates a new rule for this circuit, essentially eliminating harmless error review of Apprendi violations. Because of such unwarranted change in our sentencing jurisprudence, I must respectfully dissent.

I

A

In January 2004, the Anchorage Police Department received information that a man named "Stacy" was trafficking cocaine into Alaska by hiding it in candles. Later, law enforcement officers intercepted a package at the Anchorage airport which contained 1.2 kilograms of cocaine hidden inside candles. A controlled delivery was executed at the address listed on the package. A woman signed for the package and put it in the trunk of a car. Police then saw the defendant, Stacy Hunt, remove the package from the trunk of the car and leave with it in a Ford Explorer. The police stopped the Explorer, seized the cocaine, and arrested Hunt.

Hunt admitted to police that he ordered the cocaine and paid the woman $400 to sign for the package and to leave it for him in the trunk of the car. He then wrote a confession with his own hand stating that "Kisha called me ... to pick up [the] package," "my understanding is that Kisha would be paid $400," and a "package of 1 Kilo of coke was to be put in burgundy Mercedes S.U.V."

B

A federal indictment alleged that Hunt "knowingly and intentionally attempt[ed] to possess with intent to distribute a controlled substance, to wit: 500 grams or more of a mixture and substance containing cocaine," in violation of 21 U.S.C. §§ 841(b)(1)(B) and 846. Hunt appeared in federal court to plead guilty to the sole count in the indictment. The judge asked the Assistant United States Attorney (AUSA) to state the elements of the crime to which Hunt was pleading guilty. The AUSA stated that "the elements would be that on or about January 26th of 2004, Mr. Hunt attempted to possess a parcel that contained a little over a kilogram of cocaine... and that he did so knowingly." The court then asked Hunt if he understood what the government would have to prove in order to obtain a conviction, and Hunt said, "Yes." "And you've discussed all this with your attorney?" the court asked. Again, Hunt said, "Yes." The AUSA then interrupted, noting that he forgot an element, namely, "that Mr. Hunt attempted to possess that cocaine with the intent to distribute it." "Do you understand that additional element?" asked the court. Again, Hunt replied, "Yes, I do."

At this point, the court added a casual phrase in a simple follow up question which, as it turns out, effectively knocks fourteen years off Hunt's sentence. The judge said: "So you attempted to possess cocaine, you knew it was cocaine or some illegal drug, and you did it with the intent to distribute. I guess those are the three elements, okay?" (emphasis added). Hunt responded, "[T]o those elements, yes, I agree." Hunt then asked, "Could you give me those elements once again?" The court directed the AUSA to state the elements again, and he said "that Mr. Hunt attempted to possess a parcel which contained a little over a kilogram of cocaine.... We'd have to prove that Mr. Hunt's attempt to possess that cocaine was done knowingly and then we'd have to prove that he intended to distribute that cocaine." "Got it?" the court asked. "Okay, yes," replied Hunt. "Yes, I understand those elements," Hunt continued, "As far as the specific amount, I don't have personal knowledge of it as I never opened the package and weighed it, but I do accept responsibility for whatever was in it." Deeming this sufficient, the court accepted Hunt's guilty plea.

C

The district court sentenced Hunt for attempting to possess an unspecified amount of cocaine, pursuant to 21 U.S.C. § 841(b)(1)(B), which carries a statutory maximum of twenty years' imprisonment. The district court determined the base offense level was twenty-six and departed upward from a criminal history category of IV to one of VI to reach a Guidelines range of 120 to 150 months. The court then imposed an above-guidelines sentence of 180 months. Both the upgrade in the defendant's criminal history category and the upward departure in reaching the ultimate sentence of fifteen years were driven by Hunt's extensive criminal history. As the district court put it, Hunt has led a life "consumed with criminal activity."

This was no exaggeration. In 1984, when Hunt was just seventeen, he attacked a woman on the street, dragged her into a stairwell, and attempted to rape her. The police found Hunt exposed and on top of the woman, who was crying and pleading with him to stop. Hunt's punches left her with a bleeding mouth, a bruised face, and scratches on her neck. To avoid responsibility, Hunt told the police that the woman was a prostitute and was attempting to rob him. Hunt was convicted of attempted rape but, due to his age, received no jail time. Four years later, Hunt was arrested for sexual assault again. This time, he was accused of kidnapping a woman outside her home at gunpoint, forcing her into his car, driving her to a park, and raping her. Hunt's defense, again, was that the woman was a prostitute. No charges were filed.

A month later, in October 1988, Hunt, along with four others claiming to be members of "the Disciples," severely beat and threatened to kill a man who had refused to give them the case of beer he was carrying. Although Hunt was arrested for robbery, the case was dismissed, in part because the victim could no longer be located. In 1989, Hunt was convicted of selling cocaine, for which he received a one-year sentence.

In 1991, Hunt participated in the kidnapping and murder of a rival drug dealer. Hunt claimed that his co-defendants forced him to participate in the killing, a story which prosecutors apparently believed because they arranged for him to receive a three-year sentence, suspended for twelve months, in exchange for his cooperation. In 1993, Hunt was again convicted of drug possession, jailed for ninety days, and put on probation for three years, which he violated, causing him to serve ninety more days. Within a year of his release, Hunt violated his probation once again, this time by firing a gun in a nightclub in May 1994. Hunt was sentenced to two years in jail when he was finally convicted of this crime, after failing to appear in the original proceedings.

Just eight days after the nightclub incident, in June 1994, Hunt committed "battery with serious injury and a deadly weapon," by brutally beating his ex-girlfriend with a wooden baby cradle, and leaving her with a number of injuries, including a gash that required twenty stitches to close. He was sentenced to six years in prison. (At the same time, he was also charged with kidnapping, sexual battery, and forced oral sex, but not convicted.) Hunt went to jail for these crimes in 1996, but he was released on parole after two years, only to violate his parole three months later by testing positive for cocaine. He was arrested for another parole violation in 1999 and sentenced to six more months in jail. He violated parole once again in February 2000, for which he was not arrested until 2007.

Hunt was arrested on the current charges in 2004, but absconded to California after being released from police custody. It was not until December 2007, when he was arrested in California for beating up another women, that Hunt was finally returned to Alaska to face charges in the instant case.

Based on this vicious criminal history, the district court determined that a fifteen year sentence was necessary to "protect the public from further crimes of the defendant." 18 U.S.C. § 3553(a)(2)(C). The court added that, while Hunt's intelligence and charisma may have enabled him to avoid taking significant responsibility for his actions in the past, it would not do so this time.

II

The majority correctly recites the Apprendi rule: "Other than the fact of a prior conviction, any fact that increases the penalty for a crime beyond the prescribed statutory maximum must be submitted to a jury, and proved beyond a reasonable doubt," Apprendi v, New Jersey, 530 U.S. 466, 490, 120 S.Ct. 2348, 147 L.Ed.2d 435 (2000), but goes astray thereafter. Assuming arguendo that the district court committed Apprendi error by finding intentional cocaine possession yet failing to obtain an explicit admission from Hunt that he knew the illegal drug he possessed was cocaine, our precedent requires us to determine whether such error was harmless. See United States v. Zepeda-Martinez, 470 F.3d 909, 910 (9th Cir. 2006) ("Apprendi errors are reviewed for harmlessness."). "[A]n error is harmless if the court finds beyond a reasonable doubt that the result `would have been the same absent the error.'" Id. at 913 (quoting Neder v. United States, 527 U.S. 1, 19, 119 S.Ct. 1827, 144 L.Ed.2d 35 (1999)). The court may make such a finding where "the record contains `overwhelming' and `uncontroverted' evidence supporting" the omitted element. Id. (quoting Neder, 527 U.S. at 17-18, 119 S.Ct. 1827). Conversely, the error is not harmless if "the defendant contested the omitted element and raised evidence sufficient to support a contrary finding." Neder, 527 U.S. at 19, 119 S.Ct. 1827. Where a court must determine whether an Apprendi error was harmless, its review "encompasses the whole record including the sentencing proceedings." Zepeda-Martinez, 470 F.3d at 913 n.3 (internal quotation marks omitted). The purpose of this broad review is "to assist [the court] in determining what evidence the parties would have introduced at trial." Id. (internal quotation marks omitted). Thus, if we conclude, beyond a reasonable doubt on the basis of the record, that a jury would have convicted Hunt of attempted possession of cocaine with intent to distribute, the Apprendi error is harmless and we must affirm.

A

Here, the record contains overwhelming and uncontroverted evidence that Hunt attempted to possess cocaine with the intent to distribute it. The police received a tip that a man named "Stacy" was importing cocaine into Alaska, hidden in candles. Later, they intercepted a package that arrived in Alaska containing just over a kilogram of cocaine hidden in candles. The police then executed a controlled delivery of the package at its intended address. Sure enough, the defendant — who, as predicted, is "a man named `Stacy'" — retrieved the package hours after it was delivered.[1]

If this were not enough to convince a jury that Hunt intended to possess cocaine, Hunt confessed as much to the police. Hunt admitted that he ordered the cocaine and paid a woman named Kisha $400 to sign for the package and leave it for him in the trunk of the car. He then wrote a confession with his own hand stating that "Kisha called me to pick up [the] package" and that his "understanding is that Kisha would be paid $400," and that "package of 1 Kilo of coke was to be put in burgundy Mercedes S.U.V." Hunt's confession correctly recounted the amount of cocaine contained in the package (roughly a kilogram) and how the cocaine ended up in the trunk of the car: it was delivered to Kisha who signed for it, placed it in the car, and called Hunt to tell him it was ready for pick-up. This evidence of Hunt's intent to possess cocaine is surely "overwhelming." Zepeda-Martinez, 470 F.3d at 913.

Further, Hunt has not "controverted" this evidence, as he must to show that he suffered prejudice from the Apprendi error. See Zepeda-Martinez, 470 F.3d at 913. Nor could he. Hunt admits that he ordered the package and picked it up knowing it contained a controlled substance, but he would have the Court believe that he did not know which controlled substance he ordered and picked up. Surely it can be presumed, however, that drug dealers are not in the habit of giving each other more than they bargained for. It would therefore be absurd to suggest that Hunt — notwithstanding his confession to a "package of 1 Kilo of coke" — actually ordered a far less valuable illegal drug, such as marijuana, but the sender just decided (on his own) to mail cocaine instead, without informing Hunt or asking to be paid for the drug upgrade.

Moreover, if Hunt attempted to offer such an outlandish defense at trial, the government would likely be able to introduce Hunt's string of drug convictions in order to show that Hunt was an experienced drug dealer who would have made a point to know exactly what drug he was receiving. See United States v. Vo, 413 F.3d 1010, 1018-19 (9th Cir.2005) (holding that the defendant's prior drug conviction could be admitted to rebut his claim that he had no knowledge that a package he shipped contained methamphetamine because the "conviction tended to show that [he] was familiar with distribution of illegal drugs and that his actions in this case were not an accident or a mistake"); United States v. Howell, 231 F.3d 615, 628 (9th Cir.2000) (holding that defendant's "prior convictions for possession ... with intent to deliver cocaine [were admissible] to show that [the defendant] knew that the substance in the bag was a narcotic").

In sum, the only possible defense that is available to Hunt — that he received a free upgrade from marijuana to cocaine — is not one that "could rationally lead to a contrary finding with respect to the omitted element." Neder, 527 U.S. at 19, 119 S.Ct. 1827. Indeed, the majority has not offered a single theory that a defense counsel could possibly have argued to a jury in summation. Accordingly, there can be no reasonable doubt that, absent the Apprendi error, the result — Hunt's conviction for attempted possession of cocaine with the intent to distribute it — would have been the same.

B

The majority makes three efforts to avoid this conclusion, none of which withstand even passing scrutiny. First, the majority asserts that "Hunt's denial of his intent in this case" — which is unaccompanied by any explanation of how he accidentally came into possession of a kilogram of cocaine — meets the requirement that the defendant show "'evidence sufficient to support a contrary finding'" on the omitted element. Maj. Op. at 914-15 (quoting Neder, 527 U.S. at 19, 119 S.Ct. 1827). This, the majority explains, is because such testimony, "if credited, would raise a reasonable doubt as to his intent." Id. But evidence is sufficient to support a contrary finding only if it "could rationally lead to a contrary finding." Neder, 527 U.S. at 19, 119 S.Ct. 1827. Thus, we must ask whether a rational jury could credit Hunt's denial of intent to posses cocaine. The majority refuses to ask that question, stating instead that it "cannot conclude beyond a reasonable doubt that a rational jury would not find Hunt credible, especially where Hunt has never had the opportunity to testify," notwithstanding his conscious choice to plead guilty and to waive trial. Maj. Op. at 915.

This passage ignores the requirement that a defendant must both "contest[] the omitted element and raise[] evidence sufficient to support a contrary finding." Neder, 527 U.S. at 19, 119 S.Ct. 1827 (emphasis added); see also id. (requiring the defendant to "bring forth facts contesting the omitted element"). Instead, the majority allows a defendant to meet his Neder obligation based on the mere possibility that whatever he would have said at trial might have been credible.[2]

Next, the majority notes that "the contested fact in this case is Hunt's intent, a fact that is not subject to easy proof like the date of prior removal in Zepeda-Martinez, a fact which was proved through uncontroverted documentary evidence." Maj. Op. at 914. The implication is that harmless error analysis should be limited to cases where the error concerned an easily provable element. But this is inconsistent with Supreme Court cases which have "repeatedly recognized that the commission of a constitutional error at trial alone does not entitle a defendant to automatic reversal," Washington v. Recuenco, 548 U.S. 212, 218, 126 S.Ct. 2546, 165 L.Ed.2d 466 (2006), even where the defendant is deprived of a jury finding on an element, such as intent, which is not easily provable. See, e.g., California v. Roy, 519 U.S. 2, 5, 117 S.Ct. 337, 136 L.Ed.2d 266 (1996) (per curiam) (holding that the failure to instruct the jury that it must find intent to kill in order to convict the defendant of aiding and abetting murder was subject to harmless error analysis); Carella v. California, 491 U.S. 263, 266-67, 109 S.Ct. 2419, 105 L.Ed.2d 218 (1989) (holding that an instruction that foreclosed independent jury consideration of whether the defendant intended to commit theft was subject to harmless error analysis).

Finally, the majority relies heavily on United States v. Jordan, 291 F.3d 1091 (9th Cir.2002), which held that an Apprendi error will not be deemed harmless when a necessary element "is neither charged in the indictment nor proved to a jury beyond reasonable doubt." Id. at 1097. But Jordan's exception to harmless error analysis does not apply here because the type of drug Hunt intended to possess was charged in the indictment.

III

Near the end of its opinion, it becomes clear that the majority is not really applying harmless error analysis at all. Indeed, the majority refuses to discuss the strength of the evidence in this case. Instead, it declines to find this Apprendi error harmless for reasons that would apply to any case in which there is an Apprendi error, thereby effectively eliminating harmless error review in such case.

A

The majority reasons that "the plea and sentencing proceedings in this case provide an inadequate record because Hunt's intent regarding drug type was never litigated." Maj. Op. at 915. The majority correctly explains that harmless error review "requires us to `determin[e] what evidence the parties would have introduced at trial' had the issue been properly presented." Id. (quoting Zepeda-Martinez, 470 F.3d at 913 n.3). But it objects that, "[o]n the record before us, it is speculative at best to predict what evidence the parties would have presented at trial," and thus refuses "to speculate on how a hypothetical trial may have unfolded." Id.

These objections would apply to almost every appeal in which there is an Apprendi error since, in such cases, the omitted element will almost never have been litigated. Thus, under the precedent established today, a defendant asserting Apprendi error can avoid harmless error analysis simply by pointing out that he did not have the opportunity to litigate the omitted element. Similarly, it is always "speculative" to "determin[e] what evidence the parties would have introduced at trial had the issue been properly presented." Zepeda-Martinez, 470 F.3d at 913 n.3 (emphasis added) (internal quotation marks omitted); cf. Bryan A. Garner, Modern American Usage 780 (3rd ed.2009) (stating that the subjunctive mood is most commonly used to express states of irreality such as "conditions contrary to fact"). Therefore, while the majority may be uncomfortable engaging in a counterfactual inquiry, we are under explicit instructions from our precedents to conduct just such an inquiry.[3]

B

The Supreme Court made precisely these points in Neder when it held that the failure to submit an element of a crime to the jury is subject to harmless-error analysis. There, the defendant argued that "[t]o rely on overwhelming record evidence of guilt [that] the jury did not actually consider ... would be to dispense with trial by jury and allow judges to direct a guilty verdict." Neder, 527 U.S. at 17, 119 S.Ct. 1827 (emphasis omitted). The Neder Court explicitly rejected this argument, noting that "[t]he erroneous admission of evidence in violation of the Fifth Amendment's guarantee against self-incrimination and the erroneous exclusion of evidence in violation of the right to confront witnesses guaranteed by the Sixth Amendment are both subject to harmless-error analysis," even though such errors, like Apprendi errors, "infringe upon the jury's factfinding role" in ways that are "not readily calculable." Id. at 18, 119 S.Ct. 1827 (internal quotation marks omitted).

The defendant in Neder likewise insisted that, without "an actual verdict of guilty-beyond-a-reasonable-doubt,... the basis for harmless-error review is simply absent," requiring the court to speculate about how a hypothetical trial may have unfolded. Id. at 11, 119 S.Ct. 1827 (internal quotation marks omitted). But, again, the Court deemed this concern inconsistent with its cases which have repeatedly applied harmless error review even "where the jury did not render a `complete verdict' on every element of the offense." Id. at 13, 119 S.Ct. 1827; see also Recuenco, 548 U.S. at 221, 126 S.Ct. 2546 (rejecting the argument that applying harmless error analysis to an Apprendi error would require appellate courts to "hypothesize a guilty verdict that was never in fact rendered" (internal quotation marks omitted)).

If there is one way Apprendi errors differ from other errors to which harmless error analysis applies, it is this: where a sentence is reversed under Apprendi, the government does not have the opportunity to retry the defendant. Accordingly, Apprendi errors often result in convicted criminals receiving windfall sentence reductions. This case exemplifies such windfalls: Hunt's fifteen-year sentence — imposed chiefly because of his staggering criminal history — is effectively reduced to one year, or, more realistically, to time served.

C

The majority goes on to undermine harmless error review even further by espousing views of the judicial role that are inconsistent with the explicit limits that Congress has placed on appellate review of criminal sentences.

First, the majority categorically proclaims that "[o]ur responsibility is to see that constitutional requirements are met." Maj. Op. at 917. Congress, however, has directed federal courts reviewing criminal convictions to "give judgment after an examination of the record without regard to errors or defects which do not affect the substantial rights of the parties." 28 U.S.C. § 2111. This rule, as well as the Federal Rules of Criminal Procedure, requires that we "`disregard[]' errors that are harmless beyond a reasonable doubt." Neder, 527 U.S. at 7, 119 S.Ct. 1827 (quoting Fed.R.Crim.P. 52(a)). Since Congress need not provide criminal defendants with any appellate remedy whatsoever, see Abney v. United States, 431 U.S. 651, 656, 97 S.Ct. 2034, 52 L.Ed.2d 651 (1977), it is certainly within its power to limit appellate remedies to legal errors that likely affected the result of the proceeding in the trial court. Therefore, we do not have an unqualified "responsibility ... to see that constitutional requirements are met." Maj. Op. at 917. To the contrary, we have an explicit statutory responsibility to "give judgement ... without regard to [harmless] errors." 28 U.S.C. § 2111. This includes Apprendi errors. Recuenco, 548 U.S. at 222, 126 S.Ct. 2546.

Second, the majority insists that an Apprendi error is never a "technicality," and that "[a]voiding what the dissent calls a `windfall' sentence reduction due to an Apprendi error is achieved through a court's faithful compliance with constitutional requirements, not through appellate review." Maj. Op. at 917. This ignores the fact that the Supreme Court has applied harmless error review to Apprendi claims and has repeatedly stated that the harmless error doctrine "`serve[s] a very useful purpose insofar as it blocks setting aside convictions for small errors or defects that have little, if any, likelihood of having changed the result of the trial.'" Neder, 527 U.S. at 19, 119 S.Ct. 1827 (quoting Chapman v. California, 386 U.S. 18, 22, 87 S.Ct. 824, 17 L.Ed.2d 705 (1967)). Indeed, avoiding a windfall sentence reduction based on a "small error" (or "technicality," if you will) is the very purpose of the harmless error doctrine. See Shinseki v. Sanders, 556 U.S. 396, 129 S.Ct. 1696, 1705, 173 L.Ed.2d 532 (2009) ("The federal `harmless-error' statute ... seeks to prevent appellate courts from becoming `impregnable citadels of technicality.'" (quoting Kotteakos v. United States, 328 U.S. 750, 759, 66 S.Ct. 1239, 90 L.Ed. 1557 (1946))). So, while the majority is correct that such windfalls are ideally avoided "through a court's faithful compliance with constitutional requirements," faithful compliance with statutory requirements mandates that windfalls must also be avoided "through appellate review." Maj. Op. at 917.

Last, the majority maintains that "[a] sentence cannot be `richly deserved' under our Constitution if the facts supporting the sentence have not been proven as constitutionally required." Id. at 916. Yet Congress, under its constitutional power to regulate the federal courts, has directed us to "give judgment ... without regard to [harmless] errors," 28 U.S.C. § 2111, thereby establishing that a conviction and sentence may still be warranted even if a constitutionally required procedure was not scrupulously followed. Cf. Kotteakos, 328 U.S. at 759, 66 S.Ct. 1239 (stating that Congress passed the harmless error rule to prevent criminal trials from becoming "a game"). "The harmless error doctrine" thus "`recognizes the principle that the central purpose of a criminal trial is to decide the factual question of the defendant's guilt or innocence.'" Neder, 527 U.S. at 19, 119 S.Ct. 1827 (quoting Delaware v. Van Arsdall, 475 U.S. 673, 681, 106 S.Ct. 1431, 89 L.Ed.2d 674 (1986)); cf. Akhil Reed Amar, Sixth Amendment First Principles, 84 Geo. L.J. 641, 642 (1996) (arguing that "[t]he deep principles underlying the Sixth Amendment," and "constitutional criminal procedure generally," are "the protection of innocence and the pursuit of truth"). The majority ignores this principle by vacating Hunt's sentence despite overwhelming evidence that he committed each of the elements necessary to support it.

IV

The Supreme Court has warned that setting the harmless error standard "so high that it could never be surmounted would justify the very criticism that spawned the harmless-error doctrine in the first place." Id. at 18, 119 S.Ct. 1827. That criticism is that "`[r]eversal for error, regardless of its effect on the judgment, encourages litigants to abuse the judicial process and bestirs the public to ridicule it.'" Id. (quoting R. Traynor, The Riddle of Harmless Error 50 (1970)).

The Neder Court could have been talking about this case. Today, a defendant who has consistently evaded responsibility for his criminal conduct is once again rewarded for his labors. And today, the public sees a criminal who has shown nothing but cruelty to his fellow citizens and contempt for the law escape a richly deserved sentence based on an irrelevant technicality.

I respectfully dissent.

Notes

[1] The majority calls this evidence "circumstantial" and faults the government for not offering evidence that Hunt "looked inside the package to verify its contents." Maj. Op. at 914. This is an outrageous burden to place on the government, and one which is inconsistent with our long-standing rule that "circumstantial evidence can be used to prove any fact," United States v. Ramirez-Rodriquez, 552 F.2d 883, 884 (9th Cir.1977), and is no less inherently probative than is direct evidence, Ninth Circuit Model Criminal Jury Instructions § 1.5 (2010). Moreover, intent is almost always proven circumstantially since the only direct evidence of intent is a confession (which, incidentally, the government also presented in this case). See, e.g., Cnty. Court of Ulster Cnty., N.Y. v. Allen, 442 U.S. 140, 164, 99 S.Ct. 2213, 60 L.Ed.2d 777 (1979) (noting that "it is surely rational to infer" from the fact that the defendants were in a car which contained guns "that each [defendant] was fully aware of the presence of the guns and had both the ability and the intent to exercise dominion and control over" them).

[2] The majority is also impressed by Hunt's claim that he confessed only because that is what the police "wanted to hear." Maj. Op. at 914-15. But simply attacking one piece

of evidence (the confession) with one of the most common means by which confessions are challenged (by claiming that the confessor was just seeking to please his interrogators) is not sufficient evidence to support a contrary finding. Compare United States v. Nordby, 225 F.3d 1053, 1060-61 (9th Cir.2000), overruled on other grounds by United States v. Buckland, 289 F.3d 558 (9th Cir.2002) (concluding that the defendant brought forth evidence sufficient to support a contrary finding on the quantity of marijuana grown on his land by demonstrating that he "had been vacationing for much of the time that the marijuana crop had been in the ground, and only returned to the area five days before being arrested").

[3] Put another way, the majority's objection is either that "Hunt's intent regarding drug type was never litigated," or that it was never litigated in front of a jury. If it is the latter, then this is the end of harmless error review of Apprendi violations in the Ninth Circuit since such violations only occur where an element of a crime is not "submitted to a jury, and proved beyond a reasonable doubt." Apprendi, 530 U.S. at 490, 120 S.Ct. 2348. If it is the former, that is, if the majority only objects that the record of Hunt's intent was not sufficiently developed during the sentencing proceedings, then the proper remedy (contrary to its holding) would be to remand so that the district court can hold a hearing and make a factual finding on whether Hunt intended to possess cocaine.

Judge O'Scannlain's dissent from the denial of rehearing en banc in Hrdlicka v. Reniff (Sept 1, 2011)

O'SCANNLAIN, Circuit Judge, joined by GOULD, TALLMAN, BYBEE, CALLAHAN, BEA, IKUTA and N.R. SMITH Circuit Judges, dissenting from the denial of rehearing en banc:

The court today holds that the First Amendment mandates that county jails distribute unsolicited junk mail to their inmates, or face a burdensome lawsuit from the junk mail publisher, citing Turner v. Safley, 482 U.S. 78, 107 S.Ct. 2254, 96 L.Ed.2d 64 (1987).[1] Given that Turner decided only the standard of review to apply when a prison regulation impinges upon inmates' First Amendment rights, id. at 89, 107 S.Ct. 2254, the majority's interpretation is an extraordinary leap since all agree that no inmate rights are at stake in this case. Regrettably, the majority's opinion is completely untethered from Supreme Court precedent and in considerable tension with our own case law. It further complicates the already "inordinately difficult undertaking" of prison administration. Id. at 85, 107 S.Ct. 2254. I respectfully dissent, therefore, from the failure of our court to rehear this case en banc.

I

Ray Hrdlicka publishes a quarterly magazine called Crime, Justice & America ("CJA") that includes a number of items which may be of interest to jail inmates. Indeed, between 2002 and the publication of the majority's opinion, CJA went through fourteen editions totaling over one million copies. Which is quite impressive, until one realizes that rather than relying on subscriptions, CJA has simply blanketed jailhouses with hundreds of free copies every week.[2]

CJA's business model is fairly simple. It lures advertisers — usually bail bondsmen and lawyers — with the promise of a captive audience of thousands of inmates in immediate need of their services. It then ensures that it will fulfill that promise by pressuring jail administrators to choose either leaving stacks of CJA in common areas or allowing individual copies of CJA to be mailed directly to inmates off of an inmate roster. Either way, every seven days enough copies arrive at the targeted jails to ensure that at least one out of every ten inmates gets one. Hrdlicka is thereby able to externalize the cost of increasing his readership on the prison system.

Pursuant to content neutral department policies, officials at the Sacramento County and Butte County Jails refused to facilitate Hrdlicka's distribution scheme while allowing Hrdlicka to send CJA to any prisoner who requested it. But in an effort to minimize the risk of smuggled contraband as well as the amount of excess paper inmates could use to do things like start fires or clog toilets, these jail administrators refused to disseminate extra copies to those inmates who had not asked for them.

Hrdlicka filed a suit under 42 U.S.C. § 1983 claiming a constitutional right to pursue his business model. And now this court obliges by discovering such a right in the First Amendment.

II

Challenges to jail or prison regulations limiting outside contact with prisoners undoubtedly involve the balancing of constitutional imperatives. Turner, 482 U.S. at 84, 107 S.Ct. 2254. The majority focuses almost entirely upon those implicated by the First Amendment. But also among them is that running a jail "requires expertise, planning, and the commitment of resources, all of which are peculiarly within the province of the legislative and executive branches of government." Id. at 84-85, 107 S.Ct. 2254. Therefore the separation of powers "counsel[s] a policy of judicial restraint," particularly "[w]here a state penal system is involved." Id.; see also Beard v. Banks, 548 U.S. 521, 528, 126 S.Ct. 2572, 165 L.Ed.2d 697 (2006).

Fundamental to maintaining this balance between a prisoner's right to contact with the outside world and the State's ability to run a functional prison system is the ability to recognize when First Amendment interests are implicated. And regardless of what the majority may have found in the pages of CJA, nothing in the United States Reports or the Federal Reporter gives an outsider a First Amendment interest, let alone a freestanding right, to unsolicited contact with inmates.

The Supreme Court has certainly never found such an interest. See Jones v. N.C. Prisoners' Labor Union, Inc., 433 U.S. 119, 121, 97 S.Ct. 2532, 53 L.Ed.2d 629 (1977) (brushing aside a union challenge to a restriction against bulk mail to inmates, as "barely implicat[ing]" First Amendment rights); Pell v. Procunier, 417 U.S. 817, 822, 94 S.Ct. 2800, 41 L.Ed.2d 495 (1974) (allowing a prohibition on face-to-face interviews with inmates based on "the familiar proposition that lawful incarceration brings about the necessary withdrawal or limitation of many privileges and rights" (internal quotation marks omitted)).

Indeed, the only time the Court has ever acknowledged a publisher's "interest in access to prisoners" is when those prisoners "through subscription, willingly seek their point of view." Thornburgh v. Abbott, 490 U.S. 401, 408, 109 S.Ct. 1874, 104 L.Ed.2d 459 (1989). Only then — when jail regulations limit a detainee's access to the outside world — has the Court considered the First Amendment interests of the person with whom the detainee wished to correspond. And, even then, the Court made clear that it was announcing a rule for when the "rights of prisoners and outsiders" are at issue. Id. at 410 n. 9, 109 S.Ct. 1874. Cf. Shaw v. Murphy, 532 U.S. 223, 229-30, 121 S.Ct. 1475, 149 L.Ed.2d 420 (2001) (stating that Turner "adopted a unitary, deferential standard for reviewing prisoners' constitutional claims" (emphasis added)).

Until now, we have scrupulously followed the Supreme Court's direction and recognized the derivative nature of publishers' First Amendment interests in contacting prisoners. See Prison Legal News v. Lehman (PLN II), 397 F.3d 692, 701 (9th Cir.2005) (describing Jones as upholding "a ban on junk mail" and distinguishing a "scenario in which a publisher has [not] attempted to flood a facility with publications sent to all inmates, regardless of whether they requested the publication"); Morrison v. Hall, 261 F.3d 896, 898 (9th Cir.2001) ("Moreover, prisons can and have adopted policies permitting prisoners to receive for-profit, commercial publications, while at the same time, prohibiting prisoners from receiving unsolicited junk mail."); see also Prison Legal News v. Cook (PLN I), 238 F.3d 1145, 1146 (9th Cir.2001).

But the majority puts all of this precedent aside, and declares that "[a] First Amendment interest in distributing and receiving information does not depend on a recipient's prior request for that information." Hrdlicka v. Reniff, 631 F.3d 1044, 1049 (9th Cir.2011).

The majority tries to conceal such ipse dixit with a passing citation to two cases standing for the unremarkable proposition that laws criminalizing core protected speech in traditional public fora are subject to strict scrutiny. See Martin v. City of Struthers, 319 U.S. 141, 143, 63 S.Ct. 862, 87 L.Ed. 1313 (1943) (prohibition against summoning residents to their front doors for the purposes of distributing literature); Klein v. City of San Clemente, 584 F.3d 1196, 1204-05 (9th Cir.2009) (leafleting unoccupied vehicles on city streets). These cases are utterly irrelevant to whether Hrdlicka's First Amendment interests were implicated by the prison restrictions at issue in this case at all.

III

Even if the majority were correct that Hrdlicka had a First Amendment interest at stake, it still erred by applying the factors annunciated in Turner without taking context into account. Cf. Thornburgh, 490 U.S. at 414, 109 S.Ct. 1874(stating that the Turner factors were designed to "channel[] the reasonableness inquiry"). For example, what does it mean to consider "whether there are alternative avenues that remain open to the inmates to exercise the right" or "the impact that accommodating the asserted right will have on other guards and prisoners" when no one contends that an inmate's rights are at risk? PLN II, 397 F.3d at 699 (internal quotation marks omitted). The majority inexplicably provides special rights to Hrdlicka because he was attempting to communicate with someone who has been incarcerated.

First, a jail cell is quite clearly not a public forum. See Jones, 433 U.S. at 134, 97 S.Ct. 2532(holding that a "prison may be no more easily converted into a public forum than a military base"); accord Adderley v. Florida, 385 U.S. 39, 41, 87 S.Ct. 242, 17 L.Ed.2d 149 (1966); United States v. Douglass, 579 F.2d 545, 549 (9th Cir. 1978).[3] As such, under ordinary rules, government officials could have excluded Hrdlicka's speech on the basis of its subject matter or even his identity " ` so long as the distinctions drawn [were] reasonable in light of the purpose served by the forum and [were] viewpoint neutral.'" Good News Club v. Milford Cent. Sch., 533 U.S. 98, 131, 121 S.Ct. 2093, 150 L.Ed.2d 151 (2001) (emphasis added). "The First Amendment does not demand unrestricted access to a nonpublic forum merely because use of that forum may be the most efficient means of delivering the speaker's message." Cornelius v. NAACP Legal Def. & Educ. Fund, Inc., 473 U.S. 788, 809, 105 S.Ct. 3439, 87 L.Ed.2d 567 (1985).

Second, rather than criminalizing speech, the ban on unsolicited copies of CJA merely served to preserve the public fisc.[4] And the Court has made abundantly clear that the elected branches may set spending priorities in ways that negatively and unequally impact free speech rights so long as they do not discriminate on the basis of viewpoint. See Nat'l Endowment for the Arts v. Finley, 524 U.S. 569, 588, 118 S.Ct. 2168, 141 L.Ed.2d 500 (1998) (citing Maher v. Roe, 432 U.S. 464, 475, 97 S.Ct. 2376, 53 L.Ed.2d 484 (1977) ("There is a basic difference between direct state interference with a protected activity and state encouragement of an alternative activity consonant with legislative policy.")).

In sum, assuming Hrdlicka has an independent First Amendment interest involved in this case, that interest does not extend to commandeering public facilities for his personal gain. And it is not infringed by a "viewpoint-neutral exclusion of speakers who would disrupt [these] nonpublic for[a] and hinder [their] effectiveness for [their] intended purpose." Cornelius, 473 U.S. at 811, 105 S.Ct. 3439. Under such circumstances, the burden was on him to show that the regulations were not supported by any rational basis. See, e.g., Regan v. Taxation with Representation of Washington, 461 U.S. 540, 547-51, 103 S.Ct. 1997, 76 L.Ed.2d 129 (1983).

IV

Instead, the majority places on jail administrators the onerous burden of showing "the degree to which the[] purposes [behind the regulations] are actually served by a refusal to allow" distribution of any particular type of unsolicited junk mail. Hrdlicka, 631 F.3d at 1051.[5] Indeed, Beard v. Banks, 548 U.S. 521, 126 S.Ct. 2572, 165 L.Ed.2d 697 (2006), specifically held to the contrary, even under Turner's standard, a regulation preventing certain inmates from receiving any magazines based upon a statement and a deposition that these restrictions motivated better behavior. See also Overton v. Bazzetta, 539 U.S. 126, 132, 123 S.Ct. 2162, 156 L.Ed.2d 162 (2003) (stating that when a prison regulation is being challenged, "[t]he burden is not on the State to prove its validity, but on the prisoner to disprove it.").

Then, in a wonderful display of why federal judges should not be running jails, the majority dismisses out of hand many practical concerns that will arise from requiring jails to distribute an unknown quantity of unsolicited mail.[6]

The majority also simply ignores the impact its ruling produces beyond these jails and this publication. As Judge Smith's dissent correctly points out, one consequence of the majority's decision is to "force[] sheriffs either to allow all unrequested mail to reach inmates or to make a case by case determination of the quality of the publication." Hrdlicka, 631 F.3d at 1057 (N.R. Smith, J., dissenting). Sheriffs should not be put in this predicament. Instead, courts should give "considerable deference to the determinations of prison administrators who, in the interest of security, regulate the relations between prisoners and the outside world." Thornburgh, 490 U.S. at 408, 109 S.Ct. 1874. In applying such deference, we as federal judges must allow prison officials to "reach[] experience-based conclusion[s]" about which "policies help to further legitimate prison objectives." Beard, 548 U.S. at 533, 126 S.Ct. 2572.

V

The First Amendment does not give publishers any interest (to say nothing of a right) to send unsolicited mail to inmates. Sending such mail may be highly profitable to the publisher, but "losing [such] cost advantages does not fundamentally implicate free speech values." Jones, 433 U.S. at 130-31, 97 S.Ct. 2532. By failing to recognize this, the majority ignores the separation of powers and unnecessarily injects the federal courts into a matter "peculiarly within the province of the legislative and executive branches of government." Turner, 482 U.S. at 84-85, 107 S.Ct. 2254. And by the full court's failure to order rehearing en banc, we have needlessly muddled our First Amendment jurisprudence. I respectfully dissent from our regrettable decision not to rehear this case en banc.

Notes

[1] The majority speaks only of the rights of publishers. But because "newsmen have no constitutional right of access to prisons or their inmates beyond that afforded the general public," any rule that applies to the publishers would apply equally to anyone else. Pell v. Procunier, 417 U.S. 817, 834, 94 S.Ct. 2800, 41 L.Ed.2d 495 (1974); see also Houchins v. KQED, Inc., 438 U.S. 1, 11-12, 98 S.Ct. 2588, 57 L.Ed.2d 553 (1978).

[2] Though CJA is a quarterly magazine, it is distributed on a weekly basis so that even with the rapid turnover in county jails copies will be available to current inmates. See Distribution of Crime Justice & America Magazine, Crime Justice & America, (Feb. 27, 2011) http://crimejusticeandamerica.com/distribution-of-crime-justice-america-magazine.

[3] Indeed, the majority does not even dispute that jails are not public fora. See Hrdlicka, 631 F.3d at 1050.

[4] Recall that every piece of mail that enters a detention facility must be inspected, sorted, distributed, monitored and ultimately disposed of. Cf. Shaw, 532 U.S. at 231, 121 S.Ct. 1475(allowing jails to consider such burdens even in letters involving legal advice). Restrictions on junk mail allow jail administrators better to allocate resources to other legitimate, and more pressing concerns.

[5] In particular, the majority expects jails to prove "the degree to which allowing [the] distribution [of any particular piece of mail] in the jails would produce additional clutter in inmates cells or otherwise adversely affect jail security," Hrdlicka, 631 F.3d at 1052 and "to what degree[] the jails would be forced to expend additional resources" to handle the additional correspondence. Id. at 1054.

[6] For this among other reasons, I also disagree with the manner in which the majority applied the four-part test in Turner. See Shaw, 532 U.S. at 229, 121 S.Ct. 1475 (requiring only that the connection between the restriction and the purpose behind not be arbitrary or irrational). But such concerns are secondary to the simple fact that the majority should not have applied Turner at all.

Judge O'Scannlain's concurrence in Prellwitz v. Sisto (Sept 22, 2011)

O'SCANNLAIN, Circuit Judge, concurring in the judgment:

I agree with the court that we lack jurisdiction to consider this appeal. I write separately because I cannot join in the majority's newly-fashioned rule, which would bar the State of California from appealing district court decisions that were clearly erroneous under Swarthout v. Cooke, ____ U.S. ____, 131 S.Ct. 859, 178 L.Ed.2d 732 (2011) (per curiam). In my view, the jurisdictional question here is better resolved on mootness grounds.

I

As an initial matter, the district court clearly erred by ordering the State of California to grant Prellwitz another parole hearing. As the Supreme Court recently reminded us, federal courts may not review state parole decisions for their substance. See Swarthout, 131 S.Ct. at 862-63.

In any event, in my view the district court lacked the authority to order California to conduct a parole hearing because the writ of habeas corpus is limited to either granting or denying a release from custody. Crow v. United States, 186 F.2d 704, 706 (9th Cir.1951). "Habeas lies to enforce the right of personal liberty; when that right is denied and a person confined, the federal court has the power to release him. Indeed, it has no other power; it cannot revise the state court judgment; it can act only on the body of the petitioner." Fay v. Noia, 372 U.S. 391, 430-31, 83 S.Ct. 822, 9 L.Ed.2d 837 (1963), overruled on other grounds, Wainwright v. Sykes, 433 U.S. 72, 97 S.Ct. 2497, 53 L.Ed.2d 594 (1977); see also Picrin-Peron v. Rison, 930 F.2d 773, 775 (9th Cir.1991) (same).

Thus, if the district court determined that habeas relief were necessary because of a defective parole hearing (which it should not have), the proper remedy was to grant a conditional writ. See Hilton v. Braunskill, 481 U.S. 770, 775, 107 S.Ct. 2113, 95 L.Ed.2d 724 (1987) ("[The Supreme] Court has repeatedly stated that federal courts may delay the release of a successful habeas petitioner in order to provide the State an opportunity to correct the constitutional violation found by the court."). Then, California could have "take[n] some remedial action" of its own choosing. Harvest v. Castro, 531 F.3d 737, 741 (9th Cir.2008).

II

Regardless of what it should have done, the district court ordered a new parole hearing and that hearing has occurred. Prellwitz has received the relief he sought, and California has held the hearing it did not wish to hold. Thus, this appeal is moot, and we lack jurisdiction. See Foster v. Carson, 347 F.3d 742, 746 (9th Cir.2003) ("Where the activities sought to be enjoined already have occurred, and the appellate courts cannot undo what has already been done, the action is moot, and must be dismissed." (internal quotation marks omitted)).

By ruling on finality grounds, the majority puts states in the untenable position of being unable to appeal erroneous district court orders. I agree that "[t]o be final, a habeas decision must either den[y] the petition or order[ ] the prisoner released at a specified time." Op. at 1037 (alterations in original) (internal quotation marks omitted). But before the Supreme Court's decision in Swarthout, any number of habeas petitions were likely granted in our circuit — without a specific release date — only so that another parole hearing could be held. After Swarthout, it is crystal clear that those decisions were erroneous.

But under the court's decision today, the government could rarely — if ever — appeal such an order. If the state obeys the order and holds the hearing, the appeal (like this one) is moot. If the state does not wish to obey the order, it would have no guarantee of immediate review under the rule announced today. Nor could the state ignore the order in the hope of later challenging it in an enforcement proceeding. See Walker v. City of Birmingham, 388 U.S. 307, 87 S.Ct. 1824, 18 L.Ed.2d 1210 (1967); In re Establishment Inspection of Hern Iron Works, Inc., 881 F.2d 722, 725 (9th Cir.1989) ("In brief, the collateral bar rule permits a judicial order to be enforced through criminal contempt even though the underlying decision may be incorrect and even unconstitutional.").

Moreover, even application of the seemingly bright-line rule proposed by the majority would be difficult in practice. As in this case, it is often difficult to tell whether a district court is actually granting a writ of habeas corpus. See Alexander v. U.S. Parole Comm'n, 514 F.3d 1083, 1087 (10th Cir.2008) ("Unfortunately, not all orders state clearly whether release has been granted or denied."). Thus, closer inspection would be needed on a case-by-case basis to determine whether an ambiguous order is "the functional equivalent of a conditional release order." Id. at 1089. I think it inappropriate for us to be undertaking such an inquiry.

III

Given these difficulties with the majority's new rule, I cannot join in its opinion. I do, however, agree that we do not have jurisdiction over this appeal. Accordingly, I would dismiss for mootness and vacate the judgment of the district court. See Burke v. Barnes, 479 U.S. 361, 365, 107 S.Ct. 734, 93 L.Ed.2d 732 (1987).

Judge O'Scannlain's dissent in Silva v. Di Vittorio (Sept 26, 2011)

O'SCANNLAIN, Circuit Judge, dissenting:

Matthew Silva, a Washington state prisoner, is no stranger to the federal courts. During his incarceration, he has filed at least fourteen actions in federal district court. He has succeeded in none of them, and at least four of his suits have been dismissed for failure to state a claim upon which relief may be granted. Undeterred, Silva filed this latest suit under 42 U.S.C. § 1983 alleging violations of his First and Fourteenth Amendment rights, which too was dismissed for failure to state a claim. Silva now seeks appellate review of that determination.

Throughout his many interactions with the federal courts, Silva has proceeded in forma pauperis ("IFP"). That is, he has never had to prepay a single administrative fee associated with his many federal filings. On appeal, Silva once again seeks to proceed IFP, a privilege which he is now clearly denied under the Prison Litigation Reform Act ("PLRA"). Nevertheless, the court today holds that Silva is free to proceed IFP, and that it should adjudicate the merits of his appeal. Because such conclusion flies in the face of the plain language of the PLRA, I would dismiss this appeal unless Silva prepays the appropriate filing fees. Thus, I respectfully dissent from the court's ruling to the contrary.

I

The PLRA creates a "three-strikes rule" for prisoners seeking to proceed IFP in bringing or appealing a civil suit in federal court. Specifically, the statute provides:

> In no event shall a prisoner bring a civil action or appeal a judgment in a civil action or proceeding under this section if the prisoner has, on 3 or more prior occasions, while incarcerated or detained in any facility, brought an action or appeal in a court of the United States that was dismissed on the grounds that it is frivolous, malicious, or fails to state a claim upon which relief may be granted, unless the prisoner is under imminent danger of serious physical injury.

28 U.S.C. § 1915(g) (emphasis added). There is no claim that Silva is in imminent physical danger. If he had three or more dismissals for failure to state a claim at the time he filed this appeal, he is simply barred from proceeding IFP.

II

The majority disregards this clear statutory mandate. Instead, it observes that "[s]ection 1915(g) does not expressly state whether a prior dismissal of `an action or appeal' must be final before it can be considered a `strike.'" Maj. Op. at 1098. Although the statute does not state that a dismissal must become final in order to count as a strike, the majority opines that such a limitation is "fairly implied." Id. The majority's rationale for implying a finality limitation into section 1915(g) is unpersuasive.

A

The majority is correct that section 1915(g) does not explicitly state when or whether a dismissal must become "final" in order to count as a strike. But that is precisely the point. The fact that the statute does not state that a dismissal must become "final" to count against the prisoner counsels that we look no further than the fact of dismissal when tallying strikes. The statute is patent on this point. See 28 U.S.C. § 1915(g) (stating that IFP status shall not be granted if, on three or more prior occasions, the prisoner has filed a claim that "was dismissed" (emphasis added)); accord Robinson v. Powell, 297 F.3d 540, 541 (7th Cir.2002) (Posner, J.). A strike is not contingent in any way on the case's subsequent appellate process, which is nowhere mentioned in section 1915.

Indeed, section 1915 contemplates only one contingency that is relevant to the inquiry here — whether "the prisoner is under imminent danger of serious physical injury." 28 U.S.C. § 1915(g). Moreover, Congress has included express language in section 1915(g) indicating that this exception is the only event upon which a strike is contingent. See id. ("[i]n no event" is this court to grant IFP status to a prisoner once he has accumulated three strikes).

The majority's contrary approach transforms Congress's silence into an unspoken requirement of "finality" — indeed it mandates an assumption that all trial court dismissals under section 1915(g) were entered in error. Such an interpretation is both contrary to the ordinary and obvious meaning of Congress's language and without logical support. In short, the atextual reading advanced by the majority "has the anomalous result of allowing a prisoner to file, without payment, a frivolous appeal." Robinson, 297 F.3d at 541.

B

The majority further opines that to count a dismissal as a strike as soon as it occurs "would be a departure from the usual practice under the Federal Rules," and would "effectively eliminate our appellate function" in those cases where a third strike is being appealed. Maj. Op. at 1098 (citing Fed. R.App. P. 3). The majority implies that our "usual practice" to allow appeals of right is somehow thwarted by not automatically allowing a prisoner to appeal his third strike free of charge. But "the usual practice" of bringing an appeal under the Federal Rules includes paying the requisite filing fees. See Fed. R.App. P. 3(e). Indeed, proceeding IFP is itself an exception from the "usual practice under the Federal Rules." See Fed. R.App. P. 24(a) (governing requests for "Leave to Proceed in Forma Pauperis" (emphasis added)).

The PLRA regulates the applicability of that exception in the context of prisoners, not the "usual practice" of appellate proceedings themselves. Indeed, the "unusual" result reached by the plain text of the PLRA is simply that once a prisoner has had three suits dismissed, he may no longer avoid having to prepay the normal filing fees associated with federal appeals. Adherence to this procedure no more "effectively eliminate[s] our appellate function," Maj. Op. at 1098, than does the requirement of filing fees in general. A prisoner may still appeal just as any other party may: by prepaying the appropriate fees.[1]

III

The majority fails to appreciate the strain that its rule places upon the federal courts. Silva's case is a prime example. In his time in prison, he has filed no less than fourteen causes of action in various federal courts. Frivolous prisoner claims create inordinate pressure on the federal docket, and the course of Silva's repeated litigation is just one of many such examples. In fact, some 20,000 civil cases are brought each year by prisoners either alleging civil rights violations or challenging prison conditions. See Admin. Office of the U.S. Courts, Judicial Business of the United States Courts 145 (2010). By one estimate, nearly twenty percent of these cases are dismissed as frivolous, not to mention the almost forty percent that are dismissed because of a prisoner's failure to comply with court rules. See Bureau of Justice Statistics, U.S. Dep't of Justice, Challenging the Conditions of Prisons and Jails 20 (1994); see also Taylor v. Delatoore, 281 F.3d 844, 849 (9th Cir.2002) ("The PLRA filing fee provisions were enacted to deter the large number of frivolous inmate lawsuits that were `clogging' the federal courts and `draining' limited judicial resources.").

The rule crafted by the majority will only make the situation worse. The finality rule that the majority imports into section 1915(g) would toll consideration of the dismissal of a frivolous suit until the case has mandated and the time for the prisoner to file a petition for a writ of certiorari has expired. See Maj. Op. at 1099-100. And should the prisoner actually file a petition for a writ of certiorari, the majority would toll consideration of the dismissal until the Supreme Court has denied the petition. See id. This is more than enough time for a prisoner to file quite a few lawsuits, all the while not having to prepay his fees as most litigants must.

IV

It is undisputed that Silva had at least three prior civil actions that had been dismissed for failure to state a claim. I believe, therefore, that IFP status is inappropriate and that this appeal should be dismissed unless Silva pays the proper appellate fees.

Accordingly, I respectfully dissent.

Notes

[1] Even if section 1915(g) were read to mandate IFP status in the limited instance where the dismissal being appealed constituted the third strike itself, such a case is not presented here, as Silva seeks to appeal a claim unrelated to those constituting his strikes.

Judge O'Scannlain's partial dissent in Ralph International Thomas v. Chappell (May 10, 2012)

O'SCANNLAIN, Circuit Judge, dissenting:

The majority finds Strickland prejudice based on two conclusions: that the case against Ralph International Thomas was very close and that the testimony of three would-be witnesses would have been "extremely helpful" in corroborating the testimony of key defense witness Vivian Cercy. Maj. op. 1103-04, 1106. Neither conclusion is warranted. The case against Thomas was stronger than the majority suggests, and the insubstantial testimony of those three witnesses would not have sufficiently corroborated Cercy's testimony or otherwise undermined the State's case. Thomas is therefore not entitled to habeas relief on the basis the district court gave, and I respectfully dissent.

I

This case was not as close as the majority suggests.

Mary Gioia and Greg Kniffin were killed by gunshot wounds typical of a high-powered rifle or shotgun, but inconsistent with a handgun. Thomas owned a high-powered rifle that, based on its peculiar features, was likely to have been used effectively only by someone familiar with it. Thomas shot the rifle the night before the murders, showing that he indeed knew how to use it effectively. Moreover, Thomas was with the victims soon before they were killed and was visibly angry. His pipe placed him at the crime scene. Thomas changed clothes in the middle of the night. After the murders, his rifle mysteriously went missing, yet testimony suggested that Thomas himself returned the rifle's case to his car early in the morning after the murders.

Thomas's statements and other conduct after the murders reflected consciousness of his guilt and raised further suspicion: Thomas was able to identify Mary's body when it remained partially underwater and before its sex was apparent. After the murders, he asked another Rainbow Village resident to hold his gun-cleaning kit and ammunition. As an alibi, Thomas claimed to have walked 16.8 miles in the middle of the night. That was improbable in itself, and more improbable given that Thomas generally went to bed early (around 9 p.m.). Indeed, police officers assigned to the areas Thomas claimed to have been walking did not recall seeing him. Thomas also gave inconsistent statements to police about whether his ammunition had been stolen, about his interactions with Mary and Greg, and about his pipes. He said that he could think of plenty of reasons why someone would want to murder Mary and Greg, then could not name one.

Not only was the State's case strong, but Thomas's defense — based largely upon Vivian Cercy's testimony — was weak. Cercy's testimony was imprecise, her answers were meandering and undermined her credibility, and her statements conflicted with each other and with those of other witnesses. Cercy described the man she called "Bo" as brown-haired, then as blond. She testified that the woman she saw arguing (purportedly Mary Gioia) was wearing "dark brown pants," but the pathologist who performed the autopsy on Mary testified that she wore blue denim shorts and purple pants. One of the police investigators testified that Cercy reported having "quite a bit to drink" on August 15, raising doubts about her perception. Cercy repeatedly testified that she was minding her own business on the night of the murders and therefore was not always paying close attention to what she claimed to have observed. Her testimony was tainted by discussions she had with others, such as the notoriously unreliable "Stagger Lee" Andersen, an oft-intoxicated one-time resident of Rainbow Village. (Andersen was so unreliable that the district court did not credit his testimony.) Cercy's estimates of the timing of events that night seemed to lack any firm basis. She could give almost no description of a man who knocked on her window and spoke with her from what was, apparently, only a few feet away. Although she said that this man threatened her life, she did not drive herself and her two young daughters to safety.

In the face of this evidence, it is understandable that six California Supreme Court justices concluded that the State's case would have "established in a reasonable juror's mind" — even the mind of one who had heard all the post-conviction record evidence cited by the majority — "the near certainty" that Thomas killed Mary and Greg. In re Thomas, 37 Cal.4th 1249, 39 Cal.Rptr.3d 845, 129 P.3d 49, 67 (2006).

In casting this case as "close," maj. op. 1103, the majority emphasizes that the jury deliberated for nearly five days and asked for read-backs of testimony, maj. op. 1103. But the majority sidesteps the crucial details. Although the jury deliberated for five days, by the third day it asked about the difference between first- and second-degree murder and by the fourth day it wanted a hard copy of the jury instruction stating the difference between first- and second-degree murder. These "objective clues" (maj. op. 1103) suggest that the jury was focusing on what kind of murder Thomas committed, not on whether he killed Mary and Greg at all. (I note that none of the additional testimony cited by the majority suggests that Thomas should have been convicted of second-degree murder rather than first-degree murder; it suggests only — and feebly — that Thomas was not the killer at all. See infra Part II.) The majority is not justified in casting aside the California Supreme Court's near-unanimous determination that Thomas was, to a "near certainty," the murderer.

II

Having pitched the case to be closer than it was, the majority then finds doubt about Thomas's guilt based on the would be testimony of Jong Cheol Cho, Claus von Wendel, and Randy Turley. Their testimony, the majority maintains, would have been "extremely helpful" in corroborating Cercy's testimony and supporting the theory that someone called Bo had committed the murders. Maj. op. 1105; see id. at 1105-06.

I cannot agree. To begin with, Cercy's testimony was essentially beyond corroboration. It is hard to corroborate testimony so imprecise, at times contradictory, and often incredible, from someone who — as even the cold record shows — was not clearheaded, reliable, or perceptive. As Thomas's current counsel conceded, "Cercy was hardly a dream witness" and "her patterns of speech and thought were obviously eccentric." That understates the matter.

But even assuming that Cercy's gossamer-thin testimony was susceptible of corroboration, the three further witnesses' testimony would not create a reasonable probability of a different guilt-phase outcome. The facts those witnesses may have offered — that a "Bo" existed, that he said he had gone swimming in the bay the night of the murders, and that he left on von Wendel's boat a bag that contained no murder weapon and only some mundane, common items — do almost nothing to sharpen Cercy's self-refuting, implausible testimony. Nor do they otherwise undermine the case against

Thomas: those witnesses do not refute any of the evidence against him, such as the fact that Thomas owned a rifle that would have been difficult for anyone else to fire and that was quite possibly the murder weapon.

That a "Bo" may have said that he swam in the bay the night of the murders or picked up a bag of run-of-the-mill belongings adds little. Indeed, the swimming-in-the-bay comment may cut against James Bowen's alleged guilt: If this "Bo" had killed Mary and Greg, he would presumably have been more careful than to remark to others, hours after dumping the bodies in the bay, that he had gone swimming there. Perhaps the more natural conclusion is that "Bo" was being honest and did not realize that his comment would implicate him. And whether Cho accurately related "Bo"'s statement is open to doubt. When Cho was pressed about a discrepancy between his sworn declaration and his hearing testimony, he defended the discrepancy by stating, "English is not my native language, and therefore I miss all this." We should not overturn a jury verdict in heavy reliance upon a single sentence reported through an intermediary who may well not have understood or repeated the sentence accurately.

And the bag on von Wendel's boat shows almost nothing. Rainbow Village was a place where people came and went — where people slept in their cars, on the ground, and in others' buses. That someone staying there may have left a bag of shoes, books, a serape, and a driver's license (and no gun) in an apparently secure spot hardly merits great suspicion. The district court said that items in the bag "corresponded to the shoes and poncho that were missing from Kniffin's body when it was found." But Randy Turley testified that "Bo" liked to wear serapes. And it is no surprise that "Bo" would have an extra pair of shoes in a bag containing his belongings. Von Wendel's testimony — about an article of clothing commonly worn by "Bo" (a serape) and an article commonly worn by most American adults (shoes) — does not corroborate Cercy or undermine the other evidence of guilt.

Finally, I do not understand why the majority disregards the rebuttal testimony of Vincent Johnson. On rebuttal, the prosecutor asked Johnson, "[W]hat exactly did [Vivian Cercy] tell you regarding anything she may have seen [the night of the murders]?" Johnson replied, "She told me, basically, that everything she said was, was — she was told to say by [Rainbow Village resident and Cercy's on-and-off boyfriend] Harry Shorman, and that she basically hadn't seen anything, hadn't seen anything." Johnson's testimony makes it all the more difficult to imagine a different result in this case. Even if the three additional witnesses would have established that a "Bo" existed and that Cercy had not "made him up," Johnson's rebuttal decisively supported the prosecution's view that she was not testifying credibly and was acting as a mouthpiece for eccentric grandstander Harry Shorman.[1]

III

In sum, the evidence on which the majority relies — Cercy's narrative, Turley's confirmation of a "Bo"'s existence and description, Cho's testimony that "Bo" made a "swimming into the bay" comment, and the bag on von Wendel's boat — when set against the actual case against Thomas, does not "undermine confidence in the outcome" of his guilt-phase trial. Strickland v. Washington, 466 U.S. 668, 694, 104 S.Ct. 2052, 80 L.Ed.2d 674 (1984).

I would reverse the district court's judgment granting a writ of habeas corpus.

Notes

[1] The majority says that, during habeas proceedings, Thomas submitted a declaration in which Johnson at least partially recanted his testimony. Maj. op. 1105 n. 14. The declaration is more equivocal than the majority suggests and, in any event, Johnson testified later that he was not lying when he testified that Cercy had told him that "everything she said was" what she "was told to say by Harry Shorman" and that "she basically hadn't seen anything." The majority states that it "need not consider the effect of that declaration here." Id. But if the majority "need not consider" that later declaration, it is unclear why the majority is justified in effectively disregarding Johnson's rebuttal testimony in considering Strickland prejudice.

Judge O'Scannlain's partial dissent in Price v. Stevedoring Services of America, Inc. (Sept 4, 2012)

O'SCANNLAIN, Circuit Judge, dissenting in part:

I agree with the majority that the Director's litigating position before this court is not entitled to Chevron deference and that the proper rate of interest on past-due compensation awards under the Longshore and Harbor Workers' Compensation Act (LHWCA) is the rate set forth in 28 U.S.C. § 1961(a). That said, I cannot join the majority's discussion of these issues because, in my view, it treats several matters that are unnecessary to the outcome of this case and thus should be left for another day. See, e.g., Op. at 831-32 n. 7 (discussing whether litigating positions taken in agency adjudications are entitled to Chevron deference); Op. at 832-33 (discussing whether the position of the Benefits Review Board is entitled to deference).

More specifically, I disagree with the majority's conclusion that the Director of the Office of Workers' Compensation Programs is not entitled to deference with respect to the method of computing interest and, therefore, I respectfully dissent from the majority's conclusion to the contrary.

I

In applying the LHWCA, the Director has long taken the position that interest on past-due compensation awards should be computed on a simple basis. That position accords with the general rule of awarding only simple interest when a statute does not expressly require otherwise; it aligns with the consistent position taken by the Benefits Review Board since 1989, see Santos v. General Dynamics Corp., 22 BRBS 226 (1989); and it is consistent with the LHWCA, which is silent on the rate and computation of interest. Nor is the Director's position a novel litigating position; it has been embodied in the

Longshore Procedure Manual, used by district directors nationwide, since at least 1989. See Div. of Longshore and Harbor Workers' Compensation, Dep't of Labor, Longshore Procedure Manual, ch. 8-201, available at http://www.dol.gov/owcp/dlhwc/lspm/pmtoc.htm.

Given these features, in my view the Director's position, though informal, is persuasive enough to merit our respect. See Skidmore v. Swift & Co., 323 U.S. 134, 140, 65 S.Ct. 161, 89 L.Ed. 124 (1944) (noting consistency, thorough consideration, and valid reasoning as factors contributing to persuasiveness). We should defer to the agency's consistent, long-standing implementation of simple interest. See Fed. Express Corp. v. Holowecki, 552 U.S. 389, 399-401, 128 S.Ct. 1147, 170 L.Ed.2d 10 (2008) (deferring under Skidmore to an informal agency interpretation because it was consistent with the agency's responsibilities and had bound staff members for over five years); Tablada v. Thomas, 533 F.3d 800, 806-08 (9th Cir.2008) ("[T]he consistent and even application of the [agency's] methodology promulgated in [its] Program Statement ... since 1992 convinces us that we must accord deference to the [agency's] interpretation.").

A

To reach the contrary conclusion, the majority emphasizes the LHWCA's remedial purpose and a growing trend toward the use of compound interest. With respect, the majority's analysis is unpersuasive.

The majority first contends that simple interest does not fulfill the LHWCA's purpose of fully compensating claimants. But fully compensating employees is not the Act's only purpose. See Roberts v. Sea-Land Servs., Inc., ___ U.S. ___, 132 S.Ct. 1350, 1354, 182 L.Ed.2d 341 (2012). Rather, "the LHWCA represents a compromise between the competing interests of disabled laborers and their employers, [so] it is not correct to interpret the Act as guaranteeing a completely adequate remedy for all covered disabilities." Dir., OWCP v. Newport News Shipbldg. and Dry Dock Co., 514 U.S. 122, 131, 115 S.Ct. 1278, 131 L.Ed.2d 160 (1995) (internal quotation marks omitted). The Act is not meant always to provide a "complete remedy," but aims instead to ensure that workers receive some compensation for injuries, even if it is not "complete compensation for the wage earner's economic loss." Potomac Electric Power Co. v. Dir., OWCP, 449 U.S. 268, 281, 101 S.Ct. 509, 66 L.Ed.2d 446 (1980).

We must therefore consider the Director's position in light of the bargain the Act represents, rather than treating the Act's remedial purpose as an unbeatable trump. In this vein, the Supreme Court has cautioned against "add[ing] features that will achieve statutory `purposes' more effectively." Newport News, 514 U.S. at 136, 115 S.Ct. 1278. Whatever our views on the effectiveness of simple interest in compensating claimants, we should not add a compounding requirement to the statutory scheme just because we think it would better serve the Act's remedial purpose. See id. at 135-36, 115 S.Ct. 1278; Potomac Electric, 449 U.S. at 280-81, 101 S.Ct. 509.

B

The majority contends next that compound interest is warranted based on "changing economic realities" and a "growing recognition" that compound interest might more fully compensate plaintiffs. Op. at 841. This too is not reason enough to reject the Director's position. The Supreme Court has cautioned that a growing trend — even one that is "sound as a matter of policy" and is now a dominant view — is an insufficient basis for abandoning a settled rule. Potomac Electric, 449 U.S. at 279-80 & n. 20, 101 S.Ct. 509.

Whatever the "growing consensus," op. at 842, the Director, as administrator of the Act, is best positioned to evaluate changing circumstances and to determine whether simple interest continues to provide adequate compensation to claimants.[1] Where the Act is silent and the agency has made a reasonable choice, we should not inject our policy views into the Act's provisions.

C

The majority also faults the Director for adopting the rate set forth in section 1961(a) while not adopting section 1961(b)'s compound interest component. Again, the Director's decision is reasonable. The Director has concluded that section 1961 provides useful guidance; that conclusion should not force the Director to swallow section 1961 whole. And by declining to adopt the section 1961(b) formulation, the Director has honored the general rule that simple interest applies unless a statute expressly authorizes compound interest. See, e.g., Cherokee Nation v. United States, 270 U.S. 476, 490-91, 46 S.Ct. 428, 70 L.Ed. 694 (1926); Stovall v. Ill. Cent. Gulf. R.R. Co., 722 F.2d 190, 192 (5th Cir.1984). Because the LHWCA does not expressly authorize interest awards, it is reasonable for the Director to look elsewhere for guidance, to make a considered choice based on that guidance, and to settle on the prevailing longstanding general rule. By contrast, we have no authority to force the Director to apply a different choice that conflicts with the agency's long-standing default rule — especially given that the governing statute provides no support for such a judicial mandate.[2] Cf. Newport News, 514 U.S. at 135-36, 115 S.Ct. 1278.

D

The majority's failure to defer under Skidmore to the Director's long-standing position is made all the more perplexing by its determination that the Director's selection of the proper interest rate is entitled to Skidmore deference. The majority acknowledges that, because the LHWCA is silent on interest, the selection of interest rate is "in large part a policy determination best left to the agency." Op. at 839. The majority concludes that the Director's selection of the section 1961 rate is "consistent with the statutory framework" and that there are "[n]o clearer alternatives... within our authority or expertise to adopt." Op. at 839. But the rate of interest and the method of computing it have each been consistently applied by the Director and the Board for over 20 years and have been contained within the Director's manual for nearly as long. It is hardly reasonable to accept the one and to reject the other when the same reasoning supports both.

II

Proper application of Skidmore requires us to defer to the Director's long-standing, consistent practice of awarding simple interest, recognizing that the Director is in the best position to determine whether, as a policy matter, the method of computing interest should be changed better to align with modern circumstances.

For the foregoing reasons, I respectfully dissent.

Notes

[1] In reading the majority's opinion, one might think that the Director is an adversary of claimants who seek to receive their full entitlement. To the contrary, the Director often intervenes in lawsuits seeking interpretations or compensation more favorable to the employee than what the employee received from the Board. See, e.g., Ingalls Shipbldg., Inc. v. Dir., OWCP, 519 U.S. 248, 253, 117 S.Ct. 796, 136 L.Ed.2d 736 (1997); Stevedoring Servs. of Am. v. Dir., OWCP, 297 F.3d 797, 801 (9th Cir.2002); McDonald v. Dir., OWCP, 897 F.2d 1510, 1511 n. 2 (9th Cir.1990).

[2] The majority also suggests that we can tell that simple interest is unreasonable because the Board has indicated that compound interest might be warranted in exceptional circumstances. Op. at 842-43. But compounding interest in exceptional circumstances, such as when a party engages in willful misbehavior, accords with the general rule giving trial judges discretion to select an interest award within a range of reasonable options. See W. Pac. Fisheries, Inc. v. SS President Grant, 730 F.2d 1280, 1288-89 (9th Cir.1984); Gorenstein Enters., Inc. v. Quality Care-USA, Inc., 874 F.2d 431, 436 (7th Cir.1989) (concluding that compound interest was appropriate where the violation of federal law was "intentional, and indeed outrageous" and where the appellant had engaged in dilatory tactics); cf. also NLRB v. Seven-Up Bottling Co. of Miami, 344 U.S. 344, 348-49, 73 S.Ct. 287, 97 L.Ed. 377 (1953) (eschewing the "debate about what is `remedial' and what is `punitive'" and instead noting that a proper remedy should be formulated with the unique circumstances of the case in mind). Though we deal with prejudgment interest rather than post-judgment interest, the distinction, as the majority notes, "carries no significance here." Op. at 840.

Judge O'Scannlain's dissent in Stephan v. Unum Life Ins. (Sept 12, 2012)

O'SCANNLAIN, Circuit Judge, dissenting:

I agree with the majority that we evaluate Unum Life Insurance Company's interpretation of plan terms under an abuse of discretion standard. I cannot agree, however, that remand is appropriate. The district court did not, as the majority contends, improperly weigh evidence at the summary judgment stage. And Unum's interpretation of the plan — which is silent on whether a bonus should be counted as monthly income — is reasonable and supported by the record. I would therefore affirm the grant of summary judgment in favor of Unum.

I

The majority holds that the district court "failed to apply the traditional rules of summary judgment to its analysis of whether and to what extent a conflict of interest impacted Unum's benefits determination." Op. at 921. I disagree. The district court properly considered the evidence before it. Stephan presented no specific evidence of bias; the exhibits he filed included correspondence with Unum, an expert report, and Unum's notes from Stephan's claim folder, all of which showed consistent handling of Stephan's claim.[1] The district court considered all of Stephan's evidence, as well as hundreds of pages of evidence submitted by Unum, before concluding that "Unum's conflict of interest did not weigh heavily upon its decision-making process in this case."

Lacking support for its assertion that the district court improperly weighed the evidence before it, the majority directs the district court on remand to "permit the admission of evidence outside the administrative record" to evaluate bias. Op. at 930. This is not our law. A district court is not required to consider evidence outside the record. Rather, when evaluating the "nature, extent, and effect on the decision-making process of any conflict of interest," the district court "may, in its discretion, consider evidence outside the administrative record." Abatie v. Alta Health & Life Ins. Co., 458 F.3d 955, 970 (9th Cir.2006) (en banc) (emphasis added); Nolan v. Heald College, 551 F.3d 1148, 1150 (9th Cir.2009) (explaining that Abatie "permit[s]" plaintiffs to submit evidence outside the administrative record). We therefore cannot, as the majority suggests, require the district court to conduct an independent assessment of bias beyond the evidence presented by the parties. See op. at 929-31.

Remand thus serves only to provide Stephan a second opportunity to litigate his case. That is not appropriate here.

II

A

Nevertheless, the majority decides to remand. Having so decided, the majority's opinion should be at an end. But it is not. While purporting to "express no opinion" on whether Unum's interpretation of the plan should be found unreasonable, Op. at 934, the majority expansively opines on the correct outcome of the district court's inquiry, see op. at 934-39. In doing so, the majority mischaracterizes the record and traverses well outside the bounds of our deferential review. What is more, the majority's extensive dicta, see op. at 934-39 — which, in any event, does not bind the district court — relies on inconclusive evidence and concludes that, because it would have interpreted that evidence differently, Unum's interpretation is unreasonable. See op. at 936-39. This is not abuse of discretion review.

To take one example: the majority unfairly criticizes Unum's reliance on TWP's statement that it would "morally honor" its employment contract and posits that TWP "most probably meant" that TWP viewed the bonus as a necessary component of Stephan's salary. Op. at 937. Based on the record, which consists only of Unum's own notes of the conversation, the meaning of TWP's statement is — as the majority itself acknowledges — inconclusive. Likewise, the majority's reliance on Stephan's offer letter is misplaced. Though the letter indicated that his bonus was "guaranteed," it also said that this bonus would be paid to Stephan "provided you perform at the level" TWP anticipated for a twelve-month period. Yet the majority is confident that Unum "misreads" TWP's offer letter. Op. at 937-38. This dictum should have been left on the cutting room floor.

B

The evidence demonstrates that Unum's conclusion that Stephan's bonus was not included in the calculation of monthly benefits under the plan is a reasonable one. Unum consistently explained that it was not including the annual bonus because that bonus was contingent on Stephan completing a year of satisfactory performance, which he did not do; because the bonus was not paid on a monthly basis; because TWP had not paid premiums on the higher amount; and because it did not find TWP's expert persuasive. Its interpretation of the plan should not be disturbed. See Conkright v. Frommert, ____ U.S. ____, 130 S.Ct. 1640, 1647, 1651, 176 L.Ed.2d 469 (2010); Salomaa v. Honda Long Term Disability Plan, 642 F.3d 666, 676 (9th Cir.2011).

We may not substitute our views on how the plan should be interpreted for those of the plan administrator. The district court, after considering the evidence Stephan presented, correctly concluded that Unum's conflict of interest carried little weight in light of other considerations and that Unum had reasonably interpreted the plan. It should not have to revisit that determination.

III

It is admittedly difficult to weigh the extent to which a conflict influenced a benefits determination. See Salomaa, 642 F.3d at 675. But "district courts are well equipped to consider the particulars of a conflict of interest." Abatie, 458 F.3d at 969. The district court did so correctly in this case, and I would affirm its grant of summary judgment in favor of Unum.

I respectfully dissent.

Notes

[1] While I agree with the majority that the district court erred in denying Stephan's motion to compel certain discovery, having reviewed these documents in camera, they would not help Stephan's case. Such an error, in light of the other evidence, does not require remand. See Kaiser Found. Health Plan, Inc. v. Abbott Labs., Inc., 552 F.3d 1033, 1042 (9th Cir.2009) (explaining that erroneous evidentiary rulings require reversal only where they are prejudicial).

Judge O'Scannlain's dissent in Cudjo v. Ayers (Sept 28, 2012)

O'SCANNLAIN, Circuit Judge, dissenting:

In the forty years since it was written, Chambers v. Mississippi, 410 U.S. 284, 93 S.Ct. 1038, 35 L.Ed.2d 297 (1973), "has been used by the Supreme Court only a handful of times to overturn convictions; and the Supreme Court's standards are quite vague." Fortini v. Murphy, 257 F.3d 39, 48 (1st Cir.2001). Yet today we hold that Chambers "clearly establishe[s] that the exclusion of trustworthy and necessary exculpatory testimony at trial violates a defendant's due process right to present a defense." Maj. Op. at 754. Because "the holding of Chambers — if one can be discerned from such a fact-intensive case — is certainly not that a defendant is denied `a fair opportunity to defend against the State's accusations whenever critical evidence' favorable to him is excluded," Montana v. Egelhoff, 518 U.S. 37, 53, 116 S.Ct. 2013, 135 L.Ed.2d 361 (1996), I respectfully dissent.

I

A

All evidence in this case points to the conclusion that either Armenia Cudjo or his brother Gregory brutally murdered Amelia Prokuda after engaging in (apparently) consensual sexual intercourse. After the murder, evidence against Armenia quickly mounted. Gregory told officers that he had confessed to the crime in some detail, and he was shortly thereafter linked to the semen found on her bound, gagged, beaten, and nearly naked body. People v. Cudjo, 6 Cal.4th 585, 25 Cal.Rptr.2d 390, 863 P.2d 635, 643-64 (1993).

Unable to deny that he had been at the house — and thus would likely have left the single set of footprints found in the rain-washed ground outside her home, id., 25 Cal.Rptr.2d 390, 863 P.2d at 644 — Armenia tried to convince officers that Mrs. Prokuda had traded sexual favors for $50 worth of cocaine. Id., 25 Cal.Rptr.2d 390, 863 P.2d at 645. He then claimed to have gone on a long, slow jog while someone else committed the crime (apparently without leaving any shoe prints). This story had several gaping holes. Among the most blatant were that there was no cocaine found in the Prokuda home and that Mrs. Prokuda's "blood tested negative for alcohol and an array of illegal drugs, including cocaine." Id., 25 Cal.Rptr.2d 390, 863 P.2d at 642.

But, Armenia protested, it could not have been him. He had a goatee and several tattoos, but the only eye witness — Prokuda's five-year-old son Kevin — said that the man who attacked his mother was clean shaven and had no tattoos. Id. Though Kevin could not pick the assailant out of a lineup or identify several other pieces of evidence from the scene, Armenia asserts that he must have been talking about his brother Gregory. Id., 25 Cal. Rptr.2d 390, 863 P.2d at 645.

Armenia sought to make his story sound more plausible by calling John Lee Culver to the stand. According to Culver, Gregory confessed to the crime while the two shared a cell in the local jail. Id., 25 Cal. Rptr.2d 390, 863 P.2d at 647. Culver, however, was far from an ideal witness. He was both a criminal and a decades-long friend of Armenia, and his account of Gregory's confession did not match the physical evidence of the crime. Id., 25 Cal.Rptr.2d 390, 863 P.2d at 649. More importantly, Culver admitted that he filled in any gaps in Gregory's confession with his own speculation, see id. (stating initially that Gregory had confessed to implicating Armenia before admitting "that he merely inferred that Gregory had blamed defendant"), or through conference with Armenia's family and defense team, id., 25 Cal.Rptr.2d 390, 863 P.2d at 647 (no mention of a confession at all until contacted by defense team and none of a little boy until speaking with Gregory shortly before testifying).

The prosecutor argued that this testimony should be excluded as "inherently incredible." Id., 25 Cal.Rptr.2d 390, 863 P.2d at 648. The trial court agreed, applying a state evidentiary provision allowing it to exclude evidence whose probative value is substantially out-weighed by the danger of undue prejudice or misleading the jury. Id., 25 Cal.Rptr.2d 390, 863 P.2d at 648 (Cal. Evid.Code § 352). (The district court also decided that the evidence was insufficiently reliable to warrant admission under the hearsay exception for statements against penal interest. Id. (Cal. Evid.Code § 1230).)

B

The California Supreme Court concluded that this was an error of state law. It clarified that ordinarily only the reliability of the declarant is relevant to the admissibility of hearsay testimony pursuant to section 1230. Id., 25 Cal.Rptr.2d 390, 863 P.2d at 649. It recognized that in certain "rare instances," the trial court could exclude hearsay statements based on "doubts about the credibility of the in-court witness." Id., 25 Cal.Rptr.2d 390, 863 P.2d at 650. In this case, however, the California Supreme Court concluded that because there was insufficient proof that Culver falsely recounted what Gregory said, such questions should have "be[en] left for the jury's resolution." Id. Similarly, the court concluded the concerns about Culver's reliability should not have played a role in the prejudice calculus under section 352. Id.

It determined nonetheless that there was no constitutional error. Having reviewed the Chambers line of cases, the court concluded that "mere erroneous exercise of discretion under ... normal rules" of evidence "does not implicate the federal Constitution." Id., 25 Cal.Rptr.2d 390, 863 P.2d at 652. Chambers and its progeny, the court decided, were implicated only when "the constitutional right to present and confront material witnesses [is] infringed by general rules of evidence or procedure which preclude material testimony or pertinent cross-examination for arbitrary reasons, such as unwarranted and overbroad assumptions of untrustworthiness." Id. Because this case did not involve such an overbroad assumption, the court reviewed whether Armenia was prejudiced under the standard rule for erroneous evidentiary decisions. Id. Finding no such prejudice, the California Supreme Court affirmed the conviction.

II

The panel majority concludes that this was an unreasonable interpretation of Chambers. I disagree.

In Chambers, the defendant was accused of shooting a police officer. No one saw Chambers shoot the officer, and there was no evidence that Chambers owned a firearm. 410 U.S. at 289, 93 S.Ct. 1038. By contrast, a third party named Gable McDonald was identified as the shooter, owned a gun, and confessed to the crime three times (once in a sworn affidavit). Id. at 292, 93 S.Ct. 1038. Chambers was prevented from offering much of this evidence. He was allowed to call McDonald, but on cross-examination the government established that McDonald had repudiated at least one of his confessions. Chambers was not allowed on re-direct to give the jury reasons to credit his confession over his repudiation because Mississippi continued to adhere to the "voucher" rule, which binds a party to the assertions of his or her witness. Id. at 298, 93 S.Ct. 1038. He was not even allowed to offer the testimony of the people to whom McDonald confessed because — unlike most other states — Mississippi had not recognized an exception to the bar against hearsay for statements against penal interest. Id. at 293-94, 93 S.Ct. 1038. Deeming both of these rules to be outdated and arbitrary, the Court concluded that under the specific circumstances of that case, Chambers was denied due process of law. Id. at 302-03, 93 S.Ct. 1038.

This case does not present the same circumstances. In Chambers, there was no question about the reliability of those individuals who were recounting McDonald's confessions. McDonald also testified himself, offering the prosecution the opportunity to test the veracity of his confession. Id. at 301, 93 S.Ct. 1038. Here, by contrast, the only evidence that Gregory Cudjo admitted to the crime was the word of a witness of dubious veracity. Cudjo, 25 Cal.Rptr.2d 390, 863 P.2d at 651 (agreeing that the trial court's "doubts about Culver's credibility [were] reasonable and legitimate").

Moreover, the trial court's error was materially different from that found to be a due process violation in Chambers. There, the only question before the Court was whether the state could "mechanistically apply" two different rules that most jurisdictions had abandoned to the "facts and circumstances of [that] case." Chambers, 410 U.S. at 302, 93 S.Ct. 1038. The Court did not examine the issue here: whether a single erroneous ruling regarding state evidentiary law could render a conviction a violation of due process. The same is true of the entire line of cases on which Armenia relies. See Green v. Georgia, 442 U.S. 95, 99 S.Ct. 2150, 60 L.Ed.2d 738 (1979) (holding that due process required a statement against penal interest exception to hearsay in the penalty phase of a capital case); Rock v. Arkansas, 483 U.S. 44, 58, 107 S.Ct. 2704, 97 L.Ed.2d 37 (1987) (rule against hypnotically-refreshed testimony may not prevent a defendant from testifying in her own defense); see also Crane v. Kentucky, 476 U.S. 683, 686, 106 S.Ct. 2142, 90 L.Ed.2d 636 (1986); Washington v. Texas, 388 U.S. 14, 87 S.Ct. 1920, 18 L.Ed.2d 1019 (1967); Holmes v. South Carolina, 547 U.S. 319, 326, 126 S.Ct. 1727, 164 L.Ed.2d 503 (2006) (synthesizing this line of cases as holding that "the Constitution ... prohibits the exclusion of defense evidence under rules that serve no legitimate purpose or that are disproportionate to the ends that they are asserted to promote" but not under "well-established rules of evidence [which] permit trial judges to exclude evidence if its probative value is outweighed by certain other factors such as unfair prejudice ... or potential to mislead the jury").

The majority has not cited a single Supreme Court decision extending Chambers beyond situations where the state correctly but mechanistically applied an impermissible rule to those where it made a mistake in applying a perfectly permissible rule.[1] We therefore cannot say that the California Supreme Court's decision to uphold a verdict involving only the latter error "was contrary to or an unreasonable application of [Supreme Court] precedent." Penry v. Johnson, 532 U.S. 782, 794, 121 S.Ct. 1910, 150 L.Ed.2d 9 (2001). As we have recognized, a "state court's decision [is] not contrary to clearly established federal law... [if it] would have required an extension of [a] specialty doctrine." Benitez v. Garcia, 495 F.3d 640, 644 (9th Cir.2007). Even if we think such an extension is the logical result of existing precedent, we may grant a writ of habeas corpus only "if the refusal to extend [the Court's previous holdings] was objectively unreasonable." Id.; see also Hawkins v. Ala., 318 F.3d 1302, 1306 n. 3 (11th Cir.2003).

The California Supreme Court did not act unreasonably when it declined to extend Chambers to cover a simple error in balancing the prejudicial effect against the probative value of a piece of evidence. The rule the majority now endorses "invites federal constitutional scrutiny each and every time, on the basis of particular circumstances, [a district court decides] to exclude a defense witness as unworthy of credit." Cudjo, 25 Cal.Rptr.2d 390, 863 P.2d at 652. The Chambers line of cases did not suggest — let alone clearly establish — that the due process clause mandates such intrusive review of a state court's evidentiary rulings. Cf. Fortini, 257 F.3d at 47 ("[N]ot every ad hoc mistake in applying state evidence rules, even in a murder case, should be called a violation of due process; otherwise every significant state court error in excluding evidence offered by the defendant would be a basis for undoing the conviction.").

III

Without that extension, all that is left of this case is an error of state law, albeit a significant one. Because we lack authority to issue habeas relief based upon such an error, see, e.g., Swarthout v. Cooke, ____ U.S. ____, 131 S.Ct. 859, 178 L.Ed.2d 732 (2011); Estelle v. McGuire, 502 U.S. 62, 67-68, 112 S.Ct. 475, 116 L.Ed.2d 385 (1991); Lewis v. Jeffers, 497 U.S. 764, 780, 110 S.Ct. 3092, 111 L.Ed.2d 606 (1990), I respectfully dissent.[2]

Notes

[1] Indeed, we have already recognized that the "Supreme Court has not addressed [the] issue... [of] whether a trial court's discretionary determination to exclude evidence violated a defendant's constitutional rights." Moses v. Payne, 543 F.3d 1090, 1103 (9th Cir.2008). The majority's attempt to fill this gap with Lunbery v. Hornbeak, 605 F.3d 754 (9th Cir. 2010) is unavailing. Lunbery is hardly persuasive when it resurrected — without citation — an interpretation of Chambers that we had already rejected, Moses, 543 F.3d at 1103, and that the Court had repudiated, Egelhoff, 518 U.S. at 53, 116 S.Ct. 2013.

[2] The majority's assertion that the prosecutor's isolated reference to the defendant's race in his closing statement similarly violated Armenia's due process rights is similarly flawed. The California Supreme Court properly noted that this was misconduct, but correctly applied controlling Supreme Court case law. See, e.g., Donnelly v. DeChristoforo, 416 U.S. 637, 646-47, 94 S.Ct. 1868, 40 L.Ed.2d 431 (1974) (finding no constitutionally reversible error in improper but isolated comments during closing arguments); see also Parker v. Matthews, 567 U.S. ____, 132 S.Ct. 2148, 2153, 183 L.Ed.2d 32 (2012) (reaffirming Donnelly).

Judge O'Scannlain's dissent in Stankewitz v. Wong (Oct 29, 2012)

O'SCANNLAIN, Circuit Judge, dissenting:

To prevail on a claim under Strickland v. Washington, 466 U.S. 668, 104 S.Ct. 2052, 80 L.Ed.2d 674 (1984), a habeas petitioner must show that his attorney performed deficiently and that such performance prejudiced him. This case presents an important, recurring issue under Strickland's prejudice prong: the proper standard for evaluating whether a petitioner was prejudiced by his attorney's failure to present mitigating evidence at sentencing. When evaluating a failure-to-present-mitigating-evidence claim under Strickland's prejudice prong, Supreme Court law is clear that a court must consider not just the benefits of never-presented mitigating evidence, but also its drawbacks.

The district court did not apply that prejudice standard here. Yet, rather than remand this case to let the district court apply the right standard, the panel majority tries to apply that standard for the first time on appeal.

With respect, that effort has my colleagues flailing in the dark. The record before us is huge and the prejudice issue in this case is especially difficult. We appellate judges are ill-suited to apply the correct prejudice standard, in the first instance, to a voluminous record. A district court decision applying the right standard would have been invaluable to our review of this challenging case.

Rather than evaluating prejudice on the merits, I would clarify the standard for evaluating failure-to-present-mitigating-evidence claims under Strickland, then remand this case, once again, to allow the district court to reevaluate prejudice under the correct standard. This would do a service to circuit law — which has long been confused on that standard — and would aid us greatly if we were to consider this case on another occasion. Thus, I respectfully must dissent from the majority's decision to take a different approach.

I

When we first considered this case, we said that "[a] more complete presentation" of evidence at the penalty phase "could have made a difference" in Stankewitz's sentence. Stankewitz v. Woodford, 365 F.3d 706, 724 (9th Cir.2004). Applying that instruction on remand, the district court ruled that, "[s]ince many of Stankewitz's [mitigation] allegations are proved by official documents in the record, the requirements for his ineffective assistance of counsel claim as set forth in [our 2004] opinion are satisfied." In so ruling that Stankewitz had suffered prejudice from his attorney's performance, however, the district court failed to evaluate the potentially aggravating effect of much of Stankewitz's new evidence.

The district court therefore did not apply the correct legal standard. As the Supreme Court recently reaffirmed in Wong v. Belmontes, when evaluating Strickland prejudice "it is necessary to consider all the relevant evidence that the jury would have had." 558 U.S. 15, 130 S.Ct. 383, 386, 175 L.Ed.2d 328 (2009) (per curiam). A court may not consider just the mitigating evidence — or just the mitigating effect of any evidence — that might have been presented. See id. at 386, 390. Ostensibly mitigating evidence, after all, can be a "double-edged sword": it can also be aggravating or can invite devastating rebuttal. See, e.g., Cullen v. Pinholster, ____ U.S. ____, 131 S.Ct. 1388, 1410, 179 L.Ed.2d 557 (2011) (evidence regarding petitioner's family problems may not have been mitigating because it could have led the jury to conclude that the petitioner was beyond rehabilitation); Atkins v. Virginia, 536 U.S. 304, 321, 122 S.Ct. 2242, 153 L.Ed.2d 335 (2002). While mitigating evidence might "ma[k]e a difference" if presented, it can do so "in the wrong direction" for the habeas petitioner. Belmontes, 130 S.Ct. at 388.

That may well be the case here. Stankewitz has offered evidence of his difficult youth, of his history of mental illness, and of his substance abuse and lack of sleep before the murder. But much of this evidence "is of questionable mitigating value," Pinholster, 131 S.Ct. at 1410, and — worse yet — could well have worked "in the wrong direction" for Stankewitz, Belmontes, 130 S.Ct. at 388. As a youth Stankewitz was a violent sociopath who often hurt people. Evidence of his youth was thus "by no means clearly mitigating, as the jury might have concluded that [Stankewitz] was simply beyond rehabilitation." Pinholster, 131 S.Ct. at 1410. The same goes for the evidence of mental illness and of drug abuse, which likewise may have done Stankewitz more harm than good. See id.; Brewer v. Quarterman, 550 U.S. 286, 289-90, 292-93, 127 S.Ct. 1706, 167 L.Ed.2d 622 (2007) (evidence of mental illness and substance abuse can be a double-edged sword); Correll v. Ryan, 539 F.3d 938, 963 (9th Cir.2008) (O'Scannlain, J., dissenting) (collecting cases explaining that evidence of mental illness may harm more than help).

Yet the district court weighed the mitigating evidence wholly in Stankewitz's favor. In doing so, the court apparently believed that it was following our direction that "even a fraction of the details Stankewitz [previously] allege[d] could have made a difference" in his sentence. Stankewitz, 365 F.3d at 724. But whatever we last said about the potential effect of Stankewitz's allegations, the district court was still required to weigh both the good — and the bad — effects of Stankewitz's new evidence. That is what Strickland requires and what Wong v. Belmontes reaffirms.

II

Because the district court did not apply the correct legal standard, on appeal we have been deprived of a solidly grounded district court decision to aid us. Yet this is no matter for the majority, which, for the first time on appeal, purports to apply the right standard. But the majority's thin prejudice analysis shows only how hard it is to evaluate Strickland prejudice when the district court does not, in the first instance, apply the correct standard to an enormous factual record.

A

The majority declines to conclude "that Stankewitz was not prejudiced by [his counsel's] failure to investigate or present any of the mitigating evidence" largely because "Stankewitz's case is materially different from [Wong v.] Belmontes." Maj. op. 1174. This case is not as bad as Belmontes, the majority contends, because (1) the aggravating effect of Stankewitz's mitigation evidence might not have been as bad as in Belmontes, and (2) in contrast to Belmontes, Stankewitz's jury had already gotten a taste of that aggravating effect. Maj. op. 1173-74.

These distinctions may be accurate, but they do not show that Stankewitz was prejudiced. The majority's analysis shows only that this case may be closer than Belmontes. That does not say much. The decision in Belmontes was both unanimous and summary. It was not close. Belmontes should not be treated as though it marked the exact boundary between prejudice and harmlessness. This case may present a closer call, but that does not mean that the call must be made for Stankewitz.

B

Once we step past the majority's efforts to distinguish Wong v. Belmontes, we are left with almost no analysis of prejudice.[1] The majority lobs some conclusory assertions that Stankewitz suffered prejudice. See, e.g., maj. op. 1170-71 (contending, without analysis, that evidence of Stankewitz's "life history" would have tipped the scale). But the majority gives no persuasive grounds for concluding that Stankewitz has demonstrated a reasonable probability that his sentence would have been different with his mitigation evidence.

Rather than peddling an unpersuasive prejudice analysis, we should have used this case to clarify the law on double-edged mitigation evidence and then remanded to allow the district court to evaluate prejudice under the right standard. That approach is common to federal appellate courts. See, e.g., United States v. Bus. of Custer Battlefield Museum & Store Located at Interstate 90, Exit 514, S. of Billings, Mont., 658 F.3d 1188, 1196 (9th Cir.2011) (Fisher, J.) (vacating and remanding for the district court to apply the correct legal standard); Tamas v. Dep't of Soc. & Health Servs., 630 F.3d 833, 837, 847 (9th Cir.2010) (same); cf. Sears v. Upton, ___ U.S. ___, 130 S.Ct. 3259, 3261, 3265-67, 177 L.Ed.2d 1025 (2010) (per curiam) (vacating and remanding when lower court had not applied the correct prejudice inquiry); United States v. Lanier, 520 U.S. 259, 272, 117 S.Ct. 1219, 137 L.Ed.2d 432 (1997) ("Because the Court of Appeals used the wrong gauge in [reaching its decision]..., we vacate the judgment and remand the case for application of the proper standard.").

This approach is especially warranted where, as here, a case demands a difficult weighing of voluminous evidence — an exercise at which district courts excel. Rather than reach out to decide the merits, I would simply remand to let that exercise take its course. That is the prudent approach.

III

That approach also would have done a service to our circuit law.

Before the decision in Wong v. Belmontes, our circuit was awash with Strickland cases that ignored the drawbacks of ostensibly mitigating evidence. E.g., Correll v. Ryan, 539 F.3d 938 (9th Cir.2008); Belmontes v. Ayers, 529 F.3d 834 (9th Cir.2008); Ainsworth v. Woodford, 268 F.3d 868 (9th Cir.2001). This reasoning squarely conflicted with the Supreme Court's Strickland jurisprudence. See, e.g., Correll, 539 F.3d at 962 (O'Scannlain, J., dissenting) (explaining that, in finding Strickland prejudice, the panel majority "ignores a mountain of precedent which requires us to consider not only the benefits of the ostensibly mitigating evidence counsel failed to present, but also its potential drawbacks");

Belmontes v. Ayers, 529 F.3d at 879-80 (O'Scannlain, J., dissenting) ("In order to discern prejudice, the majority overstates the mitigating evidence, understates the properly admitted aggravating evidence, and ignores the further aggravating evidence that would have come in on rebuttal."); Ainsworth, 268 F.3d at 880 (Graber, J., dissenting) ("[M]uch of the mitigating evidence on which the majority relies presented a double-edged sword, opening the door to harmful rather than helpful inferences.").

The Supreme Court took notice and repudiated this reasoning in Wong v. Belmontes. Yet our circuit is already showing signs of backsliding. See, e.g., James v. Ryan, 679 F.3d 780, 810-20 (9th Cir. 2012) (finding Strickland prejudice based on evidence of the petitioner's dysfunctional upbringing, drug abuse, and mental illness — without citing Wong v. Belmontes or considering the potential downside of such evidence). We should have halted that backsliding by making clear that Wong v. Belmontes invalidates significant parts of our circuit law regarding failure-to-present-mitigating-evidence claims under Strickland.

IV

While I hesitate to remand this decades-old case once more, that is the prudent course. In this capital case, the stakes are high enough to take the long view, get circuit law right, and leave Stankewitz's particular case for another day.[2] If that day were to come, we would have the benefit of a better-grounded district court decision, and we could be confident that we got this case right. We cannot be confident today.

I respectfully dissent.

Notes

[1] The majority does attempt briefly to analogize this case to Wiggins v. Smith, 539 U.S. 510, 123 S.Ct. 2527, 156 L.Ed.2d 471 (2003), see maj. op. 1174-75, but Wiggins is distinguishable for the reason the majority gives: "because Wiggins did not have a pattern of aggressive behavior or a criminal history, his mitigation evidence was unlikely to pose the double-edged sword problem presented in other cases (and now exemplified by Belmontes)." Maj. op. at 1175 (citing Wiggins, 539 U.S. at 515-16, 535-36, 123 S.Ct. 2527); see also id. (admitting that "Stankewitz's history is certainly not benign like Wiggins'").

[2] It would also have relieved us from delving into whether Stankewitz's trial counsel performed deficiently. The Supreme Court has stated that, "[i]f it is easier to dispose of an ineffectiveness claim on the ground of lack of sufficient prejudice, ... that course should be followed." Strickland, 466 U.S. at 697, 104 S.Ct. 2052; see Belmontes, 130 S.Ct. at 386 (a court need not resolve whether counsel performed deficiently when a petitioner cannot establish prejudice). Rather than muscling through the record to evaluate performance, the majority should have waited to see if it needed to evaluate performance at all. Because I believe that we should have waited, I offer no view on the majority's analysis of Strickland's performance prong.

Judge O'Scannlain's partial dissent in Biocini v. Holder (June 4, 2013)

O'SCANNLAIN, Circuit Judge, dissenting in part.

While I agree with the majority that the remaining claims should be dismissed, I would hold that the BIA adequately explained its reasons for concluding that Biocini's drug trafficking offense qualified as a particularly serious crime. In its decision, the BIA cited to Matter of Frentescu, 18 I&N Dec. 244 (BIA 1982), and applied the various factors from that decision before determining that Biocini committed a particularly serious crime. Specifically, the BIA noted that Biocini had been convicted of a drug offense, that the offense involved trafficking between five and fifteen kilograms of cocaine, that she received a substantial sentence of thirty months' imprisonment, and that drug trafficking was "harmful to society" and an "antisocial activity . . . of a scope sufficient to trigger the severest immigration consequences."

Biocini argues that the BIA failed to make a specific determination that she was a danger to the community, but this argument misapprehends the BIA's decisions evaluating whether a crime qualifies as particularly serious. As the BIA clarified in Matter of U-M-, 20 I&N Dec. 327 (BIA 1991), which was decided before Biocini pleaded guilty to her offense and applied the Frentescu framework, "[S]ome crimes are inherently particularly serious, requiring no further inquiry into the nature and circumstances of the underlying conviction. . . . [T]he crime of trafficking in drugs is inherently a particularly serious crime." Id. at 330 (citing Matter of Gonzalez, 19 I&N Dec. 682 (BIA 1988)). In addition, as the BIA noted in Matter of Carballe, 19 I&N Dec. 357 (BIA 1986), once the BIA finds that a crime is particularly serious, there is no "statutory requirement for a separate determination of dangerousness focusing on the likelihood of future serious misconduct on the part of the alien." Id. at 360.

Thus, I would deny in part and dismiss in part Biocini's petition for review.

Judge O'Scannlain's concurrence in Dahlia v. Rodriguez (Aug 21, 2013)

O'SCANNLAIN, Circuit Judge, with whom KOZINSKI, Chief Judge, joins, concurring only in the judgment:

Seven years ago, the Supreme Court counseled us that we had "misconceive[d] the theoretical underpinnings" of First Amendment retaliation law. Garcetti v. Ceballos, 547 U.S. 410, 423, 126 S.Ct. 1951, 164 L.Ed.2d 689 (2006). I respectfully dissent from the majority's analysis because our court makes the same error today by rejecting what California law tells us about the professional duties of that state's police officers. Furthermore, I fear that today's new approach will lead to "judicial intervention in the conduct of governmental operations to a degree inconsistent with sound principles of federalism and the separation of powers." Id. Federal courts have no business managing the daily activities of police departments.

I

We reheard this case en banc to consider whether Huppert v. City of Pittsburg,

574 F.3d 696 (9th Cir.2009), should remain good law. That case called on us to apply Garcetti's holding that "when public employees make statements pursuant to their official duties, the employees are not speaking as citizens for First Amendment purposes" to a lawsuit brought by a California police officer. 547 U.S. at 421, 126 S.Ct. 1951. We determined that the duty of California law enforcement officers to report criminal activity meant that the officer's reports of police misconduct internally, as well as to the FBI, did not qualify as protected "citizen-speech." Although I might not preserve every line of that opinion, at its core, Huppert got Garcetti right. Two key insights emerge from that case that help illustrate how the majority in this case has gone off track.

First, Huppert correctly appreciated that the Garcetti inquiry is no trifle. Id. at 702-03. Like Connick v. Myers, 461 U.S. 138, 103 S.Ct. 1684, 75 L.Ed.2d 708 (1983), which asks whether a public employee's speech is on a matter of public concern, Garcetti delineates the First Amendment's very scope. Put differently, the speech at issue "must not be expression on-the-job and within the scope of the employee's duties; if it is, there is no First Amendment protection for the speech." Erwin Chemerinsky, Constitutional Law: Principles and Policies 1151 (4th ed.2011). Instead, a would-be plaintiff's remedy usually lies in "the powerful network of legislative enactments" that protect whistleblowers. Garcetti, 547 U.S. at 425, 126 S.Ct. 1951.[1]

Second, Huppert understood that with the "pursuant-to-official-duties" test, the Garcetti Court was charting a clear course that distinguished between citizen-speech and employee-speech. See 574 F.3d at 702.[2] There, the Supreme Court explained that

[the plaintiff] did not act as a citizen when he went about conducting his daily professional activities, such as supervising attorneys, investigating charges, and preparing filings. In the same way he did not speak as a citizen by writing a memo that addressed the proper disposition of a pending criminal case. When he went to work and performed the tasks he was paid to perform, [he] acted as a government employee.

Garcetti, 547 U.S. at 422, 126 S.Ct. 1951. The consequence of the citizen/employee dichotomy is that protection in the workplace is to be the exception—not at all the rule. See, e.g., id. at 420, 126 S.Ct. 1951 ("Employees in some cases may receive First Amendment protection for expressions made at work") (emphasis added); Morales v. Jones, 494 F.3d 590, 598 (7th Cir.2007) (noting that "the purpose of Garcetti was to allow government employers greater influence over speech that owes it[s] existence to a public employee's professional responsibilities").

With its decision to discard Huppert, and with its newly-minted "guiding principles" for identifying protected speech, the majority opinion reopens doors that Garcetti slammed shut. See Maj. Op. at 1070, 1074-76.

II

A

I cannot agree that "the Huppert majority failed to heed Garcetti's mandate" about a practical inquiry by taking stock of California courts' "description of a California police officer's professional duties." Maj. Op. at 1070. Here is the entirety of what the Supreme

Court said on this issue:

> Two final points warrant mentioning. First, as indicated above, the parties in this case do not dispute that Ceballos wrote his disposition memo pursuant to his employment duties. We thus have no occasion to articulate a comprehensive framework for defining the scope of an employee's duties in cases where there is room for serious debate. We reject, however, the suggestion that employers can restrict employees' rights by creating excessively broad job descriptions. See post, at 1965, n.2 (SOUTER, J., dissenting). The proper inquiry is a practical one. Formal job descriptions often bear little resemblance to the duties an employee actually is expected to perform, and the listing of a given task in an employee's written job description is neither necessary nor sufficient to demonstrate that conducting the task is within the scope of the employee's professional duties for First Amendment purposes.[3]

Garcetti, 547 U.S. at 424, 126 S.Ct. 1951. This passage appears near the end of the opinion, after the Court announced its conclusion of law and after it applied that holding to the plaintiff's facts. Id. at 420-22, 126 S.Ct. 1951. It is written as a rejoinder to the principal dissent's worry that "one response to the Court's holding will be moves by government employers to expand stated job descriptions to include more official duties and so exclude even some currently protectable speech from First Amendment purview." Garcetti, 547 U.S. at 431 n. 2, 126 S.Ct. 1951 (Souter, J., dissenting).

Read in context, this practical-inquiry passage simply directs us not to engage in a stilted or excessively formulaic inquiry. On the one hand, the Court is explaining that the sort of gamesmanship Justice Souter feared is not to be tolerated. On the other hand, the Garcetti Court is explaining (as cogently expressed by the Sixth Circuit) that "[s]peech by a public employee made pursuant to ad hoc or de facto duties not appearing in any written job description is nevertheless not protected if it owes its existence to the speaker's professional responsibilities." Fox v. Traverse City Area Pub. Sch. Bd. of Educ., 605 F.3d 345, 348 (6th Cir.2010) (alteration and internal quotation marks omitted). The prototypical examples of protected speech are "writing a letter to a local newspaper, as the teacher-plaintiff did in Pickering" and "discussing politics with a co-worker." Foley v. Randolph, 598 F.3d 1, 6 (1st Cir.2010) (discussing Garcetti, 547 U.S. at 423, 126 S.Ct. 1951). In Garcetti, the plaintiff did not engage in these types of actions; instead he "spoke as a prosecutor." 547 U.S. at 421, 126 S.Ct. 1951. That speech was unprotected because "[w]hen a public employee speaks pursuant to employment responsibilities" there generally is not a "relevant analogue to speech by citizens who are not government employees." Id. at 424, 126 S.Ct. 1951.

In the case before us, we confront what it means to speak as a police officer. I would not interpret the Supreme Court's caution against formalism—the "practical-inquiry" passage from Garcetti—as an obstacle to our evaluating a public-employee plaintiff's case against the backdrop of legal and professional norms. See, e.g., Tamayo v. Blagojevich, 526 F.3d 1074 (7th Cir.2008) (taking notice, in reviewing a motion to dismiss, of the oversight responsibilities of a state legislative committee and of the duties of the administrator of the gaming board); Foley, 598 F.3d at 4 (considering Massachusetts General Laws ch. 48 § 42, which spells out a fire department chief's "powers and duties," as well as the specific contract that governed the chief's employment).

B

1

California courts tell us that, "[u]nlike civilians," that state's police officers are "expected to prevent others from committing crimes, to assist in the investigation of crime, and to use their law enforcement authority to maintain the trust of the public in its criminal justice system." People v. Owens, 59 Cal.App.4th 798, 69 Cal.Rptr.2d 428, 430-31 (1997) (upholding a District Attorney's decision to single out an off-duty police officer for prosecution for engaging in a pyramid scheme because, in contrast to his civilian confederates, he had "failed to discharge" the "special obligations" of his office).

This principle was first articulated in the canonical case of Christal v. Police Commission of City and County of San Francisco, 33 Cal.App.2d 564, 92 P.2d 416 (1939). See also Titus v. Los Angeles Cnty. Civil Serv. Comm'n, 130 Cal.App.3d 357, 181 Cal.Rptr. 699, 703 (1982) (stating that Christal "enunciated the role of a law enforcement officer."). "Among the duties of [California] police officers" is the responsibility to disclose "all information known to them which may lead to the apprehension and punishment of those who have transgressed" their state's laws. Christal, 92 P.2d.at 419. The case further explained that "[w]hen police officers acquire knowledge of facts which will tend to incriminate any person, it is their duty to disclose such facts to their superiors and to testify freely concerning such facts when called upon to do so before any duly constituted court or grand jury." Id. Christal went so far as to say that "[i]t is for the performance of these duties that police officers are commissioned and paid by the community." Id. (emphasis added); compare with Garcetti, 547 U.S. at 422, 126 S.Ct. 1951 (explaining that when the plaintiff "performed the tasks he was paid to perform" he had "acted as a government employee" (emphasis added)). Dahlia has not marshaled any authority undermining Huppert's conclusion that police officers still have these obligations when speaking to external law enforcement agencies, such as the county sheriff or FBI. See 574 F.3d at 707.[4]

My colleagues deride these duties as either relics of a bygone era or judicial musing too naive to credit. See Maj. Op. at 1070 n. 9 (the "passage from Christal relied upon by the Huppert majority reads like a civics textbook"). Yet the California Government Code in force today states that public safety officers may be ordered "to cooperate with other agencies involved in criminal investigations [and] [i]f an officer fails to comply with such an order, the agency may officially charge him or her with insubordination." Cal. Gov't Code § 3304. And, numerous California cases have cited the Christal principle over the decades to express "the all-important concept of the peculiar and delicate position police officers hold in society." Frazee v. Civil Serv. Bd. of Oakland, 170 Cal.App.2d 333, 335, 338 P.2d 943 (1959). As the City of Burbank has argued to us, in a wide variety of settings the unique charge of those tasked with enforcing the criminal laws has overridden other important rights. See, e.g., Titus, 181 Cal.Rptr. at 702-03 (demanding that officers forsake attorney-client privilege in order "to cooperate in a criminal investigation"); Riverside Cnty. Sheriff's Dept. v. Zigman, 169 Cal.App.4th 763, 87 Cal.Rptr.3d 358, 361-62 (2008) (describing "a law enforcement officer's duty to report criminal activity to his or her employer," and explaining that the "statutory privilege at issue in this case, must yield when [its] exercise is inconsistent with the performance of the officer's duties").

The majority also rejects this "court-created job description applicable to every member of [the] profession" by invoking the specter of employer gamesmanship. Maj. Op. at 1070. Given its seventy-plus year lineage, the California police officer description of duty could not possibly be a reaction to the Garcetti opinion. Cf. Garcetti, 547 U.S. at 431 n. 2, 126 S.Ct. 1951 (Souter, J., dissenting) ("I am pessimistic enough to expect that one response to the Court's holding will be moves by government employers to expand stated job descriptions...."). More importantly, however, there are legitimate reasons for California to have imposed admittedly exacting obligations on its police. Just as Caesar's wife must be above reproach, "peace officers have been held to a higher standard than other public employees," because that is essential to "maintain the public's confidence in its police force." Pasadena Police Officers Ass'n v. City of Pasadena, 51 Cal.3d 564, 273 Cal.Rptr. 584, 797 P.2d 608, 611 (1990) ("[T]he public expects peace officers to be above suspicion of violation of the very laws they are sworn to enforce" (internal quotation marks and alterations omitted)).

2

Recently, the Supreme Court recalled that categorical rules have the virtue of keeping "easy cases easy." Florida v. Jardines, ___ U.S. ___, 133 S.Ct. 1409, 1417, 185 L.Ed.2d 495 (2013). In that spirit, I read Garcetti as fully compatible with a stated obligation of California police officers to report crime—a subset of which is to help expose and to assist in the investigation of crime within their ranks.[5] A California-police-officer plaintiff must engage with "California's jurisprudence defining such duties." Huppert, 574 F.3d at 707. After all, "the plaintiff bears the burden of showing [his] speech was spoken in the capacity of a private citizen and not a public employee." Eng, 552 F.3d at 1071.

When as here, a court is called on to evaluate whether a complaint states a First Amendment retaliation claim, it should evaluate its plausibility against this legal landscape. Cf. Morales, 494 F.3d at 598 ("[T]he Milwaukee Police Department requires officers to report all potential crimes. By informing A.D.A. Chisholm of the allegations against Chief Jones and Deputy Chief Ray, Morales was performing that duty as well. Accordingly, his conversation with A.D.A. Chisholm is not protected under the First Amendment after Garcetti."). In a similar vein, as mentioned above, the Seventh Circuit considered whether a complaint stated a claim for First Amendment retaliation in the context of state-law duties:

Ms. Tamayo's testimony was given to the House Gaming Committee, a legislative committee responsible for overseeing the activities of the [Illinois Gaming

Board], and her testimony involved the alleged wrongdoing of public officials in their attempts to encroach on the agency's independence. As the Administrator of the agency, she had a duty to see that the law was administered properly. This responsibility encompassed a duty to bring alleged wrongdoing within her agency to the attention of the relevant public authorities—here, the House Gaming Committee.

Tamayo, 526 F.3d at 1091. That administrator sought to "escape the strictures of Garcetti by including in her complaint the conclusory legal statement that she acted `as a citizen ... outside the duties of her employment.'" Id. at 1092. Appropriately invoking Bell Atlantic Corp. v. Twombly, 550 U.S. 544, 127 S.Ct. 1955, 167 L.Ed.2d 929 (2007), the court did not credit these legal conclusions "couched as a factual allegation." Id.

Similarly, it would be up to a California police officer to "plead[] factual content that allows the court to draw the reasonable inference that" his department imposes less stringent crime-reporting duties on its employees than California courts routinely acknowledge. Ashcroft v. Iqbal, 556 U.S. 662, 678, 129 S.Ct. 1937, 173 L.Ed.2d 868 (2009).[6] He would need to put at issue that his is a "case[] where there is room for serious debate." Garcetti, 547 U.S. at 424, 126 S.Ct. 1951. Such application of Garcetti is also in line with the rule that, in measuring the sufficiency of a complaint, "the reviewing court [should] draw on its judicial experience and common sense"; it is eminently logical that officers have precisely the duty that California courts claim they do. Iqbal, 556 U.S. at 679, 129 S.Ct. 1937.[7]

Assuming an officer's "well-pleaded facts" do suggest that Christal/Huppert are a poor fit for his circumstance, id. at 679, 129 S.Ct. 1937, then the case would proceed to summary judgment. At that stage, evidence showing that his duties are truly limited in the fashion he had alleged would need to be proffered. Discovery generally will have unearthed the relevant materials, and then the court would be free to discern which statements, if any, fell outside the officer's duties. See, e.g., Brammer-Hoelter v. Twin Peaks Charter Acad., 492 F.3d 1192, 1204-05 (10th Cir. 2007) (deciding at summary judgment which statements by teachers passed and failed Garcetti); Charles v. Grief, 522 F.3d 508, 513 n. 17 (5th Cir.2008) (considering the "factual circumstances surrounding the speech at issue" to decide "whether Garcetti applies").

The Court's mission in Garcetti was to articulate a "screening test a judge should apply" when a government employee tried to invoke the First Amendment. See Garcetti, 547 U.S. at 445-46, 126 S.Ct. 1951 (Breyer, J., dissenting). Concerned that, in practice, not every police department in California expects its officers to live up to the duties spelled out by its judiciary, the majority decides to screen almost nothing. By contrast, as I have explained, the approach faithful to Garcetti would have been to preserve Huppert as the default presumption, while also acknowledging the possibility that on occasion a police officer might be able to avoid its application.

III

With utmost respect to my colleagues in the majority, I find their "guiding principles" about implementing Garcetti similarly untenable. Maj. Op. at 1074.

First, the majority decides that if "a public employee takes his job concerns to persons outside the work place in addition to raising them up the chain of command at his workplace, then those external communications are ordinarily not made as an employee, but as a citizen." Maj. Op. at 1074. By contrast, as California courts have made clear,[8] the police have a unique role in society that makes it inappropriate to rely on case law involving other types of public employment to decide that officers' speech will be protected when delivered "to persons outside the work place," i.e., outside their own police department. Id. at 1074; cf. Kendall Turner, Dahlia v. Rodriguez: A Chance to Overturn a Dangerous Precedent, 65 Stan. L.Rev. Online 59, 63 (2012) (astutely perceiving that "[i]f a janitor cleaning Dahlia's station had noted the same illegal interrogation tactics, he could presumably enjoy First Amendment protection while reporting them because his job did not require him to expose illegal activity").[9]

The majority's third "guiding principle"—an employee is no longer carrying out his professional duties when he does so in the face of a threat or directive by his supervisor to break the law or protocol— follows the Second Circuit's misguided approach. See Jackler v. Byrne, 658 F.3d 225, 242 (2d Cir.2011). Once again, the majority resorts to the "practical-inquiry" passage for substantiation. Maj. Op. 1075. And once again, we "get[] Garcetti backwards." Bowie v. Maddox, 653 F.3d 45, 48 (D.C.Cir.2011).

There are two key problems with the Second Circuit's approach that our court adopts today. First, it conflates the "adverse-action" element of a retaliation claim and the "pursuant-to-official-duties" test. Subtly, the Jackler rule allows concern for what happened to a particular plaintiff to color the threshold question about job duties. See Bowie, 653 F.3d at 48 ("[I]t is not difficult to sympathize with the Second Circuit's dubious interpretation of Garcetti. The police chief's instruction to Jackler and the actions he ordered Jackler to take were clearly illegal. But the illegality of a government employer's order does not necessarily mean the employee has a cause of action under the First Amendment when he contravenes that order.").

Second, Jackler's holding subverts Garcetti by not applying the Court's categorical rule that the protected-status inquiry hinges on job duties, and job duties alone. Jackler involved a police officer who witnessed his sergeant lose his temper and unjustifiably strike an arrestee. 658 F.3d at 230-31. After the officer reported what had happened in a supplemental report, the sergeant pressured him to substitute his honest report for one "which contained false, incomplete and misleading information." Id. at 231. He refused, and was fired. Id. at 232.

In dismissing his claim under Garcetti, the district court determined that it was "clear on the facts as alleged by Jackler that he refused to withdraw or alter his truthful report in the belief that the proper execution of his duties as a police officer required no less." Id. at 233. The Second Circuit did not disagree that as a "police officer [he certainly] ha[d] a duty not to substitute a falsehood for the truth." Id. at 241. But then, instead of applying "Garcetti's employee-versus-citizen rule," the Second Circuit "created a significant exception to it." Caroline A. Flynn, Note, Policeman, Citizen, or Both? A

Civilian Analogue Exception to Garcetti v. Ceballos, 111 Mich. L.Rev. 759, 775 (2013).

Today's en banc court simply borrows Jackler without discussing its rationale; but as the D.C. Circuit has explained, that case is indefensible. The Second Circuit reasoned that Officer "Jackler's refusal to comply with orders to retract his truthful Report and file one that was false has a civilian analogue and that Jackler [thus] was not simply doing his job in refusing to obey those orders from the department's top administrative officers and the chief of police." Jackler, 658 F.3d at 241-42. The problem with this approach is that while Garcetti did state that its abstract ambition was to protect the kinds of speech for which there is a relevant civilian analogue, 547 U.S. at 424, 126 S.Ct. 1951, the Supreme Court unambiguously settled on a categorical rule as opposed to the potentially more calibrated (but also more subjective) proposals floated in the trio of dissenting opinions. See Bowie, 653 F.3d at 48 ("As all of the dissenting justices recognized, Garcetti categorically denies recovery ... to plaintiffs who spoke pursuant to official duties." (internal quotation marks and alteration omitted)). The principal dissent puts this matter as plain as can be, explaining that "when a law enforcement officer expressly balks at a superior's order to violate constitutional rights he is sworn to protect" the majority opinion places this "speaker[] beyond the reach of First Amendment protection against retaliation." Garcetti, 547 U.S. at 433, 126 S.Ct. 1951 (Souter, J., dissenting).[10]

I would therefore adopt neither the majority's "contrary-to-orders" maxim nor its rule about "disclosures outside the chain of command."

IV

Remaining now is the application of the foregoing framework to Dahlia's complaint.

A

1

As for Dahlia's report to Internal Affairs ("IA"), the majority states "[i]t is possible that Dahlia's professional duties required him to meet with IA at IA's insistence, but it is also plausible that Dahlia's act of meeting with IA was outside his job duties for the purpose of the First Amendment." Maj. Op. 1077. Under the Supreme Court's Twombly and Iqbal precedents, it is plaintiff's responsibility to show that his speech qualifies for constitutional protection. See Iqbal, 556 U.S. at 678, 129 S.Ct. 1937 (the Rule 8(a) pleading standard "asks for more than a sheer possibility.... [w]here a complaint pleads facts that are merely consistent with a defendant's liability, it stops short of the line between possibility and plausibility of entitlement to relief" (internal quotation marks omitted)). The majority incants the term "plausible" without pointing to allegations which make it so.

Dahlia's complaint alleges that IA initiated an investigation and came to interview him three times. Compl. ¶ 36. Dahlia does not say he sought out IA, nor does he claim that he was free either to stay silent when asked about the corruption he had witnessed, or to lie about it. Given the inherent implausibility of that scenario,[11] his complaint most certainly lacks "factual allegations that `raise [his] right to relief above the speculative level.'" Tamayo, 526 F.3d at 1092 (quoting Twombly, 550 U.S. at 555, 127 S.Ct. 1955) (alteration in original).

2

Dahlia's allegations about his "speech" to the County Sheriff's Department are similarly threadbare. The majority concludes that the protected status of his speech likely turns on "whether discovery reveals that Dahlia's supervisors instructed him to meet with and disclose information to the [sheriff]." Maj. Op. at 1078. Such construction of "pursuant to official duties" is woefully cramped. See, e.g., Foley, 598 F.3d at 6 ("In analyzing whether Foley spoke as a citizen rather than as the Chief of the Fire Department, we first note that it is not dispositive that Foley was not required to speak to the media."); Brammer-Hoelter, 492 F.3d at 1203 ("[S]peech may be made pursuant to an employee's official duties even if it deals with activities that the employee is not expressly required to perform."); Williams v. Dallas Indep. Sch. Dist., 480 F.3d 689, 694 (5th Cir.2007) (per curiam) ("Simply because Williams wrote memoranda, which were not demanded of him, does not mean he was not acting within the course of performing his job.").

Without the majority's errant gloss, Dahlia's allegations fall short. His complaint refers to no facts that suggest, let alone plausibly suggest, that in cooperating with the sheriff's investigation of corruption in the Burbank Police Department he was not "discharging the responsibilities of [his] office, [but instead] appearing as "[John] Q. Public." " Tamayo, 526 F.3d at 1092. And as already detailed, the case law and California Government Code Section 3304 indicate that cooperating with an external law enforcement agency "is a duty he `actually [was] expected to perform.'" Foley, 598 F.3d at 7 (quoting Garcetti, at 424-25, 126 S.Ct. 1951).[12]

Thus, I must conclude that Dahlia's complaint does not state a claim for First Amendment retaliation upon which relief may be granted.

B

In our circuit, though, Dahlia still would have one more chance to pursue his claim. Although the odds are long, Dahlia could conceivably satisfy the pleading standard as to the protected status of his speech by adding particular allegations about the nature of his crime-reporting duty at the Burbank Police Department. In my view, he would be entitled to be granted leave to amend his complaint, and it is on that narrow basis that I would reverse the judgment dismissing his complaint. See Lopez v. Smith, 203 F.3d 1122, 1130 (9th Cir.2000) (en banc) (explaining that the court must "grant leave to amend even if no request to amend the pleading was made, unless it determines that the pleading could not possibly be cured by the allegation of other facts"). I also agree with the majority to the extent that Dahlia's request for leave to amend to satisfy the adverse action requirement must be honored. Maj. Op. at 1078 nn. 22-23.

V

The malfeasance by officers of the Burbank Police Department which Dahlia witnessed and the threats and intimidation he endured—if true—are shocking and intolerable. Yet we must stay our collective hand, ever mindful that the "Constitution does not provide a cure for every social ill, nor does it vest judges with a mandate to try to remedy every social problem." Plyler v. Doe, 457 U.S. 202, 253, 102 S.Ct. 2382, 72 L.Ed.2d 786 (1982) (Burger, J., dissenting) (citing Lindsey v. Normet, 405 U.S. 56, 74, 92 S.Ct. 862, 31 L.Ed.2d 36 (1972)). Alongside his First Amendment cause, Dahlia brought claims under provisions of California law that (1) protect public employees from retaliation for disclosing an abuse of authority or a danger to the public safety, California Government Code § 53298, and (2) that shield employees who complain to a government agency, California Labor Code § 6310. These are the kinds of remedies that the Supreme Court has explained whistleblowers should pursue in the absence of a constitutional claim. See Garcetti, 547 U.S. at 425, 126 S.Ct. 1951. However righteous our aims, when we stretch the Constitution to match our sense of justice, we exceed "[t]he judicial power" vested to us in Article III and, by rendering state law nugatory, disserve our federal union.

While I narrowly concur in the judgment, I must respectfully dissent from the court's erroneous analysis of the First Amendment in this case.

Notes

[1] The lack of a constitutional action may sometimes be for the best, as this "complicated employment law issue ... is much better suited for a legislative solution." John Q. Mulligan, Note, Huppert, Reily, and the Increasing Futility of Relying on the First Amendment to Protect Employee Speech, 19 Wm. & Mary. Bill Rts. J. 449, 456 (2010). Many questions arise, such as "what types of complaints should be protected, whether internal or external whistleblowing should be protected, and what types of employer responses should be punished." Id. at 468.

[2] The dissenters in Garcetti, as well the academic literature since, recognize the bright-line nature of the inquiry. See, e.g., Garcetti, 547 U.S. at 432, 126 S.Ct. 1951 (Souter, J., dissenting) (majority "categorically separat[es] the citizen's interest from the employee's interest"); id. at 427, 126 S.Ct. 1951 (Stevens, J., dissenting) (similar); id. at 446, 126 S.Ct. 1951 (Breyer, J., dissenting) (majority approach described as "absolute"); Chemerinsky, supra, at 1147 (describing Garcetti as "a categorical exception from constitutional protection for speech which is on the job in the scope of the employee's duties"); Caroline A. Flynn, Note, 111 Mich. L.Rev. 759, 761 (2013) (Garcetti "replaced the balancing framework with a bright-line rule"); Monique Alexandra Bair, Garcetti v. Ceballos: Swapping The First Amendment Rights of Public Employees for Greater Government Control, 37 Rutgers L. Rec. 44, 52-55 (2010) (same).

[3] The second point the Court made is that the Garcetti analysis should not uncritically be applied when academic freedom is involved. See 547 U.S. at 425, 126 S.Ct. 1951.

[4] California law, in fact, suggests just the opposite. In one case, an Alhambra Police Department Officer who had sexually harassed a motorist went to his union representative for help in dealing with the Los Angeles Sheriff's Department investigation into his misconduct. Alhambra Police Officers Ass'n v. City of Alhambra Police Dep't, 113 Cal.App.4th 1413, 7 Cal.Rptr.3d 432, 434-35 (2003). In that meeting, the officer disclosed

incriminating details; the union representative failed to pass along evidence to his superiors and helped the officer retrieve a document with the driver's telephone number on it—a violation of several department policies. Id. The California Court of Appeal found that the union representative had an obligation to assist in bringing the officer's misconduct to light, based on Christal and its progeny. Obviously this broad duty is part of the special responsibility of police and not something characteristic to most other forms of public employment. See, e.g., Davis v. McKinney, 518 F.3d 304, 316 (5th Cir.2008) (explaining it was not within a public university's "auditor's job function to communicate with outside police authorities [such as the FBI] or other agencies [such as the Equal Employment Opportunity Commission] in an investigation"); Freitag v. Ayers, 468 F.3d 528 (9th Cir.2006) (deciding that it was not part of a correctional officer's "official tasks to complain to [a] Senator or the [Inspector General] about the state's failure to perform its duties properly").

[5] See Dahlia v. Rodriguez, 689 F.3d 1094, 1105 (9th Cir.2012) (characterizing Huppert's rule as one under which "whistleblowing on fellow officers is part of a police officer's official duties").

[6] An officer might do that by describing his employment contract, a collective bargaining agreement, or a (formal or informal) policy limiting his disclosure obligations.

[7] Simply put, "[t]here is nothing startling in the conception that a public servant's right to retain his office or employment should depend upon his willingness to forego his constitutional rights and privileges to the extent that the exercise of such rights and privileges may be inconsistent with the performance of the duties of his office or employment." Christal, 92 P.2d at 419.

[8] See supra note 7 and accompanying text.

[9] I would not adopt the majority's second principle concerning the "subject matter" of speech for the same reason. Maj. Op. at 1074-75. A police officer is not "an average public employee." Id.

[10] Although the academic literature—some of which has been cited in the briefs—has urged us to do otherwise, our duty is to apply Supreme Court precedent fairly rather than whittle it away in a case with sympathetic facts. See, e.g., Turner, supra, at 64 ("While lower courts are of course not free to ignore Garcetti, they are free to—and should—take a narrow view of what constitutes an employee's `official duties.'"); id. at 63 ("Of course, the fundamental problem may be with Garcetti itself rather than Huppert."); Flynn, supra, at 772 (although disposed to the dissenting view as a policy matter, conceding, "in agreement with the D.C. Circuit, that the Second Circuit misapplied Garcetti in Jackler: a civilian analogue exception does not follow from either the language or the logic of that decision").

[11] See, e.g., Jackler, 658 F.3d at 241 ("Of course a police officer has a duty not to substitute a falsehood for the truth, i.e., a duty to tell `nothing but the truth'....").

[12] Because our court is admonished not to manufacture arguments for parties, unlike the majority, I would not consider Dahlia's report to the Burbank Police Officers'

Association as an alternative form of protected speech. See United States v. Williamson, 439 F.3d 1125, 1138 (9th Cir.2006); Maj. Op. at 1077. Dahlia has not claimed anything beyond his statements to Internal Affairs, to the sheriff's department, and his unsubstantiated report to the FBI as constitutionally protected speech. Nor, has he even alleged that "the retaliation he faced was directly caused by this act of reporting." Maj. Op. at 1077.

Judge O'Scannlain's concurrence in In Re Application for Exemption from Elec. Public Access (Aug 29, 2013)

O'SCANNLAIN, Circuit Judge, concurring specially:

I write individually to acknowledge "the elephant in the room": to whom does one go for review when an application for an exemption from PACER fees has been denied?

We posed just this question to the Administrative Office at oral argument. Since the Judicial Conference is the body Congress tasked with writing the fee schedule, naturally, the Administrative Office suggested that comments about either the clarity or substantive coverage of the policy could be directed there. By statute, the Judicial Conference studies "the condition of business in the courts of the United States" and makes recommendations "to the various courts to promote uniformity of management procedures and the expeditious conduct of court business." 28 U.S.C. § 331. Reviewing individual applications for exemption such as Gollan and Shifflett's, however, would not be—as the Administrative Office recognized—consistent with this broad national mission.

PACER fee determinations are just one of the "increasing numbers of administrative responsibilities" being assigned to district courts "that are not subject to review by appeal." 15A Charles Alan Wright & Arthur R. Miller, Federal Practice and Procedure § 3903 (2d. ed.1992). The authors of a leading treatise on federal procedure argue that perhaps "control may be exercised by the Judicial Council of the Circuit." Wright & Miller, supra, at § 3903. Comprised of district and circuit judges, but not vested with "traditional judicial powers," the Circuit Council has been described as a "'board of directors' for the circuit." Chandler v. Judicial Council of the Tenth Circuit of the United States, 398 U.S. 74, 86 n. 7, 90 S.Ct. 1648, 26 L.Ed.2d 100 (1970); see also 28 U.S.C. § 332. Outside of the realm of judicial-misconduct allegations,[1] the Judicial Councils typically "avoid involvement with any matter specific to the decision of an individual case." Wright & Miller, supra, at § 3939. Under extraordinary circumstances not present here, i.e. a district court interpreting the fee schedule in bad-faith, the Administrative Office thought it was conceivable that those circuit bodies might appropriately deal with a PACER fee dispute. Cf. J. Clifford Wallace, Report of the Committee on Reorganization of the Circuit Conference and Conference Committees, 68 F.R.D. 469, 474 (1975) (explaining that each "circuit council has supervisory powers which are not clearly defined but do exist"). However, for more quotidian PACER applications the Judicial Councils would not be the place to turn.

Because (as the opinion discusses) there is "no right of formal appeal" to contest the amount of a Criminal Justice Act fee award, Congress decided to create an administrative "review process separate from the traditional right of appeal." In re Smith, 586 F.3d 1169, 1173 (9th Cir.2009) (explaining that "excess fees must be approved both by the presiding judge and the chief circuit judge or his delegate").

Assuming ordinary PACER-fee determinations are not reviewable by the judiciary's administrative apparatus, it will be up to Congress to decide whether to fashion an appellate-review mechanism, or whether to leave them within the exclusive purview of district courts.

Notes

[1] For a synopsis of that aspect of the Judicial Councils' work, see J. Clifford Wallace, Resolving Judicial Corruption While Preserving Judicial Independence: Comparative Perspectives, 28 Cal. W. Int'l L.J.341, 348-51 (1998).

Judge O'Scannlain's dissent in Singh v. Holder (Oct 30, 2013)

O'SCANNLAIN, Circuit Judge, dissenting.

The court's decision in Ren v. Holder, 648 F.3d 1079 (9th Cir. 2011), does not control this case. Ren states clearly that, "[i]f a credible applicant has not yet met his burden of proof, then the IJ may require corroborative evidence," and, if he so requires, "must give the applicant notice of the corroboration that is required and an opportunity either to produce the requisite corroborative evidence or to explain why that evidence is not reasonably available." Id. at 1093 (emphasis added). This rule does not mandate that every credible applicant who has yet failed to carry his burden of proof be afforded with notice and opportunity to present corroborating evidence.[1] Such a conclusion, furthermore, would be manifestly futile in this case. The IJ found that Singh credibly testified to the following facts: (1) he was hit intentionally by the jeep; (2) other people in the village told him they believed the Congress Party was behind the attack; and (3) there were no witnesses to the attack. Singh never in his testimony claimed that anyone had direct knowledge of the perpetrators' identity or political affiliation. As the IJ noted, "[Singh] even acknowledged that all the people who told him were merely relying on rumors and none of them had witnessed that these individuals [who attacked him] were members of the Congress Party." Thus, the IJ did not find that corroboration was necessary—indeed, the IJ seemed to believe corroboration would be impossible. Even if Singh obtained declarations from his friends as to the perpetrators of the attack, these declarations would still be speculative and would fail to satisfy Singh's burden of proof. The IJ did note that Singh provided "no objective evidence" to support his claims. But this is a far cry from a determination that the applicant "should provide evidence."

Furthermore, the IJ clearly stated, as an alternative ground for the disposition, that Singh had failed to demonstrate that he could have safely relocated within his native country.[2] Singh argues that this finding should be displaced because the IJ improperly placed the burden of proof on him and not on the government where it belongs.[3] Such a claim misreads the IJ's opinion and misconceives the administrative record. Before concluding that Singh "has not established that it would be unreasonable for him to relocate," the IJ had analyzed and cited the extensive evidence submitted by the United States that tended to show relocation could be both safe and practicable. During direct as well as cross-examination, Singh had the opportunity to dispute this evidence and to provide his own. He did not do so. Indeed, the only evidence that Singh presented on this issue was his own asseverations that he would have difficulty finding a job and that the individuals who allegedly persecuted him in the Punjab state would have the means and the motivation to pursue him hither and yon. Against the weight of the government's evidence, the IJ did not find Singh's testimony availing. This conclusion is not unreasonable.[4]

Because I do not believe that Ren compels remand in this circumstance, and furthermore because the IJ's alternative holding concerning relocation provides an independent basis for his decision, I would deny the petition for review.[5]

I respectfully dissent.

Notes

[1] There will certainly be cases where the applicant can present credible testimony that does not satisfy the burden of proof, and corroboration is unnecessary or futile. This is consistent with the statute, which states: "Where the trier of fact determines that the applicant should provide evidence that corroborates otherwise credible testimony, such evidence must be provided unless the applicant does not have the evidence and cannot reasonably obtain the evidence." 8 U.S.C. § 1158(b)(1)(B)(ii). This language, specifically the phrase "where a trier of fact determines," implies that the trier of fact may determine that no corroborative evidence is required.

[2] The relevant regulation states:

[A]n immigration judge, in the exercise of his or her discretion, shall deny the asylum application of an alien found to be a refugee on the basis of past persecution if . . . [t]he applicant could avoid future persecution by relocating to another part of the applicant's country of nationality . . . and under all the circumstances, it would be reasonable to expect the applicant to do so.

8 C.F.R. § 1208.13(b)(1)(i)(B) (emphasis added).

[3] See 8 C.F.R. § 1208.13(b)(1)(ii).

[4] Singh disputed the IJ's determination concerning the reasonableness of relocation on appeal before the Board of Immigration Appeals. The BIA's decision did not address the issue but, by explicitly invoking Matter of Burbano, 20 I. & N. Dec. 872, 874 (BIA 1994), incorporated the conclusions and reasoning of the IJ as articulated in her decision. In such circumstances, we may examine the IJ's determination concerning relocation as if it had been that of the BIA, see Tamang v. Holder, 598 F.3d 1083, 1088

(9th Cir. 2010); and we review for substantial evidence, see INS v. Eliaz-Zacarias, 502 U.S. 478, 481 & n.1 (1992). This court, therefore, must uphold the agency's findings unless "we . . . find that the evidence not only supports [the opposite] conclusion, but compels it." Id.

[5] The same logic that disposes of Singh's application for asylum similarly decides his prayers for withholding of removal and protection under the Convention against Torture (CAT). The procedure for denying withholding of removal on the grounds that relocation within the native country is reasonable is substantially the same as for asylum. Compare 8 C.F.R. § 1208.16(b)(1)(i)(B), with 8 C.F.R. § 1208.13(b)(1)(i)(B). Because Singh cannot overcome the government's evidence concerning the reasonableness of relocation in the asylum context, he similarly cannot prevail in withholding of removal.

On the other hand, Singh's burden for securing relief under CAT is even greater. See Hasan v. Ashcroft, 380 F.3d 1114, 1122 (9th Cir. 2004) (describing that "the legal standard for considering the possibility of relocation is different in the context of a CAT claim than in an asylum claim" and that, in the former, "the burden is on the applicant").

Singh could not prevail on the relocation question for his asylum application; he likewise cannot in these other claims.

Judge O'Scannlain's dissent in Sachs v. Republic of Austria (Dec 6, 2013)

O'SCANNLAIN, Circuit Judge, dissenting, with whom KOZINSKI, Chief Judge, and RAWLINSON, Circuit Judge, join:

Because I am not persuaded that an instrumentality of the Republic of Austria may be subjected to the jurisdiction of the United States Courts on the basis of the facts alleged in this case, I must respectfully dissent from the decision of the en banc court to the contrary.

I

The Foreign Sovereign Immunities Act of 1976 (FSIA) is "the sole basis for obtaining jurisdiction over a foreign state in our courts." Argentine Republic v. Amerada Hess Shipping Corp., 488 U.S. 428, 434, 109 S.Ct. 683, 102 L.Ed.2d 818 (1989). Under the FSIA, a foreign state is presumptively "immune from the jurisdiction of the courts of the United States" unless the plaintiff can show that his action falls within a specified statutory exception. 28 U.S.C. § 1604; see also Terenkian v. Republic of Iraq, 694 F.3d 1122, 1127 (9th Cir.2012).

Exceptions to sovereign immunity must be interpreted narrowly. Courts should guard against overly broad readings because expanding federal jurisdiction in this area can have serious foreign policy consequences. See Sampson v. Federal Republic of Germany, 250 F.3d 1145, 1155-56 (7th Cir.2001) ("In interpreting the FSIA, we are mindful that judicial resolution of cases bearing significantly on sensitive foreign policy matters, like the case before us, might have serious foreign policy implications which courts are ill-equipped to anticipate or handle.") (internal quotation marks omitted); see also J.H. Trotter, Narrow Construction of the FSIA Commercial Activity Exception: Saudi Arabia v.

Nelson, 33 Va. J. Int'l L. 717, 733-34 (1993) ("As [the FSIA] exceptions undergo judicial expansion ... the strains on foreign policy intensify."). Indeed, we have expressly recognized the restricted nature of these exceptions. Peterson v. Islamic Republic of Iran, 627 F.3d 1117, 1125 (9th Cir.2010) (describing the FSIA's exceptions as "narrow"); see also McKesson Corp. v. Islamic Republic of Iran, 672 F.3d 1066, 1075 (D.C.Cir.2012) (describing the FSIA's exceptions as "narrowly drawn").

By expanding the commercial-activity exception to encompass the facts in this case, the court, regrettably, claims jurisdiction that is denied to us by statute.

II

Carol P. Sachs, who lives in California, purchased a Eurail pass online from Rail Pass Experts (RPE), an entity located in Massachusetts. A Eurail pass enabled her to ride railways in Austria and the Czech Republic. RPE gained authority to sell Eurail passes from the Eurail Group. OBB Personenverkehr AG (OBB), a railway wholly owned by the Austrian government, is one of many Eurail Group members. OBB and Eurail are separate entities with distinct managements, employees, and purposes. While in Austria, Sachs attempted to board a moving train operated by OBB. She fell between the platform and the train such that she landed on the tracks, suffering severe bodily injuries. Sachs has sued OBB for negligence, strict liability, and breach of implied warranties.

Our analytical task in this case is made easier by the limited nature of the parties' arguments. Sachs does not contest that OBB is an instrumentality of the Republic of Austria and therefore entitled to foreign sovereign immunity under the FSIA. The majority correctly notes that "[t]he [only] exception relevant to this appeal is the first clause of the commercial-activity provision."[1] Op. at 590. The commercial-activity exception can helpfully be divided into three requirements: (1) the activity must be commercial rather than sovereign, (2) the activity must be "carried on in the United States by the foreign state," and (3) the plaintiff's suit must be "based upon" that activity. 28 U.S.C. § 1605(a)(2).

The parties do not dispute that the only relevant commercial activity in the United States was Sachs' purchase of a Eurail pass from RPE. See Op. at 591 n. 4. OBB does not contest that the sale of the Eurail pass was commercial, rather than sovereign, activity. The first requirement is therefore satisfied. It is the two other requirements that are disputed.

III

To repeat, the commercial-activity exception applies only if the activity in question was "carried on in the United States by the foreign state." 28 U.S.C. § 1605(a)(2).[2] Although the sale of the ticket by RPE clearly occurred in the United States, OBB disputes that it "carried on" that activity. Rather, OBB argues that the sale is attributable exclusively to RPE. See Phaneuf v. Republic of Indonesia, 106 F.3d 302, 306 (9th Cir.1997) ("Defendants should be permitted to argue... that they did not act: that there was no commercial activity of the foreign state.") (internal quotation marks omitted).

To determine whether the activity is attributable to OBB, it is necessary to consider the meaning of "foreign state." Because foreign states are not natural persons, they necessarily act through agents. See Op. at 595. The question is what principle limits the extent to which another entity's activity can be attributed to a foreign state for purposes of the FSIA.

Relying on Phaneuf, the majority rules that the activity of any authorized agent can be imputed to a foreign sovereign. See Op. at 593-94 ("Because we conclude RPE acted as an authorized agent of OBB, we impute RPE's sale of the Eurail pass in the United States to OBB.") (citing Phaneuf, 106 F.3d at 307-08).[3] Thus, it effectively reads "activity carried on ... by a foreign state" and "activity carried on by such state" to mean activity carried on by the authorized agents of a foreign state. This necessarily equates a foreign state and its authorized agents.

With respect, I suggest that such a reading is inconsistent with other provisions of the FSIA. Rather, "foreign state" must be interpreted more narrowly. The approach we adopted in Doe v. Holy See, 557 F.3d 1066 (9th Cir.2009), correctly interpreted "foreign state" and provides a framework with which to analyze this case. Under this narrower reading, "activity carried on ... by a foreign state" cannot include activity carried on by RPE.

A

The term "foreign state," of course, is used repeatedly in the FSIA, not just in the commercial-activity exception. The meaning of "foreign state" remains constant throughout the statute, and textual evidence from other provisions demonstrates that "foreign state" cannot be so broad as to include all authorized agents of a foreign state.

1

Courts generally presume that a term is used consistently throughout a statute. See Powerex Corp. v. Reliant Energy Services, Inc., 551 U.S. 224, 232, 127 S.Ct. 2411, 168 L.Ed.2d 112 (2007) ("A standard principle of statutory construction provides that identical words and phrases within the same statute should normally be given the same meaning."); Antonin Scalia & Bryan A. Garner, Reading Law 170 (2012) (discussing the presumption of consistent usage).[4] Here, far from indicating that different uses of "foreign state" have different meanings, the FSIA suggests that the definition remains constant throughout the statute (with the express exception of § 1608, which is not relevant here). See 28 U.S.C. § 1603(a) ("For purposes of this chapter—(a) A `foreign state,' except as used in section 1608 of this title, includes a political subdivision of a foreign state or an agency or instrumentality of a foreign state as defined in subsection (b).") (emphasis added).

Confirming this analysis, the Supreme Court has interpreted the term "foreign state" consistently. In Samantar v. Yousuf, 560 U.S. 305, 130 S.Ct. 2278, 176 L.Ed.2d 1047 (2010), the Court interpreted "foreign state" as it was used in § 1604, which grants immunity to "foreign state[s]." 28 U.S.C. § 1604. In doing so, the Court expressly relied on the meaning of "foreign state" in an exception to immunity found in § 1605(a)(5). See Samantar, 560 U.S. at 317-18, 130 S.Ct. 2278. Such approach is sensible only if "foreign state" has the same meaning in both provisions. Clearly, Supreme Court precedent indicates that "foreign state" has the same meaning when providing an exception to immunity as it does when granting immunity.

The majority, by contrast, treats the meaning of "foreign state" for the purposes of § 1604 and the meaning of "foreign state" for the purposes of § 1605 as separate inquiries. See Op. at 595 (contrasting the status required to claim sovereign immunity and the status required for activity to be attributable under the commercial-activity exception). In light of the presumption of consistent usage and Supreme Court precedent applying it to the FSIA, I cannot accept the majority's assumption that the interpretation of this term differs so greatly between provisions.

2

Given that the meaning of "foreign state" is consistent, we can turn to analyzing the meaning of that term in other provisions of the FSIA. Textual evidence from § 1605A, which also uses "foreign state," indicates that the term does not embrace all authorized agents.

Section 1605A(c) creates a cause of action against "[a] foreign state that is or was a state sponsor of terrorism ... and any official, employee, or agent of that foreign state while acting within the scope of his or her office, employment, or agency." 28 U.S.C. § 1605A(c) (emphasis added). In Samantar, the Supreme Court tells us that "the creation of a cause of action against both the `foreign state' and `any official, employee, or agent' thereof reinforces the idea that `foreign state' does not by definition include foreign officials." Samantar, 560 U.S. at 318 n. 11, 130 S.Ct. 2278 (citation omitted). Relying on § 1605A(c) and a similar provision in § 1605(a)(5), the Court invoked the rule against superfluity: "If the term `foreign state' by definition includes an individual acting within the scope of his office, the phrase `or of any official or employee ...' in 28 U.S.C. § 1605(a)(5) would be unnecessary." Id. at 318, 130 S.Ct. 2278 (citing Dole Food Co. v. Patrickson, 538 U.S. 468, 476-77, 123 S.Ct. 1655, 155 L.Ed.2d 643 (2003) ("[W]e should not construe the statute in a manner that is strained and, at the same time, would render a statutory term superfluous.")).

Just as the inclusion of "official" in § 1605(a)(5) and § 1605A(c) would be superfluous were "foreign state" to include officials, the inclusion of "agent" in § 1605A(a)[5] and § 1605A(c) would be superfluous if "foreign state" included all agents acting in the scope of their agencies (that is, authorized agents). And just as the avoidance of superfluity in another provision informed Samantar's interpretation of "foreign state" in § 1604, it similarly affects the meaning of "foreign state" in § 1605(a)(2). Therefore, by the same logic that the Supreme Court used in Samantar, the commercial-activity exception's use of "foreign state" does not include all authorized agents.

B

Because the majority's approach is inconsistent with the text of the statute, another approach is required. Our opinion in Holy See provides the proper standard for attributing the actions of third parties to foreign states. In determining whether acts taken by the Archdiocese of Portland, the Catholic Bishop of Chicago, and the Order of the Friar

Servants could be imputed to the Holy See for determining jurisdiction under the FSIA, the Holy See court relied on First National City Bank v. Banco Para El Comercio Exterior de Cuba ("Bancec"), 462 U.S. 611, 103 S.Ct. 2591, 77 L.Ed.2d 46 (1983). Bancec created a presumption of separate status for liability purposes. Id. at 626-27, 103 S.Ct. 2591. This presumption could be overcome "in two instances: when `a corporate entity is so extensively controlled by its owner that a relationship of principal and agent is created,'[[6]] or when recognizing the separate status of a corporation `would work fraud or injustice.'" Holy See, 557 F.3d at 1077-78 (quoting Bancec, 462 U.S. at 629, 103 S.Ct. 2591).

While Bancec dealt with questions of substantive liability rather than jurisdiction, Holy See decided that the standard announced in Bancec applied to jurisdictional questions as well. See Holy See, 557 F.3d at 1079. Thus, a determination of whether to attribute the actions of another entity to a foreign state for jurisdictional purposes begins with a presumption against such attribution. That presumption can be rebutted if the other entity is the alter ego of the foreign state or if failure to attribute the entity's actions to the foreign state "would work fraud or injustice." Id. at 1077-78. Other circuits have applied Bancec to jurisdictional issues as well. See Transamerica Leasing, Inc. v. La Republica de Venezuela, 200 F.3d 843, 848 (D.C.Cir.2000); Arriba Ltd. v. Petroleos Mexicanos, 962 F.2d 528, 533 (5th Cir.1992).

The standard from Holy See fits the statutory text well. Holy See counsels in favor of reading "activity ... by a foreign state" to mean activity by a foreign state, its alter ego, or an entity the recognition of whose separateness would work fraud or injustice.[7] Incorporation of the Bancec standard has the considerable benefits of not rendering any statutory terms superfluous and being capable of consistent application throughout the FSIA. An interpretation of "foreign state" that includes a foreign state's alter ego would not make any words in § 1605A superfluous. See supra Part III.A.2.

The majority purports to distinguish Holy See on the ground that Bancec and Holy See, unlike this case, arose in the context "of corporate affiliates." Op. at 594 (distinguishing "a corporate relationship" from "principles of agency"). Even assuming the validity of this distinction, the majority draws the wrong conclusion. That Holy See applies a stringent alter ego test to the activity of corporate affiliates does not suggest that we should apply a more lenient authorized agent standard to the activity of non-affiliate entities. If anything, the lack of an affiliate relationship supports application of a more stringent test because a corporate affiliate is more likely to have a close and substantial relationship with its foreign state than another entity is. That is borne out in this case: OBB may not have even been aware that RPE existed before this lawsuit. Thus, the majority's "authorized agent" standard creates an anomaly in our case law because it retains the Holy See standard for affiliates but creates a much looser test for non-affiliate entities that will often have fewer ties to the foreign state.

But the majority's distinction between the corporate affiliate context and the agency context is problematic for another reason as well: courts applying the Bancec standard have spoken expressly in terms of agency. In Bancec itself, the Court described the alter ego analysis as relevant because such extensive control creates "a relationship of principal and agent." Bancec, 462 U.S. at 629, 103 S.Ct. 2591; see also Holy See, 557 F.3d at 1079 ("[I]n applying the jurisdictional provisions of the FSIA, courts will routinely have to decide whether a particular individual or corporation is an agent of a foreign state."). Thus, at least in certain circumstances, we have held that the Bancec standard is the method for determining whether another entity is an agent of a foreign state. The majority, therefore, cannot distinguish Holy See on the ground that it applies to the actions of corporate affiliates rather than agents.

Of particular importance here is that the meaning of "agent" or "agency" varies in different legal contexts. See Holy See, 557 F.3d at 1080 ("`Agent' can have more than one legal meaning."). In Holy See, the court contrasted the typical common law agency analysis with the first prong of the Bancec standard. See id. ("The Bancec standard is in fact most similar to the `alter ego' or `piercing the corporate veil' standards ...").

The plaintiff in Holy See alleged a traditional agency relationship as the basis for attributing the actions of others to the Holy See. See id. ("Doe does directly allege in his complaint that the corporations are `agents' of the Holy See."); Pl.-Appellee/Cross-Appellant John V. Doe's Principal and Resp. Br., 2007 WL 923313, II.C.1 ("Appellants Catholic Bishop, Archdiocese and Order, were the agents of Appellant Holy See, acting in furtherance of the purposes of the the [sic] Holy See, doing the kind of acts they were engaged to perform, and were motivated, at least in part, to further the purposes of the Holy See."). Nonetheless, the Holy See court ruled that it could not "infer from the use of the word `agent' that Doe [wa]s alleging the type of day-to-day control that Bancec... require[s] to overcome the presumption of separate juridical status." Holy See, 557 F.3d at 1080. If a common law agency relationship were all that is required for the imputation of an agent's actions to the foreign state, surely the court would have treated Doe's allegation differently in Holy See. Thus, it is clear that the sort of agency relationship that Bancec and Holy See required for the imputation of actions to the foreign state (an alter ego relationship, for example) differs significantly from the all-authorized-agents standard adopted by the majority.

C

Sachs simply cannot show that RPE's actions are attributable to OBB under the Bancec standard. The first method of rebutting the presumption of separateness, the alter ego analysis, certainly cannot apply on these facts. Far from being the alter ego of OBB, RPE and Eurail are independent companies with different managements from OBB. RPE may be a subagent of Eurail, but Eurail is controlled by a group of railways, not OBB alone. The second method of rebutting the presumption of separateness—whether recognizing separate existences would work fraud or injustice—certainly does not suggest that the actions of RPE should be attributed to OBB. In Bancec, the Court found such equitable prong applicable because Bancec was attempting to recover money that would directly benefit the Cuban government while simultaneously arguing that its claim should not be subject to a set-off that would have applied if the Cuban government sued directly. Bancec, 462 U.S. at 631-32, 103 S.Ct. 2591. Here, OBB has not behaved in a comparable way. OBB has not, for example, inconsistently characterized RPE's actions to its advantage; it has consistently asserted that RPE's actions cannot be attributed to it.

If there is any "injustice" at all from failing to impute RPE's actions to OBB, it stems from Sachs' inability to sue OBB in American courts. This, however, is not the sort of injustice that validates treating RPE as if it were OBB. The inability to sue in American courts is a natural result of recognizing foreign sovereign immunity, the general rule and policy of the FSIA. See Sachs v. Republic of Austria, 695 F.3d 1021, 1026 (9th Cir.2012) ("Any injustice that results is no greater than the mine-run of cases—jurisdiction over a foreign state is, after all, ordinarily not available.").

D

The majority relies on Barkanic v. General Administration of Civil Aviation of the People's Republic of China, 822 F.3d 11 (2d Cir.1987), and Kirkham v. Societe Air France, 429 F.3d 288 (D.C.Cir.2005). These cases do not analyze when the acts of agents can be attributed to a foreign state. As acknowledged by the majority, see Op. at 592 n. 5a, the parties in Barkanic and Kirkham did not dispute that the relevant actions constituted activity of the foreign state. See Barkanic, 822 F.2d at 13 (assuming without discussion that a ticket sale by Pan American was attributable to the defendant); Kirkham, 429 F.3d at 291-92 (noting that the "sole question" before the court related to the "based upon" prong of the commercial-activity exception). Although those courts "had an independent duty to assess jurisdiction," see Op. at 592 n. 5b, their decisions "do[] not stand for the proposition that no defect existed." Arizona Christian School Tuition Organization v. Winn, ____ U.S. ____, 131 S.Ct. 1436, 1448, 179 L.Ed.2d 523 (2011) ("When a potential jurisdictional defect is neither noted nor discussed in a federal decision, the decision does not stand for the proposition that no defect existed.").

The majority makes much of the possibility that, if its reading were rejected, federal courts would not be able to exercise jurisdiction over foreign states based on the actions of travel agents. Op. at 595-97. The majority's concern seems to stem from the idea that the lack of federal jurisdiction would leave plaintiffs to sue abroad, a result the majority describes as too "chaotic" for Congress to have intended. Op. at 597. But, the general rule for the FSIA is that foreign states are immune from suit; there will be many instances in which Americans who wish to sue foreign sovereigns can only do so overseas. This is a result Congress clearly intended in many instances, so it is hard to see why the same result in this situation should strike the majority as so "chaotic."

Because Sachs has not shown that RPE and OBB have a relationship that rebuts the Bancec presumption of separate status, I would affirm the district court's dismissal for lack of jurisdiction.

IV

Even if the sale of the Eurail pass by RPE were "commercial activity carried on... by the foreign state," sovereign immunity would still, at a minimum, bar Sachs' strict liability claims because they are not "based upon" the sale of the pass, as would be required for the commercial-activity exception to apply. 28 U.S.C. § 1605(a)(2). Assuming the majority's interpretation of this requirement is correct, I agree that Sachs' negligence and implied warranty claims would be "based upon" the sale of the Eurail pass had the sale been attributable to OBB. The Supreme Court has clarified that the commercial activity in question, here the sale of the Eurail pass, must be an "element[] of a claim that, if proven, would entitle a plaintiff to relief under his theory of the case." Saudi Arabia v. Nelson, 507 U.S. 349, 357, 113 S.Ct. 1471, 123 L.Ed.2d 47 (1993). The majority understands this to mean that a claim is based upon commercial activity if that activity will establish one element of the claim. But still, a mere connection between the claim and the commercial activity is insufficient. Sun v. Taiwan, 201 F.3d 1105, 1110 (9th Cir.2000) (citing Nelson, 507 U.S. at 362, 113 S.Ct. 1471).

The majority believes that Sachs' negligence claim is "based upon" the sale of the Eurail pass because the sale evidences that OBB, as a common carrier, owed a duty of care to Sachs, a passenger. Op. at 599-601. This strikes me as a proper application of the majority's rule; however, the majority also concludes that Sachs' other claims are "based upon" the sale of the Eurail pass because the sale was the transaction necessary for an implied warranty claim or strict liability claim. Op. at 601-02.

This theory inappropriately lumps together Sachs' strict liability claims and implied warranty claims. While the majority is correct that both types of claims center on "attributing liability based on the sale of a product into the market," Op. at 602, there is a crucial difference between them. Strict liability claims do not require proof that the plaintiff entered a transaction with the defendant. Greenman v. Yuba Power Products, Inc., 59 Cal.2d 57, 27 Cal.Rptr. 697, 377 P.2d 897 (1963), which the majority relies on to explain California law on strict liability, discusses "the abandonment of the requirement of a contract between" the manufacturer and the plaintiff. Id., 27 Cal. Rptr. 697, 377 P.2d at 901; see also Restatement (Third) of Torts: Products Liability § 1 cmt a (1998) ("Strict liability in tort for defectively manufactured products merges the concept of implied warranty, in which negligence is not required, with the tort concept of negligence, in which contractual privity is not required.").

While the majority claims that Sachs' strict liability claim requires her to prove that OBB was a "seller," Op. at 602, California cases suggest that a strict liability plaintiff need not prove that the defendant is a seller. See Price v. Shell Oil Co., 2 Cal.3d 245, 85 Cal.Rptr. 178, 466 P.2d 722, 726 (1970) ("[W]e can perceive no substantial difference between sellers of personal property and non-sellers, such as bailors and lessors. In each instance, the seller or non-seller places [an article] on the market, knowing that it is to be used without inspection for defects.") (second alteration in original) (internal quotation marks omitted); Greenman, 27 Cal.Rptr. 697, 377 P.2d at 901 ("To establish the manufacturer's liability it was sufficient that plaintiff proved that he was injured while using the Shopsmith in a way it was intended to be used as a result of a defect in design and manufacture of which plaintiff was not aware that made the Shopsmith unsafe for its intended use.") Under California law, it appears that OBB's provision of train service and Sachs' use of it are sufficient to subject OBB to strict liability. Therefore, Sachs has not established that she must prove that OBB was a "seller" in order to prevail on her strict liability claim.

Because contractual privity is not an element of Sachs' strict liability claims, they are not "based upon" the sale by RPE, the only relevant commercial activity. Sachs, therefore, may not invoke the commercial-activity exception to overcome OBB's sovereign immunity. Even if RPE's sale of the Eurail pass to Sachs were attributable to OBB, the majority should affirm the district court insofar as it dismissed the strict liability claims for lack of jurisdiction.

V

For the foregoing reasons, I would affirm the district court's dismissal for lack of jurisdiction. Because RPE's sale of the Eurail pass is not attributable to OBB, Sachs has not alleged commercial activity "by the foreign state." Indeed, even if the majority's theory of attribution were valid, the strict liability claims would still need to be dismissed because they are not "based upon" the sale to Sachs in the United States.

Notes

[1] "A foreign state shall not be immune from the jurisdiction of courts of the United States... in any case ... in which the action is based upon a commercial activity carried on in the United States by the foreign state." 28 U.S.C. § 1605(a)(2). Like the majority, I use the phrase "commercial-activity exception" to refer to the first clause of § 1605(a)(2). See Op. at 590 n. 3.

[2] Congress defined "commercial activity carried on in the United States by a foreign state" to mean "commercial activity carried on by such state and having substantial contact with the United States." 28 U.S.C. § 1603(e).

[3] While Phaneuf held that an agent must have acted with actual authority in order for its actions to be attributed to a foreign state, Phaneuf, 106 F.3d at 308, it did not hold that actual authority was sufficient to allow for such attribution in all circumstances. The actions at issue in Phaneuf were taken by members of Indonesia's National Defense Security Council, rather than a corporate entity with whom Indonesia had only a loose relationship, so the closeness of the connection between the foreign state and the alleged agent was not at issue. See id. at 304, 307.

[4] The majority misinterprets this analysis as applying the presumption of consistent usage to distinct phrases, "agency or instrumentality of a foreign state" in § 1603(b), "agent of that foreign state [] acting within the scope of his or her ... agency" in § 1605A(c), and the commercial-activity exception in § 1605(a)(2). Op. at 598 n. 13. In reality, I apply the presumption of consistent usage to the term "foreign state," not to each phrase as a whole. Such application is consistent with Samantar v. Yousuf, 560 U.S. 305, 317-18 & n. 11, 130 S.Ct. 2278, 176 L.Ed.2d 1047 (2010) (interpreting "foreign state" in § 1604 in light of the use of "foreign state" in § 1605A and § 1605(a)(5)).

[5] Section 1605A(a) uses similar language to create a specific exception to immunity for:

any case not otherwise covered by this chapter in which money damages are sought against a foreign state for personal injury or death that was caused by [specified acts] if such act ... is engaged in by an official, employee, or agent of such foreign state while acting within the scope of his or her office, employment, or agency.

28 U.S.C. § 1605A(a)(1) (emphasis added).

[6] As will be discussed below, the Court used the term "agent" in a different sense than the majority does. Courts have interpreted this prong of the Bancec standard to refer to an "alter ego" analysis. See, e.g., Holy See, 557 F.3d at 1080 (comparing the Bancec standard to an "`alter ego' or `piercing the corporate veil'" standard); Transamerica Leasing, Inc. v. La Republica de Venezuela, 200 F.3d 843, 848 (D.C.Cir.2000) (noting that "in the case cited by the Supreme Court to illustrate the agency exception, various corporations were allegedly operated as a `single enterprise.'").

[7] How (or whether) this standard would apply to the actions of an individual agent, rather than entity agent, need not be addressed in this case. RPE is an entity, not an individual.

Judge O'Scannlain's dissent from denial of rehearing en banc in Moore v. Biter (Ninth Circuit) (Feb 12, 2014) [Notes omitted]

O'SCANNLAIN, Circuit Judge, joined by TALLMAN, BYBEE, CALLAHAN, BEA, M. SMITH, and IKUTA, Circuit Judges, dissenting from the denial of rehearing en banc:

Our Court defies AEDPA once again, this time by failing to distinguish one "life without parole" sentence from multiple "term-of-years" sentences. A panel of this Court holds that Graham v. Florida, 560 U.S. 48, 130 S.Ct. 2011, 176 L.Ed.2d 825 (2010), invalidates the latter, ignoring the contrary holding of the Sixth Circuit,[1] disregarding the views of state courts across the country, and flouting Graham's text and reasoning.

I respectfully dissent from our decision not to rehear this case en banc.

I

Roosevelt Moore appeals the district court's denial of his petition for habeas relief under 28 U.S.C. § 2254. Moore committed a series of forcible rapes and other offenses at the age of sixteen and was tried as an adult. In 1991, a jury convicted him of twenty-four crimes, including nine counts of forcible rape, seven counts of forcible oral copulation, and two counts of robbery, and also found that he used a firearm for most of the offenses. He was sentenced to fixed terms of imprisonment for each offense with enhancements for using a firearm, to run consecutively. Although none of the individual sentences exceeded eight years, Moore was sentenced to 254 years in prison, cumulatively. He cannot be considered for parole until he serves at least 127 years and two months.

Nearly two decades later, Moore filed state habeas petitions, pro se, arguing that his sentence is unconstitutional in light of Graham. The Los Angeles County Superior

Court summarily denied his petition. The California Court of Appeal held that Graham does not apply to Moore's sentence, and the California Supreme Court summarily denied review.

Our panel, however, granted habeas relief, holding that Graham applies retroactively to Moore's sentence and that the California state courts' decisions were contrary to Graham because Moore's case is materially indistinguishable from Graham's. Moore, 725 F.3d at 1186.

II

Under AEDPA, federal courts may not grant habeas relief on a claim that was adjudicated on the merits in state court, unless the state court's decision was: (1) "contrary to, or involved an unreasonable application of, clearly established Federal law, as determined by the Supreme Court of the United States;" or (2) "resulted in a decision that was based on an unreasonable determination of the facts in light of the evidence presented in the State court proceeding." 28 U.S.C. § 2254(d). A state court decision is "contrary to" Supreme Court precedent "if it applies a rule that contradicts the governing law set forth in [the Court's] cases or if it confronts a set of facts that are materially indistinguishable from a decision of [the Supreme] Court and nevertheless arrives at a result different from [the Court's] precedent." Early v. Packer, 537 U.S. 3, 8, 123 S.Ct. 362, 154 L.Ed.2d 263 (2002) (internal quotation marks omitted).

A state court "must apply legal principles established by a Supreme Court decision when the case falls squarely within those principles, but not in cases where there is a structural difference between the prior precedent and the case at issue, or when the prior precedent requires tailoring or modification to apply to the new situation." Moses v. Payne, 555 F.3d 742, 753 (9th Cir.2009) (quotation marks omitted). Unless the Supreme Court has "squarely address[ed]" an issue or established a principle that "clearly extend[s] to a new context," there is no "clearly established Supreme Court precedent addressing the issue." Id. at 754 (internal quotation marks omitted; second alteration in original).

The Court has consistently warned lower courts, and this court in particular, to avoid defining "clearly established" law too broadly. See, e.g., Parker v. Matthews, ____ U.S. ____, 132 S.Ct. 2148, 183 L.Ed.2d 32 (2012); Howes v. Fields, ____ U.S. ____, 132 S.Ct. 1181, 182 L.Ed.2d 17 (2012); Wright v. Van Patten, 552 U.S. 120, 128 S.Ct. 743, 169 L.Ed.2d 583 (2008); Carey v. Musladin, 549 U.S. 70, 127 S.Ct. 649, 166 L.Ed.2d 482 (2006).

A

In Graham, the Supreme Court announced that the Constitution does not permit "a juvenile offender to be sentenced to life in prison without parole for a nonhomicide crime." 560 U.S. at 52-53, 130 S.Ct. 2011. The Court's "categorical rule" was meant to give "juvenile nonhomicide offenders a chance to demonstrate maturity and reform." Id. at 79, 130 S.Ct. 2011.

To support its conclusion that the state court's decision was contrary to Graham, the panel reasoned that "Moore's sentence of 254 years is materially indistinguishable from a life sentence without parole because Moore will not be eligible for parole within his lifetime." Moore, 725 F.3d at 1191. That Moore's sentence was not likely to be completed during his lifetime, even if not labeled a "life sentence," did not distinguish it from Graham. Id. at 1191-92. Furthermore, that Moore committed serious crimes did not distinguish his case from Graham, because the Supreme Court "expressly rejected a case-by-case approach" that would take account of factual differences between crimes. Id. at 1192-93.

And there the panel's opinion stops, failing to confront the most meaningful distinction between Moore's case and Graham: Moore's term of imprisonment is composed of over two dozen separate sentences, none longer than eight years; Graham's is one sentence, "life without parole." Because the Supreme Court explicitly stated that Graham concerned "only those juvenile offenders sentenced to life without parole solely for a nonhomicide offense," 560 U.S. at 62, 130 S.Ct. 2011, it "did not clearly establish that consecutive, fixed-term sentences for juveniles who commit multiple nonhomicide offenses are unconstitutional when they amount to the practical equivalent of life without parole," Bunch, 685 F.3d at 550.

If that express limitation on Graham's holding were not enough, Graham's reasoning makes clear that the Supreme Court did not squarely address aggregate term-of-years sentences. Beginning with "objective indicia of national consensus," the Court noted that there were "123 juvenile nonhomicide offenders serving life without parole sentences," and "only 11 jurisdictions nationwide in fact impose life without parole sentences on juvenile nonhomicide offenders—and most of those do so quite rarely." Graham, 560 U.S. at 62-64, 130 S.Ct. 2011. Thus, "[t]he sentencing practice now under consideration is exceedingly rare." Id. at 67, 130 S.Ct. 2011.

But, to reach that conclusion, the Court did not consider the prevalence of sentences like Moore's—lengthy term-ofyears sentences adding up to de facto life imprisonment. See id. at 113 n. 11, 130 S.Ct. 2011 (Thomas, J., dissenting) ("[T]he Court counts only those juveniles sentenced to life without parole and excludes from its analysis all juveniles sentenced to lengthy term-of-years sentences (e.g., 70 or 80 years' imprisonment)."). Nor was Moore counted among those 123 juvenile nonhomicide offenders. See P. Annino et al., Juvenile Life without Parole for No— Homicide Offenses: Florida Compared to Nation 14-15 (Sept. 14, 2009) (listing four such offenders incarcerated in California for crimes of kidnapping and/or robbery).

If the Court did not consider aggregate term-of-years sentences adding up de facto to life without parole, it cannot have squarely addressed their constitutionality. See Graham, 560 U.S. at 124, 130 S.Ct. 2011 (Alito, J., dissenting) ("Nothing in the Court's opinion affects the imposition of a sentence to a term of years without the possibility of parole."). As our sister circuit held: The Supreme Court "did not analyze sentencing laws or actual sentencing practices regarding consecutive, fixed-term sentences for juvenile nonhomicide offenders. This demonstrates that the Court did not even consider the constitutionality of such sentences, let alone clearly establish that they can violate the

Eighth Amendment's prohibition on cruel and unusual punishments." Bunch, 685 F.3d at 552.[2]

If the Court has not squarely addressed the constitutionality of aggregate term-of-years sentences, the state court's determination that Moore's sentence is not unconstitutional cannot be contrary to clearly established federal law.

B

Unsurprisingly, in the absence of an express holding regarding such sentences, "courts across the country are split over whether Graham bars a court from sentencing a juvenile nonhomicide offender to consecutive, fixed terms resulting in an aggregate sentence that exceeds the defendant's life expectancy." Id. Some have held that Graham prohibits aggregate term-of-years sentences that amount to the functional equivalent of life without parole. See, e.g., People v. Caballero, 55 Cal.4th 262, 145 Cal.Rptr.3d 286, 282 P.3d 291, 294-95 (2012); People v. Rainer, No. 10CA2414, ___ P.3d ___, 2013 WL 1490107 (Colo.Ct.App. Apr. 11, 2013); State v. Null, 836 N.W.2d 41, 73 (Iowa 2013).[3] More have held that Graham does not prohibit aggregate term-of-years sentences such as Moore's. See, e.g., Bunch, 685 F.3d at 552-53; State v. Kasic, 228 Ariz. 228, 265 P.3d 410, 415-16 (Ct.App. 2011); Walle v. State, 99 So.3d 967, 971 (Fla.Ct.App.2012); Henry v. State, 82 So.3d 1084, 1089 (Fla.Ct.App.2012); State v. Brown, 118 So.3d 332, 341-42 (La.2013); State v. Merritt, No. M2012-00829-CCAR3CD, 2013 WL 6505145, at *5 (Tenn. Crim.App. Dec. 10, 2013).

To be sure, in many of the cases refusing to extend Graham, the sentence at issue left some possibility, however slight, that the prisoner might eventually be released. But nothing in their reasoning turned on such possibility. See, e.g., Brown, 118 So.3d at 341 ("[N]othing in Graham ... applies to sentences for multiple convictions, as Graham conducted no analysis of sentences for multiple convictions and provides no guidance on how to handle such sentences.").

The existence of such a split is good evidence that the California courts' determination here—Graham does not apply to Moore's sentence—is not contrary to "clearly established" federal law. Cf. Evenstad v. Carlson, 470 F.3d 777, 783 (8th Cir.2006) ("When the federal circuits disagree as to a point of law, the law cannot be considered `clearly established' under 28 U.S.C. § 2254(d)(1)."); Boyd v. Newland, 467 F.3d 1139, 1152 (9th Cir.2006) (holding that "in the face of [out-of-circuit] authority that is directly contrary" to our own interpretation of Supreme Court precedent, "and in the absence of explicit direction from the Supreme Court," we cannot hold that the state courts' analysis "was contrary to, or involved an unreasonable application of, Supreme Court precedent.").

Were the panel required to confront the constitutionality of Moore's sentence on direct review, or on collateral review of a federal sentence, picking one side of the dispute would have been necessary. But AEDPA precludes federal courts from settling such disputes on collateral review of a state sentence, at least without a persuasive explanation of how so many courts erred so obviously. The panel's opinion neither acknowledges the dispute nor explains how the panel divined a clearly established holding of the Supreme

Court in the face of such widespread disagreement. Instead, it concedes a tangentially related split over how Graham applies "to lengthy term-of-years sentences that provide some possibility of parole." Moore, 725 F.3d at 1194 n. 6.

C

An equally telling omission: the panel offers no justification for creating a circuit split, acting instead as though it has not done so. The only argument the opinion provides for ignoring the Sixth Circuit's well-reasoned and thorough opinion is that the facts are different. Id. But any factual distinction—Bunch will be at least 95 years old when he is eligible for parole, Bunch, 685 F.3d at 551 n. 1, whereas Moore will be at least 144—does not make a meaningful difference. Bunch, like Moore, will not be eligible for parole until well beyond his life expectancy.[4]

Moreover, nothing in the Sixth Circuit's opinion turns on the possibility that Bunch might outlive his sentence. Our sister circuit acknowledged that Bunch's sentence "may end up being the functional equivalent of life without parole." Bunch, 685 F.3d at 551. Such was the sentencing judge's goal: "I just have to make sure that you don't get out of the penitentiary. I've got to do everything I can to keep you there, because it would be a mistake to have you back in society." Id. at 548. Nonetheless, the court determined that Bunch's sentence was not contrary to clearly established federal law, because "in Graham, the Court said that a juvenile is entitled to ... a `realistic opportunity to obtain release' if a state imposes a sentence of `life.'" Id. at 551 (quoting Graham, 560 U.S. at 82, 130 S.Ct. 2011). "Graham's holding" does not apply, therefore, "to a juvenile offender who received consecutive, fixed-term sentences." Id.; see also id. at 548 (The Supreme Court "did not address juvenile offenders, like Bunch, who received consecutive, fixed-term sentences for committing multiple nonhomicide offenses.").

The panel cannot evade the force of Bunch's reasoning by noting an insignificant factual distinction, which our sister circuit assumed away. Yet the panel's opinion sets forth no other argument.

III

Respect for the California courts, for our sister circuit, and for courts across the country that have declined to apply Graham to sentences such as Moore's should have compelled the panel to declare the reasons why it found their analysis unpersuasive. Instead, the panel's opinion ignores their arguments.

But the states encompassed by our Circuit cannot ignore the opinion's holding, which requires them to ask:

At what number of years would the Eighth Amendment become implicated in the sentencing of a juvenile: twenty, thirty, forty, fifty, some lesser or greater number? Would gain time be taken into account? Could the number vary from offender to offender based on race, gender, socioeconomic class or other criteria? Does the number of crimes matter?

Henry, 82 So.3d at 1089. Also, "What if the aggregate sentences are from different cases? From different circuits? From different jurisdictions? If from different jurisdictions, which jurisdiction must modify its sentence or sentences to avoid constitutional infirmity?" Walle, 99 So.3d at 972.

Without authority to do so, the panel's opinion would force all the states in our Circuit to confront those questions; the opinion forbids them from "apply[ing] Graham as it is written," yet gives them no other "tools to work with," Henry, 82 So.3d at 1089, when answering. And each of their answers could potentially be overruled by our Court as contrary to the "clearly established" rule of Graham.

IV

As the Supreme Court has reminded us yet again, "AEDPA recognizes a foundational principle of our federal system: State courts are adequate forums for the vindication of federal rights." Burt v. Titlow, ____ U.S. ____, 134 S.Ct. 10, 15, 187 L.Ed.2d 348 (2013). We should never "lightly conclude that a State's criminal justice system has experienced the `extreme malfunctio[n]' for which federal habeas relief is the remedy." Id. (alteration in original) (quoting Harrington v. Richter, ____ U.S. ____, 131 S.Ct. 770, 786, 178 L.Ed.2d 624 (2011)). The panel has apparently concluded, without explanation, that not only the California court, but also the Sixth Circuit and courts across the country have experienced such an extreme malfunction. This "judicial disregard for the sound and established principles" that govern issuance of the writ of habeas corpus threatens to undermine "confidence in the writ and the law it vindicates." Richter, 131 S.Ct. at 780.

Because the panel's opinion defies AEDPA, creates a circuit split, and threatens frequent and unjustified intrusions into state sovereignty, I respectfully dissent from our Court's regrettable failure to rehear this case en banc.

Judge O'Scannlain's dissent in Karunyan v. US (June 13, 2014)

O'SCANNLAIN, Circuit Judge, dissenting:

Because I am persuaded that probable cause supported Sarkis Karunyan's arrest and that Agent Lauren Hanover's investigation did not violate the Due Process Clause, I respectfully dissent.

Hanover knew that someone committed fraud by convincing Medicare to pay for unnecessary medical equipment. Karunyan's complaint acknowledges that Hanover knew that the proceeds from that fraud were originally paid to Karunyan. This is sufficient to demonstrate "a fair probability that [Karunyan] had committed a crime." Grant v. City of Long Beach, 315 F.3d 1081, 1085 (9th Cir. 2002).

Rodis v. City and County of San Francisco, 558 F.3d 964 (9th Cir. 2009), is not applicable to this case. Rodis requires that an officer making an arrest for a specific intent crime "have probable cause [of specific intent] in order to reasonably believe that a crime has occurred." Id. at 969 (emphasis added). The majority does not dispute that Hanover reasonably believed that the perpetrator, acting with specific intent, committed a crime. The issue is simply whether Karunyan's receipt of the proceeds of the crime made it reasonable for Hanover to believe that Karunyan had committed that crime.

Karunyan also failed to plead a violation of the Due Process Clause. Our precedent indicates that a bad faith failure to collect potentially exculpatory evidence violates the Constitution only if "the evidence sought was of such a nature that it was not reasonably available to the defendant." United States v. Martinez-Martinez, 369 F.3d 1076, 1086-87 (9th Cir. 2004) (analyzing a due process claim for "fail[ure] to collect and preserve evidence" (emphasis added)).

The duty to collect evidence incorporates the same limitations that the duty to preserve evidence does, see Miller v. Vasquez, 868 F.2d 1116, 1120 (9th Cir. 1989) (ruling that the bad faith requirement for preservation claims applies a fortiori to collection claims), and the Supreme Court has expressly enunciated the unavailability requirement for preservation claims. California v. Trombetta, 467 U.S. 479, 489 (1984). Karunyan failed to plead that the evidence at issue was not reasonably available to him; indeed, he pled the opposite: the evidence at issue was in his own company's records.

For the foregoing reasons, I would affirm.

Judge O'Scannlain's concurrence and dissent in US v. Dreyer (Sept 12, 2014)

O'SCANNLAIN, Circuit Judge, concurring in part and dissenting in part:

Before today, "not a single federal court" had applied the exclusionary rule to violations of the Posse Comitatus Act (PCA), 18 U.S.C. § 1385, and its implementing regulations.[1] United States v. Vick, 842 F.Supp.2d 891, 894 (E.D.Va. 2012). That is no accident. As we have observed, the exclusionary rule is an "extraordinary remedy," United States v. Roberts, 779 F.2d 565, 568 (9th Cir.1986), and the Supreme Court has counseled that it is only to be used as a "last resort," Hudson v. Michigan, 547 U.S. 586, 591, 126 S.Ct. 2159, 165 L.Ed.2d 56 (2006). Yet, in a breathtaking assertion of judicial power, today's majority invokes this disfavored remedy for the benefit of a convicted child pornographer. It does so without any demonstrated need to deter future violations of the PCA and without any consideration of the "substantial social costs" associated with the exclusionary rule. United States v. Leon, 468 U.S. 897, 907, 104 S.Ct. 3405, 82 L.Ed.2d 677 (1984). Like my colleagues, I conclude that Agent Logan violated the PCA, and I concur in Parts I and II of the majority opinion. But I respectfully dissent from the majority's misbegotten remedy for that violation.

I

The exclusionary rule is "a judicially created remedy of [the Supreme Court's] own making" whose "sole purpose" is "to deter misconduct by law enforcement." Davis v. United States, ____ U.S. ____, 131 S.Ct. 2419, 2427, 2432, 180 L.Ed.2d 285 (2011) (internal quotation marks omitted). That is a worthy objective, but it "exacts a heavy toll on both the judicial system and society at large." Id. at 2427. Exclusion "undeniably detracts from the truthfinding process and allows many who would otherwise be incarcerated to escape the consequences of their actions." Pa. Bd. of Prob. & Parole v. Scott, 524 U.S. 357, 364, 118 S.Ct. 2014, 141 L.Ed.2d 344 (1998). The rule's "bottom-line effect, in many cases, is to suppress the truth and set the criminal loose in the community without punishment." Davis, 131 S.Ct. at 2427; see also Hudson, 547 U.S. at 591, 126 S.Ct. 2159 (stating that the costs of exclusion "sometimes include setting the guilty free and the dangerous at large").

For these reasons, the Supreme Court has, since the 1970s, "imposed a more rigorous weighing of [the exclusionary rule's] costs and deterrence benefits." Davis, 131 S.Ct. at 2427. Gone are the days when courts imposed the exclusionary rule in a manner that was "not nearly so discriminating." Id. Under current doctrine, the important and significant costs of the rule "present[ ] a high obstacle for those urging [its] application." Scott, 524 U.S. at 364-65, 118 S.Ct. 2014.

In short, exclusion is "our last resort, not our first impulse." Hudson, 547 U.S. at 591, 126 S.Ct. 2159.

II

Our precedents reflect this skeptical view of exclusion with regard to violations of the PCA.[2] In United States v. Roberts, we held that the exclusionary rule should not be applied to evidence obtained as a result of a PCA violation "until a need to deter future violations is demonstrated." 779 F.2d at 568. Such a demonstration requires a showing of "widespread and repeated violations" of the PCA. Id.

In announcing this rule, we adopted the approach of the Fourth and Fifth Circuits in United States v. Walden, 490 F.2d 372, 376-77 (4th Cir.1974), and United States v. Wolffs, 594 F.2d 77, 84-85 (5th Cir.1979). Significantly, none of those three cases applied the exclusionary rule to violations of the PCA, and all three referred to the exclusionary rule as an "extraordinary remedy." Roberts, 779 F.2d at 568; Wolffs, 594 F.2d at 85; Walden, 490 F.2d at 377. Indeed, in Roberts, we "consider[ed] it significant that courts have uniformly refused to apply the exclusionary rule to evidence seized in violation of the Posse Comitatus Act." 779 F.2d at 568.

Before today, that description remained true of federal courts.

III

As the foregoing survey of Supreme Court and Ninth Circuit precedent makes clear, the application of the exclusionary rule to violations of the PCA is not automatic. Rather, it is assessed by considering whether "the clear costs of applying an exclusionary rule" are outweighed by "any discernible benefits." Id. This case demonstrates that the costs of exclusion substantially outweigh the evanescent benefits. Indeed, it is not a close call.

A

Any evaluation of whether to apply the exclusionary rule to PCA violations must take into account the significant costs of exclusion. In Walden, the Fourth Circuit believed that the facts of the case before it were particularly useful in highlighting the costs of exclusion. The Fourth Circuit thought it significant that "the evidence of [the] defendant's guilt [wa]s overwhelming" and that application of the exclusionary rule would have suppressed "the bulk of the evidence" against the defendant. 490 F.2d at 376. The possibility of setting free a convicted felon was a troubling cost of exclusion, and because there was no need to deter future violations, nothing justified incurring such costs. Id. at 376-77; see also United States v. Jones, 13 F.3d 100, 104 (4th Cir.1993) (recognizing that setting free guilty defendants is a cost courts should consider in determining whether to apply the exclusionary rule to PCA violations).

In Dreyer's case, a jury convicted him of possession and distribution of child pornography. As in Walden, the evidence of guilt is overwhelming. Using specialized software called RoundUp, Agent Logan searched the state of Washington for computers trafficking in child pornography on the Gnutella file-sharing network. Maj. op. at 827. The software identified a computer bearing the Internet Protocol (IP) address 67.160.77.21 as offering several files of known child pornography to fellow Gnutella users. Id. at 827-28. We know that the files contained child pornography because they bear unique identifiers— called "SHA-1 hash values"—that match the identifiers of known child pornography files contained in a database maintained by RoundUp and the National Center for Missing and Exploited Children. Id. at 828 The IP address offering child pornography belonged to Dreyer. Id. Agent Logan, using a method that permitted him to ensure that he was downloading files only from Dreyer's computer, downloaded two images and a video, which, upon review, he confirmed contained child pornography. Id. Subsequent searches of Dreyer's seized hard drives revealed several such files. Id. at 828-29. There can be little doubt, then, that Dreyer trafficked in child pornography, an activity that is "intrinsically related to the sexual abuse of children." New York v. Ferber, 458 U.S. 747, 759, 102 S.Ct. 3348, 73 L.Ed.2d 1113 (1982).

Application of the exclusionary rule would suppress all evidence obtained by Agent Logan. Moreover, as the majority opinion observes, without the evidence obtained by Agent Logan, it is probable that "there would have been no [subsequent] search[es] and no prosecution." Maj. op. at 833. Thus, application of the exclusionary rule to the allegedly tainted evidence and its fruits is likely to result in a convicted child pornographer being released from prison.

It is impossible to state this conclusion without feeling its gravity. In this context, the Supreme Court's warning against unnecessarily "setting the guilty free and the dangerous at large" should give any jurist pause. Hudson, 547 U.S. at 591, 126 S.Ct. 2159. Yet, such a result would not be uncommon if we were to begin applying the exclusionary rule to PCA cases. Thus, the costs of exclusion are high.

B

Despite this cost, application of the exclusionary rule might still be justified if there were evidence of "widespread and repeated violations" of the PCA.[3] Roberts, 779 F.2d at 568. On this record, there is not.

The majority opinion primarily focuses on Agent Logan's ostensible violations of the relevant regulations applying the PCA to the Navy. Maj. op. at 835-36. But the actions of one agent—no matter how egregious —do not show that violations are widespread. Agent Logan's descriptions of his own practices are, therefore, of limited relevance.

Perhaps recognizing the thinness of this evidence, the majority opinion also points out that Agent Logan "began carrying out these searches with two other agents at least several months before he found Dreyer's IP address." Id. at 836. It also references another supposed violation in Kentucky. Id. at 836 n. 14. I fail to see how evidence that four agents committed violations—three of whom were part of the same investigative team— demonstrates a widespread problem. Such anecdotal evidence falls far short of what our precedents require before we will resort to the "extraordinary remedy" of exclusion, especially considering the cost of doing so in this case. Roberts, 779 F.2d at 568. Indeed, at least one of our sister circuits rejected exclusion in the face of similarly scattershot evidence. When the Eleventh Circuit was confronted with five alleged violations of the PCA within the same circuit over a ten-year period, it concluded that this amounted to only a "few" incidents that provided "no basis" for applying the exclusionary rule. United States v. Mendoza-Cecelia, 963 F.2d 1467, 1478 n. 9 (11th Cir.1992), abrogated on other grounds as recognized by United States v. Rainey, 362 F.3d 733, 735 (11th Cir.2004). The argument in favor of exclusion is no more compelling on the record before us.

Finally, the majority opinion cites the government's litigating position in this case as evidence of "a profound lack of regard for the important limitations on the role of the military in our civilian society." Maj. op. at 836. Regardless of whether that observation is true, it does nothing to show that there have, in fact, been widespread and repeated violations of the PCA; it simply shows that the government wanted to win this case and put forward the best arguments it could to justify what Agent Logan did here. From the premise that the government believes it has a certain power, it does not follow that the government routinely exercises that power. The government's litigating position is, therefore, irrelevant to the Roberts inquiry.

Thus, far from having "abundant evidence that the violation at issue has occurred repeatedly and frequently," Maj. op. at 837, we have before us a paucity of evidence that does not come close to overcoming the "high obstacle for those urging application of the [exclusionary] rule." Scott, 524 U.S. at 364-65, 118 S.Ct. 2014.

IV

Given the significant costs of exclusion in PCA cases, as well as the meager evidence of PCA violations contained in the record, I would hold that the violation at issue here does not merit application of the exclusionary rule.[4] The majority opinion's contrary holding ignores the Supreme Court's clear teaching on exclusion, our own precedents' stringent test for application of that extraordinary remedy, and the uniform rejection of exclusion by federal courts in the PCA context. Because this case provides no justification for setting a convicted child pornographer free, I respectfully dissent.

Notes

[1] To avoid cumbersome constructions, I will not distinguish between the PCA and its implementing regulations, except where it is necessary to do so.

[2] Other courts of appeals have recognized that the Supreme Court's description of the exclusionary rule in the Fourth Amendment context applies to PCA cases. See, e.g.,

United States v. Al-Talib, 55 F.3d 923, 930 (4th Cir. 1995).

[3] Roberts implied that application of the exclusionary rule in the PCA context could be justified, and I do not question that conclusion here. 779 F.2d at 568. However, I note that there is a strong argument to be made that exclusion is never justified for violations of the PCA. Several considerations might support such an argument, such as (1) the fact that Congress could have provided for exclusion had it thought such a remedy was appropriate; (2) the PCA provides for its own enforcement through criminal sanctions, see 18 U.S.C. § 1385; and (3) "the [PCA] express[] a policy that is for the benefit of the people as a whole, but not one that may fairly be characterized as expressly designed to protect the personal rights of defendants," Walden, 490 F.2d at 377. However, even assuming that the exclusionary rule could be applied to the PCA context, I believe we do not yet have a reason to do so.

[4] As for Dreyer's remaining claims, although I would affirm the district court across the board, I limit my discussion here to the issue addressed by the majority opinion.

Judge O'Scannlain's dissent from the denial of rehearing en banc in Dariano v. Morgan Hill Unified School Dist. (Sept 17, 2014) [Notes omitted]

O'SCANNLAIN, Circuit Judge, joined by TALLMAN and BEA, Circuit Judges, dissenting from the denial of rehearing en banc:

The freedom of speech guaranteed by our Constitution is in greatest peril when the government may suppress speech simply because it is unpopular. For that reason, it is a foundational tenet of First Amendment law that the government cannot silence a speaker because of how an audience might react to the speech. It is this bedrock principle—known as the heckler's veto doctrine—that the panel overlooks, condoning the suppression of free speech by some students because other students might have reacted violently.

In doing so, the panel creates a split with the Seventh and Eleventh Circuits and permits the will of the mob to rule our schools. For these reasons, I must respectfully dissent from our refusal to hear this case en banc.

I

On May 5, 2010, Cinco de Mayo, a group of Caucasian students at Live Oak High School ("Live Oak") wore shirts depicting the American flag to school.[1] Dariano v. Morgan Hill Unified Sch. Dist., No. 11-17858, amended slip op. at 22 (9th Cir. 2014). In the six preceding years, there had been at least thirty fights on campus, some between gangs and others between Caucasians and Hispanics, id. at 21, although the district court made no findings as to whether these fights were related to ethnic tensions, Dariano v. Morgan Hill Unified Sch. Dist., 822 F.Supp.2d 1037, 1043 (N.D.Cal.2011). A year earlier, during Cinco de Mayo 2009, a group of Caucasian students and a group of Mexican students exchanged profanities and threats. Dariano, amended slip op. at 21. When the

Caucasian students hung a makeshift American flag and began chanting "U-S-A," Assistant Principal Miguel Rodriguez intervened and asked the Mexican students to stop using profane language, to which one Mexican student responded, "But Rodriguez, they are racist. They are being racist. F* * * them white boys. Let's f* * * them up." Id.

One year later, during Cinco de Mayo 2010, three of the students wearing American flag shirts were confronted by other students about their choice of apparel. Id. at 22. One student asked M.D., a plaintiff in this case, "Why are you wearing that? Do you not like Mexicans[?]" Id. A Caucasian student later told Assistant Principal Rodriguez before brunch break, "You may want to go out to the quad area. There might be some— there might be some issues." Id. During the break, a Mexican student informed Rodriguez that she was concerned "there might be problems" due to the American flag shirts. Id. Another asked Rodriguez why Caucasian students "get to wear their flag out when we don't get to wear our flag?" Id. (alterations omitted). Principal Nick Boden instructed Rodriguez to have the students wearing the American flag shirts turn their shirts inside out or take them off. Id.

Rodriguez met with the students wearing the shirts, who did not dispute that they were at risk of violence due to their apparel. Id. The school officials allowed two students to return to class with their American flag shirts on because their shirts had less prominent imagery and were less likely to cause an incident. Id. at 23. Two other students were given the choice to turn their shirts inside out or to go home. Id. They chose to go home. Id. All plaintiffs in this appeal received threatening messages in the days after the incident. Id.

The students, through their guardians, brought this § 1983 action alleging violations of their First and Fourteenth Amendment rights. Id. at 23-24.

II

In Tinker v. Des Moines Independent Community School District, a group of high school students was suspended for wearing black armbands as a way of protesting the Vietnam War. 393 U.S. 503, 504, 89 S.Ct. 733, 21 L.Ed.2d 731 (1969). In what has become a classic statement of First Amendment law, the Supreme Court declared, "It can hardly be argued that either students or teachers shed their constitutional rights to freedom of speech or expression at the schoolhouse gate." Id. at 506, 89 S.Ct. 733. Of course, as the Court has subsequently made clear, "the constitutional rights of students in public school are not automatically coextensive with the rights of adults in other settings." Bethel Sch. Dist. No. 403 v. Fraser, 478 U.S. 675, 682, 106 S.Ct. 3159, 92 L.Ed.2d 549 (1986). Nonetheless, Tinker established that, "where students in the exercise of First Amendment rights collide with the rules of the school authorities," Tinker, 393 U.S. at 507, 89 S.Ct. 733, students' free speech rights "may not be suppressed unless school officials reasonably conclude that it will `materially and substantially disrupt the work and discipline of the school.'" Morse v. Frederick, 551 U.S. 393, 403, 127 S.Ct. 2618, 168 L.Ed.2d 290 (2007) (quoting Tinker, 393 U.S. at 513, 89 S.Ct. 733).

Invoking Tinker, the panel holds that the school acted properly to prevent a substantial and material disruption of school activities. Dariano, amended slip op. at 26-28, 33. In the panel's view, school officials acted reasonably given the history of ethnic violence at the school, the 2009 Cinco de Mayo incident, and the indications of possible violence on the day in question. Id. at 28. Because the officials tailored their actions to address the threat, the panel held that there was no violation of the students' free speech rights. Id. at 31. The panel also granted summary judgment with regard to the students' equal protection and due process claims. Id. at 32-35.

III

With respect, I suggest that the panel's opinion misinterprets Tinker's own language, our precedent, and the law of our sister circuits. The panel claims that the source of the threatened violence at Live Oak is irrelevant: apparently requiring school officials to stop the source of a threat is too burdensome when a more "readily-available" solution is at hand, id. at 28, namely, silencing the target of the threat. Thus the panel finds it of no consequence that the students exercising their free speech rights did so peacefully, that their expression took the passive form of wearing shirts, or that there is no allegation that they threatened other students with violence.[2] The panel condones the suppression of the students' speech for one reason: other students might have reacted violently against them. Such a rationale contravenes fundamental First Amendment principles.

A

The panel claims to be guided by the language of Tinker, Dariano, amended slip op. at 28, but in fact the panel ignores such language. Indeed Tinker counseled directly against the outcome here: relying on the earlier heckler's veto case of Terminiello v. Chicago, 337 U.S. 1, 69 S.Ct. 894, 93 L.Ed. 1131 (1949), the Court explained that students' speech, whether made "in class, in the lunchroom, or on the campus," cannot be silenced merely because those who disagree with it "may start an argument or cause a disturbance." 393 U.S. at 508, 89 S.Ct. 733 (citing Terminiello). Tinker made clear that the "Constitution says we must take th[e] risk" that speech may engender a violent response. Id. Yet, rather than heed Tinker's guidance, the panel undermines its holding, and, in the process, erodes the "hazardous freedom" and "openness" that "is the basis of our national strength and of the independence and vigor of Americans who grow up and live in this relatively permissive, often disputatious, society." Tinker, 393 U.S. at 508-09, 89 S.Ct. 733.

What the panel fails to recognize, and what we have previously held, is that Tinker went out of its way to reaffirm the heckler's veto doctrine; the principle that "the government cannot silence messages simply because they cause discomfort, fear, or even anger." Ctr. for Bio-Ethical Reform, Inc. v. Los Angeles Cnty., 533 F.3d 780, 788 (9th Cir.2008) (citing Tinker, 393 U.S. at 508, 89 S.Ct. 733). Quoting Tinker, we have explained:

> [I]n our system, undifferentiated fear or apprehension of disturbance is not enough to overcome the right to freedom of expression. Any departure from absolute regimentation may cause trouble. Any variation from the majority's opinion may inspire

fear. Any word spoken, in class, in the lunchroom, or on the campus, that deviates from the views of another person may start an argument or cause a disturbance. But our Constitution says we must take this risk....

Bio-Ethical Reform, 533 F.3d at 788 (quoting Tinker, 393 U.S. at 508, 89 S.Ct. 733).[3] Our precedents take the position, then, that far from abandoning the heckler's veto doctrine in public schools, Tinker stands as a dramatic reaffirmation of it.[4] Given the central importance of the doctrine to First Amendment jurisprudence, that should come as no surprise.[5]

B

The heckler's veto doctrine is one of the oldest and most venerable in First Amendment

770

*770 jurisprudence. See Terminiello v. City of Chicago, 337 U.S. 1, 5, 69 S.Ct. 894, 93 L.Ed. 1131 (1949). Indeed, the Court has gone far to protect speech where it might incur a hostile and even violent reaction from an audience. In Street v. New York, for example, a man was convicted for "publicly defy[ing] ... or cast[ing] contempt upon (any American flag) by words." 394 U.S. 576, 590, 89 S.Ct. 1354, 22 L.Ed.2d 572 (1969). The Court invalidated the conviction, rejecting the state's justification that the man's speech had a "tendency ... to provoke violent retaliation." Id. at 592, 89 S.Ct. 1354. The heckler's veto doctrine also protected a civil rights leader's peaceful speech during a lunch counter sit-in protest, despite the state's alleged fear that "`violence was about to erupt' because of the demonstration." Cox v. Louisiana, 379 U.S. 536, 550, 85 S.Ct. 453, 13 L.Ed.2d 471 (1965). As the Court said in Cox, "[T]he compelling answer ... is that constitutional rights may not be denied simply because of hostility to their assertion or exercise." Id. at 551, 85 S.Ct. 453 (internal quotation marks omitted).

Of course, this doctrine does not apply to all categories of speech. The Court has recognized that there are "certain well-defined and narrowly limited classes of speech, the prevention and punishment of which have never been thought to raise any Constitutional problem." Chaplinsky v. New Hampshire, 315 U.S. 568, 571-72, 62 S.Ct. 766, 86 L.Ed. 1031 (1942); see also United States v. Alvarez, ____ U.S. ___, 132 S.Ct. 2537, 2544, 183 L.Ed.2d 574 (2012) (listing types of speech that are not part of "the freedom of speech"). Where, for instance, speech constitutes "`fighting' words-those which by their very utterance inflict injury or tend to incite an immediate breach of the peace," Chaplinsky, 315 U.S. at 572, 62 S.Ct. 766; is "directed to inciting or producing imminent lawless action and is likely to incite or produce such action," Brandenburg v. Ohio, 395 U.S. 444, 447, 89 S.Ct. 1827, 23 L.Ed.2d 430 (1969); or is a "true threat," Virginia v. Black, 538 U.S. 343, 358-60, 123 S.Ct. 1536, 155 L.Ed.2d 535 (2003), such speech may be prohibited, subject to certain limitations, see R.A.V. v. City of St. Paul, 505 U.S. 377, 383-86, 112 S.Ct. 2538, 120 L.Ed.2d 305 (1992). But apart from these well-recognized categories, "the government may not give weight to the audience's negative reaction" as a basis for suppressing speech. Ctr. for Bio-Ethical Reform, Inc., 533 F.3d at 789; see also Texas v. Johnson, 491 U.S. 397,

408-09, 109 S.Ct. 2533, 105 L.Ed.2d 342 (1989) ("[A] principal function of free speech under our system of government is to invite dispute.") (internal quotation marks omitted) (quoting Terminiello) (citing Tinker).

C

Despite Tinker's emphasis on the actions of the speaker and its reaffirmation of the heckler's veto doctrine, the panel ignores these foundational precepts of First Amendment jurisprudence and condones using the heckler's veto as a basis for suppressing student speech.

The established First Amendment principles that the panel disregards exist for good reason. Rather than acting to protect the students who were peacefully expressing their views, Live Oak decided to suppress the speech of those students because other students might do them harm. Live Oak's reaction to the possible violence against the student speakers, and the panel's blessing of that reaction, sends a clear message to public school students: by threatening violence against those with whom you disagree, you can enlist the power of the State to silence them. This perverse incentive created by the panel's

771

*771 opinion is precisely what the heckler's veto doctrine seeks to avoid.

In this case, the disfavored speech was the display of an American flag. But let no one be fooled: by interpreting Tinker to permit the heckler's veto, the panel opens the door to the suppression of any viewpoint opposed by a vocal and violent band of students. The next case might be a student wearing a shirt bearing the image of Che Guevara, or Martin Luther King, Jr., or Pope Francis. It might be a student wearing a President Obama "Hope" shirt, or a shirt exclaiming "Stand with Rand!" It might be a shirt proclaiming the shahada, or a shirt announcing "Christ is risen!" It might be any viewpoint imaginable, but whatever it is, it will be vulnerable to the rule of the mob. The demands of bullies will become school policy.

That is not the law.

IV

The Seventh and Eleventh Circuits agree that a student's speech cannot be suppressed based on the violent reaction of its audience. Thus the panel is simply wrong that our sister circuits' cases "do not distinguish between `substantial disruption' caused by the speaker and `substantial disruption' caused by the reaction of onlookers." Dariano, amended slip op. at 29. In Zamecnik v. Indian Prairie School District No. 204, a student wore a t-shirt to school on the Day of Silence bearing the slogan, "Be Happy, Not Gay." 636 F.3d 874, 875 (7th Cir.2011). The school sought to prohibit the student from wearing the shirt based, in part, on "incidents of harassment of plaintiff Zamecnik." Id. at 879. The Seventh Circuit squarely rejected that rationale as "barred by the doctrine ... of the `heckler's veto.'" Id. Zamecnik made clear that Tinker "endorse[s] the doctrine of the heckler's veto" and described the rationale behind that doctrine:

Statements that while not fighting words are met by violence or threats or other unprivileged retaliatory conduct by persons offended by them cannot lawfully be suppressed because of that conduct. Otherwise free speech could be stifled by the speaker's opponents' mounting a riot, even though, because the speech had contained no fighting words, no reasonable person would have been moved to a riotous response. So the fact that homosexual students and their sympathizers harassed Zamecnik because of their disapproval of her message is not a permissible ground for banning it.

Id. The court affirmed the grant of summary judgment to Zamecnik. Id. at 882.

The Eleventh Circuit is of the same opinion. In Holloman ex rel. Holloman v. Harland, a school punished a student for silently holding up a fist rather than reciting the Pledge of Allegiance. 370 F.3d 1252, 1259 (11th Cir.2004). School officials justified their actions, in part, by citing "concern that [the student's] behavior would lead to further disruptions by other students." Id. at 1274. The Eleventh Circuit acknowledged that Tinker governed its analysis, and in an impassioned paragraph, the court invoked the heckler's veto doctrine:

Allowing a school to curtail a student's freedom of expression based on such factors turns reason on its head. If certain bullies are likely to act violently when a student wears long hair, it is unquestionably easy for a principal to preclude the outburst by preventing the student from wearing long hair. To do so, however, is to sacrifice freedom upon the alter [sic] of order, and allow the scope of our liberty to be dictated by the inclinations of the unlawful mob.

772

*772 Id. at 1275. Particularly relevant here, the Eleventh Circuit squarely rejected the claim that the heckler's veto doctrine does not apply in public schools:

While the same constitutional standards do not always apply in public schools as on public streets, we cannot afford students less constitutional protection simply because their peers might illegally express disagreement through violence instead of reason. If the people, acting through a legislative assembly, may not proscribe certain speech, neither may they do so acting individually as criminals. Principals have the duty to maintain order in public schools, but they may not do so while turning a blind eye to basic notions of right and wrong.

Id. at 1276. The court reversed the district court's grant of summary judgment to the school and reinstated Holloman's claims. Id. at 1294-95.

The panel's holding, then, represents a dramatic departure from the views of our sister circuits.[6] Yet, one would never know it from reading the panel's opinion, since the contrary decisions of those circuits are barely mentioned and completely mis-characterized.

V

Finally, the panel attempts to analogize this case to those involving school restrictions on Confederate flags. See Dariano, amended slip op. at 30-31. But these cases, dealing solely with a symbol that is "widely regarded as racist and incendiary," Zamecnik, 636 F.3d at 877, cannot override Tinker here.[7]

The panel takes the Confederate flag cases to be a single "illustrat[ion]" of the much broader "principle" that the heckler's veto doctrine does not apply to schools. Dariano, amended slip op. at 30. But as that broad "principle" is incorrect, the Confederate flag cases cannot illustrate it. Indeed, what the cases actually illustrate is a permissive attitude towards regulation of the Confederate flag that is based on the flag's unique and racially divisive history.[8] Whether or not this history provides a principled basis for the regulation of Confederate icons, it certainly provides no support for banning displays of the American flag.

VI

The panel's opinion contravenes foundational First Amendment principles, creates a split with the Seventh and Eleventh Circuits, and imperils minority viewpoints of all kinds. Like our sister circuits, I would hold that the reaction of other students to the student speaker is not a legitimate basis for suppressing student speech absent a showing that the speech in question constitutes fighting words, a true threat, incitement to imminent lawless action, or other speech outside the First Amendment's protection. See Zamecnik, 636 F.3d at 879 (rejecting the heckler's veto "because the speech had contained no fighting words"); Holloman, 370 F.3d at 1275-76 (citing Street for the proposition that "the possible tendency of appellant's words to provoke violent retaliation is not a basis for banning those words unless they are `fighting words'" (internal quotation marks omitted)).

I respectfully dissent from our regrettable decision not to rehear this case en banc.

Judge O'Scannlain's dissent in Garcia v. Comm'r of Social Sec. (Sept 23, 2014)

O'SCANNLAIN, Circuit Judge, dissenting:

The panel majority, eager to reprimand the Commissioner of Social Security for what it deems to be inexcusably sloppy practices, disregards—I suggest, respectfully—the deference we owe under law to the agency's determinations. Rather than observing the standard for harmless error that our precedents have previously prescribed, the majority has erroneously presumed that the Commissioner's ostensible error has prejudiced Stephanie Garcia, the claimant in this case. I respectfully dissent from this regrettable exaggeration of our Court's properly limited role in the adjudication of Social Security disability benefits claims.

I

Congress has carefully prescribed a minimal role for the Federal courts in adjudicating claims of disability under the Social Security Act. See 42 U.S.C. § 405(g). Accordingly, we have only limited authority to nullify the decisions of the agency and its administrative law judges with which we disagree. As the majority opinion correctly notes, we may not disturb an ALJ's denial of benefits unless "it is not supported by substantial evidence or is based on legal error." Robbins v. Soc. Sec. Admin., 466 F.3d 880, 882 (9th Cir. 2006). Legal error alone, furthermore, is not sufficient to warrant our interference: for example, we generally must stay our hand if it is "clear from the record" that any ostensible error "was inconsequential to the ultimate nondisability determination." Tommasetti v. Astrue, 533 F.3d 1035, 1038 (9th Cir.2008) (internal quotation marks omitted).

Indeed, one such error that we have identified in past cases has been an ALJ's failure "fully and fairly [to] develop the record and to assure that the claimant's interests are considered." Celaya v. Halter, 332 F.3d 1177, 1183 (9th Cir.2003). This "special" and "independent" duty of the ALJ exists in all circumstances, although, when the applicant is uncounseled, the responsibility to ensure an adequate record is heightened. See Tonapetyan v. Halter, 242 F.3d 1144, 1150 (9th Cir.2001); Smolen v. Chater, 80 F.3d 1273, 1288 (9th Cir.1996). Despite our solicitude in this regard, we have nevertheless clearly limned the outer boundaries of such responsibility. "An ALJ's duty to develop the record further is triggered only when there is ambiguous evidence or when the record is inadequate to allow for proper evaluation of the evidence." Mayes v. Massanari, 276 F.3d 453, 459-60 (9th Cir. 2001) (emphasis added).

More recently, we have refined—in the context of the ALJ's duty to develop the record—the standard by which we appraise whether any such error prejudiced the claimant. In McLeod v. Astrue, the unsuccessful applicant for disability benefits contended that the "ALJ erred by failing to develop the record adequately," specifically by not "request[ing] more explanation from two of his treating physicians" and by not obtaining "whatever VA disability rating" he may have had. 640 F.3d 881, 884 (9th Cir.2011). We determined that the ALJ had shirked this duty to develop the record, but nevertheless that this dereliction was not alone sufficient warrant for reversal. Rather, we explained that "the burden is on the party attacking the agency's determination to show that prejudice resulted from the error." Id. at 887. But "where the circumstances of the case show a substantial likelihood of prejudice," the reviewing court can remand the case so the agency may reconsider the claimant's eligibility for benefits. Id. at 888. We emphasized, nevertheless, that a "mere probability" of prejudice "is not enough." Id. Either the claimant must himself shoulder the burden of demonstrating prejudice, or otherwise such prejudice must be apparent on the face of the record or the "circumstances of the case."

II

The majority's opinion turns this duty-to-develop doctrine on its head. Even assuming, arguendo, that the ALJ committed legal error by not ordering Dr. McDonald to perform another round of IQ tests on Miss Garcia,[1] the majority misstates—and misapplies—the proper standard for assessing any prejudice such error caused.

In the first place, the majority correctly acknowledges that "[w]e will not reverse an ALJ's decision on the basis of a harmless error," which occurs "when it is clear from the record that the ALJ's error was inconsequential to the ultimate nondisability determination," maj. op. at 932 (internal quotation marks omitted). Although the majority does not expressly state that such rule is the exclusive standard by which to assess the harm caused by an error, its reasoning assumes so. For the majority detects prejudice in "a genuine probability" that a complete set of IQ test scores may have altered the medical reports or provided another basis for Miss Garcia to challenge the ALJ's determination. Id. at 933. McLeod, however, specifically forecloses this basis for reversing a denial of benefits: a "mere probability," no matter how "genuine," simply does not suffice. 640 F.3d at 888. The majority articulates an exclusive standard for harmless error that presumes prejudice unless such error appear "inconsequential" on the face of the record. Such may be the ordinary analysis for determining the prejudice caused by legal error. In the special context of the ALJ's duty to develop the record, however, our Court has already clearly explained that we cannot find prejudice unless and until demonstrated by the claimant or the record and circumstances of the case.

Furthermore, the majority offers no basis, either in law or in fact, for simply asserting that the absence of a full set of IQ test scores would have had any likely effect on the ALJ's disability determination. The majority first observes that "[b]oth Dr. Middleton and Dr. Murillo considered Garcia's incomplete IQ test results in assessing her ability to support herself through gainful employment." Maj. op. at 933. Indeed, the medical experts considered the test scores—but they also considered sundry other relevant data, such as her employment history, educational and recreational activities, financial independence, grooming, and the cooperation and comprehension she displayed during her clinical evaluation. The majority does not indicate any basis from these experts' reports that the partial test scores figured decisively in their recommendations. Nor does the majority opinion advert to any item in the record or the "circumstances of the case" that suggests the slightest chance—let alone a "genuine probability"—the ALJ would have concluded differently had he seen a full set of IQ test scores.

Even Miss Garcia's own briefing does not attempt such an argument. In her opening brief, she emphasizes only that, deprived of a full battery of test scores, she lost the opportunity to qualify for automatic disability benefits under Listing 12.05 C or D, see 20 C.F.R. § 404, subpt. P, app. 1. She does not, however, attempt affirmatively to link the incomplete IQ tests with the medical reports and the ALJ's determination of her residual functional capacity. Only in her supplemental brief does Miss Garcia clearly assert such a connection—and, even there, she does not offer any reason why we may expect the medical experts would have substantively revised their reports in light of complete test results.

The majority assures us, however, that an alternative finding by the ALJ "seems particularly plausible" based on Miss Garcia's "considerably lower" test results as a juvenile. Maj. op. at 933. But this is a non sequitur. The ALJ determined Miss Garcia not to be disabled in light of her record as a whole: he did not explain that the partial IQ test score carried dispositive weight. Nothing in the record to which either Miss Garcia or the majority point suggests a necessary connection between marginally lower IQ scores and a RFC finding that would prevent her from procuring and performing gainful employment. This "genuine probability" of a different outcome that the majority identifies, accordingly, appears little more than an unsubstantiated hunch.

In addition, Listings 12.05 C and D require not only a sufficiently low IQ test score, but also additional impairments, before the applicant may qualify for disability benefits thereunder. Miss Garcia does not, before this court, argue that she may have qualified under Listing 12.05 B, which she would satisfy simply by scoring below 60 on any of her tests without presenting any other additional impairments.[2]

Nevertheless, the majority, pointing to her substantially lower testing results as a juvenile, predicts that Miss Garcia may have scored low enough to qualify as disabled under Listing 12.05 B. For such reason, the majority finds prejudice in Dr. McDonald's failure to administer the entire battery of IQ tests and in the ALJ's acceptance of these partial scores. In effect, this reasoning says—bizarrely—that Miss Garcia wins an argument she does not make. Since she never claimed on appeal that she would have qualified under Listing 12.05 B, the possibility that she could have so qualified should not be a grounds that she suffered prejudice.

III

The majority's reasoning, furthermore, threatens to undermine the highly deferential standard under which we review the Commissioner's decisions. When presented with an appeal from an unsuccessful applicant, we may not second-guess the Commissioner's determination or reverse him simply because we disagree with the result. Our authority to order relief is more limited: if substantial evidence exists in the record to support the agency's factbound conclusions, our analysis must generally come to an end. Here the majority opinion does not suggest an absence of substantial evidence to ballast the ALJ's nondisability finding; rather, it posits that, despite any such substantial evidence, the ALJ might have reached an alternative conclusion if the record had contained a full set of IQ scores.

Such holding opens a potentially fatal breach in the substantial-evidence framework. Indeed, the majority determines that the ALJ committed legal error by not developing the record to include a full set of test scores; and, indeed, "legal error" is a basis distinct from the lack of substantial evidence for reversal. Nevertheless the relationship between these two standards, in the context of the ALJ's legal duty to develop the record, should be apparent enough. Claimants previously required to disprove the existence of substantial evidence will now plead an incomplete record and, citing the majority opinion, will assert that the outcome of their case "might have been different," maj. op. at 933. Seldom will be the occasion where the ALJ could not have examined more reports or ordered more tests. In Mayes, we specifically rejected a challenge from a claimant who contended, in effect, that substantial evidence did not support the ALJ's denial because he did not adequately develop the record. 276 F.3d at 459. The substantial-evidence standard protects against precisely such attacks on the administrative process: the courts may not overturn the agency's findings, substantiated by sufficient data, even in the presence of compelling countervailing evidence. Claimants ought not be able to circumvent this standard by invoking hypothetical evidence that the ALJ could have but neglected for one reason or another to consider. Id. Our procedure, elucidated in McLeod, for assessing the prejudice caused by an inadequately developed record reinforces these principles. The ALJ's duty to develop "is triggered only" in certain circumstances, Mayes, 276 F.3d at 459, and, unlike other contexts, we do not presume prejudice until the claimant or the record demonstrates otherwise, see McLeod, 640 F.3d at 887-88.

The majority's doctrinal innovation destabilizes this framework, substantially lowering the burden for plaintiffs seeking the intervention of the Federal courts in the Commissioner's decision-making processes and portending to make substantial-evidence review a dead letter. Such result contravenes the precedents of this Court, the intent of Congress, and the separation of powers.

IV

For the foregoing reasons, I respectfully dissent.

Notes

[1] I remain unconvinced that, at least in the circumstances of this case, the ALJ erred by not ordering a new, and complete, round of IQ tests. The majority opinion does not assert that the partial test scores constitute "ambiguous evidence" or make the "record... inadequate" for the purposes of assessing residual functional capacity. See Mayes, 276 F.3d at 460.

At most, the majority opinion gleans from the regulations an expectation of or a preference for "multiple scores" from a Wechsler series IQ test, maj. op. at 931. Whether such regulatory intimations can "trigger[]" the ALJ's duty further to develop the record, 276 F.3d at 459, does not appear compelled by our precedents. And the majority does not pause to explain why.

Furthermore, the majority scarcely indicates what countervailing constraints—if any—may defeat the regulations' preference for or expectation of multiple test scores. Dr. McDonald's purported reasons for not administering the complete Wechsler series IQ test were "the constraints of time and the slowness with which [Miss Garcia] worked." The majority simply deems this explanation an "excuse," dismissing it as "troublesome" and scolding the district court, which in its judgment "should not have accepted it in the absence of some more compelling reason." Maj. op. at 927-28 & n. 1.

I strongly resist this lecture to medical practitioners. Not only does the record lack any clear implication of either excuse-making or duty-shirking, but also it is not self-evident that the time Dr. McDonald did devote to administering the tests and interviewing Miss Garcia was insufficient or otherwise imprudent. We should be reticent to craft, in footnotes to our opinions, legal rules governing the minutiae of medical practice—such as how and when to schedule tests and interviews—where Congress has not legislated and where the agency has not regulated. And especially not where the record and the parties' briefings do not present an adequate basis for determining which sort of constraints are reasonable and which are merely "excuses."

[2] In her opening brief, Miss Garcia specifically argued that "a valid IQ score on one of the two missing IQ tests may provide satisfaction of the Listing at § 12.05(C) or (D)."

Judge O'Scannlain's dissent in Lopez-Valenzuela v. Arpaio (Oct 15, 2014) [Notes omitted]

O'SCANNLAIN, Circuit Judge, dissenting:

Today, the majority divines, under the rubric of substantive due process, that Arizona's categorical denial of bail is "excessive" notwithstanding the State's interest in mitigating flight risk. Remarkably, the majority scarcely mentions the Constitution's command that "[e]xcessive bail shall not be required." U.S. Const. amend. VIII.

I respectfully dissent from our expansion of substantive due process and neglect of express constitutional text.[1]

I

A

"[R]eluctant to expand the concept of substantive due process," Collins v. City of Harker Heights, Tex., 503 U.S. 115, 125, 112 S.Ct. 1061, 117 L.Ed.2d 261 (1992), the Supreme Court held in Graham v. Connor, 490 U.S. 386, 109 S.Ct. 1865, 104 L.Ed.2d 443 (1989), that "[w]here a particular Amendment provides an explicit textual source of constitutional protection against a particular sort of government behavior, that Amendment, not the more generalized notion of substantive due process, must be the guide for analyzing these claims." Cnty. of Sacramento v. Lewis, 523 U.S. 833, 842, 118 S.Ct. 1708, 140 L.Ed.2d 1043 (1998) (alteration in original) (quoting Albright v. Oliver, 510 U.S. 266, 273, 114 S.Ct. 807, 127 L.Ed.2d 114 (1994) (plurality opinion of Rehnquist, C.J.)). "Graham... requires that if a constitutional claim is covered by a specific constitutional provision, such as the Fourth or Eighth Amendment, the claim must be analyzed under the standard appropriate to that specific provision, not under the rubric of substantive due process." United States v. Lanier, 520 U.S. 259, 272 n. 7, 117 S.Ct. 1219, 137 L.Ed.2d 432 (1997) (emphasis added) (citing Graham, 490 U.S. at 394, 109 S.Ct. 1865).

The majority flouts this requirement. It "first" analyzes the Proposition 100 laws under "general substantive due process principles," Maj. Op. at 780, 780-90, then considers whether the Proposition 100 laws violate the specific due process prohibition on imposing punishment before trial, id. at 780, 789-91. My colleagues in the majority decline to consider—ever— whether the Proposition 100 laws violate the Eighth Amendment. Id. at 791-92 & n. 16.

One would hardly know, after reading the majority's forty-three page opinion— analyzing whether Arizona's denial of bail was excessive in light of the flight risk posed by illegal immigrants—that, under the Eighth Amendment of the Constitution itself, "[e]xcessive bail shall not be required."[2] Indeed, one might think that "[t]he Court has prohibited excessive bail." Maj. Op. at 777 (emphasis added).

B

To be sure, specific constitutional provisions do not preclude recognition of substantive due process rights that touch on related subjects. Lewis, 523 U.S. at 843, 118 S.Ct. 1708 ("Substantive due process analysis is therefore inappropriate in this case only if respondents' claim is `covered by' the Fourth Amendment."); see, e.g., Lanier, 520 U.S. at 272 n. 7, 117 S.Ct. 1219 (Graham did "not hold that all constitutional claims relating to physically abusive government conduct must arise under either the Fourth or Eighth Amendments."). Not every conceivable constitutional dispute regarding bail is resolved by the Eighth Amendment. But the question whether denying bail to illegal immigrants based on flight risk is unconstitutionally excessive is posed, precisely, by the Excessive Bail Clause. See Stack, 342 U.S. at 4-5, 72 S.Ct. 1.

The majority relies primarily on United States v. Salerno, 481 U.S. 739, 107 S.Ct. 2095, 95 L.Ed.2d 697 (1987), to justify its substantive due process inquiry, but I suggest that it has not read that case carefully enough. Salerno does not excuse the majority's disregard of the Eighth Amendment, because this case, unlike Salerno, concerns detention based on flight risk.

Two substantive due process arguments against the Bail Reform Act of 1984 were rejected in Salerno: The Court analyzed whether "the Due Process Clause prohibits pretrial detention on the ground of danger to the community." Id. at 748, 107 S.Ct. 2095. And the Court considered whether it was unconstitutional "because the pretrial detention it authorizes constitutes impermissible punishment before trial." Id. at 746, 107 S.Ct. 2095. Both claims were grounded in the Court's substantive due process precedents; they required the Court to decide whether the Bail Reform Act violated already established due process rights. See id. at 749-51, 107 S.Ct. 2095 (detention based on dangerousness) (citing, inter alia, Schall, 467 U.S. 253, 104 S.Ct. 2403, Addington v. Texas, 441 U.S. 418, 99 S.Ct. 1804, 60 L.Ed.2d 323 (1979), and Carlson v. Landon, 342 U.S. 524, 72 S.Ct. 525, 96 L.Ed. 547 (1952)); id. at 746-47, 107 S.Ct. 2095 (punishment before trial) (citing Bell v. Wolfish, 441 U.S. 520, 99 S.Ct. 1861, 60 L.Ed.2d 447 (1979) and Schall v. Martin, 467 U.S. 253, 104 S.Ct. 2403, 81 L.Ed.2d 207 (1984)). Neither claim implicated the Eighth Amendment inquiry proper to this case-whether the Proposition 100 bail laws are constitutionally "excessive" based on flight risk.

1

As to its "general substantive due process principles," the majority misreads Salerno by conflating detention based on dangerousness, which the Court considered, with detention based on flight risk, which the Court did not. In Salerno, the Court rejected the "categorical imperative"—advanced by the Second Circuit— that the Due Process Clause "prohibits pretrial detention on the ground of danger to the community." Id. at 748, 107 S.Ct. 2095 (emphasis added). Because due process does not "erect[ ] an impenetrable `wall'" to such detention, the Court reasoned "that the present statute providing for pretrial detention on the basis of dangerousness must be evaluated in precisely the same manner"—applying means-end scrutiny—"that we evaluated the laws in the cases discussed above." Id. at 748-49, 107 S.Ct. 2095 (emphasis added).

Nothing in Salerno suggests that detention based on flight risk should be evaluated in the same manner. See id. at 749, 107 S.Ct. 2095 (Detainees "concede and the Court of Appeals noted that an arrestee may be incarcerated until trial if he presents a risk of flight.").[3] Indeed, the Eighth Amendment secures the specific right not to be required to post excessive bail in light of flight risk. See Stack, 342 U.S. at 4-5, 72 S.Ct. 1. The majority's substantive due process inquiry is thus inappropriate under Graham. See, e.g., John Corp. v. City of Houston, 214 F.3d 573, 582 (5th Cir.2000) ("The purpose of Graham is to avoid expanding the concept of substantive due process where another constitutional provision protects individuals against the challenged governmental action.").

2

The Court's substantive due process jurisprudence indeed secures the specific right to be free from punishment before trial. E.g., Schall, 467 U.S. at 269, 104 S.Ct. 2403. But the majority misapplies that jurisprudence, asking under substantive due process questions properly considered under the Eighth Amendment and thereby displacing specific constitutional text.

Our role is to question whether a particular "disability is imposed for the purpose of punishment." Bell v. Wolfish, 441 U.S. 520, 538, 99 S.Ct. 1861, 60 L.Ed.2d 447 (1979). To decide whether the legislative purpose was punitive, in the absence of an "express intent to punish," we must discern whether pretrial detention is "excessive in relation to the alternative purpose assigned [to it]." Id. Answering that question, Salerno considered the "incidents of pretrial detention" under the Bail Reform Act—such as prompt detention hearings and whether pretrial detainees were housed separately from postconviction detainees—and concluded that they did not reveal an improper punitive purpose. 481 U.S. at 747, 107 S.Ct. 2095 (emphasis added). By contrast, the majority here considers the substance of Proposition 100— categorical denial of bail—and decides it is excessive notwithstanding the heightened risk of flight, the very question properly considered under the Eighth Amendment.[4]

C

The Supreme Court tells us not to rely on generalized substantive due process "because guideposts for responsible decisionmaking in this unchartered area are scarce and open-ended." Collins, 503 U.S. at 125, 112 S.Ct. 1061. The majority's incautious expansion of substantive due process confirms the wisdom of such advice. Grounded in neither text nor history, the majority's due process inquiry simply replaces legislative and popular judgment with its own, at least until Arizona provides sufficiently robust statistical analysis to suit.

If we must remove "a difficult question of public policy ... from the reach of the voters" of Arizona, Schuette v. Coal. to Defend Affirmative Action, ___ U.S. ___, 134 S.Ct. 1623, 1637, 188 L.Ed.2d 613 (2014), we should pay them the respect of grounding our decision in the textual guarantees of the Constitution, not the nebulous haze of substantive due process.

II

The question we ought to have considered is whether the Eighth Amendment contains any substantive restrictions on Arizona's authority to declare certain classes of crimes or criminals nonbailable, and, if so, whether Proposition 100 violates such restrictions.[5] Without thorough briefing on such questions from the parties, but guided by sparse discussion in Supreme Court precedent, I offer a tentative answer.

In Carlson, the Supreme Court rejected the proposition that the Eighth Amendment required certain detainees to be admitted to bail:

The bail clause was lifted with slight changes from the English Bill of Rights Act. In England that clause has never been thought to accord a right to bail in all cases, but merely to provide that bail shall not be excessive in those cases where it is proper to grant bail. When this clause was carried over into our Bill of Rights, nothing was said that indicated any different concept. The Eighth Amendment has not prevented Congress from defining the classes of cases in which bail shall be allowed in this country.

342 U.S. 524, 545-46, 72 S.Ct. 525, 96 L.Ed. 547 (1952) (emphasis added) (footnotes omitted). In Salerno, the Court reserved the question "whether the Excessive Bail Clause speaks at all to Congress' power to define the classes of criminal arrestees who shall be admitted to bail." 481 U.S. at 754, 107 S.Ct. 2095.[6]

As noted in Carlson, the Eighth Amendment echoes the English Bill of Rights of 1689. Compare U.S. Const. amend. VIII ("Excessive bail shall not be required, nor excessive fines imposed, nor cruel and unusual punishments inflicted."), with English Bill of Rights 1689 (declaring that "excessive bail ought not to be required, nor excessive fines imposed, nor cruel and unusual punishments inflicted"). But "bail was not an absolute right in England." William F. Duker, The Right to Bail: A Historical Inquiry, 42 Albany L.Rev. 33, 77 (1977). The English Bill of Rights did not restrain Parliament from declaring which classes of crimes were bailable. See Hermine Herta Meyer, Constitutionality of Pretrial Detention, 60 Geo. L.J. 1139, 1155-58 (1972); see also Duker, supra, at 81. Of course, "that Parliament classified certain offenses as nonbailable is not an absolute indication that Congress was to enjoy the same power" under the Eighth Amendment, "to define bailable and nonbailable offenses." Hunt v. Roth, 648 F.2d 1148, 1159 (8th Cir.1981), vacated sub nom. Murphy v. Hunt, 455 U.S. 478, 102 S.Ct. 1181, 71 L.Ed.2d 353 (1982).

Early American constitutions suggest, nonetheless, that their prohibitions of "excessive bail" limited the judiciary, not the legislature. E.g., Md. Const. of 1776, § 22 ("That excessive bail ought not to be required... by the courts of law."); N.H. Const. of 1784, art. I, § 33 ("No magistrate or court of law shall demand excessive bail or sureties...."); see generally, Duker, supra, at 79-83. "[B]y the time of the formulation of the Bill of Rights by the first Congress of the United States, the experience in America had been to grant bail in cases which were bailable, as determined by the legislature." Id. at 83 (emphasis added). Legislatures were free to declare horse stealing, for example, bailable or not. Compare Caleb Foote, The Coming Constitutional Crisis: Part I, 113 U. Pa. L.Rev. 959, 976-77 (1965) (describing the failure by one vote of Jefferson's bill to render horse theft bailable), with Duker, supra, at 82 & n. 293 (noting that Georgia's legislature denied bail for horse stealing despite constitutional guarantee that "excessive bail" shall not be "demanded").

The First Congress's debates over the Bill of Rights contain no hint that the originally understood meaning of the Eighth Amendment's Excessive Bail Clause was any different from the right guaranteed by the same words in the English Bill of Rights or the State constitutions. Carlson, 342 U.S. at 545 & n. 44, 72 S.Ct. 525; see also Duker, supra, at 85-86.

I tentatively conclude, therefore, based on the text of the Constitution and the history of the right to bail, that the Eighth Amendment secures a right to reasonable bail where a court has discretion to grant bail. Cf. Ex parte Watkins, 32 U.S. (7 Pet.) 568, 573-74, 8 L.Ed. 786 (1833) (Story, J.) ("The [E]ighth [A]mendment is addressed to courts of the United States exercising criminal jurisdiction, and is doubtless mandatory to them and a limitation upon their discretion."). It does not, however, restrict legislative discretion to declare certain crimes nonbailable. See Duker, supra, at 86-87 ("Although the amendment limits the discretion of the courts in setting bail, Congress is free to determine the cases for which bail shall be allowed, or whether it shall be allowed at all."); Meyer, supra, at 1194 (The Constitution "reserved for Congress the right to make legislative changes [to bail] whenever required by changed circumstances."). I have found no evidence to suggest that the Excessive Bail Clause, as originally understood, limited legislative discretion.[7]

III

During Congress's debates on the Bill of Rights, the only comment on the Excessive Bail Clause was by Samuel Livermore, Representative for New Hampshire, "who remarked: `The clause seems to have no meaning to it, I do not think it necessary. What is meant by the terms excessive bail? Who are the judges ...?'"[8] Ignoring the first question, regrettably, the majority firmly answers the second: "We are."

On the majority's chosen ground, Judge Tallman has the better of the argument, so I happily join his dissent. But I regret the majority's impulse to clash in the terra incognitia of substantive due process. Guided by text and history, we might have found surer footing by applying the Excessive Bail Clause.

I respectfully dissent.

Judge O'Scannlain's concurrence and dissent in Universal Engraving v. Metal Magic (Feb 11, 2015)

O'SCANNLAIN, Circuit Judge, concurring in part and dissenting in part:

I agree with the Court on all issues except its treatment of the post-judgment Orca decision of the Arizona Supreme Court interpreting Ariz. Rev. Stat. § 44-407. See Orca Commc'ns Unlimited, LLC v. Noder, 337 P.3d 545 (Ariz. 2014). In concluding that Universal Engraving, Inc.'s ("UEI") common law claims were preempted by the Arizona Uniform Trade Secrets Act ("AUTSA"), the district court explicitly relied upon an interpretation of the statute's preemption provision that was expressly, albeit subsequently, disavowed in Orca. I respectfully dissent from the Court's disposition to that extent.

I

The Orca court held that AUTSA displaces only claims for the misappropriation of trade secrets, such that other common-law claims—including torts based on the misappropriation of confidential information falling outside AUTSA's definition of a trade secret—remain viable. See id. at 548, 550. As UEI repeatedly alleged claims based on the misappropriation of confidential information in addition to its trade secrets claims, I am persuaded the district court erred in preventing UEI from proceeding to trial on such claims. See id. at 548 ("[B]ecause [Plaintiff's] unfair-competition claim, as alleged, is not limited to trade secrets, the superior court erred in dismissing that claim on preemption grounds." (emphasis added)). In fairness, the district judge could not have applied Orca since it came down after judgment here, but, as the majority notes, Orca is nevertheless binding and applies to this case and this appeal. See Kona Enterprises, Inc. v. Estate of Bishop, 229 F.3d 877, 886-87 (9th Cir. 2000).

II

Furthermore, I cannot conclude that the district court's error was harmless based on a single juror's question whether the jury had to conclude "that UEI suffered damages in order to vote that trade secrets were misappropriated." I respectfully suggest that we cannot base our decision on an inference drawn from such a question to the court. Cf. Floyd v. Laws, 929 F.2d 1390, 1397 (9th Cir. 1991) (explaining that courts should defer only to "legitimate or viable findings of fact"). Furthermore, even if the juror's question established that the jury did not believe misappropriation of trade secrets resulted in damages, it certainly does not establish that the jury found that UEI suffered no damages whatsoever. The jury might have found that some of the information, though confidential, was not a trade secret, and thus could not consider whether misappropriation of such information resulted in damages to UEI.

III

Because UEI was required to elect between its common-law and AUTSA claims based on an erroneous interpretation of Ariz. Rev. Stat. § 44-407, I would vacate both the judgment entered against UEI and the district court's order denying UEI's motion for a new trial. Since we are already remanding with respect to attorneys' fees, I would invite the district court to reconsider the new trial motion in light of Orca in the first instance. See Kona Enterprises, 229 F.3d at 886-87.

Judge O'Scannlain's dissent in Rudin v. Myles (March 10, 2015)

O'SCANNLAIN, Circuit Judge, dissenting:

I joined Judge Murguia's original opinion for the Court, Rudin v. Myles, 766 F.3d 1161 (9th Cir.2014), and regret that she has changed her view. She was right then, and I believe her original view is still correct. We are all agreed that Rudin is entitled to equitable tolling for the period between November 10, 2004 and August 22, 2007. See Majority at 1056-57. During that time period, Rudin faced the extraordinary circumstance of being abandoned by her lawyer, Dayvid Figler, and diligently pursued her rights. See Holland v. Florida, 560 U.S. 631, 652-54, 130 S.Ct. 2549, 177 L.Ed.2d 130 (2010). However, I cannot join the Court's new conclusion that Rudin is entitled to equitable tolling after August 22, 2007. In my view, the statute of limitations expired on April 11, 2008, over three years before she filed the instant petition.[1] Therefore, I respectfully dissent.

I

Under AEDPA, "equitable tolling is available `only when extraordinary circumstances beyond a prisoner's control make it impossible to file a petition on time and the extraordinary circumstances were the cause of [the prisoner's] untimeliness.'" Sossa v. Diaz, 729 F.3d 1225, 1229 (9th Cir.2013) (emphasis in original) (quoting Bills v. Clark, 628 F.3d 1092, 1097 (9th Cir.2010)). And even if a prisoner can show such extraordinary circumstances, she must also demonstrate that she pursued her rights with "reasonable diligence." Holland, 560 U.S. at 653, 130 S.Ct. 2549. Indeed, "the threshold necessary to trigger equitable tolling [under AEDPA] is very high, lest the exceptions swallow the rule." Bills, 628 F.3d at 1097. With these principles in mind, I turn to the relevant facts of this case.

II

The majority asserts that the events of a state court status conference, which took place on August 22, 2007, "affirmatively misled" Rudin with respect to the deadlines for her federal habeas petition, Majority at 1057-58, and therefore holds that Rudin's failure to file a timely federal petition may be excused. That conclusion, however, cannot be squared with the record or our precedents.

Even if the status conference were an "extraordinary circumstance" for AEDPA purposes, Rudin failed to act with reasonable diligence to protect her rights.[2] On August 22, 2007, Rudin, her attorney, the prosecution, and the state post-conviction court first became aware that Figler had never filed a post-conviction petition in state court. The court informed the parties, however, that due to the "extraordinary circumstances" of Figler's failure to file, it would "extend the one year deadline" to file a state habeas petition.[3] Based on these events, the majority makes the extraordinary leap that Rudin was excused from doing anything with respect to her federal petition for post-conviction relief for well over three years. See Majority at 1057-58.

In fact, however, Rudin was under a duty to pursue her rights diligently. See Holland, 560 U.S. at 653, 130 S.Ct. 2549. As the majority recognizes, as of the August 22, 2007 conference, Rudin and her new attorney, Christopher Oram, were "put on notice of the fact that nothing had been `properly filed' in either state or federal court on her behalf." Majority at 1057-58. With such knowledge, Rudin was not excused from taking action. Rather, she needed to act—with "reasonable diligence"—to preserve her right to challenge her conviction. See Holland, 560 U.S. at 653, 130 S.Ct. 2549. Indeed, the Supreme Court has spelled out precisely what steps Rudin should have taken as soon as she and Oram were aware that there were potential timeliness issues with the state petition.

In Pace v. DiGuglielmo, the Court instructed that if a state prisoner is faced with uncertainty about whether her state post-conviction petition is timely, she should "fil[e] a `protective' petition in federal court and ask[ ] the federal court to stay and abey the federal habeas proceedings until state remedies are exhausted." 544 U.S. at 416, 125 S.Ct. 1807; see also Lakey v. Hickman, 633 F.3d 782, 787 (9th Cir.2011) ("Pace also explicitly advised state prisoners . . . to file a protective federal petition to avoid a possible timeliness bar."). Rudin not only failed to file such a protective petition, she failed to file anything in federal court over the next three years.

The majority's bare assertion that Rudin diligently pursued her rights does not make it so. That "Rudin waited only three months after the Nevada Supreme Court denied her relief—from January 20[, 2011] to April 25, 2011—before filing her federal petition" is completely beside the point. Majority at 1058-59. Indeed, even if the August 22, 2007 conference were an "extraordinary circumstance" that would qualify for equitable tolling purposes, Rudin must still show she acted with reasonable diligence between August 22, 2007 and April 25, 2011. See Pace, 544 U.S. at 418, 125 S.Ct. 1807. The majority fails to demonstrate —nor could it, in light of the record —how Rudin acted with reasonable diligence for the duration of the relevant time period.

The August 22, 2007 conference did not excuse Rudin from acting, but rather armed her with knowledge that should have spurred her to protect her rights. Rudin did not file anything in federal court until April 25, 2011, over three years and eight months later. "Such a delay does not demonstrate the diligence required for application of equitable tolling." White v. Martel, 601 F.3d 882, 885 (9th Cir.2010). Thus, even if the status conference were an extraordinary circumstance, as the majority asserts, Rudin is not entitled to equitable tolling beyond that date.

III

For the foregoing reasons, I would affirm the judgment of the district court.

Notes

[1] As the majority points out, Rudin is not entitled to equitable tolling between July 1, 2004—the date the AEDPA limitations period began to run—and November 10, 2004—the date Figler was appointed. See Majority at 1056. Thus, as of August 23, 2007, Rudin had 232 days to file her federal petition. When she failed to file by April 11, 2008, the statute of limitations expired.

[2] The majority conflates the concepts of statutory tolling and equitable tolling. Here, there is no dispute that Rudin is not entitled to statutory tolling. Thus, the majority's attempt to recast a losing statutory tolling argument in terms of equitable tolling is unpersuasive.

[3] The majority says that such a ruling, "coupled with the state's failure to brief the timeliness question or move to dismiss Rudin's petition, `affirmatively misled' Rudin." Majority at 1057-58 (emphasis added). It is unclear, however, what authority supports the

position that the state's failure to do something can amount to affirmative misleading. The majority cites Sossa but Sossa actually suggests that a state, as an opposing party, has no authority to extend the statutory deadline established by Congress and therefore the state's actions (or, in this case, inactions) should not influence the petitioner. See Sossa, 729 F.3d at 1235 n. 9 (citing Johnson v. Quarterman, 483 F.3d 278 (5th Cir.2007)). In any event, the state's failure to object to the timeliness question applied to the state petition and thus would not affect Rudin's assessment of her federal petition.

For that same reason, the majority is incorrect in relying on Sossa to assert that the events of the August 22, 2007 conference were an extraordinary circumstance under AEDPA. In Sossa, we held that when a prisoner is "affirmatively misled" by a federal magistrate judge regarding AEDPA's deadlines, the petitioner may be entitled to equitable tolling. 729 F.3d at 1232 (citing Pliler v. Ford, 542 U.S. 225, 235, 124 S.Ct. 2441, 159 L.Ed.2d 338 (2004) (O'Connor, J., concurring)). We determined that when a federal magistrate judge granted multiple extensions for the prisoner to file his federal habeas petition, such extensions effectively instructed the prisoner that if he followed the court's schedule, his federal filing would be deemed timely. Id. at 1235.

In contrast, the majority here focuses on a state court's instruction regarding a state habeas petition. Unlike Sossa, neither the parties nor the court discussed the federal petition. Thus, rather than "affirmatively misle[ading]" Rudin in any way as to the AEDPA statute of limitations, if anything the status conference made Rudin aware that her state petition had not been properly filed and notified her that she should file a protective federal petition. See Pace v. DiGuglielmo, 544 U.S. 408, 416, 125 S.Ct. 1807, 161 L.Ed.2d 669 (2005).

Moreover, the majority does not explain what inaccuracy actually affirmatively misled Rudin. Sossa holds that "`[i]n order to show that he was affirmatively misled, [a habeas petitioner] need[s] to point to some inaccuracy in the district court's instructions' to him, not merely to his `misunderstanding of accurate information.'" Sossa, 729 F.3d at 1233 (quoting Ford v. Pliler, 590 F.3d 782, 788 (9th Cir.2009)). Whereas Sossa identified such an inaccuracy, see id., Rudin—and the majority— cannot. Sossa, in short, does not govern here.

Judge O'Scannlain's concurrence and dissent in Harrington v. Scribner (May 7, 2015)

O'SCANNLAIN, Circuit Judge, concurring in part and dissenting in part:

I concur in the Court's analysis of Harrington's deliberate indifference and appointment of counsel claims and join in the opinion and judgment to that extent. I must respectfully dissent, however, from the Court's equal protection analysis and conclude that the relevant jury instruction appropriately incorporated deference to prison officials' unique expertise.

I

In Johnson v. California, 543 U.S. 499, 125 S.Ct. 1141, 160 L.Ed.2d 949 (2005), the Supreme Court overturned a Ninth Circuit decision which had expressly rejected the strict scrutiny standard for equal protection claims against prison officials in favor of what the Supreme Court referred to as the "deferential" Turner standard, which asks whether the regulation was "`reasonably related' to `legitimate penological interests.'" Id. at 504, 510, 125 S.Ct. 1141 (quoting Turner v. Safley, 482 U.S. 78, 89, 107 S.Ct. 2254, 96 L.Ed.2d 64 (1987)). As the Johnson Court emphasized throughout its opinion, the two standards are fundamentally incompatible—the Turner standard requires merely a reasonable relationship to legitimate interests, while strict scrutiny requires "narrow [] tailor[ing]" to a "compelling" interest. Id. at 505, 125 S.Ct. 1141 (emphasis added). Thus, Johnson established that when evaluating equal protection claims against prison officials, strict, rather than intermediate, scrutiny is the applicable test.

Our decision in Norwood v. Vance, 591 F.3d 1062 (9th Cir.2010), does not address—and thereby does not alter—the appropriate tier of scrutiny to apply when analyzing Eighth Amendment or equal protection claims. Rather, we instructed that "[p]rison officials are entitled to deference whether a prisoner challenges excessive force or conditions of confinement." Id. at 1067 (emphasis added).[1]

Here, as the majority acknowledges, the trial court accurately instructed the jury to apply a strict scrutiny analysis to Harrington's equal protection claim. Maj. Op. at ____. The trial court then, as required by Norwood, instructed the jury that prison officials are entitled to deference in their evaluation and adoption of prison policies necessary to maintain prison security and discipline—the very goals identified in Johnson as compelling interests that might justify race-based prison policies. 543 U.S. at 512, 125 S.Ct. 1141.

According to the majority, this second instruction "pulled the rug out from under the narrow tailoring requirement" by suggesting that Harrington's equal protection claim was "competing" with the prison officials' defense on the Eighth Amendment claim. Maj. Op. at 1306-07. Such a conclusion, however, rests on the premise that deference to state officials is necessarily incompatible with strict scrutiny analysis. See Maj. Op. at 1308 ("Although one instruction recites strict scrutiny, the deference instruction introduces a new and different standard."). But the instruction's reference to "competing obligation[s]" simply reflects the reality that prison officials are forced to balance conflicting considerations—such as individual prisoner safety and the safety and security of the prison as a whole—when crafting prison policies.

Indeed, the Supreme Court has squarely rejected the view that deference and strict scrutiny are incompatible, particularly in situations in which a certain group of state officials is likely to have specialized knowledge. For instance, in Cutter v. Wilkinson, 544 U.S. 709, 125 S.Ct. 2113, 161 L.Ed.2d 1020 (2005), the Court analyzed a claim under the Religious Land Use and Institutionalized Persons Act, 42 U.S.C. § 2000cc-1(a)(1)-(2), which prohibits the government from imposing a substantial burden on prisoners' religious exercise unless the burden furthers a "compelling governmental interest" by "the least restrictive means"—the same strict scrutiny test applied in the equal protection context. Id. at 712, 125 S.Ct. 2113. In conducting its strict scrutiny analysis, the Court explained that it was appropriate to defer to prison officials' expertise when engaging in such strict scrutiny analysis. Id. at 722-23, 725 n. 13, 125 S.Ct. 2113.

Similarly, in Grutter v. Bollinger, 539 U.S. 306, 123 S.Ct. 2325, 156 L.Ed.2d 304 (2003), superseded on other grounds by Mich. Const. art I, § 26, the Court deferred to law school officials when evaluating whether the school's race-based admissions policy withstood the scrutiny analysis required for equal protection claims. Id. at 327-28, 123 S.Ct. 2325. Specifically, the Court deferred to the officials' unique ability to determine whether diversity was essential to the law school's educational mission and thereby qualified as a compelling state interest. Id. Thus, the Supreme Court has made clear that strict scrutiny and deference to state officials are by no means incompatible, even in the equal protection context.

The majority accurately quotes the crucial passage from Johnson that rejects the Turner standard of review because "such deference is fundamentally at odds with our equal protection jurisprudence." See Maj. Op. at 1307 (quoting Johnson, 543 U.S. at 506 n. 1, 125 S.Ct. 1141). But the passage must be read in light of the opinion as a whole. In Johnson, the Court rejected a lenient standard of review that fails to put the burden on state officials to articulate a compelling reason for engaging in race-based action—a standard that is necessarily incompatible with strict scrutiny. Viewed in such context, the passage simply identifies the inherent conflict between the Turner standard and the strict scrutiny standard. Here, however, there is no such inherent conflict in applying deference within the strict scrutiny framework.

Rather, such a strict scrutiny standard can, and indeed, under Norwood, must, accommodate a different form of deference—one that acknowledges the expertise of prison officials in crafting policies to promote prison safety and discipline.

II

Because the trial court's jury instructions accurately integrate such deference into the strict scrutiny analysis required by Johnson, I would affirm the jury's verdict rejecting Harrington's equal protection claim and would affirm the judgment in its entirety.

Notes

[1] The majority is correct in its observation that Norwood specifically addressed only Eighth Amendment deliberate indifference claims. Maj. Op. at 1306-07. The clear language of the opinion, however, describes the application of deference in terms of the type of activity challenged, rather than the alleged right violated, and thereby indicates that deference should be afforded any time challenges are made regarding excessive force or confinement conditions, regardless of whether the challenge alleges deliberate indifference or an equal protection violation. As Harrington challenges his conditions of confinement, Norwood, by its terms, applies.

Judge O'Scannlain's concurrence and dissent in Cummings v. Martel (Aug 11, 2015)

O'SCANNLAIN, Circuit Judge, concurring in part, dissenting in part, and concurring in the judgment:

I agree with Judge McKeown that the district court's decision to deny the petition for habeas corpus must be affirmed. Therefore, I concur in her opinion, and in its excellent reasoning—except as to Section I.A. I respectfully dissent from Section I.A., and write separately to explain why the California Supreme Court's conclusion that Deputy LaCasella was not a "key witness" under Turner must be afforded AEDPA deference.

I

I begin by noting that Section I.A. is dicta—whether it is included or excised, the result is the same because, as Section I.B. persuasively explains, Cummings cannot show that the California Supreme Court erred in evaluating Turner's second prong—the "heart of the Turner analysis."

Further, Section I.A. is not only unnecessary to resolution of this case, but is, in my view, incorrect. The California Supreme Court was not objectively unreasonable in concluding that a "key" witness under Turner must be the "principal" witness—not merely one of several witnesses whose testimony is probative of guilt. Furthermore, because its key witness analysis did not contravene Turner, and because its decision was not "so lacking in justification that there was an error well understood and comprehended in existing law beyond any possibility for fairminded disagreement," it is our obligation to defer to the state court's conclusion. White v. Woodall, ____ U.S. ____, 134 S.Ct. 1697, 1702, 188 L.Ed.2d 698 (2014) (internal quotation marks omitted).

A

The majority opinion[1] concludes that LaCasella was a "key prosecution witness" under Turner because he was important—although not necessary—to the state's case. Specifically, the majority notes that: (1) the prosecutor emphasized the importance of LaCasella's testimony to the jury, and (2) no other witness—or more accurately, no other witness of such credibility[2] —provided testimonial support for the government's precise theory of the case.

Although I agree with the majority's conclusion that LaCasella's testimony was important, I disagree with its conclusion that the California state court was thus compelled to treat LaCasella as a "key" witness under Turner, and with any resulting implications. The majority argues that a "key" witness is any witness who testifies to an important issue, beyond "some uncontroverted or merely formal aspect of the case for the prosecution," even when "other evidence [and testimony] also supports the verdict." But Turner does not establish that such "important" and "key" witnesses are the same.

While Turner "emphasized" that the bailiff-witnesses in that case were the "key witnesses" whose testimony "must inevitably have determined whether Wayne Turner was to be sent to his death," 379 U.S. at 473, 85 S.Ct. 546, this statement does not "clearly establish" that any important witness whose testimony is probative of guilt is a "key witness." If anything, Turner suggests that a "key" witness is one whose testimony is absolutely necessary to establish guilt, as was the case with the two bailiffs in Turner. See 379 U.S. at 474, 85 S.Ct. 546 (explaining that "Turner's fate depended upon how much confidence the jury placed in these two witnesses"). By contrast, as the majority concedes, LaCasella was only one of several witnesses who testified to Cummings's guilt.

Thus, the California Supreme Court's conclusion that LaCasella "was not the principal or key prosecution witness," Cummings, 4 Cal.4th at 1290, 18 Cal. Rptr.2d 796, 850 P.2d 1, is not "objectively unreasonable" and "so lacking in justification that there was an error well understood and comprehended in existing law beyond any possibility for fairminded disagreement." White, 134 S.Ct. at 1702.

II

I agree with Judge McKeown that the denial of Cummings's petition must be affirmed. However, because the California Supreme Court was not "objectively unreasonable" in its interpretation of the minimal Supreme Court guidance on the Turner "key" and "principal" witness issue, and, although I concur in the rest of the opinion, I must respectfully dissent from Section I.A.

Notes

[1] Because Chief Judge Thomas agrees with Section I.A., I refer to it as part of the "majority opinion."

[2] As the majority notes, LaCasella's testimony was not the only testimony supporting the prosecution's "first-shot" theory—"at least one eyewitness testified that the person in the back seat fired the first shot."

Judge O'Scannlain's dissent in Burton v. Davis (March 10, 2016)

O'SCANNLAIN, Circuit Judge, dissenting:

The Court affirms the grant of a petition for writ of habeas corpus in this death penalty case by holding that the California courts did not determine — in a full, fair, and adequate hearing — the merits of Andre Burton's request for self-representation during his murder trial. I respectfully disagree because I am not persuaded that the California Supreme Court decision was contrary to the Constitution and laws of the United States. Rather, under the version of 28 U.S.C. § 2254 applicable before the enactment of the Antiterrorism and Effective Death Penalty Act of 1996 ("AEDPA"), habeas corpus should have been denied.

I

A

On February 25, 1983, during a robbery, Burton shot Anwar Khwaja in the forehead and in the eye, then shot Khwaja's mother, fatally, in the chest. California v. Burton, 48 Cal.3d 843, 258 Cal.Rptr. 184, 771 P.2d 1270, 1274 (1989). Burton was "smiling or laughing contentedly" while committing these crimes and "chuckled" while escaping. Id.

Beginning on August 10, 1983, the day trial was set to start, Burton made four requests to represent himself pursuant to Faretta v. California, 422 U.S. 806, 95 S.Ct. 2525, 45 L.Ed.2d 562 (1975).[1] See In re Burton, 40 Cal.4th 205, 52 Cal.Rptr.3d 86, 147 P.3d 1014, 1024-25 (2006). The trial court denied each of those four Faretta requests as untimely. See id. The jury convicted Burton of murder and three counts of robbery, and the penalty was fixed at death. Id. at 1017.

After the California Supreme Court affirmed Burton's convictions and death sentence, Burton, 258 Cal.Rptr. 184, 771 P.2d at 1291, Burton filed state and federal habeas petitions. In state habeas proceedings, Burton alleged that he was denied the right to present a guilt-phase defense under California v. Frierson, 39 Cal.3d 803, 218 Cal.Rptr. 73, 705 P.2d 396 (1985).[2] To evaluate Burton's Frierson claim, the California Supreme Court appointed a referee to hear evidence and to make findings of fact in response to various questions, including: "Did [Burton's attorney, Ronald Slick] have reason to believe that petitioner's in court requests to represent himself were made for the purpose of delaying trial, rather than dissatisfaction with Slick's trial strategy?" Burton, 52 Cal. Rptr.3d 86, 147 P.3d at 1018.

The referee, a superior court judge appointed for this task, heard testimony from 15 witnesses over 14 court days. See id. 52 Cal.Rptr.3d 86, 147 P.3d at 1016, 1019. As part of his findings of fact, the referee concluded that Burton "tried to delay the [trial] by seeking to represent himself." In 2006, the California Supreme Court reviewed the referee's report, accepted the referee's factual finding that Burton's Faretta motions "reflected a dissatisfaction with Slick's failure to delay the trial," and denied habeas relief. Id. 52 Cal.Rptr.3d 86, 147 P.3d at 1026, 1030.

In federal habeas proceedings, the district court reviewed the state court record de novo and granted the writ, holding, contrary to the California Supreme Court, that Burton's request to represent himself was not made for the purpose of delay.

B

Whether a petitioner's request to exercise his right under Faretta to represent himself at trial is timely is controlled by Fritz v. Spalding, 682 F.2d 782 (9th Cir. 1982). In Fritz, we held that "a motion to proceed pro se is timely if made before the jury is empaneled, unless it is shown to be a tactic to secure delay." Id. at 784.[3]

As the majority observed, the district court erred when it treated the determination of Burton's purpose in seeking to represent himself as a mixed question of law and fact. Maj. Op. at 1148-49. Burton's purpose is simply a question of fact, and the district court owed deference to the state court determination of fact unless an exception enumerated in § 2254 applies. But then the majority errs when it upholds de novo review based on its conclusion that the California Supreme Court did not resolve the merits of the factual question, see § 2254(d)(1), and that Burton was therefore denied a full, fair, and adequate state court hearing, see § 2254(d)(2), (6).[4] Maj. Op. at 1148-49.

Applying § 2254(d)(1), the majority essentially concludes that the state courts did not make findings of fact regarding Burton's purpose because the California Supreme Court asked the referee to determine Slick's belief about Burton's purpose rather than asking about Burton's purpose directly. Recognizing that the California Supreme Court did make some potentially relevant findings, the majority seeks to explain away those findings by arguing that they must be considered "in context." The majority thus concludes that the state supreme court did not give a Faretta answer because it asked a Frierson question.

Applying § 2254(d)(2), (6), the majority concludes that the Frierson proceedings were inadequate to resolve Burton's Faretta claim fully and fairly because the state courts misallocated the burden of proof and because they failed to consider key aspects of the record and to apply the proper legal inquiry.

I respectfully disagree with the majority's application of these three provisions.

II

A

Contrary to the majority's opinion, the California courts did indeed determine the merits of Burton's purpose in seeking to represent himself; therefore, § 2254(d)(1) provides no basis for withholding deference. Rather than focus on the facts determined by the referee and accepted by the California Supreme Court, the majority mistakenly focuses on the context in which those facts were found.

The majority's analysis misses the trees for the forest.

1

What did the California Supreme Court actually hold with respect to the factual findings made in Burton's state habeas proceedings? There, Burton invoked "statements he made at trial in the course of his four motions for self-representation." In re Burton, 40 Cal.4th 205, 52 Cal.Rptr.3d 86, 147 P.3d 1014, 1024 (2006). In response to Burton's arguments, the court did not solely determine counsel Slick's impression of Burton's purpose in invoking Faretta; it also directly determined Burton's actual purpose.

The California Supreme Court addressed both Slick's impression and Burton's actual purpose in three key paragraphs. The court first recognized that "the referee found [that] Burton invoked and continued to invoke Faretta solely in order to delay the trial." Id. 52 Cal. Rptr.3d 86, 147 P.3d at 1026. It then discussed Slick's testimony regarding his belief that Burton's purpose was delay:

According to Slick, Burton consistently said on multiple occasions that he was not ready to go to trial, but never offered Slick a reason for a delay. In Slick's experience, it is not unusual for defendants to prefer to delay trial and to give the appearance of being able to "wait it out," and he believed that Burton, who was facing a capital trial, was such a defendant. Burton thus errs in contending that "the only reasonable inference to be drawn" from his Faretta motions is that he "wanted to defend against the state's case."

Id. Thus, the first sentence of this paragraph indicates that the referee found Burton invoked Faretta solely in order to delay trial, while the remaining sentences address Slick's impression.

In the second paragraph, the California Supreme Court discusses other evidence that "corroborates" Slick's assessment that Burton's purpose was delay:

Slick's assessment of Burton's motivation was corroborated by other evidence at the hearing. Kleinbauer testified that Burton had told her he was not ready to go to trial and that he was dissatisfied with Slick because "the trial seemed to be ... rushing forward." As a result, Kleinbauer had consulted with another lawyer, Jeffrey Brodey, who had recommended that Burton invoke his right to self-representation if he was not ready for trial and that he not settle for cocounsel status. Tellingly, Kleinbauer's notes of this conversation nowhere mention Burton's alleged desire to present a defense but say instead "tell Ron he's not ready for trial. July 25 too soon — next year some time." Kleinbauer further stated in a 1993 declaration that she had instructed Burton to tell Slick "that he was not ready for trial, and that the trial should take place next year some time, after all the investigation was done." Kleinbauer herself also felt the case "went to trial maybe sooner than it should have."

Id. Of particular note, I can think of no better example of "a tactic to secure delay" than an attorney's recommendation that a criminal defendant in a capital murder case "invoke his right to self-representation if he was not ready for trial and that he not settle for cocounsel status." While this paragraph may go no further than determining that Slick's assessment of Burton's purpose was corroborated, it does so by pointing to evidence suggesting that Slick's assessment was correct, i.e., that Burton's actual purpose was delay.

Even if these first two paragraphs address Slick's impression of Burton's purpose, the third paragraph very clearly adopts factual findings about Burton's actual purpose:

Burton's conduct and statements further confirmed his interest in delay. Burton engaged in "game playing" with Dr. Michael Maloney, who had been retained by Slick to conduct a psychological evaluation of Burton. This lack of cooperation is fully consistent with a defendant who was interested in delay for delay's sake — a conclusion additionally supported by Burton's observation in his declaration in support of his motion for new trial that "[i]n my experience in the Los Angeles County Jail, persons with death penalty cases all tended to have their cases continued for longer periods of time." Finally, we note that even the trial court seemed aware of Burton's motivation, advising him during the second Faretta motion hearing "that the trial is going to go ahead. [¶] I know you don't like the idea, but that's the idea." We therefore accept the referee's finding that Burton's Faretta motions reflected a dissatisfaction with Slick's failure to delay the trial, not a dissatisfaction with Slick's trial strategy.

Id. (alteration in original).

In sum, the California Supreme Court first recognized that "the referee found [that] Burton invoked and continued to invoke Faretta solely in order to delay the trial." Id. After discussing Slick's impression of Burton's purpose, the state supreme court moved beyond Slick's impression to the actual purpose, and it determined that "Burton's conduct and statements further confirmed his interest in delay." Id. As support for that determination, it reasoned that the "conclusion" that Burton was "a defendant who was interested in delay for delay's sake" was "supported by Burton's observation in his declaration in support of his motion for new trial" and was "fully consistent with" Burton's engaging in "game playing" with a psychologist hired by Slick to evaluate Burton. Id. Ultimately, the California Supreme Court "accept[ed] the referee's finding that Burton's Faretta motions reflected a dissatisfaction with Slick's failure to delay the trial, not a dissatisfaction with Slick's trial strategy." Id.

The referee's factual findings, as accepted by the state supreme court, squarely address the merits of Burton's purpose in invoking Faretta, and they deserve deference. If we take the California Supreme Court at face value, we are left with the clear determination that Burton's purpose in making his motion was to delay trial.

2

The majority simply ignores the California Supreme Court's accepted factual findings. Nowhere does it acknowledge the California Supreme Court's recognition that "the referee found [that] Burton invoked and continued to invoke Faretta solely in order to delay the trial." Id. Nor does it ever grapple with the finding that "Burton's conduct and statements further confirmed his interest in delay." Id.

To the extent that it does engage with the actual language of the California Supreme Court opinion, the majority regrettably misconstrues it. For example, the majority argues that the state court's statements about Burton's "game playing" and his observation about the typical length of continuances for death penalty cases "must be read in context." Maj. Op. at 1150. Those statements were made in a paragraph that begins with "Burton's conduct and statements further confirmed his interest in delay" and concludes with "We therefore accept the referee's finding that Burton's Faretta motions reflected a dissatisfaction with Slick's failure to delay the trial, not a dissatisfaction with Slick's trial strategy." Burton, 52 Cal.Rptr.3d 86, 147 P.3d at 1026. In context, the state supreme court was clearly identifying evidence that supported these two propositions, which are directly concerned with Burton's actual purpose.

Despite its exhortation, the majority prefers to read the statements completely out of context. The majority claims that the state court "was identifying evidence that `corroborated' `Slick's assessment of Burton's motivation,' which arguably refuted Burton's argument that `the only reasonable inference to be drawn from his Faretta motions [wa]s that he wanted to defend against the state's case.'" Maj. Op. at 1150-51. Yet these propositions — that "Slick's assessment of Burton's motivation was corroborated" and that Burton erred "in contending that `the only reasonable inference to be drawn' from his Faretta motions [was] that he `wanted to defend against the state's case'" — were contained in completely separate paragraphs from the statements about Burton's "game playing" and his observation about the typical length of continuances. See Burton, 52 Cal.Rptr.3d 86, 147 P.3d at 1026. When making the statements about "game playing" and Burton's observation, the California Supreme Court had clearly moved from discussing Slick's impression to discussing Burton's actual purpose.

The majority also ignores another important contextual clue that the California Supreme Court did directly address Burton's purpose: the issue of his actual purpose was a disputed factual question raised by the Frierson claim before the California Supreme Court appointed the referee. Specifically, Burton first placed his actual purpose at issue when he claimed in his state habeas petition that he "had sought on four occasions during the trial to discharge his attorney and represent himself because of Attorney Slick's deficiencies." Id. 52 Cal.Rptr.3d 86, 147 P.3d at 1017. The State responded that "the true reason Burton had asked the trial court four times to be allowed to represent himself `was to obtain a continuance to avoid going to trial, not because he wanted further investigation conducted,'" id. 52 Cal. Rptr.3d 86, 147 P.3d at 1017-18, which Burton denied in reply, id. 52 Cal.Rptr.3d 86, 147 P.3d at 1018. This factual dispute existed before the reference hearing, so it is not surprising that the referee and the California Supreme Court wound up addressing Burton's true purpose in seeking to represent himself.

Thus, the majority's attempt to explain away the California Supreme Court's findings concerning Burton's purpose — not merely Slick's impression of such purpose — by arguing they must be read "in context," falls flat. It is clear that the California Supreme Court determined Burton's purpose in invoking Faretta, and that purpose was delay for delay's sake.

B

And the California courts indeed afforded Burton a full, fair, and adequate hearing in determining his purpose in seeking self-representation.

1

Recall that Burton's motivation for invoking Faretta was a contested factual issue before the reference hearing, and Burton submitted evidence regarding that issue. In addition, Burton was aware that the California Supreme Court asked the referee to determine a closely related question: whether Slick had reason to believe that Burton invoked Faretta in order to delay trial. Of course, if Burton's actual purpose was delay, then that fact makes it much more probable that Slick had reason to believe that Burton's purpose was delay. Thus, it should have been no surprise when the California courts found a subsidiary fact — that Burton's actual purpose was delay — as support for another finding of fact — that Slick had reason to believe Burton's actual purpose was delay. Burton was not deprived of a full, fair, and adequate hearing merely because the California Supreme Court declined to specify every question that might possibly be answered in the reference hearing.

2

None of the majority's reasons are persuasive.

First, the state courts did not deprive Burton of a full, fair, and adequate hearing by misallocating the burden of proof. We have never held that the burden of proof in a Fritz inquiry is on the state or that the state must show that the evidence is not "consistent" with any other purpose than delay. Nor have we held that a misplaced burden "is reason alone not to apply the presumption of correctness" and that it would be "manifestly unfair" to bind Burton to an adverse factual determination made in proceedings in which he bore the burden of proof. Maj. Op. at 1153-54.

Moreover, with respect to Burton's purpose in seeking to represent himself, there is no indication that the burden of proof played any role in the state habeas proceedings or that the State received the benefit of the doubt. In those proceedings, nowhere did the referee or the California Supreme Court say that Burton failed to carry his burden with respect to his Faretta motions. The state courts did not deprive Burton of a full, fair, and adequate hearing on his motivation for invoking Faretta by weighing the evidence and deciding against him.

3

Nor did the state courts deprive Burton of a full, fair, and adequate hearing by failing to apply the proper legal test or to consider key parts of the record. Ultimately, these asserted errors are not errors at all. In Early v. Packer, 537 U.S. 3, 123 S.Ct. 362, 154 L.Ed.2d 263 (2002) (per curiam), a California appellate court upheld the trial court's giving a charge to a deadlocked jury under a state-law rule that differed from the federal rule. Id. at 6-7, 123 S.Ct. 362. We had concluded that the California appellate court erred in failing to apply a totality of the circumstances test and to consider key pieces of evidence:

[T]he Ninth Circuit charged that the Court of Appeal "failed to apply the totality of the circumstances test as required by Lowenfield." That was so, the Ninth Circuit concluded, because it "simply mentioned three particular incidents in its analysis," "failed to consider" other "critical facts," and "failed to consider the cumulative impact" of all the significant facts, one of which it "[did] not even mention in its analysis."

Id. at 8-9, 123 S.Ct. 362 (internal alterations and citation omitted). The Supreme Court noted that the state court had focused on three particular incidents, but set forth many facts and circumstances beyond those three incidents. Id. at 9, 123 S.Ct. 362. The Court rejected our conclusion that the state court failed to apply the totality of the circumstances test by not considering certain facts:

The contention that the California court "failed to consider" facts and circumstances that it had taken the trouble to recite strains credulity. The Ninth Circuit may be of the view that the Court of Appeal did not give certain facts and circumstances adequate weight (and hence adequate discussion); but to say that it did not consider them is an exaggeration. There is, moreover, nothing to support the Ninth Circuit's claim that the Court of Appeal did not consider the "cumulative impact" of all the recorded events. Compliance with Lowenfield... does not demand a formulary statement that the trial court's actions and inactions were noncoercive "individually and cumulatively." It suffices that that was the fair import of the Court of Appeal's opinion.

Id.[5]

Here, the majority asserts that the California Supreme Court failed to apply a "totality of the circumstances" test. Maj. Op. at 1154. Like in Early, the state court's lack of a formulary statement that it was applying the Fritz factors does not render the determination of facts improper if the fair import of the state court's decision is that it did consider the relevant factors. Moreover, the majority asserts that the California Supreme Court failed to consider various pieces of evidence that it expressly recited. Maj. Op. at 1157-58. Similar to Early, the state court's recitation of the facts shows that it did consider them.

Therefore, the state-court hearing was full, fair, and adequate, and the presumption of correctness should apply.[6]

III

For the foregoing reasons, I respectfully dissent.

Notes

[1] Faretta established that "a defendant in a state criminal trial has a constitutional right to proceed without counsel when he voluntarily and intelligently elects to do so." 422 U.S. at 807, 95 S.Ct. 2525. Subsequently, both the Ninth Circuit and the California Supreme Court held that the invocation of that right must be timely. See Maxwell v. Sumner, 673 F.2d 1031, 1036 (9th Cir.1982); California v. Windham, 19 Cal.3d 121, 137 Cal.Rptr. 8, 560 P.2d 1187, 1191 (1977).

[2] Frierson established that, "[g]iven the magnitude of the consequences that flowed from the decision whether or not to present any defense at the guilt/special circumstance phase, ... counsel could [not] properly refuse to honor defendant's clearly expressed desire to present a defense at that stage." Frierson, 218 Cal.Rptr. 73, 705 P.2d at 403 & n. 4 (relying in part on Faretta).

[3] The majority concludes that any pro se representation request is timely, regardless of whether the defendant had a purpose of delay, as long as some other permissible purpose for the defendant's motion can be found. It claims that Fritz "asks whether the defendant's actual and sole purpose was to delay." Maj. Op. at 1152. But Fritz says nothing about the defendant's "sole" purpose. Instead, Fritz employs several formulations to describe the relevant inquiry: a motion is timely unless it is "a tactic to secure delay," "unless it was made for the purpose of delay," or "absent an affirmative showing of purpose to secure delay." 682 F.2d at 784. Clearly, delay must be a purpose of a Faretta motion to make it untimely, but Fritz does not require delay to be the "sole" purpose.

[4] Pre-AEDPA 28 U.S.C. § 2254(d) (1994) provided that, in federal habeas proceedings initiated by a state prisoner,

[A] determination after a hearing on the merits of a factual issue, made by a State court of competent jurisdiction in a proceeding to which the applicant for the writ and the State or an officer or agent thereof were parties, evidenced by a written finding, written opinion, or other reliable and adequate written indicia, shall be presumed to be correct, unless the applicant shall establish or it shall otherwise appear, or the respondent shall admit —

(1) that the merits of the factual dispute were not resolved in the State court

hearing;

(2) that the factfinding procedure employed by the State court was not adequate to afford a full and fair hearing;

. . .

(6) that the applicant did not receive a full, fair, and adequate hearing in the State court proceeding;....

[T]he burden shall rest upon the applicant to establish by convincing evidence that the factual determination by the State court was erroneous.

[5] Although Early is admittedly a case governed by AEDPA, the Court made no indication that this part of its analysis was impacted in any way by AEDPA's amendments. Consequently, the principles can be applied to this pre-AEDPA case.

[6] Given the majority's conclusion that the state courts did not resolve the factual dispute on the merits and that Burton was denied a full, fair, and adequate state court hearing, the majority should not be affirming but rather vacating and remanding for an evidentiary hearing in the district court. Under pre-AEDPA habeas law:

An evidentiary hearing in federal habeas proceedings is required (1) where the merits of a factual dispute were not resolved in state hearings ... (3) the state's fact-finding procedure was not adequate to afford a full and fair hearing; ... (5) material facts were not adequately developed at the state court hearing, for which there is no cause or prejudice; or (6) for any reason it appears that the state trier of fact did not afford the applicant a full and fair hearing on the facts.

Rhoades v. Henry, 638 F.3d 1027, 1041 n. 13 (9th Cir.2011) (citing Townsend v. Sain, 372 U.S. 293, 312-13, 83 S.Ct. 745, 9 L.Ed.2d 770 (1963); Keeney v. Tamayo-Reyes, 504 U.S. 1, 8-11, 112 S.Ct. 1715, 118 L.Ed.2d 318, (1992) (modifying Townsend's fifth factor)); see also Ford v. Wainwright, 477 U.S. 399, 410-11, 106 S.Ct. 2595, 91 L.Ed.2d 335 (1986). The Townsend criteria are the same as the exceptions in §§ 2254(d)(1), (2), (3), (6). Brewer v. Williams, 430 U.S. 387, 395, 97 S.Ct. 1232, 51 L.Ed.2d 424 (1977). Therefore, the majority's conclusion that the presumption of correctness does not apply because of the exceptions in subsections (1), (2), and (6) also compels the conclusion that an evidentiary hearing is required.

An evidentiary hearing is especially appropriate when the federal district court rejects the state court's key credibility determinations. "[Section] 2254(d) gives federal habeas courts no license to redetermine credibility of witnesses whose demeanor has been observed by the state trial court, but not by them." Marshall v. Lonberger, 459 U.S. 422, 434, 103 S.Ct. 843, 74 L.Ed.2d 646 (1983). Here, the district court, on the basis of a cold documentary record, rejected the California Supreme Court's acceptance of the referee's credibility determinations, which were based on live observation of the witnesses' demeanors.

The "reexamination of state convictions that the modern writ entails implicates values of finality and comity that are important to federalism and our system of criminal justice." Gage v. Chappell, 793 F.3d 1159, 1167 (9th Cir.2015) (citing Coleman v.

Thompson, 501 U.S. 722, 731, 111 S.Ct. 2546, 115 L.Ed.2d 640 (1991); McCleskey v. Zant, 499 U.S. 467, 491, 111 S.Ct. 1454, 113 L.Ed.2d 517 (1991); Kuhlmann v. Wilson, 477 U.S. 436, 453 n. 16, 106 S.Ct. 2616, 91 L.Ed.2d 364 (1986)). Given these important concerns and the rejection of several key state-court credibility determinations, shouldn't the district court at least observe live witnesses itself before forcing the state to retry a 32-year-old capital murder case?

Judge O'Scannlain's concurrence and dissent in Calloway v. Hayward (June 6, 2016)

O'SCANNLAIN, Circuit Judge, concurring in part and dissenting in part.

My colleagues would not have dismissed Calloway's lawsuit had either of them been the judge presiding over it. Nor would I have done so—perhaps. But my colleagues are wrong to vacate the district court's dismissal order simply because we might have behaved differently. Indeed, this case is about how much discretion our district courts have to manage their dockets and to deal with uncooperative litigants. And those are topics of large importance. Yet my colleagues are unwilling to recognize the generous leeway we have always given district courts to make the difficult decisions that enable the orderly administration of justice. With regret, I cannot join such a disposition.

I

The Supreme Court long ago recognized that district courts have "inherent power" to dismiss a plaintiff's action as a sanction if he fails to prosecute his case, and that such power is one "of ancient origin" that is "necessary in order to prevent undue delays in the disposition of pending cases and to avoid congestion in the calendars of the District Courts." Link v. Wabash R. Co., 370 U.S. 626, 629-30 (1962). We review such dismissals "for an abuse of discretion," McKeever v. Block, 932 F.2d 795, 797 (9th Cir. 1991), and we may not overturn one unless "we have a definite and firm conviction that it was clearly outside the acceptable range of sanctions," Allen v. Bayer Corp. (In re PPA), 460 F.3d 1217, 1226 (9th Cir. 2006) (quoting Malone v. U.S. Postal Serv., 833 F.2d 128, 130 (9th Cir. 1987)).

In this case, I agree with the majority that the district court was within its discretion to deny Calloway's request for a continuance. The question then becomes whether the district court also had discretion to dismiss Calloway's case in light of his subsequent, repeated declarations that he could not and would not proceed to trial. I believe the district court did have such discretion.

A

To decide whether a district court acted within the bounds of its discretion, courts in our circuit typically apply a five-factor balancing test. We consider: "(1) the public's interest in expeditious resolution of litigation; (2) the court's need to manage its docket; (3) the risk of prejudice to defendants/respondents; (4) the availability of less drastic alternatives; and (5) the public policy favoring disposition of cases on their merits."

Pagtalunan v. Galaza, 291 F.3d 639, 642 (9th Cir. 2002).[1]

i

The first factor is easily met by the court's action, as Calloway and the majority both concede.

ii

Likewise for the second factor, as again Calloway and the majority both concede.

iii

The third factor presents a closer call. It asks to what extent the plaintiff's conduct risked prejudicing the other side's ability to mount a defense.

Fleshing out this factor, we have held that prejudice to the defendants is inextricably bound up with delay caused by the plaintiff. Ash v. Cvetkov, 739 F.2d 493, 496 (9th Cir. 1984); Nealey v. Transportacion Maritima Mexicana, S. A., 662 F.2d 1275, 1280 (9th Cir. 1980). And, crucially, it is well understood that district courts have discretion to consider the aggregate delay caused by a plaintiff over the course of the entire litigation; the district court need not restrict its analysis to the event immediately preceding the dismissal order. See, e.g., Link, 370 U.S. at 633 ("[I]t could reasonably be inferred from his absence, as well as from the drawn-out history of the litigation, that petitioner had been deliberately proceeding in dilatory fashion." (emphasis added)); Franklin v. Murphy, 745 F.2d 1221, 1234 (9th Cir. 1984) (explaining that "[t]he relevant time period in determining failure to prosecute . . . is the period of delay caused by the plaintiff"). And "the period of delay" need not be "particularly lengthy" to justify the district court's exercise of discretion in dismissing for failure to prosecute. Ash, 739 F.2d at 496; see also Moffitt v. Ill. State Bd. of Educ., 236 F.3d 868, 873 (7th Cir. 2001) (affirming dismissal despite "agree[ing] with [plaintiff] that there is no real record of delay or contumacious behavior on her part in this case").

In this case, Calloway caused significant delay during the five-plus years between the day he filed his complaint in 2008 and the day the district court dismissed it in 2014. After filing this lawsuit, he waited nearly two and half years before serving the defendants, and in the following years he requested at least eight extensions of time for a variety of reasons, on top of numerous failed attempts to conduct discovery and botched responses to court orders. In light of our precedents, it was not an abuse of discretion for the district court to conclude that Calloway had caused meaningful delay and hence a risk of prejudice to Hayward and Oaks.

iv

The fourth factor instructs the district court to consider the availability of less drastic alternatives. The district court did so, in compliance with our precedents, because the court repeatedly warned Calloway that he faced the possibility of dismissal before the court actually ordered it. In re PPA, 460 F.3d at 1229 (stating district court satisfies the fourth factor when it "warn[s] the plaintiff of the possibility of dismissal before actually ordering dismissal").

v

Finally, the fifth factor—the public policy favoring disposition of suits on their merits—favors Calloway, but I consider its weight to be somewhat diminished given that Calloway's own deliberate conduct triggered the district court's decision to dismiss his case.

B

The five traditional factors give the district court's dismissal order enough support to withstand scrutiny on appeal. And such conclusion is reinforced by the fact that the decision under review is largely consistent with precedent from our own court and elsewhere. As a leading treatise summarizes, there are many cases illustrating that "[a]n action may be dismissed . . . if the plaintiff, without offering some explanation that is satisfactory to the court, is not ready to present his or her case at trial or if the plaintiff refuses to proceed at the trial." 9 Charles Alan Wright et al., Fed. Prac. & Proc. § 2370 (3d ed. 2013). For example, in Kung v. FOM Investment Corp., 563 F.2d 1316, 1318 (9th Cir. 1977), we affirmed a dismissal for failure to prosecute where the plaintiff "flagrantly ignored" the district court's warning "that dismissal would result if [the plaintiff] was not ready for the pre-trial conference at the end of the last continuance." See also Moffitt, 236 F.3d 873 (affirming dismissal based merely on "the plaintiff's unwillingness to proceed on the date scheduled for trial, as opposed to the more typical failure to comply with her discovery obligations on time, or to meet some other pre-trial deadline"); Owen v. Wangerin, 985 F.2d 312, 317 (7th Cir. 1993) (explaining that cases are typically dismissed for failure to prosecute "when the plaintiff is not ready for trial or fails to appear"). Notably, Moffitt was not "a case in which sanctions less severe than dismissal had already proven ineffective as a means of preventing further noncompliance with the court's orders," nor had the court in that case "expressly warned Moffitt that it would dismiss the case for want of prosecution if she was not prepared to go forward on the scheduled trial date." Moffitt, 236 F.3d at 873.

In the present case, the district court made clear to Calloway that it would not grant him any more continuances, and warned him several times that it would dismiss his case if he continued to disavow any intention of proceeding to trial. Yet that is what he did. The district court did not abuse its discretion by following through on its warning. And while it is true that at the end of their colloquy Calloway tried to backtrack by claiming he did intend to go to trial after all, his overall course of conduct so undermined his credibility that the district court was within its discretion to enter the dismissal order.

II

The majority sees things differently. I respectfully suggest that my colleagues take an unduly cramped view of the district court's authority to sanction litigants like Calloway, and they arrive at such view only because they have overlooked several of the important lessons our precedents illustrate.

First, the majority insists that Calloway's "representations" at the March 21, 2014 hearing "did not cause an unreasonable delay in proceedings." That may be true, but as explained above, district courts are free to consider the aggregate delay a plaintiff has caused during the entire course of the litigation. My colleagues are wrong to fasten blinders on the district court; its field of vision need not be restricted to Calloway's behavior at the hearing that spurred his suit's dismissal.

My colleagues repeat the same error when they attempt to explain why Calloway's conduct posed no risk of prejudice to Hayward and Oaks. Again the majority trains its attention on Calloway's behavior on the specific date his case was dismissed, thereby excluding from view the considerable delay Calloway had caused during the nearly six years leading up to the pretrial hearing in March of 2014. As I have explained, such myopia is at odds with our precedents (and with common sense). Likewise, the majority is wrong to pooh-pooh the defendants' fear of prejudice, which, the majority claims, is "base[d] . . . solely on the continuing pendency of the case up to that point in time." What my colleagues seem to forget is that Calloway's dilatory tactics were much of the reason why the case had been pending for so long up to that point.

Finally, my colleagues simply misread the record when they say that the district court never gave Calloway any warning before dismissing his case. To the contrary, several times the district court warned Calloway (over his repeated interruptions) that if he persisted in his unwillingness to proceed to trial, his case would be dismissed. The district court did enough, under our precedents, to demonstrate that it considered alternatives.

III

I cannot say with confidence that I would have dismissed Calloway's suit if I were presiding, nor can I say that the district court abused its discretion in doing so. I regret that my colleagues have given short shrift to the district court's elemental, and quite essential, power to control its own docket in the face of uncooperative litigants. Such power is vital to the system's ability to deliver justice in a timely and careful manner—not only to Calloway, Hayward, and Oaks—but also to all those parties whose disputes were not before the court on the day of Calloway's pretrial hearing.

I therefore respectfully dissent from the majority's decision to vacate the district court's dismissal order.

Notes

[1] Judge N.R. Smith would reverse the district court because it failed to identify the five factors that govern dismissals for failure to prosecute. But we have already held that a district court's failure to identify such factors is not reversible error. Ash v. Cvetkov, 739 F.2d 493, 496 (9th Cir. 1984) ("The district court gave no indication, either orally or in writing, that it considered the essential factors [governing dismissal for failure to prosecute]. No findings of fact or conclusions of law were prepared. Such findings, although they would obviously be very helpful on review, are not required. When confronted with this situation we review the record independently in determining whether the district court abused its discretion." (internal citations omitted)).

Judge O'Scannlain's dissent in Cuero v. Cate (June 30, 2016) [Notes and

appendices omitted]

O'SCANNLAIN, Circuit Judge, dissenting:

Today, the Court erroneously orders federal habeas relief to a state prisoner on the basis of a non-existent plea agreement and irrelevant state contract law. Because the decision of the California Court of Appeal affirming Cuero's conviction was neither contrary to, nor an unreasonable application of, Supreme Court precedent, the district court's denial of the writ of habeas corpus should have been affirmed.

I respectfully dissent.

I

A

It is appropriate to recapitulate the relevant facts. While driving under the influence of methamphetamine, Michael Daniel Cuero veered off the road and crashed his car into Jeffrey Feldman, another driver who was standing outside his pickup truck on the side of the road. Feldman sustained severe injuries including a ruptured spleen, brain damage, and facial disfigurement. Cuero, a convicted felon prohibited from possessing a firearm, had a loaded firearm with him.

Over the next two weeks, the State filed a complaint and then an amended complaint against Cuero. The amended complaint charged two felonies (driving under the influence and possession of a firearm by a felon) and one misdemeanor (being under the influence of a controlled substance). The State alleged that Cuero had served four prior prison terms and that one of Cuero's prior convictions constituted a "strike" under California's "three strikes law." See Cal. Penal Code § 667(b)-(i).[1] Cuero initially pleaded "not guilty" to the charges in the amended complaint.

On December 8, 2005, Cuero appeared before the superior court to change his plea to guilty. He signed a change of plea form, which stated that he had not been induced to enter the plea by any promises of any kind and that he had no deals with the State.[2] After the court had accepted Cuero's plea on both felonies and his admissions to the "prison priors" and prior strike, the State moved to dismiss the misdemeanor count, and the court granted the motion. A sentencing hearing was then scheduled.

B

According to the State, during the preparation of the sentencing memorandum for the superior court, the probation officer discovered that one of Cuero's prior convictions constituted a strike in addition to the single strike alleged in the first amended complaint.[3] Prior to the scheduled sentencing hearing, the State moved under California Penal Code § 969.5(a) further to amend its complaint again to add the allegation of the second strike. Cuero opposed the motion. On February 2, 2006, the superior court granted the motion with the condition that Cuero would be permitted to withdraw his guilty plea, thus restoring all of his constitutional rights. The court then accepted for filing the second amended complaint alleging the additional strike.

On March 27, 2006, Cuero moved to withdraw his guilty plea entered on

December 8, 2005. The court granted the motion and set aside that plea. As part of a "negotiated guilty plea," the State filed a third amended complaint omitting the felon-in-possession charge, and Cuero pleaded guilty to the charge of driving under the influence and admitted the two prior strikes. On April 20, 2006, the court sentenced Cuero to a term of 25 years to life pursuant to the plea agreement and pronounced judgment.

C

Cuero appealed to the California Court of Appeal. Pursuant to People v. Wende, 25 Cal.3d 436, 158 Cal.Rptr. 839, 600 P.2d 1071 (1979), and Anders v. California, 386 U.S. 738, 87 S.Ct. 1396, 18 L.Ed.2d 493 (1967), Cuero's appointed appellate counsel filed a brief setting forth the evidence in the superior court, presented no argument for reversal, but asked the court of appeal to review the record for error. The brief directed the court's attention to two potential, but not arguable, issues: (1) "whether the trial court abused its discretion by permitting the prosecutor to amend the complaint to allege additional priors after [Cuero's] initial guilty plea" (citing People v. Sipe, 36 Cal.App.4th 468, 42 Cal.Rptr.2d 266 (1995); People v. Superior Court (Alvarado), 207 Cal.App.3d 464, 255 Cal.Rptr. 46 (1989)); and (2) "whether the amendment constituted a breach of a plea agreement in violation of due process, entitling [Cuero] to specific performance of the original agreement" (citing People v. Walker, 54 Cal.3d 1013, 1 Cal.Rptr.2d 902, 819 P.2d 861 (1991), overruled in part by People v. Villalobos, 54 Cal.4th 177, 141 Cal.Rptr.3d 491, 277 P.3d 179 (2012); People v. Mancheno, 32 Cal.3d 855, 187 Cal. Rptr. 441, 654 P.2d 211 (1982)). The California Court of Appeal granted Cuero permission to file a brief on his own behalf, but he did not respond. The court reviewed the entire record and the possible issues raised by counsel's Wende/Anders brief. It concluded that they "disclosed no reasonably arguable appellate issue" and affirmed, noting that "[c]ompetent counsel has represented Cuero on this appeal."

In due course, Cuero brought this petition for habeas corpus in federal district court, where it was properly denied and he timely appealed.

II

A

As a reminder, it must be observed that a state prisoner's federal habeas petition "shall not be granted with respect to any claim that was adjudicated on the merits in State court proceedings unless the adjudication of the claim —

(1) resulted in a decision that was contrary to, or involved an unreasonable application of, clearly established Federal law, as determined by the Supreme Court of the United States; or

(2) resulted in a decision that was based on an unreasonable determination of the facts in light of the evidence presented in the State court proceeding."

28 U.S.C. § 2254(d). "This is a `difficult to meet' and `highly deferential standard for evaluating state-court rulings, which demands that state-court decisions be given the benefit of the doubt.'" Cullen v. Pinholster, 563 U.S. 170, 181, 131 S.Ct. 1388, 179 L.Ed.2d 557 (2011) (quoting Harrington v. Richter, 562 U.S. 86, 102, 131 S.Ct. 770, 178 L.Ed.2d

624 (2011); Woodford v. Visciotti, 537 U.S. 19, 24, 123 S.Ct. 357, 154 L.Ed.2d 279 (2002) (per curiam)).

Contrary to the majority's suggestion that the § 2254(d) "exceptions authorize a grant of habeas relief," Maj. Op. at 883, these clauses prescribe conditions that are necessary, but not sufficient, for habeas relief under AEDPA. Other requirements exist. Most importantly for this case, § 2254(d) "does not repeal the command of § 2254(a) that habeas relief may be afforded to a state prisoner `only on the ground' that his custody violates federal law." Wilson v. Corcoran, 562 U.S. 1, 5-6, 131 S.Ct. 13, 178 L.Ed.2d 276 (2010) (per curiam).

For purposes of § 2254(d)(1), "clearly established Federal law" is "the governing legal principle or principles set forth by the Supreme Court at the time the state court renders its decision." Lockyer v. Andrade, 538 U.S. 63, 71-72, 123 S.Ct. 1166, 155 L.Ed.2d 144 (2003) (citations omitted). It "includes only the holdings, as opposed to the dicta, of [the Supreme Court's] decisions." Woods v. Donald, ____ U.S. ____, 135 S.Ct. 1372, 1376, 191 L.Ed.2d 464 (2015) (per curiam) (quoting White v. Woodall, ____ U.S. ____, 134 S.Ct. 1697, 1702, 188 L.Ed.2d 698 (2014)).

B

A threshold problem with the opinion's analysis is its failure to identify the appropriate state-court decision before us. The majority concludes that we should "look through" the opinion of the California Court of Appeal on direct review to the earlier reasoned decision of the San Diego Superior Court. Maj. Op. at 884. However, the look-through doctrine only applies "[w]here there has been one reasoned state judgment rejecting a federal claim," Ylst v. Nunnemaker, 501 U.S. 797, 803, 111 S.Ct. 2590, 115 L.Ed.2d 706 (1991), and we cannot "look through" when the federal claim at issue was not "adjudicated on the merits" in the prior reasoned decision, see 28 U.S.C. § 2254(d); Casey v. Moore, 386 F.3d 896, 918 n. 23 (9th Cir. 2004); Medley v. Runnels, 506 F.3d 857, 870-71 (9th Cir. 2007) (en banc) (Ikuta, J., concurring in part, dissenting in part) ("[W]e do not `look through' to a state decision which does not address the constitutional claim."); see also Murray v. Schriro, 745 F.3d 984, 997 (9th Cir. 2014)[4] ("[W]e `look through' to the last state-court decision that provides a reasoned explanation capable of review." (emphasis added)); Ortiz v. Yates, 704 F.3d 1026, 1034 (9th Cir. 2012) ("[W]e look through state-court summary denials to the last reasoned state-court opinion on the claim at issue." (emphasis added)).

Here, the superior court never did adjudicate the merits of Cuero's claim that the second amendment of the complaint constituted a breach of his plea agreement in violation of due process, entitling him to specific performance. In Cuero's brief in opposition to the motion to amend and in oral argument on the motion, he exclusively argued that the superior court should exercise its discretion under state law to deny leave to amend.[5] Cuero did not argue that the second amendment of the complaint would violate due process. He did not argue that any plea agreement prohibited the second amendment of the complaint, nor that he was entitled to specific performance, nor that the state court was required to construe plea agreements in accordance with state contract law. Indeed, Cuero argues to us that his trial counsel was ineffective for failing to raise Cuero's due process claim before the superior court.

Thus, Cuero never raised a due process claim, and the superior court did not decide one. As a result, Cuero's claim that the second amendment of the complaint breached a preexisting plea agreement and thereby violated due process was not adjudicated on the merits by the superior court. Such claim was indeed adjudicated on the merits by a single state-court decision: the opinion of the California Court of Appeal on direct review, the only dispositive "decision" with respect to which the petition for habeas corpus has been brought.[6]

C

Of course, "[w]here a state court's decision is unaccompanied by an explanation, the habeas petitioner's burden still must be met by showing there was no reasonable basis for the state court to deny relief." Richter, 562 U.S. at 98, 131 S.Ct. 770. In such a situation, we must ask "what arguments or theories ... could have supported [] the state court's decision" and then determine "whether it is possible fairminded jurists could disagree that those arguments or theories are inconsistent with the holding in a prior decision of" the Supreme Court. Id. at 102, 131 S.Ct. 770. "Thus, when the state court does not supply reasoning for its decision, we are instructed to engage in an independent review of the record and ascertain whether the state court's decision was objectively unreasonable. Crucially, this is not a de novo review of the constitutional question, as even a strong case for relief does not mean the state court's contrary conclusion was unreasonable." Murray, 745 F.3d at 996-97 (internal quotation marks and citations omitted).

"Adherence to these principles serves important interests of federalism and comity. AEDPA's requirements reflect a `presumption that state courts know and follow the law.'" Donald, 135 S.Ct. at 1376 (quoting Visciotti, 537 U.S. at 24, 123 S.Ct. 357). "When reviewing state criminal convictions on collateral review, federal judges are required to afford state courts due respect by overturning their decisions only when there could be no reasonable dispute that they were wrong. Federal habeas review thus exists as `a guard against extreme malfunctions in the state criminal justice systems, not a substitute for ordinary error correction through appeal.'" Id. (quoting Richter, 562 U.S. at 102-03, 131 S.Ct. 770.).

III

In order to prevail in his petition for habeas corpus, Cuero must demonstrate (among other things) that: (1) on December 8, 2005, he had a plea agreement with terms that prohibited amendment of the complaint; (2) such plea agreement had constitutional significance before the entry of judgment, so that breaching it would violate due process; and (3) rescission of such plea agreement (withdrawal of the plea) was not a constitutionally acceptable remedy for the breach of the plea agreement. Contrary to the majority's analysis, under the Supreme Court's holdings in existence at the time of the California Court of Appeal's decision, he cannot.

A

The majority erroneously concludes that, when Cuero initially pleaded guilty on December 8, 2005, he had a "written plea agreement" in which the government guaranteed that punishment would be no greater than 14 years, 4 months in prison. Maj. Op. at 882-83, 882-83, 883, 885-88 & nn. 8-9, 889-90, 891, 891. To the contrary, fairminded jurists could readily conclude that Cuero's initial guilty plea was not induced by any agreement with the State, let alone an agreement that the State would never amend its complaint.

On December 8, 2005, Cuero signed a standard change of plea form. As completed, that document states:

I, the defendant in the above-entitled case, in support of my plea of Guilty/No Contest, personally declare as follows:

. . .

2. I have not been induced to enter this plea by any promise or representation of any kind, except: (State any agreement with the District Attorney.)

STC[[7]] — NO DEALS W/PEOPLE.

Appendix A at 1 ¶ 2. Cuero's initials appear next to the line indicating "STC — NO DEALS W/PEOPLE." Id. Cuero declared that he has "read, understood, and initialed each item above ... and everything on the form ... is true and correct." Id. at 3 ¶ 13. In his plea colloquy that same day, Cuero confirmed that he had read, understood, and thoroughly reviewed with his attorney the plea form submitted, that he had signed and initialed the document, and that he had no questions about it.[8]

What about the "14 year, 4 month maximum promised by the government," Maj. Op. at 891, relied upon so heavily by the majority? Such a promise is a figment of the majority's imagination. The only statement signed by the prosecutor on the change of plea form was the following: "The People of the State of California, plaintiff, by its attorney, the District Attorney for the County of San Diego, concurs with the defendant's plea of Guilty/No Contest as set forth above." Appendix A at 3. And at the hearing prosecutor Kristian Trocha said three words before Cuero entered his plea. Those words were "Kristian Trocha" to identify himself in his initial appearance, and "Yes" in the context of the following exchange:

THE COURT: It is a sentence for the court, no deals with the People. His maximum exposure is 14 years, 4 months in state prison, 4 years on parole and a $10,000 fine. That's the most he could receive by way of this plea; true,

Mr. Tamayo?

MR. TAMAYO: It is.

THE COURT: Mr. Trocha?

[MR. TROCHA[9]]: Yes.

See Appendix B at 1, 2 (emphasis added). Thus, the court confirmed that there were "no deals with the People." And the prosecutor did not promise to refrain from ever doing anything, such as amending the complaint, that would result in a longer sentence.

He simply agreed, as a descriptive matter, that 14 years, 4 months, was the maximum prison term Cuero was facing at the time.[10]

Both Cuero's appellate counsel's brief and the California Court of Appeal's decision imply that the initial plea was not induced by a plea agreement. In his brief on appeal, Cuero's counsel stated that Cuero initially "pled guilty," with no mention of a plea agreement. In contrast, the brief states that the second guilty plea was made "pursuant to a plea agreement" and sets forth the terms of the charge bargain. Similarly, the Court of Appeal refers to the initial "guilty pleas" and the subsequent "negotiated guilty plea," which strongly implies that the court of appeal determined that no plea agreement existed for the initial plea. Such determination would not constitute an unreasonable determination of the facts.

Given Cuero's express declaration that he was not "induced to enter this plea by any promise or representation of any kind" and that there were no deals with the People, a fairminded jurist could readily conclude that the government did not promise Cuero anything, let alone that it would never amend its complaint.

B

Even if there were a plea agreement with terms that prohibited the State from amending its complaint, Cuero would still need to show that, under the Supreme Court's holdings at the time of the California Court of Appeal's decision, a fairminded jurist could not possibly conclude either that the plea agreement lacked constitutional significance before the entry of judgment or that rescission was a constitutionally acceptable remedy for a breach of the plea agreement.

In his briefing before our Court, Cuero contends that the California Court of Appeal's decision was an objectively unreasonable application of Santobello v. New York, 404 U.S. 257, 92 S.Ct. 495, 30 L.Ed.2d 427 (1971). Apparently unsatisfied with the arguments that Cuero made on his own behalf, the majority regrettably adds some selective quotation of Mabry v. Johnson, 467 U.S. 504, 104 S.Ct. 2543, 81 L.Ed.2d 437 (1984), and Ricketts v. Adamson, 483 U.S. 1, 107 S.Ct. 2680, 97 L.Ed.2d 1 (1987), to support its grant of the writ.[11]

I respectfully suggest that the Court of Appeal's decision was neither contrary to, nor an unreasonable application of, Santobello, Johnson, or Adamson.

I

In Santobello, the Supreme Court addressed "whether the State's failure to keep a commitment concerning the sentence recommendation on a guilty plea required a new trial." 404 U.S. at 257-58, 92 S.Ct. 495. There, as part of a plea bargain, the prosecution had agreed to make no recommendation as to the sentence, and Santobello had agreed to plead guilty to a lesser-included offense. Id. at 258, 92 S.Ct. 495. At sentencing, the prosecutor instead recommended the maximum sentence, which the judge imposed. Id. at 259-60, 92 S.Ct. 495. Upon certiorari, the Court vacated and remanded for the state court to consider the appropriate remedy for breach of the agreement. Id. at 262-63, 92 S.Ct. 495.

As part of its reasoning, the Court indeed made the broad statement upon which the majority relies: "[W]hen a plea rests in any significant degree on a promise or agreement of the prosecutor, so that it can be said to be part of the inducement or consideration, such promise must be fulfilled." Id. at 262, 92 S.Ct. 495.

However, this general, isolated statement does not, by itself, constitute the entire holding of Santobello.[12] With respect to the proper remedy for the government's breach, the Court remanded to the state court and held:

> The ultimate relief to which petitioner is entitled we leave to the discretion of the state court, which is in a better position to decide whether the circumstances of this case require only that there be specific performance of the agreement on the plea, in which case petitioner should be resentenced by a different judge, or whether, in the view of the state court, the circumstances require granting the relief sought by petitioner, i.e., the opportunity to withdraw his plea of guilty.

Id. at 262-63, 92 S.Ct. 495. The Court noted that if "the state court decides to allow withdrawal of the plea, the petitioner will, of course, plead anew to the original charge on two felony counts." Id. at 263 n. 2, 92 S.Ct. 495.

Thus, contrary to the majority's analysis, the Court in Santobello did not hold that literally every plea agreement offered by the prosecution and accepted by the defendant is enforceable by specific performance. Rather, the Court held that, when a trial court's judgment of conviction is based on a plea induced by a promise later broken by the state, the judgment must be vacated. The Court further held that the ultimate relief would be left "to the discretion of the state court, which [was] in a better position to decide whether the circumstances of [the] case" required specific performance or withdrawal of the guilty plea. Id. at 263, 92 S.Ct. 495.

2

The majority's grant of the petition rests entirely on the premise that "[u]nder clearly established Supreme Court law, Cuero stood convicted and his plea agreement became binding the moment the first Superior Court judge accepted his guilty plea." Maj. Op. at 884. Johnson undercuts such premise.

In Johnson, the Supreme Court addressed "whether a defendant's acceptance of a prosecutor's proposed plea bargain creates a constitutional right to have the bargain specifically enforced." 467 U.S. at 505, 104 S.Ct. 2543. There, the prosecutor proposed that, in exchange for a plea of guilty, the prosecutor would recommend a 21-year sentence served concurrently with other sentences. Id. at 505-06, 104 S.Ct. 2543. When the defendant's counsel called the prosecutor and communicated acceptance of the offer, the prosecutor told defense counsel "that a mistake had been made and withdrew the offer." Id. at 506, 104 S.Ct. 2543. The prosecutor then made a second offer to recommend a 21-year sentence to be served consecutively to the other sentences, which the defendant ultimately accepted. Id. "In accordance with the plea bargain, the state trial judge imposed a 21-year sentence to be served consecutively to the previous sentences." Id.

In its analysis, the Court reasoned:

A plea bargain standing alone is without constitutional significance; in itself it is a mere executory agreement which, until embodied in the judgment of a court, does not deprive an accused of liberty or any other constitutionally protected interest. It is the ensuing guilty plea that implicates the Constitution. Only after respondent pleaded guilty was he convicted, and it is that conviction which gave rise to the deprivation of respondent's liberty at issue here.

Id. at 507-08, 104 S.Ct. 2543 (footnote omitted). The majority completely ignores the reasonable conclusion that a fairminded jurist could draw from the first sentence of this passage: a "plea bargain ... is without constitutional significance ... until embodied in the judgment of a court." Id.[13] In other words, it is the judgment, not the acceptance of a guilty plea, that "seals the deal between the state and the defendant." Contra Maj. Op. at 885.[14]

The Johnson Court further explained that "only when it develops that the defendant was not fairly apprised of its consequences can his plea be challenged under the Due Process Clause." 467 U.S. at 509, 104 S.Ct. 2543. The Court then applied that rule:

[Johnson's] plea was in no sense induced by the prosecutor's withdrawn offer; unlike Santobello, who pleaded guilty thinking he had bargained for a specific prosecutorial sentencing recommendation which was not ultimately made, at the time respondent pleaded guilty he knew the prosecution would recommend a 21-year consecutive sentence. [Johnson] does not challenge the District Court's finding that he pleaded guilty with the advice of competent counsel and with full awareness of the consequences — he knew that the prosecutor would recommend and that the judge could impose the sentence now under attack.

Id. at 510, 104 S.Ct. 2543.

The Court concluded that Johnson's "inability to enforce the prosecutor's offer is without constitutional significance." Id. Johnson "was not deprived of his liberty in any fundamentally unfair way. [He] was fully aware of the likely consequences when he pleaded guilty; it is not unfair to expect him to live with those consequences now." Id. at 511, 104 S.Ct. 2543.

Thus, the Court in Johnson held that a defendant's inability to enforce a plea offer withdrawn before the entry of judgment is without constitutional significance, not that every breach of a plea agreement after a guilty plea violates the Constitution. Consequently, there is no due process violation so long as the prosecution fulfills the promises that induced the plea upon which the judgment of conviction is based.

More importantly, Johnson clarified the holding in Santobello. The Court noted that "Santobello expressly declined to hold that the Constitution compels specific performance of a broken prosecutorial promise as the remedy for such a plea" and that "permitting Santobello to replead was within the range of constitutionally appropriate remedies." Id. at 510-11 n. 11, 104 S.Ct. 2543 (citing Santobello, 404 U.S. at 262-63, 92 S.Ct. 495; id. at 268-69, 92 S.Ct. 495 (Marshall, J., concurring in part and dissenting in part)). "It follows that [Johnson's] constitutional rights could not have been violated.

Because he pleaded after the prosecution had breached its `promise' to him, he was in no worse position than Santobello would have been had he been permitted to replead." Id.

3

The majority also concludes, erroneously, that the state court was "constitutionally obligated to construe the agreement in accordance with state contract law" and that a "state court must supply a remedy for a breached plea agreement that comports with state contract law." Maj. Op. at 890. Although the majority relies heavily on Adamson for these propositions, I respectfully suggest that case does not support, let alone require, such conclusions.

In Adamson, the Supreme Court addressed "whether the Double Jeopardy Clause bars the prosecution of [a defendant] for first-degree murder following his breach of a plea agreement under which he had pleaded guilty to a lesser offense, had been sentenced, and had begun serving a term of imprisonment." Adamson, 483 U.S. at 3, 107 S.Ct. 2680.[15] There, the Arizona Supreme Court held that a written plea agreement[16] required Adamson to testify at the retrial of the other two individuals, that he violated the terms of the plea agreement by refusing to testify at the retrials, and that the terms of the plea agreement required the original first-degree murder charge to be reinstated automatically. Id. at 5, 107 S.Ct. 2680. The Supreme Court held that the subsequent prosecution did not violate the Double Jeopardy Clause. It reasoned that "terms of the agreement could not be clearer: in the event of [Adamson's] breach occasioned by a refusal to testify, the parties would be returned to the status quo ante, in which case [Adamson] would have no double jeopardy defense to waive." Id. at 10, 107 S.Ct. 2680. Thus, the Court held in Adamson that the Double Jeopardy Clause does not bar a state from vacating a judgment of conviction and reinstating criminal charges pursuant to the express terms of a plea agreement.

The majority does not rely on the holding of Adamson for its erroneous propositions, but rather on part of a sentence in dictum contained in a footnote of the Court's opinion. In footnote 3, the Court addressed Adamson's contention that the Arizona Supreme Court had misconstrued the terms of the plea agreement:

We will not second-guess the Arizona Supreme Court's construction of the language of the plea agreement. While we assess independently the plea agreement's effect on respondent's double jeopardy rights, the construction of the plea agreement and the concomitant obligations flowing therefrom are, within broad bounds of reasonableness, matters of state law, and we will not disturb the Arizona Supreme Court's reasonable disposition of those issues. The dissent's discourse on the law of contracts is thus illuminating but irrelevant. The questions whether the plea agreement obligated the respondent to testify at the retrial of Dunlap and Robison and, if so, whether the respondent breached this duty are matters appropriately left to the state courts....

Adamson, 483 U.S. at 6 n. 3, 107 S.Ct. 2680 (emphasis added to the clause upon which the majority relies). As the Supreme Court eloquently once stated in an unrelated context: "Most importantly, the statement is pure dictum. It is dictum contained in a rebuttal to a counterargument. And it is unnecessary dictum even in that respect." Kirtsaeng v. John Wiley & Sons, Inc., ____ U.S. ____, 133 S.Ct. 1351, 1368, 185 L.Ed.2d 392 (2013).

Even if not dictum, the footnote has been misinterpreted by the majority. The majority, consistent with precedent of our circuit,[17] focuses solely on the statement that "the construction of the plea agreement and the concomitant obligations flowing therefrom are, within broad bounds of reasonableness, matters of state law." Maj. Op. at 890. However, in context it is clear that the Supreme Court was not stating that state courts are "constitutionally obligated to construe the agreement in accordance with state contract law" and that they violate the Constitution by failing to do so. Maj. Op. at 889. And the footnote does not remotely support the contention that a state court violates the Constitution if it does not "supply a remedy for a breached plea agreement that comports with state contract law." Maj. Op. at 890. Quite the opposite. Respecting important interests of federalism and comity, the Court explained that the construction of plea agreements and whether a breach has occurred are matters of state law which are "appropriately left to the state courts." Adamson, 483 U.S. at 6-7 n. 3, 107 S.Ct. 2680. Federal courts must not "second-guess[ ] the finding of a breach" and they have no "license to substitute a federal interpretation of the terms of a plea agreement for a reasonable state interpretation." Id. Thus, the Adamson footnote, upon which the majority relies, is about deference to state courts, not about imposing new constitutional requirements on state courts.

C

The California Court of Appeal's decision was not "contrary to" Santobello, Johnson, or Adamson. "Because none of [the Supreme Court's] cases confront `the specific question presented by this case,' the state court's decision could not be `contrary to' any holding from" the Supreme Court. Donald, 135 S.Ct. at 1377 (quoting Lopez v. Smith, 135 U.S. 1, 4, 10 S.Ct. 658, 34 L.Ed. 55 (2014) (per curiam)).

In Santobello, the defendant pleaded guilty in reliance upon the promises in the prosecution's original offer, the prosecution broke a promise contained in its original offer, and the court entered judgment on the basis of the plea induced by the unfulfilled promise. Unlike Santobello, here the superior court's judgment was not entered on the basis of the initial plea, purportedly induced by unfulfilled promises. Rather, judgment was entered on the basis of the subsequent plea, which was induced by promises that have been fulfilled. In Johnson, the prosecution withdrew its original offer before the defendant pleaded guilty. Unlike Johnson, here the prosecutor purportedly breached a plea agreement after the defendant pleaded guilty. Finally, Adamson does not remotely resemble this case. There, the defendant breached his plea bargain, and the question was whether or not the Double Jeopardy Clause prohibited the state from vacating the conviction and reinstating criminal charges.

Therefore, Santobello, Johnson, and Adamson do not address the specific question presented by this case: whether the Constitution requires specific performance of a plea bargain after a defendant has pleaded guilty but before the court has entered judgment. As a result, the state court's decision could not be "contrary to" any holding from the Supreme Court. See Donald, 135 S.Ct. at 1377.

D

Nor was the California Court of Appeal's decision an "unreasonable application of" the Court's holdings in Santobello, Johnson, and Adamson. As discussed above, fairminded jurists could easily conclude that Cuero's initial plea did not rest "on a promise or agreement of the prosecutor, so that it can be said to be part of the inducement or consideration." Santobello, 404 U.S. at 262, 92 S.Ct. 495; see Appendix A at 1 ¶ 2 ("I have not been induced to enter this plea by any promise or representation of any kind, except: ... NO DEALS W/PEOPLE.").[18]

Even assuming that the State did make a promise not to amend its complaint, fairminded jurists could readily conclude that, under Johnson, Cuero's inability to enforce the original plea agreement, which was withdrawn before the entry of judgment, is "without constitutional significance." Johnson, 467 U.S. at 507-08, 510, 104 S.Ct. 2543. Moreover, fairminded jurists could conclude that, if the prosecution did breach some binding agreement with Cuero, "permitting [Cuero] to replead was within the range of constitutionally appropriate remedies." Johnson, 467 U.S. at 510-11 n. 11, 104 S.Ct. 2543 (explaining Santobello); Santobello, 404 U.S. at 263 & n. 2, 92 S.Ct. 495.[19]

Therefore, the state court's ruling on the claim presented here was not "so lacking in justification that there was an error well understood and comprehended in existing law beyond any possibility for fairminded disagreement." Richter, 562 U.S. at 103, 131 S.Ct. 770. As a result, the state court's ruling was not an unreasonable application of Santobello, Johnson, or Adamson.

IV

Perhaps the majority's faulty analysis can best be explained by its erroneous reliance on (1) perceived errors of state law; (2) circuit precedent (to bridge the gap between the Supreme Court's holdings and this case); (3) a Supreme Court decision that post-dates the California Court of Appeal's decision; and (4) issues of law framed at the highest levels of generality. Making matters worse, the majority misconstrues many of the sources of law upon which it improperly relies.

A

1

The majority erroneously relies on perceived errors of state law. Maj. Op. at 887-91 & n. 10; see Swarthout v. Cooke, 562 U.S. 216, 219-22, 131 S.Ct. 859, 178 L.Ed.2d 732 (2011) (per curiam); Wilson v. Corcoran, 562 U.S. 1, 5, 131 S.Ct. 13, 178 L.Ed.2d 276 (2010) (per curiam); Estelle v. McGuire, 502 U.S. 62, 67, 112 S.Ct. 475, 116 L.Ed.2d 385 (1991); Lewis v. Jeffers, 497 U.S. 764, 780, 110 S.Ct. 3092, 111 L.Ed.2d 606 (1990); Pulley v. Harris, 465 U.S. 37, 41, 104 S.Ct. 871, 79 L.Ed.2d 29 (1984); Rose v. Hodges, 423 U.S. 19, 21-22, 96 S.Ct. 175, 46 L.Ed.2d 162 (1975) (per curiam).

Specifically, it holds that the writ must issue because the state court failed "to interpret Cuero's plea agreement consistently with California contract law" and failed to "supply a remedy for a breached plea agreement that comports with state contract law." Maj. Op. at 890. "But it is only noncompliance with federal law that renders a State's criminal judgment susceptible to collateral attack in the federal courts. The habeas statute unambiguously provides that a federal court may issue the writ to a state prisoner `only on the ground that he is in custody in violation of the Constitution or laws or treaties of the United States.'" Corcoran, 562 U.S. at 5, 131 S.Ct. 13 (quoting 28 U.S.C. § 2254(a)). The Supreme Court has "repeatedly held that `federal habeas corpus relief does not lie for errors of state law.'" Id. (quoting McGuire, 502 U.S. at 67, 112 S.Ct. 475). "It is not the province of a federal habeas court to reexamine state-court determinations on state-law questions." Id. (quoting McGuire, 502 U.S. at 67-68, 112 S.Ct. 475) (alteration omitted).

The majority protests that these cases "do not speak to the situation where, as here, the Supreme Court has clearly held that the federal constitutional due process right is itself defined by reference to principles of state law." Maj. Op. at 902 n. 10. One would expect a citation to Supreme Court precedent to follow such a strong statement, but none exists. The majority cites our Buckley case, which cites Adamson. Maj. Op. at 902 n. 10. But Adamson held no such thing. In fact, Adamson does not contain the words "due process" anywhere in the Court's opinion. "No opinion of [the Supreme Court] supports converting California's [contract law] into a substantive federal requirement." Cooke, 562 U.S. at 220-21, 131 S.Ct. 859.[20]

2

Even if the court could grant habeas relief on the basis of state law, the majority misconstrues California state law.

California state law did not prohibit the second amendment of the complaint. Several provisions of the California Penal Code expressly permit a prosecutor to amend an information or complaint. See Cal. Penal Code §§ 969a, 969.5(a), 1009. "Under section 1009, the People may amend an information without leave of court prior to entry of a defendant's plea, and the trial court may permit an amendment of an information at any stage of the proceedings." People v. Lettice, 221 Cal. App.4th 139, 163 Cal.Rptr.3d 862, 868 (2013). Sections 969a and 969.5(a) specifically deal with amendment of the complaint to add allegations of prior felonies, and § 969.5(a), upon which the State relied, addresses amendment of a complaint after a guilty plea:

Whenever it shall be discovered that a pending complaint to which a plea of guilty has been made under Section 859a does not charge all prior felonies of which the defendant has been convicted either in this state or elsewhere, the complaint may be forthwith amended to charge the prior conviction or convictions and the amendments may and shall be made upon order of the court.

Cal. Penal Code § 969.5(a). None of these statutes indicate that a prosecutor's ability to amend the information is limited to situations in which a plea agreement has been entered.

In People v. Valladoli, the California Supreme Court interpreted both § 969a and former § 969 ½ in determining whether an information could be amended to allege prior felonies after a defendant was found guilty at trial. 13 Cal.4th 590, 54 Cal.Rptr.2d 695, 918 P.2d 999 (1996). Discussing former § 969 ½, the predecessor to § 969.5(a), the court said that if the defendant had "pleaded guilty before the magistrate under section 859a, ... the express terms of section 969 ½ would have permitted the People to amend the information to charge his prior convictions after the guilty plea." Id., 54 Cal.Rptr.2d 695, 918 P.2d at 1005; see also People v. Tindall, 24 Cal.4th 767, 102 Cal.Rptr.2d 533, 14 P.3d 207, 212 (2000) (citing Valladoli for this proposition). The court continued, "An obvious motivating force underlying section 969 ½ is to prevent one accused of a crime from quickly pleading guilty before a magistrate and thereby limiting the amount of time the prosecutor has to investigate, discover, and charge the accused's prior felony convictions." Valladoli, 54 Cal.Rptr.2d 695, 918 P.2d at 1005.

Thus, the state statutory scheme and Valladoli permit a prosecutor to request to file an amended complaint to allege prior convictions after entering a plea agreement. The majority fails to cite any California case which has definitively held that a prosecutor may not amend a complaint after the court accepts a plea agreement.[21]

Ultimately, the Supreme Court has "repeatedly held that a state court's interpretation of state law, including one announced on direct appeal of the challenged conviction, binds a federal court sitting in habeas corpus." Bradshaw v. Richey, 546 U.S. 74, 76, 126 S.Ct. 602, 163 L.Ed.2d 407 (2005) (per curiam). Here, both the superior court and the appellate court determined that amendment of the complaint was permissible under state law. We must defer to those interpretations and conclude that there was no error of state law. Rather than deferring, the majority's decision severely undermines the California Legislature's determination, in enacting sections 969.5(a) and 1009, that prosecutors should have the ability, with the approval of the court, to amend a complaint after a plea to allege all prior felonies.

B

1

The majority erroneously relies (heavily) on circuit precedent to bridge the gap between the Supreme Court's cases and this one. See Glebe v. Frost, ___ U.S. ___, 135 S.Ct. 429, 431, 190 L.Ed.2d 317 (2014) (per curiam); Lopez v. Smith, ___ U.S. ___, 135 S.Ct. 1, 4, 190 L.Ed.2d 1 (2014) (per curiam); Marshall v. Rodgers, ___ U.S. ___, 133 S.Ct. 1446, 1450-51, 185 L.Ed.2d 540 (2013) (per curiam); Parker v. Matthews, ___ U.S. ___, 132 S.Ct. 2148, 2155-56, 183 L.Ed.2d 32 (2012) (per curiam); Renico v. Lett, 559 U.S. 766, 778-79, 130 S.Ct. 1855, 176 L.Ed.2d 678 (2010).

Specifically, the majority relies on circuit precedent for the following propositions, which are not supported by the Supreme Court's decisions:

(1) The "federal constitutional due process right is itself defined by reference to principles of state law," Maj. Op. at 902 n. 10 (citing Buckley, 441 F.3d at 695); a state court is "constitutionally obligated to construe the [plea] agreement in accordance with state contract law." Maj. Op. at 889 (citing Buckley, 441 F.3d at 696); "[u]nder AEDPA, we

... must consider whether the [state court] decision is consistent with a proper application of state contract law in interpreting the plea agreement...." Maj. Op. at 888 (quoting Davis, 446 F.3d at 962).

(2) "[W]here the state has already received the benefit it bargained for — a plea of guilty and a conviction — specific performance is the best remedy, unless the defendant, whose choice it becomes, `elect[s] instead to rescind the agreement and take his chances from there.'" Maj. Op. at 890 (quoting Buckley, 441 F.3d at 699 n.11).

(3) "Because Cuero had already performed, `fundamental fairness demands that the state be compelled to adhere to the agreement as well.'"

Maj. Op. at 891 (quoting Brown, 337 F.3d at 1162).

Take the first proposition. As discussed above, Adamson does not even contain the words "due process," so the notion that the "federal constitutional due process right is itself defined by reference to principles of state law" comes solely from Buckley. Similarly, footnote 3 of Adamson says nothing about state contract law. See Adamson, 483 U.S. at 6 n. 3, 107 S.Ct. 2680 (construction and breach determinations are "matters of state law"). So the majority's restriction of the relevant state law to contract law comes solely from circuit precedent in Buckley and Davis. See, e.g., Maj. Op. at 903 n. 12 (rejecting argument under § 969.5(a) because that section "is irrelevant to the interpretation of a court-approved plea agreement under state contract principles"). Finally, no Supreme Court decisions remotely support the notion that specific performance is required when a defendant has pleaded guilty and the court has accepted that plea. Such notions are inventions of our circuit.

The Supreme Court has "repeatedly emphasized [that] circuit precedent does not constitute `clearly established Federal law, as determined by the Supreme Court.'" Frost, 135 S.Ct. at 431 (quoting 28 U.S.C. § 2254(d)(1)). "It therefore cannot form the basis for habeas relief under AEDPA." Matthews, 132 S.Ct. at 2155. And "Circuit precedent cannot `refine or sharpen a general principle of Supreme Court jurisprudence into a specific legal rule that [the Supreme Court] has not announced.'" Smith, 135 S.Ct. at 4 (quoting Rodgers, 133 S.Ct. at 1450). In the past three years, the Supreme Court has caught us three times trying to evade this rule. See Frost, 135 S.Ct. at 431 ("The Ninth Circuit acknowledged this rule, but tried to get past it...."); Smith, 135 S.Ct. at 4 ("The Ninth Circuit attempted to evade this barrier...."); Rodgers, 133 S.Ct. at 1450-51. It is unwise to think that we will slip through this time around.

2

Even if the majority could properly rely on our decisions in Brown, Buckley, and Davis, those cases not compel the conclusion that the majority reaches.

For instance, Brown and Buckley acknowledged that there are "two available remedies at law for the breach of [a] plea agreement: withdrawal of [the] plea (i.e., rescission of the contract) and specific performance." Buckley, 441 F.3d at 699; Brown, 337 F.3d at 1161. In choosing between those remedies in Buckley, the en banc court "express[ed] no view on what the proper remedy would be in a case with other facts." Id. at

699 n. 11.

Cuero's circumstances are readily distinguishable from those in Brown and Buckley. In both cases, we ordered specific performance because rescission of the contract was "impossible" under the circumstances and the petitioners could not "conceivably be returned to the status quo ante." Brown, 337 F.3d at 1161; Buckley, 441 F.3d at 699. The petitioners had "paid in a coin that the state cannot refund" by testifying and/or serving their bargained-for sentences. Buckley, 441 F.3d at 699 (quoting Brown, 337 F.3d at 1161). Here, when the superior court granted permission to amend the complaint, Cuero had not performed in a way that could not be undone. Instead, to the extent Cuero had performed, the "coin" he paid was fully refunded when his relinquished trial rights were fully restored. Thus, specific performance was not required by our precedents because rescission was still possible for Cuero.

In addition, Cuero's case differs from Davis, Buckley, and Brown because the petitioners were incarcerated on the basis of pleas induced by plea agreements that the state breached. See Davis, 446 F.3d at 959-63; Buckley, 441 F.3d at 691-93; Brown, 337 F.3d at 1157-58. Thus, those cases were much closer to Santobello. Here, the initial plea, purportedly induced by a plea agreement which the state breached, was withdrawn and does not form the basis of Cuero's incarceration. Cuero's case is much closer to Johnson. He "was not deprived of his liberty in any fundamentally unfair way. [He] was fully aware of the likely consequences when he pleaded guilty; it is not unfair to expect him to live with those consequences now." Johnson, 467 U.S. at 511, 104 S.Ct. 2543.

C

1

The majority erroneously relies upon a Supreme Court opinion — and numerous other authorities — issued after all of the state court decisions that related to Cuero. See Greene v. Fisher, ____ U.S. ____, 132 S.Ct. 38, 44-45, 181 L.Ed.2d 336 (2011); Cullen v. Pinholster, 563 U.S. 170, 182, 131 S.Ct. 1388, 179 L.Ed.2d 557 (2011); Andrade, 538 U.S. at 71-72, 123 S.Ct. 1166; see also Woodall, 134 S.Ct. at 1706.

Specifically, the panel relies on Puckett v. United States, 556 U.S. 129, 129 S.Ct. 1423, 173 L.Ed.2d 266 (2009), for the following propositions:

(1) "A state court must supply a remedy for a breached plea agreement that comports with state contract law." Maj. Op. at 890 (citing Puckett, 556 U.S. at 137, 129 S.Ct. 1423).[22]

(2) The purported breach of Cuero's plea agreement was "undoubtedly a violation of the defendant's rights." Maj. Op. at 883 (quoting Puckett, 556 U.S. at 136, 129 S.Ct. 1423).

(3) "[P]lea bargains are essentially contracts." Maj. Op. at 888 (quoting Puckett, 556 U.S. at 137, 129 S.Ct. 1423).

Section 2254(d)(1) "requires federal courts to focus on what a state court knew and did, and to measure state-court decisions against [the Supreme Court's] precedents as of the time the state court renders its decision." Greene, 132 S.Ct. at 44 (internal alteration and quotation marks omitted) (emphasis in original). "Obviously, a state-court decision cannot be contrary to clearly established Federal law that was not yet in existence." Murray, 745 F.3d at 997. Thus, because Puckett was issued after the California Court of Appeal's decision, it was not "clearly established Federal law" at the time the state court rendered its decision. Consequently, the majority cannot rely on Puckett.

The majority also relies on a number of other authorities issued after the state court's decision to state the principles of law that the state court should have applied. See Maj. Op. at 889 (relying on Doe v. Harris, 640 F.3d 972, 975 (9th Cir. 2011)); id. at 888 (relying on People v. Segura, 44 Cal.4th 921, 80 Cal.Rptr.3d 715, 188 P.3d 649, 656 (2008)); id. at 888-89 (relying on Sateriale v. R.J. Reynolds Tobacco Co., 697 F.3d 777, 791 (9th Cir. 2012)); id. at 890 (relying on In re Timothy N., 216 Cal.App.4th 725, 157 Cal. Rptr.3d 78, 88 (2013)); id. at 904 n. 14 (relying on 5 Wayne R. LaFave et al., Criminal Procedure § 21.2(e) (4th ed. 2015)). This reliance, too, was impermissible, for the state court cannot be expected to apply rules of law stated in authorities not yet in existence.

2

Even if the majority could rely on Puckett, that case cannot support the weight of the majority's argument.

The Supreme Court in Puckett stated that "[w]hen a defendant agrees to a plea bargain, the Government takes on certain obligations. If those obligations are not met, the defendant is entitled to seek a remedy, which might in some cases be rescission of the agreement, allowing him to take back the consideration he has furnished, i.e., to withdraw his plea." 556 U.S. at 137, 129 S.Ct. 1423. Clearly, withdrawal of the plea is a constitutionally permissible remedy, and Cuero received that remedy. The Puckett Court did not remotely suggest that the determination of which remedy to afford is a matter of state contract law. Also, the Puckett Court acknowledged that, although "plea bargains are essentially contracts," "the analogy may not hold in all respects." Id. This undermines the majority's proposition that only state contract law can be used to determine whether amendment of the complaint was permitted.

D

Finally, the majority erroneously frames legal issues at the highest levels of generality. See Donald, 135 S.Ct. at 1377; Smith, 135 S.Ct. at 4; Nevada v. Jackson, ____ U.S. ____, 133 S.Ct. 1990, 1994, 186 L.Ed.2d 62 (2013) (per curiam); cf. City & County of San Francisco v. Sheehan, ____ U.S. ____, 135 S.Ct. 1765, 1775-76, 191 L.Ed.2d 856 (2015) ("We have repeatedly told courts — and the Ninth Circuit in particular — not to define clearly established law at a high level of generality." (quoting Ashcroft v. al-Kidd, 563 U.S. 731, 742, 131 S.Ct. 2074, 179 L.Ed.2d 1149 (2011))). "By framing [the Supreme Court's] precedents at such a high level of generality, a lower federal court could transform even the most imaginative extension of existing case law into `clearly established Federal law, as determined by the Supreme Court.'" Jackson, 133 S.Ct. at 1994 (quoting 28 U.S.C. § 2254(d)(1)). Such an "approach would defeat the substantial deference that AEDPA requires." Id.

The majority can only grant habeas relief if the Supreme Court's cases clearly establish that a defendant has a due process right to specific performance of a plea agreement before the entry of judgment. But none of the Supreme Court's cases addresses that specific issue. See Smith, 135 S.Ct. at 4.

Instead, the best the majority can do is to point to Adamson for the general proposition that "the construction of [a] plea agreement and the concomitant obligations flowing therefrom are, within broad bounds of reasonableness, matters of state law." 483 U.S. at 6 n. 3, 107 S.Ct. 2680. "This proposition is far too abstract to establish clearly the specific rule [Cuero] needs." Smith, 135 S.Ct. at 4.

The majority treats the door supposedly opened by Adamson's general proposition as license to engage freely in de novo determination of what California contract law requires, both for the construction of the agreement and the remedy for a breach. Maj. Op. at 887-91. Again, however, no California cases establish that specific performance is required when the State amends its complaint after entry of a plea but before judgment. As a result, the majority is forced to frame principles of California law at the highest level of generality in order to conclude that specific performance is required. The majority rests its decision on the very general principle that "the remedy for breach must 'repair the harm caused by the breach.'" Maj. Op. at 890 (quoting People v. Toscano, 124 Cal.App.4th 340, 20 Cal.Rptr.3d 923, 927 (2004)). Such a general proposition obviously does not establish, under California law, that specific performance was the only remedy in this situation that could repair the harm caused by the breach.

To supply that final conclusion, the majority relies purely on its own de novo, ipse dixit analysis. Note that the key last paragraph before its conclusion section contains only a single citation to a source of law, and that citation does not establish that specific performance is required here. Ultimately, the court's decision rests on its own determinations that it would be unfair not to require specific performance, Maj. Op. at 891, and that "specific performance is necessary to maintain the integrity and fairness of the criminal justice system," Maj. Op. at 890 n. 14.[23] These conclusions are not dictated by state or federal law.

V

For the foregoing reasons, I respectfully conclude that the majority erroneously orders reversal of the district court and grant of the writ. In accordance with Supreme Court law, a fairminded jurist could conclude that Cuero's plea was not induced by any promise by the prosecutor. See Appendix A. Even assuming there was such a promise, a fairminded jurist could conclude that the plea agreement was without constitutional significance before the entry of judgment. And, even if there were a breach of a constitutionally binding plea agreement, nothing in any Supreme Court decision clearly establishes that the state court was required to order specific performance. Thus, the state court's decision was neither contrary to, nor an unreasonable application of "clearly established Federal law." 28 U.S.C. § 2254(d)(1).

For the foregoing reasons, I respectfully dissent.

Judge O'Scannlain's dissent in Jones v. Harrington (July 22, 2016)

O'SCANNLAIN, Circuit Judge, dissenting:

A suspect who wishes to invoke his Fifth Amendment right to silence must do so "unambiguously." Berghuis v. Thompkins, 560 U.S. 370, 381-82, 130 S.Ct. 2250, 176 L.Ed.2d 1098 (2010). Well into his interrogation, the suspect in this case made a single statement that, standing alone, might be characterized as an unambiguous invocation of such right. The California courts determined, however, that the suspect's statement was not unambiguous when considered in full context. Whether one believes that determination to be correct or not, it unquestionably rests on a reasonable application of clearly established Supreme Court law to the facts of the case before us — and it must therefore stand under our deferential standard of review. See 28 U.S.C. § 2254(d); Cullen v. Pinholster, 563 U.S. 170, 181, 131 S.Ct. 1388, 179 L.Ed.2d 557 (2011).

In reaching its conclusion to the contrary, the majority faults the state court for failing to apply Supreme Court precedent that post-dates the state court's decision, attempts to extend readily distinguishable Supreme Court precedent to circumstances the Court has never considered, and ultimately grants relief to Jones because the state court's decision failed to conform to the majority's preferred view of the law — all of which we are forbidden from doing under § 2254.

I respectfully dissent.

I

A

Let's begin by restating the relevant facts.

After he was identified as the potential driver in a gang-related shooting that injured two teenagers and killed a third, Kevin Jones, Jr. was brought in for questioning by the Los Angeles Police Department. LAPD Detectives Kevin Jolivette and Bill Fallon proceeded to interview Jones for a period of a few hours, beginning shortly after midnight on August 16, 2003. After being informed of his constitutional rights, Jones spoke willingly with the detectives. Throughout the interview, the detectives employed a ruse against Jones, telling him that both eye witnesses and security-camera footage identified his car as having been involved in the drive-by shooting. The officers pressed Jones on both his and his car's whereabouts the night of the shooting, and they urged him to admit his involvement in the crime.

Jones spoke at length with the detectives, and as the majority recounts, his story changed considerably throughout the course of the interview. After extensive interrogation, Jones clung to the assertion that on the evening of the crime, his car had gone missing for several hours, even though he admitted that no one other than him used the car. Jones insisted that he had noticed his car missing from its parking space that evening, but for various reasons, he thought little of it and simply assumed that the car would be returned to him. Rather than investigate where his car had been taken, Jones stated that he went to a nearby gym for a couple hours and — as luck would have it — when he returned home, his car was back.

The detectives pressed Jones on the implausibility of this story, leading eventually to the following exchange:

> JOLIVETTE: Kevin, do you think-why don't you stop this man.
>
> JONES: All right.
>
> JOLIVETTE: Stop this. The thing is you drove a car, it shows that on the tape, and that's all I'm going to put down, as far as what you were doing. You drove the car. You just didn't know it was going to happen like that. Kevin, sit up, man.
>
> JONES: I don't want to talk no more, man.
>
> JOLIVETTE: I understand that, but the bottom line is —
>
> JONES: You don't want to hear what I'm telling you.
>
> JOLIVETTE: I'm so sorry. I can't — you're mumbling, you got to speak up. I got bad hearing.
>
> JONES: I'm telling you all.

At that point, the questioning proceeded as it had for hours, and in short order Jones admitted to driving the car during the shooting. He professed innocence, however, insisting that a stranger had jumped into his car, ordered him to drive to the scene of the shooting, and then jumped out of the car, firing a gun at the victims. A few days later, police interviewed Jones again, and he again insisted on this latest version of his story.

B

Jones was prosecuted largely on the strength of his incriminating statements and was found guilty by a jury of first degree murder, two counts of attempted murder, and other lesser crimes. Jones was sentenced to 75 years to life.

Jones appealed to the California Court of Appeal, arguing, among other things, that his incriminating statements should not have been introduced at trial, because they were obtained in violation of his Fifth Amendment right to silence. The California Court of Appeal disagreed, concluding that Jones's statement that he did not "want to talk no more" was ambiguous in context and it thus did not require police to end his interrogation. Jones filed a petition for review challenging this conclusion with the California Supreme Court, which the court denied without comment.

Jones then filed a federal habeas petition under 28 U.S.C. § 2254, which was denied by the district court. Jones timely appealed.

II

Under the Antiterrorism and Effective Death Penalty Act of 1996 (AEDPA), we may grant relief only if the California Court of Appeal's[1] rejection of Jones's right-to-silence claim "was contrary to, or involved an unreasonable application of, clearly established Federal law, as determined by the Supreme Court of the United States" or "resulted in a decision that was based on an unreasonable determination of the facts in light of the evidence presented in the State court proceeding." 28 U.S.C. §§ 2254(d)(1)-(2). Time and again, the Supreme Court has reminded federal courts — and ours in particular

— that this standard is "difficult to meet" and "highly deferential," which "demands that state-court decisions be given the benefit of the doubt." Pinholster, 563 U.S. at 181, 131 S.Ct. 1388 (quoting Harrington v. Richter, 562 U.S. 86, 102, 131 S.Ct. 770, 178 L.Ed.2d 624 (2011); Woodford v. Visciotti, 537 U.S. 19, 24, 123 S.Ct. 357, 154 L.Ed.2d 279 (2002) (per curiam)).

A decision is "contrary to" clearly established law where the state court "applies a rule that contradicts the governing law set forth in [Supreme Court] cases" or where it "confronts a set of facts that are materially indistinguishable from a decision of [the Supreme] Court and nevertheless arrives at a result different from" the Court. Mitchell v. Esparza, 540 U.S. 12, 15-16, 124 S.Ct. 7, 157 L.Ed.2d 263 (2003) (per curiam) (quoting Williams v. Taylor, 529 U.S. 362, 405-06, 120 S.Ct. 1495, 146 L.Ed.2d 389 (2000)). A state court unreasonably applies clearly established federal law only if its determination "was so lacking in justification that there was an error well understood and comprehended in existing law beyond any possibility for fairminded disagreement." Richter, 562 U.S. at 103, 131 S.Ct. 770. "[A]n unreasonable application of federal law is different from an incorrect application of federal law." Id. at 101, 131 S.Ct. 770 (quoting Williams, 529 U.S. at 410, 120 S.Ct. 1495). "A state court's determination that a claim lacks merit precludes federal habeas relief so long as fairminded jurists could disagree on the correctness of the state court's decision." Id. (internal quotation marks omitted).

A state-court decision "will not be overturned on factual grounds unless objectively unreasonable in light of the evidence presented in the state-court proceeding." Miller-El v. Cockrell, 537 U.S. 322, 340, 123 S.Ct. 1029, 154 L.Ed.2d 931 (2003) (emphasis added). "While not impossible to meet, that is a daunting standard — one that will be satisfied in relatively few cases, especially because we must be particularly deferential to our state-court colleagues." Hernandez v. Holland, 750 F.3d 843, 857 (9th Cir. 2014) (internal quotation marks omitted). Thus, a "state-court factual determination is not unreasonable merely because the federal habeas court would have reached a different conclusion in the first instance." Wood v. Allen, 558 U.S. 290, 301, 130 S.Ct. 841, 175 L.Ed.2d 738 (2010).

III

All parties agree on the foundational principle underlying this case: a suspect who seeks to invoke his Fifth Amendment right to silence must do so unambiguously. See Thompkins, 560 U.S. at 381-82, 130 S.Ct. 2250. Once he does, the suspect's right to cut off questioning must be "scrupulously honored," Michigan v. Mosley, 423 U.S. 96, 103-04, 96 S.Ct. 321, 46 L.Ed.2d 313 (1975) (internal quotation marks omitted), and the "interrogation must cease," Miranda v. Arizona, 384 U.S. 436, 473-74, 86 S.Ct. 1602, 16 L.Ed.2d 694 (1966). But interrogating officers have no duty to heed a request that — either on its face or in context — is "ambiguous or equivocal." Thompkins, 560 U.S. at 381-82, 130 S.Ct. 2250.

The California Court of Appeal correctly acknowledged this rule, and determined that, in context, Jones did not unambiguously invoke his right to silence. The court explained that immediately after Jones said he did not "want to talk no more," he continued, "You don't want to hear what I'm telling you." The court opined that, "in context, considering his willingness to talk with the detectives before and after that point in the interview," Jones was not "unambiguously invoking his right to remain silent," but instead was "expressing frustration with the detectives' refusal to believe him."

There is little doubt that this factual conclusion — that, in the full context of Jones's interrogation, any invocation of his right to silence was ambiguous — is reasonable on the record before us. When strung together, Jones's statements quite reasonably read as the state court portrayed them: not as a request for silence but as an expression of frustration by a person who wished the police would believe his story. In the pivotal exchange, Jones's thoughts appear scattered and he seems upset, cutting off Detective Jolivette mid-sentence. Further, neither before nor after this exchange did Jones even obliquely mention a desire for silence. Indeed, for all but one isolated statement, Jones seemed perfectly willing to engage the detectives. In context, it is not unreasonable to interpret that singular, stand-out statement as something other than a clear invocation of the right to remain silent. Under AEDPA, that factual conclusion therefore must stand, unless it was based on an unreasonable misapprehension of clearly established law. See Wood, 558 U.S. at 301-04, 130 S.Ct. 841; Miller-El, 537 U.S. at 340, 123 S.Ct. 1029.

The majority does not seriously contest this conclusion, but instead asserts that clearly established law prohibited the state court from considering this full factual context when evaluating the clarity of Jones's statement. Specifically, the majority holds that the state court could not find Jones's statement ambiguous based on anything Jones said after the precise moment he uttered, "I don't want to talk no more, man." See Maj. Op. at 1132-33, 1136-37.

But the majority has failed to identify any case — alone or in combination with other cases — that clearly establishes anything of the sort.

A

The majority's assertion that ambiguity can never be provided by words a suspect says after he supposedly invokes his right to silence stems, at bottom, from a single Supreme Court case: Smith v. Illinois, 469 U.S. 91, 105 S.Ct. 490, 83 L.Ed.2d 488 (1984) (per curiam). But the Court's opinion in Smith has no bearing on the case before us and, in any event, does not stand for the remarkable proposition the majority attributes to it.

1

First, and most simply, at the time the state court issued its decision, Smith — a case examining the right to counsel — could not provide clearly established law for Jones's right-to-silence claim. In Miranda v. Arizona, the Supreme Court held that, during an interrogation, police must inform a suspect of both rights — his right to remain silent and his right to have an attorney present — and that they must cease all questioning upon the suspect's invocation of either right. 384 U.S. at 471-74, 86 S.Ct. 1602. But, until last December, we had refused to treat cases defining the standards for invoking one right (e.g., the right to counsel) as clearly established law governing the standards for invoking the other right (e.g., the right to silence). See Garcia v. Long, 808 F.3d 771, 777 n. 1 (9th Cir. 2015); Anderson v. Terhune, 516 F.3d 781, 787 n. 3 (9th Cir. 2008) (en banc); see also Bui v. DiPaolo, 170 F.3d 232, 239 (1st Cir. 1999) (right-to-counsel precedent did not "authoritatively answer" question in a right-to-silence case, even though the Supreme Court "likely would" apply the same standard to both rights (internal quotation marks omitted)).

We recently changed our interpretation only because of intervening Supreme Court precedent. In 2010, the Supreme Court considered whether past decisions that required an invocation of the right to counsel to be unambiguous applied equally to a suspect who sought to invoke his right to silence. In Berghuis v. Thompkins, the Court held that the same standards indeed do apply, explaining that it saw "no principled reason to adopt different standards for determining when" either right had been invoked. 560 U.S. at 381, 130 S.Ct. 2250. Accordingly, we recently held that, after Thompkins, right-to-counsel precedent now may indeed provide clearly established law in right-to-silence cases — despite our past practice to the contrary. Garcia, 808 F.3d at 777 n. 1.

But, critically, this development in the law occurred after both the California Court of Appeal and the California Supreme Court issued their decisions on Jones's claim (in 2008). Under AEDPA, we may grant relief only if the state court's decision is irreconcilable with the law as clearly established by the Supreme Court at the time the state court acted. Greene v. Fisher, ____ U.S. ____, 132 S.Ct. 38, 44-45, 181 L.Ed.2d 336 (2011); Pinholster, 563 U.S. at 182, 131 S.Ct. 1388. Before Thompkins, it was anything but clear that right-to-counsel cases governed right-to-silence claims. That very question was at the heart of the Supreme Court's grant of certiorari in Thompkins. See Thompkins, 560 U.S. at 381, 130 S.Ct. 2250. Even if one agrees with the Court's affirmative answer to that question, the point is that the answer had never been given until Thompkins. See id.; see also Anderson, 516 F.3d at 799 (Tallman, J., dissenting) ("The United States Supreme Court has never declared its right to counsel principles applicable to invoking the right to silence, and under AEDPA that precedent was not `clearly established' when the California Court of Appeal rendered its decision."). Acting before Thompkins, the state court cannot possibly have failed reasonably to apply Smith's right-to-counsel holding to Jones's right-to-silence claim. Indeed, before Thompkins, not even our court would have evaluated Jones's claim under Smith. See Garcia, 808 F.3d at 777 n. 1. Accordingly, any supposed error related to Smith cannot be a basis for upsetting the decision of the California Court of Appeal.

2

Second, even if Smith did govern Jones's right-to-silence claim, that case does not remotely stand for the sweeping propositions the majority attributes to it. Jones's case is nothing at all like Smith, and the state court's refusal to extend Smith to Jones's situation is patently reasonable. In short, even on its merits, Smith provides no basis on which to grant relief in this case.

a

In Smith, at the outset of police questioning, the suspect (Smith) stated that an unidentified woman told him to get an attorney. 469 U.S. at 92, 105 S.Ct. 490. Shortly thereafter, when asked whether he understood his right to have an attorney present, Smith responded, "Uh, yeah. I'd like to do that." Id. at 93, 105 S.Ct. 490. Rather than stop so that Smith could contact an attorney, the officers continued to read his rights, and "then pressed him again to answer their questions." Id. After a somewhat confused back-and-forth about his right to an attorney, Smith ultimately agreed to speak without a lawyer present. Id. On review before the Supreme Court, Smith argued that all questioning should have ceased the moment he requested an attorney the first time. The State countered that it was unclear to the officers whether Smith actually wanted an attorney given that he agreed to proceed without one after further questioning.

The Supreme Court rejected the State's argument, and explained that once an unambiguous request for counsel has been made, "an accused's postrequest responses to further interrogation may not be used to cast retrospective doubt on the clarity of the initial request itself." Id. at 100, 105 S.Ct. 490 (emphasis omitted). This rule was needed to prevent officers from "badgering or overreaching" to "wear down the accused and persuade him to incriminate himself not withstanding his earlier request for counsel's assistance." Id. at 98, 105 S.Ct. 490 (internal quotation marks and alterations omitted). But questioning need not end where the accused's request "may be characterized as ambiguous or equivocal as a result of events preceding the request or of nuances inherent in the request itself." Id. at 99-100, 105 S.Ct. 490.

The rule of Smith is thus: once a suspect clearly invokes his right to counsel, officers may not continue to question him and use his answers to those questions to cast retrospective doubt on the clarity of his initial invocation. That is, ambiguity cannot be retroactively manufactured through the suspect's "postrequest responses to further interrogation." Id. at 100, 105 S.Ct. 490 (emphasis added). But Jones's critical statement — the utterance that the state court reasonably determined cast doubt on what Jones meant by "I don't want to talk no more" — was not a response to further interrogation. Despite the majority's many assertions to the contrary, Maj. Op. at 1132, 1137, 1140-41, the police did not ask Jones a single question between his two statements. They did not continue "interrogating" him at all. Indeed, Detective Jolivette did not even get out a complete sentence — it is anyone's guess what that sentence was going to be — before Jones cut him off to say, "You don't want to hear what I'm telling you." Jolivette's next comment was just to ask Jones to speak louder because he was having trouble hearing him. Jones then said, "I'm telling you all." Only then — at which point an officer quite reasonably may have been confused as to whether Jones was seeking to remain silent — did questioning continue. Jones never again hinted at a desire for silence.

This is nothing at all like the situation in Smith, where officers spoke to and questioned the suspect at length after he requested an attorney. In Smith, the State contended that the suspect's earlier request was unclear based only on his "responses to continued police questioning." 469 U.S. at 97, 105 S.Ct. 490 (emphasis added). By contrast, the officers here asked Jones nothing, they did not continue interrogating him, and they certainly did not manufacture ambiguity by badgering Jones or wearing him down. See id. at 98, 105 S.Ct. 490. Instead, Jones's statement was ambiguous immediately, as confirmed by comments he made directly afterward. While those comments came later in time (barely), they were not the product of any "further interrogation" whatsoever. This situation is patently — and certainly reasonably — distinguishable from that in Smith.

If the limitations of Smith were not already obvious on the face of the Court's analysis, the Court took additional care to emphasize that its "decision [was] a narrow one." Id. at 99, 105 S.Ct. 490. That narrow decision did "not decide the circumstances in which an accused's request for counsel may be characterized as ambiguous or equivocal as a result of events preceding the request or of nuances inherent in the request itself." Id. at 99-100, 105 S.Ct. 490. And Smith certainly does not preclude the California courts from determining that Jones's situation presents just such a circumstance where the suspect's "request itself" was ambiguous. Even if on de novo review the majority would reach a different result, the majority's preferred interpretation is certainly not "beyond any possibility for fairminded disagreement." Richter, 562 U.S. at 103, 131 S.Ct. 770.

b

The majority holds to the contrary only by misattributing to Smith a sweeping rule that case in no way embraced. The majority suggests that Smith's prohibition against creating ambiguity on the basis of "postrequest responses to further interrogation" actually means that the police must disregard anything the suspect happens to say at a moment in time after he has arguably invoked his right to silence. See Maj. Op. at 1132-33, 1140-41. That is, even though context may render an otherwise apparently clear statement ambiguous, the majority concludes that such context can never be supplied by something the suspect says after his supposed request for silence.

The majority's reading not only stretches Smith to its breaking point, but it creates a rule that defies the basic logic of human interaction and which would have sweeping consequences for police officers. Consider, for example, a situation in which there is no interruption by a police officer at all. Suppose that during an interrogation a suspect said, "Man, I don't even want to talk about this anymore." Then, after an uninterrupted pause, he continued, "This is so frustrating. I'm answering all your questions, but you won't believe what I'm saying." Must an officer plug his ears and ignore the latter two sentences, merely because they came after the first sentence? Of course not. Smith does not compel such a result, and anyone who has ever held a conversation would naturally reject it. Indeed, albeit in an unpublished disposition, another panel of our court recently held that Smith allows officers to take into account the totality of just such a sequence. In United States v. Winsor, a suspect stated, "I think I'd like an attorney," which after a "couple moments of silence," he followed with, "Shouldn't I have an attorney here?" 549 Fed.Appx. 630, 633 (9th Cir. 2013) (mem.) (internal quotation marks omitted). Our court held that the suspect's two sentences — which the police did not attempt to "engineer" — should be read together as a single statement that, as a whole, was not an unambiguous request for counsel. Id. Precedential or not, that decision certainly reflects a reasonable interpretation of Smith, which, again, is the low bar the State must clear.

And if Smith would allow an officer to consider two separate but uninterrupted sentences together as a single statement, we are left with a simple question: does Smith mandate a different result merely because an officer manages to eke out half a thought between the suspect's two sentences? As explained above, plainly not. Smith spoke of "responses to further interrogation" and was concerned with ambiguity manufactured through repeated questioning and badgering. It says nothing for where, as here, an officer merely says something — but does not interrogate, question, or badger — before the suspect continues talking.

The majority complains that such an interpretation of Smith somehow obscures the "bright-line" prohibition against continuing to interrogate a suspect after he has clearly invoked his right to silence. See Maj. Op. at 1139 n. 2. The majority claims that this interpretation would "create a gray area about how much [continued] interrogation is interrogation enough," and would allow officers to continue asking a suspect "some threshold number of questions." Id. Not so. I must emphasize once again: the police asked no questions between Jones's critical statements. The only "threshold number of questions" needed to distinguish this case from Smith is the simplest threshold of all: zero. If Jones had been forced to respond to even a single question — that is, if the police had continued to interrogate him at all — perhaps that would raise more difficult considerations regarding the precise limits of the rule set in Smith. Fortunately, in this case we need to recognize only that what Smith prohibits is "continued police questioning," 469 U.S. at 97, 105 S.Ct. 490, and "further interrogation," id. at 100, 105 S.Ct. 490 — neither of which happened here.

At best, the majority's expansive rule represents an extension of Smith to a situation not contemplated by the Court in that case. Regardless how much the majority might prefer such an extension, that is not cause for relief under AEDPA. See White v. Woodall, ____ U.S. ____, 134 S.Ct. 1697, 1706, 188 L.Ed.2d 698 (2014) ("[I]f a habeas court must extend a rationale before it can apply to the facts at hand, then by definition the rationale was not clearly established at the time of the state-court decision." (internal quotation marks omitted)). Fundamentally, the question before us is not whether the majority's expansive reading of Smith is correct or incorrect; the only question we may consider is whether the state court could reasonably interpret Smith more narrowly so as to distinguish it from the situation before us. Quite obviously it could.[2]

B

Despite superficial attempts to do so, the majority cites no case that bridges the analytical gaps left unfilled by Smith.

The majority asserts that Miranda v. Arizona itself clearly established that the police could not take into account anything Jones uttered after he said that he did not "want to talk no more." See Maj. Op. at 1132, 1136-37. Cherry-picking quotations from

Miranda, the majority argues that because Jones indicated "in any manner" that he wished for silence, the police were required to stop speaking to him. See Maj. Op. at 1136-37, 1141 (quoting Miranda, 384 U.S. at 473-74, 86 S.Ct. 1602). But, despite the majority's selective quotations, it is decidedly not the law that police must cease speaking — or even questioning — once a suspect indicates that he wishes for silence "in any manner." Rather, the manner in which the suspect requests silence must be unambiguous; an "ambiguous or equivocal" request will not do. Thompkins, 560 U.S. at 381-82, 130 S.Ct. 2250. Thus, at least as subsequently clarified by the Supreme Court, Miranda would better be described to hold that questioning must stop whenever a suspect requests silence "in any [unambiguous] manner." Despite its best efforts not to,[3] the majority concedes as much. See Maj. Op. at 1139 n. 2 ("[Miranda and Smith] stand for the simple proposition that officers must stop questioning a suspect once he unambiguously invokes his right to silence...." (emphasis added)). But that simply returns us to the same question we started with: what does it mean for a statement to be unambiguous, and what sort of factual context may an officer consider when interpreting the clarity of a statement? On these questions, Miranda provides no guidance at all.

Completely beside the point, the majority makes much of the Supreme Court's commands in Miranda and in Michigan v. Mosley that a valid request for silence must be "scrupulously honored." See Maj. Op. at 1137, 1141. It is true that Miranda and Mosley state unequivocally that police questioning must cease once the right to silence is invoked. But that command simply instructs officers how to behave once the right to silence has been unambiguously invoked. This case is about whether the right was ever unambiguously invoked, or more accurately, whether the state court reasonably determined that any invocation was ambiguous in context. Neither Miranda nor Mosley speak to that question.[4]

Finally, the majority reverts to what is becoming an old habit of our court: citing federal circuit court cases to help bolster an attempt to extend Supreme Court precedent under federal habeas review. See Maj. Op. at 1137, 1139, 1140-41, 1142 (citing Garcia, 808 F.3d at 771; Anderson, 516 F.3d at 781; United States v. Lafferty, 503 F.3d 293 (3d Cir. 2007)). This we plainly cannot do. See Glebe v. Frost, ___ U.S. ___, 135 S.Ct. 429, 431, 190 L.Ed.2d 317 (2014) (per curiam); Lopez v. Smith, ___ U.S. ___, 135 S.Ct. 1, 4, 190 L.Ed.2d 1 (2014) (per curiam); Marshall v. Rodgers, ___ U.S. ___, 133 S.Ct. 1446, 1450-51, 185 L.Ed.2d 540 (2013) (per curiam). And even more, just like the majority's chosen Supreme Court cases, none of the Court of Appeals cases cited by the majority actually holds that a court can never infer ambiguity on the basis of statements made after a supposedly clear request for silence.[5] Even if these cases were relevant under AEDPA review, they would not get the majority to its preferred destination.

In sum, the majority's rejection of the factual context provided by Jones's complete statements stems from an overly broad reading of Smith that is unsupported by reference to Miranda, Mosley, or any other case cited in the majority's opinion. Under AEDPA, the State court cannot be faulted for failing to anticipate the majority's de novo extension of the law.

IV

In this case, the California Court of Appeal: (1) identified the correct legal rule applicable to Jones's right-to-silence claim, (2) reasonably interpreted the facts underlying Jones's claim, and (3) reasonably applied that legal rule to those facts in rejecting the claim. The majority does not identify a single case — let alone a relevant Supreme Court case — that holds to the contrary or that even contemplates the situation in which Jones's claim arose. Instead, the majority essentially concludes that Supreme Court precedent ought to extend farther than it currently does, and — as has unfortunately become routine for our court — chastises the state court for failing to predict and to adhere to the majority's preferred view of the law.

Because AEDPA prohibits federal courts from doing exactly that, I respectfully dissent.

Notes

[1] Because the California Supreme Court summarily denied review, we look through that denial to the reasoning given by the California Court of Appeal when it denied Jones's claim. See Cannedy v. Adams, 706 F.3d 1148, 1158 (9th Cir. 2013), amended on denial of reh'g, 733 F.3d 794 (9th Cir. 2013).

[2] Further, given the limitations of the record before us, I fail to see how we could possibly conclude that it is unreasonable to characterize Jones's comments as one continuous statement. We do not have the benefit of an audio recording, and thus we are left to guess just how rapid the exchange between Jones and Jolivette was. As the author of today's opinion suggested at oral argument, one quite reasonable interpretation of our limited record is that Jones and Jolivette spoke so quickly that they were "stepping on each other's lines." That is, perhaps the exchange was so rapid that Jones's two statements came out "as almost one sentence that has a little interruption in there."

Of course, the transcript could be read in a way to make this a more difficult case for the government — for example if we infer a dramatic pause between when Jones and Jolivette spoke. But, once again, under AEDPA we are not asked to determine what the best reading of the record is (and certainly not what reading is most favorable to Jones). We are tasked only with determining whether the state court's view of the exchange was reasonable. It was.

[3] The majority at times seems to suggest that our analysis should ignore the Supreme Court's holding in Thompkins that a suspect's request for silence must be unambiguous. See Maj. Op. at 1139-40, 1140 n. 3. The majority argues that, if AEDPA prevents Jones from basing his claim on anything the Court wrote in Thompkins, see supra Part III.A.1, then the government must likewise ignore any aspect of Thompkins that confirms the correctness of the state court's decision. See Maj. Op. at 1140 n. 3. But we have every reason to treat the parties differently in this respect, and the majority's argument to the contrary would turn AEDPA on its head.

AEDPA prohibits us from granting relief unless the state court unreasonably applied federal law as clearly established at the time the state court acted. See Greene, 132 S.Ct. at 44-45. Thus, Jones cannot receive relief based on anything in Thompkins, because Thompkins came after the state court's decision in this case. See supra Part III.A.1. The government, on the other hand, is asked only to show that the state court's decision was reasonable. To do that, the government has no need to rely on Thompkins at all. Before Thompkins, we had held that it was at least reasonable for a court to conclude that a request for silence must be unambiguous, even if the Supreme Court had not clearly established as much. See DeWeaver v. Runnels, 556 F.3d 995, 1001-02 (9th Cir. 2009). Thus, in many ways, Thompkins is beside the point for the government in this case.

But, even if reference to Thompkins is not necessary to conclude that the state court's decision was reasonable, we may of course cite Thompkins to underscore that conclusion. It would be the very antithesis of deference for us to ignore the fact that state court's conclusion about ambiguity was later held by the Supreme Court to be correct. Given the standard of review erected by AEDPA, there is no contradiction in allowing the government to rely on a case even when Jones may not. Cf. Lockhart v. Fretwell, 506 U.S. 364, 372-73, 113 S.Ct. 838, 122 L.Ed.2d 180 (1993) (state may take benefit of new rules on collateral review even though petitioner may not).

Finally, I must observe that the majority and I have referenced Thompkins for two very different reasons. I cite Thompkins merely to confirm that the state court was right to conclude that Jones's request for silence needed to be unambiguous. The majority, however, seeks to use Thompkins to sustain its otherwise unsupportable assertion that the state court was compelled to follow all of the Supreme Court's prior cases discussing ambiguity in the right-to-counsel context. See Maj. Op. at 1140 n. 3. Again, before Thompkins, the Supreme Court had never held that right-to-silence invocations are governed by the same standards as right-to-counsel invocations. Even if the state court determined that both invocations need to be "unambiguous," it was by no means compelled also to conclude that the standards governing ambiguity must be the same in both contexts. As the majority itself points out, Maj. Op. at 1137-38, there could reasonably be different standards that govern each right (even if that argument is now foreclosed by Thompkins).

[4] In the same vein, the majority discusses standards for evaluating a claim of waiver after the right to counsel has been invoked, as developed by the Supreme Court in cases such as Edwards v. Arizona, 451 U.S. 477, 101 S.Ct. 1880, 68 L.Ed.2d 378 (1981). See Maj. Op. at 1145-47. Again, the case before us is strictly about whether Jones ever invoked his right to silence unambiguously; it has nothing to do with how we determine waiver after such an invocation has occurred.

[5] Of the Court of Appeals cases, the majority relies most heavily on our en banc decision in Anderson v. Terhune, a case inapposite on its facts. There, officers ignored a suspect's "clear and repeated invocations of his right to remain silent" by feigning not to understand what he meant. See 516 F.3d at 785-86. Under AEDPA, we held that Miranda

does not allow officers to "manufacture[] [ambiguity] by straining to raise a question regarding the intended scope of a facially unambiguous invocation of the right to silence." Id. at 787. This case says nothing for how a court must interpret a one-time statement rendered ambiguous nearly immediately afterward — and before police officers can even complete another sentence.

Judge O'Scannlain's concurrence and dissent in US v. Pridgette (Aug 5, 2016)

O'SCANNLAIN, Circuit Judge, concurring in part and dissenting in part:

I concur in the court's vacatur of the sentence and restitution order and in its remand for resentencing. I respectfully dissent from the court's decision to limit the evidence that the district court may consider on remand to that which is in the existing record.

I

A

"The default rule is that `if a district court errs in sentencing, we will remand for resentencing on an open record — that is, without limitation on the evidence that the district court may consider.'" United States v. Flores, 725 F.3d 1028, 1043 (9th Cir. 2013) (quoting United States v. Matthews, 278 F.3d 880, 885-86 (9th Cir. 2002) (en banc)). "We may depart from this general rule where additional evidence would not have changed the outcome or where there was a failure of proof after a full inquiry into the factual question at issue." Id. (emphasis added) (internal quotation marks omitted). Because departure from the default rule is permissive, not mandatory, I would require the party seeking a closed remand to explain why we should depart from our default rule.

Pridgette did not address this issue at all in his opening brief. "We review only issues that are argued specifically and distinctly in a party's opening brief." Christian Legal Soc'y v. Wu, 626 F.3d 483, 485 (9th Cir. 2010) (alteration omitted) (quoting Brownfield v. City of Yakima, 612 F.3d 1140, 1149 n.4 (9th Cir. 2010)); see also id. at 487 ("[W]e won't `consider matters on appeal that are not specifically and distinctly argued in appellant's opening brief.'" (quoting Miller v. Fairchild Indust., Inc., 797 F.2d 727, 738 (9th Cir. 1986))).

"We adhere to this approach for sound prudential reasons." Loher v. Thomas, No. 14-16147, 825 F.3d 1103 (9th Cir. June 17, 2016) (quoting Ground Zero Ctr. for Non-Violent Action v. U.S. Dep't of Navy, 383 F.3d 1082, 1091 n.7 (9th Cir. 2004)). "The premise of our adversarial system is that appellate courts do not sit as self-directed boards of legal inquiry and research, but essentially as arbiters of legal questions presented and argued by the parties before them." Id. (quoting NASA v. Nelson, 562 U.S. 134, 148 n.10, 131 S.Ct. 746, 178 L.Ed.2d 667 (2011)); see also Indep. Towers of Wash. v. Washington, 350 F.3d 925, 929 (9th Cir. 2003) ("Our adversarial system relies on the advocates to inform the discussion and raise the issues to the court."); Abovian v. INS, 219 F.3d 972, 981 (9th Cir. 2000) (Wallace, J., dissenting) ("There is a risk that the court, lacking the analysis ordinarily provided by adversarial parties, will reach the wrong conclusion on the merits and create poor precedent....").

Because Pridgette did not argue anywhere in his opening brief that we should order a closed remand, he waived this issue.[1] The majority does not appear to dispute this conclusion. Given Pridgette's waiver, we should have declined to address this issue and applied our default rule of remanding for resentencing on an open record.

B

After failing to raise this issue in his opening brief, Pridgette did not mention this issue in his reply brief or at oral argument.[2] Pridgette did not even object when, after argument, the government confessed error but requested an open remand. Having failed to argue for a closed remand in his opening brief, in his reply brief, at oral argument, or in a response to the government's letter confessing error, Pridgette was granted a fifth chance to make his request when the panel sua sponte ordered him to address this issue in supplemental briefing.[3] I see no need for such solicitude.

Furthermore, I do not see why we should forgive Pridgette's failure to argue this issue in his opening brief but punish the government's failure to develop the record below.[4] If we gave Pridgette a fifth chance to argue for a closed remand, should we not also give the government a second chance to meet its burden of proof?[5]

II

Even assuming that we should excuse Pridgette's waiver, Pridgette's supplemental brief does not persuasively explain why we should depart from our default rule of an open remand.

Pridgette does not expressly delineate the exceptions to the default rule and fails to address squarely why any of those exceptions should apply in this case. Given Pridgette's citations, he seems to argue for the exception based on "failure of proof after a full inquiry into the factual question at issue." See Matthews, 278 F.3d at 886. But Pridgette neither explains what constitutes a "full inquiry," nor explains why there was a full inquiry, nor even states that there was a full inquiry. He merely argues that the government had the opportunity to meet its burden of proof and does not deserve a second chance to do so now. Seeing no adequate explanation in the briefing from Pridgette of why the exceptions to our default rule should apply in this case, I would remand for resentencing on an open record.

Undaunted by the lack of any convincing argument from Pridgette at any stage, the majority, confident as a "self-directed board[ ] of legal inquiry and research," manufactures arguments for Pridgette. But see NASA, 562 U.S. at 148 n.10, 131 S.Ct. 746; Greenwood v. FAA, 28 F.3d 971, 977 (9th Cir. 1994) ("We will not manufacture arguments for an appellant...."). Moreover, it reaches out unnecessarily to establish a prophylactic rule for our circuit because "justice so requires." Maj. Op. at 1258. Rather than adjudicate the dispute that the parties presented to us, the majority decides that, in this case, we must craft a rule to "help prevent" future errors by punishing the government. Maj. Op. at 1258. If we are so eager to set broad rules for the circuit, why did we limit the parties to 1500-

word supplemental briefs, drafted over two weeks, without the opportunity for responses, and without oral argument? Instead, we should have left this question to the next case and to parties who care enough about this issue to brief it without being ordered to do so.

III

Reviewing the record, I remain unconvinced by the majority's argument that there was a "full inquiry" into the duration of Pridgette's prior sentences. After Pridgette objected to the initial pre-sentence investigation report and the government responded, Pridgette augmented his objections in his sentencing memorandum and then referenced his written objections in passing at the sentencing hearing. The government did not file any written response to the sentencing memorandum and did not respond orally to Pridgette's passing reference to the issue at the hearing.[6]

At the hearing, the district court did not explore this issue. It offered no explanation for its decision other than its conclusion that the probation officer had sufficiently addressed the objections in his Addendum. I do not think that this minimal amount of consideration by the court constitutes a "full inquiry" into the factual question at issue. Indeed, a "full inquiry" necessarily requires a modicum of "inquiry." While perhaps the government is partly responsible for the lack of a full inquiry, that does not change the fact that there was no such inquiry.

The majority's prophylactic rule does not require any "inquiry" as part of a "full inquiry" into the factual question at issue. According to the majority, a full inquiry occurs when the government has a "fair opportunity" to present evidence and "squarely raises its arguments before the district court." Maj. Op. at 1257. In other words, the district court need not inquire into the factual question at issue so long as the government has had a chance to address such question.

While this might be a good rule to encourage the government "to present a complete record supporting its desired sentence," Maj. Op. at 1258, I am not convinced that we must establish prophylactic rules for the Department of Justice at the expense of a fully informed determination of the appropriate sentence for defendants. Like the exclusionary rule in the Fourth Amendment context, the majority's prophylactic rule will "generate[ ] substantial social costs," including setting shorter sentences for dangerous convicted felons on the basis of incomplete evidence. See Hudson v. Michigan, 547 U.S. 586, 591, 126 S.Ct. 2159, 165 L.Ed.2d 56 (2006) (internal quotation marks omitted). Given the rule's "costly toll upon truth-seeking and law enforcement objectives," we should be more cautious in establishing and applying it. See id. (internal quotation marks omitted); see also id. ("Suppression of evidence... has always been our last resort, not our first impulse.").

"The process of criminal sentencing is not a game between the government and criminal defendants, in which one side or the other gets penalized for unskillful play. The goal of sentencing is to determine the most appropriate sentence in light of the characteristics of the crime and the defendant." United States v. Matthews, 240 F.3d 806, 823 (9th Cir. 2000) (O'Scannlain, J., dissenting), on reh'g en banc, 278 F.3d 880 (9th Cir.

2002). Unfortunately, the majority loses sight of these principles and seeks to penalize the government to satisfy its own conception of justice.

I respectfully dissent.

Notes

[1] Christian Legal Society explained that, "[w]ithin the opening brief, claims must be clearly articulated in (1) `a statement of the issues presented for review'; (2) `a summary of the argument'; and (3) `the argument' section itself." 626 F.3d at 485 (quoting Fed. R. App. P. 28). In addition, an appellant's brief must include a conclusion "stating the precise relief sought." Fed. R. App. P. 28(a)(9). Pridgette did not include a request for a closed remand in any of these four portions of his opening brief.

[2] Pridgette certainly should have been aware of this issue by the time of oral argument because we ordered the parties to be prepared to discuss Flores, which addresses the scope of the remand at some length. See Flores, 725 F.3d at 1043.

[3] The majority distorts our General Orders when it asserts that, "[w]hen a panel is confronted with an important issue that was not fully addressed in the briefing, our General Orders advise that the panel should order supplemental briefing on that issue." Maj. Op. at 1258. This turns General Order 4.2 on its head. In reality, that rule provides: "If a panel determines to decide a case upon the basis of a significant point not raised by the parties in their briefs, it shall give serious consideration to requesting additional briefing and oral argument before issuing a disposition predicated upon the particular point." This is not a general license for judges to disregard the waiver of issues by ordering supplemental briefing. Rather, General Order 4.2 is a reminder that we should not decide a case on the basis of a point that the parties have not briefed. So, yes, supplemental briefing was appropriate in this case, but only as an alternative to deciding these issues without any briefing from the parties. We should have followed the parties' lead and simply declined to address this issue.

[4] Judge Kozinski has argued elsewhere that we should not treat parties disparately when they have both defaulted. See Alvarez v. Tracy, 773 F.3d 1011, 1024 (9th Cir. 2014) (Kozinski, J., dissenting).

[5] The majority concludes that the government itself waived the waiver issue by not addressing it in its supplemental brief. We ordered the parties to address "whether this case should be remanded for resentencing on an open record or on the existing record" and cited Matthews, so the government reasonably could have read our order not to permit an argument that Pridgette waived a request for a closed record. Even if the government did forfeit such an argument, we used supplemental briefing to cure Pridgette's waiver; why not order another round of supplemental briefing to cure the government's waiver?

[6] The majority asserts that Pridgette "objected for a third time at sentencing." Maj. Op. at 1255. It conveys the impression that Pridgette actually argued about this point at the sentencing hearing. He did not. His counsel simply referenced his prior briefing: "I

will stand on my previous briefing about why I think the criminal history level is actually no higher than five and that the offense level is no higher than 20." Similarly, a reader of the majority's opinion would be forgiven for thinking that the district judge was discussing the appropriate criminal history category when he said that he "ha[d] spent a lot of time thinking about this case." Maj. Op. at 1258 He was not. In context, it is clear that the district judge was talking about the case generally. Finally, the majority asserts that the government "pressed its view that the criminal-history category had been properly calculated" and "admi[tted that] the inquiry into Pridgette's criminal history was thorough." Maj. Op. at 1258. It did not. All it said about the criminal history category was: "I believe that Criminal History Category VI was also correctly calculated."

Judge O'Scannlain's concurrence and dissent in Alvarez v. Lopez (Aug 30, 2016)

O'SCANNLAIN, Circuit Judge, concurring in part and dissenting in part:

I concur in the court's determination that the Gila River Indian Community deliberately waived its non-exhaustion defense. I respectfully dissent, however, from the court's conclusion that the Community denied Fortino Alvarez his "right, upon request, to a trial by jury" when Alvarez never requested a jury. Rather than analyze the scope of Alvarez's jury-trial right under the Indian Civil Rights Act, the majority simply applies an unmoored balancing test without giving a single reason to do so.

I

As the majority recounts, in 2003 Fortino Alvarez struck his girlfriend with a flashlight, threatened her with a knife, hit her brother with the flashlight, and threatened to kill the whole family. The Community charged him with various crimes. Prior to a group arraignment, Alvarez received a copy of the Community's criminal complaint with a "Defendant's Rights" form attached. The Defendant's Rights form included the statement: "You have the right to a jury trial." The Community did not specifically notify Alvarez that he needed to request a jury trial. The rights were also read at the beginning of the group arraignment. At the arraignment, the court asked Alvarez whether he had any questions about those rights. He responded that he did not.

Later that year, Alvarez was convicted of most charges in a tribal-court bench trial in which he represented himself. At no point before or during the trial did Alvarez request a jury or even inquire about one. In due course, Alvarez filed a federal habeas corpus petition under 25 U.S.C. § 1303 challenging various convictions and sentences on the basis of nine claims. The district court, adopting the recommendation of a magistrate judge, dismissed all claims. On appeal, Alvarez challenges only the dismissal of two claims: (1) his claim that he was denied his right to be confronted with the witnesses against him,[1] and (2) his claim that he was denied his right, upon request, to a jury trial.

II

A

"As separate sovereigns pre-existing the Constitution, tribes have historically been regarded as unconstrained by those constitutional provisions framed specifically as limitations on federal or state authority." United States v. Bryant, ___ U.S. ___, 136 S.Ct. 1954, 1962, 195 L.Ed.2d 317 (2016) (quoting Santa Clara Pueblo v. Martinez, 436 U.S. 49, 56, 98 S.Ct. 1670, 56 L.Ed.2d 106 (1978)). "The Bill of Rights . . ., therefore, does not apply in tribal-court proceedings." Id. However, "persons subject to tribal authority can invoke other sources of individual rights. The two most prominent sources of these rights are tribal bills of rights ... and federal statutes such as" the Indian Civil Rights Act of 1968 (ICRA), Pub. L. No. 90-824, § 202, 82 Stat. 73, 77-78 (codified as amended at 25 U.S.C. § 1302(a)). F. Cohen, Cohen's Handbook of Federal Indian Law § 14.03[1], at 944 (2012 ed.) [hereinafter Cohen's].

ICRA, "rather than providing in wholesale fashion for the extension of constitutional requirements to tribal governments, as had been initially proposed, selectively incorporated and in some instances modified the safeguards of the Bill of Rights to fit the unique political, cultural, and economic needs of tribal governments." Martinez, 436 U.S. at 62, 98 S.Ct. 1670. Thus, in ICRA, "Congress accorded a range of procedural safeguards to tribal-court defendants `similar, but not identical, to those contained in the Bill of Rights and the Fourteenth Amendment.'" Bryant, 136 S.Ct. at 1962 (quoting Martinez, 436 U.S. at 57, 98 S.Ct. 1670).

B

"In addition to other enumerated protections, ICRA guarantees `due process of law.'" Id. (quoting ICRA § 202(8)). The majority concludes that the Community's apparent failure to notify Alvarez of the requirement to request a jury (the "demand requirement") was unfair, which sounds perhaps like a due process violation. However, Alvarez has not argued, on appeal or in the district court, that the failure to notify him of the demand requirement violated his right to due process. He argued below that numerous other aspects of his convictions violated his right to due process, but not the tribe's failure to provide notice of the requirement to request a jury.

Fear not. The majority has devised a clever way to vindicate Alvarez's due process rights: ignore the text of ICRA and instead import a due-process balancing test. Maj. Op. at 1028-29 & n.5 (concluding that we should apply the test from Randall v. Yakima Nation Tribal Court, 841 F.2d 897, 900 (9th Cir. 1988)). To its credit, the majority acknowledges that the Randall test was "developed in the context of challenges premised on" ICRA's due process right, § 202(8), and further recognizes that we have never applied the Randall test to a jury-trial claim under § 202(10). Maj. Op. at 1029 n.5.

What the majority does next, however, is both unexplained and troubling. The majority does not state why we should apply an atextual balancing test to a claim under § 202(10). Instead, it jumps straight to the conclusory determination that "the language and principle of Randall sweep beyond Section 202(8)." Maj. Op. at 1029 n.5. With respect, this is not how we should decide cases. We determine the relevant standard to apply in a given case based on reasons to do so, not the absence of reasons to refrain from adopting some standard at random (or at will).

Importantly, Alvarez did not argue that we should apply the Randall test.[2] As a result, he waived any such argument, and the majority should not expect the Community to explain why the Randall test should not apply.

Moreover, we should not apply a test designed to evaluate generalized due process claims under § 202(8) when another ICRA provision, § 202(10), specifically addresses the right to a jury trial. In general, where a specific provision constitutes an explicit textual source of protection against a particular sort of government behavior, that provision, and not more generalized notions of due process, "must be the guide for analyzing" claims that the government engaged in prohibited behavior. See County of Sacramento v. Lewis, 523 U.S. 833, 842, 118 S.Ct. 1708, 140 L.Ed.2d 1043 (1998); United States v. Lanier, 520 U.S. 259, 272 n.7, 117 S.Ct. 1219, 137 L.Ed.2d 432 (1997); Lopez-Valenzuela v. Arpaio, 770 F.3d 772, 805 (9th Cir. 2014) (en banc) (O'Scannlain, J., dissenting). We should apply this principle to analysis under ICRA because the procedural safeguards of ICRA largely mirror those of the federal constitution, both in content and the relative levels of generality of their protections.

Indeed, we have already applied this principle in construing ICRA. In Tom v. Sutton, we declined to apply the due process right in § 202(8) to find a right to appointment of counsel for indigent defendants because § 202(6) specifically addressed the right to counsel. 533 F.2d 1101, 1105 (9th Cir. 1976).

Thus, there are at least two good reasons not to import Randall's due-process test to evaluate jury-trial claims. Yet the majority adopts such test for its analysis without any countervailing reason to do so.[3]

III

Instead of shrugging our shoulders and adopting a due-process test for no reason, we should construe ICRA's jury-trial provision and determine whether the Community violated Alvarez's right under such provision.

A

Alvarez argues that ICRA's jury-trial right parallels the jury-trial right guaranteed by the Sixth Amendment. It clearly does not.

1

Congress modified the safeguards regarding imprisonment and the criminal jury trial in the ICRA. The Sixth Amendment provides:

In all criminal prosecutions, the accused shall enjoy the right to a speedy and public trial, by an impartial jury of the State and district wherein the crime shall have been committed, which district shall have been previously ascertained by law, and to be informed of the nature and cause of the accusation; to be confronted with the witnesses against him; to have compulsory process for obtaining witnesses in his favor, and to have the Assistance of Counsel for his defence.

As originally enacted, the ICRA provided: "No Indian tribe in exercising powers of self-government shall . . .

(6) deny to any person in a criminal proceeding the right to a speedy and public trial, to be informed of the nature and cause of the accusation, to be confronted with the witnesses against him, to have compulsory process for obtaining witnesses in his favor, and at his own expense to have the assistance of counsel for his defense; . . .

(10) deny to any person accused of an offense punishable by imprisonment the right, upon request, to a trial by jury of not less than six persons."

ICRA, Pub. L. No. 90-824, § 202, 82 Stat. 73, 77-78 (1968) (codified as amended at 25 U.S.C. §§ 1302(a)(6)-(8), (10) (2012)).

ICRA § 202(6) contained most of the same text as the Sixth Amendment, but it differed in key aspects. For instance, it did not provide for free counsel for indigent defendants, ICRA § 202(6) (counsel "at his own expense"), while the Sixth Amendment did so provide, see Gideon v. Wainwright, 372 U.S. 335, 83 S.Ct. 792, 9 L.Ed.2d 799 (1963). Also, § 202(6) did not provide a right to a jury trial.

ICRA § 202(10) provided a jury-trial right, but its text did not parallel the Sixth Amendment text at all. Indeed, the only commonality between the text of ICRA § 202(10) and the Sixth Amendment was that both contain the words "right to a," "trial," "by," and "jury." Subsection 202(10) expressly required a request to receive a jury, it did not require an impartial jury, and it did not require a jury "of the State and district wherein the crime shall have been committed." Compare ICRA § 202(10) with U.S. Const. amend. VI.

2

Critically, unlike the Sixth Amendment, ICRA provides a right to have a jury trial only upon request.

In 1986, Congress permitted tribes to impose a sentence of up to one year in jail. Indian Alcohol and Substance Abuse Prevention and Treatment Act of 1986, Pub. L. No. 99-570, § 4217, 100 Stat. 3207-146 (codified as amended at 25 U.S.C. § 1302(a)(7)(B)). At that time, the Sixth Amendment required a jury trial as the default for any crime punishable by more than six months in jail. See Baldwin v. New York, 399 U.S. 66, 69, 90 S.Ct. 1886, 26 L.Ed.2d 437 (1970) (plurality). In federal court, a defendant would receive a jury trial for a non-petty offense unless (1) he waived a jury in writing, (2) the government consented, (3) the trial court sanctioned the waiver, and (4) the waiver was made expressly and intelligently. See Singer v. United States, 380 U.S. 24, 34, 85 S.Ct. 783, 13 L.Ed.2d 630 (1965). The States had "adopted a variety of procedures relating to the waiver of jury trials in state criminal cases." Id. at 36-37, 85 S.Ct. 783. Without a waiver, a jury trial was the default for "serious crimes." Duncan v. Louisiana, 391 U.S. 145, 154, 88 S.Ct. 1444, 20 L.Ed.2d 491 (1968) ("The laws of every State guarantee a right to jury trial in serious criminal cases. . . .").[4]

Thus, contrary to Alvarez's argument, ICRA's jury-trial right differs substantially from the Sixth Amendment's jury-trial right. However, this conclusion merely raises the question: if the rights are different, then what right did Congress provide in ICRA?

B

1

The plain meaning of § 202(10) at the time of its enactment suggests that it did not obligate tribes to provide notice of the demand requirement. Subsection (10) provides: "No Indian tribe ... shall ... deny to any person ... the right, upon request, to a trial by jury." Thus, at least one prohibition is clear in the statutory text: a tribe cannot refuse to grant a defendant's request for a jury trial. The tribe did notify Alvarez of his right to a jury trial, and there is no dispute that Alvarez did not request a jury.

Instead, the parties' dispute centers on whether § 202(10) obligated the tribe also to notify Alvarez of the requirement to request a jury. Do tribes deny the "right, upon request, to a trial by jury" by failing to notify defendants of the need to request a jury? Obviously, the plain text of § 202(10) does not explicitly state that a tribe must provide a defendant with notice of such requirement. The lack of any textual requirement that tribes notify defendants of the need to request a jury strongly suggests that Congress did not impose such a requirement.

2

Context reinforces that the right to receive a jury trial does not include a right to be notified of the need to request a jury trial.

In 1968, there existed both tribal courts established by tribes and Courts of Indian Offenses, which "were created by the Federal Bureau of Indian Affairs to administer criminal justice for those tribes lacking their own criminal courts." Santa Clara Pueblo, 436 U.S. at 64 n.12, 98 S.Ct. 1670; see also Cohen's § 4.04[3][c], at 263-64. Congress applied § 202, including the jury-trial right, to both types of courts. ICRA §§ 201-02. In a neighboring provision, § 301 of that statute, Congress directed the Secretary of the Interior also to establish a model code to govern the Courts of Indian Offenses:

Such code shall include provisions which will (1) assure that any individual being tried for an offense by a court of Indian offenses shall have the same rights, privileges, and immunities under the United States Constitution as would be guaranteed any citizen of the United States being tried in a Federal court for any similar offense, (2) assure that any individual being tried for an offense by a court of Indian offenses will be advised and made aware of his rights under the United States Constitution, and under any tribal constitution applicable to such individual....

Pub. L. No. 90-284, § 301, 82 Stat. 73, 78 (codified at 25 U.S.C. § 1311) (emphasis added). Thus, in federally established Courts of Indian Offenses, a model code would assure that defendants there both have rights—the full slate of rights provided by our Constitution—and that they have notice of these rights. The fact that Congress provided for both in separately enumerated provisions of § 301 strongly suggests that Congress viewed rights as distinct from notice of such rights. While a model code for Courts of Indian Offenses would provide both, Congress did not impose a model code on tribal courts established by tribes, such as the court in which Alvarez was convicted. Instead, for such courts Congress only imposed the rights contained in § 202, without any notice requirement.

Consequently, I would conclude that Congress did not impose on tribes any obligation to notify defendants of the need to request a jury. Section 202(10) only required tribes to refrain from denying the right to a jury trial, but did not obligate tribes to notify defendants of the need to request a jury.

3

Substantive canons reinforce my conclusion that we should not construe § 202(10) to impose on tribes a duty to notify defendants that they must request a jury.

"Federal courts must avoid undue or intrusive interference in reviewing Tribal Court procedures." Smith v. Confederated Tribes of Warm Springs, 783 F.2d 1409, 1412 (9th Cir. 1986). In the specific context of ICRA, the Supreme Court has emphasized that "considerations of `Indian sovereignty are a backdrop against which the applicable federal statute must be read.'" Santa Clara Pueblo, 436 U.S. at 60, 98 S.Ct. 1670 (quoting McClanahan v. Ariz. State Tax Comm'n, 411 U.S. 164, 172, 93 S.Ct. 1257, 36 L.Ed.2d 129 (1973) (alterations omitted)). Most importantly, the Court has admonished, "Although Congress clearly has power to authorize civil actions against tribal officers, and has done so with respect to habeas corpus relief in [28 U.S.C. § 1303], a proper respect both for tribal sovereignty itself and for the plenary authority of Congress in this area cautions that we tread lightly in the absence of clear indications of legislative intent." Id. Absent any clear indications that § 202(10) requires the tribe to notify Alvarez of the demand requirement, we should "tread lightly" and conclude that Alvarez has failed to show that the tribe violated his rights under § 202(10).[5]

C

Based on the plain meaning of the statutory text, the statute's context, and important considerations of tribal sovereignty, I would conclude that ICRA § 202(10) prohibits a tribe from refusing a defendant's request for a jury trial, but does not impose an affirmative obligation on tribes to notify defendants that they must request a jury. Because Alvarez did not request a jury, the Community did not violate his rights under § 202(10).

I respectfully dissent.

Notes

[1] Like the majority, I do not address Alvarez's confrontation rights.

[2] Instead, he argued that the ICRA jury-trial right parallels the Sixth Amendment jury-trial right, so we should employ "federal constitutional standards" to evaluate his jury-trial claim.

[3] Further, I am not persuaded that it was unfair to require Alvarez to do something to invoke his rights. Alvarez was told he had a right to a jury trial. Alvarez failed to object, ask a question, or do anything when it was clear that the trial was proceeding without a jury. And after the trial was over, he failed to appeal. At a certain point, a defendant cannot sit on his rights and then claim unfairness when the trial does not turn out the way he wanted.

[4] The Sixth Amendment does not require a jury trial for "petty offenses," for

which the penalty does not exceed six months' imprisonment or a $500 fine, or both. See 18 U.S.C. § 1(3) (1964) ("Any misdemeanor, the penalty for which does not exceed imprisonment for a period of six months or a fine of not more than $500, or both, is a petty offense."); Cheff v. Schnackenberg, 384 U.S. 379 (1966) (A "petty offense ... does not require a jury trial."). Indeed, at the time of ICRA's enactment in April 1968, three states did not require jury trials for longer periods of imprisonment: Louisiana only granted a jury trial in cases in which capital punishment or hard labor could be imposed; New Jersey's disorderly conduct offense carried a one-year maximum sentence but no jury trial; and New York State did not provide juries in New York City for crimes with a one-year maximum sentence. Duncan, 391 U.S. at 146, 161 & n.33, 88 S.Ct. 1444. Shortly after ICRA's enactment, the Supreme Court confirmed that states need not provide a jury trial for "[c]rimes carrying possible penalties up to six months ... if they otherwise qualify as petty offenses." Id. at 159, 88 S.Ct. 1444. Thus, ICRA § 202(10) provided a greater right than those available in federal court or in state court for offenses for which the penalty did not exceed six months.

[5] We should not give much, if any weight, to the tribal decisions discussed by the parties. First, we should not base our opinion on decisions issued by unrelated tribes. Alvarez makes no argument that the Gila River Indian Community's tribal courts would handle this issue in the same manner as other courts that have addressed the issue. The Community could interpret § 202(10) differently depending on the tribe's own needs, customs, and resources. One commentator has noted:

Indian tribes are not all alike. Tribes range in size from tremendous to tiny. Some gaming tribes have per capita incomes that rival the richest towns in the United States while other tribes are some of the poorest communities in the country. Some tribes have adopted tribal court systems that largely mimic those present in the states surrounding them, while others have courts with little or no resemblance to Anglo-American justice systems.

Max Minzner, Treating Tribes Differently: Civil Jurisdiction Inside and Outside Indian Country, 6 Nev. L.J. 89, 89 (Fall 2005) (footnotes omitted). Thus, the panel should avoid imposing the decisions of unrelated tribes on the Community. To the extent that we give any weight to the tribal opinions, I note that in Confederated Salish & Kootenai Tribes v. Peone, 16 Indian L. Rep. 6136 (C.S. & K. Tr. Ct. 1989), the court stated: "In the event of a pro se defense, it is the accused's responsibility to be aware of his own rights ... and failure to act in a timely manner on his own behalf is a burden the accused must bear alone. Even when the accused intends to obtain legal counsel the need for timely advice generally is the responsibility of the defendant." Id. at 6137.

Like the majority, Maj. Op. at 1030 n.7, I question whether state-court decisions are relevant to our analysis. To the extent that we consider them, I note that several state-court decisions support the tribe's position. See State v. McClinton, 418 S.W.2d 55, 60-61 (Mo. 1967) (discussing State v. Larger, 45 Mo. 510, 511 (1870)); State v. Mangelsen, 207 Neb. 213, 297 N.W.2d 765, 767-68 (1980).

Judge O'Scannlain's dissent from the denial of rehearing en banc in Oregon Restaurant and Lodging Association v. Perez (Sept 6, 2016) [Notes omitted]

O'SCANNLAIN, Circuit Judge, with whom KOZINSKI, GOULD, TALLMAN, BYBEE, CALLAHAN, BEA, M. SMITH, IKUTA, N.R. SMITH, Circuit Judges, join, dissenting from the denial of rehearing en banc:

Our court today rejects the most elemental teaching of administrative law: agencies exercise whatever powers they possess because — and only because — such powers have been delegated to them by Congress. Flouting that first principle, the panel majority equates a statute's "silence" with an agency's invitation to regulate, thereby reaching the startling conclusion that the Department of Labor can prohibit any workplace practice Congress has not "unambiguously and categorically protected" through positive law. The dissenting opinion had it right; the panel majority's extravagant theory is more than the Constitution will bear. And it is more than our own precedents will allow. Because the panel majority reads our precedents out of existence, and opens not one, but two circuit splits in the process, I respectfully dissent from our refusal to rehear these consolidated cases en banc.

I

A

Here is a brief overview of the statutory and regulatory landscape. The Fair Labor Standards Act (FLSA), 29 U.S.C. § 201 et seq., sets a minimum wage employers must pay their employees, id. § 206(a). Employers who have "tipped employee[s]" can meet the minimum-wage requirement in either of two ways. Id. § 203(m). First, they can simply pay such employees a cash wage at or above the minimum. Id. Second, they can pay a cash wage below the minimum, but only if such employees receive enough money in tips to make up the difference. Id. Employers who choose the second option are said to take a "tip credit." In addition, for many decades it has been common practice for employers across service industries to require the people who work for them to share tips with one another, a practice known as "tip pooling." But not all employees are alike. Some, like restaurant servers,[1] are "customarily and regularly tipped," id.; others, like the kitchen staff, are not. Section 203(m) says that if an employer takes a tip credit to satisfy its federal minimum-wage obligations, it is not allowed to institute a tip pool comprising both categories of employees. Id. So, if a restaurant takes a tip credit, it cannot require its servers to share their tips with the kitchen staff (but it can require the servers to share tips with their fellow servers).

Although § 203(m) speaks directly about the tip-pooling practices of employers who take advantage of the tip credit, it says absolutely nothing about tip pooling by employers who do not take a tip credit. In Cumbie v. Woody Woo, Inc., 596 F.3d 577, 578 (9th Cir. 2010), we addressed "whether a restaurant violates the Fair Labor Standards Act, when, despite paying a cash wage greater than the minimum wage, it requires its wait staff to participate in a `tip pool' that redistributes some of their tips to the kitchen staff." We held it does not; instead, the statute's carefully calibrated scope evidenced Congress's clear intent to leave employers who do not take a tip credit free to arrange their tip-pooling affairs however they and their employees see fit. Id. at 580-83. So, if a restaurant guarantees its employees the federal minimum wage, the restaurant can (so far as federal labor law is concerned) force its servers to share their tips with the bussers, cooks, and dishwashers. Section 203(m) does not apply here — it is simply indifferent to the fate of the servers' tips.

Two background principles informed Cumbie's construction of the statute. First, it has been settled law for three-quarters of a century that "[i]n businesses where tipping is customary, the tips, in the absence of an explicit contrary understanding, belong to the recipient. Where, however, such an arrangement is made, in the absence of statutory interference, no reason is perceived for its invalidity." Id. at 579 (quoting Williams v. Jacksonville Terminal Co., 315 U.S. 386, 397, 62 S.Ct. 659, 86 L.Ed. 914 (1942)) (alterations omitted) (emphasis deleted). "Williams establishes the default rule that an arrangement to turn over or to redistribute tips is presumptively valid." Id. at 583. Second, the "Supreme Court has made it clear that an employment practice does not violate the FLSA unless the FLSA prohibits it." Id. (citing Christensen v. Harris Cty., 529 U.S. 576, 588, 120 S.Ct. 1655, 146 L.Ed.2d 621 (2000) ("Unless the FLSA prohibits respondents from adopting its policy, petitioners cannot show that Harris County has violated the FLSA.")).

After examining the statute's text and structure, id. at 580-81, we determined that the "plain text" of § 203(m) only "imposes conditions on taking a tip credit and does not state freestanding requirements pertaining to all tipped employees," id. at 581. As a result, we concluded that the "FLSA does not restrict tip pooling when no tip credit is taken." Id. at 582. "Since Woo [the employer] did not take a tip credit, we perceive[d] no basis for concluding that Woo's tip-pooling arrangement violated section 203(m)." Id. "Having concluded that nothing in the text of the FLSA purports to restrict employee tip-pooling arrangements when no tip credit is taken, we perceive[d] no statutory impediment to Woo's" tip-pooling practice. Id. at 583.

B

We decided Cumbie in 2010. Unhappy with our decision, in 2011 the Department of Labor issued new regulations addressing the very same issue. See Updating Regulations Issued Under the Fair Labor Standards Act, 76 Fed. Reg. 18,832 (Apr. 5, 2011). The preamble to those regulations confessed that Cumbie advanced a "`plain meaning' construction," id. at 18,842, but nevertheless voiced the Department's opinion that Cumbie was wrongly decided, id. at 18,841-42. The Department then announced that, statutory text and Cumbie notwithstanding, henceforth "tips are the property of the employee, and ... section [203(m)] sets forth the only permitted uses of an employee's tips — either through a tip credit or a valid tip pool — whether or not the employer has elected the tip credit." Id. at 18,842 (By "valid" tip pool, the Department apparently means a tip pool consisting exclusively of employees who are "customarily and regularly tipped.") The Department replaced this language:

In the absence of an agreement to the contrary between the recipient and a third party, a tip becomes the property of the person in recognition of whose service it is presented by the customer.

with the following:

Tips are the property of the employee whether or not the employer has taken a tip credit under section [203(m)] of the FLSA. The employer is prohibited from using an employee's tips, whether or not it has taken a tip credit, for any reason other than that which is statutorily permitted in section [203(m)]: As a credit against its minimum wage obligations to the employee, or in furtherance of a valid tip pool.

Compare 32 Fed. Reg. 13,575, 13,580 (1967), with 29 C.F.R. § 531.52.

This new regulation thus flips Williams and Christensen on their heads. It takes the longstanding rule that federal law permits employers to institute any tip-pooling arrangement the FLSA does not prohibit, and turns it into a rule that employers may only institute a tip pool if the FLSA expressly authorizes it.

II

The facts of these consolidated cases are straightforward and undisputed. The Appellees are employers who pay all of their employees at or above the minimum wage. Or. Rest. & Lodging Ass'n v. Perez, 816 F.3d 1080, 1082 (9th Cir. 2016). That is, none of them takes a tip credit. In addition, the employers have opted to institute tip pools comprised of both customarily tipped employees and non-customarily tipped employees. Specifically, Wynn Las Vegas requires its casino dealers to share a portion of their tips with casino floor supervisors, while the employers represented by the Oregon Restaurant and Lodging Association require their servers to share a portion of their tips with the kitchen staff. Id. at 1085. The question for us is whether such tip pools are prohibited by § 203(m).

So far, so Cumbie. The facts are the same. The statute is the same. But this time the panel holds that the tip-pooling arrangements just described are illegal. The only difference is that here we have a Department of Labor regulation declaring that it simply will not follow what Cumbie said was permitted. The problem for the Department is that the Supreme Court has prohibited an agency in its position from doing exactly that. That is, "a court's interpretation of a statute trumps an agency's... if the prior court holding `determined a statute's clear meaning.'" Nat'l Cable & Telecomms. Ass'n v. Brand X Internet Servs., 545 U.S. 967, 984, 125 S.Ct. 2688, 162 L.Ed.2d 820 (2005) (emphasis deleted) (quoting Maislin Indus., U.S., Inc. v. Primary Steel, Inc., 497 U.S. 116, 131, 110 S.Ct. 2759, 111 L.Ed.2d 94 (1990)).

That is precisely what we did in Cumbie: we held that § 203(m) is clear and unambiguous — and that it clearly and unambiguously permits employers who forgo a tip credit to arrange their tip-pooling affairs however they see fit. We said this explicitly no fewer than six times. Cumbie, 596 F.3d at 579 n.6 ("[W]e conclude that the meaning of the

FLSA's tip credit provision is clear ...."); id. at 581 ("[W]e cannot reconcile [Cumbie's] interpretation with the plain text of [the statute]...."); id. at 581 n.11 ("[W]e do not resort to legislative history to cloud a statutory text that is clear." (quoting Ratzlaf v. United States, 510 U.S. 135, 147-48, 114 S.Ct. 655, 126 L.Ed.2d 615 (1994))); id. at 582 (describing Cumbie's reading of § 203(m) as "plainly erroneous"); id. at 582 (refusing to "depart[] from the plain language of the statute" (quoting Ingalls Shipbuilding, Inc. v. Dir., Office of Workers' Comp. Programs, 519 U.S. 248, 261, 117 S.Ct. 796, 136 L.Ed.2d 736 (1997))); id. at 583 (reiterating that our statutory construction proceeded "[a]bsent an ambiguity").

Remarkably, we even declined to consider then-existing Department of Labor regulations — as well as an amicus brief filed by the Secretary of Labor on Cumbie's behalf — precisely because "we conclude[d] that the meaning of the FLSA's tip credit provision is clear," and hence "we need not decide ... what level of deference [the Department's interpretations] merit." Id. at 579 n.6. And, as if the substance of our holding were not already obvious beyond doubt, we cited a Chevron Step One decision to illustrate our reasoning. Id. (citing Metro Leasing & Dev. Corp. v. Comm'r, 376 F.3d 1015, 1027 n.10 (9th Cir. 2004) ("Because we conclude that [the] meaning of the statute is clear, we need not decide whether this regulation should be upheld.")).

Cumbie's teaching is straightforward: § 203(m) simply does not protect an employee's tips except when his or her employer takes a tip credit. Hence, § 203(m) unambiguously establishes that, so far as the FLSA is concerned, employers who forgo the tip credit must be left free to institute tip pools comprising servers and line cooks, casino dealers and floor supervisors, or whatever other combination of employees the affected parties decide.

III

It would take some mighty fancy footwork to get around Cumbie; if Brand X does not foreclose a contrary agency construction here, the doctrine is a dead letter. Indeed, in the panel majority's attempt to dance around Cumbie and its manifestly correct reading of § 203(m), it has stumbled off a constitutional precipice.

A

The problems begin at the beginning. The majority acknowledges that "section 203(m) does not restrict the tip pooling practices of employers who do not take tip credits." Or. Rest., 816 F.3d at 1084. That was the holding of Cumbie. As Cumbie explained, Congress wrote § 203(m) against the longstanding background norm that tip pooling is a matter of private contract. 596 F.3d at 579. Thus, given Congress's deliberate choice to subject one and only one class of employer to regulation — namely, employers who take a tip credit — the clear implication is that all other employers remain free to arrange their tip-pooling affairs without federal interference, just as they were before the statute was passed. And my colleagues say they have "no quarrel with Cumbie." Or. Rest., 816 F.3d at 1090. So we all agree that Congress has chosen not to regulate the tip-pooling practices of employers like the ones we have here; we all agree that such conduct indisputably falls beyond the outer reaches of the FLSA. But then where does the panel majority think the Department of Labor gets authority to ban the very thing Congress has decided not to interfere with?

Here is where the panel majority's analysis goes wrong, and dangerously so. The majority claims to perceive a "crucial distinction between statutory language that affirmatively protects or prohibits a practice and statutory language that is silent about that practice." Or. Rest., 816 F.3d at 1087. From that premise, it concludes that the Department of Labor can ban these employers' tip pooling because § 203(m) does not "unambiguously and categorically protect" it; instead, the statute is simply "silent about that practice." Id. at 1086-87 (emphasis added). For that reason alone, the panel majority holds, the Department has a free hand to prohibit it. Id. As the majority says, any time a statute does not "unambiguously protect[] or prohibit[] certain conduct," the statute necessarily "leaves room for agency discretion" to regulate such conduct as it sees fit. Id. at 1088.

This is a caricature of Chevron. Indeed, the notion is entirely alien to our system of laws.[2]

In one sense, the panel majority is correct: § 203(m) is "silent" about whether employers who do not take a tip credit may require tip pooling, just like it is "silent" about whether I can require my law clerks to wear business attire in chambers. Section 203(m) does not "unambiguously and categorically protect" either practice. Does that mean the Department of Labor is free to prohibit them both? Of course not; obviously, the FLSA cannot serve as a source of authority to prohibit activities it does not cover, just as a statute reading "No dogs in the park" cannot be said to authorize a Parks Department to ban birds as well. The reason is basic but fundamental, and it has nothing to do with any sort of free-floating nondelegation presumption. Rather, the point is that a statute's deliberate non-interference with a class of activity is not a "gap" in the statute at all; it simply marks the point where Congress decided to stop authorization to regulate. And while I do not question that Congress has given the Department "broad authority ... to implement the FLSA," Or. Rest., 816 F.3d at 1084, one does not "implement" a statute by expanding its domain to allow interference with conduct it consciously left alone. The Department is in reality legislating, yet that is a power the Constitution does not permit executive agencies to exercise.[3]

The problem here is that the majority has confused two very different types of statutory silence. Sometimes "[statutory] silence is meant to convey nothing more than a refusal to tie the agency's hands," meaning that Congress has given the agency discretion to choose between policy options Congress itself has placed on the table. Entergy Corp. v. Riverkeeper, Inc., 556 U.S. 208, 222, 129 S.Ct. 1498, 173 L.Ed.2d 369 (2009). But "sometimes statutory silence, when viewed in context, is best interpreted as limiting agency discretion." Id. at 223, 129 S.Ct. 1498. In other words, not all statutory silences are created equal. But you would never know that from the majority's opinion. The majority seems to think executive agencies have plenary power to regulate whatever they want, unless and until Congress affirmatively preempts them. With all due respect, that is a profoundly misguided understanding of administrative law.

An agency may not issue a given regulation unless it has a "textual commitment of authority" to do so. Whitman v. Am. Trucking Ass'ns, Inc., 531 U.S. 457, 468, 121 S.Ct. 903, 149 L.Ed.2d 1 (2001). Indeed, it is axiomatic that "an agency literally has no power to act ... unless and until Congress confers power upon it." La. Pub. Serv. Comm'n v. FCC, 476 U.S. 355, 374, 106 S.Ct. 1890, 90 L.Ed.2d 369 (1986). Thus, it should go without saying that an agency "may not construe the statute in a way that completely nullifies textually applicable provisions meant to limit its discretion." Am. Trucking, 531 U.S. at 485, 121 S.Ct. 903. And "Congress knows to speak in plain terms when it wishes to circumscribe, and in capacious terms when it wishes to enlarge, agency discretion." City of Arlington, 133 S.Ct. at 1868.

Section 203(m) speaks in plain terms, not capacious ones. To illustrate the contrast, imagine a statute that said, simply, "Unfair tipping practices are prohibited. The Secretary may promulgate rules necessary to carry into execution the foregoing prohibition." Now that would be a capacious statute. I will stipulate that a reasonable person could read it to prohibit tip pooling even by employers who do not take a tip credit; on the other hand, a reasonable person could read it not to interfere with such practice. Our hypothetical statute is "silent" in the relevant sense: in the sense that we might read it to cover the practice in question, but we are not compelled to read it that way, so the choice is for the agency to make. But § 203(m) is nothing like that hypothetical statute. It regulates tip pooling by one, and only one, specific class of employer: the employer who takes a tip credit. Hence, as we put it in Cumbie, § 203(m) "does not restrict tip pooling when no tip credit is taken." 596 F.3d at 582. There is no question, therefore, that § 203(m) stops short of regulating employers who do not take a tip credit. The Department has no power to put words in Congress's mouth when Congress has deliberately chosen to stay quiet in the face of activity it knows is taking place.

Simply put, Congress intended to control, not to delegate, when employers may require tip pooling. And there can be no question that the Department of Labor has no power to extend the statute beyond its stopping point. As the Supreme Court has said time and again, "an administrative agency's power to regulate ... must always be grounded in a valid grant of authority from Congress. And `[i]n our anxiety to effectuate the congressional purpose..., we must take care not to extend the scope of the statute beyond the point where Congress indicated it would stop.'" FDA v. Brown & Williamson Tobacco Corp., 529 U.S. 120, 161, 120 S.Ct. 1291, 146 L.Ed.2d 121 (2000) (quoting United States v. Article of Drug ... Bacto-Unidisk... 394 U.S. 784, 800, 89 S.Ct. 1410, 22 L.Ed.2d 726 (1969)).

Thus, as in Brown & Williamson, here "Congress has clearly precluded the [Department] from asserting jurisdiction to regulate" tip pooling by employers who do not take a tip credit. Id. at 126, 120 S.Ct. 1291. "Such authority is inconsistent with the intent that Congress has expressed in the [FLSA's] overall regulatory scheme.... In light of this clear intent, the [Department's] assertion of jurisdiction is impermissible." Id. Because "the statutory text forecloses the agency's assertion of authority," its attempt to prohibit tip pooling by employers like the ones before us "is ultra vires." City of Arlington, 133 S.Ct. at 1871, 1869.

The majority's reasoning flies in the face of the above principles. To prop up its theory that an agency's power to regulate surges like an expansive body of water, covering everything until it bumps up against a wall erected by Congress, the majority relies on Christensen v. Harris County, 529 U.S. 576, 120 S.Ct. 1655, 146 L.Ed.2d 621 (2000), and "Judge Souter's [sic] concurrence," Or. Rest., 816 F.3d at 1088. But Christensen and Justice Souter's concurrence give absolutely no support to the majority's radical idea that an agency can regulate whatever it wants until Congress says out loud that it must stop. Christensen says only what everybody already knows: if a statute can reasonably be read either to permit or to prohibit a given practice, then the agency has discretion to choose which reading to enforce. 529 U.S. at 587-88, 120 S.Ct. 1655; id. at 589, 120 S.Ct. 1655 (Souter, J., concurring). But the whole question is whether a particular statute can be read either way. Sometimes the answer is yes; other times the answer is no, depending on the statute. In this case, Cumbie already said, correctly, that § 203(m) cannot be read either way — it subjects to regulation only employers who take a tip credit, and nobody else. 596 F.3d at 582. The Department has no power to enlarge the statute beyond the point where Congress decided to stop regulating. The Department, and my colleagues along with it, have yet to grasp that "an agency's power is no greater than that delegated to it by Congress." Lyng v. Payne, 476 U.S. 926, 937, 106 S.Ct. 2333, 90 L.Ed.2d 921 (1986).

B

It should come as no surprise that our sister circuits have roundly and forcefully repudiated the specious theory of agency power our court now adopts. Those circuits have echoed again and again the basic reality that silence does not always constitute a gap an agency may fill, but often reflects Congress's decision not to regulate in a particular area at all, a decision that is binding on the agency.

As the D.C. Circuit has explained, "[w]ere courts to presume a delegation of power absent an express withholding of such power, agencies would enjoy virtually limitless hegemony, a result plainly out of keeping with Chevron and quite likely with the Constitution as well." Ry. Labor Execs. Ass'n v. Nat'l Mediation Bd., 29 F.3d 655, 671 (D.C. Cir. 1994) (en banc) (as amended); id. at 659 ("[T]he Board would have us presume a delegation of power from Congress absent an express withholding of such power. This comes close to saying that the Board has the power to do whatever it pleases merely by virtue of its existence, a suggestion that we view to be incredible."); id. at 671 ("To suggest, as the Board effectively does, that Chevron step two is implicated any time a statute does not expressly negate the existence of a claimed administrative power (i.e. when the statute is not written in `thou shalt not' terms), is both flatly unfaithful to the principles of administrative law ..., and refuted by precedent."); see also Aid Ass'n for Lutherans v. U.S. Postal Serv., 321 F.3d 1166, 1174-75 (D.C. Cir. 2003) ("[T]he Postal Service's position seems to be that the disputed regulations are permissible because the statute does not expressly foreclose the construction advanced by the agency. We reject this position as entirely untenable under well-established case law."); Motion Picture Ass'n of Am., Inc. v. FCC, 309 F.3d 796, 805 (D.C. Cir. 2002) (same).

Likewise, the Third Circuit has recognized that "[e]ven where a statute is `silent' on the question at issue, such silence `does not confer gap-filling power on an agency unless the question is in fact a gap — an ambiguity tied up with the provisions of the statute.'" Coffelt v. Fawkes, 765 F.3d 197, 202 (3d Cir. 2014) (quoting Lin-Zheng v. Attorney Gen., 557 F.3d 147, 156 (3d Cir. 2009) (en banc)).

The Fourth Circuit, as well, has held that "[b]ecause we do not presume a delegation of power simply from the absence of an express withholding of power, we do not find that Chevron's second step is implicated `any time a statute does not expressly negate the existence of a claimed administrative power.'" Chamber of Commerce v. NLRB, 721 F.3d 152, 160 (4th Cir. 2013) (quoting Am. Bar Ass'n v. FTC, 430 F.3d 457, 468 (D.C. Cir. 2005)).

The Fifth Circuit agrees. See Texas v. United States, 809 F.3d 134, 186 (5th Cir. 2015) (as revised) ("The dissent repeatedly claims that congressional silence has conferred on DHS the power to act. To the contrary, any such inaction cannot create such power." (citation omitted)).

Same for the Seventh Circuit: "Courts `will not presume a delegation of power based solely on the fact that there is not an express withholding of such power.'" Sierra Club v. EPA, 311 F.3d 853, 861 (7th Cir. 2002) (quoting Am. Petroleum Inst. v. EPA, 52 F.3d 1113, 1120 (D.C. Cir. 1995)).

The Eleventh Circuit piles on: "[I]f congressional silence is a sufficient basis upon which an agency may build a rulemaking authority, the relationship between the executive and legislative branches would undergo a fundamental change and `agencies would enjoy virtually limitless hegemony, a result plainly out of keeping with Chevron... and quite likely with the Constitution as well.'" Bayou Lawn & Landscape Servs. v. Sec'y of Labor, 713 F.3d 1080, 1085 (11th Cir. 2013) (quoting Ethyl Corp. v. EPA, 51 F.3d 1053, 1060 (D.C. Cir. 1995)).

Notice what the panel majority has not produced: a citation to a single case endorsing the extravagant theory of executive lawmaking our court adopts today. Meaningful silence?

At any rate we, too, once knew all of this. In Martinez v. Wells Fargo Home Mortgage, Inc., 598 F.3d 549, 554 n.5 (9th Cir. 2010), we were asked to defer to an agency's regulation of certain bank "overcharges" on the theory that the Real Estate Settlement Procedures Act did "not specifically address the situation at bar" and was therefore "sufficiently silent on the precise matter as to be ambiguous." Nonsense, we said; statutory "`silence' on the subject of overcharges does not mean that Congress's actions were ambiguous on that subject. Congress simply did not legislate at all on overcharges." Id. So, too, with tip pooling by employers who do not take a tip credit, or so I would have thought.

Oh well. Add Martinez to the heap of controlling authorities the panel majority has so casually tossed aside, placing us, here as elsewhere, directly at odds with our colleagues in the rest of the country.[4]

IV

A

Even if this case were framed in terms of Chevron Step Two, it would not make any difference to the analysis or the outcome. Precisely because the Department has not been delegated authority to ban tip pooling by employers who forgo the tip credit, the Department's assertion of regulatory jurisdiction "is `manifestly contrary to the statute,' and exceeds [its] statutory authority." Sullivan v. Zebley, 493 U.S. 521, 541, 110 S.Ct. 885, 107 L.Ed.2d 967 (1990) (quoting Chevron, 467 U.S. at 844, 104 S.Ct. 2778).

My panel-majority colleagues prove the point themselves. Notwithstanding their conviction that the Department of Labor can regulate any private activity Congress has not "unambiguously and categorically protect[ed]" through positive law, they still undertake to reassure themselves that the Department's interpretation of § 203(m) is "reasonable." Or. Rest., 816 F.3d at 1089. Yet their analysis on this score is so perfunctory that it only confirms they must really believe what they have repeatedly said, namely, that an agency does not need a discernible grant of regulatory power over a given subject matter before it can insert itself into the affairs of ordinary citizens.

Unsurprisingly, the majority never mentions the text the Department is (purportedly) executing, not even once. Here is what the majority offers instead:

First, that it was reasonable for the Department of Labor to conclude "that, as written, [§] 203(m) contain[s] a `loophole' that allow[s] employers to exploit FLSA tipping provisions." Id. Which quite obviously begs the question. But not only is it entirely question-begging, it unwittingly concedes that the statute "as written" limits the agency to regulating only those employers who take a tip credit. As explained above, an agency "may not construe the statute in a way that completely nullifies textually applicable provisions meant to limit its discretion," Am. Trucking, 532 U.S. at 485, 121 S.Ct. 1711, for otherwise it would be exercising "the lawmaking function [which] belongs to Congress... and may not be conveyed to another branch or entity," Loving, 517 U.S. at 758, 116 S.Ct. 1737.

Second, the majority invokes the FLSA's legislative history, even though in Cumbie we explicitly refused to do so, explaining that "[o]f course, `we do not resort to legislative history to cloud a statutory text that is clear.'" 596 F.3d at 581 n.11 (quoting Ratzlaf, 510 U.S. at 147-48, 114 S.Ct. 655). In any event, the primary source the majority quotes implicitly disavows the Department of Labor's interpretation. The very Senate Committee Report the majority relies on explains that an "employer will lose the benefit of [the tip credit] exception if tipped employees are required to share their tips with employees who do not customarily and regularly receive tips." Or. Rest., 816 F.3d at 1089 (quoting S. Rep. No. 93-690, at 43 (1974)). That statement makes sense only on the assumption that employers who forgo the tip credit can require tip pooling among customarily and non-customarily tipped employees, just as Cumbie had said. All the

majority can muster in response is a more general statement from the same report that §
203(m) "requir[es] ... that all tips received be paid out to tipped employees." Id. at 1090.
That's it. Even fans of legislative history should hold their noses before allowing one vague
statement from one committee report to trump not only the clear text of the statute, but
also the express interpretation of that text as set out in the very same report.

Third and finally, the majority says that "the FLSA is a broad and remedial act that
Congress has frequently expanded and extended." Id. Here we have yet one more frank
admission that the Department of Labor is "expand[ing] and extend[ing]," not
"executing," the statute Congress enacted. But notice that even on the majority's telling,
Congress is the one empowered to expand and extend the statute; the Department of
Labor emphatically is not. And whatever the majority thinks "the purpose of the FLSA"
happens to be, id. the Supreme Court has told us that "the purpose of a statute includes
not only what it sets out to change, but also what it resolves to leave alone," W. Va. Univ.
Hosps., Inc. v. Casey, 499 U.S. 83, 98, 111 S.Ct. 1138, 113 L.Ed.2d 68 (1991). In this case
there is no doubt that Congress resolved to leave employers like the ones before us alone,
at least as far as their tip-pooling practices are concerned. Neither we nor the Department
have any power to "expand or extend" Congress's decision.

B

Predictably enough, such shoddy reasoning has opened yet another circuit split on
this precise issue. By defying Cumbie and rejecting its obviously correct reading of §
203(m), the majority has created another split with the Fourth Circuit and has set us on a
collision course with several others.

Most immediately, in Trejo v. Ryman Hospitality Props., Inc., 795 F.3d 442 (4th
Cir. 2015), the Fourth Circuit expressly agreed with Cumbie that "§ 203(m) `does not state
freestanding requirements pertaining to all tipped employees,' but rather creates rights
and obligations for employers attempting to use tips as a credit against the minimum
wage." Id. at 448 (quoting Cumbie, 596 F.3d at 581). Accordingly, the Fourth Circuit held
that "it is clear that th[e] language [of § 203(m)] could give rise to a cause of action only if
the employer is using tips to satisfy its minimum wage requirements." Id. For the reasons
explained above, that holding necessarily forecloses the Department's effort to ban tip
pooling by employers who do not take a tip credit. Brand X, 545 U.S. at 984, 125 S.Ct.
2688 ("[A] precedent holding a statute to be unambiguous forecloses a contrary agency
construction.").

Looking beyond Trejo, the forecast is not encouraging for the panel majority here.
In fact, "[r]elying on Cumbie and other cases, nearly every court that has considered the
DOL Regulation has invalidated it under Chevron." Malivuk v. Ameripark, LLC, No. 1:15-
CV-2570-WSD, 2016 WL 3999878, at *4 (N.D. Ga. July 26, 2016); see, e.g., id.;
Brueningsen v. Resort Express Inc., No. 2:12-CV-00843-DN, 2015 WL 339671, at *5 (D.
Utah Jan. 26, 2015); Mould v. NJG Food Serv. Inc., No. CIV. JKB-13-1305, 2014 WL
2768635, at *5 (D. Md. June 17, 2014); Stephenson v. All Resort Coach, Inc., No. 2:12-CV-
1097 TS, 2013 WL 4519781, at *8 (D. Utah Aug. 26, 2013); see also Trinidad v. Pret A

Manger (USA) Ltd., 962 F.Supp.2d 545, 563 (S.D.N.Y. 2013) ("Because the Court is highly skeptical that DOL's regulations permissibly construe the statute, and because it is undisputed that Pret paid its employees the minimum wage without taking into account the tip credit, the Court, in its discretion, declines to conditionally certify a class based on plaintiffs' tip-pooling claims.").

The only court in the land to misread Cumbie is our own!

V

Never let a statute get in the way of a tempting regulation. That, at any rate, seems to be the prevailing mood on our court. I cannot go along with such a breezy approach to the separation of powers, and I regret our decision to let stand the majority's catalog of errors. The majority ignores binding Supreme Court and circuit precedent, allows the Department of Labor to defy the clear and unambiguous limits on its discretion written into the Fair Labor Standards Act, and creates not one, but two circuit splits in the process. Amazingly, however, those might be the least offensive things about the panel majority's opinion.

More reckless is the unsupported and indefensible idea that federal agencies can regulate any class of activity that Congress has not "unambiguously and categorically protected" through positive law. Such notion is completely out of step with the most basic principles of administrative law, if not the rule of law itself.

I respectfully dissent.

Judge O'Scannlain's dissent from the order enjoining the State of Arizona in Feldman v. Arizona Secretary of State's Office (Nov 4, 2016) [Notes omitted]

O'SCANNLAIN, Circuit Judge, with whom CLIFTON, BYBEE, and CALLAHAN, Circuit Judges, join, and with whom N.R. SMITH, Circuit Judge, joins as to Parts I, II, and III, dissenting from the order enjoining the State of Arizona:

The court misinterprets (and ultimately sidesteps) Purcell v. Gonzalez, 549 U.S. 1, 127 S.Ct. 5, 166 L.Ed.2d 1 (2006), to interfere with a duly established election procedure while voting is currently taking place, contrary to the Supreme Court's command not to do so. I thus respectfully dissent from this order enjoining the state of Arizona from continuing to follow its own laws during an ongoing election. And let there be no mistake: despite the majority's pretenses to the contrary, the order granting the injunction is a ruling on the merits, and one based on an unnecessarily hasty review and an unsubstantiated statutory and constitutional analysis.[1]

I

Some background: On September 23, 2016, the district court denied plaintiffs' motion for a preliminary injunction blocking Arizona from implementing certain provisions in Arizona House Bill 2023 (H.B. 2023). These provisions limit the collection of voters' early ballots to family members, household members, certain government officials, and caregivers. Plaintiffs appealed. A Ninth Circuit motions panel unanimously denied plaintiffs' emergency motion for an injunction pending appeal on October 11. That same panel sua sponte amended its October 11 ruling to expedite the appeal on October 14. A merits panel received briefing, heard oral argument, and issued an opinion on October 28, affirming the district court and denying the request for a preliminary injunction by a two-to-one majority. The case was called en banc the same day the opinion was issued. Eschewing our normal en banc schedule, memo exchange was compressed into five days, as opposed to our customary thirty-five. Now, just two days after the en banc call succeeded, and just four days before Election Day, the majority overturns the district court, a motions panel, and a separate merits panel to reach its desired result.

II

The Supreme Court counseled against just this type of last-minute interference in Purcell. That case also involved our court's issuing a last-minute injunction against the enforcement of a contested Arizona election law. 549 U.S. at 2-4, 127 S.Ct. 5. The Supreme Court, on October 20, 2006, vacated that injunction, which had been implemented by a Ninth Circuit motions panel on October 5 — more than four weeks before the election. Id. at 2-3, 127 S.Ct. 5. In doing so, the Court stressed the "imminence of the election" and the need to give the case adequate time to resolve factual disputes. Id. at 5-6. Despite Purcell's direct impact on this case, the majority confines that decision much too narrowly, and in its strained attempt to distinguish Purcell, disregards how this eleventh-hour injunction will impact the current election and many elections to come.

At first, it seemed that we might respect Supreme Court precedent this time around, when first the motions panel, and later the three-judge merits panel, wisely determined that no injunction should issue at this stage. Yet, after a third bite at the apple, here we are again — voiding Arizona election law, this time while voting is already underway[2] and only four days before Election Day. In doing so we depart from our own precedent, see, e.g., Lair v. Bullock, 697 F.3d 1200, 1214 (9th Cir. 2012) (staying a district court's injunction "given the imminent nature of the election"), and myriad decisions of our sister circuits, see, e.g., Crookston v. Johnson, 841 F.3d 396, 398 (6th Cir.2016) ("Call it what you will — laches, the Purcell principle, or common sense — the idea is that courts will not disrupt imminent elections absent a powerful reason...."); Veasey v. Perry, 769 F.3d 890, 895 (5th Cir. 2014) (staying an injunction "in light of the importance of maintaining the status quo on the eve of an election"); Colon-Marrero v. Conty-Perez, 703 F.3d 134, 139 n.9 (1st Cir. 2012) (noting that "even where plaintiff has demonstrated a likelihood of success, issuing an injunction on the eve of an election is an extraordinary remedy with risks of its own"). We also disregard not only Purcell, but other Supreme Court authority disfavoring last-minute changes to election rules. See, e.g., North Carolina v. League of Women Voters of N.C., U.S. ___, 135 S.Ct. 6, 190 L.Ed.2d 243 (2014) (granting stay to prevent interference with election procedures roughly one month before election).[3] In all these cases, "the common thread [was] clearly that the decision of the Court of Appeals would change the rules of the election too soon before the election date." Veasey, 769 F.3d at 895.

The majority recognizes the need to address Purcell and its progeny. But the majority's strained attempt to distinguish those cases is unconvincing — its reasoning either misrepresents Purcell or is irrelevant to the issues at hand. And it misses the main point of Purcell: the closer to an election we get, the more unwarranted is court intrusion into the status quo of election law.

A

First, the majority makes the incomprehensible argument that its injunction "does not affect the state's election processes or machinery." Order at 7. The majority cites no law, fact, or source of any kind in support of this argument, and it is dubious on its face. Of course, H.B. 2023 directly regulates the state's election processes or machinery: it governs the collection of ballots, which obviously is integral to how an election is conducted. But under the majority's Orwellian logic, regulations affecting get-out-the-vote operations are somehow not regulations of the "electoral process." (What are they, then, one might ask? The majority does not tell.) Apparently, the majority believes that only measures that affect the validity of a vote itself (or a voter herself) affect such process. Other courts, in ruling on similar regulations, have rejected the majority's view, and widely held that regulations of many aspects of an election beyond the validity of a vote affect the election process. See, e.g., Lair, 697 F.3d at 1214 (staying injunction of certain campaign finance laws); see also Harris v. Graddick, 593 F.Supp. 128, 135 (M.D. Ala. 1984) (observing that even the racial composition of polling officials could affect the election process).

Tellingly, the majority barely addresses whether enjoining H.B. 2023 will create confusion and disruption in the final days of the election — a key factor in the Purcell decision. 549 U.S. at 4-5, 127 S.Ct. 5 ("Court orders affecting elections, especially conflicting orders, can themselves result in voter confusion and consequent incentive to remain away from the polls."). And, based on this record, how could it? Factual development in the record is sparse. The majority says its injunction will be less disruptive than the Purcell injunction, but offers not a shred of empirical proof for this proposition. Order at 7-10. At this point, it appears that no one knows just how much confusion this court risks by issuing this injunction, after weeks of procedures suggested it would not.[4] What we do know is that the State has approximately four days to figure out and to implement whatever response is necessary to accommodate our latest view of the case. If requiring such action is inappropriate four weeks prior to Election Day, see Purcell, 549 U.S. at 3-4, 127 S.Ct. 5, it surely is in the waning days of voting. The Supreme Court could not have been clearer: "[a]s an election draws closer, that risk [of disruption] will increase." Id. at 5.

B

The majority's second argument — that this case is different because it involves a law that imposes criminal penalties — manages to be both irrelevant and incorrect. It is irrelevant because Purcell never says, or even indicates, that whether a law imposes criminal penalties affects whether the status quo should be upset right before an election. It is incorrect because our own circuit applied Purcell in a case involving a law that affected the electoral process and imposed criminal penalties. See Lair, 697 F.3d at 1214 (staying an injunction that applied to Montana campaign finance law enforced by criminal penalties).

C

Third, the majority misreads Purcell by inventing a supposed Purcell Court concern that the federal judiciary was "disrupt[ing] long standing state procedures" and then equating it with the majority's desire to preserve the pre-H.B. 2023 status quo. Order at 9. Nowhere in Purcell does the Court mention "long standing state procedures." Proposition 200, the voter identification law at issue in Purcell, had been approved by Arizona voters in 2004 and was not precleared until May of 2005. 549 U.S. at 2, 127 S.Ct. 5. The 2006 election was the first federal election at which it would go into effect. The voter identification law was relatively new, but, "[g]iven the imminence of the election," the Court overturned our injunction which would have returned Arizona to a pre-Proposition 200 world, the majority's so-called "status quo." Id. at 5. Obviously, Purcell was actually concerned with changes to the status quo that had occurred within weeks of an election.

And that status quo can be a law or an injunction that has been in place for just a few months. See Frank, 135 S.Ct. at 7. In Frank, the Supreme Court vacated the Seventh Circuit's September 26, 2014 stay of a preliminary injunction enjoining application of Wisconsin's voter ID law, which had been put in place by the district court in April 2014. By the time the Seventh Circuit issued its decision, the injunction had become the new "status quo," even the dissent had to concede the "colorable basis for the Court's decision." Id. at 7 (Alito, J., dissenting). The dissent noted that given the "proximity of the election," it was "particularly troubling that absentee ballots [relying on the injunction] ha[d] been sent out without any notation that proof of photo identification must be submitted." Id.

D

Fourth, the argument that "unlike the circumstances in Purcell and other cases, plaintiffs did not delay in bringing this action" continues the majority's pattern of inventing facts. Order at 9. Nowhere in Purcell does the Supreme Court discuss the timing of the plaintiffs' filing. Nowhere does it say that the plaintiffs affected their chances of success by delaying their filing. Nowhere does it use this factor in its analysis. Indeed, as recounted above, the Supreme Court is far more focused on the date of court orders that upset the status quo in relation to the date of the election. See, e.g., League of Women Voters, 135 S.Ct. at 6 (staying an injunction ordered by the Fourth Circuit a month before the election despite the fact that plaintiffs challenged the statute at issue a year prior to the election).

E

Finally, perhaps betraying its real motivation, the majority bafflingly suggests that our last-minute intervention is required now that the Supreme Court struck down the federal preclearance mechanism in Shelby County v. Holder, ____ U.S. ____, 133 S.Ct. 2612, 2631, 186 L.Ed.2d 651 (2013). But, whatever the majority might think of that opinion, Shelby County has absolutely no relevance to the Court's decision in Purcell.

The majority is correct about one basic point: in discussing the procedural history in Purcell, the Supreme Court mentioned that the regulation at issue had been precleared. 549 U.S. at 2, 127 S.Ct. 5. But the Court did not suggest that preclearance was in any way relevant to its decision. Despite the majority's oblique citation to Purcell, one will not find any support in that decision for its statement that preclearance meant the law in Purcell was presumptively valid — or that any such presumption mattered at all to the question before the Court. Quite to the contrary, the Supreme Court explicitly cautioned that it was not addressing the merits of the claim in Purcell. Id. at 5, 127 S.Ct. 5 ("We underscore that we express no opinion here on the correct disposition, after full briefing and argument, of the appeals [from the district court]....").

Even if the majority believes that courts should engage in a heightened review of voting laws after Shelby County — and I stress the Supreme Court has given us absolutely no reason to believe we should — that does not support the notion that such review matters at this stage of litigation. Purcell is plainly about the impact a court order will have on an upcoming (or in our case, ongoing) election, not the merits of the constitutional claim underlying that order. Id. Pre-clearance, Shelby County, and the merits of the challenge to H.B. 2023 are beside the point. Four days before an election is not an appropriate time for a federal court to tell a State how it must reconfigure its election process.

III

Unfortunately, though I believe the merits should not have been reached until a more thorough review of the case could have been conducted — and ideally more evidence could have been collected, including quantitative data — the majority's decision to consider and then to grant an injunction pending appeal forces the issue. In doing so, and given the current record, the majority, by adopting Chief Judge Thomas's dissent, makes various errors in both its constitutional and federal statutory analysis that further undermine its argument that an injunction is necessary. Order at 6 (adopting the reasoning of Feldman v. Arizona Sec'y of State, 840 F.3d 1057, 1085-98 (9th Cir. 2016) (Thomas, C.J., dissenting)). This situation means we are forced to reach the merits as well. See Order at 6 (citing Lopez v. Heckler, 713 F.2d 1432, 1435 (9th Cir. 1983)).

Unlike the majority, we are persuaded by the analysis of the vacated three-judge panel majority opinion and the district court opinion. Feldman, 840 F.3d at 1062-87; Feldman v. Arizona Sec'y of State, No. CV-16-01065-PHX-DLR, ___ F.Supp.3d ___, 2016 WL 5341180 (D.C. Ariz. Sept. 23, 2016) [hereinafter Feldman (D.C.)]. A few key points, some contained in those opinions, are worth highlighting. One error in the majority's reasoning stands out the most — its failure even to pretend to give any deference to the district court's denial of exactly the same request. See Purcell, 549 U.S. at 5, 127 S.Ct. 5 (concluding that the failure of "the Court of Appeals to give deference to the discretion of the District Court ... was error").

A

The majority's Fourteenth Amendment analysis falsely claims the district court improperly conducted a "rational basis" review. Feldman, 840 F.3d at 1085-87 (Thomas, C.J., dissenting). Yet, the district court never used the phrase "rational basis," instead it explicitly stated that Arizona "must show [ ] that it[s law] serves important regulatory interests," after it conducted the burden analysis.[5] Feldman (D.C.), ____ F.Supp.3d at ____, 2016 WL 5341180, at *11.

The majority argues that H.B. 2023 imposes a "substantial burden" on voting, but this cannot be reconciled with the fact six Justices in Crawford v. Marion Cnty. Election Bd., 553 U.S. 181, 128 S.Ct. 1610, 170 L.Ed.2d 574 (2008), found that Indiana's voting ID law imposed either a "a limited burden," id. at 202, 128 S.Ct. 1610 (Stevens, J., writing for three justices), or a "minimal" one, id. at 204, 128 S.Ct. 1610 (Scalia, J., writing for three justices). The majority does not even try to argue that H.B. 2023 imposes more of a burden on voters than the Indiana law, instead it just does not cite Crawford.

The majority argues that the "state's justification for the law was weak." Feldman, 840 F.3d at 1089 (Thomas, C.J., dissenting). This cannot be reconciled with Crawford's language that "[t]here is no question" that a state's interest in preventing voter fraud is an important interest. 553 U.S. at 194-97, 128 S.Ct. 1610 (holding this even though there was no evidence in the record that the particular type of voting fraud the law was trying to prevent has occurred). Arizona's interest in protecting public confidence in elections is also an established important interest. Id. at 197, 128 S.Ct. 1610. Once again the majority "solves" this problem by pretending that Crawford does not exist.

B

The majority's Voting Rights Act of 1965 (VRA) Section 2 analysis is equally shoddy. 52 U.S.C. § 10301. It concedes that no statistical or quantitative evidence exists in the record. Feldman, 840 F.3d at 1093 (Thomas, C.J., dissenting). It concedes that "the Voting Rights Act focuses on the burdens disproportionately place [sic] on minorities in comparison with the general voting population." Id. at 1093 (emphasis added). It concedes that "[t]he relevant question is whether the challenged practice ... places a disproportionate burden on the opportunities of minorities to vote." Id. at 1092. It concedes the burden lies with the plaintiffs and that "the parties seeking a preliminary injunction in this case must show they are likely to prevail on the merits." Id. at 1094.

Yet, it then argues that the district court erred by asking plaintiffs to show the burden on minority voters was greater than that of white voters. Id. at 1093-94. But the plaintiffs had the burden of showing disparate treatment. Instead of acknowledging that the current record's lack of facts showing a disparate impact is fatal to this claim, the majority invents a burden-shifting requirement. Id. at 1085-89. It argues that "once the plaintiffs had established the burden on minority voters" the district court erred by not "shifting the burden of rejoinder to the State." Id. at 1094. This burden-shifting requirement — which would require the state to prove a negative (no disparity if minorities are burdened) — has no support in the law.

IV

Finally, the unusual procedural history leading up to this decision and the contrived time pressure we placed ourselves under in rendering this decision underscores exactly why courts refrain from intervening in elections at the last minute unless they absolutely have to.[6]

After presumably fuller consideration than our own, a district court judge, a three-judge motions panel, and a two-judge majority of a separate merits panel all rejected Feldman's attempt to have enforcement of H.B. 2023 enjoined for the current election. Yet, with only three days of review (and no oral argument), a majority of our hastily constructed en banc panel has reversed course, requiring Arizona to change its voting procedures the weekend before Election Day. The record presented in this appeal exceeds 3000 pages; the parties' briefs (which now total five, after additional en banc briefing) present complex and well-reasoned arguments; and the alleged constitutional violations are serious. But our en banc panel has found it appropriate (indeed imperative) to resolve the matter in less time than we might usually take to decide a motion to reschedule oral argument.

Despite the majority's pretenses to having "given careful and thorough consideration" to the issues presented in this case, Order at 10, one wonders how much the obvious dangers inherent in our rushed and ad hoc process have infected the decision in this case. Cf. Purcell, 127 S.Ct. at 6 (Stevens, J., concurring) ("Given the importance of the constitutional issues, the Court wisely takes action that will enhance the likelihood that they will be resolved correctly on the basis of historical facts rather than speculation.").

The circumstances of this case do not inspire confidence in the majority's order. First, the majority does not appear even to have resolved what to label the relief it has determined must be handed down in this case.[7] More concerning, and as discussed above, the order fails seriously to grapple with controlling Supreme Court precedent pertaining both to appropriateness of our action at this stage of litigation and to the underlying merits of the issues in this case. The order also wholly fails to explain why it is now necessary to overrule a unanimous order from October 11 — which was approved by one of the judges who now joins the majority — denying an identical emergency motion in this same case. We are left only to wonder why that decision, acceptable four weeks ago, is now the cause for immediate correction.

Worse still is the precedent this hastily crafted decision will create. The majority purports to delay ruling on the merits of the challenge to H.B. 2023 — presumably so that this case can be carefully considered. Order at 11. But it "essentially" adopts the reasoning of a twenty-nine page dissent from the original three-judge panel opinion, Order at 6, which concludes that it is clear "this law violates the Constitution and the Voting Rights Act." Feldman, 840 F.3d at 1086 (Thomas, C.J., dissenting). If our court agrees with the essence of that dissent, what is left to decide after oral argument? The majority's framing of this issue as just a "stay," Order at 11, only obfuscates the fact that our en banc panel has blocked Arizona's voting law, declared it presumptively unconstitutional, and overturned the status quo the weekend before voting ends, all without first taking the time needed to gain a thorough mastery of the record, to hear oral argument from the parties, or to write a considered opinion.

As the majority is quick to remind us, the issues in this case are important.[8] Those issues deserved more than seventy-two hours of consideration. This court's hasty rush to decide those issues on the basis of ad hoc procedure is regrettable. I fear our action in this case will set a precedent that will harm not only the current election in Arizona, but presumably many more down the line, whenever a State enacts a voting regulation that more than half of the active judges on the Ninth Circuit simply deem unwise.

I respectfully dissent.

Judge O'Scannlain's concurrence and dissent in Nance v. May Trucking Co. (March 29, 2017)

O'SCANNLAIN, Circuit Judge, concurring in part and dissenting in part:

While I concur in the court's decision with regard to Nance's claims involving the orientation program, time spent in sleeper berths during the entry-level driver program, the excess engine idling program, and the allegedly willful withholding of wages, I must respectfully dissent from its holding with regard to Nance's claim that May Trucking Co. ("May") paid entry level drivers less than a minimum wage for on-duty hours logged before April 2011.

I

There is no reason to "remand for the district court to consider in the first instance whether Nance and Freedman preserved arguments based on this claim in their district court briefing" because it clearly was not raised below. Maj. at 5. Nance's briefing to the district court with regard to the entry level driver program focused solely on payment for hours spent in sleeper berths. In his brief in opposition to May's motion for summary judgment, Nance mentioned that May had changed its payment policy, but he did not allege that May had failed to pay minimum wage for on-duty hours logged prior to the change. Because the claim was not "raised sufficiently for the trial court to rule on it," it has been waived, and we should not entertain it. In re Mercury Interactive Corp. Securities Litigation, 618 F.3d 988, 992 (9th Cir. 2010) (quoting Whittaker Corp. v. Execuair Corp., 953 F.2d 510, 515 (9th Cir. 1992)).

II

For the foregoing reasons, I would affirm the judgement of the district court.

Judge O'Scannlain's dissent from denial of rehearing en banc in US v. Washington (May 19, 2017) [Notes omitted]

O'SCANNLAIN, Circuit Judge,[*] with whom KOZINSKI, TALLMAN, CALLAHAN, BEA, IKUTA, and N.R. SMITH, Circuit Judges, join, and with whom BYBEE and M. SMITH, Circuit Judges, join as to all but Part IV, respecting the denial of rehearing en banc:

Fashioning itself as a twenty-first century environmental regulator, our court has discovered a heretofore unknown duty in the Stevens Indian Treaties of 1854 and 1855. The panel opinion in this case enables the United States, as a Treaty signatory, to compel a State government to spend $1.88 billion[1] to create additional salmon habitat by removing or replacing culverts[2] under state-maintained highways and roads, wherever found. Pacific Northwest salmon litigation has been ongoing for almost fifty years,[3] has been before our court multiple times, and has been up to and down from the Supreme Court. Nonetheless, it apparently just occurred to the Tribes, the United States, and our court that in order to fulfill nineteenth century federal treaty obligations, the State of Washington must now be required to remove physical barriers which might impede the passage of salmon. See Washington V, 853 F.3d at 966.

Given the significance of this case — both in terms of dollars and potential precedential effect — it seemed the ideal candidate for en banc review and, hopefully, correction on the merits. But rather than reining in a runaway decision, our court has chosen to do nothing — tacitly affirming the panel opinion's erroneous reasoning.

With utmost respect, I believe our court has made a regrettable choice.

I

In reaching its conclusion, the panel opinion makes four critical errors.

First, it misreads Washington v. Washington State Commercial Passenger Fishing Vessel Association ("Fishing Vessel"), 443 U.S. 658, 99 S.Ct. 3055, 61 L.Ed.2d 823 (1979), as requiring Washington to ensure that there are a certain "number of fish" available for the Tribes, "sufficient to provide a `moderate living.'" Washington V, 853 F.3d at 965 (quoting Fishing Vessel, 443 U.S. at 686, 99 S.Ct. 3055).

Second, by holding that culverts need to be removed because they negatively impact the fish population, the panel opinion sets up precedent that could be used to challenge activities that affect wildlife habitat in other western states, which led Idaho and Montana to join Washington in requesting rehearing. The panel opinion fails to articulate a limiting legal principle that will prevent its holding from being used to attack a variety of development, construction, and farming practices, not just in Washington but throughout the Pacific Northwest.

Third, the panel opinion contravenes City of Sherrill v. Oneida Indian Nation of New York, 544 U.S. 197, 125 S.Ct. 1478, 161 L.Ed.2d 386 (2005), by refusing to apply the doctrine of laches to the United States.

Fourth, the panel opinion upholds an injunction that is overbroad — requiring the State to spend millions of dollars on repairs that will have no immediate effect on salmon habitat.

II

The Stevens Treaties[4] provide that "[t]he right of taking fish, at all usual and accustomed grounds and stations, is further secured to said Indians, in common with all citizens of the Territory." Fishing Vessel, 443 U.S. at 674, 99 S.Ct. 3055. The precise contours of this guarantee remain hotly contested but were most fully addressed by the Supreme Court's opinion in Fishing Vessel.

A

The panel opinion reads language in Fishing Vessel as requiring that there be enough fish to provide a "moderate living" for the Tribes. See Washington V, 853 F.3d at 965-66. It is true that the Court stated that "Indian treaty rights to a natural resource [i.e. fish] ... secures so much as, but no more than, is necessary to provide the Indians with a livelihood — that is to say, a moderate living." Fishing Vessel, 443 U.S. at 686, 99 S.Ct. 3055. In isolation, this statement might be read as guaranteeing the Tribes a certain number of fish, but only if one ignores the rest of the opinion. In Fishing Vessel, the Supreme Court adopted the United States' position that the Treaties entitled the Tribes "either to a 50% share of the `harvestable' fish" passing through their fishing grounds "or to their needs, whichever was less." Id. at 670, 99 S.Ct. 3055 (emphasis added); see also id. at 685-86, 99 S.Ct. 3055.

Thus, notwithstanding the significance of fish to the Tribes, the Court recognized that "some ceiling should be placed on the Indians' apportionment to prevent their needs from exhausting the entire resource and thereby frustrating the treaty right of `all [other] citizens of the Territory.'" Id. at 686, 99 S.Ct. 3055. The Court ruled that 50% of the available fish was the appropriate limit. See id. ("[T]he 50% figure imposes a maximum ... allocation.") ("[T]he maximum possible allocation to the Indians is fixed at 50%."); id. at 686, 99 S.Ct. 3055 n.27 ("Because the 50% figure is only a ceiling, it is not correct to characterize our holding as `guaranteeing the Indians a specified percentage' of the fish.").

Such ceiling makes intuitive sense. With or without pre-existing barriers, the population of fish varies dramatically from year to year and season to season. In a year with a low run of fish, absent a ceiling, the Tribes' needs could easily predominate, leaving few fish for other citizens. Thus, to protect the rights of all parties to the Treaties, the Court imposed a 50% ceiling.

Since the fish population varies, however, the presence of the ceiling necessarily entails that the Tribes may not always receive enough fish to provide a "moderate living." Indeed, the Court emphasized that the Treaties secured to the Tribes "a fair share of the available fish," rather than a certain number of fish. Id. at 685, 99 S.Ct. 3055 (emphasis added). The total number of fish that the Tribes receive indubitably will vary with the run of fish. See id. at 679, 99 S.Ct. 3055 (observing that the Treaties "secure the Indians' right to take a share of each run of fish that passes through tribal fishing areas" (emphasis added)); id. at 687, 99 S.Ct. 3055 (discussing the "50% allocation of an entire run that passes through ... customary fishing grounds").

Thus, by imposing a percentage ceiling tied to the relevant run rather than a fixed numerical floor, the Court rejected the proposition that the Tribes were entitled to a certain number of fish. Indeed, "while the maximum possible allocation to the Indians is fixed at 50%, the minimum is not; the latter will, upon proper submissions to the District Court, be modified in response to changing circumstances."[5] Id. at 686-87, 99 S.Ct.

3055. Our court has confirmed this holding multiple times.

In United States v. Washington, 759 F.2d 1353, 1359 (9th Cir. 1985) ("Washington III"), our en banc court explained:

> [T]he Supreme Court in Fishing Vessel did not hold that the Tribes were entitled to any particular minimum allocation of fish. Instead, Fishing Vessel mandates an allocation of 50 percent of the fish to the Indians, subject to downward revision if moderate living needs can be met with less. The Tribes have a right to at most one-half of the harvestable fish in the case area.

Id. (emphasis added). Likewise in Midwater Trawlers Co-operative v. Department of Commerce, 282 F.3d 710, 719 (9th Cir. 2002), we observed that under Fishing Vessel, the Makah Tribe was entitled "to one-half the harvestable surplus of Pacific whiting that passes through its usual and accustomed fishing grounds, or that much of the harvestable surplus as is necessary for tribal subsistence, whichever is less." Id. (emphasis added). Most recently in Skokomish Indian Tribe v. United States, 410 F.3d 506, 513 (9th Cir. 2005), our en banc court again described Fishing Vessel as holding that the Tribes were "entitled to an equal measure of the harvestable portion of each run that passed through a `usual and accustomed' tribal fishing ground, adjusted downward if tribal needs could be satisfied by a lesser amount." Id. (emphasis added) (quoting Fishing Vessel, 443 U.S. at 685-89, 99 S.Ct. 3055).

By holding that the Treaties guarantee "that the number of fish would always be sufficient to provide a `moderate living' to the Tribes," Washington V, 853 F.3d at 965 (emphasis added), the panel opinion turns Fishing Vessel on its head. It imposes an affirmative duty upon the State to provide a certain quantity of fish, which reads out the 50% ceiling entirely.

Instead, the panel opinion ignores the 50% ceiling, effectively adopting the position urged by the Tribes in Fishing Vessel that "the treaties had reserved a pre-existing right to as many fish as their commercial and subsistence needs dictated." 443 U.S. at 670, 99 S.Ct. 3055. Yet, as explained, the Supreme Court has already rejected this approach, following instead the United States' position that the Tribes were guaranteed the lesser of their needs or 50% of the available run. See id. at 670, 685, 99 S.Ct. 3055. Likewise, our court has rejected interpretations of Fishing Vessel that would entitle the Tribes to a "particular minimum allocation of fish." Washington III, 759 F.2d at 1359. The panel opinion's holding misconstrues not only the Supreme Court's decision in Fishing Vessel but also our decisions in Washington III, Midwater Trawlers, and Skokomish Indian Tribe.

B

To reach its conclusion, the panel points to various statements allegedly made by Governor Stevens to the Tribes at the time the Treaties were negotiated in the 1850s. Washington V, 853 F.3d at 964-65. As the Supreme Court observed in Fishing Vessel, however, "[b]ecause of the great abundance of fish and the limited population of the area, it simply was not contemplated that either party would interfere with the other's fishing rights." 443 U.S. at 668, 99 S.Ct. 3055. Indeed, the Supreme Court considered the very same statements in Fishing Vessel yet still chose to impose a 50% cap on the Tribes' share of available fish. See id. at 666-68 & nn. 9 & 11, 99 S.Ct. 3055.[6] Such cap necessarily means that the Tribes are not always guaranteed enough fish to meet their needs. If the Supreme Court considered Stevens' statements and declined to find that the Tribes were entitled to a certain minimum quantity of fish, it eludes me how a panel of our court can reach the opposite conclusion by relying on these statements now. The panel opinion utterly fails to grapple with the 50% cap imposed by Fishing Vessel.

The panel opinion further cites to the Supreme Court's opinion in Winters v. United States, 207 U.S. 564, 576-77, 28 S.Ct. 207, 52 L.Ed. 340 (1908), and our opinion in United States v. Adair, 723 F.2d 1394, 1409, 1411 (9th Cir. 1983), as supporting its conclusion that the Stevens Treaties guarantee the Tribes a specific quantity of fish. Yet, neither Winters nor Adair is factually relevant. Each involved the question of whether certain tribes were entitled to various water rights on their reservations under the treaties creating the reservations.

In Winters, the Supreme Court held that the lands ceded to create the Fort Belknap Indian Reservation necessarily included the water rights accompanying such lands. See 207 U.S. at 565, 576-77, 28 S.Ct. 207. Likewise in Adair, we held "that at the time the Klamath Reservation was established, the [United States] and the Tribe intended to reserve a quantity of the water flowing through the reservation." 723 F.2d at 1410. Thus, both cases stand for the somewhat unremarkable proposition that in the context of Native American reservations, water rights accompany land rights.

It is true that both cases found water rights that were not explicitly detailed in the text of the treaties. Nonetheless, if we read these cases broadly to mean that we can and should infer a whole host of rights not contained in the four corners of tribal treaties, the possibilities are endless. Since the Supreme Court made it plain in Fishing Vessel that the Tribes are not entitled to a certain numerical amount of fish, we certainly should not rely on Winters and Adair to hold otherwise.

III

Even if one agrees with the panel opinion that the Tribes are entitled to a specific quantity of fish, however, it does not necessarily mean that the installation and maintenance of culverts run afoul of the Treaties. But assuming that they do, it is far from clear that the drastic remedy of removal or repair should be required.

A

Before reaching its conclusion that the State violated the Treaties, the panel opinion devotes minimal treatment to showing (1) that tribal members would engage in more fishing if there were more salmon and (2) that removing culverts would increase this salmon population. See Washington V, 853 F.3d at 966 (devoting three paragraphs to these issues).[7] The panel opinion acknowledges that the State of Washington was not intentionally trying to impact the fish population when it installed culverts under state highways and other roads.[8] Id. Nonetheless, the panel opinion concludes that because there was evidence that culverts affect fish population, and because the fish population is low, the State violated the Treaties by building and maintaining its culverts. See id.

This overly broad reasoning lacks legal foundation. There are many factors that affect fish population and multiple fish populations that are low.[9] Is any surface physical activity, wherever found, that negatively affects fish habitat an automatic Treaty violation? If so, the panel's opinion could open the door to a whole host of future suits.

While such speculation may sound far-fetched, in actuality, it is already occurring. Legal commentators have noted that plaintiffs could use the panel's decision to demand the removal of dams and attack a host of other practices that can degrade fish habitat (such as logging, grazing, and construction).[10] The panel does nothing to cabin its opinion. Nor does it provide any detail for how to determine if a fish population has reached an appropriate size, making further remedial efforts unnecessary.

B

Furthermore, the future reach of this decision extends far beyond the State of Washington. As the amici observe, the same fishing rights are reserved to tribes in Idaho, Montana, and Oregon. Further, the Stevens Treaties also guarantee the Tribes the privilege of hunting. See Fishing Vessel, 443 U.S. at 674, 99 S.Ct. 3055. There seems little doubt that future litigants will argue that the population of various birds, deer, elk, bears, and similar animals, which were traditionally hunted by the Tribes, have been impacted by Western development. If a court subsequently concludes that hunting populations are covered by the reasoning of this decision, the potential impact of this case is virtually limitless.

C

Yet, our court has already held that the Stevens Treaties cannot be used to attach broad "environmental servitudes" to the land. See United States v. Washington, 694 F.2d 1374, 1381 (9th Cir. 1982) (coining the term "environmental servitude"), vacated on reh'g, Washington III, 759 F.2d at 1354-55 (but reaching similar result). Thus, in Washington III, our en banc court vacated a declaratory judgment from the district court which held "that the treaties impose upon the State a corresponding duty to refrain from degrading or authorizing the degradation of the fish habitat to an extent that would deprive the treaty Indians of their moderate living needs." 759 F.2d at 1355, vacating United States v. Washington, 506 F.Supp. 187, 208 (W.D. Wash. 1980) ("Washington II"). While the panel's opinion here deals with the specific issue of culverts, its reasoning is not so confined; it effectively imposes the same boundless standard upon the State — preventing habitat degradation — that we rejected in Washington III.

D

Once a court has decided that there has been a violation, it must address the remedy. The panel opinion acknowledges "that correction of barrier culverts is only one of a number of measures that can usefully be taken to increase salmon production."[11] Washington V, 853 F.3d at 974. And, the panel opinion further concedes "that the benefits of culvert correction differ depending on the culvert in question." Id. Yet, if culverts are only one "measure" that could affect the salmon population, what about the other measures? Why is it appropriate to require the State to correct culverts rather than something else? Since, at some level, almost all urban growth can impact fish populations, should the State be required to reverse decades of development in an effort to increase the number of fish? Is the answer that any activity that amounts to a Treaty violation must be halted or removed? The panel opinion offers no cost-benefit analysis, or any other framework, to guide future courts on what is an appropriate remedial measure (and what is not).[12]

In effect, the panel's decision opens a backdoor to a whole host of potential federal environmental regulation-making. And, it invites courts, who have limited expertise in this area, to serve as policymakers.

But the issues at the heart of this suit — development versus wildlife habitat, removal versus accommodation — are properly left to the political process. Judges are ill-equipped to evaluate these questions. We deal in closed records and have difficulty obtaining and evaluating on-theground information — for example, which culverts it would be most cost-effective to remove over the next seventeen years.

Here, the State recognizes that "[s]almon are vital to Washington's economy, culture, and diet." Prior to the injunction, the State was already working to address problematic culverts, and the State has spent "hundreds of millions of dollars" on programs designed "to preserve and restore salmon runs." There is no justification for interfering with the State's existing programs.

IV

Notably, the panel opinion does not prohibit the State from installing future culverts. Instead, it orders the State to correct existing culverts. See Washington V, 853 F.3d at 979-80. Yet, according to the State, it was the federal government, now bringing suit in its capacity as trustee for the Tribes, which "specified the design for virtually all of the culverts at issue." Further, these culverts have been in place for many decades. According to the State, "Washington's state highway system has been essentially the same size since the 1960's," and thus presumably many culverts predated this litigation, which has been ongoing for almost fifty years. Apparently, however, no one thought that the culverts might be a problem until 2001 when the Tribes filed a request for determination that such pre-existing barriers were infringing the Treaties. See Washington V, 853 F.3d at 954.

Given the United States' involvement in designing the culverts and its long acquiescence in their existence, one might suppose that an equitable doctrine such as laches would bar suit by the United States. Indeed, "[i]t is well established that laches, a doctrine focused on one side's inaction and the other's legitimate reliance, may bar long-dormant claims for equitable relief." City of Sherrill, 544 U.S. at 217, 125 S.Ct. 1478.

According to the panel opinion, however, "[t]he United States cannot, based on laches or estoppel, diminish or render unenforceable otherwise valid Indian treaty rights." Washington V, 853 F.3d at 967. The panel opinion cites several cases for this proposition, including the 1923 opinion of Cramer v. United States, 261 U.S. 219, 234, 43 S.Ct. 342, 67 L.Ed. 622 (1923) (holding that a government agent's unauthorized acceptance of leases of tribal land could not bind the government or tribe), and United States v. Washington, 157 F.3d 630, 649 (9th Cir. 1998) ("Washington IV") ("[L]aches or estoppel is not available to defeat Indian treaty rights."). See Washington V, 853 F.3d at 967.

Yet, the panel opinion's rejection of laches contravenes the Supreme Court's subsequent 2005 decision in City of Sherrill, 544 U.S. at 221, 125 S.Ct. 1478. That case involved an attempt by the Oneida Indian Nation to reassert sovereignty over newlypurchased land that had once belonged to the Nation but had been sold in contravention of federal law (although with the apparent acquiescence of federal agents) approximately two hundred years before. Id. at 203-05, 211, 125 S.Ct. 1478. In particular, the Nation sought to avoid local regulatory control and taxation of its newly-purchased parcels. Id. at 211, 125 S.Ct. 1478.

The Supreme Court analogized the situation to a dispute between states, explaining that "long acquiescence may have controlling effect on the exercise of dominion and sovereignty over territory." Id. at 218, 125 S.Ct. 1478. The Court further "recognized the impracticability of returning to Indian control land that generations earlier passed into numerous private hands." Id. at 219, 125 S.Ct. 1478. Therefore, the Court concluded, "the Oneidas' long delay in seeking equitable relief against New York or its local units, and developments in the city of Sherrill spanning several generations, evoke the doctrines of laches, acquiescence, and impossibility, and render inequitable the piecemeal shift in governance this suit seeks unilaterally to initiate." Id. at 221, 125 S.Ct. 1478.

Thus, Sherrill indicates that our court's previous holding in Washington IV, 157 F.3d at 649, that laches cannot be used "to defeat Indian treaty rights" is wrong and impliedly overruled. Cf. Miller v. Gammie, 335 F.3d 889, 900 (9th Cir. 2003). The Second Circuit has recognized as much, observing that Sherrill "dramatically altered the legal landscape" by permitting "equitable doctrines, such as laches, acquiescence, and impossibility" to "be applied to Indian land claims." Cayuga Indian Nation v. Pataki, 413 F.3d 266, 273 (2d Cir. 2005).

Yet, the panel opinion blindly cites Washington IV and sidesteps the central tenet of Sherrill by attempting to distinguish it on its facts. See Washington V, 853 F.3d at 967-68. The panel opinion tries to draw three distinctions: (1) this case does not involve the question of whether the Tribes can regain sovereignty over abandoned land; (2) the Tribes never authorized the design or construction of the culverts; and (3) the Tribes are not trying to revive claims that have lain dormant. Id. at 968.

The first distinction is irrelevant; since Sherrill made clear that laches can apply to Indian treaty rights, it should not matter whether a party is seeking to apply laches in the context of sovereignty over land or the enforcement of rights appurtenant to land (the ability to fish).

Second, as Montana and Idaho observe, it does not matter that the Tribes never authorized the design or construction of the culverts because Washington is seeking to impose the doctrine of laches against the United States, not the Tribes. And, as the Second Circuit has made plain, the logic of Sherrill applies to the United States when it is acting as trustee for the Tribes. See Oneida Indian Nation v. Cty. of Oneida, 617 F.3d 114, 129 (2d Cir. 2010).

Notably, only the United States could bring suit against Washington for alleged culvert violations because Washington is protected by sovereign immunity against suit from the Tribes. See Idaho v. Coeur d'Alene Tribe of Idaho, 521 U.S. 261, 268, 117 S.Ct. 2028, 138 L.Ed.2d 438 (1997). The panel opinion asserts that the United States cannot waive treaty rights, and this may be true as a general matter. Washington V, 853 F.3d at 967. Nonetheless, in the context of specific litigation, since the United States acts as the Tribes' trustee, such representation necessarily entails the ability to waive certain litigation rights (failing to bring a claim within the statute of limitations for example). Thus, the fact that the Tribes did not authorize the culverts is irrelevant; the United States did, and it further failed to object to the culverts for many years.

Finally, I disagree with the panel opinion's assertion that the United States is not trying to revive claims that have lain dormant. Presumably, the State's alleged violation of the Treaties was complete when it constructed the culverts (and relevant highways) in the 1960s. The United States first brought suit to enforce the Tribes' fishing rights in 1970. Washington V, 853 F.3d at 958. Yet, the United States found no problem with the culverts until 2001. While the claims did not lie dormant for 200 years as in Sherrill, they were dormant for over 30 years. And as in Sherrill, there are significant practical issues involved with asserting the claims now such as the time, expense, and efficacy of removing the culverts. See 544 U.S. at 219, 125 S.Ct. 1478.

Thus, while Sherrill may be factually distinct, it is also directly on point. The panel opinion errs by ignoring its central teaching. There is good reason to contend that the United States is barred from bringing this suit by the doctrine of laches. And, if the United States is barred from suit, the entire suit is prohibited, since the Tribes cannot puncture the State's defense of sovereign immunity on their own. See Coeur d'Alene Tribe, 521 U.S. at 268, 117 S.Ct. 2028.

Rather than taking the opportunity to harmonize our precedent, the panel opinion ignores the changes wrought by Sherrill, defying the Supreme Court's direction.

V

Even if one concludes (1) that the Treaties guarantee the Tribes enough fish to sustain a "moderate living," (2) that violation of such guarantee can and should be remedied by removing culverts, and (3) that the suit is not barred by the doctrine of laches, there is still good reason to reject the injunction itself as overbroad. As the State explains, the injunction requires it to replace or repair all 817 culverts located in the area covered by the Treaties without regard to whether replacement of a particular culvert actually will increase the available salmon habitat.

In addition to state-owned culverts, there are a number of other privately-owned culverts and barriers on the streams in question which are not covered by the injunction.

Where there are non-state-owned culverts blocking fish passage downstream or immediately upstream from state-owned culverts, replacement of the State's culverts will make little or no difference on available salmon habitat. Indeed, the State observes that

(1) roughly 90% of state barrier culverts are upstream or downstream of other barriers ... (2) state-owned culverts are less than 25% of known barrier culverts... and (3) in many watersheds, non-state barrier culverts drastically exceed state-owned culverts, by up to a factor of 36 to 1[.]

The panel attempted to address this issue in its revised opinion. First, the opinion quotes testimony from a former State employee stating that Washington itself does not take into account the presence of non-state-owned barriers when calculating the priority index for which culverts to address. Washington V, 853 F.3d at 973. What the opinion does not reveal, however, is that this same expert also testified that correcting state-owned culverts that are downstream from non-state barriers "generally" will not have an immediate impact or benefit on salmon habitat. And, according to the State of Washington, the priority index, notwithstanding its name, typically does not dictate which barriers the State addresses first; instead the State focuses on culverts in streams without barriers.

Next, the panel opinion points out that Washington law requires dams or other stream obstructions to include a fishway and observes that the State may take corrective action against private owners who fail to comply with this obligation. Washington V, 853 F.3d at 973 (quoting Wash. Rev. Code Ann. § 77.57.030(1)-(2)). Yet, what the panel opinion fails to disclose is that this law only went into effect in 2003 and specifically "grandfathered in" various obstructions that were installed before May 20, 2003. Wash. Rev. Code Ann. § 77.57.030(3). Presumably, some of the non-state barriers would fall under this exception.

Finally, the panel opinion observes that

[I]n 2009, on streams where there were both state and non-state barriers, 1,370 of the 1,590 non-state barriers, or almost ninety percent, were upstream of the state barrier culverts. Sixty nine percent of the 220 downstream non-state barriers allowed partial passage of fish. Of the 152 that allowed partial passage, "passability" was 67% for 80 of the barriers and 33% for 72 of them.

Washington V, 853 F.3d at 973.

Given the significant cost of replacing barriers, however, being forced to replace even a single barrier that will have no tangible impact on the salmon population is an unjustified burden. Even using the most conservative estimates found by the district court, the average cost of replacing a single culvert is between $658,639 and $1,827,168. Washington V, 853 F.3d at 976.[13] We do not know the precise number of state-owned culverts that are located above non-state-owned culverts which prevent all fish passage. Yet, considering that there are at least sixty-eight non-state-owned barriers blocking all passage downstream from state-owned culverts,[14] there are almost certainly more than one or two culverts whose replacement would have no impact whatsoever on salmon habitat. The panel's opinion utterly fails to explain why the State should waste millions of dollars on such culverts in particular.

Further, even if the majority of non-state barriers are upstream, the court should still take into account the location of these barriers. As noted, if a non-state upstream barrier is close to or immediately above a state barrier, replacing the state barrier will have little effect on the size of salmon habitat, but it will come at a significant cost to the State.

The panel opinion observes that the injunction offers the State a longer schedule for replacing barriers that will open up less habitat. See Washington V, 853 F.3d at 974-75. It may be advantageous to the State to have the cost spread out over a longer time period, but whether it occurs five years or twenty-five years from now, the panel opinion fails to explain why taxpayers should be required to replace barriers that will not change the available salmon habitat.[15]

Thus, significant overbreadth problems remain. There is no doubt that the record in this case is voluminous and pinpointing the specific culverts whose removal might actually impact the available salmon habitat is an arduous task. Both the panel and district court made a valiant effort to wade through the many pages of maps and statistics.[16] As it currently stands, however, the injunction is unsupportable.

VI

In sum, there were many reasons to rehear this case en banc. The panel opinion's reasoning ignores the Court's holding in Fishing Vessel and our own cases, is incredibly broad, and if left unchecked, could significantly affect natural resource management throughout the Pacific Northwest, inviting judges to become environmental regulators. By refusing to consider the doctrine of laches, the panel opinion further disregards the Supreme Court's decision in Sherrill, relying instead on outdated and impliedly overruled precedent from our court. Finally, the panel opinion imposes a poorly-tailored injunction which will needlessly cost the State hundreds of millions of dollars.

Rather than correcting these errors, our court has chosen the path of least resistance. We should have reheard this case en banc.

Judge O'Scannlain's dissent in Hahn v. Waddington (June 5, 2017)

O'SCANNLAIN, Circuit Judge, dissenting:

I respectfully dissent from the memorandum disposition because I disagree with its characterization of Washington law.

I

The majority asserts that "Washington law mandates equitable tolling when, as here, `justice requires.'" Majority at 2. However, Washington's highest court has repeatedly emphasized that "equitable tolling is allowed when justice requires and when the predicates for equitable tolling are met. The predicates . . . [are] bad faith, deception, or false assurances by the defendant and the exercise of diligence by the plaintiff." In re Bonds, 165 Wash. 2d 135, 141 (2008) (en banc) (emphasis added); see also In re Haghighi,

178 Wash. 2d 435, 447 (2013) (en banc) ("[T]raditionally we have allowed equitable tolling when justice requires its application and when the predicates of bad faith, deception, or false assurances are met, and where the petitioner has exercised diligence in pursuing his or her rights.") (emphasis added); Douchette v. Bethel School Dist. No. 403, 117 Wash. 2d 805, 812 (1991) (en banc) ("In the absence of bad faith on the part of the defendant and reasonable diligence on the part of the plaintiff, equity cannot be invoked.") (emphasis added).

Washington precedent may be read to leave open the possibility that bad faith, deception, or false assurances by a third party—as opposed to by defendants—might satisfy the predicate rule. Specifically, in In re Bonds, the court characterizes the predicate rule as "mak[ing] equitable tolling available only in instances where petitioner missed the filing deadline due to another's malfeasance." Id. (emphasis added). Nevertheless, it remains clear that bad faith rather than mere negligence is necessary for equitably tolling to apply.

II

Hahn raises no allegation that the Eastern District of Washington acted maliciously or in bad faith when it dismissed his claims against certain defendants for improper venue. Rather, he asserts that the court acted in error. Such does not constitute adequate grounds for equitable tolling under Washington's predicate rule.

III

"[F]ailure to comply with the [Washington] statute of limitations, therefore, preclude[s] maintenance of this action . . . [because Washington's] tolling rule is [not] `inconsistent' with the policies underlying § 1983." Bd. of Regents of Univ. of N.Y. v. Tomanio, 446 U.S. 478, 487 (1980).

Like the New York tolling rule at issue in Tomanio, Washington's rule is motivated by "policies of repose [which] cannot be said to be disfavored in federal law." Id. at 488. Furthermore, "[n]either [deterrence nor compensation, the principal policies embodied in § 1983,] is significantly affected by this rule of limitations since plaintiffs can still readily enforce their claims, thereby recovering compensation and fostering deterrence, simply by [filing a direct appeal that challenges a district court's alleged error]." Id. See generally In re Hall, Bayoutree Assoc., 939 F.2d 802, 805 (9th Cir. 1991) ("We review a determination of whether to transfer or dismiss for abuse of discretion."). Hahn opted not to take advantage of such opportunity to recover compensation and foster deterrence by filing an appeal, but it was readily available to him nonetheless.

IV

Because I see no reason to displace a longstanding state rule in favor of an ad hoc federal one, I would affirm the judgment of the district court.

Judge O'Scannlain's concurrence and dissent in Tsosie v. Berryhill (Dec 1, 2017)

O'SCANNLAIN, Circuit Judge, concurring in part and dissenting in part.

I

I concur in the decision to the extent it holds that the Administrative Law Judge ("ALJ") did adequately explain how Tsosie's obesity affects his residual functional capacity. I am unable, however, to join in its holding that the ALJ sufficiently justified her conclusion that Tsosie could return to his prior work.

II

Tsosie's prior job included only unskilled tasks, including moving documents and mail between buildings and lifting reams of paper. These tasks are not a good match for the specialized, skilled, and sedentary job of "membership secretary" that the vocational expert selected from the Dictionary of Occupational Titles ("DOT"). "In order for an ALJ to accept vocational expert testimony that contradicts the [DOT], the record must contain `persuasive evidence to support the deviation.'" Pinto v. Massanari, 249 F.3d 840, 846 (9th Cir. 2001) (quoting Johnson v. Shalala, 60 F.3d 1428, 1435 (9th Cir. 1995)). There is no such evidence in this record. Although there are some similarities between Tsosie's job and the membership secretary, the key dimensions on which they differ—the amount of lifting and movement required—are precisely what the parties have contested in this litigation and are the reason the ALJ could not find that Tsosie could return to his past work as actually performed.

Stacy v. Colvin, 825 F.3d 563 (9th Cir. 2016), does not salvage the ALJ's determination. In Stacy, we observed that, under the "generally performed test," if a claimant "`cannot perform the excessive functional demands . . . actually required in the former job but can perform the functional demands and job duties as generally required by employers throughout the economy,'" then the claimant is not disabled. Id. at 569 (quoting SSR 82-61, 1982 WL 31887 (1982)). If the membership secretary job were a good match for Tsosie's actual prior work, Stacy would resolve the case: although he is unable to perform the 50-pound lifting "excessive functional demand," he could perform the other duties of the membership secretary job. Instead, however, the vocational expert picked a sedentary and skilled job from the DOT that is a poor match for Tsosie's actual work, added light work to that job description, and then opined that Tsosie could perform the invented job as generally performed without any additional evidence. The ALJ therefore lacked a basis in the DOT or any other evidence to establish how Tsosie's prior job was "generally performed," much less that Tsosie could have performed it.

Perhaps Tsosie could have performed the job of a membership secretary. But that is only relevant to step five of the disability determination analysis, at which point the ALJ determines if the claimant "can perform any substantial gainful work in the national economy," not simply his own prior work. Pinto, 249 F.3d at 844 (emphasis added). "[W]e are constrained to review the reasons the ALJ asserts," and "we cannot affirm the decision of an agency on a ground that the agency did not invoke in making its decision." Stout v. Comm'r, Soc. Sec. Admin., 454 F.3d 1050, 1054 (9th Cir. 2006) (internal quotation marks omitted).

For the foregoing reasons, I would reverse the judgment of the district court and remand to the agency for the ALJ to determine, without the errors identified above, whether Tsosie could return to his past work or could perform any other substantial gainful work in the national economy.

Judge O'Scannlain's concurrence and dissent in Dylag v. West Las Vegas Surgery Center (Dec 13, 2017)

O'SCANNLAIN, Circuit Judge, concurring in part and dissenting in part.

I join in Part 1 of the court's memorandum and in the judgment affirming the dismissal of Dylag's claims against West Las Vegas Surgery Center (WLVSC). I cannot join Part 2, which reverses the dismissal of Dylag's claims against Teamworks Professional Services, Inc. (Teamworks). I respectfully disagree with the majority's conclusion that the district court wrongly held that Dylag's claims against Teamworks were so intertwined with the claims against WLVSC as to require arbitration.

I

The principal question regarding the claims against Teamworks is whether, as a non-signatory, Teamworks can still compel Dylag to arbitrate his claims under a theory of equitable estoppel. Specifically, the district court held that Teamworks could compel arbitration because "the claims against Teamworks are identical to, for the most part, the claims against West Las Vegas . . . . [T]hose claims are intertwined and the relationship between those two entities . . . [is] so close that Mr. Dylag should be estopped from denying arbitration against Teamworks." In doing so, the court relied on and followed a decision from the Second Circuit, Ragone v. Atl. Video at Manhattan Ctr., 595 F.3d 115, 127-28 (2d Cir. 2010).

The majority now holds that the district court's application of the Ragone standard for equitable estoppel was in error—although it does not even cite the case. By the majority's interpretation, equitable estoppel should not apply unless the claims against the third party are "founded in or intimately connected with the obligations underlying the agreement," Mem. at 5—a requirement imposed in some courts but not (as demonstrated by Ragone) in others. Without its really addressing the issue, the majority's view seems to be that the district court erred in applying the more lenient estoppel standard of Ragone and other cases, rather than the stricter standard preferred by the majority.

The primary difficulty with this argument is that Dylag himself has never come close to making it. On appeal, Dylag states that "the District Court erred allowing Teamworks, a non-signatory to the dispute resolution provision[,] to require Mr. Dylag to arbitrate his employment discrimination claims." But Dylag never attempts to explain how the district court's estoppel analysis was wrong, much less to argue a competing theory of equitable estoppel. Indeed, he does not discuss whatsoever whether (as the district court held) his allegations against Teamworks are so "intertwined" with those against WLVSC as to require arbitration. Instead, Dylag simply reiterates his primary argument that he never validly waived his right to sue his employers for discrimination or civil rights claims. He does not argue that Ragone is the wrong standard to apply, but rather that Ragone is distinguishable specifically because (unlike here) it involved a valid waiver of civil rights claims. That is an issue which has nothing to do with the district court's estoppel analysis, and indeed an argument the majority in fact rejects with respect to Dylag's claims against Teamworks. Mem. at 2-3.

The same was true in the district court. There, the court directly asked Dylag's attorney, "[W]hy aren't the claims intertwined . . . such that he should be estopped from denying arbitration?" Dylag's attorney responded, "The claims would be intertwined if we're not dealing with an employment discrimination case. But you have case law here that says these federal civil rights are important. . . . [Y]ou have to make sure certain things are done [to waive them]." In other words, Dylag essentially conceded that the district court's general understanding of equitable estoppel was correct and that the doctrine would apply to his case, if he raised non-discrimination claims. He once again simply reiterated his primary argument that he did not knowingly waive his discrimination claims in the arbitration agreement, and thus even if the claims were intertwined with those against WLVSC, he could not be required to arbitrate them.

In its response brief on appeal, Teamworks first noted that Dylag "completely fail[ed]" to make any argument regarding the court's estoppel analysis, and then explained why it believes the district court's application of estoppel was indeed correct. Yet Dylag did not even bother to file a reply brief to respond to these arguments. In all, Dylag has not at any point attempted to grapple with the district court's analysis of the third-party arbitration issue or the issue of estoppel.

The majority agrees that Dylag's arguments with respect to the arbitrability of employment discrimination claims are meritless. Mem. at 2-3. Because these are the only arguments Dylag has ever raised to contest arbitration of his claims against both WLVSC and Teamworks, our analysis should end there. The majority's suggestion that the district court generally misinterpreted equitable estoppel law and misapplied the test for arbitration of "intertwined" claims against a non-signatory is simply not reflected anywhere in Dylag's own arguments. Regardless of the merits of that analysis, it is not an issue we should reach. Dylag utterly failed to analyze or to argue the law underlying the district court's determination that Teamworks can enforce arbitration through estoppel, and he has not made any argument remotely resembling that adopted by the majority. He therefore has waived any such argument, and we should not build a new case for him. See, e.g., Barnes v. FAA, 865 F.3d 1266, 1271 n.3 (9th Cir. 2017) (arguments not raised in opening brief are waived); SeaView Trading, LLC v. Comm'r of Internal Revenue, 858 F.3d 1281, 1288 (9th Cir. 2017) (same); McKay v. Ingleson, 558 F.3d 888, 891 n.5 (9th Cir. 2009) ("Because this argument was not raised clearly and distinctly in the opening brief, it has been waived.").

II

Further, even if we were to consider the merits of the district court's estoppel analysis, I cannot agree that Nevada would not adopt the Ragone standard, as applied by the district court.

The majority confidently predicts that, "like most jurisdictions that apply [the equitable estoppel] framework, Nevada would require that the allegations of interdependent and concerted misconduct be founded in or intimately connected with the obligations of the underlying agreement." Mem. at 5 (internal quotation marks omitted). The problem, of course, is that Nevada itself has not said anything of the sort. And although the majority only cites cases supporting its more restrictive framework, it does not even mention those that do not—most notably, of course, Ragone itself.

Under the more lenient Ragone standard, a plaintiff may be forced to arbitrate claims raised against a non-signatory where such claims are "factually intertwined with" a dispute against a signatory, and where there is a close relationship between the signatory and non-signatory defendants. See Ragone, 595 F.3d at 127-28. There is little doubt that the district court was correct that the claims against Teamworks satisfy such standard. Indeed, Ragone itself and many cases applying it have required plaintiffs to arbitrate claims against third parties in circumstances remarkably similar to this case. See, e.g., id.; Barreto v. JEC II, LLC, 2017 WL 3172827, at *6 (S.D.N.Y. July 25, 2017); Colon v. Conchetta, Inc., 2017 WL 2572517, at *6 (E.D. Pa. June 14, 2017); Bonner v. Mich. Logistics Inc., 250 F. Supp. 3d 388, 398-99 (D. Ariz. 2017).

The majority clearly disagrees with the Ragone standard. However, that standard is not such a minority view, or so obviously disfavored, as to make it clear that Nevada would disagree as well. Furthermore, the parties have not even had the opportunity to brief which standard Nevada courts would or should apply (again, because Dylag himself never challenged this issue). Because the applicable standard may be critical to the outcome of this case, I do not believe that we should decide such issue without at least full briefing from the parties or, perhaps, certification to the Nevada Supreme Court itself.

For the foregoing reasons, I respectfully dissent from Part 2.

Judge O'Scannlain's concurrence and dissent in US v. Briones (May 16, 2018)

O'SCANNLAIN, Circuit Judge, concurring in part and dissenting in part:

As the majority opinion's detailed recitation of the facts makes clear, Riley Briones, Jr., participated in a cold-blooded murder and was a leader in a vicious gang, see Majority Op. Part I.A, so it is not difficult to understand why the district court considered a severe sentence appropriate. Notwithstanding the grievous nature of the crimes, however, the court was required to follow the Supreme Court's holding that the Eighth Amendment bars life-without-parole sentences "for all but the rarest of juvenile offenders, those whose crimes reflect permanent incorrigibility." Montgomery v. Louisiana, ____ U.S. ____, 136 S.Ct. 718, 734, 193 L.Ed.2d 599 (2016) (citing Miller v. Alabama, 567 U.S. 460, 132 S.Ct. 2455, 183 L.Ed.2d 407 (2012)).

I agree with the majority that nothing in Montgomery or Miller indicates that

Briones is categorically ineligible for a life sentence simply because he is a juvenile who did not pull the trigger, see Majority Op. Part III, and I agree that the district court was correct to begin its sentencing process by calculating the Sentencing Guidelines range, see id. Part II.A. I cannot agree, however, with the majority's holding that the district court sufficiently considered Briones's claim that he was not in that class of rare juvenile individuals constitutionally eligible for a life-without-parole sentence. See id. Part II.B.

The majority reads too much into the district court's cursory explanation of its sentence, and it divines that the district court must have adopted the rationale for its sentence suggested by the government on appeal. Although a sentencing court need not pedantically recite every fact and legal conclusion supporting its sentence, it must provide enough explanation for a court of appeals to evaluate whether or not the decision to reject a defendant's argument is consistent with law. The sparse reasoning of the district court in this case gives me no such assurance.

I respectfully dissent from Part II.B of the opinion and would remand for the limited purpose of permitting the district court properly to perform the analysis required by Miller and Montgomery.

I

The difficult question raised in this case is whether Briones is in fact one of those "rarest of juvenile offenders ... whose crimes reflect permanent incorrigibility." Montgomery, 136 S.Ct. at 734. Without any evident ruling on that question, the district court imposed a life sentence on Briones. As the majority indicates, because there is no parole in the federal system, that "sentence is effectively for life without the possibility of parole." Majority Op. at 816.

A

The majority is comfortable deferring to the district court's sentence because the court considered some of the "hallmark features" of youth identified by the Supreme Court in Miller. 567 U.S. at 477, 132 S.Ct. 2455; see Majority Op. at 817-18. I agree that the court did so, which we know because it expressly said it considered "the defendant's youth, immaturity, [and] his adolescent brain at the time [of the crime]."

But to leave the analysis at that is to misunderstand the nature of Briones's challenge to a life sentence and the importance of Montgomery's clarification of Miller. In Miller, the Supreme Court held that "the Eighth Amendment forbids a sentencing scheme that mandates life in prison without possibility of parole for juvenile offenders," explaining that a sentencing court must "take into account how children are different, and how those differences counsel against irrevocably sentencing them to a lifetime in prison." 567 U.S. at 479-80, 132 S.Ct. 2455. Left at that, Miller could be understood merely as a procedural requirement, mandating that sentencing courts must consider certain hallmark characteristics of youth and that they must be permitted to impose a sentence less than life. If that were all Miller meant, the district court likely would have complied with its dictates.

But the Supreme Court made clear in Montgomery that Miller stood for more.

Beyond procedural boxes to check, Miller recognized a substantive limitation on who could receive a life sentence:

> Miller ... did more than require a sentencer to consider a juvenile offender's youth before imposing life without parole; it established that the penological justifications for life without parole collapse in light of the distinctive attributes of youth. Even if a court considers a child's age before sentencing him or her to a lifetime in prison, that sentence still violates the Eighth Amendment for a child whose crime reflects unfortunate yet transient immaturity.

Montgomery, 136 S.Ct. at 734 (emphasis added) (internal quotation marks and citation omitted). In light of Montgomery, we know that "sentencing a child to life without parole is excessive for all but the rare juvenile offender whose crime reflects irreparable corruption" and that Miller "bar[s] life without parole ... for all but the rarest of juvenile offenders, those whose crimes reflect permanent incorrigibility." Id. (emphasis added) (internal quotation marks omitted).[1]

The heart of Briones's argument before the district court was that he could not be sentenced to life because he is not irreparably corrupt or permanently incorrigible. The "critical question" before the district court, then, was whether Briones had the "capacity to change after he committed the crimes." United States v. Pete, 819 F.3d 1121, 1133 (9th Cir. 2016).

B

Unfortunately, we cannot know whether the district court answered that question because there is nothing in the record that allows us to confirm that the court even considered it.

A sentencing court must, "at the time of sentencing, ... state in open court the reasons for its imposition of the particular sentence." 18 U.S.C. § 3553(c). In elaborating on that statutory command, the Supreme Court has explained that "[t]he sentencing judge should set forth enough to satisfy the appellate court that he has considered the parties' arguments and has a reasoned basis for exercising his own legal decisionmaking authority." Rita v. United States, 551 U.S. 338, 356, 127 S.Ct. 2456, 168 L.Ed.2d 203 (2007). "[W]here the defendant or prosecutor presents nonfrivolous reasons for imposing a [non-Guidelines] sentence, ... the judge will normally... explain why he has rejected those arguments." Id. at 357, 127 S.Ct. 2456; see also United States v. Carty, 520 F.3d 984, 992 (9th Cir. 2008) (en banc) ("A within-Guidelines sentence ordinarily needs little explanation unless a party has ... argued that a different sentence is otherwise warranted." (emphasis added)).

1

Unlike the majority, I am not satisfied that the district court "set forth enough to satisfy the appellate court that he has considered the parties' arguments." Rita, 551 U.S. at 356, 127 S.Ct. 2456. If anything, the record suggests that the district court misunderstood the applicable legal rule of Miller.

In explaining its decision to impose a life sentence, the district court indicated that it had "consider[ed] the history of [Briones's] abusive father, [Briones's] youth, immaturity, his adolescent brain at the time, and the fact that it was impacted by regular and constant abuse of alcohol and other drugs, and that he's been a model inmate up to now." The court seemingly found those facts — which it considered to be "mitigation" — outweighed by the awfulness of the murder, Briones's role in it, and his leadership in a "violent and cold-blooded" gang. "Having considered those things," the district court imposed a "sentence of life."

All of those considerations are indeed relevant to selecting a proper sentence based on the sentencing factors of 18 U.S.C. § 3553(a). But they are not directly responsive to Briones's argument arising out of Miller that he is not within the class of the rare juvenile offenders who are permanently incorrigible and hence constitutionally eligible for a life sentence. The question is not merely whether Briones's crime was heinous, nor whether his difficult upbringing mitigated his culpability. It is whether Briones has demonstrated "irreparable corruption," Montgomery, 136 S.Ct. at 734 (quoting Miller, 567 U.S. at 479-80, 132 S.Ct. 2455), which requires a prospective analysis of whether Briones has the "capacity to change after he committed the crimes," Pete, 819 F.3d at 1133.

Nothing in the district court's explanation of its sentence bears directly on the question of whether Briones is irreparably corrupt. If anything, the sentencing transcript reveals factual findings that suggest Briones has demonstrated a capacity to change. The district court observed that Briones has "been a model inmate" and that he "has improved himself while he's been in prison." Perhaps, despite that promising behavior, the district court could have determined that countervailing evidence indicated that Briones is permanently incorrigible. But the transcript does not indicate that the district court made such determination.

More troubling, the transcript suggests that the district court may have misunderstood the nature of the inquiry Briones was asking it to make. Miller "rendered life without parole an unconstitutional penalty for ... juvenile offenders whose crimes reflect the transient immaturity of youth," which the Supreme Court has instructed includes "the vast majority of juvenile offenders." Montgomery, 136 S.Ct. at 734. Yet the district court only considered the Miller hallmarks of youth as "mitigation," suggesting that it started from the inverted assumption that most juvenile offenders are eligible for life sentences and that Briones's evidence could only mitigate from that. If the district court fully grappled with Miller's rule, one would think it would have spoken of "aggravating" evidence rather than "mitigation." Moreover, in explaining that Briones's crime justified a life sentence because "some decisions have lifelong consequences," the district court suggested it misunderstood Miller entirely. The point of Miller is that "juveniles have diminished culpability and greater prospects for reform." 567 U.S. at 471, 132 S.Ct. 2455. That is why the sentencing analysis must be forward-looking and address the "capacity to change," Pete, 819 F.3d at 1133, not the static characteristics of the juvenile defendant at the moment of his criminal decisions. In fact, there are no forward-looking statements at all from the district court in its sentencing colloquy; the stated basis for the sentence was entirely retrospective.

2

To cure the deficiencies in the district court's explanation of the sentence imposed, the government asks us to infer that the district court must have found Briones incorrigible based on a lack of candor when he testified at the resentencing hearing. The majority jumps at this invitation, adopting the government's position to observe that "Briones' statements could reasonably be interpreted as not taking responsibility for his prior criminal activity, in contravention of one of the basic tenets of rehabilitation." Majority Op. at 820 (emphasis added).

The equivocal nature of the majority's statement is telling. Perhaps the district court could have thought that Briones failed to take responsibility for his actions, but nowhere in the district's court's statement of reasons for the sentence did it say as much. Although the government and the majority offer one plausible interpretation of Briones's testimony, it is hardly the only one. In fact, when I read the transcript, I see much that could support a contrary finding that Briones expressed remorse repeatedly and at length.

Briones expressed regret for his actions. He admitted the key facts of the murder and subsequent crimes and admitted that "it's probably my fault when I thought about it." He explained that he regularly asks himself "why didn't I do something at that time, why ... didn't I stop myself way before that, why didn't I do something at the court?" He explained that "the thing that haunted me so much about just living in prison was that" the murder victim was "a young Christian man," and that it "haunts me to have that on my hands." And he said, "I want to express remorse, I want to express grief."

Briones also expressed sympathy for those he had harmed. For instance, he explained that he did not believe the victim's family could ever forgive him because he was responsible for "a great offense that ... is unrepaired." He explained that "now that I'm older ... I witness not just in my own life people murdered and their killers get to go home," and he can "see[] people in pain when they've gone through their loss, [and] all of this had made me not only sympathize but to empathize with all of it." He said, "I know I have to apologize for everything and I apologize all the time to my family ..., and my apology goes out ... to the [victim's] family."

I do acknowledge that there are portions of the transcript from which one could infer a lack of candor. It is true that Briones's testimony was not crisp and eloquent. And it is true that he continued to say that he "didn't think myself a leader" in the gang and that he continued to deny that the plan from the beginning was to murder the Subway clerk.

Perhaps, hearing all the testimony and weighing the countervailing inferences, the district judge could have concluded that Briones was insufficiently honest or that he failed to take responsibility for his crimes. Perhaps those findings could be evidence of incorrigibility.

But the district court never said any of that. All the reasons that it did give for the sentence were about the nature of the crime, not the subsequent lack of remorse or acceptance of responsibility. Reading a cold transcript, the majority is willing to conclude that Briones "never actually took responsibility for any of the crimes of which he was convicted." Majority Op. at 815. I am not willing to reach such a critical factual conclusion based on an ambiguous transcript, especially when the district court made no such factual finding.

The majority accuses me of retrying Briones's case rather than reviewing it as an appellate court should. See Majority Op. at 821. But it is the majority that has invented a basis for the sentence which cannot be found in the record. The reason courts of appeals accord great deference to a district court's sentencing decision is that "[t]he sentencing judge has access to, and greater familiarity with, the individual case and the individual defendant before him than ... the appeals court." Rita, 551 U.S. at 357-58, 127 S.Ct. 2456. Unlike the majority, I would take advantage of that expertise by remanding for an actual determination of Briones's incorrigibility rather than attempting to divine one by reading a transcript through squinted eyes.

C

Another aspect of this case that gives me pause is that it is not obvious whether or not Briones fits within the class of juvenile offenders constitutionally eligible for a life sentence. If the only plausible reading of the record were that Briones is incorrigible, I could more easily assure myself that the district court reached that conclusion even though it did not specifically respond to the Miller argument. Looking at the record holistically, however, I cannot say that it necessarily betrays permanent corruption.

After Graham v. Florida, 560 U.S. 48, 130 S.Ct. 2011, 176 L.Ed.2d 825 (2010), the only juvenile offenders eligible for a life sentence are those who committed a homicide. Criminal homicides will invariably be odious crimes, but the Supreme Court nonetheless instructed that only "the rarest of juvenile offenders" may receive a life sentence under the Eighth Amendment. Montgomery, 136 S.Ct. at 734. Here, we have a juvenile felony murder offender who helped to plan a robbery-murder, who drove the getaway car, and who then was a leader in a series of subsequent violent crimes. But like one of the defendants in Miller itself, Briones "did not fire the bullet that killed" the victim; and like the other defendant in Miller, although he was involved in "a vicious murder," Briones had a difficult upbringing replete with substance abuse. 567 U.S. at 478-79, 132 S.Ct. 2455. Moreover, in this instance, we have a defendant whom even the district court called a "model inmate," which surely goes to the question of "whether [the defendant] has changed in some fundamental way since" the crime. Pete, 819 F.3d at 1133. The evidence on incorrigibility is therefore mixed, and we are ill-suited as an appellate court to say that a finding of incorrigibility is the only reasonable one.

D

As a secondary basis for affirming, the majority leans heavily on the highly deferential plain error standard of review. See Majority Op. at 820. In arguing that such review should apply to this case, the majority analogizes to cases involving defendants making purely procedural arguments on appeal that district courts insufficiently explained otherwise permissible sentences.[2]

But here, Briones is not objecting merely to a deficient explanation. Rather, his claim is substantive: that he is constitutionally ineligible for a particular sentence under Miller, a claim he did squarely argue before the district court, at length. The court's failure properly to explain its sentence requires remand not because it was procedural error, but rather because such failure prevents us from being able properly to review Briones's substantive claim. As the majority acknowledges, a district court's sentence is invalid "if the court applied an incorrect legal rule." United States v. Martinez-Lopez, 864 F.3d 1034, 1043 (9th Cir. 2017) (en banc); see Majority Op. at 818. Because the record does not allow us to determine whether the court did apply the correct legal rule, we should remand for that limited purpose.

II

A

I share the majority's concern that we ought not to conjure procedural sentencing hurdles unsupported by law. I am especially cognizant of this concern because other courts have read Miller and Montgomery to impose special procedural requirements well beyond what those opinions actually require. E.g., Commonwealth v. Batts, 163 A.3d 410, 415-16 (Pa. 2017) ("recogniz[ing] a presumption against the imposition of a sentence of life without parole for a juvenile offender" that may be rebutted only if the government proves, "beyond a reasonable doubt, that the juvenile offender is incapable of rehabilitation").

But the district court's explanation of the sentence may be faulty without requiring that it utter any "magic phrase" to justify its sentence, Majority Op. at 819, and we need impose no special procedures simply because Briones was a juvenile when he committed the murder. Instead, I would simply enforce the requirements of 18 U.S.C. § 3553(c) so that we may properly evaluate Briones's Miller claim on appeal.

The error here was not that the district court failed to apply some procedure special to juvenile offenders. Rather, the court failed to provide an adequate explanation of its sentence under the same standard that would apply to any sentencing. It erred because Briones argued that he could not constitutionally be given a life sentence, his arguments were "not frivolous," and the court did not squarely "address any of them, even to dismiss them in shorthand." United States v. Trujillo, 713 F.3d 1003, 1010 (9th Cir. 2013). Remanding for a new sentencing here would have no bearing on a case in which the defendant does not present a credible argument under Miller or one in which the district court explicitly confronted a Miller argument about the defendant's incorrigibility.

B

Comparing this case to another illustrates that we can reasonably expect more of the district court at sentencing without our being overly pedantic. In another case raising a Miller claim, submitted to our panel the same day that Briones's case was argued, the defendant-appellant had committed four murders as a juvenile — including two while facing trial — and in the process had disfigured or dismembered and then buried the victims' bodies. See United States v. Orsinger, 698 Fed.Appx. 527, 527 (9th Cir. 2017) (unpublished). Two of the victims were a 63-year-old grandmother and her nine-year-old granddaughter, and the defendant had killed the little girl by hand, crushing her head with rocks. We affirmed the life sentence because the district court made clear it had grappled with the Miller claim. See id.

The fact that another defendant committed even more monstrous crimes than did Briones does not ameliorate the tragedy of an innocent clerk's death or the terror that Briones's gang inflicted on his community. But in that second case with four gruesome murders, and where the defendant had continued to exhibit violence while incarcerated, the sentencing judge nevertheless properly evaluated the objection to a life sentence under Miller. That judge "recognize[d] that Miller permits life sentences for juvenile offenders only in `uncommon' cases" and "made a finding that [the defendant] did indeed fit within that `uncommon' class of juvenile offenders" to justify imposition of a life sentence. Id. (quoting Miller, 567 U.S. at 479, 132 S.Ct. 2455).

That is not to suggest that the district judge in Briones's case could not justifiably impose the same sentence. It only demonstrates that — even in a case that much more obviously compels a conclusion that the defendant is incorrigible — a district judge can properly address a Miller claim without invoking any magic phrase. I would require the same of the district court in this case.

III

Although I concur in Parts I, II.A, and III of the majority opinion, I must respectfully dissent from Part II.B and the ultimate judgment. I would vacate the judgment of the district court and remand for resentencing.

Notes

[1] Montgomery was decided only two months before the district court resentenced Briones, and so Briones's arguments were framed in terms of Miller. That said, Montgomery was raised indirectly by Briones's counsel at sentencing, and Briones's interpretation of Miller as a substantive prohibition on life imprisonment for most juvenile offenders is the one that Montgomery confirmed to be correct.

[2] Even if Briones were making a purely procedural objection based on the sufficiency of the district court's explanation of how it weighed the 18 U.S.C. § 3553(a) sentencing factors, our case law is not clear regarding what the proper standard of review would be. As the majority contends, in some of those cases, we have reviewed for plain error. See, e.g., United States v. Kleinman, 880 F.3d 1020, 1040-41 (9th Cir. 2017); United States v. Valencia-Barragan, 608 F.3d 1103, 1108 (9th Cir. 2010). As happens too often, however, our court has not been consistent. See, e.g., United States v. Trujillo, 713 F.3d 1003, 1008-11 & n.3 (not applying plain error review in a case where "[t]he district court did not address" the defendant's sentencing arguments). Because these cases are not relevant to considering Briones's substantive claim, however, we need not resolve this potential intra-circuit split.

Judge O'Scannlain's dissent in Pike v. Hester (June 6, 2018)

O'SCANNLAIN, Circuit Judge, Dissenting.

The majority holds that a two-month restraining order, granted by a state court of limited jurisdiction, has issue-preclusive effect with respect to a § 1983 cause of action premised on a constitutional violation and requesting compensatory and punitive damages. This cannot be right.

I

A

The saga began in the Elko County Justice Court (Justice Court), which has jurisdiction to issue protective orders against "a person alleged to be committing the crime of stalking, aggravated stalking or harassment." Nev. Rev. Stat. Ann. § 4.370(1)(q) (West 2017). The Justice Court has authority to issue temporary or extended orders of protection against stalking. See Nev. Rev. Stat. Ann. § 200.591(3) (West 2017).

On November 15, 2011, Richard Pike, an Elko County recreation director and assistant high school football coach, applied for a temporary restraining order against Elko County sheriff's sergeant J. Brad Hester. Pike applied on behalf of himself and his two children, and the application rested on several bases.

First, he alleged that Hester made false statements about Pike to others. Hester apparently told Kim Smith, the high school athletic director, that Pike was "one of the biggest potheads in town."

Second, Pike alleged that Hester improperly searched his office. See Majority Op. Part I.A. The genesis of this dispute dates back to August 2011, when Hester and two deputies conducted a search of the Jackpot Recreation Center (Center), which included walking a drug dog through Pike's office in the Center. The search of the Center lasted 10 minutes and uncovered no drugs. Hester claims that Lynn Forsberg—the county supervisor and Pike's boss—authorized him to search the Center "[a]nytime, day or night." Forsberg claims that he told Hester "if he wanted to search the recreation center, he could call me, I would come up and let him in." Pike acknowledges that, under County policy, Forsberg has authority to search his office.

Third, Pike alleged that on at least several occasions, Hester drove by Pike's house and glared at him and his family. Pike also claims that Hester drove by his place of employment in a similar manner. This final incident prompted Pike to file an application for a restraining order against Hester.

The Justice Court issued an ex parte temporary restraining order (TRO) against Hester on November 15, 2011. The TRO was converted into a two-month extended order of protection (EOP) on December 14, 2011. In granting the EOP, the Justice Court explained that it could not "conclude that the search was either lawful under the Fourth Amendment or done with NRS 200.571 `lawful authority.'" But the Justice Court also relied on "testimony about Hester's `stop and stare' activities in front of Pike's residence," finding testimony on the incident "both reliable and credible." Additionally, the court credited the testimony of Smith, to whom Hester made the disparaging remarks about Pike. Thus, the Justice Court concluded that "for all of the foregoing reasons," the EOP would be granted for two months.

B

Pike later filed this suit against Hester and other defendants in the District of Nevada, alleging, inter alia, that Hester violated the Fourth Amendment pursuant to 42 U.S.C. § 1983. Pike seeks compensatory damages expected to exceed $10,000, as well as punitive damages.

Pike moved the district court to give issue-preclusive effect to several of the Justice Court's findings. The district court, while granting issue preclusion on some findings, declined to grant issue preclusion on Pike's constitutional claim, since "the ultimate issue (whether to issue an EOP) did not require a finding of a Fourth Amendment violation, that issue was not necessarily determined." Thus, the Justice Court's conclusion that Hester did not have lawful authority to search Pike's office was not precluded from relitigation "insofar as it concern[ed] an ultimate Fourth Amendment violation."

Pike later moved for summary judgment on the question of qualified immunity. The court granted summary judgment in favor of Pike, finding that there was no genuine question of material fact that Hester's search violated clearly established Fourth Amendment law. However, the court reaffirmed that "the ultimate issue of a Fourth Amendment violation had not been directly litigated" in the Justice Court.

Pike does not argue that the district court erred by refusing to grant issue-preclusive effect to the Justice Court's Fourth Amendment determination; indeed, Pike explicitly abandons any argument to this effect, admitting that "[t]he findings by the Elko Justice Court in its extended protection order were entitled to preclusive [effect] against Mr. Hester but only as to Mr. Pike's invasion of privacy and intentional infliction of emotional distress torts, not his Fourth Amendment claim under §1983."

On appeal, Hester instead challenges the merits of the district court's order granting summary judgment to Pike on the issue of qualified immunity. Nonetheless, the majority, fashioning an argument that Pike declines to raise, affirms the district court's summary judgment order by stretching the issue preclusion doctrine to cover a situation that neither party, nor the district court, presses upon us. Because I cannot agree with the majority's opinion, I respectfully dissent.

II

A

Federal courts "can give the state proceedings no greater preclusive effect than the state courts would." Shaw v. State of Cal. Dep't of Alcoholic Bev. Control, 788 F.2d 600, 607 (9th Cir. 1986) (citing Marrese v. Am. Acad. of Orthopaedic Surgeons, 470 U.S. 373, 386 (1985)). Thus, in determining whether the EOP should be preclusive in the instant action, we are bound by Nevada law. See Allen v. McCurry, 449 U.S. 90, 96 (1980).

Under Nevada law, the following four factors are necessary for the application of issue preclusion: "`(1) the issue decided in the prior litigation must be identical to the issue presented in the current action; (2) the initial ruling must have been on the merits and have become final; (3) the party against whom the judgment is asserted must have been a party or in privity with a party to the prior litigation;' and (4) the issue was actually and necessarily litigated." Five Star Capital Corp. v. Ruby, 194 P.3d 709, 713 (Nev. 2008) (alterations omitted) (quoting Univ. of Nevada v. Tarkanian, 879 P.2d 1180, 1191 (Nev. 1994)). The burden to make this showing falls on Pike. See Bower v. Harrah's Laughlin, Inc., 215 P.3d 709, 718 (Nev. 2009).

> B

Additionally, the application of issue preclusion is premised on the widely recognized understanding that the precluded party "have an adequate opportunity or incentive to obtain a full and fair adjudication in the initial action." Restatement (Second) of Judgments § 28 (Am. Law. Inst. 1982).[1]

This fundamental exception to the issue preclusion doctrine has roots in Nevada law, as issue preclusion "is based upon the sound public policy of limiting litigation by preventing a party who had one full and fair opportunity to litigate an issue from again drawing it into controversy." Bower, 215 P.3d at 718 (internal quotations omitted) (emphasis added). And "[t]he most general independent concern reflected in the limitation of issue preclusion by the full and fair opportunity requirement goes to the incentive to litigate vigorously in the first action." 18 Charles Alan Wright, Arthur R. Miller & Edward H. Cooper, Federal Practice and Procedure § 4423 (3d ed. 2017) (emphasis added). Therefore, Nevada's requirement that a party have a "full and fair opportunity to litigate," Bower, 215 P.3d at 718, recognizes the common law concern that, in some instances, "[t]he stakes in the first action may be so small that extensive effort is not reasonable." 18 Charles Alan Wright, Arthur R. Miller & Edward H. Cooper, Federal Practice and Procedure § 4423 (3d ed. 2017).

Appreciating this concern, the Supreme Court has cautioned that "[i]ssue preclusion may be inapt if `the amount in controversy in the first action was so small in relation to the amount in controversy in the second that preclusion would be plainly unfair.'" B & B Hardware, Inc. v. Hargis Indus., Inc., 135 S. Ct. 1293, 1309 (2015) (alterations removed) (quoting Restatement (Second) of Judgments § 28 cmt. j). As the Court noted, "few litigants would spend $50,000 to defend a $5,000 claim." Id. (quoting 18 Charles Alan Wright, Arthur R. Miller & Edward H. Cooper, Federal Practice & Procedure § 4423 (2d ed. 2002)).

Following this course, every federal court of appeals considers one's incentive to litigate in the collateral estoppel context. See, e.g., Canonsburg Gen. Hosp. v. Burwell, 807 F.3d 295, 306 (D.C. Cir. 2015); DeGuelle v. Camilli, 724 F.3d 933, 935 (7th Cir. 2013); Kosinski v. Comm'r, 541 F.3d 671, 677 (6th Cir. 2008); Maciel v. Comm'r, 489 F.3d 1018, 1023 (9th Cir. 2007); Jean Alexander Cosmetics, Inc. v. L'Oreal USA, Inc., 458 F.3d 244, 250 (3d Cir. 2006); Salguero v. City of Clovis, 366 F.3d 1168, 1174 (10th Cir. 2004); Simmons v. O'Brien, 77 F.3d 1093, 1095 (8th Cir. 1996); In re Belmont Realty Corp., 11 F.3d 1092, 1097 (1st Cir. 1993); Sun Towers, Inc. v. Heckler, 725 F.2d 315, 322 n.7 (5th Cir.

1984); Cotton States Mut. Ins. Co. v. Anderson, 749 F.2d 663, 666 (11th Cir. 1984); Wickham Contracting Co. v. Bd. of Educ. of City of New York, 715 F.2d 21, 28 (2d Cir. 1983); Prosise v. Haring, 667 F.2d 1133, 1141 (4th Cir. 1981).

C

I respectfully suggest that the majority's failure to consider this foundational principle of collateral estoppel is fatal to its conclusion.

First, and most importantly, the Fourth Amendment was mentioned just once over the course of the one-day hearing and such invocation was when Pike's counsel admitted that "there was no Fourth Amendment rights violated here." If Pike's counsel conceded at the EOP hearing that Hester didn't violate the Fourth Amendment, how could Hester be said to have had any incentive—let alone a vigorous one—to litigate such question?

Second, the Justice Court is designed to resolve small claims in an efficient and prompt manner. See Nev. Rev. Stat. Ann. § 4.370 (West 2017) (limiting jurisdiction to claims under $15,000, protective orders against harassment or stalking, and certain misdemeanors). Indeed, the entire hearing over the EOP lasted just one day. And at the one-day hearing, Hester's counsel told the judge that he would not argue about "silly stuff"—such as objecting when cross-examination went beyond the scope of direct examination—so the judge could "rule and we can go all home on a Monday." In this vein, the judge noted at the outset that "[t]hese hearings are pretty darn informal." Alas, according to the majority, such a breezy proceeding, dispensing with basic rules of evidence, was a suitable setting for Hester to litigate vigorously constitutional law.[2]

Moreover, the application of issue preclusion in this setting is especially unwise, as it threatens to turn Justice Court proceedings—tailored to the prompt resolution of small claims and other disputes—into full-blown trials tasked with uncovering whether or not a purported search violated the Fourth Amendment.

Collateral estoppel "is an equitable doctrine," not an inexorable command. 46 Am. Jur. 2d Judgments § 469 (2018). Pike's counsel conceded that the Fourth Amendment was not at issue, neutering any prospect that Hester could have harbored a strong incentive to litigate vigorously the merits of that question. Therefore, I believe it improper to grant issue preclusive effect to the EOP in this setting.

III

Instead of giving preclusive effect to the Justice Court's Fourth Amendment determination, we should reverse the district court's grant of summary judgment and remand for trial. As the record shows, conflicting testimony over Hester's authority to search Pike's office plainly creates a genuine dispute of material fact. See Anderson v. Liberty Lobby, Inc., 477 U.S. 242, 248 (1986).

A

Forsberg testified that he told Hester, "if [Hester] wanted to search the recreation center, he could call me, I would come up and let him in." Hester, on the other hand, testified that Forsberg told Hester he could conduct a search "[a]nytime, day or night."[3]

As the non-moving party, evidence must be construed in the light most favorable to Hester. Tolan v. Cotton, 134 S. Ct. 1861, 1866, 188 L. Ed. 2d 895 (2014) ("Our qualifiedimmunity cases illustrate the importance of drawing inferences in favor of the nonmovant."). Yet, the district court utterly ignored Hester's testimony—not even bothering to construe it at all, let alone in a favorable light—and simply adopted wholesale Forsberg's recollection of events. Yet, Hester offered a completely different version of their conversation, which creates a genuine dispute of fact as to whether Hester was authorized to search Pike's office.[4]

B

And, indeed, whether Hester had permission to search is critical to this case. Anderson, 477 U.S. at 248 (holding that a factual dispute is material if it "might affect the outcome of the suit"). If Hester received consent from Forsberg to search Pike's office, there was likely no Fourth Amendment violation. "The Fourth Amendment recognizes a valid warrantless entry and search of premises when police obtain the voluntary consent of an occupant who shares, or is reasonably believed to share, authority over the area." Georgia v. Randolph, 547 U.S. 103, 106 (2006). Pike admitted that he understood that the County handbook policy allowed Forsberg—his boss—to search his office. We have held that an employee's privacy interest "may be subject to the possibility of an employer's consent to a search of the premises." United States v. Ziegler, 474 F.3d 1184, 1191 (9th Cir. 2007). Indeed, in Ziegler, "Frontline, as the employer, could consent to a search of the [employee's] office." Id. at 1192. And the search here involved only a drug dog briefly sniffing the exterior of a desk in Pike's office, and a file cabinet outside Pike's office— hardly Pike's personal belongings. See O'Connor v. Ortega, 480 U.S. 709, 716 (1987) (plurality opinion) ("The appropriate standard for a workplace search does not necessarily apply to a piece of closed personal luggage, a handbag or a briefcase that happens to be within the employer's business address."). Under these circumstances, Forsberg, similar to the employer in Ziegler "could give valid consent to a search . . . because the [desk] is the type of workplace property that remains within the control of the employer `even if the employee has placed personal items in it.'" Id. at 1191 (alterations removed) (quoting O'Connor, 480 U.S. at 716). As a result, under these circumstances, Forsberg could give valid consent to search Pike's office.[5]

IV

I would reverse the district court's grant of summary judgment and remand to the district court for further proceedings. Whether a Fourth Amendment violation occurred should be resolved at trial. See Tortu v. Las Vegas Metro. Police Dep't, 556 F.3d 1075, 1085 (9th Cir. 2009).

Notes

[1] The Supreme Court of Nevada has a "long-standing reliance on the Restatement (Second) of Judgments in the issue and claim preclusion context." Alcantara ex rel. Alcantara v. Wal-Mart Stores, Inc., 321 P.3d 912, 917 (Nev. 2014). It has favorably

looked to the Restatement (Second) of Judgments § 28 in the issue preclusion setting. See Personhood Nevada v. Bristol, 245 P.3d 572, 576 (Nev. 2010).

[2] Pike's attorney's statement that "the question is what was the basis for the search" is hardly illuminative, contrary to the majority's view. The attorney was referring to the basis for Hester's suspicion of Pike, not whether Forsberg consented to the search. As the attorney put it, "[t]he issue is not just a semantics having to do with day or night with Mr. Forsberg. It has to do with what information that the deputy gave to Mr. Forsberg to get him to okay the search."

[3] It appears uncontested that the search occurred within a few days of this conversation.

[4] This also corrupts the majority opinion's discussion on clearly established law. As the Supreme Court has noted, "courts must take care not to define a case's `context' in a manner that imports genuinely disputed factual propositions." Tolan, 134 S. Ct. at 1866 (2014) (quoting Brosseau v. Haugen, 543 U.S. 194, 195, 198 (2004) (per curiam)). By asking whether a "no-consent dog search of a public employee's office was clearly unlawful," the majority's opinion imports the dispute over consent into the description of the right at issue.

[5] Although Forsberg had actual authority to search Pike's office, the government may alternatively obtain valid consent from a third party when the officer "reasonably believe[s] that the third party has actual authority to consent." United States v. Fultz, 146 F.3d 1102, 1105 (9th Cir. 1998). Hester asked Forsberg's permission because Forsberg had "final say" over the building. This was not an unreasonable conclusion given that Forsberg is the county supervisor and Pike's boss.

Judge O'Scannlain's dissent in MacDonald v. Hedgpeth (Nov 5, 2018)

O'SCANNLAIN, Circuit Judge, dissenting:

The Antiterrorism and Effective Death Penalty Act (AEDPA), Pub. L. No. 104-132, 110 Stat. 1214, empowers our court to order grant of a writ of habeas corpus in this case only if the California courts reached "a decision that was contrary to, or involved an unreasonable application of, clearly established Federal law, as determined by the Supreme Court of the United States." 28 U.S.C. § 2254(d) (emphasis added). Yet despite the Supreme Court's repeated admonitions to this Circuit that AEDPA means what it says, see, e.g., Kernan v. Cuero, 138 S. Ct. 4, 9 (2017) (per curiam), the majority treats this appeal just like another State court direct review of a criminal conviction and erroneously, in my view, orders grant of the writ based on California law, rather than Federal law.

Respectfully, I must dissent.

I

Let me begin by restating the relevant facts. Felix Maquiz[1] was convicted of three counts of robbery in a California Superior Court in 2002: two counts from a 1999 robbery and one count from a 2001 robbery.

In May of 1999, Maquiz robbed an "AM/PM" minimarket in Perris, California. Two employees working in the store at the time, Betty Walton and José Lopez, reported that Maquiz pointed a shotgun at Lopez, demanded the cash from the register, and fled the store. Walton followed Maquiz outside and saw him get into the passenger side of a maroon vehicle, which then drove away. Two days later, police officers saw a maroon vehicle chasing a car down the street in Perris, and the officers pulled the maroon vehicle over. Inside was Maquiz and his friend, Ricardo Hoyos, along with a shotgun fitting the description of the one used in the mini-market robbery. Officers arrested Maquiz and Hoyos for robbing the mini-market and attempting to intimidate a witness in the car they were chasing.

In June of 2001, Maquiz robbed Kenneth Cheney at a pay phone outside of Jenny's Restaurant in Perris. With his hand held over his face, Maquiz approached Cheney from the rear with a gun and demanded that Cheney hand over his wallet. After receiving the wallet, Maquiz told Cheney to run home or he would kill him. Cheney ran to a nearby gas station, where two witnesses who had called the police were waiting. The witnesses described Maquiz as wearing a puffy black jacket, a dark beanie pulled down to his eyebrows, and dark slacks. A short while later, police officers discovered Maquiz a few blocks away from the restaurant and placed him under arrest for the robbery.

Maquiz was charged with three counts of robbery—two counts from 1999 (Lopez and Walton) and one count from 2001 (Cheney)—along with several other crimes. The prosecution also sought sentence enhancements for each robbery under California Penal Code § 186.22(b)(1), which provides for a ten-year enhancement when "any person . . . is convicted of a felony committed for the benefit of, at the direction of, or in association with any criminal street gang, with the specific intent to promote, further, or assist in any criminal conduct by gang members." Thus, whether Maquiz intended to benefit the criminal activities of a gang was a critical issue at trial.

The State's primary source of evidence to support the gang enhancements was testimony from Deputy Eric Brewer, a member of the Perris Police Department's gang unit. Deputy Brewer, having received hundreds of hours of training on gang activity over his career, testified as an expert witness on gang activity. He testified that both Maquiz and Hoyos were members of the Perres Mara Villa (PMV), the "largest" and "primary Hispanic gang in the city of Perris," which focused primarily on robberies, homicides, witness intimidation, carjacking, and other crimes. Hoyos and Maquiz were "active" members of PMV, meaning that they "actually ha[d] a potential to be out on the street and they actively r[an] with the gang." And Maquiz was known as "Mr. Lucky" in the gang, which is "a significant thing, in that most [gang members] don't obtain [a nickname] unless they're living the lifestyle."

Deputy Brewer also discussed how a robbery—even one committed alone—might benefit PMV: "[T]he fear and intimidation goes out into the community. . . . You want the people to know you're the ones that run that area and you don't want to mess with Perres Mara Villa." Likewise, Brewer testified that the fruits of the robbery could be helpful to the gang, explaining that "[w]hatever money might be obtained . . . [is] not necessarily only maintained by that individual. He's going to share [it] with other members of the gang." More generally, Brewer testified that "whether it be just . . . one [crime] or . . . two, three crimes in just a short period of time as a group, they continue to work as an organization."

Deputy Brewer then specifically discussed the 1999 and 2001 robberies.

When asked whether the 1999 robbery "constituted a benefit for the Perres Mara Villa gang," Brewer answered affirmatively, stressing the "fear and intimidation factor" and stating that "any money that was taken in the crime can be used by those gang members to further their activities."

Brewer also testified that the 2001 robbery "constitute[d] [a] benefit for the Perres Mara Villa gang." Brewer explained that the robbery "furthered knowledge of [the gang]," and he highlighted once again the "fear and intimidation factor for the gang and for [Maquiz] as a member of that gang." Brewer then described how Maquiz might have shared the proceeds of the 2001 robbery with his gang: "Out of a respect factor, he would probably have a tendency to talk about it. And as far as sharing that, if [PMV] were present while he still had that money . . . he would either share it or [PMV would] benefit . . . by what he spends the money on."

The jury found Maquiz guilty of each robbery count, and found the allegations to support the gang sentence enhancements true beyond a reasonable doubt. After several rounds of direct appeals, Maquiz was sentenced to twenty-three years in prison, with the terms of each gang enhancement to run concurrently. Maquiz then filed a habeas petition in the state court system, arguing, among other things, that (1) the superior court committed constitutional error by permitting Deputy Brewer to testify to the ultimate truth or falsity of his gang enhancements and (2) insufficient evidence supported the 2001 gang enhancement. The California Court of Appeal for the Fourth District denied the habeas petition without comment, and the Supreme Court of California—while granting the habeas petition on some grounds—did not address either of the above grounds for relief.

Maquiz then filed a federal habeas petition reasserting his arguments, and the district court denied relief. Maquiz timely appealed.

II

The majority rightly rejects Maquiz's first argument— that habeas relief is warranted because Deputy Brewer testified directly to the truth or falsity of his gang enhancements—because Maquiz can point to no law clearly established by the Supreme Court of the United States that would prohibit such testimony. Maj. Op. at 9.

But the majority runs astray in its analysis of Maquiz's second argument. The majority holds that the evidence at his trial was constitutionally insufficient under Jackson v. Virginia, 443 U.S. 307 (1979), to support the 2001 gang enhancement, and that therefore there was "no reasonable basis on which the California courts could have rejected Maquiz's [habeas petition]." Maj. Op. at 20.

With respect, I believe the majority's analysis is incorrect.

A

Jackson instructs that when assessing the sufficiency of the evidence challenge to a criminal conviction, we must ask "whether, after viewing the evidence in the light most favorable to the prosecution, any rational trier of fact could have found the essential elements of the crime beyond a reasonable doubt." 443 U.S. at 319. And, as all must agree, "Jackson claims face a high bar in federal habeas proceedings because they are subject to two layers of judicial deference." Coleman v. Johnson, 566 U.S. 650, 651 (2012). That is, "on habeas review, a federal court may not overturn a state court decision rejecting a sufficiency of the evidence challenge simply because the federal court disagrees with the state court. The federal court instead may do so only if the state court decision was objectively unreasonable." Id. (internal quotation marks omitted). So when we combine Jackson and AEDPA deference, our inquiry is whether no "fairminded jurist[]" could conclude that "any rational trier of fact could have" found sufficient evidence to support the conviction. See Yarborough v. Alvarado, 541 U.S. 652, 664 (2004); Jackson, 443 U.S. at 319. "If this standard is difficult to meet, that is because it was meant to be." Harrington v. Richter, 562 U.S. 86, 102 (2011).

B

I suggest that the majority's analysis is premised upon two core misunderstandings of how a federal court is to assess a Jackson claim under AEDPA.

1

First, the majority looks to the wrong law: rather than rely exclusively on the law clearly established by the Supreme Court as AEDPA commands, the majority turns to what it views as analogous state court decisions. More specifically, the majority disregards Deputy Brewer's expert testimony in support of the gang enhancement because some decisions from the California Courts of Appeal have held insufficient the testimony of gang experts to support enhancements in other cases. Maj. Op. at 17, 19-20. But, obviously, state courts do not clearly establish federal law on the Supreme Court's behalf. See Cuero, 138 S. Ct. at 9 (admonishing the Ninth Circuit for substituting "state-court decisions" in lieu of decisions from the Supreme Court when operating under the AEDPA standard of review).

In holding otherwise, the majority takes refuge in the Supreme Court's instruction that the Jackson standard must be applied by "reference to the substantive elements of the criminal offense as defined by state law." 443 U.S. at 324 n.16. But it does not at all follow from such premise that the sufficiency of the evidence required to meet those elements may be ascertained by reference to state law. Rather, "the minimum amount of evidence that the Due Process Clause requires to prove the offense is purely a matter of federal law." Coleman, 566 U.S. at 655 (emphasis added). Indeed, the Supreme Court reversed the Third Circuit for making precisely the same mistake as the majority makes here. In Coleman, the Court held that "it was error for [that Circuit] to look to Pennsylvania law in determining what distinguishes a reasoned inference from `mere speculation.'" Id. We should heed the same guidance in this case. To do otherwise contravenes Jackson, which "leaves juries broad discretion in deciding what inferences to draw from the evidence presented at trial." Id.

The majority offers a final reason to justify its reliance on state court cases, noting briefly that federal court decisions similarly "do not allow . . . suspicion and speculation to support a jury verdict." Maj. Op. at 18. Setting aside the heavily generalized nature of such an assertion, the majority sees fit to bolster it with cases from only our court. But as the Supreme Court has repeatedly admonished, Ninth Circuit precedent "does not constitute `clearly established Federal law, as determined by the Supreme Court.'" Glebe v. Frost, 135 S. Ct. 429, 431 (2014) (per curiam) (quoting 28 U.S.C. § 2254(d)(1)); see also Cuero, 138 S. Ct. at 9; Lopez v. Smith, 135 S. Ct. 1, 4 (2014) (per curiam).

2

Second, the majority fails to answer the only question AEDPA asks of us: whether fairminded jurists could disagree regarding the Jackson question presented in this case. That is, our inquiry here surely is not whether the California courts correctly applied the Jackson standard, but whether the State's courts applied it in an objectively unreasonable fashion. We must take significant care not to mistake the two inquiries. See Williams v. Taylor, 529 U.S. 362, 410 (2000) ("For purposes of today's opinion, the most important point is that an unreasonable application of federal law is different from an incorrect application of federal law."). The Supreme Court has emphasized that "even a strong case for relief does not mean the state court's contrary conclusion was unreasonable." Harrington, 562 U.S. at 102.

But once the majority holds the evidence insufficient under Jackson to support Maquiz's gang enhancement, it immediately concludes, as if it necessarily followed, that there was "no reasonable basis on which the California courts could have rejected Maquiz's argument that the gang sentencing enhancement . . . was unsupported by sufficient evidence." Maj. Op. at 20. Such perfunctory reasoning collapses the "two layers of judicial deference" that we must afford when evaluating a Jackson claim under AEDPA. Coleman, 566 U.S. at 651. So while the majority begins its analysis with a boilerplate recitation of the AEDPA standard of review, Maj. Op. at 10, AEDPA deference enjoys "no operation or function in its reasoning," Harrington, 562 U.S. at 104.

C

Any serious engagement with the question AEDPA asks of us mandates that we affirm the district court's denial of the writ of habeas corpus. Simply put, the question whether Maquiz's gang-related sentence enhancement is supported by sufficient evidence under Jackson lies well within the realm of fairminded disagreement.

1

A reasonable jurist could conclude that Deputy Brewer's expert testimony adequately supported both elements of the gang enhancement—specifically, that Maquiz committed the 2001 robbery (1) "for the benefit of" PMV and (2) "with the specific intent to promote, further, or assist in any criminal conduct by [PMV]." People v. Albillar, 244 P.3d 1062, 1070, 1074 (Cal. 2010).

Deputy Brewer's testimony supports the inference that Maquiz committed the 2001 robbery for the benefit of PMV; Brewer stated that the robbery "furthered knowledge of, fear and intimidation . . . for the gang and for [Maquiz] as a member of that gang." Brewer's testimony likewise supports the inference that Maquiz committed the 2001 robbery with the intent to further the criminal activities of the PMV gang. As he explained, PMV members like Maquiz "continue to work as an organization" whether they commit crimes alone or as a group, so the jury could have inferred that Maquiz committed the robbery with PMV's criminal objectives (rather than his own) in mind.

The foundation for Deputy Brewer's testimony might have been stronger, but his conclusion was far from baseless. As Deputy Brewer testified, Maquiz was an "active" member of PMV, meaning that he "actively r[a]n with the gang" and that he was "living the [gang] lifestyle." The type of crime at issue—robbery—is also probative, because Deputy Brewer testified that one of the PMV gang's "primary activities" was engaging in robberies. Deputy Brewer's testimony must also be considered in light of his extensive experience, not just with gangs in general, but with PMV and Maquiz in particular. Deputy Brewer testified that he had personally made contact with roughly 150 to 200 different PMV members in Perris, and had met with Maquiz, specifically, five or six times.

Moreover, the jury had before it evidence supporting a conclusion that the 2001 robbery took place in or near PMV territory. For example, Deputy Brewer identified various buildings in Perris where the PMV gang had marked its territory using graffiti, and such buildings are near the location of Maquiz's 2001 robbery. Because the prosecution presented evidence of the location of the PMV graffiti and the 2001 robbery, a reasonable jury could have utilized the proximity between the two locations to conclude that both incidents took place in or near PMV territory. See Jackson, 443 U.S. at 326 (holding that court must presume trier of fact resolved all inferences in favor of the prosecution "even if it does not affirmatively appear in the record"). With the robbery so located, Deputy Brewer's conclusion finds further support in his earlier discussion that criminal street gangs seek to control their territory by spreading "intimidation and fear within the community."

The California courts thus could well have reached the fairminded conclusion that sufficient evidence supported the gang enhancement.

2

The majority casts aside Deputy Brewer's conclusion that Maquiz worked to benefit PMV by intimidating the community, because Maquiz did not flaunt his PMV affiliation when he committed the 2001 robbery. Maj. Op. at 16.

So what?

Deputy Brewer discussed the extensive efforts of PMV generally to make its presence known within the Perris community by, for example, marking buildings with territorial graffiti. In light of such efforts, the 2001 robbery easily could have been attributed to PMV even without Maquiz explicitly having announced "I'm a member of PMV!" when he committed the crime. And even if the majority thinks not, the Supreme

Court has routinely rejected under AEDPA the sort of "fine-grained factual parsing" the majority must engage in to disagree. See Coleman, 566 U.S. at 655.

The majority also asserts that it cannot hold Deputy Brewer's testimony sufficient to support the gang enhancement because "[t]o hold otherwise would turn the statute into a penalty enhancement simply for committing a crime while being a gang member." Maj. Op. at 18. In so concluding, the majority makes much of the Supreme Court of California's statement that "[n]ot every crime committed by gang members is related to a gang." Albillar, 244 P.3d at 60. But Albillar's statement reflects only a state gloss on the sort of evidence needed to support the gang enhancement. Even if the majority is correct that, under California law, proof of gang membership alone is typically insufficient, by itself, to support the enhancement, it is immaterial to the federal sufficiency question presented by Maquiz's Jackson claim. See Coleman, 566 U.S. at 655. In reasoning otherwise, the majority, in essence, holds that Maquiz is entitled to federal habeas relief because the California courts misapplied California law. This is not the province of AEDPA.

III

At bottom, the majority seems simply to conclude Deputy Brewer's expert testimony is unpersuasive. But that is not the majority's call to make under Jackson, and it surely is not the appropriate inquiry under AEDPA. Taking AEDPA's command seriously, we must ask only whether a fair-minded jurist could conclude that any rational jury might have credited Deputy Brewer's expert testimony. The answer to that question is undoubtedly yes.

I respectfully dissent.

Notes

[1] As does the majority, I refer to the Appellant as "Maquiz," rather than his legal last name, "MacDonald," because all parties refer to him as Maquiz.

Judge O'Scannlain's dissent from denial of rehearing en banc in Sanchez v. Barr (April 1, 2019) [Notes omitted]

O'SCANNLAIN, Circuit Judge,[**] with whom CALLAHAN, BEA, IKUTA, BENNETT, and R. NELSON, Circuit Judges, join, respecting the denial of rehearing en banc:

In this deportation proceeding, which commenced over eight years ago, our court's opinion concedes that admissible evidence establishes Mexican citizen Luis Enrique Sanchez's removability. Current immigration law therefore required the three-judge panel to allow the deportation order to take effect. Unsatisfied with such prospect, the panel holds instead that Sanchez's entire removal proceeding now must be terminated because he was detained without reasonable suspicion—a violation of the Fourth Amendment.

Such an absurd result contravenes basic Fourth Amendment principles, defies

Supreme Court precedent, and lacks any basis in our case law (or that of any other circuit). Worse, the panel disguises the Fourth Amendment harm as a "regulatory violation" to work a simple and obvious end-run around it. At bottom, the panel fails to grasp that Fourth Amendment wrongs warrant Fourth Amendment remedies—nothing less, but nothing more. This case has languished for almost a decade, and now the government is reduced to restarting deportation proceedings, using the same evidence to achieve the same outcome that the Immigration Judge ("IJ") ordered in 2011. Our court should have reheard this case en banc to correct the panel's errant decision, a very unfortunate precedent with troublesome consequences for our immigration jurisprudence.

I

The facts are straightforward.[1] Luis Enrique Sanchez is a citizen of Mexico who entered the United States without inspection in 1988. In 2004, Sanchez applied for and received "Family Unity Benefits" from the United States Citizenship and Immigration Service ("USCIS"), which temporarily authorized him to live and to work in the United States. USCIS later denied Sanchez's request for an extension of these benefits in 2008, and at that point he no longer enjoyed lawful status to remain in the United States.

In February 2010, Sanchez and three others were marooned off the coast of California when their fishing boat's engine lost power. The Coast Guard towed their boat into port, demanded identification documents, and detained them for two hours until Customs and Border Protection ("CBP") officers arrived. The CBP officers took Sanchez to a CBP facility, interrogated and strip-searched him, and then released him. The officers prepared a Form I-213 (Record of Deportable/Inadmissible Alien), which included Sanchez's express admission to them that he had entered the United States without inspection and was undocumented.

In November 2010, the Department of Homeland Security ("DHS") issued a Notice to Appear and charged Sanchez with being removable. To prove Sanchez's removability, the government relied on both the Form I-213 prepared by the CBP officers and on Sanchez's prior application for Family Unity Benefits. Sanchez sought to have the Form I-213 suppressed and to have his removal proceedings terminated. He argued that his detention by CBP officers was based solely on race in contravention of the Fourth Amendment and 8 C.F.R. § 287.8(b), which requires arresting officers to possess a "reasonable suspicion" of the person's unlawful presence.[2]

The IJ denied the motion and ordered Sanchez removed. In 2014, the Board of Immigration Appeals ("BIA") dismissed Sanchez's appeal, leaving the deportation order in place. It concluded that, regardless of whether the Form I-213 should have been suppressed, the government could use "independent evidence . . . to establish his nationality and identity." See Sanchez v. Sessions, 904 F.3d 643, 648 (9th Cir. 2018). Sanchez timely petitioned for review in our court in 2014.[3]

II

Sanchez contends specifically that the Coast Guard detained him based on his Latino appearance in violation of the Fourth Amendment and 8 C.F.R. § 287.8(b). The threejudge panel agreed, but instead of holding merely that the evidence obtained from the arrest should have been suppressed, its opinion orders the entire deportation proceeding terminated. The opinion's irredeemable flaw is its attempt to cure an illegal arrest—a quintessential Fourth Amendment violation—with a remedy that the Fourth Amendment would never authorize.

A

If Sanchez's Fourth Amendment rights were violated, then he is indeed entitled to a Fourth Amendment remedy. Under our circuit's case law, Sanchez may (and indeed did) seek the exclusion of wrongfully obtained evidence from his immigration proceedings. See, e.g., Lopez-Rodriguez v. Mukasey, 536 F.3d 1012, 1018 (9th Cir. 2008).[4] But here, as the panel reluctantly concedes, the brute fact is that suppression does him no good: the government possesses independent (and constitutionally firm) evidence establishing Sanchez's unlawful status. See Sanchez, 904 F.3d at 653. Eager to give Sanchez some relief, however, the panel stretches our case law beyond recognition. Instead of suppression of the unlawfully obtained document, the panel awarded him "termination without prejudice," thus mandating commencement of a new round of removal proceedings with another hearing before the IJ, another appeal to the BIA, and another petition for review to our court—potentially another eight years of safe haven in the United States. Id. at 657.

The opinion seems to invoke a straightforward compensatory-justice theory. Sanchez's initial detention, the opinion reasons, resulted from racial profiling, so the subsequent deportation proceeding was "tainted from [its] roots." Id. at 655 (internal quotation marks omitted). Thus, only "full termination of the proceedings without prejudice can effectively cure any procedural defect by putting the parties into the position [in which] they would have been had no procedural error taken place." Id. (internal quotation marks omitted). Stated differently, the opinion purports to restore Sanchez to his rightful position by washing away the "taint" of his unlawful arrest. To do so, it prescribes a government "do-over," now nine years after the first round started, as if the entire eight-year-long deportation proceeding had never occurred.

B

Such approach fails. The Fourth Amendment does not authorize a court, for example, to invalidate an arrest, prosecution, or subsequent proceeding simply because it resulted from such a violation. See United States v. Morrison, 449 U.S. 361, 366 (1981) ("[W]e have not suggested that searches and seizures contrary to the Fourth Amendment warrant dismissal of the indictment."). Such limitation makes sense. The Fourth Amendment safeguards the substantive rights to "privacy and security." Carpenter v. United States, 138 S. Ct. 2206, 2213 (2018) (internal quotation marks omitted). It does not establish a right to be free from prosecution for crimes committed—even if such prosecution results from an illegal search. See United States v. Leon, 468 U.S. 897, 906 (1984) ("[T]he use of fruits of a past unlawful search or seizure works no new Fourth Amendment wrong." (internal quotation marks omitted)).

The Supreme Court's application of the exclusionary rule confirms the correct approach. Because a Fourth Amendment violation is "fully accomplished by the unlawful search and seizure," trial remedies like the exclusionary rule are "neither intended nor able to cure" the constitutional harm. Id. (internal quotation marks omitted). As such, exclusion is not designed to restore the defendant to his pre-violation position, but rather to deter future violations by offering him a windfall (i.e., the exclusion of incriminating evidence at trial). See Hudson v. Michigan, 547 U.S. 586, 591 (2006). Just as with the exclusionary rule itself, however, the panel's novel termination remedy does not "cure" the initial unlawful arrest. Thus, the opinion's core premise—that termination washes away the "taint" of the government's initial violation—contravenes the proper application of the Fourth Amendment.

To illustrate, consider whether the panel's theory would make any sense in a criminal proceeding. Suppose that a citizen is unconstitutionally detained because of his race, but law enforcement officials also discover—because of evidence obtained independently of such arrest—that he committed a drug crime and charge him accordingly. The exclusionary rule, of course, would not compel the suppression of the "independently acquired" evidence. Utah v. Strieff, 136 S. Ct. 2056, 2061 (2016). Could the court instead dismiss the criminal indictment because the illegal arrest tainted the criminal proceeding that followed? Could the court order the defendant to be released from custody? Of course not. See Morrison, 449 U.S. at 366 ("The [Fourth Amendment] remedy in the criminal proceeding is limited to denying the prosecution the fruits of its transgression."). Indeed, the panel does not cite a single case that terminates a criminal proceeding for such a reason. And if termination of proceedings would be unavailable in a criminal prosecution, then it should be inconceivable in a civil deportation proceeding.

Perhaps aware that Fourth Amendment doctrine forecloses its reasoning, the panel alludes instead to a separate justification for its remedy: deterrence. See Sanchez, 904 F.3d at 655; see also Paez Concurrence at 8-9. But whether such remedy will prevent future violations against other aliens has nothing to do with restoring Sanchez to his rightful position. Worse, the panel's indistinct reference to the remedy's deterrence value rests on contestable empirical assumptions, and the panel makes no effort to show that such benefits outweigh the costs. Cf. INS v. Lopez-Mendoza, 468 U.S. 1032, 1040-50 (1984) (balancing the benefits and costs of the exclusionary rule in deportation proceedings). Besides, the panel's subtle reliance on deterrence smuggles in the very reasoning that drives the Court's application of the exclusionary rule— reinforcing, yet again, that the Fourth Amendment should guide this case's resolution.

    C

Lopez-Mendoza, the Supreme Court's leading case on the application of the Fourth Amendment to civil deportation proceedings, also repudiates the panel's reasoning. There, government agents arrested Lopez-Mendoza "at his place of employment" even though the "agents had not sought a warrant to search the premises or to arrest any of its occupants." Id. at 1035. Below, he "objected only to the fact that he had been summoned to a deportation hearing following an unlawful arrest." Id. at 1040. Nevertheless, the Supreme Court upheld the IJ's removal order because the "mere fact of an illegal arrest has no bearing on a subsequent deportation proceeding." Id. at 1041 (emphasis added and brackets and internal quotation marks omitted).

Lopez-Mendoza rejects the opinion's core premise. Here too, Sanchez's illegal arrest has "no bearing" on his removal proceeding. Consequently, the arrest cannot "taint[]" the proceeding "from [its] roots." Sanchez, 904 F.3d at 655 (internal quotation marks omitted). The panel ignores the fact that the Supreme Court has expressly rejected the very theory on which it relies.

III

To avoid the Fourth Amendment's doctrinal dead-end, the panel mysteriously claims that its remedy seeks to cure only a "regulatory violation"—not a violation of the Fourth Amendment itself. See Sanchez, 904 F.3d at 653-55. The relevant regulation states that an immigration officer may "detain [a] person for questioning" if the officer has a "reasonable suspicion . . . that the person being questioned is . . . an alien illegally in the United States." 8 C.F.R. § 287.8(b)(2). The panel reasons that the Coast Guard's violation of § 287.8(b)(2)—again, Sanchez's detention on the basis of race—estops the government from continuing the proceeding.

But § 287.8(b)(2), as the opinion notes, exists simply to "effectuate" the Fourth Amendment and "all but parrots" its requirements. Sanchez, 904 F.3d at 651, 652 n.9; see also Paez Concurrence at 8. We may not launder Fourth Amendment violations through agency regulations to authorize a remedy that the Fourth Amendment would never allow. The panel's decision to order the government to terminate deportation proceedings because of a regulatory violation is unsustainable in theory and unfounded in precedent.[5]

A

Let's begin with a first principle that the opinion obscures: our authority to compel an agency to follow its own regulations must have its source in the Constitution itself or some federal statute. See United States v. Caceres, 440 U.S. 741, 749-55 (1979) (refusing to compel an agency to follow its own regulation because such regulations were not "required by the Constitution or by statute," and because neither the Fourth Amendment, the Due Process Clause, nor the Administrative Procedure Act authorized the Court to enforce compliance). We lack a roving commission to seek out and to redress every wrong inflicted by the Executive Branch, remediating instead only specific legal wrongs with the specific remedies authorized by federal law.

Unfortunately, the opinion never bothers to identify the legal basis for its "regulatory violation" theory. Certainly, the panel invokes the Constitution when it observes that the violated regulation "effectuate[s] the Fourth Amendment." Sanchez, 904 F.3d at 652 n.9; see also id. at 651 (regulation "all but parrots" Fourth Amendment standards); id. at 652 (regulation "reflects the Fourth Amendment's requirements"); id. at 656 n.15 (regulation "is premised on Fourth Amendment standards"). Yet the Fourth

Amendment itself cannot sustain the panel's holding. Which raises the question: what is the legal basis for the panel's remedy?

It cannot be the "Fifth Amendment due process guarantee that operates in removal proceedings." Chuyon Yon Hong v. Mukasey, 518 F.3d 1030, 1035 (9th Cir. 2008). The Due Process Clause promises aliens the "full and fair" opportunity to assert the right to remain in the United States. Montes-Lopez v. Holder, 694 F.3d 1085, 1092 (9th Cir. 2012) (internal quotation marks omitted). But here, Sanchez's unlawful arrest has no effect at all on the deportation proceeding itself. His illegal arrest does not infringe upon his ability to offer evidence, to obtain counsel, or to make his case before the IJ. No legal support there!

Nor is it the Immigration and Nationality Act, see 8 U.S.C. § 1252, or "a rule of administrative law," United States v. Calderon-Medina, 591 F.2d 529, 531 (9th Cir. 1979); see also Bd. of Curators of Univ. of Mo. v. Horowitz, 435 U.S. 78, 92 n.8 (1978) (stating that cases mandating agency compliance with their own regulations "enunciate principles of federal administrative law rather than of constitutional law"). Indeed, the otherwise-thorough opinion does not include a single sentence of textual analysis demonstrating that § 1252 authorizes us to order the government to restart deportation proceedings because of an initial unlawful arrest. Likewise, the panel cannot claim to articulate some new rule of administrative common law because its holding is incompatible with our treatment of other administrative agencies. See Caceres, 440 U.S. at 749-55.

In sum, the panel's inability to identify the legal basis for its remedy is telling, as it suggests that there isn't one. Instead, the gravamen of Sanchez's complaint is that the government violated the Fourth Amendment—not his due process rights, not a statutory right, not some rule of administrative law, and not an unidentifiable potpourri of protected interests. But if this case involves a Fourth Amendment wrong, it should be controlled by Fourth Amendment jurisprudence. Those principles, however, unambiguously foreclose the panel's extravagant remedy.

B

Unsurprisingly, no other court has imposed such a remedy. Indeed, the panel does not identify a single decision in which a federal court actually required termination of proceedings when a regulatory violation invaded Fourth Amendment interests. Instead, the panel scrounges up a single Ninth Circuit case concerning a deprivation of a procedural (not substantive) right in a criminal proceeding, see Calderon-Medina, 591 F.2d at 529; a BIA decision that (needless to say) is not precedent at all, see Matter of Garcia-Flores, 17 I. & N. Dec. 325 (BIA 1980); a Second Circuit opinion that it over-reads, see Rajah v. Mukasey, 544 F.3d 427 (2d Cir. 2008); and a smattering of inapposite out-ofcircuit decisions. See Sanchez, 904 F.3d at 654-55.

The bulk of the cases it cites in support of its theory concern regulations offering procedural protections that ensure constitutionally (or statutorily) mandated adjudicative due process.[6] But such procedural protections differ in kind from the substantive interests protected by the regulation in this case. Because the violation of a procedural right (e.g., the right to counsel) increases the risk of erroneous deportation, such violation might require a new proceeding with the procedural protection restored. Cf. Morrison, 449 U.S. at 364-65 (describing the Court's approach to Sixth Amendment remedies). By contrast, the regulation in this case—like the Fourth Amendment itself— safeguards each person's substantive right to privacy. Thus, it makes no sense to draw on cases involving defects in the proceedings themselves to address an unlawful arrest.

The panel's resort to Rajah—which did concern regulations designed to effectuate the Fourth Amendment— fares no better. The panel claims that the Second Circuit held that "petitioners may be entitled to termination of their removal proceedings without prejudice for egregious regulatory violations." Sanchez, 904 F.3d at 953 (citing Rajah, 544 F.3d at 446-47). But Rajah does not go that far. Although the Second Circuit suggested that in some other case a showing of "prejudice," "conscience-shocking conduct," or a "deprivation of fundamental rights" might justify termination of proceedings, it did not give any examples of such a circumstance. Rajah, 544 F.3d at 447. Moreover, Rajah cites to no legal authority for imposing such a remedy when the violated regulation effectuates the Fourth Amendment; instead, like the opinion here, it relies only on inapposite cases involving procedural protections. See id. (citing Waldron v. INS, 17 F.3d 511, 518 (2d Cir. 1993); Montilla v. INS, 926 F.2d 162, 166 (2d Cir. 1991)). Rajah cannot support the panel's innovation.

IV

Finally, the panel's opinion creates a host of practical problems.

A

First, the termination-of-proceedings rule creates perverse incentives for aliens and immigration lawyers to inject inefficiency into deportation proceedings. The opinion offers a windfall (termination of proceedings, no less) to those who can show that immigration officials violated their own regulations during the investigation, detention, and removal proceedings—even if such violations had no effect on the proceedings that followed. Lingering on such technicalities, however, ignores the Supreme Court's instruction that "[p]ast conduct is relevant only insofar as it may shed light on the respondent's right to remain." Lopez-Mendoza, 468 U.S. at 1038 (emphasis added).

At the same time, the panel's theory could deter the government from formulating "additional standards to govern prosecutorial and police procedures." Caceres, 440 U.S. at 755-56. The conclusion that regulatory violations authorize federal courts to terminate otherwise-meritorious removal proceedings could give the government reason to scrub from the books any regulations that benefit aliens. Perversely, then, the opinion's holding may help Sanchez only to deprive all other aliens of the benefits of the government's "own comprehensive scheme for deterring Fourth Amendment violations by its officers." Lopez-Mendoza, 468 U.S. at 1044.

B

The panel's novel termination-of-proceedings remedy also invites a wave of litigation to map its metes and bounds. The initial question, of course, is what exactly "termination without prejudice" means. Sanchez, 904 F.3d at 657. The BIA will undoubtedly dismiss proceedings, but DHS could then serve Sanchez with a new Notice to Appear and start all over again. The opinion offers Sanchez nothing more than a meaningless formality before his inevitable removal.

Perhaps, however, the panel has something more drastic in mind. Its reasoning, after all, is that the remedy must put Sanchez into his rightful position as if "no procedural error [had] taken place." Id. at 655 (internal quotation marks omitted). Such reasoning sets up a counter-factual in which Sanchez was never detained, never interrogated, and never issued the Notice to Appear. Must the BIA tear up the Form I-213 about Sanchez? Delete all records of him from the government's databases? Order each implicated government official to forget everything he ever knew about Sanchez? Doubtless, enterprising lawyers will seize on the opinion's extravagant reasoning to seek still-more intrusive remedies in civil deportation proceedings. We should not invite their spurious arguments.

C

I also fear that the decision may not be limited to the immigration context. The opinion introduces a glaring discontinuity between civil removal proceedings on the one hand and other administrative proceedings and criminal prosecutions on the other. The opinion's holding allows aliens who suffer regulatory violations to reap a windfall not present in any analogous area of law.

A criminal defendant convicted on the basis of illegally obtained evidence or a coerced confession has no similar opportunity. He can ask for a new trial with the improperly obtained evidence suppressed, but he cannot demand that the court quash his indictment. Likewise, in administrative contexts, a party can challenge an enforcement action based on procedural failures by the agency. But courts do not enjoin the agency from altogether enforcing the law against the regulated party. I am sure that criminal defendants and civil litigants would much prefer that courts dismissed their cases too. When they ask our court to punish regulatory failures the same way in other contexts, how can we deny them the same windfall?

V

This case should have been simple. The sole question in a deportation proceeding is whether the alien has a "right to remain in this country in the future." Lopez-Mendoza, 468 U.S. at 1038. Here, the government can establish Sanchez's unlawful status with admissible evidence, so the BIA correctly affirmed the IJ's removal order.

Instead, the panel's refusal to accept this outcome has produced a decision that (1) defies the Supreme Court's decision in Lopez-Mendoza, (2) ignores basic Fourth Amendment principles by ordering a more-intrusive result than the Amendment authorizes, (3) fashions a remedy to enforce agency regulations without a sound legal basis for such an imposition, (4) shows a profound misunderstanding of the difference between substantive and procedural rights and their appropriate remedies, (5) cites as authority a handful of inapposite out-of-circuit precedents, and (6) imposes serious practical costs on the administration of immigration proceedings.

Worst of all, the opinion's imposition of an extraordinary remedy wastes everyone's time, for it does nothing but delay the petitioner's inevitable removal. The en banc process exists to ensure the sound development of our circuit's case law, and we should have used it here to correct the panel's extravagant and erroneous decision.

[**] As a judge of this court in senior status, I no longer have the power to vote on calls for rehearing cases en banc or formally to join a dissent from failure to rehear en banc. See 28 U.S.C. § 46(c); Fed. R. App. P. 35(a). Following our court's general orders, however, I may participate in discussions of en banc proceedings. See Ninth Circuit General Order 5.5(a).

Judge O'Scannlain's dissent in Riggs v. Airbus Helicopters (Sept 20, 2019)

O'SCANNLAIN, Circuit Judge, dissenting:

The federal officer removal statute authorizes a defendant in a state court civil action to remove the case to federal court if it is "acting under" a federal agency. 28 U.S.C. § 1442(a)(1). In this case, the Federal Aviation Administration ("FAA") "delegate[d]" to Airbus Helicopters, Inc. ("Airbus") the authority to issue "certificates" on the agency's behalf—certificates that the FAA must otherwise issue on its own before an aircraft can be lawfully flown. 49 U.S.C. §§ 44702(d)(1), 44704. Because Airbus undertakes these duties on the FAA's behalf, I conclude that Airbus "act[s] under" a federal agency within the meaning of § 1442(a)(1). I believe that our court's contrary holding misunderstands the FAA's regulatory regime and misapplies the Supreme Court's decision in Watson v. Philip Morris Cos., 551 U.S. 142 (2007).

I respectfully dissent.

I

This case turns on the interaction between two statutes: the Federal Aviation Act, see 49 U.S.C. § 40103 et seq., and the federal officer removal statute, see 28 U.S.C. § 1442.

A

1

In the Federal Aviation Act, Congress charged the FAA with the duty to establish "minimum standards required in the interest of safety" for the "design, material, construction, quality of work, and performance of aircraft, aircraft engines, and propellers." 49 U.S.C. § 44701(a)(1). The FAA promulgated (and regularly revises) the Federal Aviation Regulations, which delineate such standards. See 14 C.F.R. § 1.1 et seq. Given the technological complexity of modern aircraft, these safety standards dictate an aircraft's design from its critical components to its smallest detail. For instance, a helicopter—or, in the FAA's parlance, a "rotorcraft"—must satisfy regulations covering everything from its "landing gear" to the "number of self-contained, removable ashtrays." Id. §§ 27.729, 27.853(c)(1).

Besides imposing substantive safety standards, the Act also creates a "multistep certification process to monitor the aviation industry's compliance." United States v. S.A. Empresa de Viacao Aerea Rio Grandense (Varig Airlines), 467 U.S. 797, 804 (1984). Before an aircraft can lawfully take flight, the FAA must issue a series of "certifications" or "certificates"—terms that the Act uses interchangeably. The first of these is called a "type certificate," which the FAA "shall issue" if it finds the aircraft "is properly designed and manufactured, performs properly, and meets the regulations and minimum standards prescribed [by the FAA]." 49 U.S.C. § 44704(a)(1). Then, before the manufacturer can mass produce an approved design, it must obtain a "production certificate." Id. § 44704(c). To do so, the manufacturer must show that duplicates of the design will, among other things, "conform to the [type] certificate." Id. Finally, the owner of each aircraft must obtain an "airworthiness certificate" by showing that the aircraft "conforms to its type certificate and, after inspection, is in condition for safe operation." Id. § 44704(d)(1). It is illegal to operate an aircraft without an airworthiness certificate. See id. § 44711(a)(1).

Together, these certification requirements prohibit a manufacturer (or the aircraft's eventual owner) from altering an aircraft's design without the FAA's approval. Instead, if a manufacturer wishes to make changes, it must seek one of two possible certificates. If a "proposed change . . . is so extensive that a substantially complete investigation of compliance . . . is required," then the manufacturer must seek a new type certificate from the FAA. 14 C.F.R. § 21.19. For less significant changes, the holder of a type certificate may seek a "supplemental type certificate." 49 U.S.C. § 44704(b)(1) (emphasis added); see also 14 C.F.R. § 21.113. Like an ordinary type certificate, a supplemental certificate authorizes the holder then to seek production and airworthiness certificates for the modified design. See id. § 21.119.

2

Perhaps because of this elaborate certification process, Congress offered the FAA an unusual tool to ease its regulatory burden: the authority to delegate its duties to the private sector. Specifically, the Act states:

(d) DELEGATION.—(1) Subject to regulations, supervision, and review the Administrator may prescribe, the Administrator may delegate to a qualified private person . . . a matter related to (A) the examination, testing, and inspection necessary to issue a certificate under this chapter; and (B) issuing the certificate."

49 U.S.C. § 44702(d)(1) (emphasis added); see also Varig Airlines, 467 U.S. at 807 ("[T]he FAA obviously cannot complete this elaborate compliance review process alone. Accordingly, [the Act] authorizes the Secretary to delegate certain inspection and certification responsibilities to properly qualified private persons.").

Since 1927, the FAA and its predecessor agency have established programs delegating its certification authority to the private sector—either to individual engineers or to organizations. Establishment of Organization Designation Authorization Program, 70 Fed. Reg. 59,932, 59,932 (Oct. 13, 2005) (codified at 14 C.F.R. pts. 21, 121, 135, 145, 183) [hereinafter ODA Rule]. In 2005, the FAA exercised its authority under § 44702(d) to institute the Organization Designation Authorization ("ODA") Program, which "consolidat[es] and improve[s]" the "piecemeal organizational delegations" previously developed. Id. at 59,933.

Under such program, the FAA authorizes "ODA Holders" to "perform specified functions on behalf of the Administrator." 14 C.F.R. § 183.41. ODA Holders act as "representatives of the Administrator," and when "performing a delegated function, [they] are legally distinct from and act independent of the organizations that employ them." ODA Rule, 70 Fed. Reg. at 59,933. Further, to become an ODA Holder, an organization must sign a memorandum of understanding promising to "comply with the same standards, procedures, and interpretations applicable to FAA employees accomplishing similar tasks." Federal Aviation Administration, Organization Designation Authorization Procedures, Order 8100.15, at A1-17 (2006) [hereinafter ODA Order].[1]

Since 2009, Airbus has been a "Supplemental Type Certification ODA." Id. ¶ 2-6, at 5. In this capacity, Airbus has the authority to "develop and issue supplemental type certificates . . . and related airworthiness certificates." Id. Airbus may issue such certificates both for its own aircraft or for those of other applicants. See id. ¶ 11-7, at 88. Although the FAA may revoke Airbus's ODA status or reconsider its issuance of a specific certificate, see 49 U.S.C. § 44702(d)(2)-(3), a certificate issued by Airbus carries the same legal consequence as one issued by the FAA: it gives the FAA's formal approval to the aircraft's design (in the case of a supplemental type certificate) or the aircraft itself (in the case of an airworthiness certificate).[2]

B

The federal officer removal statute permits a defendant to remove to federal court a state court action brought against

"[t]he United States or any agency thereof or any officer (or any person acting under that officer) of the United States or of any agency thereof, in an official or individual capacity, for or relating to any act under color of such office . . . ."

28 U.S.C. § 1442(a)(1) (emphasis added). In Watson, the Supreme Court held that a person "act[s] under" a federal officer or agency if his actions "involve an effort to assist, or to help carry out, the duties or tasks of the federal superior." 551 U.S. at 152. Although a "private firm's compliance . . . with federal laws, rules, and regulations" does not itself satisfy the statute's "acting under" requirement, id. at 153 (emphasis added), a formal "delegation of legal authority" goes beyond the "usual regulator/regulated relationship," id. at 156-57. Thus, Watson counsels that the "delegation of legal authority . . . [to act] on the Government agency's behalf" satisfies § 1442(a)(1)'s "acting under" requirement. Id. at 156.

II

Because the FAA delegates to ODA Holders its formal legal authority to issue certificates, I conclude, in respectful disagreement with the majority's analysis, that Airbus "act[s] under" the FAA.

A

1

Beginning with the text, the Federal Aviation Act compels the conclusion that the FAA delegates formal legal authority to ODA Holders. By its own terms, 49 U.S.C. § 44702(d)(1) authorizes the FAA to "delegate" a "matter related to" the "examination, testing, and inspection necessary to issue a certificate" and "issuing the certificate." To "delegate" means to "give part of one's power or work to someone in a lower position within one's organization." Delegate, Black's Law Dictionary (9th ed. 2009); see also Delegate, Webster's Third New International Dictionary (unabr. ed. 1986) ("[T]o entrust to another: transfer, assign, commit delegated by the people to the legislature> delegate] one's authority to a competent assistant>"). Congress's use of "delegate" thus suggests that the FAA may transfer its own formal legal powers to private persons, and the rest of the statute accords with such interpretation. In 49 U.S.C. § 44702(a), for instance, Congress established that the "Administrator of the [FAA] may issue" the long list of certificates mandated by the Act. See also 49 U.S.C. § 44704 (same). Accordingly, the responsibility to issue certificates falls in the first instance to the FAA, and it is this authority that § 44702(d)(1) allows the agency to "delegate."

Confirming Congress's mandate, the FAA itself describes the ODA Program as a delegation of legal authority. Under the program, ODA Holders like Airbus function as "representatives of the Administrator" and "perform[] a delegated function." ODA Rule, 70 Fed. Reg. at 59,933; see also 14 C.F.R. § 183.41 (similar). The ODA Order states that the program "delegate[s] certain types of authority to organizations," and that such designees "act on the FAA's behalf." ODA Order, ¶ 1-1, at 1. Further, these delegees "assist" the agency and "help carry out" its manifold "duties [and] tasks," Watson, 551 U.S. at 152 (emphasis removed), because the "[d]elegation of tasks to these organizations [allows] the FAA to focus [its] limited resources on more critical areas," ODA Rule, 70 Fed. Reg. at 59,933.

Altogether, Congress and the FAA expressly said—time and again—that the agency indeed "delegate[s]" to private persons (like Airbus) the authority to issue certificates, and Watson counsels that a "delegation of legal authority" satisfies § 1442(a)(1)'s "acting under" requirement. 551 U.S. at 154-57. It follows that Airbus "act[s] under" the FAA.

2

I am not alone in this view. The Eleventh Circuit came to the same conclusion in Magnin v. Teledyne Cont'l Motors, 91 F.3d 1424 (11th Cir. 1996), and the Solicitor General has endorsed that court's holding. In its briefing for Watson, the Solicitor General argued that the defendant could not seek removal under the federal officer removal statute (as the Supreme Court later held), but it cited Magnin to support the argument that "a private citizen delegated authority to inspect aircraft by the [FAA] acts under a federal officer in conducting such an inspection and issuing a certificate of airworthiness." Brief for the U.S. as Amicus Curiae Supporting Petitioners at 26, Watson, 551 U.S. 142 (No. 05-1284). "The critical point," the Solicitor General continued, "is that the individual acts on behalf of the FAA Administrator in conducting the inspection." Id.

B

Despite the clear evidence of delegation, the majority concludes that Airbus's actions as an ODA Holder constitute mere "compliance" with FAA regulations. See Maj. Op. at 16-18. With respect, I believe the majority is wrong.

1

The majority's critical error is that it conflates Airbus's two distinct roles as a manufacturer and as an FAA delegee. Specifically, an ODA Holder acts as either the regulated party or the regulator—depending on the specific function performed. It is true, of course, that all manufacturers—in their capacity as manufacturers—must comply with the FAA's numerous safety standards whenever they design or build an aircraft. But as an ODA Holder, the organization also acts as a "representative[] of the Administrator." ODA Rule, 70 Fed. Reg. at 59,933. In this capacity, the manufacturer is "legally distinct from" the organization, and its "authority . . . to act comes from an FAA delegation." Id. Put differently, the manufacturer doffs its "aviation industry hat" and dons its "FAA hat," and so clad, the ODA Holder exercises the agency's statutory authority to issue certificates.

Perhaps because the issuance of certificates so obviously constitutes an exercise of the FAA's governmental power, the majority seeks to recast the ODA Program as a "self-certification" regime. See Maj. Op. at 16-18 (emphasis added). The majority borrows such reasoning from Lu Junhong v. Boeing Co., where the Seventh Circuit compared a manufacturer's authority to issue certificates to "a person filing a tax return" compelled to certify that he reported his income "honestly." 792 F.3d 805, 809 (7th Cir. 2015). Such "certified compliance," the court reasoned, was indistinguishable from other forms of "ordinary compliance" deemed insufficient to satisfy § 1442(a)(1). Id. at 810.

Once again, the majority—as Lu Junhong before it—evinces its misunderstanding of the regulatory regime. Although an ODA Holder issuing a certificate must ensure that the aircraft complies with the FAA's safety standards, the organization's issuance of the certificate does more; it stamps the FAA's imprimatur on the aircraft. In so doing, the ODA Holder exercises a power derived from the agency and independent from its responsibilities as a manufacturer. Indeed, the FAA authorizes ODA Holders like Airbus to issue certificates "to an applicant other than the ODA Holder"—thus confirming that such power cannot be reduced to self-certification. ODA Order, ¶ 11-6, at 88 (emphasis added). And because the nature of the certification authority should not fluctuate depending on who is granted the certificate, the mere fact that Airbus certifies its own aircraft has no bearing on whether it "act[s] under" the FAA.

In short, a true self-certification regime (as with the taxpayer attesting to his income) involves an affirmation that the regulated party completed his duty; an ODA Holder's "certification" conveys the agency's formal approval to the aircraft.

2

The majority's flawed understanding of the ODA Program blinds it to the differences between this case and Watson. There, the defendant—Philip Morris—argued that the FTC had "delegated authority" to test cigarettes for tar and nicotine, and that it "`act[ed] under' officers of the FTC" when it conducted such testing. Watson, 551 U.S. at

154 (emphasis removed). But the Supreme Court "found no evidence of any delegation of legal authority from the FTC to the industry association"—the "fatal flaw" in Philip Morris's argument. Id. at 156 (emphasis added). Accordingly, the Court found no reason to treat "the FTC/Philip Morris relationship as distinct from the usual regulator/regulated relationship." Id. at 157.

Eager to fit this case into Watson's mold, the majority casts Airbus as a regulated party complying (or self-certifying compliance) with FAA rules and regulations. See Maj. Op. at 16-18. But as shown, Congress and the FAA said that the FAA delegates "legal authority" to act "on the Government agency's behalf." Watson, 551 U.S. at 156. That delegation goes well beyond the "usual regulator/regulated relationship," id. at 157, and as a delegee Airbus "assist[s]" and "help[s] carry out" the duties and tasks of the FAA, id. at 152 (emphasis removed). Under the correct reading of Watson, such a scheme satisfies § 1442(a)(1)'s "acting under" requirement. Id.[3]

III

The federal officer removal statute allows those who labor on the federal government's behalf, and are therefore sued in state court, to have such case tried in a federal forum. In this case, the FAA authorized Airbus to issue certificates that the agency would otherwise issue on its own, and such delegation satisfies § 1442(a)(1)'s "acting under" requirement. Of course, it might seem strange that a manufacturer's participation in this private-public partnership would permit it to avoid state court; § 1442's core purpose, after all, is to give federal officials "a federal forum in which to assert federal immunity defenses." Watson, 551 U.S. at 150 (emphasis added). But the statute's text is broader still, and our court has discerned a "clear command from both Congress and the Supreme Court that when federal officers and their agents are seeking a federal forum, we are to interpret section 1442 broadly in favor of removal." Durham v. Lockheed Martin Corp., 445 F.3d 1247, 1252 (9th Cir. 2006) (emphasis added). The clear consequence of Congress's handiwork is that FAA delegees perform the agency's tasks. Because Airbus is such a delegee, § 1442(a)(1) entitles it to a federal forum.

I respectfully dissent.

Notes

[1] Order 8100.15 "establishes the procedures, guidance, and limitations of authority [the FAA] grant[s] to an organization" under the ODA Program. ODA Order, at i. Since 2006, the FAA has amended Order 8100.15, see Federal Aviation Administration, Organization Designation Authorization Procedures, Order 8100.15B (2018), but the 2006 version of the Order governed at the time of the subject helicopter's manufacture and sale.

[2] In the aftermath of the recent crash of the Boeing 737 Max in Ethiopia, there seems to be some appetite on Capitol Hill to revisit the FAA's private-public partnership. See Thomas Kaplan, After Boeing Crashes, Sharp Questions About Industry Regulating Itself, N.Y. Times (Mar. 26, 2019); David Koenig & Tom Krisher, The FAA's Oversight of Boeing Will Be Examined in Senate Hearings, Time (Mar. 27, 2019). But until (and unless)

such proposals become law, we must apply the statute as it presently exists.

[3] The Ninth Circuit cases that the majority cites do not support its conclusion. See Maj. Op. at 10-15 (citing Goncalves v. Rady Children's Hosp. San Diego, 865 F.3d 1237 (9th Cir. 2017), and Fidelitad, Inc. v. Insitu, Inc., 904 F.3d 1095 (9th Cir. 2018)). Both cases apply Watson to statutory regimes quite different from the FAA's, and each decision's fact-intensive analysis defies extraction of a simple rule that resolves this case. The majority's broad assertion that the court in Fidelitad was "confronted with the identical issue" that we confront here is simply wrong, Maj. Op. at 14; Fidelitad did not address a situation where an entity had formally and explicitly been delegated authority to issue certificates on behalf of a federal agency, let alone the specific delegation that Airbus acts under here.

Judge O'Scannlain's concurrence in Gebreslasie v. US Citizenship And Immigration Services (Sept 27, 2019)

O'SCANNLAIN, Circuit Judge, concurring:

I concur in the result, but with respect I am unable to concur in the holding that 8 U.S.C. § 1252(g) withdrew subject-matter jurisdiction over Gebreslasie's claim. Instead, I would affirm the district court's dismissal of Gebreslasie's case because the complaint fails to state a claim.

I

Gebreslasie argues that the district court erred in concluding that 8 U.S.C. § 1252(g) withdrew subject-matter jurisdiction over his claim. I agree.

Section 1252(g) "applies only to three discrete actions that the Attorney General may take: her `decision or action' to `commence proceedings, adjudicate cases, or execute removal orders.'" Reno v. American-Arab Anti-Discrimination Comm., 525 U.S. 471, 482 (1999). Thus, the statute "does not bar review of the actions that occurred prior to any decision to `commence proceedings,' if any, against [an alien]." Kwai Fun Wong v. United States, 373 F.3d 952, 965 (9th Cir. 2004). Here, Gebreslasie claims that the government's failure to commence proceedings is unlawful, and such inaction is—by definition—"prior to any decision to `commence proceedings.'" Id. The district court therefore had jurisdiction to consider Gebreslasie's claim, and its conclusion to the contrary was error.

II

Nevertheless, I would affirm the district court's dismissal of Gebreslasie's case if the complaint fails to state a claim. Morrison v. Nat'l Austl. Bank Ltd., 561 U.S. 247, 254 (2010); Fresno Motors, LLC v. Mercedes Benz USA, LLC, 771 F.3d 1119, 1125 (9th Cir. 2014). Relevant here, Gebreslasie's complaint alleges that the failure to initiate removal proceedings (1) violated the Due Process Clause; (2) violated the Administrative Procedure Act ("APA"), see 5 U.S.C. §§ 701 et seq.; and (3) warranted the issuance of a writ of mandamus, see 28 U.S.C. § 1361.

Each claim fails. First, the Due Process Clause does not establish a right to compel the government to initiate removal proceedings because, at the very least, such decision is "committed to the [agency's] discretion." Morales-Izquierdo v. Dep't of Homeland Sec., 600 F.3d 1076, 1091 (9th Cir. 2010), overruled in part on other grounds by Garfias-Rodriguez v. Holder, 702 F.3d 504 (9th Cir. 2012) (en banc). Second, Gebreslasie's APA claim fails because he did not allege a reviewable "final agency action." 5 U.S.C. § 704. The failure to initiate proceedings is not itself an "action . . . by which rights or obligations have been determined, or [one] from which legal consequences flow." Bennett v. Spear, 520 U.S. 154, 178 (1997) (internal quotation marks omitted). Third, the request for a writ of mandamus fails because Gebreslasie cannot show that "the defendant official's duty [to initiate removal proceedings] is ministerial, and so plainly prescribed as to be free from doubt." Barron v. Reich, 13 F.3d 1370, 1374 (9th Cir. 1994) (internal quotation marks omitted).

For the foregoing reasons, I would affirm the district court's dismissal of Gebreslasie's case for failure to state a claim.

Judge O'Scannlain's concurrence and dissent in Ridgeway v. Walmart (Jan 6, 2020)

O'SCANNLAIN, Circuit Judge, concurring in part and dissenting in part:

I concur in all of the majority's opinion except for Part II.B.1.b, in which the court affirms the finding of liability against Wal-Mart for its failure to compensate drivers for time spent during layover periods. Specifically, I cannot agree with the majority's conclusion that the district court correctly granted partial summary judgment to the plaintiffs when it found that Wal-Mart's written pay policies necessarily establish that the company "controlled" drivers during their layover breaks. In my view, the jury should have been allowed to decide the meaning of these ambiguous policies and the extent to which the policies actually "control" what drivers may do and where they may go.

For the reasons expressed herein, I respectfully dissent from the "layover periods" portion of the majority's opinion.

I

As required by both state and federal law, Wal-Mart's long-haul truck drivers must take ten-hour breaks—so-called "layovers" —between each of their driving shifts. See 49 C.F.R. § 395.3(a)(1); Cal. Code Regs. tit. 13, § 1212.5(a). During this time, drivers formally are not on duty, and they may not drive or perform other work for Wal-Mart. See 49 C.F.R. §§ 395.2, 395.8(b); Cal. Code Regs. tit. 13, §§ 1201(u)(4), 1213(c). Trucks are equipped with sleeper berths to allow drivers to rest during their layovers, though testimony in this case indicates that drivers actually spent time performing a variety of activities including visiting family, exercising, eating, golfing, or even visiting casinos.

One of the principal claims in this case is that, under California law, Wal-Mart was required—but failed—to pay drivers minimum wage during their layover periods. The validity of that claim ultimately turns on whether Wal-Mart exercised "control" over its drivers during such periods, within the meaning of California employment law. If so, Wal-Mart needed to pay drivers minimum wage for their layover time; if not, no compensation was required. See Cal. Code Regs., tit. 8 § 11090(2)(G). At summary judgment, the district court found that, at least as a matter of written policy, Wal-Mart did purport to control its drivers during their layovers. The court entered partial summary judgment in the plaintiffs' favor on this issue, finding that "the policies in [Wal-Mart's] Driver Pay Manuals subjected drivers to Wal-Mart's control during layover periods."

In light of this ruling, at trial the issue of whether Wal-Mart was required to pay its drivers during layover periods was reduced to the question of whether Wal-Mart actually implemented these written policies. In its jury instructions, the court restated its finding of fact that the policies expressed in the pay manuals "subjected drivers to Wal-Mart's control during layover periods" and instructed the jury to find in favor of the plaintiffs if they proved "that Wal-Mart applied the [layover] policy as it is stated in the driver pay manuals." If it believed Wal-Mart did indeed apply its own written policies, the jury was instructed to award pay to compensate the plaintiffs for the full length of each 10-hour layover period.

Ultimately, the jury found that Wal-Mart owed drivers more than $44 million in unpaid wages for layover time.

II

The core problem with the jury's finding is that the district court's earlier entry of partial summary judgment short-circuited the entire layover-periods question. Although Wal-Mart's written pay policies might be understood to assert control during layover periods, that was a genuinely disputed question of fact, which should have been presented to the jury to decide. By instead answering that question itself, the district court prejudiced Wal-Mart in its ability to defend the lawfulness of its own company policies and practices.

A

Under California law, an employer must pay minimum wage for all time "during which an employee is subject to the control of an employer." Cal. Code Regs. tit. 8, § 11090(2)(G). Under this test, an employee "does not have to be working during that time to be compensated." Morillion v. Royal Packing Co., 22 Cal.4th 575, 94 Cal. Rptr.2d 3, 995 P.2d 139, 143 (2000). Even during a break period, an employee might remain under control of his or her employer if the employer imposes requirements that prevent the employee from spending "truly uninterrupted time" at his or her pleasure. Augustus v. ABM Sec. Servs., Inc., 2 Cal.5th 257, 211 Cal.Rptr.3d 634, 385 P.3d 823, 833 (2016). While an employer may freely impose reasonable restraints like requiring employees to remain on site during short breaks, it must compensate employees for break periods if it imposes more severe restrictions that effectively prevent the employee from spending the time as he or she might wish, such as by requiring the employee to remain on-call or preventing him or her from leaving the worksite for extended periods of time. See id., 211 Cal.Rptr.3d 634, 385 P.3d at 832-34.

Against this backdrop, the district court ruled that the terms of Wal-Mart's 2008 pay manual necessarily established the company's control over drivers during their layover periods. Such manual, however, says very little about what a driver may or may not do during a layover. The parties agree that Wal-Mart paid drivers a $42 "inconvenience fee," at least for layovers they spent in the sleeper berths of their trucks and away from home. The pay manual reinforces this payment but says little else about how a layover must be spent. The manual specifies that layover time is "not paid in conjunction with any other type of pay," but instead is a standalone pay category "inten[ded] ... to pay Drivers for layovers taken in the tractor cab." The manual further emphasizes that drivers "will not be compensated for a DOT [layover] break if any portion of it is taken at home." In addition to forgoing the $42 payment, in order to "take a [layover] at home" a driver must receive a manager's prior approval, safely and securely park his or her tractor and trailer, and record the break at home (and the manager's approval) on his or her time sheet. Taking an unauthorized layover at home is prohibited and "may lead to immediate termination."

Altogether, then, Wal-Mart's written policy establishes essentially two relevant restrictions on drivers' layover time: (1) they will receive a $42 payment only if the layover is spent "in the tractor cab," and (2) if they wish to take the layover at home, they must receive a manager's approval and lock the truck in a safe location. The district court and the majority seize on these basic restrictions to conclude that, because drivers were not completely free to spend their layovers at home without management approval, they must have been subject to Wal-Mart's control during that time. But none of these requirements establishes control as a matter of California law.

1

First, there can be no serious argument that the offer to pay drivers $42 for a layover taken in the truck constitutes "control" over them.

The $42 payment is simply a gratuitous offer on Wal-Mart's part—what the company asserts is a benefit to alleviate the inconvenience of spending a layover in the driver's truck. That benefit is not paid when the driver instead chooses to spend the layover in a more convenient location like his or her home, a friend's house, a hotel, or elsewhere. We have previously recognized that employers in California are free to impose such reasonable limitations on benefits like this. In Rodriguez v. Taco Bell Corp, for example, we recently held that Taco Bell did not exert control over its employees by offering them a discounted lunch, but only if they ate in the store itself. 896 F.3d 952, 956 (9th Cir. 2018). We explained that employees were free to forgo the meal discount and eat their lunch anywhere else; the fact that the restaurant required them to stay onsite to receive the gratuitous benefit did not inhibit their freedom of choice. See id. at 956-57. The same is true about the $42 inconvenience fee here.

2

Second, the manual's limitations on a driver's ability to spend a layover at home do not, as a matter of law, establish "control."

The majority suggests that these restrictions effectively direct where drivers are required to be during their layover periods. It analogizes Wal-Mart's policy to two cases in which employers were found to have exercised control by requiring their employees to spend downtime at specified locations. See Maj. Op. at 1079-80. In Bono Enterprises, Inc. v. Bradshaw, for example, the California Court of Appeal held that an employer was required to compensate its employees during lunch breaks in which the employees were prohibited from leaving the worksite. See 32 Cal. App. 4th 968, 975-76, 38 Cal.Rptr.2d 549 (1995), disapproved on other grounds by Tidewater Marine W., Inc. v. Bradshaw, 14 Cal.4th 557, 59 Cal.Rptr.2d 186, 927 P.2d 296 (1996). Likewise, in Morillion v. Royal Packing Co., the California Supreme Court held that an employer controlled its employees by requiring them to meet at a designated place and then ride employer-provided buses to the fields in which they worked. 94 Cal.Rptr.2d 3, 995 P.2d at 147. The California Supreme Court held that, even though employees could pass the time on the bus as they saw fit (for example by reading or sleeping), they were still under the employer's control during that time, because they "were foreclosed from numerous activities in which they might otherwise engage if they were permitted to travel ... by their own transportation," such as dropping their children at school, stopping for breakfast before work, or running other errands. Id., 94 Cal.Rptr.2d 3, 995 P.2d at 146.

The limited restrictions expressed in Wal-Mart's pay manual are a far cry from those in Bono or Morillion. In both Bono and Morillion, the employees were prohibited from being anywhere other than a location specifically directed by the employer. Here, by contrast, Wal-Mart's pay manual says almost nothing about where drivers can go or what they can do during a layover. At most, the policy places certain restrictions on a driver's ability to pass the layover at home. Such restrictions hardly amount to the sort of control recognized in Bono or Morillion. First, it is not clear that (as the majority suggests) Wal-Mart's pay manual prevents drivers from even visiting their homes. If drivers take any portion of their layover at home, they don't get the $42 convenience fee. But it is not clear that the policy generally requiring authorization prior to "taking" a layover at home, also means drivers needed permission to visit a nearby home even briefly, for example to eat a meal or change clothes. More to the point, the policy says nothing at all about a driver's freedom to spend layover time anywhere else. The majority points to nothing in the policy that would preclude a driver from visiting a friend, going to see a movie, going to a bar or restaurant, shopping, running errands, and so forth. Unsurprisingly, drivers testified at trial that they did—and that they understood they were permitted to do—exactly these sorts of things during layovers.

Moreover, the majority glosses over the fact that Wal-Mart's pay manual expressly allows employees to take their breaks at home as well, so long as they receive prior approval. Requiring approval before engaging in certain activities does restrict employees' ability to do those activities in some way. But it hardly prevents them. Again, the contrast to Bono and Morillion is instructive. In both cases, employers enforced policies that simply prohibited— without any apparent exception—employees from straying from their directed areas. See Morillion, 94 Cal.Rptr.2d 3, 995 P.2d at 141 & n.1; Bono, 32 Cal. App.

4th at 978 n.4, 38 Cal.Rptr.2d 549. Indeed, in Bono the court wrote that the employer would not have exerted control over its employees if had permitted them to "ma[ke] prior arrangements" to leave the worksite for lunch. See 32 Cal. App. 4th at 978 n.4, 38 Cal.Rptr.2d 549. The court observed that the lack of such a policy was "extremely significant" to its conclusion that the on-site lunch breaks required compensation. Id. Here, in direct contrast, the manual expressly informs drivers that they may spend breaks at home, so long as they receive prior approval and secure the truck while they will be away.

Just as in Bono, the availability of a policy allowing drivers to make prior arrangements to spend a layover at home should be "extremely significant" to our interpretation of the pay manual and the extent to which it purports to control drivers' activities. But instead of actually grappling with how such a policy might reduce the degree to which the manual restrains drivers' ability to go home, the majority instead quickly dismisses its relevance because the manual implicitly "reserved [Wal-Mart's] right to decline" a driver's request to take a layover at home. Maj. Op. at 1080-81. The manual itself says nothing about the grounds on which such a request might be declined. Yet, the majority appears to assume the worst, simply asserting that Wal-Mart's authority to decline a driver's request means that the policy necessarily imposed "more than a mere `burden'" on drivers' ability to take a layover at home—with no explanation for why that is so or, more importantly, how we know it from the face of the policy alone. See id. at 1080-81. At summary judgment, the manual's failure to make clear the extent of the burden imposed by the pre-approval rule should have weighed against granting summary judgment, and instead allowed this open question to go to the jury. See infra Part II.B.

In the end, the majority's interpretation of Wal-Mart's pay manual rests on a sweeping and simplistic proposition: any policy that "restrict[s] employees from complete freedom of movement during breaks" is sufficient to show "control" under California law. Maj. Op. at 1081. Unfortunately, the majority does not cite a single case that actually supports such a broad rule, and the text of the manual hardly demonstrates the sort of strict location control at issue in the only cases upon which the majority relies.

B

Because Wal-Mart's pay manual says so little about what drivers may or may not do during layovers, it leaves a great deal of room for interpretation. In attempting to parse this scant guidance at summary judgment, the district court was required to draw all reasonable inferences in Wal-Mart's favor. See Barnes v. Chase Home Fin., LLC, 934 F.3d 901, 906 (9th Cir. 2019). Instead, the court seems to have drawn every inference against Wal-Mart and assumed that the most restrictive reading of the manual must be true.[1] Perhaps a reasonable factfinder could agree with the district court that the manual could be construed as a company policy of strictly controlling drivers' whereabouts during layover periods. But the text of the manual itself does not compel such a conclusion.

1

In deciding this contested issue against Wal-Mart, the court effectively took from the jury one of the most critical questions in this case: what was Wal-Mart's official policy regarding what drivers were permitted to do during layover periods? Notably, testimony in this case shows that many drivers understood company policy to be broadly permissive, allowing them to do "whatever [they] want[ed]" during layovers. But the court significantly limited the jury's own consideration of how permissive Wal-Mart policy was by instructing them that at least the company's official written policy violated California law, and that Wal-Mart was liable if it followed such policy.

It is not difficult to see how this ruling prejudiced Wal-Mart. Wal-Mart should have had the opportunity to persuade the jury that the pay manual (and company policy generally) placed only minimal restraints on drivers' activity or whereabouts during layovers. Instead, Wal-Mart was forced to accept that its manual announced unlawful policies and then attempt to convince the jury that it had implemented practices that conflicted with those policies in material ways. In essence, Wal-Mart could win only by showing that it ignored its own company standards.[2]

2

Nor did the court eliminate the prejudice by offering a supplemental jury instruction on the definition of "control" under California law, as the majority suggests. See Maj. Op. 1081-82. Perhaps confused as to whether the court's summary judgment ruling had already declared Wal-Mart to be liable on the layover claims, the jury asked the court to clarify the "definition regarding Wal-Mart's control during layover periods." In response, the court told the jury that there "is no clear definition of control" under California law, but that the key was whether "the driver was able to use that time effectively for his or her own purposes." The court gave two examples, notably both from cases in which courts found employer control (once again, Bono and Morillion). The court gave no counterexamples from a case in which control was lacking, nor did it offer any possible limitations to the cases' holdings.

This supplemental instruction might have given the jury more detail on what "control" means under California law, but it did nothing to correct its earlier instruction that such control is necessarily demonstrated by Wal-Mart's written policy. Thus, the jury was still left to decide only whether Wal-Mart deviated from that policy in a way that materially lowered the extent to which it controlled drivers. If the jury simply decided that Wal-Mart followed its policy as written, the precise definition of control was beside the point because its command was already clear: impose liability. This was error.

III

In sum, while I join the majority in all other respects, I must conclude that the district court erred in granting partial summary judgment against Wal-Mart on the meaning of Wal-Mart's written pay policies. Such a conclusion can be supported only by drawing every inference against Wal-Mart—exactly the opposite of the court's task at summary judgment. The limited text of Wal-Mart's policies says very little about what drivers may do during their layover periods, and it does not remotely demonstrate the degree of control found sufficient in other California cases. On this scant evidence, the district court should have left for the jury the critical task of determining the extent of control exerted by Wal-Mart's layover policies and practices.

I would reverse the judgment against Wal-Mart to such extent and remand for a new trial on the "layover periods" issue.

Notes

[1] For example, the majority asserts that summary judgment was proper because it is "aware of no per se rule under California law that control will not be found when an employer creates an exception for employees who receive prior approval to engage in otherwise restricted activities." Maj. Op. at 1080. But such observation flips the burden at summary judgment on its head. In defending against summary judgment on this issue, Wal-Mart was certainly not required to show that its interpretation of the manual is necessarily correct as a matter of law. Rather, summary judgment should not have been granted unless the plaintiffs could show that Wal-Mart's interpretation was wrong as a matter of law— a conclusion that even the majority seems to recognize is not supported under California law. Regardless whether there is a "per se rule" under California law that Wal-Mart's view will necessarily prevail, such view is one with which a reasonable factfinder could agree—and thus this is a genuinely disputed question that should have been decided by the jury at trial. See Rookaird v. BNSF Ry. Co., 908 F.3d 451, 459 (9th Cir. 2018).

[2] The prejudice is especially obvious if one considers the situation of a juror who read the manual and found its policies not to be overly restrictive. Nonetheless, such a juror would have been told that, if Wal-Mart actually followed the manual, then it had violated California law. Even though such a juror found Wal-Mart's written policies to be perfectly permissive, Wal-Mart would lose unless it could persuade him or her that, in practice, the company was even more lenient with drivers.

Judge O'Scannlain's concurrence and dissent in Escobar v. Barr (Jan 7, 2020)

O'SCANNLAIN, Circuit Judge, concurring in part and dissenting in part:

While I concur in Parts 3 and 4 of the Court's disposition, I must respectfully dissent from Parts 1 and 2.

I

With respect to Part 1, the Court asserts—entirely without precedent—that the Department of Homeland Security's provision of work authorization constitutes an "extraordinary circumstance" that exempts an asylum seeker from the requirement to file an application within a year of arriving to the United States. Cf. 8 U.S.C. § 1158(a)(2)(d); 8 C.F.R. § 1208.4(a)(5). As a result, the Court excuses Diaz-Escobar's years-long failure to file an asylum application and remands only so that the Board of Immigration Appeals (BIA) may consider whether the three months Diaz-Escobar took between the denial of his work authorization and the submission of his asylum application was "reasonable."

Diaz-Escobar has never contended—neither before this Court nor before the BIA—that the provision or denial of his work authorization constituted an "extraordinary circumstance" excusing his delay. As a result, we cannot consider such an argument. See Acosta-Huerta v. Estelle, 7 F.3d 139, 144 (9th Cir. 1992), as amended (Oct. 8, 1993) ("Issues raised in a brief which are not supported by argument are deemed abandoned."); Barron v. Ashcroft, 358 F.3d 674, 678 (9th Cir. 2004) (holding that, in appeals from the BIA, this court lacks subject-matter jurisdiction over "a legal claim not presented in administrative proceedings below").

True, Diaz-Escobar made mention of the extraordinary-circumstances exception before the BIA and in his opening brief before this court; but his argument was that arriving to the United States as a minor was such an extraordinary circumstance.[1] He then argued that the denial of his work authorization was a changed circumstance, an argument the Court rightly rejects. As the majority notes, the two exceptions function differently and demand distinct analyses. Compare 8 C.F.R. § 1208.4(a)(4), with 8 C.F.R. § 1208.4(a)(5). Diaz-Escobar was well aware of the extraordinary-circumstances exception and chose not to contend that the work authorization was such a circumstance; we cannot make such an argument for him now.

II

With respect to Part 2, the Court also grants Diaz-Escobar's petition in part and remands to the BIA because, in its view, the BIA failed "to consider directly relevant and credible evidence" of his claim of past persecution. Because the administrative record, considered in its entirety, fails to supply sufficient evidence of past persecution, I would agree with the BIA's disposition of the past persecution claim.

A

According to the Court, such "directly relevant" evidence of Diaz-Escobar's past persecution is contained in two accounts. First, Diaz-Escobar's father's asylum application chronicles how, when Diaz-Escobar was no more than eight years old, guerillas sought to turn Diaz-Escobar's father into a collaborator. The guerillas shot the father, kidnapped him, and told him that his family would "suffer the consequences." Second, Diaz-Escobar testified before the IJ that he witnessed guerillas torturing his neighbors and that those guerillas sent his mother a death threat. Yet nothing in the IJ or BIA's decisions indicates that either body failed to consider such evidence. Indeed, the BIA noted that Diaz-Escobar's father was told "his family members could come to harm if he should fail to cooperate," and the IJ described how Diaz-Escobar "witnessed his neighbors being tortured" by guerillas and that those guerillas sent his mother death threats.[2]

B

Nor did the IJ or BIA draw an erroneous conclusion from such evidence. In order to qualify as persecution, unfulfilled threats must be "so menacing as to cause significant actual `suffering or harm.'" Lim v. I.N.S., 224 F.3d 929, 936 (9th Cir. 2000) (quoting Sangha v. I.N.S., 103 F.3d 1482, 1487 (9th Cir. 1997)). Threats that are "anonymous, vague, and [do] not create a sense of immediate physical violence" do not rise to the level of persecution. Nahrvani v. Gonzales, 399 F.3d 1148, 1153 (9th Cir. 2005). As the Court concedes, the threats against Diaz-Escobar were never fulfilled, were anonymous, were made to Diaz-Escobar's mother (and not to him), and were sent by mail. The threats were also vague.[3] Under our precedents, such threats do not constitute persecution. Nor does the violence faced by Diaz-Escobar's father—which occurred while the father was away from the family—convert such threats to persecution. By contrast, Salazar-Paucar v. I.N.S., 281 F.3d 1069 (9th Cir. 2002), on which the Court relies, considered threats that did "create a sense of immediate physical violence." See Nahrvani, 399 F.3d at 1153. The guerillas in Salazar-Paucar targeted the petitioner because of his civic position, specifically threatened death, executed the petitioner's political allies, came to the petitioner's house, broke down his door, and beat his parents when they could not find him. Salazar-Paucar, 281 F.3d at 1071, 1074-75. The vague threats that Diaz-Escobar indirectly experienced created general fears, not a similar sense of immediate physical violence.

C

The BIA did not err in excluding certain evidence from consideration. Hence, remand on the basis of Sumolang v. Holder is inappropriate. 723 F.3d 1080, 1083-84 (9th Cir. 2013) (remanding because the IJ and BIA each made a legal error that led each to exclude directly relevant evidence). Rather, the BIA correctly concluded that the vague and indirect threats Diaz-Escobar describes do not rise to the level of past persecution.

III

Therefore, I would deny the petition in its entirety.

Notes

[1] Contrary to Diaz-Escobar's view, arriving as a minor may not excuse his failure to file because the regulations specifically excuse only "unaccompanied minors," and Diaz-Escobar joined his father upon arrival. 8 C.F.R. § 1208.4(a)(5)(ii) (emphasis added). See Mailoa v. Holder, 510 F. App'x 576, 578 (9th Cir. 2013) (limiting the extraordinary-circumstances exception to unaccompanied minors); see also Umirov v. Whitaker, 760 F. App'x 17, 19 (2d Cir. 2019); Ali v. Holder, 434 F. App'x 342, 344-45 (5th Cir. 2011); Tambaani v. Attorney Gen. of U.S., 388 F. App'x 131, 134 (3d Cir. 2010). Yet, even were we to grant that his age constituted an extraordinary circumstance, Diaz-Escobar filed his asylum application years after attaining adulthood, far beyond the "reasonable period" allowed by the regulations. 8 C.F.R. § 1208.4(a)(5); Al Ramahi v. Holder, 725 F.3d 1133, 1135 (9th Cir. 2013) (concluding that a "reasonable period" is presumptively no more than six months).

[2] Hence, contrary to the majority's assertion, the IJ did "acknowledge[ ] Diaz-Escobar's allegations of torture."

[3] The letters to Diaz-Escobar's mother included a threat to kill her, but the record is conspicuously silent as to whether such letters threatened Diaz-Escobar. In addition, the Court erroneously states that "the guerillas told Diaz-Escobar's father that they would kill his family." There is no indication the guerillas made such a specific threat.

The father's asylum application says merely that he was told his family would "suffer the consequences." Hence, if Diaz-Escobar was threatened at all, the administrative record does not indicate that such a threat was specific.

Judge O'Scannlain's concurrence and dissent in Krishna Lunch Of Southern California, Inc. v. Gordon (Jan 13, 2020)

O'SCANNLAIN, J., concurring in part and dissenting in part:

While I concur in Part 2 of the Court's disposition, I respectfully dissent from Parts 1 and 3, which reverse the dismissal of Krishna Lunch's free speech and free association claims. In my view, Krishna Lunch has failed to state a cognizable free speech, free exercise, or free association claim, and I would affirm the judgment of the district court in its entirety.

I

In order to survive a motion to dismiss the free speech claim, Krishna Lunch must show that the distribution of its sanctified vegan food (prasada) is conduct "sufficiently imbued with elements of communication" worthy of First Amendment protection. Spence v. State of Washington, 418 U.S. 405, 409 (1974). To that end, Krishna Lunch must demonstrate 1) an "intent to convey a particularized message" and 2) that, "in the surrounding circumstances the likelihood was great that the message would be understood by those who viewed it." Id. at 410-11. "[A] narrow, succinctly articulable message is not a condition of constitutional protection," Hurley v. Irish-American Gay, Lesbian and Bisexual Group of Boston, 515 U.S. 557, 569 (1995), but the message must be "delivered by conduct that is intended to be communicative and that, in context, would reasonably be understood by the viewer to be communicative." Clark v. Cmty. for Creative Non-Violence, 468 U.S. 288, 294 (1984). I am not persuaded that there is a great likelihood that the food distribution here would be understood by viewers on UCLA's campus to be communicative. I agree with the district court that such conduct is not expressive and, therefore, undeserving of constitutional protection.

A

Krishna Lunch asserts that the viewer is likely to understand the distribution of prasada communicates a message about the harmfulness of meat consumption for humans, animals, and the environment. However, on a college campus, such as UCLA, food is distributed fairly often and for a variety of reasons generally without the intent to convey a message. Krishna Lunch notes that the "Assigned Area" where UCLA permitted them to distribute food four times per year is often used by other groups to distribute food. This fact, though, makes it more likely that viewers will simply regard Krishna Lunch's food distribution as non-communicative like that of other groups. For example, many organizations provide food for students in order to entice them to attend an event and not to communicate any message. Food can also be distributed as part of a fundraiser where the intent is simply to raise money. The fact that the Assigned Area and other areas of the campus are used for food distribution in these ways would make Krishna Lunch's conduct appear to students to be similar to other non-communicative distributions of food.

B

The majority accepts Krishna Lunch's claim that the context would allow the viewer to understand the message. This "context," though, is speech itself. Specifically, Krishna Lunch argues that the accompanying singing, chanting, banners, signage, literature, and discussions make the food distribution itself expressive conduct. Yet, "[t]he fact that such explanatory speech is necessary is strong evidence that the conduct at issue here is not so inherently expressive that it warrants protection." Rumsfeld v. Forum for Academic and Institutional Rights, Inc., 547 U.S. 47, 66 (2006), ("FAIR").

Without the explanation provided by actual speech, viewers are not likely to understand Krishna Lunch's conduct to be communicative. As in FAIR, here, the only way viewers might understand the distribution of the food to communicate a message is by hearing Krishna Lunch's articulated message. Even then, the viewer still may think that the food was a way to lure him or her to the table to hear Krishna Lunch's message, or simply a friendly offering that accompanied the group's message, and may not view the food distribution itself as communicative. Thus, Krishna Lunch's conduct fails the second part of the Spence test.

C

The majority concludes, without citing any authority, that the "context" here is not simply the accompanying pure speech but also the identity of the organization. I fear that the implications of such holding would greatly expand the dimensions of protected free speech. In essence, then, the conduct of any organization whose identity stands for some idea or purpose could be considered expressive under the First Amendment.

For example, if a Christian religious organization handed out fried fish on UCLA's campus, such distribution would not be communicating the truths of the Gospel simply because the organization itself stands for such message. Although fish might be symbolic in certain contexts, viewers likely would not understand such conduct as communicative simply because the identity of the organization is associated with a certain mission.

Neither the Supreme Court nor this Court has ever adopted such a broad view of the First Amendment. I decline to accept such an expansion here. I would affirm the district court's dismissal of Krishna Lunch's free speech claim.

II

In order to survive a motion to dismiss the free association claim, Krishna Lunch must demonstrate, as an initial matter, some underlying First Amendment conduct. Roberts v. U.S. Jaycees, 468 U.S. 609, 622 (1984). The right to free association is a derivative right that assures First Amendment rights can be exercised. Id. at 618. In other words, expressive association is "the right to associate with others in activities otherwise protected by the First Amendment." Dible v. City of Chandler, 515 F.3d 918, 929 (9th Cir. 2008) (emphasis added).

Since I conclude that Krishna Lunch's distribution of prasada is not expressive conduct warranting First Amendment protection (and I agree with the majority that UCLA's neutral policy of general applicability does not violate Krishna Lunch's right to free exercise of religion), it follows that Krishna Lunch has failed to state a free association claim because there is no underlying First Amendment activity. Therefore, I would affirm the district court's dismissal of Krishna Lunch's free association claim as well.

Judge O'Scannlain's dissent in Henri Antoine Ba v. Barr (Jan 17, 2020)

O'SCANNLAIN, Circuit Judge, dissenting:

Since I would dismiss Henri Antoine Ba's petition with respect to his request for asylum and deny his petition with respect to his requests for withholding of removal and relief under the Convention Against Torture (CAT), I must respectfully dissent from the court's disposition.

I

I believe that we lack jurisdiction to review the denial of Ba's asylum application. The Board of Immigration Appeals' (BIA's) affirmance of the Immigration Judge's (IJ's) determination that Ba is subject to the terrorism bar, 8 U.S.C. § 1182(a)(3)(B), forecloses his eligibility for asylum, id. § 1158(b)(2)(A)(v). Such determination simply is not subject to judicial review. Id. § 1158(b)(2)(D).

The majority contends that we retain jurisdiction because the IJ determined that the statutory terrorism bar applied "in the context of Ba's subsequent application for adjustment of status," not his initial application for asylum. Maj. at 2. Respectfully, I suggest that the majority is mistaken. Ba did not go through two separate sets of proceedings—one for the asylum, withholding of removal, and CAT relief, the other for adjustment of status. He was the subject of only one set of proceedings, which the BIA reopened upon Ba's request. Furthermore, there is nothing more for the BIA to decide regarding Ba's eligibility for asylum. Once the IJ found that Ba was subject to the terrorism bar, he was automatically ineligible for asylum. No additional finding was required.

II

For the same reason, I would also deny his petition with respect to his requests for withholding of removal and CAT relief in the form of withholding. Once an IJ determines that an alien is covered by the terrorism bar, such alien is automatically ineligible for withholding of removal, 8 U.S.C. §§ 1227(a)(4)(B), 1231(b)(3)(B)(iv), and CAT protection in the form of withholding, 8 C.F.R. § 1208.16(d)(2). Because the IJ determined (and the BIA affirmed) that Ba engaged in terrorist activities, he was automatically made ineligible for these other forms of relief.

III

Even though Ba is subject to the terrorism bar, he is still eligible for CAT relief in the form of deferral. 8 C.F.R. § 1208.17; see also Haile v. Holder, 658 F.3d 1122, 1125-26 (9th Cir. 2011) ("Aliens who have engaged in terrorist activities are precluded from seeking several forms of relief from removal, including asylum, withholding, and CAT protection in the form of withholding, but remain eligible for deferral of removal under the CAT."). With respect to such form of relief, I would deny Ba's petition because substantial evidence supports the adverse credibility determination and the independent record evidence does not compel the conclusion that Ba is more likely than not to be tortured if he returns to Senegal.

A

Because this is a pre-REAL ID Act case, an adverse credibility determination must be based on a material discrepancy that goes to the heart of the applicant's claim. Kaur v. Gonzales, 418 F.3d 1061, 1064 (9th Cir. 2005). The majority contends that the discrepancies in Ba's testimony regarding his involvement with the Mouvement des Forces Démocratiques de Casamance (MFDC) do not go to the heart of his claims of past persecution. Maj. at 3. Once again, I respectfully suggest that the majority is mistaken.

Ba's claims of past persecution stem from the conflict in the Casamance. The MFDC is a participant in that conflict. If the IJ found that there was reason to doubt Ba's testimony about his membership in a group that is a party to the conflict, then it was reasonable for the IJ to question the credibility of Ba's testimony about persecution that he allegedly suffered in that same conflict. See Enying Li v. Holder, 738 F.3d 1160, 1162 (9th Cir. 2013) (holding that "an IJ may use the maxim falsus in uno, falsus in omnibus . . . to find that material inconsistencies in testimony regarding one claim support an adverse credibility determination on another claim in a pre-REAL ID Act case"). For example, one of Ba's claims of past persecution is that he was injured by Senegalese soldiers in 1982 while participating in a protest for Casamance independence. If the IJ found that Ba was not truthful about his membership in a group that supports Casamance independence, then it was reasonable for the IJ to doubt Ba's claim that he was injured in a protest for that very same cause.

Granted, it is possible that Ba participated and was injured in a protest for Casamance independence but was not an active member of the MFDC. However, we do not reverse the BIA's factual findings based on the mere possibility of error. We review factual findings, including adverse credibility determinations, for substantial evidence. Lianhua Jiang v. Holder, 754 F.3d 733, 738 (9th Cir. 2014). Here, the evidence does not compel the conclusion that the BIA's adverse credibility determination was erroneous. On the contrary, in light of the material inconsistencies in Ba's testimony about his membership in the MFDC, the BIA's findings were eminently reasonable.

B

Nor does the record evidence, standing alone, compel the conclusion that Ba is more likely than not to be tortured if he returns to Senegal. Shrestha v. Holder, 590 F.3d 1034, 1048-49 (9th Cir. 2010).

For example, Ba offers up medical evaluations to prove that he was the victim of torture. But while these evaluations state that Ba has had symptoms consistent with torture, they do not establish that he was tortured, much less that he is more likely than not to be tortured in the future.

Ba presents several letters in support of his application. Unlike the majority, however, I do not think this evidence is helpful to Ba's case. Maj. at 3-4. Ba's uncle describes his own torture and imprisonment but says nothing about Ba's experiences. Ba's mother discusses her concerns about ongoing harassment from Senegalese authorities, but she does not suggest that Ba is likely to be tortured if he returns. The letter from Abbot Augustin Diamacoune Senghor appears to offer the most support to Ba's claims: It says that Ba is likely to be imprisoned, tortured, or executed if he goes back to Senegal. However, the author of the letter was the Secretary General of the MFDC—the same terrorist organization of which Ba has inconsistently claimed to have been a member, hardly compelling evidence.

Finally, although the country reports included in the administrative record suggest that Senegal is a troubled place where torture and other human rights abuses have occurred, they do not compel the conclusion that Ba, specifically, is more likely than not to be tortured if he returns.

Judge O'Scannlain's dissent in DNC v. Hobbs (Jan 27, 2020) [Notes omitted]

O'SCANNLAIN, Circuit Judge, with whom CLIFTON, BYBEE, and CALLAHAN, Circuit Judges, join, dissenting:

We have been asked to decide whether two current Arizona election practices violate the Voting Rights Act or the First, Fourteenth, or Fifteenth Amendments to the United States Constitution.[1] Based on the record before us and relevant Supreme Court and Ninth Circuit precedent, the answer to such question is clear: they do not. The majority, however, draws factual inferences that the evidence cannot support and misreads precedent along the way. In so doing, it impermissibly strikes down Arizona's duly enacted policies designed to enforce its precinct-based election system and to regulate third-party collection of early ballots.

I respectfully dissent.

I

Given the abundant discussion by the district court and the en banc majority, I offer only a brief summary of the policies at issue here and discuss the district court's factual findings as pertinent to the analysis below.

A

Arizona offers voters several options: early mail ballot, early in-person voting, and in-person Election Day voting. Democratic Nat'l Comm. v. Reagan ("DNC"), 329 F. Supp. 3d 824, 838 (D. Ariz. 2018).

1

Since at least 1970, Arizona has required that in-person voters "cast their ballots in their assigned precinct and has enforced this system by counting only those ballots cast in the correct precinct." Id. at 840. A voter who arrives at a precinct in which he or she is not listed on the register may cast a provisional ballot, but Arizona will not count such ballot if it determines that the voter does not live in the precinct in which he or she voted. Id. For shorthand, I refer to this rule as Arizona's "out-of-precinct" or "OOP" policy.

Most Arizona voters, however, do not vote in person on Election Day. Id. at 845. Arizona law permits all registered voters to vote early by mail or in person at an early voting location in the 27 days before an election. Ariz. Rev. Stat. §§ 16-121(A), 16-541(A), 16-542(D). All Arizona counties operate at least one location for early in person voting. DNC, 329 F. Supp. 3d at 839. Rather than voting early in person, any voter may instead request an early ballot to be delivered to his or her mailbox on an election-by-election or permanent basis. Id. In 2002, Arizona became the first state to make available an online voter registration option, which also permits voters to enroll in permanent early voting by mail. Id. Voters who so enroll will be sent an early ballot no later than the first day of the 27-day early voting period. Id. Voters may return early ballots in person at any polling place, vote center, or authorized office without waiting in line or may return their early ballots by mail at no cost. Id. To be counted, however, an early ballot must be received by 7:00 p.m. on Election Day. Id.

2

For years, Arizona has restricted who may handle early ballots.[2] Since 1992, Arizona has prohibited anyone but the elector himself from possessing "that elector's unvoted absentee ballot." 1991 Ariz. Legis. Serv. Ch. 310, § 22 (S.B. 1390) (West). In 2016, Arizona enacted a parallel regulation, H.B. 2023 (the "ballot-collection" policy), concerning the collection of early ballots.[3] DNC, 329 F. Supp. 3d at 839. Under the ballot-collection policy, only a "family member," "household member," "caregiver," "United States postal service worker" or other person authorized to transmit mail, or "election official" may return another voter's completed early ballot. Id. at 839-40 (citing Ariz. Rev. Stat. § 16-1005(H)-(I)).

B

In April 2016, the Democratic National Committee, the Democratic Senatorial Campaign Committee, and the Arizona Democratic Party (together, "DNC") sued the State of Arizona to challenge the OOP policy and the ballot-collection policy. The district court denied DNC's motions to enjoin preliminarily enforcement of both polices, and DNC asked our court to issue injunctions pending appeal of such denials. After expedited proceedings before three-judge and en banc panels, our court denied the motion for an injunction against the OOP policy but granted the parallel motion against the ballot-collection policy. Feldman v. Ariz. Sec'y of State's Office, 840 F.3d 1165 (9th Cir. 2016) (en banc) (mem.) (per curiam); Feldman v. Ariz. Sec'y of State's Office (Feldman III), 843 F.3d 366 (9th Cir. 2016) (en banc). The Supreme Court, however, stayed our injunction against the ballot-collection policy and the OOP and ballot-collection policies functioned in usual fashion. Ariz. Sec'y of State's Office v. Feldman, 137 S. Ct. 446 (2016) (mem.).

In 2017, the district court proceeded to the merits of DNC's suit. In May 2018, after a ten-day bench trial, the district court issued a decision supported by thorough findings of fact and conclusions of law. DNC, 329 F. Supp. 3d at 832. The district court found that DNC failed to prove any violation of the Voting Rights Act or the United States Constitution and issued judgment in the state's favor. Id. at 882-83.

DNC timely appealed, and a three-judge panel of our court affirmed the decision of the district court in its entirety. Democratic Nat'l Comm. v. Reagan ("DNC"), 904 F.3d 686 (9th Cir. 2018), vacated by order granting rehearing en banc, 911 F.3d 942 (9th Cir. 2019) (mem.). But today, the en banc panel majority reverses the decision of the district court and holds that the OOP and ballot-collection policies violate § 2 of the Voting Rights Act and that the ballot-collection policy was enacted with discriminatory intent in violation of the Fifteenth Amendment.

II

The first mistake of the en banc majority is disregarding the critical standard of review. Although the majority recites the appropriate standard, it does not actually engage with it.[4] Maj. Op. 8-9. The standard is not complex. We review de novo the district court's conclusions of law, but may review its findings of fact only for clear error. Navajo Nation v. U.S. Forest Serv., 535 F.3d 1058, 1067 (9th Cir. 2008) (en banc).

The majority's disregard of such standard and, thus, our appellate role, infects its analysis of each of DNC's claims. The demanding clear error standard "plainly does not entitle a reviewing court to reverse the finding of the trier of fact simply because it is convinced that it would have decided the case differently." Anderson v. City of Bessemer City, 470 U.S. 564, 573 (1985). Rather, we may reverse a finding only if, "although there is evidence to support it, [we are] left with the definite and firm conviction that a mistake has been committed." Id. (quoting United States v. U. S. Gypsum Co., 333 U.S. 364, 395 (1948)). To do otherwise "oversteps the bounds of [our] duty under [Federal Rule of Civil Procedure] 52(a)" by "duplicat[ing] the role of the lower court." Id. at 573. As explained in Parts III and IV, I fail to see how on the record before us one could be "left with a definite and firm conviction" that the district court erred.

III

DNC first contends that Arizona's policies violate § 2 of the Voting Rights Act. A district court's determination of whether a challenged practice violates § 2 of the Voting Rights Act is "intensely fact-based": the court assesses the "totality of the circumstances" and conducts "a `searching practical evaluation of the past and present reality.'" Smith v. Salt River Project Agric. Improvements & Power Dist. ("Salt River"), 109 F.3d 586, 591 (9th Cir. 1997) (quoting Thornburg v. Gingles, 478 U.S. 30, 79 (1986)). Thus, "[d]eferring to the district court's superior fact-finding capabilities, we review only for clear error its ultimate finding of no § 2 violation." Id. at 591 (emphasis added).

In relevant part, § 2 provides:

(a) No voting qualification or prerequisite to voting or standard, practice, or procedure shall be imposed or applied by any State . . . in a manner which results in a denial or abridgment of the right of any citizen of the United States to vote on account of race or color . . . .

(b) A violation of subsection (a) is established if, based on the totality of circumstances, it is shown that the political processes leading to nomination or election in the State . . . are not equally open to participation by members of a class of citizens protected by subsection (a) in that its members have less opportunity than other members of the electorate to participate in the political process and to elect representatives of their choice.

52 U.S.C. § 10301 (emphasis added). "The essence of a § 2 claim is that a certain electoral law, practice, or structure interacts with social and historical conditions to cause an inequality in the opportunities enjoyed by black and white voters to elect their preferred representatives." Gingles, 478 U.S. at 47. To determine whether a practice violates § 2, courts employ a two-step analysis. See Ohio Democratic Party v. Husted, 834 F.3d 620, 637 (6th Cir. 2016); Veasey v. Abbott, 830 F.3d 216, 244 (5th Cir. 2016); Frank v. Walker, 768 F.3d 744, 754-55 (7th Cir. 2014); League of Women Voters of N.C. v. North Carolina, 769 F.3d 224, 240 (4th Cir. 2014).

The first step is asking whether the practice provides members of a protected class "less `opportunity' than others `to participate in the political process and to elect representatives of their choice.'" Chisom v. Roemer, 501 U.S. 380, 397 (1991) (alteration in original) (quoting 52 U.S.C. § 10301). In other words, the challenged practice "must impose a discriminatory burden on members of a protected class." League of Women Voters, 769 F.3d at 240 (emphasis added). To prevail at step one, the plaintiff therefore "must show a causal connection between the challenged voting practice and [a] prohibited discriminatory result." Salt River, 109 F.3d at 595 (alteration in original) (quoting Ortiz v. City of Phila. Office of City Comm'rs Voter Registration Div., 28 F.3d 306, 312 (3d Cir. 1994)); see also Ohio Democratic Party, 834 F.3d at 638. If a discriminatory burden is established, then—and only then—do we consider whether the burden is "caused by or linked to `social and historical conditions' that have or currently produce discrimination against members of the protected class." League of Women Voters, 769 F.3d at 240 (quoting Gingles, 478 U.S. at 47).

The majority agrees that this two-step analysis controls but mistakenly applies it. According to the majority, DNC has shown that the OOP policy and the ballot-collection policy fail at both steps—and, presumably, that the district court clearly erred in finding otherwise. Under an appropriately deferential analysis, however, DNC cannot prevail even at step one: it has simply failed to show that either policy erects a discriminatory burden.

A

As to the facially neutral OOP policy, DNC argues, erroneously, that wholly discarding, rather than partially counting, ballots that are cast out-of-precinct violates § 2 of the Voting Rights Act because such policy imposes a discriminatory burden on minority voters related to Arizona's history of discrimination. The district court, quite properly, found that DNC failed to carry its burden at step one—that the practice imposes a discriminatory burden on minority voters—for two reasons. DNC, 329 F. Supp. 3d at 873.

1

First, the district court determined that DNC failed to show "that the racial disparities in OOP voting are practically significant enough to work a meaningful inequality in the opportunities of minority voters as compared to non-minority voters." Id. Thus, it ruled that DNC failed to show that the precinct-based system has a "disparate impact on the opportunities of minority voters to elect their preferred representatives." Id. at 872. To the contrary, the district court made the factual finding that out-of-precinct "ballots represent . . . a small and ever-decreasing fraction of the overall votes cast in any given election." Id.

Furthermore, the district court determined that "the burdens imposed by precinct-based voting . . . are not severe. Precinct-based voting merely requires voters to locate and travel to their assigned precincts, which are ordinary burdens traditionally associated with voting." Id. at 858. Indeed, the numbers found by the district court support such conclusion. Only 0.47 percent of all ballots cast in the 2012 general election (10,979 out of 2,323,579) were not counted because they were cast out of the voter's assigned precinct. Id. at 872. In 2016, this fell to 0.15 percent (3,970 out of 2,661,497). Id. And of those casting ballots in-person on Election Day, approximately 99 percent of minority voters and 99.5 percent of non-minority voters cast their ballots in their assigned precincts. Id. Given that the overwhelming majority of all voters complied with the precinct-based voting system during the 2016 election, it is difficult to see how the district court's finding could be considered clearly erroneous. See also Crawford v. Marion Cty. Election Bd., 553 U.S. 181, 198 (2008) (plurality opinion) (discussing "the usual burdens of voting"). And it further ruled that DNC "offered no evidence of a systemic or pervasive history of minority voters being given misinformation regarding the locations of their assigned precincts, while non-minority voters were given correct information" to suggest that the burden of voting in one's assigned precinct is more significant for minority voters than for non-minority voters. DNC, 329 F. Supp. 3d at 873.

As Judge Ikuta explained in her now-vacated majority opinion for the three-judge panel:

> If a challenged election practice is not burdensome or the state offers easily accessible alternative means of voting, a court can reasonably conclude that the law does not impair any particular group's opportunity to "influence the outcome of an election," even if the practice has a disproportionate impact on minority voters.

DNC, 904 F.3d at 714 (citation omitted) (quoting Chisom, 501 U.S. at 397 n.24). The "bare statistic[s]" presented may indeed show a disproportionate impact on minority voters, but we have held previously that such showing is not enough. Salt River, 109 F.3d at 595 ("[A] bare statistical showing of disproportionate impact on a racial minority does not satisfy the § 2 `results' inquiry." (emphasis in original)). A court must evaluate the burden imposed by the challenged voting practice—not merely any statistical disparity that may be shown. The Supreme Court's interpretation of § 2 in Gingles suggests the same. There, the Court observed that "[i]t is obvious that unless minority group members experience substantial difficulty electing representatives of their choice, they cannot prove that a challenged electoral mechanism impairs their ability `to elect.'" Gingles, 478 U.S. at 48 n.15 (emphasis added) (quoting 52 U.S.C. § 10301(b)). Furthermore, because "[n]o state has exactly equal registration rates, exactly equal turnout rates, and so on, at every stage of its voting system," it cannot be the case that pointing to a mere statistical disparity related to a challenged voting practice is sufficient to "dismantle" that practice. Frank, 768 F.3d at 754; see also Salt River, 109 F.3d at 595.

The majority, however, contends that "the district court discounted the disparate burden on the ground that there were relatively few OOP ballots cast in relation to the total number of ballots." Maj. Op. 43. In the majority's view, the district court should have emphasized that the percentage of in-person ballots that were cast out-of-precinct increased, thus isolating the specific impact of the OOP policy amongst in-person voters bound by the precinct-system requirements.

Contrary to the majority's assertion, however, the legal review at hand does not require that we isolate the specific challenged practice in the manner it suggests. Rather, at step one of the § 2 inquiry, we only consider whether minority voters "experience substantial difficulty electing representatives of their choice," Gingles, 478 U.S. at 48 n.15, "based on the totality of circumstances," 52 U.S.C. § 10301(b).[5] Although the majority would like us to believe that the increasing percentage of in-person ballots cast out-of-precinct demonstrates that minorities are disparately burdened by the challenged policy, the small number of voters who chose to vote in-person and the even smaller number of such voters who fail to do so in the correct precinct demonstrate that any minimal burden imposed by the policy does not deprive minority voters of equal opportunities to elect representatives of their choice. A conclusion otherwise could not be squared with our determination that a mere statistical showing of disproportionate impact on racial minorities does not satisfy the challenger's burden. See Salt River, 109 F.3d at 595. If such statistical impact is not sufficient, it must perforce be the case that the crucial test is the extent to which the practice burdens minority voters as opposed to non-minority voters. But the en banc majority offers no explanation for how or why the burden of voting in one's assigned precinct is severe or beyond that of the burdens traditionally associated with voting.

The majority argues that there may be a "de minimis number" below which no § 2 violation has occurred.[6] Maj. Op. 44. But we know from our own precedent that "a bare statistical showing of disproportionate impact on a racial minority does not satisfy the § 2 . . . inquiry." Salt River, 109 F.3d at 595 (emphasis in original). And Chisom makes clear that § 2 "claims must allege an abridgment of the opportunity to participate in the political process and to elect representatives of one's choice." 501 U.S. at 398 (emphasis in original). As such, the inquiry must require consideration of both the scope of the burden imposed by the particular policy—not merely how many voters are impacted by it—and the difficulty of accessing the political process in its entirety.

Thus, it cannot be true, as the majority suggests, that simply showing that some number of minority voters' ballots were not counted as a result of an individual policy satisfies step one of the § 2 analysis for a facially neutral policy.

2

Second, the district court made the factual finding that "Arizona's policy to not count OOP ballots is not the cause of [any identified] disparities in OOP voting." DNC, 329 F. Supp. 3d at 872. According to the OOP policy that is challenged by DNC, a ballot is not counted if it is cast outside of the voter's assigned precinct. And the district court pointed to several factors that result in higher rates of out-of-precinct voting among minorities. For example, the district court found that "high rates of residential mobility are associated with higher rates of OOP voting," and minorities are more likely to move more frequently. Id. at 857, 872. Similarly, "rates of OOP voting are higher in neighborhoods where renters make up a larger share of householders." Id. at 857. The precinct-system may also pose special challenges for Native American voters, because they may "lack standard addresses" and there may be additional "confusion about the voter's correct polling place" where precinct assignments may differ from assignments for tribal elections. Id. at 873. "Additionally", the district court found, Arizona's "changes in polling locations from election to election, inconsistent election regimes used by and within counties, and placement of polling locations all tend to increase OOP voting rates." Id. at 858.

But the burden of complying with the precinct-based system in the face of any such factors is plainly distinguishable from the consequence imposed should a voter fail to comply. Indeed, as the district court found, "there is no evidence that it will be easier for voters to identify their correct precincts if Arizona eliminated its prohibition on counting OOP ballots." Id. Although "the consequence of voting OOP might make it more imperative for voters to correctly identify their precincts," id., such consequence does not cause voters to cast their ballots out-of-precinct or make it more burdensome for voters to cast their ballots in their assigned precincts.

The majority goes astray by failing to recognize the distinction between the burden of complying and the consequence of failing to do so. In fact, the majority undercuts its own claim by citing the same host of reasons identified by the district court as the reasons why a minority voter is more likely to vote out-of-precinct. Maj Op. 14-19. All the factors the majority seizes upon, however, stem from the general requirement that a voter cast his or her ballot in the assigned precinct—not the policy that enforces such requirement. The importance of such distinction is made clear by the relief that DNC seeks: DNC does not request that Arizona be made to end its precinct-based system or to assign its precincts differently, but instead requests that Arizona be made to count those ballots that are not cast in compliance with the OOP policy.[7] Removing the enforcement policy, however, would do nothing to minimize or to extinguish the disparity that exists in out-of-precinct voting.

Consider another basic voting requirement: in order to cast a ballot, a voter must register. If a person fails to register, his or her vote will not count. Any discriminatory result from such a policy would need to be addressed in a challenge to that policy itself. For example, if minorities are underrepresented as a segment of registered voters, perhaps they could challenge some discriminatory aspect of the registration system. But they surely could not prevail by challenging simply the state's enforcement of the registration policy by refusing to count unregistered voters' ballots. Minorities in a jurisdiction may very well be underrepresented as members of the registered electorate, but the discrepancy between the protected class as a segment of the general population and as a segment of the registered voting population would not require that a state permit unregistered voters to cast valid ballots on Election Day.

Similarly, the fact that a ballot cast by a voter outside of his or her assigned precinct is discarded does not cause minorities to vote out-of-precinct disproportionately. But DNC does not challenge the general requirement that one vote in his or her precinct or take issue with the assignment of precinct locations—the very requirements that could lead to a disproportionate impact. It may indeed be the case in a precinct-based voting system that a state's poor assignment of districts, distribution of inadequate information about voting requirements, or other factors have some material effect on election practices such that minorities have less opportunity to elect representatives of their choice as a result of the system. But, in the words of the majority, DNC's challenge "assumes both [the] importance and [the] continued existence" of "Arizona's precinct-based system of voting." Maj. Op. 78. Instead, DNC challenges only Arizona's enforcement of such system. Thus, even if there were a recognizable disparity in the opportunities of minority voters voting out-of-precinct, it would nonetheless not be the result of the policy at issue before us.

3

I reject the suggestion implicit in the majority opinion that any facially neutral policy which may result in some statistical disparity is necessarily discriminatory under step one of the § 2 inquiry. We have already held otherwise. Salt River, 109 F.3d at 595. And the majority itself concedes that "more than a de minimis number of minority voters must be burdened before a Section 2 violation based on the results test can be found." Maj. Op. 44. Furthermore, I fail to see how DNC—and the majority—can concede the importance and continued existence of a precinct-based system, yet argue that the enforcement mechanism designed to maintain such system is impermissible.

Because DNC has failed to meet its burden under step one of the Voting Rights Act § 2 inquiry—that the district court's findings were clearly erroneous—our analysis of its OOP claim should end here.

B

As to the facially neutral ballot-collection policy, DNC argues, erroneously, that it violates § 2 because there is "extensive evidence" demonstrating that minority voters are more likely to have used ballot-collection services and that they would therefore be disproportionately burdened by limitations on such services. Specifically, DNC relies on anecdotal evidence that ballot collection has disproportionately occurred in minority communities, that minority voters were more likely to be without home mail delivery or access to transportation, and that ballot-harvesting efforts were disproportionately undertaken by the Democratic Party in minority communities. And, DNC claims, such burden is caused by or linked to Arizona's history of discrimination.

The district court, quite properly, rejected such argument, making the factual finding that DNC failed to establish at step one that the ballot-collection policy imposed a discriminatory burden on minority voters. DNC, 329 F. Supp. 3d at 866, 871. Once again, the question is whether such finding was clearly erroneous. Salt River, 109 F.3d at 591.

1

The district court found broadly that the non-quantitative evidence offered by DNC failed to show that the ballot-collection policy denied minority voters of "meaningful access to the political process." DNC, 329 F. Supp. 3d at 871. As Judge Ikuta observed, to determine whether the challenged policy provides minority voters "less opportunity to elect representatives of their choice, [we] must necessarily consider the severity and breadth of the law's impacts on the protected class." DNC, 904 F.3d at 717.

But no evidence of that impact has been offered. "In fact, no individual voter testified that [the ballot-collection policy's] limitations on who may collect an early ballot would make it significantly more difficult to vote." DNC, 329 F. Supp. 3d at 871 (emphasis added). Anecdotal evidence of how voters have chosen to vote in the past does not establish that voters are unable to vote in other ways or would be burdened by having to do so. The district court simply found that "prior to the [ballot-collection policy's] enactment minorities generically were more likely than non-minorities to return their early ballots with the assistance of third parties," id. at 870, but, once again, the disparate impact of a challenged policy on minority voters is insufficient to establish a § 2 violation, see Salt River, 109 F.3d at 594-95.

The majority simply does not address the lack of evidence as to whether minority voters have less opportunity than non-minority voters now that ballot collection is more limited. Instead, the majority answers the wrong question by pointing to minority voters' use of ballot collection in the past. The majority offers no record-factual support for its conclusion that the anecdotal evidence presented demonstrates that compliance with the ballot-collection policy imposes a disparate burden on minority voters—a conclusion that must be reached in order to satisfy step one of the § 2 inquiry—let alone evidence that the district court's contrary finding was "clearly erroneous."

Given the lack of any testimony in the record indicating that the ballot-collection policy would result in minority voters "experienc[ing] substantial difficulty electing representatives of their choice," Gingles, 478 U.S. at 48 n.15, the district court did not clearly err in finding that, "for some voters, ballot collection is a preferred and more convenient method of voting," but a limitation on such practice "does not deny minority voters meaningful access to the political process." DNC, 329 F. 3d Supp. at 871.

2

The district court further found that the ballot-collection policy was unlikely to "cause a meaningful inequality in the electoral opportunities of minorities" because only "a relatively small number of voters have used ballot collection services" in the past at all.

DNC, 329 F. Supp. 3d at 870-71. And, the district court noted, DNC "provided no quantitative or statistical evidence comparing the proportion that is minority versus non-minority." Id. at 866. "Without this information," the district court explained, "it becomes difficult to compare the law's impact on different demographic populations and to determine whether the disparities, if any, are meaningful." Id. at 867. Thus, from the record, we do not know either the extent to which voters may be burdened by the ballot-collection policy or how many minority voters may be so burdened.

Nonetheless, the district court considered circumstantial and anecdotal evidence offered by DNC and determined that "the vast majority of Arizonans, minority and non-minority alike, vote without the assistance of third-parties who would not fall within [the ballot-collection policy's] exceptions." Id. at 871. DNC—and the majority—argue that such finding is not supported by the record, but, given the lack of quantitative or statistical evidence before us, it is difficult to conclude that such finding is clearly erroneous. The district court itself noted that it could not "speak in more specific or precise terms" given the sparsity of the record. Id. at 870. Drawing from anecdotal testimony, the district court estimated that fewer than 10,000 voters used ballot-collection services in any election. Id. at 845. Drawing even "the unjustified inference that 100,000 early mail ballots were collected" during the 2012 general election, the district court found that such higher total would nonetheless be "relatively few early voters" as compared to the 1.4 million early mail ballots returned or 2.3 million total votes cast. Id. at 845. The majority further argues that the district court erred in "discounting the evidence of third-party ballot collection as merely `circumstantial and anecdotal'" Maj. Op. 83. But the district court did nothing of the sort. To the contrary, the district court considered whether the ballot-collection policy violated § 2 by making these estimates—and even generous estimates—from the anecdotal evidence offered. And the district court's subsequent conclusion that the limitation of third-party ballot collection would impact only a "relatively small number of voters," id. at 870, is clearly plausible on this record, see Bessemer City, 470 U.S. at 573.

The majority also argues that the total number of votes affected is not the relevant inquiry; the proper test is whether the number of ballots collected by third parties surpasses any de minimis number. Maj. Op. 84. But we already know "that a bare statistical showing" that an election practice has a "disproportionate impact on a racial minority does not satisfy" step one of the § 2 inquiry. Salt River, 109 F.3d at 595 (emphasis in original). And, even if such impact were sufficient, the record offers no evidence from which the district court could determine the extent of the discrepancy between minority voters as a proportion of the entire electorate versus minority voters as a proportion of those who have voted using ballot-collection services in the past. DNC, 329 F. Supp. 3d at 866-67.

3

As Judge Bybee keenly observed in a previous iteration of this case (and indeed in his dissent in this case), "[t]here is no constitutional or federal statutory right to vote by absentee ballot." Feldman III, 843 F.3d at 414 (Bybee, J., dissenting) (citing McDonald v.

Bd. of Election Comm'rs of Chi., 394 U.S. 802, 807-08 (1969)); accord Bybee, J. Diss. Op. 156. Both today and in the past, Arizona has chosen to provide a wide range of options to voters. But Arizona's previous decision to permit a particular mechanism of voting does not preclude Arizona from modifying its election system to limit such mechanism in the future so long as such modification is made in a constitutional manner. And, in fact, Arizona's modification here was made in compliance with "the recommendation of the bipartisan Commission on Federal Election Reform." DNC, 329 F. Supp. 3d at 855. Without any evidence in the record of the severity and breadth of the burden imposed by this change to the ballot-collection policy, we cannot be "left with the definite and firm conviction" that the district court erred in finding that DNC failed to show that the policy violated § 2. See Bessemer City, 470 U.S. at 573; see also Salt River, 109 F.3d at 591.

C

Because I disagree with the majority's conclusion that DNC has satisfied its burden at step one of the § 2 Voting Rights Act inquiry, I would not reach step two. I therefore do not address the majority's consideration of the so-called "Senate Factors" in determining whether the burden is "in part caused by or linked to `social and historical conditions' that have or currently produce discrimination against members of the protected class." League of Women Voters, 769 F.3d at 240 (quoting Gingles, 478 U.S. at 47). These factors—and the majority's lengthy history lesson on past election abuses in Arizona—simply have no bearing on this case. Indeed, pages 47 to 81 of the majority's opinion may properly be ignored as irrelevant.

IV

DNC also contends that the ballot-collection policy violates the Fifteenth Amendment to the United States Constitution.[8] To succeed on a claim of discriminatory intent under the Fifteenth Amendment, the challenger must demonstrate that the state legislature "selected or reaffirmed a particular course of action at least in part `because of,' not merely `in spite of,' its adverse effects upon an identifiable group." Pers. Adm'r of Mass. v. Feeney, 442 U.S. 256, 279 (1979). Because discriminatory intent "is a pure question of fact," we again review only for clear error. Pullman-Standard v. Swint, 456 U.S. 273, 287-88 (1982). "Determining whether invidious discriminatory purpose was a motivating factor demands a sensitive inquiry into such circumstantial and direct evidence of intent as may be available." Vill. of Arlington Heights v. Metro. Hous. Dev. Corp., 429 U.S. 252, 266 (1977).

The district court concluded that the ballot-collection policy did not violate the Fifteenth Amendment because it made the factual finding that the legislature "was not motivated by a desire to suppress minority voters," although "some individual legislators and proponents of limitations on ballot collection harbored partisan motives" that "did not permeate the entire legislative process." DNC, 329 F. Supp. 3d at 879, 882 (emphasis added). Instead, "[t]he legislature was motivated by . . . a sincere belief that mail-in ballots lacked adequate prophylactic safeguards as compared to in-person voting." Id. at 882. In analyzing DNC's appeal from such finding, the majority, once again, completely ignores our demanding standard of review and instead conducts its own de novo review. Maj. Op. 93. Our duty is only to consider whether the district court clearly erred in its finding that the ballot-collection policy was not enacted with discriminatory intent. See Bessemer City, 470 U.S. at 573. And "to be clearly erroneous, a decision must . . . strike [a court] as wrong with the force of a five-week old, unrefrigerated dead fish." Ocean Garden, Inc. v. Marktrade Co., Inc., 953 F.2d 500, 502 (9th Cir. 1991) (quoting Parts & Elec. Motors, Inc. v. Sterling Elec., Inc., 866 F.2d 228, 233 (7th Cir. 1988)).

The majority therefore fails to offer any basis—let alone a convincing one—for the conclusion that it must reach in order to reverse the decision of the district court: that the district court committed clear error in its factual findings. Given the failure of the majority to conduct its review in the proper manner, I see no reason to engage in a line-by-line debate with its flawed analysis. Rather, it is enough to note two critical errors made by the majority in ignoring the district court's determinations that while some legislators were motivated by partisan concerns, the legislature as a body was motivated by a desire to enact prophylactic measures to prevent voter fraud.

A

First, the majority fails to distinguish between racial motives and partisan motives. Even when "racial identification is highly correlated with political affiliation," a party challenging a legislative action nonetheless must show that racial motives were a motivating factor behind the challenged policy. Cooper v. Harris, 137 S. Ct. 1455, 1473 (2017) (quoting Easley v. Cromartie, 532 U.S. 234, 243 (2001)). Nonetheless, the majority suggests that a legislator motivated by partisan interest to enact a law that disproportionately impacts minorities must necessarily have acted with racially discriminatory intent as well. For example, the district court noted that Arizona State Senator Don Shooter was, "in part motivated by a desire to eliminate what had become an effective Democratic [Get Out The Vote] strategy." DNC, 329 F. Supp. 3d at 879. The majority simply concludes that such finding shows racially discriminatory intent as a motivating factor. But the majority's unsupported inference does not satisfy the required showing. And the majority fails to cite any evidence demonstrating that the district court's finding to the contrary was not "plausible in light of the record viewed in its entirety." Bessemer City, 470 U.S. at 574.

B

Second, in defiance of Supreme Court precedent to the contrary, the majority assumes that a legislature's stated desire to prevent voter fraud must be pretextual when there is no direct evidence of voter fraud in the legislative record. In Crawford, the Court rejected the argument that actual evidence of voter fraud was needed to justify the State's decision to enact prophylactic measures to prevent such fraud. Crawford, 553 U.S. at 195-96 . There, the Court upheld an Indiana statute requiring in-person voters to present government-issued photo identification in the face of a constitutional challenge. Id. at 185. Although "[t]he record contain[ed] no evidence of [voter] fraud actually occurring in Indiana at any time in its history," the Supreme Court nonetheless determined that the

State had a legitimate and important interest "in counting only the votes of eligible voters." Id. at 194, 196; see also id. at 195 nn.11-13 (citing "fragrant examples of" voter fraud throughout history and in recent years). Given its interest in addressing its valid concerns of voter fraud, Arizona was free to enact prophylactic measures even though no evidence of actual voter fraud was before the legislature. Yet the majority does not even mention Crawford, let alone grapple with its consequences on this case.

And because no evidence of actual voter fraud is required to justify an anti-fraud prophylactic measure, the majority's reasoning quickly collapses. The majority cites Senator Shooter's "false and race-based allegations" and the "LaFaro video," which the district court explained "showed surveillance footage of a man of apparent Hispanic heritage appearing to deliver early ballots" and "contained a narration of [i]nnuendos of illegality . . . [and] racially tinged and inaccurate commentary by . . . LaFaro." DNC, 329 F. Supp. 3d at 876 (second, third, and fourth alterations in original). The majority contends that although "some members of the legislature who voted for H.B. 2023 had a sincere, though mistaken, non-race-based belief that there had been fraud in third-party ballot collection, and that the problem needed to be addressed," a discriminatory purpose may be attributable to all of them as a matter of law because any sincere belief was "created by Senator Shooter's false allegations and the `racially tinged' LaFaro video." Maj. Op. 99. The majority claims that these legislators were used as "cat's paws" to "serve the discriminatory purposes of Senator Shooter, Republican Chair LaFaro, and their allies." Maj. Op. 100. Yet, the majority's reliance on such employment discrimination doctrine is misplaced because, unlike employers whose decision may be tainted by the discriminatory motives of a supervisor, each legislator is an independent actor, and bias of some cannot be attributed to all members. The very fact that some members had a sincere belief that voter fraud needed to be addressed is enough to rebut the majority's conclusion. To the contrary, the underlying allegations of voter fraud did not need to be true in order to justify the "legitimacy or importance of the State's interest in counting only the votes of eligible voters." Crawford, 553 U.S. at 196. And the majority provides no support for its inference of pretext where there is a sincere and legitimate interest in addressing a valid concern. Maj. Op. at 97-100. Instead, the majority accepts the district court's finding that some legislators "had a sincere, non-race-based belief that there was fraud" that needed to be addressed. Nevertheless, unable to locate any discriminatory purpose, it simply attributes one to them using the inapplicable "cat's paw doctrine." Maj. Op. 99. Such argument demonstrates the extraordinary leap in logic the majority must make in order to justify its conclusion.

Let me restate the obvious: we may reverse the district court's intensely factual determination as to discriminatory intent only if we determine that such finding was clearly erroneous. Thus, even if the majority disagrees with the district court's finding, it must demonstrate that the evidence was not "plausible in light of the record viewed in its entirety." Bessemer City, 470 U.S. at 574. Perhaps if the majority had reminded itself of our appellate standard, it would not have simply re-weighed the same evidence considered by the district court to arrive at its own findings on appeal.

V

The district court properly determined that neither Arizona's out-of-precinct policy nor its ballot-collection policy violates § 2 of the Voting Rights Act and the Fifteenth Amendment to the Constitution.[9] In concluding otherwise, the majority misperceives the inquiry before us and fails to narrow the scope of its review, instead insisting on acting as a de novo trial court. That, of course, is not our role.

I would therefore affirm the judgment of the district court and must respectfully dissent from the majority opinion.

Judge O'Scannlain's dissent in Edmo v. Corizon, Inc. (Feb 10, 2020) [Notes omitted]

O'SCANNLAIN, Circuit Judge,[*] with whom CALLAHAN, BEA, IKUTA, R. NELSON, BADE, BRESS, BUMATAY, and VANDYKE, Circuit Judges, join, respecting the denial of rehearing en banc:

With its decision today, our court becomes the first federal court of appeals to mandate that a State pay for and provide sex-reassignment surgery to a prisoner under the Eighth Amendment. The three-judge panel's conclusion— that any alternative course of treatment would be "cruel and unusual punishment"—is as unjustified as it is unprecedented. To reach such a conclusion, the court creates a circuit split, substitutes the medical conclusions of federal judges for the clinical judgments of prisoners' treating physicians, redefines the familiar "deliberate indifference" standard, and, in the end, constitutionally enshrines precise and partisan treatment criteria in what is a new, rapidly changing, and highly controversial area of medical practice.

Respectfully, I believe our court's unprecedented decision deserved reconsideration en banc.

I

A

In 2012, Adree Edmo (then known as Mason Dean Edmo) was incarcerated for sexually assaulting a sleeping 15-year-old boy. By all accounts, Edmo is afflicted with profound and complex mental illness. She[1] suffers from major depressive disorder, anxiety, alcohol addiction, and drug addiction. At least two clinicians have concluded that she shares the traits of borderline personality disorder. She abused alcohol and methamphetamines every day for many years, stopping only upon her incarceration. A victim of sexual abuse at an early age, she attempted suicide three times before her arrest for sexual assault—twice by overdose and once by cutting.

A new diagnosis was added in 2012: gender dysphoria. Two months after being transferred to the Idaho State Correctional Institution (a men's prison), Edmo sought to speak about hormone therapy with Dr. Scott Eliason, the Board-certified director of psychiatry for Corizon, Inc. (the prison's medical care provider). In Dr. Eliason's view,

Edmo met the criteria for gender dysphoria.[2] After the diagnosis was confirmed by another forensic psychiatrist and the prison's Management and Treatment Committee, Edmo was prescribed hormone therapy. She soon changed her legal name and the sex listed on her birth certificate. As a result of four years of hormone therapy, Edmo experienced physical changes, including breast development, redistribution of body fat, and a change in body odor. She now has the same circulating hormones as a typical adult female.

In April 2016, at Edmo's request, Dr. Eliason evaluated her for sex-reassignment surgery.[3] Ultimately, Dr. Eliason decided to maintain the current course of hormones and supportive counseling instead of prescribing surgery. He staffed Edmo's case with Dr. Jeremy Stoddart (a psychiatrist) and Dr. Murray Young (a physician who served as the Regional Medical Director for Corizon), as well as Jeremy Clark, a clinical supervisor and member of the World Professional Association for Transgender Health ("WPATH"). He also presented the evaluation and vetted it before the regular meeting of the multidisciplinary Management Treatment Committee.

Dr. Eliason, supported by Dr. Stoddart, Dr. Young, and Clark, opted not to recommend sex-reassignment surgery for several reasons, some of which are described in his chart notes and others of which were elaborated in their testimony. First, Dr. Eliason noted that Edmo reported that the hormone therapy had improved her dysphoria and Eliason "did not observe significant dysphoria." In the absence of more severe distress, Dr. Eliason could not justify the risks of pursuing the most aggressive—and permanent—treatment through surgery. Second, Dr. Eliason observed that Edmo's comorbid conditions—major depressive disorder and alcohol use disorder, among others—were not adequately controlled. Edmo had refused to attend therapy consistently in prison. She also engaged in self harm (including cutting and attempted castration) and exhibited co-dependency and persistently poor sexual boundaries with other prisoners. In Dr. Eliason's view, Edmo's other mental health disorders were not sufficiently stabilized to handle the stressful process of surgery and transition. Finally, Dr. Eliason observed that Edmo—who was parole-eligible and due to be released in 2021—had not lived among her out-of-prison social network as a woman. He noted the high suicide rates for postoperative patients and was concerned that Edmo might be at greater risk of suicide given the potential lack of support from family, friends, coworkers, and neighbors during her transition. Dr. Eliason did not rule out the possibility of Edmo receiving sex-reassignment surgery at some later point. As Dr. Eliason put it in his notes on his consultation with Edmo, "Medical Necessity for Sexual Reassignment Surgery is not very well defined and is constantly shifting." Citing the changing nature of the science and the contingent nature of his evaluation of Edmo, his recommendations were merely "for the time being."

B

About a year after her evaluation, Edmo filed this § 1983 lawsuit against Dr. Eliason, the Idaho Department of Corrections, Corizon, and several other individuals, alleging that the prison doctors' treatment choice violated her right to be free from cruel and unusual punishment under the Eighth and Fourteenth Amendments. She then moved for a preliminary injunction to require the prison to provide her with sex-reassignment surgery.

The district court held an evidentiary hearing on the motion. At the outset of the hearing, the court commented that it was hard "to envision" how a request to mandate sex-reassignment surgery could be granted through anything other than a permanent injunction. Nonetheless, the district court evaluated Edmo's motion under the preliminary injunction standard and, only out of "an abundance of caution," provided a footnote evaluating whether an injunction was merited under the more demanding standard for a permanent injunction (which the court erroneously described as "no more rigorous than that applicable to a claim for preliminary mandatory relief"). Edmo v. Idaho Dep't of Corr., 358 F. Supp. 3d 1103, 1122 n.1 (D. Idaho 2018); see Edmo v. Corizon, Inc., 935 F.3d 757, 784 n.13 (9th Cir. 2019) ("[T]he standard for granting permanent injunctive relief is higher (in that it requires actual success on the merits) . . . .").

In addition to testimony from Edmo, Dr. Eliason, and Jeremy Clark, the evidentiary hearing featured testimony from four expert witnesses. Edmo presented Dr. Randi Ettner, a psychologist, and Dr. Ryan Gorton, an emergency room physician. Dr. Ettner is one of the authors of the World Professional Association of Transgender Health's Standards of Care for the Health of Transsexual, Transgender, and Gender Nonconforming People and chairs WPATH's Committee for Institutionalized Persons. Dr. Gorton serves on that committee too. WPATH—formerly the Harry Benjamin International Gender Dysphoria Association— describes itself as a "professional association" devoted "to developing best practices and supportive policies worldwide that promote health, research, education, respect, dignity, and equality for transsexual, transgender, and gender nonconforming people in all cultural settings." World Prof'l Ass'n for Transgender Health, Standards of Care for the Health of Transsexual, Transgender, and Gender-Nonconforming People 1 (7th ed. 2011) ("WPATH Standards"). One of WPATH's central functions is to promulgate Standards of Care, which offer minimalist treatment criteria for several possible approaches to gender dysphoria, from puberty-blocking hormones to sex-reassignment surgery.

In addition to Dr. Eliason and Mr. Clark, the State presented Dr. Keelin Garvey, the Chief Psychiatrist of the Massachusetts Department of Corrections and chair of its Gender Dysphoria Treatment Committee, and Dr. Joel Andrade, a clinical social worker who served as clinical director for the Massachusetts Department of Corrections and served on its Gender Dysphoria Treatment Committee. Each set of experts had gaps in their relevant experience. Edmo's experts had never treated inmates with gender dysphoria, while the State's experts had never conducted long-term follow-up care with a patient who had undergone sex-reassignment surgery.

Edmo's experts testified that, in their opinion, Edmo needs sex-reassignment surgery. They based their conclusion on the latest edition of WPATH Standards of Care, which contain six criteria for sex-reassignment surgery:

(1) "persistent, well documented gender dysphoria,"

(2) "capacity to make a fully informed decision and to consent for treatment,"

(3) "age of majority,"

(4) "if significant medical or mental health concerns are present, they must be well controlled,"

(5) "12 continuous months of hormone therapy as appropriate to the patient's gender goals,"

(6) "12 continuous months of living in a gender role that is congruent with their gender identity."

Id. at 60. In the opinion of Edmo's experts, Edmo met all six criteria and was unlikely to show further improvement in her gender dysphoria without such surgery.

The State's experts disagreed on three main grounds. First, they did not regard the WPATH Standards as definitive treatment criteria, let alone medical consensus. In their analysis, the evidence underlying the WPATH Standards is not sufficiently well developed, particularly when it comes to the treatment of gender dysphoric prisoners. Therefore, they opined that a prudent, competent doctor might rely on clinical judgment that differs from the (already ambiguous) WPATH Standards. Second, the State's experts testified that, even under WPATH, Edmo failed to meet the fourth criterion for surgery, which requires that the patient's other mental health concerns be well controlled in order to reduce the risks associated with transitioning. In the view of the State's experts, her mental health raised the concern that she would have trouble transitioning. For their part, Edmo's experts argued that Edmo's depression and addiction were controlled enough for surgery and that some current symptoms (such as self-cutting) stem from her gender dysphoria and therefore can be alleviated with surgery. Finally, the State's experts testified that Edmo also failed to meet the WPATH Standards' sixth criterion for surgery, which requires that Edmo live as a woman for twelve months before surgery. In their view, it was essential that Edmo live those twelve months outside of prison—that is, within her social network—in order to be adequately sure that she and her social network are ready for the challenges posed by transitioning. Edmo's experts disagreed, noting that WPATH says treatment in prisons should "mirror" treatment outside of prisons.

C

Although this appeal is from a grant of a preliminary injunction, at some point the evidentiary hearing on the motion for a preliminary injunction was consolidated into a final bench trial on the merits. It is hard to know when (or if) the parties were given the requisite "clear and unambiguous notice" of consolidation. See Isaacson v. Horne, 716 F.3d 1213, 1220 (9th Cir. 2013); see also Univ. of Tex. v. Camenisch, 451 U.S. 390, 395 (1981).

The district court applied the Supreme Court's oft-cited rule that "deliberate indifference to serious medical needs of prisoners constitutes the `unnecessary and wanton infliction of pain' proscribed by the Eighth Amendment." Estelle v. Gamble, 429 U.S. 97, 104 (1976) (quoting Gregg v. Georgia, 428 U.S. 153, 173 (1976)). The State agreed that gender dysphoria is a serious medical need, so the only question on the merits is whether Dr. Eliason and his team were "deliberately indifferent" as a matter of law.

The district court concluded that the State's experts were "unconvincing" and gave their opinions "virtually no weight." Edmo, 358 F. Supp. 3d at 1125-26. Once such expert testimony was set aside, the district court held that any decision not to prescribe sex-reassignment surgery would be "medically unacceptable under the circumstances" and would therefore violate the Eighth Amendment. Id. at 1127. Accordingly, the district court entered an injunction ordering the State to "take all actions reasonably necessary to provide Ms. Edmo gender confirmation surgery as promptly as possible." Id. at 1129.

D

The panel has now affirmed the injunction. See Edmo, 935 F.3d at 803. Concluding that sex-reassignment surgery was "medically necessary" and that the prison officials chose a different course of treatment "with full awareness of the prisoner's suffering," the panel holds that Dr. Eliason and the other prison officials "violate[d] the Eighth Amendment's prohibition on cruel and unusual punishment." Id.

To reach its conclusion that sex-reassignment surgery was medically necessary, the panel spends most of its lengthy opinion extolling and explaining the WPATH Standards of Care. Because Dr. Eliason failed to "follow" or "reasonably deviate from" the WPATH Standards, the panel concluded that his treatment choice was "medically unacceptable under the circumstances." Id. at 792. To reach the ultimate conclusion—that Dr. Eliason had a deliberately indifferent state of mind and was consequently in violation of the Eighth Amendment—the panel posited that Dr. Eliason's awareness of the risks that Edmo would attempt to castrate herself or feel "clinically significant" distress "demonstrates that Dr. Eliason acted with deliberate indifference." Id. at 793. Each conclusion was legal error.

II

"Deliberate indifference is a high legal standard." Toguchi v. Chung, 391 F.3d 1051, 1060 (9th Cir. 2004). It is, after all, under governing precedent one form of the "unnecessary and wanton infliction of pain" that is the sine qua non of an Eighth Amendment violation. Estelle, 429 U.S. at 104 (quoting Gregg v. Georgia, 428 U.S. 153, 173 (1976)). Simply put, Edmo must prove that Dr. Eliason's chosen course of treatment was the doing of a criminally reckless—or worse—state of mind. Farmer v. Brennan, 511 U.S. 825, 839 (1994).

We have stated that a deliberately indifferent state of mind may be inferred when "the course of treatment the doctors chose was medically unacceptable under the circumstances" and "they chose this course in conscious disregard of an excessive risk to plaintiff's health." Jackson v. McIntosh, 90 F.3d 330, 332 (9th Cir. 1996). Yet even most objectively unreasonable medical care is not deliberately indifferent. "[M]ere `indifference,' `negligence,' or `medical malpractice'" is not enough to constitute deliberate indifference. Lemire v. Cal. Dep't of Corr. & Rehab., 726 F.3d 1062, 1082 (9th Cir. 2013) (quoting Broughton v. Cutter Labs., 622 F.2d 458, 460 (9th Cir. 1980)). "Even gross negligence is insufficient to establish deliberate indifference . . . ." Id. Likewise, "[a] difference of opinion between a physician and the prisoner— or between medical professionals—concerning what medical care is appropriate does not amount to deliberate indifference." Snow v. McDaniel, 681 F.3d 978, 987 (9th Cir. 2012) (citing Sanchez v. Vild, 891 F.2d 240, 242 (9th Cir. 1989)), overruled on other grounds by Peralta v. Dillard, 744 F.3d 1076, 1083 (9th Cir. 2014) (en banc). Although the panel organizes its opinion according to the dictum we first articulated in Jackson, it so contorts the standard as to render deliberate indifference exactly what we have said it is not: a constitutional prohibition on good-faith disagreement between medical professionals.

A

The panel first, and fundamentally, errs by misunderstanding what it means for a chosen treatment to be medically "unacceptable" for purposes of the Eighth Amendment. As did the district court, the panel concludes that the decision to continue hormone treatment and counseling instead of sex-reassignment surgery for Edmo was "medically unacceptable under the circumstances" because, in short, Dr. Eliason failed to "follow" or "reasonably deviate from" the WPATH Standards of Care. Edmo, 935 F.3d at 792. Yet such an approach to the Eighth Amendment suffers from three essential errors. First, contrary to the panel's suggestion, constitutionally acceptable medical care is not defined by the standards of one organization. Second, the panel relies on standards that were promulgated by a controversial self-described advocacy group that dresses ideological commitments as evidence-based conclusions. Third, once the WPATH Standards are put in proper perspective, we are left with a "case of dueling experts," compelling the conclusion that Dr. Eliason's treatment choice was indeed medically acceptable.

1

A mere professional association simply cannot define what qualifies as constitutionally acceptable treatment of prisoners with gender dysphoria. In Bell v. Wolfish, 441 U.S. 520 (1979), the Supreme Court rejected the argument that prison conditions must reflect those set forth in the American Public Health Association's Standards for Health Services in Correctional Institutions, the American Correctional Association's Manual of Standards for Adult Correctional Institutions, or the National Sheriffs' Association's Handbook on Jail Architecture. Id. at 543 n.27. According to the Court, "the recommendations of these various groups may be instructive in certain cases, [but] they simply do not establish the constitutional minima." Id. After all, even acclaimed, leading treatment criteria only represent the "goals recommended by the organization in question" and the views of the promulgating physicians,[4] and so, without more, a physician's disagreement with such criteria is simply the "`difference of medical opinion' . . . [that is] insufficient, as a matter of law, to establish deliberate indifference." Id.; Jackson, 90 F.3d at 332 (quoting Sanchez, 891 F.2d at 242); accord Snow, 681 F.3d at 987; see also Long v. Nix, 86 F.3d 761, 765 (8th Cir. 1996) ("[N]othing in the Eighth Amendment prevents prison doctors from exercising their independent medical judgment.").

In its discussion of the role of treatment standards, the panel fails to cite a single case in which a professional organization's standards of care defined the line between medically acceptable and unacceptable treatment. Instead, the panel cites two cases, one from the Seventh Circuit and one from the Eighth, for the proposition that professional organizations' standards of care are "highly relevant in determining what care is medically acceptable and unacceptable." Edmo, 935 F.3d at 786 (emphasis added). That may be. But as those two cases demonstrate, the range of medically acceptable care is defined by qualities of that care (or of its opposite) and not by professional associations. Medically unacceptable care is "grossly incompetent or inadequate care," Allard v. Baldwin, 779 F.3d 768, 772 (8th Cir. 2015), or care that constitutes "such a substantial departure from accepted professional judgment to demonstrate that the person responsible did not base the decision on . . . [accepted professional] judgment," Henderson v. Ghosh, 755 F.3d 559, 566 (7th Cir. 2014) (original parenthetical) (quoting McGee v. Adams, 721 F.3d 474, 481 (7th Cir. 2013) (stipulating that "medical professionals . . . are `entitled to deference in treatment decisions unless no minimally competent professional would have so responded'")). For its part, the First Circuit holds in its own sex-reassignment-surgery case that medical care does not violate the Eighth Amendment so long as it is "reasonably commensurate with the medical standards of prudent professionals." Kosilek v. Spencer, 774 F.3d 63, 90 (1st Cir. 2014) (en banc). The panel is alone in its insistence that a professional association's standards add up to the constitutional minima.[5]

2

In the words of the panel, speaking for our court, the WPATH Standards are "the gold standard," the "established standards" for evaluations of the necessity of sex-reassignment surgery, the "undisputed starting point in determining the appropriate treatment for gender dysphoric individuals." Edmo, 935 F.3d at 787-88, 788 n.16. But such overwrought acclaim is just the beginning of the panel's thorough enshrinement of the WPATH Standards. The district court chose which expert to rely on by looking at which expert hewed most closely to the WPATH Standards of Care. See Edmo, 358 F. Supp. 3d at 1124-26. And the panel uncritically approves such an approach, calling the WPATH Standards "a useful starting point for analyzing the credibility and weight to be given to each expert's opinion." Edmo, 935 F.3d at 788 n.16. By rejecting any expert not (in the court's view) appropriately deferential to WPATH, the district court and now the panel have effectively decided ab initio that only the WPATH Standards could constitute medically acceptable treatment.[6]

One would be forgiven for inferring from the panel's opinion that its bold assertions about the WPATH Standards are uncontroverted truths. But, as the Fifth Circuit has recognized, "the WPATH Standards of Care reflect not consensus, but merely one side in a sharply contested medical debate over sex reassignment surgery." Gibson v. Collier, 920 F.3d 212, 221 (5th Cir. 2019). For its part, the First Circuit, sitting en banc, has likewise held that "[p]rudent medical professionals . . . do reasonably differ in their opinions regarding [WPATH's] requirements." Kosilek, 774 F.3d at 88. Our court should have done the same.

The WPATH Standards are merely criteria promulgated by a controversial private organization with a declared point of view. According to Dr. Stephen Levine, author of the WPATH Standards' fifth version, former Chairman of WPATH's Standards of Care Committee, and the court-appointed expert in Kosilek, WPATH attempts to be "both a scientific organization and an advocacy group for the transgendered. These aspirations sometimes conflict." Id. at 78. Sometimes the pressure to be advocates wins the day. As Levine put it, "WPATH is supportive to those who want sex reassignment surgery. . . . Skepticism and strong alternate views are not well tolerated. Such views have been known to be greeted with antipathy from the large numbers of nonprofessional adults who attend each [of] the organization's biennial meetings . . . ." Id. (ellipses and brackets original). WPATH's own description of its drafting process makes this clear. Initially, the sections of the sixth version were each assigned to an individual member of WPATH who then published a literature review with suggested revisions. WPATH Standards, supra, at 109. The suggested revisions were then discussed and debated by a thirty-four-person Revision Committee, all before a subcommittee drafted the new document. Id. at 109-11. Only about half of the Revision Committee possesses a medical degree. The rest are sexologists, psychotherapists, or career activists, with a sociologist and a law professor rounding out the group. Id. at 111.

The pressure to be advocates appears to have won the day in the WPATH Standards' recommendations regarding institutionalized persons. Recall that one central point of contention between the State's witnesses and Edmo's was over whether Edmo's time undergoing hormone therapy in prison provides sufficient guarantee that she could live well outside of prison as a woman without having ever done so before. The district court resolved the debate by citing the WPATH Standards' section on institutionalized persons, see Edmo, 358 F. Supp. 3d at 1125, which tersely stipulates that institutionalized persons should not be "discriminated against" on the basis of their institutionalization, WPATH Standards, supra, at 67. Such a recommendation is not supported by any research about the similarity between prisoners' experiences with sex-reassignment surgery and that of the general public. Indeed, as Edmo's expert witness and WPATH author, Dr. Randi Ettner, admits, there is only one known instance of a person undergoing sex-reassignment surgery while incarcerated—leaving medical knowledge about how such surgery might differ totally undeveloped.

Instead, WPATH's recommendation for institutionalized persons merely expresses a policy preference. The article from which the recommendations are adapted stipulates upfront that, because WPATH's "mission" is "to advocate for nondiscriminatory" care, it presumes that treatment choices should be the same for all "demographic variables, unless there is a clinical indication to provide services in a different fashion." George R. Brown, Recommended Revisions to the World Professional Association for Transgender Health's Standards of Care Section on Medical Care for Incarcerated Persons with Gender Identity Disorder, 11 Int'l J. of Transgenderism 133, 134

(2009). Unable to make an evidentiary finding from a sample size of one, the article concludes that its presumption should set the standard of care and then proceeds to recommend revisions with the express purpose of influencing how courts review gender dysphoria treatments under the Eighth Amendment. Id. at 133, 135. As a later peer-reviewed study by Dr. Cynthia Osborne and Dr. Anne Lawrence put it, WPATH's institutionalized-persons recommendations follow from an "ethical principle," not "extensive clinical experience." Cynthia S. Osborne & Anne A. Lawrence, Male Prison Inmates With Gender Dysphoria: When Is Sex Reassignment Surgery Appropriate?, 45 Archives of Sexual Behav. 1649, 1651 (2016).

Even apart from the concerns over WPATH's ideological commitments, its evidentiary basis is not sufficient to justify the court's reliance on its strict terms. The WPATH Standards seem to suggest as much. In its own words, the WPATH Standards are simply "flexible clinical guidelines," which explicitly allow that "individual health professionals and programs may modify them." WPATH Standards, supra, at 2. Indeed, the most recent WPATH Standards "represents a significant departure from previous versions" in part due to significant changes in researchers' conclusions over the preceding decade. Id. at 1 n.2. Moreover, the WPATH Standards lack the evidence-based grading system that characterizes archetypal treatment guidelines, such as the Endocrine Society's hormone therapy guidelines. Lacking evidence-based grading, the WPATH Standards leave practitioners in the dark about the strength of a given recommendation. See William Byne et al., Report of the American Psychiatric Association Task Force on Treatment of Gender Identity Disorder, 41 Archives of Sexual Behav. 759, 783 (2012) (concluding that "the level of evidence" supporting WPATH's Standards' criteria for sex-reassignment surgery "was generally low"). For these reasons, the Centers for Medicare & Medicaid Services, an agency of the United States Department of Health and Human Services, decided, "[b]ased on a thorough review of the clinical evidence," that providers may consult treatment criteria other than WPATH, including providers' own criteria. Ctrs. for Medicare & Medicaid Servs, Proposed Decision Memo for Gender Dysphoria and Gender Reassignment Surgery (June 2, 2016); Ctrs. for Medicare & Medicaid Servs, Decision Memo for Gender Dysphoria and Gender Reassignment Surgery (Aug. 30, 2016).

3

The panel's disposition results from its failure to put the WPATH Standards in proper perspective. Had the district court understood that Edmo's experts' role in WPATH marks them not with special insight into the legally acceptable care, but rather as mere participants in an ongoing medical debate, they would have acknowledged this case for what it is: a "case of dueling experts." Edmo, 935 F.3d at 787. Instead of giving Drs. Garvey and Andrade (to say nothing of Dr. Eliason) "no weight" due to their insufficient fealty to WPATH, the district court should have recognized them as legitimate, experienced participants in that debate. And had the State's experts' criticisms of and interpretation of the WPATH Standards been given proper weight—any weight at all—the district court would have had to conclude that the State's disagreement with Edmo's experts was a mere "difference of medical opinion," not a constitutional violation. Jackson, 90 F.3d at 332.

So too with its assessment of Dr. Eliason's treatment choice. It is instructive that the worst the district court can say about Dr. Eliason is that he "did not apply the WPATH criteria." Edmo, 358 F. Supp. 3d at 1126. Focusing the analysis not on whether Dr. Eliason applied the standards of a professional association but rather on whether the treatment choice was within that of a prudent, competent practitioner, the cautious treatment selected by Dr. Eliason is plainly constitutionally acceptable.

As Drs. Garvey and Andrade explain, it is medically acceptable to offer Edmo a treatment of hormone therapy and psychotherapy but not sex-reassignment surgery. The practitioners' fear that sex-reassignment surgery would exacerbate Edmo's other mental illnesses and increase the risk of surgery was a genuine and sound fear. As Dr. Garvey put it, "[b]ased on her current coping strategies, I would be concerned about her suicide risk after surgery." Although the measured "regret rate," which refers to the proportion of postoperative patients who regret their surgery, is "low," see Edmo, 935 F.3d at 771, the district court and the panel failed to acknowledge detailed testimony that those studies neglected to follow up with such a high proportion of the observed sample that the stated figure does not "represent the full picture." In Dr. Andrade's opinion, "I think there are things she needs to work out in therapy in the short and long term before she can make a really well-informed decision about surgery." He raised the concern that Edmo is particularly at risk because of "unresolved trauma" that may stem, not from gender dysphoria, but instead from past sexual abuse.

Dr. Eliason's view that Edmo needed to have lived as a woman outside of prison in order to ensure that she would be able to adapt well after the surgery was also legitimate. Indeed, under the peer-reviewed treatment criteria developed by Drs. Osborne and Lawrence, Edmo was not eligible for sex-reassignment surgery for these exact reasons. Acknowledging the lack of evidence concerning the effects of sex-reassignment surgery on inmates, the unique challenges imposed by the correctional setting, and the significant risk of patient regret, Drs. Osborne and Lawrence proposed criteria that require a prospective patient have "a satisfactory disciplinary record and demonstrated capacity to cooperate" and "a long period of expected incarceration after [surgery]," among others. Osborne & Lawrence, supra, at 1661. This latter criterion helps to ensure that male-to-female patients have "a longer period of time to consolidate one's feminine gender identity and gender role." Id. at 1660; see also id. at 1656 ("[I]nmates with [gender dysphoria] who attempt to live in female-typical gender roles within men's prisons . . . could not effectively prepare" for life after surgery.) The district court disregarded such additional, peer-reviewed treatment criteria because they "are not part of the WPATH criteria and are in opposition to the WPATH Standards of Care." Edmo, 358 F. Supp. 3d at 1126. Had the district court taken a step back and considered not whether Osborne and Lawrence were WPATH-compliant but rather whether a competent physician could rely on their reasoning, it would have had to conclude that Dr. Eliason's treatment choice was that of a competent, prudent physician.

Perhaps recognizing such problems with the district court's definition of medical unacceptability, the panel concludes its medical-unacceptability analysis by changing the subject. Instead of considering whether Dr. Eliason's choice of treatment was medically unacceptable, the panel fixates on Dr. Eliason's chart notes, which sets forth three general categories in which he believes sex-reassignment surgery may be required: (1) "Congenital malformation or ambiguous genitalia," (2) "Severe and devastating dysphoria that is primarily due to genitals," (3) or "Some type of medical problem in which endogenous sexual hormones were causing severe physiological damage." According to the panel, such categories "bear little resemblance" to the WPATH Standards and therefore "Dr. Eliason's evaluation was not an exercise of medically acceptable professional judgment." Edmo, 935 F.3d at 791-92. In the first place, Dr. Eliason's categories are not meant to substitute for treatment standards. Such categories describe three broad pools of eligible patients; whether a particular patient belongs in a certain pool—by having dysphoria sufficiently severe to require sex-reassignment surgery, for instance— would be resolved by more detailed evaluative criteria. In the second place, conformity to WPATH is not the test of constitutionally acceptable treatment of gender dysphoria. But more broadly, the panel simply asks the wrong question. Deliberate indifference may be inferred when "the course of treatment the doctors chose was medically unacceptable under the circumstances," not when the doctors' contemporaneous explanation of the choice is incomplete. Jackson, 90 F.3d at 332 (emphasis added); see also Snow, 681 F.3d at 988; Toguchi, 391 F.3d at 1058; Hamby v. Hammond, 821 F.3d 1085, 1092 (9th Cir. 2016) (all referring to the "course of treatment," not the rationale). It does not matter that Dr. Eliason's testimony justifies his treatment choice in ways not explicit in his chart notes such that the panel calls his testimony a "post hoc explanation." Edmo, 935 F.3d at 791. So long as the ultimate treatment choice was medically acceptable, our precedents tell us, we cannot infer "the unnecessary and wanton infliction of pain" that violates the Eighth Amendment.

B

Even were the panel correct that the only medically acceptable way to approach a gender dysphoric patient's request for sex-reassignment surgery is to apply the WPATH Standards of Care, we still could not infer a constitutional violation from these facts. As the Supreme Court has explained, the Eighth Amendment simply proscribes categories of punishment, and punishment is "a deliberate act intended to chastise or deter." Wilson v. Seiter, 501 U.S. 294, 299-300 (1991). "[O]nly the `unnecessary and wanton infliction of pain' implicates the Eighth Amendment." Id. at 297 (quoting Estelle, 429 U.S. at 104) (emphasis original). Hence the commonplace deliberate-indifference inquiry, which is a culpability standard equivalent to criminal recklessness. Farmer, 511 U.S. at 839-40. Simply put, unless the official "knows of and disregards an excessive risk to inmate health and safety," he does not violate the Eighth Amendment. Id. at 837.

1

With little explanation, the panel castigates Dr. Eliason for having "disregarded" risks that he directly and forthrightly addressed. Edmo, 935 F.3d at 793. Far from disregarding the risk that Edmo would attempt to castrate herself, Dr. Eliason investigated the causes of such a risk and took concrete steps to mitigate it. Edmo's self-harm (including her castration attempts) followed closely after her disciplinary infractions and other severe stressors. Identifying this causal connection, Dr. Eliason prescribed and encouraged regular counseling to address Edmo's acting out and her ability to cope. Dr. Eliason also sought to further deter self-castration by explaining to Edmo that she will need to have intact genitals for any eventual surgery, something Edmo now understands and articulated in her testimony. Likewise, contrary to the panel's conclusion that he disregarded the risk of continued distress, Dr. Eliason opted for a treatment of continued hormone therapy and more regular supportive counseling precisely because hormone therapy had already substantially ameliorated the distress from the dysphoria.

Furthermore, the panel errs by fixating on such individual risks. Physicians ministrate to whole individuals with whole diseases. Thus, individual risks may—and frequently do—persist for the sake of the overall health of the person. Dr. Eliason and his staff clearly believed their treatment choice would mitigate overall risk, including grave risks the panel downplays. Given Edmo's long-term struggles with severe depression and addiction, coupled with the fact that she had not lived as a woman within her social network, Eliason and the other doctors with whom he staffed the evaluation were concerned that she would have trouble adjusting after surgery, which could lead to regret, relapse, or new mood disorders. Ultimately, they worried that she might attempt suicide again. Such risks are not trifling and, in light of them, Dr. Eliason's willingness to accept some risk that Edmo would try to castrate herself or would continue to feel the distress of gender dysphoria (while taking steps to mitigate such risks) is anything but deliberately indifferent.

2

None of this is to acquiesce in the straw-man argument set up by the panel: that, so long as officials provide some care, they are immunized from an Eighth Amendment claim. One may assume that some medical care is indeed so obviously inadequate that, without any direct evidence of the defendant's state of mind, we may infer that the defendant was deliberately indifferent. See Farmer, 511 U.S. at 842 (remarking that deliberate indifference is "subject to demonstration in the usual ways, including inference from circumstantial evidence" and may be inferred "from the very fact that the risk was obvious").[7] But that is not this case.

Even in a legal universe in which the WPATH Standards define adequate care, Dr. Eliason's deviations were not deliberately indifferent. He selected a course of treatment that, in light of the complex of diagnoses, the grave risks, and the rapidly evolving nature of the medical research, was not obviously inadequate. Cf. Lemire, 726 F.3d at 1075 ("A prison official's deliberately indifferent conduct will generally `shock the conscience' so long as the prison official had time to deliberate before acting . . . ."). He subjected his assessment to a review process intended to surface any possibility he was not considering, a review process that included several doctors and a full committee. And far from being an "unjustifiable" or "gross" deviation from the WPATH Standards, he departed from WPATH by raising the Standards' own concerns for the presence of comorbid conditions and the patient's limited experience as a woman. See Farmer, 511 U.S. at 839 (incorporating the Model Penal Code's definition of criminal recklessness); Model Penal Code § 2.02(2)(c) (1985) (stating that the criminally reckless individual "disregards a substantial and unjustifiable risk" and that such disregard "involves a gross deviation from the standard of conduct that a law-abiding person would observe in the actor's situation."). Indeed, the panel concludes that his deviations were simply not "reasonable"—the test for negligent malpractice, not deliberate indifference. Edmo, 935 F.3d at 792. "Eighth Amendment liability requires `more than ordinary lack of due care . . . .'" Farmer, 511 U.S. at 835 (quoting Whitley v. Albers, 475 U.S. 312, 319 (1986)).

III

The panel's novel approach to Eighth Amendment claims for sex-reassignment surgery conflicts with every other circuit to consider the issue. The panel acknowledges such a circuit split with the Fifth Circuit's opinion in Gibson v. Collier, 920 F.3d 212 (5th Cir. 2019), but tries—and fails—to distinguish the First Circuit's en banc opinion in Kosilek v. Spencer, 774 F.3d 63 (1st Cir. 2014). See Edmo, 935 F.3d at 794-95. The panel does not even address a third decision: the Tenth Circuit's opinion in Lamb v. Norwood, 899 F.3d 1159 (10th Cir. 2018).

Just as in this case, the First Circuit considered an appeal of an injunction mandating sex-reassignment surgery. But, unlike our court, the First Circuit reversed. Though the panel attempts to downplay the direct conflict between its opinion and Kosilek by pointing to minor differences between the factual circumstances in each case,[8] the decisive differences are matters of law. As to whether the care was medically unacceptable, the First Circuit held that medically acceptable treatment of gender dysphoric prisoners is not synonymous with the demands of WPATH. Kosilek first reversed the district court's finding that one of the State's experts was "illegitimate" because the district court "made a significantly flawed inferential leap: it relied on its own— non-medical—judgment" and put too much "weight" on the WPATH Standards. Kosilek, 774 F.3d at 87-88. With that expert now taken seriously, the First Circuit held that the denial of Kosilek's sex-reassignment surgery was medically acceptable because it was within the bounds of "the medical standards of prudent professionals." Id. at 90. On the question of deliberate indifference, the First Circuit applied a test, which, unlike the panel's inference from the practitioners' mere knowledge that a course of treatment carried risks, asked whether the practitioners "knew or should have known" that course of treatment was medically unacceptable. Id. at 91.

For its part, the Fifth Circuit has held that good faith denial of sex-reassignment surgery never violates the Eighth Amendment. Recognizing "large gaps" in medical knowledge and a "robust and substantial good faith disagreement dividing respected members of the expert medical community," the Fifth Circuit concluded that "there can be no claim [for sex-reassignment surgery] under the Eighth Amendment." Gibson, 920 F.3d at 220, 222. Indeed, Texas's refusal to even evaluate the inmate for sex-reassignment surgery is, in the words of the Fifth Circuit, not "so unconscionable as to fall below society's minimum standards of decency" and permit an Eighth Amendment claim. Id. at 216 (quoting Kosilek, 774 F.3d at 96).

Finally, the Tenth Circuit has upheld the entry of summary judgment against a prisoner's Eighth Amendment claim for sex-reassignment surgery. See Lamb, 899 F.3d at 1163. As in this case, the doctor who evaluated the prisoner in Lamb determined that "surgery is impractical and unnecessary in light of the availability and effectiveness of more conservative therapies." Id. Adopting Kosilek's subjective standard—that an Eighth Amendment violation would take place "only if prison officials had known or should have known" that "sex reassignment surgery [was] the only medically adequate treatment"—the Tenth Circuit held that "prison officials could not have been deliberately indifferent by implementing the course of treatment recommended by a licensed medical doctor." Id. at 1163 & n.11 (citing Kosilek, 774 F.3d at 91).

Although I am not aware of any other circuits to have directly addressed the questions posed in this case,[9] for its part, the Seventh Circuit has held that it is at least not "clearly established" that there is a constitutional right to gender-dysphoria treatment beyond hormone therapy. Campbell v. Kallas, 936 F.3d 536, 549 (7th Cir. 2019). Nor is it "clearly established" that a prison medical provider is prohibited from denying sex-reassignment surgery on the basis of the patient's status as an institutionalized person. Id. at 541, 549.

With this decision, our circuit sets itself apart.

IV

I do not know whether sex-reassignment surgery will ameliorate or exacerbate Adree Edmo's suffering. Fortunately, the Constitution does not ask federal judges to put on white coats and decide vexed questions of psychiatric medicine. The Eighth Amendment forbids the "unnecessary and wanton infliction of pain," not the "difference of opinion between a physician and the prisoner—or between medical professionals." Snow, 681 F.3d at 985, 987 (quoting Estelle, 429 U.S. at 104).

Yet today our court assumes the role of Clinical Advisory Committee. Far from rendering an opinion "individual to Edmo" that "rests on the record," Edmo, 935 F.3d at 767, the panel entrenches the district court's unfortunate legal errors as the law of this circuit. Instead of permitting prudent, competent patient care, our court enshrines the WPATH Standards as an enforceable "medical consensus," effectively putting an ideologically driven private organization in control of every relationship between a doctor and a gender dysphoric prisoner within our circuit. Instead of reserving the Eighth Amendment for the grossly, unjustifiably reckless, the panel infers a culpable state of mind from the supposed inadequacy of the treatment.

We have applied the traditional deliberate-indifference standard to requests for back surgery, kidney transplant, hip replacement, antipsychotic medication, and hernia surgery. Yet suddenly the request for sex-reassignment surgery—and the panel's closing appeal to what it calls the "increased social awareness" of the needs and wants of transgender citizens—effects a revolution in our law! Id. at 803. The temptation to stand at what we are told is society's next frontier and to invent a constitutional right to state-funded sex-reassignment surgery does not justify the revision of previously universal principles of Eighth Amendment jurisprudence.

Dr. Eliason and the State's other practitioners were not deliberately indifferent—far from it. And they certainly were not guilty of violating the Eighth Amendment. They confronted the serious risks to Edmo's health, especially the gravest one. They considered the knotty quandary posed by her overlapping illnesses and the vicissitudes of her life. Mindful of the dictate "first do no harm," these doctors determined that the appropriate treatment would be more cautious and more reversible than the one the patient desired. And they did so in the shadow of the ongoing debate about when the surgical replacement of the genitals is curative and when it is not.

Surely this was not cruel and unusual punishment.

[*] As a judge of this court in senior status, I no longer have the power to vote on calls for rehearing cases en banc or formally to join a dissent from failure to rehear en banc. See 28 U.S.C. § 46(c); Fed. R. App. P. 35(a). Following our court's general orders, however, I may participate in discussions of en banc proceedings. See Ninth Circuit General Order 5.5(a).

Judge O'Scannlain's dissent in Baker v. Ryan (March 13, 2020)

O'SCANNLAIN, J., dissenting:

The majority decides this case on the basis that there was no adjudication on the merits in state court. However, Baker never argued, either at the district court or before this Court, that the prior state court judgment was not an adjudication on the merits as to the State. And this Court "will not ordinarily consider matters on appeal that are not specifically and distinctly argued in appellant's opening brief." Miller v. Fairchild Industries, Inc., 797 F.2d 727, 738 (9th Cir. 1986). In fact, even in open court, Baker's counsel conceded that the issue was never raised and did not even attempt to make the argument, despite the Court's invitations. In respectful disagreement with the majority's statement in footnote 1, I am reluctant to overlook Baker's waiver, and thus I respectfully dissent.

In any event, I am persuaded that Ryan, in his official capacity, was in privity with the State. Ariz. Downs v. Super. Ct. of Ariz., Maricopa Cty., 623 P.2d 1229, 1232 (Ariz. 1981). Baker sought the same injunctive relief against the State that he now seeks against Ryan. Indeed, at oral argument, Baker's counsel even conceded that there was privity. Furthermore, Baker's claims stem from identical facts, and the complaints in both suits are virtually identical.

I would affirm the decision of the district court.

Judge O'Scannlain's dissent in Great-West Life & Annuity Insurance Co. v. Harrington (August 5, 2020) [Notes omitted]

O'SCANNLAIN, J., dissenting.

I respectfully dissent from Parts 1 and 3 of the court's disposition, which reverses the district court's grant of summary judgment and orders a jury trial. In my view, there is no genuine dispute that Harrington made material misrepresentations in his disability insurance application, and I would affirm the judgment of the district court in its entirety.

I

The majority ignores that it is undisputed that Harrington failed to disclose his neck pain and a paresthesia medical diagnosis in his initial application to Great-West. In his initial application, when asked if, in the past ten years he had "backache . . . disorder of the muscles or bones, including joint and spine" Harrington responded "no." Likewise, when asked if, in the past five years, he "had a checkup, consultation, illness, surgery, injury, or disease not mentioned in [previous questions]," he responded "no." Yet, the record reveals that on December 9, 2011, he visited Dr. Kristin Pena, a physician, who diagnosed him with the medical condition of "paresthesia—related to chronic neck strain." Indeed, Harrington does not even dispute that this information was not disclosed on the initial application. Such a failure to disclose constitutes a misrepresentation. Essex Ins. Co. v. Galilee Medical Center SC, 988 F. Supp. 2d 866, 871 (N.D. Ill. 2013).

And Harrington made further misrepresentations in failing to disclose his chiropractic treatments. It is undisputed that Harrington was treated by Dr. Michael Peck, a chiropractor, four times, twice for bilateral hand/finger numbness, and the other times were for back and neck problems. It is also undisputed that Harrington never disclosed any of these visits either in the initial application or in the follow-up questionnaire.

Harrington admitted in his deposition that a "consultation" includes a visit to a chiropractor. Yet, he still answered "no" on the initial application. The majority argues that it is not certain what "consultation" means, especially since the application was a "medical questionnaire," and therefore it could be disputed whether or not Harrington engaged in a misrepresentation by failing to disclose his visits to a chiropractor. Yet neither party disputes that a consultation would include a visit to a chiropractor, and the court should not read in ambiguity where none exists. See Cohen v. Washington Nat'l Ins. Co., 529 N.E.2d 1065, 1066-67 (Ill. App. Ct. 1986).

II

After Great-West received the Dr. Pena medical records, it sent Harrington a "Musculoskeletal Questionnaire" to obtain more information. Instead of providing the requested information, Harrington simply stated, "This is an inaccurate medical record and does not exist" and failed to fill out the rest of the questionnaire. Still attempting to obtain information, Great-West sent a second Musculoskeletal Questionnaire to which Harrington responded "This was a one time occurrence do [sic] to a poor nights [sic] sleep. The condition resolved the next day so no follow was indicated." Even when given the opportunity to correct his prior misrepresentation, Harrington still continued to provide inaccurate information. Particularly troubling, he even attempted to get Dr. Pena's office to change the medical record so that there would be no reference to a paresthesia diagnosis.

The majority asserts that the questions in the Musculoskeletal Questionnaire were ambiguous because it asked principally about "chronic neck strain" and only secondarily about "paresthesia." Yet, even though Harrington was sent the same questionnaire twice, he made no effort to clarify its language. Furthermore, the fact that he responded it was a "one time occurrence" and made efforts to have his medical records changed indicates that he knew of the significance of Dr. Pena's diagnosis. Harrington's failure to disclose Dr. Pena's paresthesia and neck strain diagnosis and corresponding treatment constituted a false assertion that indeed affected the risk taken by the insurer. Essex Ins. Co., 988 F. Supp. 2d at 871.

Finally, it is undisputed that Harrington did not disclose his treatments by Dr. Peck on the Musculoskeletal Questionnaire. One question specifically asked for the contact information of any treating chiropractors, but Harrington did not provide Dr. Peck's contact information even though he had been treated for bilateral hand/finger numbness (paresthesia) and neck pain, the very conditions that were the subject of the questionnaire. It appears that Harrington did indeed understand the information that the questionnaire sought because he also went back to Dr. Peck and asked him to change his records to indicate that Harrington never had hand/finger numbness or neck pain. Harrington's failure to disclose chiropractic treatments constituted a misrepresentation that affected the risk taken by the insurer. Essex Ins. Co., 988 F. Supp. 2d at 871.

III

Such misrepresentations were indeed material because, as Great-West underwriter Ami Hanson testified, had Great-West known Harrington's complete medical and treatment history, it would not have issued the coverage that it did, and the testimony of an underwriter is sufficient to establish materiality under Illinois law. Id. at 873. Great-West was entitled to rescission as a matter of law.[1] Essex Ins. Co., 988 F. Supp. 2d at 871. Summary judgment was properly granted; I would affirm the decision of the district court.[2]

Judge O'Scannlain's dissent in Harvest Rock Church, Inc. v. Newsom (Oct 1, 2020) [Notes omitted]

O'SCANNLAIN, J., dissenting:

At present, in 18 counties in California—home to more than 15 million residents and including its most populous county, Los Angeles—indoor religious worship services are completely prohibited.[1] California insists that this drastic measure is necessary to fight the ongoing global COVID-19 pandemic—a worthy and indeed compelling goal of any State. Yet, in these same counties, the State still allows people to go indoors to: spend a day shopping in the mall, have their hair styled, get a manicure or pedicure, attend college classes, produce a television show or movie, participate in professional sports, wash their clothes at a laundromat, and even work in a meatpacking plant.

The Constitution allows a State to impose certain calculated, neutral restrictions—even against churches and religious believers—necessary to combat emergent threats to public health. But the Constitution, emphatically, does not allow a State to pursue such measures against religious practices more aggressively than it does against comparable secular activities. See Calvary Chapel Dayton Valley v. Sisolak, 140 S. Ct. 2603, 2605 (2020) (mem.) (Alito, J., dissenting); South Bay United Pentecostal Church v. Newsom, 140 S. Ct. 1613, 1615 (2020) (mem.) (Kavanaugh, J., dissenting). Because California's present coronavirus-related initiatives do exactly that, I respectfully dissent from the majority's decision not to enjoin them pending Harvest Rock Church's appeal in this case.

I

I first clarify a point that is somewhat obscured by the majority's decision: we are neither bound nor meaningfully guided by the Supreme Court's decision to deny a writ of injunction against California's restrictions on religious worship services earlier this year. See South Bay United Pentecostal Church, 140 S. Ct. at 1613. That decision, which considered a challenge to an earlier and much different iteration of California's restrictions, was unaccompanied by any opinion of the Court and thus is precedential only as to "the precise issues presented and necessarily decided." Mandel v. Bradley, 432 U.S. 173, 176 (U.S. 1977) (per curiam). In that case, the Supreme Court considered whether to issue a writ of injunction under the All Writs Act, 28 U.S.C. § 1651(a), a more demanding standard than that which applies to the motion for an injunction pending appeal here. Compare Hobby Lobby Stores, Inc. v. Sebelius, 568 U.S. 1401, 1403 (2012) (Sotomayor, J., as Circuit Justice) (discussing the standard for issuing a writ of injunction, which is an "extraordinary" measure to be "used sparingly" and "only when it is necessary or appropriate in aid of our jurisdiction and the legal rights at issue are indisputably clear" (alterations and internal quotation marks omitted)), with Se. Alaska Conservation Council v. U.S. Army Corps of Eng'rs, 472 F.3d 1097, 1100 (9th Cir. 2006) ("In deciding whether to grant an injunction pending appeal, the court balances the plaintiff's likelihood of success against the relative hardship to the parties." (internal quotation marks omitted)). Without any opinion of the Court, we have no guidance whatsoever—not even in the form of "dicta" as the majority suggests, Maj. at 4—as to why the Court declined to provide such an extraordinary remedy, and we certainly have no basis to infer that a majority of the Court agreed upon some unstated rationale that somehow applies equally here.[2] Cf. Makekau v. Hawaii, 943 F.3d 1200, 1205 (9th Cir. 2019) ("[T]he mere fact that the injunction order issued under the All Writs Act does not prove that the Supreme Court . . . addressed the merits [of the underlying claim].").

II

Turning to the motion before us, I respectfully disagree with the majority's conclusion that Harvest Rock Church is unlikely to succeed on the merits of its free exercise challenge to California's severe restrictions on religious worship in the State.

There is no doubt that California's COVID-19 scheme (described more fully below) imposes direct and severe burdens on religious practice within the State. And where a State imposes such burdens through measures that are not "neutral and of general applicability," its actions must survive strict scrutiny. Church of the Lukumi Babalu Aye, Inc. v. City of Hialeah, 508 U.S. 520, 531-32 (1993). "The Free Exercise Clause bars even subtle departures from neutrality on matters of religion." Masterpiece Cakeshop, Ltd. v. Colo. Civil Rights Comm'n, 138 S. Ct. 1719, 1731 (2018) (internal quotation marks omitted). Because California's COVID-19 regulations patently disfavor religious practice when compared to analogous secular activities, I believe that the church is quite likely indeed to succeed on the merits of its challenge to such regulations.

A

First, California's complex morass of COVID-related restrictions fails even the "minimum requirement of neutrality": such restrictions discriminate against religious practice "on [their] face." Lukumi, 508 U.S. at 533.

Contrary to how California would portray its scheme, at this point there is no "neutral" or "generally applicable" State policy that one can apply to determine whether or to what extent any particular activity is permissible. Instead, California has announced a variegated and ever-changing "Blueprint for a Safer Economy," which regulates all manner of in-person activities by meticulously delineating those activities which may take place. See State of California, Blueprint for a Safer Economy (last updated Oct. 1, 2020), https://covid19.ca.gov/safer-economy [hereinafter "Cal. Blueprint"]. Despite its deceptively cohesive title, this "Blueprint" is in reality an amalgamation of dozens of independent restrictions and "guidance" documents, each of which pertains only to a specific category of activity within the State. There are, at this point, independent restrictions targeted to nearly forty categories of activity (many of them further subdivided into more categories), including retail shopping outlets, grocery stores, offices, fitness centers, places of higher education, schools, barbershops, warehouses, food packing facilities, film and television studios, family entertainment centers, museums, professional sports facilities, and "places of worship." See State of California, COVID-19 Industry Guidance (last updated Sept. 29, 2020), https://covid19.ca.gov/industry-guidance [hereinafter "Industry Guidance"]. Under this patchwork scheme, it is the State's substantive categorization of an activity that determines its level of regulation, not any "neutral" or "generally applicable" feature of that activity itself.

Relevant here, the restrictions prescribed for "places of worship" limit attendance at in-person worship services as follows: (1) at the most severe, in counties designated to be "Tier 1" risks for COVID-19 spread,[3] no in-person worship services may be held; (2) in Tier 2 counties, worship services may be held with no more than 25% of a building's capacity or 100 persons in attendance, whichever is fewer; (3) in Tier 3 counties, worship services can be held with no more than 50% of a building's capacity or 200 persons in attendance, whichever is fewer; and, finally, (4) in Tier 4 counties, worship services can be held with no more than 50% of a building's capacity, with no additional cap on attendance. State of California, Covid-19 Blueprint Activity and Business Tiers 1 (last updated Sept. 28, 2020), https://www.cdph.ca.gov/Programs/CID/DCDC/ CDPH%20Document%20Library/COVID-19/Dimmer-Framework-September_2020.pdf [hereinafter "Blueprint Tiers"]. Critically, these same parameters do not apply broadly to all activities that might appear to be conducted in a manner similar to religious services— for example, educational events, meetings, or seminars. Instead, each of these (and many other potentially similar) activities is regulated entirely separately from, and often more leniently than, religious services. See Industry Guidance, supra (providing restrictions separately governing institutes of higher education, museums, theaters, and schools); see also, e.g., State of California, COVID-19 Essential Workforce (last updated Sept. 22, 2020), https://covid19.ca.gov/essential-workforce [hereinafter "Essential Workforce"] (designating as "essential workforce"—and therefore exempt from other COVID-19 restrictions—"academies and training facilities and courses for the purposes of graduating students and cadets that comprise the essential workforce for all identified critical sectors"). Indeed, even non-worship activities conducted by or within a place of worship are not subject to the attendance parameters outlined above. See Cal. Dep't of Pub. Health, COVID-19 Industry Guidance: Places of Worship and Providers of Religious Services and Cultural Ceremonies 3 (July 29, 2020) [hereinafter "Places of Worship Guidance"].

In sum, the restrictions on religious worship services that Harvest Rock Church challenges here apply because—and only because—the activities they wish the host and partake in have been identified, substantively, as "religious" or "worship" services.

B

California contends that the many idiosyncratic lines it has drawn between activities within the State are not actually tied to the substantive content of those activities but instead reflect the State's expert judgment regarding the risk that each activity presents of spreading COVID-19. The majority accepts the State's characterization, insisting that "the Governor offered the declaration of an expert . . . in support of the claim that the risk of COVID-19 is elevated in indoor congregate activities, including in-person worship services." Maj. at 3. The problem, however, is that the very features that California's expert identified as especially dangerous in religious worship appear to have been ignored by the State in its decision to allow numerous other activities to occur, even though they self-evidently exhibit the same features.

California's epidemiological expert, Dr. James Watt, declared that the State determined church attendance to be particularly risky because: (1) gatherings of "people from different households" increase the risk of spreading the virus; (2) there have been "multiple reports" of COVID-19 spread resulting from religious events; (3) the virus is more likely to spread "when people are in close contact or proximity with one another (within about six feet)"; (4) the risk of transmission increases in groups where people speak, chant, shout, and sing in close proximity indoors; and (5) gatherings with "longer duration" increase the opportunity for the virus to spread. In his declaration, Dr. Watt distinguished the threat posed by religious services from the supposedly lesser threat posed by shopping in a store or working in an office where, according to him (but with no evidence or expertise in support),[4] interpersonal encounters are much briefer or more easily regulated.

1

The first flaw in the majority's uncritical acceptance of this "evidence" supporting California's severe restrictions on church attendance is that the bulk of the identified risk factors have already been addressed by other measures imposed by the State. In those counties where indoor worship is actually allowed to take place, congregants must observe six-foot distancing, must wear masks, and may not sing or chant. See generally Places of Worship Guidance, supra. With such measures in place, Dr. Watt's professed concerns about physical proximity and vocal projections fall flat. How would the State distinguish a physically distanced, masked, and silent congregation sitting in a church from any other setting where the same number of people are present under the same roof for any other purpose? We do not know the answer, and I question whether the State could supply one that is neutral as to the practice of religion.

2

More centrally, even if we were to accept Dr. Watt's assertion that the State has reason to find religious services more dangerous than activities like shopping or working in an office, the glaring problem for the State is that it has offered no evidence to support the notion that the myriad other activities which are less restricted than religious services are somehow safer by these same parameters. The State more freely allows an abundance activities to take place which, on their face, share the same risk factors that Dr. Watt identified as so concerning about church attendance, including: having one's hair cut and styled at a salon;[5] getting a manicure or pedicure;[6] working in a warehouse, food-production facility, or meatpacking plant;[7] playing, coaching, or broadcasting professional sports (including participating in games, practices, workouts, film sessions, and large team meetings);[8] attending college classes;[9] filming a television show or movie;[10] exercising at the gym;[11] or washing clothes at a laundromat.[12] All of these activities involve gatherings of people from different households for extended periods of time—in many cases, hours on end. Many are carried out in close proximity with others including some—like playing sports, receiving a haircut, getting a manicure, or acting out a scene in a movie—that simply cannot be undertaken while also practicing six-foot social distancing and wearing a mask. Some involve speaking loudly or shouting—for example, on an indoor television studio set filled with actors projecting lines and directors barking orders or in an indoor practice facility or locker room filled with dozens of professional athletes and coaches shouting instructions to each other—which (unlike singing in a church) the State has permitted to continue. And some have been widely reported to have resulted in significant outbreaks across the country, a fact the State itself acknowledges. See Cal. Dep't of Health, COVID-19 Industry Guidance: Food Packing and Processing 1 (July 29, 2020) ("There have been multiple outbreaks in a range of workplaces, [including at] hospitals, long-term care facilities, prisons, food production, warehouses, meat processing plants, and grocery stores."); see also, e.g., Anna Stewart, et al., Why Meat Processing Plants Have Become COVID-19 Hotbeds, CNN Health (June 27, 2020), https://www.cnn.com/ 2020/06/27/health/meat-processing-plants-coronavirus-intl/index.html; Brady Dennis & Chelsea Janes, Coronavirus Outbreak in Major League Baseball Casts Pall Over Other Reopenings, Washington Post (July 28, 2020), https://www.washingtonpost.com/health/2020/07/28/coronavirus-outbreaks-baseball-schools. Yet, despite sharing these supposedly critical features of church attendance, these activities are all more open and available to Californians. If the reason is based in some other neutral assessment of disease spread, it has not been provided to us in this case.

3

The majority makes much of the fact that, at this point, the State has imposed the same attendance restrictions on some secular "congregate" activities such as attending some academic lectures or going to see a movie in a theater. Maj. at 3. But the majority cannot dispute that not all such activities are so tightly restricted—such as participating in a college class in a laboratory or studio setting or attending a team meeting or film-review session in the auditorium of a professional sports facility. More to the point, even if it is true that the State has similarly regulated some congregate activities with analogous risks of disease spread, that does not end our inquiry. Indeed, "it does not suffice to point out that some [comparable] secular businesses . . . are subject to the [same restrictions]," if the State cannot also explain why so many other comparable secular businesses have been treated more favorably. Calvary Chapel Dayton Valley, 140 S. Ct. at 2613-14 (Alito, J., dissenting); see also id. at 2614 ("The legal question is not whether religious worship services are all alone in a disfavored category, but why they are in the disfavored category to begin with." (citing Emp't Div., Dep't of Human Res. of Or. v. Smith, 494 U.S. 872, 884 (1990))). Thus, the State cannot evade the Free Exercise Clause merely by linking its severe restrictions on worship attendance to those imposed on one or two categories of comparable secular activity; it must also justify its decision to treat more favorably a host of other comparable activities which so evidently raise the State's same expressed concerns about disease spread.

C

Finally, we cannot overlook the fact that the State's restrictions on houses of worship explicitly exempt on-site non-religious activities from the strict attendance restraints. California's guidelines for places of worship warn of the supposed danger in individuals coming together specifically "to practice a personal faith," and they make clear that the restrictions on places of worship do not apply to non-worship activities including "food preparation and service, delivery of items to those in need, childcare and daycare services, school and educational activities, in-home caregiving, counseling, office work, and other activities that places and organizations of worship may provide." Places of Worship Guidance, supra, at 3. Thus, California's framework would plainly permit a church in a Tier 1 county to host a group of people for some non-religious purpose, but the same church would be prohibited from hosting an event for the same people in the same setting for the same length of time simply if it were for purposes of religious worship. It is difficult to conceive of a more obvious form of discrimination against religious activity than that.

III

Because Harvest Rock Church is likely to succeed on the merits of its free-exercise challenge, it follows that the balance of hardships also tips in its favor. Without an injunction, the church and its congregants will be prohibited from exercising their First Amendment freedoms—the loss of which, "for even minimal periods of time, unquestionably constitutes irreparable injury." In re Dan Farr Prods., 874 F.3d 590, 597 (9th Cir. 2017) (per curiam) (internal quotation marks omitted). And, while California has a compelling interest in limiting the spread of a deadly disease, the State is not harmed by pursuing that interest—as the Constitution requires—equally against religious and non-religious activities alike. See, e.g., Legend Night Club v. Miller, 637 F.3d 291, 302-03 (4th Cir. 2011) ("Maryland is in no way harmed by issuance of an injunction that prevents the state from enforcing unconstitutional restrictions.").

I respectfully dissent from the majority's decision to deny Harvest Rock Church's motion for an injunction pending appeal.

Judge O'Scannlain's dissent in Index Newspapers LLC v. US Marshals Service (Oct 9, 2020) [Notes omitted]

O'SCANNLAIN, J., dissenting:

In the words of the majority—and I agree—"the district court has worked tirelessly to respond to a tense and sometimes chaotic situation"[1] arising from peaceful urban protest events that have degenerated into riots and destructive mob violence, resulting, inevitably, in crowd dispersal actions by law enforcement. Unfortunately, because the constitutional interests of the parties are misaligned in the provisions of the injunction before us, I must, respectfully, dissent from the order. Since the government is likely to prevail on the merits and the other requisite factors are met, I would grant the motion for stay pending appeal.

With its decision today, the majority of this motions panel validates the transforination of the First Amendment-based "light of public access" to governmental proceedings into a special privilege for self-proclaimed journalists and "legal observers" to disregard crowd dispersal orders issued by federal law enforcement officers. The district court's injunction erroneously curtails an important law enforcement tool for responding to protest events that threaten federal property and personnel, thereby limiting options available for federal officers precisely when they are most needed. While well-meaning, the district court's decision constitutes a significant and imwarranted departure from the traditional, qualified "right of public access" to criminal judicial proceedings that has been carefully delineated by the Supreme Court. In short, the majority's decision approves the mutation of a very limited historical right reinforced by a millennium of legal tradition into a broad, amorphous entitlement that finds support nowhere in our precedents or in the historical sources of the First Amendment.

Similarly, the majority's decision to uphold the injunction before us ostensibly rests on the deference that it accords to the district court's factual findings with respect to plaintiffs'"retaliation" claim, which, indeed, reveal quite a disturbing pattern of apparent misconduct by certain federal officers. But even these unfortunate facts cannot justify granting journalists and "legal observers" a unique exemption from lawful dispersal orders—orders that were neither found, nor alleged, to be retaliatory.

I

Because the facts set forth in the majority opinion do not adequately reveal the full picture, I respectfully restate them as found in the record.

A

In the early morning of July 3, 2020, the recent and ongoing political protests in downtown Portland, Oregon took a violent and destructive turn. Rioters smashed the glass entryway doors of the Mark O. Hatfield Federal Courthouse and attempted to set fire to the building. They threw balloons containing an accelerant into the lobby and fired powerful commercial fireworks toward the accelerant, which ignited a fire in the lobby. Vandalism, destruction of property, and assault on federal law enforcement officers securing the building continued throughout the Fourth of July holiday weekend, and federal agents made multiple arrests.

Before July 3rd, federal law enforcement officers at the Hatfield Courthouse had been stationed in a defensive posture, intended to de-escalate tensions with protesters by remaining inside and responding only to breach attempts on the building and assaults on personnel or to other serious crimes. With limited support from the Portland Police Bureau ("PPB"), however, federal agents struggled to contain protests that often focused on the Courthouse and frequently devolved into violence in the late evenings and early mornings.

When this pattern of violent unrest culminated in the July 3rd attack, the Department of Homeland Security ("DHS") changed its tactics and authorized federal agents to take additional action to protect the Courthouse, and to identify and to arrest serious offenders. After federal officers adopted this more assertive posture, the protests became larger and more intense. These protest events were chaotic and dynamic, and federal officers had frequent confrontations with rioters. According to DHS's Gabriel Russell, the law enforcement officer leading the federal response in Portland, 120 federal officers experienced injuries, including broken bones, hearing damage, eye damage, a dislocated shoulder, sprains, strains, and contusions. Conflict between federal officers and rioters continued until the early morning of July 30th, after which incidents diminished as a result of DHS reaching an agreement with the Governor of Oregon for the Oregon State Police to provide security in the areas adjacent to the Hatfield Courthouse.

During the period of unrest, journalists and "legal observers" ostensibly reporting on law enforcement's response to the riots were frequently interspersed with protesters when events degenerated into violence. Some of these individuals even participated in violent and unlawful conduct, including assaults on federal officers and destruction of federal property. For example, a person with a helmet marked "press" used a grinder to attempt to breach the fence surrounding the Hatfield Courthouse. Another person with a. "press" helmet entered Courthouse property and encouraged others to join, yelling to the crowd that "they can't arrest us all!" A man wearing a vest labeled "press" was seen throwing a hard object toward police. In yet another incident, a Courthouse staff member reported being kicked by someone wearing clothing marked "press."

B

Plaintiffs are a newspaper organization and individual journalists and "legal observers," some of whom are affiliated with the National Lawyers Guild ("NLG") and the American Civil Liberties Union ("ACLU"). They allege that federal law enforcement officers with DHS and the U.S. Marshals Service ("USMS") operating in Portland during the month of July (1) infringed their First Amendment "light of access" to public streets and sidewalks to observe and to document law enforcement's response to the riots near the Hatfield Courthouse; and, (2) deliberately and unlawfully "retaliated" against them for exercising their putative First Amendment right to report on those events by targeting them with tear gas, less-lethal munitions, and pepper spray.

Plaintiffs initially filed suit against the City of Portland, and unnamed individual PPB officers, in federal district court, alleging similar constitutional violations arising out of the PPB's response to the protest events. For example, Plaintiffs alleged a "broader pattern of the Portland police repeatedly and intentionally shooting, gassing, and beating journalists and [legal] observers." Among other incidents, Plaintiffs alleged that the PPB slanuned a reporter from The Oregonian in the back with a truncheon, even as she was displaying her press pass, and shoved a reporter from the Portland Tribune into a wall, after he had identified himself as media, when he initially refused to comply with an order to disperse. Plaintiffs further alleged that the PPB had publicly announced that it would use force to disperse reporters unless they had been previously selected to embed with officers. Plaintiffs obtained a temporary restraining order ("TRO") against the PPB, without the City of Portland's consent, on July 2nd, with terns similar to those contained in the instant preliminary injunction. In its order granting the TRO, the district court concluded that Plaintiffs had demonstrated "serious questions going to the merits" with respect to their claim of a First Amendment-based "right of public access" to observe law enforcement's response to protest events. The TRO specified that press and "legal observers" were exempt from any orders to disperse issued by the PPB.

After alleged retaliation by a federal law enforcement agent on July 12th, plaintiffs filed an emergency motion seeking the district court's leave to file an amended complaint describing such incident and also adding DHS and USMS as defendants in the case. The City of Portland filed an objection, arguing, inter alia, that plaintiffs' claims against the City of Portland and those against DHS and USMS raised no common questions of law or fact. The City maintained that PPB operates under fundamentally different conditions than federal law enforcement agencies, including different directives governing the use of force, different limitations on the use of force, and a separate command structure.

On July 16th, before the district court had an opportunity to rule on the motion to bring DHS and USMS into the case, plaintiffs and the City jointly filed a "Stipulated Preliminary Injunction" that substantially mirrored the TRO's tenns. The following day, the district court granted plaintiffs' motion for leave to file the operative Second Amended Complaint.

The Second Amended Complaint sets forth independent causes of action based on the First and Fourth Amendments of the U.S. Constitution and Article I, Sections 8 and 26 of the Oregon Constitution. It seeks both damages and equitable relief. The day it was filed, Plaintiffs immediately moved for a TRO against DHS and USMS, with the request for injunctive relief limited only to their aforementioned First Amendment claims.

On July 22nd, the City filed a brief in support of the entry of the TRO against DHS and USMS. The City accused both agencies of escalating violence, harming non-violent protesters, and effectively kidnapping people off of Poitland streets. Notably, on the same day, the Poitland City Council passed a resolution prohibiting the PPB from cooperating with federal officers deployed in Portland.

The district court granted the TRO on July 23rd and extended it for an additional 14 days on August 6th. On August 20th, the district court entered the instant preliminary injunction, from which DHS and USMS now seek emergency relief pending appeal.

The preliminary injunction provides, among other things, that journalists and "legal observers" are exempt[2] from general dispersal orders issued by federal officers. It further requires that federal officers refrain from using force or threatening arrest to compel such persons to disperse after an order to disperse has been issued. It also sets forth a non-exclusive list of indicia by which officers are to determine who qualifies as a journalist or "legal observer."[3]

A prior motions panel of this court entered an administrative stay of the injunction pending the adjudication of the government's motion for emergency relief. As the cowl, in its role as this motions panel, today denies such emergency request for a stay pending appeal, the injunction will go back into effect and this matter will proceed before the district court, pending disposition of the govenunent's appeal of the preliminary injunction by a merits panel of this court. Plaintiffs' Fourth Amendment and state constitutional claims did not form pan of the request for preliminary relief and remain pending before the district court, as do plaintiffs' requests for compensatory and punitive damages, attorney's fees, and costs. As the City's stipulation to a prelim nary injunction resolved only Plaintiffs' request for equitable relief, Plaintiffs' remaining claims against the City and individual PPB officers also remain pending in the district court.

II

I agree with the majority that the Nken v. Holder factors must determine our disposition of the government's request for emergency relief, but I respectfully disagree with how the majority analyzes those factors. 556 U.S. 418, 426 (2009). I address each factor in turn, beginning with the government's burden to make a strong showing of likelihood of success on the merits.[4]

The district court granted injunctive relief on the basis of Plaintiffs' two First Amendment claims: (1) a "right of public access" to public streets and sidewalks to observe and to document law enforcement officers engaged in riot control and crowd dispersal; and (2) a light to be free from "retaliation" by federal officers for reporting on law enforcement's response to civil unrest.

A

1

With respect to the "right of public access" issue, the district court purported to apply the framework articulated in Press-Enterprise Co. v. Superior Court of Cal. ("Press-Enterprise II") for evaluating "claim[s] of a First Amendment right of access to criminal proceedings[.]" 478 U.S. 1, 8-9 (1986). Pursuant to that doctrine, in evaluating a purported claim of public access to a proceeding, a count must consider: (1) "whether the place and process have historically been open to the press and general public;" and (2) "whether public access plays a significant positive role in the functioning of the particular process in question." Id. "If the particular proceeding in question passes these tests of experience and logic, a qualified First Amendment light of public access attaches." Id. "A presumptive right of access to any particular proceeding may be overcome by an oveniding govenunent interest based on findings that closure is essential to preserve higher values and is narrowly tailored to serve that interest." Id.

But the First Amendment-based right of public access and its corresponding framework have never been deemed to apply to riot control and crowd dispersal in a public street.[5] The Supreme Court has discussed only a qualified right of access to certain criminal judicial proceedings and has never recognized a right of public access outside of that context. See Press-Enterprise II, 478 U.S. at 8-9 (right of public access to preliminary hearings in criminal cases); Press-Enterprise Co. v. Superior Court of Cal., 464 U.S. 501, 503, 508 (1984) (right of public access to voir dire hearings in criminal cases); Richmond Newspapers, Inc. v. Virginia, 448 U.S. 555, 580 (1980) (right of public access to criminal trials).

In the decades since Press-Enterprise II, the courts of appeals have expanded the right-of-public-access doctrine considerably beyond its initial, paradigmatic application to criminal proceedings—including, in our court, to a variety of non-criminal, non-adjudicative, governmental proceedings, such as a horse gather on federal land, Leigh v. Salazar, 677 F.3d 892, 894 (9th Cir. 2012), and a referendum on a regulatory order conducted by the U.S. Department of Agriculture, Cal-Almond, Inc. v. U.S. Dept. ofAgriculture, 960 F.2d 105, 109 (9th Cir. 1992)—but the doctrine is not without limit. Rather, the Press-Enterprise II framework has been confined to claims of access to specific governmental proceedings and has never been applied to public spaces in general or to private events therein. Cf. Leigh, 677 F.3d at 894 (evaluating access to horse gather, not to federal lands); Whiteland Woods, L.P. v. Township of W. Whiteland, 193 F.3d 177, 181 (3d Cir. 1999) (evaluating access to town planning conunission meeting, not to town hall). Here, protests in a public street are privately sponsored and organized events, and when they degenerate into riots, the crowd control measures taken by law enforcement are spontaneous and temporary responses to ongoing criminal activity. Protests and resulting riots are simply not governmental proceedings to which a right of public access may be claimed.[6]

Similarly, even where the Press-Enterprise II framework applies, it requires a court to evaluate a claim of access by first determining whether "the place and the process" have historically been open to the public, and whether the public's presence plays a critical role in the specific proceeding at issue. 478 U.S. at 8-9 (emphasis added). Here, the district court noted that streets, sidewalks, and parks constitute traditional public fora, which have been open to speech and expression from "time out of mind," Hague v. Comm. for Indus. Org., 307 U.S. 496, 515 (1939), but it failed to evaluate any history of public access to law enforcement operations responding to ongoing criminal activity, including violent civil unrest that threatens federal property and personnel. In the absence of historical analysis regarding the proceeding, as distinguished from the place, a presumptive right of public access simply does not attach. Cf. Leigh, 677 F.3d at 894 (calling for inquiry into history of public access to horse gathers, not to federal lands).

The district court's reasoning here is reflective of an emerging pattern of lower courts expanding the right-of-public-access doctrine well beyond its original scope, with little consideration of a limiting principle. Cf, e.g., N.Y. Civil Liberties Union v. NY. City Transit Auth., 684 F.3d 286, 298 (2d Cir. 2012) (noting, with approval, that "there is no principle that limits the First Amendment right of [public] access to any one particular type of government process"). When the Supreme Court first articulated the First Amendment light of public access in Richmond Newspapers, Inc. v. Virginia, it drew on an extensive historical record of public access to criminal trials in the Anglo-American legal tradition, dating back to "the days before the Norman Conquest." 448 U.S. at 580. After canvassing more than a. thousand years of "unbroken, uncontradicted" history, the Couit felt justified in concluding that the light to attend criminal trials is "implicit in the guarantees of the First Amendment." Id. In Press-Enterprise II, the Couit limited its inquiry to post-Bill of Rights history, but nonetheless identified a "near uniform" "tradition of accessibility" to preliminary hearings in criminal cases dating back to the "celebrated trial of Aaron Bun" in 1807. 478 U.S. at 10-11.

Lower courts, by contrast, including ours, have extended the right of public access largely without extensive historical backing and without further guidance from the Supreme Court regarding the specific contours of the doctrine. If the majority's reasoning here is any indication, the doctrine is growing haphazardly, like a. weed in an untended garden, presaging conflict with more established legal lights and powers. This doctrinal disorder warrants fiuther review.

2.

Even if right-of-public-access analysis were appropriate under these circumstances, any right to access the proceeding in question must apply equally to the press and the public. See Cal. First Amendment Coal. v. Woodford, 299 F.3d 868, 873 n.2 (9th Cir. 2002) ("As members of the press, plaintiffs' First Amendment right of access to governmental proceedings is coextensive with the general public's right of access." (citing Houchins v. KQED, Inc., 438 U.S. 1, 15-16 (1978)). Indeed, it is a long-established and fundamental principle of constitutional law that "the First Amendment does not guarantee the press a constitutional right of special access to information not available to the public generally." Branzburg v. Hayes, 408 U.S. 665, 684 (1972). Cf. Erwin Chemerinsky, Protect the Press: A First Amendment Standard for Safeguarding Aggressive Newsgathering, 33 U. Rich. L. Rev. 1143, 1145 (2000) ("[The Supreme Court's] rulings, without exception, have failed to provide any First Amendment protection for newsgathering. Indeed, the Court has declared that there is no exemption for the press from general laws. In other words, while engaged in newsgathering, the press is not exempt from tort liability or criminal laws, no matter how compelling the need for reporting to protect the public's health and safety.")

But here, the district court's injunction, by its own terms, grants selfidentified journalists and "legal observers" a special privilege to disregard dispersal orders with which the general public must comply, which has no legal basis. The injunction is thus at odds with a core First Amendment principle and a common-sense rule of thumb: the media have the same rights as the rest of us.[7]

The majority opinion here rejects this characterization of the injunction and insists that it creates no special lights. According to the majority, the injunction merely prevents federal agents from seeking to disperse the press from local streets and sidewalks when the City's current policy is that press may remain there, even during riots, but does not seek to regulate crowd dispersal on federal propeity. On this view, the injunction is a wholesome exercise in federalism!

But the majority's analysis is inconsistent with the plain text of the district court's order and misapplies principles of constitutional structure. The injunction, by its own terms, appears to extend to dispersal orders issued on federal propeity, and is certainly not geographically limited in any explicit way. The injunction thus allows the press, but not others, to disregard dispersal orders that are clearly lawful. That can only be understood as a special dispensation that is not consistent with the First Amendment.

In any event, even if federal agents are located on City property when they issue, or seek to enforce, an order to disperse, principles of federalism do not justify carving out a special exemption for the press from such orders simply because City police would typically allow for one. The Federal Government is indeed acknowledged by all to be one of limited and enumerated powers, see Nat'l Fed'n of Indep. Bus. v. Sebelius, 567 U.S. 519, 534 (2012), and it is not entitled to exercise general or residual powers, see United States v. Comstock, 560 U.S. 126, 153 (2010) (Kennedy, J., concurring) ("Residual power, sometimes referred to (perhaps imperfectly) as the police power, belongs to the States and the States alone"), such as the prevention and punishment of crime and disorder on local streets, sidewalks, and parks, see United States v. Morrison, 529 U.S. 598, 618 (2000) ([W]e can think of no better example of the police power, which the Founders denied the National Government and reposed in the States, than the suppression of violent crime and vindication of its victims.").

It is an inversion of our constitutional structure, however, to require federal officers to abide by municipal policies regarding crowd dispersal when carrying out their statutory prerogative to protect federal property and personnel. Federal officials are prohibited, of course, from "commandeering" state and local law enforcement officers to help secure federal property and must instead rely on voluntary cooperation with state and local officials for this purpose. See Print: v. United States, 521 U.S. 898, 935 (1997). Where such cooperation is inadequate, the federal government must deploy its own agents. In these circumstances, the agency's laiijid directives regarding crowd dispersal, i.e., those adopted pursuant to a constitutionally enacted federal statute or rule, take precedence over state and local ones, not the other way around. Such an arrangement does not violate principles of federalism or dual sovereignty but is rather required by them. See, e.g., Alden v. Maine, 527 U.S. 706, 732 (1999) (federal government sets the supreme law of the land when acting within its enumerated powers).

The majority opinion relies heavily on the district court's conclusion, with which it agrees, that it is, in fact, tin/au:fit/ for federal agents to issue orders to disperse if they are situated beyond federal property. According to the majority, DHS and USMS have never claimed to have such authority, and the federal statute upon which they principally rely, 40 U.S.C. § 1315, does not provide for it.

The suggestion that the government has simply conceded this question is overstated. Although this issue was not adequately briefed by either pally, the government has consistently articulated the position, both before the district court and on appeal, that federal law enforcement officers may issue dispersal orders on federal property, and in several circumstances, may effectuate those orders beyond federal property, such as by establishing a secure perimeter. In particular, the government has invoked § 1315(b)(1), which provides that the Secretary of Homeland Security may designate DHS agents to protect federal property, including designating agents for duty in "areas outside the property to the extent necessary to protect the property and persons on the property."

I am inclined to agree with the government's general understanding of its statutory authority. As the government has pointed out, it would be unreasonable to require that federal officers charged with securing federal buildings wait until violent opportunists have breached the property line or entered the building before taking any protective measures. There is very likely a statutory basis for at least some crowd dispersal activity adjacent to a federal courthouse faced with violent unrest and the other challenging circumstances at issue here.

I also agree with the majority, however, that a determination of the precise scope of DHS's and USMS's statutory authority is not required for resolution of this emergency motion. Indeed, the statutory question muddles the First Amendment analysis upon which the district count's injunction is ultimately grounded. Presumably, if federal officers have no statutory basis for dispersals beyond federal property, then any such dispersals are ultra vire s, and the inquiry is at an end. There is no reason to proceed to an evaluation of the constitutional rights of persons subject to such purportedly unlawful measures, let alone to construct a complex injunction that distinguishes the rights of press and "legal observers" from the rights of other participants in a protest. Ultimately, a lack of federal statutory authority for off-property dispersals, as such, cannot serve as the sole, or even primary, basis upon which this particular injunction is upheld, given its reliance on a painstaking analysis of purported constitutional violations with respect to specific persons. Thus, even if I were to accept the majority's view that the injunction's aim is simply to prohibit off-property dispersals by federal officers, which I do not, the injunction's terms would be woefully underinclusive.

3

Even if a presumptive right of access for press and "legal observers" to witness law enforcement's response to a riot could be said to exist, the inquiry does not end there. Under Press-Enterprise II, a presumptive right of public access to any particular proceeding may be overcome by an overriding government interest based on findings that closure is essential to preserve higher values and is narrowly tailored to serve that interest. 478 U.S. at 8-9.

The district count's narrow tailoring analysis failed to take proper account of the government's interests in defense of federal personnel and property, which justify use of general dispersal orders during riot control situations that threaten federal resources, even in a public forum.[8] Here, considering the chaotic and dynamic situation during Portland's recent protest events, which have frequently devolved into riots, along with the nefarious actions by certain individuals falsely purporting to be press or "legal observers," closure of the forum through general dispersal orders is essential to the defense of federal personnel and property. Indeed, the closure of governmental proceedings has been deemed proper in several instances where the government's interest was arguably less immediate and the restriction on access was equally broad. Cf., e.g., Dhiab v. Trump, 852 F.3d 1087, 1095 (D.C. Cir. 2017) (government's interest in preventing future threats to military operations would justify closure of habeas proceedings); U.S. v. Index Newspapers LLC, 766 F.3d 1072, 1087 (9th Cir. 2014) (government's interest in secrecy justified closure of certain grand jury proceedings); ACLU v. Holder, 673 F.3d 245, 252 (4th Cir. 2011) (government's interest in integrity of ongoing fraud investigation justified sealing of complaints filed in False Claims Act actions).

Moreover, if the categories of "journalist" and "legal observer" in fact include all members of the public engaged in observation, as distinguished from speech or protest— as the majority seems to suggest—then the govenunent's interests in full closure of the "proceeding" are even more compelling. Otherwise, in the event of a riot in a public fonun that threatens federal property, federal officers could disperse only members of the public that are speaking, assembling, and protesting, but not members of the public that are observing or documenting. Peaceful protesters caught up in the riot would have to obey the dispersal order, but peaceful observers would not. This differential treatment is groundless and, in any event, would render federal dispersal orders a dead letter, even in the face of an undeniable threat to federal property and personnel. Federal law enforcement agents simply would not be allowed to clear the street. Such a prohibition is not only inconsistent with the govenunent's oveniding interest in security in cases of violent unrest that threatens federal property and personnel, it is also contrary to established law in other First Amendment settings, which permits general dispersal orders in similar circumstances. Cf, e.g., Bible Believers v. Wayne Cty., Mich., 805 F.3d 228, 252 (6th Cir. 2015) ("The police may go against the hecklers, cordon off the speakers, or attempt to disperse the entire crowd if that becomes necessary."). Carr v. D.C., 587 F.3d 401, 409-10 (D.C. Cir. 2009) ("[W]hen police face an unruly crowd they may give a dispersal order and then arrest those who, after reasonable opportunity to comply, fail to do so. We continue to acknowledge that this tactic will be invaluable to police in certain circumstances. A dispersal order might well be necessary in a situation in which a. crowd is substantially infected with violence or otherwise threatening public safety." (internal citations and quotation marks omitted)); Wise, 2020 WL 5231486 at *2 (recognizing propriety of general dispersal orders in response to Portland riots).

The only way the majority arrives at a different conclusion is by according deference to the district count's factual findings, which placed heavy emphasis on the City of Portland's consent to abide by an injunction with nearly identical teens and a declaration submitted by fonner DHS official Gil Kerlikowske stating that law enforcement officers may respond effectively to riots without dispersing journalists and "legal observers." Evaluating whether a government measure is narrowly tailored is not simply a matter of ordinary fact-finding, however. Narrow tailoring is viewed as a. mixed question of fact and law that requires a delicate balancing of legal principles as applied to specific circumstances. See Gilbrook v. City of Westminster, 177 F.3d 839, 861 (9th Cir. 1999); Gerritsen v. City of Los Angeles, 994 F.2d 570, 575 (9th Cir. 1993) ("[W]e review First Amendment questions de novo since they present mixed questions of law and fact, requiring us to apply principles of First Amendment jurisprudence to the specific facts of this case." (internal quotation marks omitted)); see also Mastrovincemo v. City ofNew York, 435 F.3d 78, 100 (2d Cir. 2006) ("Our narrow-tailoring inquiry requires us to apply principles of First Amendment jurisprudence to the specific facts of this case, and therefore we treat this issue as a mixed question of law and fact that we may resolve on appeal." (internal quotations marks omitted)); Casey v. City of Newport, RI, 308 F.3d 106, 116 (1st Cir. 2002) ("Inescapably, the application of the narrow tailoring test entails a delicate balancing judgment." (citations omitted)). Accordingly, I would revisit the district court's narrow tailoring inquiry, which I believe did not correctly balance the interests at stake.

The City's stipulation does not have the import that the district court, and the majority, ascribe to it. That the City ultimately agreed to the teens of the injunction does not show that it complied with them, let alone that it did so and managed to protect property and personnel. In any event, the City's agreeableness should not be overstated here. The PPB is still alleged to have followed until recently a policy of dispersing press and "legal observers," the TRO was entered without the City's consent, and, after the City agreed to a preliminary injunction, it suggested that modifications would be required.[9]

Moreover, as already discussed, holding DHS and USMS to the City's policies and practices reflects a misunderstanding of the relationship between federal and local law enforcement, each of which operates under a separate command structure and is typically entitled to set different enforcement priorities and to follow different directives regarding lawful crowd control tactics, including general dispersal orders. In this case, the City not only sought to distinguish the PPB from federal law enforcement, it has been explicitly adverse to the presence of federal officers in Portland, leveling serious allegations of unlawful conduct against them, and even going so far as to prohibit the PPB from cooperating with federal agents to provide security for the Hatfield Courthouse. The City's actions, and its filings in the district court, suggest that it has a divergent assessment of the severity of the threat posed to federal personnel and property by protest events that degenerate into riots, and of the proper manner of dealing with that threat. The City is entitled, of course, to utilize different crowd control tactics, but the City's choices obviously do not bind federal law enforcement agencies.

Similarly, Kerlikowske's testimony does not adequately address crowd control under the specific circumstances faced by federal officers in Poitland. For example, he deals in a conclusory manner with the evidence placed in the record regarding the involvement of putative journalists and "legal observers" in criminal acts, stating that federal officers "were not fooled" by the "press" labels and that trained officers are capable of dealing with such incidents on an individualized basis. But effectuating an arrest may not be feasible or safe in the chaotic and dynamic environment of a riot that threatens federal property and personnel, which is why dispersal orders—and related crowd control tactics, such as deployment of tear gas—are understood to be legitimate law enforcement tools in the first place. Cf. Wise, 2020 WL 5231486 at *2 (recognizing propriety of general dispersal orders in responding to Poitland riots); Don't Shoot Portland v. City of Portland, No. 3:20-CV-00917-HZ, 2020 WL 3078329, at *4 (D. Or. June 9, 2020) (allowing use of tear gas in situations where safety of public or police is at risk). Given the conclusory nature of Kerlikowske's testimony on this point, it is hardly definitive.

Accordingly, the government has made a strong showing that it is likely to succeed in demonstrating that the First Amendment-based right of public access does not support the district count's injunction.

B

With respect to the "retaliation" claim, the district court also concluded that plaintiffs were likely to succeed, largely based on its detailed factual findings indicating a disturbing pattern of unwarranted force by federal agents. The majority opinion here discusses the "retaliation" claim extensively and ultimately defers to these factual findings.

Even if plaintiffs' retaliation claim were viable, however, that claim alone cannot justify this injunction. The district comt's factual findings regarding retaliation, while apparently based on a meticulous examination of the record, bear no relation to the injunctive relief actually entered. General dispersal orders were not among the acts alleged to be retaliatory, nor did the district count make any findings to support such a conclusion. An injunction that exempts plaintiffs—not to mention, journalists and "legal observers" more generally—from dispersal orders is thus far broader than necessary to provide relief for the injuries alleged, and documented, as a result of retaliation.[10] Indeed, Judge Immergut, of the very same district court, relied on such reasoning in denying a similar request for injunctive relief based on First Amendment "retaliation" just two weeks after the instant preliminary injunction was entered. Wise, 2020 WL 5231486 at *8 (injunction not warranted where instances of alleged targeting appeared to occur when "protest medics" refused to follow dispersal orders).

Accordingly, I would hold that, regardless of whether plaintiffs' have stated a valid First Amendment "retaliation" claim, an injunction that exempts them from non-retaliatory dispersal orders is overbroad and an abuse of discretion. See Cal. v. Azar, 911 F.3d 558, 584 (9th Cir. 2018) ("The scope of the remedy must be no broader and no narrower than necessary to redress the injury shown by the [plaintiff].")

I conclude that DHS and USMS have made a strong showing that they are likely to succeed in demonstrating that the district court's extraordinary injunction was issued without an adequate legal basis. This critical Nken factor favors grant of the government's emergency motion for stay pending appeal.

III

The remaining Nken factors also favor a stay pending appeal here. First, while a closer question, the government has shown that it is likely to suffer irreparable harm during the pendency of the appeal if the injunction is not stayed, because it is unworkable for federal officers to distinguish journalists and "legal observers" in the midst of a riot that threatens federal property and personnel based on the nebulous criteria established by the district court, particularly in light of the incidents of press and "legal observer" involvement in violent unrest.

The majority rejects the government's showing on this factor, stating that the injunction is carefully drawn to avoid undue interference with DH S's and USMS's defense of federal resources, that the PPB has been operating safely and effectively under nearly identical terms, and that Kerlikowske's declaration indicates that general dispersal orders are unnecessary for crowd control. The majority's characterization of the order as carefully drawn is misleading because the order merely restates existing legal rules, such as an officer's power to make an arrest based on probable cause. And the order does not explain how effectuating arrest of individual suspects is as feasible or safe as utilizing general crowd control tactics during a riot that threatens federal property and personnel. Similarly, the City's stipulation and Kerlikowske's declaration do not warrant the treatment they receive, for the reasons discussed above.

Second, the hams to the government are serious because the injunction's curtailment of general dispersal orders will compromise the security of federal personnel and property, whereas, if there is no right of public access, as I have argued, then any harm to plaintiffs from a stay is minimal because they do not have a. right to remain in the street after they have been ordered to disperse, and the injunction does not protect them from retaliation. Third, for similar reasons, the public interest in maintenance of order and public safety also favors stay of an overbroad injunction that unduly interferes with law enforcement operations, while offering little, if any, protection for plaintiffs' actual constitutional rights. This combination of showings justifies a stay pending appeal. See Leiva-Perez v. Holder, 640 F.3d 962, 970 (9th Cir. 2011) (stay wan-anted where irreparable harm is probable, there is a strong likelihood of success on the merits, and the public interest does not weigh heavily against a stay).

IV

Because the government has made a strong showing that it is likely to succeed in demonstrating that the injunction lacks an adequate legal basis, and the other Nken factors also weigh in favor of a stay, I respectfully dissent and would grant the emergency motion for stay pending appeal.

Judge O'Scannlain's concurrence and dissent in Harvest Rock Church, Inc. v. Newsom (Dec 23, 2020)

O'SCANNLAIN, J., concurring in part and dissenting in part:

Although I have no objection to the briefing schedule set forth in the court's order, I strongly object to our failure to accommodate, even in a temporary fashion, Harvest Rock Church's request for relief from California's severe restrictions on indoor worship services by December 24.

The requested deadline is hardly arbitrary: The church seeks immediate action from our court so that its members can worship on Christmas Day, one of the most sacred holy days in the Christian calendar. And it is not the church's fault that it finds itself in this predicament. The church moved for a temporary restraining order against California's worship-related restrictions as soon as this case was remanded following a decision by the Supreme Court—yet it had to wait more than two weeks before the district court ruled on that motion. When the district court finally denied its motion two days ago, Harvest Rock Church filed a notice of appeal the same day. The next day, yesterday, the church moved for an emergency injunction from our court.

Our General Orders provide that, in exactly such a scenario, we may treat an emergency motion seeking action within 48 hours as a request for temporary relief until the panel "can more fully consider the merits of the motion." 9th Cir. Gen. Order 6.4.b. At this point—and as we are already familiar with many of the issues presented in this case— Harvest Rock Church's claims against California's restrictions appear strong. See generally

Roman Catholic Diocese of Brooklyn v. Cuomo, 141 S. Ct. 63 (2020) (per curiam) (enjoining similar COVID-19 related restrictions in New York); Calvary Chapel Dayton Valley v. Sisolak, ___ F.3d ____, 2020 WL 7350247 (9th Cir. 2020) (enjoining similar COVID-19 related restrictions in Nevada); Harvest Rock Church, Inc. v. Newsom, 977 F.3d 728, 732-37 (9th Cir. 2020) (O'Scannlain, J., dissenting) (concluding that Harvest Rock Church was likely to prevail on its previous appeal from the district court's denial of a preliminary injunction), vacated 981 F.3d 764 (9th Cir. 2020). Nonetheless, I do not object to the panel's determination that more time is needed to evaluate the merits of Harvest Rock Church's motion. But we should not deprive the church of any hope of relief during the period of time it takes our court to do so.

Even if we need more time to consider the pending motion in full, we should have granted the church at least the temporary relief it needs to ensure that its members can exercise freely the fundamental right to practice their Christian religion on one of the most sacred Christian days of the year. U.S. Const. amend. I.

Made in the USA
Las Vegas, NV
23 January 2021